EVOLUTION IN THE ARTS

EVOLUTION
IN
THE ARTS

AND

OTHER THEORIES

OF CULTURE HISTORY

THOMAS MUNRO

THE CLEVELAND MUSEUM OF ART

DISTRIBUTED BY HARRY N. ABRAMS, INC.

CONTENTS

[v]

CONTENTS

PART TWO

THEORIES OF EVOLUTION IN ART AND CULTURE

CHAPTER X

Evolutionism in Aesthetics, the History of Religion, and Particular Arts

CHAPTER XI

Changing Attitudes toward Cultural Evolutionism in Recent Anthropology and Sociology

CHAPTER XII

Stages and Sequences in Culture History

CONTENTS

PART THREE

HOW THE ARTS EVOLVE: A CORRECTED RESTATEMENT

CONTENTS

CONTENTS

CHAPTER XVII

Complication and Simplification in the Arts

CHAPTER XVIII

Regressive Trends in Art

[xi]

ACKNOWLEDGMENTS

This book has been developed in my graduate courses on aesthetics and art history, given under the friendly auspices of The Cleveland Museum of Art and Western Reserve University. My cordial thanks are extended to the trustees and officials of these institutions; to Sherman E. Lee as Director of the Museum, to Carl F. Wittke as Vice President of Western Reserve University and Dean of its Graduate School, and to Merald E. Wrolstad, the Museum's Editor, who designed the book and supervised its typography. Thanks go also to the American Society for Aesthetics, publisher of the *Journal of Aesthetics and Art Criticism*, and to Herbert M. Schueller, former Editor of *Criticism*, for permission to reprint parts of this book which first appeared in those magazines; also to the several publishers named in connection with books to which they hold the copyright, for permission to quote short passages. For timely aid in my work on aesthetics and related fields at The Cleveland Museum of Art, I am grateful to William H. Matchette, director of the Franklin J. Matchette Foundation.

Colleagues, friends, and former students too numerous to name have helped in past years by stimulating discussion of the problems dealt with in these pages. In particular, I would like to thank the following for reading and criticizing parts of the text from the standpoints of their respective fields: Max Rieser (German philosophy), Alfred Frankfurter and James R. Johnson (art history), and Olaf H. Prufer (anthropology and archeology). However, none of those mentioned is to be held responsible for the opinions expressed in the book or for any faults it may contain. Dolores Filak, my secretary at the Museum and editorial assistant of the *Journal of Aesthetics*, has given indispensable help in accurately preparing the typescript and correcting proof. My wife, Lucile, and daughter, Eleanor, have been most helpful.

It was my father, Alexander Allen Munro, who first introduced me at an early age to the wonders of evolution, and later to the Spencerian philosophy. To his memory this book is dedicated.

T.M.

INTRODUCTION

Does the history of the various arts—visual, musical, literary, and other—disclose any persistent trend or large-scale process? From its primitive beginnings to the present, in various regions and cultures, does it show any continued, over-all tendency or pattern in change? Can we observe significant analogies, recurrent types and sequences of style, between the arts of different periods and peoples? Such questions were often asked by scientists and scholars in the nineteenth and early twentieth centuries.

They were answered in very different ways: for example, by the theory of recurrent cycles, which held that art returns to a similar starting-point in various civilizations. Another theory held that art evolves or develops as part of one vast process of cosmic, organic, and cultural evolution. The theory of evolution promised much in the way of unified understanding. It claimed to link the arts with all other realms of thought by one great, all-inclusive formula.

To discuss these questions again is to venture out upon a much-traveled road—or, at least, on one much traveled in the nineteenth century but recently neglected. It may seem at first sight a rash, unnecessary venture, leading only to the same old pitfalls that have ruined many ambitious attempts at a philosophy of history. Hasty critics may assume at the start, without further reading, that this is merely one more naïve attempt at a grandiose, rigid system, one more oversimplified

formula for cultural change. Further reading will soon show that this is not the case. The errors of nineteenth-century evolutionism, which led to its rejection in the early twentieth century, are shown in detail and avoided thereafter. The tremendous diversities and irregularities of cultural change, especially in the arts, are emphasized throughout. The analogy between biological and cultural phenomena is not exaggerated.

At the same time, however, it is argued that the recent reaction against all theories of cultural evolution has been carried too far, with consequent ignoring of some true and valuable insights. So much new information has been accumulating about the history of the various arts in relation to other cultural factors that a fresh reappraisal of the controversy is long overdue. In attempting it, this book will take account of many recent developments in the philosophy of history, in the history of art, in anthropology, cultural psychology, biology and other fields.

The concept of *evolution* is widely recognized by historians of thought as the most important concept developed in the nineteenth century. It has been called the "key-idea" of that epoch. Outstanding as a focus of interest and heated argument among scholars and the educated public, it was applied in every science and branch of scholarship. There it gave rise to a host of theories about the details and varieties of evolution. It was applied not only to the development of organic life in plants, the lower animals, and man, but also to that of galaxies and solar systems, the human mind, society, culture, the sciences and arts. In all these fields, it revolutionized basic assumptions and ways of thinking. It substituted a belief in change, development, and relativity for the old belief in absolutes; for a belief in a static universe, a fixed, hierarchical society, and eternal, universal laws of goodness, truth, and beauty.[1]

The concept of evolution was, among other things, an outgrowth of the eighteenth-century theory of human *progress*: the belief that man's history has been a gradual advance from savagery and misery to a higher, better type of life; also that this advance has been, and can be in future, made by his own unaided efforts through the use of reason and science. Both evolution and progress implied a conception of human history as genetic, continuous, operating by natural causes. The belief in progress, as opposed to the older belief in man's helplessness, inherited sin, and ancient fall from primitive innocence and bliss, has been called by J. B. Bury[2] and others the most important intellectual discovery of modern Western civilization; the one which most distinguishes it from other periods and cultures. The theory of evolution added to this belief the conception of a long prehuman development and that of man's history on earth as a part of cosmic evolution.

Among other applications of the genetic, developmental approach was the theory of *evolution in the arts*. These have evolved, according to nineteenth-century evolutionists, as integral parts of man's social and cultural development. They have grown by natural processes, as a late stage in the long development of man's physical equipment, his powers of cooperation, thought and learning, his ability to transmit learned experience to later generations, and his power to adapt his environment actively to his desires and imagined goals. The arts are not miraculous, supernatural gifts of the gods, derived from a higher, purely spiritual level of being, entirely outside the material struggle for survival. They have grown out of prehistoric technics, largely utilitarian but not without aesthetic aspects, through a process of gradual differentiation and reintegration, social adaptation,

and increasing power, subtlety and complexity of means and ends.

The theory of progress affirmed the optimistic thesis that, in this development, the arts were becoming better along with other branches of civilization. The theory of evolution was at first combined with that of progress, but gradually separated so as to affirm only that art and culture had become more complex. The eighteenth-century problem of whether modern art is better than ancient was put aside for separate consideration. No particular answer to it is implied by the theory of evolution as distinct from that of progress.

A strong reaction began about 1920 against the theories of evolution and progress in art and other cultural fields. It extended not only to all general theories of art history, including that of cycles, but also to the philosophy of history in general and to all attempts at a comprehensive theory of cultural history. For several decades they received comparatively little attention from historians and cultural scientists, except to be dismissed with the comment that "evolution" and "progress" are obsolete ideas, and all philosophies of history a fruitless waste of time. Some of the reasons for this negative reaction will be examined in the following chapters.

Still more recently, after the Second World War, the pendulum started to swing the other way. In the nineteen-fifties, the interest in evolution and other theories of culture history began to revive. Anthropologists who had avoided the term "cultural evolution" as outworn and discredited began discussing it again with respect as a useful tool of thought and investigation.

Very little has been said in recent years about the *arts* in this connection, especially the arts of modern civilization. These are seldom emphasized in anthropology or other social sciences, even though they are recognized as important parts of

[1] *Cf.* John Dewey, *The Influence of Darwin on Philosophy and Other Essays* (New York, 1910).
[2] *The Idea of Progress* (London and New York, 1920, 1932).

culture and civilization. Many philosophers and general historians have only a slight acquaintance with their details. Among historians of the arts, on the other hand, especially in the United States, there is still comparatively little interest in the philosophical approach to art history, and comparatively little acquaintance with past writing in that field. No general theory of art history has replaced that of evolution in the minds of contemporary scholars. Nearly all technical writing on the history of the various arts, aside from textbook and encyclopedia summaries, is now highly specialized on some one art, period, and place; often on an individual artist or one of his works. Larger theoretical questions are usually avoided or hastily dismissed. The mistaken assumption is still current that sound scholarship must be narrowly specialized. Nevertheless, there is a persistent interest in the broader problems of art and culture history among scholars and educated laymen; a desire for new syntheses, to take account of new trends in art, recent specialized researches on the past, and present philosophic points of view.

The present book is an attempt to help in satisfying this interest, and to throw some light upon the large-scale trends and processes of art history. As yet, one can only guess at their nature, and form very tentative hypotheses. This book makes no claim to scientific exactness. But it will try at least to clarify some of the central issues with which the theory of artistic evolution deals, and to weigh what evidence is now available, for and against it. So large a field is covered that the treatment of many points must be brief and sketchy as well as frankly speculative.

One thesis of this book is that the *philosophy of history*, with special reference to the arts, is far from worthless or impossible. On the contrary, it is a rewarding field for humanistic study and reflection. Our understanding of the arts, their past, present, and probable future, has much to gain from further attention to general theory. *Part One* deals with the philosophical approach to art history, as compared with other ways of writing

about that subject. The theory of evolution is one example of this approach. It deals with questions so far-reaching that they can not be adequately dealt with from the standpoint of any one art, science, period, or other specialized field.

This book will ask again the question, asked and differently answered many times in the past hundred years, of *whether the arts evolve*, as parts of the larger process of cultural evolution in general. If so, *how and to what extent?* That depends, of course, on how we define "evolution." The answer proposed will be, on the whole, affirmative, but with many limitations and exceptions. The arts do evolve in some but not all respects, at some but not all times and places, and along various lines. Evolution is one major trend or process in the history of art and culture, but not the only one. It is sometimes opposed and overcome by counter-movements. Like some types of plant and animal, some types of art evolve up to a point and then stand still or regress to simpler forms. Change in the arts has some evolutionary characteristics in common with change in other cultural realms, but there are also important differences between them. The same can be said for cultural evolution in general as compared with organic.

The theory of evolution in the arts which is outlined in the following chapters lies between two extremes: that of the nineteenth-century evolutionists, now seen to be much too simple and rigid, and that of the extreme skeptics who deny all evolution in art and culture. The latter err as much on the negative side as the former on the positive. The former exaggerated the resemblances among cultural phenomena, the universality and regularity of cultural evolution. Anti-evolutionists exaggerate the differences. By rejecting the concept of cultural evolution, they lose a valuable tool of interpretation and organization in the field of art. They ignore the persistent trends and recurrences which appear in art history when viewed on a world scale. The blanket rejection of evolutionism in art history has discouraged investigation of these trends through the systematic comparison of different periods and styles.

Like the philosophy of history, the theory of evolution in the arts is not dead but very much alive and continually nourished by increasing historical evidence. But those who seek to rehabilitate it as an active tool of historical interpretation must guard against the common confusion of its essential principles with certain mistaken views of Hegel, Spencer, Morgan, Tylor, and other nineteenth-century writers. Cultural evolutionism in general, and especially in art, is persistently identified with the theories of these early evolutionists, brilliant for their time, but long outgrown. It would be equally misleading to identify modern atomic physics with the crude atomism of Epicurus and Lucretius.

To say that the arts evolve does not, today, imply that evolution is a "universal law," or that all artistic change is evolutionary. Certain opposite types of change, variously described as "devolution," "dissolution," and "regression," are now seen to occur much more widely than was realized a century ago. All cultural evolution, and especially that of art, must now be conceived as multilinear. The modern evolutionist is not searching for "universal laws" of art history as a basis for predicting "inevitable" future trends. He does not insist that all art-producing cultures necessarily pass through parallel stages of development, by virtue of some iron-clad, immanent determinism.

The concept of evolution in art and culture is so thickly overgrown with confusing associations from past theory as almost to defy the hope of disentangling them. One way to approach the difficult task is to trace the *history of past discussion*. This we shall attempt in *Part Two*, in roughly chronological order, but with occasional departures to follow a particular line of thought (such as the Marxist theory of art history) from its origin to the present. Arguments for and against evolution in the arts, and rival theories such as those of cycles and historicism, will be appraised.

Through association with different theories and types of phenomena, the term "evolution" has become extremely ambiguous. This makes it hard, of course, to agree on any definite statements about its reality as a historical process. Much discussion is at cross purposes because those who write about it understand the term in different senses. Not only theoretical issues are involved, but practical ones on which people feel in strongly partisan ways. To decide intelligently on the extent to which evolution occurs in the arts, one must first decide *what the term "evolution" means*, or at least choose one explicit meaning and hold to it consistently. As a means of clarifying the discussion, we shall examine in *Part Three* the chief, current definitions of this and related terms; then recommend certain ones as preferable for usage in the present context.

From the study of past discussion and the technical definitions which have emerged from it, we shall derive a set of general specifications for "evolution" in the cultural field. Whether or not any such process occurs, how would one recognize it if it did? What characteristics would entitle the history of art as a whole, or any sequence of events within it, to be called an "evolution"? One can usually get more agreement on the basic meaning of a technical term than on the other problems, involving disputed facts and values, which are connected with it. One basic, widely accepted criterion of evolution is development, growth, or increasing *complexity*. Another is *descent with adaptive modification*.

We shall go on to ask, then, to what extent these requirements are fulfilled by actual events in the history of the arts. The answer will tend to confirm the theory that artistic evolution is an actual process, a fact of cultural history.

There is a difference between (a) *describing* historical events and conditions as empirical phenomena, (b) *explaining* them causally, and (c) *evaluating* them as good or bad, progressive or decadent. Theoretical discussions of cultural history often bog down on metaphysical issues, as to the ultimate nature of reality, the primal cause and directive force of all human events. A limited amount of historical explanation can be done on a purely empirical, phenomenal level, without raising these metaphysical or theological questions. Attempts to explain on the deeper level have been too important to ignore, and will be briefly noted. But the theory of evolution is mainly an attempt to *describe* certain trends in events; not to explain them in any complete or fundamental way. Our discussion of it will be mainly on the empirical level.

Actually, such a theory as evolution can (if true) go part way toward explaining the phenomena covered by it, in the common, popular sense of "explanation." It can help us understand how certain things have come to be as they are: through what types of process and causation. The principle of natural selection helps us to understand existing plant and animal forms. It also gives a limited power to predict and control such things, as in horticulture and animal breeding. To say that present styles of art have come into being through a process of evolution, rather than as sudden gifts of the gods, is only a partial, superficial explanation of them, even if true. It leaves unsolved and perhaps insoluble a multitude of other problems as to "how" and "why." But even partial, hypothetical explanations can be useful in theory and practice.

Much of the long argument about evolution in the arts has been further confused by evaluative issues: especially whether modern art is better than ancient. To say that the arts evolve is sometimes taken to mean that they necessarily keep improving. This raises a host of additional problems, not essential to the basic question of evolution. We shall have little to say in this book about progress and other questions of value. The inquiry here is mainly concerned with facts: with the nature of what has actually happened, is happening and may happen; not with whether such events are desirable.

The aim of this book is not confined to arguing that the arts evolve. It also seeks to throw some light on many associated theories and problems, such as the comparative influence of hereditary, social, and psychological factors. It discusses the question of analogous sequences and stages in the various arts in different cultures.

One reason for reconsidering the question of evolution in art is that much more material is now available for testing it than in the nineteenth and early twentieth centuries. This includes a much wider sampling of the art of all major peoples and periods in every medium. Archeology and anthropology have brought to light a wealth of artifacts from ancient and primitive cultures, together with information about their dating, manufacture, and use. The visual arts of advanced civilizations have been likewise extensively dated, reproduced for study, and investigated as to their cultural backgrounds. Ancient, exotic, and primitive literatures have been translated and likewise investigated, including much tribal folklore which had not been previously written down. Dances have been filmed, exotic and primitive music recorded, and something has been learned about the ancient music of Greece and China. In the past hundred years, all these arts have undergone tremendous changes in Western culture and revolutionary new ones have been added, such as the film. Museums and educational institutions now facilitate advanced research in all the arts and in aesthetic theory.

In relation to the rising flood of world art a great amount of study has been done, mostly in the shape of specialized researches and monographs. But the amount of new material is so overwhelming that scholarly interpretation has not kept pace with it. Little by little, examples find their way into surveys of art history and theory, but theoretical synthesis has lagged far behind. All our previous conceptions of world art and its history must now be reconsidered in the light of new evidence.

PART ONE

THEORETICAL PROBLEMS
IN THE HISTORY
OF THE ARTS

CHAPTER I

WAYS OF WRITING ABOUT
ART HISTORY

1. "ART HISTORY" IN A BROAD SENSE,
AS INCLUDING THE VISUAL, MUSICAL,
LITERARY, THEATER, AND OTHER ARTS

The terms "art" and "art history" are often restricted to the static, visual arts, such as painting, sculpture, and architecture. In a broader sense, which we are using here instead, they include also the musical and literary arts, the theater arts of drama, ballet, and film, and many others.

"Art" as a generic term has many meanings. We shall understand it as including all culturally transmitted skills and products which are commonly used for stimulating satisfactory aesthetic experience. They may or may not be consciously so intended by the artist. They may or may not have additional ends and functions. From the artist's standpoint, art is also an attempt to express and communicate to others some of his past experience and his present attitudes, feelings, and ideas, through objectifying them in some perceptible medium. Such utilitarian skills as mining, agriculture, war, and medicine were formerly called "arts," but modern usage classes them rather as branches of applied science and technology. "Art" still includes the so-called useful and industrial arts such as architecture, furniture, pottery, clothing, armor, and weapons, insofar as these have aesthetic functions—such as visual appeal through design and decoration—in addition to the utilitarian ones. Particular arts are distinguished according to their medium or material, their tech-

nique or process, and the forms and functions of their products.[1]

The definition of "art" which we shall use is non-evaluative, in accord with present scientific tendencies in aesthetics. To be a work of art, a product does not have to be successful in pleasing people or in causing satisfactory aesthetic experience. It does not have to be beautiful, good, original, or otherwise valuable. A work of art, like an artist, can be good, bad, or indifferent. Evaluation is, of course, highly important, but it can be done otherwise than in the general concept of "art." Any product or performance can be classed as "art" if it belongs to a type which is commonly used for aesthetic functions, such as poems, paintings, statues, songs, and dances. Tattooing, though in low esteem today, is an art in this generic sense. A picture by a savage, a child, or a lunatic can be a work of art, though not necessarily a good one. This neutral sense of "art" allows us to mark off a realm of data for investigation more objectively than if we had to justify every example as good or beautiful.

The data of art history include all works of art in this sense. Many borderline questions arise, as to whether this or that object is to be classed as art: for example, a stone spear-point made with care for its design and appearance

[1] The definition of such terms as "art," "satisfactory," "aesthetic experience," etc., is a perennial problem in aesthetics and psychology. It is not discussed at length in this book. For further discussion, see T. Munro, *The Arts and their Interrelations* (New York, 1949).

beyond the requirements of utilitarian efficiency.

Within the supplementary data of art history are all clues to the date and place of origin of a work of art, its authorship (individual or group), its technique, material, derivation, functions, and relation to its physical, social, and cultural environment; the meaning and importance it had for those who made and used it at the time; its influence on later art and culture; changing subsequent attitudes toward it.

2. SPECIALIZED AND COMPREHENSIVE HISTORIES OF ART

In modern times, "art" in the aesthetic sense has come to be regarded as a distinct cultural realm, activity, and type of product. Art in general, and each particular art, now has its historical specialists who try to tell the story of that thread in the cultural process. One who deals only with ceramics or textiles is, in a way, more specialized than one who tries to cover all the arts or all the visual arts. For the sake of accurate, expert knowledge, most historians today specialize also on a certain period and people within a certain art: e.g., on Carolingian miniature painting or on architecture under the Roman republic. On the other hand, there is a growing demand for more comprehensive historical texts, outlines, and popular surveys for school and public reading.

Within his subdivision of the field, the art historian may be careful and precise as to detailed events and causal influences. Outside it, his knowledge is usually more vague. In specialized studies of art history, great advance has been made in shifting the emphasis from superficial accounts of the lives of artists and the obvious subject-matter of their art to analyses of individual and period styles and to deeper interpretations of art in terms of the artist's personality and cultural environment. Studies of historic styles necessitate some amount of generalization on the traits and tendencies involved, but these may be within a fairly small scope, such as Dutch landscape painting of the seventeenth century. Iconology, a phase of art history, also generalizes to some extent on the symbolic meanings and representational content of certain types of image. It may cover as large a field as Buddhist iconology, or may focus on the interpretation of a single statue. It notes historical changes, but does not cover all phases in the history of art.

Such studies of intermediate scope are gradually extending through the whole field of extant art, providing significant data for interpretation. But attempts to deal theoretically with world art as a whole are few and far between. Little effort has been made by American and British historians to link the particular styles and periods theoretically in terms of large-scale tendencies, underlying causal factors, and recurrent sequences. Broad surveys often give the appearance of doing so while merely narrating events in chronological order: the birth, work, and death of successive artists; the rise and decline of creative periods in various places. In recent years only a few books, such as Heinrich Wölfflin's *Principles of Art History*, have succeeded in drawing the attention of English-reading students to general problems of stylistic change over a broad area, covering various arts.

3. VIEWPOINTS FOR SELECTION AND EMPHASIS. FOREGROUNDS AND BACKGROUNDS

For the history of each art, such as painting or the drama, a partly continuous sequence of events can be traced from the earliest known beginnings. It will not be quite unbroken, for the scene of greatest creative activity shifts from place to place, with comparatively non-productive intervals. Often two or more geographically separated sequences run simultaneously, as in Chinese, Mayan, and Byzantine visual arts around the seventh and eighth centuries of the Christian era. Such local sequences may partly merge, as did the Chinese and Japanese, the Greek and Roman, the Italian and French. Separate, simultaneous processes cannot be clearly described at the same time; as a rule, the historian must trace one after the other. He may tell the story of European painting up to a certain date, and then go back in time and eastward in space to tell that of Chinese painting.

Whatever his field, he tends to see its history from his own vantage-point in time, space, and culture; to emphasize what stands out for him as most important. An oriental historian, such as Nehru, sees history in a perspective somewhat different from that of an occidental one. If one's field is a certain art, such as music, one tends to show its chief events as the main plot and action of one's drama. Its great composers are one's protagonists; its masterpieces and first performances one's main events; its rivalries and critical dissensions one's element of conflict.

Not long ago, the history of such an art could be narrated as an independent series of names, dates, and titles of works. Now, we demand more and more in the way of "background material" and "cultural setting." In a detailed history of an art, the account of events in a certain place and time is usually prefaced by a short introduction, describing event and conditions in other arts at the same time, as well as outstanding political and social events. Against such a cultural background, it is felt, the main characters and events of one's story can be more fully understood. What is "background" for the historian of music (e.g., painting at the time of Monteverdi) is foreground for some other historian. In a history of eighteenth-century French painting Louis XV, Voltaire, and Rameau stand in the background, while Watteau, Fragonard, Chardin, and Boucher dominate the foreground. Historians of music tend to rely on historians of painting for advice on what painters should be mentioned as part of music's cultural background, and vice versa. As each takes the trouble to read how other historians with differ-

ent interests have treated a certain period, all come to understand it more fully and impartially.

In a history of art, socio-economic events and conditions are a part of the "cultural background" of each style and change of style. But in a socio-economic history, the events of art are part of the cultural background, though often ignored. Art can influence the social, economic, and psychological factors, as well as being influenced by them.

As time goes on, historians change their minds somewhat, as to which characters and events are most important for both foreground and background. On the whole, the figures of kings and queens have been receding in accounts of cultural history. Greater respect is paid to obscure and shadowy figures, often anonymous, such as the bards and craftsmen who developed the Homeric epics, the musical modes, and the medieval miniature. Greater stress is laid on impersonal forces such as the rise of an urban middle class.

The criteria of "importance," upon which inclusions, exclusions, and degrees of emphasis are based, themselves change from age to age. In part, they are standards of aesthetic value, as to what artists, works of art, and styles are more or less great and hence worthy of careful study. In part, they indicate judgments as to temporal priority and originality, as in deciding what artist was the first to paint or design in a certain manner. In part, they are estimates of relative influence (a) within a certain art, as in the influence of Giorgione on Titian; (b) among different arts, such as music and poetry; (c) between art and other cultural factors, as in the influence of Aristotle's *Poetics* on French drama, or of Ptolemy and the feudal system on Dante's celestial hierarchy. Some historians stress the influence of physical environment; some that of cultural environment; some of teachers and traditions in one's art. Some stress inherited physique and psychological predisposition; some early family influence. Some stress the role of the individual artist, some that of previous art, and some that of social, political, and economic factors, to explain changes in style.

On the whole, the trend in art-historical study has been toward increasing specialization on a certain art as practiced by a small group of artists in a fairly short period of time. Advanced scholarly research is mostly of this type, while more extensive surveys are produced to fill a need and respected when done by capable scholars. In the former type the trend is toward objective analysis of works of art, styles, and movements. It makes increasing use of scientific methods, including those of physical science, social science, and psychology, in order to describe and interpret events and products more accurately and significantly.

The trend toward science and specialization in writing art history has been, on the whole, a trend away from the literary and philosophic approaches. "Sound scholarship," conceived as detailed, factual erudition, has been the dominant aim.

4. THE NEED FOR THEORETICAL STUDIES OF ART HISTORY

Comparatively lacking in the recent development has been the more theoretical approach, either philosophic or scientific. One reason for its lack is the general wave of skepticism toward philosophies of history which has spread through all branches of scholarship, the social sciences, and even philosophy itself. Another is the specialization in higher education through which, if a student enters the field of art and other humanities, he tends to sacrifice scientific and philosophic training. Later on, as a teacher and writer, he is likely to become increasingly specialized on a chosen field of artistic data, thus never gaining a thorough acquaintance with the cultural sciences. Of help to him, in writing about art history in a scientific or theoretical way, would be a basic knowledge of philosophy, logic, aesthetics, psychology, anthropology, sociology, and the general history of civilization. Lack of this knowledge weakens a great deal of art-history writing at the present time. It is manifested, not only in insufficient reference to the social and cultural backgrounds of art, but in a poverty of general conceptions and methods for the analysis of styles, and in a proneness to naïve assumptions about value in art, the psychology of artists, and related topics. It is sometimes shown in dogmatic statements about the authenticity, dating, provenance, and symbolic meanings of art, on insufficient evidence. Present art-history writing is too often limited to the mere narration of facts about more and more works of art and bibliographical references to them, with little richness of cultural background or depth of psychological interpretation.

Since a philosophic approach to art history requires a wide range of scientific as well as scholarly resources, as well as training and interest in philosophy itself, this approach to art history is scarce at the present time. Philosophic writing on the history of the arts has been hampered by uneven progress in historical studies of the various arts. Because of linguistic barriers, the study of literature as a world art has lagged in some respects behind that of the visual arts. It has had a much less clear conception of historic styles. Until a great variety of phonograph records came on the scene, the empirical study of world music was hard or impossible. Also, the products of literature, music, and dance have been, on the whole, more subject to loss and destruction. We have few data for comparing prehistoric, unwritten poetry and music with contemporaneous developments in sculpture, architecture, and handicrafts.

There is need at present for a type of history-writing intermediate between the narrowly specialized and the all-embracing history; one which risks fairly deep, extensive explanations without pretending to cover world art in a single formula; one which interrelates a few threads in cultural history, such as music and philosophy, or painting, physical science, and economic conditions, without trying to interweave all threads at once.

5. COMPARATIVE AESTHETICS:
THE MORPHOLOGY OF FORM AND STYLE

There has recently been a considerable growth of interest in the scientific approach to aesthetics as distinct from the traditional speculations about beauty. It has not lost touch with philosophy in making greater use of scientific methods and resources. Its approach to art is theoretical but it depends increasingly on a knowledge of art history, in proportion as it seeks to become empirical and inductive rather than narrowly verbal and conceptual. Those who would develop aesthetics as a science cannot ignore the genetic, historical aspects of their subject matter: the role of art in the cultural history of man. The philosophic approach to art history, whether classed as a separate subject—the philosophy of art history—or as a branch of art history or aesthetics, is likely to develop in future as a part of the general extension of scientific method throughout all studies of the cultural field.

Aesthetics, art history, and anthropology all undertake to investigate the arts, and might profitably combine forces on many common problems. But scholars in each field, for the most part, pay little attention to what those in the others are writing and thinking. Unawareness of new developments in another field may keep one at a serious disadvantage. Art historians with broad interest could profit much from recent work in anthropology, and vice versa. Aestheticians too often ignore both, and are ignored by them.

In the past, aesthetics has devoted much time to vague speculations about beauty and aesthetic value, often from a standpoint of supernaturalistic metaphysics. In recent years, it has been in transition toward the aims and methods of empirical science, approaching in a more descriptive way the phenomena of art and related types of behavior and experience. It is putting less emphasis than formerly on the concepts of beauty and "good taste." Instead, it tries to combine information from all sources about the nature and varieties of art and their place in human experience at various times and places. It is still concerned with problems of value, but tries to approach them by way of greater factual understanding. It relies heavily on art history and psychology.

Modern aesthetics, like other sciences and branches of philosophy, differs from art history in organizing its data and conclusions theoretically rather than chronologically. It does so in terms of recurrent types and tendencies; of persistent factors and configurations in the products of art and in human behavior toward them.

One branch of contemporary aesthetics is called *aesthetic morphology*. It studies the forms of art in all media, from paintings to poems, symphonies, ballets, and films in sound and color. Its aim is not to evaluate, but to analyze and compare examples as to their components and composition; then to work out a taxonomy of the principal types and variants.[2] It hopes to play a role, in the investigation of art, somewhat like that which animal and plant morphology has played in biology since the time of Linnaeus. Before the theory of organic evolution could develop on an empirical basis, it was necessary to have a systematic classification of plant and animal forms. With the whole picture of interrelated types spread out clearly before him, the biologist could hardly avoid seeing how they overlapped and how they varied from simple to complex. From this it was only a step—though a hard and epoch-making one—to the idea of change from one type to another, and from the more simple to the more complex; in short to the theory of evolution.[3]

In trying to describe the arts, we still have no systematic, empirically derived morphology of

[2] For a more detailed account of this subject, see T. Munro, *Toward Science in Aesthetics* (New York, 1956), Chs. IV ("Form in the Arts: an Outline of Aesthetic Morphology"); V ("The Morphology of Art as a Branch of Aesthetics"); and VI ("Style in the Arts: a Method of Stylistic Analysis").

[3] *Cf.* Gottfried Semper's remark on the need for an historical typology of art, analogous to that of Cuvier. One could follow the basic types, he said, "through progressive stages up to their highest point of development." *Kleine Schriften* (1884), p. 261. (Quoted by A. Hauser, *The Philosophy of Art History*, p. 146).

structural types; no taxonomy of forms and styles. There is no common vocabulary, no conceptual apparatus for describing and comparing examples of different arts and styles. Accounts of artistic form and style are still permeated by subjective evaluation, metaphysical and sometimes mystical assumptions about the ineffable spirit of art. They are gradually achieving that scientific objectivity which Taine recommended long ago. A conceptual apparatus for the descriptive analysis of forms and styles in all the arts, applied to the phenomena of past and present art, may hope to do for this field what a similar apparatus did for eighteenth-century paleontology, botany, and zoology. When we can spread out the main types and subtypes of artistic form before us in orderly array, the charting of their chronological, genetic relations can become more definite and systematic. Some steps in that direction are outlined in this book.

6. ART MUSEUMS
AND HISTORICAL ARRANGEMENT

At present, few if any art museums are arranged in a consistently historical order. This would imply having all the galleries, and all particular exhibits in each gallery, arranged in some sort of genetic sequence, so that the visitor would tend to see them in that order from prehistoric to contemporary. Labels and wall charts could further explain their chronology and historical relations. Genetic sequences on a small scale have been much used in natural history museums, as in explaining the ancestry of the horse; also in ethnological museums to show successive culture-epochs such as those of Peru and Mexico. They have not found much favor in art museums, however.[4]

This is due, not only to the comparative lack of an evolutionary attitude in the visual arts, but to special obstacles confronting it there. The difficulties and disadvantages of a thoroughly historical arrangement would be enormous. It would involve, for one thing, breaking down the present system of departments, each under a specialized expert: some according to different arts such as painting and textiles; some according to regions and main periods such as far eastern and medieval European. Contemporaneous examples for all places, or products of supposedly analogous cultural stages, would be put together in a bewildering mixture. Baffling theoretical problems of origin and influence would be encountered in arranging sequences of styles. It would be hard to study the history of a particular art, or to compare examples of a certain type without regard to chronology. For such reasons the historical approach is followed only to a limited extent, as in the sequence of Egyptian galleries within the Metropolitan Museum of New York. Even on a small scale, however, such an illustration of genetic sequence in the arts can help to stimulate a historical attitude.

In addition to disregarding historical order in its general plan, the art museum also has to detach its exhibits from their original geographic, social, and cultural settings. It seldom tries to give much understanding of these settings by connected visual displays. Thus it tends to build up the conception of a work of art as something isolated, autonomous, detached from the flow of cultural history and unrelated to events in other fields. The student or historian who seeks a larger view of art history as a part of cultural evolution must try to rearrange the parts for himself, with the aid of what few writings exist on the subject.

---

[4] Alexander Dorner, when director of the Hannover Museum, experimented with more genetic arrangements and interpretations. See his *The Way Beyond Art* (New York, 1958).

7. HISTORY-WRITING, SPECIALIZED AND GENERAL; SUPERFICIAL AND PHILOSOPHIC

The word "history" has two common meanings. One denotes all past events, especially in man's life on earth, and perhaps future events as well. Thus we say, "China has had a long history," and "Man's future history is unpredictable." In the other, more literal sense, history is historiography or the written record of these events; it denotes the attempts of writers like Gibbon to narrate them and explain their nature, sequence, and causation. Mere lists of events, as in annals, newspapers, and diaries, are rather the data of history than history itself, which implies more continuous organization and interpretation. Some historians also moralize on the past and seek to derive from it wisdom for the future conduct of life. History-writing has had many motives: among them, to preserve and glorify the memory of great men and their deeds, to justify the ways of God to man, and to explain present civilization in the light of its origins.

The historic era is sometimes distinguished from the prehistoric as the time since history-writing began, or since the origin of writing; but more broadly it includes the prehistoric era too, and even the sequence of events on earth before man came on the scene. As the whole cosmic process, occurring in time, "history" is sometimes made synonymous with "evolution" in general.

All history-writing is selective, since it is impossible as well as useless to record all past events. The historian's task is to select important events and trains of events. In this he must rely on standards of importance which are partly subjective, determined by the culture-pattern in which he lives and by his own personal attitudes. He selects, not only what seems important in general, but what seems important in his special field. Thus a history of economics tries to follow one set of threads through successive periods; a history of religion a different though connected set, and a history of marriage a third.

Art in general, as we have seen, is one complex set of threads to be followed through the total succession of events, and within it each particular art is a smaller set in itself. The events do not occur in completely distinct, continuous threads or sequences. The historian forms them in his narrative by detaching events of a certain kind from their context, and describing them in sequence. The facts themselves provide some basis for this selective organization, but historical narrative has to exaggerate the continuity of certain sequences and isolate them somewhat, though not completely, from those with which they were associated.

Early history-writing (as in Herodotus) was a mixture of factual reporting with myths, legends, and fanciful tales. Modern history tries to be wholly factual and true, but inevitably contains some debatable accounts and interpretations. At first it was largely political and military, devoted to the exploits of kings and armies. Sometimes it emphasized religious events, as in the Old Testament. As such it was specialized in a certain way, picking out the events and persons which seemed most important at the time. In modern times it has paid more attention to impersonal social, economic, intellectual, and artistic events, and to persons of humble rank. The cultural historian tries to be less specialized, more inclusive and general in his view, as he traces the interrelations of many historical threads through a series of periods, places, and peoples. But he, too, is regarded as one kind of specialist in the general field of history.

In history as in other subjects, it is always possible to *specialize on generalizing*: for example, to compare Greek and Roman civilization or Chinese and Japanese art; to characterize a period in general terms, as Gibbon did in comparing Rome during and after the time of the Antonines. If done well, with accuracy and penetrating insight, such history-writing can be profoundly enlightening; but it is more subject to argument than the cautious, narrowly factual kind which never ventures a controversial statement for fear of being found in

[9]

error. History-writing does not necessarily become more shallow or unsound as it broadens its scope. A short encyclopedia article by a good historian can be admirable as a concise summary of essentials. Greater scope usually entails more reliance on secondary sources. One may choose a fairly small area of space and time and show the interrelation of many threads within it. This tends to make the history, if done well, more broadly and deeply philosophic than a mere topical outline of greater scope. A philosophic history tends toward large scope as well as depth, but this can be achieved by implication, in using one period or even the life of one man, such as Hadrian or Charlemagne, Rubens or Goethe, as the starting-point for a commentary on human traits and problems.

Traditionally, philosophy has aspired to treat with breadth and depth such perennial problems as the source and reliability of knowledge, the world and man's place in it, the nature and values of life and conscious experience, man's history on earth, and his probable future. But much that passes under the name of philosophy fails to achieve these qualities, either because it narrows down its field excessively or because it treats large problems in a superficial way.

CHAPTER II

PHILOSOPHIES OF ART HISTORY

I. PHILOSOPHY OF HISTORY IN GENERAL. ITS APPLICATION TO THE ARTS

What is the philosophy of history? It is sometimes regarded as a branch of philosophy; sometimes as a kind of history-writing. As a modern subject, it overlaps both philosophy and history, so that books about it may be classed under either heading. It undertakes to study the whole course of human history or some large section of it, such as modern Western civilization, and to generalize about the basic nature of events therein. The philosopher of history tries to find out whether there are, in human events, any pervasive, controlling laws, tendencies, or patterns. He looks in world history for major trends, sequences, and stages, for underlying causal factors.

A philosophy of history is a particular theory along these lines, such as that of Hegel or Spencer. Most books which are classed as such undertake to discuss the whole course of human events: not in detail, but as to its main trends and explanatory principles. However, vast scope alone does not entitle a book to be called a philosophy of history. An "outline of world history," which merely lists or superficially narrates events in chronological order, would not qualify. On the other hand, a book may cover a relatively small period, as did Burckhardt's *Civilization of the Renaissance in Italy*, and take on philosophic character through the depth and cogency with which it interrelates, interprets, and explains events in that time and place. It may show significant analogies, recurrences, and causal connections among events in differ-ent fields, such as the socio-economic, religious, intellectual, and artistic. Even so, it would not fully qualify as a philosophy of history unless it tried to show how the facts within its special field were related to history in general; perhaps as typical of common tendencies. A book on the philosophy of history may not actually narrate particular events at all; it may confine itself to a theoretical discussion of the nature of history and the problems involved in explaining it.[1] Or it may be a history of *theories* of history, as in Robert Flint's *History of the Philosophy of History in France* (New York, 1894), J. B. Bury's *The Idea of Progress* (London, 1920), and Hermann Schneider's *Philosophie der Geschichte* (Breslau, 1923).

The term "historiology," long in Webster's unabridged as a "rare" word, is now coming into wider technical use. Though defined simply as "the study or knowledge of history," it now refers mainly to the *theoretical* study of history, rather than to the ordinary learning and narrating of particular events. A book of this sort may deal theoretically with history as a whole or with some part of it, such as the history of art or of Greece. Or it may deal only with an abstract theoretical problem such as "historical explanation."[2]

Modern philosophers of history usually try to

---

[1] As, for example, in Morris R. Cohen's *The Meaning of Human History* (La Salle, Ill., 1947). *Theories of History*, ed. by Patrick Gardiner (Glencoe, Ill., 1959), is an anthology of selections from philosophic and scientific theories of history.

[2] *Cf.* Patrick Gardiner, *The Nature of Historical Explanation* (London, 1952) and Arthur Child, "Thoughts on the Historiology of Neo-Positivism," *Journal of Philosophy*, LVII (1960), 665.

base their theories on established facts, so far as possible. But they venture beyond the limits of such knowledge into far-reaching hypotheses which can not, as yet, be fully supported by empirical evidence. In this tendency to bold speculation, with all its risks of error, they are carrying on a traditional role of philosophy. Since the Greeks first showed him how, man has always insisted on looking ahead, beyond the solid, clearly lighted ground of present knowledge, to speculate on what may lie beyond.

Some theories of history claim to be scientific, and some historians class the study of history as a social science. Others insist that history-writing is not and can not be a science in the full sense of the word. They point to such obstacles as these: (a) the comparative "uniqueness" of human events; (b) the complexity of historical causation; (c) the impossibility of adequate observation, experiment, and measurement; (d) the inevitability of subjective bias on the historian's part. When the historian deals with such complex and often intangible phenomena as those of art, a scientific treatment of it is especially hard, if not impossible.

Nevertheless, it is possible in history-writing, as in aesthetics, to make some steps toward scientific method. One can at least try to base one's theories on whatever direct, verifiable evidence exists at the time, and to frame hypotheses which are reasonably consistent with scientific conceptions of the universe and man. A theory of this sort should not be condemned in advance along with ancient mythologies and fictions based on *a priori* metaphysics. Having been warned of the dangers of wishful thinking and monumental system-building, the historian can try to be moderately objective and cautious. But a philosophy of history must necessarily—at least at this stage of the game—be somewhat like trying to assemble a jig-saw puzzle of which one possesses only a few parts, then trying to imagine how the picture as a whole would look. Moreover, the player in this case can not be sure that the pieces belong to any one unified picture. Even as fragments they keep

changing, and new, surprising ones keep appearing before his eyes.

A philosophy of *art* history selects one main set of threads in the total fabric of events—a certain art or group of arts—and tries to study them in some of the ways just mentioned. The historian tries to follow this set of threads through successive periods and different places, describing its main trends and stages, and explaining them as best he can. Thus to follow a particular thread, or (to change the figure) a constituent stream within the total flow of history, necessitates detaching it from its context, ignoring or minimizing most of the other factors with which it interacted along the way. The historian may do so to a greater or less extent, and this itself tends to imply a certain theory of causation on his part. To ignore or minimize outside factors to a great extent usually implies that events in art are largely caused by factors within art itself, or by factors which are basic in human nature, rather than by social, geographical, or other external factors. Heinrich Wölfflin's *Principles of Art History* and Henri Focillon's *La Vie des Formes* are of this type, whereas Taine's *Philosophy of Art* and Arnold Hauser's *The Philosophy of Art History* put more emphasis on external factors. None of these books undertakes to narrate the particular events of art history. On the other hand, Hauser's *Social History of Art* is a narrative, not a philosophy of art history, although it has a strong theoretical emphasis.

There is a difference between philosophic history-writing and the philosophy of history. It is one of degree, but can become a large one. Philosophic history-writing tends to emphasize the narration of events in approximately chronological order. It will pause at times to analyze a pervasive condition or enduring tendency, or go backward in time to take up another sequence of events; but its main mode of organization is chronological. It is a kind of history-writing, with philosophic comments as a minor though important element.

The philosophy of history, on the other hand,

is a branch of philosophy. It tends to organize its materials theoretically, in terms of general concepts, problems, and explanations. Its primary aim is not to narrate events but to analyze and interpret the whole process of human events and its place in the universe. Its data are drawn from actual events or what are supposed to be actual events. Its theoretical interpretations are drawn in part from the general philosophic or religious world-view of the writer, who seeks to discover how human history fits into that world-view and can be truthfully explained in terms of that system of beliefs. He may try to relate it to his theory of ontology, or what the universe consists of (mind, matter, or both); to cosmology, or how the universe operates (by divine purpose or the motions of inanimate matter); and to ethics (principles of good conduct, duty, and value). In part, and to a greater extent as his world-view is naturalistic, he bases his interpretation on empirical studies of events by himself and others. Since his field is vast, he must rely heavily on more specialized works by other scholars.

As a part of his discussion, the philosopher may introduce a chronological outline or a series of main stages in history as he conceives them; but the chronological approach will be subordinate. Thus Lucretius briefly summarizes the stages in the development of civilization after explaining the universe by atomistic principles. Hegel's *Aesthetics* and Comte's *Positive Philosophy* offer theories of chronological stages, but they make no attempt to describe successive happenings in detail. A book on the philosophy of history is primarily an expository treatise, not a narrative. If the philosopher's world-view is theological, as St. Augustine's was, he may try to show how history illustrates the divine plan and prefigures events to come. If he is an idealist, like Hegel, he will show the relation of events to the cosmic mind and its ideas; if a naturalist, like Lucretius and Spencer, he will try to explain them in terms of matter and motion. Comte, as an empiricist, tried to explain them in terms of gradual progression toward a scientific

or positivistic attitude as contrasted with the theological and metaphysical. Spencer's approach is largely theoretical; Spengler's is largely in chronological order, but with strongly theoretical emphasis. Toynbee is primarily a historian whose religious world-view is introduced at crucial points.[3]

In the past, the philosophy of history has often tried to show "the meaning of history." That phrase, as commonly understood, assumes that events have a supernatural, transcendental meaning in terms of cosmic or divine purpose. Naturalistic philosophers tend to believe that history as the total sequence of events has no meaning in itself. What meaning it has is produced and imputed by human minds. Man gives meaning to history, according to this view, as he comes to understand it and to influence its course accordingly, in pursuit of his own ideals and purposes.

2. RELATIONS OF ART HISTORY TO SCIENCE AND CULTURE HISTORY

There is much dispute on a single complex issue: the nature of causal explanation in history; how and to what extent the historian can "explain" any event. We shall revert to this issue in a later chapter, with special reference to historicism and the explanation of events in art.

Some historians try to be as objective as possible; to say only what can be verified or reliably documented; to make use of all available scientific resources, such as those of geology and anthropology, of astronomy, chemistry, and physics, for dating objects and events. They can, as a result,

---

[3] Most European critical philosophers of history in the last generation, says J. H. Randall, Jr., have been philosophical idealists. Most Americans have been proponents of a realistic, pluralistic, relativistic conception. The former include Windelband, Rickert, Simmel, Dilthey, Cassirer, Croce, and Collingwood; the latter, Dewey, Woodbridge, Hook, Cohen, Lovejoy, Becker, Beard, and Nevins. *Nature and Historical Experience* (New York, 1958), p. 30.

make history-writing more reliable factually and more scientific in method and content. But, as we have seen, the writing of history can never be completely so because of the need of arbitrary selection and emphasis. Other historians repudiate the wish to be scientific. They regard their discipline as one of the humanities, with a frankly personal element. They stress the sympathetic understanding and imaginative interpretation of human factors. Some stress literary style as well, making history a branch of literary art.[4] The literary approach in historiography can be further emphasized by frankly indulging one's imagination to supplement known facts. It is often hard to draw the line between imaginative history and biography on one hand, and historical fiction on the other. *Les Misérables*, *War and Peace*, and Strachey's *Queen Victoria* contain much history in fictional form.

Even when its aim is to be rigorously factual, history differs from science and philosophy in that its chief mode of organization is chronological rather than theoretical. The difference is often one of emphasis. Books on astronomy, geology, biology, and the social sciences often describe certain events in chronological order: the history of the solar system, of life, or of institutions. But they tend to describe and explain most phenomena in logical rather than temporal order.

Many sciences touch upon the arts and their history. Pliny traced the history of the visual arts as part of a treatise on various materials and their uses. Anthropology has much to say of the history of the arts among primitive peoples, prehistoric and modern. Some textbooks on anthropology contain a series of chapters on the successive periods in the arts and handicrafts from the paleolithic age to that of early urban civilization, including such types as ice-age cave painting, sculpture of clay and bone, pottery, and the development of tools and weapons from rough stone through polished stone, bronze, and iron. Some include information about other primitive arts such as music and dance. They also trace, more

or less in chronological order, the social and other cultural developments of man. To this extent, anthropology overlaps culture history and archeology. But, as a science, it also tends to organize its findings in terms of abstract types and subdivisions of primitive life, such as racial groupings, kinship and marriage systems, government, and religion. Under each of these headings, it analyzes and compares a number of different types of behavior and product, without adhering to their chronological order.

Psychology and the social sciences all deal with human acts and motives. In this they overlap the writing of history. General psychology puts more emphasis on what seems comparatively universal, basic, and enduring in human nature. It emphasizes phenomena which are common to all or most humans, rather than those of a particular group or period. The social sciences emphasize group behavior. But psychology recognizes the social and historical conditioning of all individual thought and behavior. All these human sciences now say little today about eternal laws. They realize that most of their facts and generalizations are subject to change, fast or slow. These sciences are so thoroughly pervaded by the historical, evolutionary spirit that they no longer stand out in sharp contrast with history-writing.

Culture history, as a distinct subject, is more consistently chronological, and does not confine itself to the primitive cultures. It is sometimes identified with the history of civilization; but "culture" is a broader term, including uncivilized as well as civilized peoples and periods. Any general history of culture would be sadly incomplete without frequent reference to the arts of successive epochs. While the historian of culture follows chronological order on the whole, he is quite free to depart from it at times to discuss some general subject, such as the clan system in various parts of the world. His method then shifts for a while to that of science.

[4] B. Croce, for example, insists that history is included in art, not science. *Aesthetic* (London, 1922), p. 27.

All these subjects overlap, cooperate, and use each others' methods and conclusions when it seems expedient. To realize and approve this fact today expresses an evolutionary attitude toward all intellectual inquiry. No science or discipline, no art or branch of history, has any fixed, immutable domain with rightful boundaries which must not be crossed, and proper methods to which it must adhere. All have evolved from comparatively undifferentiated beginnings. They are not marked by fences, like private property. Science, history, and art have much in common.

Science is not radically different from philosophy or scientific history from philosophic history, if the latter is pursued in a spirit of naturalistic empiricism. Philosophy in all its applications, including the theory of history, is radically different from science only when based, as it often is, on attitudes and assumptions which are hostile to science, such as authoritarian dogmatism, mystical supernaturalism, and anti-intellectualism. These are alien, not because of their beliefs *per se*, for science is not opposed *a priori* to any particular theories of history, but because they tend to obstruct free, open-minded inquiry.

The philosophy of history becomes more scientific as it limits its generalizations more cautiously to verifiable, empirical evidence and logical inference. This usually entails a narrowing of the field for more intensive inquiry. Though the historian must usually accept the decision of specialists on particular facts, he tries to rely on specialists whose methods are rigorous in their various fields. Indirectly, he thus relies on geological, physical, chemical, and astronomical information for dating events and locating the origin of artifacts. He relies on botany and zoology for identifying plant and animal remains; comparative linguistics, physical and cultural anthropology, and other sciences for ascertaining and interpreting facts in relation to their spatio-temporal and social context.

The philosophy of history also relies on the various sciences for help in explaining and generalizing. This may involve debatable assumptions about the analogy between phenomena in various fields. Is a law or hypothesis which has been developed in physics or biology applicable to cultural history? Early social philosophers likened society to a living body or an animal organism; from this they drew mistaken as well as valid inferences. Cultural evolutionists in the nineteenth century, following Spencer and Darwin, relied too heavily on biology for hypotheses. A reaction away from this ensued, but there are still some obvious analogies between the two fields. There is nothing wrong in using a biological fact as a hypothesis to be carefully and open-mindedly tested in the cultural field, to see how much actual resemblance there is. Such comparison may lead one to notice things which would otherwise be ignored. It is not merely a question of resemblance between two or more fields of phenomena. Insofar as humans are a kind of living organism, some biological generalizations are sure to apply to them, although the differences between man and other animals are more important from some points of view.

The fields of history, psychology, and sociology are not sharply separated. All these sciences look at man from different points of view and with emphasis on somewhat different types of phenomena. To apply a psychological principle in the study of history, or vice versa, is not to jump from one realm of existence to another, but to look at the same broad field from different points of view. Any valid generalization in psychology should help us better understand history, and vice versa.

Some historians rely heavily on psychological concepts and hypotheses in trying to explain the facts of history; some on sociological. The Freudian and the Marxist approach to history can both be enlightening up to a point; but neither is all-explaining. Formerly, historians relied more on theology; then on political and military concepts to explain history. Sometimes they relied on the biographies of great men. All these are still potentially revealing, since history contains all these types of factor and causal relation. Which to select

[15]

and emphasize is partly a matter of individual predilection; partly of the culture and school of thought to which one belongs. When a historian or social scientist tries to explain a complex mass of phenomena in terms of one science only, and of one or a few concepts within that science, thus producing a somewhat monistic system in that field, the result is felt today as oversimplified. It is false in attributing all events in the field to a single type of cause and discerning therein only a single type of sequence. Nevertheless, it may be enlightening if combined with and corrected by others.

The use of information and hypotheses from the sciences in the study of history will not, in itself, make that study scientific or philosophic. Everything depends on how they are used; how successfully they are synthesized. To combine the results of several different sciences on a large scale is a philosophic enterprise. The larger the scale, the more danger of error through the difficulty of dealing with such complex, diversified material. Each science has its own techniques for dealing with its own phenomena.

It is not true, as some writers have asserted, that history deals only with the concrete and particular; science only with the general, universal, and eternal.[5] History and science both deal to some extent with all these aspects of the universe. The difference is one of degree. Science tends to regard particular cases as data for generalization, rather than as important in themselves. But it often deals with particular objects and events of great theoretical or practical importance to man, such as the earth and its formation, the stars and planets. Medical and psychiatric diagnosis is devoted to ascertaining the present condition of individual persons. History emphasizes particulars—events, persons, places, temporary conditions—but seeks to characterize and explain them in terms of general concepts. It often compares particulars with each other to bring out resemblances, types, and tendencies. Both science and history keep looking back and forth between particulars and generals, to understand each better in the light of the other. Even the more distinctive aspects of a particular case, such as a battle or a ruler, can best be shown by comparing it with other cases of the same general type, as Plutarch did in his *Lives of Illustrious Men*.

3. RECENT MISTAKEN ATTACKS ON THE PHILOSOPHY OF HISTORY

The philosophy of history has been in some disfavor among scholars, especially in America, for several decades. It has been widely attacked as obsolete and discredited, impossible to deal with in terms of objective facts. Its opponents have also denounced a number of the concepts used by philosophers of history in the eighteenth and nineteenth centuries—especially those of "progress" and "evolution." Theories of cultural evolution in the field of art have been especially under fire.

These attacks, while justified to some extent by previous errors, have been exaggerated. The philosophy of history, as a general subject, implies no particular theory, true or false. It is an open field for investigation, a line of inquiry which has attracted philosophic minds in all ages, especially since modern man has developed so strong an interest in his own history and so much detailed information about it. Under one name or another, philosophic minds in the future will insist on pursuing that line of inquiry as far as the data permit.

It has been falsely charged that the philosophy of history is an attempt to prove the existence of absolute laws and regular patterns in human events. The philosophy of history does not need to start

---

[5] Reference will be made later on to the theory of "historicism" on this point. See the discussion of culture history as related to the science of culture in D. Bidney, *Theoretical Anthropology* (New York, 1953), p. 281. They are complementary, he shows; both are interested in processes and forms, variables and constants in human history. Some historic changes may be understood in terms of universal laws, while others may remain unique and unpredictable.

with any such preconceived assumption. It can and should be open-minded as to the existence of any unifying patterns or pervasive tendencies. To advance a theory in the philosophy of history does not imply that one is committed in advance to some overly regular, monistic type of explanation. Conceivably, one may hold that there is no order, pattern, or continuity whatever in human events, that all is chaos and utter diversity. Or one can accept a more moderate pluralism, holding that some approximate, irregular patterns are discernible, that analogies and recurrent sequences do occur, but not in exactly the same way everywhere. This view is supported in the present book.

Further investigation may or may not disclose more definite correlations and recurrences than we can see at present. But if we do not look for them, we are not likely to discover them. To do so requires more than a careful study of isolated events. It requires a systematic, large-scale comparison of groups and sequences of historical phenomena in different parts of the world at the same and different times, to see how much resemblance and how much diversity actually exist. No realm of historical research presents a wider range of concrete data for such study than the arts.

Why has the philosophy of history been in such disfavor? There are many contributing factors. At times, it would seem, the intellectual and cultural situation is right for producing large, comprehensive syntheses of thought; at other times, for avoiding them and gathering more data. Large systems in all branches of philosophy have been unpopular in the last few decades, especially in America, which is apparently less inclined than Europe toward philosophic systems; more toward pluralism and specialization. In historical scholarship, the reaction has been especially strong because of disappointment with the grandiose philosophies of history which appeared in the late eighteenth, nineteenth, and early twentieth centuries. Outstanding among these were Condorcet's essay on human progress, Comte's "law of three stages,"

Hegel's theory of the development of the cosmic mind, Spencer's "universal law of evolution," Taine's theory of race, environment, and moment, the "unilinear" evolutionism of L. H. Morgan and E. Tylor, and Spengler's "decline of the West." In reacting against these, American scholars have been tempted into equally excessive hostility toward the philosophy of history in general, especially in the arts. Kroeber identified it with Voltaire's idea of a universal history from the standpoint of the eighteenth-century rationalistic enlightenment; also with the works of Herder, Hegel and Northrop.[6]

Much the same can be said about the concepts of evolution and progress, although they stand for more specific theories in the field. As abstract concepts, they are highly ambiguous. They have been defined in various ways by various philosophers, some of which imply theories long since abandoned, while others are consistent with present scientific opinion. Discussions of them in art history, philosophy, and social science are sadly confused by semantic difficulties.

One occasionally hears the argument that no historian today can know all branches of history, that a philosophy of art history is bound to be shallow. This has a kernel of truth; certainly no one can know everything about any subject, especially one so vast as the history of the arts. But that has never prevented philosophers from generalizing about the universe and man, sometimes with amazing insight in spite of limited knowledge of details. A genuinely philosophic mind can learn enough of the details to form reasonable hypotheses about the whole range of facts. The kind of "synthesis" undertaken by the philosophy of history is never a mere combination of details. It is always selective, and must be increasingly so as the facts pile up. It must search for underlying

---

[6] *Style and Civilizations*, p. 110. Also A. L. Kroeber and C. Kluckhohn, *Culture: a Critical Review of Concepts and Definitions* (Cambridge, Mass., 1952), p. 145. The "philosophy of history" is there described as deductive and opposed to the recognition of many diverse cultures. It has often been so, but not always, and is not necessarily so.

tendencies, recurrences, causal sequences, broad outlines and important human implications.

Another charge against the philosophy of history is that it is necessarily *evaluative*, that it tries to tell us what is good and bad or right and wrong in past events; hence, that it can express only a personal or cultural set of standards, but cannot be objective. Certainly, most philosophies of history have been evaluative. That of Condorcet emphasized progress or improvement. Spencer began by identifying progress with evolution, and only later separated the two concepts. Most other writers who have attempted a large-scale interpretation of history have included judgments as to whether things were moving from worse to better or in the opposite direction. This has been true in histories of art as well as elsewhere. The assumption that art is getting better on the whole is not limited to philosophies of history. It is often implicit in histories of art, even when they try to specialize on a narrow range of facts. One can hardly avoid some evaluation. In any historical survey, the historian necessarily picks out events and trends which seem to him important for one reason or another. The art historian tends to give most space and illustrations to the styles and artists he considers great. He speaks of the "advances" made in each period.

There has been a fuller realization in recent years that evaluation (either moral or aesthetic) presents distinctive and peculiar problems of its own. It is not something to be casually or dogmatically undertaken. The philosopher can, if he wishes, try to write a comparatively factual, objective account, describing and explaining the main trends, without venturing any judgment as to whether they are for better or worse. The evaluative element in the philosophy of history can thus be reduced to an unavoidable minimum.

On the other hand, there is nothing necessarily wrong or fallacious about trying to evaluate history on moral, aesthetic, or other grounds. Evaluation is a legitimate part of the philosopher's task, and may be enlightening if it is done wisely and explicitly, with due recognition of the theoretical difficulties involved. A naturalistic historian today will not claim to have any absolute, eternal basis for his judgments. He will recognize that he is expressing the standards of himself and his cultural environment. He will be more relativistic than most philosophers have been in the past. There is no reason why the historian should not try to answer the question of whether or not there has been progress or retrogression in art, and in what ways. He does not need to present these personal judgments as objective facts.

Many of the sweeping attacks on the philosophy of history have been made by supernaturalists of one sort or another—dualists or idealists—who object to the naturalistic tone of much nineteenth-century evolutionism, especially that of Spencer and Morgan. Not all supernaturalists object to philosophies of history; in fact, one of the greatest of them was made by Hegel, an idealist, who believed that the cosmic mind is in the process of developing toward increasing individuality and self-realization. Art history had a prominent place in his theory. On the other hand, some supernaturalists, especially of the dualistic persuasion, argue that the essentials of art are purely spiritual and hence outside the physical processes of life in human bodies on this earth. The essentials of art, they hold, come from divine inspiration and are not affected either by previous works of art or by social and technological factors in the environment. They take the mystical view that each work of art and each genius is a bolt from the blue, which owes nothing essential to any previous artist or to the social environment. Only the superficial externals of material and technique are parts of the evolutionary process, according to this point of view. Naturalists, on the other hand, reject the view that there is any element whatever in art which is entirely detached from the natural processes of life on earth and from the evolution of physical bodies.[7]

[7] The correct and satisfactory definition of such terms as "naturalism" and "supernaturalism" is a difficult, controversial

Another objection to the philosophy of history comes from writers who go to an extreme of nominalism. As against the Platonists, they rightly argue that there is no such thing as "humanity" in the abstract, apart from the individuals who make it up; also, that there is no such thing as a *Zeitgeist* or "spirit of the age" apart from the actions, thoughts, and feelings of human individuals. But, again, it is going too far to say that one must not write about human history because "humanity" in the abstract has no independent existence. These extremists would have us write only of particular groups and periods. Arguing along this line, one might go on to say that there can be no history of a group or period, but only of single individuals, or perhaps of a single moment in the life of one of them. This is of course absurd. Humanity in the aggregate is as real as any individual, if we mean by it all the humans who have lived and will live, considered as to their generic and collective traits. Their total history as a genus is as real a set of phenomena as the history of any smaller group or individual. It can be described as to its main, common traits and sequences, without implying that all men are completely alike, or that some ghostly, independent *Zeitgeist* hovers mysteriously above them. Again, there is a moderate, reasonable position in such matters.

Anthropology is a subject with much greater claim to scientific status than either aesthetics or art history, and it has considerable prestige in the United States and Europe. Recent opinion in that subject has helped to influence American art historians against the philosophy of history in general and cultural evolutionism in particular. Several of the nineteenth-century philosophies of history, mentioned above, dealt with anthropology. They attempted a reconstruction of the stages in prehistoric and early historic culture, including the arts, and a comparison of prehistoric culture with that of contemporary primitive peoples. They conceived of cultural evolution, including that of art, as a unilinear path of similar steps everywhere.

The resemblances among different peoples were exaggerated and the diversities minimized. These faults were first clearly pointed out by the German-American anthropologist Franz Boas and his followers during the 1920's and '30's. Their attack contributed to the decline of interest in all of these lines of thought during the second quarter of the century.

Only a few of the leading American anthropologists, notably the late Professor A. L. Kroeber, have extended their studies of cultural history to the arts of civilized periods. Most anthropologists lack enough knowledge of the history of civilized arts to undertake comprehensive studies along that line. Their interests are still usually limited to the prehistoric and primitive. Hence their writings do not fill the need for theoretical studies in the arts of advanced civilizations.

A fruitful line of investigation lies open to the aesthetician with an interest in history and anthropology, and to the historian or anthropologist with an interest in art and aesthetics. There is need for cooperation among all these fields of scholarship. Most of all, there is a present need for theo-

problem in itself. It will not be attempted in this book. In a later chapter, it is discussed with special reference to the causal explanation of history. In a more general way, it is discussed with bibliography in the author's essay, "Meanings of 'Naturalism' in Philosophy and Aesthetics" (*Journal of Aesthetics and Art Criticism*, XIX [Winter 1960], 133–137; in French in *Proceedings of the IV International Congress on Aesthetics*, Athens, 1960, pp. 507–514).

Naturalism in a philosophic sense is related to humanism, empiricism, positivism, pragmatism, and metaphysical materialism. It is opposed to supernaturalism, dualism, spiritualism, pantheism, and metaphysical idealism. But important distinctions are made among these concepts. Naturalism rejects the supernaturalist theory of a transcendental realm of reality, incorporeal spirits, and the teleological interpretation of history. It conceives of "nature" as including all existence. It is based on scientific reasoning but it does not necessarily hold (as some definitions assert) that the laws and concepts of the physical sciences are "adequate to account for all phenomena." (*Cf. Webster's Third New International Dictionary*, 1961, p. 1507). This would be obviously untrue in regard to artistic and other cultural phenomena. The same dictionary defines "supernaturalism" as "belief in the supernatural; specif.: a doctrine or creed that asserts the reality of an existence beyond nature and the control and guidance of nature and men by an invisible power."

retical studies of moderate scope, which will point out hitherto unobserved connections between different fields. They need not call themselves "philosophies of art history," for that may seem to claim too much; but they can at least move in that direction. The philosophic quality in art history writing can be achieved on a smaller and more practical scale. In recent years we have had very little of it.

4. THE RETREAT FROM SYSTEM IN PHILOSOPHY AND ART

The recent trend away from philosophies of history has coincided with analogous trends in art, general philosophy, and science. To what extent they are causally connected, perhaps as varied expressions of some deeper trend in modern culture, is still obscure.

In all these realms, there has been a widespread tendency to avoid all large-scale systems; all comprehensive structures of thought and art. Searching attacks have been made on the old, traditional systems of belief; those once thought to rest on divinely established order and universal laws of truth and value. Public faith in these has been weakened or destroyed, and none of equal scope has arisen to take their place. Instead, there has been much specialization in art, philosophy, and science on details and smaller projects. Loss of confidence in the old patterns has been accompanied by extreme skepticism, pessimism, and nihilism toward traditional moral codes, ideals, and value-standards. Anxiety and despair about the future have been widely expressed in the arts.

In general philosophy, all the great Baroque and Romantic systems from Descartes, Spinoza, and Hobbes through Hegel have been undermined by the growth of Humean empiricism and existentialism. The claims of the Kantians to have built a new intellectual and moral order on the basis of empiricism are no longer convincing. To the exist-

entialists, life and the world are essentially absurd and progress an illusion. Philosophy, whose traditional function has been to try to synthesize knowledge and theory, to see the universe clearly as a whole, has largely withdrawn into its own highly specialized, esoteric researches and language-games of semantic analysis. Few attempts have been made since Herbert Spencer to construct philosophic systems based on empiricism, naturalism, and humanism. (That of Santayana is perhaps the nearest approach to one.) Many leading philosophers in the Western world, such as John Dewey, have explicitly avoided system-building. It is no longer possible, they hold, to construct a valid, comprehensive system in a world of universal change and relativity. Knowledge is now so vast and so diversified, they say, that it can no longer be covered by any single formulation. Hence they write only detached essays and treatises on separate topics, loosely interrelated. "System-builder" has become a derogatory term as applied to a philosopher, historian, or social scientist.

In the arts, the twentieth century has seen a wholesale rejection by the avant-garde of past styles and modes of organizing works of art, together with the associated theories of aesthetic value. This includes the Greek and Roman, Byzantine and Gothic, Renaissance, Baroque, and Romantic styles, all of which have come to seem obsolete and oppressive as guides to contemporary art creation. To reject the style is to reject, in part at least, the value-system which tried to explain and justify it. There has been a strong tendency to avoid the old-master type of diversified composition, as in Titian and Poussin, with its firmly integrated, complex structure, its varied feast for the eyes in line, color, mass, texture, and perspective, its approximate realism and wealth of cultural meaning, derived from Christian or classical tradition. Instead, artists tend to analyze the components of art and specialize on one or a few of them at once, such as line alone or flat color alone. Monumental, complex types of composition are dissociated into their components for separate treatment. At times the avant-garde painter combines different aspects of things as seen from different points of view at different moments, thus giving an impression of shifting instability. At other times he rejects all representation, all explicit reference to nature and man, and all definite design. Instead, he tries to express in abstract form his sudden impulses and vague, changing moods. He may try for effects of fragmentation, melting, and casual disorder which, to classical taste, would have seemed the ultimate in ugliness or triviality.

In music, too, the avant-garde composer tends to avoid the traditional frameworks of definite tonality, clear melodic line, steady meter, sonata-form, and other conventional patterns of sound. Avant-garde poetry likewise tends to avoid steady meter and rhyme as well as clear language. It prefers ambiguity, fleeting impressions, and obscure suggestiveness. Fiction and drama tend to avoid definite plot as a framework of action, as well as the depiction of stable characters; instead, they tend to stress psychological change and the instability of human relations. Persons and events are shown from different standpoints in different lights, the truth being relative to each individual point of view. Thus the boundaries between reality and illusion are progressively blurred.

These trends in various fields are somewhat parallel and mutually reinforcing. They have in common a tendency to avoid large, comprehensive, complex frameworks, diversified but firmly organized patterns in art and philosophy; in other words, the classical ideal of order in variety, unity in multiplicity. Such forms in any medium suggest rational system and control, and these classical ideals have come to seem tiresome, oppressive, and even dangerous to many moderns.

The disintegrative trend is far from universal in contemporary art. There are notable examples of large-scale organization in the cinema, in architecture, city planning, and television. These arts are closer to applied science and approach their problems more in the practical spirit of technology. They employ machine techniques and large-scale organization of personnel. They feel less hostility toward these aspects of modern civilization than do the more individualistic arts of painting and sculpture, music and poetry. They are more concerned with large masses of the population, and less disposed to react against conservative popular taste.

The sciences, too, have joined only partly in the retreat from system; less so than art and philosophy. Physical science has not hesitated to reject many particular systems—Ptolemaic astronomy, for example—which it found to be false. Science has challenged and corrected Euclidean geometry, Newtonian physics, and Darwinian evolutionism. But it has not gone on to a wholesale, indiscriminate rejection of all systems. On the contrary, it has continued the effort to build ever-larger, truer ones, as in Einstein's search for a formula broad enough to cover the valid parts of Newton's laws with new observations of light and electrons. It is rather the social and psychological sciences, especially anthropology, which have shown most aversion to systems. (The reasons for this we shall consider later.) Certainly the applications of physical science, as in rocketry and space travel, have achieved marvels of complex system in coordinating different branches of technology for the production of intricate mechanisms. Riding the crest of the military wave with vast economic and political support, they have attracted brilliant minds and launched out in bold, imaginative ventures.

The retreat from system has occurred in various ways in various times and cultures. It can be one phase in a romantic-revolutionary movement, away from oppressive rules and centralized authority. It can perform a useful task in clearing away false beliefs, oppressive restrictions, dead styles of art. This may open the way to new discoveries, better ways of living, and new kinds of aesthetic experience. After the destructive phase, a pause may ensue before the work of reconstruction can commence. It may have to wait for a later generation. For a while, people look around to survey

[21]

the ruins, take stock of the situation, and begin small pilot projects.

As everyone knows, several centuries of specialized research and experiment in science and technology have brought a rich harvest of discovery and invention. Recent art, more than that of any previous age, has shown an experimental spirit and a tendency to specialization akin to that of science. Its products, while often aimless and ephemeral, are likewise bringing a rich harvest of new forms, techniques, and styles. Its pessimistic phase, emphasizing the failures and brutalities of life, has made us recognize important evils which had long been glossed over in classic and romantic art.

These are positive aspects of the situation. There are also negative ones. Any such trend can be carried to excess before the counter-trend sets in. This occurs when rejection of the old is excessive and indiscriminate, throwing aside the true with the false, the good with the bad.

Another negative aspect can be described as "the failure of nerve." It is a sort of timidity, a lack of energy and courage to undertake new, ambitious ventures of the mind. As Gilbert Murray showed, such a trend occurred in Hellenistic culture after the deaths of Alexander and Aristotle. It is characteristic of times of trouble, when political institutions have broken down and with them the associated ideologies. Old religions, moral codes, philosophies, and styles are discredited. At such a time, things seem impossible or dangerous which had not seemed so before. People are depressed by the weakness and corruption of humanity, the apparent hopelessness of the human situation. The artist or philosopher may fear to fall upon his face if he tries any daring project. He repeats old formulas, dwells on trivialities, inflates them to look important. Large, costly works of art are made while money lasts, and long books are written, but they seldom contain original systems of thought. Occasionally such a system as that of Confucius emerges in a time of troubles as a late survival of an earlier pattern. But these are rare.

Much production in philosophy and art at such times consists in dissecting, criticizing, and epitomizing the old systems, or patching together a few small fragments in original but trivial ways.

Likewise, the present retreat from system often indicates excessive caution. The thinker is afraid to venture into bold speculations, lest he be derided as "unsound" by his colleagues.

Sometimes this attitude is rationalized as a fear of military despotism, under the mistaken assumption that philosophic systems are allied with it. Monumental styles of art are suspected for the same reason. All these have been so associated at times, but they are not always or necessarily so. The systems of Lucretius, Locke, Mill, and Spencer are quite the opposite of authoritarianism. They praise individual liberty and give strong weapons to the struggle for democracy.

Fear of systems also arises in the liberal mind from the steady advance of large-scale, mechanized industry at home. Even in liberal societies, this seems to force an increase in centralized control, especially under military pressure. Again, extreme liberals go too far in connecting complex systems in philosophy and art with those in politics, economics, and military power. There is an abstract analogy, but no essential, causal bond between them. A liberal society is not bound to express itself in dissociated fragments. Philosophy and art grew up mainly under various forms of autocracy, hereditary and dictatorial. Liberalism has had little time to work out the larger forms congenial to its modern developments. There is no compelling reason why some of these forms can not be large and systematic. A modern philosophy or a modern style of art can be firmly organized on a large scale, yet flexible, expressive of this changing world, and devoted to the freedom of the individual mind.

Systems of philosophy are not necessarily false. They are always incomplete, since it is impossible for the human mind to know or describe the infinite size, duration, and variety of the universe or even the short history of man on earth. They are always partly subjective, expressing one man's point of view in a certain changing cultural setting. But they do not have to be mere subjective fantasies. The great philosophers describe, explain, and evaluate the world as it seems to them at the time. So far as we can judge today, most of them pointed out some important, objective facts about the universe and man. It is our task to separate the true from the false in their systems; the vital from the obsolete, fact from fantasy. Some work along this line is a necessary preparation for original philosophizing. It should teach the young philosopher to avoid the chief errors of his predecessors: notably, the claim to absolute, eternal truth. He should learn that no philosophic system can be more than a set of inferences from the flux of phenomena. But this does not make philosophy any the less worth writing. In writing it, he will do well to make it as comprehensive, as logical and consistent as he can in dealing with the evidence at hand. The ever-present danger is the temptation to oversimplify the picture in accordance with some preconceived, neatly regular pattern. Modern philosophers have been amply warned against this, and should be able to avoid it. A system of philosophy does not have to attribute to the world any more regularity, order, unity, rationality, or value than is actually evident therein. The philosopher's task is to tell us just how much

he thinks is there, of what kind, and how he comes to that conclusion.

It is not necessarily foolish or misguided to attempt a system of philosophy or a philosophy of history, even in the twentieth century. To do it well is becoming harder and harder because of the vastness and rapid increase of knowledge. But one needs only to sketch the main outlines, as they appear to one person at a certain time and place. No philosopher has ever done more than that, although many have claimed to do so. Avoiding claims to certainty makes the task easier, in some respects, than when certainty seemed possible. Great systems of philosophy such as those of Plato, Aristotle, and Epicurus, of Saint Thomas Aquinas, Locke, and Hegel, are among the highest peaks of Western civilization. To emulate them in scope and surpass them in truth is not impossible, though it will challenge the best intellects of the future. Surely some of these will make the attempt, and will make new systems worthy to succeed the old.

Much the same can be said about art and about aesthetic theories for judging it. Reconstruction will involve a reappraisal of traditional forms to select the potentially vital and valuable elements; then the fusion of these with new ingredients in a wide range of simple and complex forms. Complexity is neither to be feared nor worshipped, but used when the situation calls for it.

CHAPTER III

DO THE ARTS EVOLVE?
SOME CONFLICTING ANSWERS

I. NINETEENTH-CENTURY
THEORIES OF ART HISTORY
AS A PART OF CULTURAL EVOLUTION

In 1857 Herbert Spencer published an essay entitled "Progress: its Law and Cause."[1] It was a prospectus of the huge series of books on various phases of evolution—cosmic, organic, mental, and social—which occupied the rest of his life. In this essay, he discussed the history of the arts in some detail, to show that it conformed with the "law" of increasing complexity which, at that time, he called "progress," and later "evolution." This early essay was the first detailed, systematic attempt to fit the history of art into a naturalistic theory of evolution.[2] Increasing complexity, according to Spencer, was a change from the homogeneous to the heterogeneous and from the indefinite to the definite. It included a phase of differentiation and one of integration. The development of the arts, he said, illustrated this tendency and thus exemplified the larger process of mental and social evolution. On the whole, complication was regarded by Spencer as adaptive (conducive to the survival of individuals and groups) as well as beneficial in other ways.

Spencer's theory of evolution in art was followed by a number of others, by such writers as Taine in France, Grosse in Germany, and Haddon in England. The evolutionary approach was especially favored by anthropologists and archeologists, as a way of explaining the origins and early stages of the arts. It was applied by scholars to every art, including music and literature, and to civilized as well as primitive styles. Cultural evolution was conceived as including the development of art, science, political organization, technology, and other acquired skills and institutions. As to all of these, the term "evolution" retained its main connotation of increasing complexity, growth, or development. As in biology, the process was conceived as going on through long periods of time, by descent or transmission from one generation to another. But the means and mode of transmission were recognized as very different; physical, through the germ plasm, in the case of organic descent; cultural, by imitation and instruction, in the case of artistic descent. These combined ideas —*adaptive, complicative development through cultural descent*—constituted the basic meaning of the term "evolution" as applied to art and other acquired skills and institutions.

Spencer proposed two additional theories about evolution which are much more debatable, and which have not been widely accepted as essential meanings of the term. These are, first that evolution coincides on the whole with progress in an evaluative sense, even though the two terms have different connotations; and, second, that evolu-

[1] Reprinted in *Essays Scientific, Political, and Speculative* (New York, 1892), Vol. I, 8 f.
[2] Hegel's philosophy of history was based on metaphysical idealism, and the application of the Marxist theory to art came later in the century.

tion is a "universal law of nature." One can accept Spencer's basic definition of the concept without accepting his theories about its value and the universality of its occurrence. One can accept it as the meaning of the term without believing that evolution actually occurs at all.

Many conflicting theories about it were soon advanced. Some were idealistic, some dualistic or vitalistic, some naturalistic. Some included theories of universal stages in cultural history; some explained the cause of evolution in terms of parallelism, some in terms of diffusion. Some were deterministic, others indeterministic; some teleological and some mechanistic. By association with all these different lines of thought, the basic meaning was sometimes lost, and the name "evolution" was shifted over to some controversial theory. Other terms were used as almost interchangeable with it, such as "Social Darwinism," "historicism," and "the development hypothesis."

In recent years, the confusion of terms and meanings has grown worse, along with the disagreement on what kinds of evolution really exist, and to what extent.

There is, of course, nothing sacred about Spencer's definition of "evolution." Each writer is entitled to define it in his own way, provided that he does so clearly and explicitly. No one definition can claim to be the only true, correct one. The choice of meanings must be made on grounds of established usage and expediency. But the idea of "development" or "descent with increasing complexity" is so firmly attached to it in technical usage, in biology and the cultural sciences, that it should not be ignored in favor of some other without an explanation.

Discussion at the present stage could be much clarified by agreeing that the question *do the arts evolve?* shall mean, first of all, *do the arts descend culturally with a tendency toward complication?* "Evolutionism," as applied to art and to culture in general, will thus mean primarily the belief that art and culture do descend and complicate, on the whole or to some considerable extent. It will not imply that such complication is universal or inevitable.

2. EVOLUTIONISM IN ART ATTACKED AND DEFENDED

During Spencer's life, a storm of attacks on evolutionism in art descended from many sources—theological, literary, and scientific. To hold that anything so civilized and spiritual as art could be derived from animal and savage beginnings seemed especially absurd and outrageous to conservative thinkers. Cultural evolutionism gained steadily in scientific circles throughout the nineteenth century, but not to any great extent in aesthetics. That branch of philosophy, though traditionally concerned with art, was dominated by German idealism during most of the century. Although Hegel's idealistic theory of art history had some evolutionary aspects, it was very different from the naturalistic evolutionism of Spencer, Darwin, Semper, Morgan, and Tylor. Most aestheticians would not follow the naturalists in regarding art and the spiritual life as physical in origin and subject to physical laws and processes.

The influence of Kant in aesthetics is still strong. It has usually favored an idealistic or spiritualistic conception of art. British aesthetics in the eighteenth century had made a promising start, in the works of Addison, Hume, Burke, Hogarth, and others, toward a naturalistic theory of art, including its psychological and social aspects. That approach, which has since been revived and strengthened, was temporarily overwhelmed by the influence of Kant, Schiller, and the German transcendentalists in the early nineteenth century. Kant himself inclined toward evolutionism late in his life, especially in his book on anthropology; but his views on art were distinctly pre-evolutionary. These views have been echoed by antinaturalists in aesthetics and art history-writing to the present day. Skill or talent in art, he declared, "cannot be communicated, but requires to be bestowed directly from the hand of nature upon each individual, and so with him it dies, awaiting the day when nature once again endows another in the same way."[3] Only the conditions and technics of art can be taught, in Kant's opinion, and these are never its essentials. There is a kernel of truth in this idea, which modern science would state in terms of innate aptitude resulting from organic heredity. Along this line, it would hope to explain the obvious fact that artistic genius can not be entirely due to social conditions, or be produced at will by any method of education. But this kernel of fact was exaggerated by the supernaturalists into the mystical doctrine that everything essential to art is unteachable and non-cumulative; that each step in the history of art is a special creation, a separate, divine inspiration and a bolt from the blue. Hence, it was said, the sequence of steps in art is not a connected development and is not influenced in essentials by outside events or social conditions.

Some romanticists looked with favor on the idea of evolution as a vague, universal aspiration toward growth and progress. But it was also pleasant to think of art and the artist as divinely inspired and above the mundane struggle for material necessities. There has been much resistance on the part of artists, especially in literature, to the inclusion of art in the general process of evolution. To many early romanticists, reacting against the excessive rationalism of the Enlightenment, science appeared as cold, repressive, hostile to beauty, and at the opposite pole from art. They also emphasized the role of the individual genius in art. Théophile Gautier declared, "Art differs from science in this: it begins again with each artist... There is no progress in art."[4] And Aldous Huxley in the twentieth century, member of a famous family of evolutionists but inclined toward mystical supernaturalism, agrees that "Every artist begins at the beginning. The man of science, on the other hand, begins where his predecessor left off."[5]

These arguments do not deny all cultural progress or evolution, but only that of art. Science, they concede, evolves and progresses, but is fundamentally different from art. The history of art, according to this view, proceeds along its own lines. It is outside the evolutionary process.

This oft-repeated argument against evolution in art, on the ground of art's essential difference from science, was given a typically Victorian expression by John Caird in 1887. His essay on "The Progressiveness of Art" refers with lofty eloquence to art's ineffable gifts, which can not be handed down. Art may progress, he grants after some hesitation, but in a very different way from that of science. In art, "attainment depends much more on individual ability and genius than in science." Observation, knowledge, experiment, accumulation of facts, "have in them a principle of development by which each successive age absorbs and uses up the thought of the past"; whereas "The achievements of the painters, sculptors, poets of the past are not handed on to their successors like those of the men of science... Here what a man does depends comparatively little on what others have done before him, but mainly on the quality and temper of his own mind." Accessories and traditions of craftsmanship increase, but "the perfection of a work of art lies in that which is deeper than expression,—the creative faculty, the ineffable gift of genius. It lies in that intuitive insight into the life of nature and man, that strange susceptibility to what is noble and tender and beautiful, which touches and thrills us in the works of the great masters of art and song. Now, this is an element which cannot be transmitted or handed down. It is independent of tradition and education, it comes as an inspiration on elected souls fresh from the external fount of light, and the men of

---

[3] *Critique of Judgment*, p. 170 (Meredith tr.).

[4] „Du beau dans l'art," *Revue des deux mondes*, XIX (1947) 887.

[5] "A Night at Pietramala," in *Along the Road* (New York, 1925). *Cf.* T. Munro, "Do the Arts Progress?," *Journal of Aesthetics and Art Criticism*, XIV, 2 (Dec. 1955), 186.

later times have no nearer or freer access to it than those of ages the most remote." It is the "external accessories of art," the stage properties of literature and the machinery of versification which accumulate; but this is no sign of real progress in art. The "soul of art" may shine through the most imperfect forms "with an ineffable force and fervour which at once eclipses the borrowed light of laborious culture," as in "a few rude scratches from the pencil of genius, a note or two struck from the lyre by a hand all innocent of artificial culture." Hence "great works of art do not, like the works of many great scientific writers, become in course of time antiquated and obsolete." They "have a permanence which is impossible in science." It has been said that progress in science, by dissipating the illusions of naive imagination, may be inimical to artistic excellence. In Macaulay's words, "as civilization advances, poetry almost necessarily declines." But this, thinks Caird, is fallacious, for true art does not produce its effects by illusion, and cannot be injured by science. Art and science, philosophy and religion, reveal hidden reality to us in different ways.

Thus we see, in the mind of a liberal Christian scholar of the Victorian age, an effort to reconcile the new, naturalistic view of art as progressive with the old, religious view of its mainly spiritual values. Although the main issue here is evaluative, stated in terms of progress and decline, it also raises evolutionary issues in describing great art as non-cumulative and non-obsolescent; as essentially different from science in its mental processes and methods. This concept of art, if accepted, provides an effective bar against the belief in its evolution. Art remains, as Plato and Plotinus, Dante, Blake, and other mystics would have it, a product of special creation; of a unique creative act, divinely inspired anew in each age, each artist, and each work of genius; owing nothing essential to the growth of civilization, but only external accessories.

Thus the "special creation" theory, expelled from biology and social history, fought to retain

a last stronghold in the history of the arts, against the mounting evidence for the cumulative nature of that history.

Many artists and lovers of art dislike the evolutionary conception of art because it tends to minimize the role of the individual creator and to portray him as an incident in the vast flow of cultural history. Instead of regarding his work as wholly original and creative, it stresses his debt to past art and his responsiveness to current social and ideological forces. They prefer the Platonic and romantic conception of the true artist as directly inspired from above, creating beautiful forms out of his own inmost soul or in communion only with nature. Each of the artist's precious creations seems to him utterly different from anything else ever made before. The general public tends to sympathize with this point of view; many resent the intrusion of impersonal, scientific ideas into realms of personal emotion and beauty. Such persons tend to view with hostility, not only the theory of evolution in art, but all other scientific ideas and methods in aesthetics. As J. A. Symonds observed, "Our pride and sense of human independence rebel against the belief that men of genius obey a movement quite as much as they control it, and even more than they create it. Yet this is the conclusion to which facts, interpreted by historical and scientific methods, lead us..." But Phidias and Shakespeare, he adds, are not less than they were because we know them as necessary to a series; and through historical studies "the race, the mass, from which the individual emerges, and of which he becomes the spokesman and interpreter, gains in dignity and greatness."[6]

One way to express the anti-scientific view of art is to insist that every work of art is "unique." Croce, in particular, popularized this idea. Each work of art is essentially a single, indivisible intuition.[7] Said Oscar Wilde, "A work of art is

[6] "On the Application of Evolutionary Principles to Art and Literature," *Essays Speculative and Suggestive* (London, 1893), p. 32.

[7] *Aesthetic* (London, 1922), pp. 20 f., 388 f.

the unique result of a unique temperament. Its beauty comes from the fact that the author is what he is..."[8] More recently, Peter Fingesten has written that "No work of art, no architecture, painting or sculpture can be connected to a previous one 'through generation,' nor are the recent styles together with the ancient ones 'one great system.' Every individual work of art 'was made' uniquely and did not 'grow' in the sense of the theory of evolution." This he opposes to Darwin's statement about organic evolution, that "all forms of life make together one great system, for all are connected through generation." "The history of style," he declares, "exhibits neither evolution, devolution nor involution... In art, change takes the place of evolution..."[9] Herbert Read agrees that "Art does not, in any strict sense of the word, evolve."[10]

Is every work of art "unique"? There is again a kernel of truth in this idea, which has made it sound plausible. Every work of art and every artist is unique in some respects. So is every human being, every leaf and snow crystal. But none is completely unique; each resembles others in some respects. Every work of art has many traits in common with others: not only of material and technique, but of form and style, ideas and feelings expressed, modes of appeal to the observer. Some artists and their works are more unusual than others, but the difference is one of degree. Some writers like to emphasize the difference and feel it as more important; others, the resemblance. Both must be considered in a fair and balanced theory of art.

For various reasons, the "unique" or distinguishing features of art have often been emphasized more than the resemblances. This is especially true in modern Western culture, where a great premium is placed on originality. We tend to admire the original artist and disparage the imitative one, even though we do not always agree on which is which, and are often slow to accept the original genius. But we praise originality in art as a contribution to progress. In estimating it, we look for distinguishing features and emphasize them in writing criticism and history. The resemblances we take more for granted. In the case of a living artist, it is held uncomplimentary to mention them.

Moreover, the requirements of connoisseurship, especially in the visual arts, necessitate close attention to the slight differences or nuances which distinguish a genuine work by a famous master from a copy, a work of his pupils, or a much-restored original. Prestige and large sums of money may depend on one's ability to distinguish accurately between two works which look almost alike. Even experts have been deceived, and all the resources of science are needed to protect the buyer against skillful counterfeiters.

Philosophy and science, in their search for general truths, tend to put more emphasis on similarities and continuities. This is true in anthropology, which has much to say about cultural evolution and about primitive art, prehistoric and modern. Many of the artifacts it studies are not individually notable, though some are, such as the best of the Ice-Age cave paintings. Many are ordinary products of handicraft, such as the thousands of stone tools which anthropologists classify into types and chronological sequences. But it is important also for the scientist to note peculiarities, and distinguish the real from the false.

Max Dessoir, leading German aesthetician of the early twentieth century, rightly concluded in 1927 that there is "no basic conflict" between the scientific and historical points of view towards art.[11] At the same time, he warned against losing sight of the distinctive character of a work of art in stressing only its connection with the general social consciousness of a period. This error, he felt,

---

[8] *The Soul of Man Under Socialism*, in *Works* (N. Y. & London, n.d.) Vol. 13, p. 144.

[9] "The Theory of Evolution in the History of Art," *College Art Journal*, XII, 4 (Summer 1954), 302.

[10] Art and the Evolution of Consciousness," *JAAC*, XIII, 2 (Dec. 1954), 143.

[11] "Art History and Systematic Theories of Art" (Eng. tr., *Journal of Aesthetics and Art Criticism*, XIX, 4, Summer 1961).

had been committed to some extent by Burckhardt, Joseph Nadler, Georg Dehio, and others. The historian must not, said Dessoir, lose sight of the unique in art and artists, or of the inner logic by which art forms can "lift themselves out of the general process of history, which remains irrational to a high degree."

One must agree with Dessoir that scholarship in art should pay attention to both the unique and generic aspects, the individual and the social. It should try to combine the strictly historical with the scientific and philosophical approaches. All are needed for a full and just interpretation. But it does not follow that every book and article on art should preserve an exact balance between them. Here as elsewhere, some specialization is useful and legitimate. Philosophy, science, and the larger processes in artistic change have been so persistently neglected in recent years that some extra weight on this side is needed to restore the balance. As a step in that direction, the present book will frankly emphasize the theoretical study of large-scale cultural processes.

Some highly respected anthropologists, accepting the general thesis of cultural evolution, insist that art is in some ways an exception. A. L. Kroeber agreed with the anti-evolutionists on this point at least: that art is not as cumulative as science. "Each art," he said, "or for that matter each philosophy or religion, very largely has to begin all over again, whereas each of the intermittent periods of discovery in science can begin, and generally does begin, just about where the last one left off."[12]

This is a strong argument against evolutionism in art, and the evolutionist must try to meet it in detail. Many writers reject the sharp antithesis between art and science. There is much in common between the two, they say.[13]

As against the sharp antithesis, we shall see that art is *somewhat* cumulative, even in its essentials of content, form, meaning, and style, though less so than science. Many works of art, considered great in their time, do "go out of date" later on,

as far as public interest is concerned. And each artist does not have to begin quite "at the beginning." Some try to do so, but others willingly build upon past previous art and tradition, incorporating a selection from the images, meanings, attitudes, and emotional expressions of the past. Indeed, no artist can completely "break with the past," no matter how hard he tries to do so. In rejecting one part of the great tradition of human culture, he necessarily accepts another. No artist builds completely from the ground up; he can only select, eliminate, develop, add, and rearrange in a partly original way. Even in the *je ne sais quoi* which constitutes the "essence" of each genius and the most original features of his style, there are echoes of the past and debts to society. This is nothing to be ashamed of, and it is naively egotistical for artists to deny such influence, as many do. However small the element of innovation in each artist's work, as compared with that absorbed from previous culture, it is still of great importance in the scheme of things.

It is incorrect to say, as some recent social scientists have said, that the theory of cultural evolution merely borrowed a concept from biology, in trying to show that cultural history was analogous to organic evolution. It would be quite as correct to say that the borrowing was in the opposite direction: that biologists applied social concepts to organic phenomena. Darwin's concept of natural selection was suggested in part by Malthus' book on population. Many biologists before him applied the concept of social progress to organic development. The chief danger in drawing such analogies lies in the tendency to exaggerate them and ignore important differences.

The comparison is not extremely far-fetched, after all. Man is an animal, though an exceptional

---

[12] *Anthropology* (New York, 1948), p. 303.
[13] For example, Michael A. Wallach writes in "Art, Science, and Representation: Toward an Experimental Psychology of Aesthetics" that "The difference between science and art is not as great as one may first imagine." Both control percepts, involve systems of information organized by various rules, etc. (*JAAC*, XVIII, 2 [Dec. 1960], 162).

one in many ways; his origin is an integral part of organic evolution, and his present behavior—even in the most advanced cultural realms—is strongly conditioned by his innate, organic structure and predisposition. It is still a useful approach, though not the only one, to ask how far this analogy holds true, and in what ways his behavior and history now differ from those of other animals. In recent years, there have been signs of a return in social and historical theory to the use of biological analogies as suggestive hypotheses.[14]

3. RECENT DISCUSSIONS OF EVOLUTIONISM IN ANTHROPOLOGY AND ART HISTORY

"That there has been cultural evolution from a primitive state to that of modern civilization is not doubted," says David Bidney.[15] V. Gordon Childe, British archeologist, points out some limitations to the analogy between cultural and organic evolution. But, he continues, "this is not to deny cultural evolution." "Indeed," he says, "with certain modification the Darwinian formula of 'variation, heredity, adaptation, and selection' can be transferred from organic to social evolution, and is even more intelligible in the latter domain than in the former."[16] E. A. Hoebel, American anthropologist, accepts the Spencerian formula. Cultural evolution, he says, is "The passage from simplicity to complexity, from homogeneity to heterogeneity, which, from empirical observation of living societies and the material remains and records of those now defunct, may be deduced to have occurred and to be still occurring in the world of social life among men."[17]

But, again, is art a part of this cultural evolution? Many anthropologists do not commit themselves on this point. Kroeber, who paid more attention to the civilized arts than most of his colleagues, stated that both cultures and styles of art, like organic species, "have evolved through responses to their total and fluctuating past environments, plus internal changes..."[18]

René Wellek, while pointing out the errors of past evolutionists in literary history, emphasizes that "literature has changed and developed." There is also, he says, "a development of the art of painting that is quite distinct from either the history of painters or successive appreciation of individual pictures. When we listen to a concert in which, e.g., sonatas are arranged in chronological order, we can grasp a formal development..." "The concept of evolution drawn from phylogeny," he writes, "seems nearer to the actual facts of the literary process" than the ontogenetic evolutionism of Brunetière. "The problem of development," Wellek concludes, "leads us to the heart of the theory of literary history."[19] Arnold Hauser, art historian with a sociological approach, remarks that "nothing evolves so strikingly as art."[20]

On the other hand, E. H. Gombrich, whose approach to art history is less sociological and more psychological than Hauser's, declares in sweeping terms that "Evolutionism is dead." But what does he understand by "evolutionism"? For one thing, it means to him the theory that primitives could not make better art "because they were as unskilled as children or that they did not

[14] E.g., R. W. Gerard, "Levels of Organization: Some Applications of Biological Concepts to Social Science." *Main Currents in Modern Thought*, XII, 5 (1956), 104. G. G. Simpson writes "There is a real biological and not merely an analogical relation between organic and cultural evolution... Culture is simply the behavior—or part of the behavior—of a particular species of primates." *Evolution and Man's Progress* (Special Issue of *Daedalus*, Summer 1961), pp. 514 ff.

[15] *Theoretical Anthropology* (New York, 1953), p. 282

[16] *Social Evolution* (New York, 1951), p. 175.

[17] *Man in the Primitive World* (New York, 1958), pp. 615, 648. It includes, he says, the processes of cultural differentiation along which human societies have arrived at more distinct patterns of behavior. Hoebel also quotes R. M. MacIver as saying that the main interest of evolutionary method is the "emergence of a variety of more specific forms from the less specific" (*Society: its Structure and Changes*, p. 424).

[18] *Style and Civilizations* (Ithaca, N. Y., 1957), p. 78.

[19] "Development," in *Dictionary of World Literature* (New York, 1943), p. 158.

[20] *The Philosophy of Art History* (London, 1958), p. 150.

want to do anything else because they still had the mentality of children."[21] "Both these conclusions," he rightly adds, "are obviously false." But they are not in the least essential to evolutionism in general, and have long been rejected by modern evolutionists. They are mistaken views of a few nineteenth-century writers such as Alfred Haddon,[22] when the nature and aesthetic values of tribal art were not understood.

Mr. Gombrich also suspects in evolutionism a dangerous tendency toward the "totalitarian habit of mind," which he illustrates by quotations from Hans Sedlmayer in 1927.[23] They amount, he thinks, to a "Spenglerian historicism," through talking in terms of collectives such as "mankind," "races," and "ages." But this depends entirely on how such terms are used and interpreted; on what political and social philosophy they are combined with. They are not necessary implications of cultural evolutionism in general, and they are not accepted by all or nearly all evolutionists. Certainly Marx, Engels, and Lenin believed in cultural evolution, as they believed in the atomic theory of matter and the Copernican theory of the solar system; but that does not make it false or distinctively communistic. Herbert Spencer and John Dewey, both extremely liberal and individualistic, also believed in cultural evolution. There is nothing in evolutionism *per se* to commit one to communism, fascism, liberalism, or any other particular social policy.

The belief that "collectives" or universals such as mankind or the *Zeitgeist* exist apart from individuals is derived from Platonic idealism. It is rejected by all evolutionists and other philosophers of history who base their world-view on empiricism and naturalism. Hegel combined it with an early type of cultural evolutionism, and the Hegelian tradition has been carried on until the present day, deeply affecting such writers as Wölfflin, Focillon, and Sorokin. It has produced a type of cultural evolutionism or historicism which differs markedly from that of Spencer and Darwin, in tending toward an immanent determinsm based on vitalism

or metaphysical spiritualism. Art historians and philosophers of history whose training has been under German influence often confuse it with evolutionism in general, and write as if the concept of evolution based on natural, empirical science did not exist.

The same unwarranted association of evolutionism with totalitarianism is made by James Ackerman in his essay on "Art History and the Problems of Criticism."[24] Communism, fascism, liberalism, and many other doctrines and programs of action took their starting-point from evolutionism in the mid-nineteenth century, because it was the revolutionary, key idea of Western thought in that period: an idea which stimulated further trains of thought along many different lines. Actually, the question whether the arts evolve is one of historical fact, and is not to be decided on the basis of whether we like the moral and political consequences of such a belief.

Evolutionism did help to deflate the pleasant fiction of man's central status and importance in the universe, which supernaturalist cosmology had built up. But the Copernican revolution and the discovery of the vast age of the universe and life had started this deflation long before. Romantic artists and philosophers had revived the other pleasant fiction of the transcendent role of individual artists in reconciling the material and spiritual worlds. Certainly, any individual human comes to look rather small, weak, and short-lived by contrast with the mighty flow of organic and social evolution. The social and psychological sciences

[21] *Art and Illusion* (New York, 1960), pp. 22, 108.
[22] *Evolution in Art* (London, 1895). *Cf.* R. J. Goldwater, *Primitivism in Modern Painting* (New York, 1938), Ch. I, Pt. II on "The Evaluation of the Art of Primitive Peoples."
[23] *Ibid.*, p. 20. He is not the first to make this charge. For recent discussions pro and con, see Patrick Gardiner (ed.), *Theories of History* (Glencoe, Ill., 1959), with quotations from Karl R. Popper, Isaiah Berlin, and others; also Popper, *The Open Society and its Enemies* (London, 1945) and *The Poverty of Historicism* (London, 1957). (Most of the discussion has dealt with cultural evolutionism and historicism in general; not with their application to art.)
[24] G. Kepes (ed.), *The Visual Arts Today* (Special issue of *Daedalus* [Middletown, Conn., 1960]), p. 260.

have shown the great extent to which any individual artist is shaped by his hereditary and cultural origins. These are general trends of scientific thought in recent centuries, and not peculiar to evolutionism.

Neither evolutionism nor science in general has tried to prove a complete determinism in history. Science and ordinary observation make us recognize *some* determinism in history: more than had been supposed, but not necessarily an ironclad fatalism. Evolutionary theory is not committed to either extreme: certainly not to the belief that individual choice is a mere illusion and the individual a passive puppet. His will, though caused, is also a causal factor in events. In avoiding one extreme, we are not driven to the other.[25] The moderate determinism accepted by most evolutionists is flexible enough to permit our acting, for all practical purposes, as if our wills were free. It is complete to the extent of saying that every effect is somehow caused, and part of the order of nature. It holds that certain types of effect are inevitable under a given set of conditions; but it recognizes constant change in conditions. Life on earth has had to be such as could survive under the physical conditions of this planet at the time. But that allows for considerable flexibility in detail.

However unimportant man and his works, or Giotto and Bach as individuals, may be to the universe at large, modern man has every right to say that they are and shall be important *to him*. He has every right to stress the individual aspects of artistic creation and to say that they are quite as real as the social. He is free to encourage individual freedom and creativity in art and elsewhere, so that individuals *shall not* be submerged in future. How to reconcile individual and social values is an open question for the future, as man takes more purposeful control of his cultural evolution, wisely or foolishly.

Evolutionism in general leads to a certain relativism as to values in art, but not necessarily to any collectivist policy. On the contrary, as Spencer pointed out, it tends rather to favor liberalism, through suggesting that free competition is the best means of progress. Though debatable, these are A.B.C.'s of liberal evolutionism, especially in the English-speaking world.

In the question of whether art evolves, we are dealing with an extremely complex, confused mass of concepts, affirmations, and counter-affirmations, in which semantic problems are intricately mixed with those of fact and value. When an author attacks or defends evolutionism or development in art and culture, or says that he believes or disbelieves in "the historicist theory" of art, exactly what does he mean? To what belief or line of thought is he referring? He may actually agree with someone who says the opposite, using these terms in another sense. Dictionaries provide us with a long list of different meanings, all established in technical usage. There is urgent need to restate the underlying issues clearly.

Still another question may then arise: if the term "evolution in art" is so ambiguous, so loaded with inconsistent meanings, is it usable at all in scholarly discussion? Would it be better to find another term, or a set of them? Perhaps, but none has appeared so far. In the meantime, something may be gained by a fair and fresh examination of the old ones. The question of their meaning and truth still leads us, as Mr. Wellek remarks, to the heart of historical theory in the arts.

[25] *Cf.* Ernest Nagel: "Critics of historical inevitability who have argued for either a radical or a qualified indeterminism in human affairs have rejected one extreme position only to adopt another one no less extreme and dubious." "Determinism in History," *Philosophy and Phenomenological Research*, XX, 3 (Mar. 1960), 293. Mr. Nagel here attacks the contention of Isaiah Berlin that historical determinism entails the elimination of individual responsibility. For a fuller discussion, see Berlin, *Historical Inevitability* (London, 1954) and J. W. N. Watkins, "Philosophy of History," in *Philosophy in the Mid-century*, ed. R. Klibansky, Vol. III, 158–176, with bibliography.

PART TWO

THEORIES OF EVOLUTION
IN ART
AND CULTURE

CHAPTER IV

EARLY THEORIES OF HISTORY
WITH REFERENCE TO THE ARTS

Some early conceptions of the history of the arts were contained in myths and legends dealing with the origin of civilization. These told of a primitive Golden Age when man had lived simply, by gathering food. Without tools or weapons, he had enough to satisfy his needs in a state of innocence, peace, and happiness. This age was followed by those of silver, bronze, and iron. Wealth and the desire for wealth and power grew. Cities, palaces, and fine craftwork in precious materials multiplied, but with them came also increasing unhappiness, dissension, crime, and war.[1]

It was usually taken for granted that the arts had developed from simple origins to the elaborateness of urban luxury; but this was not hailed as a blessing by ascetic poets and philosophers. Instead, they blamed it for contributing to the moral degeneration of man in later periods. Developed art was associated with sensuality and proud display. On this ground early moralists, both occidental and oriental, denounced the common assumption of both rich and poor, great and humble: that magnificent possessions, including the visual arts, and the delights of music, dance, and poetry, were altogether desirable. The better and more numerous these were, it had been suppos-

ed, the better life would become. The growth and technical improvement of the arts had been a source of pride. Now deeper wisdom raised the basic moral issue which we often state today in terms of progress: whether the growth of material wealth is really improvement from the standpoint of happiness and spiritual value. The pleasure of owning and enjoying art was often held to be outweighed by attendant evils.

These evaluative issues are not our main concern in the present book; but they are worth noticing because early discussions of them usually implied some beliefs about the facts of art history. The two lines of discussion, which we now distinguish carefully, were then commonly combined.

In respect to moral value, the Golden Age theory in Greece was the opposite of our modern theory of progress. Like the Hebrew story of man's fall from Eden, it was a theory of degeneration. But, at the same time, it contained some elements of the modern theory of cultural evolution: first, that art and civilization had in fact become more complex, diversified, elaborate, and widespread; second, that man had gone through a series of technological stages. The earliest stage was correctly identified as that of gathering wild foods. The use of bronze and then of iron tools and weapons was correctly placed in later stages. Gold and silver symbolized the supposed fineness and beauty of primitive peoples, rather than the use of these

[1] Hesiod, *Works and Days*, 107–193. Ovid, *Metamorphoses*, Bk. I, Fable III.

metals, "First of all," says Hesiod, "a golden race of mortal men did the Immortal Dwellers in Olympus fashion." There was justification for regarding the increase of wealth, including works of art, as potential causes of envy, violence, and war, although primitive man had certainly not been free from them. "Riches were dug up," says Ovid, "the incentives to vice... and gold, more destructive than iron; then War came forth, that fights through the means of both."

On the other hand the arts, especially those of music, dance, and speech, had been gifts of the gods. "By grace of the Muses and archer Apollo are men minstrels upon the earth and players of the lyre."[2] Hephaistos the Lame One, "excellent in craft," was the chief patron of the visual arts. For this he was praised, but some of his cunningly fashioned works of earth, gold, bronze, and iron have brought evil to men.

Aeschylus was closer to the modern view in speaking of the "miseries that beset mankind" before Prometheus gave men the arts and sciences. "Every art possessed by man comes from Prometheus."[3] He had taught them architecture, numbers, letters (mistress of the arts and mother of the Muses), the calendar, medicine, divination, and the use of copper, iron, silver, and gold. For this he had been punished, not for having brought evil to man, for his gifts were good; but for having given man power almost to rival the gods. In suggesting that the arts and sciences had raised man from primitive misery, Aeschylus was rejecting the Golden Age theory and moving toward the modern belief in progress. The dispute was never settled. Virgil gave an honored place in heaven to those "Whose songs were worthy Phoebus' utterance, / Or those that by discovery of arts / Made life a higher thing."[4] He flattered Augustus as one who would bring back the Golden Age.

According to the theory of cycles, which still has its advocates, humanity has gone many times through analogous sequences of stages. The nature of the cycles was variously conceived: sometimes, by analogy with the life of an individual, as one of childhood, maturity, and old age;[5] sometimes, as repeated learning and forgetting of the arts; sometimes as alternate eras of construction and destruction. To some extent, the theory of cycles in cultural history is inconsistent with that of evolution, insofar as the latter holds that man has developed and will go on developing indefinitely, with no disastrous falls and no returns to the starting-point. But, as we shall see, the two theories can be combined and were combined later on.

Plato, though not especially interested in history, proposed a cyclical theory of political changes in the past. It had some implications as to the arts. If an ideal state, a real aristocracy or government by the best had ever existed on earth, it could not have endured forever. All things human grow and die. It would be followed by a descending cycle of inferior types of state. These are timocracy (the military, Spartan type), oligarchy, democracy (in the sense of mob rule) and tyranny.[6] Each corresponds to a type of individual character, dominated by an irrational element and lacking harmony and temperance. Since artists and the masses have been given free rein, art descends to emotional excess, irrationality, vice, and intemperance. The right kind of art, properly conducted in the education of youth, could strengthen and harmonize the state and individual character. The popular kind tends to disintegrate both.

Thousands of cities have come into being and each has gone through the four imperfect types of rule many times. Disasters have repeatedly destroyed most of the human race, says Plato, and those who survived were unacquainted with arts and implements. The arts were unknown for millen-

---

[2] Hesiod, *Theogony*, 94 f. Plato says in the *Laws* (657 b) that the Egyptians believe their ancient chants to have been composed by the goddess Isis.

[3] *Prometheus Bound*, 436

[4] *Aeneid*, VI, 622, 792.

[5] Florus, *Epitome Rerum Romanorum*. In Sallust, Florus, and Velleius Paterculus, *Historical Works*. Trans. J. S. Watson (London, 1872), p. 287. F. J. Teggart and G. H. Hildebrand, *The Idea of Progress* (Berkeley, Calif., 1949), p. 109.

[6] *Republic*, Bk. VIII.

nia, and "no more than a thousand or two thousand years have elapsed since the discoveries of Daedalus, Orpheus and Palamedes—since Marsyas and Olympus invented music, and Amphion the lyre."[7]

After the last great destruction, we must suppose that the arts requiring iron and bronze disappeared. People lived simply, yet with abundance of food, clothing, bedding, dwellings, and utensils "capable of standing on the fire" (e.g., of stone or clay). Lacking gold and silver, they were simple, manly, temperate, and just. Then cities grew and multiplied; some were subjected by others.

A state arises out of the needs of man, so its first concern is normally to provide food; then housing and clothing; these give rise to various necessary occupations. But "many will not be satisfied with the simpler way of life" and will be for adding luxuries such as comfortable furniture, paintings and embroideries, works in ivory and gold, music, poetry, dancing, and women's adornments.[8] The arts have developed from simplicity to complexity, according to Plato, and this has been a change for the worse, however pleasing to the masses. Under the ancient laws of Attica, music was divided into hymns, lamentations, paeans, Dionysian dithyrambs, and citharoedic songs. Performers were not allowed to confuse one style of music with another. Noisy cries from the audience were forbidden. But the poets themselves introduced "vulgar and lawless innovation."[9] Diversified forms have arisen, "mingling lamentations with hymns, and paeans with dithyrambs, imitating the sounds of the flute or the lyre"—all through growing excess of freedom. The corrective would be a return to early simplicity, through having a council of conservative elders regulate the arts and public taste. Mythology and poetry have become more complex through combining simple narration with the imitative or dialogue style, and through diversifying the latter so as to imitate the manner, speech, and character of many different kinds of person.[10] But an artist cannot well imitate so many; moreover, it is demeaning

to imitate the lower and less rational types of person. Only the simple, unmixed style should be allowed, and the imitation of admirable characters. The style in all arts should be simple with few changes in harmony and rhythm, and without immoderate emotionalism. "We shall not want multiplicity of strings or a panharmonic scale... We shall not maintain the artificers of lyres with three corners and complex scales, or the makers of any other many-stringed, curiously harmonized instruments."[11] The flute's composite harmony is worse than any stringed instrument. Only the simple lyre and harp for city use, and the shepherd's pipe in the country, are to be approved. "Beauty of style and harmony and grace and good rhythm depend on simplicity." This is true in "the art of the painter and every other creative art... weaving, embroidery, architecture, and every kind of manufacture." Art which represents a variety of sensory and emotional phenomena tends to lure the mind from contemplation of the eternal forms of goodness and beauty to "opposite forms of vice and intemperance and meanness and deformity in sculpture and building and the other creative arts."

Between the lines of this moralizing, which expressed the philosopher's austere, intellectual tastes, one can discern the actual course of events in the arts. Plato saw what was happening and his observation is confirmed by present historical knowledge. Aside from all evaluative issues, it was a process of evolution from simple to complex, with the gradual emergence of new, more differentiated types. They contained an increasing variety of sense-qualities and forms—more different rhythms, scales, instrumental timbres in music; the expression of more different moods and emotions. In literary and theatrical representation, in the epic, tragedy, and comedy, more different types of desire, emotion, and individual personality were being portrayed. This is evident in the

7 *Laws*, Bk. III.
8 *Republic*, Bk. II, 273.
9 *Laws*, III, 700.
10 *Republic*, III, 392.
11 *Republic*, III, 399 d.

development of tragedy from Aeschylus through Euripides. Modern taste has usually, though not always, admired it as improvement. Whether one does or not, the process was evolutionary in the Spencerian sense of that word.

Aristotle described the development of tragedy more approvingly in the *Poetics*. The epic poets had been succeeded by tragedians, he said, since drama was "a larger and higher form of art."[12] "Tragedy advanced by slow degrees; each new element that showed itself was in turn developed." Aeschylus first introduced a second actor and emphasized the dialogue; Sophocles increased the number of actors to three and added scene-painting. Plots were enlarged to include more episodes or acts; iambic meter was introduced as most suited to realistic dialogue. Along with this greater differentiation of materials, integration was secured by unity of plot and other means. "A beautiful object, whether a living organism or any whole composed of parts, must... have an orderly arrangement of parts."[13] Plots can be developed from simple to complex by reversal of the situation and by recognition. Epic poetry can represent many events which occur simultaneously and thus relieve the story with varying episodes, "for sameness of incident soon produces satiety." In such comments, Aristotle not only describes the evolution of drama, but praises it. He does not, however, suggest that such evolution can or should continue indefinitely. Tragedy itself, "having passed through many changes, found its natural form, and there it stopped."[14]

Though Aristotle was impressed by the developmental process in an individual organism, somehow mysteriously directed from the seed or egg to the mature plant or animal, he stopped short of recognizing phylogenetic development. For him the species were comparatively fixed and static, though arranged in a great hierarchy of ascent from the lowest to the highest types. He was on the verge of biological evolutionism, as Linnaeus, Buffon, and Cuvier were two millennia later.[15] But Greek culture as a whole was not yet ready for a thoroughly historical, genetic reorientation or for a prolonged advance of empirical science in either the biological or the cultural field.

Pliny, writing early in the Roman Empire, traced the development of painting in a somewhat analogous manner.[16] Following Xenocrates, Apelles, and other Greek writers, he showed how that art had been progressively enriched since the time of Egyptian line-drawing. This was done through the discovery of light and shade and color contrast, by which "art differentiated itself." It was done through varying the aspect and expression of the features and the position of the limbs, through introducing folds in drapery, through showing drapery as transparent, and through covering walls with pictures of landscapes with figures. Parrhasius, says Pliny, "contributed much" as the first to give proportions to painting and vivacity to facial expression. Apelles of Cos "singly contributed almost more to painting than all the other artists put together, also publishing volumes containing the principles of painting." His inventions "have been useful to all other painters as well." Later on, it was Spurius Tadius who first introduced the fashion of "painting walls with pictures of country houses and porticos and landscape gardens," while Pausias contributed the method of painting animals in a foreshortened position.

Pliny and Vitruvius both hinted at two general ideas which later became important in the theory of cultural evolution. One was that of cumulative

[12] IV, 10. (Butcher trans.)

[13] VII, 4.

[14] IV, 12. W. H. Fyfe, in *Aristotle's Art of Poetry* (Oxford, 1940, p. 12 n.) refers to the *Poetics* as a theory of "the evolution of Tragedy."

[15] Darwin credits Aristotle with having foreshadowed the principle of natural selection. ("Historical Sketch" preceding *The Origin of Species*).

[16] *Natural History*, Bk. XXXV, V, 15 *et seq.* See also Vitruvius, *On Architecture*, on the development of architecture and scene painting (Bks. IV, V). He explains the development of the Doric, Ionic, and Corinthian orders (*genera*) in the type of building called a temple. He also distinguishes "three styles of scenery: one which is called tragic; a second, comic; the third, satyric." The first is designed, he says, with royal surroundings; the second with more realistic private buildings and balconies; the third, with rustic landscape scenes.

change; the other, that of art as a social heritage which develops through the ages. Art, they showed, is gradually built up through the contributions of successive individuals into a joint possession which is larger and more enduring than any single artist or product. The work of art is not regarded as a unique, isolated creation, but as a step in cultural development.

Of the ancient writers now extant, Lucretius came nearest to working out a general theory of evolution in organic life, civilization, and art. His amazingly modern statement of cultural evolutionism, based on the naturalistic atomism of Democritus and Epicurus, was not surpassed as a whole until the nineteenth century. Like Spencer, Lucretius offers a comprehensive story of cosmic evolution, from unorganized, undirected atoms in space through more and more complex forms of matter, life, mind, civilization, art, and science. His theory of how it happened is not far from that of natural selection. Through the chaotic, accidental swervings and assemblages of atoms at the beginning of our universe, many misshapen monsters were formed, unable to feed or reproduce themselves; these died out and left the fittest to survive. Lacking in the picture is Darwin's fuller account of the intermediate steps; of the slow, gradual process by which new forms of life arose through adaptive, environmental selection.

Lucretius rejected the legends of man's primal innocence and happiness, dwelling instead on the dangers and miseries of savage life without sufficient knowledge, skill, or social organization. This is not wholly a question for subjective evaluation: it is also one of fact, as to how prehistoric man lived, and Lucretius is much nearer than Hesiod to the present archeological account. He is nearer, not only in depicting the painful and precarious aspects of such life, but also in such details as man's use of stone and wooden tools before the invention of mining and metallurgy.[17] A future decline or cyclical recurrence is not precluded; the constructive and destructive phases of nature, symbolized by Venus and Mars, are both recog-

nized and no benign, heavenly plan is relied on to manage things for the best. But, on the whole, the history of man has been a process of development so far, with steady improvement in the arts as a means to better living, up to the present pinnacle of excellence. It is explained on naturalistic grounds as due to the inherent properties of matter.

As against the early, mythical conception of the origin of art as a gift from the gods, Lucretius credits man with having invented for himself the arts of speech, music, handicrafts, building, and other bases of civilization. "Ships and agriculture," he says, "fortifications and laws, arms, roads, clothing, and all else of this kind, life's prizes, its luxuries also from first to last, poetry and pictures, the shaping of statues by the artist, all these as men progressed gradually step by step were taught by practice and the experiments of the active mind." (*Usus et impigrae simul experientia mentis / paulatim docuit pedetemtim progredientis.*)[18] Early man was not happy or perfect, but beset by violence and fear; only gradually did he learn the arts of peace, progressing through a series of stages from the use of copper and bronze to that of iron, and from poverty to plenty through agriculture, manufacture, and social organization. The present age is the best, and not a degeneration.

MAN'S ANCIENT ARMS
Were hands, and nails and teeth, stones too
        and boughs—
Breakage of forest trees—and flame and fire,
As soon as known. Thereafter force of iron
And copper discovered was; and copper's use
Was known ere iron's, since more tractable
Its nature is and its abundance more.

[17] H. E. Barnes describes his "effort to substantiate the evolutionary and naturalistic character of the development of the universe and society, independent of any aid or interference by the gods," as "infinitely the most realistic and satisfactory of classical theories of the history of society." It indicated "the various stages of cultural and social evolution," he says, "with astonishing accuracy." *Historical Sociology: its Origins and Development* (New York, 1948), p. 8.

[18] *De Rerum Natura*, V, 1452–3. (Trans. Rouse, Loeb Classical Library). *Cf.* Horace, *Sat.* I, iii, 99.

With copper[19] men to work the soil began,
With copper to rouse the hurly waves of war,
To deal the monstrous wounds, and seize away
Another's flocks and fields. For unto them,
Thus armed, all things naked of defence
Readily yielded. Then by slow degrees
The sword of iron succeeded, and the shape
Of brazen sickle into scorn was turned:
With iron to cleave the soil of earth they 'gan.[20]

The so-called "three-stage system" which divided early history into stone, bronze, and iron ages, is still the most common one, although not universally applicable. It has since been subdivided into paleolithic, neolithic, and many other substages. Often wrongly credited to modern science, it has been described as "the cornerstone of modern archeology."[21]

The Hebrew-Christian theories of history, gradually formulated in the late Roman Empire, paid little attention to the arts and other worldly skills. They conceived of three or more stages in a single, great epic: (1) from Creation to the Fall of Man (the stage of primal innocence); (2) the age of patriarchs and prophets, from the Fall to the Incarnation or First Coming; (3) the present phase of history, to be ended by the Second Coming of Christ, the end of the world and Last Judgment. Medieval historians often thought in terms of two main periods: the Old and New Dispensations, as covered by the Old and New Testaments. St. Augustine, in *The City of God*, supplemented Biblical history and prophecy with secular history and legend to trace the concurrent histories of the "city of Men" and the "city of God" through the ancient empires and the decline of Rome up to the future end of the world.[22] This polarity between the earthly and the heavenly, the material and spiritual, ran like a pair of contrasting background themes through the medieval epic. Against them, the great Biblical cast of deities, prophets, saints, and sinners played out no evolutionary sequence, but a cyclical story with a happy ending ahead for the elect.

The conception of history as progressive and developmental, on either a naturalistic or supernaturalistic basis, died out during the late Roman Empire and the Middle Ages. It was overwhelmed by the Christian belief in the fall and inherited sin of man, from which only divine grace could save him. Early Christian thinkers such as Augustine viewed most art suspiciously, with the possible exception of music, as conducive to sensuality. By the thirteenth century a more tolerant attitude prevailed; religious art, at least, was seen as a way of glorifying God and achieving salvation.

2. FROM THE RENAISSANCE THROUGH THE EIGHTEENTH CENTURY

The revival of naturalistic humanism in art, science and general attitude toward life was a step toward the revival of evolutionary thinking, but many obstacles remained in the way, and it was long before the Lucretian train of thought could be resumed. The kind of rationalism which revived was at first largely Platonic; hence only slightly historical in approach, permeated with mysticism, and made rigid by the doctrine of fixed, eternal forms. Art and theories of art remained loaded with abstract symbolism and the burden of trying to reconcile Christian and classical ideologies. Extreme veneration of antiquity prevented great pride in the recent achievements of art.

By the early fifteenth century, however, enough had happened in the arts since Cimabue to justify some satisfaction, as in Filippo Villani's account of Florentine painting in his book on famous citizens of that town. He indicates three periods in the history of painting: (a) Greek and Latin, (b) the dark and dead art of the middle ages, and (c) the renewal by Cimabue and Giotto. Within the third

19 *Aes* means either copper or bronze.
20 Bk. V. (W. E. Leonard trans., Everyman Ed.).
21 W. D. Strong, "Historical Approach in Anthropology," in *Anthropology Today* (Chicago, 1953), p. 391.
22 Bks. XVII, XVIII.

of these are again three subdivisions: Cimabue's beginning, Giotto's restoring of dignity, and his pupils' perfecting of the art.[23]

In the middle of the sixteenth century, Giorgio Vasari could expand the story of recent progress in the visual arts to cover a long list of illustrious names from many cities and further advances (according to his standards of value) in painting, sculpture, and architecture. His conception of stages is cyclical, by analogy with those of human life and with classical theories of the cycles in political history. In their first stage or childhood, the arts are rough and sketchy. The second stage is that of youth; the third, of mature perfection. Art has then "done everything that is permitted to an imitator of Nature." It "has risen so high that its decline must now be feared rather than any further progress expected."[24] As Panofsky points out, Vasari carries his parallel with human life only as far as mature perfection; not to old age or death. As an optimistic humanist, he could not accept the idea of inevitable decline, especially since he believed the fall of Rome to have resulted from violence and Christian bigotry, including an opposition to pictures. The three stages of development occurred in classical art and again in the Italian Renaissance. In modern times, the first stage began with Cimabue, Giotto, the Pisani, and Arnolfo di Cambio; the second with Jacopo della Quercia, Donatello, Masaccio, and Brunelleschi; the third with Leonardo, Raphael, and Michelangelo. Parallels are drawn with the steps in Greek painting and sculpture outlined by Pliny and others: from the monochrome painters to Apelles, and from the hard, lifeless statues of Canachus to the perfect art of Polycletus. Vasari suggests that such developments are due to inherent factors in art. It is a "property of these arts that from humble beginning they gradually improve and attain the summit of perfection."

Vasari also contributes a discussion of styles or "manners," of which he distinguishes three kinds: those of whole periods, those of nations or peoples, and those of individual artists. Individual styles can

be improved, imitated, or abandoned. Raffaellino del Garbo's style had three stages: it opened with brilliance, became mediocre, and was wretched at the end. But Vasari does not often point out individual changes; he regards each manner as an almost invariable habit of the artist. He analyzes each in some detail with reference to its subjects, drawing, coloring, arrangement, modeling, realism, expressiveness, grace, and grandeur. National styles enable us to recognize the provenance of statues. Gothic architecture seems ridiculous to the modern eye, he says, but appeared admirable to gothic eyes.

Toward the development of cultural evolutionism, the seventeenth century made several indirect contributions. Biology, history, and social science lagged far behind the mathematical and physical sciences; but pride in the latter gave rise to a general sense of having surpassed the ancients and of being able to go still farther in future. Pascal declared in 1647 that "the whole succession of men, throughout the course of so many centuries, should be envisaged as the life of a single man who persists forever and learns continually."[25] Francis Bacon, in the *New Atlantis* and the *Novum Organum*, pointed the way to a systematic increase of knowledge through reasoning based on observation and experiment, and to its use for human welfare. This idea, fundamental to the theory of progress, became the keynote of modern Western civilization. As to whether the arts had progressed beyond antiquity, there was much more dispute than in the case of science. It became a central issue in the long and celebrated "Quarrel of the Ancients and the Moderns"—i.e., between the champions of one or the other as superior. The argument began in the seventeenth century with

[23] *De Origine Civitatis Florentiae* (c. 1400). *Cf.* E. van der Grinten, *Enquiries into the History of Art-Historical Writing* (Amsterdam, 1952), p. 20.

[24] *Lives of the Painters, Sculptors, and Architects*, Introduction to Part II (New York, 1927), p. 203. *Cf.* van der Grinten, pp. 28 f.; E. Panofsky, "The First Page of Giorgio Vasari's Libro'" in *Meaning in the Visual Arts* (New York, 1955), p. 216.

[25] "Fragment of a Treatise on the Vacuum," in *Opuscules Works*, Vol. II, trans. O. W. Wight (New York, 1859).

Fontenelle and Perrault and did not reach its climax till the end of the eighteenth.[26] At first, the belief prevailed that ancient art had reached perfection and could not be surpassed, but opinion gradually shifted to the opposite, more optimistic and self-confident view. Implicit in this changing evaluation were the ideas that history was not cyclical; that art and culture had not deteriorated and did not have to do so; that they had developed and progressed in spite of setbacks on the way. Hobbes attacked the Golden Age theory with his declaration that primitive man in a stage of war, without strong government, had "no arts; no letters; no society; and which is worst of all, continual fear, and danger of violent death; and the life of man, solitary, poor, nasty, brutish, and short."

Bossuet, in his *Discourse on Universal History* (1681) marked off twelve successive epochs in the history of culture, and recalled the attention of scholars to the subject of world history as a whole. André Félibien (*Entretiens*, 1685) carried on Vasari's approach to art history. He confirmed the belief that Italian art had declined in the early seventeenth century, as Vasari had feared and Bellori observed; but held that Poussin had revived it by returning to the classical rules.

Early in the eighteenth century, the English writer Richardson first used the term "art history" and sketched a future "history of the arts."[27] J. F. Christ, in his *Life of Lucas Cranach* (1726), used the term to indicate a special field of study. After Winckelmann, says van der Grinten, it became common property. The word "style" came into use in the first half of the century, replacing "manner" as used by Ghiberti, Vasari, and Bellori. The word "taste" was also favored, especially for the style of individual artists. Caylus (1756–64) showed that "manner" in the visual arts was analogous to "style" in literature.

Winckelmann published in 1764 what has been called "the first systematic history of ancient art,"[28] and set high standards for the subsequent development of art-historical scholarship. But his high praise for what he considered to be the spirit of Greek art prolonged the Renaissance belief that modern art had been a degeneration from it. Somewhat in the manner of Plato, he exalted its "noble simplicity and repose," its "dignity, reserve and harmonious stillness" by contrast with the restless passion and exaggeration of modern art as exemplified by the erotic sculpture of Pigalle. In his view the history of art "aims at expounding its origin, growth, change, and fall, together with the diverse styles of peoples, ages, and artists." To explain events, he took into consideration the effects of climate and of social conditions. Freedom, he said, planted lofty dispositions in the Greeks, as the prospect of the immeasurable surface of the sea enlarges our gaze.[29] Winckelmann distinguished four stages in Greek art after the formless beginning. First came the archaic stage, up to Phidias; it was hard and powerful, often minute in detail, devoid of grace. Second came the grand style of Phidias and Scopas, characterized by lofty simplicity and unity, corresponding to that of Raphael in painting. Third was the softer style of Praxiteles, beautiful and graceful, analogous

[26] *Cf.* J. B. Bury, *The Idea of Progress* (New York, 1932), Chs. IV, XI.

[27] van der Grinten, p. 6, discussing J. Richardson, *Two Discourses: an Essay on the Whole Art of Criticism as it Relates to Painting; an Argument in Belief of the Science of a Connoisseur* (London, 1719).

[28] Winckelmann's *Gedanken über die Nachahmung der griechischen Werke in der Malerei u. Bildhauerkunst* appeared in Dresden and Leipzig in 1755. *Cf.* van der Grinten, pp. 73 f. K. Gilbert and H. Kuhn credit Winckelmann with having "introduced the concept of the evolution of styles." *A History of Esthetics* (Bloomington, Ind., 1953), p. 299. E. G. Holt also calls him "the first to conceive the history of art, not merely as a sequence of anecdotes and artists' lives, but as an aspect of the general evolution of human thought." *Literary Sources of Art History* (Princeton, N. J., 1947, 1958), p. 522. This is debatable. The gradual sequence and development of styles had been shown by Pliny and others, as we have just seen. Their place in the general evolution of thought was hinted by Lucretius but not clearly stated until the nineteenth century. Winckelmann did, as Mrs. Holt remarks, think of the term "style" in relation to the art of an entire period, and as reflecting its philosophy and civilization. This included its athletics, in the case of Greece, and also the psychological effects of its climate.

[29] Addison, Shaftesbury, and Dubos had suggested similar causal theories. *Cf.* Gilbert and Kuhn, p. 302.

to that of Guido Reni. The fourth and final style was imitative, eclectic, and trivial.[30]

Meanwhile parallel studies were proceeding in music history, and here again the eighteenth century favored a neat division into stages.[31] In 1763 John Brown published his "complete" picture of the history of music and poetry from the "savage or uncultivated state." It traced thirty-six stages from the early unity of melody, dance, and song to its perfection in Greece; then its decline to the separation of melody, dance, and poetry in his own day. Brown conceived the stages in music, says W. D. Allen, according to the "fixed species" principle, in a Chain of Being. Later evolutionism was to add the idea that each stage was an "unfolding" from the previous one.

Forkel, the German romantic historian of music, writing in 1788, accepted the idea that poetry and music were originally one, but denied that they had separated. Both grew together, he said, and had the same divisions: grammar and rhetoric. Harmony is the highest development of musical grammar and expression; the fugue is the highest musical form developed by rhetoric. Forkel took a step toward evolutionism in holding that music and poetry had progressed without gaps. "Arts and sciences grow, like all creations of Nature, little by little, until they reach perfection."[32] There have been three stages in the history of music: the first, in which many people are still living, is that of rude, simple, unorganized, rhythmic sounds. The second is that of musical scales and inflected speech, with similarity between the expression of sensations and ideas. In the third, both ideas and sensations develop from the same basic potentiality in the soul. Expression must be as manifold as our sensations, and harmony makes possible the greatest variety of expressions, with the aid of newly invented instruments. Against Plato, he regards such variety as progressive.

While some writers were theorizing thus on the histories of particular arts, others were attempting a broader view of cultural history as a whole. E. B. Condillac, in 1716, suggested that language,

the dance, music, and drama had arisen out of mimetic dance and gesture for communication. Painting arose from mimetic picture writing.[33] Giambattista Vico's *Principles of a New Science* (1725) distinguished three ages in world history: first, that of religion or the gods; second, that of heroes; third, that of men. These corresponded to three kinds of "natures" (religious, heroic, and human) and three kinds of government (theocratic, aristocratic, and human). Some traits of earlier stages survive in the later. Stages in art were included in Vico's system, in that the first kind of literature was poetry; it corresponded to mythology as the beginning of philosophy. Abstract thinking develops from these; poetic wisdom was felt, imagined, and literally believed. Writing in the form of pictographs preceded speech and expressed the images formed by the poetic spirit. Primitive hieroglyphics, endowed with symbolic meaning, were used for communication. Knowledge progresses through the stages of (1) feeling without observing, (2) observing with emotion, and (3) pure reflection with clear ideas. The sequence of cultural stages is progressive to some extent, but each people declines at last through luxury, folly, waste, and madness.

Adelung, writing a German *History of Culture* in 1782, divides the history of man into eight stages, each analogous to one in the life of the individual. The third stage, from Moses to 683 B.C., is called "The Human Race as a Boy," and the eighth, from 1520 to the present, is "Man in Enjoyment of His Full Enlightenment."[34]

As the century of enlightenment, hope, and rationalism sped toward its terrible climax in the French Revolution, the champions of modernity

[30] Winckelmann used the word "style" to mean the highest achievement in art in a certain period; not to mean the artistic habit of a certain artist. He did not conceive it as capable of progress or development. (van der Grinten, p. 75).

[31] W. D. Allen, *Philosophies of Music History* (New York, 1939), pp. 82–5, 263 f.

[32] *Einleitung*, Vol. I. Allen, p. 263.

[33] *Essay on the Origin of Human Knowledge* (Paris, 1716).

[34] A. L. Kroeber remarks on how this theory anticipates that of Spengler. *Style and Civilizations* (Ithaca, N. Y., 1957).

gained a temporary victory in the "Quarrel of the Ancients and the Moderns." With respect to the arts, Turgot still had reservations in 1750. "Time unfolds continually new discoveries in the sciences; but poetry, painting, music, have a fixed limit, which is determined by the nature of languages, imitation of nature, and the limited sensibility of our organs; which they approach gradually and which they cannot pass. The great men of the Augustan era reached it and are still our models." But he found it well to hail the "Century of Louis" as having "brought minds again to that point where its progress had been arrested." About the French throne are "Rivals of Sophocles, of Menander, of Horace," inventing new arts and perfecting old.[35] As to past progress in general, Turgot advanced some ideas which Comte later developed as the "law of the three stages," the keystone of his positive philosophy. Turgot divides intellectual history into the theological, the philosophical, and the scientific stage. In the first, primitive man tries to explain events in terms of divine wills, the gods being magnified humans. In the second, philosophers do so in terms of abstract concepts such as "essences" and "faculties," which merely cover their ignorance. In the third, real explanation is done in terms of empirical observation and verified mathematical formulas.

Biology and geology had been advancing along a separate, parallel line, laying the foundations for Lamarck's theory (1809) of organic evolution through the transmission of acquired characteristics. As early as 1754, Diderot brilliantly anticipated the fusion of the two theories—cultural progress and prehuman, organic evolution—which was to dominate the intellectual life of Europe a hundred years later. Said Diderot, "Even if Revelation teaches us that species left the hands of the Creator as they are now, the philosopher who gives himself up to conjecture comes to the conclusion that life has always had its elements scattered in the mass of inorganic matter; that it finally came about that these elements united; that the embryo

formed of this union has passed through an infinitude of organization and development; that it has acquired, in succession, movement, sensation, ideas, thought, reflection, conscience, emotions, signs, gestures, articulation, laws, and finally the sciences and arts; that millions of years have elapsed during each of these phases of development, and that there are still new developments to be taken which are as yet unknown to us."[36] The ideas of beauty, order, and symmetry originated from primitive sense experience and the designing of tools to meet primitive needs. Aesthetic taste develops naturally and requires no mysterious inner sense. It consists in the perception and complication of relations in sight and sound.

It was a small but crucial step to Condorcet's explicit inclusion of the arts in "the progress of the human mind," whose history he sketched shortly before his death, while hiding from Robespierre in 1793. The arts can and do progress, he insisted. It is mere prejudice to suppose that they are condemned "to the eternal monotony of imitating the first models, since the most sublime and moving beauty has already been apprehended."[37] Enjoyment of the products of different ages will be as keen as before even though the authors deserve less credit for rising to perfection. As worthy productions multiply and become more perfect, each generation will select and admire the worthiest and let the rest fall into oblivion. Future progress in the arts will result from progress in philosophy and science, from more numerous and profound observations on the aims, effects, and means of the arts themselves, and from destruction of authoritarian prejudices which have limited them in the past—prejudices which science and

[35] *Tableau philosophique des progrès successifs de l'esprit humain.* Quoted in Teggart and Hildebrand, *The Idea of Progress,* pp. 252, 259 Cf. G. Boas, *Dominant Theories of Modern Philosophy,* p. 580.

[36] *Pensées sur l'interprétation de la nature.* Also *Œuvres Complètes,* Vols. IX, X.

[37] *Esquisse d'un tableau historique des progrès de l'esprit humain* (Paris, 1795). Trans. June Barraclough as *Sketch for a Historical Picture of the Progress of the Human Mind* (London, 1955), p. 195.

philosophy have already thrown off. Their means will not be exhausted.

As to civilization in general, Condorcet retains no trace of the old, pessimistic belief in degeneration, or in universal cycles of progress and decline. The facts reveal no limit to human improvement, he says, except the duration of the earth; no human power henceforth can stop it. Progress may be more or less rapid; it can never be reversed (*retrograde*) unless there is a general, radical upheaval in conditions on the earth. The constancy of the laws of nature seems to assure our hopes of future progress. [38] It will continue in the tenth stage of history, the first nine having brought mankind up to the creation of the French Republic. Increasing happiness and justice through knowledge, rational control, and freedom are Condorcet's main criteria of progress.

The divisions in the *Esquisse* are made primarily in terms of approximate chronological periods, not of successive cultural types or trait-complexes. He calls them *époques* (epochs) rather than stages (*étapes* or *stades*).[39] But he describes them, not as mere chronological periods, but as stages in a journey or developmental process. He calls it a *progrès*, but it comprises much of what was later called cultural evolution. It is not a completely steady movement in one direction, for some of the stages (especially from the fall of Rome to the Renaissance) are predominantly retrogressive; but on the whole the prevailing movement is forward. Cultural events and conditions in each stage are analyzed in terms of several factors, especially the political, intellectual, and technological. This is done rather briefly and unevenly, which is not surprising in view of the circumstances under which the "Sketch" was written, and in view of the limited knowledge then available.

The first stage in progress, according to Condorcet, was characterized by the formation of tribal societies. It also included the origin of the dance, music, and poetry. These had been preceded by the formation of language. In the second, the pastoral stage, languages became richer but no less figurative and bold. Song, musical instruments, and poetry were improved; men could observe their own feelings, judge and select their ideas. The third was the agricultural stage, up to the invention of the alphabet. Written literature and crafts such as textiles advanced; sciences were in their infancy. The fourth stage was that of Greece up to the division of the sciences in the time of Alexander. The fine arts then "attained a degree of perfection that no other people had known before and that scarcely any has since achieved." Some of this was due to individual genius; some to the gradual process of improvement in the arts. In the fifth stage, in Greece and Rome from the division of the sciences to their decline, Greece retained its pre-eminence in the arts except for a moment of Roman glory in Virgil and Tacitus; then followed a decline, as in Augustine and Jerome. In the sixth, knowledge and morality declined until the time of the crusades, except for the Islamic Arabs with their taste for poetry and science. The advance of science was renewed in the seventh stage, which ended with the invention of printing; in it Dante, Boccaccio, and Petrarch brought Italian literature to a high point. The eighth stage brought philosophy and science to shake off the yoke of priestly authority; their progress was swift and startling, while in Italy "the art of epic poetry, painting, and sculpture reached a perfection unknown to the ancients." In Corneille, dramatic art in France was close to even greater heights. Indeed, if an enthusiasm for antiquity claims a superiority of genius for those who created its masterpieces, it is hard to compare their works with the products of Italy and France without perceiving "the real progress that art itself has made at the hands of the moderns."

The ninth and contemporary stage carried the advance from Descartes to the foundation of the Republic. Progress has ceased to be a slow, im-

[38] *Ibid.*, Introduction, p. 9.
[39] *Époques* is translated as "epochs" in F. J. Teggart and G. H. Hildebrand, *The Idea of Progress* (1949); as "stages" by June Barraclough (1955).

perceptible affair, and has led to revolution in some nations. This must sometime spread through all humanity. The spectacle of the fine arts has brilliant results to show. Music, with its theory strengthened by physical science, has become almost a new art. The graphic arts have been more brilliant in France than they were in Italy. In painting, we still follow Raphael and the Carracci. It is long since the appearance of a genius like Raphael, but this period of sterility is not due to chance alone. Nor is it due to exhaustion of the methods of the art, nor to natural abilities inferior in France to those of Italians. "It is solely to changes in politics and in manners that we must attribute, not indeed the decadence of the art, but the feebleness of its products." French tragedy and comedy have risen in the hands of Racine, Voltaire, and Molière "to heights as yet unattained in any other nation." French, English, and German literature have learned to obey the universal rules of reason and of nature, true for all languages and peoples, which make them all delight in the same beauties and be shocked by the same faults. Though universal, they admit of great modification in relation to various environments and uses.

Man's perfectibility is indefinite, says Condorcet. The organic perfectibility or degeneration of species in the case of plants or animals is one of the general laws of nature, which extends to the human race. Through science the two chief causes of degeneracy, extreme wealth and poverty, can be eliminated, thus prolonging life and health. Pointing out that superior perceptual, moral, and intellectual faculties can be transmitted as parts of the physical organism, Condorcet seems on the verge of suggesting future progress through eugenic breeding. He ends with the hope (based on contemporary theories of evolution through the transmission of acquired characteristics) that education, in improving mental qualities, can affect the innate abilities which are physically inherited.

Here Condorcet is almost at the point of following up Diderot's insight of 1754: that of merging the theories of cultural progress and organic evolu-

tion. But, even had he lived, much spade-work had yet to be done on the empirical evidence for both organic and cultural evolution. A less Utopian, more grimly realistic conception had to be formed of the way in which both had occurred: that is, largely through bitter struggles for survival and power. This lesson was learned, in part, from the continuing struggle and disillusionment which followed the Revolution.

3. EARLY NINETEENTH-CENTURY THEORIES: HUGO, COMTE, HEGEL, AND OTHERS

More than a half century was to elapse before Spencer could unite the two streams of thought, biological and sociological, in one huge synthesis. For biology, the interval was one of detailed research and growing belief in the transformation of species. For sociology and the philosophy of history, two important, large-scale systems were produced: those of Hegel in Germany and Comte in France.

Before they appeared, Madame de Staël made a significant comment on the progress of art. Though expressed in terms of value, it had bearings also on cultural evolution. She did not assert that modern art was better than ancient in form or expression, for the ancients had achieved perfection in organizing the limited range of thoughts and feelings known to them. But now, she said, a much wider range of these psychological materials has become available. Society has changed; the sum of ideas has increased, and emotions have been more subtly discriminated. There is "a new development of sensibility."[40] Guizot, in his *History of Civilization in Europe*, developed this point by saying that in modern literature the total fund of sentiments and ideas is stronger and richer; one sees that the human soul has been moved at more numerous points and to a greater depth. Hence

[40] Bury, p. 266, citing her books on *Literature, Germany*, and *The Spirit of Christianity*.

the formal imperfections in modern writing. Along with judgments of value, these writers were observing the historical fact of increasing variety, change, and emotionality in art. Spencer was to call this "differentiation"—one of the two reciprocal phases of evolution in art. Plato, it will be remembered, had condemned the modern art of his time for much the same tendency.

Victor Hugo also emphasized differentiation in his forceful "Preface" to *Cromwell* (1827). It was primarily a defense of that controversial play from a standpoint of romanticism. But incidentally it was much more: a theory of the stages in literary history and a new conception of romantic art as the most highly developed stage yet achieved. Hugo did not say, and it would not have been true, that all romantic art is complex. Some of it is extremely simple. Many of Hugo's own works were large and complex, however, and he admired the complexity of modern literature.

The new style, he declared, is "directly opposed to the uniform simplicity of the genius of the ancients," which is often monotonous in its perfect symmetry and harmony, its repetition of the beautiful and sublime. "It is of the fruitful union of the grotesque and the sublime types that modern genius is born—so complex, so diverse in its forms, so inexhaustible in its creations." And what is the grotesque? It is infinitely varied, showing itself at times as the ugly, abnormal, and horrible; at others as the comic and burlesque. It is frightful and laughter-moving by turns, as in medieval gargoyles and witches' revels; in Dante's and Milton's demons; in the pictures of Callot and Michelangelo; in Scaramouche and Mephistopheles. The ghastly forms of vampires, ogres, ghouls, and jinns contrast with fairies and goddesses. The grotesque includes all absurdities, infirmities, deformities, blemishes, vices, passions, crimes; it is sensuous, fawning, greedy, miserly, false, incoherent, hypocritical; hence constantly presented in new but incomplete aspects.

In romantic art, said Hugo, it makes close alliance with the beautiful and sublime, each element strengthening the other by the "struggle of two opposing principles"—a dialectic, as Hegel and Marx might have called it. This struggle produces drama, the union of tragedy and comedy. Based on the Christian dualism of flesh and spirit, modern poetry is the harmony of contraries. Included within it, the grotesque is one of the supreme beauties of the modern drama, which is a complex unity of contrasting elements. In Shakespeare, who balances the two principles, we have reached the poetic culmination of modern times. He *is* the drama, says Hugo, the union of grotesque and sublime, terrible and absurd, and the drama is the distinguishing achievement of modern literature, the third epoch in literary history. Of the neoclassic, pseudo-Aristotelian "three unities," unity of plot is the only valid rule. It does not require simplicity of plot, and "does not in any way exclude the secondary plots on which the principal plot may depend." Shakespeare's plots are thus vindicated. Cromwell as an historic character, says Hugo, interested him as "a complex, heterogeneous, multiple being, made up of all sorts of contraries."

In Hugo's theory of stages in literary history, everything comes in threes, and in threes within threes.[41] We are now (1827) in the old age of civilization and of literature; youth and manhood have passed. "Poetry has three periods, each of which corresponds to an epoch of civilization: the ode, the epic, and the drama. Primitive times are lyrical, ancient times epical, modern times dramatic. The ode sings of eternity, the epic imparts solemnity to history, the drama depicts life. The characteristic of the first poetry is ingenuousness, of the second simplicity, of the third truth. The rhapsodists mark the transition from the lyric to the epic poets, as do the romanticists that from the lyric to the dramatic poets. Historians appear in the second period, chroniclers and critics in the third. The characters of the ode are colossi—

[41] Eugène Delacroix, romantic painter, agreed in 1850 that "The arts have their childhood, their virility and their decrepitude." (*Journal*, Feb. 19).

Adam, Cain, Noah; those of the epic are giants—Achilles, Atreus, Orestes; those of the drama are men—Hamlet, Macbeth, Othello. The ode lives upon the ideal, the epic on the grandiose, the drama on the real. Lastly, this threefold poetry flows from three great sources—the Bible, Homer, Shakespeare... Civilization begins by singing of its dreams, then narrates its doings, and lastly sets about describing what it thinks... Everything in nature and in life passes through these three phases, the lyric, epic, and dramatic, because everything is born, acts, and dies."

Likewise J. M. Fischer, writing on the evolution of music in 1836[42] divides it into three epochs: (1) ancient, characterized by simplicity and pure melody; (2) Christian, by harmony and brotherhood; and (3) modern, by the multiple union of harmony and counterpoint. "As the evolution of humanity from a state of nature progresses by stages up to civilization, so do art and science, the outstanding manifestations of progress... The main evolutionary periods of music coincide with the main epochs in the history of man."

Why have so many theorists thus divided history into three stages or periods? Why has the number three been so often favored in other groupings and divisions, as in the Christian doctrine of the Trinity? Many classifications of the arts follow this neat formula: for example, F. T. Vischer's "constructive, receptive, and poetic."[43] Often the facts would seem quite as amenable to a different number of divisions. These are not entirely lacking in theories of history, but "three" seems to have a special fascination. Is some unconscious, emotive symbolism involved? One remembers the Pythagorean belief in the mystical power of the number three; the common superstition about lucky and unlucky numbers such as seven and thirteen; the various ways of explaining them. There are seven days in a week, twelve months in a year. Thirteen is abnormal. Psychoanalysts have suggested a male symbolism for three, a female for two, including the idea that three or any odd number is somehow stronger,

less open in the middle, less likely to split and fall apart. This idea occurs in Chinese number symbolism. Three suggests a connecting link between two extremes, a reconciliation of opposites, a supporting column or keystone in the arch; it suggests morning, noon, and night; childhood, maturity, and old age.

Whatever may be the explanation, the present tendency in cultural science to avoid such neat divisions also calls for an explanation. Consciously, it expresses a belief that neat divisions in the past have been too often arbitrary and untrue to fact; that things do not usually happen in such simple, regular ways. But more obscure reactions may also be involved.

German speculation on the idea of progress had been growing since the time of Herder, who published works on the philosophy of history between 1774 and 1784. Unlike the French and English, most of whom inclined to a hedonistic empiricism based on Locke, the Germans favored a theistic and intellectualistic emphasis. For Herder, the goal was a full understanding of God, not social happiness, and the steps toward it were a progressive series of historic religions.[44] His own religious views inclined to deism and a rigid, physical determinism. God had created the world but does not interfere in its operation or in human history; man's destiny is determined by his physical organization and environment. Although "God exists in inactive ease," as Bury expresses it, progress is nevertheless predetermined toward the goal of final perfection.

Kant, Fichte, and Hegel all opposed taking enjoyment or happiness as the measure of progress.

[42] *Die Grundbegriffe der Tonkunst in ihren Zusammenhange nebst einer geschichtlichen Entwickelung derselben* (Leipzig, 1836). (Quoted by W. D. Allen).

[43] For more details on this question, see the author's *The Arts and their Interrelations*, pp. 179–181; also W. D. Allen, *Philosophies of Music History*, p. 94. Aristotle, *De Caelo*, Bk. I, refers to the Pythagorean doctrine that the world is determined by the number three. Beginning, middle, and end give the number of an 'all,' and the number they give is the triad.

[44] Bury, p. 240.

For Fichte, the goal is increasing conscious reason and purpose, which gives freedom from instinct. There are five historical epochs according to Fichte, and man is (in 1807) passing into the fourth. The first is that of instinctive reason and innocence; the second, that of authoritarian reason; the third, that of enfranchisement, scepticism, and unregulated liberty; the fourth, that of conscious reason, as science; the fifth, that of ruling reason in the form of art. (Hegel, on the other hand, maintained that art would be superseded by philosophy.) Fichte's theory was frankly deduced *a priori*, as a world-plan which was clear to him without the study of history.[45]

G. W. F. Hegel's philosophy of history was built, like Fichte's, *a priori* from his idealistic assumptions, but with more historical illustrations from the facts of history as he saw them. Its emphasis on art and its enduring influence on theories of art history makes it especially notable from our present standpoint. "The theory was finally to emerge," said Hegel, "that art and literature, like laws and institutions, are an expression of society and therefore inextricably linked with other elements of social development—a theory which... has discredited the habit of considering works of art in a vacuum, dateless and detached..."[46] This approach has influenced all subsequent writing on the history of the arts, although different schools of thought have put varying emphasis on the relation of art to its social context.

Whether or not one accepts the metaphysical basis of Hegel's philosophy, one must give him great credit for inaugurating the comparative study of styles in various arts, periods, and cultures; also for producing the first systematic history of the arts on a world scale, as a phase in a general theory of cosmic evolution. His concept of dialectical struggle and synthesis as a cumulative process in cultural evolution has also proven highly fruitful. His errors and limitations are obvious today, but many valid insights can still be detached from them and put to useful work.

Universal history, according to Hegel, is the process through which the world mind or spirit gradually attains full consciousness of its own meaning. In this theory, Hegel was carrying on the great Platonic tradition in Western thought, which saw reality as basically mental, in opposition to the materialistic tradition of Democritus and Lucretius. He was Platonic in seeking knowledge through the abstract operations of logical reasoning, rather than through sensory observation. But he departed radically from Plato, falling in with the modern historical, evolutionary mode of thought, in regarding change as real and progressive. Reality has not been eternally perfect; it has been gradually becoming so. Universal history involves the development of a latent germ of being, striving to realize itself. Combining these two persuasive lines of thought, one old and one new (or at least long dormant), Hegel's synthesis has made a strong appeal to those in each generation who wished to reconcile the essentials of religion and science.

Another feature of Hegel's general philosophy which has influenced later theories of art history is that of the dialectical process. Hegel developed it from Plato's conception of dialectic as a method of reasoning, in which one gradually rises toward the eternal truths by repeated contradiction and selective reconciliation. Every assertion, said Hegel, implies a denial of its opposite, and every concept has its contradictory. New ideas are derived by noting the limitations of each contradictory and combining both to form a higher idea. The assertion of one is called a thesis; that of its opposite, an antithesis; their combination in a higher unity, a synthesis. Since reality and change are fundamentally mental and logical, such relations between ideas also apply to historical and cultural stages. Each period of history is a stage in dialectical evolution; it asserts a particular type of belief or develops a certain kind of social order. This in

---

[45] Bury, p. 253.
[46] *The Philosophy of History*, trans. J. Sibree (London, 1900). The first German edition was published in 1837 from lectures delivered in 1830–31.

time leads to the assertion of an opposite type and eventually to the destruction of both through their inclusion in a higher synthesis.

In tracing the stages of world history, Hegel almost ignores the primitive and prehistoric ages and begins with the oriental civilizations, especially China, India, and Persia. The cosmic mind moves from one people to another in achieving the successive stages in its unfolding of self-consciousness: from the orient to Greece, Rome, and Germany. The three main phases of spiritual unfoldment are subjective, objective, and absolute; the first is that of childhood, the second (in Greece and Rome) that of youth and manhood; the third (of medieval and modern Europe) is old but vigorous. In the German spirit and in Hegel's own philosophy, the world spirit has achieved full self-understanding. Thus the goal of progress is already reached.[47]

The place of the arts in this process of cultural development is set forth in Hegel's *Aesthetik*, published in 1835 (after his death) and translated as *Philosophy of Fine Art*.[48] One characteristic of the historical process, Hegel maintains, is that the cosmic mind gradually individualizes or particularizes itself; thus revealing itself in sensory forms, including those of art. This is the evolution of the Ideal, or world of imagined beauty and concrete fancy. It has three successive, cumulative stages, corresponding with those of the cosmic mind's increasing self-awareness. The stages constitute three types of art: symbolic, classical, and romantic, in an ascending hierarchy of value up to the arts of Hegel's own time. The first, as in Egyptian, Chinese, and Indian art (of which he had only a slight knowledge) is called "rather a mere search after plastic configuration than a power of genuine representation." It shows struggle, aspiration, disquiet, sometimes sublimity. The second, as in Greece, achieves "free and adequate embodiment of the Idea in the shape that, according to its conception, is peculiarly appropriate to the idea itself." It creates and envisages the complete Ideal, especially in anthropomorphic art, which is suited to

reveal mind to sense. Modern "romantic" art dissolves this union between Idea and reality and reverts on a higher plane to that "difference and opposition of two aspects which was left unovercome in symbolic art." Classical art had failed in trying to objectify Mind, which is infinite, concrete universality, in concrete, sensuous shape. Romantic art seeks to escape from this bodily medium and to achieve free intellectual being, addressing itself to the inner mind.

For each stage in art history, says Hegel, a different set of arts is most suitable. Each stage finds its completest realization in some one art or group of arts. Architecture is the typical symbolic art; sculpture the typically classical one; painting, music, and poetry—especially music—are most suited for the romantic stage of the world spirit. But the other arts recur within each stage in a subordinate way, satisfying persistent needs for expression in ways not in accord with the *Zeitgeist*. Each art has a symbolic, a classic, and a romantic stage, in only one of which it can become preeminent as expressing the dominant spirit.

Later philosophers and historians who accept its idealistic metaphysics have developed the Hegelian philosophy into a major tradition. These include a number of well-known art historians and critics who dissent from Hegel on details but accept his basic premise that the history of art and culture is the unfolding of a spiritual, directive force which presses on toward realization in varied forms and styles.

Auguste Comte, French founder of positivism and the science of sociology, lived from 1798 to 1857. His major work, the *Cours de philosophie positive*, appeared in six volumes between 1830 and 1842. It brought social thought, says Alexander Goldenweiser, "to the very doors of classical evolutionism," by asserting (a) that cultural changes are slow, gradual, and continuous; (b) that they follow

---

[47] *Cf.* Bury, p. 256.

[48] (London, 1920). For a critical summary, see T. Munro, *The Arts and their Interrelations* (New York, 1949), pp. 174-177.

a fixed, determined order, and (c) that the differences between various modern cultures are due to different speed in passing through the universal stages. He was sure that the early stages of now civilized groups could be found among modern primitives in various regions.[49]

Positivism was based on a radical empiricism, recognizing the existence only of what can be observed or proved by empirical data. This, for Comte, excluded not only incorporeal spirits but metaphysical abstractions such as "mind," "essence," and "causality." Theoretically, this is different from a metaphysical materialism such as that of Lucretius in that it avoids all assumptions about the ultimate nature of reality. But in practice and in the interpretation of history its implications are similar, in that the hypothesis of a divine or spiritual cause and purposeful direction is eliminated. The church is to be replaced by a philosophical and scientific priesthood; the worship of God by the worship of Humanity, in which the arts will play an important social and aesthetic role.

Positive or scientific thinking is the highest stage in mental development, according to Comte. It observes phenomena, tests and organizes them, and applies its conclusions as rules for the guidance of life. The main thread in human history is, for Comte as for Hegel, an intellectual one; progress is reckoned primarily on this basis. However, he insists that reason and science are to be subordinate to feeling; especially to the love of others as replacing self-love. This moral element from the Christian tradition remains in the positive philosophy, and Comte is careful to praise the medieval church for its contributions to the first or theological stage of mental development. That stage has been followed by the metaphysical, which is leading to the final, scientific or positive one. Comte follows Turgot in saying that man first tries to explain things by the immediate action of imaginary spirits. In the metaphysical stage, man does so by theoretical abstractions such as "essences" and "faculties." In the third, he submits to observable facts and recognizes invariable laws in their similarity and recurrence. The growth of the individual mind recapitulates this succession of stages.

All branches of knowledge, says Comte, pass through the three stages but at different speeds. Some have become fully scientific while others remain theological, metaphysical, or only partly scientific. This gives rise to a hierarchy of the sciences according to the order in which they have attained positive status. Their relative speed and status at any one time are largely determined by the nature of their subject-matter, from more to less inclusive and from more abstract to more concrete. Mathematics, astronomy, physics, chemistry, and biology have advanced in sequence, and the next to do so will be sociology, the positive study of social phenomena. (This last includes, by implication, much of what we now class under psychology, anthropology, economics, government, and other human or cultural sciences.) Only the intellectual élite or advance guard of the population advances thus, and large remnants of the earlier stages survive in modern thinking. Kings, magicians, and priests dominate the first stage. Logicians and lawyers dominate the second, manipulating the abstractions as legal formulas. Industrialists will rule in future with the expert advice of scientists and positivist philosophers. The process of history is due fundamentally to an instinct which pushes man to improve his condition physically, morally, and intellectually. Through a tendency to cohesion or solidarity, all social and intellectual phenomena are closely tied with material development. Instinct drives man onward, not in a straight line, but with oscillations around a prevailing trend. These are produced by race, climate, and the deliberate actions of individuals.

On the whole, allowing for great differences in speed, man passed out of the theological stage around 1400 A.D. It included three phases: fetishism, polytheism, and monotheism; also a theocratic and a military phase politically. The metaphysical

[49] Goldenweiser, "Evolution, Social," in *Encyclopedia of the Social Sciences*.

stage was mainly destructive, says Comte, dissolving through the critical philosophy of Hobbes, Spinoza, and Rousseau the decaying Catholic monotheism of the late middle ages. It did so by the use of three anarchic, but at the same time, necessary principles—popular sovereignty, equality, and the right of free judgment. After this era of revolution and disorder, Comte declares, the time has come for society as a whole to enter the positive and final stage. Like Condorcet before him and Spencer afterward, Comte is optimistic about the rapid disappearance of the theological and military attitudes, the main obstacles to a rule of reason. Wars will soon cease. Industrialists guided by science will protect the working class more effectively than the church or monarchy have done. Such utopian hopes had, of course, not yet been chilled by world disasters, by the growing rivalry of capital and labor, or by the theory of organic evolution as a ruthless struggle.

The evolution of the arts appears in Comte's philosophy, as it had in Condorcet's, not as a continuous thread in itself, but as a succession of types, each characteristic of a stage in the evolution of thought.[50] Under "Fetishism" as the first theological phase, he mentions its influence on the fine arts. This was not oppressive, since a belief which endowed the whole universe with life must favor the imagination. All the fine arts originated in this period. Polytheism, the second phase of the theological stage, was also favorable to the arts. It exalted the imagination and sentiment over the reason, and employed the arts to interpret its religious philosophy concretely to the public. Each newly introduced divinity was given by the arts a costume, manner, and history suitable to his function. Through providing favorable conditions for the progress of art, polytheism helped raise it to a high peak. It is wrong to infer that man's aesthetic faculties have since declined. Monotheism, last theological phase, raised the arts still higher. The epic and dramatic works of Milton, Ariosto, Shakespeare, Corneille, and Molière are unparalleled, says Comte. Italian and German music is unquestionably superior to the ancient, which had no harmony and only simple, uniform melodies. The introduction of harmony, musical notation, and instruments like the organ was an achievement of the middle ages. Painting has advanced not only in technical methods but also in lofty moral expression, as in Raphael. Sculpture has suffered through our unfamiliarity with the human form. Architecture reached sublime perfection in the cathedral.

During the metaphysical stage, says Comte, society has been passing through a critical, negativistic state of mind, unfavorable to art. The revival of classical art in the fifteenth century was necessary and valuable in some ways, especially to help disintegrate theological thinking; but it has been retrograde in that excessive admiration of the ancients blighted the promise of the fourteenth century. Architecture fell below the medieval level. Later on, art was systematically encouraged, especially by the popes and monarchs, whose influence has been more beneficial to art than that of Protestantism and private patronage. Still more recently, industrial progress has made the artist more independent of both, as in the rise of journalistic literature. Advances have occurred especially in artistic representations of private life, as in the works of Fielding and Lesage. Dramatic music has made decisive progress in Italy and Germany, thus helping to distribute art through social life in general. The arts now suffer from unstable, transitional conditions. They are adrift from the old régime, without general direction or social destination; they await a new social and intellectual stimulus. This is not forthcoming from philosophy, which (Comte declares) has fallen into nothingness through its irrational isolation. But even amid the wildness and aesthetic vagabondism of modern Europe immortal creations have been made, such as the novels of Scott. The epic (novel) form probably indicates the mode of future renovation of

[50] *The Positive Philosophy of Auguste Comte*, trans. Harriet Martineau (New York, 1858), pp. 346–8, 552, 566, 632, 706, 738, 755.

art in general. Society will find an inexhaustible source of poetic greatness in the new, positive conception of Man as the supreme head of the economy of nature, which he modifies at will within the limits of natural law. What philosophy elaborates, art will propagate and adapt for propagation.

Comte's short book, *A General View of Positivism*,[51] devotes a chapter to "The Relation of Positivism to Art." It is concerned entirely with the possible functions and developments of art in the coming stage of scientifically ruled society. One of the most important of these is to help direct the religion of humanity through organized public festivals. Humanity itself will be the object of worship, especially the highest achievements of man, past and present. Theistic religions in the past have been adorned and given emotive appeal by the arts, and the religion of positivism will need them quite as much. "Art is the ideal representation of fact, and its object is to cultivate our sense of perfection." Where science explains fact, art beautifies it. Both evolve: their contemplations "begin with the simple objects of the external world; they gradually rise to the complicated facts of human nature." The characteristic mission of art is to construct types of the noblest kind, by the contemplation of which our feelings and thoughts may be elevated; art should surpass reality so as to stimulate us to amend it. Art begins with simple imitation, then goes on to idealization and expression. Through this last, with the development of form and style, the artist can communicate his thought effectively and completely. Positivist art will construct Utopias, limited by the knowledge of reality. It will compare the ruins of the past with prophetic pictures of the future, and idealize past achievements also. Science, poetry, and morality will be devoted to the study, praise, love, and service of humanity. "The conception of God will be entirely superseded," says Comte, by "the great conception of Humanity" and by "the principle of Love on which the whole system rests." There will be two kinds of regular festival, one static and

the other dynamic; one celebrating the love of order and the present nature of humanity; the other its progress and historical continuity. They will not be didactic, since "it is the essence of art not to instruct otherwise than by giving pleasure."

Spencer's theory of evolution resembles that of Comte in some respects, but he denied being influenced by it. There may not have been much, if any, direct influence; evolutionary ideas were in the air, and naturalistic empiricism was a British tradition. The main additional points in common between them are, first, the basic idea that history shows increasing complexity, rationality, and happiness; second, the idea that social evolution is progressive; third, that it occurs by natural law, without supernatural direction. All these ideas are older than Comte, as we have seen. In other important respects their theories differ. Spencer proposed no "law of three stages" and showed little interest in definite divisions of history. Spencer was politically more liberal and individualistic than Comte. And Comte did not include prehuman, organic evolution in his system. He was impressed by Cuvier's hierarchy of species, as a classification of fixed types. He briefly considered but rejected Lamarck's hypothesis "in which the different organic states succeed each other slowly by imperceptible transitions" so as to make a continuous, ascending series. He rejected Lamarck's theory of "the tendency of direct and individual modifications to become fixed in races by hereditary transmission, so that they may increase in each new generation." Pending further study, he said, "there can scarcely be a doubt... that species remain essentially fixed through all exterior variations compatible with their existence."

Pioneer specialized research in prehistoric archeology was done long before mid-century, especially by Sven Nilsson and other Scandinavian scientists. It did not arouse as much interest then as in later decades, when the general subject of evolution had caught the public mind, and when

51 Trans. J. H. Bridges (New York, 1957), Ch. V.

theorists were busy trying to assemble all relevant evidence for it. From fresh empirical data about 1812, the Danish archeologist Thomsen revived the Lucretian system of three stages—stone, bronze and iron—which is still, in revised form, used today.[52] Nilsson further proposed four stages of early man according to mode of subsistence: the savage or collector, the herdsman or nomad, the agriculturist, and the civilized man; this last being distinguished by coined money, writing, and division of labor.[53] Nilsson himself was aware of the broader implications of his work. He declared in 1843 that it is impossible to understand the anti-

quities of a particular country without realizing that they are "the fragments of a progressive series of civilization, and that the human race has always been, and still is, steadily advancing in civilization."[54]

[52] *Cf.* G. A. Daniel, *The Three Ages* (Cambridge, 1942); V. G. Childe, *Social Evolution* (New York, 1951), p. 17. Thomsen used it to arrange and classify exhibits in a museum at Copenhagen.

[53] G. E. Daniel, *A Hundred Years of Archaeology* (London, 1950). W. D. Strong, "Historical Approach in Anthropology" in *Anthropology Today*, p. 391.

[54] *Primitive Inhabitants of Scandinavia* (ed. Lubbock, 1868); quoted by E. B. Tylor, *Primitive Culture* (London, 1871, 1913), Vol. I, 62.

CHAPTER V

HERBERT SPENCER'S
THEORY OF EVOLUTION IN THE ARTS

I. THE "SYNTHETIC PHILOSOPHY" AS A MERGING OF PREVIOUS LINES OF EVOLUTIONARY THOUGHT

It is well known that neither Spencer nor Darwin originated the main thesis of organic evolution: the idea that new and more complex species of plants and animals originate through gradual change. After many early, partial anticipations, it received a systematic statement in Lamarck's *Zoological Philosophy* in 1809. To explain how this process might have occurred, resulting in the present diversity of living types, Lamarck relied on the theory that acquired characteristics can be transmitted to offspring, thus allowing the gradual accumulation of changes made during the life of each generation. Fifty years later, Darwin offered a rival explanation of how the evolutionary process might have occurred and might still be occurring— the principle of natural selection. Empirical evidence showed the actuality of this process but not that of Lamarckian inheritance. Darwin's explanation of the way in which species originate convinced many doubters of the main thesis itself: that evolution had actually happened, even in the case of man.

Spencer did not derive the general theory of evolution from Darwin, as some suppose. He adopted a Lamarckian version of it long before Darwin's *Origin of Species* appeared. He was convinced that evolution had occurred on a large scale and was still continuing.[1] He believed that "the

development hypothesis" was capable of far-reaching application. He shared with Condorcet an undying hope that the Lamarckian explanation would be vindicated.[2] But he soon ceased to rely on it exclusively, and accepted natural selection as well.[3] The general rejection of the Lamarckian principle was discouraging to those who hoped for rapid human progress in the future; but Spencer felt that much had been achieved and much was still possible by other methods. He went on to show that the Darwinian processes of variation and environmental selection were operative in the cultural realm as well as the organic.

Most philosophers who wrote on progress before the time of Spencer, even as late as Comte, restricted it to human history. Until Spencer, such com-

[1] Darwin, in his "Historical Sketch" preceding the *Origin of Species*, credits Spencer with having defended the development theory in 1852 "with remarkable skill and force." He also mentions Spencer's developmental treatment of psychology in 1855. Darwin modestly credits certain other writers (especially W. C. Wells in 1813 and P. Matthew in 1831) with having suggested the idea of natural selection. Spencer was somewhat influenced by Comte, but more directly by K. E. von Baer, the German embryologist who asserted that ontogeny recapitulates phylogeny (*Über Entwicklungsgeschichte der Thiere* [Königsberg, 1827–37]). For the concepts of natural selection and survival of the fittest, both Spencer and Darwin were indebted to Malthus' *Essay on Population* (1798). Both derived the concept of gradual stratification from Lyell's *Principles of Geology* (London, 1830).

[2] See his youthful essay, "The Development Hypothesis" (1852) and Hugh Elliot's biography, *Herbert Spencer* (New York, 1917), pp. 22, 45. Spencer was born in 1820 and died in 1903.

[3] "Progress: its Law and Cause," p. 53 n.

binations of the two ideas had been brief and sketchy or vaguely poetic. The social and organic phases of development had been studied separately, for the most part: one by the social philosophers, the other by the biologists, geologists, and paleontologists. Their investigation proceeded in two streams of thought, occasionally touching but mainly parallel, until the publication of Spencer's essay on "Progress: its Law and Cause" in 1857[4] —a little over a century after Diderot's prophetic comment, and two years before Darwin's *Origin of Species*. That essay, followed by Spencer's long series of books on evolution, built the two theories together into one huge system, based on the world-view of natural science. Its framework was a new, expanded concept of evolution as a universal tendency toward increasing complexity, operative in the realms of physics and astronomy, biology, sociology, and psychology. Instead of merely affirming this principle dogmatically, Spencer tried to demonstrate it inductively with an impressive mass of examples from every realm of science and history. He brought together into one system a number of ideas and theories from different fields, none of which was completely original with him, and interrelated them as names for various phases of the same cosmic process.

He grouped them, at first under the usual concept of progress, whose "law and cause" he sought to explain. When he later substituted "evolution" as the name of the law, he did not give up the idea that evolution was essentially progressive in terms of increasing morality and happiness. It was not mere complication, but beneficial complication. By thus assembling many different ideas under the single heading of "evolution," and applying it to all natural and human processes, he greatly expanded the extension of that term. In partially identifying evolution with progress, under one name or the other, he did not permanently identify or confuse the two concepts. He was aware that "progress" implied improvement, whereas "evolution" did not. He tried to describe evolution in

non-evaluative terms as an objective tendency or process in nature. But he still believed that it was, on the whole, progressive from the evaluative standpoint, and he undertook to demonstrate this on the basis of moral and aesthetic standards. He did not say or believe that every event or aspect of the process was good; he saw the reality of particular evils and failures. He was considering the general trend, and finding it good on the whole.

Evolution, he said in *First Principles* (1875), is "a change from an incoherent homogeneity to a coherent heterogeneity, accompanying the dissipation of motion and integration of matter." More briefly, it is "a change from the homogeneous to the heterogeneous" or "the simple into the complex, through successive differentiations."[5] Both *differentiation* and *integration* are involved in the total process of increasing complexity, he pointed out. Evolution thus includes (a) differentiation or increasing heterogeneity and (b) integration or coherence among the parts or functions thus differentiated. Differentiation occurs among the parts and internal relations of a single form, as in the human body, and also among types or species. Thus all the enormous present diversity of plant and animal types is said to have evolved from one or a few original, undifferentiated types of protoplasm and one-celled organism. Many of the differentiated types become specialized, or adapted in structure and function to a particular, distinctive environment or mode of life. Man is highly specialized in relying on his brain and intelligence, but this enables him to live under a great variety of conditions.

As Spencer developed it, the concept of evolution came to include the idea of *gradual* change through natural causes, as opposed to (a) the theory of special creation, which taught that all biological types including man had been created out

---

[4] First published in *The Westminster Review* for April 1857. Reprinted in *Essays Scientific, Political, and Speculative* (New York, 1892), Vol. I, pp. 8 f.

[5] "Progress: its Law and Cause," p. 10.

of nothing in the Garden of Eden, and that fossils had been produced by a series of ancient catastrophes; also as contrasted with (b) sudden, discontinuous changes in the social realm, as by revolution or autocratic mandate. It implied that such change could be *cumulative*, in that developments achieved in one generation could be at least partially preserved in later ones.

Applying the concept of evolution to cultural phenomena requires a broad interpretation of the idea of *descent*. In plants and animals, descent occurs directly through the germ plasm by sexual or other physical reproduction. In man, there is also *cultural descent*—by imitation, education, the gradual accumulation of knowledge, skills, and customs from one generation to the next.

Adaptation to environment was another biological concept which Spencer incorporated in his theory of evolution. Adaptation had been previously regarded (by Paley and other theologians) as a condition of fitness between various species and their environments, and hence as a proof of "design" or divine planning. Darwin and Spencer not only proposed a naturalistic, non-teleological explanation of it, but described it as a continuous process of adapting to changing conditions. Natural selection tended to maintain or increase such fitness by eliminating the less fit in each generation. The process of evolution was thus shown to involve continuous and (in Spencer's opinion) increasing adaptation between species and their environments. Evolution was, in other words, descent with adaptive modification.

Spencer linked the idea of adaptation with that of complication by arguing that increasing complexity of structure and function was, on the whole, a means of adaptation and survival for the species. Man's complex brain and nervous system, his hands, eyes, and powers of speech were obviously the crowning examples.

In Spencer's philosophy, "evolution" became a name for the sum total of historical events as he conceived them to be; for the historic and prehistoric process as a whole. It was a name for the

whole, vast procession of events in our universe, through countless eons when matter was inchoate, through the slow origins of life, man, mind, and civilization, in which the events of art and of written history were only the latest, brief episode. Thus to apply the name of an abstract process to the actual course of events implied that it was a true and adequate description of this course as a whole. Evolution was observable everywhere, and it was the claim of Spencer to have first disclosed it on a cosmic scale, in every realm and period.

So universal and fundamental a tendency in events must, in Spencer's view, be regarded as inevitable, automatic, certain to continue for an indefinitely long period. Progressive evolution, he thought, is not dependent on divine grace or miraculous intervention; neither does it depend on whether man is wise and moral enough to make it happen by conscious planning. In fact, efforts by man to direct his own future evolution, as through governmental control, may do more harm than good. Free variation and natural selection, even without wise planning, have resulted in progress in the past and may be counted on to do so in future. However, he believed that human wisdom, good will, artistic ability, and practical inventiveness would automatically increase as effective and successful modes of adaptation, along with justice and happiness.

A theory of evolution becomes "unilinear" when it specifies a certain sequence of stages as universal and inevitable. In this respect, Spencer's theory was less unilinear than Comte's. The French philosopher saw only one route for intellectual and social evolution: from the theological-military to the metaphysical-legalistic to the scientific-industrial. Some of Spencer's followers (notably L. H. Morgan) went farther toward a unilinear theory than he did. They regarded modern primitive, tribal peoples as being substantially like the prehistoric ancestors of civilized peoples. The modern primitive, according to this view, is only going more slowly along the same route which our own ancestors trod, and must follow it in future if he goes ahead at all. Spencer shared to some extent the common tendency of his age, to regard modern primitives as merely backward by comparison with civilized, liberal Victorians, rather than as highly evolved along different lines. But he did not propose any ironclad scheme of universal stages, in the form of specific sets of cultural traits which had to develop everywhere in a certain order. He made only a few rough generalizations: for example, that society had shifted from organization primarily for war to organization primarily for industry, and that ethical and social considerations would be more influential in future.[6]

Evolution was a "universal law," according to Spencer. It was a law in the scientific sense, as in Newton's laws of thermodynamics; not a regulative edict but an accurate description of a certain way in which things act throughout the universe. If true, as he believed, it could claim vast explanatory significance through showing how a multitude of apparently different phenomena and laws of smaller scope are examples of the same underlying process. It would not, of course, be a complete explanation. There would still remain, as in the case of Newton's laws, the metaphysical question of why nature came to behave in this way, and what makes it keep on doing so. On such metaphysical points, Spencer first accepted a teleological hypothesis in accord with liberal Christianity; then shifted to an agnostic empiricism. Ultimate reality was "unknowable"; science and philosophy could only describe and interpret the phenomena of experience. From this hypothesis he proceeded to construct his system in a naturalistic way, without introducing any supernatural agency or purposeful direction, idealistic or dualistic. In spite of his professed agnosticism, he tended to rely in effect on the immanent power and tendency of matter to organize itself into more and more complex forms, including those of life and mind. He did not hesitate to generalize about causality in the form of a basic "law" of nature

to explain evolution. "Every cause produces more than one effect"—that is, effects multiply, thus increasing heterogeneity.[7]

The term "law" was used more in Spencer's time than it is at present, to describe observed recurrences and regularities in any field of phenomena, including those of mind and culture. Today, it is usually avoided in the latter fields because it seems to imply a complete, universal regularity which seldom if ever exists in their highly variable phenomena. However, Spencer's use of the term "universal law" did not imply such absolute uniformity. Evolution was "universal" in the sense of operating in all realms of phenomena. A "law" could be simply a persistent, widespread tendency, subject to exceptions and not necessarily eternal.[8] Spencer did emphasize examples which conformed to his "law" and ignored or minimized many important, negative instances. This makes his system appear over-simplified and unilinear today. However, this again is a matter of degree. Most of his principal generalizations are not totally false, but exaggerated and one-sided. He underestimated, but did not completely ignore, the exceptions to his law. He made it clear that a contrary tendency—dissolution—also existed in the universe. Thus he did not claim that evolution was, even now, universal in the sense of operating always, without exception. Nor did he claim that it would be eternally true or dominant, like the laws of mathematics. He predicted that, sometime in the far-off future, a state of equilibrium would be attained which would be followed by a dis-

[6] On the subject of stages as treated by Comte, Spencer, and others, see H. E. Barnes, *Historical Sociology: its Origins and Development* (New York, 1948), pp. 81 f.

[7] "Progress; its Law and Cause," pp. 5–7.

[8] Darwin, in *The Origin of Species*, also used the term "law" in this way: for example, at the end of *The Origin of Species*. The many "elaborately constructed forms" of plants and animals, he says, "have all been produced by laws acting around us." These laws, he continues, are growth with reproduction, inheritance, variability, high increase leading to a struggle for life, natural selection, divergence, and extinction of less improved forms." Franz Boas also speaks of "laws" in a similar, fairly loose sense ("Anthropology," in *Encyclopedia of Social Science*, pp. 109–110).

integrative, devolutionary phase in which dissolution prevailed.

This brings his philosophy of history, to some extent, into the ancient class of cyclical theories.[9] They maintain that change pursues an alternating series of constructive and destructive phases, perhaps involving countless repetitions, past and future. They are, in spirit, inconsistent with the idea of one continuous evolution or progress lasting indefinitely into the future. But many combinations of the two types are possible, and Spencer's was one of them. For him the upward, developmental phase in which we live had lasted so long, and would last so far into the future, that the thought of an eventual dissolution was vague and remote. He did not look back with longing to a Golden Age. For all practical purposes future evolution was for him, as for Condorcet, indefinitely possible and assured by natural law.

Such a theory is optimistic by contrast with those (such as Spengler's) which prophesy an imminent decline, as must ensue if the cycles are short. It is so by contrast also with many noncyclical theories which recognize only one historic process, one long and painful struggle doomed to final failure. In his confidence that man will become happier and better, on into the limitless future, Spencer stands with Condorcet at the peak of modern optimism. He differs mainly in that his optimism claims a firmer basis of scientific evidence, and a longer backward view of prehuman progress.

2. HOW THE ARTS EVOLVE, ACCORDING TO SPENCER

The evolution of the arts had been and would continue to be, Spencer thought, an integral part of cosmic evolution, including that of mind, society, and civilization. He cited examples from the history of many different arts, both fine and applied, primitive and modern, to show that the same evolutionary tendencies had occurred there as in the development of animal, plant, and social forms. Art was becoming more complex, and in doing so it was, on the whole, improving in quality. It was evolving and progressing along with science and technology. All these developments were closely interrelated and cooperative.

Spencer was much interested in the arts and their several histories, including music and the visual arts, dance, theater, and literature. He showed considerable knowledge of their technicalities. Like other nineteenth-century evolutionists, he was interested in prehistoric and modern tribal arts as links between the animal, the savage, and civilized man. Little was known about them in his day, by comparison with all that recent excavation, exploration, anthropology, and other research have brought before us. His data were inadequate and often unreliable, but he used them skilfully to illustrate his main thesis: that the arts have descended from a few comparatively undifferentiated occupations and forms, branching out into countless different ones today. Civilized art, he contended, is more complex as well as more diversified than primitive. The history of the arts, like that of science, technology, morality, institutions, and all other mental and social phenomena, is an evolution; it conforms to the general definition of evolution, and it forms an integral part of the whole evolutionary process.

The arts have aided man to survive, and have contributed to the survival of successful groups within society. They are prominent among the distinctively human modes of adaptation. One of the functions of music through the ages has been to arouse fellow-feeling among humans through the expression and communication of basic emotions. Thus music is biologically as well as and aesthetically valuable, and its development morally contributes to evolution as well as to progress.

[9] There have been and will be "alternate eras of Evolution and Dissolution." *First Principles*, Ch. XXIII, §183.

Spencer's early and little-known essay on "Progress: its Law and Cause"[10] emphasized the history of the arts as evidence for the general thesis that everything tends to advance from the homogeneous to the heterogeneous. "Whether it be in the development of the earth, in the development of life upon its surface, in the development of society, of government, of manufactures, of commerce, of language, literature, science, art, this same evolution of the simple into the complex, through successive differentiations, holds throughout... The transformation of the homogeneous into the heterogeneous is that in which progress essentially consists."

In the development of language, words, groups of words, and whole organized languages become differentiated. Written language, painting, and sculpture are originally appendages of architecture in early theocratic government, in cave painting and sculpture, with relief carving as intermediate. Color is dropped from sculpture, so that it differs more from painting. Subjects differentiate from the purely religious to the secular; painting is divided into historical, landscape, marine, architectural, genre, animal, still-life, etc. "The evolution of the homogeneous into the heterogeneous is displayed not only in the separation of painting and sculpture from architecture and from each other, and in the greater variety of subjects they embody, but it is further shown in the structure of each work. A modern picture or statue is of far more heterogeneous nature than an ancient one."[11] An Egyptian sculpture-fresco shows all its figures on one plane rather than at various distances; all as exposed to the same degree of light. A few solid colors are used; figures are comparatively uniform in action, attitude, face, and dress. "In the pictures of our own day the composition is endlessly varied," with an infinite variety of intermediate tints. "In the coordinate origin and gradual differentiation of poetry, music, and dancing we have another series of illustrations." Music and poetry separate from dancing and then from each other; dance movements are diversified; musical instruments are multiplied. Early minstrels sang to the harp heroic narratives versified by themselves, combining the now separate offices of poet, composer, vocalist, and instrumentalist. All these arts separated gradually from each other and from religion. We see the evolution of poetry in the development of various forms of meter, rhyme, and general organization; of music, not only in more numerous instrumental tones, but also in the different modes and keys, meters, melodic parts, harmonies, and nuances of expression. In ancient literature, the Bible combines theology, cosmogony, history, biography, civil law, ethics, poetry. The *Iliad* combines religious, martial, historical, epic, dramatic, and lyric elements. In modern times these have become separate, heterogeneous divisions of art.

Science also began with "an era in which it was not yet differentiated from art, and was, in union with art, the handmaid of religion; passing through the era in which the sciences were so few and rudimentary as to be simultaneously cultivated by the same philosophers; and ending with the era in which the genera and the species are so numerous that few can enumerate them... We might do the like with architecture, with the drama, with dress."

As the history of life and society includes examples of retrogression and dissolution, so does the history of the arts. After the fall of Roman civilization, Spencer observes, the arts of Europe went back to a more undifferentiated stage in which all were again attached to and combined with each other. Architecture again dominated, and the gothic church took form. Thenceforth, the process of differentiation among the arts was resumed and has continued until the present day. It is important to notice here that Spencer considers the reversion to a less differentiated, less specialized condition in the arts as a retrogression qualitatively; a result of

[10] In his later books, the emphasis shifted to other aspects of evolution. He touched often on the arts, but never again surveyed their evolution as comprehensively as in this early essay.

[11] "Progress: its Law and Cause," p. 28.

the pathological dissolution of the Roman Empire. The path of improvement, for him, is that of increasing specialization, detachment, and separate development of the various arts, both as professions and as to the nature of the resulting products. It is a sign of progress for paintings and statues to be placed and enjoyed apart from any fixed architectural setting, and for instrumental music to be freed from the domination of a verbal text.

This phase of Spencer's theory has provoked some later critics to deny that highly differentiated arts are necessarily better than the early, undifferentiated ones. "The extreme differentiation of any art from every other art," wrote Sydney Colvin, "does not by any means tend to the perfection of that art. The process of evolution among the fine arts may go, and indeed in the course of history has gone, much too far for the health of the arts severally."[12] In the late nineteenth century, Colvin continues, a reaction against such specialization set in, led by William Morris. (Spencer disapproved of Morris, on this and other grounds.) Wagner's music dramas also exemplify this counter-trend back to a combination of the arts, says Colvin. But Spencer elsewhere speaks with admiration of the vast music dramas, and would doubtless argue that they were complex, highly evolved forms, not merely undifferentiated.

Other art historians have objected to the idea that all the modern arts are descended from one or a very few primeval types, such as the undifferentiated dance-music-drama of early Greek religion. Art, they say, differs in this regard from organic species, which are supposedly all descended from one original, undifferentiated form of life. There may have been many original sources of the arts, some specialized from the start. Spencer does not insist that all were developed from a single, undifferentiated prototype; only on the general trend of development and its value.

The history of both industrial and fine arts exhibits, says Spencer, advance in integration as well as in differentiation. To organize more parts,

and more different parts, into a unified whole is an increasingly difficult problem for the artist. The change from rude, small, and simple tools to perfect, complex, and large machines reveals this advance. In the fine arts, "Contrast the mural decorations of the Egyptians and Assyrians with modern historical paintings, and there becomes manifest a great advance in unity of composition —in the subordination of the parts to the whole. One of these ancient frescoes is, in truth, made up of a number of pictures which have little mutual dependence... The same trait may be noted in the tapestries of medieval days." But in modern paintings, "there is always a more or less distinct coordination of parts—an arrangement of attitudes, expressions, lights, and colors, such as to combine the picture into an organic whole." In music, "progressive integration is displayed in still more numerous ways," as for example in the "vast ensemble of a music drama." "In early literature, we note successive occurrences that have no natural connections; they are separate adventures loosely strung together. In modern literature, the events result from the characters and conditions, and the characters influence each other in a complex of moral and psychological relations."[13]

If he had been living after the discovery of the Lascaux cave drawings, Spencer would no doubt have used them in contrasting primitive with modern. The paleolithic drawings, able as some of them are in representing single animals and small groups, show little tendency to merge these in varied compositions with definite boundaries and unified, internal organization. As to the Egyptian and medieval arts, Spencer exaggerated their disunity somewhat, largely because he conceived of composition as necessarily realistic; he did not appreciate some of the decorative and symbolic modes of composition in ancient art. But on the whole, his generalization is not far wide of the mark.

In Spencer's theory the multiplication of effects,

---

[12] "Fine Arts," *Encyclopedia Britannica* (11th ed., 1910).
[13] *First Principles* (New York, 1895), §114, pp. 324 f.

the tendency of each event to produce many different effects, is illustrated in literature by the manifold effects of the primitive mystery play, affecting modern drama and other poetry and fiction. "The influence which a new school of painting—as that of the Pre-Raphaelites—exercises upon other schools; the hints which all kinds of pictorial arts are deriving from photography; the complex result of new critical doctrines, as those of Mr. Ruskin, might severally be dwelt upon as displaying the like multiplication of effects." Through the operation of this universal tendency to higher complication, "progress is not an accident, not a thing within human control, but a beneficent necessity."[14]

Assuming that the arts thus evolve, does this constitute a progress, and by what criterion? Spencer does not evade the issue. In an essay on "The Origin and Function of Music" (1857) he considers first the relation of vocal sound to the expression of pleasant and painful emotions in ordinary life, especially in animals and children. All music is originally vocal, he says, and variations of voice are physiological results of variations in feeling. The variations in vocal sound he analyzes in terms of loudness, timbre, pitch, intervals, and rate of variation, showing a connection between each type and certain emotional expressions. They occur in ordinary speech, but more intensely in vocal music. Song employs and exaggerates the natural language of the emotions. From the simple chant or recitative in four tones, there developed music having a range of two octaves, with increased complexity of pitch-intervals, phrases, and corresponding emotional expressiveness. Such music stimulates not only familiar but unfamiliar feelings, and becomes an idealized language of emotion. We tend to prefer sounds which habitually accompany agreeable feelings, and vice versa. The history of music illustrates the general law of progress that "alike in occupations, sciences, arts, the divisions that had a common root, but by continual divergence have become distinct and are now becoming separately developed, are not truly

independent, but severally act and react on each other to their mutual advancement."

The function of music, over and above the direct pleasure it gives, is to develop a language of the emotions. This is hardly second in importance to the language of the intellect. Joined with gestures and facial expressions, it becomes a medium of sympathy, whereby feelings in one person excite like feelings in others. Both our general welfare and our immediate pleasures depend to a great extent on sympathy. By fellow-feelings, men are led to behave justly, kindly, and considerately to each other; the civilized have more fellow-feeling than the barbarian. It is the basis of all higher affections in friendship, love, and domesticity. The tendency of civilization is to replace private, antagonistic gratifications by those resulting from or involving the happiness of others. Through the language of sympathetic intercourse we communicate to others the happiness we feel, and all can share in it. Music not only aids this process, but hints vaguely and prophetically at an ideal life of yet unrealized felicity and harmony. It takes rank, then, "as the highest of the fine arts—as the one which more than any other ministers to human welfare. And thus, even leaving out of view the immediate gratifications it is hourly giving, we cannot too much applaud that progress of musical culture which is becoming one of the characteristics of our age."

The arts as *professions*, *occupations*, and *techniques* have thus shown a persistent tendency to differentiate: (a) from religion, science, and other major types of activity; (b) from each other. In the earlier stages, they are relatively undifferentiated, vaguely combining many kinds of function. Later, they tend to specialize more and more; to split up into separate arts and even more specialized techniques. Meanwhile, on the other hand, specialized artists tend to integrate themselves into specialized groups; into guilds and corporations, with their own books, schools, and perhaps periodicals. The practice of each profession comes to be regulated

14 "Progress: its Law and Cause."

[62]

by law and custom as part of the total group activity.[15]

The *products* of these artistic professions, works of art, have shown a corresponding tendency to differentiate (a) from the products of science, religion, and other major fields, and (b) from each other, so that there are more different kinds of art. Within a single work of art, such as a painting or piece of music, there is increasing differentiation of parts: of colors, represented figures, definite musical tones and scales, rhythms, melodies, harmonies, literary subjects, emotions, etc. These multiplied effects and elements are integrated into more complex compositions, as in large murals, symphonies, and dramas.[16] Differentiation is shown in language and literature in the multiplication of parts of speech, the finer discrimination of shades of meaning.[17] Integration is shown in the organization of these words and meanings into spoken and written languages and verbal compositions.

Increasing *definiteness*, exactness, or precision is another characteristic of evolution; it is manifested in progressive differentiation, integration, or both. "Proof that all evolution is from the indefinite to the definite, we find to be not less abundant than proof that all evolution is from the homogeneous to the heterogeneous." As examples of increasing definiteness, Spencer contrasts modern tools and machines with the inexact, irregular tools and weapons of savage tribes; the modern can be made precise up to a minute fraction of an inch.[18] "Increasing accuracy of representation" in modern paintings and statues is also, for him, an example of definiteness by contrast with the indeterminate faces and figures, "devoid of individuality," in early visual art. Modern fiction and drama show a "progressive diminution of unnaturalness" and fidelity in exhibiting individual characters, by contrast with the vaguely indicated personages, the want of correspondence to the realities of life, and the predominance of supernatural events and improbable coincidences in early literature. In these judgments, Spencer shares the common assumption of his time that the aim and standard of merit

in representational art is correspondence with reality as conceived by the naturalist. He underestimates the extent to which representational art may evolve along lines of abstract conception and fantasy, and he does not realize how much succeeding generations will admire non-realistic art. But, aside from questions of value, there has certainly been a fairly persistent tendency toward naturalism and sharply individualized characterization in much Western art, especially literature. In painting and sculpture, the trend away from realism did not become strong until the last years of Spencer's life.

Is highly evolved art necessarily complex in form, and is such art necessarily the best? Spencer does not say so explicitly, but he implies it repeatedly, (a) in mentioning examples of increasing complexity in art as illustrations of the law of evolution, and (b) in praising them as better, superior, more perfect than the early, undifferentiated types. In a late essay on "Developed Music,"[19] he emphasizes the "growing complications as music develops." In all art, pleasure is derived from perceiving similarity along with dissimilarity. That of perceiving similarity is "gradually extended to larger combinations of phrases and clauses and sentences," while "the pleasure caused by contrast between one complex of notes and another comes to embrace longer and more elaborate complexes." Recognitions of variety in unity are achieved on greater scales, with variations of time, strength, key, etc. Simultaneously arises the "immense collateral development of harmony; the result being an ever-growing heterogeneity." Referring to Sir Hubert Parry's account of folk music, he contrasts it with civilized, developed music as indefinite, "imperfectly differentiated

---

[15] *First Principles* (New York, 1895), § 125-6, pp. 354-9. *Principles of Sociology* (New York, 1897), II-3, Part VIII, on Professional Institutions (dancer, musician, poet, actor, dramatist, architect, sculptor, painter; evolution of the professions.)

[16] *First Principles*, §124, pp. 350, 353-4. Cf. "The Origin of Music," in *Facts and Comments* (New York, 1902).

[17] *First Principles*, pp. 347 f.

[18] *First Principles*, p. 378.

[19] *Facts and Comments* (New York, 1902), p. 61.

into notes," and characterized by the "monotonous repetition of rude musical phrases." In some primitive music, however, we hear "the germs of those compoundings characterizing developed music." Phrases and clauses are repeated and contrasted. In more and more developed music, there are subtle variations of pitch, duration, timbre, and loudness, as well as of emotional suggestiveness. Along with this goes more integration through "subordination to the key-note" and relations among the larger parts. Also, many different kinds of music are evolved.

3. SOME WEAK POINTS IN HIS THEORY

Rather inconsistently, Spencer comments with approval on the tendency of modern plays and novels toward "abandonment of those elaborate plots which life rarely if ever furnishes."[20] That kind of complication, it would seem, is not a sign of high development; it has to be abandoned in the effort to represent the realities of life more definitely. This sacrifice of strict consistency on Spencer's part is perhaps less a fault than a concession to the facts of history—a concession which he made all too infrequently. On the whole, he was content to pile up innumerable instances of complication, in art as elsewhere, always with the implication that the more of it the better.

Too rarely did he recognize that some kinds of complexity are constantly being sacrificed, in art and life, as an obstacle to other values which are more desired at the time. An open-minded study of more such negative instances might have led him to realize that some kinds of simplification are not only desired but necessary steps in evolution itself. No kind of form, in art or elsewhere, can develop along all possible lines at once; such developments would interfere with each other. In life and art as in organic form, to choose one path of development is necessarily to abandon others, actual and possible; to sacrifice one set of values

wholly or partially to another. Spencer's failure to recognize this fact, his dogged insistence on proving his "law" at all costs, left his theory open to serious objections.

In another late essay, "Barbaric Art,"[21] Spencer almost comes to grips with this problem, and again fails to see its deep significance for his theory in general. Again, he expresses a view which seems to conflict with his basic theory, without realizing or explaining the fact. Barbaric art, he says, is the manifestation of barbaric, autocratic society.[22] Despotism seeks display in art, to awe the popular mind by "a gorgeous and highly elaborated style of art" suggesting enormous cost and labor. Examples are the elaborate decorations of Egyptian and Assyrian tombs and temples, also modern aristocratic dress and insignia in the Orient. Early European court weapons and paraphernalia were elaborately inlaid and ornamented. Only with decline of the militant régime, and correlative growth of the industrial régime, did there begin to show itself "that relative simplicity by which truly high art is characterized." But what of Spencer's basic, lifelong theory that increasing complexity is good in art as elsewhere? He does not raise this issue, which might have necessitated a far-reaching revision of his system, but goes on to denounce the current revival of medieval styles as "re-barbarization." "retrograde taste," and "reversion to the ugly." Everywhere, he says, Protestant simplicity is being replaced by Catholic elaboration in colored patterns on the walls, sculpture on the altar and reredos, heavy and glittering vestments. William Morris is an arch-reversionist in going back to fifteenth-century and Gothic type. Archaic decoration, rough-edged paper, and irregular letters on geometrically shaped book-covers remind us of the nursery: "the irregular drawings of children and those of barbarians being naturally akin." He seems not to

[20] *First Principles*, §137, p. 379.
[21] *Facts and Comments*, p. 265.
[22] St. Mark's in Venice, said Spencer, is "a fine sample of barbaric architecture." (Quoted in H. Elliot, *Herbert Spencer*, p. 39).

realize that these particular trends in style were parts of a long, far-reaching tendency to revive primitive, archaic, medieval, and oriental styles, which had been continuing ever since the Romantic movement a century earlier, and which was destined to go much farther in the twentieth century. To those who admire such early and exotic styles and are tired of the main European tradition, such "reversion" seems good and progressive.

Spencer did not make the mistake, as Inge and other hostile critics erroneously charge, of "identifying" or "confusing" mere complication with progress. He emphasized the fact that some increase in complexity is pathological, as in the morbid growths of cancer.[23] Though involving differentiation, an increase of heterogeneity, they are neither progress nor evolution. The same can be said, he adds, of abnormal social changes, as in insurrections, revolutions, famines, and pestilences. Such differentiation is really a kind of disorganization, or a step toward it. How, then, can one distinguish evolutionary, progressive complication from these unhealthy types of growth? His solution is through the additional criterion of *definiteness*, distinctness, specificity, or determination. "It is the absence of definiteness which distinguishes the multiformity of regression from the multiformity of progression." Advance from the indefinite to the definite must be recognized, then, as an essential part of the process of evolution. It is everywhere displayed, he declares, as in the evolution of the solar system from diffused matter to more definite structure.

Whether this concept of definiteness is adequate to distinguish healthy from unhealthy complication is doubtful; some kinds of morbid growth —biological, social, and cultural—may be definite enough in their own ways. But that is another question. The important thing to notice here is that Spencer leaves the door open for classing some kinds of complication in art and other cultural phenomena as devolutionary and regressive. By the same token, he might consistently agree

that some kinds of simplification in art can be evolutionary and progressive, insofar as they make for greater definiteness. But he does not pursue this line of thought. Nor does he discuss which criterion—complexity or definiteness—is to be given greater weight in deciding what is progressive and what is not when the two do not coincide. Instead, he goes on to show how the fine and industrial arts have all revealed increasing definiteness.

Putting aside once more the question of value, let us observe the relation of these trends to the concept of evolution. In terms of complexity, the simple, Protestant styles of church art which Spencer admired had themselves resulted from an earlier movement back to simplicity; a reversion from medieval and baroque ornamentation to the old ideal of the primitive Christian church, plain and humble. That movement had been, in certain respects, devolutionary or regressive. On the other hand, the revival of medieval elaboration in Spencer's time was an attempt to resume the complicative trend which had been thus temporarily interrupted. To be sure, Spencer could insist that the simple, Protestant, geometric and neo-classic art he admired was highly evolved in being precise and definite, even though less complex; that the rough, irregular art he disliked was less evolved in this respect. Thus a change in form could be evolutionary in some respects, devolutionary in other. But as a rule, complexity was his main criterion of evolution.

Using different criteria, one can thus reach different conclusions about what forms are more highly evolved than others. This is not mere inconsistency in reasoning; it indicates the deeper fact that evolutionary change proceeds in various ways; sometimes sacrificing definiteness to complexity, sometimes the opposite. The total process of stylistic change in any one period is sure to combine some of both, and some devolution as well as evolution. The regressive movement in art of which Spencer complained has not been entirely

[23] *First Principles*, Ch. XVI.

[65]

a trend toward more elaboration of ornament. Barbaric and primitive styles are not all elaborate. Some recent "re-barbarization" or primitivism in art has involved an elimination of Renaissance and Baroque details, with a new decrease in complexity.

4. AESTHETIC EVOLUTION AS A PHASE OF MENTAL AND SOCIAL EVOLUTION. THE PLAY THEORY

Not only the products of art, but also the minds, activities, and social groups in which they are produced exhibit evolution, according to Spencer. We have already noticed his account of differentiation and integration among the occupations and techniques of the various arts. It was oversimplified as usual, and was exaggerated by some of his followers into the fallacious theory that all the arts arose from a single source. But it contains a good deal of truth. On the whole, prehistoric and primitive arts were undeniably few, simple, and less differentiated by comparison with modern ones, including those of most modern tribal as well as urban-industrial cultures.

Works of art have, of course, no direct descent from one generation to another as do plants and animals; they are the products of human minds and hands in each generation. Their evolution is, in Spencer's view, at once a means and manifestation of human mental and social evolution, and is not to be thoroughly understood or described apart from the latter. Spencer devoted several volumes of his gigantic series to showing how the phenomena of psychology and sociology exhibit evolutionary tendencies.

To a present-day reader, Spencer's psychology sounds rather antiquated. It is conceived too much in terms of mental "units" of sensation, thought, and feeling; of "states of consciousness" which are supposedly put together like bricks into complex structures. It follows too closely the tradition of

British empiricism and associationism from Locke and Hume. (His extreme individualism in social philosophy is part of the same ideology.) The whole approach is too atomistic and too static for us today, accustomed as we are to conceiving psychology in terms of dynamic, total configurations in behavior and attitude. (This corresponds to social thinking in terms of groups.) Being pre-Freudian, it tends to exaggerate the extent to which human behavior is conscious and rational. It inherits from the old, dualistic epistemology the dichotomy between a conscious subject and its object, between "inner and outer relations," in spite of the attempt at a modern, biological orientation. Spencer was too much attached to the belief in physical transmission of acquired characteristics, mental as well as bodily. He overemphasized the conception of art as play, in the sense of a discharge of surplus energy, not needed in practical work. He exaggerated the simplicity and crudity of modern tribal cultures, which are far from "primitive" in many ways. As a result, contemporary psychology tends to brush aside Spencer's psychology as obsolete, like the rest of his system. Again this reaction has been carried too far in some ways, with the result that some of Spencer's valid insights are being ignored.

We have already noted some typical references by Spencer to mental evolution in general, to "more evolved intelligences" which will apprehend together things now apprehensible only in parts. "Mental evolution," said Sully, is "a progressive composition of units of feeling in more and more complex forms." Societies, too, "evolve in structure and function as in growth." As in organic form, growth or development includes that of the individual mind, as part of the total functioning of the body; also the evolution of human thinking and feeling through successive ages with the aid of civilized institutions.

The general thesis that mentality has tended on the whole to develop from simple to complex, both in each individual and in social culture, is undoubtedly correct. There is much truth in Spencer's demonstration of ways in which both types of mental development occur.[24] He points to the increasing range of discrimination and definiteness in the child's perception, desire, emotion, conception, and speech; his increasingly complex integration of differentiated movements and abstract mental processes. In the ladder of animal development, he points to the analogous widening of the range of discrimination and recognition of types and individuals; in man, to the greater power of precise, abstract, systematic thinking among civilized men. His summary of the general principle of mental development can, without too much difficulty, be translated into acceptable contemporary terms: "Every case in which an advancing intelligence distinguishes between objects, or phenomena, or laws, that were previously confounded together, implies a differentiation of states of consciousness. And every case in which such advancing intelligence recognizes as of the same essential nature, objects or phenomena or laws that were previously thought distinct, implies an integration of states of consciousness."

Such development can, in the individual or group, follow many different lines of emphasis. It can be mainly practical, scientific, or aesthetic. Spencer sees no antagonism or essential difference among them. In art as in science, there is an evolving adjustment between internal and external relations, between the thinking organism and its environment. There is greater ability to perceive, understand, feel emotionally toward, and control subtle discriminations in both realms, and to organize them in comprehensive ways. Developed science and art both involve a high degree of such differentiation and integration. One expresses it in laws and theories, the other in pictures, poems, and symphonies. Spencer was one of the first to recognize the importance of artistic activities for the mental development of the child.[25]

Spencer glorified the arts and "aesthetic culture" as "the efflorescence of civilized life."[26] He looked forward to the time when much more attention could be given to them, after the forces of nature had been more fully conquered and a healthy social life achieved. But he berated the classical "gentlemen's" education of his time for neglecting the more practical studies, necessary to human happiness—knowledge useful in making a living, in parenthood, citizenship, and health. It was a vice of education, he thought, to neglect these in favor of superficial refinements and acquaintance with the elegances of Latin verse.

The highest art of every kind, Spencer maintained, is based on science; without the latter one cannot have the best production or appreciation of art. True, very few past artists have possessed scientific knowledge in the strict sense, but as acute observers the great ones "have always possessed a stock of those empirical generalizations which constitute science in its lowest phase," and art has often suffered from the inadequacy of these generalizations. To produce good painting, sculpture, and literature, one must know facts and laws about the things which these arts represent. Here again, Spencer's taste is unduly limited to the realistic type of art; he does not recognize the value of those other types which stress fantasy, design, and emotional expression at the sacrifice of realism. Nor does he recognize the importance of non-rational processes in the mind of the artist. The romanticists had over-valued these in a mystical way, and Spencer was reasserting a new kind of rationalism; but it was far more flexible than the neo-classic, since based on a biological, evolutionary conception. "Intuition will do much, but it will not do all. Perception must be supplemented by organized knowledge." Wise for its time, this conception of aesthetic psychology is still too simple to cover the complexities now revealed by psychoanalysis in the creative process.

He is on safer ground, stating an important point which is still not sufficiently grasped in

[24] *First Principles*, §143, pp. 390 f.

[25] "The question is not whether the child is producing good drawings. The question is whether it is developing its faculties." *Education: Intellectual, Moral, and Physical* (1861).

[26] "What Knowledge is of Most Worth?" in *Education: Intellectual, Moral, and Physical*, pp. 73 f.

aesthetics, when he says that an artist needs to "understand how the minds of spectators or listeners will be affected by the several peculiarities of his work—a question in psychology."[27] "To ask whether the composition of a picture is good is really to ask how the perceptions and feelings of observers will be affected by it." Science is necessary, he says, for the full appreciation of the arts, and science itself can be poetic, not hostile to poetry; it opens up new realms to aesthetic imagination. To Spencer as to Aristotle, and to naturalistic aesthetics today, art is essentially a means to some kind of human welfare; to a good life on this earth, and especially to aesthetic enjoyment on a highly evolved mental level. It is to be judged by its effectiveness toward these ends. In this clear and simple statement, Spencer avoids the quagmires of Hegelian transcendentalism which have obstructed aesthetics to this day. He avoids also the false and artificial antithesis between art and science, by showing art to be a kind of technic which can be helped by science, and for which more scientific knowledge is needed.

The general fact that some minds are complex and highly developed, others simple and rudimentary, is obviously true and indispensable in psychology. It is not original with Spencer. Much Greek philosophy from Socrates onward is devoted to the conception of a highly developed mind and character, a true philosopher, a high-minded man, in contrast with the limited mentality of an animal, a small child, an ignorant slave, or a barbarian. The difference is not only in amount of knowledge, but also in mental ability: the power to think abstractly and logically, to control one's passions, and to achieve a harmony of mind and body under the guidance of reason. Some ethical codes have stressed single virtues such as purity, holiness, faith, or obedience at the expense of all-round development; but the Greek humanistic ideal, especially as set forth in Aristotle, is one of balanced, many-sided mental and physical growth. It includes an ability to understand and enjoy the best in art. Spencer's psychology emphasizes, in

the language of his time, this conception of a mentality which is highly developed as well as healthy, happy, and socially cooperative.

In the total process of mental development, Spencer gives an important role to the "aesthetic feelings." He resembles Schiller in deriving them from the "play-impulse," in that "neither subserve, in any direct way, the processes conducive to life."[28] However, he points out that they do yield ulterior benefits, as in strengthening the faculties, even if not so planned. He leaves room for a recognition of their indirect conduciveness to life in discussing (for example) the function of music in strengthening social sympathy. But the development of this line of thought is left to Spencer's followers. He is anxious not to exaggerate the utilitarian value of all civilized activities, and in this he avoids some of the over-simplifications of later evolutionists. His conception of both art and play differ from Schiller's in being more naturalistic, less romantic and metaphysical.

Inferior animals, and to a less extent primitive man, usually have to spend all or most of their forces in fulfilling functions essential to the maintenance of life. When circumstances make such exercise unnecessary for a while, but offer a chance for simulation of it, play occurs. Play is an artificial exercise of powers which, in default of their natural exercise, become so ready to discharge that they relieve themselves by simulated actions in place of real ones. This often involves an ideal, harmless satisfaction of destructive and pugnacious instincts, as in games. It can bring the higher mental faculties into play, as in wit-combat. "The higher but less essential powers, as well as the lower ones, thus come to have activities that are carried on for the sake of the immediate gratifications derived; ...and to such higher powers, aesthetic products yield these substituted activities as games yield them to various lower powers... The aesthetic

27 "What Knowledge is of Most Worth?" p. 79.
28 *Principles of Psychology*, II-2, Ch. IX "Aesthetic Sentiments." On the play theories of Spencer, K. Groos, and K. Lange, see Listowel, *Critical History of Modern Aesthetics* (London, 1933), pp. 27, 159.

character of a feeling is habitually associated with separateness from life-serving function." The sentiment of beauty is derived from pleasant sensations and representations which have been thus separated from biological needs.

Contemporary aesthetics relies much less upon the play theory of art than did Schiller and Spencer. We are more inclined to stress the serious, practical, and intellectual functions of art, and to regard it as a kind of skilled work. We tend to reject the aristocratic prejudice which led eighteenth-century thinkers to glorify play at the expense of paid handicraft. But it is still a valid hypothesis that art, like philosophy, science, and many other civilized activities, makes use of powers which man first developed in the animal struggle for existence. No longer needing all of these to stay alive under favorable conditions, he has a mental apparatus and a surplus of energy to use in activities which are more immediately rewarding as experience, or instrumental to remoter and less urgent needs. Some kinds of art thus come to serve a function like that of play and sport. This is far from being art's only function, however. Nor is art the only civilized activity which has playful aspects. These can be found in politics, business, and other pursuits which at times imitate and sublimate man's primitive, pugnacious instincts. These also are practiced at times for immediate gratifications.

Under the head of "aesthetic feelings," Spencer includes "states of consciousness" of all orders of complexity and of various types. Some are developed sensations, while others, such as the delight in contemplating a noble action of a fictitious character, are representative. Agreeable associations for certain colors, sounds, etc., are established in experience. Such stimuli are built up into complex forms and combinations of forms. Those felt as beautiful and agreeable tend to exercise perception without overtaxing it, through having enough variety to prevent monotony, but not enough to distract attention. Heterogeneity is thus combined with integration. For the cultured person, complex

works of art also take on pleasant associations through life experience. In the higher regions of aesthetic feeling, as in the literature of imagination, presentational elements are incidental and representative ones essential. The highest type of aesthetic excitement involves sensory impressions, the perception of ideas, and emotions. Aesthetic feelings are not, as some suppose, essentially different from others, but special modes of excitement of our ordinary faculties. In the aesthetic state of mind, the attention is released from guiding action toward ulterior ends, and allowed to contemplate images and ideas for their own sake. But strong unsatisfied wants tend to prevent this. High aesthetic development occurs, therefore, when "there is reached an organization so superior that the energies have not to be wholly expended in the fulfillment of material requirements from hour to hour." The states of consciousness (or, as we would say today, experiences) derived from the higher mental faculties (more complex functions) are then sought for their own sakes, apart from ends. Instead of the lower kind of play, involving superfluous activity of the sensory-motor apparatus and of destructive instincts, the higher, coordinating powers come to have their own such activity and pleasure, remoter from the destructive.

Savage dances and chants still contain much simulation of the predatory life, and so do the more developed arts of ancient civilizations. But long periods of peace allow the altruistic sentiments to develop, and the fine arts take forms more in harmony with them. "Aesthetic activities in general may be expected to play an increasing part in human life as evolution advances... A growing surplus of energy will bring a growing proportion of the aesthetic activities and gratifications; and while the forms of art will be such as yield pleasurable exercise to the simpler faculties, they will in a greater degree than now appeal to the higher emotions."

The development of aesthetic powers is thus a part of mental and emotional development in general, both individually and socially. Under favorable social conditions, it achieves a characteristic mode of stimulation and exercise, in the perception, understanding, and emotional enjoyment of complex forms of art. Highly evolved art is not only more complex than the primitive, but more moral and peaceful in dealing with images and ideas pertaining to a harmonious social order, in which the egoistic and altruistic impulses are reconciled. No longer needed entirely for the satisfaction of bodily wants, the complex mental and emotional functions are increasingly free to enjoy peaceful, happy experiences, including those of beauty, for their own sake. Society is far from having reached this ideal, Spencer concedes, but progress toward it is being made.

That this account is oversimplified and subject to correction at many points today is obvious to the modern reader. For example, primitive art can be complex and peaceful. But there is nothing in contemporary science to refute the general thesis that aesthetic powers and processes have evolved along many lines from primitive to modern times, as a part of cultural evolution in general. Whether they are the better for this increased differentiation and integration, for the separation of aesthetic from practical and religious experience, for the multiplication and refinement of artistic stimuli, is of course open to dispute. These are questions of value and progress. The more "highly evolved" is not necessarily better or higher in quality. It is generally agreed today that changes in the forms of art, whether developmental or not, are causally connected with changes in social thinking, feeling, and acting. Which determines which, how independent art has been, and how this interaction proceeds in detail, are more debatable.

5. LATER ATTACKS
ON THE SPENCERIAN SYNTHESIS

From the time of his earliest publications, Spencer met with bitter attacks from hostile critics. At first these attacks came mostly from conservative religionists, opposed to all evolutionism and especially to Spencer's naturalistic variety. Later, they came also from scientists who shared his naturalism and his belief in organic evolution. Each discovered numerous errors in Spencer's treatment of his own special problems. Prominent among them were anthropologists who rejected his theory of cultural evolution. His theories on art were included by implication, but have not received much direct attention in recent years.

We have already touched upon the commonest objections to his system as a whole. These and a few others can be summarized as follows:

(a) Evolution should be more sharply distinguished from progress. Spencer had not identified them completely, but had thought they coincided on the whole. Now more pessimistic thinkers emphasized the differences between them. Complication is often bad, they insisted, as in the multiplication of useless taboos in a primitive society, and in the recent growth of machine industry at the expense of human happiness. Complex works of art are not necessarily better than simpler ones. In both art and life, the path to real progress is often through simplification, loss of parts, less differentiation, less large-scale integration, at least of certain kinds. (This had been the gist of Rousseau's attack on modern civilization and its arts; it was still a strong tenet, not only of the romanticists, but also of those who compared primitive Christianity favorably with modern industrialism and scientific rationalism.) In short, some complication is retrogressive and some simplification is progressive. The concept of evolution must be detached from that of progress; the tendencies or processes to which they refer are not identical and often diverge. This does not imply that they are essentially opposed. The question still remains of the extent to which evolution is or can be made to accord with human ideals of progress.

(b) Spencer's theory of progress itself was subjected to strong attack: his optimism about inevitable, automatic improvement; his hedonistic standards of morality and aesthetic value; his individualistic, *laissez-faire* policies. His standards for judging improvement in art were those of his time, and were not considered adequate for the twentieth century. For example, he put too high a premium on realistic representation.

(c) Even from the biological standpoint of adaptation for survival, it was argued that complexity is not always the best means. Complication does not necessarily bring greater adaptation. Many complex forms of life have died out, while simpler ones persist to this day. Mammoth and saber-tooth tiger are gone, while amoeba and earthworm survive.

(d) Increasing complexity is *not* universal or necessary; it is not a fundamental "law" of the universe or of life. There are many instances of phylogenetic change in the opposite direction: notably *Sacculina*, a "degenerate" parasite in the intestines of a crab. It has lost many of the parts possessed by its more active ancestors, yet seems well adapted to its new environment.[29] On the other hand, it is answered on behalf of Spencer that such an organism is not well adapted to survive under changing or different conditions. Its adaptation is precariously dependent on a fixed environment. As Julian Huxley points out,[30] a change of this sort can not be called "progressive" in the long run, even from the strictly biological standpoint.

Spencer, to be sure, had recognized the existence of "dissolution" as a type of change contrary to evolution. He had illustrated it by the death of organisms and the decay of conquered nations. It might eventually prevail. But the present phase of history, in Spencer's view, is strongly evolutionary. What Spencer did not recognize, according to his adversaries, was that degenerative or retrogressive evolution—"devolution," as some

called it—could be as natural and adaptive a type of phylogenetic change as evolution. It is not mere dissolution in the sense of decay, death, or disintegration. Moreover, what of all the countless forms of life which had evolved up to a certain stage and then stopped, remaining in a state of "arrested development" for millions of years? In their case, too, evolution is not universal or necessary. Partial analogies can be found among extremely primitive contemporary cultures, such as the Australian aborigines and the Caribou Eskimo.

6. EXCESSIVE ANTAGONISM TOWARD SPENCER IN RECENT YEARS. THE NEED FOR A REAPPRAISAL

Influential philosophers in each century, like outstanding artists, are often denounced with exaggerated bitterness in the next. "Mid-Victorian" has long been a term of derision for nineteenth-century ideas, fashions, and morals which have seemed hopelessly out of date; but such ideas, along with styles in art, sometimes revive to some extent later on. The violence of the attack on Spencer in the first half of this century is coming to seem excessive. It was due in part to the emotional climate of the post-war era, in which pessimism was fashionable among literary sophisticates. Even a moderate hopefulness about the future of man was derided as naive, wishful thinking. Spenglerian and existentialist pessimism became as dogmatic as Spencerian optimism was in the Victorian age. Denials

[29] Twentieth-century biologists have confirmed and extended this observation: "degenerative" change or simplification during a long line of descent is not an exceptional freak of nature, but a common phenomenon. E. S. Goodrich, writing on "Evolution" in the *Encyclopedia Britannica*, 14th edition, mentions a number of types, such as barnacles and sea-squirts (*Tunicata*) which have become simplified through adopting a sedentary or parasitic mode of existence. Both "progressive" and "retrogressive" mutations occur frequently, he adds, and "which will be selected depends on the needs of the organism at the time."

[30] *Evolution, the Modern Synthesis* (New York, 1942), Ch. 10: "Evolutionary Progress."

of evolution and progress were as sweeping as Spencer's affirmation of them, and often with much less evidence than he brought forward. The contempt with which he was mentioned was out of all proportion to his faults, except from the standpoint of those who resent any attempt at a naturalistic world view. Charles Singer wrote in his *Short History of Science*,[31] "That the evolutionary philosophical system of Spencer is an object of derision is one of the few points on which all philosophers seem now to agree." He gave no definite reasons for this derision except to say that the idea of increasing complexity in future seems "a dreary prospect." He added the hope that future science will be less materialistic.

In aesthetics especially, Spencer was unwarrantably neglected in the early twentieth century. An example is Croce's contemptuous and inadequate mention of him in the *Aesthetic*, as part of his general attack on naturalistic aesthetics. Spencer's theory of art as play was overemphasized as if it were his only contribution to aesthetics. Many others are more important. Historians of aesthetics, most of whom were Hegelian and idealist in sympathy, gave only fragmentary, distorted accounts of his work in this field, and of the naturalistic approach to aesthetics in general.

Mistakes in Spencer's system are obvious today, especially on specific points in biology and social science, where research has moved on steadily. His tendency to oversimplify the processes of evolution, and to claim for his theory the status of a universal law, has been rightly attacked. But as a more modest and limited hypothesis, his theory of evolution in art retains some valid and suggestive ideas. As a whole, it has not been disproved, and in many respects it has been confirmed by later research. That some evolution goes on, of the sort which Spencer described, no one can deny. The question is, how much and where? As to the theory of evolution in general, even Singer has to admit that "any other proposed interpretation of the data is wholly incredible." Restated with corrections and additions, Spencer's theory can again become a useful instrument in the philosophy of history.

After a hundred years, the trend of opinion seems to be turning again toward a more favorable estimate of Spencer. In a recent scientific symposium, for example, mention is made of his "magnificent synthesis."[32] But what is most needed is neither praise nor derision, but an objective reappraisal and revision of his theory in the light of present knowledge.

[31] (London, 1941), p. 385.
[32] L. Z. Freedman and A. Roe, "Evolution and Human Behavior," in *Behavior and Evolution*, ed. A. Roe and G. G. Simpson (New Haven, Conn., 1958), p. 457.

CHAPTER VI

MAIN LINES
OF CULTURAL EVOLUTIONISM
AFTER SPENCER

I. NATURALISTIC
AND SUPERNATURALISTIC TRADITIONS

The developmental approach to cultural phenomena received an impetus from a few outstanding philosophers and scientists before 1860 which lasted well on into the twentieth century. Of those who followed this approach, none attempted to rival Spencer in philosophic scope as a monumental system-builder. After him, there was a period of specialization. As leading scientists accepted the main thesis of organic and social development, this issue receded from high-level controversy. Conservative elements in the general public still had to be convinced of the truth of evolution or "progressionism" as against the older doctrines of "special creation" and "degenerationism." But the interest of scientists turned more and more to the details of the evolutionary process: to the task of filling in gaps and arranging events in genetic sequence. The concept of evolution seemed to have unlimited possibilities as an explanatory principle and a means of theoretical reconstruction in every subject. It was applied to this and that institution, custom, and people; to law, marriage, government, religion, morality, science, and art. Not until after the First World War did a strongly critical, negative attitude seriously menace the authority of evolutionism in the cultural sciences. Even then, there was no considerable trend in

science back to the ancient belief in fixed forms, but rather one of skepticism toward all theories of a comprehensive, regular pattern in cultural history.

Among the specialized studies written in the late nineteenth century from an evolutionary point of view, many dealt with the arts, especially with the visual arts of prehistoric and modern tribal peoples. The visual arts and artifacts were, on the whole, better preserved and more accessible to prolonged examination than the others. Linguistics also received intensive study, and from it light was thrown on the descent of modern literature from ancient. The prehistoric and protohistoric periods were stressed as crucial for the evolutionary explanation. It was felt that one had to discover the origins of art, the missing links between artless savagery and civilized art, in order to complete the picture. Modern primitive art was stressed on the assumption (a) that it resembled and thus gave a clue to understanding prehistoric art, and (b) that it illustrated the differential speed of cultural advance: the way in which some peoples had lagged on the way, or degenerated from a higher level to which their ancestors had climbed.

As in earlier centuries, much was said or implied about the arts as developing within the general process of cultural evolution, along with social and political organization, technology, and religion. Many of the scientists who undertook to demonstrate cultural evolution brought in the development of art as a constituent thread. By the same token, when cultural evolutionism in general fell into disfavor in the twentieth century, so did the idea of evolution in art. The historians of particular arts, hearing that social science had rejected evolutionism, hesitated to speak of it in their special fields.

We have noticed two main types of evolutionism in the cultural sciences, differing as to their metaphysical basis. One, descending from Hegel to Bergson, Croce, and Collingwood, was idealistic or vitalistic, attributing evolution to the working of a supernatural, cosmic mind or life force. The other, that of Comte, Spencer, Darwin, Marx, Morgan, and Tylor, was positivistic or naturalistic. It relied more on empirical data and physical causation, seeking to explain evolution in terms of the orderly working of impersonal, natural laws. These laws were conceived as nonpurposeful and traceable ultimately to the inherent tendencies of matter or some unknowable but inanimate substance. This view came also to be known as "mechanism," especially in biology, as opposed to "vitalism" or the belief in a distinct, non-material, creative force in life and evolution. It has also been called "realism," as opposed to idealism.

Partly because of linguistic barriers, partly because of national differences in philosophic tradition, the Hegelian theory proved most influential among German-writing and German-educated scholars. It has been said that all German scholars are idealists under the skin. While this is far from true in the mid-twentieth century, it was closer to the truth in the mid-nineteenth, even in the case of scientists like Ernst Haeckel, who rejected much of the Hegelian philosophy.[1] German idealism survives in twentieth-century aesthetics and philosophy of history under many different names, such as the "phenomenology" of Husserl.

The influence of Comte had more weight in France than elsewhere, but he was soon translated and read throughout Europe. His term, "positiv-

ism," achieved wide usage as a name for the whole empiricist, naturalistic approach; for all theories of culture and history which rejected idealism and other forms of supernaturalism. It is still so used on the Continent, often with the misleading implication that all "positivists" accept Comte's views *in toto*. The "real heir" of Comte in France, according to Lévy-Bruhl, was not Taine but Emile Durkheim, who sought to develop sociology as a strictly empirical science based on "social facts," as distinct from biology and psychology. Durkheim conceived psychology as "the science of the mind of the individual; hence as separate from the study of social facts, which can not be reduced to the acts and thoughts of individuals."[2]

At the same time, a Spencerian influence is seen in Durkheim by D. G. MacRae.[3] Spencer's concept of evolution, says this writer, underlay Durkheim's classic study of the division of labor, his account of the segmentary principle of organization in primitive societies, and the development of functional specialization and interdependence in advanced industrial communities. This work remains fundamental, says MacRae, for any understanding of social change in modern underdeveloped countries.

Another predominantly naturalistic approach was that of Karl Lamprecht of Leipzig, social and cultural historian, author of a *German History* in many volumes.[4] He was influenced by Marx's emphasis on economic groups and mass movements, by Comte's theory of stages, and by Darwinist evolutionism. Opposing the older historians' concern with individuals (as in the Carlyle "great man" theory) he insisted that history was a "sociopsychological science," recording the col-

[1] Following Goethe and Spinoza, Haeckel combined some elements of materialism with some of pantheistic monism. *Cf.* H. Wendt, *In Search of Adam* (Cambridge, Mass., 1955), pp. 278–284.

[2] Bidney, *op. cit.*, pp. 87 ff., quoting L. Lévy-Bruhl, *The Philosophy of Auguste Comte* and Durkheim, *The Rules of Sociological Method*.

[3] *A Century of Darwin*, ed. S. A. Barnett (London, 1958,) p. 307.

[4] *Cf.* H. E. Barnes, *op. cit.*, pp. 115 ff.

lective psychology of the past. Following Hegel, he designated the first stage in sociopsychological evolution as the "symbolic." After that came the medieval differentiation into types of culture, the Renaissance epoch of individualism in art and other fields, the romantic epoch of subjectivism, and the modern age of nervous tension. In all these Lamprecht included the arts. He held these stages to be typical of social evolution in general, among all highly developed peoples.

The influence of Spencer and Darwin spread widely through the general public in England and the United States. That of Darwin was stronger than Spencer's in Germany. French evolutionism was at first sufficiently Comtean to provide a distinct, positivistic approach in itself. Later, it gradually merged with the contributions of Spencer, Darwin, and Taine to form a single naturalistic tradition in sociology, anthropology, and culture history. The Marxist school of thought, up to the present, is a part of this tradition in respect to its naturalism and evolutionism, but its distinctive features are so marked as to warrant putting it in a class by itself.

It is still hard for naturalistic evolutionists who admire British thought on the whole to explain Spencer's lack of influence in England. As Barnes and Becker point out, his effect on academic social science in Great Britain was "almost negligible," though he had a tremendous influence on it elsewhere. "Not only did he have enthusiastic followers on the Continent," they say, "but the early American sociologists—Ward, Sumner, Giddings, and Small—were profoundly influenced by him."[5] One cause which Barnes and Becker suggest, that the narrow and uncoordinated specialization in British social science at the time was not paralleled by a more general, systematic tendency, could be equally well applied to British and American philosophy and social science in recent years. As to other possible factors, Barnes and Becker also suggest that the type of mind in England which was inclined toward broad generalization was under the spell of T. H. Green. (He was an "ab-

solute idealist" in the German tradition.) Also, "the reformers and uplifters were repelled by Spencer's harsh, uncompromising, and mechanical individualism." Spencer was not a member of the upper class or trained at an aristocratic university, and his naturalism offended conservative British scholars.

H. G. Wells, a later British writer on history from the naturalistic point of view, had similar handicaps. Like Spencer, his influence was more on the general public than on academic scholars. L. T. Hobhouse, one of the few British sociologists after Spencer who were inclined toward systematization, disagreed with Spencer on many points, while accepting his evolutionism in general. In *Morals in Evolution* (1915), he made a statistical study of the correlation between stages in the evolution of various branches of culture. In recent years, many British social scientists have been treating Spencer with increased respect, during a time when their American colleagues were denouncing all nineteenth-century evolutionists.

2. DARWIN AND
THE NATURALISTIC TRADITION
SOCIAL DARWINISM

Darwin's ideas were, on the whole, more widely diffused on the Continent than Spencer's, so that cultural evolutionism in general was sometimes called "social Darwinism." Many of the ideas so described had come rather from Comte and Spencer. Darwin himself, while fully recognizing the developmental aspect of evolution (especially in discussing the descent of man) put his emphasis rather on natural selection as its chief mode and mechanism. This was the crucial point at issue between himself and the Lamarckians, and also a strong argument for development in general. Hence the social and cultural scientists who pro-

[5] H. E. Barnes and H. Becker, *Social Thought from Lore to Science* (New York, 1938), Vol. II, 800.

ceeded more directly from Darwin than from Spencer tended to conceive of evolution primarily in terms of natural selection and adaptation to environment, often minimizing or omitting "development" as an essential part of the concept. Some of them took the developmental phase for granted, as too obvious to need much emphasis. Others pointed to the instances where adaptive change had taken place without increasing complexity. All, they insisted, were parts of "evolution." In Germany, "social Darwinism" emphasized the struggle for survival among social groups.

Scientists in all countries respected the modest, cautious objectivity of Darwin, even when his views were later shown to need correction. His principal contributions to the theory of art history, in addition to disseminating a general, evolutionary attitude, were as follows. First, he provided the far-reaching concept of natural selection, primarily for use in biology; but it proved to be applicable also in the social and cultural fields. In culture, as in organic life, types of form and behavior such as institutions and artistic skills seemed to vary spontaneously, even to struggle for survival. The most adapted—not necessarily the best—would survive. It seemed likely, moreover, that the arts of a people, like its laws and customs, its technology and military strength, might affect its chance of biological survival.

Second and third, Darwin contributed the ideas of sexual selection and emotional expression in men and animals.[6] They were more limited and less revolutionary, but helped to bridge the gaps in aesthetic psychology between the prehuman and the human, the primitive and the civilized. The aesthetic sentiments were not necessarily a purely human, spiritual endowment; like everything else in civilization, they had developed out of animal origins. Bright natural coloring had a function in sexual selection; so had the instinctive songs and dances of certain birds. This function, important in evolution, was obviously continued and developed as a conscious art in the personal adornment

of primitive and civilized peoples; so were song and dance.

Darwin's cautious comments on these facts were soon extended by cultural evolutionists into the general hypothesis that all the arts had arisen and developed as devices for the satisfaction of basic physical desires and hence as means of physical survival; that their subsequent forms and sequences could all be explained in terms of practical utility under changing conditions, physical and social. The existence of aesthetic emotion, including pleasure in the perception and production of sensory forms, was not denied, but was itself explained as a functional trait with practical, survival value.

Many were the debates and partial reconciliations of these two opposing theories of art in the next hundred years. The evolutionary theory, leaning strongly toward the Darwinian hypothesis, had its extreme, dogmatic exponents, easily satisfied with simple, materialistic explanations of style in art, and its more moderate ones, who found some place in the evolutionary picture for selected elements from the idealistic philosophy. The artistic impulse and the love of beauty, said the latter, could not be completely explained on practical grounds or as arising wholly from utilitarian pursuits. There was in man, they said, a will to create and enjoy aesthetic form which carried the true artist, primitive or civilized, beyond the requirements of utility and practical gain. Cultural evolutionism diverged through the later nineteenth century with respect to the relative emphasis placed on one or the other of these conceptions.

Darwin realized to some extent the potentially tremendous effect of evolutionism outside the biological field, but his scientific caution restrained him from theorizing much on its social or philosophic implications. To reassure anxious religionists, he explicitly denied that biological evolutionism excluded the fundamentals of theism. He opened the way to a teleological interpretation of it for those who so desired. He was not an ex-

6 *The Descent of Man and Selection in Relation to Sex* (New York, 1871).

[76]

plicit, philosophical naturalist, nor did he clearly endorse any particular metaphysical interpretation of biology.[7] This can not be said of A. R. Wallace, who indicated his belief that the rapid evolution of the human brain was hardly explicable on any grounds other than outside, supernatural direction.

Darwin's reference to "variations which seem to us in our ignorance to arise spontaneously" avoided any assumption of a directive force therein, yet made it clear that much was yet to be learned about the genetic process. His idea of descent as proceeding "through the natural selection of numerous successive, slight, favorable variations" was later corrected by De Vries, who shifted the emphasis to sudden, large mutations. These could still be construed as "spontaneous" or "due to chance" in the sense opposed to immanent direction, although the Mendelian laws of inheritance made the whole process seem less accidental and chaotic, more in accord with regular, pre-existing patterns.

Like Darwin, innumerable scientists in the biological and social fields can be classed as naturalists on the whole, because their main conclusions tended to strengthen the naturalistic hypothesis. This can be done even when, for one reason or another, they refused to recognize these implications or explicitly kept the door open for contrary ones. Their influence was naturalistic insofar as they consistently avoided supernaturalistic hypotheses in their main researches, proceeding at each step as if natural factors were all that required consideration. Their idealistic or dualistic views, if any, were kept in a separate mental compartment or expressed so rarely or mildly as to have little effect. One might call them partial, tacit, or involuntary naturalists, by comparison with more explicit ones such as Lucretius, Spencer, and Marx. After Darwin, positivists and naturalists hailed the discovery of natural selection as a powerful argument for their philosophy, on the ground that it filled important gaps in the scientific picture of the natural world as autonomous, orderly, self-operating and self-developing.

An early example of the more positivistic, naturalistic type of evolutionist in art was Gottfried Semper, who published a treatise along this line in 1861,[8] only two years after *The Origin of Species*. It exerted a strong influence on studies of primitive art in the next generation. Dealing mainly with architecture and the useful, decorative arts such as textiles, pottery, and metals, it had little to say about painting or sculpture. Semper traced the original development of the arts to the practical needs of primitive man for shelter and clothing; only later he thought, did aesthetic feeling come in to modify the utilitarian forms. Decorative designs developed out of basic techniques in handling certain materials. This approach to art history provoked, later in the century, a strong reaction from the idealistic side. Riegl and others bitterly denounced the "materialism" of Semper, belittling the influence of external, utilitarian factors on the essentials of art, and stressing instead the concept of a psychic "form-will" in man, which led him to devise techniques and styles satisfying to his inner, spiritual urge.

Neither of these extreme interpretations is essential to the general theory of evolution in art. The latter does not stand or fall with either natural selection or the spiritual will to form as the chief causal mechanism of the process. Today, all evolutionists recognize that many structures and functions in living types, including man, can not be explained in terms of direct survival value. Some are liabilities rather than assets in the evolutionary struggle; some are variable or ineffective in this respect. An evolutionist can believe that art arose

[7] He suggested a deistic conception at the end of *The Origin of Species*, in speaking of "the laws impressed on matter by the Creator" and of "life, with its several powers, having been originally breathed by the Creator into a few forms or into one." This would imply that the divine intervention was primeval and general, not a constant, immanent direction of the genetic process. Darwin considered it "a damnable doctrine" of Christianity that unbelievers would be everlastingly punished. (Quoted from the new, complete edition of the *Autobiography* by Marjorie Grene in "The Faith of Darwinism"). *Encounter*, XIII, 5 (Nov. 1959), 48.

[8] *Der Stil in den technischen und tektonischen Künsten oder praktische Aesthetik* (Munich, 1861–63).

from primitive activities which were mainly but not wholly utilitarian, that primitive man had a taste for beauty which grew as leisure and security permitted, and that art has less practical value today; sometimes none at all.

Those who associate all nineteenth-century cultural evolutionists with a rigidly oversimplified, unilinear type of theory might well consider the work of Julius Lippert (1839–1909), whom Gumplowicz praised as a leader in sociology along with Comte, Spencer, and Bastian.[9] Murdock, his translator, while aligning him in some respects with the "classical" evolutionists, goes on to say that he has weathered the recent storm of criticism against that school "far better than Bachofen, Bastian, Letourneau, Lubbock, McLennan, Maine, and Morgan—better even than Spencer and Tylor. He avoids successfully most of the grosser errors of the earlier writers and shows himself, on the whole, surprisingly in harmony with the best of modern thought. Though an evolutionist, Lippert is not a 'unilateral' or 'monotypical' evolutionist."[10] "The early arts of man," said Lippert, "must not be regarded as conforming to a single tradition and developed in that fashion. On the contrary, human ingenuity has striven in different places to achieve the goal set by the care for life with the elements there at hand." "All these and many more combinations are conceivable and have actually occurred in fact, depending on local influences, without constituting a continuous evolutionary series."[11] Lippert criticized Morgan and others for the "category fallacy" of trying to fit cultural evolution into a series of clear-cut stages. As against the extreme parallelists, he recognized the importance of both diffusion and separate invention. He distinguished between evolution and progress as well as between social and organic evolution. While stressing economic factors and material culture (along with Keller, Wissler, Marx, and Beard), he also assigned an important role to ideas in social evolution.

3. THE INFLUENCE OF KANT AND HEGEL ON LATER THEORIES OF CULTURAL EVOLUTION. IDEALISM, DUALISM, VITALISM

The door which Hegel opened for a teleological, spiritualistic theory of evolution, and which Darwin tried to keep open despite the contrary tendency of his own and other scientific thinking, has never been quite closed. The prestige of Kant and Hegel among German-writing scholars gave rise to a long tradition of idealism in biology, philosophy of history, aesthetics, and art history. In spite of the attempts of Fechner in aesthetics and Semper in art history to develop a more empirical or naturalistic approach, idealism remained as a powerful and often dominant school of thought within the German sphere of intellectual influence. It dominated biological evolutionism in the vitalistic theories of Hans Driesch, aesthetics in F. T. Vischer, Max Schasler, and Benedetto Croce, and the philosophy of history in J. G. Droysen.[12] Elements of German idealism spread to Italy in the aesthetic and historical theories of Gentile and Benedetto Croce; to France in Henri Bergson's *Evolution créatrice;* to English philosophy in T. H. Green and F. H. Bradley; to English aesthetics in Bernard Bosanquet's *History of Aesthetic* and R. G. Colling-

[9] He did most of his writing in the eighties, and his chief theoretical work was *Kulturgeschichte der Menschheit in ihrem organischen Aufbau* (2 vols.; Stuttgart, 1886–7). An abridged translation by G. P. Murdock, with a critical introduction, was published under the title *The Evolution of Culture* (New York, 1931). On the development of the arts in relation to religion, see pp. 33–4. Ludwig Gumplowicz was himself a leading social Darwinist.

[10] *Ibid.,* Introduction, pp. xiv *et seq.*

[11] *The Evolution of Culture,* pp. 169, 234.

[12] Professor of history at the University of Berlin. His lectures on historical methodology, beginning in 1857, were published as *Grundriss der Historik* (1958–62). They were inspired by Hegel and Aristotle; but his moral view of the universe was rooted in Christian doctrine. Droysen taught that the development of humanity, whose preparatory stages are the recognition of self and the world, completes itself in the recognition of God. The lectures were translated as *Outlines of the Principles of History* (Boston, 1893). There is a chapter on "Art and [Historical] Method."

wood's *Principles of Art;* to the philosophy of history in Collingwood's *The Idea of History.*

Idealism, in the sense of metaphysical spiritualism or transcendentalism, was not merely a German importation to these countries. In the form of neo-platonism, it was already a venerable tradition throughout Western culture, increasingly aware of its kinship with Indian mysticism. In England, Coleridge had helped revive it as against neo-classic rationalism, and in America, Emerson had blended it with common-sense democracy. But the Hegelian variety, based on Kant's persuasive theory of knowledge and in tune with evolutionism, gave it a new lease of life.

To trace a broadly Hegelian tradition through the later nineteenth century does not imply that Hegel's philosophy was accepted intact, even by later idealists. It was profoundly modified by contact with subsequent religious, philosophical, and scientific influences. Croce, Collingwood, and several others, usually classed within the Hegelian tradition, sought to emphasize their points of difference from the master.[13] But they still regarded him as the starting-point for a valid philosophy of history; as incomparably more profound and closer to the truth than Spencer, whom they dismissed as a superficial empiricist.

In spite of great differences, Schopenhauer and Nietzsche can also be placed to some extent within the German, romantic tradition. They both accepted the premise of a transcendental force behind events, impelling life and man into certain historic sequences. But for them it was an irrational power, a blind cosmic will and not a cosmic mind, manifesting itself in an avid will to power and pleasure, doomed on the whole to frustration and pain. In rejecting the main Hebrew-Christian tenet of a benevolent Providence ruling the universe, they aligned themselves with the naturalists rather than the vitalists.

Nietzsche developed a somewhat dialectical theory of polar opposition between two types or tendencies in art, the Apollonian and Dionysian. The one seeks dream-like beauty and clarity; the

other ecstatic unity, the merging of all separateness in a flow of passionate excitement, as in orgiastic drunkenness and mystic trance. He saw the recurrent alternation of these two throughout the history of art and civilization, interspersed with occasional, partial balances such as that of Greek tragedy. At the same time, Nietzsche took elements from the naturalistic tradition of Darwin and Spencer, especially the ideas of natural selection and survival of the fittest. More than Darwin himself had done, he interpreted past progress as due to a ruthless struggle for power, with elimination of the weaker by the stronger. Like Thomas Huxley, he saw the Christian ethic as opposing this process through the substitution of love and humility; but unlike Huxley, he denounced the Christian ethic as a slave morality. Only through continuation of the natural, selective process, he thought, could a higher species of supermen emerge.

In metaphysics, there is an important difference between idealism and dualism. The former denies the reality of matter by reducing what seems material in our experience to some form of mind; perhaps to the thoughts of a cosmic or divine mind. Orthodox Christianity, both Catholic and Protestant, has favored dualism instead. It has maintained the reality of matter as a substance in itself, created by the divine mind but essentially different from soul or spirit. There has, however, been a strong Platonic or neo-platonic strain in Christian doctrine, as shown in the Gospel of St. John and the writings of St. Augustine, which has led many subsequent Christian thinkers to minimize the reality of matter. Sometimes these metaphysical differences have seemed important, and led to violent disputes; at other times they have been glossed over.

The rise of naturalism and positivism in the eighteenth and nineteenth centuries was a threat to both dualism and idealism: to any belief in the

---

[13] See the Introduction to D. Ainslie's translation of Croce's *Aesthetic* (London, 1922) on the extent to which Croce agreed and disagreed with Hegel.

independent reality of mind, soul, or spirit, and to any teleological theory of history as supernaturally directed. Both dualism and idealism were forms of supernaturalism, and under the new threat they tended to join forces. Fundamentalists of all faiths rejected evolutionism *in toto;* modernists looked for some reasonable way of reconciling science and religion. Some of these, and some forms of modernism, were condemned by church authorities. Catholic belief could not, for example, look with favor on any philosophy which taught that the divine mind was itself developing, increasing in knowledge and self-understanding through the ages. God is eternally omniscient and omnipotent. Nor could the church agree with Hegel that the climax of spiritual progress had been reached in his own time, country, and philosophy.

However, there were aspects of evolutionism on which liberals in both dualist and idealist camps could join hands. These were the essentials of a teleological, vitalistic conception: that, as Tennyson expressed it, "I doubt not through the ages one unceasing purpose runs." The Book of Genesis could be symbolically interpreted; the world had been created with potentialities for change. The whole story of evolution from amoeba to man was accepted by liberal Christians as true, but as subject to a deeper theological interpretation: that God had willed it so and was still directing it so, except insofar as man's free will had rebelled and caused unnecessary trouble. This teleological interpretation of the cause and process of evolution, on which dualists and idealists could agree, seemed to many more important than the question of the reality of matter, on which they differed. Thus many Christian scholars and scientists—biologists, sociologists, and archeologists—found it possible to cooperate with their naturalistic colleagues in describing and organizing the phenomena of evolution, while dissenting from them on the deeper explanation of these phenomena. A historian or social scientist could retain his theistic beliefs while giving little or no expression of them in his

technical researches and publications. It is often impossible to be sure from his writings alone whether he is a positivist, a naturalist, a Kantian or Hegelian idealist, or a Neo-Thomist. Dualistic and idealistic traditions thus partly merged in late nineteenth-century thinking to produce a vague, indefinite vitalism; a tendency to explain historical events as due to some sort of quasi-conscious willing or striving; a tendency to attack and deplore materialism and positivism, often without offering any definite substitute; an occasional cryptic hint that, behind events, there must be some kind of spiritual life force. "Call it what you will," said some, as if the exact name and nature of the mysterious, supernatural force made no great difference.

Not only did elements of dualism and idealism blend in that period, but also elements of both with naturalism and empiricism—strange as that may seem when these are defined as antithetical in principle. But the minds of philosophers, poets, and occasional scientists have been eager to combine opposites; to select and reconcile the best features of conflicting beliefs. The period was one in which innumerable theories and attitudes, new and old, consistent and inconsistent, were contending in the intellectual arena. Each thinker in whose mind a set of these conflicting views contended, especially one with a complex, divided personality, felt the need to work out his own personal synthesis.

G. T. Fechner illustrates this trait of modern thought, in somewhat unusually aggravated form, but still in a way which is typical of his age. He was, at one and the same time, a principal founder of empirical psychology and aesthetics, with a devotion to quantitative studies of sensation, and also a mystic and supernaturalist, an admirer of Schelling the idealist, and author of a philosophic work on the Persian *Zend-Avesta,* in which he expounded a fundamental dualism. The universe had not one, but a plurality of souls, and the author claimed to have discovered a mathematical relation between the spiritual and the physical worlds.[14] Needless to say, the reconciliation which thus partly satisfied its author did not last or satisfy his scientific contemporaries. Both occidental and oriental philosophers are still contending with the traditional antithesis between science and mysticism in various forms. The form in which it appeared in the long controversy over evolutionism is only one of many. But the case of Fechner should guard us against the hasty assumption that only philosophic naturalists made important empirical and experimental contributions to science in the nineteenth century. A dualistic or idealistic faith, perhaps in a separate compartment of the mind, was in practice no bar to original work along lines which, in retrospect, seem to have strengthened evolutionary naturalism. At the same time there were other psychologists such as William James, temperamentally more inclined toward naturalism, who determinedly maintained an open mind toward the possibility that empirical research—as in so-called "psychical research"—might demonstrate the reality of the spiritual world and the survival of incorporeal souls.

David Bidney sees a sharp disagreement in recent anthropology and sociology on the nature and function of culture.[15] Some definitions of it, he writes, presuppose a realistic approach, some an idealistic one. The realists, such as Tylor, Boas, and Malinowski, define it in terms of social behavior, habits, customs, and institutions; thus as having no existence apart from actual groups. The idealists, such as Cornelius Osgood,[16] define it as an aggregate or stream of ideas, conventional understandings, and communicable intelligence; thus as something conceived or perceived by minds. The realists, such as Franz Boas, hold that culture consists of artifacts plus customs and traditions. The idealists, such as Marett, Redfield, and Cassirer, hold that it consists of symbolic expressions of ideas, hence that "material culture" is a contradiction in terms. Idealism leads the study of culture to an emphasis on analyzing concepts, symbols, and stages in the evolution of cultural mentality.

Individual scientists and historians differ greatly from each other as to the extent to which they think out and express their philosophic positions clearly. Professional philosophers naturally tend to do so, especially idealists such as Cassirer and Croce. Historians and social scientists are often vague in this respect. Strictly speaking, an emphasis on material or behavioristic phenomena does not necessarily imply a realistic or naturalistic philosophy, since idealists can interpret such phenomena as manifestations of the cosmic mind.[17] By the same token, emphasis on the determining power of mind, ideas, and other psychological factors in history does not necessarily imply an idealistic metaphysics, because all these factors may be explained as activities of a physical brain and nervous system. But it is often a sign that some idealistic presuppositions lurk behind the scenes in the author's own thinking.

Idealism and dualism are often regarded as antithetical to empirical science, and there is reason to do so, for they have been traditionally opposed to the spread of positivistic methods and conclusions. Accordingly, one who entertains this view is likely to be surprised when eminent scientists who give ample evidence of empirical knowledge and rigorous inductive reasoning disclose idealistic or dualistic beliefs at the same time. Recent British and American science, especially in the social and cultural fields, has perhaps been more consistently naturalistic than that of Germany, where science is often combined with idealism, or that of France and Italy, where it is often combined with Roman Catholic dualism. In modern German physics and astronomy, the idealistic approach is often shown in a tendency to conceive of space, time, matter,

[14] Cf. J. T. Merz, History of European Thought in the Nineteenth Century, Vol. II, 508; G. Murphy, Historical Introduction to Modern Psychology (New York, 1932), pp. 85 f.

[15] Op. cit., pp. 23, 130.

[16] "Culture: its Empirical and Non-empirical Character," Southwestern Journal of Anthropology, VII (1951), 202–14.

[17] Bidney uses the term "naturalistic" in a most unusual way in speaking of the "naturalistic fallacy" as the attribution to innate human nature of thoughts and actions which are really cultural. This has nothing to do with philosophic naturalism.

and energy as basically mental constructs. In German anthropology and culture history, the influence of Kant as well as that of Hegel has persistently shown itself between the lines.

The influence of Kant has descended into contemporary anthropology and culture history in the tendency to distinguish sharply between the methods of history and of science. Kant, in a passage which deeply influenced Schiller's conception of art, had contrasted the realm of nature with that of human freedom: the former as governed by necessary laws and the latter as one in which man could make his own laws. In aesthetics, Kant applied this to the doctrine that genius in art could make its own rules, and that fine art (where the spirit could be free) was inherently superior to the useful (bound by natural laws.) David Bidney, discussing Neo-Kantian theories of culture history, notes how the philosophers Dilthey and Windelband distinguished two kinds of science: the "nomothetic," concerned with natural, universal laws, and the "idiographic" concerned with describing individual phenomena.[18] Dilthey distinguished also between *Geisteswissenschaften* and *Naturwissenschaften*, the one dealing with life forms and values which had to be understood through experience, the other with value-free phenomena which could be causally explained. Rickert proposed instead the concept of *Kulturwissenschaft* as antithetical to *Naturwissenschaft*. Culture was to be understood as including the processes of cultivation and valuation; nature as being self-originated and value-free. The human and historical branches of knowledge required a subjective approach with concrete experience of the mental symbolism involved. Contemporary idealistic philosophers such as Cassirer and Collingwood accepted this approach, which makes the methods of the human and natural sciences antithetical and opposes the attempt to explain history in terms of natural laws. For such idealists as Bastian, culture was an expression of spiritual development in ways which do not occur in nature. Comte, Spencer, and Tylor on the other hand, had thought of culture history

as a natural science and of man as a part of nature; hence of scientific method as applicable to all phenomena.

Bidney shows how Kroeber, among American anthropologists, is close to the Neo-Kantian position in distinguishing between the historical method and that of science.[19] The former method, Kroeber maintained, was not distinctive in dealing with time sequences but in attempting a descriptive integration, whereas science tries to analyze processes in quantitative terms.

4. MEANINGS OF "HISTORICISM"
IN THE PHILOSOPHY OF HISTORY.
CHANGING ATTITUDES
TOWARD SCIENCE AND EVOLUTION

The term "historicism" is applied to several of the ideas which we have been considering, but so inconsistently that its meaning presents a problem in itself. As now used, it is a highly ambiguous term which is made by different writers to stand for almost opposite conceptions. It is associated mostly with the Hegelian tradition in theories of culture history. It has been significantly applied to the history of art. As a rule, historicism is opposed to naturalistic evolutionism and to all attempts to generalize about historical phenomena in terms of the natural sciences. But some of the chief leaders in naturalistic evolutionism have also been attacked as historicists.

We may group the chief meanings of "historicism" under three headings. They overlap in actual discussion, and each writer makes his own combination of them.

[18] *Theoretical Anthropology*, pp. 250 ff. Also by Bidney, "The Philosophical Anthropology of Ernst Cassirer and its Significance in Relation to the History of Anthropological Thought," in *The Philosophy of Ernst Cassirer*, ed. P. A. Schilpp, p. 487.

[19] Bidney, *op. cit.*, p. 252. Kroeber, "History and Science in Anthropology," *American Anthropologist*, XXXVII (1935), 539–69.

A. Historicism as "historical-mindedness." Thinking in terms of change and relativity. In its broadest definition, the term refers to the whole, far-reaching tendency of modern thought since the eighteenth century to emphasize the historical aspects of things and the historical approach in describing and evaluating them. The theory of evolution is a part of this tendency. It includes the relativistic trend in philosophy, religion, ethics, and aesthetics, as away from absolutism; toward regarding all beliefs and standards as subject to change and contingent on temporary conditions. It includes an awareness of the vast age of the universe.

All of us, says Geoffrey Barraclough, including the natural scientists since Darwin, live "in an historical age, or an age of historicism." "Most of the spheres of intellectual, and often also of active life, are permeated by history." He quotes Guido de Ruggiero as saying that historicism means "the evaluation of reality as a historical process of spiritual formation." Pope Pius XII described it as "a philosophic system which perceives in all spiritual reality, in the knowledge of truth, in religion, morality, and law, only change and evolution, and consequently rejects everything permanent, eternally valuable, and absolute."[20] It rejects the rationalism of the Enlightenment, including Condorcet, says Barraclough.

But surely this is true only in part, for there is much of this broadly historical thinking in Condorcet. The relativistic philosophy defined by Pope Pius XII is rationalistic as contrasted with medieval absolutism. All modern naturalism, utilitarianism, pragmatism, and similar views are somewhat "historicist" in this broad sense. This we shall call "Type A" of historicism.

B. Historicism as belief in historical laws and predictions. This belief erects the historical approach itself into something almost absolutistic in its own way. Edmund Tylor states it as "The philosophy of history at large, explaining the past and predicting the future phenomena of man's life in the world by reference to general laws..."[21] Karl Popper defines historicism as "an approach to the social sciences which assumes that *historical prediction* is their principal aim, and which assumes that this aim is attainable by discovering the 'rhythms' or the 'patterns,' the 'laws' or the 'trends' that underlie the evolution of history."[22] Popper and Hauser both attack this belief, especially in its Hegelian form, as politically reactionary, and as substituting the ideal of a "closed society" for the liberalism of the French Revolution.

"Evolutionism" in general is sometimes confusingly identified with this type of historicism. In one respect, Spencer, Tylor, and Morgan are historicists: not in being reactionary, anti-liberal or pessimistic, but in believing that "laws" and "patterns" can be found in history. Since there is an inevitable sequence of cultural stages, according to Morgan and Tylor, we can reconstruct the general outlines of the past history of a people from comparatively little data, and to some extent predict its future evolution. Spencer undertook to predict in a general way the future course of all human evolution.

Most recent attacks on historicism refer especially to the idealistic variety. Historicism attributes a "meaning" to history, they say, a meaning based on the belief that it is divinely directed. History actually "has no meaning," says Popper,[23] although we can give it a meaning.

C. Historicism as particularizing, relativistic, and qualitative. (1) scientific, empiricist phase; (2) anti-scientific, idealist phase. What we may call "Type C" of historicism is characterized by a rejection of

---

[20] Addressing the Tenth International Congress of the Historical Sciences in 1955. Quoted by G. Barraclough in *History in a Changing World* (Norman, Okl., 1956), pp. 1–7; and by Hans Meyerhoff in *The Philosophy of History in Our Time, an Anthology* (Garden City, N. Y., 1959), pp. 28 f.

[21] *Primitive Culture* (1913), Vol. I, p. 5.

[22] *The Poverty of Historicism* (London, 1957). *Cf.* "Crypto-historicism," a review of Philip Bagby, *Culture and History* (New York, 1958) in *Times Literary Supplement* (London, Oct. 3, 1958, p. 1). *Cf.* A. Hauser, *The Philosophy of Art History*, pp. 119–120, 136–138, 167.

[23] *The Open Society and its Enemies* (Princeton, N. J., 1950), pp. 449–463; quoted by Meyerhoff, p. 304.

"Type B." It denies the possibility of universal laws and highly regular patterns in history, opposes the continued search for them, and calls for a transfer of attention in that field to the unique, particular aspects of events. It had an early stage, exemplified by Ranke, which called for some kinds of scientific method in historiography, and a later stage exemplified by Croce, which he called "pure and complete."[24]

That the same name is thus applied to more or less opposing beliefs is still an obstacle to clear discussion, both of historicism itself and of the many other ideas—such as evolution—with which it has been associated. It indicates the confusing turns and twists in theories of history, especially in Germany in the late nineteenth and early twentieth centuries. Sometimes they appear as contradictory, unreconciled ideas in the mind of a single thinker; sometimes as a conscious effort to combine different sets of values and different aspects of the truth in history-writing. Successive attempts to revise and develop the historicist approach were often carried to one extreme or the other.

Hans Meyerhoff agrees that historicism is a product of the romantic reaction against Enlightenment rationalism, as exemplified by Herder's rejection of the intellectual, philosophical approach to history. He goes on to define its basic thesis as an assertion that "the subject-matter of history is human life in its totality and multiplicity."[25] The historian, he continues, aims to portray the unsystematic variety of historical phenomena in their unique, living expressions and in constant change. Like that of art, this aim is different from the conceptual, systematic approach of philosophy and science, which is inadequate to report the concrete realities of events. History tries and should try to show the infinite variety of particular forms in time; the multiplicity of individual manifestations. All of them are unique and equally significant, "immediate to God," said Ranke. The task of history is to show "how it really happened." Imagination and sympathy are necessary in it, as

well as reason. Ranke, following Herder, attacked "Hegelian scholasticism" for trying to force the wealth of historical life into abstract concepts. "Respect for irreducible particularity" remains, according to Meyerhoff, a cornerstone of historicism.

Leopold von Ranke (1795–1886) is often credited with founding the approach to historiography which was later called "historicism." In his writings, it does not seem now as anti-scientific. It does not try to exclude scientific methods from history-writing. On the contrary, Ranke and his associates called for an increasing use of scientific knowledge and techniques, such as those of philology, numismatics, archeology, and geology. They advocated rigorous objectivity in the study of archives and other tangible records. They did insist that history should emphasize particular events and conditions in a certain time and place, seeking mainly to discover and describe "how it happened." This was in the spirit of the new, empirical type of science then emerging; it was hostile only to the older kind of science and philosophy which sought to derive eternal, universal laws from *a priori* principles, and to impose the methods and concepts of the mathematical and physical sciences on historical data. This change was necessary in an age of excessive, often dogmatic theorizing. But Ranke did not advocate ignoring general concepts or the ways in which particular events occur in large-scale combinations. He did not say that every event is *completely* unique, *sui generis*, for that would have been absurd. But he did insist that every event and historical combination of events had unique as well as universal aspects, and that the former were too commonly ignored in the search for laws and principles. Each event, he said, should be shown as an integral part of world history. He began to write a world

[24] Cf. Meyerhoff, p. 12. H. E. Barnes (*Historical Sociology*, pp. 58 f) classes Paul Radin, Wilhelm Windelband, Karl Heussi, and Ernst Troeltsch as extreme historicists in this sense. Franz Boas, Max and Alfred Weber, and A. L. Kroeber are regarded as moderate historicists.

[25] *The Philosophy of History in Our Time*, pp. 10 ff.

history in his eighty-sixth year.[26] His own philosophy was strongly religious, and he saw no conflict between it and the scientific search for truth.

In this scientific, empirical approach to historiography, Ranke was followed by such writers as J. B. Bury in England, who insisted that history was a science and tried to make it so, but without specious claim to universal laws.

Ranke's type of historicism, both scientific and particularizing, was soon followed by another which abandoned the alliance with empirical science. It re-established the traditional bonds of German historiography with Hegelian idealism, thus moving farther away from the natural sciences. But, at the same time, it preserved Ranke's emphasis on particular events and their unique aspects. It exaggerated these in a way hard to reconcile with the "unity of spirit" which idealism professed to see throughout history.

Hans Meyerhoff, in one of the introductions to his anthology on *The Philosophy of History in Our Time*, lists Wilhelm Dilthey (1833–1911), Benedetto Croce (1866–1952), José Ortega y Gasset (1883–1956) and R. G. Collingwood (1889–1943) as leaders in recent European historicism, combining it with idealism in the tradition of Kant and Hegel. For them, he writes, history was a spiritual realm whose ultimate constituents were thoughts, purposes, motives, and actions; not natural or social factors. The aim of history was to reconstruct such spiritual factors in their original meaning.[27] Historicism, for Dilthey, was to liberate man from theology, philosophy, and natural science and from three opposing world-views which could not be proven or reconciled. Croce, in the first chapter of his *History: its Theory and Practice*, attacks rationalistic, scientific, and positivistic trends in history-writing.[28]

Thus the great traditions of European thought merge, separate, grow, and converge again in part, making it hard for the chronicler to follow them in terms of "isms." At each step, the "ism" has to be redefined in accord with changes in usage.

The writing of history did not move uniformly toward a more scientific, factual description of "how it happened." It also preserved its artistic, imaginative side as a branch of literature. In the study of the arts, it joined hands with criticism. Depending on the bent and talent of the historian, it could move a long way toward fiction or essay-writing, without apology if it kept a basis of conformity to probable truth. The boundaries between history and historical fiction were often as blurred on one side as those between history and cultural science on the other. The effect of historicism as skeptical and relativistic was apparent in the common recognition that history could not, however hard it tried, achieve complete objectivity. The personal, cultural, and ideological bias of the historian was recognized as a permanent fact to be dealt with. It was always a limitation, but it could also be a creative contribution if the historian was a good one.

[26] Fritz Stern, ed., *The Varieties of History from Voltaire to the Present* (New York, 1960), pp. 54–59. Introduction to selections from Ranke on the ideal of universal history. "The historian," said Ranke, "must keep his eye on the universal aspect of things. He will have no preconceived ideas as does the philosopher; rather, while he reflects on the particular, the development of the world in general will become apparent to him." "If we picture this sequence of centuries, each with its unique essence, all linked together, then we shall have attained universal history." This differs from specialized research in that, "while investigating the particular, it never loses sight of the complete whole."

[27] P. 36. D. Krishan states the historicist idea as follows: "Social change... may be the result of immanent forces operating... within the social structure itself. Even if the consciousness of individual minds operates in a large measure, it is merely as an instrument, it has been urged, of those very immanent forces themselves. These... have a law of their own development which determines, in the main, the direction and pattern that social change has to take." "Social Change: an Attempt at a Study in Conflicting Patterns of Social Action," *Philosophy and Phenomenological Research*, XIV, 567–573 (1954). Quoted by J. W. N. Watkins in "Philosophy of History," *Philosophy in the Mid-Century* (Florence, 1958), p. 161. Historicism of this deterministic type can be either naturalistic or supernaturalistic, but it is usually the latter. So is Type C, with which it is sometimes rather inconsistently combined. Hauser calls it "mystifying" to refer all events to a superindividual origin while also stressing their uniqueness and incomparability. He classes Riegl and Wölfflin as historicists.

[28] Meyerhoff, pp. 43 ff.

Having originated in the romantic revolt from eighteenth-century philosophy and science in the field of history, historicism has retained some traces of its anti-scientific, anti-rationalistic attitude until the present day. It is still associated with the attempt to separate history from science, the insistence that history is not and should not try to be scientific; that it should not make extensive generalizations about trends and patterns. In this sense, then, historicism was anti-evolutionist or non-evolutionist, since evolution was one of the trends which science claimed to see in human events.

The attempt to separate history from natural science and empiricist philosophy, derived in part from Herder, tended on the other hand to strengthen its alliance with art and with the Platonic tradition in philosophy. One argument for this was the alleged attempt of natural science to substitute quantitative for qualitative relations; to analyze the felt qualities of experience, such as beauty and ugliness, out of existence by reducing them to their supposed elements and causes. Qualitative phenomena included all the moral and aesthetic aspects of nature and art, both emotional and sensuous; all the ideals, desires, and feelings which made life warm and colorful. Science tended to distort and falsify human life, it was said, by eliminating these and substituting cold calculation. This charge was, of course, a phase of the romantic reaction against eighteenth-century science, one which still reverberated in the early twentieth century through the anti-scientism of Henri Bergson and Benedetto Croce. To some extent it operated also against the alliance of historiography with philosophy. But idealism was more acceptable than naturalism to the historicists. It seemed to preserve the integrity of beauty, truth, and goodness, and of all spiritual life as irreducible to material processes.

That there was an element of truth in this argument, which must somehow be recognized in science, was eventually realized by many naturalists and positivists themselves. It can not be said that science has yet found a way to preserve the qualitative aspects of nature and experience, untouched by intellectual analysis. It has gone resolutely ahead with the latter. But it does not suppose that its own account of the world is the only valid one, or that it has really "reduced" the qualitative to the quantitative. It recognizes the enduring need for a sympathetic understanding of the qualitative, and for the kinds of art and history-writing which help us attain it.

The sharp dichotomy between science and history which extreme historicism tried to establish was largely bridged over by the growth of the cultural and psychological sciences during the late nineteenth and twentieth centuries. The historical and the scientific study of man as a thinking, social animal dealt with much the same phenomena. Both generalized and both had to deal with particulars. The difference of emphasis was relative, practical, and methodological. Scholars in each field were free to use as much of the other approach as seemed to be useful; many worked in the borderline area between them. The advice of nineteenth-century historicism, to pay more attention to particulars, was taken seriously by many scientists as well as historians—for example, by Franz Boas in anthropology in the 1920's. Thus, instead of widening the gulf between history and science as it often tried to do, it helped to ally them in a common trend toward cautious empiricism.

The relation between history and science as differing in emphasis, yet overlapping and cooperating, was clearly set forth by Kroeber in 1951: "I recognize," he said, "the distinction of nomothetic and ideographic method, but not as an absolute dichotomy between science as investigation of nature and history as the study of man or spirit or culture."[29] Both approaches, he said, can be applied to any level of phenomena, as in historical sciences like astronomy and geology.

The attempt to make a sharp antithesis between

[29] Introduction to Part I of *The Nature of Culture* (Chicago, 1951), p. 5.

history on the one hand and, on the other, empiricist philosophy and science, has thus been countered by important changes in the latter. Strong relativist, pragmatist, and other movements developed in them which rejected the traditional belief that science and philosophy aimed at universal laws and static, integrative systems. They, too, had been influenced by the romantic movement, by evolutionism, and by historicism in the broad sense (Type A) toward a more pluralistic view of things. Change, multiplicity, variety, particularity, were of the nature of things for them as well as for the historians. Eternal laws and unified, all embracing systems of thought were as impossible for them as for the historian. As the new approach in science and philosophy spread out more and more into cultural fields, such as anthropology and psychology, it had to take increasing note of the multiplicity of the facts, as well as of the relativity of knowledge to man's historical position. More and more, it incorporated the historical approach along with its generalizations.

This profound change in philosophy and the cultural sciences was exemplified by such men as John Dewey[30] in philosophy, Leslie A. White in anthropology, and V. Gordon Childe in archeology—all writing in the early twentieth century. As to the theory of cultural evolution, it involved a rejection of "Type B" historicism, defined above as "Belief in historical laws and prediction." Ironclad evolutionism, as belief in a universal, inevitable law, providing a basis for exact prediction, went out the window. Instead, two different trends ensued. One, extremely particularizing and skeptical, rejected cultural evolution entirely. It included both idealists and naturalists. The other, exemplified by the naturalists just named, kept it in a more pluralistic, tentative form. In this group, there was little talk of laws and predictions. Evolution in culture was, for them, real but diversified and irregular, subject to change, exception, and reversal. Such a "law", if one used the term at all, was merely a description of observed trends and

recurrences up to the present time. It might give some ground for a reasonable guess about the future, since long-term, widespread tendencies do not usually stop suddenly, but with much less reliability than in predicting the weather.

5. ORTHOGENESIS AND PARALLELISM, VITALISTIC AND NATURALISTIC. CULTURAL ORTHOGENESIS

"Orthogenesis" in biology is defined by Webster's *New International Dictionary* as "Variation which in successive generations of an organism follows some particular line, resulting in the evolution of some new type irrespective of the effect of natural selection or other external factor; determinate variation or evolution." In sociology, it is defined by that authority as "The theory that social evolution always follows the same direction and passes through the same stages in each culture despite differing external conditions."

That the term is used in both fields with similar meaning illustrates how the theory of determinate evolution has developed in both biology and sociology. Comte's evolutionism was determinate, though expressed in other terms. As against "social Darwinism," which had stressed the element of chance, determinism held that cultural evolution, like organic, was not due mainly to environmental selection, but was somehow predetermined along a certain line.

The concept of orthogenesis in sociology is closely related to that of "parallelism" or independent invention. Both are opposed on the whole to extreme cultural "diffusionism," which tends to explain analogies between the developments of different groups as due to the influence of one on the other, rather than to inherent pressure in the

---

[30] On Dewey's theory of history, see his *Logic: The Theory of Inquiry* (New York, 1938), pp. 230–239. Meyerhoff, pp. 163 ff. Also J. L. Blau, "John Dewey's Theory of History," *Jl. of Philosophy*, Vol. LVII, No. 3 (Feb. 4, 1960), pp. 89 ff.

same direction. Such influence is usually conceived as largely due to the "accidents" of location, migration, commerce, and the like. A moderate diffusionism is consistent with orthogenesis.

Those who hoped for a way to explain evolution which would keep the belief in a guiding Providence were encouraged by the theory of orthogenesis in German biology after Darwin. Indebted to Aristotle, it had its modern beginnings in the botanical researches of Carl Wilhelm Nägeli (1817–1891).[31] From his studies of the Hegelian philosophy, he derived the notion that a species is a summary of all similar individuals and, as such, an absolute idea. The plant and animal kingdoms have no transitions. Holding to the older beliefs in spontaneous generation and Lamarckism, he worked out a theory of descent in opposition to those of Darwin and Haeckel. Rejecting the idea of natural selection as the sole cause of evolution, he proposed, instead that of *Vervollkommungskraft* —that evolution is an inherent force of life, not a process thrust on living beings from outside. This internal force he also called *nisus formativus*, and defined it as one by which the development of life is led in a certain direction; not (as Darwin thought) to variations in every possible direction. However, he insisted that it was not a special life-force, but like the inertia in inorganic nature.

From Nägeli's beginning, Theodor Eimer (1843–98) developed the theory which he called "orthogenesis."[32] He also rejected Darwin's concept of variation in all possible directions, and held that the evolution of life must depend on a force operating in a definite direction. Such a force is stimulated and modified by outside influences, but provides some selection along with the material for changes. Selection alone, he said, can not produce anything new; the inner force is the true origin of life. During the late nineteenth century, this line of thought was reinforced by attacks on Darwin and Haeckel from religiously minded scientists, such as the Jesuit Wasmann, the Lutheran botanist J. Reinke, and the physiologists G. Bunge and R. Neumeister. They maintained that

the origin of life was a transcendental problem and that the psychical could not be derived from the material; hence they insisted on the need of postulating a spiritual life force, irreducible to physico-chemical factors. Most influential of this group was Hans Driesch, Hegelian metaphysician and experimental biologist.[33] Rejecting Darwinism, he called instead for a revival of Aristotle's concept of the *entelechy*—the potentiality inherent in matter, which achieves reality to the extent of matter's development into higher forms. Driesch added the idea of "something that carries its purpose within itself." He pointed to his own personal consciousness as a basis for his vitalism and "phenomenological idealism."

Support for this theory was found in the familiar dictum of von Baer that phylogeny recapitulates ontogeny. It is an obvious fact that each individual organism develops, under favorable conditions, along a predetermined course from seed or egg to mature organism. Aristotle regarded the mature, perfect form of each species as its "entelechy" or inherent, final cause. His language was not clear as to the extent to which he regarded this entelechy as purposeful in a psychological sense. Christian philosophy made it strongly so, as a manifestation of divine purpose and as a teleological theory of creation. But the concepts of predetermination and of orthogenesis can be detached from those of mental purpose and of cosmic mind or will, so as to be placed upon a naturalistic basis. The predeterminate growth of the acorn into the oak or the fertilized ovum into the human is a kind of "directedness." There is nothing necessarily mystical or spiritual about it. The geneticist explains such predetermination in terms of chromosomes and genes, combining themselves according to Mendel's formulas. He invokes no super-

---

[31] *Mechanisch-physiologische Theorie der Abstammungslehre* (1884). See the account of his work in E. Nordenskiöld, *The History of Biology* (New York, 1928), pp. 552 f.

[32] Eimer's major works were *Die Entstehung der Arten* (1888) and *Orthogenesis der Schmetterlinge* (1897). *Cf.* Nordenskiöld, p. 570.

[33] *Nordenskiöld*, pp. 608 f.

natural, vital force, and hopes to analyze the mechanism further in physico-chemical terms. Then why, it is asked, can there not be an analogous predetermination in life as a whole or in a certain lineage, along purely naturalistic lines? This may operate genetically as a persistent tendency for variations and mutations to occur more frequently and with greater power of survival along the predetermined line of development. Instead of varying equally "in all directions" as the laws of chance would seem to require, the curve of frequency would center about a certain axis. The dice, it is said, would be "loaded." Otherwise, one has to rely very heavily on environmental selection to account for the persistent continuities of evolution. And environment varies so much that it would seem rather conducive to diversity.

Naturalists as well as vitalists could thus accept the concept of orthogenesis in cultural evolution. To some of the former, it seemed reasonable to suppose a physical predisposition in the human species which impels it, under favorable conditions, to develop mentally and socially along a certain approximate line. Man inherits a physical mechanism which makes him keep on desiring more numerous and complex satisfactions, powers, and skills; also one which gives him the intelligence and learning power to achieve them. The result would be continued evolution, varying in detail according to the specific environment, but roughly constant in direction. Spencer's "universal law" of evolution was consistent with this view, although he did not use the term "orthogenesis." That term has been associated almost wholly with the vitalistic, teleological conception of orthogenesis, which has added to its present disfavor among scientists and philosophic naturalists.

Writing recently for anthropologists, the geneticist William C. Boyd[34] remarks that orthogenesis implies two suppositions: (a) that nature shows a tendency towards evolution in straight or continuing lines, as in paleontological material; (b) the

existence of some mystic, vitalistic force or principle which directs evolution along apparently predetermined lines. There can be no doubt, he goes on, "that some rectilinearity can often be observed in evolution. According to Simpson, the best part of the paleontological record is made up of lines that evolve more or less in one direction over long periods of time. Nevertheless, rectilinear evolution is far from universal."

These comments bring out a significant distinction between two related problems. One is that of the extent to which evolutionary change, organic and cultural, has actually proceeded "in straight lines" over long periods. To what extent has it followed continuous sequences of change, whereby certain characters or types of form, once begun, have kept on developing? Opinions differ on this problem. There have certainly been examples of persistent direction—the growth of the brain in man's ancestors and of scientific knowledge in cultural evolution. But it is not universal; there have been some sudden, radical changes of direction.

It is another problem to explain the causation of any such observed continuities of direction in change. Here again there is disagreement. As we have seen, one school of thought—the vitalistic— would explain it in terms of a spiritual agency. It would be a mistake to suppose, however, that all theories of cultural orthogenesis and parallelism are vitalistic. One can be a naturalist on the question of causation and still believe that an inherent, directive tendency exists in art and culture. One can explain the inherent tendency as material, inanimate, unconscious, and non-purposeful.

"Ortho-" comes from the Greek word for "right" or "true"; hence "orthogenesis" literally suggests genesis in the right direction—i.e., progressive evolution or improvement. However, the term orthogenesis has almost lost this eulogistic meaning in scientific biology. Julian Huxley

[34] *Evolution: the Modern Synthesis* (New York, 1942), pp. 38, 40, 505 f., 516, 552. *Cf.* William C. Boyd, "The Contributions of Genetics to Anthropology," in *Anthropology Today*, p. 488.

defines it as an "inner momentum" of directional change, which has been regarded as a prime cause of evolution. The existence of such a determinant, he says, is regarded by some biologists as possible when the directional change is not functional, but "of an apparently useless or even deleterious nature... So long as directional evolution is functional and adaptive, natural selection will also provide a formal explanation of it." An orthogenetic theory will be necessary if studies on mutation show that mutation "(a) is so frequent that it can override selective influences and (b) if it also tends to occur repeatedly in the same direction."

In searching for such "nonadaptive and internally-determined orthogenesis," a number of recent biologists have pointed to certain long trends for which no adaptive significance has been found. "We must," remarks Huxley, "provisionally face an explanation in terms of orthogenesis—i.e., of evolution predetermined to proceed within certain narrow limits, irrespective of selective disadvantage except where this leads to total extinction." But such cases are exceptional. To demonstrate the long continuance of orthogenetic trends, we would need to show a high mutation rate with restriction of the direction of mutation. Of this there is no evidence. Huxley concludes that dominant or primary orthogenesis, as a major factor in guiding evolution, is rare or non-existent. But "subsidiary or secondary orthogenesis is common enough." It limits freedom of variation, but merely provides limits within which natural selection still plays the main guiding role. It includes recurrent and parallel variations among different lineages of the same type, leading to convergence and parallel evolution, at least where parallel selection is also present. Huxley also quotes R. Goldschmidt in 1940 as remarking that "In many cases there will be only one direction (of possible evolutionary change). This is orthogenesis without Lamarckism, without mysticism." Again Huxley leaves room for a broad and flexible, naturalistic type of orthogenesis in remarking that "Much of the minor

systematic diversity to be observed in nature is irrelevant to the main course of evolution, a mere frill of variety superimposed upon its broad pattern."

Parallelism is the belief that cultural evolution tends to proceed in the same general direction among widely scattered groups, with or without diffusion or influence of one on the other. In widely separate parts of the earth, it is said, they tend to develop along somewhat parallel lines because all human groups have the same general predispositions. Both parallelism and orthogenesis assign a subordinate role to environmental selection as compared with that of determinate variation and mutation. Environment, they say, "trims off" the edges of the genetic process by eliminating the less fit. An extreme, rigid determinist attributes great power and steadiness to the supposed inherent drive and little power of deflection to the environment. More common today is an intermediate, modified determinism, which recognizes a small amount of inherent drive, but often weak, of short duration, and easily turned aside by local or changing conditions.

Whether or not future biologists decide that orthogenesis occurs to any great extent in organic phenomena, the question will still remain of whether something analogous to it occurs in the cultural realm. Theoretically, it could do so in either and not in the other. It would seem undeniable that the cultural development of the human species is fundamentally limited and directed by its inherited physical structure and related psychic predispositions, including powers of individual growth and conditioning. These limits and predispositions are very broad and flexible, allowing for much individual and group variation: that is, for many lines of cultural evolution, somewhat but not totally different. They do not enforce any one *specific* sequence of cultural traits, but the question remains of just how flexible they are in response to genetic and environmental variations within the total framework.

How much predisposition, of the flexible sort

which human nature imposes, would suffice to constitute "cultural orthogenesis?" This depends largely on how we define that term. Because of its strongly vitalistic associations, "orthogenesis" is not an effective term to use when these are not intended. The important fact to realize is that some kind of naturalistic determinism remains a theoretical possibility for both organic and cultural evolution, although at present out of favor in both fields.

CHAPTER VII

THE MARXIST THEORY
OF ART HISTORY
SOCIO-ECONOMIC DETERMINISM
AND THE DIALECTICAL PROCESS

I. THE "SOCIOLOGICAL APPROACH" IN GENERAL, AS DISTINGUISHED FROM MARXISM AND COMMUNISM

In Soviet Russia and other countries under communist control, the Marxist theory of art has been an influential system of thought and a basis for social action. The original propositions of Marx and Engels on art history and aesthetics have been widely applied to the various arts. Controversies have arisen within communist circles on particular aspects of the theory, and several changes of semi-official policy have occurred, especially in successive writers' congresses. No less a figure than Lenin contributed to the discussion, and the resultant formulation is sometimes called the "Marxist-Leninist" theory of art.

In non-communist countries, some writers on art frankly describe themselves as "Marxist" in a partisan sense. Others, who accept Marxist theories to some extent, avoid that label. It is not always easy, outside communist countries, to know whether they are, and should be called, Marxists in a full sense of that word. Some thorough-going Marxists avoid the label because of the common hostility toward it in capitalist countries. Some who accept only a small amount of Marxist theory in art, and who reject communism in general, have

been misleadingly classed as Marxists, merely because they emphasize social causes in interpreting artistic styles. It is quite possible to accept the Marxist theory of art history on the whole without supporting Soviet theory or practice in art or other fields. To call someone a Marxist without qualification is to suggest (perhaps incorrectly) that he follows the communist line in every respect.

Historians and critics often speak of "the method of sociological interpretation in art history," or of "the socio-economic approach to history." This is used in a specific sense by Marxists, as a name for their own method, for they recognize no other social approach as important enough to deserve the name.[1] However, non-Marxists use these terms in a broader sense, to include any kind of socio-economic emphasis or mode of interpretation, Marxist or other. Some historians are more strongly influenced by Gibbon, Hegel, Comte, Spencer, Taine, Franz Boas, or other social theorists than by Marx and Engels. It is often hard, especially in non-communist countries, to tell from a specialized book on art history or criticism whether or not a writer considers himself, or deserves to be classed, as a Marxist or communist in the full sense of the

[1] See, for example, G. V. Plekhanov's criticism of Buckle, Taine, Maine, Klüger, Hegel, and others in *Essays on the History of Materialism* (London, 1934), pp. 165 f.

word. Certainly, an emphasis on socio-economic interpretation is not, in itself, enough to indicate it. The ideas of Marx and Engels have been so widely diffused through the social sciences, as classics of past theory if not as established principles, that no one in the field can disclaim all indebtedness to them—at least as a challenge to other ways of thinking. But, for the sake of clarity, a distinction should be made between the sociological or socio-economic approach in general and the Marxist variety of it, whether or not one considers the latter to be the best.[2]

A strictly Marxist approach to the history of art and culture involves (a) a strong reliance on socio-economic explanations; a somewhat monistic approach along materialistic lines, as contrasted with the pluralism of such theorists as Taine; (b) the acceptance of certain other Marxist principles, especially the dialectical theory of history and the importance of the class struggle therein. The degree to which a historian relies on socio-economic explanations is hard to estimate; it may vary even within the works of a single author. Even among professed Marxists, there has been a difference in degree.

The issue is focused mainly on this question: "To what extent is the socio-economic factor *the* basic, controlling cause of artistic phenomena, or merely one of many contributing causes, and not necessarily the controlling one?" Even the latter, more moderate interpretation is somewhat indebted to Marx and Engels, for it was they who first clearly stated and developed the general conception of economic influence on cultural history. That such influence occurs, to a greater or less extent, is now taken for granted by social scientists and general historians. Through cultural lag and many strong resistances, this idea has been slow to penetrate the ivory towers of art history and aesthetics in the West.

The crucial issue today, from the standpoint of social science, is not *whether* economic factors influence art, but the *extent* to which they do so; the extent to which artistic styles and trends can

be explained as direct or indirect effects of this one factor. Strictly speaking, the title "Marxist" belongs only to those writers who lean farthest toward the extreme of economic determinism, along with other typically Marxist doctrines. A writer may be strongly non-Marxist in his general ideology and yet believe that the sociological approach has been unduly neglected in Western art history. He may emphasize it in his own research as a specialized method without implying that it is the only, or even the most fundamental, mode of explanation. In the realm of scientific methodology, this question can and should be discussed apart from political and emotional considerations.

To what extent the orthodox Marxist version of the sociological approach is scientifically valid remains controversial. This chapter will not attempt a comprehensive account of communist aesthetics and criticism, but will confine itself to those teachings which bear directly on the philosophy of art history. It will make some distinctions between the views of Marx and those of his chief followers in this field. It will attempt a critical summary of the Marxist-Leninist theory of art history as a continuously growing body of thought,

[2] Frederick Antal, in *Florentine Painting and its Social Background* (London, 1947-8), refers on p. 9 to his method as "the method of sociological interpretation." He has defended the sociological method theoretically in *The Burlington Magazine*: "Remarks on the Method of Art History" (Vol. XCI, Nos. 550–561 [Feb. and Mar. 1949], 49–52, 73–75). See also the comment by D. Talbot Rice, *ibid.*, p. 142. Antal does not mention Marx or Engels here and the social approach to history, as he explains it, is not specifically Marxist. He credits a number of other historians with helping to develop it in art and other fields. They include Ruskin, M. Dvořák, G. M. Trevelyan, R. H. Tawney, G. Thomson, A. v. Martin, A. Warburg, V. G. Childe, F. Saxl, Herbert Read, M. Schapiro, M. Meiss, E. Gombrich, and A. Blunt. Wölfflin is criticized as excessively formalistic. Arnold Hauser, in *The Philosophy of Art History* (London, 1959), speaks of "social history of art as a method of interpretation" (p. 268). He gives frequent credit to Marx and Engels as pioneers in this method. Other recent historians who have stressed a social approach are A. L. Guérard, *Literature and Society* (Boston, 1935) and L. L. Schücking, *The Sociology of Literary Taste* (London, 1944). An earlier American example is Upton Sinclair's *Mammonart: Essay in Economic Interpretation* (Pasadena, Calif., 1925).

consistent on the whole in spite of specific, often heated, disagreements.[3]

2. IDEAS OF MARX, ENGELS, AND LENIN ON ART AND CULTURAL HISTORY

As outlined by Karl Marx and Friedrich Engels, the dialectical theory of history made use of some Hegelian ideas, but rejected Hegel's idealism and became strongly naturalistic as a whole. So it has been ever since. Marx (1818–1883) and Engels published their *Communist Manifesto* in 1847, thus antedating Spencer's essay on "Progress, its Law and Cause" and Darwin's *Origin of Species*. It provided the basis for a general theory of history, but made hardly any reference to the arts. In the following decades, Marx and Engels applied it more explicitly to the arts, especially literature. Still later, such followers as Plekhanov, Mehring, and Lenin further developed theories of art and art history in the Marxist tradition.

The Marxist theory of art history, as part of a general theory of social history, involves a belief in cultural evolution and progress. Marx wrote of "the higher life-form toward which the existing society tends irresistibly by its own economic development," and Engels declared that "All successive historic conditions are only transitory steps in the endless evolution of human society from the lower to the higher."[4] Early Marxists praised the unilinear evolutionism of L. H. Morgan, the nineteenth-century American anthropologist.[5] Engels correlated the transition from one stage to the next in Morgan's theory with changes in the mode of production as described by Marx. Marx and Engels looked to Morgan for ethnological confirmation of their theory of history. But there are important differences between them.

Marx divided history roughly into a few main stages, based on the economic conditions of production, which "determines the general character of the social, political, and spiritual processes of life." "In broad outlines," said Marx, "we can designate the Asiatic, the ancient, the feudal, and the modern bourgeois methods of production as so many epochs in the progress of the economic formation of society."[6] The communistic stage would be the culminating one, he thought; there would be change and development, but no further revolutions.

Marxism emphasizes the dialectical conception of history, which it owes in part to Hegel. According to that philosopher, history is a process of struggle between opposite tendencies, with recurrent shifts of dominance from one to the other, followed by temporary combinations of both in gradually higher unities. This is the triadic formula of thesis, antithesis, and synthesis as steps

---

[3] For fuller accounts of Marxist aesthetics from various points of view—some friendly, some hostile—the reader may consult the following references: K. Marx and Friedrich Engels, *Literature and Art: Selections from their Writings* (New York, 1947); L. Harap, *Social Roots of the Arts* (New York, 1949); J. Somerville, *Soviet Philosophy,* Ch. IV: "The Arts: Socialist Realism" (New York, 1946); V. F. Calverton (ed.), *The Making of Society* (New York, 1937), with selections from Marx and Engels, Lenin, Thorstein Veblen, Max Eastman, V. F. Calverton, and others. F. J. Teggart and G. H. Hildebrand, *The Idea of Progress* (Berkeley, Calif., 1949) quotes from Marx and Engels on social and cultural evolution. See also H. Selsam, *Handbook of Philosophy* (New York, 1949) on "Esthetics," "Dialectic," "Hegel," "Marx," etc. On the relation of Marxism to Comte and St. Simon, see Engels' letter to F. Tönnies, 1895, in L. S. Feuer (ed.), Marx and Engels, *Basic Writings on Politics and Philosophy* (New York, 1959), p. 448. Bertrand Russell criticized the philosophical and economic principles of Marxism in Chapter XVIII of *Freedom and Organization* (London, 1934). For other discussions of Marxist aesthetics, pro and con, see the following articles in the *Journal of Aesthetics and Art Criticism:* O. Bradac, "Aesthetic Trends in Russia and Czechoslovakia," IX (1950–1951), 97; H. E. Bowman, "Art and Reality in Russian 'Realist' Criticism," XII (1953–1954), 386; V. Ehrlich, "Russian Formalism in Perspective," XIII (1954–1955), 215; Z. Folejewski, "Frustrations of Socialist Realism," XIV (1955–1956), 485; M. Rieser, "The Aesthetic Theory of Social Realism," XVI (1957–1958), 237; D. Šindelář, "Contemporary Czech Aesthetics," XVIII (1958–1959), 116.

[4] Quoted by Max Eastman in "The Marxian Philosophy." Calverton, *op. cit.,* pp. 833 f.

[5] See Engels' letter to Starkenburg of Jan. 25, 1894. Marx, *Selected Works,* I, 391–239; reprinted in Marx and Engels, *Literature and Art,* p. 11. Also Eastman, *op. cit.,* p. 858. Cf. V. G. Childe, *Social Evolution,* pp. 9–10.

[6] *A Contribution to the Critique of Political Economy,* trans. N. J. Stone (Chicago, 1904), p. 12.

in a cumulative evolution. For Hegel, the competing factors and the whole historical process were essentially intellectual and spiritual, an unfolding of the cosmic mind according to the transcendental logic of contradiction. Marx insisted that he had completely reversed the Hegelian theory of history by putting it on a materialistic basis: matter, not mind, was for him the ultimate reality and cause of evolution. "My dialectic method," he said, "is not only different from the Hegelian, but is its direct opposite. To Hegel, the life-process of the human brain, i.e., the process of thinking, which, under the name of 'the Idea,' he even transforms into an independent subject, is the demiurgos of the real world, and the real world is only the external, phenomenal form of 'the Idea.' With me, on the contrary, the ideal is nothing else than the material world reflected by the human mind, and translated into forms of thought."[7]

The persistent conflict in history, according to Marx, is not between ideas as spiritual absolutes or trends in divine thinking, but between social classes: those which own, control, and enjoy wealth and those which are made to produce it. This involves many specific conflicts along the way, between the various types of socio-economic order into which the relations between owners and workers are organized, and between the various ideologies and cultural products resulting from these types of order. The basic, determining issue is always economic; the others express it more or less indirectly and obscurely, and are decided eventually by shifts in economic control; not by rational arguments.

According to Marxism, the apparently irreconcilable opposition between two classes, such as a slave and noble class under feudalism, is eventually settled by absorption of both into a rising bourgeoisie. As the new rulers become more grasping and try to narrow their circle, a new exploited, propertyless class of proletarians is produced. Both of these will eventually disappear, according to the theory, in the classless, communist society of the future.

Marx's theory was materialistic, not only in its metaphysical basis, but in regarding the struggle for material, economic wealth and power as the fundamental determinant of social and cultural history. Darwin's theory of the biological struggle for survival seemed to Marxists as a welcome confirmation of it. Marx's own approach to social theory was, however, through economics and the German labor movement rather than through biology or archeology. Long residence in England familiarized him with its currents of thought in the mid-nineteenth century. These included, besides British evolutionism, the older empiricist philosophy of Hume, which he considered too static and passive, and reformist liberalism, which he considered too mild and utopian—a merely superficial modification of capitalism.

As to his naturalism, Marx was in the same general tradition as Comte and Spencer, but he differed greatly from both in other respects. All foresaw future progress as a result of natural law, but they differed on the nature of progress and the laws determining it. Marx emphasized a program for collective, revolutionary action, whereas Comte was rather conservative in economics and Spencer looked forward to an increasingly peaceful, reasonable kind of progress based on voluntary, sympathetic, harmonious cooperation. Future society, Spencer thought, will be flexibly integrated, but not through force or strongly centralized, collective ownership and operation. Unlike Marx, he did not heavily emphasize the economic factors in history; he did not conceive of progress as dependent on the forcible shifting of wealth and power from one class to another. Whereas Spencer and Darwin thought of evolution as gradual, through the accumulation of small variations, Marx thought of it as proceeding also by sudden, cataclysmic changes—evolution by revolution, as it was afterward called. (This can be compared with the later biological concept of mutations, which referred to sudden genetic changes.)

[7] Preface to the second edition of *Das Kapital*.

[95]

Marx did not assert that the economic determinant is the only one at work in history, but he did regard it as the most fundamental and influential one. Others which seem to be independent, he insisted, are deeply affected by the socio-economic system. Marxist theory does not say that individuals always act or try to act in accord with their own economic interests. This would be manifestly untrue, for some do sell their goods and give to the poor. Many choose a way of life which brings less wealth and power than they could otherwise secure, for the sake of different values. But the Marxist replies that even such attitudes are part of an ideology which has grown up on the basis of a certain socio-economic system. In the feudal system, there developed a hierarchical, other-worldly conception of life in this world and the next, within which sacrifice of this world's goods seemed a wise and prudent policy. Capitalism, says the Marxist, tends to make people reduce all values to cash values; to money and what it will bring. Some individuals in each system will try to revolt from it or denounce it, but the value-standards by which they do so and the ideals of heaven or Utopia with which they contrast it are also largely derived from the current ideology. Only the scientific approach (especially Marxism, according to the Marxists) achieves some objectivity; but not completely, since it, too, is involved in the dialectical struggle, and expresses a certain historical moment therein. Knowledge is always relative although the truth is absolute.

The Marxist theory is sometimes called "the materialistic determination of history." As noted above, this implies a metaphysical materialism in addition to belief in the priority of economic causes. Materialism excludes vitalistic or teleological determinism, but leaves the door open for a purely naturalistic sort of determinism. Marxists write at times like thorough-going advocates of an immanent, directive tendency in history, along naturalistic lines. Marx retained from Hegel the belief that the dialectical process would proceed "by its own self-active motion,"—by logical ne-

cessity, to reconcile opposites and achieve a higher, better unity.[8] He stressed the inevitability of a world-wide communist order as the necessary successor to decadent capitalism. In his opinion, it is not contingent on environmental accidents or on brilliant leadership, although these may help. At the same time, Marxist theory tends to emphasize the role of environment in another way, even to the point (in recent years) of flirting with biological Lamarckism. Committed to the idea that socio-economic environments determine cultural developments, it avoids belittling environment in general.

Marxism implies that there is something in the nature of man—his persistent desire for wealth and power, and his intelligent brain, ever seeking better ways to secure them—which drives him inevitably to evolve and progress. Conditions never remain static; ruling classes weaken through their own success and luxury; the oppressed rise up to take their places. There is persistent pressure on rulers and administrators to improve the techniques of production, war, government, and education. This results, whether the rulers so intend it or not, in expanding and strengthening the class of skilled technicians, intellectuals, and administrators, thus eventually undermining the power of the owners and oppressors. In this way, the rising bourgeoisie of the late middle ages gradually threw off the yoke of the feudal nobility and clergy. A ruling, owning class does not voluntarily surrender its powers and luxuries. One cannot rely, as utopians do, on moral preaching or innate kindness to achieve social justice and brotherhood. Individuals act in what appears to be a self-sacrificing way, perhaps for hope of heaven or because the ideal of self-sacrifice has been instilled in them by rulers; but such motivation is not persistent enough to insure progress.

Building on the general thesis that socio-economic conditions in each period determine its main modes of thought and action, Marx's followers applied this to all cultural phenomena, including

[8] *Cf.* M. Eastman in Calverton, *op cit.*, p. 841.

the arts. Styles in art, they declared, along with religious beliefs and practices, philosophic theories, standards of taste and value, educational and other institutions, all constitute a superstructure on the economic basis.[9] Aesthetic theories, rules and principles of art, express the interests of one class or another, usually the ruling one, whether consciously so or not. Disputes over them can not be settled in a purely logical way, but only through the superior power of those who advocate certain ones. The rise and fall of competing styles in art and theories in aesthetics are all parts of the inclusive dialectical process.

People's thoughts and desires in all realms are shaped largely by their relation to this basic system; either as members or hangers-on of the élite, exploiting class or as exploited workers. The resultant modes of thought and feeling constitute their ideology. It is never purely rational, even when it seems so. Its relation to the economic basis is largely unrealized at the time. People are usually not aware of the system they live in as one of many possible systems; they tend to take the status quo for granted. Unconsciously, people's religious beliefs and artistic productions, even their theories on abstruse philosophic and scientific topics, tend to express their satisfaction with the status quo and wish to strengthen it, or else their dissatisfaction and desire to escape or destroy it. Exploited workers, according to the theory, are often deluded by religious opiates into accepting the social system on the ground that it has been divinely ordained and that all will be made up to them in the next world.

Marxism emphasizes the role of environment, especially the socio-economic environment, in determining the main characteristics of art. Changes in it, as in the case of a revolution which redistributes wealth and power, tend to change all forms of cultural expression. The type and quality of art at any time are not due to supernatural inspiration or to innate racial superiority. Social conditions can provide themes and general directions to art, but there is always room for individual variation. They do not determine the specific details of a period or individual style. The precise ways in which genius will treat common themes can not be predicted or explained by purely socio-economic factors. But social conditions can release and inspire creativity, or the opposite.

All the arts may join, according to Marxists, in expressing the basic assumptions and attitudes which arise from the prevailing system of ownership and power. Ideas, stories, pictures, plays, customs, educational methods, and the like which tend to threaten or discredit the present system are liable to be suppressed or discouraged, while rewards go to those which strengthen the régime. In highly educated societies, there is a demand for intellectual, moral, and aesthetic means of doing so, and capable minds are thus drawn into the service of the ruling class without fully realizing it. Even the oppressed proletariat may do so through having been indoctrinated into a docile acceptance of the established ideology. Even those artists and thinkers who seem most radical, denouncing evils and calling for reform, are more or less determined by the economic conditions under which they grew up. Often they denounce imaginary evils and condone or ignore the real, social causes of human unhappiness, crime, poverty, and war. They mean well, and may have the interests of the poor and oppressed at heart; but their efforts are usually frustrated by lack of understanding, and any revolutionary movements they may try to inspire are turned off by the ruling class into ineffectual bypaths.

Culture as well as material wealth accumulates from one generation to the next, say the Marxists, especially in utilitarian techniques. In these, especially the techniques of production and commerce, there has been a fairly steady and accel-

[9] "Between the economic relationships and the styles of art," says Meyer Schapiro (interpreting Marx), "intervenes the process of ideological construction, a complex imaginative transposition of class roles and needs, which affects the special field—religion, mythology, or civil life—that provides the chief themes of art" ("Style," in *Anthropology Today*, ed. A. L. Kroeber [Chicago, 1953], p. 311).

erating progress. Those of the fine arts are not radically different; they arise largely from economic and related occupations, and serve social needs. Particular works of art, styles, rules, techniques, and theories of value are transmitted as parts of cultural evolution. But art does not show a perfectly continuous evolution, according to Marxist theory. To a large extent, it develops at each stage out of the prevailing conditions of ownership and power. When there is a new economic basis, with a new class in power, new types of art develop on it as a superstructure, instead of evolving directly out of previous styles. But art and ideas at any time contain surviving vestiges from the past as well as contemporary developments. Veneration for the past as well as current vested interests in its perpetuation may cause art to glorify ideas and attitudes more characteristic of some earlier social stage, such as Gothic architecture in modern churches. But in time, if the culture is prosperous and dynamic, a new ideology will emerge and find new forms of expression in art. Old forms of art, handed down from a previous or dying economic system, tend to become perfunctory, formalistic, and lifeless. A decadent phase of art may ensue until the control and use of wealth are taken over, suddenly or gradually, by the rising class. Extreme preoccupation with form and technique, including the ideal of art-for-art's-sake, is a sign of such decadence. Healthy art is always derived from basic utilitarian concerns and other realities of social life; it serves wide human needs. Hence the artist is respected and self-respecting in a socialist state as one who fulfills a valuable social function. The great expansion of prosperity, science, and art resulting from the early success of capitalism is now ending, say contemporary Marxists. Capitalist art is decadent, they insist, and only a workers' revolution can produce a new healthy rebirth of vigor.

On the other hand, Marx and Lenin warned against excessive belittling of past art merely because it is old or expresses a different social attitude. "We must retain the beautiful," said Lenin, "take it as an example, hold on to it even though it is old." Past cultural advances must be retained. We must understand "that only by an exact knowledge of the culture created by the whole development of mankind, that only by reworking this culture, is it possible to build proletarian culture."[10] Marx and Engels emphasized that purely didactic, obviously propagandist art is dull and ineffective. Art must have vitality, imagination, form, and skill. They admired many artists of the past who served or acquiesced in an unjust social order, for expressing the ideology of the time successfully or for expressing humanitarian ideals of permanent validity.

Art, along with religion and education, is regarded by the modern Marxist as one of the most powerful means of indoctrinating both masses and élite; for influencing their minds and emotions so as to accept and approve a certain social system or, in times of revolution, to rise up against it. Marxism is far from treating art condescendingly, as capitalism often does, as a mere amusement or surface decoration. It does not regard the artist under communism as an oddity or clown. However, the artist is not to be allowed complete freedom to express himself individually. In the communist state, he must express positive sentiments in support of working-class ideals and of the new, classless society which is to emerge. He must submit to the discipline of the party and the workers' government.

3. THE MARXIST APPROACH
AS COMPARED WITH THE FREUDIAN

Marxist theoreticians have analyzed a number of artists and period styles, especially in literature, so as to bring out their significance in the dialectic of history and in the class hierarchy of the times in which they lived. Like psychoanalysis, Marxism

10 *Selected Works*, Vol. IX, pp. 470, 471. Quoted by Somerville, *op. cit.*, p. 128.

leads the historian and critic to look beneath the surface of their obvious forms and literal meanings for deeper causes and hidden motivations, of which the artist and his public may be largely unaware at the time. Various types of subject-matter and function, of representation or the lack of it, varieties of plot, character, and situation, techniques and decorative qualities, all come to be regarded by the critic as more or less unrealized symbols of these underlying factors.

There is, however, a great difference in the two theories as to the nature of these supposedly underlying factors; hence as to the motivation and the hidden significance of art. It is not surprising, then, that their adherents have, on the whole, regarded each other with hostility, even though the two theories are not entirely contradictory. Each points to certain real causal factors in the determination of art, but neither tells the whole story. Psychoanalysis tends to minimize socio-economic variations and to stress certain well-nigh universal conflicts within the human psyche, or between it and civilization in general. Where the extreme Freudian looks in art for symbols of unconscious sexual repression, for Oedipus and other conflicts in the individual and group, the extreme Marxist looks for expressions of economic interest and class ideology. He looks in art for expressions, conscious or unconscious, clear or cryptic, of attitudes determined by the status and socio-economic role of the artist and his patrons. He implies that, once these are pointed out, the historical causation and main present importance of the artist and his work have been, to a large extent, explained. Artists of all periods have been praised, by some Marxist critics, in proportion as they seem to express a proletarian attitude of sympathy for the poor and downtrodden, with resentment toward the upper classes; in other words, for being "socialists before their time" if born before the age of Marx.

4. PLEKHANOV AND HIS CRITICS

The heavy, almost exclusive emphasis on the class struggle in explaining the cause and significance of art is exemplified by the writings of G. V. Plekhanov (1873–1918).[11] Such extreme oversimplification, implied by the overemphasis on economic factors as if they were the only influential ones, is more characteristic of some later Marxists than of Marx and Engels themselves. Engels admitted that he and Marx had at first overemphasized the economic factor, for polemic reasons. "Marx and I are ourselves partly to blame for the fact that the younger people sometimes lay more stress on the economic side than is due to it. We had to emphasize the main principle vis-à-vis our adversaries, who denied it."[12] While still insisting that the material mode of existence is the *primum agens*, Engels added that "this does not preclude the ideological spheres from reacting upon it in their turn, though with a secondary effect." Commenting on the French "Marxists" of the seventies, he continued, Marx used to say, "All I know is that I am not a Marxist." All history "must be studied afresh," Engels declared; not constructed into a neat system by dogmatic deduction on the basis of scanty historical knowledge. In addition to the material basis, the various elements of the cultural superstructure "also exercise their influence upon the course of the historical struggles and in many cases preponderate in determining their *form*." (Their content also, one might add, since local traditions and environment contribute to the subject-matter and functions of art.) There is an interaction of all these elements, said Engels, and "an endless host of accidents."

This is a moderate statement and, if accepted

[11] *Essays in the History of Materialism* (London, 1934): *Art and Social Life* (London, 1953). In the introduction to the latter book, he is called "the first Russian to apply the Marxist method to the study of aesthetics and the origins of art, to literature and to literary criticism." He began this work in the eighties.

[12] Letters to Conrad Schmidt (1890), Joseph Bloch, (1890), Franz Mehring (1893), and Heinz Starkenburg (1894), in L. S. Feuer (ed.), *Marx and Engels, Basic Writings on Politics and Philosophy*, pp. 395–412. *Cf.* Harap, *op. cit.*, pp. 10–11.

by present communist theoreticians, would go far toward making the Marxist view of art history acceptable in Western eyes. It retains Marx's essential contribution, but moves substantially toward the pluralism of Taine.

Soon after the Russian Revolution, a reaction began against extreme interpretations of the Marxist canon, together with other exaggerations of the sociological approach by non-communist writers. These were branded as "vulgar sociologism" by Mikhail Lifshitz, quoting Lenin for support.[13] He attacked Plekhanov and the current view that "Literature is an imaginative form of class consciousness... expressing itself by means of verbal images." He stressed instead "the basic historic fact that art and literature are a reflection of external reality, or a mirror of objective, all-sided human practice." Lifshitz did not deny the relationship between art and the class struggle or the importance of analyzing art in terms of social classes. He pointed out that the class situation is always an important part of the objective reality which the capable artist represents. Lenin's essays on Tolstoy were praised as examples of the best approach, in which the artist's greatness was recognized along with his social limitations. Tolstoy's art, according to Lenin, reflected the social reality of his time while his conscious philosophy and moral preachments misinterpreted it. (Marx had said much the same about Balzac.)[14] In 1954, after Stalin's death, there was a temporary relaxation of artistic censorship, and a little more recognition (at least in theory) of the diversity of factors which determine style and value.[15] But the basic, Marxist conception of art history was not abandoned or fundamentally changed; the difference was one of degree.

In evaluating art, in supporting the approved types and censoring the disapproved, present Marxist policy still strongly favors that which is (a) realistic in representation and (b) sympathetic to both the working class and the communist régime, their interests being assumed as identical. In visual representation, such as painting, this implies that scenes are to be shown more or less as they appear

to the eye, in accordance with Western traditions of perspective, coloring, and modeling since the Renaissance. In fiction and theater, it means that characters, classes, social systems, historical events and situations are to be depicted in accordance with the current Soviet conception of the facts. Persons typifying the régime tend to be idealized. Art presenting a radically different conception of the facts, and hence of realism, is not encouraged. (Pasternak's *Dr. Zhivago* is an example.)[16] Nor is free discussion or free intellectual dialectic encouraged as a means of discovering the facts, except in limited realms of technology where social theory is not directly involved. Free fantasy, expressionist distortions (except in approved types of caricature), and experiments in post-impressionist design or abstract form are not ordinarily encouraged. Exceptions are made in the case of approved versions of the folklore of Soviet peoples (e.g., as themes for ballet), folk art in costume and dance, and the like. Twentieth-century Western pessimism is discouraged and the "positive hero" is praised.[17]

[13] "Leninist Criticism," in *Literature and Marxism: a Controversy by Soviet Critics*, ed. Angel Flores (Critics Group Series, No. 9, New York). Cited by Somerville, *op. cit.*, pp. 118–119.

[14] K. Marx, "Letter to Margaret Harkness, April 1888." Reprinted in *Literature and Art by Karl Marx and Frederick Engels* (New York, 1947), pp. 41 f.

[15] A. A. Zhdanov is cited as "an extreme advocate of the subservience of culture to party doctrine" by Vincas Trumpa in "Literature and Art in the Snares of Socialist Realism" (*Lituanus*, V, 3, [Sept. 1959], 81). Zhdanov's concept of socialist realism was officially adopted at the First Congress of Soviet Writers in 1934. Accordingly, every writer was to portray reality accurately and historically in its revolutionary development and contribute to the ideological transformation of the working masses. This rule was deleted from the bylaws at the Second Congress in 1954 but restored at the Third. "To write truly," said M. Gus after that step, "means to express the objective tendencies in the development of reality. Therefore our communist tendentiousness is a higher and the only true form of objectivity" (*Znamia* [The Banner], 1959, No. 3). This thesis, says Trumpa, is based on "a blind faith in the Marxist-Leninist doctrine on tendencies in history."

[16] Successive writers' congresses have taken somewhat different positions on the extent to which "socialist realism" is to be enforced. After a brief relaxation, a stricter policy was again recommended.

[17] *Cf.* T. Munro, "The Failure Story: a Study of Contemporary Pessimism," *Journal of Aesthetics and Art Criticism*, XVII, 2 & 3 (Dec. 1958 & Mar. 1959), 143–168, 362–387. Also R. W.

Twentieth-century experiments in pure visual and musical form (as in some works of Kandinsky and Shostakovich) have been denounced as "decadent formalism" and "escape from social reality."[18]

5. STRONG AND WEAK POINTS IN THE MARXIST AND RELATED METHODS. RECENT CONTROVERSIES

It was noted at the beginning of this chapter that socio-economic factors are receiving more and more consideration by Western art historians, most of whom are opposed to Marxism and communism in general. Following Thorstein Veblen, with his principles of "conspicuous waste and vicarious expenditure," a number of American writers have discussed the popular arts—especially automobiles and women's fashions—as symbols of the desire for social status in a competitive, mobile society. Films, newspaper comic strips, and popular fiction have been extensively analyzed from both the psychoanalytic and the sociological standpoints. To the non-communist, it seems that Soviet writers are slow (for obvious reasons) to apply such interpretation to their own arts. Soviet society is not entirely classless in practice, but is developing its own bureaucracy and status symbols in the form of uniforms, orders, medals, automobiles, country houses, and other differential privileges. The restriction of painting and literature to certain approved, conservative types requires force to hold back the continuing dialectic of change.

The single-minded devotion of strictly Marxist writers to one explanatory principle has enabled them to work out imposing systems of historical interpretation. By contrast, their opponents often seem content to pile up unrelated facts and generalizations of narrow scope. Much of what non-Marxist scholars have to say about art is concerned with isolated situations; it does not combine into an integrated body of knowledge and interpretation. As Meyer Schapiro comments, "Marxist

writers are among the few who have tried to apply a general theory... The great interest of the Marxist approach lies not only in the attempt to interpret the historically changing relations of art and economic life in the light of a general theory of society but also in the weight given to the differences and conflicts within the social group as motors of development, and to the effects of these on outlook, religion, morality, and philosophical ideas."[19]

A deterministic theory of history is not necessarily false or unsound. Especially when naturalistic in orientation, it is a tenable though not a provable hypothesis. *Ex post facto*, it is easy to look through history and declare, as to everything that has happened, that it *had* to happen so. Given a certain total configuration of events and conditions at any one moment, it can be argued that those of the next are predetermined. But from such generalities and from our limited knowledge of the facts at any one moment, it is not so easy to predict just what is going to happen next. The main trend of events often takes surprising turns. Occasional successes tend to blind us to our failures in such prophecy. For explaining past events, a broad, general determinism makes us little the wiser.

Marxism, like some other varieties of historical determinism, attempts more specific explanations and predictions. This it does (a) by selecting economic factors as the basic, primary determinants, and (b) by applying the dialectical formula. Each of these works successfully to some extent and in some situations. There are cases in which a knowledge of the socio-economic factors contributes much to an understanding of cultural events, and sometimes to their conjectural prediction and control. Here one welcomes the sociological approach

Mathewson, *The Positive Hero in Russian Literature* (New York, 1958).

[18] Realism, says Pierre de Boisdeffre, "expresses the will to live of a growing society; symbolism and abstraction, on the contrary are characteristic of a society lacking in self-confidence." (*Une Histoire vivante de la littérature d'aujourdhui*, p. 736. Quoted by V. Trumpa, *loc. cit.*).

[19] "Style" in *Anthropology Today*, p. 311.

as significant and enlightening. But there are others on which it seems to throw little or no light: e.g., on the subtle but important differences between contemporary artists in the same environment. This is especially true in twentieth-century art, where wide, experimental swings of style often have no obvious connection with the artist's economic or social background. Then one tends to feel the Marxist insistence on this aspect of the problem as oversimplified and ineffective; hence a tendency to drag it in seems doctrinaire and partisan.

While the general theory of socio-economic influence on art can be stated moderately enough to achieve wide acceptance, its application in explaining particular types of art is often far-fetched and unconvincing to non-Marxist scholars. This may consist of nothing more than a series of dogmatic assertions, to the effect that certain types of art are obviously "due to" certain social conditions, or that they "express" an aristocratic or a bourgeois mentality. Sometimes this is plausible, as in Plekhanov's explanation of Boucher's paintings as due to the idle luxury of the old régime; but, even so, is this the *whole* explanation? What of previous traditions in painting and sculpture? At other times, the explanation seems even more inadequate, as in Hauser's attempt to explain the rise of individualized characterization in late Gothic literature. "The real incentive of psychological observation," he says, "comes from the fact that knowledge of human nature, the correct psychological assessment of one's business partner, is among the most essential requisites of the merchant."[20] In this case, as Richard Wollheim comments, "the psychological interpretation is obviously strained."[21]

To be convincing, the argument must show that the social condition would be sufficient to produce a psychological attitude favorable to the kind of art which ensued, and that such an attitude would not have arisen without this condition. It should also show that no other factors, existing at the time, would have sufficed to produce it. The psychological intermediary is necessary, since eco-

nomic factors can not act directly on art; they must do so through human attitudes, feelings, beliefs, and desires. To prove a close causal connection between social event A and artistic event B, one should (ideally) be able to show that A is always followed by B, that B is always preceded by A, and that B is not so correlated with any other factor. This has certainly not been shown with any exactness and would be impossible in our present state of knowledge. Too many variables are involved, many of them inaccessible to observation, and history presents too few exact recurrences. This difficulty has led some philosophers to the opposite extreme of concluding that historical explanation can never be scientific; that history is at the opposite pole from science.

This attitude may become a purely negative, sterile skepticism. As against it, the Marxist approach has a positive daring and vigor which can not be lightly dismissed with a few detailed corrections. Sociological explanations have not been disproved; they are usually inadequate and prejudiced, but deserve more thorough testing. Granting that logical proof and scientific measurement are impossible in most historical explanation, it is still possible to build up an increasing stock of reasonable, tentative explanations. If more and more apparently significant connections between socio-economic and artistic trends are found, while those of art with other trends are not, the sociological approach will be correspondingly strengthened.

The dialectical principle is oversimplified whenever the historical process is reduced to a conflict between two and only two alleged opposites, or when a cultural synthesis is reduced to two and only two constituents. Every social, cultural, and artistic situation involves many factors: some mutually opposed, some reinforcing, some mixed or variable. Any historical "thesis," any particular socio-economic order, any positive affirmation in

[20] *Social History of Art*, Vol. I, p. 262.
[21] "Sociological Explanation of the Arts: Some Distinctions," *Proceedings of the Third International Congress on Aesthetics* (Torino, Italy [1957], p. 409).

art or philosophy, can have more than one alternative or partial opposite.[22] The Marxist explanation fails as a device for explanation or prediction when it ignores the multitude of possible reactions to any given cultural situation. Assuming the disappearance of old-fashioned, laissez-faire capitalism, there are many possible successors to it other than extreme communism. Given the decline of impressionist painting, or of all the styles of art which flourished under nineteenth-century capitalism, there are many possible successors to them. No one so far, with the aid of any formula, has been able to predict future styles in the major fine arts with specific accuracy. There is no absolute law on which prediction can be based. Perhaps, by combining many lines of research, prediction as well as explanation in this field can be gradually made more reliable.[23] To predict with increasing reliability in the field of art, as is now done in regard to the weather and to business cycles, one would have to know more and more about all the main factors involved. The socio-economic would be among these, but not necessarily the most enlightening as to immediate probabilities. Much would depend, as in economics, on whether the process was centrally controlled or allowed to run a comparatively free course.

We are not concerned in the present discussion with the correctness of Marxist evaluations of art or the rightness of the policies and standards on which they are based. But they imply certain dubious assumptions about the facts of art history and their causes which are relevant to our study. It is by no means an established fact that pessimistic, non-realistic, and abstract styles of art are necessarily due to "the decadence of the capitalistic system" or that they necessarily express a bourgeois ideology. Both might flourish also under communism if not forcibly restrained. They do, to some extent, in communist Poland and Jugoslavia. On the other hand, they are not universal under present capitalism. Both may also express deeper psychological motivations, not bound up with any one socio-economic system. Communism has not entirely eliminated the causes of human unhappiness, and no social system can do so. Pessimism as a "tragic sense of life" is to some extent a perennial protest against the inevitable disappointments and frustrations of life in animal bodies on this planet, wherein man's wishes and ideals reach far ahead of his potential attainment under any social order. Some individuals are always less gifted, mentally and physically, than others. Old age and death come to communists and capitalists alike.

Formalism, decorative design, and abstractionism in art may express a negative "escape from reality" or, on the other hand, a positive, technological interest in the psychological effects of various types of artistic form, including visual design and individual, emotional expression. As free experiment with physical and chemical devices can benefit people in all classes and in any type of social order, so can free experiment with the forms and techniques of the arts. Further relaxations of control and tension in the communist sphere will probably release a new wave of experimentation and diversification in the arts, including some types now decried as "formalistic" or "pessimistic." As in the case of physical science, ways will doubtless be found to argue that they are consistent with the general communist policy of technological development, and that they are logical continuations of the historical process.

To Western scholars, it seems that Marxist critics greatly oversimplify history and overemphasize the class struggle as an influence on art. The consensus of historians and sociologists outside the

[22] "To be dialectically deterministic," remarks F. S. C. Northrop, "the negation of a thesis in time must generate one and only one antithesis. The negation of a given thesis, however, does not give rise to one and only one antithesis. One can negate the basic legal norms of the Holy Roman Empire in many different ways." Therefore, he adds, a cultural evolution which is dialectical cannot be genuinely deterministic ("Cultural Values," in *Anthropology Today*, p. 677).

[23] Karl R. Popper has attacked the Marxist and other "historicist" theories as claiming, without justification, that future trends can be scientifically predicted on the basis of laws and patterns in history. *The Poverty of Historicism* (London, 1957). Reprinted in P. Gardiner, *Theories of History* (Glencoe, Ill., 1959).

EVOLUTION IN THE ARTS

communist world would be that socio-economic factors are undoubtedly of great importance and sometimes decisive; that they are often but not always the fundamentally determining ones; that influence flows in the opposite direction also, from biological heredity and various cultural factors into the formation and change of socio-economic patterns. While the sociological approach is revealing and enlightening, it is not the only fruitful one. Not everything, especially in art, can be explained by this means. It tends to neglect those aspects of art which spring from human nature in general and from man's universal occupations and interests, rather than from his role in a certain social order. It tends to neglect individual differences, the more distinctive aspects of personality, which are (as Marx himself recognized) highly important in art and not to be explained entirely in social terms.[24] It tends to neglect the inner momentum of stylistic change within a certain art along a certain line of development or regression; the direct influence of artistic traditions on later art. Discerning Marxist historians do not ignore these phenomena, but they often underestimate them as causal factors in their own right, through attributing too much to economic causes.

Historical research, while confirming many sociological interpretations of art, also shows that very different arts and tastes can emerge from fairly similar socio-economic conditions, and similar ones from very different conditions. There is no exact correlation between artistic and socio-economic change. Other factors obviously enter and in some cases "preponderate," as Engels re-marked. What are they, and in what relative strength do they interact? Variably, of course, and their relative strength can be only roughly estimated. Much detailed comparison of different art epochs and their social backgrounds is needed at this point, including the study of oriental styles.

For an adequate theory of causation in the history of art, it is necessary to combine the socio-economic approach with the biological, psychological, and others, including the morphological analysis of styles and the history of stylistic diffusion. Extreme Marxists belittle such a view as eclectic and confused; a bourgeois misunderstanding of the historical process, perhaps arising from a concealed desire to perpetuate capitalism. This is denied by Western cultural historians, who defend their pluralism as necessitated by an open-minded survey of the facts. At the same time, they are looking with increased respect at the sociological approach as a tool of historical research.

This approach, in the broad sense not restricted to Marxism, is one important hypothesis among others. It is a program of inquiry and a device for partial explanation; not a dogma or a means of sufficient explanation. As a hypothesis, it implies a partial but limited socio-economic determinism. It is a belief that modes of production and distribution, especially the control of wealth and material power, exert an influence on art which is strong and far-reaching but not all-controlling, and not necessarily decisive in particular situations.

[24] Arnold Hauser maintains that "There is simply no other explanation of stylistic change but a sociological or psychological explanation" (*The Philosophy of Art History*, p. 258).

CHAPTER VIII

TAINE'S THEORY
OF THE DETERMINING FACTORS
IN ART HISTORY

I. COMMON MISUNDERSTANDINGS
OF HIS THEORY.
HIS CONTRIBUTION TO AESTHETICS
AND THE PHILOSOPHY OF HISTORY

Taine's theory of evolution in art was narrower in scope than Herbert Spencer's, but dealt with a crucial problem which Spencer had left almost unanswered. Spencer's vision had encompassed the whole, vast process of cosmic evolution, in which the history of art was but a small, recent chapter. Taine's was focused on the question of what causes the arts of different peoples to develop along different lines. This led him to a general theory of the determining factors in cultural history.

Spencer had been content, for the most part, to demonstrate the *fact* of evolution: how the arts exemplified the "universal law" of increasing complexity. He threw little new light on *why* they had done so: through what specific agencies or mechanisms. He had emphasized the uniformities in art history: how all the arts, in all periods and peoples, had obeyed the same cosmic law; hence he paid little attention to the diversities in art among different peoples. Taine's theory was more multilinear. Like the Marxists, he tried to fill in and strengthen the naturalistic account of cultural evolution by explaining its causal mechanism. His explanation was similar to theirs in some respects, but more pluralistic. Like them, he had little interest in the cosmic process or in the pre-human evolution of life, but much in civilization and its divergences. More than Marx, Engels, or Spencer, Taine sought to analyze and explain the growth of distinctive styles of art.

Like Spencer, Hippolyte Taine has been attacked and misrepresented by opponents of naturalism and evolutionism in aesthetics and cultural history. He has been falsely charged with trying to reduce all environmental influence to that of climate,[1] whereas he made it abundantly clear that physical climate is only one of many factors in the *milieu*. He laid more emphasis on the psychological or cultural "climate" in which a style of art arises. It is also untrue that he attributed everything to environment, for he also emphasized heredity. Like most other French and English aestheticians, Taine is commonly underestimated by scholars under the influence of German idealistic philosophy, who belittle him as a mere empiricist or naturalist.[2]

[1] *E.g.*, in R. H. Stoddard's Preface to the English translation of Taine's *History of English Literature* (trans. H. Van Laun, New York, 1891). It was H. T. Buckle, in his *History of Civilization in England* (London, 1857–62), rather than Taine, who put extreme emphasis on geographic and climatic factors. *Cf.* M. Cohen, *The Meaning of Human History* (La Salle, Ill., 1947), Ch. 5, "The Geographic Factor in History."

[2] The common misrepresentation of Taine's work is exemplified in K. Gilbert and H. Kuhn, *A History of Esthetic* (Bloomington, Ind., 1953), p. 479. "Taine goes a step further," they say, "urging that the work of art is a product of its environment

Taine's influence on succeeding generations in aesthetics, criticism, sociology, and cultural history has been strong and far-reaching, but largely unacknowledged. As it often happens, those who wrote about him have chosen to emphasize his mistakes and limitations. Those who followed his lead have often done so without realizing it, being more preoccupied with new empirical research than with giving credit to past thinkers. The "sociological approach" to art history and criticism, for which most of the credit (or blame) is now given to the Marxists, springs quite as much from Taine as from Marx and Engels. His moderation and pluralism have tended to make his ideas less dramatic than those of many extremists.[3]

One of the principal arguments against Taine's theory in his own day was that he neglected the importance of the individual personality; that the genius of the artist was lost from sight through "reducing art to social and environmental factors."[4] This same charge was brought by supernaturalists against all cultural evolutionism and all attempts at scientific aesthetics. It has been carried to extremes in the attempt to portray all art as due to individual genius, divinely inspired. But it is not wholly unjustified in Taine's case. In emphasizing social aspects, he did neglect the individual somewhat. Later theories have tried to deal fairly with both on a scientific basis. They recognize the unique aspects of the individual artist as well as those he has in common with his group. Even the "unique" ones are found to be affected by social and environmental factors. Taine gave some recognition to the importance of great artists and their subtle differences in style. But in his time the chief need was for more attention to the larger social and cultural processes. The role of individual genius had long been overstressed by romantic philosophers and artists.

Taine's analyses of style in painting have since been overshadowed by the more intensive analyses of visual style in German *Kunstwissenschaft*, as in the works of Fiedler, Riegl, and Wölfflin. His theories of racial and national psychology have been largely superseded by later research in anthropology and sociology. This is the way of science; but it should not involve excessive belittling of the pioneers. Taine was a pioneer in the scientific, naturalistic approach to both these fields. Far more than Fechner, whose chief work did not appear until 1876, Taine deserves the credit for initiating the scientific movement in aesthetics.[5] His approach was much broader, more socially and historically minded, whereas Fechner's was largely focused on individual taste, with a premature attempt at quantitative measurement. Marxist theoreticians berated Taine as eclectic and superficial because of his pluralism; he had not, they said, sufficiently emphasized the socio-economic factor.

Taine's pluralism in causal explanation is modern in avoiding the more rigid, unilinear types of historical determinism. It indicates a wide range of variable factors, including the physical, biological, psychological, social, and cultural. It allows for their interaction in various ways and with different relative strength at different times. Thus it avoids the mistake which so many philosophers of history have made: that of attributing the course of history wholly or mainly to some single factor or supposed law. It avoids the overly simple method, still common among art historians, of attributing all innovations to the individual artist plus the influence of his immediate predecessors in the same art. Taine offers no single, simple formula. At the same time, he avoids the opposite weakness, more common today, of evading the

and nothing else." Taine is absurdly underestimated also by B. Croce (*Aesthetic*, Ch. XVII) and by Lionello Venturi, an Italian historian strongly influenced by German idealism, in *History of Art Criticism* (New York, 1936), pp. 229 f.

[3] For a fair and informative summary of his influence, see Sholom J. Kahn's *Science and Aesthetic Judgment: a Study in Taine's Critical Method* (London, 1953): especially Ch. XIV, "Our Heritage from Taine."

[4] *Cf.* H. A. Needham, *Le développement de l'esthétique sociologique* (Paris, 1926), p. 219, citing critiques of Taine by P. Rousselot, G. Barzellotti, and C. Péladan.

[5] See Listowel, *A Critical History of Modern Aesthetics* (London, 1933), p. 109. But Gilbert and Kuhn say with approval, "The book generally considered to mark the beginning of the new science was Fechner's *Vorschule der Ästhetik*..."

whole problem of historical causation and thus suggesting a complete, skeptical indeterminism. All events have their causes, in Taine's view. The general types of cause are not infinite in number. They can be classed in a few main groups, each capable of specialized investigation. Their interaction is diverse in different periods and cultures, but not so completely diverse as to prevent all scientific generalization.

Taine's life, from 1828 to 1893, overlapped the lives of Malthus, Lyell, Darwin, Spencer, Huxley, Marx, and Engels. Emile Zola (1840–1902) wrote of him with respect and acknowledged his influence; he applied Taine's sociological approach in portraying fictional characters within the grip of a social milieu. As a youth, Taine eagerly read Hegel, who stimulated him toward a philosophical, historical view of things. He has been called "basically a Hegelian."[6] But, like Marx, Taine soon outgrew the Hegelian influence.[7]

His mature works are naturalistic and empirical, with little trace of metaphysical idealism or dualism. His theory of causation is naturalistic, as contrasted with supernaturalist theories since Plato, in that it does not rely upon divine inspiration or a cosmic mind or will as an explanation of events in art. Taine is concerned with natural, phenomenal causes and effects, open to empirical study by science. Like Spencer, he does not speculate on first causes or ultimate realities. Although he groups his types of cause under three main headings, each comprises a multitude of different variables.

2. VARIATION AND ENVIRONMENTAL SELECTION IN ART.
THE PSYCHOLOGICAL CLIMATE

Taine received little direct influence from Comte, Spencer, or Darwin; but positivism and "social Darwinism" were in the air and his writing was permeated with both. Early in the important "In-troduction"[8] to his *History of English Literature*, where his key ideas are concisely formulated, was a reference to Darwin's *Origin of Species*. It was followed by one of many comparisons which he made between organic life and national character. Both, he declared, are affected by environment in developing specific needs, activities, habits, and aptitudes. In the *Lectures on Art*,[9] he went on to apply the principle of natural selection to the arts. Temperature and physical circumstances make a choice, he said, amongst various species of trees, allowing some to propagate and excluding others; they act "by natural selection... a law as applicable to moral as to physical conditions, to history as well as to botany and zoology, to genius and to character, as well as to plant and animal." It operates through a "moral temperature," consisting of the general state of minds and manners, and sometimes called the "spirit of the age," which selects "among different species of talent, allowing only this or that species to develop, to the exclusion more or less complete of others." It does not produce artists, for talent and genius are like seeds. A country will probably produce at different times about the same number of potential

6 R. Wellek, "Hippolyte Taine's Literary Theory and Criticism" (*Criticism*, Winter 1959), p. 11. Plekhanov also called him "an idealist in his conception of history" because he said that "history is a problem of psychology." *Essays in the History of Materialism* (London, 1934), p. 235. This ignores the fact that psychology can itself be conceived in a naturalistic way, and that it was so conceived by Taine in his mature works. It also ignores the psychological basis of socio-economic behavior. Plekhanov has been criticized by other Marxists for underestimating psychological factors in the milieu. Taine was rather an empiricist or positivist than a materialist. "I am so little a materialist that in my eyes the physical world is nothing but appearance." (Quoted by Wellek, p. 9).

7 See Sholom J. Kahn, *op. cit.*, pp. 24 f., 222. Taine "had serious reservations when he first read the German thinker," and was basically more in accord with Spinoza. "By 25 February, 1852, the disillusion with Hegel was complete." Taine then wrote, "Alas! another illusion destroyed!" From Spinoza, it seems, Taine derived his hope of reconciling descriptive science with a hierarchy of values; material with mental activity.

8 P. 18. The "Introduction" was first published as an article, "L'histoire, son présent et son avenir," in December 1863. The *History* itself was originally published in 1863–4.

9 (Trans. J. Durand, New York, 1875). Contains *The Philosophy of Art* and other series in two volumes.

talents; but a different proportion and different varieties of these will develop according to the prevailing psychological environment.

Along with this cultural Darwinism, Taine found room (as Spencer had done) for the Lamarckian principle. Man's character, adapted to his circumstances, becomes more stable in proportion as the external impression is made upon him by numerous repetitions, "and is transmitted to his progeny by a more ancient descent." At any moment, the character of a people is "an abridgement of all its preceding actions and sensations."[10]

Taine was not much interested in the Spencerian problem of whether art history as a whole was a process of increasing complexity. He was much more interested in the development of national styles and art-producing groups. But he defined a masterpiece of art along somewhat Spencerian lines as "that in which the greatest force receives the greatest development."[11] Taine did not attempt, as many evolutionary theorists have done, to establish a universal sequence of stages in art as a whole. His interest was usually focused on the development of particular schools of art, and he saw these as following evolutionary principles. In each, he emphasized a repetitive cycle of short stages from primitive through mature to decadent. He sought to show that in Greek, Dutch, Italian, and English art distinctive styles had arisen, each from a distinctive character.

In conceiving history mainly in terms of divergent racial or national groups, each with a distinct psychological character, Taine's theory was more multilinear than the Marxist one. In his emphasis on the cyclical pattern of art history and on the distinctive, persistent character of each national civilization, Taine was starting on a line of thought which Spengler was to carry to extremes in the twentieth century. In Taine's account, however, there was none of Spengler's mystical vitalism or his rigidly monistic, immanent determinism. Taine and Spengler both oversimplified their accounts of the various ethnic cultures. They overestimated the constancy of character within a people and the

cultural differences among peoples. Both underestimated the extent of cumulative cultural development from one people and one civilization to the next.

Setting out to explain why different peoples have developed different kinds of art, and to do so without relying on the concept of an immanent spiritual force, Taine was drawn to look mainly in the environment of art for determining factors. Here he had to look for conditions which had differed notably from people to people, and which could be causally connected with the kind of art each one produced. Working backward from the national styles of art to find their causes, he found a direct, all-inclusive cause in the distinctive psychology or dominant, motivating character of each people. This is variously described as a "master faculty," a "moral temperature," a "particular system of inner impressions and operations," and as the "birth, growth, energy, and connection of ideas and emotions." It operates to provide a psychological environment which may be favorable to production in one art and one style of art but not in others. It is concretely expressed by each people in visual and literary representations of certain imaginary characters, such as the Greek athlete, Don Quixote, or Faust.

What Taine calls a "moral temperature" is somewhat analogous to what the Marxists call an "ideology." The modern concepts of "culture-pattern" and "value-system" also refer to related phenomena. Taine's concept is more concerned with race and nationality[12] than with socio-economic status.

[10] *History of English Literature*, p. 18.

[11] *The Ideal in Art*, p. 353. (*Lectures on Art*, Vol. I).

[12] National character in relation to art and taste was discussed in ancient and in modern times, notably by François Ogier in *Preface to Tyre and Sidon* (1628). See the quotation in B. H. Clark, *European Theories of the Drama* (New York, 1947), pp. 117 f.

3. RACE, ENVIRONMENT, AND MOMENT

What produces such a moral or psychic "climate"? It is traced back to three interacting factors: *race*, *milieu*, and *moment*. Each is rather a heterogeneous set of factors than a single one. They are roughly classed under these three names, but they overlap and interpenetrate. The whole psychological climate acts as part of the *milieu* of art, but it has its own environmental determinants also. "Moment" is not a distinct factor or set of factors, but a name for the particular way in which other factors organize and present themselves at any one time, thus exerting a peculiar, temporary influence.[13] In reality, there are only two sets of factors, which would be called today "heredity" and "environment." The importance of the concept of "moment" is to call attention to their ever-changing contents, forms, and trends: especially in the case of cultural environments.

At any time and place, the sum total of active, present factors will display a certain distinctive nature and transitory configuration. This is a *moment* in history. It is conceived as of indeterminate length and scope. It may be a brief epoch in a single art, such as "French tragedy under Corneille," by contrast with the same under Voltaire. It may "embrace one or more centuries, like the middle ages," in which "a certain dominant idea has held sway" throughout thought and action. Even though the physical and cultural *milieu* remains constant on the whole, the situation is very different just before and just after the work of a great artist. Just afterward, that work is part of the total, cumulative tradition which shapes an artist of the next generation. "One artist is the precursor, the other the successor; the first has no model, the second has; the first sees objects face to face, the second sees them through the first." Likewise with a major period of history: each is influenced by its predecessor. Moment is "the acquired momentum" of history. It is a name for the fact that race and environment operate at any one time, not on a *tabula rasa*, but "on a ground

on which marks are already impressed. According as one takes the ground at one moment or another, the imprint is different, and this causes the total effect to be different."

By the concept of moment, Taine called attention to the fact that a cultural environment which seems to be fairly stable and constant may change radically from year to year or day to day, as to its influence on art. Social moods, fashions, attitudes, may be short-lived but powerful while they last. Through this concept, Taine was reaching for the same historical insight which Marx and Engels expressed in terms of dialectic. This is, that the significance of any event or production, any individual or social trait, can not be fully grasped apart from its historical context. Likewise the value of a work of art, as great or trivial, is not an absolute rank above the shifting currents of history, but something to be estimated in relation (a) to its own contemporary situation, its users, predecessors and successors; what it achieved in its day, and (b) to our present situation, insofar as we consider using or enjoying it.

What Taine called a "moment" or "epoch" is close to what other philosophers of history have called a *Zeitgeist* or "spirit of the age." That term is too often meant and taken literally, as denoting a real entity in the supernatural sense, or a stage in

---

[13] In the idea that artistic talent is influenced by surroundings and epoch, Taine had been anticipated by the Abbé Dubos (1719), Madame de Staël, and Stendhal. Herder, V. Cousin, Guizot, H. Hallam, Sismondi, and Jouffroy had stressed the role of physical environment in political and literary history. The influence of the social environment on art had been emphasized by romantic critics such as L. de Bonald (*Réflexions critiques sur le beau moral*, 1807) and G. P. de Barante (*Tableau de la littérature française au XVIIIe siècle*, 1809). The latter declared that "literature is the expression of society," and always conforms to the nature of society. "Tel société, tel art," said Michelet. In 1838 L. Dussieux published *L'art considéré comme le symbole de l'état social, ou Tableau historique et synoptic du développement des beaux arts en France. Cf.* H. A. Needham, *op. cit.*, pp. 34–35, 108, 210; also T. Brunius, *Alexis de Tocqueville* (Uppsala, 1960). Taine developed this sociological approach into a more general systematic theory of the genesis of art. *Cf.* E. Grosse, *The Beginnings of Art* (New York, 1900), p. 12; K. Gilbert and H. Kuhn, *A History of Esthetic* (Bloomington, Ind., 1953), p. 278.

the unfolding of a cosmic mind. Taine's emancipation from Hegelian metaphysics is evident in his careful empiricism on this point. He claimed no more reality for the spirit of the age or "moral temperature" than can be observed in the actions and expressions of human beings, in art and otherwise. By the concept of moment he also called attention to the variable speed, momentum, and dynamic movement of historic process, as affecting each successive change. The "spirit of the age" is no static thing or condition.

Taine's emphasis on the temporary configuration among causal factors at any one moment is a valuable contribution to historical methodology. It indicates a line of research which is indispensable in any attempt to explain a complex event or process. Today it seems rather obvious, but it was not so at the time. We see now, for example, that what appears to parents and outsiders as a constant family environment may be radically different for the second child from what it was for the first, simply because he *is* the second child, with all the difference that implies from his point of view. We see that, to the artist who follows Giotto or Palestrina, the range of possibilities is very different from what it was for Giotto or Palestrina. They have opened certain paths that can be traveled farther, but at the same time they have closed others. To do what they did, however independently, will now be considered as mere imitation, to be unfavorably compared with the pioneer work. Giotto closed two doors, partly and temporarily. That is, he made it harder for a while to achieve greatness in either of two directions; (a) the Byzantine style, which he helped to put out of fashion; (2) the style of Giotto himself, which no one could repeat too closely without being an imitator. Masaccio found a third door. After Titian or Beethoven, it was hard for a young artist to find a new road to greatness. However unwillingly, he had to follow them in some respects, if only because they had covered so wide a range of what was possible in their time. If he tried too hard to avoid their influence, he might drift into

trivialities, blind alleys, or strained exaggerations.

What produces a historical moment? It results, says Taine, from the combined, previous interaction of race and environment; of innate, national character and surrounding circumstances. One must therefore analyze each of these into its components.

4. RACE AND HEREDITY
IN RELATION TO CULTURE

Taine's conception of *race* has been attacked as leading to the Nazi ideology which preceded World War II.[14] This is unjust, for it lacks the worst features of that ideology: the belief that one race is inherently superior to others, and that it has the right to rule over others by force. So strong has been the postwar reaction against "racism" that any emphasis on this term in a philosophy of history now seems obsolete and dangerous; but there is much in Taine's conception of it which has to be preserved under one name or another.

The important thing is to distinguish the valid elements from the obsolete. "What we call the race," he says, "are the innate and hereditary dispositions which man brings with him into the world, and which, as a rule, are united with the marked differences in the temperament and structure of the body." So far so good. But Taine goes on from this to an extreme and untenable theory of racial continuity. A race like the old Aryans, he says, after thirty centuries in every clime from the Ganges to the Hebrides, and passing through every stage of civilization and revolution, "nevertheless manifests in its languages, religions, literatures, and philosophies, the community of blood and of intellect which to this day binds its offshoots together. Different as they are, their parentage is

---

[14] On this point, see Wellek's defense of Taine, *op. cit.*, pp. 1–3. "Taine's race is simply the old *Volksgeist*, the genius of a nation."

not obliterated;... the great marks of the original model have remained." This statement exceeds the evidence, and is unacceptable today.

The traits which Taine classes under "race" include many which, today, would be classed as cultural rather than as hereditary. In approaching Dutch art, he begins with what he considers to be common characteristics of the Germanic race as opposed to the Latin. Some are physical and undoubtedly hereditary, such as a whiter skin, blue eyes, blond hair, large bodies, irregular features. They are not to be found in all Dutch and Germans, however. Taine exaggerates the resemblance of individuals in a given race or nationality. Some of the traits he mentions would now be classed as partly or wholly cultural, even if based on innate predisposition, such as a "voracious appetite for meat and drink" together with "sluggishness and torpidity of impressions and movements." The cold, damp climate, he remarks, contributes to such traits. "Huge white bodies," he says of the Saxons (in tracing the sources of English literature) "cool-blooded, with fierce blue eyes, reddish flaxen hair, ravenous stomachs, filled with meat and cheese, heated by strong drinks; of a cold temperament, slow to love, home-stayers, prone to brutal drunkenness: these are to this day the features which descent and climate preserve in the race, and these are what the Roman historians discovered in their former country."

In such a list of "racial" traits,[15] Taine sees no need to distinguish clearly between the innate and acquired, since, as a Lamarckian, he assumes that both can be organically transmitted. Today, of course, a scientific historian would insist on making that distinction, and he would not class as "racial" anything so strongly influenced by culture as eating habits. Nor would he, so casually, jump from "racial" to "national" traits as if there were little differences between them. The former are now described, so far as possible, in terms of innate, genetic transmission; the latter are essentially political and social even when they coincide to some extent with racial groupings.

Today, the idea that any significant connection exists between biological race and artistic or other cultural traits is now rejected by most geneticists and anthropologists. Any observable cultural differences between racial groups are usually attributed to environment, not heredity. This attitude is partly supported by empirical evidence, to show that there is little difference between the races as to innate predisposition for specific cultural traits and achievements; also to show that there is more such difference among individuals of the same race. But the evidence is not conclusive; there has been little controlled experimentation.

The present attitude toward race is partly a phenomenon of "moment"; it is a wave of reaction away from the Nazi overemphasis on race and on the myth of Nordic superiority. As such, it may have gone too far in influencing scientific beliefs. There is still a possibility that, along with racial differences in hair and skin, there may be at least a slight, organic predisposition toward certain lines of cultural development. Such a hypothesis does not necessarily imply any general superiority or inferiority. In the individual, a special aptitude for music is often based on measurable, physiological differences in auditory acuity and memory, and on the power to imagine sounds. There is nothing inherently impossible in the idea that certain clusters of such predispositions, organically based, have a slight correlation with racial differences, subject to wide individual variation. However, such an idea is purely speculative at the present time, and there is little or no empirical evidence to support it. The consensus of biologists, as reported by Julian Huxley, is that "cultural evolution in *Homo sapiens* is essentially independent of genetic differences between human subgroups or races."[16]

---

[15] *History of English Literature*, Vol. I, p. 41.

[16] In *Issues in Evolution*, ed. S. Tax (Chicago, 1960), p. 220. Clyde Kluckhohn commented on this that "Virtually all anthropologists would be in complete agreement with Huxley." In corroboration, see also Margaret Mead, "Cultural Determinants of Behavior," in A. Roe and G. G. Simpson, *Behavior and Evolution* (New Haven, Conn., 1958), p. 480.

Although Taine's theory of racial predisposition to specific culture-traits is now discredited, some of the other ideas which he set forth under the concept of race are more valid. Today, they are included in the general concept of heredity, without special reference to races or nations. Heredity and environment, innate predisposition and nurture, endogenetic and exogenetic factors, are still recognized under one name or another as the two great classes of cultural determinants. Different scientists emphasize one or the other. Little was known about the relation of genius to heredity when Taine wrote.[17] But in spite of all the great advances in genetics from Mendel to the present, little has been done to isolate the genes and predispositions which determine artistic or intellectual aptitude, as apart from the influence of culture. Everyone recognizes their decisive importance in the individual and in certain family lines. They seem to have little or no correlation with race or nationality as such. They descend in lines which cut across these groupings, to produce certain hereditary types of aptitude, physique, and temperament which recur in various races. Occasionally, they can help to produce a genius in any race. No one disputes the importance of heredity in *Homo sapiens* as a whole: his culture is what it is, with all its strengths and weaknesses, mainly because of his organic endowment. No one disputes it as a factor in producing the individual artist, specialized or versatile, healthy or sickly, sane or insane. To this extent, what Taine called "race" is still to be reckoned with as a determinant of artistic evolution.

5. PHYSICAL AND CULTURAL ENVIRONMENTS

The other main cause of psychological character, and hence of artistic achievement, is *milieu*—surroundings or environment. Taine distinguishes between what we now call "physical" and "cultural" environment. Man, he says in the "Intro-duction," is surrounded by nature and his fellowmen; physical and social circumstances disturb or confirm the primitive tendencies committed to their charge. "Sometimes the climate has had its effect." But climate is not all, even of the physical scene: there is also topography, food supply, raw materials, relation of land to water, mountains and valleys, routes for travel. That such physical factors influence culture, including art, is today unquestioned as a general fact. Their influence on styles of architecture and clothing is too obvious for argument.

What has aroused most objection is Taine's attempt to connect specific traits of land and climate with specific traits of painting: for example, the emphasis of early Renaissance painting on line and mass, as connected with the Italian air, light, and hilly countryside; the emphasis of Venetian and Dutch painting on coloristic atmosphere, as connected with the actual lights and colors of these watery regions. It has taken little effort to discover negative instances: different sorts of painting in the same region; similar styles in very different lands and climates.[18] But again, the attack has gone too far. One can hardly deny that some amount of influence along this line occurs; it must follow from the very effort to represent one's visible surroundings accurately, aided by the accumulation of suitable materials and techniques for doing so. The mistake would be to regard this as the *only* determining factor, and Taine did not make it. He often pointed out that any single factor can be outweighed by others. For an explanation, the sum total of knowable factors must be considered, as converging at any one historical moment.

[17] It was shortly to receive more intensive, scientific study by Francis Galton (*Hereditary Genius—an Inquiry into its Laws and Consequences*, 1869) and T. Ribot (*L'Hérédité-Etude psychologique sur ses phénomènes, ses causes, ses conséquences*, 1873). Included in the latter was a chapter on the creative imagination as capable of hereditary transmission. Galton stressed the idea that individual personality was not a supernatural addition to nature but a selection from it by normal processes.

[18] E. Grosse, in *The Beginnings of Art*, mentions a number of such negative instances. (p. 14).

Milieu is also social, psychological, and artistic, according to Taine. Previous works of art provide part of the civilized environment, physical and intangible, within which new art originates. They are among its determining causes, directly and as contributing to the surrounding "moral conditions." On the whole, however, he regards the influence of *milieu* as limiting and superficially disturbing; as forcing compromises, rather than as actively directing the course of art. That course is directed primarily by innate racial character. But racial character, as we have seen, is not sharply separated by Taine from the social and psychological *milieu*, except that the former is carried wherever the people migrates, while the latter may radically change, as in migration or conquest.

Besides other art, what cultural factors operate in the environment of art? He includes political and social conditions, as in the results of Aryan conquest in producing "intolerable oppression, the subjugation of the individual, utter despair, the thought that the world was cursed." This was the psychological state which led to the growth of metaphysics and myth, "so that man in this dungeon of misery, feeling his heart softened, begot the idea of abnegation, charity, tender love, gentleness, humility, brotherly love—there [in Asia], in a notion of universal nothingness, here [around the Mediterranean], under the Fatherhood of God." Protracted situations and pressures, such as the eight-hundred-year crusade of the Spanish against the Moors, have their effects on national character, as does English and French democracy. As compared with Marx, Taine alludes to socio-political events and forces rather casually, not as main determinants, and with little attention to class conflicts.

In applying the theory of socio-economic causation to particular artists, styles, and periods, Taine was comparatively brief and impressionistic. He dealt with it suggestively in a section on Greek social institutions, which begins, "If ever the correspondence of art with life disclosed itself through visible traits, it is in the history of Greek statuary."

His essay on Balzac begins, "Balzac was a business man, and a business man in debt." In his discussion of Florence in the fifteenth century, he correlated social changes with changing ideas, states of mind and types of art.[19] He related art to political conditions in contrasting ancient Rome with Renaissance Italy and in analyzing the effects of the Norman conquest on English literature. Many of Taine's perceptive hints along these lines have been developed in detail by later historians, usually without acknowledgement.

In the discussion of individual artists, Taine often goes into some detail; but mainly to show the relation of their works to the national character and *milieu*, whether Greek, English, Dutch, or Italian. One can hardly expect, in 1864, a psychoanalytic study of an artist's family *milieu* in infancy, or of his racial and family heredity. Yet these approaches to the causal explanation of an artist's style, which have greatly attracted later historians and biographers, are logical extensions of Taine's theory of race and *milieu* as contributing factors. Each factor has its limitations as a principle of explanation; each has been, by turns, overemphasized and underestimated. Taine's brief survey of them is vague and superficial by our scientific standards; necessarily so because of the small amount of detailed knowledge at the time. He deserves respect for having stated problems, which are still unsolved and growing in importance, and for his general hypotheses, which are still useful, rather than for his sketchy applications of them.

6. NATIONAL STYLES AND THEIR CAUSAL EXPLANATION

We have followed Taine's reasoning backward in historical time, from the works and styles of art which constitute the end results, within the limits of his investigation, to the psychological conditions which produced them; then to the causes of these

[19] *Voyage in Italy*, II, Book III, Ch. II.

conditions—first *moment*, as the immediate set of causes, then *race* and *milieu* as more lasting influences or trains of events leading back into the ancient past. He usually presents them in a different order: from race, *milieu*, and moment to the resultant styles of art. He states his theory first, as in the "Introduction" to the *History of English Literature* and in the introductory pages of each set of lectures on the visual arts—Italian, Dutch, and Greek.

The description of styles and examples is thus an application and illustration of the theory. This has its advantages and dangers. Insofar as the theory is true and illuminating, it leads him to notice traits in art which are genuinely characteristic of a national style and of the mental and emotional attitudes behind it. But this approach also leads him, inevitably, to emphasize those traits in art which conform to his idea of the national character, thus confirming his general theory. Further study has led us to a much less simple, uniform conception of Italian art and civilization as compared with Dutch or English.[20] But it does not invalidate Taine's general theory of causation. It calls rather for more intensive, openminded research along the lines he suggested: on the specific, distinctive traits of national and other styles in art, and their relation to other traits of the groups wherein they flourished.

Taine's observations on English literature are discerning and enlightening. Those on Italian and Dutch art are still stimulating and, on the whole, in accord with present views on the subject; but they are comparatively brief and general. As usual in his day, they emphasize the represented subject-matter and emotional expressiveness of painting and sculpture more than the purely visual aspects of design, form, and style. The focusing of critical and historical interest on these aspects of art was still to come. Taine was sensitive to the formal or "mathematical" aspects of visual art, in the representational arts and also in architectural design. He saw the value of organized proportion and composition among the constituent lines, masses, and colors of a work of art. The ideal work of art,

for him, had to make a number of varied elements "converge" harmoniously, in what Spencer called complexity through differentiation and integration. But his emphasis, in both describing and evaluating art, was in the neo-classic tradition of moral idealism.

7. CHANGING CONFIGURATIONS IN HEREDITY AND ENVIRONMENT

Corrected and extended in the light of modern knowledge, Taine's three concepts still provide a most useful starting-point for historical explanation in art and other fields. It is hard to imagine any other kind of naturalistic cause or explanation which can not be included under one or more of these concepts, as broadly redefined. They are flexible enough to include all the contributions of recent psychology and psychoanalysis, for all the determinants recognized therein pertain to heredity, environment, or their changing interactions. For example, Freud has called our attention to the strong influence of the family environment in infancy; of the child's relation to parents and siblings. He recognizes also the importance of innate predisposition, as in making one child resist an unfavorable situation while another becomes neurotic.

In overemphasizing the racial and national aspects of heredity, Taine underemphasized their individual, family, and local aspects. Likewise, he underestimated the local aspects of environment, as in the immediate, family and neighborhood influences which play upon the future artist in early childhood. The crucial, differentiating factors are not heredity and environment in general, or as

[20] E. Hennequin criticized Taine for oversimplifying the conception of a racial or national climate of taste. *La Critique scientifique* (Paris, 1888), p. 116. An active modern civilization like the French, he argued, has great diversity of taste. Grosse added that most great works of art are created, "not conformably to, but against, the prevailing taste." (p. 15). It now seems obvious that there are many diverse elements in a national climate of taste. Different ones tend to encourage and preserve different kinds of art.

common to a whole race or nation through the ages, but the peculiar selection and arrangement of genes and local, temporary influences which produce a certain individual or subgroup at a certain time and place.

In this respect, the concept of *moment* or temporary configuration is as applicable to heredity as it is to environment. Through selective migration, conquest, intermarriage, mutation, or other factors, the genetic constitution of a subgroup or family lineage may change substantially with consequent effects on the individuals produced.[21] Taine did not pursue his inquiries along this line, or recognize the importance of what we may call the hereditary or genetic "moment."

8. PSYCHOLOGICAL AND SOCIOLOGICAL APPROACHES TO ART HISTORY

It is now evident that Taine's account of the social *milieu* fails to pay sufficient heed to economic factors, class conflicts, and the shifting control of wealth and power. But his conception of the *milieu*, in general and at any one moment, is flexible enough to be developed along such lines to a moderate extent. On the other hand, the sociological approach could usually profit from more psychological analysis along the lines proposed by Taine. The two must be combined for best results.

What is the relation between *psychological* and *socio-economic* factors in history? Neither Marx nor Taine explained this clearly. It depends largely on one's conception of "psychology." In Taine's day, psychology had not yet become a science. Taine's thinking did much to bridge the gap between the old, metaphysical psychology and the new, empirical science by that name. As we have seen, he helped to place it within a naturalistic, empirical, and evolutionary framework. He did the same for aesthetics and the scientific study of the arts, later called by the Germans *allgemeine Kunstwissenschaft*. Works of art, said Taine, should be studied as

botany studies plants; styles of art, such as Dutch or Italian, should be studied objectively, like species of trees, to discover their nature, development, and varieties.[22] Personal evaluation and mysticism were to be avoided. He took the same attitude toward social or folk psychology, trying to discover the objective traits of racial and national cultures instead of merely praising one as superior to another. Individual artists were to be analyzed as exemplifying the spirit of the group, with distinguishing features observable in their works and lives. Like Spencer and Comte, Taine saw the history of art as an integral phase of cultural evolution, not a series of bolts from the blue. All parts of a civilization were, for him, interconnected and changed together. True, he did not avoid evaluation entirely. He felt that fact and value, description and judgment, must be somehow reconciled in one consistent system of thought. But he tried not to confuse the two, and dealt with evaluation mainly in a separate book, on *The Ideal in Art*. His main approach was descriptive and empirical.

Traditional psychology, as "the philosophy of mind," had been dealt with mainly in terms of the supposed "faculties of the soul"—reason, will, sensation, and emotion—and mainly through introspection, not the observation and interpretation of behavior. It was conceived largely in terms of the supposed relation between a static Subject and Object, self and external world. The main problems were not factual description but epistemological, theological, and moral: how the isolated self could know the outside world and God; how reason could adjust itself to faith and control the lower self. Psychology was usually based on a dualistic or idealistic metaphysics until the skeptical analysis of Hume; a naturalistic approach was rare until the nineteenth century. The psychologist paid little attention to such mundane affairs as the struggle for wealth and power. He thought in

[21] See the discussion of "genetic drift" by S. L. Washburn in "The Strategy of Physical Anthropology," Kroeber, ed., *Anthropology Today*, p. 719.
[22] *The Philosophy of Art*, p. 38.

terms of an abstract, generalized sort of individual soul, dealing with an abstract universe; in terms of Platonic "essentials," not of such "accidents" as individual peculiarities, changing folkways, reactions to climate and food supply.

It is not surprising, then, that Comte, Marx, and other social theorists found little help in the psychology of their time; little contact between what passed for "psychological causes" in history and the concrete realities of social and cultural history. No wonder that Plekhanov charged Taine with being an "idealist" for saying that "history is a problem of psychology."[23] He agreed with Taine that the "subjective" or psychological side of history, "the human spirit, the sentiments and ideas of men" must be explained. But he felt that Taine had not done so; that it could not be done except in the Marxist way, "by the material conditions of men's existence, by economic history."[24]

This antithesis implies that economic history is in itself not psychological; not a process of ideas and sentiments, but something outside which controls the psychological phenomena. This is justifiable if we understand "psychology" in the old sense, as a branch of philosophy having little to do with socio-economic behavior. Taine understood it more broadly, however, as comprising the whole mass and succession of reasonings, emotions, sensations, and conceptions which constitute the inner, invisible personality, and which can be investigated only through observing its expressions in his behavior and possessions. "You consider his writings, his artistic productions, his business transactions or political ventures; and that in order to measure the scope and limits of his intelligence, his inventiveness, his coolness, to find out the order, the character, the general force of his ideas, the mode in which he thinks and resolves."[25] If, as Taine says, the data of psychology are to include all types of civilized behavior and production, such as works of art, commercial and political activities, house, furniture, dress, and conversation, then man's socio-economic behavior is *not* a thing apart. It is but one variety of psychological

phenomenon; one way in which man expresses his inner thoughts and feelings; one type of situation which helps to shape the inner, psychic man.

Some differentiation of approach is necessary along such lines, as a practical step in dividing phenomena into fields for specialization by the various sciences. Theoretically, the psychologist might well claim them all as his province. The experience of the farmer and the physicist, the painter and the politician, each toward his own kinds of object and situation, is all psychological. Taine is right, for his purposes, in envisaging this all-inclusive realm for psychology; it is consistent with the philosophy of empiricism. But for the practical management of psychology in relation to other specialized sciences today, narrower limits are necessary. Without making sharp divisions where the field is continuous, psychology and the social sciences try to emphasize different aspects of it.

This broad conception of psychology is in accord with modern usage, as in Webster's definition of it as "The science which treats of the mind (of man or other organisms) in any of its aspects; ...the study of the organism and its activities... esp. in relation to its physical and social environment."[26] From this standpoint, the antithesis between the "psychological" and the "socio-economic" becomes invalid; the issue between Taine and the Marxists is that of whether one set of psychological factors—the socio-economic—is basic and determining in relation to the others. The "socio-economic" should not be excluded from the "psychological" by limiting it to the purely material, external conditions—e.g., to climate, food supply, and mineral resources. Their historical importance always lies, not in themselves, but (as Marx himself realized) in how humans respond to them or to the lack of them. Such responses develop into organized socio-economic systems. The "psychological" approach to them, as narrow-

[23] *Essays in the History of Materialism*, p. 235.
[24] *Ibid.*, p. 243.
[25] "Introduction" to *History of English Literature*, pp. 6 f.
[26] *Webster's New International Dictionary* (Springfield, Mass., 1936, 1961).

ly understood, tends to emphasize their inner, subjective aspects, while sociology and economics tend to emphasize their external, collective forms. Both approaches are necessary for a deeper understanding of the psychological and cultural climate as Taine broadly conceived it, and also for understanding the individual artist and his style.

General psychology still focuses on the more universal, innate functions, abilities, and tendencies, observable to some extent in every normal individual. The social sciences emphasize relations among individuals and groups: some comparatively universal, such as the family; others peculiar to certain times and places, such as the tribe. On the border between them are such subjects as social psychology, cultural psychology, and cultural anthropology. The psychologist who studies widespread phenomena such as auditory discrimination or the Oedipus complex tends to work along lines comparatively remote from the socioeconomic, although even here he discovers changing social influences. Likewise the economic historian, studying types of property ownership, or gathering statistics on the business cycle, feels remote from psychology, though even here he discovers human nature, its changing emotions

and desires. All these approaches and many others, both psychological and sociological, can be fruitfully applied to causal explanation in the arts.

Taine was moving toward the kind of scientific inquiry which we now call social or cultural psychology, concerned with group behavior and its mental, affective, experiential correlates. Today, as in Taine's work, this inquiry includes a study of objective products and expressions, such as works of art, along with a study of other data regarding the psychology of the groups concerned. Within this approach, he included a conception of great individual personalities, actual and imaginary, as embodying concretely the distinctive traits and ideals of the group. He did so, rather unfortunately, in terms of "race" and "nation," whereas "group" or "culture" would have been more broadly inclusive. He approached these phenomena with a special interest in the genesis and etiology of modern cultures, and most of all in the history of the arts. The paths of research and explanation to which he pointed have not yet been adequately explored. Workers in the field could profit from a re-examination of his stimulating and suggestive hypotheses.

CHAPTER IX

THE UNILINEAR EVOLUTIONISM
OF MORGAN AND TYLOR

I. ITS RELATION
TO CULTURAL EVOLUTIONISM IN GENERAL.
ITS THEORY OF ART

In recent anthropology, a distinction has been made between "unilinear" and "multilinear" theories of cultural evolution. The former type, now attacked as false, is attributed chiefly to Edward B. Tylor and Lewis H. Morgan. Tylor was English, Morgan American.

The full title of Tylor's chief work indicates the scope of his system: *Primitive Culture: Research into the Development of Mythology, Philosophy, Religion, Language, Art, and Custom.*[1] Morgan's chief work was published in 1877 under the title *Ancient Society: Researches in the Lines of Human Progress through Barbarism in Civilization.*[2]

Morgan and Tylor both accepted the general thesis of cultural evolutionism. Tylor stated it in Spencerian terms: "On the whole it appears that wherever there are found elaborate arts, abstruse knowledge, complex institutions, these are results of gradual development from an earlier, simpler, and ruder state of life. No stage of civilization comes into existence spontaneously, but grows or is developed out of the stage before it."[3] This thesis was developed at length by Morgan and Tylor, in opposition to the traditional "degeneration theory."[4] As a general statement of cultural evolutionism, it has never been refuted or weakened by later evidence. Later attacks were directed rather at the associated theory of how—by what

specific modes and stages—the process had occurred. Serious confusion has arisen from identifying this special theory with cultural evolutionism in general. Because of the charge by some American anthropologists that "evolutionism" and "the evolutionists" are now refuted and discredited (especially Morgan and Tylor), it is important to distinguish those ideas which have really been refuted from those which have not.

Morgan proposed an exact, regular formula for the details of cultural evolution. Tylor was more aware of past philosophic theories and problems in the field; of the difficulties involved, and of how his own ideas fitted into the development of evolutionary thought. Morgan had little to say on the fine arts. As an anthropologist, he was interested mainly in primitive social and political organization. He proposed a comprehensive pattern of early cultural history, with the implication that it covered the arts; but he did not work out a detailed account of their place in it. Tylor did not propose so elaborate a pattern, but he wrote at

[1] Its first edition (London, 1871) was a continuation of his *Researches into the Early History of Mankind*, published in 1865.

[2] He had previously published *Systems of Consanguinity and Affinity of the Human Family* (1869).

[3] *Anthropology* (New York, 1891), p. 20. He scarcely mentions Darwin or Spencer, however, and insists on the difference between his work and theirs. (Preface to Second Edition, 1873).

[4] Tylor argued especially against Joseph de Maistre, who had restated that theory early in the nineteenth century. See Tylor's *Primitive Culture* (London, 1913), Vol. I, p. 35, referring to de Maistre's *Soirées de St. Petersbourg*, Vol. II, p. 150.

greater length on the fine and useful arts, both primitive and civilized.

2. TYLOR'S CONCEPTION OF ART AND CULTURE

To Tylor we owe the basic definition of "culture" in its broad, objective sense, now accepted in science, as distinguished from the popular sense which had glorified nineteenth-century European refinements. "Culture or Civilization," he said at the start of *Primitive Culture*,[5] "taken in its wide ethnographic sense, is that complex whole which includes knowledge, belief, art, morals, law, custom, and any other capabilities and habits acquired by man as a member of society. The condition of culture among the various societies of mankind, insofar as it is capable of being investigated on general principles, is a subject apt for the study of laws of human thought and action." That savages or "benighted heathen" could be considered as having "culture" was a rather incredible notion in mid-Victorian London and Paris. But the new conception facilitated objective research on the development of man's acquired heritage from its beginnings.

Instead of making "culture" synonymous with "civilization," Morgan distinguished the latter as the third and most advanced stage, beginning with the use of writing. This is a useful distinction, now widely accepted.

Tylor's definition of culture also implied a broad, objective concept of "art" and "the arts." It was illustrated in his chapters on the primitive arts. His contemporary, Taine, was independently arriving at the same conception; but to most writers on art and aesthetics the term "art" still meant something refined and beautiful by Greek standards. That the "crude" drawings, carvings, and chants of primitive peoples could be classed as art at all seemed highly questionable. The older, eulogistic conception of art as inseparable from classical beauty was a formidable barrier (not wholly overcome to this day) against the scientific study of art. Under it people could never agree on what was really art, or hence on what the data of aesthetics and art history should be.

Like Taine, Tylor likened cultural traits to "the species of plants and animals studied by the naturalist." To ethnography, he said, "the bow and arrow is a species, the habit of flattening children's skulls is a species, the practice of reckoning numbers by ten is a species. The geographical distribution of these things, and their transmission from region to region, have to be studied as the naturalist studies the geography of his botanical and zoological species." Mechanical invention gives examples of the development of species, he said, as in the evolution of the modern breech-loading gun from the wheel-lock by way of the flintlock and muzzle-loading percussion-lock. The cross-bow is obviously "a development arising from the simpler instrument," the long-bow. Later instruments are more powerful and efficient, handier, less wasteful.[6] This conception, if applied to art and followed out, might have led to an evolutionary study of the fine arts; but neither Tylor nor Morgan did so in detail.

In the *Anthropology*, Tylor gave a concise summary of what was known of primitive and early civilized art in his day. Using "art" in the old sense of "useful skill," as Morgan did, he included under that heading the development of tools, weapons, and machines, farming and cattle-raising, architecture and dress, ships, navigation, cooking, lighting, glass, metalry, and commerce. These are "arts of life," and their decorative, aesthetic aspects were not ignored. Under "arts of pleasure," he traced the evolution of poetry and drama, music and musical instruments, danc-

[5] (London, 1913), Ch. I, "The Science of Culture," p. 1. Tylor sometimes makes "culture" coextensive with "civilization" and at other times contrasts them. "The dull-minded barbarian," he says with characteristic Victorian pride, "has not power of thought enough to come up to the civilized man's best moral standard." (*Anthropology*, p. 407).
[6] *Primitive Culture*, Vol. I, p. 8.

ing, painting, sculpture, and games. The development of oral and written language was separately traced. The emphasis throughout, as in Spencer's theory, was on the ways in which the arts had increased in variety, subtlety, organization, power, and understanding of life and nature. Like Spencer, he overemphasized the criterion of realism in judging primitive art, and underemphasized design. He recognized to some extent the merits of primitive art, including prehistoric drawings on bones and cave walls. He avoided many controversial points, such as the priority of particular styles. He assigned some achievements in art to the savage, barbarous, or early civilized stage without trying to correlate them exactly with traits in other fields. His general scheme of history was fairly flexible, and he refrained from trying to force art history into any single, rigid sequence of steps.

3. "NEARLY UNIFORM CHANNELS." IMMANENT DETERMINISM AND PARALLELISM

Both writers made contributions of value to the theory of evolution; but both made mistakes, natural enough in relation to the limited knowledge of their time, but serious in the light of subsequent research. Their enthusiasm for the new, epoch-making theory of evolution, with its claim to be a universal law of life and civilization, led them to exaggerate the uniformity of the process and to underestimate its irregularities. Their theories were similar and involved much the same errors; that of Morgan shows them in a somewhat more extreme form.[7] The errors appeared especially in two aspects of their work; two general features of the evolutionary process as they conceived it. One had to do with the *course* or *direction* of cultural evolution, which they conceived as mainly along a single line or sequence of predetermined changes. This underestimated its variations. The other had to do with the *stages* or

successive steps through which evolution had pursued its course. These they conceived as three in number, according to the traditional sequence of "savagery, barbarism, and civilization." The error here lay in the extent to which they regarded each of these stages as substantially the same everywhere. This, too, underestimated the actual diversity; the difficulty of dividing past cultural change into three distinct, contrasting stages, or any other definite number, because of the irregular overlapping of specific changes.

Let us first consider their conception of the course of cultural evolution as uniform, and of its causation as inwardly determined. Morgan's main thesis, in *Ancient Society*, was that "the principal institutions of mankind have been developed from a few primary germs of thought; and that the course and manner of their development was predetermined, as well as restricted within narrow limits of divergence, by the natural logic of the human mind and the necessary limitations of its powers. Progress has been found to be substantially the same in kind in tribes and nations inhabiting different and even disconnected continents, while in the same status, with deviations from uniformity in particular instances produced by special causes. The argument when extended tends to establish the unity of origin of mankind."[8]

As to the main cause of evolution, this thesis clearly affirms an immanent, psychological determinism, based on the "natural logic" and "limitations" of the human mind. It affirms a parallelism in cultural history, in that separate groups will tend to evolve independently along similar lines. It does not, however, go on to explain that process in terms of idealism, by a supernatural, spiritual cause. Morgan's treatment throughout the book is on the whole naturalistic, although he makes the usual Victorian acknowledgment of divine Providence at the end of the book, in a rather perfunctory way. The labors of our ancestors were

[7] Tylor's early works may have influenced Morgan. See D. Bidney, *Theoretical Anthropology*, p. 209.
[8] Ch. II, p. 18, on "Ethnical Periods."

"a part of the plan of the Supreme Intelligence to develop a barbarian out of a savage, and a civilized man out of this barbarian." The main course of cultural evolution, says Morgan, is determined inwardly; not by chance variation or particular environmental conditions. Such "special causes" merely produce occasional "deviations from uniformity," and uniformity is the basic, normal character of the process. Thus Morgan's conception, though undeveloped philosophically, leaned toward orthogenesis in explaining the causation of cultural change.

Morgan said also that "the experience of mankind has run in nearly uniform channels... in virtue of the specific identity of the brain of all the races of mankind... The germs of the principal institutions and arts of life were developed while man was still a savage." This statement, though exaggerated, contains some truth. All man's civilized experience and culture is certainly determined within broad limits by the nature of his brain and physical endowment, as distinct from those of other species. It is "uniform"—i.e., of one general form or type—to the extent that it is basically human. But Morgan underestimated the high plasticity and variability of human thought and behavior within those limits. Its specific channels are not "nearly uniform." Only in the most general, potential way does savage experience contain "the germs of the principal institutions and arts" of civilized life. Once again, it is a question of degree.

E. B. Tylor stated a similar thesis in 1888: "The institutions of man are as distinctly stratified as the earth on which he lives. They succeed each other in series substantially uniform over the globe, independent of what seem the comparatively superficial differences of race and language, but shaped by similar human nature acting through successively changing conditions in savage, barbaric and civilized life."[9] This again seems to imply an immanent determinism and parallelism, but elsewhere Tylor shifted the emphasis toward natural selection. History and ethnography, he said, "combine to show that the institutions which can best hold their own in the world gradually supersede the less fit ones, and that this incessant conflict determines the general resultant course of culture."[10] He also assigned an important role to cultural diffusion. Many races, he said, whose history can not be brought into connection by present evidence, "may have grown up under one another's influence or derived material from a common source." But he also cautioned against an error which was afterward made by extreme diffusionists such as Elliott Smith and W. J. Perry: "that the civilization of the whole world has its origin in one parent stock." Culture probably originated independently in various places, he thought, but it involved much inheritance from common traditions.[11]

As to "the course which the civilization of the world has actually followed," Tylor proposed five descriptive concepts. "Progress, degradation, survival, revival, modification, are all modes of the connexion that binds together the complex network of civilization."[12] He explained them all in a unilinear way. "Progress" and "degradation" stand for movements forward and backward along the one main avenue of change. "Survivals" are "processes, customs, opinions, and so forth, which have been carried on by force of habit into a new state of society," remaining as examples of an older condition of culture. In "revivals," old thoughts and practices "burst out afresh" in a world that thought them dead or dying; for example, modern spiritualism. "Modification" suggests the possibility of divergent alteration of

9 "On a Method of Investigating the Development of Institutions: Applied to Laws of Marriage and Descent," *Journal of the Royal Anthropological Institute of Great Britain and Ireland*, Vol. 18 (1888). (Quoted by Hoebel, p. 611). A. Goldenweiser remarks that the early evolutionists derived their theory of mankind from such writers as J. G. Herder, A. Bastian, and T. Waitz. ("Evolution, Social," in *Encyclopedia of the Social Sciences*). Tylor acknowledges a debt to Bastian and Waitz in the Preface to *Primitive Culture*.

10 *Primitive Culture*, Vol. I, p. 69.

11 *Researches*, p. 374. (Quoted by Bidney, p. 199).

12 *Primitive Culture*, Vol. I, pp. 16–17.

what has been received, but Tylor did not develop this idea.

"Progress" was understood by Tylor and Morgan, as it was by Spencer, to imply the two ideas of "development" and "improvement." He did not confuse or carelessly identify the two meanings, but gave his reasons for believing that, on the whole, the more recent is the better in the evolutionary process. "From an ideal point of view, civilization may be looked upon as the general improvement of mankind by higher organization of the individual and of society, to the end of promoting at once man's goodness, power, and happiness... Thus a transition from the savage state to our own would be, practically, that very progress of art and knowledge which is one main element in the development of culture."[13] The same criteria suffice to measure both past progress and the degree of culture among living peoples. In seeking "a definite line along which to reckon progression and retrogression in civilization," we can find it in "the absence or presence, high or low development, of the industrial arts, especially metal-working, manufacture of implements and vessels, agriculture, etc., the extent of scientific knowledge, the definiteness of moral principles, the condition of religious belief and ceremony, the degree of social and political organization, and so forth." The main tendency of human society has been to pass from a savage to a civilized state, and this has been, according to Morgan and Tylor, an improvement as judged by all these criteria.

Tylor's progressionism was only a little more moderate than that of Gibbon, whom he quoted with general approval. Gibbon, he thought, had exaggerated the lowness of savage life and dwelt too much on the brighter side of civilization.[14] There are virtuous, happy savages, and "The onward movement from barbarism has dropped behind it more than one quality of barbaric character which cultured modern men look back on with regret, and will even strive to regain by futile attempts to stop the course of history, and restore the past in the midst of the present." In early Christian times, men fell away in intellectual life while advancing in the new religion of duty, holiness, and love. But these are exceptions. "On the whole the civilized man is not only wiser and more capable than the savage, but also better and happier, and the barbarian stands between." The examples Tylor gives of "degeneration," "retrogression," or "degradation" all tend to show that such a movement in social change is (a) unusual, a secondary process, and (b) for the worse. He does not recognize, on any important scale, the possibility of a healthy, beneficial regression toward earlier, simpler conditions, or a beneficial revival of them.

4. STAGES IN CULTURE HISTORY

This problem had been somewhat neglected since Comte and Hegel. It had been a central one in the philosophy of history since the early Greeks. Whether a philosopher conceived the main trend of history as progress or decline, evolution or cyclical recurrence, he was seldom content to think only of its general direction, its beginning and end. He wondered also about its intermediate chapters. By what steps did man proceed from his first state, in Eden or the jungle, to his present one? What will be his next, perhaps his final one? The theory of evolution is not complete without some answer to this question, though not necessarily in terms of any fixed number of uniform stages.

It was the task of Tylor, Morgan, and their contemporaries to explore this problem in a naturalistic way from the standpoint of anthropology and archeology, in the field of prehistory and early history. This was a crucial field for the evolutionist to explore, in search of missing links between the origin of man and the complex civilizations of Egypt, Greece, and Rome. A vast amount of specialized researches had provided

[13] *Ibid.*, p. 27.
[14] In *Decline and Fall*, Ch. XXXVIII. Tylor, *loc. cit.*, p. 35.

masses of data, which Morgan and Tylor tried to synthesize with special emphasis on the sequence of steps in primitive culture. They did so on a larger scale than ever before, with a detailed account of the interrelation of culture-traits in various activities and institutions on each level.

Morgan and Tylor conceived the three stages as differing from chronological periods in that a given stage (such as barbarism) had occurred at different times in different places. The early stages, they believed, still exist among "primitive" tribes today, whereas the ancestors of modern civilized peoples passed through them thousands of years ago. Isolated, modern savages, they declared, are so like our early ancestors as to show us with considerable accuracy how the latter must have lived.

In marking off his list of stages or "Ethnical Periods," Morgan indicated that these were not mere arbitrary time-spans. Each "covers a distinct culture"; it represents "a distinct condition of society," and is distinguished by a peculiar mode of life. The Danish conception of stone, bronze, and iron ages is still useful for classifying artifacts, he said, but inadequate to mark off main stages. "The successive arts of subsistence which arose at long intervals will ultimately, from the great influence they must have exercised upon the condition of mankind, afford the most satisfactory bases for these divisions." But, he continued, we do not know enough about them yet, and must use for the present other inventions or discoveries as tests of progress to mark the beginning of epochs. He distinguished the following stages in the arts of subsistence, the first two as originating in savagery, the last three in barbarism: (1) Natural subsistence upon fruits and roots on a restricted habitat; (2) Fish subsistence; (3) Farinaceous subsistence through cultivation; (4) Meat and milk subsistence; (5) Unlimited subsistence through field agriculture.

To the modern reader, there is something suspiciously neat and regular in the longer list of stages and substages which Morgan worked out.

Savagery and barbarism were each divided into three: as periods, into older, middle, and later; as conditions, into upper, middle, and lower. The middle status of savagery begins with a fish subsistence and the use of fire; the upper with the bow and arrow. Lower barbarism begins with pottery; middle with domesticated animals in the East and irrigated agriculture in the West; upper barbarism with iron smelting and iron tools; civilization with writing and a phonetic alphabet.

Examples of all the main stages in past cultural history are to be found today, Morgan believed. "So essentially identical are the arts, institutions, and mode of life in the same status upon all the continents, that the archaic form of the principal domestic institutions of the Greeks and Romans must even now be sought in the corresponding institutions of the American aborigines." "The Grecian and Latin tribes of the Homeric and Romulian periods afford the highest exemplification of the Upper Status of barbarism." They were on the verge of achieving civilization.

Morgan defined savagery, barbarism, and civilization in specific, objective terms. Savagery had developed "organization into gentes, phratries, and tribes; the syndyasmian family; the worship of the elements in its lowest form; syllabical language; the bow and arrow; stone and bone implements; cane and splint baskets; skin garments; the punaluan family; the organization upon the basis of sex; the village, consisting of clustered houses; boat craft, including the bark and dug-out canoe; the spear pointed with flint, and the war club; flint implements of the ruder kinds; the consanguine family; monosyllabical language; fetichism; cannibalism; a knowledge of the use of fire; and lastly, gesture language."[15] Late, advanced barbarism, as portrayed in the *Iliad*, included poetry, Olympian religion, marble temple architecture, field agriculture, stone-walled cities with advanced municipal life, plank ships, nails, wagons, chariots, metallic plate armor, iron swords and tools, wine, mechanical powers except the screw, potter's

[15] P. 35.

wheel and hand-mill, woven linen and wool, iron metallurgy, the monogamian family, military democracies, the popular assembly, and individual property.

Both Morgan and Tylor felt the urgency of combating the traditional religious theory of degeneration or degradation, in explaining particular ethnic phenomena. Based in its Christian form on the Old Testament account of early Semitic tribes, this theory considered their pastoral life, patriarchal organization and religion as typical of primitive culture. But what of living peoples who seem far inferior to the Biblical standard? The hypothesis of degradation led, says Morgan, to "regarding all the races of mankind without the Aryan and Semitic connections as abnormal races—races fallen away by degeneracy from their normal state." It was supported by the researches of Sir Henry Maine on ancient law, which adopted the patriarchal family of the Hebrew and Latin types as the oldest form of the family and the earliest organized society. Modern groups practicing some less ideal system, promiscuous or incestuous by our standards, must have degenerated from the patriarchal family according to this conservative view.

As against it, J. J. Bachofen and Morgan argued that the earliest type of social organization, after the primitive "undivided horde," was based on the clan as a unilateral, matrilineal structure. In opposing the old theory of universal degeneration, along with the universal priority of patriarchy and patrilineal descent, Bachofen and Morgan had the facts on their side; but they went too far to the other extreme in affirming the universal priority of matriarchy and matrilineal descent. Since Morgan's time a few anthropologists have continued to support the matrilinear theory, but the weight of present evidence indicates that the sequence was different in different places.[16]

There is nothing false or "unilinear" in merely dividing past history into a certain number of arbitrary periods, such as "early, middle, late," or "prehistoric, ancient, medieval, modern." These headings may be understood in a purely formal way, as a succession of chronological time-spans. They may be marked off by important events such as the advance and recession of glaciers or the fall of dynasties. Such concepts are empty and unspecific as to the nature of cultural change within the periods.

The concept of a stage in cultural evolution implies more than this. It is more like the concept of childhood or adolescence as a stage in the life of an individual, which implies both (a) a certain period within the development of an individual, and (b) a certain set of traits regarded as characteristic of that period. Thus adolescence comes between childhood and adulthood, and is characterized by sexual maturation and emotional sensitivity. Evolutionist theory assumed a partial analogy between individual and generic development, ontogeny and phylogeny. Thus the stages in cultural evolution were often conceived as analogous to those of individual life: savagery as "the childhood of the race"; prehistoric art as "the childhood of art," and so on. "We may, I think," said Tylor, "apply the often-repeated comparison of savages to children as fairly to their moral as to their intellectual condition."[17] Savagery as a cultural stage thus implied not only a set of cultural traits, including the lack of barbarous and civilized ones, but also a double temporary reference. It referred (a) to a certain epoch in calendar time and human prehistory: roughly, from the origin of the human species to a few thousand years B.C., when all mankind presumably had savage traits, and (b) to the time within the life of a particular group, during which it lives in a savage way. This, according to the theory, could last until any chronological date, and is still lasting in the case of many contemporary, primitive tribes. Normally, it is the stage preceding barbarism; but some have never progressed that far and may never do so.

[16] The case for diversity in summarized by R. H. Lowie in *Primitive Society*, p. 185. *Cf.* H. E. Barnes' discussion of Morgan and the matriarchal theory in *Historical Sociology*, pp. 86 f.

[17] *Primitive Culture*, Vol. I, p. 31.

Some may retrogress from a later stage to savagery. Thus the temporal reference of a cultural stage, as of a stage in individual life, is relative rather than absolute.

As a theory, the Tylor-Morgan version of evolutionism implied more than a set of three abstract concepts. It implied, first, certain debatable propositions about the facts of history; about the dates and temporal order in which different sets of traits have actually developed. Second, it implied a value-judgment to the effect that the later and more developed are, on the whole, better. Third, insofar as the analogy between savagery and childhood was insisted on, it implied a debatable conception of both. Today, we are more impressed by the differences between children and adult savages.

The terms "savage" and "barbarous" are usually meant as condescending and derogatory, at least by those who admire civilization; sometimes as admiring, by those who prefer the "noble savage." These associations, and the incorrectness of many past theories about primitive life, have led to their partial abandonment as technical terms in recent anthropology. They can still be safely used in a loose, non-technical way, provided one does not try to define them too specifically. One can recognize that there are many different kinds of savagery, of barbarism, and of civilization; also that life in the first two stages is sometimes preferable, on moral and other grounds, to so-called "civilization." Many present anthropologists have ceased to use the terms "primitive," "savage," and "barbarous" because of their vague and disparaging tone. For much the same reasons, "heathen" and "pagan," "crude" and "degraded" are avoided, and more objective terms preferred. However, it is not easy to find satisfactory ones of equal breadth.

Tylor defined them fairly simply and objectively in his *Anthropology*:[18] "The lowest or savage state is that in which man subsists on wild plants and animals, neither tilling the soil nor domesticating creatures for his food." The materials used for

tools are found ready at hand; people "cannot extract metal from the ore, and therefore belong to the Stone Age." (Tylor credited John Lubbock with dividing the stone age into paleolithic and neolithic.) Barbarism occurs when people take to agriculture or, as pastoral tribes, have a constant supply of milk and meat. "Lastly, civilized life may be taken as beginning with the art of writing." Difficulties arise, however, when we ask such questions as these: Are people still to be called "savage" if they use metals but not agriculture or domesticated animals? Are there such peoples? If so, how sharply can the stages be divided?

5. UNIFORMITY AND DIVERGENCE

Strictly speaking, no theory of evolution is, or can be, purely unilinear. That would imply that all animals and plants, all societies and cultures, all styles of art, have followed exactly the same path throughout the history of life. Exceptions to this are too obvious to be ignored. All theories of evolution, biological and cultural, have recognized the fact that *some* divergence exists. This was taken for granted, even when no such term as "multilinear" was used. There was no need to stress diversity in the mid-nineteenth century, for that was the main phenomenon to be explained: the origin of different species. In the world of animals and plants, what could be more obvious than the differences between types? Man and ape, insect, bird, and fish, seemed worlds apart; so far that the notion of their common descent was at first incredible. True, the Bible taught the descent of all mankind from Adam and Eve; all men were brothers in a sense, but the gulf between the educated Londoner and the Australian aborigine was too evident to need underlining. The urgent need, in establishing the general thesis of evolution, was to demonstrate the underlying connections of all these types as parts of the same inclusive process,

[18] (New York, 1891), p. 24.

and as now possessing some basic characteristics in common. It is easy to see how excessive zeal for this phase of the inquiry could have led some theorists to exaggerate the uniformities.

Morgan was one of those who went farthest along that line. He maintained that all human groups, insofar as they evolved at all, had gone through the same sequence of stages. Some had died out along the way; some had changed slowly, some had stopped, and some retrogressed. This would help explain the diversity of living groups. But there was only one main road for cultural evolution.

One's theory becomes more and more unilinear and controversial as one tries to correlate each period of time, each step in historical sequence, with more and more specific traits in more and more different peoples throughout the world. This implies more uniformity, and less room for variation. Carried to extremes, it would imply that all savages were substantially alike, all barbarians alike, and all civilized peoples alike. Cultural evolution would be conceived as a tightly integrated, multiple process, in which every phase of human activity developed along with every other in a cluster of parallel sequences. At every moment, predetermined changes in social and political organization would accompany predetermined changes in technology, religion, art, and other phases of culture. Given any one major trait of a people, according to this view, it should be possible to infer the others and the general stage of evolution reached. Aside from minor variations due to environmental differences, evolution would proceed everywhere along parallel lines, (a) as to the main course followed by different peoples, and (b) as to the concurrent developments of different branches of culture within a given people.

Morgan did not go to this extreme, but he went much closer to it than any present anthropologist will go. He implied that variations from it were comparatively minor and due to exceptional outside conditions. By contrast, later theorists regard the various branches of culture as more loosely interconnected and more capable of divergent change; also as more responsive to environmental conditions, including diffusion from other groups. The elaborate lists of traits which Morgan assigned to each stage are not totally false, although subject to correction at many points.

What is to be done with such a theory as knowledge develops? One possible course is to treat it as a hypothesis and try to correct it, bit by bit, at points where it is shown to be mistaken or exaggerated. This was done throughout the nineteenth century, and is still being done. The mode of investigation practiced by Spencer, Morgan, Tylor, J. G. Frazer and other cultural evolutionists came to be called "the comparative method." It involved a search through countless sources for examples of stages and substages, preconceived along certain lines. One of its weaknesses was the human tendency to look especially hard for examples which confirmed one's theory. At the same time, it should be granted that the wealth of data which Tylor (and to a less extent Morgan) assembled and organized is too valuable to be ignored in any subsequent theory of cultural evolution. Although often unreliable in detail and interpretation, it constitutes a major achievement for their generation; one of the useful, though never final, syntheses which each century of science constructs with the data at hand, only to be superseded by the next. The preferred method of anthropology today is toward a different method of organization: under the heading of specific areas, social groups, and periods as organic wholes, rather than under such abstract classifications as "magic," "animism," "myth," "language," "counting," "the family," and others of the sort, which were favored by Tylor, Frazer, and their contemporaries. The danger of the latter was to suggest that peoples everywhere are more alike, in each of these categories, than they really are. But every mode of classification, every way of organizing and interpreting knowledge, has its limitations and distortions in addition to the aspects of truth which it reveals. The present method tends to overestimate the diversities. Though requiring extensive revision in the light of present knowledge, all the great evolutionary syntheses of nineteenth-century Europe have certain lasting values, to which later theorists must return with a critical, selective eye.

6. MORGAN AND THE MARXISTS.
RISE AND DECLINE OF HIS INFLUENCE

Although not philosophically materialistic, Morgan's theory appealed strongly to the early Marxists, largely because of its emphasis on the influence of property and social organization on culture, and because it taught (in opposition to the Biblical theory) the evolution of society from primitive beginnings. Says V. F. Calverton, "Almost every radical thinker in the nineteenth century cited Morgan as a final authority. Friedrich Engels built his whole book, *The Origin of the Family*, on Morgan's thesis. Kautsky used Morgan's evidence in his *Enstehung der Ehe und Familie*, and Plekhanov made frequent reference to Morgan in his various studies of primitive art and culture."[19] In time, his popularity with Marxist writers contributed to the reaction against him in other quarters, especially among anticommunists today. This is somewhat unjust, since he himself was not a Marxist, and there is nothing distinctively communistic in his theory.

Morgan's work was "bitterly repugnant" to many conservative Victorians because it pictured early man as sexually promiscuous.[20] It pleased the conservatives in other ways: notably, by showing monogamy and private property as characteristic of the highest stage of progress yet achieved. Westermarck, another evolutionist,[21] pleased them more by disagreeing with Morgan on the history of marriage. "Monogamy," said he, "prevailed almost exclusively among our earliest ancestors," and "Human marriage, in all probability, is an inheritance from some apelike ancestor." This theory was, in turn, attacked by Robert Briffault in *The Mothers*.

On the whole, Morgan's ideas appealed to radicals and reformist liberals by explaining marriage and property, as well as the conventions of morality, law, and justice, as products of gradual evolution; hence as possessing no eternal, absolute authority and as subject to still further change. These ideas, now taken for granted in social science and naturalistic ethics, were revolutionary extensions of "social Darwinism" in Morgan's day. Encouraging to socialist and other reformers was the sentiment expressed in Morgan's discussion of property: that the "burdensome character upon society" of privileged classes had been demonstrated. The growth of property has been so immense as to become, on the part of the people, an unmanageable power. The time will come, he said, when human intelligence will master it and define the relations of the state to the property it protects. "The interests of society are paramount to individual interests," and "The dissolution of society bids fair to become the termination of a career of which property is the end and aim; because such a career contains the elements of self-destruction."[22]

Morgan's importance for the philosophy of art history is not in what he said about it himself, but in the indirect bearing on art of his general theory of cultural evolution. As long as his theory enjoyed a tremendous vogue among the intellectual public, it encouraged an evolutionary approach to the particular arts and also to religion, science, and other phases of culture which he had not discussed in detail.[23] That vogue was gradually weak-

[19] *The Making of Man* (New York, 1931), p. 6.

[20] Calverton, *op. cit.*, p. 6, quoting W. H. R. Rivers.

[21] *History of Human Marriage* (1891); *Origin and Development of the Moral Ideas* (1906–8).

[22] *Ancient Society*, p. 561.

[23] H. E. Barnes lists a number of later writers who applied evolutionism to primitive culture: in America, J. W. Powell, F. H. Cushing, W. J. McGee, and D. G. Brinton. *Historical Sociology* (New York, 1948), p. 32. He describes Sir J. G. Frazer, author of the celebrated *Golden Bough*, as an uncritical evolutionist. "Perhaps the most extreme and uncritical exem-

ened in anthropology by attacks on his matrilineal theory of the evolution of marriage and kinship, and later by a reaction against his system and method as a whole. His decline in favor also had wide repercussions on thinking in the field of art history: it tended to discourage all evolutionary theories there, both "unilinear" and otherwise.[24]

plification of the unilineal evolutionary anthropology and historical sociology," Barnes declares, "was contained in the numerous works of the French writer, Charles J. M. Letourneau (1831–1904). "He summarized his ideas in *La Sociologie d'après*

ethnologie (1892) and treated many branches of culture in this manner. The history of sociological theories of culture stages from Comte to the present day is summarized by Barnes. (pp. 81 ff.). Those of Bagehot, Kovalevsky, W. Wundt, Durkheim, Greef, Novicow, Ratzenhofer, Tönnies, Giddings, and Ellwood are included.

[24] Further details regarding Morgan, Tylor, and unilinear evolutionism can be found in recent surveys of anthropological theory. Among the most informative of these are: David Bidney, *Theoretical Anthropology* (New York, 1953), Ch. 7; E. A. Hoebel, *Man in the Primitive World* (New York, 1958); A. L. Kroeber (ed.), *Anthropology Today* (Chicago, 1953); V. Gordon Childe, *Social Evolution* (New York, 1951), Ch. I. Some of the recent attacks on Morgan and Tylor will be mentioned later.

CHAPTER X

EVOLUTION IN AESTHETICS,
THE HISTORY OF RELIGION,
AND PARTICULAR ARTS

I. EVOLUTIONARY THEORIES OF AESTHETICS
(ALLEN, SULLY, GROOS, GUYAU)

During the last three decades of the nineteenth century, there appeared a host of articles, monographs, and books of smaller scope which undertook to fill in the details of the evolutionary account of art at various points. They specialized more or less intensively along different lines. Some dealt with a single art or medium such as music or language; some with a certain period or cultural stage, such as modern tribal arts; some with a particular concept, such as that of art as play. Some accepted and pursued a particular theory of evolution, such as that of Spencer, Taine, or Morgan; some presented new examples of development with little theoretical interpretation. Different conceptions of evolution were not always clearly distinguished; vague terms like "the development hypothesis," "progressionism," and "social Darwinism" were used interchangeably. Many writers were so eager to defend evolutionism in their own fields, as against "special creation" and "degenerationism," that they felt no need to define theoretical terms with precision.

Out of the many evolutionary studies which appeared during the late nineteenth and early twentieth centuries, a few may be selected to represent different lines of thought.

Grant Allen's *Physiological Aesthetics*[1] was a short treatise on general aesthetics from the standpoint of naturalistic psychology. It was dedicated to "the greatest of living philosophers, Herbert Spencer," as an "attempt to extend in a single direction the general principles which he has laid down." Its author, at Oxford, acknowledged indebtedness also to the works on physiological psychology of Bain, Helmholtz, Hermann, and Bernstein. Like other naturalistic approaches to aesthetics, it has been scornfully attacked by supernaturalist aestheticians.[2] In trying to explain the nature and development of aesthetic experience on a physiological basis, Allen was attempting one of the hardest

[1] (New York, 1877).

[2] For example, by Gilbert and Kuhn in *A History of Esthetic* (Bloomington, Ind., 1953), p. 526. It seems to these writers an absurd "confession" for Allen to say frankly that he is "not an excessive devotee of fine art"; that he should regard this as an asset in science because "the worshipper of art is liable to bring with him into the consideration of its simplest elements those enthusiastic feelings which are aroused in him by its highest developments." But Allen is not far wrong in saying that such a person "will probably regard with contempt every species of aesthetic emotion except those most elevated ones which are capable of gratifying his own fastidious and educated taste." (Preface, p. xiii). Allen shows in later chapters that he is by no means ignorant of the fine arts or lacking in appreciation. He is correct in saying that "excessive worship" of them can obstruct clear thinking, especially in accepting the unwelcome idea that art has developed from a physical, primitive basis. "The subject of Aesthetics," he rightly charges, "has so long been given over to transcendental rhetoric and vague poetical declamation, that the name alone upon a cover is sufficient to deter most scientific readers." That remark could still be made with some truth.

tasks in either psychology or metaphysics. It has certainly not been accomplished yet. Neither naturalists nor supernaturalists can claim to have explained aesthetic experience in any thorough, conclusive way. The shortcomings in Allen's attempt are obvious but understandable if one remembers that scientific psychology was in its early infancy in his time. He added something of value to the British tradition of empiricism and evolutionism in psychology and aesthetics. This was to apply new information about the physiology of sense-perception, hedonic tone, and emotional conditioning to the phenomena of aesthetic experience. He did so in an evolutionary way which would have been impossible for Burke, Hume, Kant, or other eighteenth-century thinkers, and which Spencer had only briefly suggested.

Rejecting the conventional dualism which had hampered British empiricism since Locke, Allen frankly adopted the naturalistic conception of mind. Without the ambitious claims which Fechner was making at the time to quantitative exactness in aesthetics, he carried certain basic hypotheses of naturalistic aesthetics a step farther toward explicit formulation. His basic, metaphysical outlook was that of Greek and modern materialism: "the functions of the higher co-ordinating nervous centres *are* consciousness itself, every other nervous function being only definitely cognised when brought into relation with that system of energies in the higher organs which constitutes the psychical life."[3]

Allen's aesthetic psychology was evolutionary, first, in the general attempt to show how the complex inner, ideational experiences of art, including literature and painting, had developed out of man's physical equipment and animal inheritance. Rejecting the view of Ruskin and Darwin that we cannot explain why some forms and colors are pleasant and others not, he undertook to show "the general relation of pleasure and pain to our organism and its circumstances," and the fact that "our existing likes and dislikes in aesthetic matters are the necessary result of natural selection." His

aim was to "exhibit the Aesthetic Feelings as constant subjective counterparts of certain definite nervous states," and to proceed from the study of "such simple pleasures in bright colour, sweet sound, or rude pictorial imitation, as delight the child and the savage" to "the more and more complex gratifications of natural scenery, music, painting, and poetry." Derived from British empiricism was Allen's emphasis on pleasantness and painfulness as capable of being transferred from direct physical sensation to ideas of imaginary things and actions. When the gratification derived from nervous organs is connected in thought with one's own personality, as part of an imaginary plan of action, it does not reach the aesthetic level. "But when that gratification is the product of exercise unconnected in thought with our own personality, and wholly cut off from actuality, it becomes a subject for aesthetic employment, both in poetical and pictorial representation."[4] After a detailed discussion of the higher and lower senses as sources of pleasant and unpleasant feeling, he went on to a brief survey of the "imitative arts," likewise in terms of psychological hedonism. Here he commented suggestively on the "emotion of the sublime," plot-interest, the use of emotive words and images, and other topics of perennial concern to the aesthetician.

Allen accepted Spencer's "play theory" of the origin and nature of art.[5] The greatest physical pleasures, he said, are normally derived from eating, drinking, and procreation as functions necessary to preserving life in individual and species. The object of work is to procure the necessities of life, and it may incidentally produce pleasures. But play is activity entered upon for its immediate gratification; it is purposeless with respect to life-giving needs, and results from an accumulation of energy in a fully-nourished, healthy nervous structure of high efficiency. This is discharged, in play under leisure conditions, on any appropriate object

[3] P. 201.
[4] P. 211.
[5] P. 31.

[130]

at hand. Common to both play and art, said Allen, is their remoteness from life-serving function and their having pleasure alone as their immediate end.

Here he oversimplified the facts more than Spencer had done. Spencer did not say that pleasure was the only immediate end of art. Play differs from aesthetic feeling, according to Allen, in that it is active while the latter is passive and receptive, mainly through the eyes and ears. It is the business of art, then, to combine as many as possible of pleasant visual and auditory sensations, with as few painful ones as possible. And "the aesthetically beautiful is that which affords the Maximum of Stimulation with the Minimum of Fatigue or Waste, in processes not directly connected with vital functions." The aesthetically ugly fails conspicuously to do so. In either case, the emotional element is weak, and mainly cognized as an intellectual discrimination. Hence, Allen says, we get the idea of aesthetic feeling as noble and elevated, since not directly traceable to any life-giving function. (Here again he oversimplifies the nature of art, which is certainly not devoted entirely to getting pleasure without pain, or to stimulation without fatigue.)

The extreme contrast between work and play, associating art with the latter, is not essential to the general theory of evolution in art. There is a kernel of truth in the idea that art, like many other civilized activities including science and philosophy, sport and practical affairs, makes use of functions developed in the prehuman struggle for existence for ends and enjoyments not strictly necessary for survival. It is psychologically true as well that, although art and play often have important indirect values, these tend to be ignored at the time in both types of activity. But the differences between art and play are so important that the two are no longer coupled as basically similar. Nevertheless, the hypothesis appealed to a number of nineteenth-century aestheticians, eager to find some bridge between the primitive struggle for necessities and the supposedly disinterested, impractical, serenely "useless" contemplation of art.

Karl Groos, while accepting the play theory in part, held it firmly within the evolutionary conception by showing how play itself was biologically useful. In *The Play of Animals* (1898) and *The Play of Man* (1901), he argued that the play of young animals and children had survival value as a preparation and practice for necessary activities in later life. He denied that play was merely a release of surplus energy detached from necessary ends; nevertheless he accepted Schiller's idea that art and play are alike in being ends in themselves, while work is a means to some ulterior end. Art arises especially from impulses of love and combat.

Whereas Taine was attacked for exaggerating the social, and neglecting the individual aspects of art, Allen was attacked for the opposite reason—by the psychologist J. Sully, in a review in *Mind*.[6] Like Spencer, Sully argued that art fulfils an important social function through arousing sympathy. Later on, in *The Colour-Sense: its Origin and Development*[7] and an article on "The Aesthetic Evolution of Man,"[8] Allen remedied this lack. Following Darwin, he attributed to animals the rudiments of a sense of beauty, and held that aesthetic perception has evolved along with the rest of human nature. The sense of color, from its original connection with sexual functions, extends to become more delicate and active in the arts. In general, the aesthetic faculties become through evolution more broad, disinterested, and social, as in the development of architecture as an expression of religious and national feeling.

Sully also followed Spencer in regarding the evolution of art as progressive from a standpoint of value. He pointed out a practical application of this theory in art criticism, thus adding emphasis to an important step which Spencer had made only vaguely and confusedly. Evolutionary psychology, Sully wrote,[9] gives us a criterion for judging art; that is, a method for comparing the

6 Vol. II (1876), 387. Cf. Needham, *op. cit.*, p. 236.

7 (London, 1879).

8 *Mind*, Vol. V (1880), 445–464.

9 "L'art et la psychologie," in *Revue philosophique*, Vol. II (1876), 321–334; also *Sensation and Intuition: Studies in Psychology*

different kinds of aesthetic enjoyment in relation to the corresponding forms of art. The principle of evolution implies an extension and development of our faculties. The law of this development provides, said Sully, a criterion for aesthetic judgment.

The brilliant, short-lived Jean-Marie Guyau (1854–88) helped to clarify the evolutionary, naturalistic approach to aesthetics in the seventies and eighties. Following Taine, he combined the psychological and sociological points of view. Without the broad scope of Taine or Spencer, he went directly to certain crucial issues, correcting previous errors and achieving a moderate, empirical theory of art and aesthetic experience.[10] He attacked especially those basic tenets of idealistic aesthetics, descending from Plato through Kant, which blocked the way to a naturalistic account of artistic phenomena. These all combined to reinforce the supernaturalist conception of art and beauty at their best as purely spiritual, disinterested and abstractly contemplative, entirely apart from the needs, desires, and practical activities of man. Naturalistic evolutionism was basically committed to the opposite view; that art and all the varieties of experience involved in it had developed continuously out of the primitive struggle for existence; that they had helped man to survive, and had remained in manifold contact with practical life. Marx, Engels, Taine, and Spencer were supporting this view, each in his own way, but with special details which Guyau could not accept. The Kantian obstructions to scientific aesthetics, still strong today, were stronger in Guyau's time. Spencer's moderate, partial analogy between art and play was not inconsistent with evolutionism. A partial dissociation of some kinds of art from the struggle for physical survival had obviously occurred through the advance of civilized leisure. Some partial detachment of art from other concerns was desirable today, as the advocates of "art for art's sake" had insisted. The artist must have some freedom from distracting moral and utilitarian considerations, to work out his own problems. The full development of art, said Guyau,[11]

required a "cult of beauty" around the artist. In Spencerian terms, differentiation or specialization was an essential phase in the evolutionary process itself, and had occurred throughout the history of art. But it was always partial and relative; not founded on a complete, metaphysical dichotomy.

Guyau was not much impressed by either Schiller's or Spencer's theory of art as play. To conceive of art as a vain, though hygienic, exercise of our highest powers, he argued, would tend toward dilettantism and ignore the vital, serious nature of great art. In trying to place art above life, he said, Schiller's conception of ideal art tends to lower it beneath science and everyday life. Art is not a kind of play, although play contains aesthetic elements. In evolving from the primitive stage, art ceases to be playful and becomes a form of work. Grant Allen's distinction between play and art is unsound, said Guyau: pure sensation can not be divorced from action; all perception is active, in muscles as well as nerves; it is never entirely contemplative. Even if art detaches itself for a time from certain aspects of the life around it, the separation is not necessarily permanent. Art may return as a result of its independent growth to become more necessary to the rest of life than before. "Human civilization, which multiplies in each of us capacities of every sort and… divides our functions excessively, needs to compensate by the various types of artistic play for the work it forces on our organs."[12]

Guyau went on to attack the Kantian divorce between beauty and utility, with its depreciation of the latter. According to this theory, he said, everything which is not "art for art's sake" is necessarily lacking in beauty; industry and art move in opposite directions. (Ruskin and Morris were protesting this dislocation, in art and life as

and Aesthetics (London, 1880), Essay XIII. Needham, op. cit., p. 243.

[10] L'art au point de vue sociologique (Paris, 1887); also Les problèmes de l'esthétique contemporaine (Paris, 1884), Needham, pp. 243 ff.

[11] Problèmes, p. 92.

[12] Problèmes, p. 10.

well as in theory.) Along with this, he attacked the related Kantian theory that true beauty answers to no real need and excites neither desire nor fear; that aesthetic experience is, accordingly, "disinterested" in the sense of being devoid of all interests but that of contemplation itself. This theory, said Guyau, would exclude beauty from the most real and vital aspects of life. On the contrary, he insisted, all the main human needs or desires, corresponding to functions essential for life, can take on aesthetic quality. These are breathing, moving, eating, and reproducing—all modified and refined by civilization, as in modern love and expressions of ideal love in art. There is no aesthetic emotion, Guyau declared, which does not awaken in us a multitude of desires and needs, more or less unconscious. The beautiful and desirable cannot be separated. (Psychoanalysis confirms Guyau's theory in this respect.) "At the origin of aesthetic evolution," he maintained, "among inferior beings, agreeable sensation was gross and wholly sensual." Man introduced a distinction between the merely pleasant and the beautiful; animal and human pleasures. In a future stage of progress, the pleasant and the beautiful will again be identified within the latter; as life becomes more harmonized, all our joys will take on the character of beauty.

Like Spencer, Guyau laid stress on the social aspects of aesthetic enjoyment, especially as to the function of music and poetry in arousing sympathy. Art must identify itself with the forces which tend to unify society. Literature, in the past, has followed the evolution of society, and "every evolution brings on a dissolution."[13] Literary decadence, he said, is connected with biology and sociology; one can find in an epoch the traits of old age—an enfeeblement and perversion of vitality, of the forces resisting death. Excessive freedom and riches, selfishness, luxury, envy, and the like are social maladies which lead to dissolution and decadence in society and art. The literary decadents tend to disintegrate society.

Guyau criticized the sociological approach of Taine and Hennequin as oversimplified. Three kinds of society interact with genius, he said: first the real, previously existing society which conditions and partly sustains the genius; second, the ideally modified society which the genius himself conceives; third, the consequent formation of a new society, that of his admirers, who partly realize his innovation through imitation.

Unlike the romanticists and *décadents* of his generation, Guyau did not think of art as opposed to the machine or to science. Machinery itself has an aesthetic quality.[14] (Here spoke the France of *La Tour Eiffel*; not that of Baudelaire.) The mystery and poetry of the universe, he continued, will always last, along with the scientific explanation of its phenomena. Science, like poetry, is born of wonder, and there will be an eternal poetry in science itself. Human evolution has intellectualized all man's faculties, including his sensibility, thus leading to the progress of ethics and aesthetics.[15] In future this will increase, and "The artist will acquire, more and more, on one hand the scientific spirit which shows reality as it is, and on the other the philosophic spirit, which goes beyond such reality and raises eternal, fundamental problems."

The general thesis that art is influenced by social factors was still further reinforced by the Finnish writer Yrjö Hirn.[16] Although there exists, he said, a purely aesthetic impulse in art which aims at no outside end, many outside forces also act upon it. These appear in the primitive arts, including ornamentation, dance, and drama. Art, said Hirn, has a positive social function in allowing man to intensify his emotional experiences, pleasant and painful; also as an emotional sedative in calming and soothing too powerful feelings. Following Adam Smith and Spencer, he stressed the value of art as a means of communicating emotions and thus establishing collective sympathy within larger and larger groups.

13 *L'art au point de vue sociologique*, p. 355.
14 *Problèmes*, pp. 115 ff.
15 *Ibid.*, pp. 155, 161.
16 *The Origins of Art—a Psychological and Sociological Inquiry* (London, 1900).

2. SOCIOLOGY AND ETHNOLOGY APPLIED TO THE NEW "SCIENCE OF ART" (GROSSE)

The need for scientific study of such problems, and thus for a new "science of art" (*Kunstwissenschaft*) was set forth by Ernst Grosse, ethnologist and sociologist of Freiburg. In *The Beginnings of Art*,[17] he called for greater attention to primitive art, not only because of its important role in cultural evolution, but also because of its relative simplicity. He outlined the aims, methods, and limitations of a genuine science of art, then surveyed the principal arts of contemporary primitives with occasional references to prehistoric examples (such as the European and Bushman cave-drawings), and ended with some generalizations on the arts of various peoples.

Like Taine and Fechner, Grosse devoted considerable thought to the requirements of the new science of art.[18] It is sometimes regarded, he began, as a combination of the history and philosophy of art; but neither of these deserves to be called a science. The history of art cannot become so until its individual facts have been grouped in logical connection. The philosophy of art has been too speculative; that of the Hegelians and Herbartians has today (1893) "only a historical interest." Art criticism is too subjective. No science can hope to explain any phenomenon completely; science has to content itself with demonstrating the normal sequence of phenomena in its general aspects. It remains on the empirical surface of things. A science of art will have accomplished its purpose when it has shown "that regular and fixed relations exist between certain forms of culture and art."

Within empirical limits, said Grosse, the science of art must try to describe and explain the individual and social phenomena of art. The individual ones, though usually considered more interesting, can not be explored to any great extent since the data are insufficient, especially from early periods. The sociological approach is more promising: to "relate the aggregate character of the art groups of a period or a district to a whole people or a whole age."[19] One should begin with the simple arts of primitive peoples, which the science of art "still disdains to honor with a glance." Ethnology can be of great help in this study. Only from a knowledge of savage art can we come to understand the civilized complexities. The first step is to collect examples of the arts of all primitive peoples. Next, one must try to define and compare their aesthetic characters in general and in detail, to grasp the special meanings and feelings the primitive artists intend to convey, and to relate these to the various stages and types of social evolution. This, Grosse conceded, would be a long and difficult task.

Reviewing the history of the subject, Grosse declared that Abbé Dubos and Herder had been the first to attempt an account of art as a social phenomenon. They had also paid some attention to primitive art. Taine had been given too much credit for starting the sociological approach to art history. Both he and Guyau had confined themselves to the civilized periods. Moreover, Taine's theory was unsound: he had, for one thing, overlooked the fact "that art not only passively but actively opposes taste." As Hennequin had shown, Taine overestimated the unity and distinctive character of race, climate, and public taste. "Nearly every great work of art is created not conformably to, but against, the prevailing taste. Nearly every great artist is not chosen but rejected by the public."

Here Grosse himself, like the man he attacked, was oversimplifying the facts. There are many "publics" in a large, civilized nation, some one of which—perhaps a small, sensitive, critical avant-

---

[17] *Die Anfänge der Kunst* (Freiburg, 1893). English trans. (New York, 1897, 1900). The term *Kunstwissenschaft* had been in use among scholars for a number of years, but there was still much disagreement about its meaning and scope. See T. Munro, *Toward Science in Aesthetics* (New York, 1956), p. 143.

[18] Chs. I, II.

[19] P. 12.

garde—may accept and foster a new genius while most of the population rejects or ignores him. Without some such fostering, how will he ever be recognized? Taine's basic thesis—that the climate of public taste acts as a selective and determining *milieu* in the evolution of art—was not wrong, but needed qualification. One must go on to show the various influences on art of different subgroups and attitudes within a society, and the influence of various kinds of art upon them. This has not yet been done with any approach to thoroughness.

"The unity of primitive art," Grosse affirmed, "stands in the sharpest contrast to the diversity of primitive peoples."[20] The Australians and Eskimos are extremely unlike, but their ornaments (said Grosse) are often similar. So are the rock drawings of Australians and African Bushmen, in spite of racial differences. This Grosse took as an argument against Taine's racial theory. (Contemporary stylistic analysis would not agree with Grosse on the high resemblance between the arts of primitive groups.) He went on to argue that "The uniform character of primitive art points undubitably to a uniform cause," and that this unifying factor is the method of securing food among hunting peoples. Climate he considered a secondary factor, effective only through the mode of production.

As against the play theory of art, in its extreme form, Grosse upheld the evolutionary view that art had been an active means to social survival. He rejected the common tendency of civilized nations to treat art more and more as idle play. It is inconceivable, he said, that a function to which so much energy has been applied should be without influence in maintaining and developing society. Natural selection would "long ago have rejected the peoples which wasted their force in so purposeless a way, in favor of other peoples of practical talents; and art could not possibly have been developed so highly and richly as it has been."[21] The social and educational importance of art has continuously increased: partly as a means

to social welfare, partly as a means to individual development, which is the main goal of social evolution. Art frees the individual from the bonds of social connection. "Thus art is no idle play, but an indispensable social function, one of the most efficient weapons in the struggle for existence," and destined to be even more richly developed through that struggle. It is now maintained for its indirect social value more than for its immediate, aesthetic appeal. We have the right to demand, said Grosse, that art should serve a social and broadly moral function; but this it can do best while serving artistic interests, not by moralizing.

Primitive art has practical importance for hunting peoples. Ornamentation promotes technical skill; personal adornment and the dance influence sexual selection; personal decoration may also serve to frighten an enemy. Poetry, dance, and music inspire warriors to defend the group. All art extends and strengthens social bonds, but to an unequal extent—dance and poetry greatly, music very little. (Here Grosse parts from Spencer.) The hegemony passes from one art to another as society evolves: the dance loses influence as the social group enlarges. Poetry has gained through the invention of printing, and its soothing voice "resounds mightily over the clash of arms." (Later events have hardly sustained this optimistic view.) As to each art, Grosse thus considered various practical and social explanations of its primitive and prehistoric phenomena. Why did men of the reindeer age display more skill in naturalistic representation than their successors? Because hunting peoples need more skill in observation and manual execution. "Neither the agriculturists nor the herdsmen require for their maintenance so high a perfection of the power of observation and of skill with the hand; consequently these faculties deteriorate among them, and with these the talent for naturalistic representation."[22]

[20] P. 309.
[21] P. 312.
[22] P. 199.

Do the sources of music lie, as Dubos and Spencer believed, "in the cadences of impassioned speech," or was Schopenhauer right in calling music "quite independent of the visible world" and of any world outside itself? Was Darwin right in thinking that music arose as a means of sexual attraction? Grosse found all of these theories unverified by the available facts. He leaned a little toward Schopenhauer in admitting that no satisfactory social explanation or connection could yet be found for this art: music is "an emotional movement unique in its nature." The music of a people, said Grosse, is independent of its civilization, and its civilization is independent of its music. Unique among the arts, music "serves essentially the objects of art alone." Other sociologists were quick to challenge Grosse on this point, and to insist that music, too, had been an integral part of social evolution.

3. EVOLUTIONARY THEORIES OF PRIMITIVE VISUAL ART. CHILDREN'S ART. STAGES AND SEQUENCES (HADDON, BOAS)

As the question of the "missing link" between ape and man perplexed biologists before the discovery of *Pithecanthropus* and other intermediate types, so that of primitive art perplexed the cultural evolutionist. On the basis of archeological data, how could prehistoric art be shown as transitional from the first stage of human life, presumably cultureless, to the art of ancient civilizations? To what extent were the arts of contemporary "primitive" peoples analogous to the prehistoric, thus providing data for the theoretical reconstruction of prehistoric art?

Many archeologists and anthropologists had helped to build a mass of information about primitive culture by the last quarter of the nineteenth century. Most of them had not tried to detach material bearing on the arts and related aesthetic phenomena from that on other aspects of primitive culture. Some of the major works we have been considering, such as that of L. H. Morgan, showed only a minor interest in art as such. It was generally realized that the evolution of art could not be completely detached from that of the rest of culture, or studied to advantage in complete isolation. Nevertheless, keen public interest in the origin of the civilized arts directed some attempts to select and draw the artistic threads of early history together. One by one, the civilized arts were considered from an evolutionary point of view. How could music, poetry, painting, and the rest have developed in prehistoric times—before Homer, before the Egyptians? In each art, what types had come first, and what had been the subsequent stages? What were the causal relations between such types of art and other historical factors? How were the stages in primitive art related to the stages in social development?

We have already noticed the attempt of Gottfried Semper to explain the origins of art on evolutionary lines. This included the theory that decorative motifs in architecture and the useful arts had evolved primarily from early technical processes required by the nature of the materials used and the functions intended. Later ornamentation was derived, according to this theory, by copying primitive motifs long after the technical processes which originated them had disappeared. Motifs derived from basketry and textiles had been, in some cases, applied to pottery and metal. Semper denied that realistic imitation of natural flower and plant forms had played much part in the early evolution of ornament.

This theory was applied to other arts by his followers, such as Von Conze,[23] who held that the most geometric, stylized, unrealistic stage in any art must be the earliest, since it was closer to

---

[23] *Beiträge zur Geschichte der griechischen Plastik* (Halle, 1869). See also Listowel, *op. cit.*, p. 229, on later theories of M. Hoernes and K. Woermann, giving priority to the decorative arts, especially self-adornment.

the original techniques. Such a theory was hard to reconcile with the realistic paleolithic drawings and paintings which were being gradually discovered throughout the late nineteenth and twentieth centuries, but these were often conveniently ignored. Current ideas of ancient painting and sculpture, based largely on a partial knowledge of Egyptian, Greek, and Roman styles, still assumed that the main order of evolution, the "progress of art," had been and must be toward more and more realistic representation. The belief that art was more highly evolved and better in proportion as it was more realistic or naturalistic usually involved a condescending, superior attitude by the modern historian toward primitive art.

In the eighties and nineties, the general problem of sequence and priority in the visual arts was focused on this single issue: which had come first, realistic representation or abstract, decorative symbolism? In relation to the whole, complex subject of evolution in the arts, this seems a rather minor issue, but it has received great emphasis in anthropology. The issue of priority here is still considered so important in anthropology that, in a recent survey of that field,[24] it is the only topic to be mentioned under the broad heading of *Evolution in Art*.

As against the commonly accepted view, W. H. Holmes and Alfred Haddon presented empirical evidence to show that realism had, in some cases at least, come first. The study by Holmes in 1888 was comparatively specialized.[25] In Chiriqui art, he maintained, an evolution from realistic through stylized to abstract symbolic forms had taken place. He showed examples of what seemed to be a progressive conventionalization and abstraction of certain motifs, such as the alligator. But he had no proof that the more realistic examples were actually earlier.

A few years later, Haddon defended a similar thesis with respect to a much larger field of distribution.[26] He brought forward a wide array of examples from contemporary primitive and ancient civilized cultures, to show again that realism

had come first. A zoologist and anthropologist, Haddon claimed to apply biological methods, as Darwin and Spencer had done. Stylization and simplification in decorative art had occurred everywhere, he declared, through the "degeneration" of realistic forms by repeated, unskilful copying. The original, realistic meanings would still be attached to the conventionalized forms, so that the latter would act as symbols. Haddon accepted the current assumption that a savage could not "copy or adapt a certain design because it promises to develop into a more pleasing pattern,"[27] and that anyone with artistic skill would certainly use it to copy nature. In a neat, comprehensive table,[28] Haddon diagrammed three main "stages of development" in art, information, wealth, and religion. They were, rather, stages in a life cycle from realistic "origin" through "evolution" to "decay." Passing through this cycle, under the heading of "Art," were four types descending from "Solitary Decorative Figures." The first, *Pictures*, had degenerated through incompetent copying. The second, *Groups*, had received conventional treatment for decorative purposes. The third, *Series of Patterns*, had been simplified through repeated copying. The fourth, *Combinations or Heteromorphs*, had shown degradation resulting from the monstrous in art. Under the heading of "Information," three types were shown in parallel descent from early, realistic *Pictographs*. One had gone from phonograms to alphabetical signs; another from abbreviated pictographs to arithmetical signs, and a third from emblems to personal and tribal signs or symbols. Religious symbols and ornamented useful objects had likewise gone from comparative realism to what we should now call "abstract" or non-representative

[24] E. A. Hoebel, *Man in the Primitive World: an Introduction to Anthropology* (New York, 1958), pp. 270–273.

[25] *Ancient Art of the Province of Chiriqui* (Bureau of American Ethnology, Annual Report 6, 1888), pp. 13–186.

[26] *Evolution in Art* (London, 1895). *Cf.* H. Balfour, *The Evolution of Decorative Art* (London, 1893).

[27] P. 317. *Cf.* Goldwater, p. 18.

[28] P. 8.

signs. A number of contemporary scholars accepted Haddon's views.[29]

So the situation remained until 1908, when Franz Boas pointed out that, in some cases, the evolution of style had actually proceeded from geometric to realistic. His study was based on Eskimo needlecases, in which ancient, geometric motifs were shown to have evolved into naturalistic animal figures.[30] Boas did not assert that this had always been the order of development; rather, he emphasized that no particular sequence could be assumed as universal without adequate stratigraphic or historical evidence to that effect.

At present, it seems that both types of sequence have occurred in different times and places; which has been more common can not yet be stated with assurance. Nor can we be sure at the present time of just what sequences of change preceded the high development of realistic drawing, painting, and sculpture in the Cro-Magnon epoch. Was there a comparably high development of abstract, symbolic decoration before it or along with it? The evidence is still too incomplete to write the full story of early evolution in the visual arts, and many alternations of emphasis may have occurred, of which nothing is now known. Yet the undoubted antiquity of ice-age realism, and the lack of any known high development of abstract design before it, still offer some support to Haddon's theory. It seems to be accepted, moreover, that the use of conventionalized visual symbols for written language is largely a product of the neolithic period. Roughly, the sequence was from realistic animal representations to highly simplified symbols, as in the mesolithic culture of Le Mas d'Azil in France. It did not necessarily occur in the same race of men as a continuous process. Furthermore, it was not necessarily a decline or "degeneration" in the derogatory sense employed by Haddon. "The so-called degenerate figures on the painted pebbles are the rudiments of an embryonic system of writing," says Hoebel,[31] and why should we deplore the invention of writing,

which—more than anything else—distinguishes civilized from primitive culture?

Be that as it may, the broader issue involved in this dispute about priorities is the same as that which we have noted in regard to Comte, Morgan, and Tylor—whether or not cultural evolution passes everywhere and necessarily through any uniform sequence of stages. Both Semper and Haddon thought it did, though disagreeing on the sequence; Boas called for suspended judgment until more evidence could be assembled.

Another disputed issue in the early twentieth century was the common association of primitive art with children's drawings.[32] It was gradually realized that primitive art (prehistoric and modern) was not merely a crude, groping attempt at realistic representation but, in many cases, a radically different kind of art, sophisticated in its own way, with different aims and standards such as those of symbolism, design, and expression.

The new understanding of primitive art was well summarized by Ralph Linton, American anthropologist.[33] The arts of living, uncivilized peoples, he declared, are not really primitive: not simple, generalized, or ancestral to our own. An African mask or Haida totem pole is no more a "spontaneous childlike expression" than the Parthenon sculpture is. The so-called primitive art of

[29] Notably, Colley March, who denied "the geometric origin of pattern-making." "Evolution and Psychology in Art," *Mind*, V (1896), 441. Goldwater (p. 41) also lists Charles Read and W. H. Goodyear in this group.

[30] *Decorative Designs of Alaskan Needlecases* (United States National Museum, Reports, Vol. 39, 1908), pp. 221–344. *Cf.* Hoebel, p. 272. Boas further developed his position in *Primitive Art* (Oslo, 1927). Among other studies in the visual arts, Boas referred to these in his article on "Anthropology," § on "Art": F. A. van Scheltema, *Die altnordische Kunst* (Berlin, 1923); H. Stolpe, *Collected Essays on Ornamental Art* (Stockholm, 1927); E. Wilson, *Das Ornament* (Erfurt, 1914).

[31] P. 273.

[32] Grosse had protested against it in 1893 (*op. cit.*, p. 193) pointing out that children's art lacks observation. But as late as 1912 a book could be called *The Childhood of Art* (by H. G. Spearing, London) which undertook to cover the history of drawing and painting from prehistoric times through the early Greek.

[33] *American Magazine of Art*, Jan. 1933, pp. 17–24.

today is of two types—angular (as in textiles) and curvilinear (as in most painting and carving). Its aims are very different from most European art, which has been predominantly naturalistic. It refers to thought-images instead of visual images. It prefers rigid stylization to naturalism. Any impulse toward the latter is usually checked by the requirements of utilitarian form, of magic or of religion.

During the early twentieth century, drawings made by young children in European cities were analyzed intensively. They were compared with drawings of similar subjects by primitive adults, and found to be significantly different. They were differently motivated when spontaneous and not too much influenced by adults. A drawing of a man by a young child is usually built up of separate units such as the head, the body, the two arms, the two legs, the hat, each visually conceived and executed as a distinct act, with emphasis on each part according to its felt importance. Primitive adult art, prehistoric or modern, when executed with developed skill, tends to conceive the outline of the figure more as a continuous whole, whether realistically or not.[34] Nevertheless, there were undeniable resemblances between some primitive drawing and that of children in modern Western civilization. In both, there seemed to be a recurrent progression from weak or chaotic scribbling to controlled form of some sort; from the more schematic, conceptual type to the more realistic; from simple to complex in form and meaning. This was most noticeable if one did not take the best paleolithic drawings as the beginning of the story, but started rather with some of the more "degenerate" (simple and stylized) neolithic figures made much later.

Detailed observation of the changes in drawing by a particular child over a period of years seemed to some psychologists to confirm the hypothesis of recapitulation. This was developed into a theory of art education, based on the assumption of a normal, orthogenetic sequence in the artistic growth of each individual. Teaching would then be at its best, according to this theory, if it brought the child step by step through a recapitulation of the principal stages in past art.[35]

The idea of a detailed, universal recapitulation, like that of the human embryo in ontogeny, has not been proved for art and is doubtless exaggerated. But there is undeniable significance in the mass of experimental data produced by psychologists and art educators before the Second World War, through patiently preserving and analyzing the drawings of individual children over a period of years. This significance has never been fully assessed. There is certainly some analogy between the physical maturation of an individual and his artistic or other cultural maturation. Both are a kind of ontogeny. Though different, they must be intimately connected. The analogy is limited, however, not only by the vast difference between organic and cultural, but also by the fact that individual growth in art is always influenced by the surrounding culture. It can be directed in radically different ways merely by ordinary exposure to popular art in magazines and city streets, even when the teacher tries his best to protect the child from all outside art or explicit direction.[36] Hence the apparently universal tendency of modern Western children toward realism may have

[34] Pioneers in the understanding of children's art were: C. Ricci, *L'arte dei bambini* (Bologna, 1887; Leipzig, 1906); G. H. Luquet, *Les dessins d'un enfant* (Paris, 1913), *Le dessin enfantin* (Paris, 1927); G. Kerschensteiner, *Die Entwicklung der zeichnerischen Begabung* (Munich, 1905); S. Levinstein, *Kinderzeichnungen bis zum 14ten Lebensjahr* (Leipzig, 1905); W. Stern, "Die zeichnerische Entwicklung eines Knaben vom 4. bis zum 7. Jahre," *Zeitschrift für angewandte Psychologie* (1909), pp. 498–526; H. Eng, *The Psychology of Children's Drawings* (New York, 1931).

[35] Henry Schaefer-Simmern, *The Unfolding of Artistic Activity* (Berkeley, Calif., 1948). Gustaf Britsch, says this author, in his *Theorie der Bildenden Kunst*, shows that artistic activity as a general attribute of the human mind reveals itself in children's untaught drawings and in the first stages of art in all periods. "He demonstrates," says Schaefer-Simmern, "the existence of definite evolutionary stages by which artistic configuration develops gradually from simple to more complex relationships of form." (p. xi)

[36] Cf. T. Munro, "Franz Cizek and the Free Expression Method." In *Art Education: its Philosophy and Psychology* (New York, 1956), p. 237.

been largely due to the surrounding realism of Western adult art. Now Western art has, to a large extent, gone off on other paths, sometimes emulating the art of primitives and sometimes (e.g., in Klee) that of children. Abstract art avoids all representation. Under these new conditions, one may well ask what will be the "spontaneous" course of Western children's art in the next few decades.

The condescending attitude toward primitive art did not disappear until well along in the twentieth century, when artists and critics discovered the aesthetic virtues of African and other primitive sculpture, exalting it as more advanced in design than the realistic products of the classical tradition. Leo Frobenius had praised it (somewhat too fancifully) in a series of books on African masks, rock carvings, and fetishes. Gauguin had drawn attention to Polynesian art through his own paintings in the nineties, and Parisian artists were emulating African Negro sculpture before 1910.[37] When science stopped assuming that primitive art was necessarily inferior to modern, one result was to cast more doubt on the whole theory of cultural evolution. If paleolithic and tribal art was really better and more highly evolved in important ways than that of modern civilized art, what happens to the "development hypothesis?" Had art really "degenerated" after all?

Whether or not the trend of Greek and Renaissance art to increasing realism had been a "degeneration" remained in dispute. Paleolithic art was now admired for its realism; African Negro art for boldly sacrificing realism to design. But in any case, the path of evolution seemed, in the twenties, less and less straight and unilinear.

4. EVOLUTIONARY THEORIES OF RELIGION, MYTHOLOGY, AND MAGIC (MÜLLER, FRAZER).

We are not especially concerned in this book with theories of the early evolution of religion and magic, except as they relate to the arts. But the

bonds between religion and art have been so close as to warrant a brief look at evolutionism in the field of religious history.

In the nineteenth century, as we have seen, cultural historians were on the whole less specialized than at present, and less cautious in advancing comprehensive theories. They were still excited by the rapid accumulation of data in various fields of research. Their minds ranged widely and imaginatively from field to field, advancing bold hypotheses which often outran the data then available. Scholars in the history of religion collaborated with those in comparative mythology and folklore, linguistics and comparative literature. A few, such as Max Müller, combined vast erudition in several of these fields. Like other cultural evolutionists, they sought for analogies among widely separated peoples, and sometimes jumped to extravagant claims for universal principles of origin.

One of these was the theory of solar, seasonal, and other natural origins for myths and conceptions of deities. Mannhardt and Müller were among the leaders in this approach, and in the general science of comparative mythology. A hundred years or more of preliminary work lay behind them in the gathering of folklore by such men as Herder, Bishop Percy of the "Reliques," and the brothers Grimm.[38] Now the science of linguistics and comparative philology had provided a mechanism for the systematic exploration of analogies in word and meaning among all the great language-systems and the peoples who had used them. Müller proposed his own theory of solar and other

---

[37] See Robert Goldwater's summary of this shift in theory and taste: *Primitivism in Modern Painting* (New York, 1938), Ch. I, pt. II. Leo Frobenius' best-known work was *Das Unbekannte Afrika* (Munich, 1923). H. Kühn's *Die Kunst der Primitiven* (Munich, 1923) was the first general survey of primitive visual art from the new and more favorable point of view. It was succeeded, with more aesthetic analysis of sculptural form, by P. Guillaume and T. Munro in *Primitive Negro Sculpture* (New York, 1926).

[38] Jacob Grimm (1778–1865) and Wilhelm (1787–1825) helped to develop scientific linguistics out of the study of early literature and folklore. Association with the romanticists at Heidelberg drew their interest to German myths and sagas.

natural origins in 1856. He followed it with a massive system of volumes on the sciences of language, religion, and thought, as well as important translations from the Sanskrit and other oriental classics.[39] He brought forward countless examples of similar names of gods and natural phenomena in various languages, to show the Indo-European origin of many Greek, Roman, and Germanic deities and their primal reference to sun, storm, and spring revival. The two subjects of chief interest to the Vedic poets, he said, were (1) the sunrise, when light conquered darkness, and the annual triumph of spring over winter, and (2) the thunderstorm, with a bright god as victor over dark clouds and the rescue of fertilizing rain from its prison during heat and drouth. These subjects had given rise, said Müller, to two schools of modern interpretation, the solar and the meteorological, seeking to explain hymns and episodes in various Aryan mythologies as poetical metamorphoses of the sunrise or the thunderstorm. "I have always considered the solar and vernal phraseology," said Müller, "as the more important and the more primitive in the growth of mythology."

Mannhardt, who published *Die Lettischen Sonnenmythen* in 1875, died in 1880. At the end, he came to feel that both of these interpretations had been overdone. "I am very far from looking upon all myths as psychical reflexions of physical phenomena, like Kuhn, Schwartz, Max Müller and their school," he wrote. Müller disclaimed any such extreme view.[40] He insisted that, like Mannhardt, Oldenberg, and others in the field, he had felt "uncomfortable" at the way in which more and more myths had "rushed in and claimed their place as myths of a solar and auroral origin." The idea of a marriage between the sun and the earth, with the harvest as result of that union, he had found in the traditions of widely distant races, unconnected historically.

Müller believed that the ambiguity of language, its inadequacy for the expression of thought and description of phenomena, was a main cause of the development of mythology. In the highest sense, he said, mythology is "the power exercised by language on thought in every possible sphere of mental activity."[41] Cassirer attacks this view as implying that myth does not rest upon a positive power of thought, but on a mental defect, a pathological influence of speech. From this point of view, he says, "all artistic creation becomes a mere imitation, which must always fall short of the original." And even idealization and style, measured by the truth of the object depicted, are "nothing but subjective misconception and falsification."[42] Müller himself, however, did not draw from his theory any inferences so extreme and so derogatory to art. And the substitute theory which Cassirer offers is a return to Kant and Hegel: that the forms of thought themselves contain the measure and criterion for their own truth and intrinsic meaning, instead of having to be measured by the extraneous facts which they are supposed to reproduce. Straight from Hegel comes the dictum of Cassirer: that, in the realms of myth, art, language, and science, "the spirit exhibits itself in that inwardly determined dialectic by virtue of which alone there is any reality, any organized and definite Being at all." Every form of existence, Cassirer continues, has its source in some intellectual grasp of meaning, and the realms just mentioned "function organically together in the construction of spiritual reality." On this spiritualistic basis, Cassirer builds a theory of "the successive phases of religious thought," according to the way in which gods are conceived: first the anonymous, impersonal stage, then the stage of polynomy

---

39 He summarized his work and some principal controversies with other scholars in the Preface to *Contributions to the Science of Mythology* (2 vols.; London, 1897). See esp. Vol. I, p. 142.

40 *Op. cit.*, p. xx.

41 "The Philosophy of Mythology," in *The Science of Religion* (London, 1873), pp. 353–355, quoted by E. Cassirer in *Language and Myth* (New York, 1946), pp. 5–8. Cassirer here attributes to Spencer the view that the mythico-religious veneration of natural phenomena, such as the sun and moon, originates in "nothing more than a misinterpretation of the names which men have applied to these objects."

42 *Ibid.*, p. 6.

wherein each god unites a wealth of attributes and names, then the stage of attaining a unified God-idea through the unity of the word, then the further striving for a concept of unlimited Being.

Certainly Müller's concept of the inadequacy of language is itself inadequate to explain myth, art, and science, and he did not propose it as sufficient in itself. Subsequent research on language makes it seem even less adequate for the purpose. But naturalists will also find the idealistic explanation inadequate, as relying too much on the supposedly all-creative, all-encompassing power of mind. As against this monistic idealism, the naturalist insists that only through the interaction between thinking organisms and their natural environments do myth, art, language, and science evolve; and that all may be fairly judged for truth by their power to help us in dealing with the outside world. But art, for the naturalist, has other functions and values beside the accurate imitation of nature. Cassirer's emphasis upon the Platonic *logos* has helped to strengthen the contemporary interest in semantics, with metaphysical implications, as an approach to aesthetics and the philosophy of art history. It is one more instance of the perennial ability of supernaturalism to find new ways of asserting itself against empirical science.

Under the influence of Max Müller, many archeologists of the late nineteenth and early twentieth centuries proceeded to interpret the visual arts of early cultures in terms of solar and seasonal myths. A reaction then ensued, as often does after the over-use of a theory.

A more recent tendency is to emphasize symbols of fertility, such as the Tree of Life, the Earth Goddess (Ishtar and her equivalents) and related phenomena in primitive art. Psychoanalysis, along Freudian and Jungian lines, reinforces the historian's battery of interpretive tools. But symbols of sex and fertility are obviously related to those of seasonal birth, death, and rebirth.

In describing "what is now called the evolution of mythology, and indirectly of religion,"[43] Müller also stressed the process of syncretism—the fusing of different deities, or substituting of one for another—and also anthropomorphic development. The Greek gods, he pointed out, had advanced beyond some of their Vedic, Egyptian, and South Sea Island relatives in assuming human or superhuman form, including ethical virtues. Yet they did retain traces of their early derivation from natural phenomena. After early anthropomorphism came the idea of one great god above all other gods, and eventually the monotheistic idea of a single God.

The founders of the scientific history of religions according to Solomon Reinach (who followed them closely on that path) were W. Mannhardt, William Robertson Smith, and Max Müller.[44] William Robertson Smith, author of *The Religion of the Semites* (1889) was deposed from a professorship in Scotland and tried for heresy for his scientific approach to religion. He pointed out that so-called histories of religion had been almost entirely a study of Christian beliefs, other religions being regarded as mere heathenism.[45]

In contrast with the scientific approach, Reinach discussed two earlier, mistaken theories of the origin and nature of religions: (1) that of divine revelation, the Biblical, orthodox Church doctrine,[46] and (2) that of imposture, the anti-clerical view of such eighteenth-century *philosophes* as Voltaire and Rousseau. These men shared, said Reinach, "the strange idea that man... lived for centuries without any religion, and that human societies were purely lay societies before the spirit of domination and fraud introduced the worship of the gods." More correct, he showed, were the

[43] P. 149.

[44] S. Reinach, *Orpheus: a History of Religions* (New York, 1930; trans. from the 38th French edition), p. 26. His bibliography includes W. Mannhardt, *Wald- und Feldculte* (1875–77); *Mythologische Forschungen* (1884); Max Müller, *Introduction to the Science of Religion* (1875); S. Reinach, *Cultes, mythes, et religions* (5 vols.; 1904–23); M. Jastrow, *The Study of Religion* (1902); W. R. Smith, *The Religion of the Semites* (new ed., 1906); Frazer, *Totemism* (1898).

[45] J. Murphy, *The Origins and History of Religions* (Manchester, 1949), p. 5.

[46] *Orpheus*, p. 8, referring to an 1810 statement of it by Creuzer, a Hellenist of Heidelberg.

theories of Fontenelle and De Brosses. The former, about 1694, surmised that primitive man had invented fables to explain the causes of natural phenomena such as lightning, wind, and wave; also that he had imagined his gods in his own image at successive stages of civilization. De Brosses, in 1760, had introduced the concept of fetishism as the worship of small devotional objects such as stones, shells, or carvings.

Reinach summarized current scientific theories of the origin and history of religions. Animism and taboo were the original, essential factors in religion and mythology, he said. A little later came totemism and magic, associated with the worship of animals and plants and with increasing social organization. Animism included the worship of the dead. Magic he regarded as "the strategy of animism," since "by the aid of magic, man takes the initiative against things," becoming the conductor in the great concert of spirits which surround him. All great primitive inventions had been made under the auspices of magic and religion. Involved in taboo was *mana*, the latent power in a person, a thing, or a word, which could be evoked in magic.

In subsequent decades, the advance of historical research has amplified and corrected Reinach's account at many specific points. But there seems to be little tendency to doubt his main evolutionary conclusions: (1) that the advanced, civilized religions developed gradually out of primitive types, somewhat like those found in modern tribal cultures; (2) that they all retain vestiges of their primitive antecedents; (3) that animism, taboo, *mana*, and fetishism were early types; organized totemism emerged later, along with more complex social organization; (4) that the organized polytheistic pantheons of the Egyptian and Greek types represent a later stage of social evolution, and thorough monotheism a still later one. The close relation between such religious phenomena and those of visual and literary art is further corroborated. It seems increasingly evident that the history of religions has been intimately bound up with that of the arts, especially in their early periods, before the arts became largely secular. Art at each stage has not only expressed religious attitudes, beliefs, and activities, but has helped to determine their forms and lines of development.

Sir James Frazer was one of the most influential of British cultural anthropologists at the close of the century. He was widely read by the general public and provided colorful themes to literary artists. His famous work in many volumes, *The Golden Bough*,[47] followed the "comparative method" practiced by many evolutionists, including Spencer. This was to assemble innumerable examples of similar cultural phenomena from a wide range of peoples, periods, and places; to classify them under certain general headings, and to show on this basis that cultural evolution had followed certain analogous paths throughout the world. The comparative method fell into disfavor among anthropologists later in the twentieth century, but Frazer's main conclusions, though attacked by supernaturalists, have not been disproved. He did much to spread the new belief that all religions, including the Christian, have evolved from primitive beginnings by a natural, gradual process, and that certain primitive survivals exist in advanced religions, such as the common myth of the god who periodically dies and is reborn. Frazer's prodigious learning was conveyed in graceful literary style; it was equally at home in the archaic rituals of early Rome, the Norse myths of Balder the Beautiful, and the magical practices of contemporary African tribes. He showed the close connection between magic and religion: the one as involving an attempt to control the forces of nature directly, the other as appealing for divine favor through prayer and other means, including the arts. He explained the psychology of imitative and other types of magic, as based on incomplete knowledge but reasonable and progressive at a primitive stage. His view that magic is closer than religion to modern science, because of its attempt to control phenomena directly for human ends,

47 (London, 1900).

has been questioned as too flattering to magic, but it is not without a kernel of truth. His belief that magic preceded religion on the whole has also been questioned, especially during the recent attack on all theories of uniform sequence. Certainly, much primitive art involves both magic and religion. It is hard to find magic apart from some elements of religion, as Frazer himself noted. Often the two are mixed, as in an attempt to control minor spirits by appealing for the aid of more powerful ones.

Wilhelm Wundt (1832–1930), one of the chief founders of psychology as a unified, empirical science, disagreed with Frazer's theory of magic and mythology as ancestral to science. He stressed the differences in psychic method between them. Alexander Goldenweiser, agreeing, added that science corrects its beliefs and methods in the light of experience, while magic is proof against experience. Science eventually destroys both magic and mythology, these critics agreed.[48]

Nevertheless, there is much enduring validity in Frazer's analysis of the types of magic and of its main difference from religion—its attempt to control nature directly, as by charms, spells, and amulets—as contrasted with the offering of prayers and inducements to a powerful spirit. The question of the nature of magic and primitive religion, including the order in which they developed, is important for all theories of art history because of the intimate involvement of primitive art in both. Evolutionism in general does not insist on any particular sequence, or on a sharp division between magical, religious, and scientific stages.

Concepts of magic and primitive religion, based largely on the study of contemporary primitives, were applied by many nineteenth-century writers to archeological data such as the paleolithic cave drawings and sculptures on the usual assumption of a correspondence between the two. Thus the multiplication of realistic animal forms, often with marks of spear thrusts upon them, was explained as imitative magic for purposes of hunting. No better explanation has been offered. This illustrates

the way in which evolutionists from various fields cooperated in establishing the details of prehistoric culture.

References to evolution in histories of religion, though somewhat fewer in recent years, are not lacking. John Murphy, of the University of Manchester, begins his survey of *The Origins and History of Religions* (1949) with a discussion of the biological analogy, the physical evolution of man, and the stages in prehistoric culture. These are three main methods in the history of religions, he declares: the comparative, historical, and cultural. The comparative method classifies religions, according to their similarities and differences, into the monotheistic, polytheistic, monistic, animistic, and mana types, all of which are intermingled. The historical method is evolutionary, he says, "since it is a comparison between the lower or more elementary and the higher stages in the evolution of religion in general, and between the lower and higher stages in the evolution of a particular religion."[49] Degeneration occurs, and lower types may occur later in time. Religion as a whole evolves from such a primitive form "as the dim belief in a future life which can be guessed from the burials of Paleolithic or Old Stone Age Man to the complex beliefs and rituals of civilized people." Religion is among the customs and practices of primitive man which anthropology and comparative religion both observe; here the two sciences overlap.

The third method, the cultural, arranges the materials in "horizons." It is similar, Murphy explains, to the German method of *Kultur-Kreise* or culture-circles. A horizon is the circle upon which a man looks out when he contemplates his life and the world, including all the objects and

[48] Wundt, *Elements of Folk-Psychology*, pp. 93–4; Goldenweiser, *History, Psychology, and Culture* (New York, 1933), pp. 167, 190. Wundt also wrote what Goldenweiser calls "a psychological history of art," in which religion and mythology are shown as "a projection into the external world of the ideas and fantasies of the human mind." *Völkerpsychologie*, Vol. III, p. 559, on art.

[49] P. 4. Ch. II is on "Evolution and Anthropology"; Ch. III on "Man in Evolution."

instruments of his culture; also habits, customs, and ways of thinking and acting. Horizons "mark stages in man's history and in the evolution of his culture," says Murphy; "but this method has lately been taken in reaction from the evolutionary method," because it seemed that the great evolutionists (Frazer, Tylor, and Spencer) had led their followers into partly erroneous theories. Hence the movement to "let each culture-horizon speak for itself... without stressing... its having evolved out of something else, or its passing onwards into something different."[50]

In Murphy's account, the essentials of evolutionism are preserved along with the change in terminology from "stages" to "horizons." He distinguishes five main religious horizons: the Primitive, Animistic, Agricultural, Civilized, and Prophetic. These are based on general social and cultural conditions. The Primitive, that of early food-gatherers and hunters, is an emotional attitude toward objects possessing mana; it tends to be anthropomorphized into worship of personal spirits. The second, Animism, is belief in independent spirit-beings, separate from body. It occurs in tribal society on the level of simple garden and village cultivation. The Agricultural horizon involves domestication of plants and animals on a large scale; often flocks and herds. More personalized worship includes the mother-goddess and the personification of natural phenomena. The Civilized horizon is that of the ancient cities and empires; it reflects the political and social system it embraces and is commonly polytheistic, with an organized, monarchical society of gods. A civilized type of mind emerges here, with powers of abstract thought, social principles and increasing individuality. The fifth or Prophetic horizon is developed out of it, with growing capacity for conceptual thought and the emergence of great individuals—prophets, philosophers, ethical and religious teachers, especially from the ninth to the third centuries B.C.

This scheme is obviously in the main tradition of British evolutionary anthropology from Tylor to Gordon Childe, but considerably more flexible than the systems of Morgan and Tylor.

5. EVOLUTIONARY THEORIES OF LITERATURE. ORIGIN AND DESCENT OF LITERARY TYPES. STAGES IN WORLD LITERATURE. (BRUNETIÈRE, SYMONDS, MOULTON)

Attempts to apply the evolutionary hypothesis to the history of literature and music have labored under the serious handicap of lacking all prehistoric examples in the original state. By contrast with the rich and ever-growing supply of prehistoric visual art, the beginnings of literature must be surmised from indirect, later evidence, including early written versions. By the usual definition, "prehistoric" refers to a stage or period before the use of written records. "Literature," in the broad sense not restricted to writing, must have had a long prehistoric stage which was entirely oral, and a protohistoric stage which was largely so. Early writing, as in the first Sumerian and Egyptian inscriptions, includes little that can be classed as literary art. The unwritten part of world literature was, no doubt, much larger than the written until after the invention of printing. It is still large among primitive peoples, although civilized observers are fast recording it in print and phonographically.

The usual method of reasoning by analogy has been applied here as in other arts: that is, to assume that prehistoric literature must have been somewhat like that of modern primitives, and to reconstruct the former from a study of the latter. When uncritically applied, this method is obviously dangerous. In some respects, to be sure, modern primitive literature must stand between prehistoric and modern civilized: especially as to the degree to which it uses abstract, logically systematized concepts, and as to the size of its vocabulary. But anthropologists have recently been emphasizing

[50] P. 9.

the fact that modern primitive languages are not as small in vocabulary as had been supposed, or as lacking in abstract ideas. They are often richer than ours in concepts of qualities and relations which are important in their own mode of life, such as types and degrees of kinship and descriptions of jungle phenomena.

Another assumption which has had to be modified is that ancient written literature, such as Homer, Hesiod, and the Vedic hymns, represents "the childhood of literature," "the dawn of poetry," and the like. In many respects, these are now seen to be complex products of highly civilized societies. Hence any comprehensive theory of stages must be pushed back much farther chronologically.

Theories of literary evolution since Taine have dealt especially with the following problems:

(1) The development of spoken language from animal sounds; its modes of change and lines of differentiation throughout the world, including modern primitive languages. The gradual differentiation of the main language systems and of particular languages and dialects within them.

(2) The origin and development of literary art as a whole out of ordinary thought and verbal expression; its main stages and lines of differentiation and integration.

(3) The evolution of literary types or *genres*, such as the lyric, epic, drama, and novel.

(4) The development and decline of particular styles or movements, especially national and period styles in one or more genres (e.g., Greek tragedy).

(5) The histories of the main national and racial literatures (e.g., English) as manifesting evolutionary traits. Periods and stages in each.

(6) Comparisons of analogous stages or periods in the literary history of various peoples: e.g., the "heroic" stage in Greek and in Welsh poetry. Extent to which various literatures manifest such recurrent analogies.

(7) Causal factors in literary change: environmental or immanent, economic, social, etc. Relation of literary change to social change and trends in other arts.

Much of the discussion has been focused on the question of *genres* and their descent. In the nineties Ferdinand Brunetière, critical follower of Taine, attracted wide attention with his theory that a literary genre develops and declines as an organism does, and that (like a biological species) it can be transformed into another genre. Thus, said Brunetière, French tragedy was born with Jodelle and died with Voltaire. The lyric genre was transformed at the start of the seventeenth century "entre les mains de Malherbe," into the genre of eloquence; only to be changed back again by Rousseau in the eighteenth century.[51]

Much of the argument about genres and their descent has been confused by failure to distinguish clearly between genres as persistent or recurrent types (e.g., tragedy, the song, the portrait, the temple) and *styles* as characteristic of a period, artist, nationality, or other space-time division. Greek tragedy and Elizabethan tragedy have been called, simply, "genres," whereas they are actually stylistic variants of a persistent type. A style such as "romantic" may characterize a number of genres at a certain time and place.

Brunetière's discussion of genres was further obscured by the unusual meanings which he gave to certain terms. In his theory, three traits or conditions make a work "classic": the perfection of its expressive means, the fidelity of the artist to the genius of his race and country, and appearing at the moment of perfection of its type. The work must be born when the specific form of the genre is at the peak of its vital parabola; for genres "have only one time." The artist born too early or too late cannot achieve greatness.[52]

This theory, like Taine's, thus deals with the supposed life cycles of particular types, rather than with the evolution of literature as a whole. René

[51] Brunetière, *Études critiques sur l'histoire de la littérature française*, 3rd series, 2nd ed., p. 300. *Cf.* E. Caramaschi, "Brunetière critique," *Revue d'Esthétique*, XI, 3-4 (July–Dec. 1958), p. 48.

[52] Caramaschi, *op. cit.*, p. 40.

Wellek has criticized it as based on a faulty analogy between the life of an individual and that of a literary genre. Biological ontogeny, he says, has no such literary parallel. Brunetière did a disservice to the study of types by exaggerating the continuity of their descent and transformation into other types. "The concept of evolution drawn from phylogeny," says Wellek, "seems nearer to the actual facts of the literary process."[53] This point is well taken. The career of an artistic type such as the epic is more analogous to that of a biological type, such as the mastodon, than it is to the life cycle of an individual. The latter is comparatively regular, symmetrical, and inevitable. By contrast, some biological and some artistic types last on indefinitely: e.g., the fern, the mollusk, the adventure story, the love song.

The concept of literature as an evolving social phenomenon, briefly outlined by Spencer in the fifties, had been further developed by Taine in France. Both streams of influence were present in the literary studies of Leslie Stephen and John Addington Symonds. Said Stephen, "Literature is the noise of the wheels of history"; it is a by-product of social change and a function of the whole social organism; natural selection and environment determine the survival of literary species.[54]

In the eighties and nineties, Symonds developed in England a theory of types, based on that of Taine and somewhat like the one which Brunetière was advocating in France.[55] He raised the same question of why "a certain type of literature or art manifests itself, apparently by casual occurrence, in a nation or a given epoch. If favorable conditions for its development are granted, it runs a well-defined course, in which every stage is connected with preceding stages by no merely accidental link; and when all the resources of the type have been exhausted, it comes to a natural end. Such types suggest the analogy of natural growth." What the art historian has to explain is "the development of a complex artistic structure out of elements existing in national character, which structure is only completed by the action of successive generations and individual men of genius, all of whom in their turns are compelled to contribute either to the formation of the rudimentary type, or to its perfection, or to its decline and dissolution." As an outstanding example, Symonds pointed to "The rise, progress, decline, and dissolution of what we call Elizabethan drama." Gothic architecture, Italian painting and sculpture, Italian Romantic poetry, medieval stained glass and chivalric epics, and many other species present analogous problems. Symonds' theory was that "a clearly marked type of national art, when left to pursue its course of development unchecked, passes through stages corresponding to the

[53] "Development," in *Dictionary of World Literature*, ed. J. T. Shipley (New York, 1943), p. 157. Also R. Wellek and A. Warren, *Theory of Literature* (New York, 1942), pp. 246, 268, referring to Brunetière's *L'évolution des genres dans l'histoire de la littérature* (Paris, 1890). *Cf.* L. L. Schücking, *The Sociology of Literary Taste* (London, 1944), p. 1.

[54] L. Stephen, *History of Thought in the Eighteenth Century* (London, 1876); *English Literature and Society in the Eighteenth Century* (1904). *Cf.* F. W. Maitland, *The Life and Letters of Leslie Stephen* (London, 1906), p. 283; Wellek and Warren, *Theory of Literature*, p. 263; P. Appleman, "Evolution and Two Critics of Art and Literature," in *Proceedings of the Third International Congress on Aesthetics* (Venice, 1956), p. 236; D. Pizer, "Evolutionary Ideas in Late Nineteenth-Century English and American Literary Criticism," in *Journal of Aesthetics and Art Criticism*, XIX, 3 (Spring 1961), pp. 305–310. The two critics whom Appleman discusses are J. A. Symonds and Leslie Stephen. Pizer distinguishes three periods in the influence of evolutionism on criticism. First, in the 1870's and 1880's, such writers as S. Lanier and E. C. Stedman adapted Spencer's individualism and optimism to confirm their romantic conceptions. Second, during the eighties and nineties, T. S. Perry, Hamlin Garland, W. M. Payne, J. A. Symonds, and H. M. Posnett applied the historical relativism and environmental determinism of Taine and Spencer to build evolutionary systems. Third, from the eighties until now, such critics as B. Matthews, H. H. Boyesen, Edward Dowden, W. D. Howells, and G. Pellew retained only a few evolutionary by-products. In general, says Pizer, evolutionism led to the belief that literature grew and changed according to natural law and could be understood only in relation to the previous development. It also emphasized the milieu and fostered a scientific attitude in criticism.

[55] *Essays Speculative and Suggestive* (London, 1893), esp. "The Philosophy of Evolution," "On the Application of Evolutionary Principles to Art and Literature," and "Notes on Style." He paid homage to Taine (p. 7), but criticized him for not sufficiently recognizing the resistance of individuals to the *milieu*, specific strains of atavism in the artist, and the phenomena of mental hybrids.

embryonic, the adolescent, the matured, the decadent, and the exhausted, in growths which we are accustomed to regard as physiological." Such progressions are so inevitable, he thought, as to show a definite "law of sequence" whereby historical criticism approaches scientific certainty.

Despite the emphasis on cultural milieu, as in Taine, the causal explanation of the "well-defined course" of each type is again one of immanent determinism. Without explicitly stating either a mechanistic or vitalistic determinism, Symonds likens the life cycle of a type in art to that of an organism. Environment can provide, at best, only "favorable conditions for its development." It is no mere accident of outer circumstances that, when the inner potentialities of the type are "exhausted," old age and death must ensue.

Symonds went on to discuss the concept of style as a national and personal phenomenon. In literature, it is "the adequate investiture of thought with language."[56] It derives from the tongue one uses, he said, from the artist, and from that of his race. But Symonds, like Brunetière, failed to distinguish clearly between historic styles such as "Elizabethan" or "Gothic" and persistent types such as "drama" or "cathedral."

Symonds did not ignore the larger processes of cultural evolution, or of literary evolution within it. He did not confuse the life cycle of a type with evolution in general. "Evolution in its largest sense," he said in Spencerian terms, "may be defined as the passage of all things, inorganic and organic, by the action of inevitable law, from simplicity to complexity, from an undifferentiated to a differentiated condition of their common stock of primary elements."[57] One can not, he cautioned, apply this and other concepts of biology to mental and social phenomena "in the same way," for "each requires its own species of analysis, a different system of investigation, and a separate nomenclature." If properly developed, anthropology (including psychology, morality, and all branches of history) "will tend more and more to become an evolutionary science."

The origin and development of persistent types such as the epic and lyric have been the subject of much theorizing. The lyrical interjection, expressing joy, sorrow, hunger, or sexual desire, has been called the 'germ' of all higher lyrical forms.[58] Narrative and dramatic poetry came later, says Listowel. Between the mimic dance and the imaginative drama came the religious mime.

Among epics, what is the origin of such examples as the *Odyssey* and the *Ramayana*? The older explanation tended to attribute each to the creative genius of some one man, real or legendary, who had fashioned it out of whole cloth. The later, more evolutionary hypothesis attributed them to a slow, gradual coalescence of anonymous folktales of diverse origin. These might have dealt with different heroes, whose exploits were later assigned to one man as a connected heroic cycle. Centuries later, perhaps, one or more individual poets might have reorganized them into more complex unities, each with the stamp of personal genius. The latter view has been confirmed as a general tendency, but there is still controversy as to the extent to which particular works like the *Odyssey* were individual creations. The Platonic, supernaturalist approach (as in Kant) assigns by far the greater share to individual genius and divine inspiration; the scientific, to gradual social production.

The latter view was developed in detail by Richard G. Moulton, an English writer who worked in the United States during the early twentieth century. In *World Literature and its Place in General Culture* (New York, 1911, 1930), he outlined a "simple scheme of epic evolution," to show the descent of written poetry (fixed by writing, individually authored, original) from oral poetry (floating, changing, collective, with conventional echoing). Within this general process, he said, ballad stories had been fused into heroic cycles such

[56] P. 183.
[57] P. 30.
[58] H. Werner, *Die Ursprung der Lyrik* (Munich, 1924). *Cf.* F. von der Leyen, *Das Märchen* (Leipzig, 1925); Listowel, *op. cit.*, pp. 231–2.

as that of the Argonauts, and later into the organic epic, through amalgamation of numerous stories in a common plot. In *The Modern Study of Literature*,[59] Moulton included a valuable analysis of literary morphology and a chapter on "Literary Evolution as Reflected in the History of World Literature." The latter described the differentiation of poetry and prose and evolution in the epic, drama, and lyric. Evolution, along with inductive observation, was for Moulton one of the "two master ideas of modern thought," too little used in the study of literature. He conceived it in Spencerian fashion as differentiation and reunion in new combinations. The evolution of world literature had been a continuous movement, its first stage being in ancient Greece and Rome. (Moulton paid little attention to modern primitive folklore.) Poetry had at first included philosophy and mythology, proverbs, riddles, and practical technology. Prose literature had arisen later, he said, and itself differentiated into history, philosophy, oratory, and other types.

A more recent approach to the origin of genres is that of André Jolles,[60] who lists the primitive or elementary genres as: *Legende, Sage, Mythe, Rätsel, Spruch, Kasus, Memorabile, Märchen, Witz*. These, says Jolles, are compounded and developed into all the others. The eighteenth-century novel was preceded by the letter, the diary, the imaginary voyage, the memoir, the essay, comedy, romance, and other types. Some writers have urged that literature needs periodically to renew itself by "rebarbarization,"[61] with the transformation of popular expression into serious literary art.

On the heroic and other stages in literary evolution, H. M. Chadwick is often cited for his comparative study, *The Heroic Age*.[62] To decide whether the folk epic is a recurring expression of a certain stage in civilization, this work and its sequels compared ancient Greek and early Teutonic heroic poetry; also that of several oriental and primitive peoples. This type of poetry, said the author, makes its appearance in widely separated nations and periods. His conclusion was that such resem-

blances are due primarily "to resemblances in the ages to which they relate and to which they ultimately owe their origin." The study of such ages, said Chadwick, is essentially one of anthropology.

One contemporary anthropologist, A. L. Kroeber, has studied the novel as to its appearance at various points in history.[63] Novels, says Kroeber, are somewhat long and complex, realistic in representing life and individual characters; they avoid the poetic, heroic, grandiose, and supernatural. Successful, fully realized novels, he asserts, have appeared only three times: in Japan, China, and the modern West. Unlike the course of sculpture, drama, and science (which branched out east and west from the Near East with much traceable diffusion), that of the novel shows a minimum of historical connection by diffusionary influence. Its manifestations seem to be parallel products of long independent cultural developments, when these reached a certain phase or stage.

One approach to the scientific study of folktales has been called the "Finnish method," from the technique developed in Finland by Kaarle Krohn and Antti Aarne. A particular tale is studied in both oral and written versions; sometimes as many as six hundred of the former. These are arranged geographically as to origin, while the latter are

[59] (Chicago, 1915). *Cf.* C. M. Gayley and B. P. Kurtz, *Methods and Materials of Literary Criticism* (Boston, 1920), p. 594, on "The Evolutionary Theory" of the origin of the folk epic. This implies that, unlike *Paradise Lost*, the folk epic is "composed of many more or less anonymous parts finally arranged by some bard or editor whose task was one of compilation." Scholars differ as to the nature of the parts and the method of compilation.

[60] *Einfache Formen* (Halle, 1930), quoted by Wellek and Warren, *op. cit.*, p. 246. *Cf.* A. H. Krappe's list of literary folk-types in *The Science of Folk-lore* (London, 1930): the fairy tale, the merry tale or fabliau, the animal tale, the local legend, the migratory legend, the prose saga, the proverb, the folksong, the popular ballad, charms, rhymes, and riddles.

[61] M. Lerner and E. Mims, *Encyclopedia of the Social Sciences*, IX (1933), pp. 523–43; Wellek and Warren, p. 340.

[62] (Cambridge, 1912). It was a part of the monumental series on *The Growth of Literature* by H. M. and N. K. Chadwick (Cambridge, 1932–40). *Cf.* Gayley and Kurtz, *op. cit.*, p. 619.

[63] "The Novel in Asia and Europe," in *The Nature of Culture* (Chicago, 1952), p. 409.

arranged chronologically. From a study of regional and chronological variants the attempt is made to reconstruct in theory an original prototype. It is correlated with different sources of information about folk migration, commerce, and other influences. Substitution of local names, incidents, and culture-traits is noted. Inconclusive as such inquiries may be in a particular case, they combine to show a process of continuous, adaptive change.

The descent of a certain type of literary character —the folk hero such as Achilles and Robin Hood— was explained from an anthropological point of view by Lord Raglan.[64] He opposed the common "euhemeristic" theory that such characters are based on real, historic persons, and also the theory that they are freely imaginative fictions. Instead, he argued that such characters, together with the myths and heroic folk-tales in which they appear, are derived from primitive ritual drama or dramatic ritual. In the tradition of Frazer, he related them to the common primitive practice of killing the king and replacing him with another as a symbolic rebirth. Such rituals had magical and religious functions in early cultures. Late forms of myths and fairy-tales, he maintained, are altered descendants of early myths in which the ritual connection was more obvious. As to their primal source, Raglan favored an extreme, centralized diffusionism, according to which all or most of them have descended from some one central source, perhaps a culture older than the Sumerian and Egyptian and ancestral to both. Their later differentiation, he said, was affected by environmental change. For example, a people having only chariots may imagine the sun as riding in one, while a people having only boats will substitute a boat. The conception of a ritual hero, as in ancient tragedy and epic, may descend to the level of a trivial folk-tale by a sort of devolution, surviving for amusement or literary values.

Raglan's theory is controversial (a) in postulating a central source for cultural diffusion, and (b) in emphasizing the similarities among folk tales, myths, and their heroes throughout the world.

Contemporary anthropology has, on the whole, favored a belief in many independent origins along with some diffusion; also more attention to diversities. Raglan went unusually far in denying practically all historicity to folk heroes, except where it is confirmed by written or other tangible records. Oral tradition, he thought, is extremely short-lived and unreliable. Evolutionism in general does not require this extreme position. One can believe that conceptions of folk heroes develop for the most part from early religious imagining, and at the same time that they are often merged with traditional accounts of real persons.

Though Raglan minimized diversity in the usual nineteenth-century manner, the analogies which he pointed out (following Andrew Lang and other predecessors) are striking enough to demand some explanation. In analyzing the imaginary careers of a number of heroes such as Oedipus, Theseus, Romulus, Heracles, Perseus, Jason, Asclepios, Dionysos, Apollo, Joseph, Moses, Elijah, Arthur, Siegfried, and several Javanese and other lesser-known characters, he found a striking list of recurrent details. For example, the hero's mother is often a royal virgin; his conception is unusual and he is said to be the son of a god; an attempt is made to kill him, but he is taken away and raised by foster-parents in a far country. Nothing is told of his childhood, but as a man he returns to his kingdom, conquers a king or monster, marries a princess, gives laws, but loses favor with the gods and is driven out to meet a mysterious death, often at the top of a hill. The combination of twenty-two such traits constitutes a basic pattern. Not all, but a varying selection recur in different cases. Raglan stressed the persistently dramatic features of such folk tales, as contrasted with pure narratives. As against a theory of independent origins, Raglan pointed to the fact that folk tales of a tribal people often contain reference to kings, cities, and other culture-traits unknown to their own experience.

To explain such recurrences there are, of course,

[64] *The Hero* (London, 1936; New York, 1956). Also *Jocasta's Crime* (London, 1933).

other hypotheses. One may resort to Jung's theory of archetypes, whereby certain widely recurring images arise spontaneously from the collective unconscious, which is itself derived from past collective experience. Or one may rely on the Hegelian theory of immanent, spiritual determinism. Each of these explanations encounters its own difficulties, and the problem is still with us. Recent theories of literary history have tended to ignore or belittle the recurrences instead of trying to explain them.

Looking back before the origin of literature to that of its first medium, spoken language, science finds itself baffled by an apparently uncrossable gap between animal and human. David Bidney has called it "an irreducible gulf between the actual or potential human power of conceiving and symbolizing and the mental functions of man's nearest animal relatives."[65] All attempts to reconstruct the origin of language, he continues, have proved futile, and linguists find in such data "little or no evidence about the origin of human speech."[66] Edward Sapir defines language as "a purely human and non-instinctive method of communicating ideas, emotions, and desires by means of a system of voluntarily produced symbols."[67] Nevertheless, says Bidney, we may assume that human language originated from man's desire to communicate. Even if, as Cassirer has suggested, it resulted from a sudden mutation and not by gradual, Darwinian change, it must have evolved in some way from animal sounds and gestures. Metaphysical idealists tend to insist that man's mental powers came first and led him to devise linguistic means of expression; naturalists tend to regard the two as concomitant and interacting.

The noises made by our primitive ancestors, says Harry Hoijer, and perhaps those accompanying primitive tasks, came slowly to symbolize the actions and ends involved in such tasks.[68] The two main theories of the origin of language are the interjectional and the sound-imitative or onomatopoetic.

Typical of many attempts in the early twentieth century at a developmental survey of world literature was A. S. Mackenzie's *The Evolution of Literature*.[69] The writer, who had studied in England, paid homage to Edward Caird and Jebb, and cited a wide range of English, French, and German sources on anthropology, archeology, linguistics, and comparative literature. From Spencer's essay on *Progress: its Law and Cause* he drew the concept of evolution as "from the simple to the complex, with an increasing unification of the whole and specialisation of the parts." Complexity, he noted, has no value in itself, and progress depends on increased ethical, intellectual, and aesthetic satisfaction. Literature is a product of social life, he said, and its evolution is dependent on that of society; but the economic factor is not enough to explain its history. The structure of Mackenzie's system was in the tradition of Tylor, and he marked off four conventional "stages of social development" as the framework for his history of literature: primitiveness, barbarism, autocracy, and democracy. "If literary specimens be arranged in connected order from primitiveness to representative democracy," he said, "we may gain a more vivid conception of the constant interplay of society and literature."

Among the potential resources for this study was linguistic paleontology, a branch of philology. Attempts had been made on that basis to reconstruct prehistoric literature.[70]

As a part of the general trend toward specialization in scholarship and away from philosophies of history, there has recently been less theorizing

[65] *Theoretical Anthropology* (New York, 1953), p. 4.

[66] *Ibid.*, citing E. H. Sturtevant, *An Introduction to Linguistic Science* (New Haven, 1947), p. 40.

[67] *Language* (New York, 1921). Bidney, p. 3.

[68] "Language and Writing," in *Man, Culture, and Society*, ed. H. L. Shapiro (New York, 1956), pp. 200, 203.

[69] (New York, 1911). Mackenzie was professor of English and comparative literature at the University of Kentucky.

[70] Mackenzie refers to these among other works: T. Benfey, *Geschichte der Sprachwissenschaft* (Munich, 1869); H. A. Strong, W. S. Logeman, and B. I. Wheeler, *History of Language* (London, 1891); W. D. Whitney, *History of Language* (New York, 1899); O. Schrader, *Reallexicon der Indogermanischen Altertumskunde* (Strassburg, 1901).

about the history of literature as a whole (so-called "universal literature") and more about that of particular types, periods, and other subdivisions. While the word "evolution" is now less current, there has been little tendency to deny the basic fact of literary evolution in a broad sense. T. S. Eliot rejects it sweepingly from the standpoint of his supernaturalist philosophy, but he has little company in this attitude among contemporary scholars. "The whole of the literature of Europe from Homer," he asserts, "has a simultaneous existence and composes a simultaneous order."[71] On the other hand, the essence of evolutionism is reaffirmed by René Wellek and Austin Warren in the brief statement that "In literature, there is a gradual transition from simple statements to highly organized works of art." We must conceive of literature, they add, "as a whole system of works which is, with the accretion of new ones, constantly changing in its relationships, growing as a changing whole." But Wellek is on more dubious ground in holding that "this postulates an aim for the series of changes," and that the series of developments will be constructed in reference to a "scheme of values or norms."[72] To speak of evolution as having an "aim" suggests the old philosophies of teleology, idealism, and vitalism, from which science has been trying to escape. To describe evolution in terms of any "scheme of values" tends to complicate the issue unnecessarily with subjective value-judgments. These can be more effectively dealt with in such terms as "progress" and "deterioration."

6. EVOLUTIONARY THEORIES OF MUSIC: STAGES, ORIGINS, DEVELOPMENTS. (ROWBOTHAM, COMBARIEU, LALO)

Questions similar to those in literature have been discussed in regard to music. One outstanding difference is the present lack of definitely written ancient music, comparable to the mass of ancient

written literature. The nature and development of early music must be conjecturally reconstructed from such scanty clues as the following: (a) modern tribal music, folk music, and other comparatively primitive types; (b) surviving ancient musical instruments; pictorial and sculptural representations of such instruments and persons playing them, such as Orpheus, Krishna, Pan, and ancient Egyptian and Mesopotamian musicians; (c) a few verbal inscriptions and manuscripts, especially of hymns, with marks which were probably meant to guide singing and playing; their exact significance usually not clear today; (d) verbal descriptions and evaluations of music and its effects, as in Homer, Plato, the Bible; (e) a few ancient treatises and scattered comments on the theory of music, such as those of Aristoxenus, Aristides Quintilianus, and St. Augustine; all rather obscure to the modern reader.

As in the case of other arts, there has been a gradual discovery, during the past hundred years, that not all music outside the main European tradition is "primitive" or merely crude folk music. The West has had to learn that its own lines of musical development, especially the harmonic and contrapuntal, are not the only ones along which music can become a mature, complex art. It is surprising today to find the Hindu *ragas* classed, in an early twentieth-century history of music, under "First Primitive Period," and discussed mainly in terms of their supposed magical powers.[73] In music as in other branches of culture, the historian now looks back on a longer, wider vista into the past. He sees there, not one single

---

[71] Quoted by R. Wellek and A. Warren, *Theory of Literature*, p. 265, from Eliot's *The Sacred Wood* (London, 1920), p. 42. W. P. Ker is also quoted as saying that we do not need literary history, since its objects are always present and eternal, thus having no real history. (*Essays*, London, 1922, Vol. I, p. 100). Both these statements reveal an extreme Platonism. Chapter XIX on "Literary History" in the above-mentioned book by Wellek and Warren contains a good discussion of literary evolutionism with a bibliography.

[72] "Development," p. 157. *Theory of Literature*, p. 268.

[73] J. Combarieu, *La Musique, ses lois, son évolution* (Paris, 1907), p. 108.

line of evolution through Palestrina, Bach, and Beethoven, but many divergent ones, analogous in some ways and different in others. Even among the tribal cultures loosely classed as "primitive," he finds considerable difference in type and in degree of development. As African Negro tribes surpassed modern Europe in the complexity of some of their sculptural designs, so they did also in complexity of rhythmic counterpoint with drums and other instruments. One can no longer assume, as the early evolutionists did, that prehistoric and modern primitive music are alike at the beginning of the genetic sequence: uniformly crude, monotonous, undifferentiated, and unorganized. Even the subtleties of Gregorian chants were little known to the general public until recent years, when the phonograph brought them to a wider audience.

In this great extension of the music historian's horizon, the invention of the phonograph and other recording devices, such as the film and magnetic tape, has played a revolutionary part. Countless exotic styles of music, from advanced and primitive peoples, are now available for comparative study which were out of reach a half century ago. Most of them can not be written down exactly in our present notation, but they are nevertheless preserved and reproduced for students everywhere.

The nineteenth-century system-builders, such as Spencer, Tylor, and Grosse, included a few speculations on early music to illustrate the application of their formulas in this field. The exciting promise of this approach gave rise to a long list of more specialized treatises on music history as an evolution in itself.[74] They dealt with the following problems, all of which were being raised in other arts as well: (1) the general question of whether and how music history exemplifies the concept of evolution in the broad, Spencerian sense; (2) the question of the origin and descent of types; (3) the question of stages and sequences; (4) educational applications. As to the first of these, there has been little denial of the general fact that music as an art has grown more complex

through differentiation and integration. Most of the argument has been about the last three.

The history of evolutionary theories of music is well reviewed by Warren D. Allen in *Philosophies of Music History*.[75] With the evolutionary theories which emphasize growth and social influence, he contrasts the earlier, "great man" theory, which we have noted under various names. It implied the old, romantic, supernaturalist belief that musical creation and advance were largely the work of individual, inspired composers, owing little to past music or to outside conditions. Examples of the great-man theory are found by Allen in the music histories of Michael Praetorius[76] and Georg Kiesewetter.[77]

Herbert Spencer, as we have seen, gave a prominent place to music in his scheme of cultural evolution. In 1854 he published an essay on "The Origins of Music," as one of the *Illustrations of Universal Progress*. Music history was no longer to be a mere chronological list of composers and their works, for music was like an evolving species: creating, developing, and changing itself "by virtue of various principles which are unfolded, each in its turn."

One of the first music historians to adopt and elaborate Spencer's theory was Frederick Rowbotham.[78] He proposed a fixed sequence of pre-

[74] For example, J. F. Rowbotham, *A History of Music to the Time of the Troubadours* (London, 1885–87); C. H. Parry, *The Art of Music* (London, 1893; later republished as *The Evolution of the Art of Music*); R. Wallaschek, *Primitive Music* (London 1893); J. Combarieu, *op. cit.*; C. Stumpf, *Die Anfänge der Musik* (Leipzig, 1911); M. H. Glyn, *Analysis of the Evolution of Musical Form* (London, 1909; with considerable attention to Hindu, Gregorian, and primitive music); L. A. Coerne, *The Evolution of Modern Orchestration* (New York, 1908); A. Casella, *The Evolution of Music* (London, 1924); E. C. Bairstow, *The Evolution of Musical Form* (London, 1943). P. A. Scholes, *The Listener's History of Music* (London, 1932) contains a chart of the "Evolution of Music" (p. 100).

[75] (New York, 1939), esp. pp. 104 ff., 110 ff., 231 ff. The present section is much indebted to Allen's account, which also discusses theories of progress and gives an extensive bibliography.

[76] *Syntagma musicum* (Leipzig, 1615).

[77] *History of the Modern Music of Western Europe* (Leipzig, 1834).

[78] *Op. cit.*; Allen, p. 110.

historic stages, three as usual: those of the Drum, Pipe, and Lyre. (Wallaschek later argued that the pipe must have antedated the drum.) Rowbotham also accepted the theory of Rousseau, Herder, Burney, and Spencer: that "the origin of vocal music must be sought in impassioned speech." Another series of stages, he declared, was that of one-note, two-notes, three-notes, and five-notes, involving the development of melodic scales. Henri Lavoix in France and C. H. H. Parry in England subordinated composers' biographies to the evolution of musical forms. Parry described the seventeenth-century rise of secular music as an example of the Spencerian "tendency of all things from homogeneity towards diversity and definiteness."[79] Man had progressed from simple intervals to definite, heterogeneous scales and melodies; also to increasing variety of chords—fourths and fifths, then thirds and sixths, then additional consonances and discords. Further complications ensued in the combination of melodic lines, as in the fugue. Another series of three stages, according to Parry, is from the unconscious and spontaneous to the self-conscious and analytical; then to the synthetic.

Spencer held that poetry, music, and dancing had had a co-ordinate origin and had later differentiated; rhythm in speech, sound, and motion have only gradually been separated. Ernst Grosse began his chapter on music, in *The Beginnings of Art*, by reaffirming that "Music appears, at the lowest stage of culture, in the most intimate connection with the dance and with poetry." He agreed with Spencer that music had evolved from simple to complex in pitch relations, as in modern polyphonic and symphonic compositions. But he rejected Spencer's idea that the sources of music lie in impassioned speech. Modern primitive music, he argued, is sharply different from emotional speech; it is not characteristically loud, rapid, excited in pitch and timbre, but often monotonous and soft. Grosse was more favorable toward Darwin's theory that the power to produce musical tones and rhythms was first developed by our animal ancestors as a means to attract the other sex. For this, he remarked, there is more evidence in the sounds made by certain animals, including the anthropoid gibbon. But he found no evidence among humans "that music in any form plays a part in the lowest grades of culture in the intercourse of the sexes." On the other hand, he said, music does play a limited military role in these lowest grades, and a greater one as accompaniment to the dance.

More than most evolutionists, Grosse followed Schopenhauer in regarding music as detached from the rest of life. "If the music of a people is independent of its civilization, so inversely the civilization of a people is essentially independent of its music."[80] He quoted Fechner with approval for saying that musical talent occurs in connection with every degree of mental endowment.[81] It is often lacking in persons of high intellectual and artistic ability, and vice versa; some otherwise low cultures are highly developed musically, and vice versa. "Music serves essentially the objects of art alone." According to Grosse, it develops in individuals and in civilization generally, but somewhat apart from the rest of cultural evolution. While dance and poetry tend to strengthen and widen social bonds, Grosse thought that music did not. (Here he parted from Spencer).

The psychologist W. Wundt[82] also held that music and poetry were the offspring of the dance; that these three were originally united, as they often are today in the tribal dances of primitives. Instrumental music was first, in his view, a rhythmic accompaniment for dancers. Fixed scales arose from magical numbers (as among the Pythagoreans). Homophony led to polyphony and thence to harmony. The earliest types of song were the exclamatory, the ritual, and the work song, while the earliest dance types were the individual, ecstatic dance and the collective, magical, mimetic dance.

[79] Parry, *op. cit.*, 1893, p. 169.
[80] P. 303.
[81] Fechner, *Vorschule der Ästhetik*, Vol. I, p. 163.
[82] *Völkerpsychologie* (1900–1920), Vol. III, pp. 110–336.

Wallaschek and K. Bücher emphasized the rhythm of bodily movements in work and dance as the source of music, while C. Stumpf[83] suggested instead that both vocal and instrumental music had come from the action of signalling to people at a distance. The earliest lyrical utterances of primitive peoples, according to H. Werner,[84] were meaningless words or sounds together with gestures, sung at tribal dances to express joy after a successful hunt or hearty meal, unsatisfied hunger or sexual desire, or lament for the dead. The addition of words came later.

Historians have differed considerably as to whether music evolved as an integral part of cultural evolution, or as a separate process. Some have even regarded the history of instrumental music as largely separate from that of song and opera.[85] The romanticists had insisted on the organic nature of culture, as something which evolves together. If instrumental music separates itself from other factors, according to Spencer, this is not necessarily permanent or desirable; it exemplifies the differentiating phase, after which reintegration may occur. Wagner was eager to help in that reintegration himself, through opera. Others preferred instrumental music alone. Not only romanticism, but also the synthetic approach of Spencer, Tylor, and others favored the view that music had interacted with other cultural factors at every stage of its development. Cultural evolutionists have tended to emphasize examples of such interaction, as in the relation of Gregorian music to the medieval church, and of the troubadours to chivalry. The Marxists sought to show how music, like other arts, had always arisen from socio-economic conditions and expressed them in its forms. They saw two main currents in musical evolution: one from the folk-songs and dances of the exploited workers, the other, more refined and artificial, from the palaces of the rich and noble. Middle-class music had at first been revolutionary, as in Beethoven, but has later become conventional and decadent.[86] On the whole, later historians have accepted the general thesis of interaction between music and other outside factors in art and culture; but such interactions have been hard to trace in detail. Less has been done along this line than in the history of literature and the visual arts.

Combarieu in France, Parry in England, and Daniel Gregory Mason in America applied to music history the evolutionary ideas of Spencer and Tylor. Among the ideas thus applied were (a) that of three general cultural stages: the savage, barbarian, and civilized; within these, the stages of music history were to be fitted; (b) the assumption that such evolution had been a progress, so that savage and barbarian music were altogether inferior to civilized. Parry classed not only oriental music, but also medieval church music, as "primitive" or "semicivilized." He wrote condescendingly of the "primitive melodic music of the church," where "there were no bars," and when singers "did things very much by ear."[87]

Combarieu devoted sections of his history to "L'Évolution musicale et l'état social" and "L'Évolution musicale et les êtres vivants." In the latter, quoting Lamarck and Darwin, he invoked the biological analogy in comparing the modern orchestra to "some gigantic and powerful animal." It had at first an indeterminate stage; then, in the seventeenth and eighteenth centuries, specialization of functions began to appear. The orchestra is now adult and clearly differentiated. Daniel Gregory Mason wrote in similar terms of the evolution of music from simple to complex, from Scarlatti through Beethoven.[88] Like all evolutionary processes, he said, it was marked by increasing differentiation. "The first movement of Beethoven's Hammerclavier Sonata, op. 106, is to Scarlatti's Pastorale as a dog or a horse is to an oyster." Such absurd comparisons could only help to discredit the theory in general.

Combarieu was rather vague in regard to the

[83] *Die Anfänge der Musik*, pp. 7–34.
[84] *Die Ursprünge der Lyrik* (1924), pp. 8 ff.
[85] Notably H. A. Haweis, in *Music and Morals* (London, 1871).
[86] N. Slonimsky, *Music Since 1900* (New York, 1937), p. 549.
[87] Parry, p. 98.
[88] *From Song to Symphony* (Boston, 1924), p. 126.

social contacts of musical evolution, as in the gradual freeing of music from the church and the organ, and the mingling of national folk-tunes during the Thirty Years' War. He was influenced by Comte in saying that music had known a theological age with plainsong; a metaphysical age with the symphonists, Bach, Haydn, Mozart, and Beethoven; and the present age, positivistic in its realism.[89]

Various triple schemes of periodization, analogous to those for other arts, were proposed by other historians. Often each of the three was divided into three more. Hugo Riemann is one of these historians, along with C. V. Stanford, C. Forsyth, and Arnold Schering. Alfred Casella saw three periods in harmonic evolution up to the twentieth century: those of absolute diatonism (to 1650), of modulation and modern scales (to 1750), and of chromaticism: a fourth, of atonality, was developing. Guido Adler[90] divided the three as follows: the monodic-choral (to c. 1000); polyphonic (9th through 16th centuries); homophonic (1600–1900), with monody and the harmonic style. Each art has its own periodization, Adler thought, and they do not necessarily correspond. Obviously historians do not agree on the main stages and their chronological boundaries.

The cycle theory was applied to music by Alfred Lorenz.[91] Revolutions in musical style, going alternately toward the melodic and harmonic principles, occurred about 400, 1000, 1300, 1600, and 1900 A.D., according to this theorist.

The recapitulation theory, according to which each individual student should traverse the successive stages from ancient to contemporary in his own development, has been applied in musical education in a way analogous to that which we have seen in visual art. Vincent d'Indy and Edward MacDowell used it, and Satis N. Coleman applied Rowbotham's evolutionary formula in American education.[92] The one-note, two-note, and three-note order was to be followed in teaching little children. "Being little savages, they can understand savage music... The natural evolution of

music shall be my guide in leading the children from the simple to the complex." Beginning at the drum stage, children were to go on to ways of making tones. (But are children really savages?)

W. D. Allen noted the ambiguity of the word "evolution"—meaning, for various writers, development, progress, differentiation, or new growth.[93] He noted also the comparative fixity of certain types, such as the plainsong in the Catholic Church, as an exception to universal change. He went on to show examples of the opposite process, from complex to simple. Progressive simplification has occurred, said Allen, in the Lutheran chorales of the late eighteenth and early nineteenth centuries, as compared with richer harmonization for double chorus in the seventeenth century.[94] Some American courses in music appreciation now work backwards from Stravinsky and "the complicated musical arts of Bali" to simple folksongs.

From the standpoint of naturalistic aesthetics Charles Lalo, professor of aesthetics at the Sorbonne, proposed a critical evolutionism in his treatise on music theory.[95] He considered the psychological, sociological, and formal aspects of music, as well as the historical. While not disputing the general complication of the art from prehistoric times to the present, he cautioned against assuming that either Greek or Gregorian music was really simple or primitive, if one considers the complexity of their many modes. As against Spencer, Lalo declared that the "law of increasing complexity" is not continuous in its operation in music, while "in certain respects the general development can present the aspect of an inverse, regu-

[89] 1907 ed., p. 201.

[90] In *Handbuch der Musikgeschichte* (Frankfort, 1924). Allen, p. 266.

[91] *Abendländische Musikgeschichte im Rhythmus der Generationen* (Berlin, 1928).

[92] *Creative Music for Children: a Plan of Training Based on the Natural Evolution of Music, including the Making and Playing of Instruments* (New York, 1922).

[93] *Op. cit.*, p. 285.

[94] P. 271.

[95] *Éléments d'une esthétique musicale scientifique* (2nd ed.; Paris, 1939).

lar passage from complex to simple."[96] The complicative tendency is continuous in the primitive period, when acquisitions accumulate pell-mell; they continue to do so in the techniques and instruments of music. But the classical age eliminates many of these accumulations, proceeding rather in a dialectical series of specific oppositions and reconciliations. (Here Lalo shifted from the Spencerian to the Hegel-Marx formula.) The aesthetic organism begins by complicating, he went on, only to turn later on toward simplicity. "In art, complication is artifice, convention, stylization; simplicity is naturalism. After the infantile or primitive period, stylization comes first and naturalism at the end." (But can not early stylization be simpler than later naturalism?)

Reminiscent of Taine and the cyclical formula was Lalo's "law" of three recurrent states or ages.[97] With the confident exactness of a Morgan or Tylor, he marked off four main stages in occidental music history from the Greeks on down: those of Greek recitative (mélopée), Christian melody, medieval polyphony, and modern harmony; each with fairly definite chronological boundaries. Each was divided into the same "three stages"—pre-classic, classic, and post-classic—and each of these into two similar subdivisions. The "pre-classic" contained "primitives" and "precursors"; the "classic," great and pseudo-classics; the "post-classic," romantics and decadents. Each was shown as centered in a certain region; hence the evolution was spatial as well as temporal.

Every art which develops freely and uninterruptedly, said Lalo, will normally pass through them, over and over again. The classic phase is characterized by "purity of tastes, honesty of techniques, separation of genres, and clear, rational compositions." Both early and late extremes show an excessive mixture of types, impure and complicated effects, and dubious tastes. The Venetian school of painting was primitive in Vivarini, classic with Titian and Veronese, romantic with Tiepolo; then followed decadence and death. Late classic becomes pseudo-classic, as in the eighteenth centu-

ry; then a romantic reaction brings new life by raising supposedly inferior types and by an unruly exuberance. It dissolves into decadence in the next period: an incoherent mixture of realism and symbolism. After the decadence of Mallarmé's generation, said Lalo, the early twentieth century entered upon a new primitivism, the start of a new cycle, with naïve and barbarous mixtures, Negro styles, popular arts, mixtures of types and arts, dadaist anarchy. In occidental music, Lalo's elaborate table distinguishes all six phases in the Greek, in the early Christian, in the medieval polyphonic, and in the modern harmonic eras. (Medieval post-classicism, for him, lasts through Bach and Handel into recent academic counterpoint.)

Lalo's theory is more naturalistic, less rigid, and less pessimistic than those of Spengler and Toynbee. He does not insist on any supernatural determinism or on the necessary decline and fall of a whole civilization once it reaches the end of a cycle. Having passed through a romantic and decadent phase, any art can easily renew itself by finding some new source of energy and inspiration; some new cycle whose primitive phase it can enter.

More in the twentieth-century spirit was Lalo's insistence, in the chapter on "Les Évolutions divergentes," that musical evolution is not unilinear. Within a single art, he said, the developments are not exactly parallel throughout a particular society. The various arts, "even if they have without doubt the same direction, do not always follow the same route, with the same speed or the same approaches." They diverge in spite of the identity of their common destinations, as many currents flow within the same river. Their periods do not always correspond; they do not always arise in the same order. Literary people, said Lalo, think that music, as the most superficial, is the last to evolve; but musicians think it comes last because it is the most

---

[96] Pp. 250, 252.

[97] P. 255. A footnote quotes C. Bayet, *Précis d'histoire de l'art* (Paris, 1905) on the recurrence of periods of infancy, youth, maturity, and decadence in the plastic arts.

personal and profound. But does it come last? The classical age of Greek music preceded by over two hundred years, according to Lalo, the fifth-century flowering of literature and plastic art. Attempts to correlate the periods of medieval architecture with those of music are unconvincing; only occasionally has the apogee of a musical age coincided with that of the literary one. In modern harmony, whose classical development is German, Lalo held that the musical apogee coincided with the finest period of German literature and philosophy.

7. THE EFFECTS OF EVOLUTIONARY IDEAS ON ART AND ARTISTS

Considering the tremendous influence of evolutionism on the intellectual life of Western civilization, including science, philosophy, religion, and theories of art, one might expect to find a similar effect on art itself. On the contrary, the effect seems to have been comparatively slight and somewhat negative. This is not surprising if one remembers that the late romantic hostility toward science had throughout the nineteenth century, and still has, a far-reaching influence on the arts. This contrasts with the warm reception given the idea of progress by some of the earlier, German romanticists, by Shelley in *Prometheus Unbound*, and by Hugo in *La Légende des siècles*.

Around mid-century a number of prominent authors wrote of evolution as an extension of progress. Most of them rejected or ignored the naturalistic conception of it, preferring instead the teleological one. From this point of view they rhapsodized about the spiritual purpose and fulfillment of life through evolution. Toward the end of the nineteenth century, and still more as world disasters multiplied in the twentieth, the prevailing mood changed to pessimism. The belief in progress was widely rejected and evolution was treated instead in terms of the possible "atavism" or degeneration of man. On the whole, very little

attention has been paid to either idea in twentieth-century art, except for occasional, contemptuous references to "the illusion of progress." Even to those artists who showed no explicit hostility to scientific theory, the idea of evolution was on the whole unattractive. It may have seemed to some, like the Grand Canyon of Colorado or the starry sky above, as too vast, impersonal, and overwhelming a subject to be adequately treated in contemporary styles. The day of Miltonic sublimity had passed, and art preferred to deal with smaller, more intimate aspects of nature and the inner self or with the evils of modern civilization.

Tennyson, one of the few major Victorians to concern himself with evolution, could be sure in 1842 (*Locksley Hall*) that "thro' the ages one increasing purpose runs, / And the thoughts of men are widen'd with the process of the suns." He could see "the wonder that would be" when "the war-drum throbb'd no longer, and the battle-flags were furl'd / In the Parliament of man, the Federation of the world." But by 1886 (*Locksley Hall Sixty Years After*) he was looking doubtfully at "Evolution ever climbing after some ideal good, / And Reversion ever dragging Evolution in the mud." "Is it well," he asked, "that while we range with Science, glorying in the Time, / City children soak and blacken soul and sense in city slime? / There among the glooming alleys Progress halts on palsied feet, ..."

Browning, whom Georg Roppen links with Tennyson as an evolutionist "in the Platonic tradition,"[98] expressed as early as 1835 (in *Paracelsus*) a vision of life and nature as permeated by the divine spirit, climbing from their lowest forms to distant glories. "Progress is the law of life," he proclaimed. In later poems, especially *Fifine at the Fair*, he became alarmed at the rise of naturalistic theories of evolution in Darwin, Tyndall, and Thomas Huxley. He attacked them with savage

[98] *Evolution and Poetic Belief* (Oslo, 1956). A detailed analysis of evolutionary ideas in the works of Tennyson, Browning, Swinburne, Meredith, Hardy, Butler, Shaw, and Wells.

sarcasm, along with the claims of science to solve cosmic problems hitherto left to theology.

Swinburne's conception of evolution expressed a more positivistic world-view. In *Genesis*, he defined God as a notion created by man, and as having no part in the development of life. Yet he had little faith in natural science either, and played with images of oriental pantheism, especially in *Hertha*. Life, he thought, is vertical movement, progressive intelligence, climbing through organic evolution to liberty and perfection. George Meredith, too, inclined toward pagan agnosticism, and was happily untroubled by the warfare between science and religion. There are echoes of romantic pantheism in his *Ode to the Spirit of Earth in Autumn*, with its worship of "Great Mother Nature." Evolution for him was a spiritual conquest of physical nature and of the bestial instincts in man. Accepting Spencer's "struggle for survival" and Darwin's natural selection, he combined them with an Aristotelian sort of determinism, not conscious or planful, but directed as in the growth of a seed, and eventually ascending to conscious reason.

Poets who wrote of evolution with enthusiasm after 1900 were mostly minor ones such as W. H. Carruth, author in 1909 of *Each in His Own Tongue*. Its opening lines affirm the religious interpretation: "A fire-mist and a planet, / A crystal and a cell, / A jellyfish and a saurian, / And caves where the cavemen dwell; / Then a sense of law and beauty, / And a face turned from the clod— / Some call it Evolution, / And others call it God." Such a picture seemed naïve and oversimplified to leaders of early twentieth-century thought.

Thomas Hardy rejected the optimism of the early Victorians and emphasized the tragic spectacle of the individual, doomed to struggle and pain within a joyless, hopeless universe. His loss of idealistic Christian faith under the influence of Darwinism affected him profoundly. Unlike Darwin and many other scientific evolutionists, he could not reconcile the idea of unplanned, natural evolution with a faith in the purpose and value of life. In the eighties and nineties he drew closer to Schopenhauer's doctrine of an immanent Will in the universe: a blind, unconscious, cosmic "Mother." In his blackest moods, Hardy felt that man was a prisoner in a web of chance and circumstance; that consciousness was a curse. In *The Dynasts* and in a letter of 1902, his conversion to pantheistic idealism led him to some slight hope that the unconscious will of the universe might eventually become conscious and sympathetic. But the emphasis remained on pessimism and fatalism. Samuel Butler, on the other hand, rejected the idea that life is governed by chance and blind natural selection. In *Life and Habit* (1877), he sided with Lamarck and added a vitalistic doctrine of life as an autonomous power which conquers matter and creates itself according to its own will and faith.

Bernard Shaw derived much of his optimistic vitalism from Butler, thereby transforming Schopenhauer's "world as will" into something driving upward toward the Superman. (*Back to Methuselah; Man and Superman*). In this, he was close to Henri Bergson's philosophy of "creative evolution," which appeared in 1907. Shaw agreed with Nietzsche that man as a species should be overcome and superseded, but argued that the way to do so was through eugenics or selective breeding. He emphasized the value and power of creative intelligence more than love or beauty; he looked to the "philosophic man" to raise life to higher levels, as in the past man had outlived the dinosaur by his brain. Throughout Shaw's paradoxical combination of agnosticism and mysticism, paganism and Puritanism, idealism and worldliness, he retained his confidence in life as rising through intelligence and will toward a Utopia of continuing creativeness.

H. G. Wells, in *A Modern Utopia* (1905) and *Men Like Gods* (1923), built an evolutionary conception more on the Darwinian basis of struggle, including the class struggle for power. He retained his basic naturalism throughout his long career, but saw it as no bar to believing that, in man, a purposive force has taken hold of life; man is no longer a slave of chance or material determinism. As to its practical implications, Wells' concept of the creative will was close to that of Shaw, though lacking the latter's vitalistic metaphysics. However, he played with the conception of a God who was himself growing and evolving along somewhat Hegelian lines. Through most of his life Wells was an optimist about progress, but not a naïve one. He warned with frank, unsparing realism that it might miscarry. He insisted above all that the value of the individual as unique and free be not submerged in exclusive preoccupation with vast, impersonal, social movements. Science and invention fascinated him, and he was one of the pioneers in the modern wave of science fiction, as in *The Time Machine* (1895). Here he contrasted two kinds of human degeneration through mechanical progress, thus anticipating Capek's robots and Aldous Huxley's *Brave New World*, the antitheses of utopian perfection. He stressed the insecurity of existence and the fact that "anything may happen." Progress is not assured and man must work for it through imposing ethical control upon the blind workings of natural selection. After these cautions, Wells offered a specific, positive, and challenging picture of what the Utopia of the future might be, as to social organization, physique, personality, and way of life. In his early Utopias, Wells relied on the hope that man might raise himself to an ethical, progressive mode of life as against the crudely selfish, violent one—perhaps through the forceful direction of a superior, "samurai" group. But later, as the Second World War came on, he lost this hope and instead imagined (in *Star Begotten*, 1937) a beneficial mutation in man, caused by cosmic rays projected from an older and wiser race of Martians.

Across the Channel from England, Émile Zola carried on the naturalistic tradition as Bergson carried on the vitalistic one. He classed himself, and Tennyson condemned him, as "a positivist, an evolutionist, a materialist." His declared aim was to move through the world observing human behavior as one would observe the forms of animal life. He was impressed by the disastrous effects of heredity. The naturalistic fiction-writers in America, whom Zola and evolutionism influenced, emphasized the theme of "the beast within." Says Malcolm Cowley,[99] referring especially to Frank Norris and Jack London, "When evolution is treated in their novels, it almost always takes the opposite form of devolution or degeneration. It is seldom that the hero evolves toward a superhuman nature, as in Nietzsche's dream; instead he sinks backward toward the beasts." This theme of atavism has been treated more recently in William Golding's novel, *Lord of the Flies*.

Strangely enough, in view of their importance elsewhere in modern civilization, the ideas of evolution and progress are almost ignored in the visual arts of the past hundred years. One exception, typical in its negative attitude, is that of the French mural painter, Paul Chenavard.[100] Almost forgotten today, he was chief painter to the Republic of 1848, a friend of Baudelaire, and like the poet a pessimist on the subject of progress. He conceived and sketched a grandiose project for a series of paintings, mosaics, and sculptures to be placed in the Panthéon, depicting the whole history of man from Adam to Saint-Simon. The approach was secular and pessimistic, in that civilization was to be shown as declining and facing imminent death. It was never executed because of the Catholic return to power in 1851, but Baudelaire discussed it favorably in an essay on "Philosophic Art."

Thenceforth, painting and sculpture were to move far away from philosophy and the ideas of evolution and progress. (There were a few exceptions, such as Rodin's *Man of the Bronze Age*.) Walt Disney's *Fantasia*, a film in animated painting, contained a fantasy of evolution from the origin of the earth through the disappearance of the dinosaurs, set to the primitivistic music of

[99] "Naturalism in American Art and Literature," in *Evolutionary Thought in America*, ed. by S. Persons (New York, 1956), p. 315.

[100] *Cf.* J. C. Sloane, "Baudelaire, Chenavard, and 'Philosophic Art,'" in *Journal of Aesthetics and Art Criticism*, XIII, 3 (Mar. 1955), 285.

Stravinsky's *Sacre du Printemps*. The animated film is fairly well suited to deal with a fantasy of vast change through long eons of time; but so far Disney's experiment has had no notable successors.

A positive effect of evolutionism in American architecture is noted in the work of Louis Sullivan, Frank Lloyd Wright, and Walter Gropius. All of these, says Donald D. Egbert,[101] are believers in the idea of "organic expression," and this is an evolutionary concept. Sullivan and Wright, he continues, reiterate that great architecture must evolve organically out of the specific architectural problem, and must express its function directly. It should be natural, intuitive, and not based on abstract, rational principles as in Renaissance architecture. Environmental conditions, physical and social, should determine its design, said Wright, "as a plant grows out of soil... both unfold similarly from within." Form changes with changing conditions. Technology and machine industry, democracy and nationalism, are characteristic of American life and should therefore be expressed in its architecture, though without subordinating the personality of the artist or the user. In America, Egbert adds, the optimistic idea of evolution as continuously progressive influenced Sullivan and Wright; also the interest in primitivism, the revival of early, "natural" arts and crafts. These architects incline to a belief in cycles of growth, maturity, and decay in art. Other recent architects have been more influenced by the Hegel-Marx theory of dialectical progress, with a spiral or zigzag development. The Darwinian idea of natural selection was used to support Sullivan's belief that architectural styles of the past are unfit to survive. Adaptive evolution would result in beauty through the "integral simplicity of organic nature," as Wright phrased it. In sculpture Horatio Greenough, who died in 1852, was an early exponent of the evolutionary ideas of organic expression and functionalism. Walt Whitman, admired by Wright and Sullivan, believed that first-class poems, also, "grow out of circumstances, and are evolutionary."[102]

These examples suggest that, in recent years, the ideas of evolution and progress may have helped to make artistic change more consciously evolutionary. They helped to make artists and the public welcome change and seek originality, in addition to striving for a functional adaptation to changing conditions. This would supplement the influence on intellectual attitudes which John Dewey has pointed out.[103] To some slight extent, this eagerness for change may have speeded up the process of artistic change. Otherwise, it would seem that the idea of evolution has so far exerted comparatively little influence on the actual process of evolution in the arts. That idea is itself a product of cultural evolution: of growing knowledge about the processes of change in nature and culture.

However, before the idea of evolution emerged into social consciousness, and along with its early anticipations in the seventeenth and eighteenth centuries, the arts themselves were vaguely expressing the new interest in pervasive change and development. They did so through increasing emphasis on forms which unfold, differentiate, and integrate in time, especially in music, the novel, and the theater. This trend in art eventually led to the cinema, which transformed pictorial art from a static, spatial medium to one of spatio-temporal progression. Romantic literature, early in the 1800's, was gradually putting into words, with strong elements of Neo-Platonism and vitalism, the new ideas of universal growth and aspiration toward fully conscious life. These helped to stimulate evolutionary theorizing in biology and anthropology. Thus art and science cooperated in the discovery of evolution. But art, having preceded science in this case as in many others, lost interest in it and moved off on other lines. A little later science, too, showed signs of turning away from it.

[101] "Organic Expression and Architecture," in Persons (ed.), *Evolutionary Thought in America* (New York, 1956), p. 336.
[102] "A Backward Glance o'er Travel'd Roads," in *Leaves of Grass*.
[103] *The Influence of Darwin on Philosophy*.

CHAPTER XI

CHANGING ATTITUDES
TOWARD CULTURAL EVOLUTIONISM
IN RECENT ANTHROPOLOGY
AND SOCIOLOGY

I. EARLY TWENTIETH-CENTURY ATTACKS
ON THE THEORY

We have noted the following trends in various contexts, and will now examine them in more detail within the social sciences. Here, too, we shall see the counter-trends which afterwards developed.

First, a wave of pessimism set in during and after the First World War, including attacks on the belief in progress. These came from sources as diverse as Dean W. R. Inge, who attacked it from a theological point of view, and Oswald Spengler, who offered instead a new theory of inevitable, cyclical decline. The belief in progress, while distinct in theory from that of evolution, had been so closely connected with it by Spencer and others that the skeptical reaction spread to both.

Second, doubts were cast on Spencer's "universal law" of evolution even in the nineteenth century, by scientists in various fields who were neither pessimists nor supernaturalists. Among other weak points, they dwelt upon the fact that some lines of adaptive, organic change have been regressive, toward greater simplicity. Greater complexity, they argued, does not insure survival or better adaptation to environment. Many com-plex forms, including early varieties of man and the higher apes, have died out while simple forms persist. This tended to reinforce a skeptical attitude toward evolutionism in general. It was further strengthened by De Vries' criticism of Darwinism.

Third, the acceptance of naturalistic evolutionism in the cultural field by Marxist thinkers led to its association with Soviet communism in the minds of many Western liberals after 1917. Later on, some also associated it with Fascist totalitarianism. Both were anathema to Western liberals.

Fourth, the rapid development of historical scholarship in the various arts, with stricter standards of objectivity and factual accuracy, led to a phase of specialization in Europe. This spread to America, where such scholarship was still in its infancy at the beginning of the twentieth century. On the higher educational levels, this often involved a divorce of art-historical scholarship from philosophy, psychology, biology, and the social sciences, in which evolutionary theory had flourished. Many art historians neither knew nor cared much about the philosophy of art history, or about the relation of their chosen field to the wider context of humanistic knowledge and theory. The same wave of specialization affected these other fields also; hence many of their leaders neither knew nor cared much about the history and theory of the arts.

Fifth, as noted above, the discovery of highly skilled, realistic paintings and carvings from the Ice Age seemed to cast doubt on the theory that art had developed.

2. THE "BOASIAN REACTION" AGAINST UNILINEAR EVOLUTIONISM

The opinions of anthropologists in regard to cultural evolution have had an influence far beyond their own domain. The respect in which anthropology is commonly held, as a cultural science with rigorous standards, based largely on objective, empirical data, has given its pronouncements considerable authority in other fields, such as the history of the arts. Nineteenth-century anthropologists, and philosophers speculating on anthropological data, had been largely responsible for the wide public acceptance of cultural evolutionism.

In the early twentieth century the tide began to turn against it in anthropology itself. When Franz Boas and other scientists of like prestige appeared to be attacking evolutionism, the news spread quickly. Not only the younger anthropologists, eager to break with past authority, but also younger historians of art and culture, passed the word around that "evolutionism" was now disproved and discredited. Many of them took pains to avoid the word "evolution" entirely except to attack it, using instead such neutral terms as "cultural change" and the "social process."

What theory took its place? None of equal scope and definiteness, answering the same broad questions. Instead, there was a conscious effort to avoid all large-scale theorizing. Evolutionism had been enjoying such pre-eminence as *the* modern, scientific explanation of the past, replacing all the old philosophies of history, that if it, too, had to be rejected, what hope was there for any other,

or for the philosophy of history as a field of scholarship?

The attack of Boas and his school was not an attempt to revive pre-evolutionary theories, such as that of special creation and degeneration, which Tylor had so vigorously opposed. That fight was over as far as science was concerned, and the traditional religious theories of biology were no longer at issue. The new argument was among the scientists themselves, many of whom were naturalistic in world-view. It was not only between an older and a younger generation, but also between the more theoretical type of anthropologist, which had flourished in the nineteenth century, and the more cautious, rigorously factual, highly specialized type, which came to the fore in the 1920's.

The anthropological attack on cultural evolutionism is so commonly attributed to Franz Boas of Columbia University that it has come to be known as the "Boasian reaction." Yet Boas' own published comments on the subject are, on the whole, comparatively mild and moderate, directed toward specific aspects of the theory. The most extreme attacks came from some of his students and followers.[1] Boas did not reject all cultural evolutionism, but rather the oversimplified, Morgan-Tylor version of it, which he called "single unilineal development." "It is safe to say," he declared, "that the critical study of recent years has definitely disproved the existence of far reaching homologies which would permit us to arrange all the manifold cultural lines in an ascending scale in which to each can be assigned its proper place."[2]

[1] The most complete attempt to refute Morgan is in Robert H. Lowie's *Primitive Society* (1920), according to H. E. Barnes (*Historical Sociology*, pp. 31, 63, 89). Earlier criticisms of Morgan had been made by Tylor, Lippert, Kovalevsky, and Vierkandt. But the thorough repudiation of unilinearism and the establishment of scientific, historico-analytical anthropology are due to Boas and his followers, especially Clark Wissler, A. L. Kroeber, R. W. Lowie, A. Goldenweiser, E. Sapir, Fay-Cooper Cole, Ruth Benedict, and Paul Radin. "Marett espoused similar ideas in England," says Barnes, "albeit less rigorously, as also did Vierkandt, Ehrenreich, and Thurnwald in Germany."

[2] *Primitive Art* (Oslo, 1927), pp. 4, 5.

"On the other hand," he conceded, "dynamic conditions exist, based on environment, physiological, psychological, and social factors, that may bring forth similar cultural processes in different parts of the world," so that some historical events can be viewed "under more general dynamic viewpoints." Thus he did not deny significant analogies among cultural processes, or the possibility of explaining them in general terms. One way of studying them, he continued, was that of geographical distribution, which he himself had applied to the analytical study of folk-tales in 1891.[3] There is, he believed, "a certain homology between universal distribution of cultural facts and their antiquity." Archeology confirms that stone implements, fire and ornaments are found in the paleolithic period, while pottery and agriculture, which are less universally distributed, appear later; metals are still more limited in space and later. In effect, this seems to be a recognition of universal cultural stages; but Boas deplored "recent attempts to raise to a general principle this point of view which, with due caution, may be applied here and there." Such attempts by Herbert Spinden and Alfred Kroeber appeared to him as "quite untenable." That the local developments of most limited distribution are the youngest is, he argued, "only partially true."

Boas' main concern in these remarks was in regard to scientific method; not with the truth or untruth of evolutionism as a general principle. "It is obvious," says Marian W. Smith, "that his rejection did not apply to the facts of evolution, which he and his students continued to document in physical anthropology as well as in technological fields. Rather, it was directed toward evolution as a doctrine. The acceptance of evolution had become so general that there was a disposition to view field data in its terms. Boas' arguments were directed against this use of evolution as a basic premise capable of coloring observation and interpretation."[4] He was anxious that no general hypothesis, such as that of a relation between distribution and antiquity, should be assumed without

sufficient evidence to be always true. The same caution applied to unilineal evolutionism: "we may not start our inquiries and interpretations, as though the fundamental thesis of a single unilineal development of cultural traits the world over, of a development that follows everywhere the same lines, had been definitely proven." Such an assertion must be supported by detailed studies of single cultures, revealing analogies in their development.

Both of these cautions were eminently justified by the conditions of evolutionary theory in the early twentieth century: the more general one against over-reliance on any single hypothesis, and the more specific one against assuming unilineal evolutionism in the face of adverse evidence. The advice had salutary effects in stimulating an attitude of open-minded empiricism in anthropology, along with a program of energetic fieldwork including complete "immersion" in primitive living cultures. From armchair philosophizing, with little attention to the diversity of cultures, the approach was shifted to a cautious pluralism with emphasis on local details. From the "comparative method" of gathering and pigeon-holing scattered notes about culture-traits which seemed analogous but might not really be so, the approach was shifted to a study of the functional importance of each trait in its particular total context. These inquiries were especially needed at the time because of the rapid disappearance of the few primitive cultures which remained in a relatively pure, indigenous state amid the standardizing forces

[3] *Journal of American Folk-Lore*, Vol. IV, pp. 13–20; also *Science*, Vol. XII (1888), pp. 194–196.

[4] "Boas' 'Natural History' Approach to Field Method." In *The Anthropology of Franz Boas*, ed. W. Goldschmidt (Memoir 89 of the American Anthropological Association, Vol. 61, No. 5, Part 2, Oct. 1959), p. 49. Boas, it is said, was never much interested in the Darwinian theory of evolution. "One cannot help feeling," says E. H. Ackerknecht, "that Boas' arguments against social evolutionism are to a large extent transcriptions of Virchow's polemics against Haeckel in the question of biological transformism." Quoted by C. Kluckhohn and O. H. Prufer, "Influences During the Formative Years," in *The Anthropology of Franz Boas*, p. 22. However, Boas speaks in *Primitive Art* (p. 1) of man's mental equipment as "evolving from a condition similar to that found among the higher apes.'

of urban civilization. Now there is again a need for armchair—or at least for deskchair—philosophizing, to synthesize the mass of data collected; also for more attention to cultural similarities.

Boas retained the historical approach, as in considering "every cultural phenomenon as the result of historical happenings." His insistence on the "fundamental sameness of mental processes in all races and in all cultural forms of the present day" was not inconsistent with evolutionism in general, but only with the condescending attitude toward modern primitives which prevailed in mid-Victorian society. By the 1920's, the assumption that modern tribal cultures were extremely crude and simple, radically different from European civilization, was being generally abandoned by the evolutionists themselves; it was not at all essential to their thesis.

Nor was it essential in the evolutionary philosophy to hold that realistic art had always preceded abstract, symbolic decoration, or had always followed it. Boas was not attacking evolutionism in general, when he found no evidence in contemporary primitive art to establish either sequence as universal. He saw examples of both in primitive cultures, sometimes in the same tribe.[5] They spring from distinctive sources, he believed, and neither develops into the other. Boas could not have proved, and did not try to prove, that the geometric and the realistic were equally old, or unrelated genetically. His data were mostly from recent primitive art, and he was too cautious to hazard a generalization about prehistoric events on insufficient evidence. Whether there was any universal prehistoric sequence in the types of visual art, whether any one type came first everywhere and if so which one, is still an unsolved problem. Both are found in paleolithic art. The present tendency is to believe in diverse origins; but this view is not proved.

At the end of *Primitive Art*, Boas explicitly reaffirmed the main thesis of Spencerian evolutionism in the arts: the fact of increasing complexity and differentiation. "What distinguishes modern esthetic feeling from that of primitive peoples," he said, "is the manifold character of its manifestations. We are not so much bound by a fixed style. The complexity of our social structure and our more varied interests allow us to see beauties that are closed to the senses of people living in a narrower culture".[6] On the subject of increasing complexity, Boas had some words of praise for the much-derided Victorians.[7] "The early anthropologists," he said, "like Tylor, Morgan, and Lubbock, who developed their theories under the stimulus of Darwinian evolution, observed correctly the increasing complexity of cultural forms, the progress of knowledge and the elimination of antiquated forms... They erred in assuming a single unilinear evolution..." But they were not entirely wrong in believing that cultural evolution is sometimes determined along a certain line. "It seems possible," Boas wrote, "that laws exist that determine the development of a given culture in a given direction... As long as a certain trend of activity or thought persists it will proceed on the lines laid down, toward an increasing intensity or complexity."

---

[5] *Primitive Art*, pp. 352–355.

[6] Bidney states that "Boas was opposed to the thesis of the cultural evolutionists that cultural development is always from the simple to the complex," but he does not document this statement. (*Theoretical Anthropology*, p. 215). The question is partly a verbal one: if "development" and "evolution" are defined in the usual way, as implying some sort of complicative growth, then by definition they must be always from the simple to the complex. But this does not mean that all cultural change is necessarily complicative, and the early evolutionists did not say that it was. Spencer, as we have seen, recognized a contrary movement. Bidney, in criticizing early evolutionism, remarks that cultural evolution sometimes goes from the complex to the simpler, in the sense of the clearer and more rational, especially in the intellectual realm. (P. 218). This implies a different definition of "evolution."

[7] "Anthropology," in *Encyclopedia of the Social Sciences*, pp. 102 ff.

3. EXAGGERATED ATTACKS
BY FOLLOWERS OF BOAS
ON CULTURAL EVOLUTIONISM IN GENERAL

In view of the moderate, limited nature of Boas' criticism, why did so many of his followers misrepresent it as a total, unqualified rejection of cultural evolutionism? Why did so many of the younger anthropologists and art historians, in the twenties and thirties, vie with each other in more and more indiscriminate blasts at the concept of evolution? No single answer can be given. Such swings of opinion from one extreme to the other, from excessive reliance on a theory to equally excessive rejection of it, are common enough in the dialectic of history. So is the spectacle of a wise, cautious leader who states his views in a balanced way, with necessary qualification, only to be followed by smaller men who exaggerate and oversimplify them. In any case, a number of Boas' followers filled the air with much more intemperate statements; some even before he had published his views, and while he was still expressing them in lectures and seminars.

One of the most extreme was Berthold Laufer, who said in 1918, "I must confess that I am in a state of mind where I would no longer give a dime for a new theory, but I am always enthusiastic about new facts." Linear evolutionism, he continued, was "the most inane, sterile, and pernicious theory ever conceived in the history of science."[8] The usually moderate Ruth F. Benedict also indulged in some overstatements, as in saying that "the idea of evolution" has to be "laid aside in the study of culture"; that the order of events with which psychology, history, and anthropology deal "is best studied without the implications of any evolutionary arrangement."[9] As the attack spread, C. Kluckhohn had to say in 1939 that "To suggest something as 'theoretical' is to suggest that it is slightly indecent."[10]

At the height of the war on unilinear evolutionism, the mistakes of nineteenth-century evolutionists in this respect were exaggerated for polemic

reasons. We have seen that Spencer's theory of cultural evolution was less unilinear than is commonly charged, and that even Morgan and Tylor, though admittedly the worst sinners in this respect, were not quite as rigid as some later critics have made them out to be. All of these men wrote at a time when, to defend the basic theory of evolution, one *had* to emphasize resemblances and continuities. The diversities were evident enough and provided a strong argument for special creation.

The evolutionist had to argue against the firmly-rooted belief in "miraculous interferences, abrupt leaps and bounds in Nature," and for the new conception of an "unbroken chain of sequences" from elemental matter to Shakespeare.[11] Even so, Spencer also emphasized the universal tendency to differentiation in both organic and social evolution. Human culture, being basically limited by man's inherited psychophysical endowment, could not be expected to diversify as widely as organic species; but even here, a wide range of variations was possible within the general process of social evolution as Spencer defined it.

The word "unilinear" is of course a metaphor, to describe cultural change in terms of spatial movement. No one can deny that all cultural change by the human species as we know it has to be somewhat unilinear, along lines determined by its inherited nature. But (to develop the me-

[8] Review of R. H. Lowie's *Culture and Ethnology* in *American Anthropologist*, Vol. 20, (1918), p. 90. Quoted by Hoebel (*Man in the Primitive World*, p. 612), who calls this statement "immoderate" and "an outburst of antievolutionistic fanaticism."

[9] "The Science of Custom," *Century Magazine*, April 1929; reprinted in V. F. Calverton, ed., *The Making of Man* (New York, 1931), p. 809. Hoebel calls her statement "purblind." In contrast with it, an essay by Ruth Benedict, finished in 1948 and edited by Margaret Mead, says that "Although a large part of the history of any given culture is due to accident, an evolutionary process may be traced... Evolution can be well illustrated in two fields, the technological and the political." "The Growth of Culture," in *Man, Culture, and Society*, ed. by H. L. Shapiro (New York, 1956), pp. 192–193.

[10] "The Place of Theory in Anthropological Science," in *The Philosophy of Science*, Vol. 6 (1939), p. 333. *Cf.* Hoebel, *ibid.* Kluckhohn did not endorse that attitude toward theory.

[11] *Cf.* J. A. Symonds, *Essays Speculative and Suggestive* (London, 1893), p. 29.

taphor) it has gone along a broad avenue or valley, not a narrow path, within which there has been room for much divergence, as well as for some convergence and some approximate parallelism.

Even the error of regarding modern primitives as similar to prehistoric ones is an error of degree. Here, too, some emphasis on similarities was justifiable at the time. It is undeniable today that prehistoric cultures resemble some present tribal cultures in significant ways, such as the lack of writing and of metal tools, science, machinery, city life, and symphony orchestras. Such modern tribes are actually like our prehistoric ancestors in certain respects. No nineteenth-century evolutionist said they were alike in *all* respects. The mistake was not to realize, or emphasize, the extent of the differences. By now, most tribal cultures have absorbed some traits from surrounding civilization.

Alexander Goldenweiser helped to aggravate the confusion in 1933 by entitling a section in his *History, Psychology, and Culture* "The Downfall of Evolutionism."[12] In his text itself, however, it soon appeared that the downfallen theory was not evolutionism in general, but the particular kind which he described as "the simplist evolutionary scheme" or "evolution and environmentalism in their crude classical forms." These were the doctrines of "the early evolutionists" or "classical anthropologists." As against these, he reviewed the errors which had led to their downfall. Their "comparative method" had been unsound in assuming without sufficient evidence that apparently analogous traits from different cultures were really analogous. Their notion of a "primal matriarchate" had no factual basis. Eduard Hahn had attacked their dogma of the three stages by showing that wherever man hunted, women gathered wild plants; that the pastoral stage did not necessarily follow hunting; that agriculture had developed in two forms—one with the hoe only, performed by women; one with domestication and the plow, performed by men. The belief in universal, primitive communism was untrue. Animism and magic had been equally primitive, and ancestor worship had occurred under advanced conditions. Other early errors, Goldenweiser charged, were the clangens succession, the priority of realistic art, the universality of pottery in high civilizations, the frequency of parallel development, and the belief in evolution as progressive in the sense of improvement.[13]

But if all these had been the faults of "early, crude, classical evolutionism," as almost everyone now agreed, what then was *modern, refined, corrected evolutionism?* That there was, or could be, such a thing was clearly indicated by Goldenweiser at the end of his chapter on "Cultural Anthropology" (p. 164). Here he hailed a new tendency in anthropology: "a more constructive analysis of developmental trends in history pointing towards a revised evolutionism." What it was he did not explain; but apparently something had survived the downfall.

4. "MULTILINEAR" VERSUS "UNILINEAR" EVOLUTIONISM

In the late nineteen-forties in America, the pendulum began to swing back to a revival of interest in cultural evolution and a disposition to theorize in terms of it. One leader in this revival was Julian H. Steward. The negative side of his argument—the attack on unilinear evolutionism—was supplemented by a positive call for more attention to developmental sequences of smaller scope and more diversity than those of nineteenth-century theory. The existence of such sequences, and hence of more diversified kinds of evolution, had been suggested but not emphasized by Spencer, Tylor,

[12] (New York, 1933), pp. 132 ff. He also misrepresented Spencer (p. 126) by saying that he touched "only indirectly" upon material science and art.

[13] Goldenweiser lists these errors also in "Social Evolution," in *Encyclopedia of the Social Sciences*, p. 660. See also B. Malinowski, "Culture," in the same work, Vol. IV (1931). D. G. MacRae described Malinowski as chief leader of the antievolutionary reaction, especially against Frazer. *A Century of Darwin*, ed. by S. A. Barnett (London, 1958), p. 308.

and others; usually without a distinguishing name. In the nineties, G. J. Romanes had distinguished in biology between "monotypic" and "polytypic" evolution, the latter being divergent, along different lines.[14] J. M. Baldwin and G. F. Stout, discussing this distinction in an article on social evolution and progress, commented that "Social evolution is polytypic; it expresses the social growth when hemmed and conditioned by physical, biological, and psychological situations and events, and is in many diverging directions." Before the Boasian reaction, however, the need to emphasize divergence had not been widely felt. Steward supplied the emphasis and an appropriate name to contrast with the now rejected unilinear type. It caught the attention of a new generation of anthropologists, and encouraged a cautious return to evolutionary theory.

"Multilinear evolution," said Steward, "is essentially a methodology based on the assumption that significant regularities in cultural change occur." It is concerned with the determination of cultural laws and with historical reconstruction, he added, "but it does not expect that historical data can be classified in universal stages."[15] It is, he said elsewhere, "like unilinear evolution in dealing with developmental sequences, but is distinctive in searching for parallels of limited occurrence instead of universals."[16] Among the errors of the unilinear scheme, Steward asserted, had been (a) to try to force the data of all precivilized human groups into the two categories of savagery and barbarism, and (b) to postulate the priority of matrilinear patterns over the other kinship patterns. Multilinear evolutionism has no such assumptions, he said. It recognizes that cultural traditions may be different in different areas, and merely asks whether any significant resemblances between cultures can be observed and described. It is interested mainly in particular cultures and in their observable resemblances and differences, thus working out specific parallels of form, function, and sequence.[17]

Multilinear evolutionism is, according to Steward, open-minded toward recognizing independ-

ent development, as in Lowie's studies of moieties, dual systems of numbers, and messianic cults; also in accepting a kind of necessity in cultural development, in that certain achievements presuppose others. "If a tribe practices metallurgy it is clearly not on the plane of savagery; only stockbreeders and farmers forge metals."[18] A. L. Kroeber granted that "culture relations or patterns develop spontaneously or from within, probably more frequently than as a result of direct taking-over... The same type is frequently evolved independently."[19]

The multilinear approach goes a little farther toward generalization than those whom Steward calls the "relativists and particularists."[20] "Its major categories are primarily developmental stages applicable to all cultures," while theirs are limited to "culture areas or traditions." The relativists and particularists are, on the whole, those still stubbornly opposed to all theorizing, especially about evolution; the multilinearists have moved a step or two in the direction of such theorizing, with a firm resolve not to go too far. By pointing out one middle course, Steward performed a valuable service. Hoebel noted in 1958 that, whereas con-

[14] *Darwin and After Darwin* (Chicago, 1892–7); quoted in "Evolution" and "Social Evolution," in J. M. Baldwin's *Dictionary of Philosophy and Psychology* (New York, 1902, 1925); esp. Vol. I, p. 354 and Vol. II, p. 536. L. T. Hobhouse had also remarked that "the course of social evolution is not unitary but that different races and different communities have... diverged early, rapidly, and in many different directions at once." (Quoted by H. E. Barnes, *op. cit.*, p. 54, from *Morals in Evolution*, pp. 1–2).

[15] Steward, "Evolution and Progress," in A. L. Kroeber (ed.), *Anthropology Today*, pp. 313 f.

[16] *Theory of Culture Change: the Methodology of Multilinear Evolution* (Urbana, Ill., 1955), pp. 14–15. It is, perhaps, a little confusing to call "evolution" a method or methodology, and to say that it "deals with" sequences or "searches for parallels." Evolution itself, unilinear or multilinear, is a process or supposed process in the historical phenomena themselves. It is evolution*ism* or a *theory* of evolution which functions in science as a concept, hypothesis, or method.

[17] Hoebel, *op. cit.*, p. 613.

[18] R. H. Lowie, *An Introduction to Cultural Anthropology* (New York, 1940), pp. 40, 376. (Quoted by Steward). Also "Evolution in Cultural Anthropology: a Reply to Leslie White," *American Anthropologist*, XLVIII (1946), p. 223.

[19] *Anthropology* (New York, 1948), p. 241.

[20] *Theory of Culture Change*, pp. 19, 28.

structive work in evolutionary analysis had been in abeyance since 1949, this was no longer the case. This was, he believed, "one of the most significant changes in anthropology in the current decade."[21] Hoebel preferred to state the new issue as between multilinear and "general" (not "universal") evolutionism. "Universal" seemed to claim too much, and more than its leaders intended.

As the argument over "multilinear evolution" grew in force, one scientist after another insisted that he, or someone before him, had advocated something of the sort. "I myself pointed out years ago," said R. H. Lowie, "that multilinear evolution is involved in such a scheme as that of Father Schmidt." From the primeval level, according to that scheme, three independent developments proceed: one of farming, one of higher hunting, and one of pastoralism.[22] Leslie A. White, always a steadfast evolutionist, protested against the idea that "multilinear evolution" was something new and original. He had some kind words to say for the much-belabored Victorians. Spencer, Tylor, and Morgan, said White, had all recognized multilinear evolution as well as unilinear. They had never said that every people had to go through the same series of developmental stages.[23] Daryll Forde of London charged that Steward had made "a false dichotomy between universal and multilinear evolution." The "universal" approach of White and Childe, he suggested, was simply on a different level of abstraction, and there was nothing inconsistent between them. White welcomed both, but insisted on the possibility of over-all, comprehensive generalization.[24]

The cultural stages proposed by White and Childe are, in Steward's opinion, so general as to be neither very arguable nor useful. Who can deny, Steward asks, that hunting and gathering (Childe's conception of savagery) preceded plant and animal domestication (his conception of barbarism) and that the latter was a precondition of large urban populations, writing, mathematics, social differentiation and specialization (his conception of civilization)? The generalizations that culture changes from the simple to the complex, and that increasing control of energy underlies cultural achievements, have (says Steward) "long been accepted." Childe's transfer of Darwinism to cultural evolution "also will not evoke challenge."[25] Steward's objection to such generalizations was that they do not "explain particular features of particular cultures." To be sure, he granted, the same can be said of the biological use of evolutionary principles. Organic variation, heredity, and natural selection cannot explain a single life-form, since they do not inform us about the particular circumstances that help determine biological determination. To understand specific cultural forms, one must trace the history of each in detail.

To these objections one may answer, first, that if the validity of applying general evolutionary principles to cultural phenomena is now to be accepted without challenge in anthropology, this at least marks a notable change from the sweeping negativism of the Boasian extremists. In the second place, it hardly justifies the belittling of such evolutionary principles as variation, heredity, and natural selection to say that they do not, in themselves, fully "explain" the characteristics of any one individual or species. They have contributed profoundly to our understanding, not only of history of life as a whole, but also of the development of species and the nature of each individual.

---

[21] Op. cit., p. 614.

[22] An Appraisal of Anthropology Today (Chicago, 1953), pp. 70–71, referring to W. Schmidt, Handbuch der Methode der Kulturhistorischen Ethnologie (Münster, 1937).

[23] An Appraisal of Anthropology Today, p. 71.

[24] Ibid., p. 72. White, says H. E. Barnes, "has vigorously criticized the Boas school for its alleged adherence to the negative attitude of the extreme Historicists." Historical Sociology, p. 65. Cf. White, The Science of Culture (New York, 1949), p. 338. Cf. Steward, Theory of Culture Change, p. 16; Childe, Social Evolution (New York, 1951), pp. 35, 160.

[25] Childe, op. cit., p. 175; Steward, p. 18.

5. RENEWED SUPPORT
FOR CULTURAL EVOLUTIONISM.
THE MID-CENTURY COUNTER-REACTION

Throughout the American attack, many British social scientists remained unshaken in their acceptance of cultural evolutionism. These included archeologists such as V. Gordon Childe, social anthropologists such as A. R. Radcliffe-Brown, and sociologists such as Donald G. MacRae. Among the most influential was Julian Huxley, whose main work was in biology, but who also won respect in anthropology for his writings on the cultural, social, and ethical aspects of evolution.

Radcliffe-Brown's scornful attitude toward the American anti-evolutionists, especially Laufer, was typical though expressed with unusual vehemence. He had not discussed their views in his book, he said, because "Their writings show an amazing confusion of thought and ignorance of the theory of social evolution."[26] Accepting a Spencerian concept of evolution, he emphasized that there had been divergent development in the form of social life in different portions of mankind, and also uneven advance in organization.

Childe, on the other hand, was more impressed by the applicability of Darwinian principles (variation, heredity, adaptation, and selection) to social and cultural evolution. While pointing out the differences between organic and cultural, he concluded "this is not to deny cultural evolution... Cultural change is an orderly and rational process that can be understood by the human intellect without invoking any necessarily incalculable factors and miracles." All the divergent development among societies in the Old and New Worlds "does not invalidate the use of the term 'evolution' to describe social development, nor even the implied analogy between social and organic evolution." Convergence and diffusion, he said, distinguish social from organic evolution.[27]

Donald MacRae praised Spencer's contribution to social science in having first used the terms "social structure" and "social function" in their modern sense, and in having put the classification of institutions on a firm basis.[28] The period of reaction against cultural evolutionism, especially the inclusion of a historical element in social science, "is now coming to an end," he commented.[29]

In forming a new evolutionary synthesis for the mid-twentieth century, the writings of Julian Huxley were clear and far-reaching. Where many writers were vague or inconsistent on the meaning of "evolution," he offered a new definition in the tradition of Spencer. Evolution is, he said, "a one-way process, irreversible in time, producing apparent novelties and greater variety, and leading to higher degrees of organization." "Higher," he added, means "more differentiated, more complex, but at the same time more integrated."[30] In an essay on "Evolution, Cultural and Biological,"[31] he declared that an evolutionary approach to culture is essential. "We shall never fully understand human culture unless we look at it as a portion of the evolutionary process—both a product of past evolution and a basis for possible future evolution." But this approach in anthropology has been "bedevilled by false starts and false premises," such as Comte's unilinear "straitjacket for culture." Culture has both mental (subjective) and material (objective) components; both can be studied naturalistically and scientifically. Culture consists of artifacts, socifacts, and mentifacts, all of which comprise the self-reproducing or reproducible products of the mental activities of a group of human individuals in a society. A piece of pottery,

26 *Method in Social Anthropology* (Chicago, 1958), pp. 189, 181
27 *Social Evolution* (New York, 1951), pp. 166, 169, 175.
28 *A Century of Darwin* (London, 1958), p. 307.
29 Robert Briffault should also be included in the list of British cultural evolutionists, although his extreme views set him apart from most of them. In his monumental work on *The Mothers* (New York, 1927), he held stubbornly and with copious evidence to the matriarchal theory, now rejected as a universal principle by most anthropologists. See also his *Rational Evolution* (New York, 1930), first published in 1919 as *The Making of Humanity.*
30 *Issues in Evolution*, p. 44. Vol. III of *Evolution After Darwin* (Chicago, 1960), ed. by Sol Tax and Charles Callender.
31 Reprinted in *New Bottles for New Wine* (London, 1957), pp. 76, 79, 91.

said Huxley, can be both a useful artifact and a beautiful mentifact. The arts produce mentifacts as "organized constructions of significance to be communicated from one human mind to another." Evolution operates in man overwhelmingly as a cultural process, rather than biologically. It shows adaptation, long-term advance, divergence, limitation (resulting in stabilization or regression), a rise in the upper level of achievement, and an increased realization of possibilities. Cultural evolution differs from biological as to selection and mechanisms of change, as to the presence of diffusion and convergence, as to the accumulation and organization of knowledge, and in other ways.

Whereas most anthropologists have neglected art, especially civilized art, Huxley referred to it often and emphatically, as an integral part of cultural evolution. "In the light of evolutionary humanism," he wrote, "art appears not as an instrument of the State, but as an organ of the evolving human species."[32] Art, along with science, religion, and law, is a product of psychosocial (cultural) evolution.[33] Man's destiny is to make possible greater fulfillment for more human beings and fuller achievement by human societies. "The important ends of man's life include the creation and enjoyment of beauty, both natural and man-made;... the feeling of active participation in embracing and enduring projects, including the cosmic project of evolution."[34]

"Theories of aesthetics do not emerge," said Huxley, "until after millennia of the practice of art."[35] Religion develops from fluid, non-rational myth to precise, rationalized theology. Science grows "from a mere recognition of empirical regularities into an elaborate system of theories and laws capable of increasingly precise mathematical formulation." Complex languages develop long before their systems are described in rules of grammar and syntax. Thus latent cultural pattern-systems develop in various fields and receive their conscious formulations later on. Huxley classified the material components of culture on a functional basis according to the human needs and desires

they serve—nourishment, health, shelter, clothing, enjoyment, adornment, communication, etc. The arts evidently function under several of these types, notably communication, where they provide "mentifacts—organized constructions of significance to be communicated from one human mind to others." With other mentifacts, said Huxley, works of art express and organize experience aesthetically, symbolically, and intellectually, and transmit these organizations to others, thus building the psychological framework of social culture.

Among the persistent upholders of cultural evolutionism in America, L. A. White, Robert Redfield, and A. Lesser should be mentioned. Attacks upon them have been largely directed toward their attempts to correlate stages in different cultural components such as kinship organization, technology, property rights, class structure, and political integration.[36]

Ralph Linton[37] entitled one of his chapters "Cultural Evolution," while expressly disavowing the unilinear variety. The processes of cultural change, he said, can be regarded as evolutionary only insofar as they show some definite, fairly consistent direction. In general, they have been "directed toward a better adjustment of the social organism to its environment," although there are examples of degeneration, non-functional elaborations, and hypertrophies. "The existence of a definite direction in the development of culture," Linton added, "would seem to be fairly well demonstrated by the numerous parallels between the Old and the New World cultures."[38] David Bidney clearly distinguished between the notion of fixed stages and "the idea of evolution itself as a method of studying cultural phenomena."[39] "That there has been cultural evolution from a

[32] *New Bottles for New Wine*, p. 307.
[33] *Issues in Evolution*, p. 213.
[34] "The Evolutionary Vision," in *Issues*, p. 259.
[35] *New Bottles for New Wine*, pp. 78 f.
[36] *Cf.* G. P. Murdock, *Social Structure* (New York, 1949), p. 187.
[37] *The Tree of Culture* (New York, 1955), pp. 49 ff.
[38] P. 59.
[39] *Theoretical Anthropology*, p. 282.

primitive state to that of modern civilization is not doubted. But how to evaluate cultural progress is in doubt, and the assumption that there are fixed, necessary laws governing the development of all peoples is rejected."

Typical of the changing climate of opinion in America was a statement in 1956 by Harry Hoijer. In an article on "Language and Writing," he said "that the history of man's cultures shows a continuous and cumulative development extending from their earliest beginnings to the present means of course that man has possessed language as long as he has possessed culture."[40]

In 1958, Margaret Mead reviewed the past "period of low interest" in cultural evolution and dated its end at 1952.[41] At that time, she said, the Wenner-Gren Foundation International Symposium on Anthropology helped to end the divergence between biologists and anthropologists, especially those interested in child rearing and learning. Defining culture as "the system of behavior characteristic of a human group which is transmitted through experience," she recommended the study of "inventions which survive" as "the mainstream of a cultural evolution in which the various items are arranged in an ascending sequence of levels of organization." In such terms, "directional evolutionary change in culture may be viewed as inevitable and the only variable is the time at which a next stage will occur. In this approach, theories of orthogenesis become relevant."

If 1952 was a turning-point, 1959 may be noted by future historians as the date of a substantial victory for cultural evolutionism in American anthropology. In that year, a series of panel discussions was held at the University of Chicago to celebrate the centennial of Darwin's *Origin of Species*. To it were invited a galaxy of noted participants from both sides of the ocean, as authorities on all phases of evolution. Sol Tax, professor of anthropology at the University, chief organizer of the conference and editor of its published report, summarized its findings in a concluding paper.[42]

Panel Five on *Social and Cultural Evolution* had been under the chairmanship of Clyde Kluckhohn and Alfred L. Kroeber. The panelists had been Robert M. Adams, Edgar Anderson, Julian Huxley, Hermann J. Muller, Fred Polak, Julian Steward, Leslie A. White, and Gordon R. Willey. Its general conclusion, said Tax, had been "that we all now believe in cultural evolution." At the same time, he remarked that some other anthropologists, not present, might be less committed to that belief; hence the endorsement should be qualified. "However," Tax continued, "all anthropologists recognize both the general rise of culture from an almost non-existent form in animals to the human stage, where culture seems to be everything." "We are thus evolutionists for the species, including its developments of culture..."

This estimate by Dr. Tax of present anthropological opinion is important in two ways for the main subject of the present book, evolution *in the arts*. The panelists here assembled were not, and did not claim to be, authorities on art, aesthetics, or art history. Most of them expressed no opinion on whether the arts evolve. But a great obstacle to belief in the evolution of the arts was removed when American anthropology ceased to reject cultural evolutionism in general. No one denies that art is, on the whole, a part of culture. Whether it evolves along with the other parts is now an open question, to be decided by empirical evidence from art itself; not by deduction from ideas developed elsewhere. The whole question can no longer be casually dismissed by saying, "Of course art does not evolve, since culture in general does not evolve."

Kluckhohn gave a keynote by saying, "Everyone concedes that cultural evolution is an extension to biological evolution, yet different from it. But

[40] In H. L. Shapiro (ed.), *Man, Culture, and Society* (New York, 1956), p. 198.
[41] "Cultural Determinants of Behavior," in A. Roe and G. G. Simpson, *Behavior and Evolution* (New Haven, 1958), p. 480.
[42] "The Celebration: a Personal View," in *Issues in Evolution*, Vol. III of *Evolution After Darwin* (Chicago, 1960), p. 281.

different to what degree and in what respects?" He mentioned the difference in ways of transmission, and called for better taxonomic bases for a cultural typology. Huxley remarked that the products of psychosocial evolution, such as science, religion, art, and law, are new and unlike anything produced by biological evolution.

There was much discussion of the need for a "macrodynamic" or large-scale approach to cultural science instead of the recent "microdynamic" one. Cultural macrodynamics, said Polak, is "the long-term process of the recurrence and the rise and fall of civilizations." He also emphasized the influence of man's non-technological creations, including art and philosophical ideas, value-systems and ideologies. Throughout the discussion the arts were assumed to be "non-technological," rather than a kind of technic or technology. "Technology" was understood in the usual sense as concerned with utilitarian implements and methods. Art was classed rather vaguely with "values," "ideal goals," and "stylistic innovations."

In another session of the same conference,[43] Gordon R. Willey, specialist in American archeology and ethnology, declared that art, religion, science, world-views—all constituting the realm of ideas or the "moral order" (as Redfield had called it)—develop along with the technological and social order. Their evolution is causally related to that of these other orders, but is not well understood.

Along with the revival of cultural evolutionism, the prevailing attitude toward the nineteenth-century evolutionists became more favorable; even toward Morgan, whom the Boasians had singled out as arch-offender. Robert M. Adams endorsed the view of Leacock that a trend is in prospect "toward the synthesis of the historical empricism associated with the name of Boas and the theoretical evolutionism associated primarily with Morgan."[44] A sympathetic biography of Morgan by Carl Resek in 1960 was favorably reviewed by Marshall D. Sahlins, anthropologist of the University of Michigan.[45] Now that evolu-

tionism in anthropology is being rehabilitated, the review began, it is necessary to rewrite the history of the science. Morgan had been "stoned outright by Western scholars and then buried under an avalanche of indifference," but now his books were being republished. The changes in his influence, Resek held, might well reflect turns in American thought and life. The reviewer noted in this connection the difference between Resek's book and Bernhard Stern's less sympathetic biography in 1931. The new book, said the reviewer, verified Francis Parkman's prophecy in a letter to Morgan: "The more advanced we become in intellectual progress, the more your labors will be appreciated."

In 1960 Sahlins and three colleagues published an enthusiastic affirmation of cultural evolutionism in anthropology. Their book of essays, *Evolution and Culture*,[46] paid tribute to Tylor and Spencer while criticizing the Boasian reaction as a mistake. They defined "general cultural evolution" in Spencerian terms as "increase in organization, higher energy concentration, and... increased heterogeneity." (P. 8). They said little about the arts, but did not rule them out of the process.

Cultural evolutionism in its new form is not merely the revival of a nineteenth-century theory. It asks that this and other hypotheses be actively tested by empirical and, if possible, quantitative methods. Just how and to what extent is a general, evolutionary trend in culture shown by concrete evidence? In line with this approach, Robert L. Carneiro has proposed an application of "scale analysis" to the study of cultural traits and their

[43] *The Evolution of Man*, Vol. II of *Evolution After Darwin*, pp. 112, 136.

[44] "The Evolutionary Process in Early Civilizations," in *The Evolution of Man*, Vol. II of *Evolution After Darwin*, pp. 158-159, quoting E. Leacock, "Social Stratification and Evolutionary Theory," in *Ethnohistory*, V, 193-199.

[45] *Lewis Henry Morgan, American Scholar* (Chicago, 1960). Reviewed in *Science*, Vol. 131, 13 (May 1960), p. 1435.

[46] Sahlins, M. D., and E. R. Service (eds.), *Evolution and Culture* (University of Michigan Press, Ann Arbor, 1960). Essays by T. G. Harding, D. Kaplan, M. D. Sahlins, and E. R. Service.

developmental sequence in various societies.[47] Granting that there is no unilinear sequence to which all societies have adhered exactly, he asks, "but may there not be an evolutionary sequence which *most* societies have followed *most* of the time?" The scaling method will show, he believes, "that along with the development of new forms there is retention of old ones" and "a normal course" of development in such traits as agriculture, pottery, loom weaving, smelting, and stone architecture.

To what extent any quantitative method can be usefully applied to the history of the arts, especially those of advanced civilizations, must be experimentally decided. Premature, excessive quantification leads to oversimplified conclusions. Many of the most important artistic phenomena are still inaccessible to measurement or statistical treatment. But some cautious steps in that direction can safely be made (a) in developing a more objective typology of artistic traits; (b) in refining rough estimates of more and less; and (c) in counting or measuring what *can* be significantly counted or measured, without assuming that this tells the whole story.

[47] "Scale Analysis as an Instrument for the Study of Cultural Evolution," *Southwestern Journal of Anthropology* (Albuquerque, N. M.), Vol. 18, 2 (Summer, 1962), 149–170.

CHAPTER XII

STAGES AND SEQUENCES IN CULTURE HISTORY

1. THE MEANING OF "STAGE." CONFLICTING THEORIES OF CULTURAL STAGES

The basic concept of cultural evolution, as we have seen, implies no particular theory of stages or parallel sequences. Evolutionism in general does not stand or fall with the belief that all humanity passes through uniform channels of cultural development, or that matrilinear kinship always precedes patrilinear, or that living primitives are exactly like prehistoric ones, or any other of the errors for which nineteenth-century evolutionism has been blamed. Spencer, Darwin, Taine, and many other leaders in that movement had little interest in the problem and advanced no definite theory of general stages. Cultural evolution can be conceived as a process which is so continuous and gradual as to present no well-marked stages. Or the evolution can be so divergent, as in that of animals and plants, that no definite stages are common to all the lines of development.

Two other traditions in evolutionary thought did emphasize theories of stages, and the ensuing controversy has focused wide attention on the problem. Hence it is often confused with that of whether culture evolves at all. Any thorough discussion of cultural evolution today must take it into account and indicate its present status. Contemporary answers to it usually take their starting-points from one of the two traditional approaches: from the naturalistic one, descending from Lucretius, Nilsson, and Comte to Morgan and Tylor,

or from the spiritualistic one, descending from Plato, Kant, and Hegel.

The sequence of trends in theorizing about cultural evolution, including the question of stages, has assumed a somewhat dialectical form: first the nineteenth-century thesis of a highly regular, universal pattern; second, as antithesis, the Boasian rejection of that pattern in the early twentieth century; and now the attempt at a synthesis, retaining the best elements of both. This would retain those elements of the thesis which are found to be true, along with the cautious empiricism and pluralism of the Boasian reaction. In its broad outlines, the present situation is fairly simple. No scientific writer on the subject advocates an extremely rigid, unilinear theory of stages, and no one denies or could deny all analogies between the histories of different cultural groups. The truth is somewhere between these extremes, and the present task is to discover more specifically where it lies.

Much depends on how one understands the word "stage." It is sometimes taken to imply a great deal in common; a high degree of uniformity between distant cultural sequences. But this is not a necessary meaning. There are also cultural stages of a much more limited, partial kind. Because of its ambiguity, some present writers avoid the term; but the substitutes they employ (such as "levels of integration") are not much clearer. Webster's *New International Dictionary* defines "stage" in a general sense as "a place of rest on a regularly traveled road"; hence, "a degree of progression in any pursuit, development, process, or the like; as, a stage of one's life." In biology, it means "One of several periods (whose beginning and end are usually marked by some important change of structure) in the development and growth of many animals and plants." In social science, it is "One of the steps into which the material development of man or a race is divided; an economy; as, the pastoral, agricultural, barter, or nomadic stage." (The restriction to *material* development is not in accord with present usage). In these dictionary definitions, we can see how the idea of a stopping-place on a journey has been transferred to that of a period or temporary condition in a process. A stage in this sense is somewhat like a period, era, or epoch, but is not conceived in purely chronological terms such as centuries or millennia, or even in such terms as dynasties and Olympiads. A cultural stage is conceived as a span of time in which a certain group remains for a while in a basically similar cultural state or mode of life such as "Neolithic." Different groups may reach a similar state at different times. Having reached that state by some comparatively drastic changes, the group remains for a while to elaborate, refine, or otherwise vary it in detail (e.g., in the chipping of flints) before going on to another phase of radical changes. The latter may also be described as a "stage," but one of transition rather than of equilibrium.

A cultural stage is never actually a "place of rest" or complete equilibrium. On the contrary, the revolutionary "break-through" to a new stage is usually followed by intensified activity along many related lines. New sources of energy may be discovered and put to various tasks; latent human energies may be released by dissolving old bonds; previous folkways and value-systems are abandoned and new ones are worked out. The historian may mark off a stage in terms of one new trait which lasts a while, such as the use of bronze for tools and weapons. But this may actually have been accompanied by other, far-reaching changes.

2. CULTURAL COMPONENTS; COMPONENT AND COMPOSITE SEQUENCES

Culture, as conceived by anthropologists, consists of many branches or components. Each is itself a complex of many different but closely related activities, institutions, customs, skills, ways of thinking and feeling. They are not in reality separate entities, but are distinguished conceptually for purposes of study. They come down through successive stages in varied forms. Kinship and other forms of social organization, material technology, government, religion, and art are main components or broad divisions of culture and culture history; within each are many subcomponents, as in the many practical skills which make up technology. "Art" contains many specific arts, techniques, and styles. Some components, such as magic, tend to dwindle or die out, while others of more recent origin, such as science, develop.

Regarded as diachronic or descending through time, the components of culture are variously described as "threads" or "strands" by comparison with those in a tapestry, and as "streams" or "currents" like those in a river. They are said to run through history like the "strains" of melody through a symphony. A cross-section of a culture, or of human culture as a whole at any one time, would disclose a multitude of such components, intricately mingled.[1]

The history and successive changes of a single component may be described as a *component sequence*. The change from rough to smooth stone, to bronze and then to iron, would be a sequence in the component of material technology. Scientists are also interested in the other traits, the whole modes of life, which have accompanied certain kinds of tool and weapon. They are interested not

[1] For a discussion of the components, categories, or elements of culture, see A. L. Kroeber and C. Kluckhohn, *Culture: a Critical Review of Concepts and Definitions* (Cambridge, Mass., 1952), pp. 95 ff. They are variously distinguished. For example, N. K. Bose in 1929 analyzed culture into Speech, Material traits, Art, Mythology, Knowledge, Religion, Family and Social Systems, Property, Government and War.

only in component stages and sequences, but in what we shall call "composite sequences." When archeologists refer to the "Neolithic" stage, they often mean the whole mode of life which, they think, was correlated with the use of smooth or polished stone implements. The same is true of such a concept as "savage" or "barbarous," which does not refer to any one component but to a certain general stage of culture. Either can be defined in terms of a trait-complex or syndrome of traits and types in many components. A "composite sequence" is, accordingly, a temporal succession of composite stages in culture, each of which is a more or less integrated complex of traits. It can be defined and studied with reference to the history of one people or environment.

How long does a group or culture stay in one composite stage? That is extremely variable. In some respects, the stages have been getting shorter. That is another way of saying that culture changes at an accelerating rate, now that we have acquired the desire and the means to make it do so. This acceleration has been highly selective, with some peoples changing much faster than others; but all are now being swept to some extent into the torrent of cultural change. Certain general traits persist, however: the stage of iron and urban industry has lasted a long time.

Do all the components in culture change together, with all arriving at the next composite stage at about the same time? Some such view was approximated, though not to this extreme extent, by Morgan and the unilinear school. It is now recognized that they do not all change together or at the same rate of speed, in the life of any people. Some components lead the way and bring related changes in others, sooner or later. Some go much faster, as physical technology has done in modern industrial civilization. Others are more inert or obstructed, exemplifying "cultural lag," as in international political control today. "All cultures grow irregularly," said Ralph Linton. They have certain foci of interest which have induced them to develop to a high degree those elements which seem important to them and to lag behind in the development of others or to reject them completely. In borrowing from other cultures, ...they select only those elements which fit into their interest patterns."[2]

To call a sequence "evolutionary" or "developmental" implies, in Spencerian terms, that it is moving toward greater complexity and definiteness. If so, the later the stage, the more complex would be the form of culture, on the whole. But Spencer and other evolutionists have recognized that an actual historic sequence is never completely and regularly developmental.

Historians usually specialize on one particular historic sequence or a group of closely related ones: that is, on certain chapters in the life of a group, large or small, which are connected biologically, politically, or culturally. They tell of achievements and adversities, developments and declines. Taine was much interested in these small-scale evolutions. But the general theory of cultural evolution deals rather with humanity as a whole, and with its total history (including prehistory), regarded as a single, large-scale sequence. Are there definite, comprehensive stages in that sequence too? Is the sequence one of over-all development, at least for the present, as Spencer thought? The only way to demonstrate these propositions would be to analyze and compare at least a fair sampling of the major component sequences in different parts of the earth. Early progressionists and evolutionists, such as Condorcet and Comte, based their statements about all humanity (le progrès humain) on the few familiar sequences which were then fairly well known: those of the Mediterranean region and Northern Europe. Here a developmental trend on the whole, in spite of setbacks like the fall of Rome, was fairly evident. But now the histories and prehistories of a great many more peoples in both hemispheres, including Asia and Africa, are partly known to science. Hence, to be substantiated, a statement about cul-

[2] *The Tree of Culture* (New York, 1955), "Preface" by Adelin Linton, p. vi.

tural evolution in general must take their stages and sequences into account. Their great diversity, especially in civilizations long dead such as those of the Scythians and Mayans, makes generalization still very difficult—at least for the present, until more definite patterns appear. We are now at the point where many specific, partial analogies are becoming obvious in a spotty, discontinuous way. The over-all trend of complication is becoming more obvious, and also the wide recurrence of certain types like smooth stone tools, domesticated animals, and geometrically decorated pottery.

3. HOMOTAXIAL SEQUENCES

The general question, on which an authoritative answer is awaited with impatience, can be stated in terms attributed to T. H. Huxley. Referring to geological strata, he described certain sequences of fossils within them as "homotaxial." Certain types of fossil occur in similar sequences from one stratum to another, in different localities. The sequences are not necessarily contemporaneous but are analogous in order, spatially and (by inference) temporally. A cultural sequence is homotaxial, says V. G. Childe, when each stage always occupies the same relative position in it wherever the whole sequence is available.[3] (In New Zealand, the bronze age was missing.) In general, then, we may ask "to what extent are cultural stages and sequences among various peoples or environments homotaxial?" It is a separate but related question to ask "to what extent does homotaxial recurrence indicate that the sequence concerned is necessary and inevitable?" To argue that it does implies a causal inference which writers of the past have been all too quick to make on insufficient evidence.

Certainly, the general trend of recent research is to confirm the hypothesis of *partial* analogy or homotaxis among the main developmental sequences of history and prehistory, along with much divergence and convergence. The concept of convergence has received increasing attention as a way of recognizing the fact that similarities do not necessarily imply a previous parallel development. The peoples concerned may have diverged widely, then become more similar because of new factors such as diffusion or migration to a similar environment.

The fact of partial analogy or parallelism can be further described in either of two ways. (a) One can say that a certain type of "general" or cross-cultural stage such as "barbarism" recurs in some but not all traits, wherever the sequence goes that far. The few basic traits by which the concept of barbarism is defined—its "core" or "primary" traits—recur most widely. Others, the more variable "secondary" traits, recur in some but not all cases of barbarism. (b) Without using any such concepts of general stages, one can simply describe and classify the specific analogies which occur on a smaller scale, here and there. If any such analogies are to develop into almost universal stages, that is for the evidence to show.

4. RECENT APPROACHES
TO THE PROBLEM OF STAGES

The two types of description just mentioned are examples of two opposite approaches to theoretical problems. Some writers tend to follow one or the other persistently; some change back and forth. The first is more deductive: it applies some general hypothesis, such as Morgan's theory of stages, and tests it in relation to new data.

This mode of thinking was emphasized by the British archeologist V. Gordon Childe in his short treatise on *Social Evolution*. He began with a restatement of Morgan's theory as revised by Engels and others, especially certain Russian archeologists. Although it is now untenable in detail, he said, it is still the best attempt of its kind. "I shall

[3] *Op. cit.*, p. 20, quoting T. H. Huxley, Address to the Geological Society (1862); *Collected Essays*, Vol. VIII.

use Morgan's terminology as a provisional basis of classification, though I shall, of course, propose new criteria."[4] Applying Morgan's sequence of savagery, barbarism, and civilization to recent archeological data, he had to revise not only the criteria but the details of sequence. But, on the whole, he found this triple division into main stages to be still substantially correct and usable.

Childe was especially interested in the transition from barbarism to civilization in contrasted natural environments. The starting-point, "early barbarism," was somewhat similar in all places, being based on cultivation of the same cereals and breeding the same animals. Also the final result, "civilization," though not uniform, showed everywhere the aggregation of large populations in cities, the differentiation of primary producers, full-time specialist artisans, merchants, officials, priests, and rulers; an effective concentration of economic and political power; the use of writing, conventional standards of weights and measures of time and space, some mathematical and calendar science. But the intervening steps in development diverged widely. The plow was not used by the civilized Mayas; hence it could not be used to define a necessary stage on the way to civilization. Other technological criteria used by archeologists, such as tool materials and means of transport, are not suitable to define general stages in evolution since peoples diverge too widely in these regards. The same is true, said Childe, of the development of social institutions in the several sequences, such as the rule of chiefs and the position of women.[5] Thus fairly definite, composite stages were found at both ends of this transition, but not between them.

It is important to distinguish in general between traits such as agriculture and writing, which can be used to define a stage because they recur almost everywhere in the same general sequence, and the highly variable ones. The former seem basic and determining in that a complex of other traits tends to gather about them. Certain institutions, says Steward, can be distinguished as basic or constant, whereas those which lend uniqueness are secondary or variable. Examples of the former in the American high civilizations are agriculture, social classes, and priest-temple-idol cult. Steward remarks that the present classification of developmental periods can make little use of technological features such as the use of metals. The presence of iron in China had minor importance; it could not change peasant-like folk communities into larger systems.[6]

The concepts of savagery and barbarism are usually avoided by American anthropologists, as suggesting not only the unilinear fallacy but such derogatory meanings as "wild," "uncouth," and "cruel." "Civilization" is often avoided in the sense of a definite stage, perhaps because it seems too flattering. More objective, neutral terms are sought, but the word "primitive," which is often applied to what Morgan called either savage or barbarous, is no great improvement. Its vagueness is obvious, and it wrongly suggests that the peoples so described (both prehistoric and modern) represent the first, original state of man. However, the American anthropologist E. A. Hoebel retains all four of these traditional terms, defining them briefly and objectively, in a way not far removed from that of Tylor.[7] "Savagery," he says, means "a state of cultural development marked by the absence of gardening or agriculture and written language." "Barbarism" means "possessing gardening, agriculture, or domesticated herds but devoid of written language." "Primitive" would apply to either: "not characterized by the inclusion of a written language; therefore, nonliterate or preliterate." "Civilization" is "possessing gardening, agriculture, or domesticated herds, and a written language." (There is room in this classification for intermediate or transitional stages such as "semi-barbarous.")

Wilhelm Schmidt of Vienna, whom we have

[4] P. 11.
[5] Ibid., pp. 161–5.
[6] Theory of Culture Change, pp. 184–7.
[7] Man in the Primitive World (New York, 1958), pp. 644 ff. On Tylor's definitions, see Bidney, op. cit., p. 191.

already noted as a critical evolutionist in ethnology, combined technological and social criteria in the following scheme:[8]

    I. *Primitive* cultures (foodgatherers, preliterates): (1) Central, exogamous, with monogamy; (2) Southern, exogamous, with sex-totems; (3) Arctic; exogamous, equal rights.

    II. *Primary* cultures (foodproducers, preliterates): (1) Exogamous, patrilineal; totemistic, higher stage of hunting; "city" culture; (2) Exogamous, matrilineal, horticulturists, "village" culture; (3) Patrilineal, with undivided family; including pastoral nomads who became ruling races.

    III. *Secondary* cultures (picture writing): (1) Free patrilineal cultures (Polynesia, Sudan, Hither India, Western Asia, Southern Europe, etc.); (2) Free matrilineal cultures (Southern China, Farther India, Melanesia, etc.).

    IV. *Tertiary* cultures (alphabet): The oldest civilizations of Asia, Europe, and America.

Schmidt was a member of the *Kulturkreis* group in Vienna, which took its starting-point from Frobenius in 1898 and Graebner in 1904. It advanced the theory of several distinct, original cultures, each with a set of characteristic traits. Their survivals and diffusions were, it said, still to be found in present cultures. This "culture-historical" method has been criticized by American anthropologists as too schematic and anti-historical, in that the factors into which it analyzed early cultures were "selected arbitrarily... and received their validation only secondarily during the resolution."[9]

The opposite mode of investigation is more inductive. It is also more in accord with the Boasian reaction, since it stresses the unprejudiced gathering of new data from a variety of sources, without applying any general theory at the start. Hence it has been favored in America. Both methods are empirical and reciprocal. They supplement each other in the logic of scientific reasoning. The former is more likely to retain some general concepts from the past, rightly or wrongly. The latter strives for new ones, but slowly and cautiously;

hence it may remain a long time without any broadly integrating principles. It spends much time refuting previous general theories, and often overstates its case by ignoring the elements of truth in them. It patiently gathers data about particular cultures, their histories and prehistories throughout the world. If, after much separate observation and dating, a comparison of two or more cultures seems to show some analogous sequences, it is careful not to suppose more analogy than the evidence proves.

Will the two approaches meet in the middle? In principle they should, eventually; but it will be a long time before complete agreement is reached. In the meantime, the inductive approach tends to develop its own terms, avoiding those of the other. The following theories of stages emphasize the inductive approach from empirical data, although they make some use of older terminologies.

Working from stratigraphic data in Peru, W. D. Strong[10] proposed in 1948 this sequence of culture epochs: (1) the prehorticultural, (2) the incipient horticultural, (3) the formative (of local civilizations), (4) the florescent, (5) the fusional, and (6) the imperial epochs. These, he adds, have been variously defined in terms of changing economic, political, militaristic, and artistic configurations within the so-called Peru-Bolivian co-tradition. The scheme, says Strong, has also been applied to the record in Mexico-Guatemala with close correspondence, and Steward has suggested that a similar one may fit the archeological and early historical periods of the Near East, Egypt, India, and China. This widely distributed series of similar pre-industrial patterns strongly suggests, in Strong's opinion, "cultural growth regularities of considerable magnitude extending over wide areas and many millenniums."

[8] *The Culture Historical Method of Ethnology* (New York, 1939), p. 350.
[9] A. L. Kroeber and C. Kluckhohn, *Culture: a Critical Review of Concepts and Definitions* (Cambridge, Mass., 1952), p. 160.
[10] "Historical Approach in Anthropology," in *Anthropology Today* (Chicago, 1953), pp. 393 f.

Another system of stages based on American archeology is that of Gordon R. Willey and Philip Phillips.[11] It is comparatively simple, running from "lithic" through "archaic," "formative," and "classic" to "postclassic." These names are not especially informative, but they are defined with care in terms of several components. The "formative" cultures are based on agriculture, and make abundant use of ceramics and weaving. Houses are durable and there are pyramidal temples. Urban life begins in the "classic" stage, characterized by large, elaborate temples and great art styles limited to well-defined regions. Crafts are specialized and differentiated. These great styles break down in the "postclassic" stage, about six hundred years before the Spanish conquests.

Willey and Phillips quote with approval Alex Krieger's distinction (1953) between "stage" and "period," to the effect that "a stage is a segment of a historical sequence in a given area, characterized by a dominating pattern of economic existence." A "period" depends on chronology. A stage may include several locally distinctive culture-complexes and minor time divisions. In New World culture-history, say Willey and Phillips, there are only two basic technological and economic divisions: hunters-gatherers and agriculturists; these are analogous to the Old World stages of (a) Paleolithic-Mesolithic and (b) Neolithic and later. The criteria for dividing pre-agricultural stages are technological, referring to artifacts, while those of later stages are more diversified, including the moral, social, political, religious, and aesthetic.

These authors add some useful comments on cultural lag, a problem which, they say, inheres in all developmental interpretation. They distinguish two kinds of lag situation: belated and marginal.[12] In the former, a culture shows the essential traits of a certain stage long after the time usually considered appropriate for it. In the latter, "a culture shows significant characteristics of a given developmental stage in a configuration which, as a whole, fails to measure up to the definition of that stage." The former shows a lack of change; the latter, change that is incomplete or one-sided. The second type may be due to developmental regression. Some cultures are simply belated, while others are both belated and marginal.

Elsewhere,[13] Willey declares that New World culture evolved "in an essentially independent manner," whatever the contacts may have been with the peoples and cultures of the Old World. Paralleling subsistence increase, he says, the social unit enlarges and becomes more stable. Sedentism and food surpluses make possible the creation of material wealth and the expression of religious and aesthetic feelings in art and architecture. Great skill and sophistication, including monumental art, were attained well before the rise in power of cities and states.

Steward has summarized the different names and criteria for major types and stages of cultural development. Many specialists on the Old World, he points out, cling to outmoded technological concepts such as mesolithic, neolithic, bronze, and dynastic; whereas Americanists are now using such terms as formative, developmental, classical, florescent, empire, and conquest, as names for a cultural typology and sequence.[14] Steward prefers to speak of "eras" and "levels of sociocultural integration," rather than of "stages," but this seems to make no great difference. In a table of "major eras," he shows the recurrence of a certain sequence of levels in Egypt, the Near East, China, Meso-America, and Northern Peru. These divide the period from about 9,000 B.C. to the present into the following eras of cross-cultural types: Hunting and Gathering, Incipient Agriculture, Formative (peasant communities to states), Regional Florescent States, Initial Empire, Dark Ages, Cyclical

[11] *Method and Theory in American Archaeology* (Chicago, 1958), esp. Ch. 3, "The Historical-Developmental Approach in American Archaeology." Also pp. 200 f. *Cf.* Willey, "Archeological Theories and Interpretation: New World", in *Anthropology Today*, esp. p. 378.

[12] *Ibid.*, p. 74.

[13] "Patterns in New World Culture," in *Mind, Evolution, and Culture* (Vol. II of *The Evolution of Man*), p. 136.

[14] *Ibid.*, p. 186.

Imperial Conquests, Iron Age, and Industrial Revolution. This sequence, in spite of its novel nomenclature, corrects and refines the nineteenth-century conception of cultural stages, instead of abandoning it entirely.

5. IRREVERSIBLE STAGES AND SEQUENCES

After all the vehement rejections of nineteenth-century evolutionism, present anthropology seems to be coming around again to a belief in general cultural stages. "No one doubts," says Steward, "that hunting and gathering preceded farming and herding and that the last two were preconditions of 'civilization,' which is broadly characterized by dense and stable populations, metallurgy, intellectual achievements, social heterogeneity and internal specialization, and other features."[15] It is a significant return toward nineteenth-century evolutionism if not only the general fact of evolution as a process, but also the concept of a normal sequence of stages, is being re-established.

What does "irreversible" mean in this context? It must be understood in a relative, partial way. A sequence such as "hunting and gathering, farming and herding, urban civilization" is irreversible in the sense that no people can go directly from the prehuman to the civilized stage, or to settled agriculture, without passing through the stage of hunting and gathering. No people can go directly to metallurgy without first using non-metallic implements. But these are not completely irreversible, for it is possible to regress from any cultural stage to something like an earlier one. Instances are known of reversion, as from agriculture back to hunting among certain American Indian tribes.[16]

Some kinds of sequence appear so necessary and inevitable by the nature of things that one must believe they happened so, whether or not there is enough historical evidence to prove it. This is not *a priori* reasoning in the metaphysical sense, but a deduction from known psychological facts about human nature and its environment, which we may assume to have been much the same in prehistoric times. Thus it is hard to imagine large cities before the development of food production on a large scale. In the development of writing, Kroeber distinguishes three irreversible stages: pictures (including ideograms), rebus or transitional, and wholly phonetic writing. "Not only do the historical facts show that the succession has been pictograph-ideogram-rebus-phonogram in the known instances," he says, but "that order is psychologically irreversible in a free internal development uninfluenced by alien inventions."[17] It is conceivable psychologically to go from the visible picture to the symbolic pictogram or ideogram; thence to the spoken word for the object or idea, and thence by transfer to a similar-sounding word symbolizing another idea, and finally to any similar sound-group irrespective of semantic meaning. To go directly from a visual symbol to a sound-cluster "makes no psychological sense." The argument is convincing in this case but the method is a little risky for common use. Many statements about primitive man have seemed equally unquestionable, only to be refuted by historic evidence.

This "irreversible" sequence is irreversible only in regard to the prehistoric origins of written language. For it is always possible to regress in language: either through the loss and destruction of what has been learned, or in a voluntary, selective way. A modern civilization can revive the art of picture-writing if it wishes, after a period of disuse, and employ it along with phonetic writing.

The comparative regularity, necessity, and irreversibility of such sequences appear most clearly in what we have called "component sequences." It appears in the development of a single cultural component or a closely related set of them, such

[15] *Ibid.*, p. 28.
[16] Linton, p. 53: "after the introduction of the horse, a number of Indian tribes, who had previously been agricultural, reverted to a purely hunting existence."
[17] *The Nature of Culture* (Chicago, 1952), ch. on "History and Evolution," p. 98.

as writing or material technology. It appears in the sociopolitical component, in the apparent necessity of a small-unit, kinship stage before that of large, urban empires. Many such component sequences are comparatively invariable among all peoples who evolve at all. As to other components, either there is no universal sequence or we have not yet discovered it. These include, as we have seen, the realistic-geometric contrast in visual art and the matrilineal-patrilineal contrast in social organization. The stages and divisions in the various component sequences do not necessarily coincide, within the same culture or among different cultures. There are partial correspondences, such as the frequent origin of writing in the neolithic stage; but this is not universal. When we think in terms of a total cultural sequence —of the highly composite stages in the total culture-pattern of a given people—we find still less of the necessary and the irreversible. As between various peoples, the proportion of apparent divergence among secondary traits, and even in some which are often primary (such as material technology) tends to increase as we compare these all-inclusive sequences.[18]

The limited extent to which cultural evolution is directional or deterministic is well described by Linton, in saying that "the technological basis of any society does not indicate a single form for each of the other associated institutions, but limits the number of possible forms and rules out certain forms altogether."[19] Margaret Mead states the fact more generally: that each stage is subject to the previous state of knowledge, which "may limit the alternative innovations but cannot determine which of many possible innovations will appear."[20] This anthropologist, whose interests have covered a wide field, lists the "irreversible" patterns as including language, the family, tool using, provision of food, shelter, and protection, a group organization of families, a system of relating man to the perceived universe, and (in relation to art) "some idea of the elaboration of ornamentation (including some form of patterned movement and

sound, and patterned decoration of the surfaces of the human body and of artifacts)." Such gained patterns are irreversible, she writes, insofar as they concern types of cultural behavior which are shared by every group of human beings, so that at least a small group of human adults would preserve and re-establish them in case of a holocaust. Certain inventions survive as the "mainstream of a cultural evolution in which the various items are arranged in an ascending sequence of levels of organization." These include what we are calling component sequences in the following: technology, the use of energy, social organization, and religion. On this basis, "directional evolutionary change in culture may be viewed as inevitable and the only variable is the time at which a next stage will occur."[21]

It is well to remember again, as we note the views of anthropologists on these various aspects of cultural evolution, that they are thinking mainly of the early stages, including the basic traits of urban-industrial civilization but not the specific traits of advanced cultures. Therefore, what is said about invariable, irreversible sequences does not necessarily apply to the fluctuations of civilized art. The "directional" element there may turn out to be much less than in primitive art and culture generally.

However, tentative generalizations are now being made in anthropology on a much larger scale than heretofore in recent years. In the Chicago conference on Darwin's centenary (1959), the statement was made for discussion that four major, critical breakthroughs or revolutions have been discerned through empirical evidence.[22] These

[18] To ignore this fact by postulating "uniformity of culture history for a given stage of development" is called by Bidney "the evolutionistic fallacy." (It is certainly a fallacy, but not in all evolutionism.) *Theoretical Anthropology*, p. 218.

[19] *The Tree of Culture*, p. 50.

[20] "Cultural Determinants of Behavior," in A. Roe and G. G. Simpson, *Behavior and Evolution* (New Haven, 1958), p. 484.

[21] *Ibid.*, pp. 483-4.

[22] *Issues in Evolution*, Vol. III in *Evolution After Darwin* (Chicago, 1960), pp. 209, 226 f. The statement was attributed to Kroeber, but credit also given to Childe and White during the discussion.

were "(1) food production, beginning gradually about 7,000 B.C.; (2) a syndrome centering around 3,000 B.C., in which writing, metallurgy, urbanization, and political structures were first evolved; (3) from about 600 B.C., religions organized both doctrinally and institutionally; (4) beginning about A.D. 1600, the rapid and progressive development of science, technology, invention, industry, and wealth." These concepts of stages are the product of much generalization on observed sequences in different cultures, especially but not exclusively in Europe and the Near East. They are composite rather than component sequences; they describe change along many lines. The shift in emphasis from one component and direction of change to another is also described: as concerned with subsistence in the first stage, with general civilization in the second, religion in the third and secular activities in the fourth.

6. CULTURAL STAGES
AS CONCEIVED IN VARIOUS SCIENCES:
ARCHEOLOGY, ANTHROPOLOGY, SOCIOLOGY

These and many other sciences and branches of scholarship cooperate today, as in the nineteenth century, to throw some light upon the emerging patterns of cultural history. In all of them, there is difference of opinion on what patterns really exist. Writers differ on the subject of cultural stages, not only because of the epoch or moment of history in which they write, but also because of their philosophic world-view, whether naturalistic, idealistic, dualistic, or otherwise.

Some, though not all, naturalistic writers have based their conception of stages on types of implement and technological process, such as "bronze" and "metallurgy." They have been called "materialistic," although they are not necessarily philosophic materialists. They do not ignore mental phenomena or depreciate the value of art and science, but they tend to regard these as largely determined by material and economic factors. Even in speaking of art, they tend to stress its material and sensory aspects. Some of this group of writers are Marxists, some are not.

On the other hand, the idealistic or spiritualistic type of evolutionism tends to mark off stages in terms of mental development, conceptual and symbolic modes of expression. In art, it tends to stress these mental or spiritual elements. Hegel's three stages, the symbolic, classic, and romantic, were thus based on the relation between the world mind and the sensory forms of art in successive periods. This tradition tends to minimize the sensory media of art and all distinction sbetween arts or styles which are made on a sensory or material basis. Thus Croce belittles all attempts to classify the arts. Scientific anthropology has usually emphasized the naturalistic or positivistic tradition, but with occasional dissenting voices such as that of Kroeber, calling for more direct attention to ideas and artistic styles as influential factors as well as goals and values. On the other hand, philosophy has usually been dominated by dualistic or idealistic supernaturalism. Most of its leaders have been men of books and armchair discussion; words and ideas, rather than material objects, have provided the main subject-matter for their theorizing.

One's theories of history are thus influenced, not only by one's philosophic or religious background, but also by the scientific field in which one works. A philosopher or historian of ideas, even if he is a naturalist or positivist, is likely to think of cultural stages in terms of intellectual development. Comte saw them as theological, metaphysical, and positive or scientific. A historian of religion tends to emphasize the sequence from primitive animism and magic through organized polytheism to monotheism and naturalism. These appear to such a thinker as the core traits, the main distinguishing features, of the stages in cultural history. A sociologist or political scientist will tend to define the stages in terms of social and political types and institutions; an art historian, in terms of different styles of art such as "realistic," "romantic," and "decorative." Such disagreement is aggravated by the specialization of scholars in the various fields concerned, and by the lack of effective liaison between them.

V. Gordon Childe was primarily an archeologist and as such mainly interested in the recurrent traits of material objects. This conception of culture he contrasted with the anthropological, which "comprises all aspects of human behavior that are not innate reflexes or instincts," including language and logic, religion and philosophy, as well as the material expressions of these immaterial aspects.[23] His approach, as we have just seen, retained Morgan's triple division into savage, barbarous, and civilized, but he tried to redefine each in accord with later evidence. Archeology has proved everywhere, says Childe, that stone was used before metal for tools and weapons, and copper or bronze before iron.[24] Also, he asserts, in both new and old worlds the earliest societies always lived exclusively by hunting, fishing, or collecting, while farming invariably begins later. Illiterate farmers always precede literate citizens. Childe's theory of stages thus embraces several component sequences, each regarded as invariable or identical throughout the world. Furthermore, these sequences correspond: a certain stage in one component always or usually coincides with a certain stage in the others. Hence Childe accepts in principle Morgan's general sequence: "Savagery," he says, "is older than Barbarism, Barbarism older than Civilization."

This is a composite sequence, including several component ones. But it does not embrace all the components of any one culture; it is a partial composite sequence. Also, it does not insist that all the traits associated with these three categories are invariable. Childe goes on to ask, in *Social Evolution*, "whether any similar generalization can be inferred from the observed successions in respect of other aspects of culture such as kinship systems."[25] In other words, how far can we truthfully go toward affirming that an all-embracing sequence of cultural traits or stages is invariable?

Those in tool-making and food-production correspond to some extent but not completely. Neither of these corresponds exactly with the kinship sequence, for there is no invariable sequence as between the matrilinear and patrilinear, or between matrilinear descent and matriarchal rule. Childe concludes that "archeology does not hold out much prospect of correlating social institutions with stages of cultural development as defined in economic terms."[26]

Anthropologists often point out the inadequacy of archeological data as material from which to build a complete framework for a system of general stages. But can they do better with their own more diversified field of phenomena? Their field is broader in comprising, besides material artifacts, non-material traits such as kinship and language. They cover a longer time-span, coming down from prehistoric to modern primitive cultures. But they have comparatively little to say about the higher civilizations, ancient or modern. Hence their sequences do not provide an adequate skeleton for marking off stages in the civilized arts. Steward's nomenclature, as summarized in the previous section, shifts from one component to another. "Iron Age" refers to material, "Agriculture" to a method of food-getting, "Empire" to political organization, and so on. This is quite justifiable if the basic, determining factor is different in different periods, which may well be the case.

7. SOCIAL AND POLITICAL STAGES

Some anthropologists, like the sociologists, tend to emphasize social organization. Thus Robert M. Adams describes the rise of civilization mainly in terms of the contrast between independent temple-

---

[23] *Social Evolution*, pp. 30 ff.
[24] *Ibid.*, p. 29.
[25] P. 29.
[26] *Ibid.*, p. 165.

centered communities and the stratified, militaristic, urban state."[27] Morton H. Fried chooses "social differentiation" as the main evolutionary determinant. In his opinion, there is a "historically inevitable transition" from egalitarian to rank, stratification, and then state society.[28]

From the standpoint of historical sociology and political science, H. E. Barnes outlines as follows the "main stages in the political evolution of mankind." He presents the outline as a joint product of sociologists from Gumplowicz to Giddings and MacLeod.[29]

I. Tribal society
    Kinship basis
    Personal relations in politics
II. The transitional stage of feudalism
    Personal bonds in social organization
    Quasi-territorial basis of politics
    Rise of property in political considerations
III. The territorial state and civil society
    City-states
    Patriarchal empires of antiquity
    The national state
        Absolutistic
        Representative
        Democratic (usually republican)
IV. The functional and regional political society of the future
    Political federations and spheres of interest
    Functional or vocational representation.

This outline omits all mention of tools and material technology. It is based on another component: that of social and governmental organization. The question remains, then, of the extent to which technological and other component stages could be fitted into these in conformity with the facts. Assuming the accuracy of the outline in regard to socio-political stages, does it provide a skeleton into which we can place corresponding stages in the history of art, religion, and intellectual development? Is there a certain style or set of styles in painting, sculpture, architecture, music, poetry, and so on, which corresponds to "feudalism"? To the city state? To the patriarchal empire?

Such questions remain to be answered, and we shall return to them in a later chapter. Various historians provide us with a few particular correspondences, but not with any complete, systematic correlation. Perhaps there is none; perhaps we do not know enough about the facts as yet.

In any case, there is this to be said for H. E. Barnes' outline. It reaches from the prehistoric to the present chronologically, thus offering a longer framework than any provided by recent archeology or anthropology. In respect to the length of its time-span, it is one into which the whole history of all the arts might conceivably be fitted. Beginning with the kinship tribe at an unspecified date, it can include both ancient and modern tribes. Successive stages in technology from hunting and food-gathering to machine industry, from stone to steel and nuclear power, can all be listed in a parallel column beside it, as a step toward finding the extent of correlation. The whole history of each art can be summarized in another set of parallel outlines, for the same purpose. To pursue this line of investigation, beginning with a socio-political system of stages, would be to proceed deductively, as in Childe's revision of Morgan's system.

The extent of correlation which one might reveal between the various component sequences would neither prove nor disprove the general fact of evolution in art and other branches of culture. A low correlation would simply indicate a large, multilinear divergence, not only among different peoples and places, but among the several component developments which together make up cultural evolution as a whole. Like those of animals and plants, such developments would be seen to fan out along many different paths, only loosely held together by causal connections and convergences. This is another way of saying that the various branches of human culture evolve to some

[27] *The Evolution of Man*, p. 155.
[28] "On the Evolution of Social Stratification and the State." *Paul Radin Memorial Volume*.
[29] *Historical Sociology* (New York, 1948), p. 98. *Cf.* W. C. MacLeod, *The Origin and History of Politics* (New York, 1931).

extent together, to some extent independently, and do not necessarily arrive at their main stages or revolutionary break-throughs at the same time. Such a discovery would not be at all surprising, for it has long been surmised. Only the most extreme of unilinear parallelists (a breed almost extinct today) would expect to find an exact, point-to-point correspondence between the histories of all branches of civilization. No one expects to find that poetry has radically changed its style when each new source of physical power was introduced. But it is also true that poetry and other arts show the effects of the industrial revolution. Even the Marxists, who go farther than most in affirming social influence on art, do not affirm a completely rigid integration. On the other hand, even a low and partial correlation would be significant, as helping us to see and understand more fully the interacting processes in cultural change.

Sociologists and historians will undoubtedly provide us with more exact and enlightening outlines of stages from their own points of view. That of Barnes is extremely brief; it needs detailed definition of each stage in terms of socio-political and other traits, primary and secondary. It needs subdivision and reference to historical examples—peoples, dates, and places which illustrate each stage. Many writers have offered such outlines, but none has won general acceptance. One reason is that, in trying to subdivide and amplify the outline, one often runs into controversial issues such as that of matrilineal priority.[30]

To what extent does the list of types in Barnes' outline correspond with the actual sequence of chronological development? On the whole, perhaps, but with the usual qualification: that examples of many "earlier" types still exist along with the "later" ones. A cross-section of contemporary culture throughout the world reveals many apparent survivals of archaic types, more or less modified by diffusion from the advanced ones. This is true of the technological and socio-political components in these modern primitive cultures, and it is true of the artistic components also. To what extent, then, do artistic types characteristic of the tribal and other less evolved social orders persist today, and with what stylistic modifications from outside influence?

[30] "There is no evidence," says Barnes, "that maternal kinship is correlated with lower material culture or paternal with more advanced economic life." (*Op. cit.*, p. 90).

CHAPTER XIII

RECENT THEORETICAL WRITINGS
ON ART HISTORY

During the first half of the twentieth century, the theory of evolution in the arts received little favorable attention from Western historians. What little they said about it was mostly adverse. In art history, as in the social sciences, the issue was still confused by disagreement on the meaning of "evolution" and its implications in regard to cultural phenomena. Those who defended and those who attacked it were often thinking of very different things without realizing the fact.

Minute research and meticulous documentation were the order of the day, and all theorizing was under suspicion. The "Boasian reaction" in anthropology had its counterpart in the history and criticism of all the arts, including music and literature, in a common disposition to avoid philosophic issues or dismiss them casually. Students of art history were warned that sound scholarship required intensive concentration on one art and period. By the mid-twentieth century the theory that art develops as a part of cultural evolution was almost ignored except for occasional brief denials of it.

Let us now go back a few years, to pick up some threads of nineteenth-century German thought. All present historical scholarship in the visual arts is indebted to the *Kunstwissenschaft* movement in German-speaking countries during the late nineteenth and early twentieth centuries, even though its name, translated as the "science (or knowledge) of art," has never won much international acceptance. Its limits have not been precisely defined, but such men as Semper, Burckhardt, Grosse, Fiedler, Riegl, Dvořák, and Wölfflin are often listed as leaders in it. Their influence has spread to English-speaking historians as well as French and Italian, not only through their own works, but also through the teaching and writing of younger German-trained scholars who emigrated to the United States and England, there to teach future college professors and museum curators.

Some of the leaders just named accepted the theory of evolution in art; others did not. We have already noticed the work of Semper and Grosse as fitting directly into the stream of naturalistic evolutionism. Both were much occupied with anthropology and primitive art; both emphasized the effects of material and social environment on art. Both theorized on the aims and methods of the new "science of art," for which they had high hopes.

Others dealt more with the visual arts of advanced civilizations. Among these, too, some accepted the evolutionary approach. A notable example was Max Dvořák, who wrote on the relations between art history and the history of ideas (*Kunstgeschichte als Geistesgeschichte*).[1] He insisted on the continuity of artistic evolution, which he saw especially as a progressive ability to represent nature accurately. Like previous evolutionists, he has been criticized for overemphasizing the importance in art of the power to represent nature. Certainly, it is not the whole of the history of art or of painting, and perhaps not the greatest part; but in showing evidence of its continuous and cumulative nature during long periods, Dvořák seriously weakened the current theory that each epoch is unique and incomparable, without real continuity from one to another.

The latter theory is associated in art with the name of Alois Riegl, but is a lineal descendant of the "historicist" movement in the philosophy of history during the nineteenth century. Riegl and others applied it to the visual arts. As noted in a previous chapter, that movement was on the whole anti-evolutionist. As to the arts, historicism inclined to the belief that each period style, and each particular work of art, was essentially unique and incomparable with others. Each had its own absolute value. Although all styles aim at faithful reproduction of nature, said Riegl, "each has its own mode of apprehending nature." It is hard or impossible for an artist in one epoch to see or paint in the mode of a previous epoch, he continued, or for us today to understand its art. The history of art is a history of successive conceptions of nature, different modes of seeing and representing it, and there is no progress or continuity from one to another.

Followed out consistently, this would preclude any real science of art and any conception of art history as having a pervasive trend or pattern, evolutionary or otherwise. However, it was not carried to this extreme. As Arnold Hauser shows, historicism as applied to the arts carries the inconsistency of "referring every historical event to some superindividual—ideal, divine, or primeval —origin," while combining with this "an individualizing treatment that asserts not simply the uniqueness, but also the absolute incomparability of historical structures, and so concludes that every historical achievement, and thus every art-style, must be measured only against its own acknowledged standards." The distinctive will or intention of each individual artist is the key conception in Riegl's view of art.

On the other hand Wölfflin, also influenced by historicism, tends to minimize the role of the individual artist, holding that his intention and stylistic trend are the product of his age and limited by it. Visual forms and modes of representation have, in Wölfflin's theory, their own history and power to dominate the individual and national inclinations of the artist. This version of historicist theory in the field of art is less opposed to evolutionism in that it thinks in terms of types and sequences. In other respects, as we shall see, Wölfflin does separate from evolutionism.

The historicists, in writing of art, never consistently adhered to the theory of complete uniqueness, whose absurdity reveals itself on the slightest analysis. Riegl himself pointed out the similarity between imperial Roman and seventeenth-century portrait painting, as varieties of the baroque, and attributed it to a higher law.[2] No work of art and no style can be completely unique, since each has obvious traits in common with others of its kind. They are, at least, works or styles *of art*, and skilled human products. All works in a certain

[1] First edition, 1923. *Das Rätsel der Brüder van Eyck* appeared in 1904. For a summary and appraisal of his work, see A. Hauser, *The Philosophy of Art History* (London, 1958), pp. 222 f. Hauser's discussion of Fiedler, Riegl, and Wölfflin is also valuable (pp. 120, 137, 222 ff.). On the place of the *Kunstwissenschaft* movement in the history of aesthetics, see Listowel, *A Critical History of Modern Aesthetics*, esp. pp. 201 ff. ("The Theory of the Science of Art").

[2] *Kunstgeschichte als Universalgeschichte* (1898); quoted by Hauser, p. 195.

medium such as paint have at least that medium and its requirements in common. If the phenomena of art were really unique there could be no description of similarities between the works in a certain style. These obvious truths are either ignored by the historicists or brushed aside with the facile pseudo-argument that all the similarities are merely external and superficial, while the "inner essences" are unique. But the absurdity of historicism when taken literally has been no bar to its wide, enduring influence as a haven for those who wish some avenue of escape from scientific naturalism in cultural subjects. When repeated without a qualifying term such as "partly" or "somewhat," the half truth is easily turned into a falsehood. As we have seen, unique and generic traits in art are both important to the art historian and aesthetician. Insofar as events of art resemble other events and fall into sequences, such as the products of a certain artist or school of art, valid historical generalizations can be made.

On the other hand, the constructive phases of the historicist approach as made by Riegl and other *Kunstwissenschaft* scholars should receive due credit. The real half truth in the theory of uniqueness lies in the actual diversities of art, which are are quite as real as the similarities and often more interesting. They help to distinguish artistic evolution from organic, where distinctive individual traits also exist but are usually of small concern to science. Previous exaggeration of the similarities in art, by evolutionists and others, had falsified the picture. Art historians in the nineties were justified, as Franz Boas and his students in anthropology were a generation later, in calling for intensive, empirical studies in particular arts, cultures, and periods.

As a would-be science, *Kunstwissenschaft* involved a partial revolt from aesthetics and philosophy as they had been developed in Germany. Both had been much preoccupied with questions of value: Kantian aesthetics with the establishment of *a priori* norms of beauty and good art, related to those of moral rightness; Hegelian metaphysics

with historical development as a divinely directed, spiritual progress. The more scientifically minded scholars saw the need for putting such evaluative considerations aside to some extent in the attempt to build up the descriptive, specialized study of the arts.

Who started the "science of art"? The answer depends somewhat on one's national, as well as ideological, point of view. Naturalists and positivists, especially in France and England, tend to credit Taine and to agree with Lord Listowel that, in the arts, he was "a founder of the empirical, historical, and comparative method proper to the natural sciences, as opposed to the deductive method of the nineteenth-century metaphysicians."[3] Comte, Spencer, and Semper could also claim to have had a hand in it, along with other early naturalists in aesthetics and criticism. Marxists would date its origin from Marx and Engels. Some writers credit Konrad Fiedler (1841–1895) and Alois Riegl (1858–1905). Thus Lionello Venturi, an Italian art historian in the Hegelian tradition, writes that Fiedler "renounced reflections on the beautiful to occupy himself only with art, and in that way he is the founder of the science of art, distinct from aesthetics."[4] Fiedler also objected to discussing "art" in general, on the ground that only the specific arts were aesthetic realities. To what extent such abstractions as the *Zeitgeist* or spirit of an age stand for any definite reality was a moot point in *Kunstwissenschaft*. It was characteristic of historicist thinking to deal in such vague metaphysical generalities on the one hand, while on the other insisting that scientific attempts to generalize about history were invalid.

In any case, the ideal of separating the science of art from aesthetics and philosophy was only half-heartedly attempted. Even those devoted to "pure visibility" approached it with a vision that was far from innocent of metaphysics. That

---

[3] *A Critical History of Modern Aesthetics*, p. 109.

[4] *History of Art Criticism* (New York, 1936), pp. 278, 285. Fiedler's chief work, *Schriften über Kunst*, was published in 1913–14.

would have been impossible in the heavily idealistic intellectual climate of prewar Germany, and these scholars did not seriously attempt it. Neither did the naturalists such as Semper and Allen. It is impossible to avoid all philosophical presuppositions in science. From a pragmatic standpoint, the main question is: to what new, positive insights and discoveries does one's philosophical orientation lead? The partial withdrawal of *Kunstwissenschaft* from academic philosophy freed the scholar for more direct observation and limited generalization in a special field. Both idealists and naturalists profited from it to build up an impressive mass of information about the arts. But contacts with aesthetics and philosophy were actively maintained until Hitler and the Second World War disrupted humanistic scholarship. "It was necessary," says Venturi, "to build a bridge between aesthetics and the empirical notation of the artistic fact, and that bridge was called the science of art."[5] It was a two-way bridge, for even the idealists admitted the necessity of going out to explore some of the phenomena in which the world spirit expressed itself, especially in the domain of art where aesthetic appearance was the principal "reality" to be explained. One's philosophy provided the maps and tools for such exploration. But the travelers returned laden with new materials which helped to transform aesthetics and philosophy themselves.

In 1906 Max Dessoir began editing the *Zeitschrift für Ästhetik und allgemeine Kunstwissenschaft*, whose "double-barreled" title expressed the desire to reunite philosophic aesthetics with the more general, theoretical activities of the science of art. Still later, the short and single term "aesthetics" replaced the double-barreled one as a name for the combined subject, now strongly empirical in approach, but not ignoring traditional philosophical and psychological problems.

The need to avoid or minimize evaluative assumptions in the new historical research led away from both the naturalistic and the idealistic varieties of evolutionism. The naturalistic variety, as we have seen, had in the nineteenth century its own evaluative presuppositions. It was slow in abandoning its optimistic heritage from Condorcet and Spencer, expressed in the belief that evolution was necessarily progressive. It was slow in abandoning the sense of European, mid-Victorian superiority in art and culture; in learning that accurate representation was not the only value, even in the "representative arts," and that so-called "primitive art" could claim superiority in some respects.

Hence there was an implied revolt from both schools of evolutionary thought in the demand of Alois Riegl that each style and period be examined for what it was: not as merely decadent or merely a step toward the perfectness of Athens or Florence. Each, said Riegl, expressed its own "mode of seeing and apprehending," which the historian should try to understand with sympathy. In *Stilfragen* (1893), Riegl protested against the common disparagement of the so-called "minor arts" of mere ornamentation, by contrast with the "major" ones which represented man and his actions. He applied this approach in tracing the history of ancient ornamentation and in analyzing a style of late Roman art which had often been disparaged as "baroque."[6] Neither Riegl nor his followers consistently tried to eliminate all value-judgments from art history-writing. That would be almost impossible in the first place, since the historian tends to imply, by his very choice of certain works of art to write about, that they are somehow worthy of attention. In addition, Riegl made a positive contribution to value-theory by showing that an apparently decadent age and style often has aesthetic values of its own, besides leading to a new, major style.

Thus the almost irresistible impulse to evaluate prevailed over the wish to establish a descriptive science of art. The fruitful aim of specializing on the visual, formal, and stylistic traits of art, which led to a great expansion and refinement of aesthetic

[5] *Op. cit.*, p. 272.
[6] *Die spätrömische Kunstindustrie nach den Funden in Österreich-Ungarn* (1901).

vision, was later exaggerated into the dogma, still current, that purely visual, abstract values are the only ones worth having in visual art; that represented subject-matter has no importance there, and that even in observing a realistic work of art one should ignore the subject-matter as much as possible.

The movement led by Riegl turned away from nineteenth-century evolutionism, not only as to the value of past styles, but also in reducing the emphasis on their genetic sequence. To the nineteenth-century evolutionist, the most important thing about a style or culture was how it fitted into the whole developmental process, not what it was in itself. Distinctive traits were overlooked in favor of those which illustrated larger sequences; the peculiar character and flavor of an epoch in art was missed; short-lived but notable phenomena were obscured by long-range trends. Particular works were regarded too much as merely "leading up to" some later work. The new approach was perhaps no truer, but it was a needed corrective. It was time to forget the vast genetic sequences for a while and look without distraction at the products of a certain place and time by themselves, as one might see them displayed in a museum gallery—timelessly, as different expressions of the human mind. Books were written on "timeless art" and "art without epoch," in the attempt to restrain students of art from thinking too much about dates and influences and to make them look more carefully at each work of art as it is today.

3. THE "NEW CRITICISM" IN LITERATURE. THE "AUTONOMY OF ART."

One of many similar movements in scholarship related to the arts was the so-called "New Criticism" in literature during several decades after the First World War. It is sometimes identified with "contextualism" as a literary theory. Protesting against excessive use of the evolutionist, historical,

and other genetic approaches to literature, it called for closer attention to each individual poem as an independent whole. By the nineteen-twenties, both the psychoanalytic and sociological schools of criticism had been so eager to show the influence of biographical and social factors on the artist and his work that they sometimes neglected the inherent qualities of the work itself, or forced them into some preconceived theory of its cause and genesis. In calling for close, undistracted, aesthetically responsive reading of each work by itself, this phase of the anti-historical reaction was again a salutary corrective. It led to much intensive study of the words, thought patterns, verbal sounds, and types of imagery used by various poets. This was sometimes microscopic and pedantic, but contributed to the growing science of formal and stylistic analysis.[7] However, contextualism was carried to excess in its turn by those who denounced all attempts to link the work of art with outside biographical or social factors. They did not see that these various approaches were supplementary, not exclusive or conflicting, and could be combined in the total enterprise of understanding and appreciation.[8] In its more excessive form, contextualism has stood for what Walter Sutton calls "the currently accepted idea of the poem as an inviolable whole, the product of the synthetic creative imagination, and of art as a unique realm of experience... an integrated symbol and the vehicle of a pure knowledge, mystically apprehended."[9] The poem is to be experienced in a state of rapt contemplation, not linked causally with the outside world. Sutton points out the relation of the contextualist "new criticism" to the romantic, organic theory of Coleridge, the mysticism of Yeats, the idealism of Croce, and other anti-

[7] Cf. "Criticism, The New," in J. T. Shipley (ed.), *Dictionary of World Literature* (New York, 1943), p. 137.
[8] This pluralistic view has been well set forth by R. P. Blackmur in "A Critic's Job of Work," in *Language as Gesture* (New York, 1935).
[9] "Contextualist Theory and Criticism as a Social Act." *Journal of Aesthetics and Art Criticism*, XIX, 3 (Spring 1961), 317-325.

naturalist tendencies. It can also be linked in this respect with nineteenth-century historicism.

The extreme avoidance of all genetic approaches can not easily be maintained in a historically-minded age; certainly not by the art historian himself. The place of a work of art or style in its limited, neighboring sequence is seldom completely ignored. But the place of these in the larger sequences of evolution have been ignored to a large extent up to the present time.

The implied revolt from evolutionism, and the analogy with later trends in anthropology, had still another aspect. The evolutionists had overstressed the resemblances between all cultures and their styles of art on a given level. L. H. Morgan had been clear as to the differences between the successive stages, but on a particular stage such as the neolithic or the early civilized, he had given the impression that all cultures were much the same. As to the styles of civilized art, historians had been greatly impressed by such resemblances as that between Mayan art and Egyptian. They tended to think of each style mainly as transitional between an earlier and a later style. Now the art historians and, a little later, the anthropologists, were calling for more attention to the differences.

Evolutionism had also emphasized the intimate connection of art with other branches of culture, including science, and that of each art with other arts. This tendency was inherited from the romantic conception of the "unity of art" and the "unity of the spirit." It had been strengthened by studies of primitive culture, in which the arts and other branches of culture had not yet become clearly differentiated or separately conducted. It was shared by naturalists and some idealists, though on different grounds, as both strove to demonstrate a universal process of cultural development. "Historicism," on the other hand, appealed to some idealists as well as dualists in drawing a line between science (especially natural science) and the spiritual realm of art, history, and religion. Benedetto Croce stressed the independence of art and history from science, while at the same time at-

tacking those who try to differentiate the arts from each other on a basis of medium, techniques or sensory form. Art is one, he insisted, though separate from natural science. Fiedler also called for recognition of the "autonomy" of art from science and practical life.

Those who called for the autonomy of art had various things in mind. Some meant "art for art's sake," the right of art to be judged for its own distinctive values rather than on moral and other external grounds. Some meant that art should not be controlled by political or other outside agencies. As to the problem of what determines events in art, an emphasis on its autonomy meant that it was not merely the result of outside forces, physical or socioeconomic; that it had its own internally determined kind of growth. If patterns and recurrences appeared in its history, these might be due to something in its own inner character and laws. The concept of autonomy was not so hostile to idealism, which had long proclaimed the freedom of art in its spiritual aspects from the laws of material necessity. For the idealist philosopher, the autonomy of art did not imply a complete freedom from moral responsibility or from causal interrelation with other mental activities, all being ultimately traceable to the same cosmic mind or will. Nor did it imply that the material and technical aspects of art were free from material laws, needs, and functions. These might still be explained in such material terms, with the constant reminder that such aspects were merely superficial and external. So the art historian under idealist influence, pursuing the "inner essentials" of art, was often impelled to look for them in "pure form," where beauty was pure and not merely adherent. Riegl insisted on the worth of abstract Arabian ornament, and Focillon in a later generation saw an inner logic in the mathematical play of Celtic interlace and Gothic façade. True, such form was necessarily embodied in visible materials and often in a context of stylized natural representation (as in Carolingian miniatures) or physical use (as in the cathedral). But, like music, ornament could free itself to a considerable extent from these incidental contacts and approach the purity of the Idea, as Plato had hinted in the *Philebus*.

Strictly speaking, naturalistic aesthetics could reply that all such relatively "abstract," non-functional or non-representational forms were equally the products of material brains, and no more free than any other kind of art from the requirements of perceptible embodiment. But in fact the naturalist seldom did think along these lines in the nineteenth century. Except among the Marxists, naturalistic aesthetics was, on the whole, weak and intimidated by the majesty of Kant and Hegel. Marxist aestheticians often treated abstract form and decorative ornament with some condescension as "mere formalism," the effete expression of a decadent feudal or capitalistic hedonism. Hence they discussed it mostly in a negative way, if at all, bestowing their praise instead on those kinds of art which deal more realistically with the socioeconomic interests of the worker. In the nineteenth century the naturalistic approach to art history was directed more through anthropology to a study of the primitive arts and useful crafts, as part of the whole evolutionary process. This left the intensive study of pure form, design, and style in civilized visual arts and music largely in the hands of scholars trained in the German idealistic tradition. Even when ostensibly avoiding philosophic issues and referring to the sensory, material, practical aspects of art, their philosophic creed could usually be read between the lines.

4. STYLISTIC ANALYSIS AND PERIODICITY.
WÖLFFLIN'S CONTRAST
OF CLASSIC AND BAROQUE;
ITS NON-EVOLUTIONARY CHARACTER

The work of Heinrich Wölfflin dealt with painting, sculpture, and architecture as well as with the decorative arts, but with strong emphasis upon their formal aspects, considered in abstraction.[10]

Unlike the older art history and criticism, the new paid scant attention to the subjects represented or the moral sentiments conveyed. In architecture and the useful arts it emphasized the visible and formal rather than the structural, functional, and social aspects. The representational and functional were not entirely ignored. Wölfflin often alludes to them, but mainly as examples of some abstract stylistic trait.

Such emphasis upon the sensory and formal aspects of art can be quite consistent with evolutionism. Form and style can be held to evolve, along with functional efficiency, emotional expressiveness, and the power to represent nature accurately. But in the hands of Wölfflin and many of his contemporaries, it took a non-evolutionary form.

No item of German art theory has received more attention from Western students of art history than the five pairs of opposite concepts by which Wölfflin contrasted the "classic" art of the Cinquecento throughout Europe with the "baroque" of the Seicento. They stood not only for a contrast, but for five modes of historical development from the one style to the other. These were translated as "from the linear to the painterly," "from plane to recession," "from closed to open form," "from multiplicity to unity," and "from absolute to relative clarity." By contrast with German philosophy, Wölfflin's treatment seemed refreshingly empirical and stimulating to further observation. Though limited in his work to the static visual arts, they soon suggested to scholars in other fields analogous contrasts and developments in music, literature, theater, and elsewhere. They led to an expanding concept of "baroque" as covering the whole culture and *Zeitgeist* of the seventeenth century. Others protested that not all sixteenth-century art was as Wölfflin described it, and that not all seventeenth-century art was "ba-

---

[10] *Kunstgeschichtliche Grundbegriffe* (Munich, 1915), translated as *Principles of Art History: the Problem of the Development of Style in Later Art* (New York, 1932).

roque" in his terms. The proper definition of this and other stylistic terms is still controversial.

Wölfflin's concepts were widely applicable because the traits to which they referred were general and also derived from observation. They were easily discernable in a wide range of visual art, regardless of the subject or use. They were not pure abstractions, but ways of treating concrete subject-matter in art. A *Last Supper* became a certain arrangement and lighting of figures in space. This was not purely sensory, for the suggestion of depth and solidity depends on the observer's imagination. Reference was also made to dramatic actions and emotional expressions; but with consistent emphasis upon their formal aspects. Likewise, in architecture, the structural and functional aspects were mentioned, but mainly as presenting one visual trait or another, such as multiple clarity or picturesqueness.

This deliberate narrowing down of the focus of vision by scholars in art, this ignoring of much that critics and the public had previously held most important, was related to the contemporary revolt from "subject-matter" and "associated literary values" in the visual arts themselves. The impressionists and post-impressionists were deliberately choosing uninteresting subjects as vehicles for form, or distorting normally interesting subjects like the human face or body into semi-abstract designs. Purely abstract painting was to be the next step.

Meanwhile, something was lost and something was gained by the narrowing down of the historian's vision. As always, the specializing approach permitted an intensive, microscopic vision, such as that of Bernard Berenson, to explore the nuances of individual style and incidentally to show the subtle differences between real and counterfeit, the work of the master and that of his assistants or copyists, in the growing market for authentic art. At the same time, the problem of the larger sequence, of the place of each style in artistic and cultural history as a whole, was often neglected.

Wölfflin himself was not a man of microscopic vision. In the "Introduction" to his *Principles*, he took note of the "much-trodden" paths of individual and national styles, then passed to the larger subject of period styles in Europe as a whole. But, needed as it was, his concentration of study on the visual aspects of style helped to spread among scholars a somewhat narrow conception of style itself, as something involving only a few of the elements in art. Style was often conceived by the specialist as something different from representation, expression, technique, and use or function; something to be described in purely abstract, visual terms, rather than as a distinctive way of selecting and organizing *all* the components. The historiography of art was correspondingly narrowed.

Wölfflin was interested in the larger sequences of art history, although he refrained from speculating on them in detail. In the "Conclusion" to his *Principles*, he mentioned the fact that the change from classic to baroque in the visual arts was not peculiar to sixteenth and seventeenth-century Europe, but had happened many times. It was evident in the change from high gothic to late gothic architecture and sculpture, the former of which was linear and "classic" in Wölfflin's sense, the latter painterly and "baroque." He quoted the view of Burckhardt and Dehio that "a periodicity in the history of architecture was to be assumed," and that "every occidental style, just as it has its classic epoch, has also its baroque." In the representative arts too, he continued, it is uncontested that "certain homonymous developments from linear to painterly have taken place more than once in the occident." Moreover, this sequence is at times reversed. About 1800, for example, a new "linear" vision arose in opposition to the eighteenth-century "painterly" mode. It was praised in the criticism of Diderot and F. Schlegel. In such renewals of an earlier mode, Wölfflin observed, it often seems that art has been able to "begin again at the beginning." But a closer look shows that it never returns exactly to the point where it previously stood; there are always diversities and mixtures.

This concept of periodicity in the history of styles brings Wölfflin close to the ancient theory of cycles, armed with new evidence from the analysis of trends in European visual art. It can be reconciled with evolutionism, but as Wölfflin left it, it is non-evolutionary if not anti-evolutionary.

5. WHAT CAUSES CHANGE IN ART? IMMANENT DETERMINISM AND THE IDEALISTIC TRADITION. RIEGL, FOCILLON, KRAMRISCH

In the same concluding chapter, Wölfflin raises again the question of *why* such periodic changes should occur in art and related modes of apprehending the world. He touches briefly on some traditional answers. All are inadequate, as he realizes; they leave us still asking why the forces of history should operate in this particular way. But they are starting-points for speculation.

There are two main possibilities, he thinks. "Is the change in the forms of apprehension the result of an inward development, ...of the apparatus of apprehension fulfilling itself to a certain extent of itself, or is it an impulse from outside... which determines the change?" We must not suppose an internal mechanism running automatically to produce a certain series of forms under any and all conditions. "Certain forms of beholding pre-exist as possibilities; whether and how they come to develop depends on outward circumstances." Thus, Wölfflin surmises, there may be a partial predetermination, presenting a limited range of alternative forms, from which external conditions select certain ones for actual development. In the 1800 return from the painterly to the classic, "the main impetus lies certainly in outward circumstances," but these circumstances consist of a general "revaluation of being," a change in attitudes of thought;—in other words, Taine's "psy-

chological climate." The emphasis in Wölfflin's thinking is toward a rather vague, immanent determinism, as in his praise of Dehio for believing "in a history of form working itself out inwardly." The history of forms is to be explained, declares Wölfflin, "by the fact that every form lives on, begetting, and every style calls to a new one." "The effect of picture on picture as a factor in style is much more important than what comes directly from the imitation of nature."

Riegl was more explicit on this question than Wölfflin. As against the naturalism of Semper, he proposed a new theory of the genesis of styles: that of *Kunstwollen* or the will to art. Lionello Venturi, himself an idealist, praises Riegl for having substituted this "idealistic affirmation" of the creative spirit for Semper's naturalistic reliance on function, material, and technique.[11] Riegl did not define it explicitly, but applied it as antithetical to mere techniques for imitating nature. It is not a mere synthesis of the artistic intentions of a period, but a real dynamic force; a will to a certain style. "I left the art-history seminar of Adolf Goldschmidt in Berlin," writes Alexander Dorner, "a staunch partisan of Alois Riegl's dialectical concept of history, ...which harnesses the evolution of art to the traditional eternal polarity of body and spirit. According to that concept, the spirit and its pure, general ideas eat, as it were, through the crust of sensory images. By virtue of its eternal divine properties the soul was supposed to rise from the haptics of objective sensory notions to the optics of subjective intellectual concepts, from the palpable plane to the higher intellectual representation of space."[12] On Kantian lines, Riegl sought to discover *a priori* the possible directions and categories of the will to art, and thought he had done so in terms of tactile and optical form. He based his categories on observation and analysis of historic styles of ornament, abstracting from them certain basic motifs and arranging them in genetic order. For this slight

[11] Venturi, *op. cit.*, p. 285.
[12] *The way Beyond Art* (New York, 1958) p. 15.

concession to empiricism, the idealist Venturi chides him for having "lost the consciousness of the eternity of the human spirit."

One of the few philosophical discussions of art history in the second quarter of the twentieth century was the essay by Henri Focillon, *La Vie des formes*.[13] From his special field of study in the medieval visual arts, Focillon asked again what regularities, if any, appear in the ever-changing forms and styles of art, and what causes them. He saw only partial, approximate regularities, with diversity enough to preclude explanation by any simple formula. He applied several theories and found none completely adequate: neither an iron-clad determinism nor a chaos of chance variations. His conception of art history was fairly pluralistic, but with a strong inclination toward immanent determinism. Like many French writers on art, he often sacrificed clarity of statement to poetic metaphors and graceful turns of phrase, leaving some doubt as to whether he intended his statements to be taken as literal truth. If taken with any approach to their literal sense, they express a basically idealistic metaphysics in the main tradition from Plato through Kant and Hegel, but with individual modifications.

As to what causes change in art, Focillon answers with a shower of imagery suggesting that the forms of art have an independent life and power of their own. "We are entirely justified in our assumption that [plastic] forms constitute an order of existence, and that this order has the motion and the breath of life." Each change in art leads on to other changes. In each work of Moslem ornament, "a sort of fever seems to goad on and to multiply the shapes." "Form is a mobile life in a changing world." A style is "a development... whose essential harmony is in many ways testing itself, building itself, and annihilating itself." Forms "comply with an internal, organizing logic." Its dialectic "accepts and demands new contributions, according to its own needs." "The life of forms is not the result of chance. Nor is it... called into being by historical necessities. No; forms obey

their own rules—rules that are inherent in the forms themselves, or better, in the regions of the mind."

Focillon mentions the arguments of Bréal against attributing reality to form as such, or construing it as a living entity. Yes, he concedes, forms that live in space and matter live first in the mind, and their external activity is but the projection of some inner process. This Crocean conclusion leaves unanswered the perennial question of the nature of mind and how forms "live" there, but Focillon seems quite content with the idealistic explanation.

Against evolutionism Focillon is explicit. He warns against "the dangers of 'evolution'; its deceptive orderliness, its single-minded directness, its use, in those problematical cases in which there is discord between the future and the past, of the expedient of 'transitions,' its inability to make room for the revolutionary energy of inventors."[14] These charges make it clear that Focillon is thinking, not of evolutionism in general and in the larger sense, but of some extremely rigid, unilinear type. It soon appears that he means by "evolution" the organismic theory of the development of particular styles, as Taine and Symonds did; not that of art or culture as a whole. He means by it the "activity on the part of a style in the process of self-definition, i.e., defining itself and then escaping from its own definition." It can be regarded, he says, as a dialectical or experimental process. (To say that a style "defines" itself in a logical and dialectical way is to follow strictly in the footsteps of Hegel.)

Focillon is also emphatic in rejecting Taine's theory in general, which he finds not only inadequate but "offensive." Nevertheless, he follows Taine in several respects, such as the concept of a "psychological landscape" in which both geography and artistic style play a part. He repeats with approval the familiar theory that a style, when able to develop, goes through four suc-

[13] (Paris, 1934). Translated as *The Life of Forms in Art* (New York, 1948).
[14] P. 8.

cessive stages, states, or ages: the experimental, the classic, the age of refinement, the baroque. He praises Waldemar Déonna for showing that these states "present the same formal characteristics at every epoch and in every environment." Hence the analogy between Greek and gothic archaism, Greek art of the fifth century B.C. and early thirteenth-century sculpture, flamboyant or baroque gothic and eighteenth-century rococo. "The history of forms cannot be indicated by a single ascending line," he rightly observes as against the unilinear fallacy. One style comes to an end, another comes to life. Like Wölfflin, Focillon thinks in terms of an indefinitely extended periodicity; a cyclical, somewhat varied recurrence of style after style without any over-all direction or development.

Focillon disclaims too rigid a determinism which might "isolate works of art from human life and condemn them to a blind automatism and to an exactly predictable sequence." There is a spiritually free diversification and experimentation in art. (Kant and Schiller had emphasized freedom in the play of genius, making its own rules.) It is due, says Focillon, not to Taine's "race, environment, and time," but in part to the fact that each stage in the development of a style opens up a new range of formal possibilities, from which the artist is free to choose.

Also, in part, it is due to a "spiritual ethnography" composed of diverse, recurrent types of personality or "families of the mind" which cut across all races. The artistic milieu is favorable to different types of mind, different types of artist, at different times. Minds of a certain spiritual family feel a certain affinity with each other beyond all restrictions of time or place. Each style seeks out a certain spiritual family. Artists of the same stamp recognize and call out to each other, and tend to express themselves in similar types of form regardless of the "moment" in which they are born. They often react against their cultural climate.

This is perhaps Focillon's most original, positive

contribution to the subject, and one which can be accepted on a naturalistic basis. It is a tempting hypothesis that certain innately predisposed types of personality may tend to produce certain types of art, if only variations on the current styles or selections from current alternatives, wherever and whenever such persons are born. William James, to whom Focillon referred, had suggested that some are born "toughminded" and others "tender-minded"; some stubbornly empirical and skeptical, some predisposed to other-worldly faiths. Some are born little liberals, said Gilbert and Sullivan; some little conservatives. Some may be natural classicists, others romanticists or mystics. Recent theories of psychological types, such as the "introvert and extrovert" of Jung, point in that direction. A congenital mystic would be more at home, presumably, in medieval Italy than in modern America; and his type of art would be more likely to win favor. His mystical tendency would be liable to counteraction by the prevailing rationalism and pragmatic naturalism of the latter.

Focillon believes in an "immense multiplicity of factors" in opposition to the "harshness of determinism." All these are said to interact with the "moments" of civilization, with natural and social environments, and with the life of forms itself, which thus turn out to be not quite as self-propelling, not quite as predirected, as the author seemed at first to imply. But he consistently minimizes the role of environment.

There is nothing essentially inconsistent between the theory that art history is influenced by external factors and the theory that events within a certain art often follow a certain trend for a while, even under changing and diverse conditions; that they seem to acquire a certain momentum along that line, at least until something powerful happens to deflect them. Artists are particularly sensitive to events in their own field. Those in a certain art or group of arts—such as architecture, sculpture, and painting in the Renaissance—may naturally want to carry farther a certain kind of task begun; to develop farther one of the possibilities which, as

Focillon says, each stage in the growth of a style reveals. A naturalist may, if he likes, describe this phenomenon figuratively as a kind of "life" within the forms. But he can not accept Focillon's belief that they have, in sober truth, a life of their own.

Among the more recent historians and critics of art who have leaned toward supernaturalism, some have stated their creed explicitly. If they denied evolution and progress in art, they did so on metaphysical grounds. Among these, we have mentioned Aldous Huxley as a devotee of the so-called *philosophia perennis*, which is a summary of the mystical, pantheistic transcendentalism common to Indian, Persian, neo-Platonic, and medieval European thought. Ananda Coomaraswamy was another of this school, closer to its Indian origins. His empirical descriptions of style, as in Rajput miniature painting and Buddhist sculpture, are quite acceptable to Western naturalists, whose aesthetics he detested. They include his interpretation of the iconographic symbolism of Eastern art, whose importance as a factor therein can not be denied. But this led him to a serious misunderstanding of modern Western art and aesthetics, as concerned only with "sensuous" values. The more he shifted from the factual interpretation of oriental art to its value and truth as expressions of the true religion, the more unacceptable to Western scholars his writings on art history became.[15]

The same is true of Stella Kramrisch, his younger co-worker in the interpretation of Indian art to the West. Like him, she mingles profound historic knowledge, a sensitive eye to the subtleties of style, and devotion to the art of India with a mystical attitude in which few Western scholars can follow her. In the aesthetics of India, which she accepts and applies, the artist is a medium through which Deity reveals itself, and his individuality is thus overshadowed. His ego is detached from the creative process, stands aside and is astonished at the working of a greater force. A Western reviewer of her comprehensive work on Indian art[16] remarks on how, in spite of her vast observation, her method makes the technical,

"positivistic" factors of art history seem to her irrelevant. Hence she remains apparently indifferent to technical issues and to recent datings of Indian art by Western scholars. To what degree, he asks, are such imaginative and metaphysical interpretations inimical to empirical judgments based on objective methods?

Granted that this metaphysical view is one on which Indian art itself partly rests, to what extent does it provide interpretations of that art acceptable to the Western mind? The answer must be a selective one. The historian imbued with religious supernaturalism is led by his world-view to observe and understand many traits and hidden meanings of religious art which a skeptic, however acute and learned, would probably ignore. Western scholarship must accept these with gratitude: not only the subtle distinctions in visible style, but also the clues to an understanding of those "psychic" elements in oriental art which are actual, cultural phenomena. As such, these will be open to an ultimately naturalistic interpretation.

6. OTHER THEORETICAL DISCUSSIONS OF ART HISTORY. HAUSER AND THE SOCIOLOGICAL TRADITION

We have observed in previous chapters how the supernaturalistic theories of art history were countered in the nineteenth century by several varieties of naturalistic evolutionism. The naturalistic approach, which suffered a temporary decline through the anti-evolutionary trend in anthropology in the early nineteen hundreds, has been gradually reviving. Aesthetics in general has developed along increasingly naturalistic lines, especially in the United States, and so have specialized studies

[15] Among Coomaraswamy's chief theoretical writings on art are *The Transformation of Nature in Art* (Cambridge, Mass., 1934) and *The Dance of Siva* (New York, 1924).

[16] John M. Rosenfield, reviewing *Indische Kunst* (Köln-Marienburg, 1955) in *Erasmus* (Feb. 25, 1957, p. 95). *Cf.* Kramrisch, *The Art of India through the Ages* (London, 1955), pp. 9 ff.

of art history. But theoretical discussions of art history from the naturalistic point of view, including the question of evolution, have been few and far between.

There was little systematic scholarship in art history or aesthetics in English during the late nineteenth and early twentieth centuries, by comparison with the impressive output in German. British and American universities were slow in establishing chairs in these subjects and in offering courses on any art except literature. Of the little writing on art in English at the time, the greater part was journalistic and superficial. Some was explicitly anti-evolutionist. Some, in the traditions of Coleridge and Emerson, inclined toward transcendentalism.

Two avant-garde critics of the visual arts in the early twentieth century were Clive Bell and Roger Fry. Both were informal essayists rather than systematic theorists. Bell exploded into violence in denouncing evolutionism. "To criticise a work of art historically is to play the science-besotted fool. No more disastrous theory," he said, "ever issued from the brain of a charlatan than that of evolution in art."[17] Giotto was not a creeping grub that merely led to Titian as a butterfly. To think of any artist as leading to the art of someone else is to misunderstand art. When we "begin to consider a work as anything else than an end in itself we leave the world of art." In such terms, extreme German and Crocean historicism was finding its way into English aesthetics before the First World War.

Fry, whose thought and language were more temperate and based on detailed analysis of examples,[18] likewise took an unfavorable view in 1917 of the "view of works of art as crystallised history." He was an early exponent of that school of criticism which called for more attention to particular works of art for their directly perceptible, visual forms: for "structural design and harmony" as opposed to historical and literary associations. He found no regular correspondence between the great historical movements in art and those in political and religious thought; sometimes they coincided, sometimes not. The rhythmic sequences of change in art were determined more by art's own internal forces, he thought, than by external ones such as the economic. The two rhythms are distinct, and often play against each other.

During the twenties Albert C. Barnes, art collector with a background of biochemical science and influenced by Dewey's naturalistic pragmatism, carried form analysis in painting farther along historical lines than either Bell or Fry. His emphasis, like Fry's, was on the clear perception and comparison of visual forms, but with more attention to continuities of influence from one painter and period to another. He pointed out, even in the greatest artists, traits "borrowed" from previous ones, but transformed into new syntheses and thus not examples of mere imitation or eclecticism. Artists should not fear to borrow from the past, he said. His major work, *The Art in Painting*, was roughly chronological in sequence after a long introduction on the principles of "plastic form."[19] He did not develop an explicit philosophy of cultural history or try to explain events in terms of immanent determinism, but the influences he traced were almost all within the art of painting, rather than external. They were inferred from observable similarities in relation to chronology.

In *Art as Experience*,[20] John Dewey acknowledged his indebtedness to Barnes, who had shown him a great deal about how to look at pictures. In an earlier book (*The Influence of Darwin on Philosophy*), Dewey had praised the liberating influence of evolutionism on civilization. But in his only book on art, he did not discuss its relation to evolution. He did try to show the continuity of art with ordinary experience and with the adaptive interaction between organisms and environment. As to art history, he saw the art of each period as an

[17] *Art* (London, 1914, 1923), p. 102.
[18] *Vision and Design* (London, 1920), pp. 1–15.
[19] (New York, 1925, 1928).
[20] (New York, 1934).

aid to understanding its civilization. He restated the familiar problem of "recovering an organic place for art in civilization." This, he said, "is like the problem of reorganizing our heritage from the past and the insights of present knowledge into a coherent and integrated imaginative union."[21] These words have an evolutionary tone. But Dewey was like most other American philosophers in ignoring the evolution of art as a specific problem in the philosophy of history.

In 1928, the present writer argued that genetic and comparative psychology, "by locating the human mind in an evolutionary process," had "confirmed the hypothesis of the rise of art out of primary organic functioning, and its continuity with the rest of human behavior."[22] At the same time, he warned against some of the errors and limitations of Taine and other early evolutionists, and called for more "patient description of observable genetic sequences." Art history shows moves toward simplicity as well as toward complexity, he noted. Again in 1949, in a treatise on comparative aesthetics,[23] he discussed the "evolution of art forms" with special reference to the differentiation and reintegration of types.

The present revival of interest in the philosophy of art history, including evolution, owes much to Arnold Hauser's recent book on the subject.[24] He had previously published a two-volume work, *The Social History of Art*[25] in which the sociological approach was applied to a wide range of artists and works in historic sequence, but with little theoretical discussion. Both of these books were charged by some reviewers with too close adherence to the sociological approach. Hauser paid tribute to Marx and Engels as pioneers in this method, but did not confine himself to strictly Marxist doctrines. Hauser's writings did much in the mid-twentieth century to help revive an interest in the philosophy of art history and in the possibility of a naturalistic approach to it, based on the social and psychological sciences. He accepted the general thesis of evolution in art without the unilinear fallacies.

After exposing some of the weaknesses in the idealist theory of immanent determinism in art, Hauser goes on to show an element of empirical validity in it. He rejects Wölfflin's conception of the autonomous evolution of forms and his theory that the history of style is not conditioned by external circumstances, but governed by an immanent system of laws. That writer does not succeed, he says, in showing that the evolution of art is completely free from the pressure of external circumstances. Nevertheless, a craft has its own history, which is, says Hauser, "on the whole one of continuous progress attributable to immanent causation... It is still quite reasonable to speak of an autonomous development here." In any particular historical case it is a problem, says Hauser, to decide which set of factors is more decisive. In general, he emphasizes the external, and within these the socioeconomic, which he considers most influential. Their influence extends, he thinks, even into the factors which seem most "immanent," as in the way the attitudes of artists are affected by their social training, status, and craft organization. A work of art, he writes, is the result of at least three lines of causation: the psychological, sociological, and stylistic. Each affects the other. "Sociological concepts do not enable us to comprehend the essence of art," he concedes, and art is only "among other things" a product and a cause of social events.[26] Thus the door is left open to other historians to show the causal relation between these "other things" and art; their methods may compete with the sociological as well as supplement it.

The "psychological" factor is treated more sketchily, except for psychoanalysis. As a psy-

---

[21] P. 338.

[22] T. Munro, *Scientific Method in Aesthetics* (New York, 1928), pp. 49, 64. Reprinted in *Toward Science in Aesthetics* (New York, 1956), pp. 37, 51.

[23] *The Arts and their Interrelations* (New York, 1949), pp. 377, 412–413.

[24] *The Philosophy of Art History* (London, 1959), esp. Chs. I, II, and IV on the sociological approach.

[25] (London, 1951).

[26] Pp. 275–6.

chological being, says Hauser, the individual retains freedom of choice among the possibilities presented by social causation. He can, within limits, create some new possibilities not prescribed by his society. But what he does along this line is also influenced by social conditions. Sociology tries to find the "preconditions of thought and will which derive from a man's social position." It assumes the ideological character of thought, including self-deception, as revealed by Nietzsche and Freud no less than by Marx.[27] However, Hauser criticizes Freud's approach to the psychology of art and artist as being "unhistorical." Freud does not realize, he says, the extent to which the conflicts and repressions from which all moderns suffer, including the artist—conflicts which help to motivate and form his art—are due to a particular set of social conditions.

Only the most naïve materialism, says Hauser, views art simply as a direct reflection of socio-economic conditions. There is no regular thesis-antithesis rhythm in the sequence of styles. Theories of the uniform, periodic sequence of styles are "pure fiction." Although the sociological method in history-writing is scientific, it does not claim to be predictive; there are no universal laws in the social history of art.[28]

"Nothing evolves so strikingly as art," says Hauser. He rejects the statement of E. M. Forster that history evolves while art stands still. We must avoid, he says, the naïve evolutionary belief that the simple and undifferentiated always precedes the complex and undifferentiated. But historical research and criticism must try to discover and explain "the position occupied by each particular work of art in the whole process of evolution."

In view of Hauser's evolutionism, including strong attacks on historicism, it is strange to find him repeating some of the anti-evolutionist clichés of historicist writers. One work of art, he says, "does not continue another or supplement another; each begins at the beginning and attains its goal as best it can... works of art are in fact incomparable."[29] His hostility toward periodic the-

ories leads him to exaggerated denials of recurrence, as in speaking of each artistic tendency as "a unique situation in the historical process" and of each stage as "totally different" from previous ones.

7. NEW CYCLICAL AND QUASI-CYCLICAL THEORIES OF ART HISTORY. CONTRASTIVE POLARITIES AND THEIR PERIODIC RECURRENCE. SPENGLER, SOROKIN, KROEBER

Early in this book, it was noted that one of the oldest theories of history is that of cycles. It has often been applied to the arts. After some thousands of years, it is still preferred by some philosophic historians. Those who try to develop such a theory usually try to answer two main questions: first, what is the specific nature of the cycles or other recurrences? Second, what causes them?

As to the second, many writers avoid a definite answer, especially those who wish to treat the subject in an empirical way, without metaphysical speculation. Those who do answer it usually suggest some sort of immanent determinism, with a parallelism between the various components of culture; all these proceed together through the cycles, impelled by the same inherently directive force. Environmental factors are usually regarded as too diverse, irregular, and accidental to produce a cyclical recurrence on the vast scale which is said to exist. A belief in the supremacy of environment and cultural diffusion does not usually accompany a belief in cycles, and vice versa. Most thinkers opposed to immanent determinism simply do not see the cycles or believe they exist in any highly regular, inevitable way. They usually agree, however, that some striking analogies do occur between the arts of peoples widely separate in

[27] Pp. 13, 17.
[28] Pp. 270-2.
[29] Pp, 36, 73, 194.

space and time; also that these call for more research, and, if possible, some explanation.

Many believers in historic cycles explain them on a supernaturalist basis, as due to a cosmic will or vital force. A few are naturalists. Spencer attributed the great cosmic cycles of evolution and dissolution to the inherent, unpurposeful tendencies of matter. Those physicists who tell us that the universe is running down, through the dissipation of energy, still leave us with the question of what will happen when it is all dissipated. Will it somehow wind itself up again? Has it charged and discharged its energies innumerable times in the past, or is it still doing both in various parts of space? Here the scientist leaves us in the hands of metaphysics; but the cyclical conception is perhaps no more unreasonable than any other.

Periodicity in nature is a common phenomenon, and man has learned to accept it as a fact even though unable to explain it in any thorough way. His whole life has always moved with its rhythms: with day and night, sleep and waking, the cycle of the seasons, the orbits of the planets, the birth, maturity, and death of living organisms, the rise and fall of empires. He has celebrated these in the arts. The forms of art are frequently periodic, as in the recurrence of a musical refrain. In modern times, man has noted other cyclical returns, such as the business cycle. Hence it has often seemed natural and plausible, even without attempting an explanation, to extend and reapply this concept to other phenomena where it is less obvious: to styles in art, whole civilizations, and human history in general. In these larger applications, it is usually recognized that the recurrence is only partial and somewhat irregular, with more or less diversity among the cycles.

As to the nature of the recurrences, there is considerable difference of opinion. We may arrange the types of theory from the extremely grandiose, speculative philosophies of history to the very cautious, empirical generalizations on a small scale. The former type undertakes to include all cosmic history, or at least the human part of it,

in the wavelike rhythm. It conceives of the recurrence as highly regular and as comprising all branches of culture. Spencer and Spengler both exemplify this grandiose extreme, though Spencer did not elaborate his concept of cycles much, and he did not (like Spengler) believe that each civilization goes through a separate cycle. Wölfflin and many other art historians have conceived of the recurrence in a much more limited way: as comprising only certain abstract traits of style in a single art or group of arts, and as somewhat irregular and diversified. They have not asserted that this periodicity is part of a universal law or inevitable sequence. Finally, Kroeber exemplifies the cautious empiricist, who tries to observe and plot specific resemblances, to see whether they actually recur in any significant way. He thinks they do, and in some cases with a fair amount of regularity. Kroeber rejects the theory of immanent determinism, but he has no other general explanation to offer. Since the term "cycle" tends to suggest a large amount of size and regularity, it is commonly avoided by those who do not conceive recurrence in that way.

Let us begin with some of the more ambitious theories, covering human history in general. A number of modern social philosophers, following Plato, have stressed the analogy between society and the individual, the species and the single organism, phylogeny and ontogeny. These theories have been called "organismic." They maintained, says H. E. Barnes, "that a society tends to grow, flourish, decline and wither away. In this way, they offered socio-biological confirmation of the old cyclical theory of social development."[30] Among them, in addition to Spencer, were Paul von Lilienfeld, A. G. F. Schäffle, and René Worms, all of whom lived from the nineteenth on into the twentieth century. The idea that whole cultures or civilizations grow and die like individual organisms, later developed by Spengler, was proposed by the Russian scientist Nikolai Danilevsky (1822–85) in *Russia and Europe* (1869). His purpose was

[30] *Historical Sociology*, p. 24.

to show that Russia would eventually take over the civilization of the world, as indicated by the history of former civilizations.[31] There have been about twelve great civilizations or culture-historical types, according to Danilevsky, each a fundamental type of life with a distinctive plan of organization. They do not blend or pass on their fundamental plans to successors, he said, although they transmit specific achievements. They grow slowly, flower briefly, and die. Our European or Germano-Romanic civilization culminated artistically around 1700 and scientifically in the nineteenth; it will soon be replaced by the Russian, in Danilevsky's opinion.

Shortly after the First World War, Oswald Spengler impressed a wide, international circle of readers with his dramatic, cyclical philosophy of history entitled *The Decline of the West*.[32] Even then, it seemed prophetic with its prediction of future wars, dictatorships, and social chaos. In some but not all respects it has been verified by subsequent events. It is the latest philosophy of history to maintain a highly regular, predetermined pattern in the course of events. Since then, the trend of opinion among historians has been strongly away from this type of theory.

Spengler combined, as H. E. Barnes remarks, "the cyclical theory of historical development, a wholehearted acceptance of the organismic theory of society and social evolution, and the Romanticist idea of a culture-soul which dominates the traits and activities of any people... Every culture is a self-contained organism that passes through a pre-ordained and inevitable life-cycle in response to the power of Destiny."[33] The Hegelian, romantic element is obvious in this theory of a "soul" in each civilization; also the debt to Schopenhauer's pessimism and to the biological concept of the organism with its predetermined life-cycle. Nothing important is carried over from age to age, according to Spengler. There is no general evolution of culture. The accumulation is merely superficial and technical; surviving ideas and devices are given different meanings and functions in the

later culture. Each culture is a unique, integrated whole.

There have been six great, historic cultures, in Spengler's view: the Egyptian, Old Chinese, Classical, Indian, Arabian, and Western or Faustian. Each goes through a parallel sequence of four stages: birth, youth, maturity, and old age; or spring, summer, autumn, and winter. Different cultures resemble each other somewhat in their corresponding stages, but the culture-souls and their products are essentially different. "Civilization," as he defines it, is the late, decadent stage of each culture, when it has lost its creative power. Our society reached it in the nineteenth century, with the growth of great cities, materialism, skepticism, imperialism, and war; its extinction through Caesarism and chaos is near.

Spengler lays great emphasis on the arts of every culture and on their consistency at every stage with its characteristics in other fields. His analogies are often illuminating, pointing out real resemblances in form and underlying attitude between phenomena in widely separate realms. But he exaggerates, in the interest of his neatly regular pattern, the differences between the great historic cultures and the resemblances within each culture. He persistently ignores negative instances which do not fit into his formula. Also, he underestimates the extent to which cultural achievements accumulate from one culture to another throughout the whole course of history.

Spengler's conception as a whole is now regarded more as a work of imaginative fiction than as one of sober fact; but the cyclical type of theory is far from dead. Arnold Toynbee, one of the most widely read historians of the mid-twentieth century, based his gigantic *Study of History* upon

[31] On cyclical theories of social history, see Kroeber, *Style and Civilizations* (Ithaca, N. Y., 1957), esp. pp. 112, 158.

[32] (New York, 1929). Translated from *Der Untergang des Abendlandes* (Munich, 1917, 1921). See the discussion by H. E. Barnes, *op. cit.*, p. 103 and that by Kroeber, *op. cit.*, pp. 83 ff., 163 ff.

[33] Kroeber (p. 97) minimizes the organismic aspects of Spengler's theory, but most critics think otherwise.

it. He is classed as a "new Spenglerian" by Stuart Hughes, and Kroeber agrees that "The rise-and-fall concept, analogous to organic growth and decay, is as basic in Toynbee as in Spengler."[34] Each civilization, according to Toynbee, is divided into Genesis, Growth, Breakdown, and Disintegration, with an emphasis on the last of these stages. He gives little space to the arts, but makes it clear that he regards the archaism and primitivism of recent visual art as a sign of decadence, analogous to that of Hellenistic sculpture.[35] Readers who dislike contemporary art, science, materialism, and rationalism, as a falling away from early religious faith and as bound up with our social troubles, will find some confirmation in Spengler and Toynbee, but not much comfort. All such trends, good or bad, are seen as largely inevitable, and cultural decay as not to be averted by any simple return to primitive faith. The longing for such a return is itself regarded as a sign of cultural senescence.

Pitirim Sorokin, an idealist, asserts an alternation between what he calls the ideational, idealistic, and sensate styles of art.[36] The first is predominantly religious, the second religious-secular and heroic, the third secular and skeptical. Ideational art is created, according to Sorokin, mainly by the priesthood; idealistic by the chivalrous, noble aristocracy; sensate by the materialistic bourgeoisie and intellectual proletariat. (He does not attribute them causally to these social conditions, however.) We are now at the close of a sensate era, and an ideational "spring" may soon develop. Among serious scholars in art, Sorokin asserts, "there are very few now who fail to notice the 'cyclical' or the erratically recurrent direction of the change of art phenomena." He does not agree with Spengler's conception of cultures or civilizations as completely integrated. He emphasizes instead two other kinds of construct: (1) systems, such as language, science, art, and religion, and (2) supersystems, which transcend civilizations: the ideational, idealistic, and sensate. These are qualities or ways of thinking and acting which pervade all departments of a culture at a certain time, those of art being connected with those of religion, philosophy, and social organizations. Thus European civilization from the sixteenth century on is said to be, on the whole, capitalistic, democratic, Protestant, individualistic, contractual, utilitarian, and sensate, in science and philosophy as well as art.[37]

Let us now return to some theories of smaller scope, such as that of Wölfflin: those restricted to a single art or set of related arts. Within this limited field, they seek to show that certain traits recur periodically. Some are further restricted to the art of a certain place and time while others consider it on a world scale. Most have been based primarily on European art from the Greek period onward. Possible analogies with Asiatic art are occasionally suggested, but this fertile field has been little explored by theorists of art history.

A. L. Kroeber uses the term "contrastive polarities" for the supposedly recurrent rhythms, "back and forth movements between extremes" such as classic-romantic, Apollonian-Dionysian, and others.[38] They usually originate, he says, in the attempt to describe typical products of a certain phase of style. Sometimes they are extended to cover analogies with other arts in the same civilization or to the same art in other civilizations. Thus romanticism is found in literature, painting and music in early nineteenth-century Europe, while classic stages are found in Latin literature of the Augustan age, in seventeenth-century French and in eighteenth-century English.

That some degree of oscillation between opposite pairs of traits occurs from time to time in many arts, periods, and civilizations is now fairly well agreed by art historians. Even though what we call "romantic" or "Dionysian" never occurs more than once in exactly the same way, there is

---

[34] *Style and Civilizations*, p. 119.

[35] *A Study of History*, Vol. VI (London, 1939), pp. 59 f.

[36] *Social and Cultural Dynamics: Fluctuation of Forms of Art* (New York, 1937), pp. 75 n., 678 ff.

[37] Kroeber compares and criticizes Sorokin and Spengler in *Style and Civilizations*, Appendices I–III.

[38] *Style and Civilizations*, p. 138.

enough resemblance between cases to warrant using the same descriptive terms with caution. There is nothing especially controversial about saying that such approximate "polarities" do occur occasionally, but that is only the start for theorizing on the subject. The chief moot points from then on are (a) how regular is the alternation as to the length of each phase, the intervals between phases, the similarity between corresponding phases, etc., and (b) what causes the alternation? The theorist goes out on thinner ice in proportion as he claims to see a highly regular periodicity, and seeks to explain it through some one causal agency. Another difficulty for theorists is to reconcile the supposed "uniqueness" of each style and its cycle of life with the idea that certain polarities, stages, and sequences recur in similar ways.

Curt Sachs, historian of music and other arts, has proposed a formula based on the alleged alternation of "ethos" and "pathos" types of art. These terms, he argues, are preferable to the older antithesis between classic or static, on the one hand, and baroque, romantic, or dynamic on the other. He prefers them also to Nietzsche's contrast between Apollonian and Dionysian "or wisely moderate and passionately immoderate."[39] Style proceeds everywhere and always, according to Sachs, between serenity, strictness, and moderation on the one hand and, on the other, passion, freedom, and exaggeration. Denying the reality of evolution and progress in art in the eighteenth-century sense, Sachs proposes instead a continuous succession of ethos-pathos cycles. There are giant cycles, he believes, and smaller ones within them, each including opposite phases. He uses the word "evolution" loosely, as in stating that "two main rules of evolution follow" from his discussion.[40] These are, that "Every cycle starts on an ethos phase and ends on a pathos phase" and that "every phase develops from ethos to pathos." Striving to bring several arts into the alternating pattern from prehistoric to modern, Sachs has to force the facts considerably along the way. He has little to say of other cultural factors; his approach is that of the art historian rather than that of the social or cultural historian.

H. W. Janson, reviewing Sachs's theory in the *Magazine of Art*,[41] comments that it is far too symmetrical to fit the material it seeks to contain. "His ethos-pathos cycles have no biological foundation—an indispensable requirement since man's past and future are but a tiny segment of the evolution of all living organisms on this planet. Dr. Sachs's theory is superior to its predecessors only to the extent that one strait-jacket, within its own peculiar limitations, may be more comfortable than others."

Arnold Hauser rightly criticizes most of the so-called polarities as exaggerating the antithetical character of styles. This has been done, he says, since the early nineteenth century, as in Schiller's contrast of the naïve and sentimental, Riegl's haptic and optic, Wölfflin's linear and painterly, and Worringer's abstraction and empathy.[42] Such thinking gives a false impression of art history as consisting of violent contests, of dilemmas in which there are only two alternatives. Certainly one can agree with Hauser that all these antitheses have been oversimplified, with the usual ignoring of diversities. Nevertheless, there is a kernel of truth in them. Stylistic traits do recur in part, though never exactly.

Besides criticizing past theories of periodicity in art, Kroeber developed some of his own. His major work on the subject, *Configurations of Culture Growth*,[43] was a survey of several main branches of civilization in which creative production occurs —philosophy, science, philology, sculpture, painting, drama, literature, and music—in all the great civilizations including the orient. In each, he examined the chief types of product, their values, and their individual geniuses where known. His quest throughout this extensive survey was for

[39] *The Commonwealth of Art: Style in the Fine Arts, Music, and the Dance* (New York, 1946), pp. 199, 202, 334.
[40] P. 363.
[41] April 1947, p. 164. See also Kroeber, p. 140.
[42] *Philosophy of Art History*, p. 164.
[43] (Berkeley and Los Angeles, 1944).

recurrent patterns of cultural growth and decline, as shown in the spatial and temporal distribution of great creative epochs. He described many "growth curves" of rise, florescence, climax, decadence, and death.

Kroeber also published several more specialized studies of periodicity in art: among them, one on the novel and one on women's dress-fashion styles.[44] In the latter, he and Jane Richardson found "long-term drifts" in the fundamental diameters of dress, such as width and length of skirts and proportion or place of the waist. These lasted about half a century, and after reaching an extreme reversed themselves for about the same time in the opposite direction, giving about a century for the full two-way oscillation of the pendulum. Moreover, he found certain steady, tranquil periods of low fashion variability, alternating with agitated, rapidly fluctuating ones. The latter were correlated with decades of social and political unrest. Periods of tension also seemed to favor more radical departure from the basic, ideal pattern favored in a particular culture, which is partly determined by racial body build.

8. ORGANISMIC THEORIES; RECURRENT SEQUENCES OF STAGES IN THE HISTORY OF STYLES

A number of organismic theories have been proposed in art history. On a smaller scale than Spengler's, they deal only with styles in particular arts; not directly with whole civilizations. (At the same time, a style or trend in art may be interpreted as "expressing its age" in a broader way.) The comparison of the history of a style to the life of a plant or animal can be meant only in a figurative sense, as in speaking of the "birth of the Gothic" or the "ripe" stage in Greek vase painting. Or it can imply real, detailed analogy between the two types of process in respect to the sequence of stages which both must go through. As in the writings

of Taine and Symonds, this view may be quite positivistic, implying no mystical attribution of real life to the style as such. The early, groping, experimental stage of a style is felt to be actually similar to that of childhood; that of classic balance and control to maturity, and that of excess or weakness to old age. It is recognized that many styles, like organisms, do not live through a whole life cycle and that some are affected by outer conditions. But any seriously intended theory of style as having a normal life cycle implies some degree of inherent determinism; environment alone would not suffice to produce it.

As motivated by idealism and historicism, the organismic conception of style becomes more metaphysical and supernaturalistic. The spirit of the age expresses itself in various national and individual styles, each of which may go through its own life cycle as a part of the larger one. Here the determining force is conceived as definitely immanent and spiritual.[45]

Kroeber, whose point of view is on the whole naturalistic and liberal, finds several ways in which the organic analogy to style seems to hold.[46] A style, like a species or genus in biology, "has a history. It represents an achieved evolution, which is unique, not repetitive in itself." Species, society, and culture exist as a stream of essentially repetitive individuals down the generations. The species or genus is a "form common to the individuals," and so is a culture. Species, styles, and civilizations are full of adaptation and consistency of form, whose efficient causality we do not understand.

Kroeber goes on to consider the further analogy between the history of a style and the life of an

[44] Summarized in *Style and Civilizations*, pp. 7–27.

[45] Historians emphasizing the socio-economic approach connect the organismic theory with political and social conservatism as a reaction from the French Revolution. To conceive the state and its culture as an organism, they say, implies that it should grow peacefully and cumulatively within its present, pre-established form, without internal conflict. Hauser so interprets Wölfflin. (*The Philosophy of Art History*, pp. 132–5). However, later organismic theories of style do not necessarily imply that political orientation.

[46] *Style and Civilizations*, pp. 77 f.

organism. He makes a distinction between (a) the independent recurrence of a certain quality at non-corresponding phases of different styles and (b) its appearance at corresponding phases.[47] The former would be less significant. If an impressionist quality is found haphazard in the painting of various peoples, but at no consistent place in a sequence of qualities, it may be due to all sorts of different contingencies. In the other case, it would be interpreted as due to immanent factors in the growth of styles generally, as a toddling gait is a function of infancy and tumultuousness of adolescence. To show that such predetermination exists, one would have to find enough independent, parallel examples occurring in definite sequences. Kroeber cites with interest the attempts of Paul Ligeti[48] to do so, but finds them inadequate. The same can be said of Ligeti's theory of alternating waves, a hundred forty years long, between linearity and impressionism. But he does believe that certain sequences in architecture and sculpture hold for the arts generally: a frontal posture and fixed stare and smile in the incipient stage. Rococo, Churrigueresque, or flamboyant architecture would come late. (Kroeber does not distinguish here between successive styles and successive stages in the history of a single style.) Like Focillon, he is impressed by the work of Waldemar Déonna in successfully piling up examples of similarities in corresponding phases of Minoan, Greek, and European sculpture.[49] Déonna distinguishes archaism, classicism, and decadence as a recurrent sequence, with examples of each in Greek sculpture and again in that of medieval and renaissance sculpture. With these sequences, Déonna interweaves an alternation between the idealistic and realistic polarities.

9. PERIODIC RECURRENCE IN ART AS RELATED TO EVOLUTION

The belief that art history presents a cyclical or periodic pattern is usually interpreted as inconsistent with that of evolution in art, but it is not

necessarily so. In Spencer's theory, as we have seen, the whole evolutionary process was only one phase in a vast, alternating cycle of evolution and dissolution; but it was so incalculably vast in itself as to be, for all practical purposes, the only one deserving much consideration. Man could do nothing much to change the pattern, and for the indefinite future the trend was upward. On the other hand, Spengler imagined the cycles as much shorter, lasting only for a few centuries each, with a separate cycle for each civilization. Western man has been on the downward trend for some time and his final dissolution is not far off, according to Spengler. Other cyclical developments elsewhere in the world were not ruled out, but none was definitely in sight, so the present picture was gloomy. Both Spencer and Spengler imagined the cyclical rhythm as the larger, dominant one, with development fitting into it as one of the alternating phases.

Most evolutionists have rejected the theory of great cycles, preferring to think of the developmental process as lasting indefinitely into the future. All of them have recognized some amount of minor, periodic repetition within the evolutionary process and subordinate to it, but they usually avoid the term "cycle" as implying too much large-scale regularity. Obviously, the flow of historic events includes the familiar rhythms of nature. It includes the life cycle of each individual organism. Phylogenesis includes the growth and spread of various types of organism, such as the fish and reptile, followed by their decline or arrested development and in some cases their extinction. We do not know yet whether man and other mammals face the same eventual downturn of their phylogenetic cycles. The growth and decay of empires and civilizations is an obvious fact, often repeated, and constitutes an irregular, quasi-cyclical movement in history as a whole. It is not

[47] P. 142.
[48] *Der Weg aus dem Chaos* (1931).
[49] *L'Archéologie, sa valeur, ses méthodes.* 3 vols. (Paris, 1912), esp. Vol. III, "Les Rhythmes artistiques." Kroeber, p. 145.

at all sure, however, whether all empires and all civilizations must continue going through that cycle to destruction, or whether the cycle is inherently predetermined as in the case of individual organisms.

A theory of recurrent stages and sequences in style is quite consistent with evolutionism. That a type of art such as Greek vase painting or French tragedy should go through a series of stages somewhat like the growth and decline of an organism would imply only a minor periodicity in art. It would not be inconsistent with an over-all evolutionism in which certain elements of style were held to be transmitted and accumulated. This theoretical possibility should not be ignored, even though some organismic theories of style (such as Taine's and Spengler's) have ignored or rejected general evolutionism. However, those who believe that styles in art must, and always do, go through a regular life cycle have the burden of proof on their hands. So far, they have shown us only a few examples of a definite full cycle. These have occurred mainly where there were few competing stylistic influences in the same art. As world-wide diffusion spreads in modern times, it becomes harder and harder for a style to go through a long, uninterrupted cycle. One can always point to the growth and decline of an individual artist's style, when he lives long enough. Any social or cultural movement, or any rainstorm, must necessarily have a beginning, a moment of height, and a decline; but this does not justify, except as a figure of speech, the inference that it has a real "life cycle" of its own.

Art history and cultural history are full of such minor pulsations, and it is a necessary task of twentieth-century evolutionism to describe them; to see how they fit into the larger trends and processes. The kind of periodicity in art which Wölfflin described, and which Kroeber called "contrastive polarities," can be regarded as minor fluctuations within an over-all process of cultural evolution, or in some cases as temporary deviations or regressions in the main process itself.

10. THE BEARINGS OF PSYCHOANALYSIS ON THEORIES OF ART HISTORY. FREUD AND JUNG

Freud wrote nothing at length on theories of art history or of history in general, but he was keenly interested in the arts and their place in civilization. His comments on them are suggestive and in line with naturalistic evolutionism, even though he said little directly about it.

The criticism by Marxist historians, that Freud's thinking was unhistorical, has some basis in fact but is exaggerated. He was not much interested in the differences between types of social order such as the capitalistic and communistic, but very much in those between early primitive life and modern civilization in general. He was not much interested in the struggle between classes, religious sects, artistic movements, or other subdivisions of society; much more so in the inevitable conflict and partial reconciliation between civilized society and the original nature of man. He was not much interested in the intermediate stages of cultural history, although he knew a good deal about Egyptian, Greek, and renaissance arts; much more so in the present stage, with all its hope and menace for the future. In present culture, he was less interested in the larger institutions often stressed by sociologists—in nations, churches, industries, and the like—but more so in the family as an influence on the young child; as an agency through which moral standards and restraints were poured into each child, and as the scene of a recurring drama with lifelong mental and emotional effects. The change from one type of socio-economic system to another, as from capitalism to communism, seemed to him to promise very little in solving man's fundamental psychic problems. He did recognize that some cultures (and some circles within modern culture) were more severe and rigid in their moral and religious restraints, more hostile to the natural desires of man, than others. Also, he recognized the aggravating effects on anxiety of severe competition for wealth, status, love, and self-esteem, together with the artist's peculiar difficulty in attaining them in modern times.

One evolutionary aspect of historic change interested him especially: that of the increasing complexity of civilized life, resulting largely from man's growing knowledge and power over physical nature. Man had achieved the ancient dream of godlike power, he said, without the wisdom or happiness of the gods. Physical science had increased man's power of oppression and destruction and consequently his anxieties, while his knowledge of himself and his ability to regulate his public and private life by conscious reason remained immature.

In this pessimism, based on recognition of the failure of benevolent reason so far to achieve human happiness, Freud inherited the late romantic reaction from the optimistic Enlightenment and Revolution. But his pessimism was not hopeless and he did not advocate the surrender of reason to faith or passion. On the contrary, the only hope he saw was in increasing the power and scope of conscious reason and science to harmonize the demands of instinct and civilization within the individual ego and society. He did not, as Jung and some of his followers have done, place a romantic faith in the unconscious, irrational, primitive levels of human nature. But he did see in them sources of life and death, good and evil, and above all of an animal vitality which can not be successfully ignored or drastically suppressed. His attitude toward the animal and primitive in man was objective, avoiding the extremes of contempt and idealization to which previous generations had gone. Freud distinguished clearly between evolution and progress, but did not go to the reactionary extreme of holding them to be opposed and irreconcilable. Increased complexity in civilization had brought some benefits and might bring more in the shape of order, beauty, and happiness; but the outcome was far from certain.

The chief difficulty, as Freud saw it in his late book on *Civilization and its Discontents*,[50] lay in the perennial struggle between two basic instincts

in man: the Eros instinct, making for social unity, cooperation, constructive effort, sympathy, kindness, and cultural development; and the Thanatos or death instinct, making for cruelty, disintegration, and destruction. These two were ever at war, with partial compromises. The death instinct had not been eliminated or permanently harnessed by morality and refinement; it was apt to break out at any time in redoubled fury among the most civilized peoples.

The arts have played an important role in the perennial struggle between these two tendencies in man, and in the related effort to reconcile his primitive physical impulses with the moral, aesthetic, and rational demands of civilization. Freud stressed their role as expressions of the Eros instinct and as contributing to beauty, order, and unity. Others since Freud have emphasized the fact (confirmed by psychoanalysis) that art itself contains a destructive impulse in various forms. It can symbolize destructive wishes on the part of the artist and his group toward the social order, one's family and associates, and oneself. It can also express in symbolic form the wish to restore and rebuild; to compensate and atone for such death wishes.

Freud himself did not stress the point that the impulse to destroy and disintegrate is not necessarily bad in the long run. The impulse to preserve social unity is not always good. Man owes his survival as an animal, in part to both. He attacked his enemies and sometimes cared for his friends and family. Some if not all of the social unities he builds become in time restrictive and oppressive; some one has to break them down to make room for growth. The same is true of intellectual forms, such as philosophic and scientific beliefs, and of artistic styles. Humanitarians hope that civilization will make the process of destroying or changing the old as painless to individuals as possible, and it has already done so to some extent. To Freud the greatest need was not for destruction, or for the complete suppression of any natural impulse, but for the redirection of all natural

[50] Tr. J. Rivière (New York, 1930).

[210]

impulses into socially beneficial channels. This is done to some extent in the psychological process of sublimation. At least, the impulses are thus turned into socially approved channels, though not always beneficial ones. There they can become a source of social rewards and of self-esteem.

Art is one of the main channels of sublimation, both for the artist himself and for those who respond to his work sympathetically. It provides approved, symbolic substitutes for repressed and condemned desires, and thus a partial satisfaction of them. It also provides a fantasy-fulfillment of approved but frustrated desires, and a partial escape from the miseries of life. This can be a source of direct happiness, at least for the moment, in addition to bringing tangible rewards to the artist—his "way around to reality." It can be used to excess as a chronic evasion of responsibilities and more lastingly effective ways to improve the situation. The commercialization of "dreams for sale" can provide a numbing opiate for the public mind. It can be used as an implement of indoctrination, whether intentionally or not, so as to develop attitudes of passive acceptance or revolutionary antagonism toward present social and cultural conditions; of mutual respect or intolerance and hatred toward others. Freud did not think it possible, or even desirable to try to "love all others as oneself." Hence he did not look to art as a means for attaining that Christian ideal. But he did see it as a potential means to the Greek ideal of self-knowledge and rational self-control. A great work of art, such as the tragedy of *Oedipus*, can help us understand our personal problems, to see them as shared by others, and to cope with them on a conscious, intelligent level. It can also suggest possible solutions of them.

The images and forms of art, including sense qualities, shapes, colors, sounds, types of design, plot, and character, even types such as classic and romantic, Apollonian and Dionysian, can become symbols to the artist and his public of strongly emotive meanings, some consciously and some unconsciously. With the aid of psychoanalytic theory, the historian and critic of art can thus find hitherto unsuspected meanings and causes of emotional effect in art.

To find in civilized art symbolic expressions of primitive as well as infantile thought does not provide a full causal explanation of the civilized product. It does not explain the distinctive traits of any civilized style. It tends to lead us away from the fascinating, perplexing diversities of civilized art, which seem to many critics as the true "essence" of art and genius. It leads us back to a prehistoric age when all men and all artists were more alike. (Even though some paleolithic artists seem to have been much better than others, there is no sign of great individuality comparable to that of modern times.) This may seem like a failure of the psychoanalytic approach if one's only aim is to explain modern diversity. But from another point of view it is no more a failure than organic evolutionism was in explaining the diversity or living animals and plants. It traced them all back genetically to certain simple, relatively undifferentiated types. This is what psychoanalysis tries to do, not with all the aspects of art, but only with certain symbolic and motivational elements in it. In doing so, it tends to confirm the belief that the over-all trend in both art and society has been, on the whole, one of development from simpler to more complex.

The psychoanalytic approach, as developed by Freud, Jung, and their followers, is starting to provide a useful bridge between the animal, primitive, infantile, and irrational depths of the psyche on the one hand, and on the other the complex refinements of art and civilized custom. It can help us understand the arts of all peoples and periods. This results especially from comparing primitive art, including folklore, with the civilized treatment of similar subjects. We can often see the progressive disguise and distortion of a crudely physical image beneath the developing symbolic form. Creative social processes of this sort, analogous to dream-work, go on through centuries, as in the modification of certain deities and fairy-tales. In such a process we have a clue to the differentiation of specific types of art. Moreover, psychoanalysis can help us understand our own emotional responses to art, whether favorable, unfavorable, or ambivalent, and thus provide one ground for evaluating it as a source of aesthetic experience.

One is likely to underestimate the historical relevance of Freud's theories because he so often works backward in time. This is true of his clinical work with individuals, in which he sought to discover certain causes of the patient's neurosis by retracing the sequence of steps which led up to it; down through layer after layer of concealing memories, perhaps to an infantile trauma. (He made it clear that such an early stage, and the whole sequence of events, were not the whole explanation). Some persons react to a certain experience by building a neurosis; some by creating art or in other approved, "normal" ways. Organic predisposition is also a factor. In exploring the general nature of unconscious and preconscious thinking, Freud found himself working back to phenomena analogous to those of primitive thought. In this connection, he tells of his great interest in reading a recent book on primitive language, and finding phenomena there described which resembled the language and imagery of dreams and neurosis. Unconscious thinking, he said, is "archaic" in that it tends to use abstract conceptual and logical material from waking life, transforming it into concrete images. It often ignores or distorts the rational meaning by substituting some merely sensory connection, such as a punning relation between words, which seems far-fetched and absurd on the conscious level.

Finally, Freud worked back in time from his analysis of modern, civilized thinking, normal and neurotic, to a hypothetical reconstruction of certain aspects of prehistoric life. This brought him into the field of anthropology and culture history, as in *Totem and Taboo*.[51] From his observations of the apparent universality of the Oedipus complex today, he developed the hypothesis of an actual, often repeated primal drama in which the sons overthrew and killed the father, took his women, and later felt a remorseful desire to atone for the guilt. This happened so often, perhaps, that it became a part of the inherited, collective unconscious of the human race. Freud realized the conjectural nature of this hypothesis, and advanced it more as a suggestive myth, with some possibility of truth, than as a reasoned theory.

Meanwhile, some cultural psychologists found reason to doubt that the Oedipus complex is really universal. There seems to be little or no evidence of it in some Pacific Island cultures.[52] Even so, its prevalence in Western culture as an apparently inborn tendency remains a problem. It is related to art through the widespread representation of certain aspects of the family drama in realistic or symbolic form, including much religious art. No doubt it is also related to the power and frequent severity of the patriarch in many cultures, such as the Hebrew, Roman, and Japanese.

Jung, Freud's former supporter and afterwards leader of a dissident school of psychoanalysis, developed it more along supernaturalistic, vitalistic lines through his conception of the libido as a spiritual force. He, too, worked backward from present-day individual and cultural phenomena to certain supposedly archetypal patterns in prehistoric thought. Jung and his followers have had considerable success in finding them in the arts, dreams, and religious expressions of various cultures. This offers a partial explanation of recurrent analogies.

Psychoanalysis or depth psychology is only one of many recent developments in building up our knowledge of the "psychological factor" in art history—that is, in the narrow sense of "psychological" as distinct from "sociological." In this sense, it is also distinguished from the "stylistic" or strictly art-historical approach, which seeks for causes of particular styles and sequences of style within art itself.

[51] (1912–13).
[52] *Cf.* A. Kardiner and R. Linton, *The Psychological Frontiers of Society* (New York, 1945).

PART THREE

HOW THE ARTS EVOLVE:
A CORRECTED RESTATEMENT

CHAPTER XIV

MEANINGS OF "EVOLUTION"
AND RELATED CONCEPTS
AS APPLIED TO THE ARTS

We now turn from a historical survey of past theories to a direct consideration of the problem: "Do the arts evolve? If so, how and to what extent?"

The first question encountered is that of the meaning of "evolution" as applied in the cultural field. By what criteria could we recognize it? Whether or not it actually occurs in art, how could we recognize it if it did occur?

That question, one would think, should be decided in advance, at least in a tentative way, before going on to statements about the reality of the process. But most of the discussion passes over it lightly, assuming that everyone knows what "evolution" means. Unfortunately, the meanings assumed are usually vague and inconsistent. What we need at this point is a set of abstract specifications as to what the term implies with reference to the arts. With these in hand, we can then examine some of the known phenomena of art history, and ask to what extent they fulfill the criteria of evolutionary change.

The foregoing historical summary shows that the word "evolution" has been applied to art and culture in many different senses. When a writer says that he believes or disbelieves in cultural evolution, when he attacks or defends "evolutionism" in art history, he may mean any one of a number of things. If he understood the term in a different sense, he might take a different position with regard to it.

From the standpoint of modern lexicography and logic, there is no one right meaning for any word or conventional sign. A word is a man-made instrument of thought, inquiry, communication, and recording. We are free to define and redefine it so as to improve its efficiency for these functions. While ambiguity has its values in literary art and conversation, science chooses rather to reduce the meanings of each term so far as possible, to avoid ambiguity. It can not reduce them in each case to a single meaning; that would involve a needless multiplication of terms, and the context usually indicates which of several meanings is intended. But each of the main theoretical terms which have been argued about for generations has become confused by associated ideas, residues of the many different, conflicting schools of thought. "Evolution" is not one of the oldest of these, but it has been applied in many different sciences to widely different types of phenomena, by theorists with very different beliefs, each eager to construe the word in some way favorable to his own point of view.

As a general policy, it is not wise to include very controversial theories in the basic definition of a concept: e.g., to define "religion" in a way which would be accepted only by members of a certain sect, or to define "government" in a way acceptable only to members of a certain party. This hampers all communication of ideas. It is usually possible to define such common, much-used words in a fairly neutral way, more or less acceptable to all schools of thought. Then one can state one's controversial ideas as beliefs or assertions *about* the thing specified; e.g., as to which religion is the true one or which type of government the best.

Writers actively engaged in polemics tend to include their own beliefs and attitudes as part of the definition, explicitly or by innuendo. When they are attacking a certain belief, they tend to distort and caricature the terms in which it is expressed; to suggest that its main concepts have a ridiculous or preposterous meaning. Thus the theory of organic evolution was at first caricatured as a belief "that one's grandfather was a monkey." The theory of cultural evolution is now being caricatured as implying all sorts of extreme, disproved beliefs; in fact, every mistake or exaggeration ever made by an early evolutionist.

One way to treat such ambiguous terms in writing is to choose a fairly well established definition from some dictionary or other neutral reference work; then to state clearly which meaning is being used and hold to it consistently. From the standpoint of the lexicographer, who is presumably objective on most theoretical points, the problem is one of picking out, from the tangled mass of alternative, inconsistent meanings, one or a few which are most suitable. They should be (a) fairly well established in authoritative usage and (b) neutral enough for common acceptance, yet (c)

without entirely ignoring major controversies. One way to handle this is to say, in the definition, that some persons believe this or that about the thing referred to, or that, according to a certain theory, it is thus and so. Such issues often focus on the question of reality: whether the thing, event, or personage referred to actually exists or existed in the past, or whether it is merely imaginary; whether the belief in it is false. On many such topics there is now enough consensus to permit a categorical statement in the definition: a centaur is a mythical or fabulous creature, part man and part horse. But there is still some disagreement in physics about the reality of ether as "a medium postulated in the undulatory theory of light as permeating all space." Hence, says Webster, "its existence is at present denied by many." The same dictionary defines "spontaneous generation" in biology as "The generation of living from non-living matter; abiogenesis"; then adds, "from a belief, now abandoned, that organisms found in putrid water arose spontaneously from it." The first of these statements defined the basic concept in a neutral way; the second truthfully reported current disbelief in the reality of the process it refers to.

The concept of evolution in the biological field can be likewise objectively defined by stating, first, its basic connotations: what "evolution" means in general and in reference to organic phenomena; second, what principal theories have been advanced about it as a real process; third, what the consensus in biology is about these theories. One can say that evolutionism in general is now almost universally accepted in biology, though Darwin's theory of gradual variation has had to be corrected somewhat. Such a fair statement helps to correct the common misapprehension that Darwinism and evolution in general have been "disproved" and "abandoned."

3. BIOLOGICAL DEFINITIONS OF "EVOLUTION"

J. T. Merz, in his *History of European Thought in the Nineteenth Century*,[1] contrasts the "genetic view of nature" in the later nineteenth century with the "morphological" period of 1800 to 1860. That had been mainly concerned with classification and description of specimens (p. 274), whereas the later decades emphasized change and development. Scientific interest turned to how things have come to be what they are, and what is their history in time. Leibnitz had anticipated this view of nature in the seventeenth century.

The English word "evolution," says Merz, came to be applied in this way of regarding things, and to mean "the continuous and orderly development of states and forms of existence."[2] It came to be used interchangeably with "development" and "Entwickelung" for the series of genetic changes exhibited by human beings.

Karl Ernst von Baer (1792–1876) demonstrated in 1834 the limited transformation of certain animal forms in the succession of generations.[3] He also contributed the important concept of *differentiation* (Sonderung) as a phase of development. By "development," von Baer meant what Haeckel later called "ontogenesis" (individual growth) as distinct from "phylogenesis," that of phyla, genera and species. "Evolution" came to be applied mainly to the latter.

The dated quotations in the *Oxford English Dictionary* summarize the principal meanings of "evolution" before, during, and after Spencer's time. From this source we learn that an essay on biology in 1670 contained the sentence, "by the word Change [in Insects] is nothing else to be understood but a gradual and natural Evolution and Growth of the parts." This refers to the growth of an individual organism from a rudimentary to a mature condition; not to the transformation of species. In 1832 Lyell extended the term "evolution" to cover the new idea of the gradual transformation of species and the origin of new ones, as opposed to special creation. "The testacea of the ocean existed first," he said, "until some of them by gradual evolution were improved into those inhabiting the land." And, again, "The orang-outang, having been evolved out of a monad, is made slowly to attain the attributes and dignity of man." Spencer was following this usage when, in 1852, he denounced those who "cavalierly reject the Theory of Evolution."

The *Oxford Dictionary* (Vol. III, 1897, p. 354) gives a long list of definitions of the term, under three main headings which stand for different types of meaning. Of these I 6c is the most relevant here: "The origination of species of animals and plants, as conceived by those who attribute it to a process of development from earlier forms, and not to a process of 'special creation.' Often in phrases, Doctrine, Theory of Evolution." Accordingly, one definition of *evolve* is "...to originate (animal or vegetable species) by gradual modification from earlier forms; in wider sense, to produce or modify by evolution."

Joseph Needham, writing on "Evolution" in the *Encyclopedia of the Social Sciences* (New York, 1931), concludes in Spencerian language that "Evolution, then, means primarily the passage from simplicity to complexity, from homogeneity to heterogeneity, which, from empirical observation of living creatures and their remains, may be deduced to have occurred and to be still occurring in the world of life." Two factors are necessary, he says: organisms and their environments.

Lamarck, Spencer, Darwin, and others have regarded the adaptation of living forms to their environment as a major tendency in organic evolution. This idea is sometimes but not always expressed in defining evolution as "descent with adaptive modification." Thus Evolutionism, ac-

---

[1] (Edinburgh and London, 1903), Ch. IX, esp. pp. 278–9.
[2] On previous biological usage of the term, Merz cites the article on evolution in the *Encyclopedia Britannica*, 9th ed., by T. H. Huxley. In the early eighteenth century the word "evolutio" was used by Leibnitz, Harvey, and Haller in a different biological sense, opposed to "epigenesis."
[3] Merz, pp. 301, 305–7.

cording to the *Dictionary of Philosophy*, holds "variety of species to be the result of change and modification and growth and adaptation rather than from some form of special creation of each of the myriads of organic types and even of much in the inorganic realm." Adaptive change is conceived as change conducive to the survival of the type concerned, whether by changing itself or its environment. Some writers rely exclusively on this criterion, omitting complexity. Thus Ronald Fisher declares that "Evolution is progressive adaptation and consists in nothing else."[4]

In these wordings, two basic ideas or groups of ideas recur: (1) *development, growth, or increasing complexity*, and (2) *phylogeny or descent with adaptive modification and origination of types.*

4. BASIC DEFINITIONS OF "EVOLUTION" AS APPLIED TO PHYSICAL, MENTAL, SOCIAL, AND CULTURAL PHENOMENA

As the *Oxford Dictionary* shows, the term "evolution" was applied to mental, social, and cultural phenomena long before Darwin and Spencer, as an appropriate term for describing certain modes of change. This was not a late, far-fetched extension of a biological term outside its proper sphere. In 1677 a certain Hale applied the term to human nature, in the sense of working out in detail what is potentially contained in principle. "It must have potentially at least," he said, "the whole systeme of Humane Nature, or at least the Ideal Principle thereof, in the evolution whereof the complement and the formation of the Humane Nature most consist." In 1807 it was applied by Knox and Jebb to the growth of a social institution, the British constitution, to imply a gradual, natural development as opposed to production by a specific act. Grote, in his history of Greece, wrote in 1847 of "the great evolution of Scythian power." Spencer was building on established usage when he wrote in 1873 (*Study Sociol.*, v. 98) that "Psychology...

deals with the evolution of the faculties... by what processes... ideas grow from concrete to abstract and from simple to complex." "Societies," he declared, "are evolved in structure and function as in growth." James Sully, in the *Encyclopedia Britannica*, 8th ed., 1878, declared that "Mental evolution is a progressive composition of units of feeling in more and more complex forms," and Clodd, writing on myths in 1885, wrote that "evolution is advance from the simple to the complex." By 1884 Spencer was predicting that "by future more evolved intelligences, the course of things now apprehensible only in parts may be apprehensible all together."

Oxford generalizes on this usage by two related definitions: "7. The development or growth, according to its inherent tendencies, of anything that may be compared to a living organism (e.g., of a political constitution, science, language, etc.); sometimes contrasted with revolution. Also, the rise or origination of anything by natural development, as distinguished from its production by a specific act; 'growing' as opposed to 'being made'... 9. In recent philosophical speculation used in a more comprehensive sense... According to Herbert Spencer... all the changes in the universe, whether material or psychical, are phenomena either of Evolution or of the reverse process of Dissolution." *Oxford's* definition 9, which follows Spencer in including cosmic, physical processes, is still used by astronomers. For example, in an article by C. H. Payne-Gaposchkin on "Why Do Galaxies have a Spiral Form?"[5] "Do the spiral galaxies give us clues to the evolution of the universe?," the author answers that their forms do suggest an evolutionary sequence of dynamic growth.

In the phylogenetic sense, the anthropologist E. A. Hoebel follows and extends the definition by Needham, quoted in the previous section. Like

[4] *Genetical Theory of Natural Selection* (London, 1930). Quoted by Marjorie Grene in "The Faith of Darwinism" (*Encounter*, Vol. XIII, No. 5, Nov. 1959 p. 49.

[5] *Scientific American*, Sept. 1953, p. 89.

biological evolution, he says, "cultural evolution may be taken to mean the passage from simplicity to complexity, from homogeneity to heterogeneity which, from empirical observation of living societies and their material remains may be deduced to have occurred and to be still occurring in the world of social life among men."[6] This explicitly follows the Spencerian wording. The *Dictionary of Sociology* likewise defines "evolution, cultural" as "The development of a culture (or of given culture traits) from simpler, less integrated forms to more complex and integrated forms, by a continuous process."[7]

Webster's *Third New International Dictionary* (Merriam Co., Springfield Mass., 1961) first restates the common definitions for general and biological use. Evolution, it states, is "a process of continuous change from a lower, simpler, or worse condition to a higher, more complex, or better state." (We have rejected the evaluative meanings.) It then goes on to add two definitions for the cultural field. One is "the progressive development of civilization and social institutions in a fixed sequence of stages—called also unilinear evolution." (Since this implies a special, discredited theory, it is unsatisfactory for our purpose.) The other is "a process of cultural change determined especially by technological factors and marked by a movement from simplicity to complexity and the gradual increase of man's control over his environment."

In definitions of this sort, which recognize established usage in the cultural field, the same two basic ideas recur. Whether applied to organic, mental, social, or cultural phenomena, "evolution" has two main connotations: (1) *development or increasing complexity* and (2) *the gradual, adaptive modification of earlier types with origination of new ones*. The first is in the Spencerian tradition, the second in the Darwinian. Some writers emphasize one, some the other, as the essential meaning of cultural evolution. Some use only one and reject or ignore the other. Thus Hoebel follows the Spencerian wording, while A. G. Keller prefers

the Darwinian. In taking evolutionary theory over into the social domain, he thinks, Spencer's formula should be replaced by that of "variation, selection, transmission, and adaptation."[8] Julian Steward asserts that "complexity as such is not distinctive of the evolutionary concept" (*Anthropology Today*, p. 314). But he substitutes a theory of "developmental levels" in which the later are usually found to have "not only greater internal heterogeneity and specialization but wholly new kinds of over-all integration." This brings us back fairly close to the Spencerian formula.

The two ideas are not inconsistent, and can be regarded as indicating complementary aspects of the same process. One way to combine them would be to say that evolution *in the full sense* has *both* characteristics, while a process having only one is only partly evolutionary. We shall consider both in relation to the arts.

5. CULTURAL AND ARTISTIC EVOLUTIONISM. WHAT "EVOLUTION IN THE ARTS" MEANS AND DOES NOT MEAN

An important distinction can be made between "evolution" as an abstract concept and "evolutionism" as a belief or theory. As an abstract concept, it does not necessarily imply any belief or

---

[6] *Man in the Primitive World* (New York, 1958), p. 615.

[7] H. P. Fairchild, ed. (New York, 1944), p. 110. It introduces a controversial note, however, in specifying that "evolutionary change" is "continuous, orderly change in a definite direction..." Such words suggest a unilinear type of movement toward a predetermined goal. Most contemporary writers do not regard this as an essential meaning.

[8] *Societal Evolution* (1915), quoted by H. E. Barnes, *Historical Sociology*, p. 21. Another who prefers this Darwinian formula is V. G. Childe in *Social Evolution* (New York, 1951), p. 175. G.P.Murdock limits it to "processes of orderly adaptive change" in culture and social structure. (*Social Structure*, New York, 1949, p. 184). *Cf.* Robert Scoon, "The Rise and Impact of Evolutionary Ideas" in *Evolutionary Thought in America*, ed. by Stow Persons; New York, 1956, p. 5): "I am ready to propose that by evolution we mean strictly a continuous process of change in a temporal perspective long enough to produce a series of transformations."

statement as to whether the process it refers to actually occurs. Two persons can agree on the meaning of the concept and disagree as to whether any such process occurs or has occurred. Scholars can agree on the abstract meaning of the Fall of Man, the Sleep of Buddha, or the Last Judgment, without agreeing on whether these concepts refer to real or imaginary events. Debate on the subject could be facilitated by some agreement on the basic definition of "evolution" as a concept. Then we could go on to discuss the extent to which it is a true description of the facts.

Needham and Hoebel, in the definitions quoted above, first describe evolution in terms of increasing complexity, then add that such a process "may be deduced to have occurred and to be still occurring." It would help in technical discussion to call the belief or theory "evolutionism."

Cultural evolutionism is the belief that present cultural forms have come into existence through a long process of descent with gradual, adaptive modification, the origination of new types of form, and a tendency to increasing complexity.

Art is a branch of culture, and the same general theory can be applied to this branch by substituting "artistic" for "cultural." The title of this book, "Evolution in the Arts," refers to such a process, conceived in relation to artistic phenomena. *Artistic evolutionism is the belief that a large-scale process of descent with adaptive, cumulative, complicative change has occurred and is still occurring in the arts.*

It does *not* mean (1) that evolution is the only, or the universal, process in the arts, (2) that it is always or necessarily dominant, (3) that the arts are progressing or getting better, or (4) that they are developing uniformly along a single line, or (5) that they obey a universal law of evolution, or (6) that they are all determined by some one causal factor, or (7) that they go and must go through parallel series of stages in all parts of the world, or (8) that they will necessarily go on developing in future. It does not mean (9) that they evolve continuously, always and everywhere, without interruption or new beginnings, or (10)

that all recent art is more highly evolved than earlier art. Whether true or false, these ideas can be more clearly expressed as specific supplementary theories than in definitions of the basic, general concepts.

In defining a concept, one has to consider the connotation or abstract meaning and the denotation, the range of particular instances or varieties covered by it. We have just restated the connotation. The denotation proposed by Spencer covered the whole cosmic process, past, present, and far into the future; on the whole, and except for minor dissolutions, past history exemplified the evolutionary tendency. However, as we have seen, later theorists showed that examples of regressive simplification and arrested development were much more numerous than Spencer had realized. Some of these non-evolutionary changes were adaptive. Evolution, in the sense of complication, could not be truly called "universal."

But confusion then arose from the fact that so many people, scientists and general public, had formed the habit of referring to all past history as "evolution." There was no difficulty here for Spencer. But if the two were not the same, which should be called "evolution"? Two alternatives were open. First, one could redefine "evolution" in a looser, vaguer way, so that it would still cover the whole historical process. Second, one could retain the definite connotation of the term but recognize that it did not cover the whole process. *Both* of these alternatives have been followed, with much resulting confusion.

Especially in the social and cultural realm, where exceptions to the complicative trend were being stressed, some writers insisted that "evolution" meant only "change," or "descent with modification," or, in Goldenweiser's phrase, "the idea of a changing and transmuting society." The only thing then ruled out was the old conception of a fixed order, produced by special creation. Thus loosely defined, the concept could still be applied to all change; organic, cultural, or other. But it had now lost much of its distinctive meaning, and the Spencerian idea of complication was hard to eliminate. So the term "evolution" gradually fell out of use, as being hopelessly unsound and misleading. This solution, which inflates and thins out the concept excessively, is condemned in Joseph Needham's article, cited above. "The word evolution," he writes, "has been applied by many writers to any process of change or becoming, but this use of the expression is not defensible."

The other alternative, followed in this book, is to retain the Spencerian idea of *complication* as one basic criterion of evolutionary change, but eliminate some of the others, especially those of universality, necessity, and progressiveness. Evolution is *not* co-extensive with all history, change, or becoming; not equivalent to the whole cosmic, organic, or cultural process, but only one phase or constituent tendency within them.

To what extent it is the *dominant*, prevailing trend of the universe or of life and culture is open to argument. One can say without risk that it is a widespread, long-enduring one which has dominated many lines of descent up to a certain point.

6. SPECIAL, SUPPLEMENTARY THEORIES ABOUT EVOLUTION IN VARIOUS FIELDS

In the biological field, there are several such theories, past and present, about the specific processes and factors by which evolution is said to operate: e.g., the transmission of acquired characteristics, natural selection, small "Darwinian" variations, mutations, and Mendelian laws of heredity. We have seen how religious and metaphysical theories have attempted to explain evolution on a deeper level with respect to biological and other phenomena. Some of these are: the development of the Cosmic Mind, according to Hegelian idealism; modern Christian, teleological interpretations of evolution, as by Tennyson; vitalism and creative evolution (Bergson): emergent evolution (Alex-

ander); materialism and mechanism (Lucretius, La Mettrie, Jacques Loeb, and others).

As to cultural evolution, including artistic, we have reviewed a number of associated theories, ancient and modern. These are listed or discussed in many articles on evolution, but usually without distinguishing them from the basic concept and general theory. Alexander Goldenweiser's article on "Evolution, Social," in the *Encyclopedia of Social Sciences* (the only one devoted to the cultural phase of the subject) gives no definition of "evolution" or of social or cultural evolution. After stating that "The idea of a changing and transmuting society was foreign to primitive culture"—which was certainly not true of Lucretius—it criticizes various theories of cultural stages and about matriarchy, parallelism, etc., as if these were essential, fatal weaknesses of evolutionism in general.

7. "EVOLUTION" AS DISTINCT FROM "PROGRESS."

As we have seen, Spencer used these terms almost interchangeably. He first applied the name "progress" to the cosmic process of increasing complexity, then the name "evolution." He came to prefer the latter as more objective and more descriptive of the mode or "law" by which the process operated. Either one, it is now believed, can occur without the other, and there is no exact correlation between them. Whether the arts evolve is largely a question of fact, to be settled by observing and describing the nature of successive changes in them. Whether the arts progress is essentially an evaluative question, involving standards for judging improvement or deterioration. Thus to separate the two concepts does not imply that they refer to two entirely separate processes. What we call "evolution" and what we call "progress" may still coincide in whole or in part. But increasing complexity in life or culture does not necessarily make for improvement in its quality. Adaptation to environment, as judged in terms of fitness for survival, does not always coincide with improvement in the moral, intellectual, or aesthetic quality of life.

To say that changes are "adaptive," in the sense of being conducive to survival, does involve a limited kind of evaluation. Biologists say that a certain organ, limb, or habit of life has or has not "survival value." This is related to value in general, insofar as all possibility of good conscious living is dependent on physical life and health. But it is a very limited kind of evaluation, which makes no distinction between good and bad, better and worse, in the quality of life. If the words "value" and "progress" are used in this limited biological sense, it should be made clear that they do not imply other kinds of value as well. All reference to moral, aesthetic, and other human values can be removed from the concept of evolution, thus making it cover changes which seem deplorable from a human standpoint, such as the development of poisonous fangs, predatory habits, or parasitic degeneration as a successful mode of survival.

To distinguish evolution from progress does not imply that there is no evaluative difference between simple and complex forms; that amoeba is as good as man, or that a degenerate parasite is as good as its livelier ancestors. The aim is to separate the idea of the process itself from all judgments of its value. Each raises a set of difficult problems which must be dealt with separately. By the human standards in which value is judged, a trend toward developing the necessary physical equipment for good experience is progressive; a trend for the better, or toward the better. A partial loss of it is a trend for the worse—potentially, at least, even if no actual difference in consciousness or sentiency occurs. But such alleged differences in value are expressions and projections of a human, anthropocentric point of view; not objective properties of the universe. By the biological standard of fitness for survival, the survival of *Amoeba* and *Sacculina* seems to indicate their superiority to the mammoth and to *Pithecanthropus Erectus*.

They may even prove their biological superiority to *Homo Sapiens* by outliving him.

But even by this standard something can be said for man, and for his evolution as progressive. Julian Huxley has recently restated the question of what kind of organic evolution deserves to be called "progressive." He answers it, both from the biological standpoint and from that of human values.[9] From the former, he takes as the "criterion of biological progress" greater control over the environment and greater independence of the environment. These trends have not, he shows, been characteristic of organic evolution as a whole, but only of the various dominant groups of animals which have successively emerged—trilobites, fish, reptiles, birds and mammals, and now man—to dominate the earth in various periods. Man's evolution can be judged as progressive, he says, from this biological standpoint; also from the standpoint of human value, because it involves an increase of aesthetic, intellectiual, and spiritual satisfaction. Likewise one may ask about art history, not only whether it has been an evolution, but whether it has been and probably will be a progressive evolution.[10]

8. "RETROGRESSION" AS THE OPPOSITE OF "PROGRESS"

The same care should be devoted to the concepts used as opposites of "progress" and "evolution." If, as here proposed, we use the former in the

[9] *Evolution: the Modern Synthesis* (New York, 1942). Progress, he says elsewhere, is a series of advances which do not stand in the way of other advances. (*Evolution in Action*, London, 1952).

[10] See, for example, C. L. Morgan, "Evolution and Mind," *Encyclopedia Britannica*, 14th ed. Another example of this type of definition is quoted by Lalande: "The word evolution does not, by itself, imply any idea of progress or of regression. It indicates all the transformations which an organism or a society undergoes, independently of whether these are favorable or unfavorable." *Vocabulaire technique et philosophique* (Paris, 1947), p. 301; quoting Demoor, Massart, and Vandervelde, *L'Evolution régressive*, p. 17.

sense of "large-scale improvement," it seems consistent to use "retrogression" in the sense of "large-scale deterioration" or return to a lower, worse condition.

The words "progression" and "reversion" have also a different, less evaluative sense. They refer to changes of smaller scope, not necessarily involving any increase or decrease in value or complexity. A *progression* is defined as "A continuous and connected series, as of acts, events, or steps; a sequence whose continuity suggests movement or flow; as, the slow progression of incidents in a play; a period of progression rather than of progress in industry." (Webster). A *reversion* is "A return toward some ancestral type or condition; the reappearance of an ancestral character or characters." (Webster). *Regression* is also used at times in this non-evaluative sense, as return to an earlier form or condition, which may be better or worse, simpler or more complex.

9. CONCEPTS MORE OR LESS OPPOSITE TO "EVOLUTION"

Since the history of art contains many countermovements, reversing to some extent the main trend of evolution, it is necessary to find terms for describing them. No single term is adequate. All have taken on confusing associations, which we must try to guard against.

The chief theoretical rivals of evolutionism, and in that sense its opposites, were the theory of *special creation* (that all organic types were created, fully formed, in the Garden of Eden and have not changed essentially since) and the theory of *degeneration* (that man and his culture have deteriorated since the Fall of Adam). These are not, however, direct antonyms of "evolution."

If "evolution" is defined without implications of improvement, its opposite should not imply deterioration. If the essential meaning of "evolution" is "increasing complexity," then its antithesis should mean *decreasing complexity*. It is hard to find such a term. All the words in common use for this purpose have taken on evaluative, derogatory connotations, partly from Spencer's theory. His favorite term, *dissolution*, suggests decay and death, and Spencer applied it to phenomena of decline and disintegration, as in the fall of an empire. Not realizing the extent to which regression and simplification could occur apart from dissolution, he saw no need of a neutral term for so describing them. Other terms in common use, such as "degeneration," "retrograde evolution," and "decadence," have likewise taken on pejorative meanings.

Undevelopment is a fairly neutral term for change in a direction opposite to growth. Etymologically, the best antithesis for "evolution" would seem to be "involution" or "devolution," and both these words have been so used.[11] We shall use *devolution*, without any evaluative implications. Devolution and regression can be good, bad, or indifferent.

The opposite of "complexity" is usually understood as "simplicity." The opposite of complication, then, is simplification. "Simple" is also an antonym for "compound" or "mixed"—i.e., for having different parts or elements. A thing is simple if it has few parts or little differentiation of its parts. A solid sphere, cube, or pyramid of uniform texture is simple by comparison with a tree or bird. But it is also definite, and thus not entirely unevolved. To change from a complex form to a simple, definite form would be only a partial devolution. However, persons who wish to reverse the evolutionary process often call for a return to "the simple life."

Evolutionary complication includes both differentiation and integration as reciprocal phases. Either can dominate at times, but if it is not even-

[11] *The Dictionary of Sociology* (Fairchild, ed.) defines "devolution" as "the reverse of evolution in the Spencerian sense," from a more complex to a simpler condition. The *Oxford Dictionary* quotes H. S. Carpenter in 1888 as writing, "If there be e-volution, there surely is de-volution, a degradation of the species."

tually balanced by the other, full development does not occur. Differentiation can be increased through increasing the number of parts. Conversely, it would be a partial devolution to decrease either (a) the number of parts or units, (b) the differences between them, (c) their integration or unity, or (d) their definiteness, individually or collectively. A process including all these tendencies would be thoroughly devolutionary. If carried far enough, it would lead to the dissolution and extinction of the form or type. It would be a return to the homogeneous, vague, and formless, as in the decay of a dead animal.

The history of art and of other cultural components discloses many examples of *partial* evolution or development, along certain lines only. Some show only differentiation, or only integration. There are also partial devolutions, including only certain constituent parts or phases of the form concerned. Such partial developments and undevelopments often proceed concurrently. They may reinforce or counteract each other. Visual realism may increase in painting at the expense of surface decoration. In such cases it is often hard to estimate the total, net change in terms of complication or simplification. Growth in one respect may require diminution in its opposite.

10. SUMMARY

The term "evolution" has acquired several different meanings through association with the theories of different writers. In arguing that evolution does or does not exist in the arts, it is well to indicate what one means by the term. As applied to both organic and cultural phenomena, two basic definitions have achieved wide, authoritative usage. They avoid many controversial issues raised by individual writers, and will be used in the following chapters. They state two general specifications, as follows: (1) *development or increasing complexity* and (2) *descent with adaptive modification and origination of new types.*

To deserve the name "evolution" in the full sense, a process of cultural change would have to manifest both characteristics to a considerable extent. The next few chapters will try to show that the history of the arts has been an evolution in this sense. A large-scale process of cultural descent with adaptive, cumulative, complicative change has occurred and is still occurring in them. This process is not universal, uniform, or necessarily permanent. It is subject to many exceptions and counter-movements.

The opposite of "evolution" is "devolution" or "regression." These terms imply simplification or reversal of the previous direction, but not necessarily change for the worse.

CHAPTER XV

TYPES OF ART: THEIR DESCENT
WITH ADAPTIVE MODIFICATION

I. THE NEED FOR SYSTEMATIC DEFINITION AND CLASSIFICATION OF ARTISTIC TYPES

That which "descends" in evolution is the type rather than the individual. In the biological realm it is the species, genus, or other type of organic structure and functioning. In the social realm it is the type of acquired skill and of collective, interpersonal behavior, as in the institution of marriage. As to whether art evolves, then, one must ask what types of art exist and are capable of descending from generation to generation.

Extreme historicism dismisses the question all too simply by denying that there are any types of art, at least in the essentials of art. Rejecting this answer as false, our next step must be to distinguish some types which will be at least as valid for the realm of art as those of "vertebrate" and "mammal" are for animals.

A few artistic types have been distinguished in aesthetics ever since the Greek period, as in Plato's concept of "imitative" (representational) art and in Aristotle's contrast between the epic, tragic, and comic. These and a few other traditional genres, mostly in literature, were far from enough to cover, even superficially, the tremendous variety of forms and functions in world art. Up to the present time, they have too often been conceived in a pre-evolutionary way as static, fixed, and mutually exclusive categories. Other traditional "aesthetic categories" such as the beautiful, sublime, and ugly have been so strongly evaluative

and controversial as to unfit them for use in objective classification.

In recent years, many other concepts of artistic types have come into use, such as the "sound film" and the "animated cartoon film," but no systematic taxonomy or typology has been worked out to cover all major types in all the arts. That is a task of aesthetic morphology, which is still in a rudimentary state. The present chapter undertakes to sketch out a method for developing such a system. It must be empirical and flexible, allowing for future changes and for the impossibility of forcing works of art into any simple, rigid system.

As noted in a previous chapter, aesthetics is now in a state somewhat analogous to that of biology at the time of Linnaeus in the eighteenth century, when no satisfactory nomenclature or classification of organic types existed. It was impossible to demonstrate the evolution of types when the types themselves had not been systematically distinguished. As Merz points out, the eighteenth and early nineteenth centuries in biology and related fields were mainly devoted to such a survey and classification of the phenomena. With such a map before them, it was only a step (though a crucial and difficult step) to add the temporal dimension and to recognize change within the system of types. The multiplicity of subordinate types under each main heading suggested a genetic relationship among them on the basis of analogous structures and functions. It suggested the multilinear differ-

[225]

entiation of subordinate types from the few main, relatively undifferentiated ones. The impossibility of drawing sharp lines between all plant and animal types and the frequent occurrence of borderline cases further suggested a process of transition from one to the other. Without assuming too confidently that history will repeat itself in the realm of art, it is not unreasonable to strive with this in mind for a more adequate typology of art. To clarify existing methods of nomenclature and classification in this field would have many other values, theoretical and practical.

2. GENERIC AND RECURRENT TRAITS OF ART AS CONTRASTED WITH UNIQUE, INDIVIDUAL ONES.

We have referred several times to the anti-evolutionist argument that every work of art is unique, the product of a unique creative act, and possessing a mysterious X which differentiates it from all others. This X, the essential spirit of the work, does not, it is said, descend in time; there is no continuity of influence or growth in it from earlier to later, and no evolution. As against this mystical view, science tends to stress the resemblances and continuities throughout nature, history, civilization and art.

Both views can be carried to excess. The very fact that we can distinguish recurrent traits and types in art—the realistic and the decorative, the epic and the portrait, the hymn and the dance— implies some resemblance and persistence through time. As we have seen, every work of art is unique in some ways, like every individual star, plant, and animal. In other ways it resembles others, at least to the extent that it can be classed as a work of art; perhaps also as a poem, a temple, a symphony, or a ballet. Through the stylistic analysis and comparison of forms, one can further observe that any two poems, any two paintings or symphonies, resemble each other in specific ways, such as language, rhythm, subject, key, coloring, instrumentation, and emotional tone, while differing in others. Point by point, the observer who begins by proclaiming, "They are utterly different; they can't be compared," is forced to recognize that every work of art resembles others in a multitude of ways. The same general types of line and color, of rhythm, scale, and melodic figure, of rhyme and imagery, recur again and again with variations in the art of peoples remote in time and place. Not only techniques and sensory qualities but "spiritual qualities"—ideals, beliefs, hopes, feelings, meanings, aspirations, all appear and reappear. Not only details but modes of composition, ways of organizing the whole—as into sonnets, novels, temples, or symphonies—are recurrent configurations in the history of art.

As morphological analysis becomes more refined, we can state more precisely what distinguishes the art of Chopin from that of Schumann, and one Chopin mazurka from another. Sometimes the differences are so slight as to deceive the experts, as in early copies of Chinese paintings. Sometimes they are great and susceptible to fairly objective description, as in comparing Shakespeare's plays with those of other Elizabethan dramatists and with earlier versions of the plots he employed. Titian's style is fairly close to Giorgione's; consequently it is sometimes hard to distinguish between their works. But neither could be confused with Fra Angelico. Every painting by Titian is unique in certain ways and in certain ways similar to other works by Titian and the Venetian school.

The progress of morphological and stylistic analysis involves increasing ability to perceive and describe the subtle nuances of resemblance and difference. It helps us to distinguish more exactly between the unique and the generic in each case, and to put both into words. This includes much which was formerly regarded as indescribable, an utterly mysterious *je ne sais quoi*. Much remains which cannot yet be clearly described, but it is steadily decreasing in scope.

The artist and the lover are characteristically devoted to the unique and particular, or what seems to them to be so. Each lover is sure that his beloved is "like no other woman in the world." A mother feels strongly the uniqueness of each of her children; an artist, that of each of his works. They tend to resent and resist an emphasis on similarities, as somehow derogatory. The artistic attitude toward life and the world usually stresses the qualitative, concrete, and particular, though not exclusively so. Art does, at times, deal with generalities; with universalized abstractions as in symbols of Everyman, his vices and virtues. But it usually tries to present these through concrete embodiments, leaving pure abstraction to science and philosophy. Even so-called "abstract painters" try to create unique, original products; they often resent the suggestion that their works resemble, or are derived from, those of other artists.

Supernaturalist philosophers like Croce are akin to the artist, the lover, and the parent in insisting on the uniqueness of each work of art and in denouncing aesthetic analysis. The latter, says Croce, "annihilates the work." (*Aesthetic*, p. 20). To the naturalist, this seems absurd. How can any kind of thinking about art injure the work itself? It remains just as it was. Analysis may interfere, at least at the moment, with rapt, emotional contemplation. But the chief aim of aesthetic analysis is not immediate enjoyment but knowledge and understanding; not of a single object alone, but of art as a realm of human activity and product, in relation to other such realms. To gain this end, scientific aesthetics must describe the similarities and social, long-range aspects of art.

At the same time, the aesthetician should not ignore the unique aspects, but give a fair account of both. Overemphasis on similarities and continuities may lure him into some new variant of the "reductionist fallacy." Because A is somewhat like B, or somewhat influenced by B, one assumes that it is "nothing but" a case of B, or that it can be fully described and explained as "merely a result" of B. Since art often emphasizes the unique and particular, the concrete and personal, scientific accounts of art should be especially careful not to underestimate them by "reducing" all its phenomena to a few general types.

All attempts at a philosophic or scientific study of art, including the Platonic and Christian, the aesthetic, moral, religious, and social points of view, tend to emphasize certain types and traits, rather than the whole, individual work of art as unique and isolated. The evolutionary approach also tends to emphasize the long-range, large-scale sequence of events, the succession of types and stages, rather than the particular object viewed intensively. The psychoanalytic approach to art tends to minimize the highly differentiated, civilized, adult, expert characteristics of an artist and his work in tracing them back to infantile, primitive, and sub-rational causes, in which all humans are more alike. The tendency thus to look beyond the present moment to its context in the total flow and fabric of things is necessary for the sake of broader understanding, evaluation, and control. Those who attack it fundamentally are attacking reason, science, and philosophy in general.

3. TRAITS AND TYPES IN ART AS COMPARED WITH ORGANIC TYPES. AESTHETIC TAXONOMY

Any observable characteristic of a work of art, or any of its culturally established meanings, is a *trait*. Thus redness and rectangular shape can be traits of a painting; slow tempo and violin-tone, of a piece of music. A cross, in certain contexts, symbolizes Christianity. Such a meaning or suggestive power in a work of art is a *trait*, as in a picture of someone kneeling before a cross. A distinctive mode of selection or of organization involving many details can also be a trait, such as "polyphonic" in music and "tragic" in drama. It is a compound trait if it has to be defined in terms of several characteristics.

[227]

A trait is an abstract quality, having no existence apart from the concrete object, sound, or other phenomenon to which it belongs. A round, red, smooth layer of paint in a picture is a concrete object, a concrete detail or compound part of the picture. Roundness, redness, and smoothness are abstract component traits, distinguished by the human mind through comparative analysis, and given a different name in each language. As an object of aesthetic experience, the picture is not a physical object but a total, visual configuration, which the educated observer can analyze into a complex of diversified traits, each with its own name and conceptual meaning. A given trait will differ somewhat according to the complex in which it occurs. In ordinary aesthetic experience one analyzes only to a very slight extent if at all, but for scientific study the process of analysis and conceptualization must be carried farther.

A *type* is a class, group, or kind, distinguished on the ground that its members possess a certain trait or traits in common. Any trait may be used as the basis of a type: the type or class of things which have that trait in common. Large works of art are a type, and small ones are another. "Rectangular paintings" constitute a type, and brown ones another; so do violin music, polyphonic music, and tragedy. A type may be conceived in terms of one or many traits. In the latter case it is a compound type. To define a symphony requires several specifications: Webster's dictionary defines it as "An elaborate instrumental composition in sonata form for a full orchestra." The word "type" is roughly equivalent to "kind," as in saying "a man of his type." In technical usage it suggests a kind or category which has been explicitly recognized and defined with some precision. The French word *genre* is almost synonymous, in the sense in which the *fabliau* is a literary genre. In Webster's terms, it is a category applied to literature or art as falling into distinctive groups with respect to style, form, purpose, etc. The words *genus* and *species* are also closely akin to "type" in their broad senses, derived from the

Latin. All are roughly equivalent to "kind" or "class." But "genus" and "species" have come to take on more restricted meanings in biology, as designating certain kinds of type: those on certain levels in the system of classification. A species is then intermediate in breadth between a genus and a subspecies or variety. But in the expression "origin of species," it refers more loosely to organic types in general. "Genus" and "species" are not much used in reference to art. In this field, the terms "genre," "style," and "manner" are often used in special, restricted senses, but not consistently so. In the present book, the word "type" will refer to any kind of class, organic or cultural, which can be defined in terms of some fairly objective trait or traits.

As biological taxonomy has developed, increasingly precise meanings have been assigned to various kinds of structural type, class, or phylum in the system from broadest to narrowest groupings. Thus a dog belongs to the Kingdom Animalia, the Phylum Chordata, the Subphylum Vertebrata, the Class Mammalia, the Subclass Eutheria, the Order Carnivora, the Family Canidae, the Genus Canis, and the Species Familiaris. Each group or type is defined in terms of a set of distinguishing characteristics: e.g., the vertebrates have an internal skeleton with a backbone and skull; the eutheria nourish their young, while in the womb of the mother, through a placenta.

Biologists have developed a *taxonomy* based on significant structural characteristics: those connected with a number of basic, far-reaching differences in form and function. To say that an animal is a vertebrate or invertebrate, a mammal or reptile, is significant in this way. To say that it is carnivorous or herbivorous, a marine or land animal, is less significant as a way of characterizing its structure and functioning. These are nonstructural types. Many different kinds of animals and plants inhabit the sea, including air-breathing mammals as well as fish. Many different kinds of animal—insects, fish, reptiles, birds, mammals, etc., and even insectivorous plants—eat flesh and thus belong to the type "carnivore," in a broad, non-structural sense of that term.

Types of art are not, and can not be at present, defined or classified with any approximation to the clarity and system of biological taxonomy. They change, divide, and merge rapidly in modern culture. Nevertheless, there are partial analogies. Literature, for example, is a type of art which includes prose and verse; fiction is a type of literary prose; the novel, short story, and anecdote are types of prose fiction. Some types of art are distinguished on structural or morphological grounds: for example, the sonata, the sonnet, and the arabesque. Some are distinguished functionally, in terms of use—e.g., the dwelling, the hat, the sword, the cup—but these imply certain structural traits as means to the functions. However, a certain need or function can be filled by different types of form in culture as in organic life.

For the development of an adequate *system of types in art*, one must consider the various possible bases of division and classification. Common to aesthetics and biology are the concepts of form and function, including the shape, arrangement, and dynamic interaction of parts; also mode of interaction with the environment. The concept of function leads us, in biology, to examine the utility of an organ or instinct for survival of the individual and type. In aesthetics, it leads us to examine the way in which a work or type of art or one of its parts operates in the social environment; how it succeeds or fails in satisfying human needs and wants, including aesthetic ones. This may lead to its survival or abandonment, and to the survival or destruction of its users.

Many bases and differentiae, commonly used to distinguish types, are too vague, subjective, or evaluative to serve well descriptively. Such are "fine art," "beautiful arts," "belles lettres," "creative arts," "liberal and servile arts," "major and minor arts." Some of these derive from ancient class distinctions in an aristocratic society. Some imply greater spiritual value. "Popular art," "élite art," "official art," and "avant-garde art" may refer to the kind of public or patronage, rather to the form or function of the art itself. Consequently, they include a great many different structural or formal types. Such various ways of defining and classifying types have their uses, including the evaluative. Different systems of classification are needed for different theoretical and practical purposes.

Every work of art belongs to several types in respect to different traits. For example, a picture can be at once a mural painting, a fresco, a crucifixion, a decorative design, and an example of fifteenth-century Florentine style. Some types of art are defined so as to be mutually exclusive or almost so: for example, visual art and auditory art. A mural painting belongs entirely in the visual type, a piano sonata in the auditory. But this does not prevent some works of art from having traits in common with both types. Thus the opera is an audiovisual type, and mobile color is sometimes called "color music."

Some ways in which works of art are classified refer to their external connections. One of these is in terms of *provenance:* the geographical, chronological, and social origins of the product. Thus we speak of oriental and occidental, North and South American, ancient and medieval art, or more specifically of Southern Chinese art in the Sung dynasty. Specifying the social and cultural context, we may distinguish between a Florentine nobleman's costume in the fifteenth century and that of an eighteenth-century peasant woman in Saxony. Such terms give no direct indication of the nature of the product, although, to one who knows the period, they will suggest certain definite types of product.

One of the commonest ways to classify works of art is in terms of the *art*—in the sense of *skill or process*—by which it was produced. Often the same word, such as "painting", is used interchangeably for the process and the product. But the meanings of these words are variable. "Sculpture" now includes, not only works produced by carving, but statues, reliefs, abstract three-dimensional designs, mobiles, and other types of form, produced by many different technics in a great variety of materials. "Architecture" also includes a great variety of materials and of designing and building processes. It is distinguished from other arts partly in terms of the form and function of its products, as consisting of buildings large enough to be entered, lived in, or used for some other active purpose. The art of furniture-making has likewise become so diversified in material and process that it must be distinguished mainly on the basis of form and function in the product. Music is performed by a great variety of instruments and reproduced by others.

As the name of a traditional art comes to cover more and more different kinds of material, tool or instrument, process, form, and function, it becomes less exactly descriptive; it ceases to stand for any one particular type or set of characteristics. One has more and more difficulty in tracing its history as a continuous thread or set of threads. This shows that some evolution is taking place: the products classed under each of these traditional names are becoming more differentiated. Being more diverse and scattered in process, product, and use, the art becomes less integrated as a single area of culture. Such a term as "handicrafts" becomes increasingly vague as partly or wholly machine-made products are classed within it. "Decorative arts" in a museum is a catch-all term for countless types of product, from small sculpture to pottery and textiles, jewelry and miniature painting. Although histories are written of such heterogeneous realms of art, they find it difficult to trace the continuities in development.

4. DESCENT
WITH MODIFICATION IN THE ARTS

There is no definite limit to the number of possible types in art, from the standpoint of modern aesthetics and art history. New ones such as free verse and the documentary film are constantly appearing, derived in part from older types. The film drama is descended from the stage drama and the still photograph. A belief in the fixity of a limited number of artistic types went along with that in fixed animal species in the pre-evolutionary world-view, including that of Aristotle. The evolutionary conception of art implies a belief in the "origin of species" in that realm: in the continuous, unlimited *transformation* of older types of art into newer ones, through small gradual steps or larger mutations.

Types of art, like those of plants and animals, overlap in many cases so that sharp distinctions between them are impossible. Modern tragi-comedy is on the borderline between tragedy and comedy in the classical sense. So is the "failure story,"[1] a new type of drama and fiction involving some features of tragedy, but not its classical nobility and magnitude. No stigma is now attached to such hybrid types or *mélanges des genres* if they prove their worth in other ways.

The conception of a type, in art as elsewhere, is abstract and general. From the standpoint of a nominalist philosophy, it can have no existence apart from its concrete embodiments: from examples possessing the traits by which it is defined. To say that a type recurs here and there, at different times, can in fact mean only that examples possessing these traits occur at various times and places.

When a biologist speaks of "descent" among animals and plants, he refers to the processes of physiological generation, sexual or otherwise, by which younger individuals are derived from older ones. Individual organisms thus "descend" from their ancestors, and modern types of plants and animals from ancestral types. The class of birds (*Aves*) is said to be descended from that of reptiles, with *Archaeopteryx*, a primitive reptile-like bird of

[1] See "The Failure Story: a Study of Contemporary Pessimism" and "The Failure Story: an Evaluation," by T. Munro. *Journal of Aesthetics and Art Criticism*, XVII, 2 (Dec. 1958), pp. 143–168; XVII, 3 (Mar. 1959), pp. 352–387.

the Jurassic period, as an intermediate type. Cultural descent resembles organic descent in that certain types of form and functioning are transmitted from one generation to the next through long periods of time. Similarities in the costumes, products, dress, language, laws, beliefs, attitudes, and social institutions of a people endure through centuries. They undergo adaptive modification in the process, and new or altered types emerge.

The fact that types of art descend through time in this sense would seem obvious enough to require no argument, were it not for some of the objections made by anti-evolutionists. We have noted Aldous Huxley's assertion that all art "begins with each artist"; also Peter Fingesten's, that "No work of art... can be connected to a previous one 'through generation'" since every work of art "'was made' uniquely and did not 'grow' in the sense of the theory of evolution."[2] It seems hardly necessary to say that no evolutionist ever thought of works of art as "generating" or reproducing themselves directly as do plants and animals; certainly a statue does not divide in two or mate with another to produce offspring. Cultural descent proceeds through imitation and education, preserving and symbolic recording, transmitting skills, knowledge, aims, and beliefs from one generation to the next. Only in a figurative way can any work of art be said to produce or influence another. It can do so only indirectly, through the intermediary of some human individual, whose perceptual, imaginative, affective, and motor functions it stimulates in a certain way. It may thus inspire an artist to produce a work somewhat similar.

Cultural descent, unlike organic descent, proceeds entirely through the transmission of acquired characteristics, although it can be influenced by genetic, physiological variations along the way. By definition, only acquired traits and types are classed as artistic or cultural; the constructive instincts of the bee, the bird, and the ant are not artistic or cultural, regardless of the beauty of the product. Artistic and other cultural traits can be transmitted only through being acquired or imitated by someone else; thus "acquirement" or learning characterizes the manner as well as the content of cultural descent. But this power to learn, accumulate, and transmit culture is an inborn, distinguishing trait of man, transmitted in varying amounts through his physical genes.

The idea of "heredity" is somewhat ambiguous. Heredity can be physiological or cultural. In contrast with "environment," it refers to the inborn, endogenous heritage of an individual or species. But we also speak of a "cultural heritage," including the arts, and of cultural inheritance as a continuous process; it is the same as "transmission," but from the inheritor's point of view.

Particular works of art, such as the Egyptian Sphinx and pyramids, can be handed down as parts of the cultural heritage. A single work of art, thus enduring through the ages, can undergo a sort of evolution in its own history. The Homeric epics are thought to have developed from simpler beginnings into complex literary forms. These forms, as first declaimed and then written down in Greece, have been modified by much editing and translation into other languages, to adapt them for study in different countries. The same words come to mean somewhat different things.

A *type* of art, being a class or species, descends in a different way: in the fact that works of art possessing the traits by which it is defined are produced in temporal sequence and with some causal connection; not as totally detached, independent inventions. In addition to such descent, many types and traits in art are invented independently. The causal connection is close when the maker of the later work not only sees or hears the first work, but learns about its making from the man who made it. There is somewhat less connection when he only sees or hears it, or perhaps a poor reproduction or description of it, without knowing the artist or his methods. The connection is presumably close when successive examples are made by members of the same family

[2] See also previous references to W. P. Ker and T. S. Eliot.

(e.g., the Bachs) or by master and apprentice in the same guild or studio. The influence can be very indirect and long delayed, as when a statue is buried for centuries, then dug up (as in the Renaissance) to resume its influence. It is not implied that the earlier work is the sole or sufficient cause of the later. Many other factors will necessarily influence the later work and the whole process of cultural descent. In the organic realm also, many factors in addition to physical heredity cooperate to determine the total process of descent with adaptive modification. We shall return in a later chapter to the subject of causation in cultural descent.

The descent with modifications of a certain basic type such as the axe, the animal drawing, or the sculptured human figure can be traced through millennia, with some continuity in spite of many gaps. To say that the jade ceremonial axe "descended" from the bronze utilitarian axe, and the bronze from the neolithic stone axe, involves much arbitrary simplification, but is true to some extent. In this way, quasi-genetic sequences have been worked out for various types of sword, polearm, helmet, shield, and body-armor.[3] Such diagrams are necessarily much more simplified and inadequate to represent the facts than similar charts of biological descent, such as those for the ancestry of the horse. To represent the sequence as a single or branching line of descent ignores the constant pressure of external influences from the physical and cultural environment, including other arts. For example, some renaissance shields are influenced by renaissance sculptural reliefs; some sword decoration by Near Eastern enamels. But even a highly abstract schematic diagram can be suggestive and partly accurate. Similar sequences have been worked out for types of house, temple, church, chair, women's clothing, portrait, and landscape painting. The ritual hymn, the hunting dance, the work-song, the heroic cycle, and various types of folk-tale such as that of the clever animal, likewise descend with modification through time. Their descent involves frequent splitting into sub-

types and merging with others into combined ones. To trace the process accurately, the type must be analyzed into its constituent parts and traits, such as the blade, hilt, grip, and pommel of a sword, its materials, dimensions, shape, hardness, flexibility, and ornamentation. In terms of these, continuities and modifications are measured and changes explained, as in the increase of surface ornamentation when swords became a decorative feature of aristocratic costume, rather than a necessary weapon. The type thus adapts itself to a changing cultural environment.

In music, a sequence of changes was assembled in chronological order by the Italian composer Alfredo Casella.[4] To include whole musical compositions would have rendered the sequence confusingly large and hard to follow; but Casella restricted it to a hundred examples of the perfect cadence from the thirteenth century to Schönberg in the twentieth. Continuous, gradual change, over and above individual stylistic traits, is evident in the manner of proceeding from the subdominant to the dominant to the tonic tone or chord. There is a prevailing trend toward extension and elaboration of the cadence, and of enrichment by harmonic, rhythmic, and instrumental coloring.

Many progressions have been pointed out in the history of architecture; for example, in Banister Fletcher's chart of "The Evolution of Gothic Vaulting."[5] Others could easily be made in sculpture and painting: for example, in Greek sculpture

---

[3] Bashford Dean prepared a series of diagrams, based on the armor collection of Metropolitan Museum of Art in New York. They showed the descent of each type through successive periods which he compared to geological horizons. While pointing out the difference between such "evolution of objects" and organic evolution, he stressed the analogies also. They were, he said, especially close "when objects represent the work of the brains and hands of generations of the same family of artists." *Bulletin of the Metropolitan Museum of Art*, Vol. X, No. 8 (Aug. 1915), p. 173 n., with diagram of the development of helmets, p. 175. He made a similar one for daggers in *Catalogue of European Daggers* (New York, 1929), p. 7, and for swords in *Catalogue of European Court Swords and Hunting Swords* (New York, 1929), p. 7.

[4] *The Evolution of Music* (London, 1924).

[5] *History of Architecture* (London, 1931), p. 328.

from Myron to Praxiteles; in Italian painting from Giotto through Raphael and Veronese. This last was, indeed, prolonged in some respects well into the seventeenth century and beyond, in spite of concurrent changes from "classic" to "mannerist" and "baroque" style. Such a sequence is not necessarily continuous in all respects, and seldom is over a long period. As to colors and contours, such radical shifts as that from "linear" to "painterly" could be made, while in other respects pictorial innovation held to a fairly persistent course.

From Giotto at least as far as Bruegel, Poussin and Claude Lorrain, this course can be summarized as the *development of the single vista*. Giotto's massively modeled figures were few in number, arranged in shallow space with fairly even lighting. Masaccio and Uccello complicated the scene with more diversely lighted figures in different, active postures, and with more elaborate perspective to a farther distance. This approach was still further elaborated by Raphael in the Vatican frescoes, and the great Venetians enriched it with subtle variations in color, surface texture, and luminous atmosphere. In Bruegel's "Winter, the Return of the Hunters," we see a vast expanse to far-off peaks and chilly skies, over a valley populous with skaters, houses, and other details. The light of nearby fires is smoothly adjusted to varying natural illumination. Throughout this long progression, the underlying trend is toward developing a complex, imaginary, realistic view into space, as if from a single point of view, at a single moment of time, under a single set of atmospheric conditions.

A somewhat similar progression was made in Hellenistic painting, at least up to such an elaborate, subtly lighted vista into deep space as that of the "Combat with the Lestrygonians" in the *Odyssey* series, now in the Vatican. But that kind of painting was almost unknown in the early renaissance. The emphasis on developing the single vista distinguishes European renaissance painting from the chief Byzantine, Persian miniature, and Chinese sequences. It involved gradually eliminating the simultaneous portrayal of different moments or episodes in a story, although this practice appears as late as Veronese's "Rape of Europa." It involved the elimination of multiple perspective, as in the Indian Buddhist wall-paintings at Ajanta; of unrealistic differences in the scale of figures, and of views through a stone wall, as in Byzantine and Sienese painting. By the seventeenth century, the main outlines of the spacious, complex vista had been perfected. The next two centuries tended to specialize on smaller, more intensive aspects of the scene with figures, and at the end of the nineteenth century a radical shift in direction occurred.

Artistic and other cultural traits differ from organic traits in being much more easily detached and recombined, often with traits from other sources. Geneticists are making some advance in rearranging particular genes, but it remains a difficult process. Natural evolution does it in a slow and limited way.

Much Greek sculpture was colored; later, color was usually omitted, but when any sculptor wishes to reintroduce it he can easily do so. Instrumental music can be combined with poetry and song or separately developed. The pictorial aspects of painting and photography are combined with the temporal, mobile aspects of drama and music in the film; but they can easily be detached again and fitted into some different combination. This ease of rearranging traits in art does not, of course, guarantee that the new arrangement will catch public favor and thus endure as a type.

Organic descent with modification is multilinear, but cultural descent is more so and increasingly so, as man develops power to select and recombine his cultural traits more consciously. Particular combinations of traits do descend in culture, but less tenaciously than organic ones. They are much more fluid and floating, increasingly variable as urban civilization develops, being less rigidly determined by physical structure and environment. This is especially true of artistic characteristics, and most of all in modern Western civilization. Here they become increasingly free from lasting, urgent requirements of a utilitarian, religious, social or ideological nature, and more susceptible to the capricious fluctuations of artistic impulse and public taste. Such increasing diversity makes it harder to discern the relatively constant factors or correlations in artistic phenomena.

5. ADAPTIVE MODIFICATION IN THE ARTS

Change in the forms of culture proceeds in relation to environments, both physical and cultural. The physical environment includes the natural setting and resources in which the group lives at any one time, and also the physical features introduced by man, such as roads and buildings. These last are partly cultural, but the cultural environment includes also the more intangible setting of customs, beliefs, attitudes, and activities. A special branch of culture, such as art, religion, or science, has for its environment at any one time all the rest of the culture-pattern of the people concerned. Each part is affected by every other part, directly or indirectly. Changes in the types of form within any particular area, such as education, must to some extent adapt themselves to those of other areas. Reciprocal influence is constant in a closely knit culture, with different parts exerting more or less influence on the whole at different times and places.

As cultural traits and groups of traits in art descend through time, they often travel socially and geographically as well, from one class, region, and people to another. In the process, they become altered by adaptation to the new and changing environments, physical and cultural. Buddhism and Buddhist art underwent extensive modifications in traveling from India to Indonesia, China, Tibet, and Japan. Christianity and Christian art developed along different lines in the Western and Eastern Roman Empires, in feudal Europe, Protestant Germany, and American industrial democracy. The necessary adaptation of architecture to climate,

topography, materials, and functions was pointed out long before Taine, by Vitruvius and others. A type of functional form such as the wheel is modified in going to different physical environments such as water, ice, and sand. In one cultural environment it may become a Buddhist prayer-wheel, and in another the landing-wheel of an airplane. Such changes are adaptive, not only in responding to environmental influence, but in doing so in ways which tend to favor the persistence of the wheel as a utilitarian type, and of the culture in which it functions. Symbols such as the swastika change meaning as they migrate.

Various kinds of artistic type descend through time. There are, first, the *arts* themselves as types of skill and occupation: painting, sculpture, architecture, poetry, singing, dancing. Each involves a certain set of *technics*, exercised in dealing with a certain type of material or medium such as paint, stone, words, or musical tones. Their descent through the ages is shown in their products from the Ice-age to the present, and in contemporary descriptions and representations; for example, in Egyptian pictures and Biblical descriptions of dancers and musicians. Each of these traditional skills has been adapted to changing environments. As time elapsed, many of them were organized into occupational classes, guilds, craft unions, and professional organizations; also into schools and academies. Sculpture has changed its technics in relation to the *materials* available, such as bone, stone, wood, clay, bronze, gems, and gold; in relation to general *technology*, such as the development of metallurgy and casting; and in relation to the *social* and *religious* patterns of Egypt, Greece, Rome, and medieval Europe.

"Adaptation" in general is defined by Webster as "adjustment to environmental conditions." "To adapt" is "to alter so as to fit for a new use" or "to render fit, by changing, to meet the demands of a new environment." The migration of this concept into the cultural field has required some adaptation in the concept itself. It has led to a distinction between several different kinds of adaptation, including "passive" and "active." Practically all pre-cultural adaptation, it is said, has been passive in the sense that the species of plant or animal (including man) has undergone the changes in its own bodily structure which are necessary to fit it for survival in a new environment, or to fit it more perfectly for survival in the same environment. This has occurred through genetic variation and natural selection.[6] Man as a genus originated in this way. But since then, his power to think, learn, transmit, and accumulate skills has allowed him to change his environment instead, so as to fit his needs more perfectly.

Most of the efforts of human culture have operated to change the environment in one way or another: primarily, so as to insure food and water supply, the right amount of body warmth, safety from disease and enemies, and other things necessary for survival as a species. Man's inherited bodily equipment has changed little since his appearance as *Homo Sapiens*, according to present opinion. He has seldom tried to change it through eugenics, but has tried to make it healthier within the same innate, generic pattern. Meanwhile, he has radically changed and developed his earthly environment in a lasting, cumulative way through technology. His physical environment is now, to a large extent, a cultural one, as wild nature is changed into farms and cities. In addition, he has built up a mental environment in the form of transmitted ideas, knowledge, and attitudes. These are preserved and transmitted through linguistic and other symbols. Much of man's attention and waking life is directed toward this complex mental environment, along with the symbolic forms in which it is expressed. Some of these are scientific, some religious, some artistic. Much of the new environment, both tangible and intangible, belongs to utilitarian technology, as in coal mines and drainage systems. Some is definitely artistic, as in art museum collections and symphony concerts.

No one can deny that the arts, including literature and music as well as the visual arts, have played a major part in the active adaptation of the earth to serve man's needs and wishes. A great deal of the new environment, both tangible and intangible, can be classed as art, whether good, bad, or indifferent. In cottages and palaces, newspapers and magazines, radio and television programs, it is so intended and received by millions. In other words, a large part of man's control of his environment has been through the arts, along with more purely utilitarian skills and products.

As to what is strictly "adaptive" and what is not, the usual criterion is the biological one—conduciveness to survival of the species. So far, the passive modifications which gave man a complex brain and an opposable thumb have proven highly adaptive, though his stubborn aggressiveness may eventually bring about his downfall. The utilitarian portion of his cultural achievement has also proven adaptive in helping him to conquer the earth and multiply profusely. His arts, too, can be appraised on this biological basis. Spencer and others have made a good case for music and for art in general as helping to build up social sympathy, communication, and solidarity. They argue that music, dance, and theater have provided recreation, release, and pleasure, thus making life more healthy, attractive, and worth trying to maintain.

The opposite case has also been well argued, especially as to luxurious, civilized art. Ancient philosophers and prophets denounced it for causing war and crime. It has stimulated greed, divided people into hostile religious, political, and racial groups. (Even so, the biologist may insist, the resulting struggles have contributed to natural selection and the survival of the fittest.) Plato and others have said that some kinds of art make people soft, indolent, unfit to serve as soldiers or vigorous leaders. Religious art which glorifies the chaste, celibate life seems hardly conducive to the survival of the species. Yet this and other means of birth control may, within limits, be adaptive in preventing overpopulation, and hence favorable to the species as a whole. Modern critics such as

---

[6] Some animals, such as the beaver, modify their environments, but only to a slight extent and not cumulatively.

Ruskin have deplored the ugliness and unhealthiness of industrial civilization which defaces the countryside with smoking chimneys. Instead of beautifying it, we often fill it with hideous billboards and monotonous suburban slums. On the other hand, literature and other arts undertake to tell us forcibly of our mistakes: of slums as breeders of crime and disease; of wars as unnecessary evils. Painting at times presents us with symbols of beauty and harmony; at other times with those of anger and anxiety. Art often attempts to improve itself and the civilization around it by negative images and attitudes. It dramatizes evaluative problems and helps us think them out.

The effect of art on human survival can thus be regarded as beneficial in some respects, harmful or uncertain in others. Much modern art seems to have little effect on survival one way or another. It is interesting, enjoyable, sometimes educational, but far removed from the basic problems of health and survival. (Some poster art serves these ends today.) Those we leave rather to scientific technology, education, and government. Through increasing specialization and division of labor, the arts have been left to some extent in a realm apart, welcome to some and distasteful to others, of "art for art's sake" and art for aesthetic values. From the biological standpoint, they become increasingly non-adaptive as they separate themselves from vital concerns. Totalitarian régimes seek to harness them again to the quest for survival and power of some particular government or form of government. As cultivated for purely aesthetic values, they may not operate either for or against survival as much as art in earlier epochs did.

Julian Huxley finds no difficulty in turning from the strictly biological aspects of evolution and progress to their aesthetic, intellectual, and humanistic ones. He is careful not to confuse the two, or to project a cultural, anthropomorphic point of view into biological considerations where it has no place. Without confusing them, we may note that common language recognizes a kind of adaptation which is concerned with aesthetic and other psychological needs, rather than with mere physical survival. One speaks frequently of psychological "adjustment" between individuals, or between an individual and his environment. A slum environment may be emotionally and spiritually depressing to a sensitive, humanitarian artist, as it was to Dickens and Zola. In that situation, he can either adapt himself passively to it, through developing a callous, indifferent attitude, or try to change it actively, or move away to a different one. A man who tries to beautify the physical surroundings of himself and others is an artist; he is actively adapting the physical milieu to his own and their aesthetic needs. The result may be adaptive in the biological sense, or only in the psychological sense, or both. The two are intimately connected even though they vary somewhat independently.

It is not far-fetched, then, to say that the development of art has, on the whole, been adaptive in transforming man's environment so as to enhance the aesthetic and other psychological values of life, in addition to strengthening his physical hold on life itself. At the same time, we must grant that it has not done either with uniform success, or to the fullest possible extent. It can become not only non-adaptive but maladaptive when developed to excess in ways harmful to physical survival.

6. TYPES OF ARTISTIC PRODUCT, ACCORDING TO MODES OF TRANSMISSION, COMPONENTS, SPATIO-TEMPORAL AND CAUSAL ORGANIZATION

Modern aesthetic morphology, through analyzing and comparing the products of all arts, periods, and places, formulates certain basic principles of description and classification. It distinguishes many more types of art, in every medium, than were recognized in the traditional *genres*. Some of these cut across the older classifications based on particular arts. Certain concepts of material (physical and psychological), of process, form, and style, apply to all or many arts and serve as bases for the systematic description of artistic types.

(a) A work of art operates by *transmitting* certain sensory stimuli and suggested meanings to the observer. (The "transmission" especially referred to here is not general, cultural transmission from one generation to another but from the work of art to the observer and, indirectly, from the artist to the observer. General cultural transmission operates through such particular transmissions and in other ways.) Two main *modes of transmission* are distinguished: *presentation* and *suggestion*. The *presented* factor in a work of art includes its stimuli to direct, sensory perception: especially to sight and hearing, but sometimes to the lower senses of touch, smell, and taste. On this basis, types of art are distinguished and works of art classified according to the sense primarily addressed: e.g., as visual forms or auditory forms. Sculpture, textiles, clothing, and furniture are primarily visual arts, but can be perceived tactually to some extent, as by the blind. Music is, of course, predominantly auditory, although a trained musician can read a musical score visually as others read literature. Literature was an auditory art before the art of writing, and still is when spoken aloud; but it is now transmitted more often visually. Opera and the sound-film are audio-visual.

The *suggested* factor in art is that which the object tends to call to the mind of a suitably educated and conditioned observer: its meanings and culturally established associations, but not its purely private, personal associations for a single individual. It includes suggested sense-imagery, as in a poem; also concepts, inferences, desires, emotions, and the expression of all other psychological processes. Three main types of suggestion are distinguished: mimesis, arbitrary symbolism, and common correlation in experience. Red may suggest a rose, fire, or blood by visual mimesis. An oval line or mass may suggest a human head. Music may imitate the song of a bird or a child crying, by auditory mimesis. Verbal onomatopeia is another kind of auditory mimesis. Ar-

bitrary symbolism, usually without mimesis, occurs in written language, religious and other emblems, such as the cross for Christianity. (Various kinds of symbol and sign will be distinguished later.)

There is correlation in experience between the visual image of a fire and the tactile image of heat; between the sound of a crying child and suggestions of grief or pain. Several of these modes of suggestion can be combined in the same work of art.

On the transmissional basis, works of art can be described and classified in terms of their relative *emphasis on one or another mode of transmission*, or on several at once. Some are mainly presentative and visual, with little suggestive meaning, as in abstract decorative patterns. Some, especially in printed literature, depend mainly on suggestion. Some are highly specialized in mode of suggestion, depending largely on some one mode such as arbitrary symbolism; others are diversified.

(b) The *components* of art are also distinguished in psychological terms. They are names for types of imagery or other psychological content. Some of them, such as color, can be either presented (as in a painting) or suggested (as in a poem). Others, such as conation, emotion, and reasoning, can be only suggested. Under each are classed certain *component traits*, specific varieties of it. Some components are relatively simple or *elementary*, such as hue and pitch. A specific variety of one is an *elementary component trait*. Thus "red" is an elementary component trait under the component "hue," and "high" or "low," "middle C" or "f above middle C" is an elementary component trait under "pitch." Joy and sadness are traits under the component "emotion"; desire and aversion, welcoming and rejecting, are traits under the component "conation." There are many traits under each component; in other words, the component is a type or heading under which a certain set of traits can be classed. Every trait can be used as the basis for conceiving a simple type or types: e.g., dark pictures, soft music, sad stories, rapid dancing.

Types of art are also distinguished according to the relative emphasis given to one or another component: e.g., paintings, as linear or colorful; plays as emotional or intellectual. They are also distinguished according to the emphasis upon a certain trait: e.g., an angular or curvilinear type of statue or design.[7] Music and painting are called "expressive" when they emphasize the suggestion of emotion and desire.

The lower senses give rise to their own components, traits, and types. They can be presented or suggested. E.g., flavor is a gustatory component and scent an olfactory one; salty and bitter, lemon and pineapple, are gustatory traits; the scent of roses or burning leaves is an olfactory trait. These can be presented directly, as through food and perfume, but in literature and pictorial art they are suggested as kinds of imagery. They all give rise to types, such as rose perfume.

(c) *Spatio-temporal and causal organization.* Most painting is presented in two dimensions of space (unless collage or heavy impasto gives it a third), but it can suggest the third dimension through mimesis and perspective. Sculpture, architecture, landscape design, furniture, and clothing are developed presentatively in three dimensions of space, but to a variable extent. Music is organized in a certain temporal order and, on the whole, is intended to be heard in that order; so are literature, dramatic performance, and ballet. Most sculpture and painting are static as stimuli to perception. To perceive them is a temporal process, but they do not move, or have to be perceived in any exact temporal order. (In Chinese and Japanese handscrolls an approximate temporal order is determined.) A static painting can suggest movement and temporal sequence. Mobile sculpture and mobile color involve temporal change; the film is a moving picture, determined in temporal order. The plot of a play or novel involves causal organization in addition to spatial and temporal, all suggested. Certain events seem to occur as a result of previous events; actions are supposedly performed in order to achieve certain effects. In musical

and decorative visual design, causal interrelation is less emphasized.

In terms of these frames of reference, the arts have been traditionally classified as "space arts," "time arts," "arts of rest and motion," etc. Such classifications are over-simplified, and do not adequately cover the great variety of forms in art. One must not assume that, because painting has traditionally been an art of space and of rest, it will always and necessarily be so. In the animated cartoon, such as those of Disney, it has become an art of time and motion. There are many mixed and intermediate types of art in terms of these frames of reference. For example, landscape architecture is mainly a static art, presented in three dimensions of space. But wind and falling water can introduce motion, and there is temporal determination when flowers are planted so as to bloom or show red leaves at certain seasons.

(d) *Developed components and traits.* For analyzing and describing very complex works of art, especially those which change rapidly in time or space, developed components are distinguished in each art. They involve some development in space, time, or both, and perhaps in causal relations. Under various names, they are used by artists for organizing a work of art, and by critics for interpreting and evaluating it. A developed component may involve the combined arrangement of several elementary components. Melody in music involves the arrangement of notes of different pitch, loudness, rhythm, etc., in temporal sequence. Perspective and modeling in painting involve the arrangement of many details of shape, size, overlapping, and perhaps of light and dark, hue, etc., to produce an illusion of the third dimension. Literature and drama involve plot, characterization, etc. Motion picture films involve photography, plot, settings,

[7] For example, Ralph Linton writes that "All art can be divided, on a purely objective basis, into two great types: that in which the designs or representations of natural objects are angular and geometric, based upon a use of straight lines, and that in which the designs or representations employ curves... European art is predominantly curvilinear." ("'Primitive' Art," in *American Magazine of Art,* Jan. 1933, p. 18).

editing, montage, etc. A particular variety of any of these is a developed component trait. Thus a symphony can be analyzed into its developed traits of melody, harmony, meter and rhythmic phrasing, counterpoint, dynamics, orchestration, etc. A progressive sequence of different color-harmonies in a ballet or color-film involves developed coloration.

Any work of art can be analyzed as to its psychological content into a certain set of component traits, presented and suggested, elementary and developed. Accordingly, works of art can be classified as to the selection and diversity of components and component traits which they involve. Ballet and film involve visual movement, presented and suggested. Types are distinguished as to the developed components emphasized. Some music is melodic (i.e., specialized on melody) and some predominantly rhythmic (e.g., African drumbeats). Such component development cuts across the arts. For example, Shakespeare's plays and Rembrandt's paintings both emphasize characterization; the plays have meter and rhythmic phrasing in common with a Beethoven symphony. Sculpture and architecture involve solid shape as a presented component; painting, as a suggested one.

All these types evolve, to the extent of descending through historic time from one generation to the next, with adaptive change along the way. New types originate from old, sometimes by gradual change, as painting developed suggestive three-dimensional perspective; sometimes by more radical leaps, as in the invention of the cinema toward the end of the nineteenth century. The development of the photograph from painting, and of the motion picture from the photograph, are quick and radical enough to be compared with biological mutations.[8]

7. COMPOSITIONAL TYPES:
UTILITARIAN, REPRESENTATIVE,
EXPOSITORY, AND THEMATIC

Four main modes of composition are distinguished in aesthetic morphology: four ways of organizing the component traits, compound details and interrelations of art. They are: utilitarian, representative, expository, and thematic. All of them are used in all the arts, though with different emphasis at different times. Types are distinguished on this basis. This classification of works of art cuts across the classification of whole arts in terms of medium and technic.

A particular work of art may be composed in two or more of these modes at once, with varying emphasis on one or another. When it is, the results appear as compositional factors within the work of art: for example, a chair may involve a utilitarian factor (also called "functional") and a thematic (design or decorative) factor. A representative factor may be introduced by the carved, painted, or woven portrayal of animal or other figures; an expository factor by a motto or group of symbols expressing some general idea. A cathedral usually involves all four modes, but most works of art specialize on one or two of them. Painting has usually combined representation and design, but recently has tended to subordinate or omit the representative factor. Furniture and architecture have tended to specialize on the utilitarian or functional, omitting non-functional ornament but achieving an effect of design through the utilitarian structure itself. Music usually specializes on thematic design, but sometimes introduces representation (as of a storm or battle) through auditory mimesis. Music can also be utilitarian, as in bugle-calls, marches, and work-songs to stimulate and coordinate bodily movements.

In general, *utilitarian* composition is the ar-

---

[8] For further details on the morphological principles summarized in this chapter and in Ch. XVI on Styles, see T. Munro, *The Arts and their Interrelations* (New York, 1949) and *Toward Science in Aesthetics* (New York, 1956).

rangement of details in such a way as to be instrumental (or at least apparently or intentionally instrumental) to some active use or end. It tends to aid or guide overt bodily movement or preparation for it; to serve the ordinary business of life, rather than to serve only as an object of aesthetic or intellectual contemplation. Insofar as a thing is organized in a utilitarian way, its form can be described in terms of the fitness of parts and detailed arrangements for some active use, as in the legs and seat of a chair, the blade and handle of a sword, the walls and roof of a house. Literature can be utilitarian, as in advertising, propaganda, guide-books, prayers, speeches, letters, sermons, and other compositions aimed at influencing or guiding action. Some works of art, especially primitive, are adapted for utilitarian ends on a basis of supernaturalistic beliefs, as in a dance with rattles to bring rain, an amulet to ward off disease, or a clay figure of the earth goddess to be buried and make the crops grow. The ineffectiveness of the means does not prevent it from having utilitarian composition, as in an early flying machine which would not fly. Naturalistic technology is often mixed with supernaturalistic, especially but not exclusively in the prescientific stage of cultural history.

Representative (or representational) composition arranges details so as to suggest, to a willing and suitably educated observer, a fantasy of some concrete object, person, scene, or group of them, in space. Some representation suggests a series of events in time. There are two main varieties of representation: mimetic and symbolic. In mimetic representation, the presented images (visual, auditory, or tactile) resemble the set of images called up in imagination. Thus the lines and color-areas on a canvas may represent a valley with trees. Mimesis may be very simple, pertaining to one detail; representation is a mode of composition, involving some complex development. Symbolic representation occurs mainly in literature, where the spoken or printed words combine to suggest and guide a fantasy. There is usually no resemblance between the presented and suggested images, except for onomatopoetic words. However, mimesis and arbitrary symbolism can both be used, as in pictographs. Representation is static in most paintings, mobile in the film, ballet, and dramatic enactment. Either mimetic or symbolic representation can be realistic or unrealistic in relation to current conceptions of reality.

Expository composition arranges details so as to suggest or explain some general relationship, abstract idea, pervasive quality, or underlying principle, as of a causal or logical connection. Today, such composition appears chiefly in the literary essay, such as a discussion of honor, love, or beauty; also in meditative lyrics and passages of abstract discussion in the course of fiction and drama. In the past, it was more common in the visual arts such as painting, sculpture, and stained glass, where it was used to convey religious and moral ideas through combinations of visual symbols. A single symbolic image is not enough to constitute expository composition; a number of symbols must be juxtaposed with a joint effect of general significance.

Thematic composition is an arrangement adapted for stimulating and guiding aesthetic experience through the repetition of presented or suggested traits or combinations of them, and usually also through the variation, contrast, and integration of such traits. When visually presented, it is sometimes called "decoration" or "ornamentation." Any trait or unit thus repeated or contrasted with others in a work of art is a *theme*. Angles and curves or blue and red areas, as in a painting or textile design, are contrasting themes. Two or more angles of slightly different shape or size, or two spots of a different blue, are variations of the same theme. Integration is produced by subordinating all the units to some framework scheme or pattern.

A thematic composition which is developed with some complexity, as by involving several variations and contrasts within a unifying framework, is a *design*. Music produces designs of auditory themes such as chords, melodic figures, and instrumental timbres. Poetry produces designs of word-sounds and also by arranging images and other suggested ingredients thematically. Variations on the theme of war in a story, contrasted with those on peace, contribute a thematic factor.

Some works of art are highly specialized on thematic composition, while in others it is rudimentary and incidental to other modes. It is hard to avoid some thematic relationship, as in the four legs of a chair or the repetition of a musical phrase in simple songs. Two eyes in a face or two elbows in a human figure are the rudiments of thematic composition. In some styles such as primitive Negro sculpture, this factor is further developed by emphasizing and intensifying other bodily similarities.

Where two or more compositional factors are developed in the same work of art, they are sometimes merged so closely as to be almost indistinguishable. Each detail then functions in several different compositional factors. In other works of art they are more or less separate and even conflicting, as when a piece of ornamentation is superficially applied to a very different basic structure: e.g., nineteenth-century gothic ornamentation on a machine.

When two or more compositional factors are developed in the same work of art, one usually provides a *basic framework* for the whole, the other or others being fitted into it as accessory factors. In a chair, the utilitarian factor gives the basic framework, determining the overall outlines of the form. Within it, as we have seen, accessory developments of a representative, expository, or thematic nature may be developed. In the Statue of Liberty in New York, on the other hand, the basic framework (from an aesthetic, perceptual standpoint) is representative: a statue of a goddess. Within it utilitarian details are inserted, to make it serve as a lighthouse. Thematic details can be inserted in a representative painting, as in repeated linear shapes and color-areas within a landscape. Or representative details can be inserted in a

thematic framework, as in the small pictures of animals and plants used as decorative motifs within a Persian rug design. The framework factor is not necessarily the most important aesthetically, and is often the least original.

Many types of art can be distinguished in terms of these modes of composition and their interrelations. Each mode produces a number of persistent, compositional *framework-types*. *Utilitarian* types include, for example, the axe, chair, cup, dwelling-house, temple, sword, hat, boat, and cart. (Other modes can be introduced as accessory factors in any of them.) *Representative* types include the portrait (drawn, painted, or sculptured), the human figure in the round, the landscape painting, the landscape with figures, the still life, the epic, ballad, prose tale, novel, drama, tragedy, and comedy. *Expository* types include the essay, treatise, proverb, meditative lyric, and certain types of diagram or symbolic image such as the Hindu yantra and the medieval table of consanguinity. (In the "Tree of Jesse," both representative and expository schemes are involved.) *Thematic* types include the fugue, sonata, and symphony; the sonnet and other conventional verse patterns; the arabesque, plaid, checked, and other types of visual surface decoration. Many other types involve almost equal emphasis on two or more modes: for example, the "Tree of Jesse" in Christian iconography involves certain specifications along representative, expository, and thematic lines. Conventional variants of each compositional type develop in different cultural traditions: for example, the Nativity and Crucifixion as representative types in the Christian context; the Birth of Buddha; Krishna Dancing with the Cowgirls. (These may involve expository and thematic development also.)

In addition to those based wholly or mainly on one mode of composition, there are other types based on *relations among compositional factors*: as to which are used and with what relative emphasis. As noted above, some works of art are highly specialized and others diversified compositionally. Specific varieties of these arise in different arts and cultures. For example, music which specializes on thematic development is often called "pure" or "absolute" music, while that involving some representation (e.g., "Forest Murmurs," "The Combat of David and Goliath") is called "descriptive" or "programmatic." Painting which involves little or no representative development is called "abstract," "non-objective," or "non-representational." Types of painting and sculpture are distinguished as to their relative emphasis on realistic representation, decoration, or stylization. A "stylized" work may emphasize design or symbolism at the expense of realism.[9] Decorative painting emphasizes visual development rather than realism or emotional expression. Expressionistic painting sacrifices realism to emotional suggestiveness. Poetry (in the sense of verse) involves more thematic development of word-sounds than prose ordinarily does. "Rhythmic prose" is an intermediate type. Furniture and architecture which emphasize utilitarian fitness and have little added ornamentation are sometimes called "functional." But ornamentation has its own aesthetic and other functions, such as that of showing social status.

Any work of art can be described in terms of many traits and types pertaining to its modes of transmission, elementary and developed components, spatio-temporal and causal development, and modes of composition. To bring out the distinctive and important aspects of a work of art, one must notice (a) how the various traits are combined, how and to what extent they are unified in this particular case; (b) how it differs from others of a similar art, general type, and provenance. A detailed morphological description of any complex work of art, as of any plant or animal, could be continued indefinitely, beyond any useful length. Hence it is necessary to abbreviate and summarize selectively; to omit or minimize the ways in which a work is like many others, emphasizing instead what appear to be its most distinctive and important traits from a standpoint of originality, historical influence, or other criteria. Under present conditions, there will always be a subjective element in such selection, but it can be gradually reduced.

8. INTERNAL SEQUENCES AND PROGRESSIONS. HISTORIC SEQUENCES, PROGRESSIONS, AND TRENDS

To describe a work of art in detail, one may need to point out sequences within it. In music, the term "sequence" usually refers to a succession of melodic or chordal phrases which go up or down in pitch by regular diatonic degrees in the same scale. But in a broader sense, music contains many other kinds of temporal sequence or succession: e.g., of "variations" in a "Theme with Variations," or of different orchestral effects in the same passage. In drama and fiction, one can speak of a sequence of scenes or events. In painting, there are static sequences of units so arranged that one sees them in a certain temporal order: e.g., trees in a Chinese handscroll. A garden path, or a line of rooms along a corridor, may present a sequence of vistas. These are all *internal* sequences, within a single work of art or the perception of it. If such a sequence moves definitely from one point, theme, or condition to a different one, it can be called a "progression": e.g., from a red or major tonality to a blue or minor one.

Another kind of sequence, important in theories of art history, is a *historic* or *genetic* sequence. This is a succession of changes from one work of art or one style to a later one. It can be described in terms of traits and types: e.g., as a gradual *progression* from a certain type such as "archaic" or "geometric" to another such as "classic" or "biomorphic." (The term "progression" here does not imply improvement or progress). It can be described as change from a high degree or frequency in some respect (e.g., in the number and size of curves) to a low one, or vice versa. Change back to an earlier type is a *regression*. A genetic sequence

[9] Linton, *op. cit.*, p. 18; Franz Boas, *Primitive Art* (Oslo, 1927).

implies a considerable amount of continuity of descent or influence from earlier to later products.

Both internal and historic sequences can be analyzed and described as to component, compositional, and other types of trait and type. In music, one *component* sequence may involve successive changes in melodic theme; another, changes in rhythm. Combining the two, we have a compound rhythmic-melodic sequence. A *compositional* sequence is one involving changes in the mode of composition or the relations between various modes: e.g., from narrative representation to exposition in the course of a novel. These can occur within a single work of art.

In addition, large-scale historic sequences can be analyzed in the same way. From the Gregorian chant through the romantic period in music, there is an overall tendency to increase melodic, harmonic, rhythmic, and orchestral complexity, which usually gives a more richly sensuous quality to the whole. From Beethoven and Berlioz through Wagner, there is a development of programmatic composition, sometimes through mimetic representation.

9. THE EVOLUTIONARY DESCENT OF ARTISTIC TYPES; THEIR DIFFERENTIATION AND REINTEGRATION

All the above-mentioned traits and types descend with adaptive change as part of the cultural process. Their changes can be described in terms of one or more modes of composition: e.g., as increasing or decreasing ornamentation and representation within a utilitarian framework such as the axe or chair. In the long history of the axe, some changes have made it more effective and durable along naturalistic lines, perhaps for a special function, as in the battle-axe. Others have sought to make it more effective along supernaturalistic lines, as by carving certain magic symbols on it. Some axes are carved

to represent animals. These may function also as thematic decoration.

New compositional types are constantly evolving from the old. The folk dance provided one source of instrumental music. "During the sixteenth century," says Percy A. Scholes, "the linking of a couple of pieces in dance style (especially Pavan and Galliard) opened the way to the development of the extended suite—a string of pieces based on dance rhythms and styles."[10] In the same period, the sonata developed from the dance type along more abstract lines, as pure concert music. "The introduction of the opera in the seventeenth century," Scholes continues, "led to the evolution of the Overture and this, in turn, to that of the Symphony."

Detailed historic studies of such evolutionary changes show them to be often correlated with changing social and cultural environments, such as feudalism and the rise of a wealthy urban middle class, chivalry and the courts of love, troubadours and minnesingers, and the pervasive secularization of culture in modern centuries. It must not be assumed, however, that changes in art are due entirely to such external factors.

A certain type may disappear from the élite levels of serious, fine art for a while, only to reappear on another cultural level. For example, today's "comic strip" in the newspapers, mainly for children and usually dealing with rather trivial subjects, is a representative type which descends indirectly from the serious picture sequence of other days. Its essence is the telling of a story in temporal order by representing one situation after another, in a series of pictures arranged in spatial order. It is found in the Japanese narrative scroll, in medieval pictures of the lives of saints, and in Egyptian wall paintings and reliefs. It never died out entirely, being preserved in book illustrations and in narrative sequences such as Hogarth's *Marriage à la Mode*.

For an understanding of the larger outlines of

[10] "The History of Forms," in *The Oxford Companion to Music* (London, 1938), p. 340.

artistic evolution, it is important to trace the history of the *modes of composition* in their mutual relationship. Each has a history, which can be traced somewhat independently: the history of utilitarian forms; of expository forms; of representative forms; of thematic and decorative design. Each of these cuts across the histories of the particular arts, since each involves many different arts and media. At various times, it concentrates more heavily in one or the other. For example, expository form has concentrated especially in literature in modern times. Before the spread of literacy, it was strong in the pictorial and sculptural arts. Utilitarian music was more important in past ages than at present: when armies made more use of bugle calls, drum-beats, and martial music, and when group work was often done with song, as in sailors' chanteys and cotton-picking rhythms. Much concert music emphasizes design.

The histories of the modes of composition, and of types distinguished on this basis, tend on the whole to verify Spencer's theory that *art evolves from the less to the more differentiated*. More types and subtypes of it continue to emerge. This is not uniformly true, for exceptions exist; but it has been a widespread tendency. The realm of culture which the ancients called "techné" or "ars" was less differentiated than its modern descendants. It included, not only the ancestors of what we now call "arts," but prototypes of what we call "philosophy," "pure science," "applied science," "engineering," and "industrial technology." Only from the eighteenth century on was "art" gradually limited to skills and products with an aesthetic function, while those without it were grouped apart under some of the other names just mentioned. Aesthetic art as a realm or type of skill and product became increasingly differentiated from pure and applied science. Ancient and medieval products, as we have seen, were often highly diversified compositionally. They might combine, as in the temple and cathedral, utilitarian, expository, representative, and thematic factors with considerable development of each. Many ancient

examples can be found which combine two or more, as in ornamental tools and weapons. (Whether such forms should be called "undifferentiated" or not depends on their previous history: where they result from a reintegration of previous differentiated types, that word should not be used.)

In ancient and medieval art, the expository or utilitarian development was comparatively easy to keep within aesthetic bounds. It could be balanced by sufficient representative or decorative development to preserve the aesthetic fitness of the whole. The beauty or aesthetic value of the whole was not limited to representation or decoration; the utilitarian and expository factors themselves could function aesthetically, as parts of a total form which was still regarded in an undifferentiated way, with an attitude at once aesthetic, intellectual, and practical. But as time went on, the growth of scientific interests involved a huge increase in both expository and utilitarian composition. Expository writing tended to specialize more intensively on logical reasoning and intellectual explanation: thus to become pure science, as in Euclid, or a more prosaic, non-literary type of philosophy, as in Aristotle's *Prior Analytics*. In other words, as expository writing developed more intensively, it tended to pass out of the ancient realm of aesthetic art and to enter the new realm of pure science. As utilitarian composition developed more intensively, it, too, tended to leave the realm of art and to become scientific invention or non-aesthetic manufacture and management.

Comparatively undifferentiated forms remained and still remain, mostly within the realm of art, which has been slower to specialize intensively. A modern work can include some expository and/or utilitarian development and still be classed as art because of its visual or literary appeal. It may be on the borderline between literature and science or philosophy, or between practical invention and decorative art. But to develop exposition or utility beyond the point where it is readily grasped as part of an aesthetic form tends to push it beyond the frontier of art and into that of philosophy, science, or practical invention.

Theoretical exposition at a prescientific stage is often combined with poetry, drama, and fiction. It tends to discard these in approaching modern scientific method, as distracting irrelevancies. A more purely intellectual, logical response is desired and stimulated instead of a partly aesthetic one. We have already noted the significance of certain early, relatively undifferentiated literary types, such as the philosophic poems of Hesiod and Lucretius. Hesiod's *Works and Days* involves some utilitarian development as a manual for farmers and husbandmen; some expository development in wise generalization about life, men, and gods; some representation in myths, legends, and descriptions of the countryside in various seasons; some thematic arrangement of both word-sounds and ideas. It includes some poetry along with prescientific germs of what was later to become agricultural technology, astronomy, meteorology, physics, biology, sociology, psychology, and ethics. The same can still be said of Lucretius' *On the Nature of Things*. Although it is nearer to science, and the realms of thought are more clearly distinguished in it, the whole is still philosophical poetry, containing an undifferentiated mixture of artistic and protoscientific thinking on a wide range of subjects. Plato's dialogues combine dramatic form and poetic imagery with prosaic discussion of problems which were later to be taken over by the sciences, and by frankly prosaic philosophizing based on science. In Aristotle's writings, the artistic, literary factor is much less evident; the sciences are separating from art and from each other.

An analogous tendency has operated in the utilitarian, visual types of art. More or less undifferentiated examples are found in the ancient and medieval periods, as in ornate armor and weapons, houses and furniture. Prescientific buildings, tools, and furniture often combine utilitarian form with representation and thematic decoration, as in carved, painted, modeled, or woven images of animals, flowers, warriors, and goddesses on swords and shields, helmets, garments, chairs, and tables, houses, dishes, chariots, and harnesses. As modern weapons, tools, and furniture are refined by scientific technology for greater efficiency, they tend to discard such "non-functional" elements as cumbersome, dust-catching "gingerbread." Houses tend to become more severely "functional," and factory buildings still more so. Complex visual design tends accordingly to be relegated to places where it will not interfere with some desired efficiency, as on ornamental textiles.

Utilitarian writing tells people how to do things, or tries to aid or influence them to do certain things and not others. We find it today in railway timetables, traffic regulations, manuals on parliamentary law, and similar books and pamphlets on "how to do it" in every field from golf to gardening. Most of this writing makes no attempt at literary art, and is not so classed. But outstanding utilitarian works which do so qualify have come down to us from previous centuries: for example, Isaak Walton's seventeenth-century treatise, *The Compleat Angler*. Its framework is utilitarian, on how to fish, and it lives up to this title; but in addition, it is studded with accessory bits from other modes of composition—short stories, dialogue, songs and verses, expository digressions on life. They make up a compositionally diversified piece of literature. Of like diversity are Robert Burton's *Anatomy of Melancholy* and some of Montaigne's essays.

Thematic and representative composition are, apparently, more essential to aesthetic art than exposition or utility; less likely to pass over into science when intensively developed. Thematic development can be carried out in isolation, apart from any of the other modes, to extreme levels of complexity as in the music of Bach, Mozart, and Brahms, without sacrificing aesthetic to intellectual or practical considerations. Some textile design, as in Persian rugs (the surface design, not the rug itself, which is utilitarian) develops in a similar way within the visual realm. Science has made but little progress, so far, in charting or guiding such thematic development. In a diversified product, the presence of a strong design factor, visual or auditory, is the surest guarantee of artistic status and aesthetic appeal in what could otherwise be treated as purely intellectual or practical.

Representation also has been a persistent factor in the aesthetic arts. It has not been indispensable, for "abstract" or non-representative art is at least as old as geometric pottery decoration. It goes back to early neolithic times, although some design which seems to us purely abstract was descended from stylized representation and perhaps understood as such when made. Some primitive music represents natural sounds such as thunder and the cries of animals; some is devoid of representative meaning so far as its performers and practioners know. But certainly representation, in its visual, auditory, and literary forms, is widespread and constitutes a basic factor in art which has shown no tendency to be taken over completely by science, no matter how intensively it is developed. It has utilized scientific technology, as in printing stories and making films, but for its own aesthetic ends. To stimulate and guide an acceptable fantasy in the mind of a watcher or listener has been a major aim and function of art, as the enjoyment of such a fantasy has been a major type of aesthetic experience.

However, representative art has not been exempt from the general tendency toward compositional differentiation and specialization. Some phases of it have passed over from art into scientific technology. In much primitive painting and sculpture, the representation of human and animal forms is combined with thematic development, so as to produce a relatively undifferentiated, stylized, unrealistic form. As such, it may fit into a larger composition involving symbolic exposition and magico-religious utility. In the art of the early empires and of Byzantium, representation was combined with magnificent decoration and often subordinated to it. In Greece, in the early Roman Empire, and again in the Renaissance, an intellec-

tual trend toward scientific naturalism was accompanied by increasing specialization on visual naturalism or realism in painting and sculpture. Accurate representation of anatomy, posture, perspective, natural coloring, and atmospheric light became dominant aims, and to them were sacrificed the more obvious, ornate types of gold and mosaic decoration. Design persisted as a more subtle factor in thematic arrangements of the realistic shapes and surfaces themselves throughout the Renaissance and on into the nineteenth century. But the tendency of painting to specialize on representation was shown in the abandonment, not only of Byzantine decoration, but of medieval, symbolic exposition. This last persisted through the seventeenth century, but with decreasing importance. In the mid-nineteenth century, a new scientific trend appeared in the naturalistic painting of Courbet and the naturalistic literature of Zola. In it, the interest in design and decoration dropped accordingly. In the seventies, impressionist painting was influenced by physical theories of light and color. It produced new decorative coloring, but largely in the interest of representing the reflections of sunlight on colored objects out of doors.

At this time the camera was coming into increasing use as a device for pictorial representation. It rapidly showed itself capable of performing quickly and easily, first in black and white, then in color, feats of realism which would have taken a painter hours of work and years of training. By the end of the century the cinema was making pictures move, thus outdoing all previous pictorial art in this type of realism. In other words, the intensive development of visual representation had taken it largely out of the hands of the artist and into those of the engineer. At the same time, it produced a new type of artist. The camera replaced the pencil, pen, and paint-brush for the great mass of pictorial needs in which an accurate record was the prime consideration. Much of this was for utilitarian purposes, as in the scientific identification of criminals by their portraits, finger-prints, and Bertillon measurements. The art of painting responded to the camera with a rapid series of experiments, in search of some new type of picture-making which the camera could not perform, or not so well. These led it, now into reviving primitive and archaic stylizations for the sake of thematic design; now into expressionist distortions in the tradition of El Greco; now into surrealist fantasies; now into borrowing some characteristic effects of snap-shot photography itself (as by Degas and Toulouse-Lautrec); now into cubist dissections of familiar objects; now into reducing all representation to the vanishing-point, and recently into abstract or non-objective painting.

To this extent, avant-garde painting has willingly surrendered representation to scientific technology. Sculpture also has become increasingly abstract in recent years. Like experiments have been made in the film and in literature, but with less success so far. There is still a great demand for representational art, and it is increasingly focused upon literature. Story-telling and other representational features are classed as "literary values," with the disparaging implication (quite unjustified by historical precedent or aesthetic evidence) that they have no place in the visual or musical arts.

Literary representation itself has undergone a period of intensive, specialized development, with increasing influence from science. The rise of the prose novel and short story in the nineteenth century was partly at the expense of poetic narrative: of the epic, the ballad, and other forms of story-telling in verse—that is, of representation along with thematic development of word-sounds. The intensive interest in detailed, realistic representation now impelled, as in expository writing, an abandonment of word-sound design as distracting and irrelevant. Poetic narrative persisted, as in the work of John Masefield, but on a smaller scale. In the film and drama likewise, a strong desire for realism has kept artificial design and stylization in a surbordinate place.

In all these ways, the differentiating tendency has been strong and widespread throughout the history of the arts. But it would be a mistake to regard it as universal; there are major exceptions.

In the first place, one must not suppose that all primitive or prehistoric art is compositionally undifferentiated. On the contrary, the great mass of primitive artifacts is specialized along utilitarian lines. Many prehistoric tools are comparatively undifferentiated *as tools*: that is, they can serve as a hand-axe, a scraper, a weapon, and so on. Some are fairly specialized as utilitarian devices, such as spear-points, arrow-points, bone fish-hooks, needles, and the like. Those which are not, which involve strong thematic design as in the Venus of Lespugues and some of the ice-age cave paintings, are the exception and not the rule. The early artifact whose superior decorative quality wins it a place in the modern art museum is not to be taken as fully typical of the art of its time; it may be one piece out of many thousands, selected precisely because it involved some thematic as well as utilitarian or representative composition. Ancient art abounds in portrait heads and clay figures whose visible development is limited to the representative mode, whether or not they were used for magic, religious, or symbolic purposes. The ordinary soldier had a plain sword, lived in a plain, humble house or tent, and ate from coarse dishes. Many early tales were told in plain prose, and simple melodies piped with no elaborate meaning. The example of any ancient art which now stands out as richly diversified in sensory form and meaning is likely to be one on which exceptional care and expenditure were lavished, as a religious offering or as the future property of some exalted personage.

But this very fact is significant: that such major works, on which exceptional care and creative power were lavished, tended to become more diversified compositionally than modern works of similar status. An ancient legend, genealogy, history or set of moral precepts which was held in respect by the group was likely to be put in verse and rhythmically declaimed. As such it was easier to remember as well as aesthetically moving.

Whether the work was basically utilitarian, representative, or expository, one could express one's sense of its importance by clothing it in richly decorative form. Expository development through applying symbolic images was itself a way of enriching a utilitarian or representative form, as in a cathedral or a statue of Siva with his flame, drum, skull, and other attributes. In pre-modern times, on the whole, creative genius was not forced to choose between aesthetic art, pure theory, and practical ingenuity. No one of these seemed to offer an adequate channel, and creative genius tended more to grow along several lines at once. Now our whole civilization has become more specialized, educationally, professionally, and psychologically. The gifted youth is under pressure to choose a specialty: to become either an artist or a theorist or a practical technologist; to narrow down more and more intensively within each of these realms. If he chooses pure science or philosophy he is under pressure to make it more purely intellectual and factual, avoiding all claim to fine writing. If he chooses to build houses or furniture, he must make them more purely functional, with no unnecessary embellishment. Art, as we have seen, offers its own range of specialties. Each of these fields has now become so vast and competitive, with so many rewards to the successful specialist, that diversification presents no great allure. The result of compositional diversity today is often a work which seems merely odd and overloaded, hard to classify, hard to appraise by any simple standards; as if trying to ride several horses at once.

Nevertheless, there are forces within the arts which stubbornly oppose and resist this universal specialization. The very fact that extreme specialization on utility or exposition takes the product entirely outside the realm of art leaves art full of less specialized products, made along more traditional lines. Here and there, we notice definite countertendencies: to reintegrate compositional types which have been somewhat separated. This not only produces compound arts, like the opera, ballet, and sound-film, but types with more than one mode of compositional development.

It is well known that, in the Industrial Revolution, a strong emphasis was placed on utilitarian manufacture with little or no thought of beauty, filling England with smoky factories, slums, and ugly implements. Victorian aesthetic taste often followed a separate course, into fussy and elaborate, cumbersome and useless ornamentation in the home, church and palace, and especially in women's clothes. Certain "aesthetic" literary artists detached themselves as far as possible from contemporary reality, while other writers plunged into its ugliest depths.

As against this detachment, Ruskin and Morris led an enduring movement to combine utility and simple decorative (thematic) beauty in the visual arts. Others have tried to reintegrate literary realism and rhythmic prose. Poetry keeps raising its head in a prosaic world, and finds a new aid in phonographic reproduction. Some philosophers, such as George Santayana, refuse to write in a coldly, narrowly expository manner; they insist on expressing their most abstruse thoughts in rhythmic, euphonious prose. Bernard Shaw's plays combined a great deal of theoretical discussion with a representative framework, and T. S. Eliot's lyric poems are heavy with expository symbolism. Attacks on program music as obsolete romanticism did not succeed in excluding the representative factor completely from that art. It took a new lease on life with Debussy, Ravel, and Stravinsky, while Schoenberg and others pushed ahead with new types of pure, thematic music. Highly specialized experiments in art are never enough to satisfy the taste of connoisseurs or public permanently. The attempt to reduce music or painting to pure design, while welcomed as one kind of art, is always accompanied or followed by more diversified types, conveying several kinds of value in a single work of art. In contemporary art, specialized and diversified types exist side by side, with the trends of taste favoring now one and now the other. If the old, diversified types do not all reappear on the serious, élite levels of fine art, they may be found elsewhere in our culture. Expository pictorial art finds a new place in educational texts and graphic displays, to convey abstract ideas easily and pleasantly to children and the general public.

10. CHANGING RELATIONS BETWEEN ART AND OTHER BRANCHES OF CIVILIZATION.

When culture was less differentiated than it is at present, art was on the whole more closely allied with religion, government, and moral education. It was often their handmaid, receiving from them its chief support, its main themes, and directions as to how to treat them. It also influenced these institutions in return. From prehistoric times, art had been used for important, non-aesthetic functions, especially magical, religious, and political. It was accordingly developed in ways considered suitable to such ends. During the ancient and medieval periods, most major works of serious art were to some extent religious, moral, or political in aim and subject; often all of these at once. Later on, cultural differentiation brought a progressive detachment of the arts from these other activities. Under the influence of naturalism and secularism, art turned its main interest away from religion and religious ethics. Under the influence of liberalism, it turned toward the individual and away from glorification of the state or ruling class.

In the "art-for-art's sake" movement, such detachment was demanded by artists and their spokesmen as a rightful, desirable liberation; as an opportunity to specialize at last on their own proper concerns. This is still the prevailing attitude in Western culture. On the other hand, the devotees of patriotic and religious art deplore the change as impoverishing art and lowering its dignity to the status of mere entertainment, sensuous pleasure, and decoration. There is some

ground for both attitudes. Art has certainly lost or rejected some of its rich former content, together with its claims to transcendental value as a revelation of the higher world. But in compensation, the freedom to specialize has allowed it to develop and differentiate hugely along its own, preferred lines. It still lacks the old, close integration with the rest of life and culture. But some new kinds of loose, voluntary integration are developing. These are being achieved through professional organizations of artists, through the growing role of art in education and scholarship, through a growing demand for art by the general public, and through various types of democratic social patronage. In the Western democracies, art is often placed at the service of commerce and industry through advertising and design. Meanwhile, the totalitarian states have revived some of the older types of political domination, in which art becomes again a tool of some political régime.

11. SUMMARY

One criterion of evolutionary change is "descent with adaptive modification and origination of new types." Does the process of change in the arts fulfill this criterion?

In the arts as in organic life, that which descends through long periods of time is the *type* rather than the individual. In both fields, it has been necessary to distinguish and classify a considerable range of types in order to trace effectively their descent with modification. Until recent years, few artistic types had been clearly and objectively described. Many others are now recognized, such as the portrait, the temple, the symphony, the mimetic dance, and the novel.

Historical study of such types reveals many progressions or *sequences of change*, each in a more or less consistent direction from one type to another. They show the origin and development of new types, such as the realistic single vista in painting and the sound-color film in cinema.

The *traits* which constitute artistic types are often detached and differently assembled. The resulting new types may or may not survive. Descending types often migrate and change in adaptation to new physical and cultural environments.

Types of art can be distinguished on many bases, such as technics, materials, cultural settings, modes of transmission, spatio-temporal and causal organization, psychological components, and modes of composition (utilitarian, representational, decorative, etc.).

Types of art tend to differentiate and reintegrate in new ways. Many early, relatively undifferentiated types, such as the philosophic poem and the religious drama with dance and song, have divided and developed along more specialized lines. Art as a whole has tended to differentiate from other cultural activities, but some reintegration is occurring.

CHAPTER XVI

THE DESCENT OF STYLES
AND TRADITIONS

I. THE NATURE OF STYLE IN VARIOUS ARTS

"Style" is one of many ambiguous terms in aesthetic theory. It has meant different things in different arts. Only recently has there been a persistent effort to redefine it in a way which is applicable to any art and even outside the arts. It has become a major concept in the history and theory of the arts and has found its way into anthropology, especially as applied to primitive artifacts.

The main idea, now called by that name, is not new. Vitruvius and Pliny called it *genus*, as in writing of the Doric, Ionic, and Corinthian *genera* in architecture. (It is significant that the same term was used for biological types.) This name has persisted in the French term *genre*. Italian Renaissance writers used the word *maniera* for a similar idea. The English word "style" comes from the Latin name for a stylus or writing instrument, whose meaning was extended to cover "mode of writing or expression." Under these different names a great variety of artistic styles or types has been distinguished, such as the pastoral style, the grand style, the classic, bombastic, satiric, tragic, comic, witty, painterly, polyphonic, etc. They are conceived on various bases: some with reference to the dominant mood or attitude, some to the kind of formal composition, and so on. The word "style" has been used as a term of praise, as in saying, "he writes with style," or "that painting has style." Calling an artist a stylist can also be

derogatory, implying that he has little content or that he follows past styles too imitatively.

In literary criticism, "style" has had a rather narrow meaning by comparison with that in other arts. It has referred primarily to the linguistic component of literature rather than to literature as a whole; to the choice of words, the syntax, punctuation, word-sounds, and general use of the medium, as distinguished from the psychological content of ideas and attitudes and also from the formal design, such as the sonnet pattern.[2] Thus a description of the style of a work of literature was far from characterizing the work as a whole. Literary theory is now gradually accepting a broader conception of style.

The newer conception is applicable to any art and any component in art: to that which is expressed or represented as well as to the manner of expression; to the choice of ideas and attitudes as well as to the choice of words or other handling of the medium. It is descriptive rather than evaluative, implying no critical judgment. Practically all works of art—good, bad, and indifferent—have at least some characteristics of a style or styles. There is no merit or demerit in doing so. The

[1] The theory of style set forth in this chapter is based on the author's essay, "Style in the Arts: a Method of Stylistic Analysis," *Journal of Aesthetics and Art Criticism*, Dec. 1946. Reprinted in *Toward Science in Aesthetics* (New York, 1956), pp. 192–226.

[2] On literary style in this sense, see R. Wellek and A. Warren, *Theory of Literature* (New York, 1949), Ch. XIV. The Modern Language Association has published *The MLA Style Sheet* on punctuation, footnotes, paragraphing, etc. *PMLA*, LXVI (1951), 3–31.

concept of a particular style is a way of describing and classifying works of art, not of evaluating them.

As such, a style is a kind of artistic type. It differs from some other kinds in that it involves a *recurrent cluster or complex of interrelated traits in art. It is a characteristic way of selecting and organizing the ingredients of art, capable of being repeated with variation in many otherwise different products.* It thus serves to classify and characterize these products as a group or sequence.

A style is a *compound* type of art as contrasted with a simple type such as "large pictures" or "round pictures." To define a style adequately, one has to mention a number of traits, usually referring to various components, parts, and aspects of the art concerned. Some styles are defined in terms of many traits: for example, Wölfflin's conception of classic and baroque: others more simply. Superficial acquaintance with a style may lead one to think of it too simply, in terms of one trait alone: e.g., to think of "romantic" art as merely "sentimental." Deeper study tends to reveal a more complex group of correlated traits, all significant for an understanding of the distinctive nature and historical position of the style.

2. PERIOD STYLES; INDIVIDUAL STYLES; RECURRENT STYLISTIC TYPES

A period style or historic style is conceived as occurring mainly or wholly in the art of a certain period of history, such as the Renaissance or the Sung Dynasty. It is named and defined with special reference to the art of that period: e.g., as "Renaissance style" or "Louis XV style." By implication, this relates it also to a certain place and people, in which and by whom the style is supposed to have been produced. Sometimes the name refers to the place, as in "Florentine" or "Venetian" style, with implied reference to the time when the style was at its height. A historic style is one which

has actually occurred, but one can imagine a period style which has not, as in a story about the future. Historic styles are sometimes named in terms of a nationality or people (Japanese style, Scythian style), or of a religious or cultural group (Buddhist or Islamic style). Thus we have national, religious, and other kinds of historic style; all tending to imply an approximate place and time as well. "Paleolithic style" has a long period or cultural stage, while "Lascaux style" refers to the place where certain paleolithic drawings were made and found. Some styles, especially of costume, are restricted to a social class or occupational type such as the nobility or clergy.

An *individual* style, that of a single artist such as Michelangelo, is a historic, period style of very small extension: the "people" concerned are limited to one person, and the period is limited to his working life. It may, however, be imitated by others and thus prolonged or revived in part. We speak thus of the "Miltonic" or "Byronic" style; the Giottesque or Chopinesque. The style of an individual artist is, to some extent, an example or substyle of the larger period style through which he lives, and to whose history he contributes.[3] It tends to differ in some respects from the styles of other artists in that time and place. It may differ so much as to appear atypical, a revolt from the prevailing style rather than an example of it. Usually an artist works in different styles in different periods of his life. Some very versatile artists—Picasso, for example—develop a long sequence of different styles or substyles during the course of their careers.

The conception of a particular historic style is derived, to a large extent, from observing and comparing different works of the same or closely

[3] "A historical style," says Kroeber, "can be defined as the co-ordinated pattern of interrelations of individual expressions or executions in the same medium or art." (*Style and Civilizations*, p. 32). Kroeber errs here in limiting style to the same medium or art. *Cf.* Hauser, *Philosophy of Art History*, p. 208: an elementary criterion of style is "an agreement in respect of a number of artistically significant traits among the works of a certain limited cultural area or period." Another criterion is fairly wide diffusion of these traits.

related arts (e.g., painting, sculpture, and architecture) from about the same period, place, and people. It is an attempt to characterize them collectively as to their most important and distinctive traits, by applying some name (such as "baroque" or "classic") which has general connotations of its own.

By extension, the word "style" is also applied to a complex mode of thought, behavior, and personality which flourished at a certain time and place in history: for example, that of "renaissance man." The concept of "baroque style" can be applied, not to art alone but to the distinctive features of European culture in any and every field during the baroque period. "Style" in this sense is a temporary pattern or configuration in culture as a whole, including philosophy, science, religion, government, and industry.

While most styles in art are conceived with reference to some specific period, place, and people, some are not. Such terms as "classic," "romantic," "pastoral," and "comic" are applied to works of many different periods and cultures. This may be true even though we associate them especially with some one period. We associate "romantic style" especially with Europe at the beginning of the nineteenth century, and "classic" with ancient Greece and Rome. But these concepts are also applied to art in other times and places which is thought to possess the essential traits of romanticism or classicism. A style which is not associated definitely with any one period may be called a *non-period style* or a *multi-period style*. It can also be called a *recurrent stylistic type*.

Many other ways of designating styles are in current use. One hears the expression "peasant style," "official style," "avant-garde" or "experimental style," and the like. Any of these may be understood with special reference to a certain place and time (e.g., "official style" to ancient Egypt) or in a broader sense as applicable to similar kinds of art at various times and places.

Many such conceptions of style are vaguely defined, as to historical reference and also as to the trait or traits supposed to characterize them. The effort is now being made to mark them off more clearly by defining each principal style-name in terms of some definite period, place, and people, art or arts, and distinguishing traits. But this involves many problems of nomenclature, historical fact, and morphological analysis.

3. STYLES AND COMPOSITIONAL TYPES

Each period style is a distinctive way of treating or varying one or more persistent compositional types. "Chair" and "doorway" are utilitarian types which descend through many centuries, many cultures, and many styles of art. On the whole, they descend more continuously and persistently than styles, which are usually rather short-lived variations of them. They can be treated in an imperial Roman, gothic, baroque, rococo, Ming Chinese, or twentieth-century functional style. The same can be said of countless other utilitarian types, such as the axe, sword, helmet, cup, and dress. Landscape painting, a representational type, can be treated in the ancient Hellenistic style or in that of the Southern Sung dynasty, seventeenth-century neo-classicism, or nineteenth-century impressionism. The essay is an expository type in literature. The ritual hymn, the love song, the work song, the war dance, and the fable are persistent types in other arts. Successive styles within the history of a people or of mankind as a whole can be regarded as ways in which such persistent compositional types as these descend with adaptive modification.

In relation to the history of styles, a persistent compositional type such as the palace (utilitarian) or the epic (representational) is a flexible framework, a somewhat indeterminate vehicle for stylistic development. By its essential nature and function, it tends to require certain basic parts and traits. The epic involves a series of exploits of a hero; the palace, magnificent residential quarters and protective walls; the map, a small drawing of geographical features. Stylistically, the compositional type is somewhat neutral and flexible in that it can be treated in various ways at various times and places. Many of its details are optional and variable. Over and above its basic specifications, the fullness of the concrete form is filled in by the cultural and artistic determinants in some particular place, period, people, stylistic tradition, and individual artist. Some style is almost unavoidable. Even an attempt to have no stylistic development at all, by restricting the product to its bare, functional essentials, produces its own kind of style when achieved consistently. Artists who associate the idea of style with ornateness or conservative traditionalism, and therefore wish to avoid it entirely, may find themselves creating a new, severely "functional" style in spite of themselves, and perhaps approximating some older functional style.

A very long-lived, widespread compositional type, such as the axe, the chair, the sculptured human figure, or the animal-drawing, has undergone so many stylistic variations that it is not exclusively bound up in our minds with any one period style. We can therefore define it more neutrally as to its non-stylistic essentials. With many other types the opposite is true. The fugue, for example, is so strongly associated with J. S. Bach and the polyphonic style of the renaissance and baroque periods that we may regard it almost as a period style of music: the fugal style, as a phase of baroque polyphony. From this point of view, any later composition in fugal form may be regarded as a revival of the polyphonic style, which declined after J. S. Bach. Polyphony can also be regarded as a developed component in music, available to any modern composer and not limited to any one period. It can be emphasized in one movement of a symphony and not the others.

Thus styles can not be sharply distinguished from types and components; all these concepts overlap because the phenomena to which they refer are so closely intermingled. The fugue itself can be regarded, from the morphological standpoint instead of the historical, as a thematic compositional type. As such, it is not bound up with any one period. It has proven capable of varied treatment in such varied styles as those of Bach, Mozart, Beethoven, Brahms, Franck, and Reger. There are *fugato* passages in Stravinsky and Prokofieff. Much the same can be said of the sonata and the sonnet as thematic types. From this point of view, stylistic traits consist in the distinctive ways in which each period and individual treated the fugue, sonata, or sonnet. In a modern fugue, one would try to notice especially its differences from the ways in which Bach and Handel treated that basic framework-type. The individual styles of Bach and Handel were the culminating stages in the career of polyphony as an extensive, period style which spread over Europe from the late gothic through the baroque period. It was exemplified, not only in fugues, but also in masses, cantatas, oratorios, concertos for chamber orchestra, and many other persistent types. When Brahms writes a fugue, as in the *Variations on a Theme by Handel*, it develops certain late romantic traits along with those inherited from early styles.

Each period style is the resultant of an interplay of many factors, including those in the physical, social, and cultural environment, upon one or more persistent types. Stylistic variations in the armchair are affected by the materials admired and available, such as marble, ivory, oak, mahogany, wool, silk, steel, and plastics. Social conditions, such as feudal restrictions on who shall sit in armchairs, or the influence of feminine, upper-class taste, affect the style. The essay as an expository type of literature is affected by inherited ideologies: by Greek ideas in Cicero and Roman ideas in Montaigne; by Enlightenment liberalism in Voltaire and Hume. The essay as a type adapts itself to these changing climates of thought and to related modes of verbal expression—neo-classic, romantic, naturalistic, or otherwise. The personality and ability of the artist are among the determinants of style in each case; but these too are affected by cultural conditions and manifest historical styles in other ways than through the media of art. In their whole modes of life and ways of thought and feeling, as well as in their essays, the men just mentioned were characteristic of their times. The dance suite, sonata, symphony, concerto, string quartet, and other thematic types of music have been treated in various styles by Haydn, Beethoven, Schumann, Debussy, Schoenberg, and Prokofieff.

It is an essential part of each style and of the culture-pattern within which it flourishes that certain persistent types are singled out for special emphasis and development, as main channels for temporary drives and interests, while others are neglected and remain either static or atrophied. The process and its causes are largely unconscious and unrealized at the time; even in retrospect they are hard to explain. But as a result, the style of art at a certain time and place is always practiced, and historically remembered, as associated especially with certain arts and compositional types. Gothic, from the standpoint of the modern historian, is characteristically the style of the cathedral, along with the furnishings and manuscripts produced in connection with it. The static, visual arts have thus stood out in retrospect with greater prominence, partly because of their durability, than music, theater, dance and oral literature. If we could reconstruct past cultural eras more completely, we would see their arts in somewhat different perspective.

4. STYLISTIC TRAITS AND SUBTRAITS

A style, and hence the traits which make it up, may occur in any art or medium. It may consist of visual, auditory, or lower-sense traits. Styles are distinguished in cuisine and dress, in fine and useful arts, and in areas of culture outside the realm of art. The traits which constitute it may be directly presented (as brownness is in a painting of wood and leather) or suggested (as in a literary description of those materials). The tendency to use various tones of brown is a stylistic trait of Rembrandt and his school, while the use of more bright, contrasting hues is a stylistic trait of Monet and the impressionists.

In general, a stylistic trait is a trait regarded as especially characteristic of a certain style and used as one of the specifications in defining it. In a particular work of art, it is a trait which serves to identify it as an example of a certain style or styles. The definition of a style, as we have seen, requires a comparatively large number of such specifications; it cannot be reduced to a single trait such as red, loud, fast, realistic, or geometric. However, the presence of one such trait which is essentially inconsistent with a certain style may be enough to show that the work of art in question does not belong to that style, and that it could not have been produced at the time or place in which the style originated. A bright, flat blue circle in a Rembrandt painting would probably seem incongruous. Although some styles are named for brevity in terms of a single trait, such as the "geometric" style, the "animal" style, or the "red-figured" style, other traits are always understood as correlated with it. Such traits may refer to different components and modes of composition: e.g., to the linear traits of red-figured vases or to the position and distortion of animal figures.

Certain traits of a style are regarded as more typical and essential than others: for example, pointed arches in gothic architecture. These are felt to be more expressive of the spirit of the style and more indispensable in deciding whether a work of art belongs to that style. They are comparatively constant and emphatic in the works so classified; others are more optional or variable. Some occur often but not always or necessarily in the style. Flying buttresses are characteristic of some divisions of the gothic style, but are not universal or necessary in all gothic architecture.

They are more characteristic of the French than of the Italian substyle of gothic.

Not all the traits of a work of art are stylistic traits, but only those which serve to identify it as an example of a style; those which it has in common with many others of the style, and which do not occur to any great extent in other styles. Some of the traits in a work of art which are highly praised and valued, which seem to the untrained eye as most distinctive, may not be definitely stylistic. Most of its stylistic traits will be present in other examples of the same style. The most distinctive and important traits in a work of art can often be described as unusual ways of varying a familiar style; of giving it an original twist or achieving its potentialities to an extent not reached by other examples. A completely unique trait would be non-stylistic, but it is hard to imagine one. A trait which occurs in so many different styles that it is not distinctive of any is a non-stylistic trait: for example, the mere fact of representing the human body in stone or using rhythm and melody in music. Selectiveness, unity, and contrast in general are not stylistic, but some particular degree or variety of each could be.

When two styles are similar in a certain respect —e.g., in having curved lines and surfaces—they must be differentiated in terms of degree, quantity, or some other slight variance; perhaps in the way they are combined. Louis XVI furniture is straighter than Louis XV. Classic and romantic poets both use imagery from nature and express emotions. To distinguish their styles, some scholars count and compare the number of times a certain kind of image or emotion is used. The same can be done with the frequency of certain dissonances or modulations in music. To some extent such differences can be measured or estimated. Critics often describe stylistic traits in roughly quantitative terms, such as more and less curvilinear, or more or less inclined to attribute human feelings to plants and animals. Rembrandt uses, on the whole, less contrast of hues than Rubens does. It would be hard but not impossible to measure this sta-

tistically. Many of the traits involved in style, such as "mystical" and 'idealistic," are much harder to estimate, and so is their combined, aesthetic effect. In trying to do so, one runs the risk of projecting one's own attitudes and habits of thought into the style, thus giving it meanings quite different from its original ones.

The definition of a style may include not only traits of perceptible form and meaning, but also those of materials, tools, and technics, which may not appear directly in the final product. They must be inferred from the perceptible traits with the aid of outside information. Such information is important to the anthropologist in comparing styles of tool or pottery. At all stages of culture, style is influenced by the materials, tools, and technics available at the time and place. But in modern civilization people tend to think out, more in advance, what kinds of form and style they want to produce; then to import or invent the materials and means which are necessary to that end. Conceptions of a desired form and style tend more to determine the material and process. Some styles try to conceal the nature of the raw material and technical process; others to emphasize them and adapt the form to them. Unwanted, perceptible traits of the material can be concealed and others substituted, as the natural wood is often concealed in rococo furniture by paint, carving, or inlay. Certain perceptible traits which are wanted, and which could formerly be produced only by certain materials or processes, can be imitated with increasing exactness. Thus the appearance of water-color on paper is produced in printing; that of stone or bronze patina is imitated on plaster casts. The sound of violins and voices is reproduced by radio and phonograph. Aesthetically, the perceptible qualities are more important than the physical. This ease of change and substitution in material or physical medium is important for an understanding of modern styles.

Some traits and types in art are more directly perceptible to the senses than others: some can be measured and others not. A conception of style based only on measurable traits, as in the size, shape, linear decoration, and surface textures of a clay pot, is closer to the ideals of exact science than one which deals with intangible suggestions like mysticism, romanticism, and pessimism. But without attention to the latter also, no conception of style is adequate to deal with the more highly evolved types of civilized art. For a deeper understanding of the "spirit" of a style, as well as of particular works of art, we must take account of abstract meanings and emotional expressions insofar as they can be inferred with some assurance as socially established in the culture concerned. Ideas as to what is beautiful and what is not can be established meanings—e.g., in a picture of Aphrodite and Hephaestus or a poem about them. Evaluative and emotional suggestions in the work of art itself can thus be stylistic traits, but not the observer's personal feelings toward the work or style in question. Literary style consists very largely of suggested traits or meanings, conveyed by verbal symbols. When a literary work is read silently, even the sounds of words are suggested by the text and imagined by the reader. Characteristic traits in either sound or meaning can be stylistic.

Style is not separate from meaning or content, although the two can be distinguished in theory and in morphological analysis. It is incorrect to think that a certain set of ideas or represented subject-matter can be expressed with only superficial change in various styles, as a man puts on a different set of clothes. Certain ingredients may persist throughout the change, but to change the verbal or visual form of expression is sure to change, in some degree, the ideas and feelings suggested. A religious, Christian, otherworldly content of ideas, images, and attitudes is an important trait of style in most medieval European art. Stylistic analysis requires a study of the relation between these and the more obvious, sensory traits of art, to see what consistency or inconsistency may exist between them.

Something of the sort must be included, with due caution, in all attempts at a thorough charac-

terization of modern, civilized styles. This is not true of stylistic research in anthropology and archeology, where such interpretations usually seem too subjective. It is necessitated by the fact that the scope, complexity, and diversity of associated meanings in modern art and civilization are so much greater than in prehistoric culture. (There has been some attempt to prune away such associations from recent art, but it has not gone very far.) Even though we do not know in detail what associations prehistoric art had for its makers, and must assume considerable development along this line in late paleolithic times, it is probable that civilized art is on the whole more complex and diversified than primitive art in both presented and suggested factors. Thus some description of the cultural meanings and affective qualities of style is more necessary, as well as more verifiable, in the study of civilized than of early primitive art.

Traits and terms implying evaluation or the expressing of likes and dislikes do not serve well to define a style; they are too subjective and debatable. Such words as "beautiful" and "ugly," "delightful" and "disagreeable," "superb" and "over-decorated," though suited to critical evaluation, are not ordinarily suited to the scientific description of styles or works of art. They may become so only when these words themselves are given a special, objectively verifiable meaning. "Beauty," for example, can be defined, not as high aesthetic value, but as conformity to the Greek canons of balance, proportion, and classical repose. These are still somewhat vague and debatable, but are more susceptible to objective (intersubjective) observation. Tastes change toward styles, so that the gothic and baroque may seem "excessively ornate" at one time but not at others. Without saying "too much" or "too little," one can indicate a comparatively high or low degree of the trait indicated. A style should be objectively defined, after which the critic may evaluate it in any way he sees fit. The names of many stylistic traits such as "heavy," "harsh," "crowded," etc., are often used with evaluative coloring. The attempt should be made to avoid this in morphological description.

It is impossible to define a style in purely objective terms, or to describe a work of art without some report of one's own subjective experience in observing it. Even a description in terms of direct sense-qualities such as red and blue, square and round, contains a subjective element. To describe a line as waving, drooping, firm, decisive, limp, or balanced, involves some projection of the observer's empathic and imaginative responses. The subjective element is likely to increase when one tries to characterize the suggested feelings, emotional attitudes, implicit beliefs and inferences in a work of art or style, in such words as tense, calm, wild, erratic, unified, passionate, cold, austere, wistful, sentimental, cynical, ascetic, neo-Platonic, and the like. Without doing so to some extent, one can not include what seem to be, from the standpoints of aesthetics and art history, among the essentials of art. But there is a middle course between describing these essentials as objectively as possible and, on the other hand, emphasizing one's own emotional responses and personal preferences. This is a problem which confronts, not only stylistic theory, but all writing on the history and morphological analysis of art.

The trained eye, ear, and mind can find much to do in describing those aspects of art which are directly perceptible to the senses or attributable to the object as culturally established meanings. Among these, one may include as essentials of a style any of the main groups of traits discussed above: those pertaining to the modes of transmission (presented and suggested), to spatiotemporal and causal organization, to elementary and developed components, and to the modes of composition.

Stylistic traits have been classified in various ways. Kroeber distinguishes three "ingredients of style" in the representational fine arts. First, he says, is the objective subject matter dealt with; second, the artist's concept of the subject, including its emotional aura and value toning; third, the

specific technical form and execution—the artist's diction, rhythm, or brush stroke.[4]

The kinds of trait which are most significant in defining styles vary considerably from art to art and style to style. Sometimes the material and technic are distinctive and influential in determining the total form, sometimes not. The same can be said of represented subject-matter and utilitarian function. It is an integral part of some styles to give special weight to the subject of a painting or the function of a piece of furniture or architecture. A painting of the *Entombment* may be rendered in a different, graver style than that of the *Nativity* or *Marriage at Cana*. A sword or other implement whose military function is important may be fashioned more severely than an ornamental staff or scepter. Our present age is inclined to stress utilitarian function, and to feel as a fault any lack of harmony between the form and the function or subject-matter. But this itself is a stylistic trait. Some periods (e.g., the rococo) and some artists have been more inclined to ignore the usual requirements of a functional or representational type, and to treat all sorts of them in about the same style. Van Gogh's late works treat many subjects in a similar style. Such an apparent detachment of style from subject or function can itself be a stylistic trait. One may then feel that style (in a limited sense of the word) does not take in the whole work, but acts as a separate, somewhat independent part of it, as in spreading surface ornamentation over a sword or shield. Usually there is a reason for the divorce, other than mere lack of artistic ability. An artist such as Van Gogh may be so much moved by his inner feelings and his interest in certain qualities of color and brushstroke that the differences in external subject-matter seem unimportant. In a relatively safe, luxurious milieu, a sword or shield may have actually lost its

[4] *Style and Civilizations*, p. 30. Meyer Schapiro lists three "aspects of art" to which the description of a style usually refers: form elements or motives (such as the round or pointed arch), form relationships (such as ways of combining motives), and expressive and other qualitities (such as cool and warm, gay and sad). "Style" in *Anthropology Today*, p. 289.

previous functional urgency and become itself an ornament rather than a weapon. The subjects of religious paintings may no longer be taken very seriously, at least by the patrons of art, so that sad and happy ones, religious and secular, have become mere vehicles for a style which is mainly aesthetic and ornamental in spirit. The aim of stylistic analysis is not to evaluate, but to describe such traits and, if possible, their relation to surrounding social attitudes and conditions.

A trait in aesthetic form and style is not an independent, discrete unit or element, capable of maintaining its identity without change in different combinations. It is a product of perceptual and intellectual analysis, and always occurs in a configuration or gestalt, large or small. Within a large, complex configuration like a picture or symphony, the observer can distinguish smaller, simpler configurations, such as the combination of shapes and colors making up a face in a group, or the combination of pitch and rhythm traits which make up a melodic figure. Any trait such as redness or dissonance is somewhat affected by its surroundings; it may appear as brighter or duller, more or less dissonant, according to its immediate and total context in the work of art.

Accordingly, the description of a style—in abstraction or as manifested in a work of art—can not be a mere listing of separate traits. It must give some account of the way traits are interrelated, in the work as a whole, in the large parts, and in smaller parts within these. Red and blue will be very different when they occur as tiny streaks within a mottled texture, in equally small details within a complex textile design, or as large, contrasting areas of plain color. They will be different when presented as pure decoration or as symbolic details in a coat of arms. Essential to the concept of a style is its characteristic way of combining concrete details and traits within them, so as to produce a distinctive total effect. While this will vary to some extent within each particular work and substyle, it can maintain enough identity in different contexts to be abstracted, named, and

recognized. There can also be a perceptible difference between the style in its purest form, occurring in its most typical examples, and the same style in mixed, impure, atypical versions.

Practically any trait or type—even those commonly regarded as simple and elementary, can be analyzed psychologically into a small cluster of related subtraits. Any particular case of redness can be analyzed into a certain hue, intensity or chroma, and brilliance or value. The subtle differences which come from varying colors in these ways may or may not be significant in defining a style. In making rough, sweeping contrasts of style between "classic" and "baroque" painting, one may use Wölfflin's concepts of "linear" and "painterly" as single, elementary traits. But in comparing two "baroque" painters such as Rubens and Vermeer, it may be important to distinguish various constituents of painterliness. Wölfflin does this in general terms in his brief definitions of the five opposing pairs.[5] The trait called "painterly" is itself a joint product of such subtraits as "depreciation of line," "merging of objects," and "apprehension of the world as a shifting semblance." Two painterly artists may exhibit these in different degrees.

The difference between traits and subtraits is only relative, a device for classifying them in some orderly way. The "subtrait" is not necessarily smaller or less important.

5. THE EXTENSION OR DISTRIBUTION OF A HISTORIC STYLE

As a set of traits which recur in certain works of art, every historic style has a certain extension or field of occurrence. This is the realm of space, time, and social culture in which it is or was

[5] Introduction, p. 14, in *Principles of Art History* (New York, 1932). *Cf.* Wylie Sypher's discussion of these as "polarities... in discussing the evolution of renaissance styles..." *Four Stages of Renaissance Style*, p. 19.

produced and used. This realm is also called its "provenance"—the place and time in which a style or work of art originates; the person or persons who produced it. The field of production may be the same as that of use or very different, as when a kind of art is made in one region for export to another, or by one sex or one social class for use by another. Works of art are often found as "trade pieces," far from their original provenance. The group which makes it may stay in a certain place or, like the Celts, wander far. A style may originate in one field, travel to another, and die out in the first; these are its primary and secondary fields.

The distribution of styles in modern civilization changes rapidly and, on the whole, with increasing speed. Contributing causes are the speed of communication, commercial enterprise, and fickleness of taste, impelling a constant desire for novelty. In advanced civilizations and especially in periods of individualism, greater attention is paid to individual artists and their styles. People tend to think of art as something which progresses or should progress. Ancient and medieval art was not as anonymous as is sometimes thought, but less emphasis was placed on originality and the expression of individual personality than in the contemporary, Western world. Artists themselves are now more conscious of their styles and eager to work out new, distinctive ones, better than the old or at least different from them.

In various ways, a style can grow and spread as it wins favor; then decline and contract. Its changes in distribution, or its distribution at any one time, can be charted much as biologists chart the distribution of certain types of living or fossil organism, and as anthropologists chart that of certain types of axe or clay pot.

The distribution of a style, and any changes which occur in it, can be described in various ways. It has a certain *cultural* extension, a *social*, a *geographical*, and a *chronological* extension. It may change, and differ from other styles, in any or all of these ways:

(a) *Culturally:* as to its occurrence in one or more arts or other branches of culture. Analogous trait-complexes and trends like those in art may occur in such fields as religion, philosophy, science, politics, economics, ethics, and general mode of life.

(b) *Socially:* as to its occurrence in one or more social, political, ethnic, or religious groups, classes, or subdivisions of them. A style may originate in one nation or religion and spread to another; in the upper, courtly class and spread to the lower, or among men and spread to women, or among city-dwellers and spread to peasants, or among soldiers and spread to civilians. It may be made by slaves or humble artisans for the rich and noble.

(c) *Geographically:* as to the place or places in which it is made and used. Some are local or narrowly distributed; others spread over whole continents or hemispheres.

(d) *Chronologically:* as to its active production and use in certain periods of time. Some are short-lived, such as futurism in painting; some endure for centuries, such as Doric architecture.

To describe thoroughly the changing distribution of a style, one should note all these possible modes of occurrence. One should distinguish also between the production or performance of a style and its use or enjoyment. One should note the gradual rise of a style in activity and favor, so that it spreads over larger areas, is made in greater quantity and perhaps by better artists, and is used by more élite groups; then its gradual or sudden decline and contraction.

6. NAMING AND DEFINING
PARTICULAR STYLES.

The development of aesthetic morphology requires the eventual adoption, by a consensus of scholars, of standard names for each style and accepted, fairly uniform definitions for each. We are still far from achieving it. There are serious difficulties in the way, but some progress is being made.

A single word, such as "rococo", can take the place of much detailed description for those who understand it. It can be further qualified in various ways: e.g., "a rather plain, heavy version of rococo," or "rococo with a few Louis XVI characteristics." "Rococo" is defined in Webster's *New International Dictionary* as "A style of ornamentation developed in France chiefly under Louis XV (1715–74) and carried to extremes in Italy and Germany in the eighteenth century, characterized by curved spatial forms, light and fantastic curved lines, often flowing, reversed, or unsymmetrical, and ornamentation of pierced shellwork. Hence, any style of ornamentation marked by extravagant curvature and ornament." (The word "extravagant" is debatable as an evaluation). "Gothic," in architecture, is defined in terms of pointed arches, high vaults, pitched roofs, slender piers, thin walls, large stained glass windows, flying buttresses, etc., although a building may be classed as gothic without having all these traits.

To define a period style as clearly as possible, showing its nature and difference from others, one should specify (a) its approximate field of distribution or provenance, thus marking off a group of art products within that field, and (b) the traits which are believed to characterize them. Historians sometimes begin with the idea of a certain field, such as France in the eighteenth century, and then try to list the distinctive traits of art in that field. They may find several different kinds of art within it, so that no one style or set of traits will characterize the whole. They may have to distinguish several styles within the period, some more important and some less. The other way to begin is with the idea of a set of traits, an abstract style conception such as "baroque" or "romanticism," and then ask where and when it is to be found in art. This may lead one far afield. Both approaches are needed, to supplement each other progressively: one is inductive and synthetic; the other deductive and analytic, using the style-concept as a hypothesis.

Styles can seldom if ever be marked off from each other with absolute precision. They are constantly changing, growing, and declining. As to their fields and the traits in which they are defined, they overlap and shade into each other. This is true even of styles which, as abstractly defined, seem antithetical and incompatible. Someone is likely to try to combine the best elements of both or to change gradually from one to the other, producing what historians may describe as a mixed or transitional style.

To define the field or extension clearly, one should indicate the *period*, the *place*, and the *people*. The "people" concerned may be very numerous —the whole population of a nation or continent— or comprise only a small school or *coterie*, such as the Barbizon painters, futurists, or cubists. The group may be few in number but scattered over the world, as are contemporary abstract expressionist painters. It was mentioned above that the "people" may be only a single artist, as in the style of Raphael or Milton. But if imitated or practiced by others, such as the artist's apprentices or assistants, it becomes the style of a "school," atelier, movement, or other grouping. A Raphaelesque picture was not necessarily made by Raphael.

The extreme of narrowness in the productive field of a style is in the works of a single artist such as Picasso, in a single medium such as painting, in a single period of his life such as the "blue period." Historians refer to El Greco's early style under the influence of Tintoretto, and to his late style, more like some late Byzantine frescoes; highly individual, mystic, and unrealistic, with much elongation of the figures and glowing, vaporous colors.

Sometimes it is impossible to locate a period style geographically or chronologically because of inadequate information about its provenance. Partial information, or partial resemblance to known styles, may suggest a hypothetical provenance, or several possibilities. Pending further information, one may identify it only roughly, as for example in Asia Minor during the first millennium B.C., with possible Hittite influence. The effort of the historian will always be to place it as exactly as possible in a spatio-temporal-cultural setting, but for the time being it must be conceived as unlocated, undated, or both; a detached, floating complex of traits without known provenance.

In working out a new conception of style (of a new style or a newly distinguished old one) scholars often disagree on what name should be used and what the name should imply. In the case of impressionism, is the attempt to record a quick, fleeting impression of passing phenomena the most essential characteristic? If so, Whistler and Degas —the former with his butterfly as symbol of this aim—can claim to be impressionists. If "broken color," as a means to representing the vibrant sunlight reflections on colored objects out of doors, is the most essential aim, then Whistler and Degas are not typical impressionists, but Monet and Sisley are. The latter conception of impressionism is now emphasized. It tends to restrict the term to pictorial art, and hence to be less useful when the term "impressionism" is applied to music or poetry. Similar issues arise in respect to almost every major concept of style.

What works and types of art, what schools and artists, are to be classed as examples of a certain style such as "baroque"? To say "the baroque style occurred in these places at these times" implies a certain definition of the word "baroque"; a certain conception of the baroque style. If we change the definition, a change in denotation is almost sure to follow. This is essentially a verbal, semantic problem, but closely related to the description of historic facts.

The concept of a style has its own history, apart from that of the style itself and often hard to trace. The word "baroque" was formerly traced to the name of an irregularly shaped pearl, and is now traced to the name of a type of syllogism in scholastic logic. In either case, the spread of such a name and concept to cover broad and very different areas of culture is an important thread in cultural history. As a rule, it follows considerably after the spread of the style itself, which usually has no single, accepted, general designation at first. The problem of what to call the style, and of what examples shall be classed under it, receives increasing attention as historians examine its career in retrospect. Only in the twentieth century has the interest in styles of art become so keen that we try to name and classify contemporary styles in detail in their early, experimental stages, and eagerly anticipate future changes in style. How a current name was first attached to a certain style is often hard to trace, and apparently due to a series of accidental associations, not rational choice. The etymology of the name and its early meaning may be far removed from the significance later given it by theorists. "Irregularity" and "strangeness" are traits attributed to both the pearls and paintings called by that name; but the analogy is rather far-fetched. The resemblance to "baroco" syllogisms is even more so. "Rococo" comes from "rocaille" and "coquille," meaning rock and shell, which were often used as motifs in eighteenth-century French decoration; but they give no profound clue to the nature of the style as a whole. Such terms may be first applied in a casual, metaphorical way to a some vaguely designated kind of art, then gradually come into technical use, the original meanings being almost lost. The same can be said of "gothic," in which the early reference to Goths was overwhelmed by other ideas, and of "romantic," with its reference to the medieval romances, the romance languages, and ultimately to Rome. More precise names for styles could no doubt be worked out afresh, together with more clear, objective definitions; but established usage is hard to brush aside. Accordingly, much present effort is devoted to correcting the definitions and denotations of traditional, ambiguous style-names. In the case of gothic, baroque, rococo, and many others, evaluative connotations of extravagance, overdecoration, bad taste, and the like have had to be eliminated and more objective traits attached in their place.

Logically, the connotation or abstract definition

of a style-name should be consistent with its supposed denotation or extension. If we define "rococo" abstractly as "light," "curving," and "unsymmetrical," we cannot consistently apply the term to an object which is heavy, rectilinear, and symmetrical. If we define it in a way which excludes typical examples of the Louis XVI style, we cannot consistently use "rococo" as equivalent to "eighteenth-century French." If we define a style in terms of certain traits, and classify certain works of art, schools, artists, or periods under that style, the specified traits should be observable in those examples. It can hardly be expected that *all* the examples will exhibit *all* the specified traits, for there is too much variation in any modern period. One can allow for this by saying that the specified traits are "common in," or "characteristic of" the style in its most typical form, without saying that they are essential, universal, or necessary. But if the exceptions are numerous and important, the application of the term becomes doubtful. One has the choice, then, of redefining the term so as to cover the exceptional examples, or of classing them under some other style-name. Some amount of inconsistency and ambiguity between the connotation and the denotation of style-names does no great harm in casual conversation and even in popular writing on art history; but it hampers exact communication on a more scholarly level. Present confusions in stylistic terminology are a serious barrier to research on the history and evolution of styles.

Confusion arises especially from the double reference of each style-concept to (a) a set of *traits*, regarded as characteristic of the style, and (b) a certain *period* or *provenance*, marked off in terms of specific dates, places, and people, including individual artists and their works. Early discussion of the style under one name or another is usually based on a fairly limited group of objects, produced by artists of a certain locality within a limited span of years. The concept of the style is then a sort of greatest common denominator of the characteristics which seem important in these particular

works. Thus Wölfflin worked out his new conception of "baroque" by contrasting certain examples of European painting, sculpture, and architecture, mostly from the sixteenth century, with certain others, mostly from the seventeenth century.

Some incautious readers inferred that *all* seventeenth-century art had *all* of Wölfflin's five baroque characteristics, and that *no* art of other centuries had them. This, in spite of his explicit statement that some "Seicento" characteristics are to be found in the sixteenth and eighteenth centuries. It has been pointed out that some sixteenth-century artists such as Tintoretto are, at times, more baroque (in Wölfflin's sense) than some seventeenth-century ones, such as Poussin in his more classical moments. There is nothing incorrect in making the concept of a style refer both to a certain period in art and to the main, distinctive traits of art in that period. To do so is an essential task in writing the history of art. The error comes only in oversimplifying the facts: in assuming that all the art in that period is of one style, and that examples of that style never occur outside the period.

If one starts out with the idea of baroque as a period and also with the idea of a certain style as characteristic of it, one is tempted to interpret as many artists and works of the period as possible in terms of that style. One tends to exaggerate the ways in which they conform to it, and minimize the non-conformities.

It is not always easy to decide what actually was the most characteristic style of a place and period. Is it the one which actually dominated art at the time? But this may have been a conservative survival from the past which no longer seems to us as the real, creative expression of the age. Is it the avant-garde style which later came to dominate a subsequent age? But what right have we to call a somewhat neglected, minority style most typical of its own age? In such cases, our judgment is necessarily influenced by knowledge of later events and our own value-judgments.

[263]

7. MAJOR STYLES IN WESTERN ARTS:
CHANGING CONCEPTIONS
OF THEIR NATURE AND SCOPE.
THE TAXONOMY OF STYLES

In the recent history and theory of styles, there has been a tendency (much influenced by German-writing scholars) to enlarge the extension of a few selected concepts. This is due partly to the desire of philosophers of history to extend their systems (as in Spengler's conception of Faustian art); in part to the discovery of more actual similarities and influences among the various arts than had been realized. Carl J. Friedrich cites Ludwig Curtius, the archeologist, as thus extending the meaning of "gothic." "I mean by Gothic," said Curtius, "not merely the youthful experience of a gothic cathedral or of late gothic altar shrines, but the whole world of the late middle ages, its religious, spiritual and ethical essence, which lives on in... the music of Johann Sebastian Bach."[6]

Such an extension of the term "gothic," to cover a much longer period and greater variety of styles than usual, is no mere careless confusion. It expresses a reasoned belief that there is a far-reaching "spirit" which pervades this larger field, and which deserves the name "gothic" more than do the small styles to which it is usually limited. This is debatable, and in any case it raises the question of how such different meanings can be reconciled. Can "gothic" in the broad sense be defined in terms of observable traits as well as of "spiritual essence"? If so, what traits do Bach's music and the gothic altar have in common? Are they both substyles of gothic art, and what exact period does gothic style cover?

Through this process of expansion a few style-concepts have been given vast scope, while being vaguely defined and overlapping. Many others have been narrowed down or abandoned. "Renaissance," though still a broad concept, was used in the nineteenth century (e.g., by Banister Fletcher in his *History of Architecture*[7]) to cover what is now called "mannerist" and "baroque" in addi-

tion to its present meaning. "Rococo" used to be roughly equivalent to "Louis XV" and restricted to French decorative style in that reign. Now it is often applied to all the arts throughout Europe in the whole of the eighteenth century. A short list of major style-concepts, such as renaissance, baroque, mannerist, neo-classic, and romantic, has thus been used to cover all modern styles in all the arts. "Louis XV" thus becomes a substyle of "rococo."

At the same time, this list (with slight variations) is used by some historians as the basis for a system of periodization for modern Western culture history. "Baroque" comes to mean, not so much a style or set of styles, as an all-inclusive chapter of history during a certain period: a spatio-temporal section in the total flow of human events, within which all art styles are mere constituent patterns.

By classing certain styles under others from the broadest to the narrowest, an effort is made to work out a systematic *taxonomy* of styles. But it is still hampered by the double reference: to abstract traits and types, and to main periods of art and cultural history. Which shall be emphasized? Biology also has that problem, in distinguishing between a formal classification of animals and plants, both living and extinct, and a chronological account of their evolution. Problems of stylistic nomenclature are constantly arising: for example, whether to class "Chinese Chippendale" as a subdivision of "rococo," in a very broad, international sense of the latter term. The Chippendale and other, contemporary English styles can be classed as "English rococo," as the Dresden *Zwinger* has been called "German rococo."

Thus to transfer the idea of "rococo" from its original French provenance, in ornament, furniture, and architecture under Louis XV, to partly similar styles in the same arts across the Channel or in Germany and Austria, involves an extension of the concept along geographical and social lines,

[6] "Style and Historical Interpretation," *Journal of Aesthetics and Art Criticism*, XIV, 2 (Dec. 1955), p. 143.
[7] (London, 1896).

in terms of places and peoples. In this case, the period of the style is obviously due in large part to the diffusion of tastes and patterns, by imitation and in some cases by the travel of artists back and forth from one country to another. As the denotation of the concept is thus extended, one must redefine its connotation accordingly. What must "rococo" mean if we are to speak of Italian and Spanish rococo? If "rococo" is to cover Chippendale furniture, what stylistic traits has it in common with the French? Louis XV emphasizes lightness in shape and color, gilt and pastel tints, light brocaded silk upholstery with unsymmetrical designs. Chippendale tends rather to mahogany and walnut; to darker colors and heavier shapes. Both have in common an occasional use of *chinoiserie*. Chippendale is often but not always curvilinear, and sometimes lighter in shape than previous English furniture. As one expands the extension of such a term to cover more and more different varieties, more and more space and time, the abstract definition must become more simple and general, in terms of fewer traits. Is all eighteenth-century French art of the old régime, including Regency and Louis XVI, to be classed under the main generic name "rococo"? Are Sheraton and Hepplewhite to be classed, along with Chippendale, as English rococo? If so, we must not specify wide curvilinear shape, as in cabriole legs, among the essential traits of rococo in general.

In thus expanding the denotation of such a style-name farther and farther in space and time, the historian runs the risk of once more oversimplifying facts to fit a concept. He is tempted to overlook the increasing multiplicity and diversity of the field it is supposed to cover. He is tempted to imagine some mysterious, intangible, unifying spirit beneath all these differences. This is the persistent error of Platonizing historians and philosophers. It has been especially notable in concepts of supposed national styles such as the Greek, Italian, or German, which nationalistic or racially conscious historians try to erect into major histori-

cal divisions. Taine and Symonds drifted into this error. Both generalized too sweepingly about such broad fields as Greek drama, Italian painting, and Dutch painting, with insufficient recognition of the diversities involved.

8. POLYTECHNICAL AND WHOLE-CULTURE STYLES. THE "SPIRIT" OF A STYLE AND OF ITS AGE

Through a process of cultural extension within the same approximate period, place, and people, a style may spread from one art to another and perhaps through all the arts of the epoch. It thus becomes a pervasive, far-reaching cultural movement. Related movements may occur in different fields such as religion, philosophy, science, political and social behavior, all combining into one vast cultural trend such as the romantic movement of the late eighteenth and early nineteenth centuries in Europe. Certain abstract traits, such as the love of freedom, change, nature, and emotion, link its typical products in all these diverse fields. As a style of art, life, and thought in all their manifestations, romanticism is thus highly extensive culturally. As displayed in many arts, many skills and media, it can be called a *polytechnical* style. A style limited to one art is monotechnical. In terms of the sense or senses addressed, a style can be unisensory (as in music), bisensory (as in opera) or multisensory (as in a religious ritual with incense). As displayed in non-artistic fields as well, it can be a *whole-culture* style;[8] a temporary but far-reaching configuration within the total culture-pattern of a people at a certain place and time. It is less extensive than the total culture-pattern, since that includes also many non-stylistic traits: ways in which the culture of the period is not distinctive or differs from the main, typical style.

At an early stage in the study of a certain period,

[8] *Cf.* Kroeber, *Style and Civilizations*, pp. 70, 151, on "whole-culture styles."

one may feel only a vague, intangible flavor in common among the diversified manners and products of an age. Modern stylistic analysis can gradually trace it down to more objective traits if it is real and not imaginary. But there are many difficulties in doing so. It is hard to discern and describe in words an abstract resemblance between music and painting, or music, food, and odor. But such analogies can and do exist, because of the basic unity of the human organism, including all its senses, and because of the close association of all arts in a given culture-pattern. Some particular emotional attitude may pervade the whole pattern at a certain time, such as revolt or docile obedience, ascetic simplicity or lush sensuality. With a set of related ideas and behavior-traits, it may be expressed and symbolized in various arts, thus constituting an extensive style. But it is not easy to distinguish a comparatively objective analogy of this sort from the more subjective illusion of kinship or causal relation due to contiguity in space and time. Hasty inference interprets Van Gogh's style as an expression of his incipient madness; it attributes the detachment of bodily parts in analytical cubism to the "disintegration" of modern civilization. The traveler associates certain styles of cooking, such as the Italian and Chinese, with the national cultures and artistic styles with which they have been historically connected; he associates certain "heavy" perfumes, such as amber and sandalwood, with the ornateness and sensuous eroticism of the East; light, fresh, cool flower scents with the healthy, outdoor ideals of Western femininity. To what extent are these mere accidental or occasional associations, and to what extent expressions of deeper attitudes, fixed or transitory? We are on firmer ground in associating the restrained simplicity of the Gregorian chant with that of the romanesque and early gothic churches in which it flourished; the more complex, exuberant church music of the late renaissance and baroque with its architectural styles. But any single trait may have different meaning in a different context: the heavy scent of oriental incense becomes religious when it proceeds from a censer in church.

The field of denotation of the concept "romantic," as conceived by Goethe, the Schlegels, and others in the early nineteenth century, was mainly literary. Byron was regarded as a typical romantic poet. As it happened, many artistic and intellectual leaders of the romantic movement were men of broad vision, interested in all the arts and regarding them as essentially one; as varied expressions of the same, underlying spirit of man. Hence the concept spread quickly through the visual arts, music, and ballet; through painting and sculpture, garden design, and rustic cottage architecture. Poets felt a kinship with the philosophers and biologists who were working out the grand conception of cosmic evolution as embracing all of life and culture in its drive toward physical and mental progress.

In recent decades, historical studies of the arts have become more specialized, not only detaching one art from another in research and education, but often detaching the art of each period and place from that of others for intensive study. As we have seen, this trend has sometimes obstructed philosophic theorizing about the arts, including the development of broad conceptions of style, based on the discernment of underlying affinities among the various arts at a particular time and place. In the effort to correct this, concepts of all-inclusive styles have been loosely used and vaguely defined. Terms like "baroque" have been flung about from art to art with oversimplified analogies. Western scholars now distrust such terms as "spirit of the age," beloved by German philosophers of history. Nevertheless, it seems obvious that some kinship, some distinctive set of attitudes, beliefs, aesthetic tastes, and expressive symbols does bind together examples of different arts in each epoch; not all of them, but enough to justify one in classing them under the same general styles.

It is also highly important for style-theory to develop a numerous list of narrower concepts for describing the immense variety of substyles, past and present. The larger and more diversified the field which a style-concept has to cover, the more its meaning tends to thin out; to become more vague, abstract, and remote from the concrete individuality of specific, local styles. In the personal style of a single artist at a single moment of his career, we encounter the full, unique, distinctive richness of a style, and hence we tend to say, "Le style, c'est l'homme même." Both the generic and the specific are important in the classification of styles, as in that of biological types.

Faced with this problem, critics and historians have responded in different ways. Some hold the essentials of style, as of aesthetic value, to be indescribable in words; once more the mysterious *je ne sais quoi*. Some resort to vague expressions such as "the romantic spirit," which are mere restatements of the problem; for in what does the romantic spirit consist? Some use descriptive terms in a broad, metaphorical way, as in calling music "linear" or "colorful." Thus a great novel is "orchestrated," and architecture is "frozen music."

Aesthetic morphology seeks more objective terms and concepts for describing styles, some applicable only in one art and some in many. These are emerging from the detailed comparison of works in all media, as to their component traits and modes of organization. It is never possible to achieve complete objectivity in describing art. One can approximate it more, for practical purposes, in talking about the presented, directly observable, traits of form and style, such as "gilt," "unsymmetrical," and "curvilinear" in rococo ornament. Many other abstract terms, such as large and small, simple and complex, regular and irregular, are fairly objective and applicable to the whole field of art. But when we try to describe the subtle, emotional and ideological suggestions of art, and to distinguish styles on this basis, we tread on thinner ice. To what extent, for example, is renaissance literature to be called "naturalistic," by analogy with renaissance painting, in spite of its strong infusion of neo-Platonism?

Early attempts at stylistic differentiation often emphasized somewhat vague, debatable qualities of emotional suggestiveness, as well as value judgments. Winckelmann saw noble simplicity, dignity, and harmonious stillness as essentials of Greek art. Later style-theory has shifted the emphasis to perceptible traits in the visual and musical arts, and in literature to specific meanings of words instead of those vague qualities which have to be felt "between the lines." Alleged stylistic traits have been subjected to a much more rigorous testing in application to a wide sampling of the objects said to manifest them. (Winckelmann, for instance, knew comparatively little of early Greek art.) Wölfflin's five contrasting pairs of traits have seemed objective, partly because they avoided the intangible, emotional "auras" of art and focused the attention either on directly visible images, such as sharp or blurred lines, or on directly represented physical appearances, such as perspective in shallow planes or in continuous recession. It has been comparatively easy to apply these concepts within the visual arts, and even in music and literature they have been suggestive. To call baroque and romantic music "painterly" is not without objective reference; it suggests the blurring of "melodic lines" and strictly metered rhythms by means of harmonic and orchestral "coloring." Likewise, one can point to "closed" and "open" forms in literature: the one in tightly unified, neo-classic plots and simple types of character; the other in stories which present an unfinished, ragged slice of life with human beings full of inconsistency and change.

To achieve its maximum utility, the concept of a style in terms of abstract traits should serve as a verifiable hypothesis in observation and comparative analysis. Even the more subjective concepts, such as "serene repose" and "nervous energy" can be illuminating in a contrast, let us say, between Phidias and Donatello. Still more widely, the concept of each polytechnical or broadly cultural style should act as a chart and flashlight in one's travels through the arts of different periods, calling attention to qualities one might otherwise ignore and which, though perhaps between the lines, can be discerned by different readers as actually present and distinctive. Each word, such as "heavy and powerful" for baroque and "light and delicate" for rococo, should be a *mot juste;* not a mere flight of fancy on the critic's part, but a precise clue to recurrent traits which can, on demand, be sensed or reliably inferred in perceiving the objects indicated. Having found each trait as specified, separately and in combination, one should feel that one has not been dealing with superficial accidents or anomalies, but with the inmost character of the style, as in penetrating beneath the psychic reserve of a human individual. As an extensive map and revealing torch, Wölfflin's set of traits is less illuminating than some later definitions of baroque; less so, for example, than Carl J. Friedrich's phrase "restless search for power." That search in all its forms, says Friedrich, "spiritual and secular, scientific and political, psychological and technical, is the only common denominator which enables us to conceive of them as varied expressions of a common view of man and his world."[9]

One must not remain content with such a single, abstract quality in isolation; it must be linked up with all the main, diverse types and examples which embody it. A step is taken in this direction when we see and describe the peculiar ways in which each art expresses the supposedly essential quality or qualities. For example, baroque painting suggests power through heavy, swirling masses and sweeping curves of drapery and gesture. The common field of baroque feeling, says Friedrich, "was focused on movement, intensity, tension, force. Baroque art found its richest fulfillment in the castle and the opera, two creations for the completion of which many arts have to be worked into a harmonious whole."[10]

The aim in stylistic analysis and in cultural history as a whole is not limited to saying just how people felt about their own art and culture. Even if we could do so, it would not satisfy us. In some ways, we understand their cultural pro-

ducts less than they did, in other ways more. They were too close to them to achieve the necessary perspective, the necessary comparison with other styles and cultures before and after theirs. In saying that "a restless search for power" was a keynote of baroque art, we do not imply that baroque artists necessarily realized the fact, or stated it explicitly. Artists expressed it in metaphors and symbols, often obscurely. With our greater knowledge of their time as a whole, in addition to our developed techniques of historical interpretation, we can reasonably attribute meanings to their art which they themselves felt only vaguely and half-consciously; which many of them failed to grasp at all, yet which were profoundly active at the time.

With no mystical or supernatural implications, it can be truly said that the "form-will" or "spirit of the age" in each period of the life of a people tends to express itself in some favored, especially suitable art or group of arts. Sculpture, which was major for the Greeks, is much less important for us today. Tattooing, degenerate and despised by the élite today, was a major art for the Maori. Our age, on the contrary, felt impelled to invent and develop the cinema and vehicles of rapid transportation. The impulse is largely unconscious at the time, or at least unaware of its reason and direction. It becomes, as Hegel well understood, increasingly conscious as it evolves. It is an important phase in the history of styles, and of culture in general, to examine the special fitness of certain media and technics for expressing the distinctive attitudes and ideas which each culture-epoch tries to express. In the past, this could only be found through trial and error on the part of groping innovators, not clearly aware of what they wanted to achieve in a refractory medium.

[9] *The Age of the Baroque* (New York, 1952), p. 65. Several discussions of the meaning of "baroque" in various arts have been published in the *Journal of Aesthetics and Art Criticism.* See especially R. Wellek, "The Concept of Baroque in Literary Scholarship,"; W. Stechow, "Definitions of the Baroque in the Visual Arts"; W. Fleming, "The Element of Motion in Baroque Art and Music"; and R. Daniells, "English Baroque and Deliberate Obscurity," all in Vol. V, No. 2 (Dec. 1946).

[10] *The Age of the Baroque,* p. 40.

There is no spirit of a style apart from concrete works of art and from the humans who make, perform, and experience them; but within these embodiments it is a real concurrence in the ways of selecting and organizing the materials of art. Neither the spirit of the age nor that of the style exists, fully formed, before its expressions in art. These help to determine its nature as well as to make it conscious. But something there must be, prior to the achievement of the style, which impels many cultural leaders, at about the same time, to make similar choices and emphases, affirmations and denials. It is for the critic and historian of art to grasp the underlying spirit of each style, in this wholly naturalistic sense; to see how it fits into the enveloping spirit of the age, and how it is displayed in specific works of art.

As this task is accomplished, often through several generations of study, we come to see more clearly the relation between the abstract "spirit," sensed or intuited between the lines, and the visible, audible, tangible, perhaps measurable traits of form and content in particular arts and other cultural phenomena. The relation is partly one of means and ends, in which the perceptible traits function as means—more or less unconscious—to the fuller expression and realization of the style's distinctive spirit. Wölfflin's perceptible baroque traits could function, whether or not the artists so intended them, as means to the fuller expression of baroque power, intensity, movement, and magnificence. One can see, in this connection, how the "classic" style of linear detail and detachment, the neat, self-contained little patterns, the static array of objects in planes parallel to the picture, would all impede a drive toward stronger expressions of power: then how the overflowing of these bounds by light, color, composition, and represented motion into one united channel could help release the accumulating energy of a new and larger world. This is not to say that every artist who contributed to baroque style felt all these drives or shared the general love of abstract power. Rembrandt, though baroque in his paint-

erly coloring and lighting, usually suggests quiet reticence and gentleness. Even when an artist is in some ways unsympathetic to the main trends of his time, he may contribute to them in other ways, directly or indirectly.

9. PROLONGED AND REVIVED STYLES

Historic styles in art are more or less transitory phenomena, associated with a particular period, long or short. Some are so short as to seem mere passing fads or fashions, such as the Dadaist movement or the hoop-skirt. This in itself does not imply that they are unimportant. Outside conditions may impel a rapid fluctuation of styles. On the whole, most modern styles show a tendency to become shorter-lived, along with the general acceleration of cultural change. Many artists try to avoid conforming exactly to any one recognized style. Other styles endure for millennia, such as the Doric, Ionic, and Corinthian in architecture. They express a conservative tradition in public taste, and help to sustain it. In comparatively stable cultures like that of Egypt, the basic traits of an official style may last for centuries.

A style is more ephemeral, as a rule, than a persistent compositional type such as the portrait, landscape, dwelling, chair, heroic tale, and hymn of worship. A certain style may spread like fire through hundreds of them in a generation, then die out and be replaced by another way of treating the same basic types. Kroeber emphasizes the function of style as "a way of achieving definiteness and effectiveness in human relations by choosing or evolving one line of procedure out of several possible ones, and sticking to it." Thus habits are channeled, he adds, and skills acquired.[11] While this is undoubtedly true of many primitive and other long-lived styles, some modern ones are so ephemeral as to be of little use in habit-formation. They are hardly placed before the public before

[11] *Anthropology* (1948), p. 329. *Cf.* Bidney, *op. cit.*, p. 95.

the demand arises, among public and artists, to replace them with others.

As a style spreads out to new physical and cultural environments, it is sure to change—perhaps so much as to be called a new style. National self-esteem and perhaps commercial interest may cause the importers to call it by a new, local name. This raises a problem for the historian and critic, who may try to link it up with its origins as a variant or substyle of the original one.

Even in the place of origin, a style can not remain active long without changing. New generations of artists and patrons, new determining conditions, tend to keep it constantly in flux. It may change in its home environment faster than abroad. In modern times especially, metropolitan taste tends to weary of each fashion while, or even before, it spreads through the provinces and backward areas. If yesterday's style is to endure in its main outlines, it must be altered in detail enough to give an air of novelty. Long duration in time, within the same art, place, and people, thus tends to introduce some variety.

Thorough study of a period style, such as romanticism in the early nineteenth century, tends to lead the historian *backward* in time to its forerunners; to previous art which manifests its traits, and which may have influenced its later growth. Thus, in retrospect, Shakespeare seems in some important ways to be romantic: especially in his irregular, complex plots, which often violate the three neo-classic unities. His works, neglected by some neo-classicists, inspired romantic writers such as Hugo, many of whom admired him warmly. In painting, Jacob van Ruisdael and Salvator Rosa now seem romantic in their wild, irregular landscapes and fitful lighting. Strictly speaking they can better be classed as *pre-romantic* or *proto-romantic* than as fully romantic.

At the same time, they are of their own epochs in other respects. Shakespeare is in some ways a renaissance mind, and in some ways mannerist and baroque. As with Goethe and other towering figures, it is often impossible to pigeon-hole them

in any single style; they combine many, even antithetical ones, in the same and different works. While a certain style is at its height, as baroque was in the seventeenth century, the germs of other styles are groping into embryonic life; some destined to develop it, some to oppose and conquer it. To set chronological boundaries for the life of a style is always somewhat arbitrary. The sensibility and sentiment which provide a restrained factor in Mozart, and even in Bach, anticipate the more passionate emotion of Beethoven, Berlioz, and Chopin.

By the same token, it is possible to find romantic traits all through the nineteenth century and up to the present day: in Walt Whitman's free verse, in Debussy's impressionist program-music; in the personal, abstract, often self-conscious expressionism of contemporary abstract painters. But romanticism here is a somewhat minor note amid the rising chorus of naturalistic and later trends. It can be regarded as a romantic revival or as a late phase in the romantic movement itself.

A style often dies out for a time, to the extent that it is no longer actively practiced or purchased by the élite, then is revived or comes again into such favor. It is then a *revived period style*, and is often designated with the prefix "neo-," as in neo-gothic and neo-classic. For some purposes, as in buying a chair or painting, it is important to distinguish between one which is "an authentic period piece," an "original Chippendale, of the epoch," and one which is merely, "in the style of" though recently made. Loosely speaking, both have the "period style," or parts of it, though one is of the original provenance and the other a late imitation. Some revived period styles are imported from a distance, as in the American architecture called "Gothic revival" and "Greek revival."

What we call the "revival" of a style is never an exact revival of the whole style; it is the imitation of certain selected traits of the original one. The same is true of a style which endures a long time without a lapse. New needs, tastes, materials, and technics impel variations, so that an expert can easily distinguish them. This can not always be said of counterfeits or exact reproductions, whose aim is to deceive experts and patrons by imitating the original materials and technics to the last detail. It applies rather to the free, normal career of a style which retains its creative vigor.

Revivals of a style are often limited to applied ornament or other superficial appearances, while the underlying structure is influenced by other factors such as new uses, materials, and technical methods. This has been the case in some New York skyscrapers, where gothic ornament was spread over a steel-and-stone or reinforced concrete structure. There is some consistency between structure and ornament where both point skyward; but the whole form, externally as well as internally, would have been impossible in the gothic period. It is a mistake, however, to think of the gothic ornament as the only style present or of the whole as a mere counterfeit, lacking all real style. There may be a groping, embryonic style in the new use of structural steel, now struggling to free itself from an older ornamental tradition, and destined to produce later on a more pure and original style.

The combination of two or more styles in the same work of art is no exception, but common in civilized art. Every period in civilized art, and every modern artist with a long career, produces some diversity of styles. In some of these, the constituent styles remain somewhat distinct, each a separate stylistic factor or cluster of traits, inconsistent or conflicting. In others they are merged in what we feel, with the aid of familiarity and habit, as a single, homogeneous style. The merging is incomplete in such painters as Gentile da Fabriano and the fifteenth-century Germans who retain gilt embossing and flat gold backgrounds along with realistic, solid figures. This is not to say that such pictures are bad or lacking all unity, but only that in them the constituent style-factors are comparatively distinct. This is characteristic of transitional periods, in which one style is yielding to another. It is also characteristic of periods in which a single building, such as Chartres Cathedral, remains in process of construction over a period of several generations, so that different parts are built in different styles. In many European cathedrals, gothic in period and predominantly gothic in style, one finds romanesque parts, early and late gothic parts (as in the two towers at Chartres), and even renaissance and baroque parts, especially in the accessory fixtures, wood-carving, and paintings which were added inside at a later date. This does not necessarily affect the experienced observer as a fault or anomaly, for he comes to realize that such diversity can be itself a trait of style. The same is often true of the interior decoration and furnishing in English country-houses which have been lived in for centuries; a piece being added here and there with no desire to eliminate everything old. In spite of the diversity, a loose consistency of style can still be maintained by the dominance of typically English objects from successive generations. Thus a single work of art can epitomize successive periods in the history of styles.

Contemporary taste, in an age of wealth and great mobility, tends on the contrary to build and furnish quickly from the ground up, making a clean sweep of everything old. The thirty-year-old New York skyscraper is torn down to make room for a larger one, neatly consistent in the style of the day. The design and furnishing of each room are worked out consistently by an interior decorator, with everything new and in the latest modern or revived, adapted "traditional" style. Nevertheless, a trained eye can usually see the influence of various historical traditions, such as the Japanese, even in the newest, occidental "modern." As no modern, civilized nation can claim complete racial purity, no great modern style can claim to be completely pure and original.

10. TRADITIONS, SUBTRADITIONS, AND CO-TRADITIONS. TRADITIONAL STYLISTIC FACTORS IN A WORK OF ART

"Tradition" is a name for that which is transmitted culturally; especially that which comes down through long periods of time. In a broad sense, without the prefix "a" or "the," tradition is the whole mass and force of old, inherited practices, attitudes, institutions, beliefs, and value-standards which largely determine the life of each new generation. It is often felt, by innovators and rebels, as a dead, oppressive weight to be rejected and destroyed. Conservatives venerate it on the whole and moderate liberals regard it as a necessary, valuable but not sacred, basis for gradual progress. Even the rebellious, anti-traditional attitude is itself a tradition, inherited from previous rebels and revolutionists. Moreover, modern tradition as a whole is so extremely diversified and flexible, especially in the liberal democracies, that it allows great leeway for the individual to select and combine for himself. If he does not, the failure is due not to tradition in general, but to some local or personal limitations and pressures.

Tradition includes not only art but custom, religion, philosophy, science, and utilitarian technology. Each of these has its particular traditions as parts of the total cultural heritage. They are preserved, exemplified, and symbolized in the real and imaginary characters, lives, and works of great individuals. Within tradition as a whole are a multitude of more specific, major traditions, and minor traditions or subtraditions within each of them: those of each region, religion, nationality, social class, occupation, and field of knowledge. Though intermingling, they come down as partly separable currents in cultural history. The historian of each field tries to detach its traditions from those in other fields, bringing them out in relief as partly distinct lines of cultural descent. At the same time he shows how each interacts with other factors along the way.

Art as a whole is becoming one diversified tradition, a constituent stream or set of merging streams in the total flow of cultural change. In recent centuries, it has been partially detached from the other main streams such as science and religion, in practice and as a field for study. Each art and group of arts, such as theater, has its own traditions. In these, the local and recent individuals and works are usually the most conspicuous, but their cultural ancestry can be traced. Through the development of communication, recording, and education, local traditions throughout the world are gradually diffused and blended. Sometimes the indigenous ones are overwhelmed and lost, but usually elements of them remain along with the new importations.

There is a growing tendency to synthesize and interrelate all local traditions within a world tradition for each art or branch of learning—a world tradition of painting, one of poetry, one of music, and so on, while all these specialized streams pour into the total stream of world civilization—the Great Tradition, as it is sometimes called. This tendency is part of the integrative phase in cultural evolution. The Great Tradition is that of world culture in its dynamic, descending, inherited, and cumulative aspects. The constituent streams which now converge into it were largely separate until modern centuries, although some diffusion existed in prehistoric times. They are now converging at an accelerating rate. The resultant impacts produce strong tensions and clashes: e.g., between the growing communist tradition, the older ones of Western capitalism, and the Eastern caste and clan systems. They involve conflicting traditions in art as well as in politics, social structure, religion and philosophy. Some of these conflicts are gradually adjusted in larger syntheses.

The opposite phase, that of increasing differentiation and definiteness, occurs not only in specialized practices, but also in the greater clarity with which historians in each field trace back and describe its particular traditions.

There are powerful forces in our time which make for uniformity, standardization, and regimentation on a world scale, in art as elsewhere. They are strengthened by the unprecedented resources of modern technology. At times they threaten cherished humanistic values of individual freedom, variation, and multiformity. But the impulse to these is also deep rooted in human nature. All particular forms of social and cultural organization break down eventually, and the differentiating trends burst forth again with new vigor.

The total tradition of each art such as music or painting, as detached and interpreted by the historian, includes not only its successive styles but also its supply of materials, instruments, functions, and technics, its persistent compositional types, its ideal goals and standards of value. All these evolve together, in the sense of descending with adaptive modifications. They are diffused together at times, dwindle and revive, split and merge again.

Style in art is never a wholly separate factor; it becomes more so in theory as we gradually distinguish its functions and varieties. It becomes more so in practice as artists and art teachers become aware of the existence and value of many styles, as alternative ways of treating the same basic types. This awareness is gradually replacing the old assumption that there is only one correct style or tradition such as the Greek in sculpture, and that all the rest are mere crude bungling. As research proceeds, the history of styles appears more clearly as an ever-changing, multicolored thread in the history of each art and as different from the basic types and technics over which it plays.

The whole temporal sequence of styles in each art, which its historians narrate, is the *stylistic tradition* of that art. Some of it, now lost, they try to rediscover. It can be distinguished in theory from the history of tools and technics, although these are bound up with it.

As we have seen, certain styles or elements in style recur from time to time in the history of a given art: sometimes within a direct line of descent, as in English literature, and sometimes at wide spatio-temporal intervals. Those in the same line are largely inherited culturally; those at wide intervals may be due in part to independent parallelism, even though some general cultural diffusion links them indirectly. But even these, as observed and published by historians, are now flowing into the common stream of stylistic tradition. In written history, we link observed examples of each type into groups and sequences, under such titles as "The Romantic Tradition in European Poetry" or "The Mystic-religious Strain in Greek and Roman Art."[12] Such a persistent "strain" is a particular stylistic tradition; a constituent trait-complex within the total tradition of each art. In the larger view of cultural history, the romantic-Dionysian tradition is a major stream which descends along with its antithesis, the classic-Apollonian tradition, flowing into all the arts and influencing their successive period styles. Each gushes forth with renewed strength at times, then diminishes at others. An important tradition can be dormant or latent for centuries, as Greek naturalism in art and science was during the early Christian centuries, then revive in a new form.

What is the relation between styles and traditions in art? A style becomes a tradition when it is not totally lost and forgotten, but lives on as a part of the cultural heritage. New, contemporary styles are not yet traditions, but they may become so quickly, as by the death of a celebrated artist. An old style is an active, productive tradition when it is still practiced by artists, perhaps after an interval of disuse. But even when no longer produced, it can still function in the cultural heritage of a people through being remembered and contemplated, venerated or disliked. It can be a somewhat active force through being only written about and studied, especially when examples

[12] For example, Gilbert Highet's *The Classical Tradition: Greek and Roman Influences on Western Literature* (New York, 1949). It deals with styles, patterns, ideas, words, beliefs, attitudes, themes, and stories. Jean Seznec, *The Survival of the Pagan Gods* (New York, 1953) describes "the mythological tradition in Renaissance humanism and art," including its modifications by successive artists and centuries.

are shown in museums, read in books, or played by musicians. As such, it can influence the minds of the young, including artists, even if not directly imitated. As a subject of continued thought and different emotional attitudes during successive generations, it changes even when no longer practiced. The memory and present conception of an old style may be very different from the style as originally regarded. It has its ups and downs in critical esteem, as in the case of Hellenistic sculpture, the plays of Shakespeare, the music of Bach, and the painting of El Greco. It is reinterpreted, perhaps neglected and forgotten for a while, then rediscovered and admired for different reasons. It can live on, if not as an active force in later art production then as an influence on thought and feeling in other realms.

As a period style persists and becomes a tradition, its field of extension changes along with changes in its constituent traits. The tradition as a tight or loose assemblage of traits may expand or contract geographically and ethnically as its timespan extends. It may spread to more areas of art and culture or die out in some and remain in others. Traditions in the modern world are unstable, dynamic configurations in the total cultural process, ever tending to dissolve into the general flow. As against this disintegrative tendency, accelerated by the perpetual modern demand for novelty, there operates a conservative tendency of growing strength. Based originally on the forces of habit and custom, on the normal veneration of things old and cherished, it is aided by the development of specialized occupational and scholarly groups; also by institutions and technics for recording and preserving past art, as in museums and libraries, phonograph records and films. It is harder and harder for a style or tradition to die out completely, aside from the possibility of world disaster. Extinct and vanishing styles are dragged back by explorers and scholars into the light of historical knowledge, there to influence public education, and perhaps to inspire some young artist to revive them completely or in part.

What is the difference between a major and a minor tradition? It is not necessarily one of importance, of value or cultural influence. From our present standpoint, it is one of size and scope; within a large, diversified tradition in culture, or within a single art, there are many specific ones. Each of these is a minor tradition or *subtradition* in relation to the larger one of which it is a part. It is a constituent stylistic trait or trait-complex which descends through the art and culture of successive generations. It corresponds to what we have distinguished above as a "substyle" in relation to a more extensive style, but with the further distinction that this is a substyle which descends for a considerable time.

A major, extensive period style such as the baroque includes many substyles. It can be divided into varieties of baroque, on the bases we have noted. Correspondingly, the baroque tradition as a more or less active style and influence up to the present time can also be divided into subtraditions on the same bases.

Any trait, such as the emphasis on power and heavy masses in swirling or diagonal motion, becomes a subtradition of baroque insofar as it is handed down and actively practiced. It may be practiced in the art where it originated or in another art; the style of Rubens can influence photography and mobile color in the film. It may operate as one of several stylistic factors in a single work of art. It may be introduced as part of a form which is prevailingly baroque, or as a minor, subordinate factor in a form which is stylistically diversified: e.g., a contemporary, functional building with a small amount of baroque ornamentation over the doorways, or a neo-baroque stage setting for a modern drama, or a passage of neo-baroque polyphony in a modern symphony.

The life and influence of a subtradition may cut across all cultural compartments as between the arts and other realms. The magnificence of baroque palace architecture can be used to stimulate respect for a communist government. It may inspire monarchical ambitions in a dictator. An impulse toward the grandiose and pompous in any realm may express itself, unless restrained by contemporary inhibiting influences, in a revival of baroque palatial style. A stylistic subtradition may consist of *any stylistic trait or trait-complex* which is transmitted and kept alive through successive generations. The trait or complex which persists may retain its identity and be easily discernable in other contexts, or may be almost indistinguishably merged with others as a vague, pervasive quality.

Examples of the former are the shell as a conventional motif in eighteenth-century French furniture, the theme of the clever animal in folklore, the pentatonic scale and the Dorian mode in music. The "Palladian motif," says Banister Fletcher, is sometimes to be found within Italian Renaissance architecture; it consists of "superimposed Doric and Ionic orders which, under the main entablature, frame intervening arches supported on smaller free-standing twin columns, and there are circular openings in the spandrels."[13]

As the trait-complexes descend through time and diffuse through space, they keep separating and recombining with others, yet never to the extreme of dissolution into unitary traits. Small and large clusters persist and retain some identity along with different concomitants through centuries and millennia, as in the Greek classical orders and the still older swastika, wave, and fret motifs of early pottery decoration.

Anthropologists use the concept of an area *co-tradition* to mean "the persistence of a number of combined and closely related traditions within a specified area."[14] In the Peruvian or central Andean co-tradition, says Gordon R. Willey, all cultural phases partake of certain traits and trait complexes: agriculture, pottery, weaving, and architecture. Tradition in general implies, says Willey, a deeply channeled, patterned activity in which the vitality of a culture prefers to express itself. Maya calendar lore, a complex, tightly unified tradition, lasted over a thousand years, with recognized stylistic and technical period subdivisions. As a tradition in

limited facets of culture, Willey mentions the white-on-red ceramic painting of Andean South America. A tradition includes specific lines of continuity and persistence in cultural ideas through time, by means of which the archeologist traces culture growth. The North American tradition of cord- and fabric-marked pottery expanded and contracted geographically with slight internal changes, while the Peruvian red-and-white tradition evolved a number of very different pottery styles, linked together by the same color scheme.[15]

In a particular work of art, as we have seen, two or more traditional strains are often present, either distinct or merged. They constitute, from the standpoint of morphology, *traditional stylistic factors* in that work of art. Examples are the Greek factor in Gandhara Buddhist sculpture; the romanesque and gothic factors in Chartres Cathedral; the primitive Negro factor in cubist sculpture; the Persian and impressionist factors in a painting by Matisse; the Arabian factor in a Spanish Gypsy song and dance; the classical tradition in Dante's *Divine Comedy;* medieval modes in Stravinsky's music.

These factors are often described as "influences" or "derivations." The critic sees what he regards as the influence of Rubens in a painting by Renoir; he hears "echoes" of Debussy in a passage by Ravel or Respighi, notes the debt of Milton to Dante and of Dante to Virgil, feels that certain characters in Faulkner may be partly derived from Dostoyevsky. These modes of expression assume certain causal relations of influence and derivation among artists which are often debatable and impossible to verify. It is less controversial to describe them as stylistic analogies; as the observable presence, in two different works, of similar stylistic factors.

That traditional stylistic factors can be found in

[13] *History of Architecture on the Comparative Method* (New York, 1931), p. 659.

[14] G. R. Willey, "Archeological Theories and Interpretation: New World," in *Anthropology Today*, p. 374. (He credits W. C. Bennett for the term.)

[15] Willey, p. 373.

a work of art or in the total output of an artist does not imply that his work lacks originality or greatness. They can be found in the greatest works of the greatest artists; a completely new trait of material, technic, content, or form in art is almost inconceivable. Originality is always a matter of degree. It may consist largely or wholly in a new selection and arrangement of traditional traits and subtraditions. Traditionalism is eclectic in a derogatory sense only when the traditional elements are too inconsistent or too weakly integrated to become a new synthesis. In an age which sets so great a premium on originality, artists tend to resist and deny the suggestion that they have borrowed anything from the past, even though the debt is obvious to experts. They often claim to have learned directly from nature, forgetting that art has shown them how to look at nature and to learn from it.

Any one of the baroque traits discussed by Wölfflin can be detached, handed down, and incorporated as a stylistic factor in later art. All the five or more traits which made up the baroque as a seventeenth-century period style need not be handed down together; any selection from them can be handed down separately. An impressionist painter can carry on and develop the painterly trait as opposed to the linear, while avoiding the oblique, recessional trait which characterized much seventeenth-century composition. He can, as Monet did, make his coloristic light-reflections play over a comparatively flat surface, such as the façade of a cathedral, represented as approximately parallel to the picture plane. A composer can emulate Bach's interweaving of voices in a fugal passage, while substituting more dissonant chords and sudden, polytonal modulations. Matisse can incorporate Persian traits of flat color-pattern from the miniatures, without the small size and sharp lines which originally accompanied them, combining them instead with large brushstrokes and some impressionist lighting.

It may be misleading to describe the use of flat color-pattern as "Persian," unless the resemblance

is marked in other respects. Flat color-pattern is a traditional stylistic trait, but it is found in Egyptian, Chinese, and other local traditions in addition to the Persian. Many traits which Wölfflin called "baroque" or "Seicento" are much older.

II. RECURRENT STYLISTIC TYPES; NON-PERIOD OR MULTI-PERIOD STYLES

The historian who surveys the whole known history of his art from the vantage point of a particular age and style is often struck by surprising resemblances between works of widely separate periods and places, coming from different social, cultural, and religious environments. They are not parts of one continuous tradition.

Beneath obvious differences in material, technic, use, and subject-matter, the historian may discern a pervasive kinship of style, form, and expression; more so than between many works of the same time and place. It is natural for him to describe such analogous works in terms of the familiar, nearby styles which they resemble. Historians now speak of a "baroque" phase in Roman sculpture and architecture, and of "romanticism" in the pastoral poetry of Theocritus, Bion, and Virgil. Likewise, reference is made to Gothico-Buddhist sculpture in Central Asia, because of its similarity to medieval Gothic.[16] Other writers speak of "Baroque style in East Indian sculpture and architecture."[17] Indian sculpture and architecture of the Gupta period have been described as "classic" by contrast with the later baroque and rococo types. Some Japanese sculpture in the Kamakura period (of guardian spirits, not the Buddha image) is "baroque-like" in its tendency to large, irregular,

---

[16] See R. Grousset, *Civilizations of the East* (New York, 1931, 1934): "India," pp. 124 f.; "China," pp. 177 f. J. Strzygowski, "The Afghan Stuccos of the N. R. F. Collection" (New York, Stora Gallery, n.d.).

[17] W. Cohn, *Indische Plastik* (Berlin, 1923), p. 45. G. Jouveau-Dubreuil, *Archéologie du sud de l'Inde* (Paris, 1914).

swirling masses, suggesting violent energy and movement. Similar Chinese figures come from the 'ang and other early dynasties.

A Japanese historian, not influenced by Western scholarship, might rather call Bernini's and Puget's sculpture "Kamakura-like." We tend to call the Moribana school of flower-arrangement "romantic," because it suggests our romantic, picturesque gardens in its movement away from rigid, geometric formalism and toward a more natural, informal, highly textured style. Both Japanese and Western picturesque gardens of the eighteenth century and later have been influenced by Chinese gardens and landscapes. We in the West have, strictly speaking, no right to impose our own stylistic concepts on every aspect of oriental art which resembles ours. If for no other reason, it suggests occidental priority and derivation. However, some terminology is urgently needed for describing these transcultural analogies, and almost any name will do if it is objectively defined and applied.

The first and basic task in studying these apparent analogies is to observe and analyze them empirically, in terms of stylistic traits. How and to what extent are the so-called "Gothico-Buddhist" sculptures of Western Asia really similar to European gothic ones? What are the traits of style which the quasi-baroque, Hellenistic and imperial Roman sculptures have in common with seventeenth-century European baroque?

If we apply to such a type the name of a well-known period style, the latter concept must now be redefined more broadly and simply, as in other cases of widening extension. Its definition as a non-period type or style must omit those traits which are peculiar to any one period, and reduce them to those few, highly abstract qualities which actually recur at various times and places. A period style never recurs completely and identically. The definition of a recurrent type will usually need to mention fewer traits than that of a period style, but more than that of a simple type such as "round pictures" or "soft music." On the whole, a simpler,

more abstract, recurrent type will have a larger extension (field of occurrence) than a period style. It can be regarded as a genus within which many subtypes and period styles can be classed as species or examples.

"Decorative art" can be defined in a comparatively simple, general way as that which emphasizes presented visual qualities and thematic arrangements, rather than realistic or idealistic representation, symbolic meanings, or suggested emotions. It covers many specific ways of doing this, as in Chinese, French rococo, and Islamic decoration; hence its basic definition cannot specify any traits peculiar to one of these variants. But the concept of "Japanese decorative art" narrows down the field somewhat. Its definition should specify traits consistent with the decorative type in general, but distinguishing the Japanese variety from others. To narrow the field still further, the "Yamato-e style" is a period style of Japanese decorative art, beginning in the late Heian period and carried on as a "tradition" in the fifteenth century. Lee (1961, pp. 28–29) describes it in painting as follows: "The compositional devices depend upon use of all the available space from the bottom to the top edges of the scroll. Horizon lines are almost nonexistent for the painters wished to decorate the entire surface... Arbitrarily placed cloud-bands, originally derived from T'ang painting, are used inside as well as outside of rooms, as boundaries or ties between adjacent areas... Diagonals of screens, shutters, walls, mats, or flooring create dominant patterns and directional movements... Sudden little vignettes of decoratively arranged nature or of representations on painted screens vary the dominance of more arbitrary patterns. The pure colors, mauve, malachite, azurite, cinnabar, and red lead, are carefully applied with emphasis on their flat decorative quality... Gold and silver, in powder or cut shapes, are sprinkled on the calligraphic sections, written in the cursive Japanese manner."

The terms "Apollonian" and "Dionysian" refer to two contrasting stylistic types. They derive from Nietzsche's essay on *The Birth of Tragedy*. Nietzsche defined these terms with special reference to early Greek drama; hence primarily to one art and one period. But he developed them with such far-reaching, philosophic scope as to suggest their application to other arts and periods as well. They have come to stand, in modern discussion, for two polar, alternating strains or tendencies in all art and civilization. "Dionysian" is close to "romantic" in its emphasis on the emotional, the irrational, and the mystic sense of oneness. As such, it is sometimes preferred to "romantic," being less bound up with a modern movement. "Apollonian" coincides with one phase of what we now call "classic"—its emphasis on clarity and calmness; but not with another—that on rational understanding, analysis, and purpose. The latter emphasis Nietzsche attributed rather to Socrates, and regarded as, on the whole, unfavorable to art. In this attitude, he expressed his own romantic traits.

These pairs of opposite concepts are useful in describing and classifying art, and will be more so when more sharply defined. One must not expect to find in art many examples of either extreme; they are theoretical polarities rather than types of actual phenomena. Most art, whether called classic or romantic, Apollonian or Dionysian, lies somewhere between the two and shows some trace of both qualities, if only for internal contrast. Nietzsche himself showed how classical tragedy achieved a partial reconciliation between the Apollonian and Dionysian extremes. In one way or another, that effort has continued ever since, and it began before the age of Greek tragedy. Classical sculpture, as in the Parthenon pediment, involved a combination of rigid geometry with naturalistic, biomorphic shapes; the two held firmly but flexibly under the control of a dynamic reason, not a set of frozen rules.

In such forms, the recurrent stylistic type operates as a developed component, appearing and reappearing in ever-new contexts of art and culture. André Gide remarked, "the struggle between classicism and romanticism takes place in every mind."[18]

The idea of "classic" as a type involving balance, moderation, and unity is applied to the relation between the basic structure of a work of art and its ornamental enrichment. Whereas the archaic is conceived as somewhat bare and severe, or lacking in unity between the functional, representational, and decorative elements, the classic is conceived as uniting all with balance and restraint. The baroque is conceived as leaning toward extravagant or excessive, heavy ornamentation or functionally unnecessary swirls and protuberances; the rococo as likewise over-ornamented, but in a lighter, more delicate way. Idea and form, or emotional meaning and sensory expression, are likewise conceived as reaching perfect balance in the classic, with a consequent effect on the beholder of repose and quiet strength. The classic type is conceived as emphasizing reason and order, both in what it expresses and in how the artist works; the romantic type as emphasizing impulse, imagination, and direct intuition, also in the product and the creative process. Obviously, these criteria are all partly subjective and evaluative: opinions differ widely on what is "overdecorated" or "perfectly unified." But there is also an objective element in them which can be roughly expressed in terms of degree and proportion between the various factors in form.

12. PARTICULAR STYLISTIC ANALYSIS

We have been considering styles as a kind of complex type in art. They are distinguished in terms of style-concepts, each designated by a style-name. To define these satisfactorily, in relation to a set of traits and also to a field of extension, is a difficult task. But aesthetic taxonomy is in an infantile stage and is receiving little systematic study. To analyze a style-concept as to its meaning and rela-

[18] Quoted by Hauser, *Philosophy of Art History*, p. 107.

tion to works of art is *general* stylistic analysis. It is a branch of aesthetic morphology.

A different but closely related kind of problem arises when we seek to identify a work of art as belonging to some style or styles. This is *particular* stylistic analysis. To analyze the Parthenon as a particular object, noting the traits in which it fulfills the specifications of "doric architecture," is analysis of this sort. It is often useful to compare two or more works in respect to their stylistic affiliations: e.g., the Parthenon and the Erechtheum.

The aim of particular stylistic analysis is, first, to locate the work in relation to a certain style or styles. These may be traditional or other extensive styles, practiced by other artists, or individual styles, characteristic of this artist only. The problem is to note and describe the traits in which it conforms to the specifications of a certain style, fully or partially. These are its conformities with respect to that style. Second, the aim is to point out its non-conformities also, with respect to the same style, and thus to estimate the extent of conformity. Is it a typical and pure example of the style or mixed, borderline, transitional, hybrid? By comparing two or more works in relation to the same or similar styles, one can sharpen such estimates of their stylistic affiliations: for example, the Parthenon and Theseum as doric; Chartres and Amiens cathedrals as gothic; Rubens and Vermeer as baroque.

Along these lines, one may hope to approach a recognition of the comparatively distinct, unique nature of a particular work of art, or of the works of a certain artist. This may require attention to very slight nuances of difference between similar traits in different styles and examples. However, it is not to be assumed that all such nuances can be expressed in terms of conformity or non-conformity to well-known styles. The non-conformities or differentiae should be described in positive terms, and this is not easy to do, especially in the case of new, unfamiliar works. Concepts of style are helpful in describing a particular work of art,

however, in that one such concept may take the place of many words, many references to specific traits. To the connoisseur, it is informative to say that a certain work is "in the rococo style, but with unusually flat and simple curves," or "in the style of Monteverdi, but with a few unusually modern dissonances."

In classifying examples, critics and historians often speak as if the artist, not the work of art, were the example. They may argue, for instance, about where to place J. S. Bach in relation to the baroque; Chardin in relation to the rococo style. This is convenient as an abbreviation for "the works of Bach" or "the paintings of Chardin," for it is they, more than the artists, which manifest style. From the standpoint of morphology and historiography, the products are the primary data. Style is not the man, but an aspect of his work. In many cases, we know and can know nothing about the man, and even when we do, it is his work which makes us regard him as important for art history. No doubt he possessed psychological traits related to those of the style his works exhibit. These are also important in cultural history, but the relation between them takes us far outside the realm of aesthetic morphology and the history of art, strictly speaking.

The attempt to characterize a particular work in its most distinctive aspects is not directly relevant to the theory of evolution, which is more concerned with general types and trends. It is mentioned here primarily to show that evolutionism does not deny or ignore the unique aspects, and that morphology can include them both.

Another way in which it is relevant is to emphasize the fact that styles and traditions descend, not as independent abstractions, but only as repeated traits of concrete, particular works of art. The way in which a work of art embodies or exemplifies a certain style or tradition tends to function as a factor within that work. It may help to give unity and harmony to the whole, but two or more different stylistic factors may do the opposite unless merged and reconciled somehow.

Then they may give a total effect of mild, dynamic tension and contrast.[19]

The much-abused term "unique" has been applied not only to particular works of art and artists, but also to styles of art. Here again, it is often used as an objection to evolutionism as well as to the theory of cycles. If each style is completely unique, there can be no gradual development of styles and no continuity in art history. There can be no recurrence of a style in different periods and cultures.

"A style cannot be repeated," says Kroeber; "it is too individual and unique. Another style may take its place and run a generically similar course; but they differ so substantively in quality that it would be farfetched to speak of their relation as cyclic. Styles always are concrete."[20] Hauser speaks of a work of art as a "unique, unmistakable, incommensurable spiritual achievement," and adds that "any artistic tendency is in a way the result of what has gone before, and this creates at any time a unique situation in the historical process as a whole."[21] (In other words, as Taine showed, any style is partly the result of a historical moment.) Each stage, says Hauser, presupposes the achievements of the previous one, and so becomes "totally different." Hence Greco-Roman and late-gothic 'baroque' are not parallel to seventeenthcentury baroque. Styles cannot recur, so there can be no cycles.

Both of these writers exaggerate the difference between styles and the impossibility of their recurrence. It is true that styles and the cultural situations which give them birth can not be repeated exactly; but it is also true that no style or cultural stage is "totally different" from all others. The similarities and differences are a matter of degree. Styles can be repeated in part; in certain respects. Likewise social situations can be repeated

in certain respects: e.g., the transition from feudalism to bourgeois capitalism.

Kroeber accepted three analogies between style in art and organic species. "Both a species and a culture and a style have evolved through responses to their total and fluctuating past environments, plus internal changes—mutational innovations and inventive or creative innovations respectively."[22] The limited sort of "uniqueness" which Kroeber predicates of both styles and organic species does not in the least preclude their evolutionary descent. A species, he says, like a culture and a style, "represents an achieved evolution, which is unique, not repetitive in itself."[23] No one can deny that the oak tree and the tiger are unique and nonrepetitive in some respects, and in the total configuration of traits which makes each a distinctive type. Each species is defined (a) by classing it within a genus or phylum, all of whose members have certain basic traits in common; and (b) by stating its differentiae or unique characteristics as compared with others of that class. Both the

[19] Thus Sherman E. Lee points out that Chu Ta (1626–c. 1705) painted in two styles: one rapidly and economically brushed in paintings of rocks, fish, birds, or plants; it is daring, cold, brilliant, almost whimsical, often attributing human values to animate and inanimate objects; the other is complex, tentative, careless, abbreviated, antitraditional. The first is immediate and intuitive, the second constructive and rational. A cold and rational mood common to both unites them, and so do occasional lapses from the second to the first style in landscapes. The first style emphasizes the parts and unites them partly by literary means; the second emphasizes the construction as a whole. Both styles are exemplified in Chu Ta's "Landscape after Kuo Chung-shu," in the Cleveland Museum of Art, where the painter undertakes a liberal interpretation of the Northern Sung monumental style. ("The Two Styles of Chu Ta," *Bulletin of the Cleveland Museum of Art*, Nov. 1958, p. 215). Elsewhere, the same author and Wen Fong distinguish five sequential styles in "the evolution of Chinese landscape art": the Courtly, Monumental, Literal, Lyric, and Spontaneous. They find traits of several in a Northern Sung landscape handscroll. The painter was somewhat eclectic and transitional. His effort to combine the monumental, epic style with the newer romantic, miniature, Southern, lyric style involves some conflict, the authors think. *Streams and Mountains Without End* (Ascona, Switzerland, 1955), pp. 21–29.

[20] *Style and Civilizations*, p. 129.
[21] *Philosophy of Art History*, pp. 73, 193 f.
[22] *Style and Civilizations*, p. 78.
[23] P. 78.

similarities and the differences, the continuities and variations or mutations, are results of evolution. Renaissance styles resemble those of Greece and Rome in some respects, showing their descent therefrom. In other ways they differ.

Kroeber errs in saying that styles are always concrete. A style is always an abstraction, conceived by distinguishing certain recurrent traits in different works of art. But some conceptions of style are closer to the concrete level than others. As we have seen in this chapter, there are different kinds of style. Period styles are conceived and defined with direct reference to some particular historic situation; to the products of some particular place, time, and person or persons. If the situation thus marked off is relatively small and brief, the chances are that a fairly large cluster of stylistic traits in common can be discerned within it. Original individual styles are of this sort. By the same token, the style thus conceived will be relatively unique; there will be little chance of finding exactly this cluster of interrelated traits in any other style or situation.

Gordon R. Willey analyzes the meaning of "uniqueness" more carefully in discussing Kroeber's concept of "horizon style."[24] This, he says, is "a widespread art style which is registered in a number of local sequences." The various sequences in the appearance of the same style from one locality to another are synchronized. "The significance of the idea," says Willey, is in the phenomenon of the style as a unique entity... Establishment of the uniqueness of the style depends upon three factors: its technical quality, is content or representation, and its configuration." Two specimens might be similar in technique (fine-line carving on stone) and content (a jaguar) but different in the delineation of the jaguar (configuration). This would make the two styles distinct, Willey comments. The "configurational aspect of style" is the crucial factor, in his opinion.

It should be further noted, however, that even in such a linear "configuration" there may be traits in common from one specimen to another.

Indeed, there certainly will be. The "fineness" or uniform sharpness of an incised line is not merely technical; it is also a visible trait of form and a factor in determining the total aesthetic configuration of the object. If the two representations of the jaguar resembled each other in a general mode of schematic stylization, neither would be quite unique. There are similarities of delineation in representing jaguars, even between such distinct, extensive styles as the Mayan, Toltec, and Aztec. Intensive comparison of any two representations of the same subject is likely to disclose both similarities and differences in form.

Webster's *New International Dictionary* (Merriam) defines "unique" as "Being without a like or equal; single in kind or excellence; hence, loosely, unusual, notable." Some styles are unusual and notable, some are not. No style is "without a like" in the sense of being without any resemblance to any other.

14. STYLES AND ORGANIC TYPES. THE FUSION OF TRADITIONS. HYBRID STYLES

The partial uniqueness of styles is thus no bar to their participation in the evolutionary process. Both styles and organic types can come into being as transformations of previous types. At one time and place a certain animal species thrives and appears in many examples crowding out other, competing species. At another, it may dwindle and die out as did the great Jurassic reptiles. These statements can be applied to styles in art. Here, as in organic types, there are many borderline and transitional subtypes, produced in the course of evolutionary change. Both change gradually and also, at times, by large, sudden steps.

These analogies, long denied or belittled, have recently been confirmed by A. L. Kroeber. There

[24] "Archeological Theories and Interpretation: New World." In *Archeology Today*, p. 375.

is a close organic parallel to style, he writes, in the consistent form of organisms; especially that which is basic to a characteristic functioning of the animal or plant, giving it typical powers of habitus, temperament, or ethos.[25] This congruence of form and function differentiates greyhound and bulldog, the streamlining of fish and birds; it is analogous to the coherence of assimilated form and quality in culture.

Some organic types are styles of art, in strict and literal fact. These are the varieties of animal and plant which have been artificially bred for beauty; for aesthetic qualities of some specific kind. They include modern breeds of dog, horse, cat, bird, goldfish, flowering tree, shrub, and perennial. Some are ornate, some plain and severely functional; styles and tastes change in them from culture to culture and period to period. They are imported and exported as parts of the total diffusion of culture and of art.

Ideally, the classification of unknown examples requires the existence of a well-developed, established system of taxonomy with standard nomenclature and accepted specifications for each category. This did not exist in biology while the foundations of that science were being laid and evolution discovered. It developed there along with the analysis of particular examples and on the basis of empirical research, as a set of hypotheses for organizing the growing mass of biological data. The system of Linnaeus, a pioneer step, was much altered later. Concepts, definitions, and systematic interrelations were constantly changed to fit the growing knowledge of the facts. So it must be in aesthetics and art history. At the present stage, it would be impossible to work out a permanently satisfactory system of style-concepts, but a start can be made.

In one respect, the relation between persistent compositional types and styles in art is somewhat like that between the main inclusive types and the smaller subdivisions in biology. Styles act, as we have seen, as transitory variations on the more inclusive, stable types. The Louis XV and Louis

XVI styles are ways of varying the chair, the house, the woman's costume, the woven textile, and the statue of the human figure; these types or basic patterns persist through many styles. Likewise each of the main biological types—plant and animal, vertebrate and invertebrate, crustacean, reptile, bird, fish, and mammal; in botany the spore-plants, naked-seed and fruit-seed plants, and so on—has differentiated into a multitude of genera, species, and varieties. These are, on the whole, more transitory than the main types, although this is not always true.

Organic types, being hard and slow to change, are comparatively irreversible. Once an animal species has died out, it is hard or impossible to revive it. But the death of a style is only provisional. Since its "life" consists only in being actively admired, used, and emulated, a "dead" or dormant style may at any time be restored to active favor; even one long buried like the Pompeian, and suddenly rediscovered.

Classic and neo-classic theory held, on the whole, to the belief that the principal types or genres in art were and should be fixed, clearly distinct, and essentially unchanging. For each main type, according to Aristotle, there was a certain line of development, aimed at achieving its own characteristic excellence. This was analogous to the fixity of organic types: e.g., the tree, shrub, and herb. Comedy had one proper set of effects and values; tragedy another, even though (as Socrates cryptically remarked) their genius was the same. To mix them, or produce a hybrid tragicomedy, was a violation of the order of nature and of art. In the eighteenth century, we find Lessing still arguing that painting has one proper, limited field and purpose, poetry another; that each errs if it trespasses on the other's domain. This mode of thinking is an integral part of the pre-evolutionary world-view. It belongs with the assumption that God has organized the universe, once and for all, into a fixed hierarchy of levels and differentiated types, including social classes and occupations;

[25] *Style and Civilizations*, pp. 77 f.

[282]

that to seek for radical change, or to climb above one's station, is immoral. Types of art are and should be eternal; each has its fixed laws and limits, within which only slight stylistic variations are permissible.

It is now evident that the arts have always been changing and overflowing their boundaries, with or without philosophic approval. Something of the old attitude persists in the attitude of the modern purist, who resents all mixture and variation of traditional styles. But since the evolutionary attitude swept in during the nineteenth century, aesthetic theory has been gradually, reluctantly, adjusting itself to the necessary reorientation. In evaluation, it has been tending toward a relativistic tolerance for variety, novelty, and unlimited experiment in art. In aesthetic morphology, it now conceives of types and styles as constantly changing and overlapping, as do biological species. Thus, from a modern standpoint, it is easy to conceive of many acceptable varieties of tragedy, and of intermediate types combining tragedy, comedy, pathos, and farce.

Since prehistoric times, man has been challenged by the fixed differences in type among natural phenomena, and fascinated by dreams of mixing them. Since the Ice Age at least, his art has given form in costume, dance, and cave painting to fantasies of hybrid creatures such as men with birds' heads. They were not sterile, like most real hybrids, for they begot a long line of angels, sphinxes, centaurs and the like throughout the history of art. In fairy-tales of magic, frogs turn to princes and back again. Such fantasies have eventually stimulated efforts to realize them in one way or another: e.g., to fly like birds and swim under water like fish. They show a perennial rebellion in man against the fixity of types, and especially against the limitations of his own type, which he has been able to surmount to a large and growing extent through science and art. Having escaped from the self-imposed delusion that it was aesthetically and morally wrong to alter the divinely fixed system of types, he tends to challenge

the dogma that basic types in art can not be mixed, and that hybrid styles are in bad taste. Modern man insists on experimenting with the most bizarre combinations, to see whether they will work functionally, aesthetically, or both.

Hybrid styles often arise more or less spontaneously, especially through the mixture of social groups, as in Gandhara sculpture. They are often short-lived. A very obvious hybrid is still likely to be regarded as a corrupt monstrosity and ridiculed by connoisseurs. Thus a combined bookcase, radio, desk, and liquor cabinet may be scorned unless it meets a genuine need for versatility and compactness. A house or church in mixed gothic-baroque-Chinese style will arouse the ridicule of purists and of all who fear to be accused of bad taste. At the same time, a European cathedral or a nobleman's house furnishing may be approved even though it contains many styles. The rightness or wrongness of such judgments does not concern us here; only the fact that hybrid examples are much easier to produce in art than in plants or animals. Some survive as types while others fail; some are ridiculed at first by those who like "pure" types, then accepted as people get used to them. In all the great historic styles, there has been some mixture of influences—for example, in the Greek blending of Dorian, Ionian, Egyptian, Mycenean, and other sources; in the Spanish blending of Classic and Moorish; in German Renaissance painting with gold backgrounds; and in the Chinese blending of Indian Buddhist and native styles.[26] There have been

---

[26] Thus H. Goetz remarks that "The form development of Indian art is... rich and diversified. Incessantly new inspirations from the outside world have been absorbed, and new forms have been evolved by their fusion with the already existing indigenous tradition. Ancient Near Eastern, Iranian, Roman, Chinese, even Islamic elements have been digested. Especially Achaemenian and Roman art have exercised an enormous influence. Gupta art, in fact, represented a complete revolution, thanks to the incorporation of the late Roman architectural and figural typology. But at the same time these foreign elements were dissected and reinterpreted so thoroughly that something completely different, purely Indian, emerged from them." ("Tradition and Creative Evolution in Indian Art'," in *Marg*, Bombay, XIV, 2, Supplement, March 1961, p. 5).

artistic migrations and assimilations since the dawn of history, even in paleolithic and neolithic times.

Artistic hybrids tend to be offensive while they are new and felt to be eclectic, composed of inconsistent, conflicting elements. Later on, they may be admired as richly diversified, either because the constituent factors are more smoothly harmonized or because people are used to them and no longer feel them as discordant. It is hard and sometimes impossible to distinguish clearly between "conflict" or "disunity" as a defect in art and "contrast" or "variety" as something desirable. The distinction may rest (a) on the extent of difference between the factors, or (b) on the extent to which they are integrated by other means, or (c) on the extent to which the observer can and will integrate them perceptually and intellectually.

It would be hard or impossible today to find a purely indigenous, regional culture or style of art. As we become one world, art styles and culture-patterns everywhere tend to merge to some extent, though strong local differences remain. Most connoisseurs of art deplore this obliteration of distinctive styles and cultures, and would regard it as a retrogression rather than a progress from the standpoint of aesthetic value.

Cultural importation and assimilation are highly selective processes. At any one time, a group will be receptive toward certain importations, for which it is socially and psychologically ready, and hostile or impervious to others, which it rejects as ugly, evil, or merely absurd and trivial. Later on, having changed internally, it may make a very different selection. Artistic importations and the resultant hybrid styles are often quite fertile, as for example in the repeated adoption of Chinese influences by European art since Marco Polo, and indeed since the Han Dynasty, when silk came to the West. How good the resultant mixtures are as art is always debatable; some will prefer the unmixed, ancestral style. But at least, new styles result, as *Chinoiserie* did from the importation of certain Chinese traits into eighteenth-century French and English art. In migrating to Europe, the Chinese styles were profoundly modified in adaptation to their new environment; parts of them were ignored, and others merged with more indigenous styles such as those of Louis XV and Chippendale in furniture. Likewise, Spanish baroque architecture and sculpture changed in migrating to Latin America, into the hands of local Indian craftsmen.

A *historic sequence* in art history is a succession of connected events in that field; especially one occurring more or less continuously in the same art or group of arts, in the same region and social group or culture. A *stylistic* sequence is one involving successive changes in style. It consists of a chronological succession of trait-complexes, each a style or substyle in itself. To call them *stages* implies that there is a fairly definite, consistent direction in the sequence; that it is a progression or regression from one style to a very different one, either by gradual or sudden changes. Thus the "archaic" stage in Greek sculpture is said to have occurred between the late seventh or early sixth century B.C. and about 480 B.C., being preceded by the "geometric" and followed by the "classical" stage or style.

A stylistic *trend* is a persistent direction in stylistic change; an underlying tendency from one style or set of traits toward another: e.g., from neo-classic to romantic; from visual realism to abstract expressionism or decorative design. A general stylistic trend such as this will necessarily involve many *component trends* with respect to various components in the art concerned; e.g., in painting, directional sequences in line, color, texture, modeling, perspective, subject-matter, composition, etc. Each can be separately described in terms of successive traits; their interrelations form the general trend.

A stylistic sequence may or may not involve a definite trend; the style may stay about the same or change in various directions about equally. To say that there is a prevailing trend does not mean that all the phenomena concerned are changing in the same way, but that a considerable number or important group of them are doing so. Sometimes a few influential leaders can set the trend for a while, as in women's fashions. Statistical study of many phenomena, changing in various ways, may reveal an underlying and increasing trend within them: e.g., to lighter, simpler, more comfortable clothes. In a diversified field of phenomena such as art, simultaneous trends can be noted in various media, styles, and components. Some will run more or less concomitantly, in parallel curves, while others run in opposite directions or in apparently unrelated ways.

A comprehensive trend such as evolution or devolution can include at the same time a multitude of constituent trends and subtrends, some approximately parallel and some not. An important problem is to discover the extent to which such constituent sequences are correlated with each other, for this may indicate the extent of causal connection between them. Certain sequences, the behavior of certain variable factors, may have a high positive correlation and others a high negative one, either of which suggests some causal connection. Such study will also indicate the extent to which a certain main trend, such as evolution or cycles, is (a) universal and constant, (b) partial and opposed but dominant, (c) sporadic, indecisive, (d) increasing or decreasing.

Such quantitative studies may be confined to changes within art or a certain branch of art, or may deal with the relations between art and other cultural factors. By means of them, we may hope in future to bring the question of the relative influence of different factors (e.g., the psychological and socio-economic) down from the level of speculation and partisan doctrine to one of empirical demonstration. But that time is far off. Before the variables can be correlated, they must be distinguished and defined with some accuracy. Many specific sequences and trends must be charted, in various arts, places, and peoples. These must not be limited to broad, vague generalities, such as "from mysticism to naturalism," but focus on particular morphological components and traits. For example, the trend from Gregorian to renaissance music involves specific sequences of change in regard to meter and rhythm (as in *musica mensurata*), in mode and key, in melodic and harmonic structure, in vocal and instrumental coloring, in relation to verbal text, in liturgical function, and in range of emotional expressiveness. It is not enough to say that music grew more sensuous and worldly; the total sequence of stylistic change must be analyzed into a number of concurrent, interrelated sequences, involving increase in some traits and decrease in others. Considerable information of this sort already exists in histories and monographs on the various arts, but it is not brought together or arranged so as to bring out the larger trends and recurrences. Too much of the study is devoted to individual artists, styles, and periods in isolation.

All the biological and cultural sciences, including aesthetics, try to compare the various trends which occur or have occurred within their fields of phenomena. Where exact measurement is possible, as in economics, they chart and graph such trends as rises and falls in price with accuracy, noting which curves are parallel or analogous and which move in contrary directions. Various degrees of conformity or non-conformity among such trends can be measured in terms of positive or negative correlation. These lead to estimates of causal influence among the factors concerned, and the amount of causal influence itself is often described in terms of a high or low correlation.

One great obstacle to doing this in aesthetics and art history is the difficulty of defining traits and types in a way which can be measured. Sensory qualities such as shape, color, pitch, and loudness, and the number or frequency of certain words and images, illustrate the kinds of trait which can be

[285]

counted and measured. But they are not always very significant or revealing as to the essentials of style or the differences between great and trivial art. Attempts to apply statistical methods to the more general, intangible traits such as "sensate" and "idealistic" have been inconclusive, as in P. Sorokin's *Fluctuation of Forms of Art* (1937). However, where exact measurement is impracticable, rough estimates and informal correlations can often be made in the spirit of science, though without claims to proof.

A major style-trend, such as that toward increasing naturalism during and since the Renaissance, includes the rise and decline of many substyles, such as that of Florentine painting in the fifteenth century. Some are steps in it or manifestations of it. Other contemporary styles are partly opposed to it, as in the persistence of Byzantine traits in Sienese painting. During a major, long-range trend, someone is likely to stage a revolt: perhaps a throw-back to some older style. Modern naturalism, in the broad sense, has been growing on the whole for centuries, along with secularism, democracy, utilitarian functionalism, and other trends. It has involved important traits in the work of such diverse figures as Giotto and Masaccio, Chaucer and Rabelais, Stendhal and Courbet. Against it have moved certain tendencies in the work of modern mystics such as El Greco and Blake. The growth of a certain trend is usually at the expense of competing trends or previous conditions.

For a deeper understanding of art history in all its branches, we need more detailed, objective accounts of apparent analogies between various arts and period styles in each. We need especially those involving distant times and places, so that direct diffusion is unlikely. To what extent, for example, does the sequence "geometric-archaic-classic-baroque-rococo-romantic-decadent" actually recur in various arts, periods, and cultures?

H. Goetz (loc. cit.) maintains that Indian visual art has passed through the same cycles as in the West and in "all other arts of mankind." At the start, he says, there are helpless, naïve forms, expressing a plain, boorish mentality, then simple, natural forms expressing a healthy, vigorous one, then complicated, studiedly involved forms, expressing an elegant and then a decadent, morbid mentality. These vast cycles, he continues, reflect the general trends of cultural progress and contain style epicycles which express the mentality of successive prominent dynasties. The early dynasties gather and mix eclectically the various art traditions already present, then evolve their own imperial styles, at first grandiosely barbarian and finally effeminate and decadent. Along with these changes goes a parallel transformation of the concept of divinity from a cosmic force to an idealized super-image of man, then to a pretext for human frivolities and at last to a superficial, dead routine. Goetz compares the practice of later Indian and Chinese nobles in having their concubines painted as Buddhist and Hindu deities with that of European ones in posing their mistresses as Madonnas.

Suggestive as it is, such a summary is arbitrarily simplified into a formula which needs empirical verification at every point. (Did Indian religion, for example, begin with "the vision of an incomprehensible but overwhelming cosmic force" or with nature spirits and totems as in other parts of the world?) The alleged sequence of stylistic types —helpless, eclectic, naïve, simple, natural, grandiose, elegant, decadent, etc.—needs to be tested for correctness against the dated sequence of objects, apart from its relation to concurrent sequences in religion, government, and morals.[27]

The conception of analogous types and stages is

[27] Goetz further proposes a chronological analogy between European and Indian style-sequences. In both, he says, there was a three-century interval between "early" and "mature" style. Hellenistic art lasted three to four centuries, later Buddhist art also three; Roman Hellenistic and Gupta art both four. Romanesque art lasted three and gothic art two to three, while in India the early and late medieval periods totalled four or five. The final alleged analogy is between the two or three centuries of renaissance art and Indian art to the end of the seventeenth century. All these chronological and stylistic divisions are open to question, apart from theories of cause (such as the influence of dynasties) and of value such as the "decadence" of late stages in a sequence.

still too vague to provide a solid basis for theory. What, for example, does "archaic" mean as a recurrent stylistic type? It calls to mind some definite images of early Greek sculpture such as the Apollo of Tenea (sixth c. B.C.). Few historians define it in terms of specific traits, yet broadly enough to be applicable to various arts and periods. According to Webster, as applied to objects of art it means "belonging to an early conventional stage but of too advanced a style to be called primitive." But this merely indicates its position as a stage in a sequence, without defining it in terms of traits. W. R. Agard in the *Encyclopedia of the Arts* (1946) defines it with reference only to Greek sculpture, as a "combination of human bodies rendered with increasing naturalism, yet still held firmly in the grip of formal design." But "formal design" can be very flexible and variable. Classic and baroque sculpture also holds its figures firmly in the grip of different, more complex and curvilinear types of design. So do the later periods of Chinese and Japanese sculpture.

Such concepts as "primitive," "savage," "barbarian," and "early empire," which refer to general cultural stages, are also used to designate types and stages of art. But can any definite types or styles of art be correlated with them? We have seen that Morgan's theory of a tight correlation among all cultural components in each stage must be abandoned. Subsequent research has disclosed much more diversity in each than he realized. There are many kinds of "savage" art, including the naturalistic and the decorative-symbolic. There are more kinds of barbarian and still more of early urban and imperial art. But there is not an infinite number in any cultural stage. There may still be a limited range of types and styles in each, within which certain traits are most recurrent. In the meantime, scholars keep on using such obviously ambiguous terms as "primitive art" as a catch-all for a wide miscellany of styles outside the main academic traditions of East and West. Such extremely different ones as paleolithic, neolithic, modern equatorial African, Polynesian, Melane-

sian, and Mayan are included. Even the art of Henri Rousseau and other self-taught modern Parisians, along with that of the Italian Trecento, has found a place there. Obviously, no very specific group of stylistic traits can be found in common among all these. We need a new set of terms and concepts for the various main stylistic types which occur in these many environments. They should be based primarily on morphological analysis, with related information on provenance.

Among the concepts deserving redefinition is that of "decadent art." Does it have any meaning other than "the art of a sick or dying culture" or "art which we disapprove and consider unhealthy"? This derogatory term is applied by various theorists to a wide range of types and styles. Ascetic supernaturalists of East and West have branded all naturalistic, sensuously pleasing art as "decadent." They place the beginning of decadence where others see a great creative rise, as in the renaissance. Hellenistic, Byzantine, baroque, and rococo art have all been called "decadent" by those who see in Phidias and Giotto the summits of progress. By others, they have been praised as different but equally healthy. It is not to be assumed that the art of a weakening culture is necessarily weak itself, any more than the art of a neurotic person is necessarily neurotic. These are partly evaluative questions, but they involve certain issues of historic fact and others of morphology. Can certain observable traits of form and style be accurately associated with the concept of decadence?[28]

The description of change in art and culture is often expressed in terms of rather vague linear metaphors. Morgan's account is said to be "unilinear"; Steward's "multilinear." We speak of movements, regressions, changes of direction, cycles; all referring literally to some sort of physical motion in space. People and works of art do move, to be sure, but this is not what we mean. We are thinking of different kinds of qualitative,

[28] *Cf.* R. L. Peters, "Toward an 'Un-definition' of Decadent as Applied to British Literature of the Nineteenth Century." *Journal of Aesthetics and Art Criticism*, XVIII, 2 (Dec. 1959), 258.

formal, and aesthetic change; complex processes which are hard to describe. A "cycle" is simply the recurrence of a somewhat similar sequence of traits and changes.

Any unilinear conception of changes in art must be highly simplified, arbitrarily selecting certain aspects of the process, but it is not necessarily completely false. There are elements of truth in nineteenth-century unilinear evolutionism, as we have seen. They express the fact that there has been some overall persistence of development in evolution, over and above all divergences, diversities, and regressions. A single line is not necessarily a straight line; it can be a graph of rises and falls, as in a statistical chart. If we are dealing with only one abstract variable, such as complexity, it becomes easier to chart its historical rises and falls than when we try to follow many variables at once. Complexity is a fairly objective trait and hence more susceptible to quantitative estimate than a controversial one like "beauty," "decadence," or "spirituality." "Realism" as a stylistic type can also be defined in a fairly objective way, in terms of the relation between representational form and current standards of the nature of reality. It includes a complex of related traits, however, and each of these can vary separately. A picture can be realistic in shape and not in color; in psychological implications and not in visual perspective. Estimates of the ups and downs of any such traits in art over a period of years require constant simplification, the ignoring of countless minor variations, but they can be useful nevertheless. They can be done in all arts: e.g., in tracing the increase of dissonance and orchestral diversity in music; of rhythmic irregularity in verse; of pessimistic and nihilistic attitudes in recent fiction and drama.

Doubtless future historians and aestheticians will employ giant computers and other mathematical devices in such study; but these are of little use until we have a clearer conception of what to count and measure: that is, of what specific variables most deserve measurement if possible. Fortunately, there are many intermediate steps toward exact measurement, and in the meantime rough quantitative estimates in linear terms can be useful as applied to specific, morphological variables.

At present, our limited knowlege of art history discloses no universal movement in any one direction among all the main variables concerned, but rather a baffling diversity of movements. They are rather zigzag or interweaving than unilinear. Cultural history from this point of view seems more like the writhing, struggling growth of a tropical jungle than an orderly parade. Styles and tendencies are constantly competing with each other for support and survival. They split, radiate, diverge, and reconverge bewilderingly. Countless influences pour upon them. But within the whole, it now seems possible to discern a prevailing trend of development. Most plants strive upward toward the sun, though some are negatively phototropic. A new forest becomes larger and more complex under favorable conditions, over and above the cyclical careers of particular organisms and organic types. Many incidental breaks and radical changes of direction are to be seen, as when a fire, flood, or earthquake changes the previous trend of forest growth. But there is little sign, in art history as a whole, of that universal periodicity, that complete and regular return to "begin at the beginning" of which the cyclical theorists talk. In art as in other realms of culture, something is carried over from stage to stage, sequence to sequence, as the generations come and go.

16. SUMMARY

A *style* of art is a kind of type: one involving a set of interrelated, recurrent traits. It is a characteristic way of selecting and organizing the ingredients of art, capable of being repeated with variation in many otherwise different products. A historic or period style is associated especially with some particular period, place, and social group or individual artist. It is one way of varying a persistent type such as the temple, the hymn, the epic, the headdress, or the armchair. A non-period style is a recurrent stylistic type such as "romantic" which occurs in various forms at various times and places.

A style can be analyzed into a set of constituent *traits* and subtraits, some of which are essential or typical while others are optional or variable. Stylistic traits include not only those directly perceptible to the senses but also characteristic ideas, beliefs, types of attitude, desire, and feeling.

Every historic style has a certain changing distribution or field of occurrence in space, time, and cultural setting. The study of changes and descents in style is now hampered by the ambiguity of style-names and by disagreement on the traits and provenance (geographical and chronological) of major styles such as the baroque. Polytechnical styles, such as "romantic," appear in many of the arts of a period. Some pervade the whole culture and are sometimes regarded as expressing the "spirit of the age." Some styles are short-lived; others live on for centuries or die out and then revive in altered form.

Styles and groups of styles descend through history as traditions, subtraditions, and co-traditions. Two or more may appear as constituent factors in a single work of art, as in a church containing both gothic and classical features. Traditions in the arts, along with those in religion, philosophy, and other cultural components, descend with modification as currents in the "great tradition" of world civilization. They are converging on the whole in spite of continued differentiation and conflict. Stylistic analysis disproves the theory that each style and each work of art is completely unique.

Empirical study of the descent of styles and traditions discloses analogies, partial but striking, between the sequences of styles in times and places remote from each other. This raises difficult problems of explanation.

CHAPTER XVII

COMPLICATION AND SIMPLIFICATION
IN THE ARTS

1. DOES ART BECOME INCREASINGLY COMPLEX?

We have now to consider the second requirement of evolution in art, the one which Spencer regarded as the essential characteristic of evolution. The question whether art becomes more complex can be asked in regard to several aspects of art history: namely, (a) world art as a whole from its beginnings, including the whole body of skills, occupations, products, and technical knowledge now classed under that heading; (b) specific types and examples of art in different periods, ancient and modern; (c) specific trends and sequences in the history of styles.

As to all these, our thesis in this chapter is that complication—and hence evolution—does occur in the arts on a large scale. On the whole, it has been and still is the prevailing tendency. But one can find important examples of the opposite trend, toward increasing simplicity. How do these affect the main process of evolution?

Considered in isolation, trends toward simplicity in art are in some ways devolutionary and regressive. In view of their importance, we can not say that art history is uniformly or steadily evolutionary. But they appear at present to be minor, subordinate pulsations, eddies within the main stream. Some of them are necessary to evolution itself, in clearing a way for larger developments.

The total process of art history, including minor simplifications but predominantly compli-

cative, can be called *synthetic evolution*. This term implies a combination of different trends in a comprehensive development. It also refers to the dialectical nature of art history as a continuing synthesis of conflicting tendencies.

2. THE NATURE AND VARIETIES OF COMPLEXITY IN THE ARTS

To review Spencer's concept: complexity is differentiation plus integration or coherence. Increasing complexity involves a change from the more homogeneous or undifferentiated to the more heterogeneous, differentiated, and definite. Differentiation may be found within a single object or process, in the fact of having many unlike parts or ingredients. It may be found among separate objects or processes when each as a whole is different from others. One kind of complexity in art occurs when a particular work of art is internally differentiated and integrated; when it has many different parts or qualities which are organized in some unifying way. Another occurs when various arts and their products—skills, occupations, styles, and particular works of art—have become very different from one another, and yet are socially interrelated.

Simplicity in art is not the complete antithesis of complexity. A very simple work of art, with few parts or little difference among its parts, may be highly integrated, definite in form, and very different from other forms. Complex types and simple but definite types may both result from evolution. Antithetical to the highly evolved condition, and preceding it on the whole, is an undifferentiated, vague, indefinite, unintegrated condition, as in a field on which miscellaneous objects have been thrown at random. By increasing the definiteness and differentiation of parts, we take one step toward complexity; by linking parts together more firmly we take another. Either may be taken separately. Both together, or alternately, tend to produce a complex form. Some works of art are comparatively low in both differentiation and integration; some have much internal differentiation but little integration. Some have much of both, and are highly complex.

The early Greek philosophers wrote in other terms of this antithesis and its possible reconciliation: they spoke of the One and the Many. Plato's ideal Republic involved a harmony and unity of diverse individuals and classes. The classical ideal in art has stressed unity in variety, order in multiplicity. Romantic trends in art have called for more freedom and variety; for a partial relaxing of the order imposed by reason and mathematics. They have seldom if ever gone to the extreme of disorder and disunity; all art involves some integration. Before the theory of artistic evolution was proposed, Coleridge and others called for a combination of unity and contrast as an ideal in art.[1]

A work of art can be complicated in many different ways. It can be complex in some respects and simple in others. This makes it hard to estimate the total, relative complexity of works which have been developed along different lines and in different media. Nevertheless, rough comparisons can be made, especially between very high and very low degrees.

One way in which a work of art can be diversified is to have many different, concrete parts: for example, a building with many rooms, windows, doors, halls, corridors, etc., of different shapes and sizes. A story or play can have many different characters and episodes; a picture can have many different human figures and objects in the background; a symphony can have several movements. Such diversity and multiplicity of parts can be achieved through adding and assembling previously separate units, as in combining separate folk tales into a connected series. This is the method of addition. The opposite method is division, in which an existent form or design is divided and subdivided into part within part and group within group.

One way of estimating the degree of complexity in a work of art is in terms of the number of definite inclusions it contains: the number of designs within designs; of patterns, motifs, or other definite forms within larger ones. Certain gothic cathedrals, certain Persian carpets and modern symphonies can be classed as ultracomplex in this respect. Beginning with the total form as an organic whole, one can analyze it first into its main, coordinate parts, such as the walls, roof, and spire of a cathedral; the border and central field of a rug; the movements of a symphony. In the cathedral, somewhat smaller design-units are: the portal with sculptured ribs and tympanum relief, the rose window, the arcade, the altar, and the carved, wooden choir stalls; each containing many designs within designs, down to the smallest, undifferentiated surface of stone, wood, or glass. In the same way, thematic analysis can descend in music from the whole movement through large sections of the movement (such as exposition, development, and recapitulation) to periods, phrases, and figures, down to single notes and chords. The number of inclusions is not the total number of units, although many inclusions usually require many units. It is the number of times or distinct levels of size through which one can descend, in the same general area, from a larger, inclusive form to smaller but still definite forms or patterns within it.

Complexity can also be found among abstract qualities and relations: a picture can have many different colors and linear shapes; a symphony,

[1] *Biographia Literaria*, Ch. XIV.

many different instrumental tones and key modulations. In aesthetic morphology, we study the various possible ways in which form can be built up in any art, to any desired degree of complexity.[2] For example, a picture can be complicated in regard to line alone, as a pen-and-ink drawing, into a highly intricate arabesque. A musical composition can have a complex melodic pattern, but little development in rhythm, chord-structure, or instrumentation. A story can be complicated in terms of action alone, with little development of character, local color, or intellectual commentary. Such works have low component diversity; they are developed in few components. Development can also be made in one or more modes of composition; in the utilitarian, representative, expository, or thematic alone, or in two or more of these. Such developments can be thoroughly integrated, or only slightly so. A cathedral has high compositional diversity because it is developed along utilitarian lines (as a building for active use), along representative lines (through portrayals of divine, human, and animal figures in sculpture and stained glass), along expository lines (through symbolic expression of general theological and moral conceptions), and along thematic or decorative lines (through building designs by the repetition, variation, and contrast of themes in line, mass, color, and other components).[3] Styles such as the gothic and baroque can also be analyzed and compared in these ways, as to the degrees and modes of development they employ. Some cathedrals have high stylistic diversity and comparatively little integration in this respect. That is, different parts are made in different periods and styles.

Organic development also proceeds along various lines, such as digestion, circulation, respiration, locomotion, and reproduction. A species can be more highly evolved in one respect than in another. The dinosaurs were less highly evolved as to brain and nervous system than in some other respects. Cultures can be compared as to the complexity of various components: i.e., as to political, social, economic, technological, religious, philosophical, scientific, and artistic development. Naturally, the many different lines which evolution can follow make it hard to compare two types which have developed along very different lines. Nevertheless, rough comparisons can be made between such two diverse types as a tribe and a city-state, a plain vase or plain carpet and a sonata. Rough estimates can be made as to the net or over-all degree of complexity which each contains. But such estimates, necessarily somewhat vague and arbitrary, are of little value without an understanding of the specific ways in which each object is relatively complex or simple.

In the evaluative criticism of art, judgments of "too much" and "too little" are frequently made, often with scanty observation on which to base them. Critics are impatient to announce that a certain work "lacks unity" or is "tiresomely crowded with details." But they seldom explain how much is too much, how unified or how complex a work of art should be. Tastes differ on these questions. However dogmatic or unsupported, such judgments are worth studying in themselves as expressions of taste. They help decide what kinds of art shall find favor and survive.

3. COMPLICATIVE TRENDS IN VARIOUS ARTS. HIGHLY COMPLEX WORKS OF ART

It seems obvious that the world's artistic heritage has grown enormously more complex since its prehistoric beginnings. This evolution appears in its multiplicity of arts, technics, occupations, institutions, types of product, styles, and traditions.

Since Spencer wrote *Progress: its Law and Cause* in 1857, the multiplication of arts and distinct skills and occupations has proceeded rapidly. It is ob-

[2] See T. Munro, "Form in the Arts: a Method for Analysis," in *Toward Science in Aesthetics* (New York, 1956), p. 160.
[3] *Ibid.*, pp. 170 f.

jectively recorded in statistical surveys of occupations by governmental and institutional specialists.[4] So immense an artistic industry as the cinema was unknown to the mid-nineteenth century. It has already split into hundreds of distinct but related occupations, from producers, authors, and directors to scenario writers, actors, musicians, cameramen, script girls, costume and make-up experts, and editors who cut and reassemble film. It is developing more and more distinct types of product, such as the news, documentary, advertising, animated cartoon, and educational film. Individual and national stylistic traits are appearing, as in the Italian, Russian, and Japanese film; the styles of Griffith, Eisenstein, René Clair, Disney, Hitchcock, and Bergman. Architecture is likewise an expansive, rapidly evolving art. So much technological knowledge, both aesthetic and scientific, is now demanded of architecture that large metropolitan firms maintain staffs of specialists on different phases of the work and on various types of building such as commercial and residential. These consult with other experts in heating, lighting, air conditioning, fireproofing, telephone service, and so on. Construction, labor relations, procurement of materials, and coordination of processes in a large building are managed by contractors in consultation with architect and patron. At the same time, much that was included in architecture in Vitruvius's day, such as the designing of water-pumps and military engines, has been detached from it and assigned to various types of engineering.

The integrative side of such evolution is closely bound up with differentiation. Each new skill or occupation develops its own internal organization, as in corporations, labor unions, employers' associations, and training schools. Separately and collectively, the various arts are explained and guided by lectures, courses, books, and articles from technological, critical, historical, and theoretical points of view. Museums, concert and theater bureaus, libraries, publishers, and university faculties contribute to their intellectual integration. In many countries, national and local governments are active in supporting and, in some degree, influencing the arts. UNESCO is an ambitious international experiment in cultural cooperation, including the arts.

This cumulative process of differentiation and integration occurs, not only in world art as a whole, but also in each particular art. Among musicians and music-lovers the world over there are many and growing international contacts, associations, music festivals, broadcasts, contract and copyright agreements, trade unions, concert bureaus, and the like. The world of music is a little universe of its own; it overflows many boundaries of language and national antagonism, some of which hamper other arts. But in these also the trend exists: as soon as travel and communication revive after a war, artists and scholars in each art begin traveling and exchanging ideas. Exhibitions are circulated, films distributed, conventions of writers, painters, and critics held.

Some arts are much more active than others in the twentieth century. They expand, develop, differentiate, and reintegrate more rapidly, as if great social forces were flowing into and feeding them. In addition to the film and architecture, these include the artistic aspects of radio, television, popular magazine and newspaper publication, transportation, furniture and clothing. These are often described as industries or mass media rather than as arts. They are often regarded with disdain by conservative critics and aestheticians. But all can claim to be arts in the broad sense, whether their products are great or trivial, insofar as they involve aesthetic aims and functions. Many of the most dynamic arts today are classed as "useful" or "applied" rather than "fine" arts, in that they involve utilitarian as well as aesthetic functions.

Among the more purely "fine" arts, some are more actively differentiating than others. Poetry is comparatively inactive in this respect: it is not

4 Cf. T. Munro, *The Arts and Their Interrelations* (New York, 1949), pp. 274 f.

rapidly subdividing into specialized branches and occupations, based on different skills and types of product. It has evolved few new types or styles in recent years. Painting, on the other hand, which is also classed as a fine art, has been prolific in developing new styles, isms, and controversial movements, many of them short-lived. Post-impressionism is a loose name for several different styles of the late nineteenth and early twentieth centuries, such as those of Van Gogh, Gauguin, Seurat, Cézanne, Matisse, Rouault, and Picasso. It is variously subdivided into, or supplemented by, other style-concepts such as pointillism, expressionism, fauvism, cubism, futurism, vorticism, dadaism, constructivism, abstractionism, non-objectivism, and many more. Some of these are redivided or succeeded by variants such as abstract impressionism, abstract expressionism, and the like. No previous age has so avidly tried to create new styles in pictorial art, each with a distinctive name and claim to high originality; each eager to replace all others in the public favor. For each, there is a fickle, short-lived public of *avant-garde* critics and admirers.

In addition to these indigenous Western styles, there has been a steady influx of exotic importations, archaic and primitive revivals, such as Persian miniature painting, Japanese prints and paintings, primitive revivals, primitive Negro sculpture, Mayan architecture, Egyptian and Minoan painting. Brought into Western culture by travelers, archeologists, and collectors, these have influenced European art and been partly incorporated in it. In turn, European artists and critics have helped to develop a taste for the exotic in the general public, so that foreign styles are still more eagerly imported. Much the same can be said of exotic and primitive music and dancing, now enjoyed by Western audiences not only in direct performance but in television, phonograph records, and color-films. In many parts of the far and near east, especially Japan, there has been an equally ardent importation and absorption of Western arts and practical technologies, by all classes of society. In each case, there has been a partial grafting of these upon the native cultural stock.

Picasso's different "periods"— rose, blue, cubist, paleontological, and others yet unnamed—are equivalent to a whole galleryful of ordinary, individual painters in diversity and specialization. At one time he will paint in flat colors alone, at another with massive modeling of figures; at one time in line alone and with color reduced to a dull monochrome; at another, with boldly contrasting hues. He has absorbed and transformed "influences" from countless exotic and primitive sources such as African sculpture, Greek vase-painting, and sculpture, medieval stained glass, and Coptic embroideries.

All this involves differentiation of styles on an unparalleled scale, and at the same time a partial integration, as Orient and Occident, North and South hemispheres, pour examples of their native styles into one common heritage. Yet it is not a complete melting-pot, which would destroy them all. For determined, expert services are used to keep them distinct in the public mind; to cultivate an understanding and appreciation of each tradition for what it is, in addition to experiments at eclectic combination. The integration of art on a world scale is still extremely loose and fragmentary. It is much less evident than differentiation, but it is proceeding as a part of the general, cultural assimilation which goes on in spite of wars and political rivalries. It has gone far since Spencer's day.

Specific sequences within a given art usually involve some development. Some reveal the gradual evolution of a certain definite style, such as that of realistic, three-dimensional painting in the Italian renaissance. Some but not all of these involve increasing complexity. If one follows the development of gothic church construction in France, from such early examples as St. Severin to the finished cathedrals of Notre Dame, Chartres, Amiens, and Rouen, one perceives not only a gradual clarification of the gothic style but on the whole a complication of the form.[5] Each step ahead suggests and makes possible a train of others. The transfer of weight and thrust from walls to piers and buttresses, plus the decreasing need for thick walls as defense, allowed thin walls, high vaults, large windows, and stained glass. Growing wealth and ambitious display, along with the need to admit larger crowds, helped to motivate the multiplication of parts. Useful elements of structure like the flying buttress won favor also for their visual appearance, and were developed beyond the requirements of strength into huge three-dimensional designs around the apse and sides. Towers and steeples, arcades and sculptured portals, chapels, aisles, balconies, windows, clustered piers, floor designs, ornate metal grills and carved woodwork, all contributed to the late gothic cathedral an unparalleled multiplicity of parts. Along with it went a profusion of symbolic and representational meaning, as theological, historical, and moral concepts were expressed in visible form. The whole was more or less integrated, in spite of frequent differences in style among successively added parts. It was unified from a structural, utilitarian standpoint by the building design as an architectonic whole; as a strong, lasting, protected hall for large assemblies and ceremonies. It was held together as a visual form by many continuities of visual theme and pattern. Small details in the façade, apse, and choir were grouped in subordinate patterns. The cathedral was integrated as a symbolic form by the coherence of the religious ideas which its various parts expressed.

Certain particular works of art stand out as peaks of complexity. Wagner's *Ring* cyle, Michelangelo's Sistine frescoes, Rodin's unfinished *Gate of Hell*, the plays of Shakespeare, James Joyce's *Ulysses*, Thomas Mann's *The Magic Mountain*, André Gide's *The Counterfeiters*, are all complex in different ways. Complexity is not the same as cultural richness; it can be formed exclusively from contemporary elements, and on the other hand, much cultural baggage can be poorly organized. But the examples just mentioned qualify as highly

evolved on both counts. To these we may add J. S. Bach's *Art of the Fugue* and *St. Matthew Passion*, some ceiling paintings by Tiepolo, and Bosch's fantasies of Heaven and Hell. One thinks of the heavily sculptured temples of central and southern India, such as the great complex of buildings at Madura. One thinks of the Taj Mahal with its delicate lacework of carved and inlaid stone, its minarets, gardens, and pools. On the other hand, the *Book of Kells* is small but complex in a more limited, specialized way, especially that of linear design on a flat surface. In each of these examples, there is a multiplicity of parts, which are given coherence by pervasive continuities of theme and by subordination to some comprehensive design.

History does not show a steady, continuous, unilinear increase in the complexity of particular works of art. It shows an over-all tendency to complication in that civilized art has produced works far more complex than any produced in prehistoric cultures. Some recent examples, such as Wagner's *Ring* series (when fully staged as a combined audio-visual-literary form) probably exceed in complexity any previous work of art. But history also shows that many very complex works were produced in antiquity, such as the *Odyssey* with its intricately woven design of episodes and characters. On the other hand, some very simple forms are produced today: in abstract painting, for example.

Within every civilized period and style, there

[5] As to architecture, Max Rieser comments that "Evolution of style shows as a rule increasing complexity, i.e., internal differentiation tied up by correspondence. Thus, for instance, in the course of evolution the half circle of an apsis is broken up into corresponding segments as units of a more intricate organization while the basic shape of the apsis is unimpaired." ("The Language of Shapes and Sizes in Architecture or Morphic Semantics," *Philosophical Review*, March 1946, p. 155). As examples, he mentions the change from the early romanesque apse at Aulnay de Saintonge to that of the cathedral of Amiens or the renaissance apse of St. Pierre in Caen. See also P. A. Michelis, "À Propos des plans d'Hagia Sophia," on the development of Byzantine architecture, especially of the dome on pendentives. (*Acts of the XIth International Congress of Byzantinists*, 1958, Munich, 1960).

is a considerable range of variation as to degrees of complexity. Any style can be complicated indefinitely by combining more and more different parts. Some Egyptian and Babylonian temple-complexes, including their surrounding parks and gardens and their painted, carved, or tiled wall-decorations, were fairly elaborate; yet these cultures also produced very simple figurines, vases, and jewels. The degree of complexity required of a work of art is variable at any time; it depends partly on the intended location, size, and functions of the work. A royal palace, an opera or pageant, will tend to be elaborate at any time; a vase or love-song, simple. The Pompeian mosaic of *Alexander and Darius* is complex, but many Greek vase-drawings are limited to a few significant strokes. A portrait is usually simpler than a landscape with figures. There are simple Byzantine mosaics and enormously complex ones, as in Santa Sophia in Istanbul and St. Mark's in Venice. The same can be said of romanesque reliefs and gothic book illuminations. Rembrandt's earlier works, such as the *Night Watch* and the Biblical prints and paintings, have more figures, elaborately arranged in deep space, than his late portraits. The latter are complex in some other ways, however: e.g., in organizing subtle nuances of light and characterization.

It is also true that some styles and some periods have been more inclined than others to build complex forms when the opportunity for it arises. The baroque age was at home in the grand manner and took kindly to large, ornate forms, especially in the Catholic South. This is true not only of its architecture and surrounding parks, but of its paintings also. Throughout the Flemish renaissance there had been a tradition of landscape painting with many small figures, arranged in groups at different distances in imaginary space. The Ghent altar-piece by the brothers Van Eyck is of this type, especially the *Adoration of the Lamb*. Patinir, Hugo van der Goes, and Lucas van Leyden developed the tradition farther by introducing more elaborate subdivisions of space, more action and

variety in the figures. In their use of perspective and realistic coloring, these artists added components which had been only slightly developed in Byzantine and early gothic painting.

In the late renaissance, mannerist, and baroque periods, this tradition was carried to a peak of complexity by Tintoretto, Bruegel, Poussin, and Claude Lorrain. As to the number of figures in a single scene, the first two of these outdid all the rest, and few subsequent painters have tried to equal them. Bruegel's *Winter, the Return of the Hunters*, covers an enormous landscape, minutely subdivided into farms and fields, roads, icy ponds, and groups of trees and figures, far and near. Tintoretto attempted an imaginary view of Dante's heavens in his sketch for the *Paradiso*, now in the Louvre. Here and in several other paintings, such as *The Gathering of Manna* and *The Miracle of the Loaves and Fishes*, he employed the device of grouping the countless figures into small subvistas. The main suggested vista through the window-like frame of the picture is divided into partly distinct scenes, far and near, each a little picture in itself with figures and background. They are separated from each other as views through some opening—perhaps through a clearing in the woods, perhaps through a door or gap in ruined masonry. Albrecht Dürer (in his wood engravings), Filippo Lippi, Ghirlandaio, and Carpaccio had done this to some extent, but in a more sharply linear way. Tintoretto, as a late Venetian, added the subtlety and richness of painterly color and light. In the work of these mannerist and baroque masters, the landscape with figures reached a height of complexity seldom attempted before or since in any still painting.

When the cinema gave pictures a temporal dimension, new avenues for complication were opened in Western art. In China, a somewhat analogous avenue was opened by the development of the handscroll and its use for landscape painting in the Sung dynasty. This could be extended horizontally to any distance and viewed in temporal sequence from right to left, as if from a moving boat, car, or airplane. Each small section could exhibit a profusion of minute details. Mountains, streams, lakes, trees of a few distinctive types, tiny houses, bridges, and human figures would move by as the scroll was turned; not haphazardly, but in organized designs suggesting music through the variation of themes, division into movements, and rising to climaxes.

Theoretically, the possibility of complication increases as the form is developed in more and more dimensions of space and time, and to greater size within them. Greater size in space or greater duration in time allows a greater number of perceptible parts and details, other things being equal. Among the static visual arts, painting is usually presented in two dimensions only; this restricts its development along that line. But it can suggest or represent a vista in three dimensions of space. Sculpture can present a form in three dimensions, and this gives it many different aspects from different points of view. Architecture has the further resource of internal spatial development, with many different vistas as in a cathedral. Landscape design and city planning can increase the range still further in space, and to some extent determine the temporal order in which the parts are seen.

When the presentation is controlled in temporal order, the possibility of complication is vastly increased. Each moment in a symphony, a different complex form is presented to the ear. One hears, and strives to perceive organically, a rapid flow of intricately varied and connected tones, chords, figures, phrases, movements; each organized in rhythm, pitch, and timbre and fitting into a comprehensive design. The possibilities are somewhat similar in ballet, drama, opera, film, and other temporal arts.

In modern urban civilization, most people learn to grasp some of these complexities with increasing skill from early childhood onward. They can easily follow and understand a motion picture or a television program which would overwhelm a primitive observer. Individuals differ greatly, by nature and training, in ability to perceive complex

forms. But for every human a limit is eventually reached, beyond which organic perception and interpretation are too difficult and finally become a vague blur.

Among all human inventions, the most complex single, physical product today is perhaps the modern battleship or aircraft carrier, including its fleet of attendant planes, each a marvel of intricate mechanical and electrical equipment in itself. This can hardly be classed as a work of art, however, because it lacks almost entirely an aesthetic aim or function. It may seem beautiful to some observers, and the sailors work to keep it clean and neat; but this is not enough. Within the class of useful works of art we may safely class the transatlantic passenger ship; not because it is peaceful, but because it shows, inside and out, a conscious effort to develop aesthetic aspects: in the shape of the vessel and in the design and decoration of its rooms and equipment. It is a highly diversified type of mobile architecture, for which the cooperation of many minor arts has been secured. Much the same can be said of a huge metropolitan hotel. Lavish expenditure is devoted to making these gigantic devices for residence or transportation seem beautiful as well as comfortable to their patrons. Even musical and theatrical facilities are included

In terms of sheer size, number, and variety of parts, these examples are far more complex than the cathedral, and each is highly organized as a whole. But from the standpoint of aesthetic perception, they are in one respect less complex: one cannot see much of their complexity at any one time. Their exterior designs are rather simple and regular, especially that of the conventional hotel with its rows of identical windows on flat walls. Inside, there are no great, diversified vistas as in the cathedral. People go through one comparatively small, box-like room after another. Even huge ball-rooms present no such elaborate subdivision of interior space and surface quality as does the cathedral, with its arcaded aisles, intersecting nave and transept, chapels, balconies, and luminous, colored windows. In the hotel, bedrooms and

[297]

corridors are all much alike; one is not tempted to look at many of them; they do not build up into a complex aesthetic form.

Still larger types of useful art, combining utilitarian emphasis with some amount of aesthetic development, are developing before our eyes. One of them is the city plan or planned community, small or large. From the village to the metropolis, the city as a human product is or can be made a work of art.[6] In theory and in occasional examples, such as Paris, the aesthetic aspects have been highly developed. More can be done along this line whenever people wish to do so. In the meantime the development of complex urban and regional design proceeds along more exclusively utilitarian lines, directed by considerations of traffic, finance, industry, commerce, health, and social welfare. It is proceeding into ever-larger complexes like the Tennessee Valley region, linking together many towns and villages with their intervening roadways, waterways, forests, and farmlands. Smaller than these, but larger than any single edifice, is the organized group of buildings with attendant grounds, lawns, and gardens, as in a large university, an exposition, a zoological, botanical, or amusement park, or a shopping center. To a varying extent, their designers take account of aesthetic factors and plan the whole complex with an eye to visual harmony. The buildings of a modern university are more diversified than those of their medieval prototype. They often contain a stadium and outdoor theater, concert-hall and art gallery in addition to lecture halls, dormitories, laboratories, greenhouses, and observatories. Other types of complex, such as the hospital or the shopping center, involve different kinds of utilitarian structure, which are turned to decorative advantage when this is desired.

High complexity in a particular work of art indicates the ability to organize, in a comparatively purposeful, conscious way, many different details—such as shapes, tones, rhythms, words, ideas, characters, or incidents—into a unified composition. Such a work may be described as "highly

evolved." As there are many degrees and kinds of variety, there are many degrees and kinds of unity. Through instinct, the bee and the spider build fairly complex combs and webs. Plants and even inanimate snow crystals are often complex; the human body itself is more complex than any work of art. From such complexity and functional adaptation, theologians inferred a divine Artist; this is the "argument from design." But man's instinctive drives are not sufficiently fixed and specific to produce art in a purely mechanical way. Only through long cultural development has he learned to make works of art which are comparable in complexity to his own body; to the crystal, the web, and the honeycomb. On the whole, and aside from exceptions which prove the rule, prehistoric art was relatively simple and undifferentiated.

We know that comparatively primitive, modern, tribal artists often produce fairly complex designs, as in African Negro drum-beats and sculpture. Some civilized observers could not at first believe that they had done so intentionally; so widespread was the fiction that the "savage" is purely instinctive and emotional. It was even more surprising to find examples of somewhat complex form in the paleolithic cave-paintings. Here again, we must assume that such complexity is the result of conscious, purposeful action. It indicates a surprisingly high level of artistic development in certain respects, for that early date. But we should not attribute to the paleolithic drawings more complexity than they actually possess. They are, as one would expect, less complex on the whole than the drawings of modern, civilized artists. Some of the Lascaux drawings are highly evolved in terms of definiteness; of clear perception and selective representation of animals; they give a vivid impression of the structure and movement of a certain species of animal. Some show also a developed power of rhythmic line and shading in single units. But only the rudiments of pictorial composition appear, in a few small groups of over-

[6] Mumford, 1938.

lapping animal figures. In sculpture, there are paleolithic figurines with a strong sense of unified design on a small scale, but no organized composition of sculptural forms comparable to those achieved in the Parthenon pediments and the Ghiberti doors. It is not impossible that some paleolithic artists achieved the power of complex organization, and that their works may sometime be found. Art may have repeatedly achieved high stages of evolution along certain lines, long before the historical period. Complex types of modern tribal art are exceptional; much of it is simple, repetitious, and monotonous. Our art museums tend to misrepresent it by showing only the best examples. In music so highly developed as the Balinese, there is little if any building up toward a climax or foreseen conclusion; often the musicians simply stop in the midst of things when they feel that they have played enough.

To grasp in full the complexity of a highly evolved, civilized, and sophisticated work of art, one must pay attention not only to concrete parts and their interrelations, but also to the subtle differentiation of qualities. Modern music involves regular differentiation of pitch in scales and keys; of rhythm in meters. Phrasing and incidental variations further differentiate rhythm in more irregular ways. In the work of Debussy, Ravel, Stravinsky, and Schönberg, music has continued to evolve new subtleties and modes of organization in polytonal and twelve-tone harmony; in frequent changes and minute subdivisions of rhythm, as in Debussy and Stravinsky; in varied blends of tone color and orchestration, as in Rimsky-Korsakow. Modern musical notation specifies these traits more definitely. In painting, impressionist and post-impressionist color introduced a greatly extended range of tints, shades, and luminosities.

Literature, depending on the medium of words, displays in Proust, Henry James, and Joyce a meticulous concern for the precise shade of meaning conveyed by each word and phrase; its aura of ambiguous suggestiveness; its power to differentiate subtle moods and sensations.

Many primitive languages and literatures consist mostly of nouns and verbs; those of advanced civilizations have added thousands of modifying terms—adjectives, adverbs, descriptive phrases, etc. Many translations of primitive literature, intended for the enjoyment of civilized readers, are edited and developed linguistically to the point where they lose much of their original quality. The same is true of many phonograph records and other adaptations of primitive music for the urban listener. When translated into our diatonic scale with European keys, chords, and melodies, perhaps for playing on a piano, they are no longer primitive. Some of the difference in quality between primitive oral literature and sophisticated modern writing may be found in contrasting this excerpt from a Bantu folk-tale (translated fairly literally) with one from a story by Henry James:

The Bantu folk-tale:[7] "This is what some people did. The son said: 'Mother, go and find a wife for me, as I am now grown up.' The mother said: 'My child is now grown up.' The mother got up and went to look for the wife. The wife gave birth to a child, and later on to another. At last she said to her husband: 'Let us get up and go and see my mother.' The husband said:' We will go.' They got up, both of them. It happened to be a time of famine. On the way they found wild figs. The woman then said: 'Do climb up and give me some figs.'...."

The story by Henry James:[8] "Nothing had passed for half an hour—nothing, at least, to be exact, but that each of the companions occasionally and covertly intermitted her pursuit in such a manner as to ascertain the degree of absorption of the other without turning round. What their silence was charged with, therefore, was not only a sense of the weather, but a sense, so to speak, of its own nature. Maud Blessingbourne, when she lowered her book into her lap, closed her eyes with a con-

[7] From J. Torrend, *Specimens of Bantu Folk-lore from Northern Rhodesia* (London, 1921), p. 9.

[8] From "The Story In It," in the collection entitled *The Better Sort* (Scribner, New York, 1903).

scious patience that seemed to say she waited; but it was nevertheless she who at last made the movement representing a snap of their tension..."

There are further possibilities of subtle suggestion through variations of syntax and word order. Approximate synonyms from ordinary, colloquial, poetic, or scientific diction have different flavors. Some of the living tribal peoples whom we wrongly call "primitive" are intermediate in general linguistic development. While their range of words and ideas is usually less on the whole, they often make finer distinctions than we do in realms of special importance to them: for example, different kinds of snow and light reflection on them; the tracks and odors of different animals.

Few European or American writers use the richness of their languages to the full in conveying subtle shades of meaning; some deliberately avoid doing so, for reasons we shall consider later on. But in the work of those who cultivate subtlety (e.g., Henry James or Marcel Proust), a short passage may be enough to reveal a highly evolved, sensitive, mature, and educated mind; one able to describe slight differences and blends in quality; one widely versed, perhaps, in world history and literature and able to draw significant analogies between ordinarily remote ideas. This sort of writing and thinking fits into Spencer's formula for evolution in terms of differentiation, definiteness, and reintegration.

The ways of integrating a work of art have multiplied in recent years. No longer is the artist required to follow a narrow range of rules and patterns. He uses, with critical approval, not only more varieties of form and design, but often more flexible, loose, shifting unities such as those of Debussy, which appeared to early critics as "formless." The same can be said of James and Proust, in whose stories there is often little plot or overt action.

Insofar as there is high complexity in certain modern works of art, there must have been a gradual or sudden complication in the stylistic sequences which led up to them, perhaps through centuries. Many of the intermediate steps are lost to us, but certainly the peaks of complexity did not appear all at once by individual flashes of genius. As for the late gothic cathedral, so for the modern novel or symphony, the historian can trace a gradual development through many generations. He often describes it explicitly as an "evolution"—the evolution, let us say, of dramatic plot construction from Aeschylus to Shakespeare, with its increasing range of characters, action-threads, and subplots. One can trace that of polyphonic music from the late Gregorian chant through Palestrina to Bach and Handel. Separate historical studies have traced the development of the modern armchair with upholstered padding and springs from the plain, stiff, wooden chair of the gothic period; that of the film from Porter's *Great Train Robbery* to *Gone with the Wind* and later sound-color giants.

It was Madame de Staël, as we noted above, who saw in the greater psychological understanding of modern writers a reason to believe that literature had progressed beyond the Greek and Roman. We need not assume that such an increase is necessarily an improvement; i.e., that complication is progress. But it is certainly a kind of evolution. World art as a whole, since the renaissance, undoubtedly expresses more varieties of human experience than that of any previous age. In accordance with the Faustian ideal, the psychological materials of modern art include both good and bad experience, the pleasant and the painful, happy and unhappy, sane and insane, healthy and diseased, virtuous and vicious, wise and foolish, savage, barbarous, and civilized. Modern art represents every conceivable kind of character, including the poor and humble, who were usually caricatured in the art of aristocratic ages. The forms of art, being more diversified than ever before, can arouse a greater variety of direct perceptual and imaginative experiences. They can make us imagine how it feels to be godlike or demonic, saintly or cruel, a person of the opposite sex, or even another kind of animal. In recent years, the arts have helped us realize more fully and poignantly how it feels to fail miserably in life; to suffer in an abject, unheroic way. They have portrayed the inner, subjective world of individual experience far more subtly than ever before.

All this multiplicity and ceaseless change in experience, real and imagined, is partly integrated in particular works and styles of art. They help a thoughtful observer to organize it further for himself, in terms of his own world-view and personality. But they are infinitely flexible, adapted to many types of mind and levels of education, and capable of many interpretations.

4. MYSTIC SYMBOLISM AND RELIGIOUS ICONOGRAPHY. THE MULTIPLICATION OF SYMBOLS AND MEANINGS

The development of religious art involved a tremendous elaboration of symbols and meanings. Each ethnic group and each local religious cult had its own set of them, descended from prehistoric times and used to distinguish its own deities by their peculiar forms and attributes. Symbolic images in art were used for purposes of magic and worship in sculpture, painting, and ritual drama. Totemism contributed animal and plant symbolism, as in the theriomorphic deities of Egypt and Babylonia. Astrology and calendar lore contributed symbols of the heavenly bodies and constellations. The cycle of the seasons offered imagery from the birth and death of plants, the mating and reproduction of animals. As local cultures merged into larger ones with the formation of great empires and the growth of trade and travel, religious syncretism brought together masses of symbols and meanings, ikons of religious personages, myths and legends of cosmic events and processes.

Any familiar visual image or type of phenomenon in nature could be treated as a mystic symbol. To treat it so was to regard it with awe and emotion, veneration or fear, as having a deeper, supernatural meaning beneath its obvious appearance and meaning. The symbol came to be regarded as a key to the understanding of divine truths and hence, under certain circumstances, to the exertion of supernatural powers. Any mystic symbol could have countless meanings at the same time. As used in different religions, it could refer to innumerable gods, demi-gods, and minor spirits. In the great, synthetic religions such as Hinduism and Mahayana Buddhism, enormous masses of symbols and meanings flowed together in the shifting iconography of the great gods, their avatars, consorts, vehicles, attributes, attendant spirits, cosmic acts, and powers.

An example is the sculptured figure of the dancing Siva Nataraja, whose dance personifies the rhythmic energy and movement of the cosmos, whose fire symbolizes his destructive power, and whose foot upon the prostrate dwarf symbolizes his victory over a demon. Also commonly represented in the dancing figure are the braided locks of a yogi, a cassia garland, the skull of Brahma, the cobras, the figure of Ganga (the river lost in Siva's hair), and the different ear-rings, male and female. Together, they signify the five activities of Siva: creation or evolution, preservation and support, destruction, illusory embodiment, and release or salvation. Separately, they are the activities of the gods Brahma, Vishnu, Rudra, Mahesvara, and Sadasiva.[9] These images and meanings, along with thousands of others such as those of Krishna playing his flute, Krishna and Radha, Krishna and the cowmaids, and the like, abound in Indian visual art, poetry, dance, and drama. The elaborate technics of the various schools of Yoga are also full of symbolic names for different parts of the body, physical and psychic functions, and states of mind.

For Christian theology, the basic conception of

[9] Ananda Coomaraswamy, *The Dance of Siva* (New York, 1924), p. 59.

universal symbolism was set forth by St. Augustine in *On Christian Doctrine*, especially as an aid to interpreting the imagery, events, and personages of the Bible. It also guided artists in literature and the visual arts through the middle ages and to some extent up to modern times. In addition to the established symbolism of orthodox religious organization, many other types may flourish in the same culture, more or less under cover. Thus vestiges of old magical, animistic, and polytheistic cults remained in Israel long after they were officially banned and expurgated from the Bible. In Christian Europe, vestiges remained of old pagan cults, as in the Walpurgisnacht. Satanism and the Black Mass remained alive along with local superstititions of elves, fairies, banshees, poltergeists, leprechauns, and the like, each with its own set of magical or mystical symbols. Cabbalism, alchemy, astrology, and related forms of mystic lore, combined with bits of science, descended from the ancient world through Jewish and Arabic scholars and attracted a considerable Christian following in the renaissance, in spite of their unorthodox teachings. Each had its own huge mass of symbols, some of them cryptic and reserved for the initiate. Pico della Mirandola, Paracelsus, Jakob Boehme, and Robert Fludd were among the scholars who mixed Christian theology with ideas from these unorthodox sources.[10]

There are also counter-trends within the ideology of mystic symbolism. At a certain stage in each of the great religions, sages and scholars have tried to bring some order into its iconography, beliefs, and practices. Within a single, organized theology such as that of St. Augustine, the range of meanings for a given symbol is not infinite, since it is limited by the context of the Scriptures and the official church interpretation thereof. But taken all together, the traditional iconographies of the world's religions present an intricate maze of symbols and meanings which modern scholars try in vain to interpret exhaustively.[11]

Each scholar, as a rule, confines himself to the iconography of a single religion or sect. But many have commented on the recurrence of certain symbols in different religions and parts of the world, such as the Tree of Life in Buddhist, Christian, Hindu, Norse, and Mayan religious art. They provide what seem to be connecting links among the religions, and, as some evolutionists believe, evidence of their common origins. Not only types of symbol, but meanings also, recur in various cultures. Many of them deal with the common, important facts of human life, such as birth, sex, reproduction, war, death, hunting, crops and herds, rain and sunshine, and mythical explanations of these in terms of supernatural personages. The repetition of such ideas keeps the number of meanings down within finite limits; but there are countless ways of attaching them to the names of different gods and spirits, their deeds and characteristics.

Instead of regarding the ambiguity of symbols as an intellectual fault or source of confusion, and hence trying to correct it, mystics revere it as a sign of the mysterious, inner unity of the cosmos. It seems to show the far-reaching connection among the symbols which deity has placed everywhere as clues to supernatural truth, morality, and salvation. This contrasts with the attitude of science and rationalism, wherein the logical ideal is maximum precision of meaning. In mathematics, so far as humanly possible, each concept such as "three" or "triangle," and each sign such as "plus" or "minus," should have but one meaning. This way of thinking strives toward simplicity and economy, whereas mystic symbolism encourages the indefinite proliferation of images and meanings. Clarity of definition is sacrificed to profusion of symbolic associations. Ancient Greece contained both the mystic and the rationalistic type of art.

[10] *Cf.* G. De Givry, *Witchcraft, Magic, and Alchemy* (Eng. Tr., London, 1931), p. 208. This book contains many symbolic illustrations from the works of Robert Fludd (*Utriusque cosmi maioris et minoris historia*, 1619).

[11] As in such treatises as A. Coomaraswamy's *Elements of Buddhist Iconography* (Cambridge, Mass., 1935); T. A. Gopinatha Rau's *Elements of Hindu Iconography* (Madras, 1914–16) and Louis Réau's *Iconographie de l'art chrétien* (Paris, 1955).

The former is exemplified in the Orphic and Eleusinian mysteries; the latter in the Parthenon.

Early religious symbolism was based in part on real analogies and causal connections in nature, as confirmed by modern science. They exist between spring in temperate climates, the growing of plants, and the reproduction of animals; between sunshine, rain, and good harvest. Early symbolism also contained the rudiments of valid classifications of phenomena into types and realms, genera and species, as in the animal, vegetable, and mineral realms and the "four elements" of earth, air, fire, and water. These developed gradually toward scientific taxonomy, as in the classification of geometrical forms and Aristotle's philosophical categories. Magical methods of controlling nature through symbolic, ritual acts, as in hunting, farming, and medicine, worked often enough to maintain some faith in them. But they were mixed with poetic fancies, myths and legends, unsupported dogmas, vague and far-fetched analogies, such as that between the Milky Way and mother's milk. These could be joined as symbols of the Egyptian sky-goddess Nut and of Hathor, whose symbols were the cow's horns and the moon. The phases of the moon were vaguely analogous to those of woman's menstrual cycle; hence associated with chastity and lunar goddesses from Hathor to Diana. So fluid were these connections that the same image could stand for opposite ideas. Diana was a descendant of older moon goddesses and earth mothers; she symbolized at one time chastity, at another fertility and reproduction.

A comparatively systematic, organized example of the multiplicity of meanings is the fourfold symbolism of Dante's *Divine Comedy*, wherein each major image is said to have four meanings of different kinds: the literal, allegorical, tropological, and anagogical. This itself was considered as symbolical of the way in which Christ accomplished his mission through his earthly, mystical, sacramental, and glorified bodies.[12] Although the fourfold symbolism used in the poetry of Dante seems multiple today, it is simple by comparison with the unrestrained, tropical profusion of Hindu and Buddhist symbolism. The restriction of each symbol to four types of meaning, and the classification of all symbolic meanings under these main headings, showed a modern Western tendency toward logical clarity and system. The development of the system was the product of centuries, from Clement and Origen to the medieval scholastics.

On a more primitive level, the ambiguity of symbols and concepts was accompanied by relative indifference to logical reasoning. There was no demand for laws of correct inference, such as those worked out by Aristotle and the scholastic logicians. Contradictory beliefs could be held at the same time and the fact justified, if necessary, by the relativity and illusory character of all supposed knowledge. Low esteem was placed by mystics such as Tertullian on sensory evidence or logical demonstration. *Credo quia absurdum; certum est, quia impossibile est.* In early Christian thought, as in the Far East, elements of rationalistic demonstration were merged with poetic visions and ecstatic revelations.

Early mystic symbolism, with its related tendency to illogical inference, is multiple rather than complex or highly evolved. Dante's is less multiple but more truly complex because more definite and logically organized. In the thirteenth century it is on the way toward modern rationalism. The evolution of symbolic thinking included, not only this increasing clarity of definition and

---

[12] H. F. Dunbar, *Symbolism in Medieval Thought and its Consummation in the Divine Comedy* (New Haven, Conn., 1929), pp. 263 ff. "Not only is one symbol to be used in many senses, but its appropriateness for the expression of any given reality is manifold... The Virgin is the sun, not only through her union with the Divine Sun, but also because she outshines all other saints as the sun does the stars, because she illumines the world..., because her love for mankind is like the heat of the sun, because she put to flight the shadows of heathendom, and so forth... Christ's function as Logos and as the limit of an infinite progression of symbols is fulfilled literally before the eyes of man in his earthly body, allegorically to humanity in his mystical body through empire and church, tropologically in his sacramental body, through which the gift of grace is extended to each soul." These are all included in his glorified body, by the sight of which Dante was blinded for a time.

inference, but the differentiation of logical thought as in science and philosophy, from artistic thought, where fantasy might reign forever unchecked. Prescientific indifference to logic had its advantages, as in allowing the oriental mind to accept several religious creeds at once without caring about their apparent inconsistency. Hebrew tradition, on the contrary, had instilled a careful respect for the letter of Mosaic law, and the Greek inheritance encouraged some respect for definite statements.

Complex, systematic iconography was at its height in medieval Christian art, as interpreted by such historians as Émile Mâle and Réau. But by the early fourteenth century, Occam's famous razor was cutting away the intellectual foundations on which it was based. Occam expressed the growing antipathy of philosophers and scientists toward unnecessary multiplication of ideas. "It is vain," he said, "to do with more what can be done with fewer." (This is, says Bertrand Russell, "a most fruitful principle in logical analysis.") Much Christian symbolism remained in renaissance art, along with growing naturalism. It was even complicated to some extent, as in Michelangelo's Sistine frescoes, by the infusion of more Greek and Roman imagery. Ovid's *Metamorphoses* and other classical sources were ransacked for images to use as symbols in painting, especially on classical subjects. But on the whole the profusion of symbolic images was gradually pruned away in the renaissance, along with that of gothic ornament in the churches. It dwindled slowly after the Council of Trent. Poussin, Rubens, Velázquez, and Rembrandt showed comparatively little interest in it. A few belated works of mystic symbolism appeared in the seventeenth century, such as Robert Fludd's curious treatise on cabbalism, astrology, and alchemy; but the old mode of thought could not flourish in the cold light of the French *Encyclopedia*. In the Far East, it remained powerful until the advent of Western ideas, and still exists there in traditional art and thought.

The pruning away of mystic symbolism from Western art in the seventeenth century was a drastic simplification of both images and meanings. This devolutionary trend was outweighed in Western culture as a whole, however, by the release and stimulus it gave to scientific thought. Here, images and meanings were to be linked more in terms of logical relations or verifiable causal connections, as in the mathematical and experimental sciences. A drawn or painted triangle is a concrete example of the concept "triangle"; an isosceles triangle is a species of the genus "triangle." A falling apple is an example of the law of gravity; its behavior can be predicted and verified on that basis. In art, new lines of development took the place of mystic symbolism; simpler at first but with endless possibilities of growth. One was the naturalistic landscape with figures, expressing the new interest in accurate sensory observation of nature under variable conditions.

5. TENDENCIES TOWARD SIMPLIFICATION. PEAKS OF COMPLEXITY IN THE ART OF VARIOUS PERIODS. WHAT CAUSES A SIMPLIFYING TREND?

Along with examples of complexity, there persist in the modern world many simple types of art and trends toward further simplification. Examples of art can be found on every degree of development from the ultra-simple to the ultra-complex. At the opposite pole from the symphony is the tolling of a single church-bell. In our shops can be found plain, colored brooches, glazed or enameled, for women's wear, and simple, glazed animal figures much like those of Egyptian faïence. Some of Constantin Brancusi's sculptures (e.g., *Bird in Space*, 1919) are reduced to simple geometrical forms such as the oval and cylinder. The abstract painting, *White on White*, by Casimir Malevitch (1918) consists of two white rectangles of slightly different tone, one placed obliquely on the other. Some recent paintings by Pierre Soulages contain only a few broad strips of black on white. (E.g.,

Painting, 1953, in the Solomon R. Guggenheim Museum, New York).

The sequence of changes in formal costume from the court of Louis XIV to the present, for both men and women, is one of great simplification. Gone are the ruffs and huge skirts, the laces, plumes, heavy brocades and embroideries. The man's usual costume is now comparatively plain and colorless; the woman's, simple and functional by day, and even on festive occasions far less ornate than in the baroque period. Such examples can be found in every branch of art.

Stylistic sequences are not always wholly or even mainly complicative. They may seem so if we arbitrarily limit them to those examples which best illustrate the growth of a certain style, and if we notice only their positive, constructive phase. But as a rule, as we have seen, they involve some sacrifice of features derived from a previous style. These features may persist in the early examples of the new sequence, making them as complex on the whole as later ones, or even more so. Thus the complex polyphonic style declined in eighteenth-century music to make room for the homophonic development of the sonata form in the younger Bachs, Haydn, Mozart, and Boccherini. Modern music as a whole is undoubtedly more complex than ancient, if only through the development of modern harmony in chord-relations and chord-progressions. This involved a great elaboration of tonality or key-relations within two or three modes, the major and the melodic and harmonic minor. But along with this development, there went a sacrifice of the other ancient and medieval modes, which (as we know from Aristoxenus and Augustine) were considerably developed as to pitch relations and emotional expressiveness.[13]

In Italian painting, the development of pictorial form from Cimabue to Tintoretto and Veronese appears as a steady increase in complexity if one thinks only of its positive achievement: the realistic, single vista into deep space, with many solid objects arranged therein. But this is not the whole story. Some of the paintings and pictorial mosaics in the Byzantine style by predecessors of Cimabue were quite as complex in their own ways as Tintoretto's paintings were in theirs. In some ways, Giotto's Assisi frescoes are simpler than their Byzantine predecessors. Gold haloes, flat backgrounds, sharp outlines, stylized figures, and other Byzantine traits gradually disappeared. The evolution of one style often involves the dissolution of another, and the final result may be a net simplification.[14]

During the past three centuries, Western painting has undergone a series of drastic simplifications through eliminating or reducing elements previously emphasized. This tendency took as its starting-point the late renaissance, mannerist, and baroque styles. These included some surviving elements of the medieval synthesis of Christian symbolism, used for moral, religious, and other instruction, in addition to the new naturalism. By the end of the seventeenth century, the medieval elements and functions were practically abandoned in the work of style leaders. Instead, there was a great development of the three-dimensional vista into imaginary space on earth. Fairly realistic perspective, anatomy, and coloring were combined with neo-classical traits of composition, subject-matter, and sensuous appeal. Dutch genre painting of common people tended to eliminate idealistic representations of nobility and divinity; the grandiose, park-like landscape followed these out, giving way to scenes of ordinary life. The emphasis on represented subject-matter (stories, noble or picturesque characters, and dramatic situations) gradually diminished during the late nineteenth century in impressionism and post-impressionism. Emphasis shifted to the more purely visual, but a new interest in thematic design arose, often com-

13 *Cf.* Casella, *op. cit.*, p. xxii.
14 Arnold Hauser remarks that, if one starts with Giotto, "the course of events shows a tendency to complication"; but from fifteenth-century naturalism, "the tendency is evidently towards simplification, clarification, and serenity." In the Carolingian period a more complicated, painterly, baroque trend preceded a severe classical, archaic one. (*The Philosophy of Art History*, pp. 130, 255).

plex in its free distortions of anatomy, perspective, and surface coloring. Twentieth-century abstract and non-objective painting, founded chiefly by Kandinsky, eliminated all represented subject-matter. In Kandinsky, Gorky, Miro, Mondrian, and some others, it retained an interest in design and definite thematic relations, but this too has dwindled in recent years.

However, as we look back over the series of eliminations, one notable fact emerges: that something positive has usually arisen in the art of painting to take the place of what was omitted. A new line of development has occurred, and the evolutionary process has continued. Being dropped for a while from one art does not mean elimination from culture as a whole. The educational functions, performed by pictures before the age of public schools and general literacy, are now assigned to other agencies. Photography has come in to satisfy the demand for visual realism. Even in painting, the discarded elements are discarded only in the work of contemporary artists; they remain in books and museums, ready to be revived when called for. Thus even the most drastic, negative aspects of artistic simplification are relatively slight and temporary. They operate on the whole, not to destroy artistic or other cultural achievements; not to reverse the main evolutionary trend, but to diversify, liberate, and enrich it for further development.

At the dawn of human culture, there may have been gradual or sudden progressions in art and culture where only development occurred; where there was not much to reject or subordinate in making room for the new. But such a situation becomes increasingly unlikely as culture develops. There is always something of the old to put aside, destroy, or subordinate for a while. Settling into the sedentary village life, neolithic man had to put aside the immemorial habits of a hunting, wandering life. Now tradition is everywhere, seeming to overwhelm and stifle originality. Everything seems to have been tried; what more can the young artist do? At present, there is no

development, no evolution in art without concomitant dissolution. The latter is as necessary as catabolism, the breaking down and elimination of old tissue in bodily life. One cannot grow in all respects at once, always accumulating and never rejecting. All art is selection and emphasis, and selecting one thing means rejecting another. There is this difference, however, from bodily metabolism: what we reject today may be missed and sought once more tomorrow; perhaps in a different form.

At any stage of its evolution, a culture will show some of its components in process of development, while others are dwindling. The net result may or may not be unhealthy. On the contrary, people may be struggling to free themselves from a system which has outlived its usefulness and come to be a burden. Thus the kinship and marriage system at the tribal stage, and the manorial system of land tenure and farming at the feudal stage, had to be abandoned in favor of simpler and more flexible ones.

Ralph Linton remarks that each society has certain dominant interests about which it tends to elaborate behavior.[15] This tends to produce hypertrophy in certain areas, he adds, such as physical technology in our culture at the expense of social invention. The Southwestern Indians developed ceremonial rituals to the point where they took up most of the time not used in getting food. We may further add that certain types of art sometimes hypertrophy to the point of weakening the whole social order or at least the strength of the ruling class. The *Tale of Genji* seems to show this in the Fujiwara period, where the Japanese nobility developed a delicate aesthetic sense and a love of decorative beauty in rituals and furnishings to a high degree. At the same time athletic, military, and administrative strength declined. What should be called "hypertrophy" or overdevelopment is an evaluative term, and opinions differ on the best proportion or balance among component developments—in society as in a work of art. Prudence

15 *The Tree of Culture*, p. 52.

urges that basic securities be first attained, then aesthetic luxuries; but people are reluctant to postpone the latter for the sake of the former. Advances in the more aesthetic and intellectual fields had to be initiated first in a few small, relatively isolated cultures and privileged classes, then spread to others. No culture can develop in all fields at the same rate, and humanity can not evolve in all groups at the same rate. It seems to have been necessary to have uneven growth at the expense of much inequality, suffering, and conflict; then to give some other groups, classes, and components their opportunity to forge ahead while the previous leaders paused or declined. The same is true among various arts and types of art. As between the large and ever-increasing number of possible developments at any one time—possible arts, persistent types, and styles—each culture chooses one or a few to carry farther than the rest for a while.

In view of this uneven rate of evolution, and the frequent moves in some components backward toward simplicity, one must be careful in generalizing about the dominant trend. Comparing Amiens cathedral with a modern, small-town church, one sees a tremendous simplification, a devolution or undevelopment. Comparing a Gregorian chant or troubadour song with an opera of Wagner or Verdi, one sees a tremendous complication.

When an old, complex style has recently been rejected, there is often a period of comparative simplicity before the new development goes very far. This occurred in early renaissance architecture, in Brunelleschi's Pazzi Chapel as compared with previous gothic and later baroque complexities. For a time, no new elaborations may be desired; there is a sense of relief at escaping the old complexities, as into fresh air. But then, in an atmosphere of creative industry, the impulse to elaborate along the new line is apt to be irresistible. Young artists wish to explore its possibilities, vary its themes. If a little is good, will not more be better? Growing love of luxury leads again to ornateness.

Accordingly, complication prevails over simplification. This may constitute the so-called "baroque phase" of that particular progression.

It is not to be assumed, however, that the middle or late stage of a progression is necessarily more complex than the first. Its sequence of steps is not rigidly evolutionary. It may bend with every cultural wind that blows, within and without the art concerned. Unpredictably, some strong individual genius, some artist, ruler, or moral reformer, predisposed toward the simple and austere, may impose his tastes on an age otherwise inclined toward luxurious ornament. A wave of moral asceticism, of scientific rationalism, or of practical efficiency may restrain the growth of an exuberant style.

Where styles compete and merge, it is often hard to disentangle the beginning, middle, and end of a progression from other styles with which it has been associated. Its beginning may be found as a minor note of inconsistency in a previous, highly complex style, such as the slightly rounded figures in a Cimabue madonna, otherwise mainly Byzantine. Only gradually does it detach itself from the old context, realize its own distinctive aim and character, achieve its independent growth. The end of that growth may be in some respects simpler than its beginning; evolutionary only in its increasing definiteness, its single-minded economy of statement.

Consider the main course of Greek sculpture from the Aegina pediments to Praxiteles. On the whole, though not steadily, it detaches itself from the architectural setting, to focus on an independent type of form, the free-standing statue in the round, which can be moved from place to place and viewed from different angles. As such, it develops in certain respects: especially the traits involved in visual realism and humanism; in the portrayal of living flesh, animated posture and expression, individualistic portraiture. This is its evolution. But concurrently, it tends to sacrifice many traits which are or seem incompatible with these: participation in a complex architectural design; angular stylization of the single figure, again with emphasis on design; expression of the abstract, superhuman ideals of deity. The statue by Praxiteles is not in all respects more complex than the Aegina pediment; certainly not as a design of lines, planes, and masses. But it is an integral part of the newer, late Greek culture-pattern of more naturalistic humanism, which was more highly evolved in many ways than the previous, naïvely religious one. The Hellenistic culture-pattern included, for example, the biological knowledge of Aristotle and the psychological insights of Euripides and Socrates.

As to the general history of the arts from the paleolithic to the present age, there can be no doubt that a tremendous complication has occurred. The obvious fact is that no works of art, comparable in complexity to the cathedral, the symphony, the long novel, the sound-color film, or the modern city plan, are known to have been made in prehistoric times. It is hard to conceive of any on the basis of what we know about prehistoric and modern tribul cultures. We have found no great complexity in Mohenjo-Daro, Sumeria, or early Egypt. In other words, *there has been a process of evolution in art, and on the whole it has prevailed over contrary tendencies.*

This is not to say that such complication has been steady and uniform, so that an early work is necessarily simpler than a later one. On the contrary, *there are complex works from early civilized periods, and simple modern works.* The peaks of maximum complexity in the various arts, so far as we know them, have not all occurred in recent times, or at any one time in the history of civilization. They are scattered irregularly through the various periods and places in which a fairly advanced, urban culture has been achieved.

Reference was made above to cities and to large complexes of buildings with attendant grounds, as in a modern university. Few early cities were as populous as ours, or as complex in terms of public utilities, highways, and other utilitarian features. But from the visual, aesthetic point of view, there is often little design or unity in the modern city; still less in larger regions. Such planning is worked out in theory, but is obstructed in practice by *laissez-faire* traditions and opposition to large-scale social planning, especially in America. Cities and sparsely populated regions here often grow in a sprawling, unplanned, and uncoordinated way; hence do not achieve much complexity from either the utilitarian or aesthetic point of view. Ancient cities were mostly small and simple in basic plan, but were often highly unified by order of the king and his architects. Old, crowded sections were ruthlessly torn down. No expense was spared to make the palace, or complex of palace buildings and gardens, a wonder of the world like the hanging gardens of Babylon, for the glory of the monarch. Some religious groups amassed great wealth and built themselves elaborate structures, such as those of Lhasa in Tibet. Most of these great architectural complexes were destroyed, but from contemporary descriptions and surviving ruins we can reconstruct, in imagination at least, the past glories of Luxor and Karnak, Knossos, Athens, Alexandria and Rome, Persepolis, Byzantium, and Chichen-Itza. Versailles remains.

The type of art which we are now considering was not necessarily a whole, planned city, for the city as a whole might be largely an agglomeration of slums and hovels. The work of art would in that case be only a city within a city, a palace-complex or a residential quarter for the king, his nobles, their wives and servants. Such, for example, were the Forbidden City of the Manchus, with the Winter and Summer Palace in and near Peking. Around the gates of Xanadu the rabble might starve or die of plague; within, a stately pleasure-dome was reared, to last until the mob or enemy broke through, as in time they always did. Hence glories of this sort have been ephemeral, as Kipling observed: "one with Nineveh and Tyre." For this reason, it is hard to take proper account of them in the history of art. Lost were not only the buildings, but most of their contents: veritable art museums in many cases, with pictured walls, sculpture, tapestries, books and manuscripts, magnificent furniture, gold and silver utensils, ceramics, glass, jewelry, court costumes, musical instruments, carriages, pleasure-boats, ornate armor, and weapons. The knowledge that they existed should make us cautious about claiming for present art a completely higher level of evolution. But at least they show a tremendous evolution up to their time.

In ages of great and highly concentrated luxury and power, pageants and palaces have assumed a size, complexity, and magnificence unknown to modern, democratic cultures. History describes in detail the extravagant constructions ordered by an Emperor Yang of the seventh century. Over three million men were made to dig a canal a thousand miles long and to line it quickly with willow trees. Down its length, fifty dragon-shaped barges were drawn, including the Emperor's own, with four decks, two thousand feet long. It contained a lavish throne room as well as a miniature private palace and a hundred twenty sumptuous cabins, decorated in gold and jade, for the royal attendants. Thousands of men, dressed in silk, drew the barges while young girls pulled on brightly colored cords and scattered flowers and perfumes. Yang also built enormous parks and palaces with artificial lakes and islands, and a "traveling town" with palaces on wheels. Much later, such Chinese novels as the *Chin P'ing Mei* (seventeenth century) and the *Dream of the Red Chamber* (eighteenth century) contain vivid descriptions of the palaces, parks, furniture, costumes, and luxurious entertainment of wealthy families under the Empire. Palaces and luxuries quite as fabulous existed in the Roman and Byzantine Empires, with different styles of art. The pageantry of Venice and of France under the Bourbons was magnificent in its way, but often less extravagant.

Our knowledge of the early history of art in many cultures is so incomplete that a complex style whose date seems early may represent the outcome of a long development. This is the case with some aspects of Chinese art. As to painting,

George Rowley maintains that "the gradual development from simplicity to complexity enables the art historian to date his monuments with considerable accuracy," and that "Chinese painting evolved through a real process of change from the simplicity, regularity and uniformity of earlier times toward the complexity, irregularity and diversity of advanced civilizations."[16] There is undeniably some truth in this, if one compares what little we have of Han dynasty painting with the three-dimensional scope, the variety and subtlety of design and representation, the richness of suggested meaning, of Sung painting at its height. Yet Han painting is by no means crude or primitive; its drawing is deft and animated, precise and rhythmic within its apparently narrower limits. Holger Cahill, reviewing this book, questions its evolutionary principles on the ground that Chinese design "is complex, irregular, and diverse when we first come in contact with it (the Shang-Yin bronzes)."[17] But we do have neolithic Chinese pottery, decorated with simple geometrical designs, and prehistoric artifacts which show that here, too, complex design did not spring suddenly into being from the brain of some Shang dynasty genius.

Another puzzling instance, for one who expects modern art to be more highly evolved in all respects, is the *Odyssey*. In complexity of action and plot, it has few equals in subsequent literature. As R. G. Moulton has shown,[18] it organizes the multiplicity of characters, motives, and episodes (mostly assembled from earlier legends) into a firm, symmetrical design. In addition, it is rich in verbal music and incidental imagery. Yet scholars tell us that it was probably written about 800 B.C., long before the classical period of Greek literature. To be sure, urban civilization had already existed in the Mediterranean area for some two thousand years or more; literature had long written and oral traditions behind it. Soon after the rise of

---

[16] *Principles of Chinese Painting* (Princeton, N. J., 1947).
[17] *Magazine of Art*, Nov. 1947, p. 292.
[18] *The Modern Study of Literature* (Chicago, 1915), pp. 132 f.

wealthy and moderately secure city-states in that favorable environment, pioneer artists were able to develop certain arts along certain lines to a peak of complexity which has seldom if ever been surpassed. Their ancestors must have already evolved, not only the necessary technics such as written language and prosody, but (concretely if not in theory) the concept and ideal of organized form; of unity in variety and multiplicity. They must, through long experimentation, have found it possible to build more and more complex forms in certain media.

Having done so up to a certain point, they refrained from going farther. Many such developments were lost, forgotten, and made again elsewhere. Some followed parallel lines; others merged into cumulative traditions. Rather than to develop along any one line indefinitely, different cultures and different artists have often preferred to start on new ones. But in spite of this "beginning over," there has been a gradual tendency to pour individual and local traditions into larger ones— national, racial, religious, and linguistic. With the knowledge and skill available in modern times, it would have been possible to produce far more complex works of art than have ever been produced. But the tendency toward complication has been resisted and arrested at various points by an opposite set of factors, which we are shortly to consider.

In organic evolution also, as we have noted, the complicative tendency has been very unequal in different types and strains. The fact that animals and plants with every degree of complexity exist today indicates that, in every hereditary line, a complicative tendency persisted up to a certain stage. (Even the *amoeba* is complex by comparison with inanimate matter.) Thereupon it ceased and the type remained at that stage, varied without much net rise or fall in complexity, or in some cases regressed to a simpler stage. Man and his ancestors reached the highest level in this respect, but apparently ceased evolving physically, for a while at least, with the advent of man some million

years ago. They adopted instead the mental, cultural mode of evolution. Within cultural evolution itself the various types of activity and product have likewise developed unequally: some to ultra-complex stages with no sign of stopping, while others proceed to various stages of complexity and stay there, and still others regress to simpler forms.

As one observes these diversities in the historical process, the question arises, "why?" Certainly, the modern artist has the power to build up far more complex forms than he does build. In theory, it would seem that houses, pictures, novels, symphonies, and other types could be almost indefinitely elaborated by adding more and more parts and subdividing each of them, up to the limits of the space, time, and materials available. This the artist might do if his only creative drive were along the line of complication. The result, of course, would soon be regarded as a monstrosity. Long before that extreme was reached, modern taste would soon be protesting: "It's too big and crowded; too busy, over-decorated; heavy, tiresome, pretentious, ostentatious," and the like. But there is another set of uncomplimentary epithets for works of art which do not seem complex enough: they are "too bare and severe; empty, uninteresting, trivial, lacking in variety," and so on.

What is it, in the mind of an artist, critic, or patron, which makes him feel that a certain amount of development is not too much or too little, but just right? Why, after achieving a type so awe-inspiringly complex as the cathedral, widely acclaimed as a peak in human progress, does art so often turn away from it in favor of something plainer, smaller, and simpler? There is no reason to suppose that modern architects could not make a cathedral as complex as Amiens if they wished, or more so. Modern dressmakers could make a court dress as elaborate as that of the Infanta in a painting by Velázquez. Why do they not wish to, and why does the public not ask them to do so?

The artist does not usually think the problem out in these terms, as a choice between more complexity and more simplicity in general. His attitudes have been influenced by contemporary tastes and fashions, probably long before embarking on this specific project. As a result, he feels that a certain kind and quantity of development is "just right" for this sort of thing. Contemporary taste approves a certain range of individual choice and variation in this respect, on the part of the artist. He works out a compromise, more or less unconsciously, between his personal impulses and the attitudes of his group. If he produces something outside this approved range, he runs a risk of having his product ignored or condemned. He may do so and win eventual approval if he is unusually strong or lucky, and appeals to some latent, potential desire within the public. This happened in the case of Wagner, who complicated his products far beyond the usual norm, and in the case of Klee and Mondrian, who simplified theirs far beyond the usual norm for their time. But it is no explanation to refer the compromise to changing social pressures, for these also need explanation.

We have ruled out the view that complication is the only normal, healthy process, and that its arrest is necessarily symptomatic of general dissolution. The breaking down of complex styles and the deliberate restraint of growth in others is so widespread as to bear no implication of social or individual decline.

Complication is construction, and Freud refers it ultimately to the Eros or constructive impulse in man. It has been man's way of adapting to environment and of surviving. Its opposite is the Death or destructive impulse. But simplification is not necessarily destructive; it also operates as an attitude of restraint and clear purpose in construction; a disposition to build only what seems needed and fitting; to stop when one has gone far enough, as ants stop building when the hill is large enough. It is also a disposition to prune away superfluous parts. Instinct tells the animal when to stop, but in man we must look for consciously acceptable reasons. For the artist there is joy in building, and in continuing to build as long as strength endures.

But there is also joy in finishing each particular task, and in keeping it within bounds; in trimming off unneeded parts. For the observer, there is joy in continuing to see or hear something he likes. So Schéhérazade tells one more story every night. But eventually, fatigue sets in as regards any one kind of stimulation; one demands an end to this one—for a time at least—and something else to enjoy for a while. Again the question is, "why does fatigue or disapproval toward continued building set in at that particular point, for that kind of art?"

6. SPECIALIZATION ON CERTAIN LINES OF DEVELOPMENT. PREROGATIVE ARTS AND TYPES OF FORM; THEIR TENDENCY TO COMPLICATION

In the animal world, various lines of descent come to specialize on distinctive modes of adaptation and survival; some on voracity, some on defensive shells, some on mobility, some on profuse reproduction, some on intelligent behavior. Why or how different ones in the same environment select different lines, no one knows. Some philosophical biologists, as we have seen, try to explain it by teleological predestination, some by mechanical orthogenesis, and some by the blind play of chance variation. Even on this last hypothesis, one must postulate some inertia or momentum which impels a certain organic strain to keep on trying the particular mode of adaptation, the kind of structure and behavior which has proven successful so far. In concentrating its efforts along that line, it may develop increasingly complex mechanisms for coping with the environment in that general way. The ant and the bee thus developed complex but different, instinctive patterns of behavior.

Each human strain, insofar as it maintains biological and cultural identity, tends to resemble all others in some respects, but also to select in a largely unconscious way some distinctive forms of organization and behavior. This often includes emphasizing a certain art or arts and certain styles therein.

In every creative culture and period, some art or arts and some type or types of product are selected as major channels for the creative energy of the group concerned. We shall call these *prerogative arts and types of art*. The choice is gradual and mainly unplanned, but is furthered by the work of great individuals in those channels or in others (e.g., religious) which can be merged with them.

Why these channels are chosen, and why a certain group becomes creative in them at a certain time, we cannot fully explain. Abstractly, Hegel's theory has some truth: that in each stage of cultural development certain arts are most suited to express the mentality of a people. His metaphysical explanation of it is less convincing. The rise and fall of different arts in prestige within their cultures is more variable than he realized.

Whatever the causes may be, these prerogative arts and types of form become the foci of enduring, collective interest and emotional concern; of desire, effort, pride, and admiration from the whole group, or at least from élite subgroups within it. They acquire emotive power as aesthetic objects through being endowed with important symbolic meanings and associations, connected with the dominant hopes and fears, loves and hates, desires and aversions, of the group. Works of art of this sort have often had magical, religious, or political significance (perhaps all three) as symbols of *mana* and of spiritual or temporal rank and power. In a tribal village, a carved wooden totem or fetish or a portrait of a royal ancestor may occupy such a position. In a more advanced culture, that position may be held by a temple, a palace, a throne, an altar, a reliquary, the statue of a god or demigod, a crown, noble or ecclesiastical robes, a ritual hymn, dance, drama, or epic dealing with the legendary origins and notable events of the group and its heroes. In a versatile, broadly creative

culture, many of these types of art may acquire some degree of such prestige. In the Athens of Pericles it was widely distributed through several channels, but the Acropolis was its chief focus. In the large medieval town, it was the cathedral, with the castle, palace, or city hall often holding equal or strong secondary interest as the focus of temporal power. The cathedral, especially, involved a concentration of cultural means and expressions, often in a poor and ignorant environment. As such, it was a cynosure of interest and admiration as well as of hope for the future life. Another prerogative type in the medieval world was the religious book in manuscript, illuminated with decoration and pictorial illustrations, such as the missal, psalter, or book of hours. It was a favorite gift and treasure of nobility and clergy. Still another was ritual music, especially the Gregorian chant.

A prerogative art tends to attract, by high prestige and rewards, a large proportion of the best artists and craftsmen. These tend to give the art still higher prestige and often make it a style-leader within its culture. New ideas, interests, attitudes, winds of doctrine, cultural trends of all sorts, tend to find their first expression here. Stylistic traits, capable of adaptation to various arts, spread from the major arts of the time to lesser ones. Thus renaissance visual style spread, on the whole, from painting and sculpture out into stained glass, tapestry, ornate furniture, and the smaller decorative arts, replacing in each case belated medieval survivals.

For an art or work of art to occupy such exalted social status is a condition which tends to favor the elaboration of decorative ornament; not, perhaps, the maximum of which the group is financially and technically capable, but the maximum which it considers to be in good taste, and more than it accords humbler products. Local cultural factors may restrain the proliferation of ornament in a particular case, as did the Greek antipathy toward Persian luxury and preference for mathematically proportioned forms. Since great ornate development is usually costly in work and money, the ability to concentrate a large share of labor and wealth upon it often indicates great inequality of wealth and power. Many must toil, and many others go hungry, to build and furnish the palaces and temples and support the armies of entertainers. This inequality is usually rationalized and justified in some way by the prevailing ideology, as by the need to glorify gods and kings for the welfare of the state. Greater power of the masses tends to favor arts of mass entertainment such as the Roman circus; even the Emperor has to keep the masses pacified. Power of a more educated, free-thinking class, as in Athens and Florence, favors development along more intellectual lines, as in the essay and the psychological and moral drama.

When a people reacts against a previous social order which was characterized by elaborate, luxurious display, it may assume an opposite attitude toward the main visible and auditory symbols of what it now hates. In iconoclastic fervor, it may try to destroy all art, all "idols" and odious formalism; to avoid ornate temples and rituals. Instead, it may venerate in simple rites a plain, undecorated relic of the Founder, a rough stone or a fragment of dress associated with some saint or martyr, as in the Christian catacombs and in the holy place at Mecca. This is in some ways a regressive movement.

Such simple tastes tend to disappear as the new régime lives on, becomes more prosperous, and seeks a worthy outlet for its creative energies. Then the relic of the saint is enshrined in a gold, bejeweled reliquary of the finest goldsmith work, and this, perhaps, within an inlaid marble tabernacle. The piece of the true Cross, or the tooth of Buddha, must have a worthy setting. Thus the late Buddhist temples and Islamic mosques and palaces, like the late medieval churches and castles, become the foci of rich ornamental development, each along lines congenial to the group. The western Islamic development, from which the representation of human and animal subjects is largely taboo, tends to stress elaborate arabesques

and geometrical or floral designs on every available surface: wall tiles, carved stone and stucco, textiles, metalry, leather, and ceramics.

7. LOSS OF PREROGATIVE STATUS AS FAVORABLE TO SIMPLIFICATION. DIVISION OF COMPLEX TYPES; THE CATHEDRAL

When the conditions which have singled out a certain type of art as a focus for social effort no longer operate, the natural consequence is neglect and degeneration of that type. This is often delayed by social inertia, during a period in which the old, magnificent forms are imitated in a perfunctory way, while the main creative interest of the group has moved elsewhere. Even greater financial support than before may be given to these older forms by conservative groups, anxious to perpetuate the *status quo ante* for which they stand as hallowed symbols. A great conservative artist may pour new life into them for a while, but only briefly. Lavish rewards are insufficient as a rule to attract the greatest talents into forms which seem to them obsolete and exhausted. Meanwhile, artists and patrons of the avant-garde are experimenting with new types and styles, often under heavy difficulties. Most of these experiments will lead no farther, but a few will turn out to be the main lines of advance for the next generation.

If great concentration of wealth, power, and the opportunity for cultivating aesthetic taste lead to the high development of certain arts, social leveling tends in the opposite direction, at least for a while. Ordinary conquest or the substitution of one despot or demagogue for another does not have this effect, since the new rulers tend to appropriate and imitate the luxuries of the old. They may even follow the styles of the conquered (as in the Yuan Dynasty) unless they have already developed their own. Ordinary mass uprisings and local revolutions are usually quelled, and a new unequal order introduced, without much deep effect on the arts.

A deeper effect, though often slow and temporary, is that of altruistic and ascetic moral reforms like the Buddhist and early Christian. They challenge the rightness of concentrated luxury at the expense of so much misery and encourage more equal distribution of wealth. Such a reform is often short-lived, soon giving way to a new concentration of magnificence, as in Christian church and palace architecture after Constantine. But repeated waves of reform and revolution have in modern centuries produced a more lasting effect on art and culture. They gradually reinforce the growing power and determination of popular leaders to remake the social order on a more permanently democratic basis. Humanitarianism and democracy together have long operated in Western culture, and are now doing so in the Orient, to prevent the lavish growth of decorative and luxurious arts on anything approaching their former level. In the world as a whole there is perhaps a higher total of arts and luxuries than ever before, but it is less concentrated in the elaboration of a few outstanding, original works of art for the enjoyment of privileged groups. The smaller, more numerous substitutes are monotonously repeated through cheap mass production.

Perhaps democracies in future will be able and willing to sacrifice more private enjoyment for the sake of great public art. Perhaps, through improved technology, vast wealth and democratic sharing will combine to produce a new flowering of decorative and luxurious art, both public and private. It may then excel the ancient in complexity of design as well as in comfort and efficiency, on a broader basis of popular enjoyment.

Great simplification in the arts of costume and furniture has reflected the leveling trend of recent centuries. Democratization, in eliminating the palace, tends to eliminate also the need to display aristocratic status at great expense. Decrease in the number of servants available has increased the need for simplicity and easy maintenance in house-keeping and laundering. Dust-catching sculptural ornamentation on furniture, laces and velvets which are hard to clean, are not needed to show one's socio-economic status. They become a mere burden to housekeepers. Instead, costly automobiles and mink coats are somewhat analogous, but in general the display of status is a less compelling motive than it was in the age of hereditary aristocracy. Many persons of high status do not try to display it. Science and the naturalistic spirit have reinforced this trend by stressing health, comfort, convenience, freedom for active work and exercise for men and women, boys and girls. The results appear not only in the making and wearing of simpler clothes, but in related changes of aesthetic taste. The old, heavy, elaborate costumes now seem appropriate only in a museum, on the stage, or at a fancy-dress ball. For ordinary wear, they would seem ridiculously overdressed and pompous.

Art forms can become so complicated, so loaded with past accretions of meaning, symbolic and emotional associations, new functions and means to them, as to seem oppressive and cumbersome. People feel an impulse to divide them and deal with their constituent parts and functions separately. Observing them, one feels almost that they are being forced by some internal pressure to divide, like pregnant animals or fruit-trees heavy for the harvest.

The fact that a certain type or style of art has dwindled through comparative neglect does not imply that artistic power in general has dwindled, even in the art and medium concerned. The decline of the cathedral is often regarded as indicating a decline of modern architecture, or of all modern art. Aside from all questions of beauty and value, this oversimplifies the events. What happened after the zenith of cathedral-building was not a general flagging of architectural production, but rather a *splitting up* of the cathedral into many specialized types of building. Although highly evolved in some respects, the cathedral was relatively undifferentiated in others: that is, in combining so many functions and devices in one building. From the modern functional standpoint, many of these appear as primitive and rudimentary. The cathedral, with its attendant structures, functioned not only as a sheltered meeting-place and auditorium, but also to some extent as a concert hall, an art gallery, a library, an educational institution; sometimes as a center for craftwork and scholarly research, as a fort in time of need, and as a center for political influence. As the seat of a bishop, a cathedral symbolized his high status in the churchly hierarchy. A fortified monastery like the Grande Chartreuse, near Grenoble, contained even more of the requirements for self-sufficient living by an organized community, with individual cells, gardens, kitchens, and refectories. Outside disorder necessitated the crowding together of many such functions in a small, compact mass, often on a hilltop.

Scholarship was confined mainly to the clergy; books were in manuscript and had to be guarded. Pictorial and sculptural iconography performed an important task in mass education, in morals, doctrine, and Bible stories. Hence the importance, for more than decorative reasons, of covering walls, windows, floors, and furniture with a profusion of symbolic forms.

After the Middle Ages, these conditions were gradually replaced by others, favorable in some respects to decentralization. The very concentration of power in the national monarchy weakened the self-sufficiency of individual towns. Security under the king's protection reduced the need for close crowding and concentration of architectural means under a single roof. Buildings were dispersed for convenience over wider areas. The rise of secularism and rationalism favored the independent growth of universities, schools, and libraries. The growth of each specialized activity, formerly housed within the cathedral, forced it to leave and seek more elbow room, more flexible quarters for expansion. Some insisted on the chance to do so under secular auspices. Artists and their patrons were less interested in conveying religious beliefs and attitudes through art; more in portraying nature and expressing pagan and modern attitudes toward life. The heavy accumulation of symbolic images disappeared from architectural and other forms of art, and with them the educational importance of such iconography. Printing diffused cheap books; the rising wealth of the middle class diffused the ability to read and own books and to embellish one's house or place of work. More comfortable dwellings took the place of the hovels that once surrounded many cathedrals. Secular buildings such as town halls, guild halls, noblemen's palaces, gardens, and country villas, drew a larger share of artistic embellishment. The cathedral was no longer the focus in an increasingly secular culture. After the revolutions of the late eighteenth and nineteenth centuries, wealth and artistic expression spread still further down the social scale. The palaces of kings and nobles also declined as centers of prestige and magnificent life.

No single structure, no single art or type of art has replaced the cathedral or the palace in a democratic age as a channel for artistic genius, supported by public or institutional funds. Instead, we have innumerable houses and apartments for persons of small and moderate means, simpler and less impressive in appearance but fairly cheap and comfortable. We have extensive surburban developments and a great variety of specialized utilitarian structures, most of them with some artistic pretensions: churches, theaters, schools, hotels, hospitals, post-offices, court-houses, libraries, playgrounds, office-buildings, country clubs, factories, garages, laboratories, barns and silos, grain elevators and gasoline filling stations. Wealth, labor, and architectural ability are diffused horizontally through all this multiplicity of types and examples, many of them through mass production and prefabrication; vertically, to nearly all income-brackets. The grandiose production of vehicles for locomotion, especially automobiles and airplanes, has taken a large share of our constructive ability. The motion picture film has also taken some. The whole process is so broadly diffused and rapidly changing that no sign appears yet of any general convergence into one channel or focus. It is not surprising, then, that no single type of building can rival the cathedral in compact elaboration of form and function, aesthetic and utilitarian, or in attracting so high a concentration of artistic genius. National and international cultural centers like the Unesco building in Paris may do so in future.

If we emphasize the negative side of these chapters in architectural history—that is, the disappearance of the cathedral and palace as dynamic types and channels for creative genius—evolution seems to be giving way to dissolution. But the disappearance of certain types, made unfit to survive by changing environments, is an essential phase in evolution itself. The continued fecundity and vitality of art appears, not necessarily in the active perpetuation of old types, but also in the production of new ones. In such development, it is normal for comparatively undifferentiated types to split or differentiate into several independent ones, whereupon each of these goes on developing and perhaps dividing into still more specialized types. Some of these die out while others survive.

This has happened with the theater. A specialized type in the ancient world, it declined for a time and some of its functions were taken over by the church. Once more breaking away in the renaissance, it flourished anew under secular conditions, then split into the many contemporary varieties of the covered and outdoor theater: the opera-house (center of Paris and an ornate focus of secular French culture in the nineteenth century), the motion picture theater (including the outdoor "drive-in"), the metropolitan theater for stage plays, the small, experimental theater for community or university, the large covered auditorium for mass assemblies, and so on. Each of these becomes a complex type in itself. A similar process of continued fission and separate development can be found in the history of the theater arts themselves, from the Molpai or undifferentiated, early Greek religious play with music and dance through

the separate later careers of each of these arts, and their occasional recombination as in the modern opera.

Decentralization and the exodus of population from large urban centers to the suburbs, aided by fast transportation and good roads, have recently tended to break up such large architectural types as the metropolitan hotel. Instead, great numbers of smaller motels have sprung up along the main highways. Large metropolitan department stores give way to smaller branch stores and suburban shopping centers. But all these newer types, along with the small suburban dwelling-house, tend to grow and complicate again, especially in utilitarian functions such as heating, lighting, plumbing, air conditioning, telephones and television. The new types also have some aesthetic appeal in external design, textured walls, furniture, draperies, windows, and television sets. Thus they qualify as useful art, though of uneven quality.

8. THE REINTEGRATION OF DIVERGENT TRENDS

Architecture since the gothic period has displayed constant reintegration along with differentiation. This appears in the internal organization of specialized types and in their social interrelation along the various lines already discussed. One of these is the planned region or city, comprising many arts but basically architectural in nature.

The division of a type, followed by separate development for a time, is often followed still later by a new partial merging, a different synthesis. This has happened in the useful arts, including furniture, during and since the Industrial Revolution. All through the nineteenth century, many types of furniture and household utensil combined some utilitarian fitness with heavy, non-functional (or even anti-functional) ornamentation, which obstructed performance of the main intended service. Machines with neo-gothic ornament, weakly constructed chairs with uncomfortable, carved ornaments in the back, and the like were common. Mechanization increased the gulf between the work of the artist and the engineer, sending the former into escapist dreams of medieval legend while the latter often manufactured purely utilitarian, grimy factory towns and cheap, unaesthetic utensils. The twentieth century has seen a new, partial reintegration between the artistic and engineering phases of manufacture, as in the electric refrigerator and other kitchen equipment and in radio and television appliances. The new synthesis, though never final, is unlike the early, undifferentiated stage in that the relations between the aesthetic and utilitarian factors are more clearly thought out, each definitely planned so as to achieve its own goals while not interfering with the other. Often the utilitarian basis of the form is adapted for aesthetic purposes, to make a decorative design, instead of having a non-functional design imposed upon it.

Another integrative trend in art, which has spread throughout the world in the twentieth century with accelerating speed, is the convergence of local, national, and regional styles into one great tradition. For uncounted millennia, the human race has been spreading over the globe; different groups have lost touch with all but their near neighbors. Some diffusion always continued, occasionally on a large scale as in the East-West trade of the early Roman Empire (Han dynasty in China). Since Marco Polo and the Crusades helped to revive it after a lapse, the convergence has been increasingly active, partly through imperialism, colonization, missionary zeal, and world commerce. Now technology has made us into "one world" through rapid transportation and communication, with all the dangers of mass extermination. International organizations like the United Nations and Unesco, grants and scholarships for study abroad, and the growth of international professional organizations in every field, have reinforced internationalization. The spread

of world communism, while divergent from the non-communist world, has helped to spread Western thought and institutions of the Marxist type in Asia, Africa, and South America. Competing cultural propaganda from the free world, including radio-television broadcasts, magazines, and exhibits, tries to spread a different Western ideology.

In this cultural diffusion and convergence, the arts have played a minor but significant role. Illustrated books and magazines, traveling art exhibits, traveling orchestras, dance and theater groups, films, and records have all spread the art of every region to every other part. Already the destructive effects of this are apparent, as well as the constructive. They appear in the steady, relentless decline—the slaughter, one might say—of local traditions in every art by Western innovations. The damage is most notable in the useful arts, especially architecture, furniture, clothing, and house furnishings, where cheap mass production together with functional efficiency make the imported wares outsell the traditional handicrafts. But even in the fine arts, Western music and films, Western literature and painting, invade and conquer almost everywhere. Such international exhibitions as the Venice Biennale in painting, sculpture, and decorative arts show year by year the trend toward an international style. Sometimes it is eclectic, combining some local with some Western features, and sometimes almost wholly Western. Modern Japanese architecture, whose traditional styles helped make the Western international style in the early twentieth century, has in turn borrowed much from the West in technological improvement and the use of large steel structures. Contemporary Japanese literature and music are also eclectic, combining elements of both civilizations which sometimes appear to represent the best of each, sometimes the worst. Communist China is now in the throes of a determined effort to stamp out most of the Confucian-Taoist-Buddhist heritage and substitute the Marxist type of Western thinking. Meanwhile the

West is discovering previously unknown riches in traditional Chinese fiction, poetry, philosophy, and primitive science. India and Pakistan are grafting Western arts and ideas on their Hindu and Islamic traditions. The exportation of Western art and culture by the liberal democracies is partly private, partly governmental; that of the communist variety, almost wholly the latter. The communist is more actively and consciously hostile toward the older traditions; the non-communist, more tolerant and sympathetic to the point of sentimental admiration. But in either case, the exported occidental product seems usually strong enough to crush or seriously weaken the local.

In many cultures, including our own, there is differentiation between the sexes in regard to aesthetic interests and attitudes. Within each sex, there is of course much individual variation; but many men and women regard the fine arts and the aesthetic side of life as women's special province. Although most professional, creative artists have been men, women are expected to have more interest in the appreciation, purchase, and encouragement of art; to be more sensitive to beauty and ugliness in the environment, and disposed to use their influence in doing something about it. More than men, they provide an audience for museums and exhibitions of the visual arts, for theaters, concerts, and fiction. They direct a growing share of family and institutional income to the arts. In larger numbers they are becoming professional artists in all fields, and even as home-makers their work takes on artistic quality insofar as they select and arrange furnishings or plan a garden. Interior decoration and dress tend to be favorite arts for the more feminine type of woman, and when circumstances permit she tends to elaborate both to the extent which she considers to be in good taste. The more masculine type of man or woman tends toward greater plainness in both of these arts. (Fashion dictates some exceptions, as in men's sport wear.) Although social attitudes are changing, a young man with strong interest in the fine arts and interior decoration still runs some risk of being considered effeminate, at least outside of urban intellectual circles. A man is expected to take more interest in the practical, utilitarian aspects of things than in the aesthetic. Automobile advertisers appeal to the man by emphasizing mechanical features, and to the woman by emphasizing style, color, and upholstery. Both like comfort, but the woman is more apt to sacrifice it for appearance. The very masculine youth has his own aesthetic interests, as in papering his wall with pictures of bathing beauties and athletes. He tends to enjoy them as means to wishfulfillment fantasies, rather than for any specifically artistic treatment. Meanwhile, he may be indifferent to visual ugliness elsewhere.

Feminism, co-education, and art education tend to counteract extreme sex differences in art, and produce a more broadly synthetic taste in which each sex develops some appreciation for the other's traditional interests and attitudes. Insofar as the differentiation lasts, it tends to favor different lines of development in the arts addressed primarily to men or women, boys or girls. Within the same art, such as clothing and furniture, types of product addressed to feminine taste tend to receive more complex decorative development, or at least the use of rich materials and delicate finishing, while those for masculine taste tend to be plainer and simpler, with the accent on comfort, durability, and efficiency.

Ancient writings, as we have observed, often combined speculation on the nature of things or on practical technics with literary art. Pythagoras and his followers, who invented geometry, the first science, and who also described the mathematics of pitch in music, were deeply mystical, aesthetic, and religious in their attitude toward life. Lucretius' poem *On the Nature of Things* is a treatise on physics, astronomy, biology, psychology, anthropology, and ethics as well as a poem full of lyrical passages. Plato's dialogues, pregnant with the social philosophy of today, were in semidramatic form. The undifferentiated types of verbal expression which these works represent have tended to split into separate lines of descent: into non-literary science on the one hand and non-scientific literature on the other, including types (such as the novel) which were almost unknown to the ancients. Partial reintegrations occur, as in the scientific elements in Dante, Milton, and Thomas Mann; the literary element in scientists and philosophers such as Thomas Huxley, William James, Bertrand Russell, and George Santayana. Modern science fiction is a partial combination. But, for the most part, science goes one way and art another. At the rebirth or awakening of science after its thousand-year sleep, another great, versatile mind appeared in Leonardo da Vinci, in whom the spirit of science was merged with that of visual art. It is no proof of lesser genius in Titian and Copernicus that they specialized, one on art and one on science. Though some rare genius might be versatile enough to follow both, a social division had to be made between them, to allow each growing enterprise a freer, fuller development.

A central motive in the separation between science and art was the gradual differentiation between two basic attitudes toward life. One was the emphasis on fact; on the testimony of reason and careful sensory observation; on exploring and conceiving of reality by their means; on trying to accomplish things efficiently with their aid. The other was the emphasis on fantasy-building, mysticism, and faith in revealed authority. Both sought the truth, and claimed to discover it; but they sought it by different paths, and reported very differently on what they found. Both used the senses in one way or another: the former to study and control nature; the latter to give pleasure, or to mortify the flesh, or to symbolize a supra-sensory reality. Long before science began, there were individuals of both types; but the birth of science and rationalistic philosophy in Greece was the start of a long, persistent effort to detach it from the influence of fantasy, mysticism, and authority. Before that birth, there was no clear conception of fact and truth as distinct from imagination and tradition. Early historians reported

events as they were said to have happened, or as one might imagine their happening. The writing of history was often indistinguishable from that of myth and legend. Myths were attempts to explain the nature and origins of things, and as such precursors of science and philosophy; but they did so largely in terms of fantasy and tradition, without systematic empirical verification.

The arts served powerfully to express and implement religious world-views, and in return the arts were enriched by vividly colorful, inspiring themes to be expressed: stories of gods, angels, saints, and devils, of heavens and hells, of the origin and future of man, as well as by the opportunity to beautify divine worship in every medium, and thus to win divine favor. Religion and religious art gave some scope to all types of mind, including the intellectual, the active, the aesthetic, and the dreamer.

The myth-making power, a perpetual source of vitality in the arts, is said to have died out in modern man. Science, it is said, has not only deprived art of its old religious content, but has failed to supply anything adequate in its place. The scientific view of life is said to be so cold and depressing, the universe it discloses so ugly and heartless, the progress it achieves so unsatisfying to the soul, that the true artist recoils from expressing or glorifying it.

This attitude, though widely expressed today, is not the only one which has been felt toward the breach between art, religion, and science. Many religious sects and individuals feel no need for either art or science. Many modern artists and critics feel that they are doing very well indeed without benefit of clergy, or of the laboratory. Nature is still there to be enjoyed for its beauty, immortalized in the landscapes of Claude, of Turner, and of Monet. To a mind that feels at home in modern culture, it is quite satisfactory to be able to specialize along the lines which art has taken. One may look back upon the old, undifferentiated types with admiration, yet with no desire to be involved again in all their confusing religious and philosophical issues; in all their heavy symbolism. Least of all does the scientist or engineer wish to confuse and complicate his products by reintroducing artistic and religious considerations. If he has to cooperate with an artist, as in designing a refrigerator, let each make his own distinct contribution. If he is religious, let him go to church on Sunday; if artistic, to the art museum or an evening sketching class. These are common attitudes today. Science, art, and religion, once divorced, can not easily be reunited. But, though distinct and different, they can all be combined as parts of life. If myth-making is a function of art, it can be done frankly and consciously as such, with no claim to factual truth except in an indirect, symbolic way, and hence with no claim to religious or scientific credence.

This solution, however, fails to satisfy those who feel that myth for myth's sake, or for art's sake, can be only a trivial amusement; it must, to be taken seriously, deal with vital problems of belief and conduct. Hence the poetry of T. S. Eliot. And there have been philosophers, from Plato and Plotinus to Aquinas, Hegel, and Bergson, who refuse to surrender philosophy entirely to the scientific, rationalistic, or empirical approach. In each new generation they strive to reconcile some of its beliefs and methods with those of religion, and its insights with those of art.

9. PRESSURES TOWARD EFFICIENCY, ECONOMY, AND SPECIALIZATION AS FAVORING SIMPLICITY OF FORM

One persistent factor, conducive to simplification, is the increasing desire for efficiency in any practical device. People want means which will be as successful as possible in achieving their purposes. This attitude is taken toward weapons, tools and machines, and also toward the utilitarian functions of the useful arts, such as architecture and furniture.[19]

In philosophy and pure science as well as in technology, the intellectual value of simplicity has long been realized. Within his own mind and in his published writings, the scientist or philosopher is engaged in an unceasing struggle to achieve simplicity of thought and statement, in handling the multiplicity of materials which come to his attention—problems to be solved, data to be organized and interpreted. In quest of adequate data, he may take in more and more, but always in the hope of explaining and arranging them in the simplest possible way consistent with the facts. We have seen how William of Occam, toward the end of the middle ages, helped to revive the scientific spirit with the bold demand that explanations be not multiplied beyond necessity. In geometry, the simplest possible proof of a theorem is the most elegant and the ideal of scientific reasoning. Such proofs have been called "beautiful." The Copernican theory overcame the Ptolemaic, not because either could be proved or disproved at the time, but because the Copernican explained the observed phenomena more simply; the Ptolemaic required one to suppose innumerable epicycles in the movement of the heavenly bodies, and eventually came to seem absurdly complicated.

It is not to be assumed, however, that the simplest theory is always truest, for the facts to be explained may require a complex one. This is the case with culture history, where the unilinear theories of the nineteenth century turned out to be much too simple. An acceptable theory must also work well—be efficient—as a tool of explanation, prediction, and control.

The pressure toward simplification is most obvious in the case of utilitarian forms, and especially in military devices, where immediate life or death may be at stake. Military technics, according to

19 Under the rather vague term "etherealization," Toynbee discusses the tendency of civilizations toward simplification for increased efficiency. (*A Study of History*, III, pp. 174 ff. *Cf.* Kroeber's review in *The Nature of Culture*, p. 374). An example is the reduction of mixed-system writing to alphabetic by systematic omissions.

some historians, have shown more consistent progress through the ages, in terms of increasing efficiency, than any other human skill. Here false beliefs, laziness, ultraconservatism, and stupidity tend most surely to eliminate the group which manifests them. In art, these traits can persist for centuries without, apparently, doing much vital damage. It is well known that military evolution parallels in some respects the evolution of animal methods of attack and defense. The giant armadillo, now extinct, relied on heavy body armor; so did the medieval knight. In the urgent quest for efficient defense and offense, some complex types have been abandoned entirely after long evolution: heavy body armor has gone the way of the rapier and the catapult. The modern foot-soldier's costume is simpler than the knight's, for the sake of mobility and because bullets penetrate thin steel. But new types develop, such as those for space travel.

In many types of device there is continuous pressure toward increasing efficiency. It is highly selective, neglecting some types while impelling rapid improvement in those given cultural priority. Where it operates, it takes both a positive and a negative form. Positively, it urges the inventor and producer to build complex machinery for ever-greater power and versatility, as in the automobile and airplane. Each has a growing "program" of related ends or functions, such as speed, safety, comfort, and economy in locomotion. These require more and more parts, intricately organized. On the other hand, there is a counter-pressure to eliminate unnecessary or obstructive parts, to avoid cost, friction, danger of breakdown, and heavy, cumbersome performance. The whole, and each part retained, is to be made as simple in shape as possible; to be streamlined for the utmost economy, efficiency, and fitness for its particular task.

A machine or a part so simplified can assume a special kind of visual charm and beauty in the eyes of one in tune with mechanical ideals. They are often compared with the efficiency of a gull's wing and other functional devices in nature. An-toine de St. Exupéry, French aviator, has a lyrical passage in *Wind, Sand, and Stars* on the beauty of the propeller and on the constant pressure toward simplified economy in mechanical form.

As parts are eliminated, or made simpler and smaller, the pressure to add new parts continues. People ask new services of this type of mechanism or ways of doing the old ones still more effectively: the automobile must be made increasingly fast, comfortable, safe, easy for women and others without mechanical knowledge to operate. Accessories such as windshield-wipers, electric horns, heaters, air-conditioners, radios, air-filters, oil-filters, automatically adjusting headlights, cigarette-lighters, power brakes and power steering are installed to meet demand, thus requiring more and more parts. These the engineer must simplify in their turn and fit into a compact whole. More and more demands are whipped up by advertising and salesmanship. They often interfere with each other, as in the case of speed and safety. The aesthetic charm of streamlined efficiency, which may appeal to the élite, has to compete with the opposite charm of decorative complication, the adding of differently colored and chrome-plated, ornamental parts which are not otherwise necessary, so as to please popular taste. Again a compromise is reached. The evolution of such a functional type as the automobile is thus a continuous compromise between complicating and simplifying tendencies, both motivated by the desire to satisfy a set of public demands (including the aesthetic) as efficiently and cheaply as possible.

Historians trace the several, interlacing developments of many such types, often describing them as "evolutions." Some begin with very different ancestors: e.g., from the sundial to the modern clock. The evolution of clockwork[20] shows the gradual incorporation of more efficient devices for performing the main task of measuring time, together with supplementary ones such as sounding an alarm at the desired moment. The product

[20] E.g., J. D. Robertson, *The Evolution of Clockwork* (London, 1931).

often becomes more complex on the whole, as more and more finely adjusted parts are interrelated in a smoothly working mechanism. In the history of the clock we note the successive inventions of pulley-weights, escapement-wheels, pendulums, mainsprings, etc. But old parts are constantly being eliminated as new ones do the same job more efficiently. Electric clocks, run by alternating currents, dispense with many parts.

As a utilitarian form becomes too complex and cumbersome, while the demand for more different services continues, recourse may again be had to the expedient of dividing the form into several simpler, more specialized types, to be made and used separately. Thus the automobile as a genus is divided today into many different species: the passenger car for various income-levels, various kinds of bus, truck, van, tractor, trailer, army tank, jeep, bulldozer, and so on. Each of these is more highly evolved than the early horseless carriage in being more definitely adapted to a special set of functions. Thus the prevailing trend toward complication is kept from producing unwieldy monsters by being diffused through more and more different channels, all interrelated as parts of the same evolving, mechanical civilization.

Extremely simple devices, when highly specialized and definite in form and function, are as characteristic of our highly evolved, scientific technology as are the complex ones. Among a surgeon's instruments are distinctive scalpels, probes, and the like, extremely simple in form, each designed for a special type of operation. Another example is the Johansen gage, used in precision manufacture to measure the size of an opening within very small limits of tolerance. It is only a small oblong block of metal, completely plain, but of a certain exact size and shape, and made of metal which will change its shape as little as possible. Very complex machines are sometimes used to turn out very simple products cheaply and effectively: for example, those for making pins, nails, bolts, and screws. By itself, the highly definite product may be highly simple. But such

a product is desired and fashioned only in a civilization which has reached a high level of evolution along that line, as ours has along mechanical lines. Though detached and independently movable, it is an integral part of this larger technological and cultural complex. A specialized, definite device of this sort is far more highly evolved than an equally simple device in prehistoric culture, such as a stone tool or wooden staff which can be used for many functions, but is not specifically adapted to any one of them. However, a device can be versatile—suited to a plurality of functions—and still definite, if its fitness for each and all of them is clearly worked out.

Inspecting a simple artifact in isolation, without knowledge of its cultural setting, one may not be able to interpret its function or the degree of evolution it represents. But on the whole, visible clarity and refinement of form in an artifact are *prima facie* evidence of some definiteness in functional planning. A single drawn line, like the perfect circle which, according to the legend, Giotto drew as a child, may demonstrate high manual dexterity under definite, mental control. A single stroke on a Buddhist temple bell, full of mellow overtones and dying slowly away, exhibits definite control of sound for partly aesthetic reasons. It fits smoothly into its visual and auditory context of ritual, and as a symbol of transitory life, into the Buddhist philosophy. With a minimum of complexity in itself, it indicates the high evolutionary level of its artistic and cultural context, as would a single spring from a finely made Swiss watch.

10. THE AESTHETIC APPEAL OF SIMPLICITY AND ECONOMY. PSYCHOLOGICAL ASPECTS

Works of art are usually under less pressure to be efficient than are tools and machines. On the contrary, the fact that "efficiency" and "success" are favorite slogans of our business world and machine age has made these words anathema to many artists. But art can be efficient in its own way, though usually not so described. It may be so in ways quite different from those of machinery. If the aim of a palace is to show the owner's status, wealth, and magnificence, a lavish profusion of parts and ornaments may be more efficient toward that end than a severely "functional" one. Such display and self-aggrandizement can itself be a kind of psychosocial function. So can the achievement of a certain kind of beauty as measured by prevailing aesthetic tastes. At times, taste favors complex decoration for its own sake, as in Islamic textiles, mosaics, tiles, and stucco surface designs. Fashion sometimes calls for women's clothes and hats to be loaded with "non-functional" ornament; if so, then the aims of feminine beauty and sex appeal may be most efficiently served in this way. Usually the aims of art—especially fine art—are not clearly thought out; hence it is hard to decide what means to them are most efficient. But to some extent, Occam's law applies here also. The most efficient work of art is one which uses just the amount and kind of elaboration which will best achieve the desired result and avoid undesired ones. There is usually an optimum point, after which more details will give diminishing or undesired returns.

Perfect fitness and bare, economical efficiency in a utilitarian device often please the observer aesthetically. Awareness of the fitness of the object and of the skill of the maker, along with a sensuous delight in seeing and perhaps handling the object, may fuse together into a unified, aesthetic experience. A sensitive observer may thus admire what seems to be a perfectly balanced, sharp and flexible steel sword in a glass case, even if he has no desire to use one. The beauty attributed to such forms may then be transferred to any object of similar shape, texture, and associations. In the early twentieth century, there was a wave of enthusiasm for "machine forms" in painting and sculpture. Closely related to the cubist movement, which emphasized geometrical shapes, it was exemplified by Charles Sheeler's photographs and Léger's paintings of machines, industrial landscapes full of sharp rectangles and rigid cylinders, and even farmhouse interiors, likewise severe and geometrical even without actual machinery. Actual machine parts were admired and exhibited by art museums in the 1930's. In the eyes of enthusiasts, a steel disk or ball-bearing could be more beautiful than an old-fashioned "fuzzy landscape" or soft human figure. Machine forms and geometrical designs analogous to them were constructed in sculpture, pottery, furniture, and textile designs. Houses were built to resemble "machines for living." Composers represented machine sounds in music (for example, those of a train in Honegger's *Pacific 231*). There were even ballets with mechanical movements, sometimes to show that these had their own kind of beauty and sometimes to show that man was a prisoner of the machine.

In the minds of some persons, geometrical and mechanical forms were associated with simplicity, economy, and efficient functioning, but others admired them for different reasons. A design or landscape of machine or factory forms could itself be complicated *ad lib*. A painting of such forms was not "functional" or efficient in the same way as a machine. Indeed, when applied to the back of an armchair, straight lines and sharp angles might defeat the function of comfort. Admirers of airplane design demanded ornaments on their cars and elsewhere, borrowed from airplanes but having no use on a car. Streamlined forms were demanded where streamlining had no particular function. It requires a grasp of deeper aesthetic analogies to see that functional efficiency is not necessarily connected with shiny metal or hard, geometrical shapes. In plants and animals, it occurs in soft, colorful textures and irregularly curving shapes. But we live in an age when efficient invention is associated especially with steel machinery, and pure science with mathematics and physics. By association, images taken from steel machinery tend to suggest efficiency and power, and as such to be admired or detested in accordance with one's feelings toward efficiency and power. Likewise, simple geometrical diagrams suggest rational order, scientific knowledge, clarity and cogency of thought, even to one who does not understand their mathematical meaning. Plato himself admired them aesthetically, in the *Philebus*, and Edna St. Vincent Millay wrote that "Euclid alone has looked on Beauty bare." Mondrian's extremely simple paintings, mostly straight, black lines and rectangles on white surfaces, owe part of their appeal to such associations; to suggesting the bare precision of geometrical thought; the static equilibrium of forces in a framework of enameled metal. Scientific diagrams can, of course, be highly complex and irregular; then their aesthetic effect is likely to be different.

Though considerations of efficiency tend to make for relative simplification, extreme simplicity itself is no guarantee of efficiency, and is not necessarily connected with it. A simple device, intended for some practical use, may fail as did the wings of Icarus. Though intended to give aesthetic pleasure, it may be too simple to attract or hold anyone's interest. *Economy* in art may be simple or complex. It implies that, whatever the work attempts, it accomplishes with a minimum of parts, motions, and energy-consuming efforts. A good golf player can thus, with ease and grace, hit a ball far and accurately.

Certain kinds of literature and music are praised for their terse economy: the Japanese *Haiku*, for example. It is a very short poem, often restricted to a single emotive image, in which the poet seeks to produce a concentrated aesthetic effect with the minimum of means.[21] Such effects were sought by the Japanese in many media, such as a brush-drawing in ink of a single bamboo spray, a tea-bowl, a flower-arrangement, a few tones on a flute. Admirers of their terse, restrained economy of form could find somewhat analogous qualities in a Greek vase, a Bach chorale, a Chopin prélude, or a Shakespeare sonnet. For them, "simple" and "economical" are terms of praise; the opposites, such as "fussy," "involved," "overdecorated," "grandiose," "wordy," "diffuse," are terms of opprobrium.

Such examples of economy are by no means completely simple. They are small and relatively simple in the total realm of art. But on close analysis, each reveals itself as a *multum in parvo*, a little world of delicate nuances and definite, organized form. Centuries of experience were necessary to show the artist how to say and hint so much in so small a compass; how to prune away so much that would not be necessary for this particular effect.

Certain kinds of desired aesthetic effect may require a very different kind of form: not the severely geometrical but the lush, ornate, or profusely irregular. The tea-bowl may be definitely contrived to look indefinite, rough, and casual. A scientific approach to art and aesthetics does not necessarily imply a preference for mechanical forms and hard, steely qualities in art. If one is designing a décor for *Tristan und Isolde*, and wishes to enhance its mood of heavy, romantic passion, what will be the most efficient style of décor for this purpose? If one wishes a stage background to suggest that the characters are inefficient, fumbling, confused, fond of miscellaneous bric-à-brac and cheap decoration, how can this be done most effectively? The paradox is clear: inefficiency can be efficiently suggested; stupidity can be intelligently suggested. And even here some economy of means may help. A sense of vulgar, excessive ornamentation can be conveyed with relatively few ornaments, of the right bad kinds, well disordered.

Efficiency, broadly understood, is simply success in achieving whatever one sets out to achieve. If one's aesthetic aim requires means which are very different from those of mechanical invention, real artistic efficiency will demand their use. When mystics and romanticists denounce the modern Western ideals of success and efficiency, they are using these words in a very narrow sense.

21 On the mountain road the sun arose
   Suddenly in the fragrance of plum-flowers. (Basho)

However, the intellectual and logical spirit of science does tend to involve a preference for plain and simple forms, insofar as they are consistent with the ends in view. It is no accident that the Greeks of sixth and fifth-century Athens, who created science and philosophy, praised restraint in art and life, or that they often left large surfaces empty and undecorated. Horace agreed with Epicurus in preferring a simple country villa to Persian luxuries. The desire for extreme austerity in one's surroundings, as found in a monastery, expresses a general asceticism; a will to exclude from life all sensuous pleasures. In more moderate degree, and with no general disapproval of sense pleasure, austerity is characteristic of the scientist's laboratory, the philosopher's study, and even of the artist's studio. At least during working hours, and perhaps at all times, such men do not wish to be distracted by a profusion of sensory stimuli, however interesting. The more interesting, the more distracting and obstructive to one's own thoughts. A passively aesthetic or dreamy person may find no conflict in being surrounded by attractive and suggestive sights and sounds, as in a Persian palace with its overall decoration, its musicians and dancing girls; but anyone who wishes to develop his own line of thought must relegate them, however regretfully, to hours of leisure. If any art is to be around him, it must be of the simplest, plainest, and quietest. If it is inescapably conspicuous, he must learn to ignore it.

When one is trying to sleep, one wants darkness and quiet. During illness, one prefers plain walls and inconspicuous furnishings. Convalescent, one may enjoy flowers and a little soft music or conversation. If one's work has been arduous, one may wish to rest quietly for a while, then go out in the evening for a different kind of stimulation, such as a musical show at the theater. The desire for strong, sustained aesthetic stimulation comes and goes as do physical appetites. It is somewhat periodic and determined by one's general physical and mental condition. But some individuals and some cultures demand more on the whole than others do. They range from the extreme ascetics who want none at all at any time to the avid pleasure-seekers who must be surrounded in all waking hours by lights, colors, music, people moving and talking. Either extreme may indicate some inner, psychic difficulty; normally, there is some fluctuation between moderate degrees of aesthetic appetite. In this, a condition of relative satiety or resistance to outside excitement calls for the simplification or complete avoidance of art or any other powerful stimuli in the environment. It is impossible in a civilized environment to avoid all art, in the broad sense of that term. A completely plain, white wall can be a work of art, as is the bell which calls the monks to prayer, but both are extremely simple and unobtrusive. The language and the modulation of tone in which one speaks can be artistically controlled. For one who has acquired a taste for carefully designed surroundings in the home and office, plain and unobtrusive art will probably be less distracting than none at all; less so than confusion, bleakness, or wild nature.

The motives for simplification which we have just been considering are all connected with the basic pressure toward efficient functioning, a pressure which long antedates human art and the human species itself. It operates as a brake on the opposite pressure, toward filling up one's mind and one's surroundings with as many things as possible, each interesting in itself; with complex things to look at, listen to, read, make, and do; with complex problems for attention, thought, and action at every moment of the day. It operates as a pressure, variable according to the person and situation, toward clearing away, cutting down and restraining complication in art and elsewhere. Without it, we should be overwhelmed and exhausted, able to enjoy or accomplish nothing. With it, we keep clearing the field for that which seems most important. We keep destroying, forgetting, ignoring that which interferes with the main job at hand, be it work, rest, or play. We keep forgetting thousands of numbers for which we have no further need: the number of the hotel room one has left; the time of a train one has taken. Such a forgetting or excluding from consciousness does not necessarily indicate neurotic repression or conflict; the neurotic has added reasons for forgetting, and forgets or ignores things which a normal person would not. Instinct and limited powers of perception make the animal notice only a few of the stimuli which are pouring in upon him when awake. Man notices more and thinks about more, and is less guided in his selection by instinct. More and more, his selection must be conscious and purposeful, based on intelligent evaluation. He tries to preserve a flexible balance between the complex and the simple, in his surroundings and in his inner experience, in order to achieve what seem to him the highest values under changing conditions. Only by resolutely simplifying life where complexity is not needed can he complicate it most effectively where it is needed. On this, his judgment is groping and fallible.

The desire for more complexity or simplicity in art varies widely according to the general culture-pattern and the waves of fashion; it varies according to age and sex, occupation and personality type. It varies according to the time of day and one's state of energy or fatigue. One can tire of too much of either, and want the opposite for contrast. Strong specialized interest can hold the adult observer's interest through the effort needed to grasp a complex form, and he will not feel it as hypertrophied. Let his interest shift, and his judgment of what is too complex will shift with it.

II. PSYCHOLOGICAL LIMITS
TO THE COMPLEXITY OF WORKS OF ART

A work of art is not only a means to self-expression on the part of the artist and an outlet for his constructive impulses; it is also a means of stimulating and guiding some kind of aesthetic experi-ence in the observer. Most types of product classed as art are addressed to his sense of vision, to that of hearing or (as in opera) to both. They undertake to stimulate and guide his perceptual responses and others related to them, such as imagination, understanding, and emotion.

Since art is addressed to sense-perception and other psychophysical mechanisms, its operation is conditioned by the nature of these mechanisms in the observer. A blind man cannot directly enjoy a painting, or a deaf man a symphony. Limits are set by the structure of the human eye and ear to the range of light-waves and of sound-waves which can be sensed; hence to the effective ranges of color and pitch in art. Too intense stimuli are intolerable; too slight are imperceptible. To some extent, the limits of development in art are thus set by man's hereditary, organic structure. In the individual, it expands with normal growth, thus extending the range of effects in art which can be perceived. Even though the sense organs change little, the power of the brain to interpret what they sense develops greatly. Education, including special training in art, can further expand the individual's power to perceive, understand, imagine, feel, desire, and reason in response to a work of art. A small child cannot comprehend a drama of adult passions; an ignorant man cannot understand a wide range of historical, mythological, or scientific references. If a fugue has more than a few voices, or a play more than a few main characters and subplots, it becomes too complex for the average listener to follow. This had happened in polyphon-ic music by the time of Johann Sebastian Bach's *Art of the Fugue*. To any but the musical specialist, the countless ways of varying each theme—by contrapuntal inversion, diminution, and the like—presented an insuperable problem for untrained ears to follow in detail. Others might enjoy it more vaguely, as a rapidly moving, closely woven texture of sound; but the question was increasingly asked, whether all this complexity was worth while. Simpler kinds of music, such as the single melodic line with accompaniment, now made a more direct sensuous and emotional appeal on all social levels.

On the whole, other factors being equal, the more one complicates a work of art the harder it is to apperceive as an organic whole; to grasp all or most of its details and constituent relations both individually and collectively, as parts of whatever unifying form exists. Other factors affect the ease of apperception, such as one's familiarity with the kind of material involved, including sensory images and meanings; also one's interest, mood, condition, and surroundings at the time. If a subtle, mature, and intricate work of art is presented to someone who cannot perceive and understand it thoroughly he may grasp only a part of it, as when a small child notices a kitten somewhere in the corner of a huge Rubens painting. He may grasp the whole thing in a vague, superficial way, as when a tired business man drowses through a long symphony; or he may turn away from it entirely, as too difficult and boring.

The difficulty of perceiving and understanding art is not exactly proportional to its complexity. Much differentiation of parts with little integration makes it hard to co-perceive them as a whole. A definite, comprehensive framework pattern makes it easier. A simple work may be hard to grasp because of the unfamiliarity of its contents, form, style, or symbolic meanings. But on the whole, increasing complexity puts an increasing strain on one's powers of co-perception, interpretation, imagination, and memory.

The degree of complexity which will be welcomed in a work of art is roughly proportional to the mental and aesthetic development and mood of the individual or group concerned. The harder it is to apperceive a work of art thoroughly, the more incentive is required to motivate the necessary effort. An external, non-aesthetic motive may suffice, as in the case of a student hoping to pass an examination. If there is none, one must rely on internal, aesthetic interests, such as a developed taste for some difficult kind of art. Such an interest can turn the difficulty and the effort into an exhilarating challenge and a pleasant exercise of powers, as in playing a competitive game.

Under present conditions, the incentive necessary for working hard to apperceive a complex work of art is often lacking. The speed of modern living and the number of claims to one's attention in the course of a day tend to favor simple, "streamlined" forms, like the half-hour condensations of a long play or novel for radio or television presentation. There is a constant pressure for the layman, not especially devoted to some difficult medium, to confine his aesthetic enjoyments to simple, easy forms which can be taken in quickly, between other activities, like sandwiches at a quick-lunch counter. In urban environments the time is past when people had few things to do beyond their daily work, few claims to their attention in the long winter evenings; when they could spend long hours in leisurely conversation or listening to interminable epics of heroism and romance.

Awareness of the present taste for brevity tends to restrain whatever impulse an artist may have toward composing ultra-complex forms. If he does not, his publisher, dealer, or producer will usually do it for him, or the critics will point out his mistake. Further development, unless justified by manifest genius, will tend to cut down his potential audience more and more, limiting it to a smaller group of connoisseurs with a special interest in this sort of thing.

On the other hand, he usually realizes also that he must develop the form to some extent, combining some variety with some unity, in order to attract and hold the attention of possible observers; even of fairly young children under present urban conditions. (Newspaper comic strips for children require a considerable amount of perceptual ability and information.) Since the tastes and abilities of various sections of the public vary considerably in this respect, he may try to adapt his work to those of some intended audience, making it somewhat more or somewhat less complex and difficult without going to one extreme or another.

Other factors also affect the situation: notably, which art or medium is concerned and the circumstances under which it is to be experienced. Some kinds of art, such as painting, music, and lyric poetry, often rely on the concentrated, forceful effect which comes from experiencing a small form all at once, or in close succession. But a cathedral, a city, or a group of buildings and gardens can be indefinitely complicated, partly because it does not have to be perceived completely, all at once. One can live with it, grow up with it, walk here and there on different days and grasp it part by part, learning slowly to perceive its general plan. One can be vaguely aware of its complexity, enough to admire and enjoy it, without ever working very hard to grasp it in detail. The *Odyssey* would be hard to grasp thoroughly at a single reading or hearing; but one does not have to do so. Growing up in ancient Athens, the son of a citizen would probably hear excerpts from it read on many different occasions, thus gradually coming to know the structure of the whole. Many of its episodes could be heard separately as independent units. On the other hand, when a complex play or symphony is intended to be heard completely at a single sitting, it makes a heavier strain on one's apperceptive powers. Aristotle knew this in recommending certain "unities" or restrictions in the scope of action. Shakespeare seemed much too full of confusing actions and characters to French audiences with neo-classic tastes. Modern audiences have learned to follow Shakespeare with little effort. In a popular film, where the action skips about rapidly from scene to scene, time to time, and character to character, even youthful audiences have little trouble in following the story. From early childhood, they now learn to interpret the conventions of rapid cinema technique.

It is often a temptation for a young, ambitious artist with grandiose ideas of his genius to plan a colossal masterpiece, combining all the great ideas, all the best features of previous works, in one tremendous composition. One might as well hope to make the supreme masterpiece of culinary art by combining all possible flavors in a single dish, or the greatest possible tool by combining all shapes of blade, point, hammer, and corkscrew in a single handle. The advantages of complex unity are counterbalanced by the difficulty of using, apperceiving, or enjoying so many diverse elements together. It is easier for the human mind to grasp the same materials in smaller combinations at different times, with intervals of rest and change in between. Many will prefer to make their own selection and arrangement, as of short pieces on a concert program or small pictures on a wall, instead of having to take a gigantic "package deal" *in toto*.

The psychological limits to complexity in works of art are all more or less flexible and variable. They vary from person to person and change in cultural evolution. Man's history gives ample proof of his ability to learn, not only to perform very complex tasks, but to enjoy the process, and to keep seeking new, harder problems to solve for the pleasure of doing so. Some people enjoy as a leisure pastime the solution of intricate problems in chess or higher mathematics. Difficult art offers to those who like it a somewhat similar challenge. Conditions may change so as to motivate, on a large scale, public interest in the apperception of complex art in many media. When it does, artists will be encouraged to make and perform it.

12. SPECIALIZED EMPHASIS, OMISSION, AND SUBORDINATION

To permit the constant development of art along new, original lines, and at the same time to keep the size and complexity of each single work within acceptable bounds, something has to be diminished or omitted. Thus, as we have seen, each new development entails some loss or simplification of previous developments. Often this can be described in terms of the components in a particular art.

The specialized emphasis on light and color by impressionist painters, such as Monet, entailed a blurring and softening of linear contours, solid shapes and space relations. Atonal music such as that of Schönberg entails a sacrifice of tuneful melody and definite key structure. Emphasis on the subtle analysis of mood, personality, and the stream of thought in James and Proust entails some sacrifice of the overt action which one finds in the *Iliad*, *Macbeth*, and *Cyrano de Bergerac*. Trends in style consist largely in such shifts of emphasis from one set of components and modes of composition to another, along with new developments in the set now given greater emphasis.

It is well to realize, in comparing a great artist with his predecessors and contemporaries, what he omitted or minimized; what materials and ways of organizing them he might have used, since they were there before him, but which he felt as obstructive to the things he most wanted to do. Art being a process of selection and emphasis, it has its negative side in rejection and subordination, which often pass unnoticed. The individual artist at the same time may reject with violent hate; it is the complement of his passionate love for what he accepts and affirms. But from the standpoint of civilized society, the rejection is often temporary and provisional. It is a necessary phase in the division of labor and the specialized attempt to do a certain job as well as possible, that other valued things must be put aside for a while. Later on, posterity may find a way to recombine them.

Our culture is permeated by the spirit of applied science and invention, eager to push ahead on a variety of lines. Each artist wants to do something new and original, which no one has done before or is doing at the present time. This attitude appears in the great diversity of twentieth-century art; its innumerable styles and isms, most of them short-lived; the great difference between individual artists. Some specialize on line alone, omitting color; some on color alone, omitting line; and so it goes. Some go through a series of radically different, highly specialized styles, achieving both complex and simple forms.

Some of the old masters, such as Giorgione and Titian, Shakespeare, Goethe, Beethoven, and Brahms, achieved a more evenly balanced development than most contemporaries try to do. This gives them power to appeal in many different ways to an observer of equally varied interests. But in general, both period and individual styles tend to differentiate by stressing various components, traits, and modes of composition.

In composing a particular work of art, one tends also to differentiate the concrete parts, and one way of doing this is to emphasize certain ones more than others—the traditional principle of dominance and subordination. It is not an ironclad rule of good art, and some kinds of art do very little of it; but most do so to some extent. A certain tree in a landscape, an apple in a still life, a character in a play, a theme in music, will be emphasized in one or more ways: for example, by large size, bright color, conspicuous position, loudness, or more elaborate development. The main protagonist in a play is likely to appear more often in the center of the stage, and to have his character more fully displayed through speech and action. He tends to hold our attention longer. He is shown more "in three dimensions," while the minor ones are, in varying degree, flattened out or simplified into mere vague silhouettes. In the *Odyssey*, most of the suitors are of the latter type. They are like figures in the background in a Goya bullfight, or apples near the edge of a Cézanne still-life. One tends to apperceive them marginally. In a Tchaikowsky concerto, besides the main themes are many subordinate ones which receive less repetition and variation.

Other things being equal, a plain textile is likely to attract less attention than one with may different large, contrasting figures. Its simplicity fits it for a subordinate place in a room: e.g., as a background for pictures. Some styles and cultures, such as the Islamic, like to decorate all available surfaces and objects in a room. Italian churches and palaces of the late renaissance and baroque were often lavishly decorated throughout. But contemporary taste runs more to large, plain surfaces, often in solid, subdued color, with only a few accented areas here and there. One of these areas may be a painting; another an ornate textile on a wall or cushion. These stand out from plain walls and floor coverings. Sometimes an inexperienced person buys each piece of furniture separately, with no thought of the *ensemble*, choosing in each case an ornate example merely because he likes it in isolation. Putting them together, he is surprised how they seem to clash and compete for attention, making the whole room look more "busy" and overdecorated than he had intended.

When current taste favors an organized contrast between the emphatic and the unemphatic, there is a call for simplification in many items of furnishing which might otherwise be elaborately designed. In spite of standardization, our culture encourages variation to suit individual taste, from house to house and from room to room in the same house. Thus the owner or decorator can choose which parts of the room and which objects within it shall be complex or otherwise accented. Painting enjoys high priority in this respect. A complex, colorful painting, such as one by Van Gogh or Renoir, may be made the focus of visual interest in a room, its color-scheme being followed out more softly elsewhere. Bright ceramics, enamels, and silks are often given a similar function. But for those who prefer, a wall can still be papered in an ornate landscape or abstract design, or a floor can be covered with a Persian carpet. This may lead to the choice of a simpler or darker painting or none at all, and to plain, drab ceramics. An area of moving pictures or colored lights, projected on the wall or on a television screen, provides even stronger, localized emphasis. Soft luminescence in a darkened room can bring out intermediate accents and patterns.

One who studies the history of a single art such as wall-paper, carpets, or pottery may be puzzled by the great variety of styles now available in it, and by its wide range from plain to ornate, simple to complex. These testify to the flexibility of contemporary style, its many divergent experiments, and the interplay within it of pressures toward various ways of balancing complex and simple areas. In some arts no further net increase in the complexity of particular works is likely in the near future. In others, such as the design of a city or a larger geographical unit, complication may increase indefinitely.

13. SUMMARY

The question whether the arts evolve depends in part on whether they tend to *develop* or become increasingly *complex*. Present knowledge indicates a large-scale tendency along this line in the history of the arts. They have become more complex on the whole and are still doing so. Art in general, as a major part of civilization, has developed hugely in size and complexity. In modern centuries it has produced countless types such as the opera, the symphony, the color-sound film, and urban architecture, which surpass in complexity all or most of the art of previous ages. Even when not individually more complex, modern works often contain more subtle differentiation of qualities and relations than ancient or primitive ones. Modern art contains a much greater variety of content, form, and style than the ancient or primitive.

However, the tendency to complication in art is not steady or universal. Later works are not always more complex. Some highly complex examples are found in ancient and medieval art (e.g., the *Odyssey* and Chartres cathedral). Some modern art is highly simplified. The tendency to complication, though widespread and persistent, is opposed by contrary tendencies. These often prevail in certain arts for a time. We cannot be sure which will dominate in future.

Tendencies to simplification, regression, or devolution in the arts are not necessarily a sign of decadence. Many social and psychological factors tend to favor simplification. Among these are (a) the loss of prerogative cultural status by a type such as the cathedral; (b) pressures to divide a complex type and produce its elements independently; (c) pressures toward greater clarity, efficiency, and economy in thought and action; (d) innate psychological limits to the perception and understanding of complex forms; (e) the need to eliminate or subordinate some aspects of art as a means to the further development of others.

CHAPTER XVIII

REGRESSIVE TRENDS IN ART

The decline and fall of nations and of civilizations is a frequent spectacle of history. Spencer called it "dissolution," the opposite of evolution. Evolution being progress or change for the better from his point of view, dissolution is retrogression or change for the worse. It involves a breakdown of previously developed, complex and definite forms in art and culture; a tendency to simplification, indefiniteness, and disorder. "Retrogression" commonly implies not only a change for the worse but also a reversal in the direction of change; a going back to earlier types of form. Spencer's theory failed, as we have seen, to recognize that regression and simplification in organic structure may be good from the biological standpoint of fitness for survival.

In further correction of Spencer's theory, we have just been considering some types of simplification in art which do not necessarily involve dissolution or decadence; which are, on the contrary, phases of evolution itself, running hand and hand with complication and helping to balance it. Later on, we shall examine some cases of regression in art which are likewise healthy rather than decadent. To express these distinctions we have had to distinguish between "regression," in the neutral sense implying any reversal in direction or return to previous types, and "retrogression" in the sense of deterioration. Whatever terms are used, it is important for the understanding of

history to realize that a return to previous conditions is not necessarily a change for the worse.

Three main types of regressive movement in art and culture, all involving some simplification, must be distinguished. The first is that of the large-scale dissolution of an advanced civilization and its arts, as in the fall of the Roman Empire. It is involuntary, uncontrollable, and predominantly destructive. It involves some regression to simpler forms but the positive element in these is not enough to outweigh the destructive.

Many rich cultures have ceased to exist as distinct social groups. In some, such as the Hittite and Scythian, the people themselves have perished or been absorbed by other groups. Even if all are slain, important elements of the culture may survive through being transmitted to another group; perhaps to the conquerors. Such elements are sure to change considerably in being fused with foreign culture-traits, so that the old pattern as a distinctive whole will have ceased to exist. This may be the case whether or not some biological strains survive, as among the modern Mayans or the descendants of Roman citizens who lived among the ruins after the destroyers had done their work. They called themselves "Romans," and the fiction of a Holy Roman Empire lived on for centuries; yet the old Roman civilization had ceased to exist. Its successors in the West, though indebted to it, were substantially different.

In such disasters there is never an exact return to earlier cultural forms. The small social units after the fall of Rome were different from those before its origin. Those which assembled as heterogeneous groups of survivors and stragglers lacked the well-knit kinship organization and tradition of the ancient tribal and urban units. They looked back on greatness, not ahead to it. But important analogies exist in the general mode of life. In the era of great expansion under the Republic and the early Empire, the Pax Romana guaranteed some protection to peaceful subjects in their homes and artisans in their shops; to far-flung commerce by road and sea, including importation of exotic works of art; to the builders of great public works such as theaters, baths, and temples. In spite of constant wars somewhere in the Empire, there were large areas of comparative security. These lasted long enough to permit a detailed adjustment to life on a highly evolved social level, with institutions adapted to managing art, commerce, education, and administration on a large and complex scale. Such an evolution does not go so far under a weak, uncertain hegemony, such as that of Athens in the Mediterranean. The fall of Rome under the blows of repeated invasions and domestic upheavals eventually forced regression to something like the early stages of social life: to the sedentary village, precariously dependent on the protection of some warlord, and (at worst) to the nomadic or pastoral tribe or horde, driving some sheep or cattle, but eking out a living by robbery under short-lived chieftains.

As to the arts, many of the phenomena of primitive stages appeared in reverse; the disappearance of the great superstructure of large, complex, refined imperial art; the building of cramped, thick-walled little towns, houses, tombs, and churches out of fragments of old buildings; the concentration of effort on small handicrafts, utilitarian and decorative, such as weapons, costumes, coins, and jewelry, which could be easily moved or hidden in times of danger. During great and prolonged disorder, nearly all art-production ceased. During the repeated devastation of Italy by the barbarians, one could not expect major works of city-planning, architecture, drama, poetry, music, or theater. What products appeared were mostly simpler and cruder, with little effort at aesthetic refinement. The whole range of art production which had expressed the Roman spirit, the evolution of the Greek inheritance into something more huge, magnificent, and powerful, almost ceased to exist.

There had been many signs of inner decay before and while the barbarians flowed down the peninsula. For centuries, Rome had shown increasing inability to function, to stay alive and carry on its normal economic activities, to protect its borders from the invader and its citizens at home from riotous mobs. The fall of Rome involved an unparalleled loss of accumulated cultural evolution; of institutions, buildings, great works of art, skills and traditions, books of classical literature and scientific knowledge. Many of the cultural treasures which came down to later ages were preserved in devious ways almost by accident, under the ruins of houses, or in the translations of Arabic and Jewish scholars.

Catastrophic regressions have occurred repeatedly in the histories of Egypt, Mesopotamia, India, and China. Egypt had several periods of feudalism under weak central monarchies. After the death of Charlemagne, the dissolution of his empire led to small, independent kingdoms and a loose, shifting feudalism. Often a change of dynasties at the top makes little difference to the people below; they pay taxes and tributes to a different set of oppressors. But where a wholesale disintegration of the collective mode of life ensues, it is inevitably destructive to complex forms of art. Nowhere in recorded history has the extent of cultural dissolution been as terrible as in the decline and fall of Rome.

Somewhat analogous disasters occurred in Mexico in the successive destructions of the Mayan, Toltec, and Aztec cultures. As one compares the grandiose, carved and painted temples of Chichen-Itza with the huts of the modern Mayan Indians, descendants of the temple-builders, one sees the results of a tremendous cultural regression from the urban-imperial to the sedentary village level.

[333]

No doubt, similar villages existed in the imperial age, with a mode of life not unlike that of the contemporary villagers, except for modern importations; but the highly evolved superstructure of knightly aristocracy, scientific learning, and complex art is dead and only the skeleton remains. When the Mayan empire decayed from disease, crop failure, and war, some of its culture was handed on. This fell at the hands of the Spaniards, who destroyed much of the accumulated art and learning through greed and religious fanaticism. In many regions of the Far and Near East today, people live on apathetically in the shadow of the monuments their ancestors produced in the creative epoch of their culture. They repeat a few craft processes in a routine way, but lack (at least for the present) enough ambition or ability to develop new ones.

Smaller involuntary regressions are to be found throughout the history of civilization. One occurred in the fall of Athenian democracy, followed by a reversion to oligarchy and tyranny, as a result of the defeats by Sparta, Macedonia, and Rome. Politically, it was a setback for the evolution of free institutions, but other types of social order evolved instead. There was much less loss of cultural values than in the fall of Rome. Artistic, philosophic, and scientific production continued actively. There was much destruction, as in the sack of Corinth by Mummius. But the basic skills, traditions, and activities of art were not destroyed. Through the interpretations of Lucretius, Cicero, and other literary men, and through the work of Greek artists in Italy, the bulk of the Greek inheritance was safely transmitted to new soil.

The story of the fall of Rome and the centuries which followed was oversimplified by early historians. One must be careful not to reduce them to a single pattern of barbarian destruction and enforced regression. On the one hand, the so-called Dark Ages were not as completely dark as formerly believed; they show many gleams of light in art and learning. On the other, the destruction of art and culture was not entirely the work of barbarian invaders. During the centuries after the accession of Constantine, quantities of pagan art —temples, statues, paintings, manuscripts, and decorative arts with pagan motifs—were destroyed by zealous Christians, many of whom believed that the pagan gods were evil demons trying to seduce their souls. (See Gibbon on this point.) The degrading and final extinction of Greco-Roman polytheism with most of its arts—literary, musical, and dramatic as well as visual—involved an extensive cultural dissolution by imperial Romans themselves. It had regressive aspects, but these were partly outweighed in art by the rapid development of new, Christian tendencies.

The history of coins in this period, roughly 500 to 1000 A.D., yields significant data on the evolution and devolution of styles. Coins were preserved in great number, whereas larger gold, silver, and bronze objects were often melted down. They were easily transported to outlying regions and hidden in *caches*, to be preserved in the ruins of houses for centuries. They were small and fairly simple in design, and could be copied or adapted without too much trouble by provincial or semi-barbarous artisans.

André Malraux, in *The Voices of Silence* (pp. 132 ff.), reproduces a series of magnified photographs of Celtic and Gallo-Roman coins minted in various parts of Europe after the Roman *débacle*. He traces them all back in subject to a stater of Philip II of Macedon in 350 B.C., with a late classic profile of Hermes. Showing the gradual disintegration of this form in later coins, farther from Greece and Rome, he remarks that new, positive qualities of form appear amid this disintegration; bold, expressive stylizations of the profile and the transformation of it into a lion-head. The figure of a horse and rider is likewise changed into forceful, non-classical designs which suggest contemporary art. It is incorrect, says Malraux, to class all such art as "retrograde." Art is retrograde or regressive (he does not distinguish the two) only when the inherited forms, drained of their previous significance, are more evident in it than the new ones being developed. Some Gallo-Roman art, he finds, is retrograde in this way, having merely disintegrated into ideographic signs.

One may question whether even the division of an early, representative form into ideographic signs is necessarily retrogressive in the derogatory sense. It is certainly a reaction toward early Iron, Bronze, and Neolithic types of form, which often stressed ideographic symbols; but these too can be developed artistically, as in early Chinese and Egyptian characters.

To decide how regressive in style a certain work of art really is, one should know something about its makers; the history of the tribe which made it and their relations to other cultures. In the strictest sense, a regression involves fairly direct descent from the more highly evolved type. Thus the inhabitants of Italy, long exposed to imperial art, could regress from it to older, simpler types. But we know little of the extent to which the outlying, Celtic and Germanic tribes had ever been civilized. Some individuals and groups were thoroughly Romanized. Some had a thin veneer of Roman culture and could to that extent regress from it to their earlier, indigenous culture. Others, with little or none, might be simply altering an exotic design in their own traditional way, in making a coin somewhat like the Macedonian stater.

In any case, our conception of a regressive art, in the strictly non-evaluative sense, should not be extended carelessly to include everything made after the great disaster by people far from the center of things. The farther one goes in space and time from the scene of crucial events, the less one sees of purely regressive phenomena, and the more these are mixed with external, local processes and new collateral developments.

2. VOLUNTARY REGRESSIONS TO A SIMPLE, PRIMITIVE MODE OF LIVING. THEIR EFFECTS ON ART

The second type of regression is very different. It is a somewhat voluntary adoption, in actual ways of life, of a set of cultural traits characteristic of an earlier era. It is not necessarily disastrous or destructive. It is to some extent controllable and reversible. In accordance with our previous definitions, we shall call this type a regression or reversion but not a retrogression or dissolution.

A case in point is the reversion of some American Indian tribes from the agricultural village stage to that of hunting and pillaging. This occurred especially after the introduction of the horse and gun. (Linton, 1955, p. 53). So far-reaching a change naturally tends to destroy some of the arts of the higher stage. But unlike biological changes, it is not irrevocable. (Roe and Simpson, 1958, p. 22).

A somewhat different kind of voluntary regression appears in the departure of English, French, and Dutch emigrants to seek frontier life in small, simple communities in the New World. Some had been simple peasants before, but others sacrificed the amenities of urban life in a modern nation. They brought much of their traditional culture with them, especially in religion, local government, and the useful arts. What they left behind was not permanently lost, but could be imported later on. The discontented could return to civilization. The Puritans had already renounced a good deal of modern, ornate art in their homes and churches, thus regressing to earlier ideals of austerity. The Calvinists had eliminated much church music. Some old-world ties were maintained. But in the rigorous environment of early Massachusetts and Virginia, the colonists had to become almost self-sufficient in small groups, and to cluster at a moment's warning to the stockades for protection. In course of time the regressive phase gave way to new cultural developments.

Such movements are not necessarily primitivistic in thought or desire. Those who engage in them often have no longing for savage or exotic ways of life as such. Their main desire may be to escape from irksome restraints and compulsions at home; to find a place where they can build another modern, civilized society under their own control. They might prefer a liberating revolution at home; but, believing this impossible, they are willing to sacrifice urban comforts for the sake of freedom. They accept primitive, frontier conditions perforce, in the hope of outgrowing them as soon as possible.

Somewhat different examples are provided by the many small communities which were established in the eighteenth and early nineteenth centuries, such as the Oneida community and others set up by Shakers and Mennonites. Some were conscious regressions to primitive Christianity; some were experiments in utopian socialism. The two ideals were consistent, since the community of property among early Christians was often cited as a model. Opposition to new-fangled inventions was characteristic, as in the rule of the Amish of Ohio against automobiles. When the Mormons under Smith and Young trekked west through small towns, farms, and open Indian country into the wilderness of Utah, they were inspired by the Bible account of similar wanderings under Abraham and Moses; by the escape of the Chosen People from Egyptian and Babylonian captivity and the search for a promised land. That escape, like that of the Mormons, had been in some ways a regression from complex urban to simple pastoral life; from the hateful luxuries, idolatries, and harlotries of the teeming city to find peace and freedom for worship under the stars. Once at the Great Salt Lake, the regressive phase of Mormonism ceased and the growth of a new urban culture began.

Countless individuals have obeyed the call to turn their backs on city life and live as hermits or isolated families in the wilderness. Many have taken native women and tried to "go native," even to the extent of being adopted by a primitive tribe. Comparatively few reports come back to

civilization from these experiments. Many such adventurers have become drunken beachcombers, unable to adjust themselves constructively to any social pattern. It is impossible for any adult, conditioned in the tastes, beliefs, and attitudes of modern urban civilization, to leave these all behind when he goes from Paris to a South Sea island. His dislike for civilization is not enough to make him think and feel like a native tribesman, however eagerly he tries to act like one. He may achieve a synthesis, as Gauguin did, of a few selected elements from both artistic traditions; but he will always be to some extent an outsider in the primitive group.

Without leaving his home town at all, an individual such as Diogenes may himself stage a one-man regression to the primitive. He lived in a tub, says the legend, rejected all the comforts and conventions of civilization, and tried to show that the life of animals was better than that of men. Few have the courage to act this part consistently, but many pose as children of nature, especially in communities like Paris and Los Angeles, which are tolerant toward eccentricity.

The arts of early colonial and frontier groups have in the past shown a strong tendency to simplification. The great traditions of large-scale architecture, city-planning, painting, sculpture, literature, music, and theater have been left behind. Replacing them have been simple, utilitarian handicrafts, naïve drawings and carvings, and hymn tunes in unison. The Bible is often the only literature. Today, it is easier to bring urban refinements and machinery into the wilderness, and harder to escape from omnipresent civilization.

Does regressive art of this second type involve a deterioration in quality? Critics and historians praise selected examples of colonial handicraft, as in houses, furniture, pottery, metalry, and textiles from New Amsterdam and Massachusetts Bay before 1700. Some were made by awkward bunglers, some by sensitive artists. Critics praise a strong, plain functionalism, an honest strength of design, a direct, individual approach in the best pieces, as contrasted with ordinary city products. American colonial workmanship of the later eighteenth century, in the eastern cities, belongs in a different category. It was no longer the expression of a regressive move away from European culture, but rather of new local developments, constantly nourished by imported models from the European capitals.

3. PRIMITIVISM IN ART.
FANTASIES OF REGRESSION TO SIMPLICITY.
REVIVALS OF
ARCHAIC AND PRIMITIVE STYLES

A third type of cultural regression occurs in art and ethics. This also is comparatively voluntary and reversible. It is limited in scope, usually involving no overt attempt to destroy or escape from modern civilization completely, and affecting only a part—perhaps a small part—of the lives of individuals. For every individual or group that actually left civilization to adopt a primitive life, there have been millions who dreamed of doing so but never did. They left no impact on history except when they expressed and communicated their wishful dreams in some outward medium or gesture. Then these dreams ceased to be merely subjective and became a kind of overt action, capable of influencing the lives of others and forming a part of contemporary civilization itself. The outward expressions of primitivism include religious and ethical teachings and reforms. If carried out in action, these belong to the second type of regression, discussed in the previous section.

Primitivism in the various arts has assumed many forms and many degrees of regression. On a rather superficial level, it is content with fantasies of primitive life and love away from civilized conventions. In story, verse, or picture, these may be executed in a thoroughly modern, urban, academic style and technique. Similar escapist fantasies deal with happy young people in a rustic

environment. More thoroughly regressive tendencies appear (a) in the use of styles, techniques, and instruments from an earlier age, as in William Morris's archaistic handicrafts; (b) in the imitation or adaptation of actual, tribal styles such as those of African sculpture; (c) in stylistic traits which suggest abstractly a savage or infantile attitude such as wildness or destructiveness, perhaps apart from any primitive subject or tribal style.

Robinson Crusoe and *Swiss Family Robinson* expressed only a partial regression. They satisfied the contemporary taste for fantasies of adventure under primitive conditions. Here the imaginary regression was involuntary, due to shipwreck; the Europeans did not "go native" but maintained their civilized mode of life as well as possible under the circumstances. In the novels of Herman Melville (*Omoo* and *Typee*) and others, the European visited primitive and exotic communities as a tourist or sailor, enjoying its beauties and unconventional loves without surrendering his civilized mentality. Later, especially in the twentieth century, fantasies of regression became less idyllic. As we have seen, they stressed man's "atavistic" tendencies; his underlying brutality and destructiveness.

Pre-romantic fantasies of primitive life were mixed with contemporary details, as in pictures of Old Testament life by Italian renaissance masters and by Poussin and Claude Lorrain, with shepherds garbed in Florentine fashions or in Roman togas. It took a long time to reach the art of Gauguin, in which primitives were shown, not only more realistically, but in a style more akin to the primitive. In the eighteenth century, primitivistic fantasies in drama, fiction, lyric poetry, painting, and music, were popular in the French court. The whimsical play of Marie Antoinette and her courtiers, in having dairy cottages built and in dressing and acting like dairy-maids and shepherds, made artistic history. It dramatized the pictorial, rococo fantasies of rustic life by Watteau, Boucher, and Fragonard.

Likewise the small, ceremonial tea-houses of

Japanese Samurai, studiously plain and rustic like the carefully roughened tea-bowls of the ceremony itself, expressed a symbolic regression. This was no mere play, but an effort to compensate for the burdensome complexities of urban duty and etiquette by a relaxing, yet still artistically stylized, return to nature. Lao-Tzu and the Taoist tradition, Chinese Ch'an and Japanese Zen, all taught escape from courtly convention and burdensome knowledge, back to primitive simplicity, directness, and vigor. Their teachings have profoundly influenced Far Eastern art. Chinese gentlemen-artists of the late Sung and Yuan periods expressed their distaste for civilization (especially under the Mongol conquerors) by exquisite paintings and lyrics of country life. Theocritus, Virgil, Horace, and Longus (in *Daphnis and Chloe*) expressed in literature other phases of this recurrent wish for escape from urban artificialities; for a return to the woods and fields as simple, amorous swains and shepherdesses. For the modern city-dweller, such pastimes as hunting and fishing are playful regressions to once necessary occupations. Competitive sports among teams representing various cities are symbolic re-enactments of the former warfare among independent city-states, with feelings of loyalty and rivalry now directed into harmless channels. Gandhi's hand spinning-wheel, on the other hand, was no game or hobby but a serious symbol of return to primitive industrial methods.

The antiquity of backward longing for the good old days, when manners and morals were uncorrupted and children well-behaved, is shown in ancient Egyptian literature.

Yesterday is perished,
And violence is come upon all men.
To whom should I speak today?
Men do not as they were done by nowadays.[1]

A similar mood is voiced by Henry Vaughan in the seventeenth century:[2]

O how I long to travel back
And tread again that ancient track!

That I might once more reach that plain
Where first I left my glorious train...
Some men a forward motion love,
But I by backward steps would move.

We have already noticed the relation of primitivism to the ancient theory of an early Golden Age of bliss and innocence, from which man had fallen into crime, disease, and war; also to the Hebrew-Christian doctrine of the fall of man from Eden. Historically, these beliefs have been opposed to those of progress and evolution, which taught the rise of man from a previous state of bestiality, not at all blissful or innocent. So revivals of primitivism are to some extent reversions to ancient, prescientific theories of history. They certainly run counter to Spencer's evolutionism, in which progress and evolution were closely linked with increasing complexity, while simplification was linked with retrogression and dissolution. However, a moderate primitivism is not inconsistent with twentieth-century conceptions of evolution and progress. These are no longer conceived as unilinear, but as including many changes of direction. Among these there may be minor backward movements to recapture lost values and thus correct the evolutionary process without reversing it entirely.

Various names are applied to such regressive movements in art. "Archaism" implies any conscious return to or imitation of an earlier style, such as that of the so-called archaic period in Greek sculpture and vase-painting. "Archaistic" art is different from genuinely archaic art. "Primitivism" usually suggests a farther return, to the savage or tribal stage of art and culture. "Atavism" suggests a reversion to savagery or animalism.

Lovejoy and Boas define cultural primitivism as "the belief of men living in a relatively highly evolved and complex cultural condition that a life

---

[1] From the Middle Kingdom poem, "Dispute of a Man with his Soul." J. Mayer and T. Prideaux, *Never To Die* (New York, 1938), p. 70.
[2] Quoted by Toynbee in *A Study of History*, VI, p. 505.

far simpler and less sophisticated in some or in all respects is a more desirable life."[3] They distinguish between chronological and cultural primitivism in that the former places the best condition of man in the remote past, and holds out slight hope of future improvement through some recovery of what has been lost. The latter (which may be combined with it) is the discontent of civilized people with civilization or some important feature of it. "The cultural primitivist's model of human excellence and happiness is sought in the present, in the mode of existing primitive, or so-called 'savage' peoples." Some of the main ideas of modern primitivism originated in antiquity, such as the noble savage, the superiority of the animals, and the simple life as an Epicurean ideal. (Lovejoy and Boas, Chs. IV, XI, XIII).

Robert J. Goldwater, after analyzing many varieties of primitivism in recent painting, and in the praise of it by critics, finds one common assumption therein.[4] It is that "externals, whether those of a social or cultural group, of individual psychology, or of the physical world, are intricate and complicated and *as such not desirable*." Reaching under the surface, it is supposed, will reveal something simple and emotionally more compelling than surface variations. Simplicity and basicness are "things to be valued in and for themselves." It is the assumption, Goldwater continues, "that the further one goes back—historically, psychologically, or aesthetically—the simpler things become; and that because they are simpler they are the more interesting, more important, and more valuable."

It would seem that anyone who rejects the theory of progress, maintaining that art and life were better in the olden days than now, must logically infer that regressions can be good. In fact, he should believe that regression is the only way to improvement. However, this is not the case. Some of the most notable pessimists among recent philosophers of history, such as Spengler and Toynbee, while denouncing as an evil illusion much that Western man regards as progress, have

little good to say about regressive movements either. These they regard as mere symptoms of decadence; the old age and approaching disintegration of a culture. Such movements are not, they imply, real recoveries of lost value; they are futile attempts at such recovery, as in the pathetic or absurd attempts of an old man to act like a young lover. Says Spengler: "The 'return to nature' which already thinkers and poets—Rousseau, Gorgias and their 'contemporaries' in other cultures—begin to feel and to proclaim, reveals itself in the form-world of the arts as a sensitive longing and *presentiment of the end*."[5] Archaism is defined by Toynbee as "an attempt to get back to one of those happier states which, in times of troubles, are regretted the more poignantly—and perhaps idealized the more unhistorically—the farther they are left behind." After belittling its examples in art, such as the gothic revival which "desolated" nineteenth-century architecture and the "perverse attempt" to revive dead languages, he concludes that an air of failure or futility surrounds them all. The reason is that the archaist tries to reconcile past and present, which are "incompatible."[6]

James Baird, in a study of literary primitivism, has a higher opinion of it. "Aesthetic primitivism," he says, is "... a creed springing inevitably from a state of cultural failure." Though society may fail and die, "the inventiveness of the individual endures." When new symbols are substituted for old, as in replacing the 'lost' symbols of Protestant Christianity, there is necessarily a "regression to primordial, as opposed to "civilized," forms." The result, as in Herman Melville's creative use of oriental and Polynesian symbolism,

[3] A. O. Lovejoy and G. Boas, *Primitivism and Related Ideas in Antiquity* (Baltimore, 1935), p. 7. On primitivism in various periods, see also G. Boas, *The Happy Beast in French Thought of the Seventeenth Century* (Baltimore, 1933) and M.-S. Rostvig, *The Happy Man* (2 vols.; Oslo, 1958).

[4] *Primitivism in Modern Painting* (New York, 1938), p. 172.

[5] *The Decline of the West* (New York, 1929), Vol. I, p. 207.

[6] *A Study of History* (1-vol. ed.; New York, 1947), pp. 505–515. Toynbee quotes J. B. S. Haldane as likening the archaism of contemporary art to that of the declining ammonites (spiral cephalopods of the Mesozoic era). Toynbee, VI, 60 n.

can be important art, "a new affirmation of life."[7]

Primitivism can indeed achieve these positive values, although it does not always do so. Much depends on what elements of early culture it tries to revive. It does not always spring from actual cultural failure. Sufficient to motivate it is the fact that some persons dislike contemporary culture, believe it has failed, and wish to revive a different one. Those who think modern technological civilization has failed have not proved their case. But certainly the artistic symbols of Christianity have lost some of their appeal, and modern man is in quest of others. It is unlikely that he will find adequate substitutes in oriental or Polynesian tradition.

Whether a regressive movement can ever succeed in producing good art is another evaluative question, which we may only notice briefly in passing. Those who admire primitivism, as in the paintings of Gauguin, will feel that it sometimes can and does. Different opinions are possible, and it should not be assumed without more evidence that such movements are always and necessarily futile, pathological, or signs of decrepitude. True, old people and old civilizations often think back with longing to the distant past, when they were young and vigorous. But they are not the only ones who long for the past or wish to recapture something good which has been lost. It is not necessarily morbid to do so, especially if one lives in a time of troubles when important values have actually been lost. When the Vandals were plundering Rome, sacking and killing as they went, it was not a pathological symptom to wish that Rome were strong once more. When a certain art seems to have reached a dead end, to have exhausted the possibilities of a certain line of development and be searching for a new inspiration, it is not unreasonable to look over its past history, to see whether some of the older experiments deserve to be resumed and carried farther. It may be healthy and constructive to revert to these experimentally, as starting-points; but only if this is done selectively and in moderation. The regressive

trend becomes immoderate and unhealthy, for the individual or the group, when the past is longed for in excess, with corresponding neglect or underestimation of the present; when the present is rejected *in toto* and desires are channeled into really unattainable fantasies. It is doubtless immoderate, as Toynbee holds, to try to revive a dead language as a living vernacular, in substitution for an established modern tongue. But it is not immoderate to encourage a limited revival of such a neglected language as Gaelic or Provençal, as a subject for scholarly research or as a second language for those who enjoy it and wish to preserve its distinctive cultural values.

There is ample historical evidence to show that an ancient style can not be revived as a whole, or an exotic one imported, to the extent that it will satisfy the present group as an adequate expression of its own present interest and attitudes. The modern culture-pattern is sure to be different enough to make that alien style somewhat inadequate. If the old style catches on at all, as something performed, it will have to be modified to suit present tastes. This is now being done in our borrowings from primitive art. But to observe and perform it with all possible sympathy, to try with all one's learning and imagination to feel it as its originators did, is neither futile nor pathological. It can be an agreeable enlargement of one's present experience, and also a source of hints for new composition, as in performing a seventeenth-century play or string quartet, learning to sing a Gregorian chant or to paint in the Persian style. The artist can then select from it certain elements of form or content, to be combined with modern ones. Archaic and exotic scales and rhythms are used by Debussy, Prokofieff, and Stravinsky. When done creatively, this can result in a viable new style. One reason is that a modern culture-pattern, within an advanced, heterogeneous civilization, is itself a compound of old and new, foreign and domestic elements. It is not pure and uniform, but full of inconsistent attitudes and anti-

[7] *Ishmael* (Baltimore, 1956), pp. 3 f.

thetical, emotive symbols. Some of these are almost incompatible, as in the Apollonian, Dionysian, Socratic, and Epicurean strains which we inherit from the Greeks. Nevertheless, they can be loosely integrated into the shifting, unstable pattern of modern art and culture, and even into a single work of art whose aim is to contrast them as irreconcilable.

One may question, not only whether primitivism and archaism are necessarily bad in themselves, but whether they always reveal a bad condition of society. In a "time of troubles," when actual life is worse than usual, the longing for previous happiness would naturally be reinforced. But there is always trouble of some sort. Men have had regressive fantasies even when actual conditions were good; in times of creative growth as well as of decadence. On the other hand, Confucius and Aristotle, whose ideas were not regressive, lived in times of trouble. As Macaulay remarked, "It may at first seem strange that society, while constantly moving forward with eager speed, should be constantly looking backward with tender regret. But these two propensities, inconsistent as they may appear, ... spring from our impatience of the state in which we actually are. That impatience, while it stimulates us to surpass preceding generations, disposes us to overrate their happiness."[8]

In its sweeping contrast between past and present, primitivism tends to exaggerate the goodness of the one, the badness of the other. But it is often right in pointing out specific faults in present life from which early man was relatively free. "The more complex a culture becomes," says Bidney, "and the larger the society to which it pertains, the less opportunity there is for the individual to participate actively and fully in the life of the community, so that social culture tends to impoverish rather than to enrich the life of the individual."[9] While this is not always or inevitably true, it is true enough to make a case for those who would turn the clock back to simplicity in some respects at least.

Extreme primitivism and quietism in religion usually tend, as we have noticed, to discourage all but the most rudimentary forms of art, especially visual art which smacks of luxurious display. They lead instead to voluntary poverty; to the hermit or monastic temper; to prayer and preaching within bare walls or in the open fields. But milder forms of primitivism have encouraged the expression of its ideals in simple, austere types of art. Religious meditation on the earthly paradise before the Fall, and on the days when Jesus lived among the humble folk of Bethlehem and Galilee, led to new versions of the Gospel story in art, aids to dreaming of what it must have been like to live then. Much of the later Christian art, from the Gospel miniatures and tympanum carvings of the romanesque to the frescoes of Giotto and the early renaissance, was inspired by this desire to recapture a beautiful past, not of warrior kings and palaces, but of simple peasants visited by Deity, as in the story of the disciples of Emmaus. Later on, these same Biblical themes were treated in no regressive spirit, but as bases for another ornate superstructure of complex, pictorial form and aristocratic elegance.

Any revival, of a style in art or a custom in life, is in a sense a regression; a return to that way of thinking and acting. But a historical movement would hardly be called "regressive" unless the negative phase, the rejection in fact or fantasy of the new in favor of the old, were comparatively strong. If the new is on the whole approved and retained, the old being merely taken off the shelf and added to it, the net effect is developmental. The early renaissance had a negative phase in rejecting and disparaging the gothic, which was in 1350 "contemporary civilization." Then the cry was "back to the ancients." By contrast with flamboyant gothic ornament, early renaissance style was and seemed refreshingly simple, orderly, and quiet. But soon, while still reviving classical culture, the renaissance moved away from its

8 T. B. Macaulay, *History of England*, I (1848), Ch. III.
9 *Theoretical Anthropology*, p. 13.

classical models while hardly daring to do so; its regressive phase outgrown in a new synthesis of classical and Hebrew-Christian culture.

Regressive movements are not necessarily from the complex back to the simple. If one lives in a drastically simplified age, like that of Otto I in A.D. 962, where catastrophic regression has already taken its toll, one may long instead for past complexities. Otto's "Holy Roman Empire" expressed by its name the dream of reviving the empires of Charlemagne and ancient Rome. But, since the prevailing trend of history has been complicative, most regressive wishes are in contrary motion

4. ROMANTIC PRIMITIVISM AS REGRESSIVE

Some of the most important examples of primitivism in modern civilization are connected with romanticism. As a cultural movement and a style in art, romanticism is usually defined as beginning in the mid-eighteenth century and ending in the mid-nineteenth. But the beliefs and attitudes it emphasized did not die out entirely then. Under various names, some of them retain a strong influence today. There are strong romantic traits in Walt Whitman, Pierre Loti, Gauguin and Gustave Moreau, Ravel and Debussy. Primitivism is displayed in Gauguin's flight to Tahiti and the pictures which he made there in a semi-primitive style. It usually involves a return to simplicity, or a wish to do so; this too is evident in Gauguin's flattening out of three-dimensional shapes and perspectives; his substitution of broad areas of bright contrasting color; his use of rather heavy, blunt linear shapes instead of the sinuous curves of academic art.

Both romanticism and primitivism can take many forms, not all of which involve the tendency toward simplification. Romanticism led at times to complex forms of its own, as in the novels of Hugo and the music of Wagner and Tschai-

kowsky. It admired the intricacies of gothic architecture. (We have seen how Herbert Spencer denounced this as "rebarbarization.") Primitivism, in imitating tribal art, has taken some fairly complex models, such as those of African and Melanesian sculpture.

The savage and the animal in man are sometimes conceived and expressed in modern art in terms of wild passion, confusion, violence, and bestial lust. Accordingly, romantic art often manifests its regressiveness in forms associated with these traits, such as jagged, irregular lines, broken curves, rough surfaces, blurred edges, and unbalanced compositions. Such effects appeared in European art during the mannerist period; they persisted through romanticism, impressionism, and post-impressionism. They were paralleled in literature by verbal images of moonlight, storms, ghosts, mystery, and magic. Romantic music was somewhat analogous in its richer instrumental and harmonic coloring and broken rhythms, blurring the previous Mozartian clarity of melodic and chordal structure. All this was often associated with the return to primitive, Dionysian wildness and occultism.

Effective as these devices are in suggesting the desired moods, they represent a fictitious rather than an actual, historical regression in art. Comparatively little primitive art, so far as we know it, is of this type. The tribesman is not always in a state of wild excitement; he is often at rest or going stolidly about his work. It often takes much dancing, music, and alcohol or drugs to rouse him to a state of excitement. Animals, too, are not wholly free, emotional, or impulsive; their lives are largely fixed by inherited patterns of reflex and instinct. Much primitive human art, like the honeycomb, is firmly geometrical. Neolithic art coincides with the rise of written language and of settled village life, with its developing social order. Geometrical design required some feeling for visual order, sharp linear precision, regularity and control. It may have been admired for these qualities amid a world of insecurity, sudden dangers, and unknown spirit enemies. Even paleolithic art shows at times a love of fine symmetrical form in chipped stone tools, and of carefully realistic animal figures. Some romanticists, for whom rational order is an old and tiresome story, a symbol of oppression, associate the supposed freedom of primitive life with symbols of irregularity, wildness, and disorder.

Is the romantic love of indefiniteness in form and content an example of devolution? That would seem to follow if we accept Spencer's use of increasing definiteness as a criterion of evolution. Certainly, it has a regressive aspect in reacting against neo-classicism. But paradoxically, indefiniteness can itself become a definite aim of art; a definite concept of certain types of psychological effect which romanticism emphasized.

It would be a mistake to regard romanticism as essentially anti-evolutionist, when it did so much to foster early theories of evolution. In particular, it stressed the unity of all life and the universal striving for growth and progress; the kinship of modern man with animals and savages in spite of the veneer of civilization. In rejecting the evils of civilization, it did not suggest that man return to savagery and stay there forever; but rather that by casting off civilized corruptions he could resume with greater vigor the onward march toward perfection. Perfection was still conceived as simple rather than complex, and primitive man was nearer to it than modern man. "We cannot reflect on the morality of mankind," said Rousseau, "without contemplating with pleasure the picture of the simplicity which prevailed in the earliest times... As the conveniences of life increase, as the arts are brought to perfection, and luxury spreads, true courage flags, the virtues disappear..."[10]

Ideal simplicity was exemplified by the noble savage, the peasant, and the child, in contrast with the urban, sophisticated, wealthy, upper-class adult. It was something to be envied and admired, not for its own sake, but for its association with moral virtue, courage, innocence, beauty, health, and happiness. Likewise, complex civilization had

been admired, not for its own sake, but for the blessings it was thought to bring. To some extent they were the same: virtue, happiness, and beauty in addition to knowledge, power, wisdom, and refinement. Opinions differed as to whether complexity or simplicity was the better means to the ends on which all agreed in principle—virtue and happiness. Book-learning and power, being associated with civilization, were disparaged by the primitivists.

Detailed portrayals of the savage, the peasant, and the child emphasized different virtues and blessings to be envied and admired. The peasant appeared as spiritually noble in Goldsmith's "Deserted Village," Robert Burns's "Cotter's Saturday Night" and "A Man's a Man for a' That," and in Thomas Gray's "Elegy Written in a Country Churchyard." In painting, Millet portrayed the simple, devout peasant in "The Angelus."

Wordsworth showed the "simple child" as tender, naïve, and trusting (*We are Seven*) and as trailing clouds of glory from his previous life in heaven (*Ode, the Intimations of Immortality from Recollections of Early Childhood*). Wordsworth's attempt to simplify poetic diction into something closer to ordinary speech was not altogether successful. Adult poets, trying to think and write like children, or in a form apparently meant for children yet conveying a deeper message, often produced an intermediate type which was neither adult nor childlike. By analogy with Gauguin as quasi-primitive, it can perhaps be described as quasi-naïve or (in some cases) pseudo-naïve. It appears at its best in William Blake's *Songs of Innocence*, whose introduction sounds the keynote:

Piping down the valleys wild
Piping songs of pleasant glee,
On a cloud I saw a child,
And he laughing said to me:

[10] J. J. Rousseau, "A Discourse on the Moral Effects of the Arts and Sciences" (1750). In *The Social Contract and Discourses* (Everyman ed.; New York, 1932), p. 145.

"Pipe a song about a Lamb!"
So I piped with merry cheer.
....
And I wrote my happy songs
Every child may joy to hear.

Poems like this are simplified and quasi-naïve in the following respects: the short, end-stopped lines with regular rhymes and rhythms as in a nursery rhyme; the restriction to one and two-syllabled words with obvious primary meanings; the child and lamb as main subject of the real and imagined songs; the happy mood and simple images throughout. Like *Alice in Wonderland*, they have a deeper meaning for adults.

In *Scenes from Childhood*, a set of short sketches for piano, Robert Schumann undertook to express varied moods of a young child's day, his play and dreams, and even the pleading tones of a childish voice. Drawing and painting were slower to emulate the childish touch. Sentimental, Greuze-like pictures of pretty children, sad or smiling, abounded in academic painting through the nineteenth century. But it was not until the twentieth century that artists and psychologists showed much interest in the spontaneous visual art of children. Ricci, an Italian writer, had discussed children's art in the 1800's. "Progressive education," in the romantic tradition from Rousseau's *Émile* and Froebel's kindergarten, had urged that children be allowed to express themselves freely in visual media. Franz Cizek, in Vienna, conducted a famous school along these lines in the 1920's. But it was not until Paul Klee and Miro that adult, sophisticated artists turned their major efforts into quasi-naïve drawings and paintings, often with a subtle hint of deeper meanings on the adult level.

After the Second World War the regressive trend spread more widely, especially in abstract expressionist painting. It was regressive, not in the sense of returning to any definite, previous style, but in trying to avoid all traditional styles, forms, and techniques derived from either civilized or primitive art. It was often regressive in producing extremely loose, blurred, irregular forms suggesting dissolution and disorder. This went to the opposite pole from classical unity and monumentality; also from rational planning, scientific mechanization, and social control. Instead, the artist relied on spontaneous impulse, automatism, and the release of primitive forces in the unconscious. He felt himself as highly individualistic. Appropriate new techniques were tried, as in throwing or dripping paint upon the canvas from a distance, or riding a paint-covered bicycle over it.

While conservatives scoffed, the international popularity of abstract expressionism outside the Iron Curtain showed that it satisfied, for a time at least, some widespread psychological need. This might be a temporary one, connected (as some critics thought) with the revolt from science and the machine; with social revolt and the breakdown of traditional value-systems. In any case, it attracted large numbers of "self-taught" painters, since no formal, technical training was necessary. No definite standards of value being generally accepted, each could claim to be as good as any other. Different ones achieved wide but usually short-lived fame.

The resemblance of some abstract expressionist painting to that of young children was often noted. In the work of adults, this was regressive in terms of individual growth, though not necessarily bad or pathological. For experimental purposes, chimpanzees were provided with finger paints and paper and allowed to make pictures.[11]

[11] On the psychology of contemporary expressionism, see J. P. Hodin, *The Dilemma of Being Modern* (Routledge and Kegan Paul, London, 1956), esp. pp. 57 ff. Expressionism "appears in times of great spiritual tension," this author maintains. It asserts itself sombrely and passionately "against the tyranny of mathematical thought, belief in causality and technical progress, in fact against the mechanization of civilization." *Cf.* Herbert Read, *The Philosophy of Modern Art* (Horizon Press, New York, 1953), esp. p. 56: "in the work of the expressionist school generally, there is an element of despair, leading to remorseless analysis and masochism..." On experiments with painting by chimpanzees as compared with that of children and adult abstractionists, see Desmond Morris, *The Biology of Art* (Knopf, New York, 1962). "As modern painting has progressed away from the representational," writes this author, "it has unknowingly regressed backwards through the various phases of a child's graphic differentiation." (p. 154).

Again the resemblance to some (not all) abstract painting was obvious. The comparison was resented by some artists, but was not unreasonable in view of the strong anti-rationalism expressed and displayed by some artists themselves.

From its beginnings in Kandinsky, however, abstract painting varied greatly. Some artists such as Mondrian, Gorky, and Afro showed mature, purposeful control in both simple and complex forms. As such they were not regressive. Moreover, as we have seen, even the most regressive movements in art may lead to new, unforeseen developments. While a single abstract painting may be too simple to hold the observer's interest long, a series of them can easily be used as sketches for abstract color-films, animated paintings with temporal development analogous to that of music.

Glorification of the child and savage in art, with its implied depreciation of old age and advanced civilization, was in line with the early romantic belief in evolution and progress. Old age symbolizes the past and the heavy hand of oppressive tradition; it is something to be put aside and surpassed. It may be sentimentally cherished, as in the image of a dear old grandparent; but its advice is not to be trusted or obeyed. The same is to be said of all former styles in art and established principles of aesthetics. To the religiously minded romantic, the child was innocence; to the progressive, he was infinite possibility for the future. He was something to be admired, envied, given freedom to grow and express himself; to realize his innate potentialities. This attitude has helped to make modern Western civilization almost the opposite of the Confucian Chinese in many ways. On its negative, simplifying side, it calls for the rapid elimination of old people from authority, rapid change of styles and abandonment of yesterday's leaders, yesterday's favorites in art, as soon as they show signs of age. It involves a possible contradiction, however, in that unlimited freedom for the child implies the right to sexual precocity. Much contemporary art, with its frank portrayals of sex (including precocious examples as in V. Nabokov's *Lolita*) operates to accelerate the maturity of children in this and other respects. On the other hand, progressive education calls for preserving the values of childhood and resists the premature imposition of adult attitudes and responsibilities. Really good, wise, beneficent old and middle-aged persons are comparatively infrequent in contemporary art, especially popular film and fiction. Older persons are often portrayed as stupid, selfish, oppressive, ridiculous, perpetually trying to obstruct the freedom and happiness of the young.

Perhaps the greatest change in artistic primtivism from the early romantic type to the present is the changed conception of what it means to be primitive. "Simplicity" is no longer seen as its most essential trait. More accurate knowledge about prehistoric and modern tribal life has been gained from archeology, anthropology, and travel. More knowledge of the infantile in man has been gained from psychology and psychoanalysis. The peasant as a picturesque type has almost disappeared and the modern farmer is very different; more urbanized and civilized, as a rule. Neither savage, child, nor peasant is imagined in the sweetly idyllic fashion of early romanticism. The true picture of primitive man appears to be somewhere between this and Thomas Hobbes' unflattering description, but nearer to the latter. The savage was not always nasty or brutish, but was often cruel and violent, inclined to cannibalism, prone to disease, and valuing human life cheaply. His cruelty and violence are not far beneath the surface in civilized man. But the fact that primitivism was not wholly accurate in its conception of primitive life does not invalidate it as an ideal for the future. Even if they never existed in the past, some of the virtues it attributed to early man may still be worth striving for, and capable of reconciliation with the values of civilization.

The back-to-nature and back-to-the-primitive ideals have become an integral part of modern, urban culture, so that we no longer feel them as regressive or as radically hostile to classicism. *Atala* and *René*, along with *Paul and Virginia*,

Robinson Crusoe, *The Swiss Family Robinson*, and Melville's *Omoo* and *Typee*, are established literary classics. It makes no essential difference whether the story is one in which city-dwellers revert to a primitive life, or one in which primitive people lead their own idyllic lives (as the writer imagines them), untroubled by outside visitors. In the latter type, the urban reader can easily project himself into the tribal scene and identify himself with some of its characters. Neo-primitive art such as that of Gauguin, along with romantic, rustic landscapes, now holds a firm place in our museums. It has not displaced classicism, but is there beside it; our culture has expanded to take in both. Neo-classic, romantic, and contemporary music likewise complement each other on the same concert programs. What once was felt as a regressive escape from the bonds of civilization has now been accepted as contemporary, and as an integral part of a freer, more diversified civilization.

5. SYMBOLS
OF DESTRUCTION AND DISSOLUTION

The infantile in man, the repressed "id" in his individual psyche, now seems to psychoanalysts as rather violent and destructive. It is not simple, but a writhing mass of undisciplined, irrational desires. Rightly or wrongly, it is this wilder aspect of primitivism which appeals more to twentieth-century art. Its expressions are less idyllic than *Paul and Virginia*, less politely Victorian than the pre-Raphaelites. They appear more abstractly, not as explicit representations of savages or infants; they appear in connection with any subject at all or with no subject, as in abstract painting and sculpture. They appear in the bodily distortions and dissociations of post-impressionism and cubism. Blurred, jagged, explosive shapes and ragged blotches abound in abstract painting. In music, a much more violent, pounding, savage kind of primitivism appears in Stravinsky's *Sacre du Prin-*

temps. Its shifting rhythms and dissonances are far from simple.

Contemporary art expresses this new kind of regressive primitivism through symbolic images of violence, harshness, destructiveness, and disintegration in every medium. It no longer dwells upon the ideals of simple happiness and virtue. There is another kind of devolution in its fantasies and symbols. It is closer to the kind which Spencer called "dissolution" than to the escapist and reformist kinds produced by early romanticism. Stories of crime, including murders, rapes, and suicides, abound in contemporary film and fiction. They are often presented, not as in former epochs, with the implication that these are reprehensible or pitiable violations of eternal moral law and natural order, but (a) as more or less justifiable in that no such law and order exists, or (b) as cynical examples of the absurdity and futility of life. Their protagonists usually come to grief, not in the manner of classical, tragic heroes, but ignobly and often contemptibly. Characters symbolizing age, authority, law and order, rank, wealth, success, knowledge, conservatism, and the like are satirized as hypocritical, tyrannical, dishonest, and inwardly miserable.

In Freud's terminology, this type of art seems to express the Thanatos or death instinct in man, rather than the Eros instinct which usually predominates in artistic creation. It is regressive and devolutionary insofar as it expresses wishful fantasies of disintegration toward the products of previous cultural evolution and toward traditional styles in art. Whether it is so completely depends on whether it opens the way, perhaps unconsciously and unintentionally, to renewed evolution by clearing away outworn, obstructive patterns in life and art.

Not all contemporary art is of this negative, regressive type. Some of it is tightly geometrical, as in the work of Mondrian and some of Kandinsky, thus expressing an orderly, rationalistic type of simplification. Kandinsky, founder of abstract painting, and some of his followers often produce firmly integrated forms, expressing positive moods and vigorous attitudes. But at present the negative, destructive, and rejective attitude seems prevalent. It is especially notable because of the high esteem in which many of its leaders (artists and critics) are held. Negatively, it continues the symbolic protest against both classical and scientific civilization and established styles of art. It often implies that modern civilization is a failure. But, in contrast with the early romantic type as in Wordsworth, it does not substitute a dream of quiet, simple rustic life and happy childhood. In fact, it does not offer any definite substitute for what it rejects; it is largely negative and often destructive in its imagery. It suggests hatred for the present world, but does not try to imagine a better one, past or future, in religious or naturalistic terms. It satirizes what it regards as a false conception of success and progress, but does not offer any better, truer conception of them.

Since the Second World War, during the years of cold war tension and anxiety, the negative, destructive phase has been more in evidence than attempts at reconstruction. It is manifested, not only in explicit and symbolic rejections of traditional moral standards, religious and philosophical beliefs, but in the breakdown of empires and social orders, entailing great actual destruction of life, property, and institutions. Along with this there has been a symbolic rejection of both classic and romantic styles in art; both being associated with the old order and the kind of art which hides social evils with a specious beauty. Both are rejected as falsifying life. Even the traditional idea of "art" is derided in favor of "non-art"—which turns out to be only another kind of art. In rejecting all the traditional styles, the extreme rebel tries to avoid not only beauty and realism in representation, but also all organized design and unity of composition. Whether by intention or not, he sometimes achieves a different kind of unity through consistency of texture, coloring, and arrangement, in images suggesting destruction, frustration, failure, and exclusion. But the total forms are mostly very simple in comparison with baroque complexity.

The term "regressive" has also been applied to the life and work of individuals. Psychoanalysis has shown that many neurotic persons wish, more or less unconsciously, for a return to their lost childhood when life was simpler and happier under parental protection. When frustrated, they relapse into a childish attitude. Normal persons may do this to some extent, but usually develop some ability to deal with adult problems on an adult level. Dreams of childhood can motivate the normal artist to creative fantasies along that line. As E. H. Gombrich shows in the case of Picasso, a mature artist's work may deal in a more or less disguised way with emotionally charged memory-images from childhood.[12] Picasso pours into regressive forms, says Gombrich, "all the aggression and savagery that was pent up in him," in the symbolic "smashing" of objects by cubism. (Cf. the Demoiselles d'Avignon). Such individual regressive impulses may find a sounding-board in the public demand of the time. The stage had been set, Gombrich adds, by a series of "regressive" moves in European painting since the impressionists: notably in the use of loud, bright colors which had been banned as too crude and primitive. The imagery of Van Gogh and Gauguin, says Gombrich, was "crudely and aggressively regressive."

Since Goethe, romantic art has often been called "sick art." Recent writers have taken up the charge with added evidence from psychiatry and psychoanalysis. They find in late romantic art (e.g., in Baudelaire), expressions of sadism, masochism, and sexual inversion.[13] Similar diagnoses have been made of post-impressionism and abstract expressionism. It is easy to link such artistic regressiveness with psychopathic regression in the individual. Van Gogh's insanity is often used as evidence. No doubt psychological connections do exist. But we should not go too far in branding all art we do

[12] "Psychoanalysis and Art," in B. Nelson (ed.), *Freud and the Twentieth Century* (New York, 1957), pp. 186 ff., 204-5.
[13] Cf. Mario Praz, *The Romantic Agony* (London, 1933).

not like as psychopathic. Insanity in the artist does not prove that his art is insane.

Art of a classical or geometrical type may also have psychopathic origins and associations. It may be an overcompensation against destructive impulses. Some kinds of neurosis and psychosis manifest themselves in compulsive neatness and orderliness. Some neurotic and psychotic art is tightly integrated, symmetrical, precise in technique.[14]

Though regressive art may have pathological associations, expressed in obvious or cryptic symbols, it is not necessarily harmful or unhealthy. Unlike the catastrophic, involuntary type of regression, it is usually content with a symbolic gesture of destruction or rejection toward the world. It may serve a therapeutic purpose for the artist and society through this symbolic release. It may serve as a warning signal of real social maladjustment, thus arousing efforts at reform even though the artist's attitude is wholly negative. We must not assume that portrayal of ignoble, frustrated characters in literature and drama, or expression of negative, destructive feelings in abstract art, will necessarily tend to produce the same kind of feeling or character in the observer. The effects may be quite opposite. Also, it should not be assumed, along Marxist lines, that negative art is the expression of a decadent, capitalistic civilization. That remains to be seen. The frustrated, negative tone of much contemporary art may change with changing international conditions and give way to a new, constructive phase. The encouragement of subjective expressionism by the individual artist, a continuation of "art-for-art's-sake" romanticism, may again liberate valuable psychological ingredients for a new, complex artistic development. Apparently formless, confused, and disintegrated expressions may once more prove to be only the rudiments of a new, flexible type of form—perhaps with added temporal development through the film or other suitable media.

Symbols of violent emotion, positive or negative, have a way of losing their emotive force with the passage of time. The objects toward which the feeling was originally directed cease to move later generations as strongly; they take on the pathos of distance, as in Wordsworth's "old, unhappy far-off things, and battles long ago." No doubt we experience much less pity and terror than the Greeks did from the tragedies of Oedipus, Orestes, and Medea. We tend to regard them in a more detached, aesthetic way. Images which suggested violence and hate to the artist and his generation may assume a very different quality a few years later. Thus Van Gogh's *Night Café*, whose coloring he is said to have felt as evil, now seems agreeably decorative to many observers. Dissonances which would have shocked a thirteenth-century listener now provide a pleasant contrast, like seasoning in food. *Frankenstein*, Poe's tales of horror, and similar fantasies have come to seem only mildly thrilling. Thus the most negative attitudes in art, however hostile in intent to evolution and progress, are soon toned down, absorbed, and gently fitted into the total development of art along with their hated adversaries. However hostile to tradition, they themselves become a part of it.

6. SYNTHETIC EVOLUTION IN ART AND CULTURE

We have accepted the idea of *complication*, or differentiation and integration, as a basic meaning of "evolution." We have asked whether this process occurs in the arts, and if so to what extent. The answer was "yes." It occurs on a large scale over long periods of time; from the origins of art until the present. But evolution in this sense is not the only major trend in art history: we have seen contrary, simplifying trends of considerable magnitude, and other movements hard to estimate as to change in total complexity.

As to the history of art in general, we have found no reason to doubt that it has been, on the

[14] *Cf.* C. G. Jung, *Symbols of Transformation* (New York, 1956); Margaret Naumburg, *Psychoneurotic Art* (New York, 1953).

whole, predominantly complicative or evolutionary. As including the sum total of skills, products, institutions, ideas, and attitudes concerned with the arts, it now forms a cultural heritage of tremendous magnitude and differentiation. It is loosely and partially organized in theory and practice; increasingly so on a world scale as main traditions and human contacts merge.

As to particular works of art, the products of advanced civilizations are, on the whole, far more complex than anything achieved by prehistoric cultures. On the other hand, the art of modern centuries includes extremely simple forms and others on all intermediate levels of complexity. In this respect as in many others, the evolution of art is analogous to that of animals and plants. Many persistent types have evolved a certain distance, then stopped; a few have then regressed toward greater simplicity.

The evolution of art, like the total cultural evolution of which it is a part, contains many smaller movements, trends, and sequences which historians describe in detail. It is necessary to distinguish in theory between these processes, though they actually interpenetrate. The evolution of art as a whole is the evolution of one cultural component among others such as religion, science, and social organization. It is a compound or composite evolution in relation to the many component processes which make it up: the evolutions of the various arts, national schools and traditions of art; also of the persistent types of art (such as the chair and portrait) and of particular styles and stylistic traditions.

In the evolution of a certain style, such as gothic architecture or baroque polyphonic music, one can trace that of various subcomponents such as interior vaulting and exterior sculpture in the cathedral; of harmony, counterpoint, and instrumentation in music. These can be described as component stylistic sequences and trends. Some are evolutionary in the sense of increasing complexity, and thus form component stylistic evolutions; some are simplifying or devolutionary.

Many large sequences, such as that of European pictorial style from 1300 to the present, contain both evolutionary and devolutionary trends or phases.

Of the simplifying trends and movements, many contribute indirectly to the total, complicative growth of art. Some tend to correct or prune away hypertrophies: types and styles of art which now seem burdensome, oppressive, and tedious. They clear the way for new developments. Even those which consciously oppose the main process of evolution as a whole, and try to reject all art up to date, tend to be accepted by posterity as one more kind of art, one more style, ideology, or possible mode of production added to the total cultural heritage. However antithetical or violently hostile they may feel themselves at the time, posterity tends to feel them as less so. Later artists can use them as alternative styles to be practiced at will, or as mere contrasting themes in a complex form. Thus Goethe used the symbols of romanticism and classicism in *Faust*. Simple songs can be introduced in complex dramas such as Shakespeare's *Twelfth Night*. The values of simplicity in particular works can thus be combined with those of complexity; there is no irreconcilable antagonism between them. The world of art embraces both and tries to synthesize them cumulatively.

The total process of art history, and that of each particular art, can be described from this point of view as a *synthetic evolution*, in the sense that it includes and loosely reintegrates a great number of divergent trends. It combines many minor, more or less antithetical sequences in style, some of which are evolutionary while others are devolutionary. The whole process can be called "evolutionary" on the whole, only as long as the complicative, developmental trend appears to dominate; in future it may become a synthetic devolution, with complicative trends in the minority.

One distinctive trait of modern cultural evolution is the greater multiplicity of elements in each great national and ideological synthesis, together with greater freedom for each to express itself; to make itself felt in the total pattern. Ancient

Egypt, like many tribal and early empire societies, was simpler and more rigid. It showed less pulsation, less give and take between rival pressures in art, religion, and government. Innovations and unorthodox practices in art and elsewhere were sternly suppressed, as in the case of Ikhnaton. Throughout the rise and fall of many dynasties, including foreign conquests, Egypt's cultural continuity endured with impressive strength. But simple unity is increasingly hard to maintain in a world which has come to expect increasing freedom of thought, action, and artistic expression.

7. SUMMARY

This chapter has distinguished three recurrent types of major trend in art and other areas of culture which are to some extent regressive and devolutionary. One is catastrophic and deserves the Spencerian term "dissolution." The second is a voluntary regression to simpler, more primitive types of life and art. The third is romantic primitivism as expressed in the arts of complex, civilized societies. The last two may have constructive effects in helping to revive lost values of an earlier age.

The destruction and elimination of unwanted aspects of the old is a necessary part of all life and growth, as in bodily metabolism. It may destroy more values than it helps to create. But cultural evolution in a broad sense includes both a developmental, complicative phase and a simplifying, eliminative phase. When the latter dominates, the whole process tends to become devolutionary.

CHAPTER XIX

CUMULATIVE CHANGE IN ART
AND SCIENCE

I. IS SCIENCE CUMULATIVE,
ART NON-CUMULATIVE?
EXTREME AND MODERATE ANSWERS

An often-repeated argument against evolution in the arts, as noted in an early chapter of this book, is that art is constantly "beginning at the beginning" whereas science preserves and incorporates the discoveries of previous generations. Science accumulates and develops through the ages, it is said, while art is essentially non-cumulative. This argument does not deny all cultural evolution, and some of those who advance it agree that evolution occurs in cultural fields outside the arts.

As fully stated in extreme form, the argument includes six alleged contrasts between art and science, all said to be fundamental and permanent. First, art has to keep "beginning anew" or "going back to the starting-point," whereas science does not. Second, art does not retain and incorporate previous achievements as it goes along. Each work and style of art is a completely new creation in itself, whereas science does incorporate its discoveries progressively. Third, works of art do not become obsolete; they retain their value indefinitely, whereas works of science (such as textbooks) have to be constantly replaced as new discoveries supersede them. Fourth, the methods of art are radically different from those of science; they are emotional, imaginative, subjective, and non-rational, whereas those of science are logical, ob-

jective, and rational. To these it is sometimes added, fifth, that art deals with values while science deals with reality or fact; sixth, that art deals in particulars while science deals in generalities or universals.

These assertions merit careful answer by the evolutionist. They have been repeated so often as to be widely taken for granted, with little attempt to analyze and check them with the evidence. If true, they would force us to conclude that evolution in art has never occurred and never can occur, since art is by its very nature non-developmental: a mere succession of discontinuous starts and stops or independent cycles.

Our thesis in this chapter is that all these alleged contrasts, and the whole sharp dichotomy between art and science, are greatly exaggerated. Each contains a small element of truth in referring to certain actual differences in degree. These are not basic or permanent, and are gradually diminishing. They constitute no fundamental obstacle to the evolution of art or disproof of its reality. The theory of evolution does not imply that art has been steadily cumulative from the first, always and everywhere, or that it is so now. It does insist that there is nothing in the nature of art to prevent it from developing cumulatively; if not now, then in future. In addition, it maintains that art has done so to some extent in the past. To refute the absolute antithesis, one need only point to a few examples of artistic accumulation.

In its most extreme form, this argument usually expresses a supernaturalist world-view. It proceeds from the idealistic tradition—from Plato by way of Kant—which we have observed at various stages of the discussion. It is closely related to the historicist belief that each artist and each work of art is unique and incomparable, a separate product of divine inspiration; also to that of romantic dualism, that art is purely spiritual and outside the physical struggle for survival.[1] Recently, the alleged antithesis has been most sharply stated by such supernaturalists as Aldous Huxley. We have already noted Huxley's statement that "Every artist begins at the beginning" while "The man of science, on the other hand, begins where his predecessor left off." To this he adds that works of science become obsolete while works of art do not. "To find out about electricity we read contemporary scientists, not Faraday; but a work of art such as *Macbeth* is not replaced or rendered obsolete." Some recent scientists have also repeated this familiar statement. "Scientific activities," said George Sarton, "are the only ones which are cumulative and progressive."[2]

Social and cultural scientists appear, however, to be less sure than physical scientists that science is the only cumulative part of culture. Margaret Mead, anthropologist, writes that "it seems necessary to discard the distinction once made between the cumulative character of technology and the noncumulative character of other aspects of human culture."[3] In any culture, she thinks, certain aspects may be non-cumulative because of failure to recognize them or to develop adequate techniques for transmission, so that a direct apprenticeship relation may be the only form of cultural transmission. The arts are not the only cultural components for which cumulative techniques have been slow to develop. Any part of culture is potentially cumulative. The "elaboration of ornamentation," including patterned movement, sound, and decoration of bodily surfaces and artifacts, is an "irreversible gain" according to this author. The arts, says Mead, are among the kinds

of cultural pattern which would be maintained and reinstated if only a small group of adult humans survived a holocaust.

A. L. Kroeber's comments on this question are especially noteworthy. He began by repeating the traditional antithesis, but went on to modify it considerably in his later years. We have noted his quasi-cyclical theory that high productivity in art and science comes in intermittent bursts or pulses. In each of the intermittent periods, he said, each art "very largely has to begin all over again, whereas each of the intermittent periods of discovery in science can begin, and generally does begin, just about where the last one left off."[4] Science and technology, he continued, are accumulative by nature, while philosophy, religion, art, empire, and nationalism are substitutive: a new product replaces the old one. A pulley or water wheel, geometry and the laws of the lever, are not wholly forgotten or abandoned even in times of destruction. In 1957 he still saw "considerable truth" in the idea that "the great arts soon wither away and have to begin all over again."[5] Utilitarian knowledge and invention, concerned with subsistence and survival, must "face reality", whereas the fine arts "face values, not reality, and do not grow cumulatively; or at least they have not generally grown cumulatively

---

[1] See the quotations above from Kant, Gautier, and Caird.
[2] *The Life of Science* (1941, 1948); quoted by R. B. Perry in *Realms of Value* (Cambridge, Mass., 1954), p. 308. See also J. B. Conant, *On Understanding Science* (New Haven, Conn., 1947), p. 20.
[3] "Cultural Determinants of Behavior," in Roe and Simpson, *Behavior and Evolution*, pp. 490, 485, 492. See also C. H. Cooley, "Art, Science, and Sociology," in *The Making of Society*, ed. by V. F. Calverton (New York, 1937), p. 725. The alleged gulf between art and science, he declares, on the ground that the sciences are cumulative while the arts "bloom and die like flowers," is not so sharp as commonly supposed. Each art has a related science, and each science has related arts. There is much in common in their processes of thought. The *Dictionary of Sociology* (New York, 1944), p. 110, does not limit "cumulative evolution" to science. It is "the resultant growth, modification, and development of associated and related aspects of society, whose combined changes terminate in a general effect."
[4] *Anthropology* (New York, 1923, 1948), p. 303.
[5] *Style and Civilizations*, pp. 36, 61 ff.

through their recorded history."[6] "They mostly borrow but little from the arts of other civilizations. Some accumulation may take place, but it is not a typical or conspicuous process in art history generally."

While thus holding to part of the traditional antithesis, Kroeber modified it significantly in other respects. It is only the utilitarian, practical phase of science that grows cumulatively, he conceded in 1957. The history of pure science is much like that of fine art. When its aim is understanding rather than utility or profit, "the course of science runs much like that of the arts." It comes in bursts, each dedicated to a particular set of problems, and when these have been solved by the methods available the science slackens until a new orientation, a new set of important problems, is discovered. Then the front of creative activity in science "runs its own course anew." Fundamental or pure science thus progresses "in not too different a way from development in the arts." Applied science develops in a more even, less pulsating course than does pure science. The latter, as in Greece, is often unaccompanied by much technological progress. In modern times, however, pure science has tended to progress "more uniformly and steadily," perhaps because of its massive organization and success.

More significantly still, Kroeber finally conceded that the arts might do so too. "There are indications that a similar change is impending in the visual arts, and possibly in music; but is being delayed in literature by language diversities."[7] He did not amplify this important statement, which brought him close to recognizing explicitly that the arts evolve. If they have already shown some cumulative change, and may do so more uniformly and steadily in the near future, if science is not always cumulative but only so in recent years and in its pure, creative phase, then what is left of the old antithesis? No permanent, absolute difference in this respect remains, but only a time lag in art and pure science because of their lesser urgency from a practical standpoint. In the past there has

been less motivation for preserving and developing these less urgent skills, and hence less continuity in their growth from one culture to another. Art is no longer off by itself as the sole exception to cultural evolution. The behavior of styles in fine art, Kroeber concluded, is quite similar to that of movements in philosophy, scholarship, mathematics, and pure or fundamental science. "Intellectual creativity and aesthetic creativity behave alike historically."

Kroeber was right on the whole in his final statement of the facts: there is no absolute contrast between art and science in respect to their evolutionary growth, but only a difference of degree which is gradually being overcome. One must agree with him that pure science has not, until recent centuries, been as cumulative and continuous as utilitarian technology; also that art, though still far less so, is at last becoming more cumulative and may tend to develop further in this direction. Kroeber did not go far enough, however, in perceiving the cumulative aspects of art history in the past. He overemphasized the "intermittent bursts" of creativity and underestimated the extent to which achievements are passed on from one creative epoch to another. He did not sufficiently realize the factors in common between art and science, which invalidate any sharp dichotomy between them and suggest that both may develop along more similar lines in future.

Even today, science and philosophy are not as steadily cumulative as they might be. Wars and disasters, revolutions and new controlling ideologies, all tend to break the continuity and redirect workers into different paths. There is often more continuity in applied science, where practical needs stimulate maximum effort, than in pure science, where it depends more on the love of intellectual

---

[6] This is another exaggerated antithesis: the fine arts often face what people consider to be reality at the time, and their conception of it often agrees with the scientific conception of the time. Attempts at utilitarian control are likewise based at times on a false conception of reality, as in magic and primitive religion.

[7] *Ibid.*, p. 152.

discovery. In philosophy, the cumulative process is even more uncertain; often subject to social and religious pressures, and (like art) lacking accepted, reliable criteria of validity. Santayana mentions, in an essay on "The Progress of Philosophy,"[8] how unsteady this progress is. Modern philosophers, he says, tend to split apart the heritage of philosophy and specialize on narrow problems, instead of trying to synthesize progressively. Since his time, philosophy has become even more specialized along semantic and linguistic lines, often ignoring its traditional problems. Scientists, too, can be so much preoccupied with urgent contemporary problems as to ignore past achievements in their field. It is rather the historian of science or philosophy who carefully combs through old documents to find neglected insights of permanent value. Textbook writers summarize what seems fundamental for the student today, but needs and opinions change on this question. Last year's textbooks are sometimes put aside, not because their ideas are all permanently superseded, but because of a temporary change in interest and emphasis among writers and teachers.

2. CUMULATIVE PHASES IN ARTISTIC CHANGE

Authors who say that art is non-cumulative seldom specify exactly what aspects of art history they have in mind. Sometimes they refer to particular works of art, such as *Macbeth*, or artists such as Homer; sometimes to the whole course of past art as compared with that of sience; sometimes to particular styles or bursts of creativity in different places. But all of these have cumulative aspects.

Art as a whole—the sum total of man's artistic products—is obviously cumulative in a simple, literal sense. "Cumulative," says Webster's *Dictionary*, means "formed or becoming larger by successive additions." In this sense, art is cumulative now, and has been so throughout the history

of civilization. The term in this sense does not require that such additions be linked together as an organic whole. No one can deny that works of art have been accumulating for thousands of years: the mere multiplication of paintings, statues, churches, poems, and symphonies would suffice to make art "cumulative" in this respect. In addition, new materials, tools, technics, and media for the arts have been invented by the thousand during the past five millennia.

In neither art nor science has the accumulation been a mere disorderly piling up of unrelated products. Experts in the arts have been at work for centuries, classifying and arranging both old and modern works, evaluating, interpreting, and managing them; the results are stored and actively used in museums and libraries, theaters, schools, films, and phonograph record collections. In short, the world's total heritage of art has developed in a cumulative way, as has that of science. Though less organized than science, it is partly and increasingly so. The myriad styles and traditions which make it up are being socially reorganized as they pour into one reservoir of world art.

This, however, is not all that is meant by calling science "cumulative" and art the opposite. A more important meaning is that works of science at any one time tend to preserve and incorporate what is considered best in the achievements of previous generations, while works of art do not.

One half of this antithesis is undeniable: science is now highly cumulative. In this respect, it is analogous to the growth of an individual organism, and to the evolution of life. The man retains and develops the bony and muscular structure, the nervous system of the child; the higher vertebrates have retained and developed the spinal cord, the digestive, respiratory, and other systems which were gradually evolved by their ancestral species. A treatise on physics incorporates what is considered most true and important in previous treatises on the subject, including the methods of in-

[8] In *Soliloquies in England and Later Soliloquies* (New York, 1922), p. 49.

vestigation and the general organization of ideas. Even a concrete product of applied science, such as a machine, is often a selective epitome of past inventions along the same line. In the modern dynamo, an electrical engineer can point out features derived from earlier, cruder dynamos and from the simple induction coils and electro-magnets which preceded them. Science as a whole, as a body of knowledge and of technics for con-trolling nature, develops continuously through preserving past, verified discoveries, eliminating errors, adding new knowledge and theory, revis-ing and reorganizing the whole, and transmitting it to the next generation.

The other half of the antithesis melts away on close inspection. As we have already seen, artistic styles and traditions are also cumulative, though to a less extent. The "beginning anew" is only partial and occasional. Baroque style in visual art, music, and literature preserved and incorporated what the age found best and most congenial in the classical tradition up to the time. It merged this inheritance with new developments. To be sure, some traits of baroque style have been abandoned (for a time at least) by later artists. But the same can be said of baroque science. Modern scientists now tend to reject the *a priori*, deductive absolutism which kept so long a hold on European science.

The main difference is that tastes in art, including what is best in previous styles, are constantly changing. We have not yet found a permanent set of standards in art for what to preserve and what to reject, whereas we have (or think we have) found one in science. But later generations of scientists may not agree with us entirely on this point.

As to an individual artist, it can always be said that his early life is cumulative mentally. He learns, grows, experiences nature, art, and people, inter-acts with his environment, experiments in differ-ent styles and media, gradually "finds himself" in deciding on what he wants most of all to say and make. In maturity he selects and organizes elements from these into a new synthesis. Early

insights and achievements are, in varying degree, preserved and incorporated in his mature products. Hence these products can be said to "express" his personality; not the whole of it in any one work or perhaps in all of them, but important parts of it which have been a long time growing. *Macbeth* or *The Tempest* is in this sense a cumulative work of Shakespeare, containing a quintessence or se-lective residue from his previous growth as an artist up to that point. However sudden and detached a particular flash of inspiration may be, as if out of a clear sky, the finished work will include psychological materials drawn from the storehouse of the artist's life experience.

The detailed conception of the work of art develops gradually in his mind. Its execution deve-lops on his paper or canvas, through minutes, hours, or years. In some cases, a series of sketches or preliminary rough drafts has been preserved, lead-ing up to a form which the artist regarded as finished. More and more ideas may have been incorporated along the way. In other cases the opposite occurs, as in certain series by Matisse (paintings of a girl with embroidered blouse) and Picasso (drawings of a bull). The first type is more definitely cumulative; the second is in a way eliminative, as unwanted details are left out. But both involve a cumulative power to select, reject, and reorganize. In later years, the artist may aban-don so many of his previous interests and specialize on so few effects that the creative process now seems to be largely one of elimination, of free-ing oneself from excess baggage. This phase can be called de-cumulative or dispersive; but again it implies a previous accumulation. In time, if the artist keeps on living, he will undergo a more fundamental loss or dissolution of what he had learned.

Each artist also builds on the work of previous artists, whether he realizes it or not. Thus each art, each style, and each sequence of styles is cumulative to some extent. Unlike scientists, many artists do not consciously and intentionally build on past achievements, and they often like to think of themselves as completely original. In this they have been encouraged by false aesthetic theories. To the expert observer, there is no such thing as a completely original artist or work of art. All mature artists have been influenced by the past and present works of art about them, whether great and serious or popular and trivial. The connoisseur of music can detect much of Bach and Handel in Haydn and Mozart; much of all these in Beethoven, Chopin, and Brahms. To the connoisseur of painting there is much of Tintoretto and of late Byzantine painting in El Greco; there is much of Giorgione and Titian in Tintoretto; there is much of Giotto and Masaccio in Raphael and Leonardo. Traits of the Sung Chinese landscape tradition persist in later Chinese and Japanese landscape painting. Of course, something new is added; the style as a whole is different, but elements of past achievement remain. This does not mean that a style always develops in descending from one artist or period to a later one. On the whole, Rubens' style was attenuated in Van Dyck, although some personal traits were added. Much the same can be said of any art. Even when leading artists try consciously to "break with the past," they usually find themselves reviving some remoter style or tradition, such as that of African or Polynesian sculpture. Sometimes they do so consciously and purposely; sometimes they incorporate vague, unconscious memories of something seen, heard, or read long ago.

The cumulative character of a modern building is evident, not only in its functional and engineering features, its understanding of the properties of materials, the necessary conveniences for a building of a certain kind, but in the aesthetic form and style itself, whether ornate or bare and geometrical as a machine. The cumulative character of a poem such as the *Divine Comedy* or the *Canterbury Tales* is not, as the anti-evolutionists maintain, a matter of "superficial technique" alone. It extends to all the ideas and feelings expressed; to the form and style of the whole. The debt is not only to previous works in the same language or medium, or

only to previous art. Michelangelo is indebted to Greek and Hebrew religion, philosophy, and literature, as well as to previous Italian painters. Dante is indebted to the Ptolemaic system of astronomy as well as to Virgil's *Aeneid* and to contemporary Tuscan verse.

We have seen how such indebtedness is brushed aside by anti-evolutionists as "merely superficial and external"—mere "accessories," "machinery," and "stage properties," as Caird put it. The essential "soul of art," they insist, is quite different, "independent of tradition and education, it comes as an inspiration on elected souls fresh from the eternal fount of light," and so on.

This type of argument is impossible to refute by empirical evidence. It can always have the last word, for any and every namable quality, form, idea, feeling, meaning, or attitude in art which can be shown as culturally transmitted is immediately set aside as "non-essential," while the "soul of art" still hides untouched within the work of true genius. It is always something else, unique and ineffable, a *je ne sais quoi* eluding all analysis, discernable only to persons of superior taste. If confronted with a work which seems deeply influenced by accumulated culture, one can even brush the whole of it aside as "non-art" or, in Tolstoy's words, mere "counterfeit art." The whole question, including the definition of "art," is thus shifted to a level of dogmatic and personal evaluation where no objective discussion is possible.

Art history contains many breaks and discontinuities. If one looks only at these, art will appear less cumulative. All the arts, and many sciences as well, did have to "begin over" to a large extent, in western Europe after the fall of Rome and the centuries of insecurity. Such breaks in art were due in large part to breaks in social, economic, and political organization; to the large-scale disruption of society as a whole in a certain area. When the disruption is smaller and briefer, when the new owners and rulers are similar in racial and cultural background, they can pick up the pieces and continue the arts with these as models, especially if a few craftsmen survive. The archeology of the Near East discloses innumerable destructions of cities, layer upon layer, with the probable slaughter or enslavement of most of the population. But many durable artifacts such as stone and ivory carvings survived in the rubble or were carried off as plunder, there to exert a silent influence on the art of the conquerors. Hence there is considerable continuity of artistic tradition in the Mesopotamian and Syrian regions during the first three millennia B.C.

In Europe after the fall of Rome, artistic traditions were kept alive in the monasteries, and cultural importations from the Middle East began long before the fall of Constantinople in the fifteenth century. We do not know how much Giotto profited from earlier painting in the "Roman style," much of which (since lost) was extant in his day. (The armies of Charles V destroyed much ancient art in Rome in the sixteenth century). As the Renaissance progressed it profited more and more from classical art through translation, import, and excavation.

On the other hand, the rise of many national and period styles has been comparatively continuous, with much cumulative influence. Consider, for example, the spread of Buddhism and Buddhist art from India through China and eventually to Japan. In Wei and Kamakura Buddhist sculpture, the influence from one to another is apparent, along with the inevitable variations. Japanese art does not "begin at the beginning," but builds on Chinese foundations in almost every medium, as does Japanese Buddhism. Is it true, as Kroeber maintains, that each religion and philosophy, too, has to "begin all over again"? It would be hard to show this in the case of Buddhism, emerging from early Brahmanism, or of Christianity, emerging from Judaism. What medieval or modern philosophy, in the Western world, does not contain a large infusion of Socratic and Platonic theory? St. Thomas explicitly relies upon Aristotle. Santayana makes clear his indebtedness

to Lucretius, Plato, Spinoza, and Indian philosophy as well.

It is a common and commendable practice for scientists as well as philosophers to refer explicitly to earlier authorities in their fields, in part to acknowledge debts and in part to help the reader connect the present work with its antecedents; to see just what has been accepted from the past, and what rejected; to make it clear what the present writer claims to have added of his own. Sometimes, but less frequently, a composer writes at the start of a piece of music, "Hommage à Lully," "Variations on a Theme by Palestrina," or the equivalent. When the modern composer sets out to write in some older style and add a contemporary twist, the audience is thus helped to realize that (a) the partial imitation is intentional and frank, not a surreptitious or unconscious plagiarism; and (b) that the claim to originality lies in certain alterations—for example, modern dissonance and polytonality in harmonizing an eighteenth-century theme. His attention is thus directed to significant relations between past and present, and his appreciation aided. To be sure, one's debt to the past can never be fully acknowledged; a learned artist like Stravinsky, Picasso, or James Joyce would have to list almost the whole history of his art. But if at least the more notable, specific debts are acknowledged, the public can be helped to perceive what some historians and philosophers miss: the prevailing, widespread continuity of artistic evolution.

The cumulative nature of scientific invention is well illustrated by the problems confronting the Patent Office. A modern, highly developed machine such as an automobile is not invented all at once, but gradually, perhaps through many generations. One or more basic patents are issued for an early form of it: e.g., for a combustion engine and a device for transmission of power to a wheeled carriage. (Even this idea was probably not entirely new, but developed from older types of engine and carriage, perhaps never patented. Hero of Alexandria constructed a steam engine, and probably others before him.) After the first patent, an indefinite number of others may be issued, year after year, for improvements in the basic mechanism and for added appliances such as the self-starter and windshield-wiper. The modern automobile is a selective epitome of many such contributions.

In the arts, analogous problems are raised in the nature of copyrights, as well as of patents for technical instruments and processes. The latter, as in the motion picture camera, are works of applied science in addition to being artistic in aim. But the problem of copyrights for literature and music is more distinctively artistic. In the vast majority of cases, where no great stakes of money or fame are involved, it is never raised. In a work of painting or sculpture, some critic may point out a debt or derivation from a previous artist; but the case seldom comes to court. More and more, however, high financial stakes are involved in best-selling plays and novels; in musical shows, radio, and television productions. Taking an idea for a story, an incident, a joke, or a tune from some other work and dressing it up with slight variations as an original creation will not always pass unchallenged. The case may come to court, and it will be up to a judge and jury, perhaps unversed in art, to decide just how much of work A has been taken over into work B; how much it has been altered "creatively," and whether the material taken was really original with A's reputed author. Perhaps he took it from someone else, or from the vast public domain of art history; from works never copyrighted, or on which the copyright has now expired. Laws and jurisprudence in the realm of art are less highly developed than in scientific technology, and it is harder to decide there on questions of originality. But in general it is obvious that older works of art are constantly being ransacked for ideas to be altered, combined with others, and included in newer ones.

On the whole, the history of art constantly involves accumulation from the past, of ideas and skills, forms and styles, ends, means, tastes, and standards of value. When an individual artist produces a work of art, he necessarily accepts and incorporates some of this traditional accumulation. But at the same time he often feels it as an oppressive burden. "Tradition" may seem to him as a hateful, dead weight of authority and custom which hampers his original genius, and from which he wants to escape completely. In the desire to sharpen up this particular work of art, so that its message or impact will be as forceful and unimpeded as possible, he is highly conscious of rejecting and avoiding certain traditional practices; more so than of those he retains. Such a conscious emphasis on elimination or decumulation, as opposed to accumulation, is especially characteristic of regressive, primitivistic movements in art, where the artist feels himself as rejecting modern civilization and recent, civilized art as a whole. In reviving some earlier style, he is accepting some previous accumulation of world art, recently neglected.

Neither in art nor in science can any single product or style epitomize the whole of previous evolution. In both realms, cumulative change has diverged along many different lines. Intensive development along any one line is necessarily selective and exclusive, crowding out other potential developments whose seeds were present in the previous, less differentiated form. This is true of organic evolution, whose cumulative nature is widely recognized. After the early stage of marine life some living strains took to the land, others to the air, while still others stayed in the sea. Each abandoned some of its marine heritage while substituting another line of evolution. The ancestors of birds, in developing avian traits, had to give up some reptilian ones. A modern bird does not epitomize the mammalian line of development or vice versa, though both have some traits in common. The human embryo, in its prenatal growth, develops temporary traits reminiscent of its prehuman ancestry, but rapidly discards them in its rigidly determined progress toward the infant human type. In other words, organic evolution is cumulative only to a limited extent and along selected lines.

The same is true of evolution in art and science. One would not expect a treatise on chemistry to include all that is in a treatise on psychology, or vice versa. A dynamo is the result of cumulative invention along one line; a vaccine against poliomyelitis, along another. At the same time, there are overlappings: the vaccine and the psychological text profit implicitly, directly or indirectly, from what is known about chemistry. This is one world, and all its factors interact, though some more directly and obviously than others. By the same token, one would not expect a modern symphony to epitomize the development of drama, or a painting that of orchestral music. Each has evolved along somewhat different lines, and is cumulative mainly with respect to its own ancestral strain. Nevertheless, each art has contributed to the others.

3. PARTICULAR WORKS OF ART
AS MORE OR LESS CUMULATIVE.
HEAVY-LADEN CULTURE-CARRIERS

As in scientific invention, so in art, some products are more richly and elaborately cumulative than others. The great astronomical observatory at Palomar is a concentrated summary and application of much of the physical and mathematical science of its day. The *Odyssey*, the *Mahabharata*, the *Divine Comedy*, Chartres cathedral, Wagner's *Ring* cycle, Tolstoy's *War and Peace*—each of these is not only complex but an epitome, a symbolic résumé, of large areas in the culture which preceded and surrounded it. Michelangelo's Sistine frescoes symbolize a wide range of Greek, Hebrew, and Christian tradition. *Macbeth* embodies a good deal of Scottish history, legend, and witchcraft. Such a work is a *culture-carrier* in a way in which simpler or more specialized works of the same period are not. The same can be said of certain artists such as Leonardo and Goethe. It can be said of certain styles such as the baroque, by contrast (let us say) with the impressionist.

When successful, the man and his work are often regarded as "great," but distinctions of value are not necessarily implied. A highly specialized, simple work may be as good in a different way; a heavily laden culture-carrier may be dull, badly organized, or ineffective in other respects. The main distinction is objective: some works of art are so profusely endowed with different images, descriptions, references to persons, places, events, and customs, with diversified pictures and designs, or with a wide range of musical or dramatic effects, that the beholder can learn a great deal from them about the whole culture in which they were produced; about previous works of art in this and other media; about past moral and emotional attitudes, ideals, beliefs, and traditions. All this can most easily be made explicit in literature and other arts involving verbal text; but some of it can be symbolized in the visual arts and, to a less extent, in music. An old but living city such as Rome or Kyoto is an epitome of many traditions and many stages in each, including both visual forms and their associated meanings.

For art to be cumulative, its products do not have to be complex. The accumulation may consist of growing skill, experience, and knowledge in the minds of artists and the public. It may consist in knowing what to omit and avoid, what is unnecessary and superfluous from a functional or aesthetic standpoint, or both. Elimination can be as important as addition: for example, in pruning away dust-catching ornaments from furniture and architecture; in omitting high-flown, artificial figures of speech from poetry and drama. What will seem superfluous depends in part on changing tastes and conditions; but throughout such change in taste and style there develops a growing awareness of specific causal relations in the realm of art; of what artistic devices will probably succeed in producing a certain desired effect under given circumstances, and what will tend to frustrate it.

The sketch of a flower by Leonardo, a plain porcelain bowl of the Sung period in China, a short Japanese poem of the *Haiku* type, a lyric by Heine or Verlaine, a song by Schubert—these, however perfect in their way, are not explicitly and heavily loaded with diversified cultural references. They are highly evolved in being highly "definite," in the Spencerian sense. An expert can point out how, in each case, the work involves and suggests to the initiated mind a certain context of advanced civilization. Long, cumulative social experience was required to teach the artist how to create so simply and surely in just this highly specialized way, with no superfluous details. As a "flower in the crannied wall" results from, and therefore signifies to the botanist, the whole previous history of its evolution, so the tiny Leonardo sketch implies, in a figurative sense, all previous Western art and science. But here we are reading into the sketch a great deal of cultural context which it does not explicitly state, represent, or symbolize. The cumulative process does not always show itself in highly cumulative, particular products.

By the same token, it can be said that some cultures, and some great traditions in the arts, are more syncretistic, more replete with accumulations from varied sources in the past, than others. All the advanced, urban-industrial civilizations of the present day are so, by contrast with the more isolated, tribal and village cultures which most anthropologists prefer to study. The modern Mayans of Yucatan have forgotten much of their ancestral culture; the meaning of symbols, the astronomical lore, and the like. They have absorbed some of the simpler features of Spanish Catholic culture; of Western mechanization and democratic institutions. But on the whole their present culture includes a much smaller sampling of world culture, past and present, foreign and domestic, than does that of modern England or Japan. Western civilization has for many centuries been absorbing Far Eastern elements, such as the art of silk manufacture in the early Roman Empire. Nineteenth-century European and American philosophers were much impressed by oriental thought. Our music has absorbed certain features of the Arabian and African Negro traditions; our painting and sculpture are indebted to the Negro, the Mayan, the Polynesian, the Near East and the Far East, as in the works of Gauguin, Matisse, Picasso, Modigliani, and Henry Moore. Our architecture, as in Frank Lloyd Wright, is indebted to Mayan and Japanese sources. In short, Western art as a whole and each particular art, including those as recent as the film, is richly and diversely cumulative. This does not and can not appear completely in any one artist or work of art; but particular aspects of it appear in different ones. Some appear, for example, in the exotic tales of Pierre Loti, Rudyard Kipling, and Joseph Conrad, portraying exotic life; some in Debussy's use of the whole-tone and pentatonic scales; some in the erudite allusions of Ezra Pound and T. S. Eliot.

On the other hand, the very diversity of Western art, its partial absorption of so many exotic traditions, makes it possible for Western artists to differ radically from each other, and even to adopt radically different styles at different times, as Picasso has often done. Without going outside the limits of the expanded Western tradition as a whole, they can choose to follow, now the archaic Greek style of the black-figured vase, now that of the Celtic or Carolingian miniature. They can retell the Arabian tale of Sinbad the Sailor (descending from Egyptian and Indian sources) or combine a Gregorian mode with tribal rhythms. Whether all this borrowing results in a hodge-podge or a genuine synthesis depends on the ability of the artist. For better or worse, it is going on. To the uninitiated, contemporary art seems as a result madly confused and heterogeneous, lacking any continuity of development or consistency of style. To the evolutionist, cumulative growth is evident on every hand, even though the elements have not fused into a single style.

4. OBSOLESCENCE IN ART AND SCIENCE. DEGREES OF CULTURAL VITALITY

By those who attack evolutionism in art, the idea of science as cumulative is associated with that of its rapid obsolescence. Science progresses so fast, they say, that any particular scientific treatise is soon superseded. This is increasingly true at present, although it was not true of early science. The other half of the antithesis is more questionable. Is it true that works of art do not go out of date? That a prehistoric love song, if we could hear one, would be as much alive now as when it was first uttered? This would be hard to prove. Works of art *can* become obsolete; some do so rapidly, some slowly. Their obsolescence is not as regular and universal as that of science, but again the difference is one of degree.

As we have seen, it is somewhat misleading to compare a work of art with a treatise on pure science. In the field of art, a treatise on aesthetics is more comparable to one on physics. Both depend for their validity on the accumulation of knowledge and theory; both become obsolete as the accumulation proceeds. The one on aesthetics does so more slowly because that subject is progressing slowly, being largely prescientific. In applied science, that which corresponds to a work of art is a concrete utilitarian device; a weapon, tool, or machine such as a spear, axe, or dynamo. An industrial process such as the smelting of silver corresponds in part with a ritual dance or other work of temporal art which can be repeated exactly or with variations an indefinite number of times. Some utilitarian devices go out of date quickly, especially the modern types which are steadily improved by science. Before the age of science, many utilitarian types remained basically unchanged for centuries: for example, the spindle and distaff, the plow, the yoke, the bowl, the knife, the cloak. Some ancient works of art can satisfy perennial aesthetic tastes almost as well today as when they were first made. This is true of the *Odyssey* and *Oedipus*. If not valued for the same reasons, as in the Lascaux paintings, they are valued for something else. Other works of art have a wide appeal at first but lose it rapidly; they satisfy short-lived tastes and interests.

Changing fashions and fluctuations of taste occur not only in the popular arts of dress and dance music, but also in more serious arts. Impressionist painting is out of fashion as a style to be actively practiced, although people still like to look at impressionist works of the 1870's. Obsolescence, or the fact of being superseded by something else of a similar kind, is never an inherent characteristic in the product itself, either of art or of science. It is an expression of social attitudes and behavior toward the product. When a thing is considered obsolete, people cease using and prizing it; they put it aside, neglect and disparage it, perhaps destroy it to make way for the substitute.

In different periods and cultures, people act very differently toward their products in this respect: toward their own, and those of their ancestors. The cultures in which things become obsolete very slowly, if at all, are on the whole static, ultra-conservative cultures. Prehistoric cultures were more so, on the whole, than modern, urban ones. They were in the grip of rigid patterns of custom, from which they broke away slowly and often unwillingly and fearfully.

When a culture is very mobile, with a strong faith in the value and possibility of progress along certain lines, it tends to reject the old impatiently along those lines and to substitute eagerly something new which it considers superior. Different cultures act in this way toward different kinds of things; they are fickle and substitutive along different lines. Modern Western culture, especially in the United States, is so in regard to utilitarian inventions; not only minor gadgetry but major technics such as building, transportation, communication, mass production of food, clothes, and shelter, printing, medicine, and educational methods. Last year's automobiles, hats, and television sets become quickly obsolete, at least for typical, upper-and-middle-bracket citizens who can afford to keep up with the times. Always to possess the new model is a mark of status and prestige in many circles. The same citizens may be consciously and proudly conservative or reactionary in religious, political, or economic views and behavior, maintaining that what was good enough for their ancestors is good enough for them.

Eager adoption of the new entails ruthless discarding of the old. The old automobile or refrigerator goes to the scrapheap, perhaps after a period of use by less opulent citizens, and no tears are shed over it. The old textbook on physics may be sold second-hand for a while, or given to charity, but it will probably end before long as waste paper. There are notable exceptions in the case of inventors' first models and machines with publicized historical associations, such as Lindbergh's airplane. Some of these are carefully preserved and viewed with respect in the Smithsonian Institution. The public attitude toward them is not entirely unlike that toward old works of art. People respect the pioneer work as a step ahead for its time, even though it is now outmoded. They also like to dwell on something with glamorous associations, such as Napoleon's sword, the relic of a saint, or a statue of Joan of Arc. A manuscript or first edition of a famous book of science or literature may be similarly honored. Though obsolete in regard to its first and main functions, it takes on new social functions as an object of interested study. Even a treatise by Faraday is still important for a historian of science. An old invention may be instructive to the modern student or inventor.

In the aesthetic realm, we behave differently toward different arts and types of art. In many popular arts, obsolescence is almost as rapid as in automobiles. People, especially the young, want to see the latest films and musical shows, hear and dance to the latest tunes, read the latest novelists and see the latest newspaper comic strips. Older ones are quickly discarded, except when someone with an antiquarian turn of mind (perhaps a museum director) exhibits for a brief moment the popular arts of yesterday. Then they are greeted by the public with mixed feelings: mild admiration, perhaps, along with condescending amusement toward the quaintly ridiculous.

Is the new product better? Are all the values of the old preserved in the new? Opinions often differ in both art and science. There are technical developments in the contemporary film or automobile, not found in those of 1910. New scientific treatises usually have more solid grounds for claiming superiority, but the latest theory is not always confirmed. Promising medical "cures" and dietary regimes, backed by plausible evidence, are often discarded. In astronomy conflicting theories persist for centuries, such as those about the nature of light and the origin of the solar system. The consensus fluctuates between them.

In other ages, people acted toward certain types of art in much the same way that moderns act toward science and invention. They impatiently threw aside or destroyed the old to make room for the new. Sometimes this was done on religious grounds, as when the Christians after Constantine destroyed pagan temples, paintings, and statues, often using the stones for Christian churches. For similar reasons the Spanish conquerors destroyed Aztec and Mayan art. Sometimes it is done on more aesthetic grounds; much ancient and gothic art was destroyed in the Renaissance. Such ruthlessness toward past works of art is often shown in great, creative periods, as well as by others without that excuse. Artists and patrons are so confident of being able to make a better one tomorrow, that they destroy the old without a qualm. In arts where this attitude prevails, works of art become rapidly obsolete, for a time at least.

Whether they should be so, or are really so by higher standards, is often debatable. Tastes often change, and reverse themselves. Trained artisans are now busy scraping off the later frescoes in Italy and France, to reveal what remains of the earlier ones. Some historians, such as Spengler, maintain that a disposition to cherish and revere past works of art, as shown in filling art museums, is a sign of diminishing creativeness. From this standpoint it would appear that modern rapid obsolescence in science and invention is a sign of our creative exuberance there. The same might be said of our popular, secular arts, such as the film. On the contrary, our disposition to cherish certain old examples of religious art—temples, churches, paintings, carvings, stained glass—may be connected with the fact that we no longer actively produce much that is original in this field. Modern creative ability has turned into other channels.

Planned, rapid obsolescence is today a recognized policy in kinds of mass-produced, useful art, such as clothing and automobiles. It affects not only the structural and utilitarian aspects of the product, but the aesthetic also. Parts and materials are not made to last forever, but to wear out in a comparatively short time, so that the owner will want to buy a new one. A poorer man may use the old one for a while, but will have to pay increasing sums for repairs. Even while it is structurally usable, its appearance becomes obsolete. Extreme, ornate, or odd designs are made, so as to be the latest, fashionable mode one season and absurdly old-fashioned the next. So-called "classic", simple, timeless forms are often avoided, especially by youthful and fashion-conscious groups. In reaction some élite groups, such as students in aristocratic colleges, are conspicuously conservative in dress.

Rapid obsolescence is the negative side of an eager quest for novelty, originality, and progress. Both may be misguided, pursuing false values, but the process is an objective fact and a trait of modern Western culture. In the more serious "fine arts" for the élite, it is likewise manifested in a constant urge to be original; not to imitate any previous style or artist; not even to repeat one's own established style for fear of falling into a formula. As against this tendency, there is a frequent counter-pressure by the dealer and public to make the artist repeat a successful type of product as long as it is in vogue. It expresses the same desire for wide distribution that has led to cheap mass production and communication in other fields, and which is leading in painting and small sculpture to the manufacture of cheap but increasingly faithful reproductions. Also, there are always groups in the population with more conservative tastes. Some are middle-aged and anxious not to seem radical or faddish. Some are learned intellectuals and connoisseurs, who react against the popular taste for new fashions by ostentatiously condemning and ridiculing the new in their field, while praising some antique work of art or traditional belief. Certain violent denouncers of "modern art," devotees of oriental and medieval mysticism in art and philosophy, have a passion for the latest automobiles and mechanical gadgets. From this type of élite subgroup, ultraconservative in certain realms, there comes a strong denial of progress in art; strong insistence on the idea that past works of art do not become obsolete. They delight in exalting, as unexcelled masterpieces, little-known and difficult works which are not popular with the masses or even with the majority of learned critics. To be different, and to attract attention as original minds, they attack accepted old masters such as Shakespeare; revered historic styles such as late Greek sculpture.

There are various types and degrees of obsolescence in art, from the standpoint of social attitude and behavior. A work or style of art can be more or less alive, active and influential within a culture at any particular time. It is never equally so throughout the world, but is more active in certain groups, usually but not always the ones in which it originated. The great Indian epic, the *Mahabharata*, permeates Indian culture but is little known as a whole in the West. The present tendency, however, is for influential works in each culture to become more widely and rapidly known in others.

The highest level of cultural vitality for a style is to be actively practiced and produced by leading artists, the style leaders of the group. For a work of art, it is to be actively imitated or emulated;

not exactly copied, but followed in important respects, as were the paintings of Giotto and Masaccio in the early Renaissance in Italy. The Elizabethan style of drama, as exemplified by Marlowe and Shakespeare, was thus active in England in the late sixteenth and early seventeenth century. Louis XVI furniture was actively produced during the reign of that monarch in France, and Chippendale furniture in eighteenth-century England. Often a style does not reach its maximum influence until after the death of its originator. It is often impossible, at the time, to be sure which artists will have the most enduring influence; which styles are ephemeral fads and which are the main achievements of the period.

On the second, somewhat lower level of vitality are those styles which are still extensively produced, but not by the chief style leaders, whose interest has turned elsewhere. To this extent the Greek architectural orders are still alive, though less so in recent years. Neo-gothic churches, impressionist paintings, Louis XVI and Chippendale chairs, are still being made with original variations. Artists and critics of the avant-garde may consider them as out of date, "old hat," while they are still rising to a peak among the more conservative and provincial groups. Sometimes a style which seems *passé* is raised to the top level again by a great artist, as polyphonic music was by J. S. Bach.

On the third level of animation are those works and styles which are no longer produced in new examples to any considerable extent, but are still actively admired, published and read, performed, or conspicuously shown to an interested public at some cost of money, time, and energy. They are alive in appreciation but not in production. Reproductions without claim to originality, such as colorprints of old-master paintings and mechanical copies of Chippendale chairs, are made in increasing quantity. To this extent Homer, Phidias, Euripides, Dante, Shakespeare, Corneille, Racine, El Greco, Vivaldi, Beethoven, and a host of other great and minor masters are still strongly alive in our culture. Their styles are, at the present moment, not actively practiced by any considerable group or number of artists, and to this extent they are obsolete, as the horse-drawn chariot is obsolete. But, as objects of active study and admiration, they exert an influence on present art. To some extent the spirit of their genius pervades contemporary culture, and selected traits from their work can be discerned therein by expert analysis. Its unique, unduplicated features seem to contemporary taste so valuable that it is still actively preferred over later versions of the type to which it belongs. At any moment such a work or style may be "revived" as a mode of still more direct, thorough-going emulation, perhaps in some other medium. Thus women's fashions have recently drawn inspiration from Egyptian, Greek, and Roman sculpture and Italian painting.

The fourth level, still more obsolete, contains those artists, works, and styles which are known only to a few historians and other scholars. They have disappeared from the public consciousness, even as objects of perception. They are mentioned briefly in the larger histories of art. They are shown inconspicuously in side galleries of museums, and are liable to removal when the space is needed. They are not republished, performed, or recorded on phonograph records.

The fifth is the limbo of total oblivion, for those unfortunates that have been totally destroyed, buried, forgotten, or ignored. It is highly populated, perhaps by some of the greatest masters of all time.

In this mobile age when reputations are constantly being reappraised, none is certain of a permanent place on any one level. Forgotten works may be excavated or drawn into the spotlight by some influential critic. Former idols such as Tasso, Giulio Romano, Goldoni, the *Song of Roland*, and the *Romance of the Rose* sink into brief or lasting decline. "No one reads Byron today," it is said. The invention of the long-playing phonograph record has raised a large number of half-forgotten composers and their works from the fourth to the third level. Lost works of Schubert, Haydn, and Rembrandt have been discovered. Once properly made or recorded in lasting materials, art can live for centuries in a state of suspended animation, as did the Venus of Melos, waiting to exert its old charm on demand.

In this process of almost universal obsolescence, with occasional survivals and revivals, the social functions of a work of art often change considerably. It is preserved, admired, and perhaps imitated for different reasons from those which prevailed at its first appearance. In modern times there has been a wholesale reappraisal of past art on the basis of new standards, mainly those of aesthetic form and design. Prehistoric cave paintings, tribal masks and fetishes originally made for magical purposes, ancient and medieval religious painting and sculpture, have been reappraised as great on this more strictly aesthetic basis. The original claims to merit on magical, religious, moral, patriotic, or sentimental grounds have been largely brushed aside, with the consequent raising of some works from oblivion and the degradation of others. Many a damaged, faded old painting of some subject now devoid of interest, lacking even the aesthetic qualities to make it function (for most observers at least) as a stimulus to visual enjoyment, is now cherished in a museum largely for its historical importance; because it represented a step ahead for its time, or was made by a famous painter. Thus an "old master" may be assigned an honorable place on the third level of activity because his works have the power to appeal strongly in some way—perhaps a new way, unsuspected in his time—to the present generation of cultural leaders. What is called "greatness" is thus manifested as a power to arouse the admiration of cultural élites through many generations, perhaps in different ways and for different reasons.

Although some works of past art are preserved and respected, the vast majority of them obviously are not. Those who say that works of art do not become obsolete are thinking of a few—infinitesi-mally few—examples, which have been fortunate enough to survive destruction as well as changes of taste. Next to nothing remains of Greek mural painting of the classical period. How many songs, stories, poems, instrumental compositions, dances, jewels, costumes, dishes, and palaces are lost in proportion to each one that remains in the heritage of world art? Many were destroyed by accident or in waves of indiscriminate vandalism; many others were destroyed as obsolete, worthless, by art-lovers who preferred some new style. Our public libraries become crowded with old novels and magazines, many of which must be thrown away to clear the shelves. European libraries contain huge masses of manuscripts and old editions of forgotten works: grandiose epics, artificial lyrics, bombastic tragedies imitating some great writer. Unread by the public, they are known only to a few librarians and historians. Occasionally, a neglected masterpiece is found among them, but for the most part they are dead from the standpoint of cultural activity. They have been superseded by a few outstanding works which are accepted by experts and the public as containing all the essential values of their various types and periods.

Nothing could be more untrue, in the light of historical fact, than Aldous Huxley's statement that "The artist does not go out of date because he works with materials that do not change," and that "The instinctive, emotional side of man, being hereditary, remains the same." Art never deals only with the purely hereditary, relatively unchanging basis of human nature; always with cultural modifications of this basic, instinctive, and emotional nature. Art is itself an acquired alteration of instinctive tendencies. It expresses and appeals to the acquired attitudes and tastes of some cultural group, at some stage of social development. To do so is its life, while that cultural climate endures. When the climate changes, or the work or style of art is transported to a different one, the chances of its continued appeal are few; most of them perish. If one takes root and survives in other cultures, generation after generation, it is through appealing to some widespread, enduring, cultural modification of man's original instincts. All cultures are alike in some respects, different in others. Insofar as the work or style of art expresses and appeals to merely local or transitory cultural interests, it tends to die out elsewhere.

Modern Western civilization is extremely diversified in its interests, catholic in its tastes. To an unusual degree, it can understand and enjoy the products of exotic cultures, remote in place or time. The interest in tribal and far eastern visual arts, folklore, music, and dance (now available on films and records) is high and growing. But the taste for large doses of extremely exotic or primitive art is still confined to small sections of the intelligentsia. Many who exalt it in theory, perhaps above modern art, spend little time in actually observing it. Many prefer modernized, refined, abridged versions. The "prehistoric love-song," which Huxley thinks would still be moving, would probably not hold the attention of modern listeners very long. Authentic, original versions of primitive literature tend to be hard to understand, narrowly limited in content, and often tiringly repetitious, as in the endless genealogical records (like the "begats" of Biblical chronicle) and the monotonous exploits of folk heroes. Tribal music also tends to be highly repetitious, lacking temporal development, even where it has certain complex features, such as rhythmical drum-beats. Listening to it in an urban apartment, rather than dancing to its hypnotic rhythms while naked around some campfire, the civilized hearer soon loses interest. Masks and fetishes require less sustained attention as parts of an interior ensemble. One can easily enjoy them for their obvious decorative quality alone.

The power of a work or style of art to hold interest is not necessarily proportional to its nearness in time or place. One is surprised and delighted by the modernity of some ancient Egyptian writings, such as the "Song of the Harper." Certain Egyptian love-lyrics sound a perennial note of simple affection. But from these exceptional cases, featured in the anthologies, it is a mistake to generalize about all ancient and primitive art. Most translated Egyptian and cuneiform literature has little interest today except for specialized scholars, since it deals mainly with local and ephemeral concerns.

Contemporary critics deplore the popular tendency to enjoy and evaluate art for sentimental reasons; for personal associations with the piece itself—who owned it, and the like—and for the interest of the subject represented. The directly perceptible form, the mode of treatment, should be the sole basis for evaluation, they say. But it is a deeply rooted psychological tendency to be emotionally moved by the human associations of an object heard or seen, whether it is Napoleon's sword or a painting of the Madonna and Child. If we judged only the visible form, we would logically rate an ancient work of art no higher merely because it was ancient, or had glamorous historical associations. But as a matter of fact people are commonly moved by such associations. As a result an ancient work which has survived the centuries, or even one of grandmother's day, tends to become actually more powerful as an object of interest and enjoyment—and not only for the ignorant layman. Connoisseurs also are moved by such factors, more than they care to admit. The mere fact of being a relic of the memorable past thus tends to confer upon those fortunate, few works of art which have survived a new and growing social role. They become emotive images, charged with the pathos of distance, standing serenely in the rush and turmoil of mechanical civilization as symbols of a lost Golden Age of cultural youth. Upon them we project our idealistic fantasies of the past as happier, more beautiful, and more creative than the present. This in turn tends to make us magnify the greatness of ancient works of art, and deny the obsolescence of art in general.

Obsolescence in art and other human products is closely related to the processes of natural and artificial selection. What is culturally alive and functioning is what has been selected either by nature or by human planning; by accident or intention. What we call "obsolete" is what we tend to eliminate, wholly or partly. In organic evolution also, there are many intermediate degrees of vitality and obsolescence. A species may stay alive, though not very numerous or healthy, for long ages in spite of maladjusted parts or traits, perhaps survivals of once useful ones. Man is somewhat hampered by several of these useless vestiges. Many species have dwindled to a few survivors, living precariously just short of extinction. Man and the mosquito, on the other hand, have conquered vast stretches of the earth, as the squid pervades the sea. These are dynamic and expansive, very much alive as species.

So at present are the automobile and airplane; so is the motion picture film. These are new types; along with them are hosts of simpler, more primitive types of art and artifact which have come down through the ages with little change. They are not hyperactive culturally; do not hold the spotlight of interest; are not channels for the greatest creative enthusiasm. The unglazed clay vessel, as in flower-pots, is one of them; the wooden mallet is another, as in the game of croquet. Some children's games, dances, and fairy-tales are ancient in origin, yet still actively practiced. They are surpassed as products of cultural evolution by other products, but not superseded or obsolete. Likewise in the organic world innumerable species live on, in prolific or precarious ways, which have been surpassed by human and other mammalian development. They have reached dead ends, and change little. Only along a few exceptional lines does evolution, organic or cultural, proceed at high speed as if impelled by some impetuous but wandering Cosmic Will. Elsewhere, established patterns may endure for geologic eras.

5. SUMMARY

This chapter has examined the argument of anti-evolutionists that art can not evolve because it is not cumulative. Art, they say, is fundamentally different from science in that (a) it is constantly "beginning at the beginning," (b) does not retain and incorporate its innovations, and (c) does not become obsolete.

There is a real difference between art and science in these respects, but it is one of degree and is gradually diminishing. It is an example of cultural lag which is due to temporary causes. Science was not systematically cumulative in its early stages. Art is becoming more so as modern methods of preserving and transmitting its products, aims, and techniques develop. It could do so more rapidly if those concerned with art desired to make it more cumulative. That they do not is partly due to the hostility of romantic art toward science and technology.

A closer look at the history of art shows that it is often highly cumulative. Innovations in its form, style, and mental content as well as those in technique have been transmitted from one generation to another on a vast scale. Few artists or schools of art really "begin at the beginning." They build on the work of previous artists. Elements of older styles are obvious in later ones.

Particular works of art in each period differ greatly as to the amount of previous art and culture which they directly incorporate and re-organize. Some, such as Michelangelo's Sistine frescoes, are richly packed with traditional forms, conceptions, and attitudes. Types and examples of art in each age also differ as to the extent to which they become obsolete. This is true also of scientific inventions and treatises. The modern tendency to rapid obsolescence in all fields, including art, is correlated with accelerating change and desire for progress.

CHAPTER XX

THE ARTS
AS PSYCHOSOCIAL TECHNICS

I. AESTHETIC AND UTILITARIAN TECHNICS. THE TECHNOLOGY OF ART

That the arts are less cumulative on the whole than utilitarian technics is generally agreed, although, as we have just seen, they are more cumulative than is commonly realized. By contrast with the applied sciences, they lack the means and methods to continue selecting, preserving, and re-employing the fruits of past experience in a systematic way. Apparently they lack the motivation for such an effort. At least, there is no insistent call to make the arts more cumulative, but rather a satisfaction with their present state in this regard. If anyone urged them to emulate science in striving for cumulative progress, the answer might well be that one great value of the arts is their great variety, their personal touch, their striking contrasts in style. If they have to begin all over again every few centuries, well and good.

We are not primarily concerned with what is desirable or undesirable in art, but rather with the facts and trends of its history. From the standpoint of evolutionism, it is challenging to find this huge, important area of culture which seems to defy the main trend. What is the reason for this low degree of cumulativeness? Is it permanent, unalterable, or a condition which is likely to change in the course of general cultural evolution? These questions are not often asked; but one answer is implicit in the traditional view that art is radically different from science, and that no convergence or

cooperation along this line is possible. We have already rejected this overly simple explanation.

Our thesis in this chapter is, first, that the arts are not radically different from the utilitarian technics, but are in fact another kind of technic, partly utilitarian; that the modern gulf between them is temporary and exaggerated by some theorists; second, that the arts or aesthetic technics have lagged behind the utilitarian in adopting scientific ways of thinking; third, that this helps to explain their comparative lack of cumulativeness; fourth, that scientific methods are gradually entering the field of art as well, and may do so more in future, for better or for worse; fifth, that art will become more cumulative if this change in methodology proceeds.

This does not mean that art will abandon its own methods completely and substitute those of the present exact sciences. What it does mean we shall try to see in the next few sections. The change will be partial and optional; not binding on any artist to follow unless he wants to. Whether or not it will be harmful or beneficial depends, as in all applied science, on what sort of persons direct the process, and how they use the greater power which science gives.

What is meant by saying that the arts are a kind of technic, and in this respect analogous to farming, pottery, writing, and the making of tools and weapons? Simply that they are all socially developed ways of getting things done; of controlling some kind of phenomena in order to achieve desired results. They are patterned, acquired, culturally transmitted skills and processes, involving certain types of functional device.

The difference between aesthetic and utilitarian technics is important but relative and partial. Utilitarian technics aim, to a large extent, at supplying man's physical needs by controlling various types of physical phenomena. They deal mostly with inanimate and organic phenomena such as stone, clay, wood, metal, coal, electricity, atomic power; sometimes with plants and animals; also with the human body, as in medicine. They aim at such general ends as health, comfort, and security; at getting and distributing food, clothing, shelter; at civil order and protection from enemies. Some other utilitarian technics are more social and psychological: for example, laws and governments; financial, commercial, and educational methods and institutions. Educational lectures and textbooks are psychosocial in their aims and in the types of phenomena which they endeavor to control and direct.

Art and aesthetic satisfactions are often included among these; art operates at times as a part of education. Art is a psychosocial technic rather than a physical one. Psychiatry and psychotherapy are also psychosocial technics, but with some attention to the physical basis of mental health. They also use art to some extent. Art, like education, deals with physical as well as mental and emotional phenomena; it employs physical objects, light-waves, sound-waves, or the like as stimuli to the eyes, ears, or other sense organs. It produces psychological effects on the brain of the percipient, arousing aesthetic and other kinds of inner experience there. It is also a means of expression on the part of the artist and of communication between him and other persons. As in songs and rituals, it is a means of communication between the users of art, and of shared experience among them. It often helps to develop group solidarity and common attitudes, though not necessarily so. Art operates by presenting to the human senses more or less complex combinations and sequences of sensory

details in space, time, or both. Through innate human predisposition and cultural conditioning, these have the power to arouse complex responses, somewhat similar from person to person and culture to culture but highly variable in detail. They stimulate not only perception but understanding, imagination, desire, emotion, pleasant or unpleasant feeling, and many other types of response in complex, diversified configurations.

The arts and utilitarian technics have much in common. They overlap and cooperate frequently, especially in the so-called "useful arts" of architecture, furniture, pottery, textiles, clothing, and utensils. These involve both utilitarian and aesthetic ends; artistic designers and scientific engineers collaborate in producing them. Fitness for some utilitarian function can be part of the meaning of a work of art. Botanical science and garden art collaborate in horticulture and landscape design. Science and art inhabit one world, and the gulf between them is bridged in many places. Artists and engineers collaborate in radio and television, motion pictures, and pictorial color-printing. Attempts at sharp dichotomies between art and applied science in such terms as "useful-beautiful," "rational-emotional," "practical-aesthetic," and "physical-psychological" ignore many borderline types and combinations. Nevertheless, there is a difference in emphasis. Those classed as "art" tend to emphasize aesthetic appeal, while the others do so to a less extent or not at all, as in coal mining and urban drainage systems.

One way in which art differs from utilitarian technics is in the greater vagueness and multiplicity of its ends and functions. Its means or functional structures are also multiple and vaguely defined. Utilitarian technics and devices are commonly made and used for a specific purpose or set of purposes, as in arrow-heads and fish-hooks. "Art" as a general realm is vague and controversial in extension, being limited by some to "beautiful" or otherwise superior productions, while others make it cover all human products with a socially established aesthetic function. Within this loosely defined field, a multitude of functions and values are pursued. Artists do not ordinarily think out and state their aims precisely and explicitly; often one can only infer them from the nature of the product and the way it is actually used and regarded. Many arts and particular works of art are versatile or multifunctional; each has many possible uses. A certain picture, song, or poem can arouse many different responses in different individuals, or in the same one at different times. It is hard for the artist to be sure, even if he wants to know, how his work will impress different parts of the public today or a generation hence. They may find his serious works funny, his daring works too conventional, his bold designs tame, his supposedly trivial pot-boilers greater than what he thought were his masterpieces. The same play or piece of music seems exciting to some, relaxing to others; boring to some, and to others intellectually interesting.

Hence the difficulty in adapting artistic means to specific, aesthetic ends. Different cultures and periods use the same arts for different ends and functions. Sometimes the chief use is magical, as in amulets and spells; sometimes religious, as in temples, statues of the gods, hymns, and ritual dances; sometimes political and social, as in art which glorifies a king, noble, warrior, or revolutionist; sometimes commercial, as in modern advertising; sometimes military, as in arousing terror in the foe and martial vigor in one's army. The same song, dance, or picture may be used for different values at different times, as when a primitive fetish is taken from its jungle village setting and placed in an art museum.

By contrast, applied science tries to adapt specific devices to specific ends or functions, more and more definitely. If these are multiple, as in an automobile, the engineer thinks out a definite program of intended functions and means to them. If a new need is to be met, or an old one under new conditions, the means are changed accordingly. In art, people become attached to a certain style or object and use it for different values.

Artists offer new kinds of art to the public with little if any clue as to what they are intended to do or why they are expected to be valuable. The public accepts or rejects them, perhaps for no explicit reason. Critics disagree, and often fail to make it clear why they regard a certain work as successful or unsuccessful. The whole relationship between means and ends is increasingly confused in art as traditional rules and standards are abandoned. Meanwhile, applied science clarifies its immediate ends and means as it develops, although their ultimate value is often obscure and debatable.

The concept of technics, as including both aesthetic and utilitarian skills, the arts and applied sciences, is broader than that of "techniques" in art. The latter covers only one factor in art; one usually not regarded as the most important. It refers to basic skills in handling the tools and materials of each particular art or craft. It refers to a facility or dexterity which may exist apart from creative, imaginative, inventive, or interpretive ability. In piano-playing, technique may imply rapid finger-work; in dancing, agility in executing conventional dance-movements; in painting, facility with the brush and knowledge of the necessary steps in laying on paint to get certain general effects. It is often said that, to be a real artist, in composition or performance, one needs a great deal more than mere technique; that some artists have achieved greatness with very little technique. They had something important to express in their art, and found the necessary means of expressing it without brilliant virtuosity.

The word "technics," also derived from the Greek word for "art," can be defined more broadly as covering all the acquired abilities and processes involved in art. In making a decorated boat or pot, it includes the aesthetic as well as the utilitarian skills and aspects of the product. It includes inventiveness, if any, in thinking up new functional or decorative features. It includes local and period styles as well as basic, functional necessities. It includes the "creative" phase of designing or composing and whatever powers of sensitive interpretation are required for successful performance. It includes the basic techniques of each medium and the ability to use them in ways desired by the tastes of the time. It includes the tools and devices of art as well as the mental abilities employed in inventing and using them. The technics of art include selecting and organizing all traits of meaning, form, style, suggested emotion and attitude, which can cooperate toward producing a desired psychological effect.

In a primitive stage, many of these skills and processes are comparatively undifferentiated, often executed by the same person. The painter may make his own paints and brushes; the musician his own flute and the song he plays upon it. The maker of the spear may hunt with it and the maker of the house may live in it. One result of increasing differentiation has been to separate the concept of technique from those of creation, invention, and expression.

That techniques of this limited sort can be taught is not seriously questioned. One sees it happen daily in art schools, piano lessons, the training of apprentices. They are easily transmitted and accumulated culturally, diffused and exported from one place to another, as from Florence and Venice to the Paris academies. Pliny, Vitruvius, Cellini, and Leonardo da Vinci passed them down from one age to another, to be used by future generations of artists. But, it is said, these are not the essentials of art; they are only its mechanical, superficial externals. They are mostly concerned with physical tools and materials and with rules for manipulating them. The essence of art consists in using them well, and "that cannot be taught."

There is some truth in this argument, but it goes too far. The processes of art cannot be divided into a simple dualism between physical and mental, mechanical and creative. One can be creative in devising better techniques and instruments for the arts. (Stradivarius and Disney are examples.) Furthermore, techniques of a mechanical, instrumental sort are not the only phase of artistry which can be taught and handed down. The lessons of a great

teacher, such as Leopold Auer on the violin, the advice of great artists such as Leonardo, Hugo, Wagner, Stravinsky, and Kandinsky to young artists, are not confined to mechanical techniques; they deal directly with what these masters consider as the highest aesthetic values in art. They discuss personal ideals and creative processes. The wisdom of philosophers, critics, psychologists, and sociologists on art from Socrates onward has been handed down in aesthetics, criticism, and texts for students on the practice of their crafts. These deal with styles, values, ideals, and standards of excellence. They form a considerable body of cumulative wisdom and scholarship, in spite of disagreements. They constitute what may be called *prescientific technology*. In architecture, the proportion of science in artistic technology is larger than in poetry, perhaps because architecture involves a larger utilitarian factor. The technics and technology of art include, not only mechanical tools and techniques, but whatever advice on "how to do it" has accumulated in each art. Artistic or aesthetic technology is roughly equivalent to "applied aesthetics" and analogous to "applied psychology."

Artistic technics include all the abilities and processes of art which are acquired and culturally transmitted. They are, in varying degrees, teachable and cumulative. They do not, however, include another important factor in art, which is heredity or innate ability. Genius or talent, the total personality and creative ability of a Goethe or Titian, that which makes him different from all others, is undoubtedly due in large part to some individual combination of genes. As such it can be distinguished in theory from that which he learned and developed through the experience of art and life. Such hereditary factors cannot be classed among the technics of art or of culture. But they are inseparably merged in the artist's personality and art. Only through developing them in a cultural context and expressing them in technical forms can he manifest them to the world. If the science of eugenics is ever successfully applied to the breeding of artistic aptitudes, the hereditary factor will itself be brought within the scope of cultural control.

2. TECHNICAL VS. EXPRESSIONIST THEORIES OF ART

That the arts are *aesthetic technics*—i.e., skilled methods and devices for producing certain types of experience in the beholder—is a very old idea. Aristotle states it several times in the *Poetics*. "Each art ought to produce," he says, "not any chance pleasure, but the pleasure proper to it." Tragedy, as compared with epic poetry, "fulfills its specific function better as an art."[1] A tragic plot, he says elsewhere, "ought to be so constructed that, even without the aid of the eye, he who hears the tale told will thrill with horror and melt to pity at what takes place."[2] Horace in Rome and Le Bossu in seventeenth-century France are among those who continued this Aristotelian approach to the technology of art.

Crude as these premature attempts at aesthetic technology seem today, they were on a track which might have led to valuable insights with the aid of advancing psychological knowledge. But the strong hold of transcendentalism on aesthetics has discouraged attempts along that line until recent years. The technical view of art, in spite of its respectable lineage, has been overshadowed by one which flatly denies that art is a means to any outside end or function at all; certainly not to pleasing or influencing any observer. Art, according to this other view, is an end in itself; it is to be explained and justified as a mode of expression on the part of the artist. Whatever effect it may have on the observer is incidental, and is not its essential aim or function. Said Oscar Wilde, "The moment that an artist takes notice of what other people want, and tries to supply the demand, he ceases to be an artist."[3]

The issue is relevant to the theory of evolution in that, if art is a social technic, it may possibly become more cumulative. Those who restrict the concept of art to individual expressions of emotion usually deny that it evolves in this or any other way.[4]

The Platonic tradition, combined with Christian asceticism, belittled the importance of pleasure-giving as a function, and of anything aimed at making sensory experience more enjoyable. (St. Thomas Aquinas inclined toward Aristotle on this point, seeing no harm in the right sort of visual pleasure). Plato had disparaged the taste of the masses and the value of any art which pleased them by representation or sensuous luxury. The value of art was not to be judged by the extent to which people liked and enjoyed it, but rather by the way in which it led the mind upward to an understanding of the eternal forms of perfection. This itself might have been considered as a technical function, along with that of inducing religious piety and helping the soul to find salvation. In practice, religious art has been so regarded by the Christian church, but in theory the technical conception of art has been associated with naturalistic hedonism and avoided by supernaturalist aestheticians.

---

[1] Butcher translation, XXVI, 7. 1462 b 12.

[2] *Ibid.*, XIV, 1.

[3] "The Soul of Man under Socialism."

[4] A statement of the expressionist theory which has had much influence in England is that of R. G. Collingwood, an idealist and follower of Croce. In *The Principles of Art* (Oxford, 1938), he states the issue in a way which merely caricatures the technical theory, then dismisses it by the simple expedient of saying that what people call "art" in this sense is really "pseudo-art," The technical theory is a "vulgar error,' he says (p. 19) although it is believed by most people, including economists and psychologists—notably I. A. Richards. Art is not a psychological stimulus, Collingwood declares, or a means to arousing a state of mind or emotion in the audience. "What the artist is trying to do is to express a given emotion." (P. 282). A bad work of art is one in which the agent tries to express a given emotion but fails. But "expression is an activity of which there can be no technique." (P. 111).

The chief work by I. A. Richards, which Collingwood denounces for its technical theory of art and language, is *Principles of Art Criticism* (London, 1926). Richards speaks there of the "emotive use" of language: i.e., to evoke emotion, as distinguished from the scientific use.

Many of these have preferred to take the artist's point of view, rather than the observer's, and to think of art as a process by which the artist expressed his inner visions. These, in turn, could be explained as emanations of divine radiance or manifestations of the cosmic mind, in which the artist was only an instrument. In any case the essence of art was the process of conception and expression; not the causing of any specific effect on other humans. Croce went on to belittle the whole sensory, external aspect of art; not only its conception and imagination but even its "expression" were held to be essentially mental. Kant had stressed the essentially "useless," "purposeless" character of art and pure beauty, associating "use" and "purpose" mainly with the world of material laws. To the naturalist, it seems that what is valid in Kant's analysis of art and beauty can be expressed in functional terms: that art is a means of producing an experience of beauty in human observers, along with other functions. But the traditional ideology of aristocracy weighed heavily against any interpretation of art and beauty in terms of use, however broadly "use" might be conceived. Use and beauty were antithetical, along with work and play; one was the function of a working class and the other of those who did not need to work. The production of art had been a kind of work, and artists had usually been low in social status, especially those who worked with their hands.

In the early nineteenth century the romantic movement was claiming for artists a high moral, spiritual dignity, which seemed attainable through dissociating art from practical and material concerns. Schiller, from the artist's point of view, glorified the transcendental role of art as spiritual play. "Man," he said, "is only completely a man when he plays." Schiller praised the gods of Greek art as free from all labor, effort, purpose, desire, and will. Indolence and indifference, he said, are their envied condition[5]. Such an ideal resembles the Indian conception of Siva Nataraja, the divine dancer, one of whose aspects is total activity—"life's energy, frantic, aimless, and play-

ful."[6] He dances, not to please any mortal, but as an expression of his inner nature. "All his gestures are own-nature-born, spontaneous, and purposeless—for his being is beyond the realm of purpose."[7] But, however enviable in a god, such lofty self-sufficiency is beyond the reach of human artists and questionable even as a human ideal. The human artist is a social animal like other humans, and is often at his best when cooperating or contending with his fellows. He is an intelligent animal and, when awake, cannot long avoid some sort of purposeful action.

"Art for art's sake," the romantic slogan, has been construed in many ways. It can be consistent with the technical, functional view of art, as a defense of the artist's right to specialize on distinctively artistic problems of technique, form, and style without serving any moral or other outside end. He does not even need to aim at beauty; art is free to determine its own ends. From the spectator's point of view, "art for art's sake" can also be taken as the right to enjoy and evaluate art for distinctively aesthetic values, whatever these may be. So interpreted, the doctrine has been a liberating influence in the evolution of art along many experimental lines.

However, it has also been used by those who wish to deny all active functions to art; all concern with its effects on others, whether moral, political, or aesthetic. When asked about the possible effects of his art on others, a modern artist often answers that he has no interest in such effects, and no obligation to have any. Fine art is, and should be, "useless," without any social function at all. Any suggestion that he take an interest in psychological effects is apt to be taken as a covert move to impose the whole ancient burden of moral, political, and perhaps religious duty on the artist; perhaps as a mask for totalitarianism.

Meanwhile, art goes on having effects, whether

[5] *Letters on the Aesthetical Education of Man*, XV.
[6] H. Zimmer, *Myths and Symbols in Indian Art and Civilization*, p. 167.
[7] A. Coomaraswamy, *The Dance of Siva*, p. 64.

the artist or his friends wish to think about them or not. These effects are partly aesthetic, immediate, and brief; partly social, economic, political, far-reaching and long enduring. The power of art on the public mind and on attitudes and tendencies to action or inaction is obvious and great. For artists and theorists to reject all interest in such effects is like putting chemical elements together and giving them to the public, without knowing or caring whether the combination is explosive or poisonous. Art is a causal agency for good or bad, whether by purpose or blind accident.

The technical theory of art is a conscious recognition of this fact, with the implication that artistic functions can be scientifically studied and planned if anyone chooses to do so. It does not urge that art should be devoted to any particular function, aesthetic or moral, or to any particular psychological effect, that of beauty and pleasure or the opposite. It does not imply that artists themselves should necessarily investigate and plan, but suggests that scholars concerned with understanding art might do so. A clear recognition of the technical nature of art would be an advantage to social and cultural scientists in helping them to study and describe artistic phenomena as they now describe utilitarian technics. For centuries they have been on the verge of doing so, and some have made the attempt, only to be denounced by artists, critics, and aestheticians as ignorantly demeaning the sacred realm of art. Needless to say, this obstacle has stood in the way of a comprehensive evolutionism and, more importantly, of actual, cumulative advance in the arts. It has obscured and rejected the main conception on which such accumulation could be based.

To say that art is a psychosocial technic does not imply that artists in the past have always thought of their art as a means to some effect on the beholder. The actual effects of art, which patrons value and which scientists regard as social functions, may not be consciously intended by the artist. He may have a different aim or none at all. At certain periods of history, most artists have modestly sought to please and satisfy their individual patrons. Some have sought to please the gods; some have created to please a divine observer, like those pious medieval sculptors who placed their work where no other eye could see it. Some artists had to please so as to make a living; some were rich and independent enough to create as they wished, to please themselves. A man who has developed a love for creative work in his medium might well go on practicing his art if he knew he was the last human alive. Some artists scorn the public and create for some "choir invisible" of truly appreciative souls or for posterity. Some insist that they paint or write only to please themselves, or to release a pent-up impulse. They may be quite sincere even though, a little later, they put their works on exhibition.

The technical conception of art does not imply that an artist necessarily aims or should aim at producing a specific effect on some particular person or kind of person. He often does aim at a more general one. He may have, somewhere in the back of his mind, a vague hope of winning respect from discerning people who are interested in the sort of thing he is trying to do. To win respect is to influence them in a certain way; to produce a psychological effect on them.

Sometimes the artist thinks rather of communicating something to the outside world in general—some image or idea which he feels as tremendously important, so that he must publish it abroad whether people like it or not. But communication requires someone to receive as well as someone to send out. To make someone receive and understand the communication is to arouse a response in that other mind. Expression without communication is unfulfilled, a mere soliloquy as on a desert island. Its human fulfillment is in making someone else perceive, understand, and if possible sympathize. This is not inconsistent with the fact that many of art's finest expressions have been addressed to an imagined, supernatural being, or to oneself in the double role of speaker and listener.

The artist may disregard all other persons, thinking only of his own impulse to express. Thus Walt Whitman sounded his "barbaric yawp over the roofs of the world." That will indeed relieve the artist's pent-up energies and emotions, and he may be quite indifferent to the effects of his voice on possible hearers. Many artists have likened the process of creation to that of giving birth to a child, the emphasis in both cases being on the need to expel something from within, rather than to communicate with anyone outside or to affect the outside world in any way. This is, no doubt, a very real, basic, primitive motivation toward artistic expression. The expressionist theory is right in calling our attention to it. This leads the psychoanalyst to ask why such a pent-up urge to express ideas and images of visual, musical, or, verbal form ever develops in the first place; why a certain form becomes so strongly affect-laden as a symbol for the artist concerned.

However, it is probable that few adult, civilized artists are completely indifferent to the effect of their utterances on the outside world. They may not care whether their work is liked or respected; they may even prefer to anger, shock, or displease; but most of them seem to want their expressions to be noticed, understood in some degree, and perhaps to move people out of bored indifference. One who yawps with total unconcern for public reaction today may not like the actual effect, and may try next day to produce a different one. Whitman, like most other artists, labored carefully over his choice of words, his rhythms, and his imagery. He wanted his words to move people in certain ways, and rearranged them to that end.

At one moment the artist may pound the piano-keys at random to relieve his feelings, or splash paint recklessly upon a canvas; at the next, he may start to listen or look more critically, wondering how the effect could be improved. This phase of the creative process differs obviously from childbirth, which requires little or no planned adaptation of means to end on the part of the prospective mother. It is not purely automatic

and impulsive; it raises the problem of how best to achieve a desired, perceptible form by means of one's chosen medium. Such thinking may be largely experimental, qualitative, *ad hoc*, with little or no preconception of the final form to be achieved. That conception often emerges through fumbling trial and error, after many changes of aim and direction. Blind trial and error may then change gradually into systematic pursuit of a goal: the objectification of a clearly imagined form.

Whatever the precise configuration of thought and action in a particular case, the creative process tends to develop some reflective adaptation of means to ends, even when not concerned with effects on anyone but the artist himself. When it is concerned with others, the technical character of art becomes more obvious and its problems more varied, since the artist must then consider the psychology of possible observers and how his devices are likely to affect them. But even when it seems to be purely self-centered, it can hardly remain as wholly spontaneous, unpremeditated action when it enters the stage of critical polishing, revision, and development.

Advocates of the expressionist theory of art tend to ignore this wide occurrence of reflective elements in the creative process, through their eagerness to make a sharp dichotomy between art and applied science. There is indeed a difference in degree, but not a complete one. Certainly the welling up of unsought fantasies from the unconscious often plays a major role in art, more often than it does in the useful technics. The same can be said of impulsive expression, as in automatic writing and musical extemporizing. In all of these the tendency to think of means and future ends diminishes, perhaps to the vanishing point. But enough is known of the methods of impulsive, romantic artists to indicate that most of them do a good deal of reflective thinking at times. The expressionist theory, by obscuring this aspect of art, tends to make society ignore the effects of art and the possibility of achieving better ones through intelligent planning. It tends to justify the artist in disclaiming all responsibility for the effects of his work on other humans. The technical approach calls attention to such effects and holds that artistic creation is quite compatible with intelligent thinking.

The technical theory of art does not imply that an artist *should* plan ahead to produce a certain effect on observers, and think about it while he works. That could, of course, easily destroy his art. To wonder how people will like it could distract his imagination, and to adapt his work to their taste could lower its quality. Some artists and entrepreneurs do think along these lines, with good or bad results, but science imposes no obligation to that effect. Rather it begins with the pragmatic assumption that whatever method leads to the best results is the best method, at least in relation to specified aims and conditions.

The fact that an artist may compose or perform at times only to express himself or to satisfy a creative urge is quite consistent with the technical nature of art. As we have seen, art has many functions; different ones for different kinds of person and situation. If art can help an artist to achieve inner peace and harmony by expressing himself, objectifying his fantasies, and communicating with others, this is itself one of the functions of art. Whether consciously so planned or not, the process of creation, of handling a medium and forcing it into a desired form, is a technic for expression and communication on the part of the artist. For children in school, and for neurotic patients, art is systematically used as a technic for self-expression, to aid in achieving inner harmony and balanced growth in personality. It is no contradiction for a work of art to exercise one function for the artist, another for the élite public, another for the masses, and still others for those who deal in or manage his work. The fact that an artist thinks of his work primarily as self-expression or creation for its own sake may, in the long run, make his work more valuable to others than if he sought to please them.

The expressionist and technical theories of art

are consistent and supplementary when both are placed on a naturalistic basis. In the work of creative and interpretive artists, expression is so important as to require elaborate, subtle technics. Simple, primary emotions can be expressed without technics by animals and new-born infants; but not the complex moods and sentiments which civilized artists want to express. The arts provide these technics through attaching culturally established meanings to presented and suggested images. They are subject to some cultural and individual variation, but contain much that is widely understood. Appreciation also develops its own technics in the effort to grasp or explain with sympathy the varied expressions of art. Thus the technics of art include means of expression and communication. Broadly conceived, the technical theory of art includes all that is true and valid in expressionism.

The difference in point of view between artist and appreciator often has important consequences. One of these is shown in Tolstoy's view that any communication of feeling, such as an ignorant peasant boy's account of his escape from a wolf, can be as good a work of art as a product of highly sophisticated technique. Right or wrong, this approach led him to disparage many of the artists commonly regarded as great. Artists sometimes assume that their own exciting experience in producing a work makes it good art and entitles it to be praised and rewarded by the public. It may fulfill its function for the artist and not for anyone else. The appreciator will insist on evaluating art in terms of its value *to him*. Mere success in expression from the artist's standpoint is not enough to justify the work to the receiver. He will ask whether it is successfully communicated *to him* (which requires technique), and also whether the emotion or other experience communicated is worth accepting.[8]

The fact that art is used as a means to an end

---

[8] Collingwood obscures this fact by insisting that bad art is merely failure to express a given emotion, or disowning one's actual emotions. (Pp. 282, 284).

does not imply that it is *only* a means to an end, in the sense of being merely instrumental to some deferred, terminal value outside the process of creation or perception. It does not imply that the artist or observer should always regard the product so, and keep thinking of its ultimate purpose. The concept of art refers not only to the finished product but also to the process of making or performing it. That process can be intrinsically good as experience, although it is not always so. It can have many different ends and values; some achieved during the process, some long afterwards; some in direct aesthetic perception and others through its indirect, deferred effects. Art has been multivalent, versatile, throughout its history. Different ends and values have seemed most important at different times. Different ones have been consciously emphasized by artist and public. For many artists, the process of creation or performance, in spite of its unhappy moments, outweighs in importance anything that the product can do afterwards. Fame, applause, rewards, even the work itself which they finished yesterday, may bore them; they are off on some new venture. Small wonder that, for such an artist, the process of expression and execution seems to be its own reward, conducted "for art's sake," and that he rejects any theory which would subordinate the doing to the after-effects of the product.

Appreciators often prefer to think of a work of art as "good in itself"; as an intrinsic rather than an instrumental good. They feel that it demeans the work of art to regard it as a mere means to one's enjoyment. At the same time, they may actually like and admire it largely because of the pleasure it gives them. There is a strong resistance in Western culture, mainly derived from its ascetic moral tradition, against admitting that the chief purpose of a work of art may be, at times, to give pleasure. One feels under obligation to look for some loftier, more unselfish, spiritual justification.

The appreciation of art has its own techniques, not always the same as those of creation and performance. But in this they are similar: that thinking too much about the enjoyment one hopes to give or get can defeat its own purpose. It is usually necessary to forget oneself and one's feelings to some extent; to focus one's attention on the object; to act and feel for the moment as if the work of art were an intrinsic good. This is not hypocrisy or inconsistency, but a necessary technique in enjoying art: that of projecting one's imagination wholeheartedly into it. Later on, or in analyzing the behavior of others, one can recognize the importance of the subjective response in evaluation, and in motivating the production of similar works.

It is misleading to define art as "the expression of values"[9] or contrast it in this respect with utilitarian technics and technology. Art does produce and develop new kinds of value, but utilitarian technics and applied sciences do this also. Fundamentally, all human values are given to man by nature; especially by his favorable earthly environment and the complex physical equipment evolved by his ancestors, including powers of feeling, thought, learning, sympathy, and varied enjoyment. The technologies of nutrition and medicine increase his ability to enjoy the values of life, and so do those of industry, law, and education. The values provided by the arts are somewhat but not entirely different from these. Many of them are immediate values, to be enjoyed at once in direct perception. But many kinds of object and activity, in addition to the arts, provide immediate satisfactions, perceptual and otherwise. The arts provide somewhat new values by devising new kinds of form and style; by increasing the variety and richness of our perceptual and imaginative world and its emotive meanings. The sciences also create values. They make life more significant and interesting by helping us to understand ourselves and the world we live in. Art and applied science both give us increasing power over nature, ourselves, and each other, which we may use to in-

9 As in M. Rader's *Modern Book of Esthetics* (New York, 1952), p. xiv, and C. W. Morris's "Science, Art, and Technology."

crease the values of life or to injure and decrease them.

In relation to the general trends of culture history, it is the user's or consumer's point of view which determines the chief role of art in society, rather than the artist's. The very tendency to take a special interest in artists' personalities, in how they live, feel, and create, is modern and inspired by romanticism. Through the centuries, artists have been greatly outnumbered by the users and enjoyers of art. Their patrons—kings, priests, nobles, officials, rich men and women, and in recent years a wider purchasing public—have exerted more political and economic power than they. If art has flourished, been encouraged and rewarded as a way of making a living, it is mainly because of the values it has given to consumers through some kind of enhanced, emotionally satisfying experience. Art would never have been kept alive at great economic cost, merely as a means to self-expression for artists. They are paid to express themselves and perhaps to satirize or castigate their patrons at will, because they usually deliver adequate values to justify it. Regardless of whether artists and theoreticians consider art as a psychosocial technic, society at large has persistently treated it so. It has gone to works of art for all manner of psychic foods, delights, and comforts. To get these, it has paid heavily in time, energy, money, and praise for what it likes. It has been increasingly tolerant toward the vagaries and inadequacies of individual artists and schools of art, from the conviction that artists in general deserve to be fostered and given considerable freedom to experiment, for the eventual benefit of art and civilization.

3. HISTORICAL RELATIONS BETWEEN THE ARTS AND UTILITARIAN TECHNICS. PRESCIENTIFIC AND SCIENTIFIC TECHNOLOGY

The extreme divorce between artistic and utilitarian technics, which has given rise to much misunderstanding of art, is largely modern. In part, it is an actual divergence in their activities and organization; in part, a fictitious divorce in theory, which exaggerates the actual differences.

It is well known that the modern distinction between "arts" and "utilitarian technics" did not exist in antiquity. The Greek word "techné," roughly translated as "art" or "craft," included both. It was applied to utilitarian skills such as mining, agriculture, medicine, and war, as well as to dancing, poetry, music, and painting. The "liberal arts," to which we still refer in our degrees of bachelor and master of arts, included some disciplines now called sciences. That some arts aimed at beauty or aesthetic pleasure while others did not was recognized, but was not considered as dividing them into radically different groups. Dance and song were among the "arts of the Muses," led by Apollo, while Hephaestus was patron of the visual arts combining use and beauty, as in a well-wrought shield with figures in relief.[10] Daedalus was the legendary prototype of inventors; some of his products were beautiful as well as practical. Until well along in the eighteenth century, the word "art" and its equivalents in other languages were used in this broad sense.

From the Renaissance on, the concept of "art" was gradually split in two. The skills and products aimed at beauty or aesthetic pleasure were classed as "beautiful," "elegant," "polite," or "fine" arts, while those aimed mostly at utility were called "useful," "mechanic," "industrial," or "applied" arts. Still later, in the nineteenth and twentieth centuries, the term "art" without any prefix was gradually limited to those of beauty or aesthetic satisfaction, including the visual, musical, literary,

[10] *Cf.* Hesiod, *The Shield of Herakles*, 111–142.

and theater arts. Those which had both kinds of aim, as in furniture and clothing, were called "useful arts." Those which had little or no aesthetic appeal were not called "arts" at all, but "industries," "applied science," "engineering," or "technology." Mining, agriculture, and medicine thus went out of the realm of arts, except for such subdivisions as horticulture and plastic surgery, which still laid considerable emphasis on aesthetic aims.

In recent years the word "technics" has been increasingly used. As distinguished from "technology," it means the active skills and processes themselves, whereas the latter word refers more to the knowledge, theory, or science developed in connection with such skills. The chipping of flint is a technic; a particular chipped arrow-head is a technical device; the knowledge of how to chip flints is a kind of primitive technology. On the prescientific level they are not clearly distinguished, since technology is undeveloped. But on the advanced level there is considerable difference. An example of technology would be a treatise on mechanical or electrical engineering. A technical or technological device would be a machine such as a dynamo. "Technics" in this realm include the skills of trained "technicians," as in medicine, who know how to apply certain difficult methods worked out by scientists, but do not necessarily understand the scientific principles involved and could not apply them in original ways. Like artisans or craftsmen as distinct from creative artists or managing designers, they can carry out difficult orders, but their powers of invention are supposedly limited to relatively simple phases of the process. A technologist may have less manual skill in execution, but more theoretical knowledge of why certain technics will succeed and others not. Broadly conceived, a utilitarian technic such as farming includes all the skills, methods, and practical knowledge involved in that occupation. It can exist on a primitive level without scientific technology, as farming did in the neolithic period, or on an advanced level. Here a scientific technology

has been developed, as in agriculture as taught at a modern university. Through applications of chemistry, biology, and other sciences, technology has transformed the active steps of the process as executed by farmers and farm laborers. Utilitarian technics in many fields, such as medicine, war, and manufacture, have been thus developed from the primitive, prescientific stage into the scientific.[11]

Some primitive utilitarian technics and devices were supernaturalistic in relying on magical and religious means of securing desired ends. An example is the planting of small images of the Earth Mother to insure success in agriculture. They have been gradually but not completely replaced by naturalistic, applied science, as in the use of chemical fertilizers and hybrid plants to secure the same result. Supernaturalistic technics are still employed for utilitarian ends, as in the use of prayers and amulets to cure disease. The chipping of an arrow-head and its use in hunting are naturalistic technics, even though they may have been accompanied by appeals to magic or divine help. Their operation does not have to rely on any supernatural agency.

The concepts of technology and engineering are often restricted to the physical sciences involving mathematics and exact measurement. Applied biology, as in plant and animal breeding, is sometimes added. Physical scientists are frequently reluctant to accord the honorable name of "science" to such upstarts as sociology and psychology, or to grant that their practical applica-

11 The terms "technology" and "technics" are now commonly restricted by anthropologists and cultural historians to the utilitarian, physical varieties. The aesthetic arts and their products are classed apart. Polak, for example, speaks of the influence of non-technological creations, including art. (Sol Tax, ed., *op. cit.*, Vol. III, p. 232). Adams writes, "I am very skeptical about the contrast of a rate of accumulation in technology and science with another rate in values or political institutions." (P. 222). Willey (p. 223) contrasts "technological innovations" with "innovations in style' of art. Julian Huxley writes (p. 242) that we must create a world "based on science, but not one entirely technological." It must also involve moral and religious values, art and literature, he says, This terminology obscures the technical aspects of art and other institutionalized skills and processes.

tions (as in welfare legislation and psychiatry) can be a kind of technology. The idea of social or psychological "engineering" now has a vaguely shocking, totalitarian sound, as if it implied a desire to "regiment" and "brain-wash" people. (It does not, of course, necessarily imply anything of the sort, but the association is historically significant.) Any suggestion of "aesthetic technology" or of "scientific planning in art" now seems even more preposterous if not a downright threat to beauty and liberty.

If the word "technology" were used in the original sense of "techné" and "logos," it would now include the science or systematic knowledge of both kinds of "art," the aesthetic and utilitarian. It would cover not only the various branches of engineering and applied science, but also "poetics," in the Aristotelian sense, and "aesthetics" as the study of perception in the field of art. In modern usage, the applied utilitarian sciences have taken over the term "technology." There is no good name for the scientific study of aesthetic skills and products. "Aesthetics" is the nearest approach to it, but it has confusing associations.[12]

The subject of aesthetics is still distinguished at times from "poetics," the name employed by Aristotle, in accordance with the Greek words from which they are both derived. "Poetics," in this sense, refers to artistic making or doing in general, in any medium. A book on poetics would be a kind of technology, a manual for the artist on how to produce good art. "Aesthetics," on the other hand, would be restricted to a study of perception, especially the aesthetic contemplation of beauty in art, nature, and elsewhere. It would take the standpoint of the beholder and not try to advise the artist. This distinction has found little acceptance in recent years. On the contrary, the concept of aesthetics has been expanded to cover both the making and the perceiving of art and beauty, along with other relevant phenomena. It has become a name for the general, theoretical study of all the arts and related types of experience and behavior.

[12] The monumental *History of Technology*, edited by Charles Singer and others in five volumes (Oxford, 1954–58), surveys this subject from the paleolithic period onward. It is somewhat vague about the meaning and extension of "technology." The scope of the series is defined in the Preface as "a history of how things have been done or made." A rather dubious etymological definition is ventured: "the systematic treatment of any thing or subject." From the seventeenth century, it is said, the English meaning was "systematic discourse about the (useful) arts," and from the nineteenth the term became "almost synonymous with applied science." "Technology should mean," adds V. Gordon Childe, "the study of those activities, directed to the satisfaction of human needs, which produce alterations in the material world." (Vol. I, p. 38). The survey is mainly devoted to material technics, but the aesthetic and linguistic ones are not excluded. There are chapters on prehistoric graphic and plastic arts, fine ancient craftsmanship in ivory, wood, and metal, the culinary and cosmetic arts, pottery and figured textiles, printing, and photographic arts including cinematography. Architecture and medicine are omitted. The emphasis is on technical methods, but the aesthetic qualities of the product which distinguish "fine" from ordinary workmanship are not ignored. A section on "Technology and the Arts" by A. Fleck deplores the "unfortunate trend" of the eighteenth and nineteenth centuries to divorce "fine art" from life, industry, and the social scene and to confine them in Academy and Salon. Romantic poets and novelists, it continues, turned to neo-Gothic and other fantasies. Photography helped turn painting to abstract design, but stimulated impressionist experiments. Printed posters and illustrations (e.g., by Daumier) stayed closer to social reality. Some but not all architects profited from steel construction. The implication seems to be that the arts are not necessarily outside the realm of technology; that many past arts were a part of it, and that the modern separation is due to a retreat by art itself from other kinds of technology as exemplified by machine industry. Since this *History of Technology* emphasizes material technics, it says little about the literary, musical, theatrical, or other arts where materials are less in evidence. Social technologies such as law are hardly mentioned. Supernaturalistic technics receive only incidental mention. This tends to restrict the concept of technology to effective, naturalistic methods and to obscure the importance of magic and religion as ways of trying to get things done.

George Sarton's *History of Science* (2 vols., Cambridge, Mass., 1959) deals with pure science and philosophy as well as technology from the prehistoric through the Hellenistic period. It includes the visual arts, especially sculpture, architecture, and painting as well as the "Aristotelian humanities" of ethics, politics, economics, historiography, rhetoric, and poetics. Sarton explains that the *Rhetoric* and *Poetics* are outside the field of science, but that they exemplify Aristotle's effort to analyze all knowledge in scientific terms. They were not written for poets, whom they cannot help, Sarton thinks, but for men of science and lovers of objective truth. He adds that artists are wrong to object to scientific analysis of their work if that study is unpedantic, does not try to regulate them, and "is willing to accept them in the same spirit as it accepts the creations of nature." (Vol. I, pp. 581–2).

4. THE SPREAD OF SCIENCE THROUGH SUCCESSIVE FIELDS OF PHENOMENA. ITS CHANGING AIMS AND METHODS

It is an error, derived from pre-evolutionary thought but surviving today, to regard the arts and sciences as permanently separate fields, each fenced in like a private or national domain. Not only art and science in general, but also the particular arts and sciences, are shifting, overlapping types of human activity. They correspond to no sharp divisions in nature or in human experience. Systematic classifications of them, worked out by successive philosophers such as Aristotle, Francis Bacon, and Auguste Comte, have all been outgrown by the evolution of the activities themselves, including new directions of inquiry and attempted control. The same types of phenomena recur in different contexts, interpenetrating those of different sciences and examined by them from different points of view. Those of physics and chemistry, for example, such as matter and motion, heat and light, atoms and molecules, occur in living organisms and as such form part of the subject-matter of biology. Biology considers them only as entering into living organisms or affecting them; physics considers living organisms as systems of atoms and molecules, electrically charged, behaving in some respects like inanimate matter. Sociology considers living, thinking organisms as they enter into social groups and activities; it also has to consider the physical and biological realms as environments of man. Culture history considers much the same phenomena with emphasis on temporal sequences in the life of cultural groups, institutions, and technics.

Art and science do not occupy separate fields of phenomena. All the main types of phenomena which science studies and describes, such as numbers and triangles, stars and lightning, plants and animals, human affairs, have at one time or another been treated by the arts. Both have had similar goals at times: to find and tell the truth about the world and to control it in certain respects. Art has been studied by science and the products of science have been admired by artists. Geometrical forms occur in architecture, sculpture, textile design, and painting.

Even today, different as they are in method, they are not entirely so. Science has no monopoly on reasoning, or art on feeling and imagination. Both lean heavily on sense perception. Both deal with concepts and with particular images and objects. Both count and measure at times, and at other times employ less exact methods. Both serve to guide life, well or ill, and both contribute values to it.

The combined history of art and science shows several long-range tendencies. Some of these are especially relevant to our study. One, much the oldest, is the converging development of many local cultures, including the ancestors of civilized art and science, into larger and larger traditions. Early science had not yet been separated from art, magic, and religion. Here and there, by diffusion or independent invention, we see the beginnings of science in various parts of the world, such as Babylonian and Mayan astronomy and calendar lore, Indian mathematics and psychological aesthetics, Chinese chemistry and medicine, Greek geometry and physics. Most of these did not develop very far. In Greece and Rome the scientific movement burned low in the early Christian era, but sparks were preserved in a few manuscripts such as those in Arabic on optics and pharmacy. The arts, on the other hand, continued to flourish with intermittent breaks in many of these cultures, under the protection and in the service of organized religion, the state, and concentrated wealth.

Mathematical and physical science revived in Europe as part of the Renaissance of classical civilization, gathering force as it developed in complexity from the fifteenth century on. Now we are also rediscovering the beginnings of philosophy and science in many distant cultures and trying to separate these from their art, religion, and other cultural components. Thus we try to describe the history of Chinese science and technology as a component sequence in that of Chinese culture as a whole.

Another great movement, beginning in Greece, was the spread of the scientific attitude through successive fields of culture. This was partly geographic, from Greece and Italy to North Europe and outward through the world. It was also a spread within European culture itself, from one field of phenomena, one area of intellectual inquiry, to another. Modern science revived and continued the outward movement from mathematics and physics into biological, social, moral, psychological, and aesthetic investigation.

Among the ancestors of European science was the nature-philosophy of Thales and the Milesian school, which led to Democritus and the atomic theory. Another was the mathematics of Pythagoras and his followers. Both began around 600 B.C. The Pythagorean theorem was an early attempt at general proof without relying on individual assent or detailed empirical corroboration. It appealed to universal reasoning as to what must be true. In Athens a little later, the main interest of leading philosophers turned to the study of life, mind, society, moral conduct, art, and education. Socrates, Plato, Aristotle, and Epicurus laid the foundations of what were later to become the biological, social, psychological, and aesthetic sciences.

The work of these philosophers contained much unverified speculation, but it made a crucial step toward science in trying to base conclusions on rational inference instead of custom, tradition, faith, and authoritarian dogma. The struggle between rationalism and primitive modes of thought was to be a long one and is not yet finished. Another basic step toward science in Greek philosophy was the foundation of logical method, especially by Aristotle.

The scientific attitude or spirit, as distinct from any particular method, subject-matter, or conclusion, consists primarily in the desire to discover true knowledge about the world and man through observation and logical reasoning. It is more than a wish; it is a faith in the possibility and value of such knowledge and a sustained determination to seek and express it in spite of opposition, no matter how disagreeable the truth may be in relation to one's personal desires and interests. It involves also a persistent effort to extend the scope and improve the methods of this enterprise, including the systematic integration of new discoveries with previous ones and the continuous testing and correcting of assumptions and hypotheses. In the Greek period, the main expressed motive of this quest for truth was the love of wisdom for its own sake (philosophia). It was also pursued as a guide to the good life, the elevation of spirit, and the understanding of divine perfection.

Pure science developed out of rationalistic philosophy in Greece as a gradual change from speculative and dialectical reasoning to attempts at more cogent proof by inference from self-evident premises, from empirical evidence, or both. Aristotle worked out a deductive method in detail and a partial step toward an inductive one. Induction was developed by Bacon in the seventeenth century and by J. S. Mill and others in the nineteenth. Statistical methods have developed it still further for use with numerous data. Science now uses both induction and deduction, especially deduction from hypotheses to be verified experimentally. Science also relies on precise definition of concepts when possible, on laboratories for controlled experiment, and on devices for accurate observation and measurement such as microscopes, telescopes, and computers. These are used more in the older, more exact physical sciences than in those relating to man, society, and culture, but are extending even there.

The ancient advance of science through successive fields was halted until the Renaissance. Galileo and Copernicus revived it in the physical realm; Vesalius and Harvey extended it in anatomy and physiology. General biology as a science began its rapid growth in the seventeenth and eighteenth centuries with Linnaeus, Buffon, and Cuvier. The social sciences arose in the late eighteenth and early nineteenth centuries, in the work of such men as Adam Smith, Montesquieu, and Auguste Comte. Psychology was added in the late nineteenth century.

As Comte himself showed, the sequence was to some extent natural and necessary. The sciences developed, on the whole, in order of the increasing complexity and difficulty of the phenomena to be described. Those of mathematics and physics are none too simple, but mathematics specializes on the numerical and quantitative aspects of nature and human thought; physics on matter, motion, atomic structure, energy, gravity, heat, sound, light, and related phenomena. Scientific study could more easily make a start with these than with the more complex, subtle, and often intangible ones of life and mind. Each new science, moreover, helped to pave the way and provide useful tools for the next one. Sooner or later, all subsequent sciences made some use of mathematics. Although biology did not at first rely heavily on physics and chemistry, it did so later. The social and psychological sciences have come to need biology.

Before the sciences of life, society, and mind had laid a naturalistic foundation for the study of art and aesthetic experience, it was impossible to develop an empirical science of aesthetics. It is now becoming possible, but science has not yet made much headway there. Among the chief fields of inquiry, not yet transformed by science, are those concerned with value, such as ethics and aesthetics. They deal with types of phenomena vaguely described in such terms as beauty, goodness, rightness, and moral obligation.

Wherever science spread, it tended to displace the more primitive modes of thinking from which it had begun to free itself in Greece. But they proved to be stubborn adversaries. Entrenched, anti-rational tradition fought to keep its power with every means at its command, including the stake and torture. Giordano Bruno lost his life to it, but by the nineteenth century the scientific attitude had so far pervaded European civilization as to insure a fair hearing for Darwinism after bitter attacks. Emotional resistance to it is still strong in the fields of art and social conduct; in aesthetics, ethics, economics, and politics. Repeated efforts have been made in philosophy and science to achieve a rigorous objectivity, as in Descartes' attempt at a skeptical beginning, only to have the dogmas of supernaturalist tradition re-enter by the back door. Francis Bacon warned against the danger of wishful thinking with his "idols" of the cave, tribe, forum, and theater. But philosophy and science have never been entirely immune to socio-economic pressures and the will to believe. In spite of all attempts at objectivity, they always show to some extent the bias and limitations of contemporary culture. Seen in the light of historical dialectic, they can claim only relative truth; but in spite of their weakness and misuse they constitute man's chief hope of attaining wisdom and welfare on earth. As the total body of scientific beliefs and methods accumulates from age to age and culture to culture, the elements in it which are most culture-bound, most subservient to local, transitory interests, tend to be eliminated; thus leaving what we hope will have more claim to widespread, lasting validity.

Another major trend in science has been the increasing emphasis on technics and technology. Before the advent of science, primitive technics and technologies had already been developed in every main field. Since then, when the scientific exploration of a field has gone a considerable way, the new knowledge has been gradually used to transform the practical technics and technologies in that field.

Pure science grew partly out of practical technology, as in the rise of geometry from surveying and of astronomy from calendar lore. It always kept some relation to the conduct of life. But it was soon turned away from utilitarian emphases, partly through the influence of Plato and his school. The Hellenistic Greeks were on the verge of recognizing the value of science in industry. They made some practical applications of physical science in invention; for example, in the works of Archimedes and Hero of Alexandria. Many factors, however, prevented their accepting this as a major goal of science and philosophy. Among these were the aristocratic ideology of most intellectuals, the usually ample labor supply (so that there was no great call for labor-saving devices), the Athenian interest in humanistic studies, and the anti-scientific tendencies in both pagan and Christian religion. The fate of Prometheus, Phaethon, and Icarus for trying to rival the gods in power was never forgotten.

According to Plutarch, "Archimedes did not think the inventing [of military engines] an object worthy of his serious studies, but only reckoned them among the amusements of geometry. Nor had he gone so far, but at the pressing instances of Hiero of Syracuse, who entreated him to turn his art from abstracted motions to matters of sense, and to make his reasonings more intelligible to the generality of mankind, applying them to the uses of common life. The first to turn their thoughts to mechanics, a branch of knowledge which came afterwards to be so much admired, were Eudoxus [fl 366 B.C.] and Archytas [428–347 B.C.], who confirmed certain problems, not then soluble on theoretical grounds, by sensible experiments and the use of instruments. But Plato inveighed against them, with great indignation, as corrupting and debasing the excellence of geometry, by making her descend from incorporeal and intellectual to corporeal and sensible things, and obliging her to make use of matter, which requires much manual labour, and is the object of servile trades. Mechanics were in consequence separated from geometry, and were for a long time despised by philosophers."[13]

During the Renaissance Leonardo da Vinci was ahead of his time in applying scientific knowledge to particular inventions and in calling for more scientific study of nature. But it was not until the seventeenth century, in the philosophy of Francis Bacon, that the technological ideal of science was given a clear and general statement.

"The end of our foundation," said the head of scientific research in Bacon's prophetic fantasy, *The New Atlantis*, "is the knowledge of causes, and secret motions of things; and the enlarging of the bounds of human empire, to the effecting of all things possible." We cast about, he said, "how to draw out of them things of use and practice for man's life and knowledge, as well for works as for plain demonstration of causes..." Among the types of phenomena to be studied and controlled were those of plants and animals, including human physiology as well as those of matter, sound, light, tastes, and odors. The aims included not only health, longevity, and power, but also new beauties of sight and sound. The cinema is foreseen, as we "imitate also motions of living creatures by images of men, beasts, birds, fishes, and serpents." Instruments of sweet music and the conveyance of sound to a distance are foretold. Among the prophetic hints is one of evolution and genetics, as men learn "to make divers new plants, differing from the vulgar, and to make one tree or plant turn into another."

This new orientation did not exclude the older, Greek ideal, the love of knowledge and rational inquiry for their own sake and as a typical human activity. It did not rule out, as a motive, the thrill of scientific discovery and the adventure of extending the frontiers of human knowledge. These motives still persist and are uppermost in the minds of some scientists and philosophers. But modern science is inspired, far more than ancient science was, by the Baconian ideal of understanding and controlling nature for the benefit of man through observation and experiment. At the same time, scientists realize that the goal of useful technology can best be achieved by putting it aside at times in order to conduct basic research without thought of immediate applications. Practical usefulness can

---

[13] (Quoted by A. R. J. P. Ubbelohde, in C. Singer (ed.), *History of Technology*, Vol. IV, p. 666).

be a general aim without being always an immediate end in view.

5. TECHNICS, TECHNOLOGIES, AND PURE SCIENCES IN VARIOUS FIELDS. THEIR RELATION TO THE ARTS

Among the important distinctions made in Greek thought was that between *theoria* and *praxis*, now roughly translated as "theory" and "practice." *Theoria* meant primarily seeing; also mental contemplation or reflection. *Praxis* meant doing, action, business. Philosophy was of course theoretical, but was also related to practice. In and after Socrates, it was directed largely toward guiding action and thought on a high intellectual and moral level, including the higher types of art, but not labor-saving mechanical devices. Physical and biological science, which the Platonists belittled and almost ignored, was then largely theoretical rather than practical, although some biological technics such as medicine were developed in a partly scientific spirit by Hippocrates and his followers. Most ordinary praxis was conducted without the benefit of philosophy or science.

In modern times, the growth of science has involved a recognition of practical technology as one of the two main divisions of science in every field. The other, "pure" or theoretical science, is defined as "unbiased by practical considerations; not directed toward the solution of practical problems" (Webster). However, this is a difference in degree, since even pure science is somewhat influenced by practical considerations and directed toward eventual use. Pure science does tend to state most of its findings without explicit reference to possible use, in the form of laws, formulas, or other descriptions and explanations of phenomena.

The division between pure and applied science (technology) does not correspond exactly with that between theory and practice. All four have branched out and interwoven. Both pure and applied science involve highly abstract, theoretical considerations. Technology is not so much the actual *doing* of things (farming, bridge-building, making war, etc.) as the guidance of such doing by verbal and numerical explanations, rules, and advice. It guides not only the technical processes but also the making of complex devices to aid them, such as mechanical cultivators and chemical fertilizers. On the other hand, both pure and applied science involve their own kinds of doing. Both involve overt activities of research, observation, experiment, discussion, publication, and the like, and for these purposes both have developed elaborate devices, such as laboratories, cyclotrons, and "mechanical brains" for complex calculation. In modern science, the "pure" and "applied" phases are often so closely coordinated as to be almost indistinguishable. In principle, pure science describes and explains phenomena in its field without reference to practical use; but in fact the discoveries of pure science often grow out of technological experiment, as in recent electronics, and new theoretical advances are quickly put to use by someone. The actual difference is one of degree, as to how much the aim of quick utility guides the direction of research and the way in which knowledge is organized and expressed— with or without explicit reference to possible uses outside science itself.

What in science is analogous to the work of the artist? An artist is characteristically a *doer*, a maker or performer, rather than someone who tells how things are done or should be done. Of course, theorists and critics do things too, especially if they teach or publish; but artists are, in a fuller sense, practitioners of the art with which they are concerned. In this respect they are analogous to practicing farmers, builders, soldiers, and physicians, rather than to those who investigate and write books about these occupations. Sometimes there is an obvious personal similarity. Many physicians and surgeons are also amateur painters or violinists; in both fields they need and develop sensitive, delicate fingering and a love of fine craftsmanship. But we must not oversimplify the analogy. Artists differ greatly as individuals. Some are introverted dreamers and rarely emerge as overt doers, writers, makers, or performers. Some write books on aesthetics, criticism, and art education. Some are creative designers and composers, analogous to creative inventors in applied science, while some only operate, perform, or execute the works of others. One cannot say, therefore, that an artist is necessarily like any particular kind of scientific worker. The types of person and process in art are much more variable than those in science and often more unspecialized, with the same person doing many things or turning easily from one to another.

As we have seen, a treatise on physics and one on aesthetics are somewhat analogous. They differ, not only as to their fields, but also as to degree of scientific development. One is a product of pure science while the other is largely unscientific or prescientific. The treatise on aesthetics, at the present stage of evolution in its field, is likely to be a mixture of generalized art criticism, history, philosophical speculation, value theory, semantics, and miscellaneous bits of fact and theory about art from psychology and sociology. Both are cumulative and obsolescent; a textbook on aesthetics thirty years old is somewhat out of date. But one on physics goes out of date more rapidly because it belongs to a more scientific and rapidly developing subject, with a systematic procedure for testing and accumulating knowledge. Aesthetics is still vague and confused as to its basic aims, assumptions, and methods; as to the extent to which it wants to be descriptive or evaluative, empirical or dogmatic, scientific or gracefully literary and personal. But the need for pure science in aesthetics is becoming obvious: the need, that is, for a systematic pursuit of generalized knowledge about the arts and related types of experience and behavior. Its main future outlines and divisions are taking shape, in the form of related inquiries on the psychology, morphology, and sociology of art.

The most significant analogue in science to *Macbeth* or any other work of art is a particular technical *device*, a tool, instrument, weapon, food, medicine, or other concrete means of getting something done. A dynamo is a concrete means of getting something done in the realm of physics —a typically modern way, as Henry Adams pointed out in his autobiography. He compared it to a statue of the Virgin, as a typically medieval source of artistic and spiritual power. To anyone who knows art history, the statue is a product of previous cumulative development. A poem, dance, or symphony is also a technical device, a complex mechanism for producing certain psychological effects. The performance of a piano sonata and that of a surgical operation both involve complex manual skills, directed by a purposeful brain.

Physical technology has its analogue in artistic or aesthetic technology, which is a generalized explanation, based on technical knowledge and experience, of how to get things done in some field of art. In this respect a manual on electrical engineering is analogous to one on water-color painting, violin-playing, musical composition, or short-story-writing. Both emphasize techniques: the nature of the medium; the materials to be controlled and the instruments for controlling them, the difficulties to be encountered and possible ways of overcoming them. Also, both usually mention the chief ends and values which are sought in the field and the best ways of achieving them under present conditions. Some kinds of musical technology, such as notation and the rules of classical harmony, are loosely described as "theory," by contrast with instrumental and vocal practice. Other kinds of music theory are closer to pure science, such as the psychology of musical perception.

Criticism of the arts has technological implications in judging the success or failure, merit or demerit, of particular works of art. It evaluates them by certain standards, explicit or implicit. These are always debatable but significant as expressing contemporary cultural attitudes. Criticism often describes the effect the work in question had on the critic and his response to it, favorable or unfavorable. Thus it tends to imply beliefs as to what would be a better way to achieve similar ends, or what ends would be better to aim at. Art criticism and books on art appreciation also involve technology for the appreciator on how to perceive, understand, and enjoy a certain kind of art.

Aesthetic technology differs greatly from physical as to its degree of scientific development. Physical technology applies scientific knowledge while the aesthetic type has little of such knowledge to apply. Aesthetic technology is largely prescientific, which means among other things that it is vague as to ends and means, unreliable in generalizations, personal and speculative. Such prescientific technology is often expressed in an antiquated way in terms of supposed laws of beauty and good taste, rules of good art or correct design. It often specifies no ends at all, or only empty, high-sounding generalities. Its traditional "laws" are derived more from metaphysics, past authority and custom than from open-minded experimentation and free choice.

Scientific technology is seldom expressed so dogmatically. It claims no moral or metaphysical authority. It does not tell the prospective user or technician, "you must" or "you ought" to do thus and so; but only that *if* he wishes to build a certain kind of bridge under certain conditions, or cure a certain disease in a certain kind of patient, *then* this is probably the most effective way of doing it, so far as we know at present. All modern, scientific technology is of this sort. Its "rules" are all relative and tentative. They are potential aids to the practitioner, who is free to use them or not, so far as science is concerned. On the whole, scientific technology has prevailed over its primitive forerunners, not by coercion, but by demonstrating to potential users that its methods are more effective than theirs for doing what one wants to do. The "rules" of nutrition and hygiene are not morally or legally binding,

except where society wishes to make them so; but people usually find it wise to obey them on the whole, in their own self-interest.

The prescientific status of aesthetic technology appears in the slowness and reluctance of art to develop "rules" of this wholly relative, optional, and tentative sort, offered for the voluntary use of artists and public, with no claim to be binding. Its "rules" could easily be restated so as to remove all threat to the artist's freedom: simply as generalizations, based on past experience, on how to do most effectively whatever he wants to do. Of course, even this would be unacceptable to an artist who wants to do *only* what has never been done before, or to one who wishes to avoid all planning in terms of means and ends.

If any compulsions, rewards, or penalties are to be introduced, that is a question for social policy. Technology at any given time and place usually emphasizes ways to do the things which society most wants to do or has to do under the circumstances, and these underlying goals are always debatable. Sometimes moral, religious, and political considerations are mixed with physical or biological ones. All of these involve different kinds of technology, with different aims and standards. The technics of contraception and sterilization, nuclear weapons and the bombing of cities, are often discussed from the standpoint of what is right or legal; but such questions are external to the science directly concerned. This is not to say that any such technology is or should be entirely independent, operating autonomously in a vacuum.

On the contrary, one great source of trouble in the present world is the way in which physical technologies have been allowed to develop far beyond the social and psychological ones, without effective control by policies aimed at general human welfare. But the issue is not strictly between technological and non-technological thinking, or between science and a return to supernaturalist authoritarianism. It is rather a clash between different technologies, all more or less autonomous or demanding to be so. There are specialized technologies, especially the physical and social, and broader ones whose function (not always exercised) is to help direct and coordinate the others. Each specialized technology accepts hypothetically certain goals and value-standards for its own field, which it takes over from the value-system of its culture. Thus health and longevity are accepted without question as goals of nutrition and medicine. Other technologies may challenge these, as social science now questions the value of large, increasing populations. These must be argued out on some broader, higher level.

The choice of ultimate social goals and comprehensive policies is, in theory, a problem for ethics and axiology. Science can not prove any definite answers to it, but neither can any other method, and science can throw some light upon it if asked to do so. However, specialists in ethics and aesthetics do not usually think in these terms. Meanwhile the technics concerned, including both art and physical invention, tend to operate autonomously or under the control of arbitrary social and economic forces. Ethics, as a search for wise goals and standards of human conduct, is potentially a kind of psychosocial technology, all-embracing in that field. One of its functions is to consider how the other, narrower technologies, including art and physical invention, can be most wisely fostered and interrelated for the common good.

As aesthetics develops, it will tend to distinguish more clearly between its pure, descriptive phase and its applied, practical phase. Pure aesthetics will not undertake to advise the artist directly on how or what to produce or perform. The ideas it provides can, however, be so applied in aesthetic technology. Bernard Bosanquet exaggerates the gulf between theory and practice here in stating that aesthetics "exists for the sake of knowledge and not as a guide to practice" (*History of Aesthetic*, Preface). This goes too far when applied to aesthetics as a whole. Even in its narrow, traditional sense as a branch of philosophy, aesthetics cannot avoid influencing practice to some extent, and it has often tried explicitly to do so. It becomes a

potential guide to practice whenever it defines beauty or aesthetic value in a certain way, thus indicating how, in the opinion of the writer, these qualities can be found or produced. Philosophers writing on art and beauty from Plato to the present have offered advice on practice to those who make art and to those who use, criticize, or manage it. Art has sometimes followed this advice, as in the allegiance of French baroque drama to Aristotelian principles; at other times it has rejected theoretical guidance. Even as a purely descriptive quest for knowledge, aesthetics has much to gain from closer association with practice in the arts. Whether they also can profit from the association depends on the kind and quality of guidance it offers.

Technology prescribes no unconditional ends. It tries to implement the main desires of its time and place. This does not imply that all ends are equally good. Science and technology do not ignore or belittle the importance of directing one's desires and efforts toward the best possible goals. In the course of evolution, technology has come to specialize on means and methods, accepting most of its ends from the dominant value-systems of contemporary cultures. It has enough to do without debating general ends and values in detail. But the choice of ends and values does not have to be left to irrational or ancient, authoritarian methods. This is important and difficult enough in theory to deserve the full attention of associated disciplines, such as ethics and aesthetics. In both of these, axiology or value-theory has a large and vital place. It can be approached in the spirit of scientific naturalism even though science cannot establish, and does not seek to establish, any absolute system of values.

What is now called aesthetic axiology or value-theory can be studied from both points of view, the descriptive and the practical or technological. From the former, one can try to describe and explain the phenomena of evaluation in the arts: their history, psychology, and sociology; the arguments and evidences used in defending and attacking different aims and standards. From the technological standpoint, one can try to compare ways and means of pursuing different, specific ends in and by the arts. For this purpose, many actual experiments are needed on the effects of different kinds of art, including aesthetic and non-aesthetic effects, immediate effects and later consequences. The results of such study can be placed at the disposal of artists and others concerned with decision-making, to be used or rejected.

6. PRESCIENTIFIC MODES OF THINKING IN VARIOUS FIELDS; THEIR PARTIAL REPLACEMENT BY SCIENCE

The fields of the particular sciences, arts, and technologies are marked off in different ways. Their boundaries are constantly changing. As we have seen, they correspond to no fixed, eternal divisions in the universe, but reflect evolving types of human experience, interest, and activity. Those of the pure sciences correspond, on the whole, to different types or aspects of phenomena: e.g., number and quantity for mathematics; plants for botany. Those of the arts are made partly in terms of the sense addressed, such as visual and auditory; partly in terms of the medium used, such as painting and literature; partly in terms of the process used, such as sculpture; partly in terms of the type of product and function, such as architecture and furniture. The fields of the various technologies are distinguished partly in terms of the pure science or sciences applied in each. Chemical engineering is an application of chemistry. A certain technology may employ several pure sciences and other technologies, as agriculture uses chemistry, biology, biochemistry, electrical and mechanical engineering.

Ancient thought made various rough divisions in the universe and human activity, such as the animal, vegetable, and mineral "kingdoms." Along with these naturalistic ones, it imagined supernatural and paranatural realms, such as those of gods and demons, often assigning them special abodes in the universe from which these spirits could sally forth to interfere with the lives of men. Augustine distinguished the earthly and heavenly "cities" in history. Medieval society tried to organize itself into two parallel hierarchies, the spiritual and the temporal. The nature of each realm and its supposed occupants was explained in myth and legend, such as those of the seasons and the constellations. Human needs, hopes, and fears connected with each were recognized by primitive sages. They motivated various types of technic and technology, such as those for securing the health and fertility of food-plants and domestic animals.

Some of these, as we have seen, can be classed as naturalistic; some as supernaturalistic. (The latter term we shall take to include the "paranaturalistic" —that is, all kinds of spirits and occult phenomena, supposedly not subject to the ordinary laws of nature, whatever their grade or merit in the spirit world.) In primitive cultures the naturalistic and supernaturalistic were not clearly distinguished. Many important technics included both aspects: the building of a house or the carving and launching of a boat was attended by magico-religious rites. Histories of technology which include only the naturalistic phase tend to give a false impression of primitive culture and of technology in the broader sense. The supernaturalistic phase was often closely identified with the artistic: for example, a house would be made or a ritual performed with extra care and decoration so as to win divine favor for the enterprise in view. Without reference to the supernaturalistic phase, one cannot fully understand the motivation for artistry along with material efficiency. Spells and charms, prayers and sacrifices, rites of exorcism, were magical and religious technics. An amulet for apotropaic purposes was a magical device; a temple a religious one. In trying to satisfy man's basic needs, they often gave aesthetic satisfaction too, and aroused a desire for more of the latter.

In relation to each main set of technics and devices, there grew up a prescientific technology which undertook to provide a generalized, quasi-rational basis for it; an explanation of what to do and why. It was often expressed in terms combining magic, religion, and naturalistic understanding of causes and effects. Said Hesiod: "Pray thou unto Zeus the Lord of Earth and unto pure Demeter that the holy grain of Demeter may be full and heavy: thus pray thou when grasping in thy hand the end of the stilt-handle thou comest down on the backs of the oxen as they draw the pole by the yoke-collar. And let a young slave follow behind with a mattock and cause trouble to the birds by covering up the seed... If thou plowest late, this shall be a charm for thee: When first the cuckoo uttereth his note amid the leaves of the oak and rejoiceth men... then may Zeus rain on the third day and cease not, neither overpassing the hoof of an ox nor falling short thereof."

All technics are naturalistic as to the means which are actually employed, since man has no other means to use. (To modern psychology, man's thoughts and feelings are natural phenomena.) In other ways, they can be supernaturalistic: (a) in aiming at supernatural goals, such as heaven or Nirvana; at some kind of future life on a transcendental plane; (b) in assuming that supernatural agencies may affect the success of an undertaking, so that efforts must be made to gain the help of benign ones and avert the power of hostile ones.

What aim could be more important than an eternity of bliss instead of torment? Clues to the necessary means were found in ancient scriptures and prophecies claiming divine inspiration; in revelations and mystic visions, and in official church decisions. Often the attempt to please a divine ruler was based on the kind of steps which had been found effective in pleasing earthly ones. Much of the best technological thinking of past

ages, on a high intellectual level, has been supernaturalistic and otherworldly.

Some kinds of it have been essentially magical, such as alchemy, astrology, necromancy, and cheiromancy. Today they are usually classed as pseudo-sciences, but this does not fully characterize their positive aspects or their occasional contributions to science. Supernaturalistic technics could succeed for reasons quite different from those believed in by the user; in other words, the technic could work although the technology was false. Actual cures have been made by the sorcery of shamans, and actual deaths have been brought about by sticking pins in a figure of one's enemy —at least when the enemy knew about it and could die of fright. Likewise the technology of art can be false and yet serve as an effective guide to the artist, as when he believes that he is being divinely inspired and is stirred by that faith to supreme imaginative flights.

Prayer and worship were essentially religious technics, rather than magical, in that they strove to please a god too powerful to be directly controlled. Art functioned, in part, as one kind of religious technic. Much thought was devoted to producing the kinds of art which would please divine taste. Much religious technology, as in Hindu yoga, Buddhism, and Neo-Platonic mysticism, was devoted to self-discipline; making oneself worthy or capable of attaining divine enlightenment. Elimination of sensuous desires and attachments was a favorite method. This could lead the devotee to elaborate feats of bodily and psychic self-control, beyond the reach or desire of Western culture. In Western Christianity, such books as Thomas à Kempis' *The Imitation of Christ* are examples of religious technology. Art was often used as a means of elevating the mind, as in Indian mandalas and yantras, Christian crucifixes for contemplation, rosaries to be told, and verses to be repeated. But extreme ascetics feared that art might be a dangerous influence, leading rather in the opposite direction.

St. Augustine labored long and anxiously with

this problem in his *Confessions*. Especially to be feared were luxurious and erotic types of art, but all sensuous enjoyment was suspected. Simple, devotional literature and music were usually allowed. Later on, the majesty and brilliance of religious art lent an extra dignity and prestige to religious technology. For centuries, this helped religion and the church to resist the competition of science, through inspiring faith in religion as a means of attaining one's desires in this world and the next. In the baroque period church and state, religion and science, reason and faith, seemed for a time to be reinforcing each other as technics of material and spiritual power.

In utilitarian fields, naturalistic technology developed greatly in Europe, long before the advent of science. But its evolution was hampered by many obstacles. Since this life was theoretically regarded as a vale of tears and a mere testing-ground for the future one, there was little incentive to invention for material, worldly use. Throughout the feudal age, aristocratic prejudice forbade the upper-class intellectual from engaging in useful, material work, or devoting his mental powers to improve its methods. Military technology was the main exception, and its progress was comparatively steady. Architecture also had claims to social dignity, as Vitruvius maintained. Law, government, commerce, road-building, transportation, agriculture, manufacturing, grammar, and rhetoric all evolved considerably with little or no aid from science. As Childe and other archeologists have shown, a series of revolutionary break-throughs in sources of power brought in a series of proliferating advances in material technology from the neolithic period onward. Each great invention, once fixed in a stable culture, tended to beget a long line of improvements. The bow and arrow, the wheel, pottery, smelting, glass-making, brick-making, paper-making, bronze and iron tools, sailing, clocks, the Roman road, the yoke, harness, saddle and stirrup, the padded horse collar, button-holes, gunpowder, the printing press, steam and electricity—each of these was the start of many

radiating, cumulative sequences. Among them were artistic instruments and technics, such as painting in tempera, fresco, and oils, the lyre, the flute, the pipe organ, bronze casting, the arch, the camera.

Rapidly cumulative as utilitarian technology seems now, by contrast with aesthetic, it must have been relatively slow and sporadic for countless millennia. While under the stigma of low caste and subordinated to otherworldly technics, there was little motivation to hasten its advance. While mixed with magic or religious technics, the naturalistic ones were not subjected to rigorous testing. Failures were too often wrongly explained, as due to some small slip in performing a ritual, some sin of oneself or one's ancestors, some angry goddess unintentionally slighted. When things went right, as they might by accident, the wrong means were often credited, the false beliefs confirmed. The claims of otherworldly technology to assure salvation could not be empirically tested. Only in war and in the basic essentials of health, nutrition, social organization, and care of young were mistaken technics quickly punished by elimination of the group. The whole conception of experimental research and discovery, with testing, recording, communication, and funding of knowledge for transmission to posterity, was almost unknown before the seventeenth century. Some great discoveries were widely diffused; others were made and forgotten innumerable times; some were tabooed and suppressed as impious. The same steps had to be made repeatedly, in different parts of the world, generation after generation. Major catastrophes, as in Rome and Alexandria, could destroy vast areas of accumulated theoretical and practical wisdom. Long after science had proven its case and won in some fields, primitive thought and "empirical" methods—those based on craft experience, rule of thumb, without a scientific basis—prevailed in others. Thus prescientific technologies, mixtures of truth and falsehood, were transmitted cumulatively for centuries in every field including the arts. They were often transmitted through secret brotherhoods and priest-hoods, only slowly and partially escaping into public knowledge.

Even in the seventeenth and eighteenth centuries, when science had prevailed in theoretical physics, astronomy, and chemistry, there was comparatively little use of it in industry. Until the seventeenth century, technological advances were based largely on craft experience, personally transmitted as "craft mysteries."[14] The transition to scientific technology was then aided by the leadership of men with high social position, such as those of the Royal Society in England, many of whom wished to explore new economic resources. They attracted men of ability to applied science, made scientific surveys of technologies, supported experimental research, and published the results internationally. But even then, long after scientific technology was available, the tradition-bound methods of industry and agriculture resisted them until the Industrial Revolution started a rapid chain reaction. This was only in the utilitarian realm, and on the whole the fine arts held aloof from it, retreating into their romantic dream-worlds as the nineteenth century came in.

With reference to each natural and supernatural realm, the ancient civilizations developed theories about the character and origin of the beings within it. As expressed in myths and legends (such as Hesiod's *Theogony*) and illustrated in the visual arts, these are now valued chiefly for aesthetic reasons. But they are also significant as efforts to describe and explain the workings of the universe and man. As such, they are predecessors of metaphysics and of pure science, even though their methods and conclusions are radically different. The explanations grew up along with the technologies, sometimes as developments of these. In the minds of poets and philosophers, especially in Greece, the attitude of wonder and curiosity seems also to have motivated early theorizing, more or less apart from immediately practical considerations.

For uncounted centuries the animistic, totem-istic, dualistic, and other forms of supernaturalistic theory ruled unchallenged. Free imagination was checked, not so much by empirical evidence as by custom and social pressures, including the fear of new ideas.

The revolutionary steps toward pure science in Greece involved, as we have seen, an attempt to substitute reason and empirical observation for faith and fantasy; also, in the tradition of Democritus, an attempt to explain phenomena in terms of natural causes instead of spirits, magic, and miracles. But the older type of explanation persisted in the mystic-religious strain from Pythagoras through Renaissance Neo-Platonism, substituting a depersonalized system of eternal ideas for the deities of popular religion.

Many types of ancient thought were ancestral to the pure sciences. We have mentioned technology as one, and Egyptian surveying as an ancestor of geometry. Belief in the magical power of numbers and experiments with the strings of the lyre also contributed to Pythagorean mathematics and the theory of harmony.

In all fields, naturalistic theories have had to compete with supernaturalistic ones, especially in astronomy, chemistry, biology, and psychology. The dualistic and idealistic traditions have proven flexible in adapting themselves to some aspects of science. Dualism was briefly reconciled with mathematics and primitive physiology in Descartes; idealism with evolutionary biology in the Hegelian vitalists through Bergson. Both are still trying to keep a foothold in physics, biology, and psychology, by retaining the concept of an independent soul or life force.

Thus the victory of scientific empiricism, naturalism, and rationalism has been slow and gradual, outside as well as inside the realm of art. Science has had to compromise for centuries with supernaturalism in each successive field, though prevailing little by little. Individual thinkers have expressed this compromise with varying emphasis

[14] Singer, C. (ed.), *The History of Technology*, Vol. IV, pp. 663 ff.

[392]

on one or the other component. The division of thought and action into fields or compartments, such as "church" and "state," reaches deeply into contemporary life. A man may be a naturalist on week-days, a supernaturalist on Sundays; a naturalist in physics, a supernaturalist in psychology and ethics; a naturalist in biological technology, yet a believer in mythical explanations of biological phenomena.

In view of the ancient origins of pure science —at least twenty-five centuries ago—it seems at first surprising that so long a time elapsed before its systematic application in the field of physical technology. Surprising at least until one realizes what formidable obstacles have delayed its growth. Similar obstacles, and others in addition, remain to block the acceptance of scientific thought in the social, psychological, and aesthetic fields. Pure science, as organized knowledge, research, and theory, is developing in these fields. The world could perhaps be managed reasonably and peacefully in accordance with its teachings. But the attempt to introduce it in the actual technics of control meets with stubborn resistance, not only from the selfish and predatory, but from men of good will who remain attached to prescientific modes of thought in human affairs.

7. PAST ATTEMPTS AT A TECHNOLOGY OF ART IN EUROPE

Our discussion up to this point has shown that science and art are not directly antithetical. They do not occupy permanently separate fields. They often cooperate. Science is basically an attitude of mind, a way of thinking and acting, which can be applied in any field of phenomena or human activity. It has been partly accepted and applied in the arts, but much less there than in other fields.

The term "art," in the modern aesthetic, non-evaluative sense, stands for a diversified group of technics and devices which are used for many purposes, especially that of stimulating and guiding certain types of psychosocial response which are called "aesthetic." These are managed to some extent, and have long been managed, with the aid of scientific knowledge and technology, especially in certain arts such as architecture and horticulture. Science can be used in this way, not merely with respect to physical techniques and materials, but for the determination and achievement of aesthetic and other psychosocial ends such as beauty and healthy social life through city-planning. When an art does make use of scientific knowledge and methods, it tends to become more rapidly cumulative as the physical, utilitarian technics have done. But in some of the fine arts, especially poetry, music, and painting, the attempt to use scientific thinking has encountered strong emotional and ideological resistance, which has caused a return to prescientific thinking. This has been especially true in the practice of the arts concerned, as to both performance and creative composition; less so in aesthetics, since this is more completely intellectual in its aims. But in aesthetics it has operated to prevent the development of a practical, technological approach, as in Bernard Bosanquet's remark, cited above. Bosanquet, a metaphysical idealist in the tradition of Plato and Hegel, assumed that any attempt on the part of aesthetics to guide or aid the artist would be to "commit the impertinence of invading the artist's domain with an *apparatus belli* of critical principles and precepts," an impertinence which has drawn upon aesthetics "much obloquy." Hence the aesthetician must disclaim all desire to "interfere with" the artist, and pursue his studies only "to satisfy an intellectual interest of his own."

In thus identifying help or guidance to the artist with some sort of coercion—"invasion" or "interference"—Bosanquet was partly justified by previous attempts to lay down absolute laws of beauty and good art; attempts made chiefly by philosophers of his own idealistic school. But he misunderstood the spirit of modern technology, which (as we have just seen) is not to prescribe specific aims or binding rules, but to show the practitioner in any field how to do more successfully, effectively, and certainly whatever he wishes to do. So far as technology is concerned, the technician is free to accept or reject such aid and advice. On the whole technicians in other fields have finally decided to accept it, perhaps with reservations and modifications. If aesthetics were conducted in an empirical, descriptive way, pointing out that certain kinds of art tend to produce certain kinds of effect on certain kinds of person under certain conditions, then it would be only a step for the artist (if he so desired) to apply this knowledge in practice. He could use the appropriate means to produce the effect he desired, or modify it so as to produce a different one.

The fact that aesthetics and related subjects have no adequate, reliable body of such technological advice to give the artist is not surprising, since there has been no serious, concerted attempt to build it up in recent years. It is due in part to the opposition of scholars such as Bosanquet. We have rejected some of the arguments on which the reaction was based, such as the theory that art and scientific technology are radically different—one spiritual and the other material, one purely logical and the other purely emotional and imaginative, etc. But the question still remains as to why the emotional resistance to technology in the field of art is still so strong, in spite of the rapid advance of science in related psychosocial fields in the twentieth century. To answer it, we must look briefly at some of the previous attempts to develop art along the lines of rationalistic technology.

In the words of Julian Huxley, noted in a previous chapter, "theories of aesthetics do not emerge until after millennia of the practice of art." Artistic technics developed thousands of years before the philosophy of art, now called "aesthetics," achieved explicit statement in the works of Plato and Aristotle. No doubt there developed also, even in paleolithic times, the rudiments of artistic technology in transmitted oral instructions as to how to draw a bull or chip a leaf-shaped flint. These were empirical, rule-of-thumb technologies, far from scientific but later systematized in craft mysteries and written down for public information.

Plato's philosophy of art includes a technology, partly naturalistic and partly supernaturalistic. The latter appears in his *a priori* belief that certain kinds of art can lead the soul upward from the sensual to the transcendental level. These are not the imitative kinds but those expressing ideals of perfect beauty, harmony, goodness, and truth. The divine madness of the artist is one possible mode of ascent; intellectual dialectic the other. The more naturalistic technology appears in his advice on the use of art (especially music and poetry) in the education of the guardians. Proceeding on the psychological assumption that a certain kind of art will tend to produce a similar kind of mood and character, he prefers the simple, stately, vigorous, old-fashioned kind of music to the kind which expresses and causes luxurious softness. This is the prototype of all Western aesthetic technologies in which art is used as a means to some social, political, ethical, psychological, or military end, rather than for its own sake or the immediate satisfaction of perceiving it. In his earlier works, Plato disparaged pleasure as an end, especially that derived from popular art; but later he became a little more tolerant.

There must have been many books on the practice of various arts in the time of Aristotle. His pupil Aristoxenus wrote one on music (the *Harmonics*), which is one of our few extant examples of ancient musical technology. It was not remarkable that Aristotle himself should have treated poetry (and by implication other arts) in a functional way. He did the same for oratory in the *Rhetoric*. But the *Poetics* is far more than a working manual on "how to do it." The beginnings of aesthetic morphology as a pure science are present in his brief allusion to the components of poetic form, such as plot, character, thought, diction, and song. His discussion of poetic ends and means, pleasures and displeasures, is an application of the psychology of his day. His "rules" are stated in no absolutistic spirit, but rather as reasonable generalizations on current practice. Aristotle granted the right of the masses to enjoy their own kind of art. There was a place, he said, for "highly strung and unnaturally colored melodies" played by professional musicians before mechanics and laborers, although the free and educated would listen elsewhere to their own kind of music.[15] While aristocratic in tone, this was a step toward recognizing the relativity of tastes.

What might have been a scientific aesthetics and technology of art, as part of a general development of technology in Hellenistic Greece, went down in the ruins of Greek culture. Steps toward a Roman revival appear in Vitruvius, Pliny, and a few others, but with no great philosophic mind to guide them into broadly humanistic theory. Horace's *Art of Poetry* is explicitly technological as a guide for poets, by showing them how to "inform and delight" the reader. But its rules are comparatively dogmatic and restrictive, erecting the tastes of an educated Roman gentleman of the time into universal principles. An oversimplified psychology, unaware of the variability of individual responses to the same kind of art, is evident from the first in Horace's assumption that a grotesque combination of human and animal parts is necessarily ridiculous. There is no hint at possible change or development in art or of problems to be solved by empirical study. The Dionysian strain of divine madness in art, to which even Plato gave cautious recognition, is obscured by a meticulous Apollonian classicism, emphasizing unity, order, clarity, and perfection of finish.

The Renaissance revival of classical aesthetic theory was at first strongly Platonic, then more Aristotelian and naturalistic. Castelvetro in the late sixteenth century, Corneille and Boileau in the seventeenth, revived with variations the technological approach to poetics. It was not confined to mere techniques as such. There was much discussion of the ends of poetry and other arts—whether chiefly for pleasure or for moral elevation—and also of the necessary means to them, such as the three dramatic unities of place, time, and action. Castelvetro recommended verse on the stage because the voice can be raised more easily in poetic speech, so as to arouse emotional states. The poetics of Aristotle and Horace was used by poets and dramatists much as treatises on anatomy, perspective, and proportion were used by painters, so as to achieve the desired effect: a balanced, unified representation, improving on nature while basically true to it. François Ogier, in his *Preface to Tyre and Sidon* (1628), made a step toward relativism in calling attention to the differences of taste between nations and periods. He recommended that the writers of his day adapt their work to their own country, language, and point of view, instead of imitating the ancients too exactly.[16]

Aesthetics in the Renaissance and early seventeenth century was still much under the influence of Platonic absolutism, with its *a priori* laws derived from a transcendental conception of goodness, truth, and beauty. This was one type of neo-classicism, but very different from the empirical, relativistic type, based more on Horace and the Epicureans, which arose in the late seventeenth and eighteenth centuries. This latter type rejected *a priori* rules and relied instead on the concept of "taste"—i.e., *good* taste, the taste of superior persons. Leaders in this transition were the Abbé du Bos, Voltaire, and David Hume. (See, for instance, Hume's essay on "The Standard of Taste.") It was aristocratic in assuming the superiority of the taste of innately sensitive persons, well-read, well-traveled, and cultivated in the arts. These, it was assumed, would usually be wealthy gentlemen of the upper classes, who had been able to develop their taste through the enjoyment of good art. "Taste" was conceived as sensuous rather than intellectual, hence not to be conveyed in general rules; more akin to good taste in wine, cuisine, and manners than to geometry. It

---

[15] *Politics*, VIII.

[16] Quotations from Castelvetro and Ogier are contained in B. H. Clark's *European Theories of the Drama* (New York, 1918, 1947).

was not restricted to art of Greek and Roman origin, and a man of taste could enjoy (for example) rococo chinoiserie.

In this trend, Epicurus outweighed Plato. In theoretical minds, however, it led to a search for empirical generalizations on what will please the person of good taste. "Genius" was not to be bound by such rules, but would not want to go far from them. This late phase of neo-classicism was still far from the romantic glorification of emotion and the common man—peasant, child, or savage.

R. Le Bossu, in the late seventeenth century,[17] tried to develop aesthetic technology still further on a psychological basis, through adapting specific poetic means to specific mental and emotional effects. Following Aristotle, he assigned certain "passions" to certain types of drama. "Comedy has for its share joy and pleasant surprise" while tragedy has terror and compassion. The epic, he added, comprehends all passions, including joy and sorrow, but each epic has its own emotive effects which distinguish it from others of the species. Achilles contributes anger and terror to the *Iliad*, while Aeneas is tender and gentle. Incompatible emotions should not be stirred up, said Le Bossu, and the audience should be gradually led from tranquillity to stronger feelings. This approach influenced Dryden and Pope in England and in general the neo-classic art of the eighteenth century. Increasing emphasis was placed on the role of individual genius and its right to disregard past rules and practices. Neo-classical rationalism amplified the ancient list of emotions to be sought in art, and also the range of artistic devices for producing them.

A related movement in eighteenth-century music was the theory of affects or affections (*Affekten-lehre*). According to J. Quantz and P. E. Bach, the chief aim of music is "to portray certain typical emotions, such as the tender, the languid, the passionate, etc."[18] It was realized in the "sensitive style" of music in the late eighteenth century, which tended to replace the Italian "gallant style."

"In spite of its rationalistic nature and schematic methods," says W. Apel, "it paves the way for the free expressiveness of the Beethoven style." Bukofzer explains that the doctrine was based on the ancient analogy between music and rhetoric, attempting to develop concrete musical figures to correspond with figures of speech. A system of "topics" was conceived as a "guide to invention" (*ars inveniendi*) which would facilitate the choice of a particular figure to represent a particular affection. However, Bukofzer comments, the musical figures were in themselves ambiguous apart from a musical or verbal context. They did not "express" affections, but only presented or signified them. Hence one cannot classify an isolated figure as meaning joy, beatitude, or the like. The affections were conceived as static attitudes. J. S. Bach used such figures metaphorically, together with other devices. According to baroque thought, says Bukofzer, a musical idea could present an abstract affection in concrete form.

While romanticism abandoned the rationalistic, schematic nature of *Affektenlehre*, it retained the desire to portray or express in music the emotions of ordinary life. This led through early romantic music to Wagner's leit-motifs and to the program-music of Debussy and Stravinsky. It was the formalistic school of E. Hanslick (*Vom musikalisch Schönen*, 1854), in most ways closer to the neo-classicists, who led the attack on all such attempts to express outside, non-musical emotions in music. Hanslick admitted that adjectives such as "powerful," "graceful," "tender," and "passionate" can be used to describe the musical character of a passage, but not to suggest a specific feeling in the composer or listener.[19]

[17] *Traité du Poème Épique* (Paris, 1708). *Cf.* Gilbert and Kuhn, pp. 214, 233 f.

[18] *Affektenlehre*, in W. Apel, *Harvard Dictionary of Music* (Cambridge, Mass., 1950). M. F. Bukofzer discusses the subject more fully in *Music in the Baroque Era* (New York, 1947), pp. 388 f. He mentions Nucius, Bernhard, Vogt, and J. Mattheson (*Der Vollkommene Capellmeister*, 1739) as leading exponents of the theory.

[19] "Aesthetics of Music" in *Harvard Dictionary of Music*, pp. 18–19.

In most of this discussion, there was a failure to distinguish clearly between (a) the expression, suggestion, or representation of an emotion and (b) the production or stimulation of that emotion in the listener. Even as to "expression," it was not made clear whether the composer himself must feel it inwardly, in addition to presenting the musical stimuli which suggest or mean it. Following Plato, it was often assumed that the expression or representation of a feeling would necessarily arouse the same one in listeners. Coupled with the idea that expression was the chief aim of art in general, this led to an emphasis on how to find the appropriate "language" to express each feeling, mood, and sentiment. The question of what effect it would have on observers was thus left to take care of itself. Proper expression by the artist would automatically insure the desired feeling in the listener, it was often assumed. On the same ground, it was assumed that adequate portrayal of noble, moral characters in painting or poetry would tend to make the observer more noble and moral. Plato makes the same assumption in condemning Homer and Hesiod for their "immoral" gods. Now we realize more clearly that the effects of art are more complex and variable than this. A certain feeling or type of character may be clearly expressed in the work of art, successfully communicated to a percipient and understood as such by him, yet arouse a very different emotional effect in him, depending on his own character and temporary mood.

8. ARTISTIC TECHNOLOGY IN INDIA. THE THEORY OF RASA

Indian aesthetics was close to the Greek in conceiving art as a means to certain ends.[20] It excluded the doctrine of art for art's sake. Coomaraswamy quotes the *Sahitya Darpana* as saying, "All expressions, human or revealed, are directed to an end beyond themselves; or if not so determined are thereby comparable only to the utterances of a madman." Pleasure was not condemned, for aesthetic experience is an ecstasy or delight of the reason, and the work of art serves as a stimulus to the release of the spirit from all inhibitions of reason. It can only come into being as "a thing ordered to specific ends." (P. 57).

The basic conception of art as having only instrumental value is capable of wide variation as to the specific ends to be sought and the most effective means to them. The former can be worldly or otherworldly, sensual or spiritual, social or individual, objective or subjective. Whichever ends are chosen, the appropriate means and technological theory will of course be different. One chief aim sought may be, as in modern romanticism, the individual self-expression of the artist. But this aim, and consequently a great deal of modern aesthetic technology, was foreign to Platonic and Indian aesthetics. "Least of all," says Coomaraswamy, "has it [the Asiatic view] anything to do with functional self-expression." "To glorify rebellion and independence, as in the modern deification of genius and tolerance of the vagaries of genius, is plainly preposterous." (P. 23).

Traditional Indian aesthetic doctrines were an integral part of the religious, moral, and social system of India. This was not entirely rigid. It allowed different aims and methods to various types of person; many cults, philosophies, and theories of art arose. Some were more naturalistic then others in granting the worth of earthly pleasures such as physical love and sensuous art, at least on certain levels of experience. These were not held incompatible with a rise to transcendental levels, and could symbolize divine attributes. Some techniques of yoga are life-rejecting from the standpoint of Western psychology and ethics, while others, milder and more positive in nature, are intended to enhance the richness of sensuous and fantasy life on this earth. There is some dispute as to the relative values of art and yoga in attaining

20 "The Theory of Art in Asia," Ch. I of *The Transformation of Nature in Art* (Cambridge, Mass., 1934), pp. 47 ff.

desired spiritual states. Some lovers of art praise it above the extreme, unnatural, and constrictive exercises of Hatha Yoga as a means to liberation of the spirit.

The Indian technology of art was intended for the guidance, not only of the artist, but of the spectator as well. Abhinavagupta discusses the ends and means of the drama from four standpoints: those of the spectator, the dramatist, the stage manager (including actors and musicians), and society, including its moral and cultural ends. (Pandey, p. 385). "The audience is to be instructed," says Abhinavagupta, "not only in regard to the empirical and semi-empirical aims of human life... but also in regard to the transcendental and highest aim, namely, the final emancipation." (Pandey, p. 228). On a somewhat lower level, the aesthetic attitude is described psychologically as a type of experience and a series of steps toward the state of mind which is necessary for the fullest enjoyment of a dramatic presentation. One begins the rise from the ordinary sense-level to the aesthetic one by an "attitude of play" on going to the theater. One anticipates a succession of beautiful sights and sounds. One becomes self-forgetful when the music starts, and inhibits ordinary, worldly ideas. The introductory scene helps develop this attitude into one of "facing the entire production" and "identifying with the focus of the situation." Ordinary consciousness of time, place, reality, right and wrong, doubtful and possible, are inhibited in apprehending the presented action. The percipient goes on to identify with the hero, ignoring the actor's personality and rejecting all that is conflicting in the presentation. Identification is reached when the percipient "evaluates the entire situation in which the hero is placed, exactly as does the hero himself." (Pandey, p. 170). "The Indian dramatist aims at presenting an emotive experience and not action, as do the European dramatists." The physical situation is introduced only to present an inner state. It is impossible to appreciate an Indian drama fully, says Pandey, merely through perceiving the external, physical situation; it is only a means to an end. The inner experience can be known only by identification. Aesthetic experience includes experience of basic emotions as organized in the dramatic situation, with mimetic changes and transient emotions, and with the peculiar flavor given by harmonious mixture of all these ingredients. (Pandey, p. 183).

The Indian technology of art was focused on the concept of *rasa*. Its earliest extant text is the *Natya Sastra* of Bharata (fourth or fifth century A.D.), and it was further developed in the tenth century by Abhinavagupta.[21] Bharata's text, says Gnoli, is a collection of rules and instructions, mostly concerned with the production of drama and the education of actors. In drama, the visual and auditory arts collaborate in arousing in the spectator a state of consciousness or "flavor" called rasa, which pervades and enchants him. Aesthetic experience is the act of tasting rasa and immersing oneself in it to the exclusion of everything else. It is also that which is tasted. In such experience, Abhinavagupta added, the consciousness is freed from external interference and practical desires; it has no end outside itself and is pleasure, bliss, or rest. Rasa breaks the chain of causality and is manifested rather than caused by the poetic word. It belongs to the poet, who expresses what he sees in the form of a generalized feeling or passion, which is transferred to the spectator.

Rasa is not only a generalized state, but includes a list of specific rasas, eight or nine in number, corresponding to the permanent feelings or mental states of human nature (Gnoli, p. 29). These feelings are: delight, laughter, sorrow, anger, heroism, fear, disgust, astonishment, and serenity. As transformed in aesthetic experience, they are: the erotic, the comic, the pathetic, the furious, the heroic, the terrible, the odious, the marvelous,

[21] His commentary on Bharata is translated and annotated by R. Gnoli in *The Aesthetic Experience According to Abhinavagupta* (Rome, 1956). Rasa and other Indian aesthetic theories are discussed in detail by K.C. Pandey in *Comparative Aesthetics*, Vol. I, *Indian Aesthetics* (Varanasi, India, 1959). See also A. Coomaraswamy, *The Transformation of Nature in Art*, Ch. I, "The Theory of Art in Asia" (Cambridge, Mass., 1934).

and the quietistic. The feelings correspond to some extent, but not exactly, with the "affects" or "passions" of neo-classic aesthetics; the rasas or aesthetic transformations, with the aesthetic types or categories distinguished in traditional Western aesthetics. In ordinary life, each mental state is manifested and accompanied by certain causes, effects, and concomitant elements. The same causes, etc., do not arouse the corresponding sentiment exactly when presented on the stage or in poetry. They manifest an aesthetic pleasure or rasa, which is colored by the nature of the mental states which they would arouse if they were real. As elements in poetic expression, they are called determinants, consequents, and transitory mental states. Of these last there are thirty-three varieties such as discouragement, weakness, contentment, joy, etc. Rasa will produce certain effects in the spectators, such as making them mutter in fear, making their hair stand on end, and the like. The causes of rasa are the effects of the permanent mental states.

"The relation between the Determinants, the ordinary mental states, and Rasa," says Gnoli, "is the central problem of Indian poetics." It dealt with the relations between the basic emotional and conative mechanisms of human nature, the power of poetic words and dramatic situations to arouse certain partly similar feelings, and the way in which aesthetic experience combines and transforms them into a specific, pleasant "flavor." The musical ragas (modes) and their pictorial illustrations express specific moods and dramatic or poetic situations, loosely related to the various rasas.

Although the theory of rasa is prescientific, it is based on empirical observation and introspection as to the emotional effects of art on human nature. As such, it goes far beyond most Western psychology in subtlety of analysis and classification of types. It is part of a mystic-religious ideology, in which the experience is conceived as having five levels, the last being transcendency. One is to rise from the ordinary sense or empirical level to the aesthetic or cathartic level, with self-forgetfulness and a universalized subject-object relation;

thence to a subconscious level of intense introversion. (Pandey, pp. 166, 142). The mystical context makes it difficult to compare this theory of art with those of Western naturalism, but there is undoubtedly a common basis of observed aesthetic phenomena, psychological inquiry, theoretical explanation, and practical application.

9. WESTERN ATTITUDES TOWARD AESTHETIC EXPERIENCE.

Modern Western theories of the aesthetic attitude are somewhat analogous to the Indian, especially as to (a) the necessary detachment from outside concerns and (b) identification and empathy. But Western aesthetics has not developed them in much detail as to the necessary steps for attaining the aesthetic attitude or as to the varieties of "flavor" such an experience may contain. Western methods of teaching art appreciation tend to neglect the inner, subjective phase of the experience, the attainment of a suitable attitude of mind; this being left to the observer as something that will take care of itself. The same phase in artistic creation—achieving a state of inner harmony and freedom from anxiety before action—is likewise ignored in the Western education of artists. Modern Western technology in both these realms deals almost wholly with objective, externally observable phenomena: with the artist's overt skills and knowledge in handling the medium; with the way he represents a natural object or makes an observable design; also with the observer's power to see or hear and recognize these things; to perceive sensory forms and interpret their meanings, representational or symbolic. The feelings which can be expressed in art and those which can be aroused by it are alike supposed to be so infinitely varied and so indescribable in words that any attempt to classify them abstractly is sure to be inadequate. Scientific psychology has certainly not gone far in that direction, or tried to do so. Western languages are richly endowed with terms to express and describe subtle feelings. They are used in literary art itself and in critical writings about art. But as long as Western psychology is so strongly extroverted and behavioristic in approach, it will not be able to help much toward a technology for achieving through art specific emotional experiences. We expect the artist to try to move us in certain ways, and reserve the right to resist, comply, or respond in any other way we choose. Often we are impatient, in perceiving art, to judge its value and originality; to comment on it verbally and exhibit our own connoisseurship. Thus we lack the self-forgetfulness and identification which oriental theory considers so important.

This difference is no doubt correlated with our general emphasis on the control of external nature and on accurate observation of the empirical world. Western culture in general is more extroverted; Eastern (especially Indian) has been more introverted, and still is so in conservative intellectual and artistic levels, in spite of recent social changes. In Europe, the romantic tradition tended to correct the neo-classic by a stronger emphasis on the subjective in art and theories of art. Contemporary Western art is increasingly subjective in certain respects and psychoanalytic science has begun to explore the inner world in its own way. The Freudian technique of raising inner situations to the conscious level for intelligent adjustment is farther from the oriental approach than the Jungian technique. All of these approaches could be utilized in working out a naturalistic aesthetic technology, in pursuit of the kinds of experience which are most highly esteemed in Western culture.

We in the West have hardly begun to recognize the extent to which "art appreciation" (as it is vaguely called) can be developed into a complex technique of its own. Too often we assume that (a) all art is, or should be, easy enough for anyone to understand and enjoy, and (b) that the only things worth studying about it are historical facts. We are now beginning to teach children how to see pictures, hear music, and read poetry so as to grasp the form, style, and subtle nuances of individual expression. Experts differ on the best ways of doing so. There is a gulf here, as in the technology of art production, between those who pin their faith on verbal, rational analysis and explanation as a means to appreciation and those (the more romantic or mystic) who insist that real appreciation must be immediate, intuitive, nonverbal, a sudden flash of enlightenment and identification with the work of art as a unique, indivisible unity.

There is some truth in both sides of this argument, as usual. Intellectual analysis and information can be overdone so as to prevent aesthetic apperception; but without some of it the experience is likely to be vague and superficial. Since much depends on the state of mind of the observer —for example, whether he is free, relaxed, and attentive or distracted by irrelevant thoughts and worries—our technology and educational procedure for art appreciation may profit from the oriental emphasis on this phase of the experience. Many intermediate courses are possible between the extreme, Kantian conception of aesthetic experience as purely contemplative, detached and disinterested, and the Deweyan conception of it as continuous with ordinary life. Without condemning all feelings of "interest" or desire toward the subject of a picture (an erotic nude, for example) and all practical thinking in relation to it, one can agree that there is a certain type of experience, relatively free from outside distraction, which has its own distinctive values. To achieve a full, complex and satisfactory experience of a work of art some technical training is necessary, and the technology of appreciation in various arts is still to be worked out on a scientific level.

To a modern reader, all past attempts at a psychological technology of art and aesthetic experience are apt to seem oversimplified, rigid, and mechanical. We have learned that the range of emotional and other effects produced by art is too great to be covered by any simple list. As to what artistic devices will produce a certain effect, we have learned that many hidden, unpredictable variables may affect the outcome. People differ individually and culturally too much for us to assume that a given device will always have the same effect, even on persons of similar social and educational background. Assuming that one aim of aesthetic technology is to advise an artist how he can produce certain psychic effects—immediate or deferred, aesthetic or otherwise—there is much to be learned about how to produce them in different kinds of person. Part of the effect may be unconscious and inexplicable to the person concerned.

Yet the task is not impossible. People and their responses are not completely different or unpredictable. Within a certain culture at least, one can sometimes predict with fair success what the most common response will be in persons of a given type. Dealers, publishers, film producers and the like must do so in order to make a living. The fact that prescientific aesthetic technology now seems absurdly oversimplified and rigid does not prove that it was totally false or unworkable. It seems to have worked fairly well as long as artists and their patrons willingly thought and felt in this way, and while it coincided with the general climate of baroque culture. People had not yet acquired the romantic aversion to rules and mechanical devices. These were never sufficient in themselves to guarantee good art, but could be put to good use by a Racine or J. S. Bach as a part of his total resources. If artists and critics again look more favorably on science, these eighteenth- century attempts at an aesthetic technology can be corrected, developed, and refined.

Meanwhile, musicologists and psychologists of the various arts have not ceased to experiment and theorize on the "expressiveness" and emotional effects of various types of art. They have done so, as Bosanquet would say, "for the sake of knowledge" and "to satisfy an intellectual interest," without much hope that such knowledge would be of use to artists. Other writers, some of them

composers and performers, address themselves more directly to other artists and prospective artists in discussing musical expression. If you want to express a certain mood or feeling, they say in effect, this is how to do it.[22] But the methods are much freer than those of the past centuries, and less aimed at arousing specific emotions in the listener.

Any generalization about the effects of art runs the risk of oversimplifying human nature. Authors often say, "this is pleasant" or "that is ugly," "this is harsh and dissonant" or "that gives one a feeling of serenity," without realizing that the kind of art concerned may have a very different effect on different persons. Various cultures, periods, age-levels, sexes, educational levels, respond in different ways, and we have no right to assume that any one is correct or superior. Research must take account of the diversity in actual responses, and also in the kind of experiences which are preferred. The "ends" or desired effects in art are enormously variable, though perhaps not infinitely so.

Our modern awareness of the variability of aesthetic experience throws some light on the question of why the arts so often have to "begin again" in successive civilizations. Aesthetic needs and desires are not as stable and constant as those for basic physical satisfactions. Even if the knowledge of how to produce certain aesthetic effects had been more cumulative, successive cultures would not want exactly the same ones. Differences in milieu and social order tend to produce different responses. For example, feudal loyalty is a strongly emotive theme in Japanese literature; jealousy in Western literature. These tendencies change from generation to generation, and so plastic is human

22 On expression in music and other arts, see for example M. Schoen, *The Effects of Music* (New York, 1927); *The Psychology of Music* (New York, 1940). R. W. Lundin, *An Objective Psychology of Music* (New York, 1953), esp. pp. 164 ff. on "Theories of the Aesthetic Response." A. R. Chandler, *Beauty and Human Nature* (New York, 1934), esp. Chs. 6 ("The Expressiveness of Color"), 12 ("The Expressiveness of Music"). K. Liepmann, *The Language of Music* (New York, 1953), Ch. 15. F. Nicholls, *The Language of Music or Musical Expression and Characterization* (London, 1924), Chs. IV–VII on expression through harmony, movement, melody, and variation in tone.

nature that the same ones never seem to recur exactly. People do not know exactly what they want from art until a new kind is presented to them; then they like it or dislike it, or perhaps learn to like it in time. What they want is not sufficiently clear or constant to allow a cumulative technological formulation of the ways to provide it. At least, that has been the situation up to date, and if changing at all it is changing slowly and uncertainly.

10. ROMANTIC REACTIONS AGAINST RATIONALISTIC TECHNOLOGY IN ART AND LIFE. OCCIDENTAL AND ORIENTAL EXAMPLES. ZEN AS A METHOD

Attempts to develop a rationalistic technology of art in various periods and cultures have been followed by reactions against that approach.[23] As rationalism has gone to extremes at times, the reaction against it has at times been equally extreme; at other times the issue has been milder, a question of degree. Many varieties of rationalism and irrationalism or anti-rationalism have arisen in philosophy and theology.

We are now considering the issue with special reference to aesthetics and the arts, where it is often stated in terms of "rules" and "reasoning" in the creation of art. Rationalism has sought to establish such rules and principles of beauty and value in art through reasoning, by *a priori* or empirical methods or both. Anti-rationalist movements have attacked not only the particular rules proposed, such as the three unities, but also all reliance on rules and reasoning in the creation of art. The artist, they say, is not bound by them and can not learn from them how to create good art. The better course for him is to trust to his own intuition, feeling, and imagination, or perhaps to some supernatural inspiration. Even if he could produce a certain effect on the observer at will by the simple means

of presenting to him certain recognized artistic devices, that success would have nothing to do with good art. (So the argument runs.) No real artist would work in that way; it is too mechanical, too cut and dried. It is not hard to arouse a desired emotion; the masses are easily swayed to tears or laughter by what is now called "hokum". A skilled experienced craftsman in the theater can pull the audience this or that way at will, without feeling the emotion himself. But this, in Tolstoy's words, is mere "counterfeit art" if practiced *à froid*, as a mere bag of technical tricks. A genuine artist, it is said, is above all sincere; he expresses his own experience, present or remembered. His approach is entirely different from the one proposed by neo-classical technology. He does not begin with thoughts of how to influence a possible observer. He begins from within, from his own inner vision, which he mentally conceives and then expresses communicable form. Whether the public or the patron likes it or not is a minor consideration.

Which approach is better, more productive of good art, has never been conclusively decided. It can hardly be settled as long as standards differ so widely on what artists and what works of art are really great. As neo-classical methods worked fairly well in the neo-classical period, so romantic methods worked fairly well in the romantic age. Perhaps a really great artist can use either or both; Shakespeare could appeal to the judicious and also to the groundlings. Without creative ability, neither method is infallible. But certainly the romantic attack did much to discredit the whole idea of extending scientific technology into the arts.

[23] The term "rationalism" is used here in a broad sense, to mean the practice of basing one's opinions on reasoning; also the theory that human reasoning is a more reliable source of true knowledge than mysticism, revelation, authoritarian dogma, emotion, unconscious fantasy and impulse, and other non-rational methods. In this sense it does not imply a reliance on *a priori* principles at the expense of empirical testing. Such reliance is an extreme form of rationalism, sometimes called "a priori" or "dogmatic" rationalism. It is inconsistent with empiricism, which relies also on sense data. A moderate rationalism, such as that of experimental science, is allied with empricism in that it uses sense data as well as logical inference in deriving and testing opinions.

Romanticism collided head-on with neo-classical rationalism in Blake's marginal comments (c. 1808) on Reynolds' *Discourses*.[24] "We ought to distinguish," the classicist had said, "how much is to be given to enthusiasm, and how much to reason... taking care not to lose in terms of vague admiration, that solidity and truth of principle, upon which alone we can reason, and may be enabled to practise." To which Blake the romanticist replied, "What has Reasoning to do with the Art of Painting?" "To generalize is to be an Idiot. To Particularize is the Alone Distinction of Merit." To Reynolds' assertion that "mere enthusiasm will carry you but a little way," Blake answered hotly, "Mere Enthusiasm is the All in All! Bacon's Philosophy has Ruin'd England." And later, "If Art was Progressive We should have had Mich. Angelos and Rafaels to Succeed and to Improve upon each other. But it is not so. Genius dies with its Possessor and comes not again till Another is Born with It."

As a recurrent attitude and movement, romanticism has occurred many times in the world's history, often as an explicit attack on rigid rules and too much thinking. In China, the reaction against Confucian formalism began early, around the time of Confucius himself, in the teachings of early Taoism. It was not a short-lived movement but an enduring attitude and way of life which persisted along with Confucianism down to the present century in China and Japan. Reinforced by certain elements in Buddhism from the Wei dynasty on, it acted as a balance and a corrective, a relaxing, and at times a liberating force. Individual artists and schools of art, as well as scholars and officials in all fields, could work out their own syntheses from all three traditions.

As we noted in the previous chapter, romantic anti-rationalism is often associated with primitivism: with a call for return to the old days when people lived more simply and freely, without having to think so much or act so carefully. Men in those days, it is supposed, did not have to obey so many conventions of morality and etiquette, to

scheme and contrive so anxiously in order to hold their heads above water. This mood of revolt and longing finds a regular channel today in annual vacations or more frequent trips to the country. One can get away from city responsibilities, put on old clothes, and go fishing. The Chinese artist-scholars who painted rustic landscapes in the spirit of Ch'an during late Sung and Yuan times, and the collectors who prized their works, often expressed such desires in poetic inscriptions on the paintings themselves. Under the Mongol emperors, court life and official responsibility became so irksome to many in the north that they escaped entirely to the south of China, where they had more freedom to pursue a life of art or meditation under rustic conditions.

The fact that rules and reasoning are felt as oppressive in such movements is significant. It indicates that, for many persons at least, the rules are no longer means of attaining a good life or good art, but are obsolete and cramping. Reasoning is felt, not as an enjoyable exercise of man's mental apparatus or a means to worthwhile understanding and discovery, but as a difficult, anxious, never-ending attempt to get things which turn out to be unattainable or worthless; of trying to solve problems which cannot be solved. Hence the delightful allure of anything which promises to let one stop thinking and worrying, to live immediately and vividly in peaceful relaxation. Rules and reason in general are blamed for the trouble. Says Omar Khayyam,

You know, my Friends, with what a brave Carouse
I made a Second Marriage in my house;
   Divorced old barren Reason from my Bed,
And took the Daughter of the Vine to Spouse.

But the poet uses some adroit reasoning in defense of his Epicurean philosophy, and he is not without a technology of his own for achieving Paradise on earth. It calls for a simple life, but includes several kinds of art: a book of verses, a jug of wine, and "Thou beside me singing." Likewise Blake, in

[24] *Poetry and Prose of Willam Blake* (London, 1939), pp. 786 ff (London, 1904), pp. 30 ff.

spite of his tirade against reasoning, used a good deal of it in organizing his complex mythology.

The moral and aesthetic rules against which romanticists revolt are one kind of prescientific technology. Those who revolt against them usually want no technology at all: no rules, no tiresome reasoning, no abstract principles or policies. In the long run, however, this always turns out to be impossible. Someone has to think and plan; some regular procedures for bodily health and social cooperation are unavoidable. Paradoxically, the movement to escape from rules and reasoning usually leads in time to a new set of rules and quasi-rational methods for attaining the desired ends. It requires sustained, purposeful effort to live without purpose or planning. The effort leads to a new technology, at first a little simpler than the old, then more and more complex and restrictive along its own lines. The impulse to plan for the morrow, to work out a generalized policy of action, seems too deeply rooted in human nature to be easily suppressed. The leaders of the movement feel impelled to preach their gospel to the world, or at least to demonstrate their non-conformist behavior to a few disciples. Of the latter, some will ask the master to explain his attitude: what values he seeks and how. Others will write down his answers if he does not. Successors will try to clarify or improve the method, and before long a systematized technique has evolved, the regimen of a school or cult, with its own *raison d'être* and *rationale*. If carried far enough, this leads to a deadening routine and the need for another revolt.

In the Taoist classic we can see the beginning of one such involuntary technology for life and art. "The Sage occupies himself with inaction," said Lao Tzu, "and conveys instruction without words. Attain complete vacuity, and sedulously preserve a state of repose... Desire not to desire, and you will not value things difficult to obtain. Learn not to learn, and you will revert to a condition which mankind has lost. Leave all things to take their natural course, and do not interfere."[25]

"Banish wisdom, discard knowledge, and the people will be benefited a hundredfold... Banish learning, and there will be no more grieving."[26] "Discard the stimuli of purpose," said Chuang Tzu,[27] and "free the mind from disturbances."

"The sources of Ch'an Zen," says Coomaraswamy, "are partly Indian, partly Taoist... Its discipline is one of activity and order; its doctrine the invalidity of doctrine, its end an illumination by immediate experience. Ch'an Zen art, seeking realization of the divine being in man, proceeds by way of opening his eyes to a like spiritual essence in the world of Nature external to himself." The Ch'an Zen artist, Coomaraswamy continues, "has been trained according to treatises on style so detailed and explicit that there would seem to be no room left for the operation of personality... and yet immediacy or spontaneity has been more nearly perfectly attained in Ch'an Zen art than anywhere else." (P. 41). Alan Watts, another enthusiast for Zen, is sure that it has not degenerated after 1400 years into the formal observance of precepts; that its criterion is an unmistakable spiritual experience, and that it has found a way to pass on its teaching which can never be explained away by the intellect. The experience is Satori or "sudden realization of the truth of Zen." The Koan, a riddle-like problem which must be answered in a certain, apparently nonsensical or irrelevant way, is "a means of breaking through a barrier." It aims, says Watts,[28] not at destroying the intellect but at controlling or surpassing it. Another technique is a sudden blow of the master's stick at the student's head or back.

Some Western observers, after examining the techniques and interviewing practitioners of Zen, are not so sure of how important the experiences attained really are, or how free the techniques are

[25] L. Giles (tr.), *The Sayings of Lao Tzu* (London, 1904), pp. 30 ff.

[26] A. Waley, *The Way and the Power: a Study of the Tao Te Ching* (London, 1956), pp. 166, 168.

[27] *Musings of a Chinese Mystic* (L. Giles, ed.) (London, 1911), p. 105.

[28] *The Spirit of Zen* (London, 1946), p. 72.

from stultifying routine.[29] Nor are they sure how "immediate" and "spontaneous" are the works of art produced under the stimulus of Zen. Thousands of Haiku (short poems, mostly about nature in symbolic images) are stereotyped in form and meaning; thousands of brush drawings of bamboo and other conventional subjects are much alike. Watts asserts that the first important influence of Zen on Chinese art appears in the T'ang dynasty, in the work of Wu Tao-Tzu, whose paintings are all lost except for one doubtful example. It combines "serenity" and "liveliness" with "a foundation of complete rest," says this author. The spirit of Taoism and Zen, he adds, is found in the Sumiye Japanese style, where the brushstrokes are laid on swiftly and irrevocably, with no possibility of correction. (Pp. 111-13). Watts and D. T. Suzuki, who have written voluminously on the teachings of Zen, have done much to spread an interest in it among American artists and would-be artists. These have used some of its techniques with debatable success, along with other anti-rationalistic methods.

Even if the claims of Zen and Yoga to stimulate good art production are exaggerated, these technologies are enduring and important enough in their own cultures to deserve careful, open-minded study. Granting that they have done something to foster peace of mind and other values, the fact remains that they are fairly elaborate, systematized technologies, involving purposeful planning and regulated sequences of steps. Zen differs from Yoga in certain ways: for one, that it is aimed more at vigorous, conscious, immediate experience, while Yoga seeks a gradual escape from sensation and desire. Insofar as both regard escape from the chain of rebirths as the highest goal, they are supernaturalistic and hence unsusceptible to empirical verification. As to the nature and value of their contribution to artistic creativeness, one must always ask what other factors have been present in the success of the greatest examples, and why the method has not been sufficient to insure success in all cases. If success depends mainly on differences

in innate ability, the value of the method remains questionable, as in most Western methods of art education and techniques for artists. No doubt some followers of Ch'an and Zen have produced good art, and so have Christians, Moslems, romanticists, and neo-classicists. In each case, it is well to inquire, not only what power the belief or technology had to foster creativeness, but also what kind of art it produced.

One function of Zen, according to Koestler, has been to provide a channel of release in Japanese culture from the excessive pressure of conventional duties, moral debts and obligations with their attendant anxieties. Ch'an Zen is certainly correlated with the development of several great styles of landscape painting in China and Japan which express in various ways a love of nature and a sense of union with it. The "flung ink" and Sumiye techniques of painting, even though actually the result of long, planful practice and obedience to rules, do succeed in suggesting the opposite. They may thus arouse a sense of freedom, spontaneity, and easy vigor in the onlooker. Western art might profit from the oriental method of long observation and practice, the cultivation of a harmonious mental state before using the medium, and then a quick, impulsive act of execution.

Some non-rational techniques for stimulating artistic creation are supernaturalistic, relying on trances, prayers, fasting, and other austerities in the hope of divine inspiration, and regarding art as only a step toward further salvation. Others are more naturalistic, employing drugs and intoxicants, as in the case of Coleridge and De Quincy (opiates) and Poe (alcohol). Various drugs such as opium, bhang, mescal, and hashish have been used for centuries in combination with bodily and mental disciplines in the hope of blissful enlightenment. Rhythmic breathing may have a similar effect. The results from an artistic standpoint are always doubtful, and the price in other values is

[29] For example, Arthur Koestler's unfavorable report on Japanese Zen and Indian Yoga in *The Lotus and the Robot* (Macmillan, New York, 1961).

[405]

enormous. Apparently a richly stored imagination can be further stimulated by such means for a while. Romanticists have looked with sympathy or admiration on physical and mental disease and abnormality, as being not only departures from the tiresomely normal but favorable to the release of unconscious impulses and dreams. Disease, insanity, sadism, and suicide through passion have been treated by romanticists with sentimental glamor.[30]

II. CHANGING ATTITUDES TOWARD SCIENCE IN VARIOUS ARTS.

Other strains in the romantic tradition kept a firmer hold on normal life throughout the nineteenth and early twentieth centuries, retaining some elements of naturalism and neo-classicism to make a stronger synthesis. Goethe, whose Werther and young Faust were in some ways prototypes of romantic youth, turned from extreme romanticism to a synthesis of classic and romantic. The mature Faust turned to useful, technical works. Goethe never lost his interest in science and evolution, biology and color-theory. Wagner theorized about the complex, synthetic art-form of the future in addition to creating great examples of it. Coleridge and Poe, both romantic dreamers, sought to whip up their fantasy-lives through artificial stimuli, but both theorized rationally about art. Poe, far from avoiding reason, invented the modern detective and mystery story, in which the intelligent solution of practical problems is the basis of plot.

The nineteenth and early twentieth century was a period of diversity, change, and conflict in styles and theories of art. Scientific naturalism and experimentalism flourished in art by the side of fin-de-siècle decadence. The scientific attitude toward art, not in the form of classical rules but of open-minded, objective study and reporting, revived in the sociological novels of Zola, in the pictorial naturalism of Courbet and in the social criticism of Daumier. Jules Verne developed "science fiction" with prophetic enthusiasm for the wonders of future technology. Eiffel made his tower, itself a triumph of mechanical technology, into a symbol of modern Paris. Far from rejecting reason and science, many of the avant-garde hailed it as an exciting subject for art and an aid to the artist. From Monet to Seurat, impressionists and pointillists made use of the new physical theories of light and color. Some twentieth-century painters, such as Léger, used mechanical themes for decorative design. Architects and furniture designers thought in terms of structural steel, glass, and reinforced concrete as materials; in terms of social functionalism and organic form as aesthetic principles.

Many of the new trends in various arts, even when the artist himself was indifferent or hostile toward science, were in line with those of modern science itself. Functionalism was another name for intelligent technology in art. Other trends in common between art and science were (a) secularism or naturalism; (b) specialization on various types of form and psychological effect, as in futurism; (c) the experimental attitude toward art as a field where any new unconventional device was to be given a fair trial; and (c) cosmopolitanism, the adaptation and synthesis of many exotic and primitive styles, as in the music of Debussy, the oriental tales of Kipling, the cubist use of African Negro sculpture.

Among the arts, a sympathetic attitude toward science and technology was strongest, on the whole, in those combining aesthetic with utilitarian functions, such as architecture and furniture. Here some knowledge of engineering was increasingly needed. These arts rapidly developed their own cumulative technologies in terms of form and function, means and end. The ends were not merely physical, but psychological and sociological also, including the production of desired moods and attitudes of mind through interior design. The scientific spirit flourished also in certain types of

[30] Cf. M. Praz, The Romantic Agony (London, 1933).

art criticism, such as the application of psycho-analysis to art. It flourished for a while in the Fechner tradition of laboratory experiment on the psychology of art, and in evolutionary theories of art history. Gyorgy Kepes, artist and writer on art at the Massachusetts Institute of Technology, remarked that "the widely held belief that art and science are polar opposites, mutually exclusive in aims, methods and results..., will not bear close scrutiny." These two creative activities are interdependent, he added, and "each achieves stronger growth when nourished by the other."[31]

The arts where sympathy for science was weak-est, and anti-rationalism correspondingly strongest, were the more purely aesthetic arts of poetry, music, and painting. Here science seemed to offer least to the artist, either in technological help or in acceptable ideas and images for artistic treatment. On the contrary, while a few artists painted machines and factory chimneys, more and more came in the twentieth century to view them with a hostile eye as symbols of deadly mechanization. Here the very fact of science's apparently irresist-ible march, the ubiquitous, inescapable effects of standardized mass production, seemed to repel more artists than it attracted, and with them the patrons and critics of art. How intolerable, they thought, would be a world in which everything, even the arts, had been reduced to mathematical formulas and automatic routines.[32] Let art at least resist as long as possible, and stay as different from science as possible in its methods and its products. Even the inquisitive scrutiny of psycho-logists, in trying to study the artist under a mi-croscope, aroused the indignation of Amy Lowell, imagist poet of the twenties. Let the artist be allowed some privacy for his sensitive feelings and his fragile visions.[33]

Attacks on science and mechanization, including the belief in evolution and progress, had been frequent in late romantic art: in the essays of Baudelaire, for example. But they received a tremendous impetus from the First and Second World Wars and the great depression of 1929

and following years, with the ensuing arms race and cold war. Mistaken as it was to blame the world's troubles on science, rather than on society's misuse of science, it was common practice to make science the whipping boy. "Science fiction" itself turned from glamorous dreams of future Utopias to horrifying scenes of automatic "robots," re-pression and destruction, as in Aldous Huxley's *Brave New World* and George Orwell's *1984*. Some visual artists consciously developed an abstract or semi-abstract symbolism of revolt from science, reason, and the machine age, as in the deliberate infantilism of dadaist poetry, Schwitters' collages of discarded refuse, and Dali's "paranoiac art."

The use of art by communist and fascist dictators as a means of propaganda and indoctrination aroused the especial hostility of Western liberals toward any technological approach to art, even in support of freedom and democracy. It proved almost impossible to secure support for the United Nations, Unesco, and other idealistic projects from the artists of the West. To the Soviet regimenta-tion of artists for political purposes, many liberals saw only one alternative: the complete detachment of art and artists from all intellectual and practical concerns, all interest in social protest or reform or even in the expression of ideal goals. Many ab-stract and surrealist painters withdrew more and more deeply into subjective worlds of private symbolism. In the effort to avoid all planning, all purposeful construction, they cultivated automa-tism, the immediate, impulsive action toward a canvas. Painters disclaimed any interest whatever in pleasing the public, although they still exhibited and sold their works. The more esoteric and ap-

[31] "Art and Science," in *Art and Architecture*, Oct. 1956, p. 18.
[32] Walt Whitman expressed this attitude in "When I Heard the Learn'd Astronomer." After seeing the figures, diagrams, etc., "How soon unaccountable I became tired and sick, / Till rising and gliding out I wander'd off by myself, / In the mystical moist night-air, and from time to time, / Look'd up in perfect silence at the stars." *Leaves of Grass.*
[33] "To a gentleman who wanted to see the first drafts of my poems in the interests of psychological research into the workings of the creative mind." *Selected Poems* (Boston, 1928), p. 73.

parently formless these works became, the more the public, led by avant-garde critics, flocked to admire and buy them—proving that such art satisfied some kind of public need: perhaps for a brief illusion of escape from the trap of destructive technology which seemed to be closing fatally on everyone.

We have already noticed the persistent vogue of German idealism in aesthetics and the philosophy of art history, through such writers as Croce, Bosanquet, and Collingwood. Maintaining high prestige in English, French, Italian, and American university circles until recent years, it has operated to prevent the spread of scientific modes of thought in either art or aesthetics. Other forms of supernaturalism have cooperated with it in this respect, as in *The Illusion of Progress* by W. R. Inge, an English cleric.

Thus it appears that a number of powerful tendencies, social and cultural, have operated in the twentieth century to block once more the naturalistic attempt to revive a technological approach to art and aesthetics. By the same token, these forces have tended to strengthen the ideologies in art and aesthetics which are hostile to naturalism and rationalism: namely, extreme romanticism and supernaturalism. As these forces prevail, the power of art and aesthetics to become systematically cumulative, like the older technologies, tends to diminish. More primitive modes of thinking and acting tend to revive, especially in the more purely "fine" or aesthetic arts.

At the present time, the methods of these arts are comparatively primitive by comparison with those of applied science. ("Primitive" implies less highly evolved, but not necessarily worse or inferior.) They resemble modes of thought which were used in the early stages of utilitarian technology and in prescientific speculations about the nature of the world and man. As we have seen, primitive technics in all fields were a mixture of realism and fantasy, reason and emotion, planning and capricious impulse, empirical inference and the will to believe. The utilitarian technics have gradu-

ally abandoned primitive modes of thinking in accepting those of science; but the aesthetic technics have resisted this transformation after several unsuccessful attempts at it.

12. POSSIBLE EXTENSIONS OF SCIENCE AND TECHNOLOGY IN THE FIELD OF ART.

In previous sections we have noted that science is primarily a way of thinking and acting, an attitude toward the world and its phenomena; not a particular field or set of fields. It is not limited to the exact sciences, such as mathematics, physics, and biology. It has been introduced in one field after another, with some difficulty and resistance at first as it encounters new kinds of phenomena and established habits of primitive thinking. As it enters each new field, it gradually replaces the older modes of thought. Scientific methods are not entirely different from ordinary thinking, but constitute a development of man's innate powers of intelligent reasoning. Thinking and behavior can gradually become more rational, thus moving in the direction of science, long before they achieve full scientific status.

When certain types of phenomena, such as those of art and aesthetic experience, are too complex and difficult to be measured or described in exact laws, some preliminary steps toward science may nevertheless be possible and useful. Scientific method is not limited to the specific concepts and procedures of the old, exact sciences. Its partial extension in art and aesthetics would not necessarily involve, at first, any increase in exact, quantitative measurement, laboratory experiment, or statistics. The ability to measure, predict, and control with numerical exactness is rather an ultimate hope of each new science than an indispensable method. In the early stages of a new science, to rely heavily on attempts at measurement is usually premature and disappointing; the most important aspects of the new field of phenomena cannot be measured immediately, if ever. To concentrate on what can be measured may involve an emphasis on the less important, marginal aspects. There is usually a need for considerable spade work in surveying the field, roughly classifying and correlating phenomena, selecting what seem to be their most important and distinctive features, forming and testing hypotheses about their main causal interrelations. Little by little, rough quantitative estimates of "more" and "less" can be refined into measurements, but there is danger of self-deception in specious claims to exactness or logical proof.

The advance of science into a new field is not merely a reduction of the new phenomena to the concepts, laws, and causal explanations of the older ones. Some overlapping between the older fields and the new will be evident from the start. Living bodies obey the laws of physics, and so do works of art. The perception of art is a physiological as well as a psychological process. Music consists of soundwaves, and can be produced by scraping horse-hair over catgut. But it is, of course, much more than that. The aspects of the new field which can be adequately described in terms of older sciences usually turn out to be the less distinctive and important ones. To describe and study the more important ones, a new terminology must be developed, involving: (a) some transfer of concepts from the older sciences, (b) some prescientific concepts, traditionally used in discussing the new field, and (c) some freshly coined technical terms. The third kind tends to grow in importance, replacing many older terms which are found too ambiguous or misleading.

In entering each new field, science has had to change and develop new methods in adaptation to the different phenomena encountered, and to different social desires for controlling them. Freud found the methods of medical psychiatry and nineteenth-century psychology quite inadequate to deal with the phenomena of unconscious symbolism in dreams, art, and the neuroses. He had to develop new ones, but in a basically scientific spirit of observation, hypothesis, and control. To

be found adequate in dealing with the phenomena of art and aesthetics, science will have to develop much more sensitive, complex methods than it has ever used up to date.

The growth of scientific methods in a new field does not imply that everyone who works there uses them. Agriculture and stock-breeding have become more scientific on the whole, but not all farmers and stock-breeders are scientists. Some can use scientific aids, with or without understanding them fully; some can not.

There is no serious question here of art being "invaded" or "taken over" by science, or of artists being forced to adopt unwelcome scientific methods. At least, if that occurs, it will be due to outside social policies and pressures; not to science or technology itself. Liberal democracy can use the arts and scientific knowledge about them in its own interests and in that of free artistic progress on a world scale if it chooses to do so. If an artist in a free society makes use of science and technology, it will be because he finds them helpful in creating as he wants to create.

Further use of scientific methods in art and in thinking about art does not imply that works of art themselves will become more scientific, rationalistic, or naturalistic in form or content. They will not necessarily be geometric or classic in style. Insofar as romantic, Dionysian, and other non-classic types of art have their own values, technology can be directed toward their attainment.

The creation and performance of art will always require, at times, methods quite different from those of science: less intellectual and planful, more imaginative and emotional. An intelligent use of science there will not try to substitute its own methods where these are less suitable, but will ask how the methods already used in art can be made more effective in achieving their desired aims.

As to how much irrational or non-rational thinking is needed in the creation of art, opinions differ. As to whether and how the appropriate emotional attitude can be artificially produced, there is a long history of past efforts, from Zen to laudanum and marijuana,[34] but again little verified knowledge. To investigate the question might well be one aim of aesthetic technology. Aldous Huxley, who combines the mystic, artistic, and scientific attitudes, has written and experimented on the psychological effects of certain drugs in stimulating visual fantasies. Some of the drugs now used in psychiatry have been given to normal persons with effects akin to psychosis. Perhaps there is a better way than Zen or drugs to achieve the desired states of mind and the desired artistic results.

In principle, the Taoist doctrine would seem to imply letting nature take its course instead of trying to accomplish things artificially; but in practice mankind (especially in the West) has insisted on looking for better ways to achieve what it wants, in art and elsewhere. If what we want in art is the "personal touch," and if we are losing it through standardized mechanization, then it is a problem for technology to analyze that value more empirically, and to ask how best it can be attained in a modern, industrial society.

One possible approach to technology in the arts is to ask what problems confront an artist in this age, and how they might be solved, at least in theory. Artists are aware of some of them and feel strongly about what should be done; but these are not necessarily the most far-reaching problems. Further inquiry is needed on what different kinds of artist really want to accomplish, what different sections of the public want from works of art, and what is standing in the way of these achievements.

Some problems of the artist—those of which he is usually most conscious—are external. They have to do with his economic, social, and professional status; with patronage, public and private support for his work; with subsidies for his education, travel, materials, and leisure for creative work without the need to sell his wares at once in the open market. They also have to do with his freedom to create and express himself as he wishes, without undue censorship or coercion from state,

church, or pressure groups. One recurrent problem is that of how public or corporate support can be given to the arts without "regimentation" or pressures to conform to official taste. These are many-sided problems, involving not only aesthetic and moral issues, but also economic, political, and institutional ones. In spite of widespread disagreement on ends and means, an objective technological approach could seek to discover areas of substantial agreement, and possible institutional devices for attaining commonly approved goals without the disadvantages which are feared.

Other problems of the artist are more internal, subjective, personal; they have to do with his own desires and mental processes. These cannot be entirely separated from those of his relations with other individuals and society as a whole; but they involve his inner life and cannot be solved completely by changing his environment.

Aside from the question of what he *should* try to do (which technology cannot settle), certain questions of fact remain. What do artists want most to do, and to what extent do they actually aim at affecting or influencing any observer, actual or ideal? Is there any kind of mental discipline which can help in marshalling, liberating, and concentrating all one's creative forces toward one end? How can one avoid self-consciousness and project oneself wholly into the task in hand, the ideal goal?

Such questions are fundamental to any technology of art, whether the approach is rationalistic or the opposite. Technology thinks in terms of means and ends. If we cannot clarify to some extent the ends in view, we cannot ask technology for means to them. Neo-classic technology, with its doctrine of affects, conceived the problem too narrowly and rigidly in terms of specific devices for expressing and arousing certain "passions". If a modern technology thinks in terms of more diversified goals, its means must be accordingly

---

[34] On the use of drugs by contemporary jazz musicians, see Allsop, K., "Jazz and Narcotics," *Encounter*, XVI, 6 (June 1961), 54–58.

variable, but there must be at least a flexible relation between them. Present-day art is too often in the position of having a wealth of means—of instruments, techniques, and knowledge of styles—but no clear notion of what to do with them. Experiment thus becomes aimless, a shot in the dark. Criticism also is often in the dark as to whether the experiment has succeeded. Hence there is little accumulation of wisdom.

Can any sort of technology help one to get original, important ideas, in art or elsewhere? Probably not. "Having new ideas" is largely the result of innate ability and general life experience; it cannot be reduced to any simple, psychological technique. Though everyone has ideas of some sort, only a few have ideas which posterity will recognize as new and important. This much can be said, however: that there are two, or perhaps three, main ways of treating the problem. One, the simplest, is to do nothing but wait in the hope of getting an inspiration from some inner or outer source. In principle, this is the way of Tao, of inaction, of drifting with the current, letting nature take its course. For some profuse geniuses, it works very well. Their minds are unfailing springs of great ideas, bubbling up without apparent effort. But many others have tried this, only to be disappointed by the failure of inspiration to come. The Muse is reluctant and must be wooed. From this need, two kinds of technology have arisen: the rationalistic and the romantic. Though at swords' points in theory, they supplement each other in some respects. Both can be developed scientifically.

13. RECENT ROMANTIC AND RATIONALISTIC APPROACHES TO ARTISTIC TECHNOLOGY.

Romanticism often looks, not to the conscious, daylight levels of the mind, but to the unconscious and semiconscious levels of dream and waking reverie. It looks for a sudden impulse from behind, not fully understood by him who feels it. In social culture and tradition, it tends to ransack the records and survivals of primitive, undisciplined desire and passion, as in ancient myths and legends, rustic superstitions, tales of mystery, witchcraft and, demonology. Anything in music, words, or visual forms which can evoke this twilight world of the imagination is welcomed. Much material of this sort can be found, as Coleridge found it, in odd books of ancient lore and distant travel. To collect it is part of the "storing of the well," and must be done in a fairly alert, understanding way. But then how does one perform the essential step, the creative flash that merges selected elements from all one's past experience into the pregnant image of a new work of art? The impatient artist's answer, we saw, was to try to whip up his imagination with some artificial aid such as drugs, asceticism, prayer, Zen, or Yoga. Do such methods work? Apparently, to a limited extent, but in some cases only, where the artist already has a rich fantasy life; only for a limited time and at a heavy cost in health and social adjustment. Romanticists do not try to investigate the question systematically, again because of their opposition to science and rationalism in art.

Certain diseases and pathological conditions may also, as Thomas Mann believed, have the power to stimulate creative imagination. Epilepsy, tuberculosis, and the many types of neurosis and psychosis warrant study from this point of view, to see whether they actually do have such effects and if so, whether the valuable factors in them can be detached from the pathological and harmful.

Attempts by Western artists to cultivate automatic writing and painting have so far had little demonstrated value. So have attempts at exploiting one's own unconscious for valuable dream material. Such attempts in Western culture are often correlated with an egotistic, self-conscious subjectivism; a desire to express one's own personality and prove one's originality. But the mere discharge of inner feelings and fantasies is not necessarily valuable to others. Such methods lack the sense of supernatural guidance which has inspired Eastern and Christian mystics with a feeling of the transcendental importance of art. In rebelling against logic, the mystic anti-rationalist (St. Paul, for example), is not merely asserting his little ego, but is joining forces with something he feels to be much greater than himself. It is questionable how much of the oriental or medieval technology can be profitably used by the Western naturalist apart from the religious faith with which it was originally connected.

The rationalistic approach, aspiring toward scientific status, has at present no specific aids or methods to offer the artist in this crucial phase of his work. Very little has been done with it in recent years, although such collateral sciences as medicine, psychiatry, psychoanalysis, and pharmacology have amassed a good deal of relevant knowledge on the subject. What science could do is to resume the empirical, experimental investigation of aesthetic psychology with special reference to the creative imagination and the processes of art. Even if artists themselves do not now initiate or want such investigation, the field is open for pure and applied aesthetics to pursue it for the sake of knowledge and possible future use. The scientist could reasonably ask whether there are any better methods than the ones already tried for stimulating imagination in the ways desired, and whether certain elements in the old ones could be used to more advantage without their harmful consequences.

Rationalistic technology would not be limited to studying the methods of romantic artists and asking how these can be improved upon. It would also study the more conscious, planful types of creative process, as used in the past and present, asking how these also could be aided or improved as means to ends.

One common type of artistic process which deserves investigation is like intelligent reflection in any field. It involves an attempt to analyze the problem at hand in terms of general objectives, needs, resources, and conditions (e.g., in planning a monument, a theater, or an opera for a small cast). One then goes on to survey a number of possible solutions and to select a few as promising. This usually involves recall and appraisal of past works of art made to solve a somewhat similar problem. Elements can be selected and rearranged from these, along with newer ones, to form an original conception of the intended work. It is then tested out in practice, in the medium, and revised as one goes along. Many works of art are made in this way. It is too planful and plodding to suit the extreme romanticist. But the two approaches can be combined to some extent, or used at different times. The rationalistic one can be developed into a method of education as well as of artistic production. Material aid can be given the artist along this line by providing him with ready access to works of art in all media, types, and styles, along with commentaries on them. There can be no guarantee, of course, by this or any other method, that the results will be original or important. That still depends on variables beyond the present reach of technology.

14. VARIETIES OF ARTIST AND CREATIVE PROCESS

How acceptable would any such technical assistance be to artists? Again, that depends on the type of artist. They are more different than is commonly supposed, and some would welcome it more than others. Past discussion has been oversimplified by stereotyped conceptions: those of "the artist" and "the creative process" as contrasted with "the scientist" and "scientific method." One popular image of the artist is still the romantic one of a pale, solitary dreamer in his humble garret, working by candle-light on the wings of some mysterious inspiration. The scientist is thought of as a cold-blooded man in a white coat, manipulating dials and test-tubes in a laboratory or pushing buttons in a giant computer. Actually, of course, there are many different kinds of scientist and of persons who make use of scientific devices. Some of them, such as psychiatrists and teachers, have to deal with the delicate, subtle, and immeasurably complex phenomena of the human psyche. They do not work entirely by logic or mathematical formulas. They have flashes of inspiration and are not entirely unemotional. Individual genius is important in science as well as art, although scientists are on the whole more cooperative.

There are many kinds of artist also, and of creative process. The total field of art contains a great variety of occupations, if we include not only painters, sculptors, poets, and composers, but others who contribute to the production of art. We must then include craftsmen and artisans who execute the designs of others, performers such as actors and pianists, orchestra conductors, film producers and directors, publishers, editors, dealers in art, engineers and camera-men in radio, television, and film. Which of these are "artists" and to what extent is a question of semantics. But it is evident that the occupations and the methods used in the total field of art production, performance, and distribution are highly diverse. Authors and composers, painters and sculptors, architects and designers, are presumably among the most creative, although not all of them are really original, and people in other branches of art often contribute original ideas. Some creative artists work alone in a studio or office; some contribute stories, pictures, or designs for wider reproduction and circulation; some work directly in large organizations where they cooperate with engineers and other presumably non-artistic persons.

Types of personality and mental process vary considerably from one art to another. On the whole, workers in the useful arts of architecture, furniture, ceramics, and textiles tend to be more sympathetic toward scientific technology than those in the purely aesthetic arts. Those in the more collectivized, cooperative arts such as film and television tend to be more so than the solitary artists. Even if they do not understand the details of applied science, they see how useful it can be, and learn how to cooperate with trained technicians. In these fields, there is already a fairly close rapprochement between art and science. Art is already partially transformed by scientific influences.

This has nothing to do with the style or expression of the works produced. A motion picture studio is quite as ready to produce a romantic film as a neo-classic one; perhaps more so because of popular demand. An urban architect can design a thatched cottage with a picturesque garden in the best romantic tradition. But one who designs urban buildings today must know something about a variety of technologies, such as steel construction, heating, and lighting, or work with specialists who do. The visual aspects of his work must be closely integrated with the structural and functional. He works out a "program" of intended functions and adapts the design to them. On the other hand, the lonely rebel or dreamer, bent only on emotional expression, can get along more easily in poetry, painting, or serious music.

Even here the romantic type of artist is not universal. It was mentioned above that some solitary painters, such as Seurat, make careful use of scientific knowledge and plan their works meticulously. In a modern, open society, where individuals are comparatively free to follow their inclinations, every major art is likely to attract various types of personality; some planful and analytical, some the opposite. This is true whatever the dominant style and ideology may be. As Focillon explained, artists of a certain innate predisposition feel an affinity with others of the same type across the ages, over and above the differences in culture and style. But the predominant type will differ from age to age and place to place according to fluctuations in the culture-pattern. The introduction of a "classic" or "romantic" period may be due in large part to a few non-conformist individuals, in advance of their time; but, as it comes to dominate the scene, more and more individuals of the ascendant type are attracted into arts in which that type is admired and rewarded.

More and more young, uncertain, plastic individuals are influenced to ride the ascending wave to its crest. In Marxist societies at the present time, the romantic, isolated dreamer is not encouraged. In present liberal societies, this type is more active and respected. It is hard for us to realize that artists have not always hated science; that Leonardo, though a precocious genius, was not the only artist who saw nature also with a scientific eye or liked to plan his work with the aid of geometry, proportion, anatomy, and optical perspective. More artists may wish to do so in future.

In avoiding extreme anti-rationalism, art does not need to go to the opposite extreme of coldly objective, logical reasoning; to mechanical, push-button controls, or docile obedience to rules. There are countless intermediate types of artistic process in creative production, performance, and appreciation. They are already in use to some extent, and may be used increasingly in future. Each has its values and limitations.

In the perception and appreciation of art, including ways of teaching it to various age-levels, an intermediate attitude is now common. Studies in the history and theory of art are highly intellectual and analytical. The teaching of art appreciation to children in Western schools is less abstract and theoretical, but involves some discussion of styles and values. Absolute rules are avoided, but there is a search for principles which will be valid at least in relation to certain styles and periods.

The common conception of the "creative process" in art includes only a small part of what an artist actually thinks and does. Even the most wildly romantic is not in a frenzy of passion all the time. He is not always swept along by sudden impulse and inspiration. Even those who go farthest along this line are usually content to relax and think normally in between creative episodes.

Broadly conceived, the creative process in art includes much that happens before and after the "flash of inspiration." It includes the long previous accumulation of selected materials—sights, sounds, ideas, feelings—and of experience in translating these into terms of a particular medium. Many good artists never have a flash of sudden inspiration; they work along steadily and gradually toward a foreseen goal. Details fall into place little by little, not all at once. In any case, after the flash (if any), there is commonly a phase of elaboration and a final one of correction, trimming, and polishing. The first and last stages of the process tend to be a good deal less excited and impulsive, more rational and planful, than the middle one.

Planning and reasoning do not have to be in verbal form. We know very little yet about the non-verbal types of thinking which a painter or musician carries on. But certainly many artists form tentative, imaginary conceptions of a projected work, at first in vague, sketchy, or fragmentary form, then more and more definitely. Such a preliminary image, visual or auditory, may act as a tentative purpose to be achieved in one's chosen medium, subject to alteration on the way. The more purely impulsive painter will step up to the canvas and start painting automatically, with no preliminary conception. Even so, the first accidental strokes may suggest an imaginary form which will henceforth direct the process. In pure improvisation, the pianist may sit down at the piano and let his fingers wander aimlessly over the keys. But in doing so, he is partly determined by his previous musical experience and habits. As he proceeds, the apparently accidental notes may suggest a theme, to be developed into a familiar pattern such as a sonata.

The preliminary conception of an intended work, if any, is somewhat like a hypothesis in scientific investigation, in that it constitutes a tentative, proposed solution to the artist's present problem of construction or expression. As he tests it out in a particular medium and materials, in relation to other requirements such as the intended function, location, or audience, he may find it advisable to modify the original idea or substitute a different one. The idea "works" for him if it leads to a final product which satisfies him. All this can be done with very little verbalization. For the literary artist, of course, the tentative form or "germ" of the product includes a vague assemblage of meaningful words. Artists vary as to the extent to which they analyze their work into specific problems and alternative solutions, definite goals and means to them. For those who do analyze, each detail of the work may present a minor problem in itself: how to fit it consistently into the total complex form and psychological effect one had in mind.

15. "RULES OF ART" FROM THE STANDPOINT OF NATURALISTIC TECHNOLOGY

The so-called "rules" of art can also be verbal or non-verbal. Artists differ greatly in their attitude toward them, between the two extremes of docile obedience and utter flouting. When a period of dogmatic rationalism is at its height, such a verbal rule as the three unities of drama may be taken as an absolute law, almost as cogent as the moral law of God or the statutes of a state. But even at the height of neo-classical rationalism in Europe, there was some recognition of the artist's right to depart from aesthetic rules, and some disagreement as to their precise nature and authority. They were never enforced with complete rigidity. This was partly due to the fact that the Bible says practically nothing about good and bad art, aside from denunciations of idolatry and immorality. In any case, the "rules" never covered the whole of the work of art; they specified as to certain abstract traits only, and left much room for choice and innovation to the artist. More cogent in practise might be (a) the tastes and orders of patrons and officials, and (b) the particular works of ancient art which were taken as models of perfection. These were sometimes verbal, sometimes not. Observing what a patron bought and rejected could provide a wordless rule for the hungry artist. A memory-image of Praxiteles' *Hermes* could be a visual rule and standard for the sculptor. For any artist today, the composite memory-image of past works and styles which he habitually admires can act as a tentative guide, encouraging this and discouraging that, while leaving him free to reject it entirely if he wishes to.

On the basis of a naturalistic world-view, rules for art can never be absolute. Their authority is derived from no transcendental source, but from human tastes and preferences, which are increasingly variable and relative to particular individuals, cultures, moods, and situations. Insofar as these exhibit recurrences and constancies, and are satisfied by certain types or traits in art, there is a possibility of tentative rules analogous to those of nutrition and medicine. If the person to be addressed by the work of art is of a certain kind, and if one desires to arouse a certain kind of response in him, then this or that artistic means will probably succeed under the circumstances. Because of our present ignorance, such generalizations are never completely reliable, but most artists find it worth while to use them at least as a point of departure. Through controlled experiment, they can be developed in the direction of scientific technology.

Even without reference to any particular kind of observer, tentative general rules are possible. Many rules of art are relative to a certain historic type and style, such as the Gregorian chant or Byzantine wall-painting. They are analogous to the rules of a game such as tennis or football. No one is obliged to play it at all, but if one does so, it is usually more enjoyable to play it according to accepted rules. In art, anyone is free to invent a new game or change the rules of an old one. The result may justify it, but the effect will be different. Sometimes an artist, however original, wants to convey the effect of a particular style—perhaps as a stage or film setting for a scene in a Byzantine cathedral. If one wants that effect, there are certain things one must do in drawing, coloring, modeling, perspective, backgrounds, facial expressions, etc. Many original artists, such as Joyce, Picasso, and Stravinsky, know how to produce in various historic styles and often do so up to a point. They like to establish a certain stylistic atmosphere, such as that of Raphael or Mozart, then depart from it in subtle ways, giving a new tang to the flavor without spoiling or destroying it. Aesthetic technology can be developed indefinitely along these lines, to show the essentials of various styles without prescribing to the artist exactly what he should do with them. Such knowledge, combined with perceptual experience, can be useful to the artist and appreciator alike. Sometimes a work of art will seem vaguely disturbing to the latter because he does not understand it stylistically. It may help one to apperceive it and adjust to it aesthetically if one can locate the work in relation to past styles: as to just how it conforms and how it breaks away from them.

Past styles and examples of art can be a potent stimulus to the imagination. Trying to be completely original and creative only from within, the artist often finds he has nothing to say; his mind and canvas are blank. Something in nature or in art will start him on a train of fantasy: perhaps as to how that existing form could be improved upon. The same technique operates in scientific discovery, invention, and theory. Here the original thinker usually begins with the present state of affairs in a certain realm or persistent problem; the point at which previous advance left off. He sees the machine or reads the book of another thinker, and sees inadequacies, inefficient or doubtful details, unfinished lines of thought which could be carried farther. In science one is limited by the facts; in invention by facts and human desires. In art, though cultural pressures may favor one line of imagination rather than another, the artist is more free to imagine as he wishes.

Some of the fantasies which feed the creative imagination are comparatively spontaneous, motivated from within and in a largely unconscious way. Others can be stimulated in a wholesale, indiscriminate way, as by drugs or other artificial techniques. Still others consciously begin with the observation of some existing work or works of art or with some actual scene, event, or situation in the outside world. Here the artist's characteristic mode of perceiving and thinking differs from that of others in tending toward some active alteration of the subject-matter perceived. Certain things may be added or emphasized, others omitted or minimized; the whole is reorganized, perhaps translated into a different artistic medium. Such a process may be comparatively conscious and planful or the opposite. It may be largely automatic, dreamlike, undirected save by unconscious or half-conscious motives and memories which blend with present perception and build a new form out of all these ingredients. Such artistic dreamwork can continue long after the external stimulus has ceased. It can go on intermittently for days or years; now as aimless reverie, now directed into some definite, artistic form.

The technological approach to such phenomena is exemplified in modern art education. It is not one of trying to substitute a logical or other radically different method, but of asking how the actual processes of art—both rational and nonrational—can be made more vigorous, more genuinely creative, more successful in achieving their own freely chosen goals.

Such an approach in art and education may seem at the opposite pole from science and technology to those who think of these in terms of the older, exact sciences. But "free association" is already an established psychological and psychiatric technique. In those sciences, it is practised in certain ways for certain ends, which differ partly but not entirely from those of art. Psychoanalysis has given us some insight into the fantasies of artists and normal people as well as of neurotics. Any understanding of their nature, causation, and effects can be applied in artistic technology, so as to utilize the phenomena concerned in the interest of the ends desired.

As there is a kind of art which conceals art, so

there is a kind of control which limits control. In art education, it is the kind which arranges things so as to facilitate and stimulate the maximum amount of free, creative imagination. Each culture will encourage it along the lines it deems most valuable, but these lines can be broad and flexible enough to allow a large amount of individual self-determination.

Along such lines we may expect in the art of the future an increasing rapprochement between the rationalistic attitude and the romantic, anti-rationalistic one. This will probably involve some extension of scientific technology in the arts, overcoming present resistances; but not completely. A strong effort will be made to preserve the values of romanticism where they are most needed.

Practical technologies, analogous to the present applied sciences but different in aim and method, will develop further in the arts. They will accumulate experience as to the most effective ways of accomplishing in and by the arts whatever ends are desired. There will be, as now, specific technologies for each art in terms of its distinctive media, technics, aims, and functions; also a more generalized technology for art as a whole. In the arts themselves, there will continue to be a great variety of technics and mental processes: some voluntarily moving farther in the direction of technology than at present, while others remain where they are or move toward the opposite, non-rational extreme. In aesthetics and criticism, there will be more understanding of the interaction between opposing attitudes and of the values sought by each.

The spread of scientific thinking meets with less resistance in aesthetics than in art itself, but even there the prestige of romantic spiritualism and other anti-scientific traditions is still strong. There too, the idea of scientific method is persistently misrepresented as a disposition to measure beauty and to establish laws of taste. The accumulation and testing of empirical knowledge about the arts and related psychological and social phenomena goes on apace, but more slowly and sporadically

than it does in fields where that enterprise is deliberate and cooperative. Meanwhile, persons and institutions with scientific interest do not, to any great extent, embark on studies of the arts. These are left mainly to a "humanistic" approach, which is often deliberately unscientific. But the spread of scientific method in aesthetics has proceeded greatly in the first half of the twentieth century and shows every sign of continuing. As it spreads, it will accelerate the cumulative preservation and transmission of practical knowledge in the arts.

16. POSSIBLE VALUES AND DANGERS OF SCIENCE AND TECHNOLOGY IN THE FIELD OF ART

This chapter has not argued for a wholesale, indiscriminate extension of scientific methods in art or aesthetics. It has argued that a moderate extension is probable in future: not in all branches of art, but in a few where the aid of science is most easily acceptable. In pure aesthetics, there is everything to be gained by such extension, provided new methods appropriate to the phenomena are developed. Aesthetic technology or applied aesthetics, if developed with due attention to specific needs and to new knowledge about the effects of art on human beings, can greatly increase the power of art to achieve the ends toward which it is directed.

If this increased power is used wisely, the results can be highly beneficial to art and life. But, to repeat a basic distinction, evolution is not necessarily progress. The increased power which science gives to any technical activity is always a two-edged sword. In art, as in physics, it increases the power to do harm as well as good. Technology as such is neutral; its goodness or badness depends on the ends to which it is directed more than on the success or efficiency of its methods. The choice of ends will depend on the kinds of individual, group, and social system which control it. The world has amply seen the dangers of physical technology in the pursuit of selfish, aggressive, partisan ends. Attention is now being drawn to the application of aesthetic technology in political, military, and commercial propaganda, as in the "hidden persuaders" of advertising. Such use has just begun and seems sure to grow rapidly. Its present effects are doubtful; a mixture of good and bad, wise and foolish, with alarming possibilities for evil. It can lead to a neglect and deterioration of aesthetic, intellectual, and ethical values, a leveling and lowering of standards, and a further prostitution of art to mercenary or aggressive ends. It can be an instrument of social and mental regimentation and oppression.

But the same dangers exist in regard to all other branches of technology: physical, biological, social, and psychological. In all, it seems impossible to turn the clock backward, even if we wished to do so. It is a futile gesture to urge, in one field after another, that science should be kept out and only prescientific, personal, emotional, irrational methods used. The main result of this romantic attitude in art and aesthetics is to surrender the field and all the new power to those who would use it selfishly and perhaps harmfully. The only promising way to secure the values of science and avoid its dangers is for men of good will to foster the growth of scientific knowledge in all fields, and to see that its direction is controlled by men of the same sort, responsible to public control and working in the public interest. The details of social policy toward art can then be adjusted in a reasonable spirit, somewhere between the extremes of centralized control and complete individual irresponsibility.

The ultimate theoretical question is, of course, how the aims and uses of art, toward which technology is directed, are themselves to be chosen. That question lies outside the province of the present book. Neither philosophy, science, nor technology is able at present to demonstrate the rightness or superiority of any specific set of goals,

aesthetic or ethical. But no other agency or method, naturalistic or supernaturalistic, can do so. Scientific ethics and aesthetics can at least throw some light on the problem by helping us to understand the alternatives more clearly, along with the probable consequences of each mode of action and each kind of art. They can help us understand the arguments on all sides of each disputed issue as to which effects are better or worse, how and for whom. They can help us understand the psychological and social processes of evaluation, decision, and choice; how we acquire our standards and how we can make these processes more intelligent and broadly humane if we so desire. With or without such understanding, the actual decisions are largely acts of will, which science can neither prove nor disprove. We can only hope that power will come and stay in the hands of those most able to choose in a manner which posterity will consider wise and just.

From the standpoint of art, it is to be hoped that these will be persons of broadly developed aesthetic tastes, sympathetic toward the values of different kinds of art, artist, method, and experience, disposed to open doors for new, free experiment, rather than to hold the arts within a few old channels. It is to be hoped that they will seek to increase the role of the arts in cultural evolution, the respect in which they are held, and the rewards conferred on those who do good work in them. But the arts will still be only one avenue for cultural progress. Their activities must be fitted into larger plans and at times subordinated to other interests, while at other times taking the lead in holding up ideal goals for evolution and progress. Aesthetic values are only one among many kinds of human value, but a kind which has been neglected recently by science and social policy. To help realize the potential values of art more fully in theory and practice, while avoiding its potential evils, can be the chief aim of scientific effort in the arts.

17. SUMMARY

Works of art are man-made instruments for producing psychological effects on observers, individually and socially. These include perceptual, imaginative, rational, conative, and emotional responses; also the formation of attitudes toward certain kinds of action and belief. Works of art are so used and always have been, even when not consciously so intended. This is not inconsistent with their being also used as means of self-expression by the artist.

Ancient writers and many modern ones have clearly recognized the technical nature of art, which has been mistakenly denied in recent years. Both artistic and utilitarian technics were classed under the general name of *techné* (art). Their kinship has been obscured by the recent restriction of the word "technology" to utilitarian skills and products, and of "art" to aesthetic ones. Although their specific aims and methods are somewhat different, they have much in common and have evolved together.

The arts or aesthetic technics have been slower to adopt scientific ways of thinking, including the intelligent planning of means to specific ends. This helps to explain their comparative lack of cumulativeness. They are now increasingly pervaded by scientific ways of thinking and will probably be more so in future, for better or worse. The change will be partial and optional; accepted voluntarily, if at all, as a way to achieve more effectively whatever one wants to achieve in art. Some kinds of artist are more favorably disposed than others to rational methods. The results can be good or bad; this depends on the ends sought and the means employed. "Scientific thinking" does not necessarily mean the use of quantitative measurement, machinery, or coldly logical methods to the exclusion of personal emotion, fantasy, and unpremeditated impulse. It does not mean that an artist should think about the effects of his work while creating it.

The concept of "technic," as applied to artistic skills and devices, is broader than that of "technique" as commonly defined. It includes the forms, styles, and psychological content of art, as culturally acquired and transmitted. The technology or "poetics" of art, which is still largely prescientific, consists of accumulated theories and rules as to how to do things. It includes aesthetic ideals and standards of value. Some of it is now included in the subject of aesthetics.

Science and rational thinking are more suited to aesthetics (pure and applied) than to the practice of art, but even in the latter they are increasingly used. This constitutes a partial reaction against the extreme anti-rationalism of early nineteenth-century romanticism. As science advances through successive fields, it tends to adapt its methods to the new types of phenomena, needs, and problems encountered there. Scientific thinking in the field of art is different from that in the physical and mathematical fields. The belief that art and science are necessarily hostile rests on a misunderstanding of both.

In the past, premature attempts were made at both rational and anti-rational technologies of art in Europe and Asia. The anti-rational methods, as in Ch'an-Zen, tend to develop their own quasi-rational rules. More psychological knowledge is required for an adequate technology of art. Its rules can be analogous to those of present applied science: not commands, but suggested ways of doing effectively whatever one wants to do.

CHAPTER XXI

LEVELS OF EXPLANATION IN THE HISTORY OF ART

I. EXPLANATION AND DESCRIPTION. PARTIAL EXPLANATIONS

A mature, inquiring mind is not content to observe events without trying to understand their causes and effects. Since Francis Bacon, the quest for causal explanation in science has been increasingly linked with that for means of control. When the course of events appears to affect us for good or ill, to satisfy or frustrate our desires, we wonder how it could be redirected so as to satisfy us more completely. Long before Bacon, the study of history was undertaken for the purpose (among others) of helping man to act more wisely in the light of past experience; especially through understanding the causes of past trouble and how to avoid it in future. Even when control is remote or impossible, thoughtful observers like to find some plausible explanation for great events like the fall of Rome or important processes like evolution.

Since Hume, most philosophers have recognized that what we commonly regard as causal explanation is, fundamentally, an inference from observed associations among events in human experience. We cannot know with certainty the essential nature of causation in ultimate reality. But, for all practical and many theoretical purposes, people are usually satisfied with more superficial, partial explanations on the empirical level, in terms of observed relations among phenomena.

Several kinds of explanation and of causal rela-

tion are distinguished in philosophy and science. They differ somewhat in relation to the kinds of thing for which an explanation is sought; also in relation to the context of inquiry and the special interests of the inquirer. Some of the things to be explained are particular events such as the assassination of Julius Caesar. In art history, one may ask what caused a change of style: e.g., El Greco's increasing distortions of anatomy. Was it due to astigmatism (as some academic critics used to say) or to his early, Byzantine influence, or to the intense religiosity of Spain, or to the fact that this style seemed the next step ahead after Tintoretto's mannerism? Or to a combination of many different factors?

In the philosophy of art history, we are not concerned so much with the explanation of particular cases as with that of general processes and trends; also with general methods of explanation and theories of causation. This chapter deals with the problem of explaining evolution in art and with the chief proposed answers to it.

Evolution has been regarded in the past, not only as something to be explained, but as a way of explaining other things, including art. Spencer's "universal law" of evolution was advanced as an explanation of development in every field. Darwin's "natural selection" was accepted as explaining a great variety of biological phenomena, such as fossils, protective coloring in animals, and similarities in structure and function among apes and men. In criticism of this view, Thomas Huxley remarked that evolution is not an explanation of the cosmic process, but merely a generalized statement of the method and results of that process. It is certainly not a complete explanation; it does not explain what power or powers originated, directed, and still direct the evolutionary process. Huxley's dictum implies a sharp distinction between explanation and description; that no matter how full the description, the process cannot be "explained" in terms of "how" alone; explanation demands an answer to the question "Why? By what controlling power?" This distinction gave a welcome loophole, in Victorian Europe, for the reintroduction of religious faith, which claimed to answer the "why?"; also for naturalism and agnosticism, as in Spencer's doctrine of the Unknowable.

Huxley's distinction has also been applied to the problem of explaining evolution itself, in both the organic and cultural fields. If it is no explanation at all to tell *how* things happen, if we cannot show why or by what ultimate agency evolution proceeds, then (it is said) we cannot explain evolution at all, but only describe it.

Some distinction along these lines is valid and useful. We have followed it so far in trying only to show *that* evolution in art has occurred, and some of the principal *ways* in which it has occurred —e.g., through processes of cultural descent, accumulation, complication, and simplification. This main thesis, that evolution in art occurs in certain ways, can be discussed and supported without introducing any theory whatever about the *cause* of evolution. Discussing it so has enabled us to avoid many distracting issues along the way. However, to avoid them entirely would be to content oneself with the mere shell of a theory, and to ignore some of the most interesting, controversial aspects of the discussion.

We have summarized the leading theories up to date and touched occasionally on causal issues in the last few chapters. Without offering any radically new solution, the remaining chapters will briefly weigh and interrelate those theories which

seem to retain some vitality at the present time. No single theory of cause will be found sufficient. There seem to be elements of truth in several and they are not completely exclusive. For the present a moderate pluralism, in which many hypotheses are weighed, seems the only reasonable course in the philosophy of history.

The explanation of historical events encounters special difficulties, many of which we have considered in previous chapters. Unlike the artificially controlled situations in a clinic or chemical laboratory, historical situations do not repeat themselves exactly enough to permit the formulation of precise descriptive laws, in terms of which a particular effect can be explained or predicted with assurance. It is impossible to observe past historical events directly; what happened and what led up to them must be inferred from fragmentary, often unreliable evidence. It is impossible to experiment with human behavior in the large on any extensive scale. Experiments are tried, as with a new system of government or a new style of art; but hardly ever under standardized conditions, permitting objective analysis of causes and effects in comparison with a control group. The enormous complexity and diversity in cultural events make it hard to discern exact recurrences within them. Cultural phenomena seem to be constantly changing their behavior. Unknown and unexpected variables constantly upset our predictions. In view of the lack of adequate "covering laws," some theorists have argued that the only complete explanation of a given event would be the full description of all previous events, which is of course impossible. Philosophers have often warned us that an event or condition is not fully explained or evaluated merely by tracing its genesis, especially through a single sequence of events leading up to the present one.[1]

The sharp dichotomy between description and

[1] For critiques of the "genetic method" in historicism, by Sidney Hook and others, see J. H. Randall, *Nature and Historical Experience* (Columbia U. Press, New York, 1958), pp. 64 f.; also Patrick Gardiner, *Theories of History*.

explanation is still being used as a means of attacking evolutionism in the cultural field. As such, it is largely a revival of the old, extreme type of historicism, which tried to make a sharp distinction between history and science. Since historical events are unique, it argues, there can be no laws of history; hence no explanation and no prediction. Evolution is attacked on the ground that it can neither explain anything nor be explained itself.

Although containing the usual elements of truth, this argument again goes too far. So sharp a dichotomy between description and explanation, like that between history and science, is excessive and unwarranted. It is agreed that *complete, certain, ultimate* explanations are now impossible in history as they are in science and philosophy. But *partial, tentative, empirical* ones are not. They are more difficult in theories of history than in the exact sciences, and must be accordingly modest in their claims. With this due caution, explanatory hypotheses are as possible in regard to cultural history, including that of art, as elsewhere in the empirical sciences. They can be gradually tested out against empirical data and strengthened, weakened, or corrected. A true but partial explanation is better than none if it is not mistaken for the whole, the necessary and sufficient explanation; if it does not give us a false, distorted picture of the whole sequence of events.

What is explanation? To what extent does it require a demonstration of causal relationship? As usual, there are different meanings and opinions. In the ordinary sense, "to explain" is "to make plain or clear to oneself; to reach an understanding, as of a cause or origin." (Webster). Any way of helping toward an understanding may qualify as explanation in this popular sense. Sometimes the emphasis is on cause or origin, sometimes on interpretation of a term or idea, sometimes on a statement of motive or purpose, and so on. The *Philosophical Dictionary* (1942) likewise defines "explanation" in a general sense as "the process, art, means or method of making a fact or a statement intelligible; …the result or expression of what is made intelligible." This may be the meaning attributed to a thing or a genetic description of it.

There is also a much more rigorous, exacting concept of explanation in logic and the mathematical and physical sciences. Webster states it as "to demonstrate (a phenomenon) as determinable from known conditions and stimuli or deducible from accepted premises." According to the *Philosophical Dictionary*, explanation in a technical sense is "the method of showing discursively that a phenomenon or a group of phenomena obeys a law, by means of causal relations or descriptive connections." There are three kinds of causal explanation, according to this authority: genetic (in terms of the direct, immediate conditions producing a phenomenon), descriptive (material elements of the phenomenon), and teleological (the end intended or to be attained). Explanation does not need to emphasize cause, for it can be "the search for generalizations whose variables are functionally related so that the value of any one variable is calculable from the value of the others, whether or not causal relations are noticeable or ultimately involved…"

There has recently been much discussion of the nature of explanation in writing history; especially as to whether it can approach that of the natural sciences in being based on general laws. In opposition to those who would separate history and science as radically different, Carl G. Hempel in a much-quoted paper (1942) has argued "that general laws have quite analogous functions in history and in the natural sciences, that they form an indispensable instrument of historical research, and that they even constitute the common basis of various procedures which are often considered as characteristic of the social in contradistinction to the natural sciences." He defines a general law as "a statement of universal conditional form which is capable of being confirmed or disconfirmed by suitable empirical findings." It is about the same as a "universal hypothesis" and asserts a regularity of the following type: "in every case where an event of a specific kind *C* occurs at a certain place and time, an event of a specified kind *E* will occur at a place and time which is related in a specified manner to the place and time of the occurrence of the first event." Such hypotheses are used, says Hempel, in historical explanation and prediction; they imply that whenever events of the kind described in the first group occur, an event of the kind to be explained will take place. There is no difference in this respect, he continues, between history and the natural sciences; "both can give an account of their subject-matter only in terms of general concepts, and history can 'grasp the unique individuality' of its objects of study no more and no less than can physics or chemistry."

Patrick Gardiner (1959, p. 270) mentions some objections to this theory: especially that attempts to state the "laws" presupposed in historical explanation have often been vague and unspecific, or else so highly determinate and particularized as not to qualify as laws. W. H. Walsh, in an essay on "'Meaning' in History," (Gardiner, p. 303), goes farther in charging that "despite everything that has been said on the subject in the last 200 years, no one has yet produced a reputable example of an historical law." (Comte's, Marx's, and Toynbee's attempts do not qualify, he thinks.) Even those who advance such laws seem unsure of the circumstances in which they can be expected to apply. Hempel himself points out that many of the explanations offered in history are based on "probability hypotheses" rather than on universal, deterministic laws. They are therefore "explanation sketches" rather than complete explanations; that is, vague indications of the laws and conditions which would be relevant. They need "filling out" to become full-fledged explanations.

We need not, perhaps, regret too much the lack of universal laws in historiology, for they would not, in themselves, give complete understanding of events which exemplify them. As Gardiner remarks, it is part of the task of an explanation to make something intelligible, and this is seldom if ever achieved "merely by showing that it is the sort of thing which can always be expected to happen under certain types of circumstance. (1959, p. 270; *cf.* W. Dray, *Laws and Explanation in History.* Oxford, 1957). This limitation applies, however, to almost all kinds of attempted explanation. They show mainly that the event or idea in question is part of some larger type or causal tendency; that it fits into some larger complex of interacting factors. This always leaves us with the question, "how and why did this larger state of affairs come to be so in the first place?"

Since it is unrealistic to hope for exact historical laws at present, it seems advisable to get along with something less ambitious. We can accept as a partial explanation anything which seems to promise greater understanding; to make the fact in question more intelligible. Lacking universal laws, we can try to develop a number of "probability hypotheses"; not necessarily of a formal, mathematical sort, but as rough, informal generalizations, subject to correction in the light of more careful research.

Such generalizations can be stated cautiously as apparent *tendencies* under certain conditions. One can say that A often *tends*, under conditions B and C, to be followed by D. This implies that, in the light of observation up to date, A seems to exert an influence in the direction of D, or to be otherwise positively correlated with D. The influence may be slight or strong, steady or occasional, dependent on few or many contributing factors. It is said that a people whose conditions of life are too easy, with few enemies, ample food and temperate climate, tends to become lazy and luxury-loving. Long concentration of wealth in the hands of a well-entrenched aristocracy with traditions of refined enjoyment seems to favor development of the arts of decoration, entertainment, and ritual, as in the Japan of the *Tale of Genji.* But how strong and regular these tendencies are cannot be stated without much comparative study. "Necessity is the mother of invention" is a half-truth at the most; it is true only under certain conditions, with certain cooperating causes—e.g., when people have the desire, initiative, courage, basic knowledge, and skill to invent what they need. But it has enough truth to be a partial explanation in many cases and in the general development of technology. If not a full-fledged hypothesis, it is at least a start toward one. "History repeats itself" is a partial truth; "history does not repeat itself" is also partly true.

Many of the generalizations advanced as laws by such philosophers as Comte, Marx, and Spencer, and later branded as false, contain an element of truth or probability. They describe types of sequence in events which happen often though not always. They deserve empirical testing rather than wholesale acceptance or rejection. The same can be said of the theory that successive discoveries of new sources of energy have led in the past to deep, far-reaching cultural changes and developments, amounting to new stages in cultural evolution.[2] This can be restated as a causal hypothesis to the effect that major increases in the control of energy tend to produce more highly evolved cultural stages. But, as often happens, the influence is reciprocal: such discoveries are also the result of a higher cultural development, as in scientific technology. Whether continued evolution will result is problematic: the discovery of nuclear power may lead to annihilation or genetic weakening.

Hypotheses and partial explanations of history are not limited to explicit theories of cause, although most of them contain some causal implications. Some of them take the form of describing persistent and recurrent processes in history, modes and mechanisms by which historic change occurs. If it is true that art and culture evolve, this knowledge helps increase our understanding of history although it is not a complete explanation. Any knowledge of how the major processes of history are interrelated is explanatory in a broad sense of that term. It would help us understand both history and evolution to know that evolution is (or is not) one phase in a larger cyclical pattern. It helps explain evolution to know that it contains several

widespread processes, such as natural selection and cultural diffusion. These are modes and mechanism by which evolution proceeds. They can also be regarded as contributing causes of evolution. Sometimes they operate and seem to have great influence; at other times not. Like the behavior of electrons and protons in the atom, such a mode is usually not directly observable to the casual eye. Though conceived as phenomenal and not an exact picture of ultimate reality, it has to be inferred from sense-evidence by refined and complex techniques. It operates on a deeper level than ordinary sense-experience reveals. The modes thus discovered, such as the chemical elements and their behavior, are much fewer in number and more regular in operation than the profusion of sensory phenomena as seen in ordinary experience. What seem to the casual observer as utterly diverse, remote phenomena, such as the perfume of a tropical flower and the bones of a fossil reptile, are shown to be instances of the same basic process operating along somewhat different lines under different conditions. Thus discovering the hidden analogies and recurrent patterns beneath phenomena, reducing apparent chaos and diversity to relative order and simplicity, partly satisfies the understanding. This is true especially when, as in the case of natural selection, the causal principle can be used as a tool for prediction and control.

The process of natural selection is one of the ways in which evolution operates, another being artificial selection as in animal breeding. The concept of natural selection helps explain evolution by showing how the latter works. Natural selection does not always coincide with evolution, however. As we have seen, it sometimes favors devolution, when simpler types are fitter for survival. Evolution and natural selection are somewhat distinct processes, which coincide on the whole. The knowledge of both helps to explain a multitude of still smaller processes, by showing in detail how these work; especially by showing the

[2] Hoebel, p. 619. Cf. L. A. White, "Energy and the Evolution of Culture," *American Anthropologist*, Vol. 45 (1943), 335–356.

intermediate steps and obscure mechanisms involved. The theory of evolution as a total process postulates a development from the extremely simple and indefinite to the extremely complex and definite (as in man, culture, and art). But, until Darwin, its obscure, intermediate steps had not been understood; therefore the whole process seemed unlikely. Darwin's description of natural selection was further filled in and corrected by the descriptions of mutation and Mendelian inheritance. These help explain how genetic change occurs. The other phase of natural selection, that of environmental influence, has been clarified by accounts of many changes, such as the drying of the swamps which had favored reptilian life. Geology, biochemistry, botany, ecology, anthropology, and other sciences contribute their shares to filling in the total picture. Science and historiography cooperate in building up a systematic description of the cosmic process, including man's role in it, as seen from our limited viewpoint with our limited powers. Science emphasizes the recurrences, history the uniquenesses; but both deal with both. Thus to describe the cosmic process more and more fully is to explain it more fully, though with no expectation of completeness or complete objectivity.

As we increase our understanding of the cosmic process, we automatically increase our power to predict the future; never certainly, but tentatively as in weather forecasting. From the fact that the earth has spun around the sun so long, we cannot be completely sure that it will do so tomorrow, but it is safe to assume so for all practical and many theoretical purposes. The same is true of evolution in life, culture, and art, with this difference: the process itself being so diverse and inconstant, so often arrested or reversed, we cannot be nearly so sure that it will continue. Its past length and persistence in certain areas give considerable ground for expecting that it will. But so many more variables enter the picture than in astronomy that we cannot, with present knowledge, predict specific lines of artistic evolution with any assur-ance. There is no good reason to suppose, however, that reliable prediction cannot be gradually increased along these lines as we learn more about the causal factors and persistent tendencies involved. This has occurred in meteorology and economics. Increased knowledge will also, theoretically, give increased powers of control, but society may decide not to use them to the full.

The question will always remain of why or how there came to be an evolutionary process in the first place. Any specific answer to it extends the story backward in time, with the possibility of an infinite regression of such questions and answers. In trying to explain what started the process or makes it continue as it does, we enter a path along which science can take us but a little way. Beyond it, we enter the realms of metaphysics and of fantasy.

2. LIMITS AND LEVELS OF CAUSAL EXPLANATION IN SCIENCE AND METAPHYSICS

If "metaphysics" is conceived in a traditional way as the branch of philosophy which seeks to gain certain knowledge of ultimate reality, that attempt is hopeless in the opinion of empirical science and philosophy since Hume. The subject of metaphysics in this sense has declined in recent years. This can also be said of aesthetics as an attempt to explain the ultimate nature of beauty as a transcendental category.

However, some newer conceptions of aesthetics and metaphysics are more in accord with modern scientific empiricism. Both subjects can be conceived as limited to the interpretation of phenomena. Modern aesthetics limits itself to a theoretical interpretation of phenomena within the realm of art and aesthetic experience. Art history describes artistic phenomena chronologically with some attempt at causal explanation, as in estimating the influence of one man or school on another and that of social conditions on the styles of art. Such explanations are inadequate to explain the specific nature of styles, trends, or individual genius. But, as we have seen, historiography can gradually become more philosophic as it delves more deeply and broadly into problems of general type and trend; of correlations between artistic and nonartistic phenomena. It can become comparatively philosophic without making any claim to penetrate beneath the phenomenal level of knowledge, or to transcend it by *a priori* logic or mystic intuition.

Modern metaphysics itself, as an empirical subject, makes no claim to transcend human experience or to attain knowledge of first or ultimate causes (ultimate in the sense that the train of causation cannot be traced back farther). It seeks only to analyze and interpret experience itself—including scientific data from the observation of nature—as deeply and carefully as possible. It sometimes tries to make reasonable guesses about the nature of underlying reality. It is not committed to any particular theory in this regard. Metaphysics in a modern sense has been defined as "Any scheme of explanation which transcends the inadequacies or inaccuracies of ordinary thought." (*Dictionary of Philosophy*, p. 196). Webster remarks that writers since Schopenhauer have largely held the empirical view that metaphysics is concerned with the analysis of experience, in the broad sense. Some who insist on restricting the term to its older sense regard the notion of empirical metaphysics as a contradiction in terms. They would prefer to call the newer subject "philosophy of science." Under any name, what we are calling "empirical metaphysics" is based on science. It is an attempt to extend scientific lines of reasoning beyond the point where definite verification is possible, and to speculate in the spirit of science on what may lie beyond.

From the standpoint of empiricism, there is no sharp, absolute division between the metaphysical and empirical levels of explanation. All thinking is and must be empirical whether it recognizes the fact or not. All philosophy, science, and practi-

cal wisdom are "phenomenology," in a literal sense of that term (not in the current sense of Husserl's idealism). All are studies of the phenomenal world, which they cannot transcend except in unverifiable speculation. But within this phenomenal, empirical realm of thinking there are many levels of profundity, breadth, logical precision, and systematic organization. The deepest is that of empirical metaphysics, the most superficial that of naïve, uncritical, popular thinking.

Between them is the level of science, which itself has many degrees of depth and precision. Science now avoids attempts at ultimate explanation and stays fairly close to the empirical evidence in each field. It deals with proximate rather than first or ultimate causes. No single science, such as anthropology, cultural history, or aesthetics, can spend much time on metaphysical speculation; not because the latter is false or idle guesswork, but because each science has enough to do in studying its own special phenomena. Moreover, each science tends to develop rigorous standards of accuracy and proof, which tend to restrain it from speculation on metaphysical problems. Although intermediate between metaphysics and naïve thinking as to the scope of its inquiries, science is more exact and rigorous than either in its methods and standards of probability. Although science and metaphysics cooperate, they work on somewhat different levels of interpretation and require somewhat different types of mind.

On the naïve, superficial level of empirical thinking, one stays close to the concrete, sensuous, affective surface of experience; to the here and now. Naïve explanations are usually in terms of persons and familiar natural phenomena. Mysterious events are often explained as caused by good or bad persons or spirits who want to help or hurt one. Primitive thought erects such figures from the local scene of human and animal friends and foes into deities controlling all events for good or ill. Even in modern civilization, the naïve mentality tends to explain historical and scientific phenomena in terms of such familiar, human or animal agencies and actions. As to the question, "Why did Rome fall?", a naïve answer (expressed in recent films) is that Rome fell to punish its people for their wickedness and cruelty to Christians. A slightly less naïve explanation, based on some historical knowledge, is that Rome fell because the barbarians invaded it. But, though factual as far as it goes, it does not go very far in telling us why the barbarians tried to invade or succeeded in doing so. On a more scientific, but still empirical level, one tries to show the many different factors and trains of events which led up to the fall, including the social, economic, political, ethnological, geographical, technological, military, religious, and ideological.

Within the framework of an empiricist worldview, naturalistic philosophers continue to think about metaphysical problems. They are not content to brush these problems aside as Spencer did, merely because they are "unknowable," or to ignore them in favor of mere linguistic analysis. Instead, they try to infer from recurrent aspects of phenomena some reasonable hypotheses about the realities which must underlie and cause them. No such hypothesis can ever be proven or disproven; but some appear at least to work better pragmatically within experience itself, as intellectual tools for dealing with life and with the growing mass of scientific data.

The metaphysics of naturalistic empiricism continues to speculate upon the traditional problems of ontology and cosmology: that of the fundamental substance or substances (mind, matter, or both?); also that of the origin of motion, the operation of the universe, the first cause and ultimate explanation of what happens in the universe and human experience. Idealism holds that what seems to be matter is essentially mental, consisting of ideas in the cosmic mind. Naturalism holds that mental or psychic phenomena are essentially activities of matter, the motions of complex brain cells and nervous systems. It does not deny the existence of mental, psychic, or spiritual phenomena as such, or as types of activity and experience. It

does not depreciate their value for humans. But it does deny that they are actions of any independent soul or mental substance which can exist apart from bodies. It denies that mind has a prerogative status in the universe. Dualism regards both mind and matter as real, distinct, independent substances. For the idealist and dualist, the first cause and origin of motion is psychic and purposeful. For the naturalist it is material and purposeless. Purposeful action, in his opinion, occurs only in living, highly evolved, animal bodies such as that of man. It is one of the activities of matter in a state of complex, organic functioning.

Dualism, idealism, and their many equivalent or related beliefs (vitalism, teleology, spiritualism, etc.) are forms of supernaturalism in the sense defined by Webster: "any doctrine or creed that asserts the reality of an existence beyond nature and the control and guidance of nature and men, by an invisible power or powers." "Nature" is defined by the same authority as "the system of all phenomena in space and time." Naturalism holds that this is the only system or level of reality and that its behavior is determined only by its own character as partially described in scientific laws. Nature is viewed as self-contained and self-dependent, as having no supernatural, rational, psychic, or purposeful cause or government. Life, mind, and spiritual activities such as art are said to be only incidental and occasional products of natural agencies; they hold no pervasive or preeminent position in the universe, and may cease to exist as in the death of a plant or animal organism. Naturalism denies "that nature is derived from or dependent upon any transcendent, supernatural entities" (Runes, 1942, p. 205). It does not, of course, hold that everything real or natural can be perceived by man, for electrons are not directly perceptible. But they are conceived as integral parts of the order of nature, not as transcendental spirits. There is direct, cogent evidence for their existence as physical phenomena.

There is another sense of the ambiguous word "nature" in which dualism, idealism, and related theories could claim to be naturalistic rather than supernaturalistic. In this sense, as defined by Webster, nature is "The totality of powers or agencies which determine the character and process of things, in general and in detail; that which is the ground of existing phenomena and determines the order of causes and effects, whether conceived as a plurality of formative agencies or as a single and unitary principle governing all reality in space and time." So conceived, "nature" is not limited to the phenomenal world or to that which occupies space and time. It includes also whatever spiritual or other incorporeal agencies, creative and directive powers, may underlie and cause phenomena. The pantheist or panpsychist, such as Hegel and Wordsworth, may prefer to think of all nature as sentient; the rocks and streams as alive; plants and animals as striving toward perfection. This has been a favorite theme in romantic art and in early vitalistic theories of evolution. The panpsychist includes all apparently physical phenomena in his conception of reality as wholly spiritual. "Nature" is then equivalent to "reality," "being," or "the universe as a whole." Dualists tend to think of "nature" as physical and passive, acted upon by a creative, active spirit, both in the universe as a whole and in living human bodies. Spirits are thus supernatural or (in the case of petty and evil spirits) praeternatural. In spite of these ambiguities, the term "naturalism" is coming to be more commonly associated with the materialistic, atomistic tradition from Democritus to Dewey and Santayana.

Naturalism does not hold that nature is now or ever can be completely controllable by man. This would be absurd, not only because of the infinite magnitude of the task, but also because man is himself a part of nature and always subject to its basic modes of behavior. Naturalism denies most forms of theism, but Lucretius and other naturalists have believed in gods who were parts of physical nature. There may be natural organisms in other planets, more highly evolved than man. To believe in "nature gods" in the sense of in-

corporeal beings such as nymphs, dryads, and other spirits behind natural phenomena is a form of supernaturalism. Naturalism denies that the causal order of natural events can be interrupted or invaded by outside agencies of a radically different sort, as supposed in theories of magic, miracles, and creation *ex nihilo*.

Modern naturalism does not hold necessarily that all *being* is material. As in Santayana's *Realms of Being*, it may recognize an immaterial realm of essences or potentially existent qualities and relations such as those described by mathematics. Such a realm would be part of "being" but not of "existence," and not mental or spiritual in basis as Platonists believe. According to this theory, essences come into existence temporarily as matter embodies and exemplifies them. Existent nature does not include all the conceivable possibilities in the realm of essence. This is but one of many debatable points in naturalistic metaphysics, on which its advocates disagree. Each traditional theory has its main tenets and a margin of optional, variable ones.

Each metaphysical theory tends to imply a certain type of answer to basic questions in the philosophy of history, with some margin for individual variation. Each answers, in a different way, such questions as "What is the first cause of evolution and of human history as a whole? What is and has been their main determining, directive agency?" Supernaturalist theories try to do so in terms of spiritual creation and control. Naturalism tries to do so in terms of agencies within the general system of nature.

This system is conceived by naturalism as physical in basis, but not as limited to the kinds of phenomena studied by the physical sciences. It also includes life, mind, and art. These are conceived as integral parts of physical nature, from which they emerge in the course of evolution as special, complex developments of matter. They are not *completely* new and different as some theories of emergent evolution hold. They behave in ways which are significantly different from those of inanimate matter. Each emergent level of such evolution has its distinctive modes of behavior in addition to those it had on previous levels. The thinking of an artist or scientist remains subject to the basic tendencies of matter and of living animal organisms. Emergence does not, according to the naturalist, involve the entrance or origin of any radically new agency or causal principle inconsistent with the previous ones. It is largely a process of complication along certain lines. When matter reaches a new degree and type of complex structure, it becomes capable of new functions such as those of living and thinking. Naturalism denies that matter or nature has any mental or vital character apart from such structure.

However, the differences between animate and inanimate matter, thinking and unthinking animals, civilized and uncivilized thought, are obviously vast and supremely important to man himself, though not to the universe at large. Hence it is wise to observe and describe these differences in great detail and if possible control them in accordance with our standards of value. Once we have recognized their common basis and membership in physical nature, there is less value in trying to "reduce" the higher to the lower levels of emergence, except for purposes of further understanding and control. The higher, more evolved levels must be, primarily, studied and explained so far as possible in their own terms, as total configurations. Admittedly, to trace the evolutionary genesis of art or describe its psychophysical mechanisms is not to explain it completely. Nevertheless, it may add something to our powers of understanding and eventual control.[3]

3. THEORIES OF THE FIRST OR ULTIMATE CAUSES OF EVOLUTION

Anyone whose thirst for explanation reaches to metaphysical levels, even within the limits of empiricism, is doomed to some disappointment.

No theory of causation can be complete. Whatever is said to be the cause of something, one can ask what caused that cause, and so on indefinitely. This has led to metaphysical guesses about an uncaused "first cause," the unmoved mover to which all effects must be originally traceable, the ultimate substance or substances beneath phenomena. Theories of the first or ultimate cause attempt to explain, at least in part, the origin and the present motive and directive power of all events. Whether God, matter, or something else is taken as the first cause, we are left with the question why He or it should be so, and should ever have been so, possessing a certain inherent nature, powers, and tendencies throughout eternity. We are left, as Santayana remarks, with the ultimate mystery of why there should be any universe at all. In particular, why should it be as it is, with its luminous galaxies and green, inhabited earth, so favorable to human life?

As to the fundamental cause of evolution, the explanations offered by rival schools of thought all leave something unexplained. Various forms of supernaturalism hold that events occur as they do because God, the gods, or Fate wills it so. But on asking why the prime mover wills it so, we are told that this is an inscrutable mystery, perhaps dangerous to pry into with our feeble intellects.

To give more satisfaction to the curious, the world's religions have developed myths and cosmogonies such as those of Hesiod and the first book of Genesis. Theories in which the first cause is divine and spiritual usually offer a quasi-psychological explanation such as God's displeasure at Adam's disobedience. This seems to make the course of history intelligible from a human point of view.

The various forms of naturalism attribute evolution and all other phenomena ultimately to the nature of matter, in a broad sense of that term; not exclusively to matter in some complex form, such as atoms, but to whatever ultimate

[3] For further details on the implications of naturalism, see Index references to this term.

particles, electrons, units of energy, waves in ether, or other physical entities may be the basic, space-occupying substance. Matter, in this broad sense of the term, is constantly reorganizing itself into countless different forms. These keep interacting with each other; some reinforcing and helping to build each other up, some counteracting and tending to break each other down. Any partial description of these interactions is a partial explanation of their joint results. Matter, says Santayana, has certain inherent "tropes" or tendencies to move in certain ways, including what we call gravity, chemical affinity, and the like. Why it does, or whether it has always had or will have the same ones, is not known. That it often acts in much the same ways for long periods allows us to describe and predict its behavior in physical laws. But we cannot be sure how long these will hold true. Our laws of physics are not necessarily eternal or operative throughout the universe, of which we can observe only a small part.

Among the inherent tendencies of matter, according to the naturalist, is that of organizing itself into more and more complex forms such as those of atoms, molecules, protoplasm, plants, animals, societies, artists, and symphonies. This is cosmic evolution, in Spencer's terms. Lucretius attributed the origin of such forms to a primeval "swerve" of some atoms, making them collide and assemble. But modern thought pictures them as always "swerving" in the sense of moving spontaneously in various orbits and systems. Spencer considered the organizing tendency of matter as universal, though granting that it might reverse itself some day. Contemporary naturalists are not sure of its universality. Matter evolves at certain times and places but not in others. In some strains of life it evolves up to a point and then stops or regresses. In certain respects the physical universe seems to be "running down" or losing its stored-up energy. How it stored this energy in the first place and whether it can do so again after dissipating it are questions for which physics has no definite answer. Such apparently inconsistent behavior in various

realms may indicate no basic inconsistency in the inherent tropes of matter, but rather the interaction of some of its differently organized forms, such as genes and physical environments. This might conceivably produce a different joint result in different cases: continued evolution in some cases, devolution in others.

Metaphysical explanations often seem to be no explanation at all. "Matter evolves at times because that is its nature," says the naturalist. "This is mere tautology," says the supernaturalist. "Matter evolves at times because the World Mind wills it so." And why does the World Mind will it so? "Because that is its nature." "Equally tautologous," replies the naturalist.

Metaphysical explanations are so general that, even if true, they do not help much in explaining specific events and phenomena. If we want to know why the romantic movement occurred or why Byron, Berlioz, or Delacroix created as he did, it does not help us much to be told that the World Mind willed it so or had reached the romantic stage of its development. Nor does it help us much to be told that matter has the inherent power to organize itself gradually into a Byron and his poem, *Don Juan*. Either may be true as an ultimate explanation of universal causality; but we need something more specific and selective, as to how and why events turned in this particular way and not others. Both theories need to be filled in with credible accounts of intermediate steps, specific modes and mechanisms. Otherwise the sequence (e.g., from "dead matter" to a symphony) seems quite incredible.

In the nineteenth century, much discussion focussed on the "argument from design" or teleological argument, associated with the theologian Paley. It held that the fact of complex adaptation, as in the human eye and hand, implies a purposeful creator as it would in a watch, discovered lying on a beach. Evolution must therefore, in Tennyson's words, have an "unceasing purpose" through the ages. Certainly, replied the naturalists, matter does not take on complex, adaptive form all at once; but fossil evidence, spontaneous variations, and other data suggest that it can do so gradually through millions of years. Furthermore, "purposeful action" is a phenomenon which occurs, so far as we know directly, only in living human bodies and to some extent in the higher animals; never in an incorporeal way.

In the present state of philosophy, neither of the two basic explanations can be proved or disproved. All the phenomena and all the specific, causal explanations of biology, social science, and culture history can be given a naturalistic or a supernaturalistic explanation. Historically, it is a fact that naturalism has gained increasing scientific acceptance during the last three centuries. A determined effort was made to explain evolution on a basis of liberal theology during the Victorian age, and it was never directly refuted. But the teleological hypothesis lost support in later years because it did not seem very helpful in explaining or predicting specific phenomena, especially the existence of evil and suffering. The naturalistic hypothesis gained ground because more and more phenomena (including those of art) seemed explicable in physiological, psychological, and socio-economic terms without resort to supernatural agencies.

Scientists and practical men of affairs tend to dismiss metaphysics as mere idle speculation, getting nowhere. Some scientists and historians claim to avoid all metaphysics and to deal only with verifiable facts. They do not realize the extent to which philosophic assumptions can be implied in the interpretation of scientific data. It is hard indeed to develop a theory of cultural history without showing some philosophic bias toward naturalism or supernaturalism. A persistent effort to explain events without reference to supernatural direction is *ipso facto* evidence of a naturalistic or positivistic inclination.

In theory, many compromises can be made. One can lean a little toward dualism or idealism by supposing an emergent level of cultural and mental phenomena, the outcome of organic evolution but transcending it and essentially different from it. The supernaturalist in science, however rigorous in certain limited fields of research, tends to reveal himself as Darwin's rival Wallace did, by resorting to supernatural explanations when no other type is immediately available. The naturalist expects a natural one sooner or later and is willing to wait for it.

Neither naturalism nor supernaturalism provides an adequate explanation of the history of art. No past or present theory does so; each has its weak spots. The weaknesses of supernaturalism concern the relations of art and culture with the natural world of matter, organic evolution, the physiological and economic bases of life. Those of naturalism concern the subjective, introspective aspects of artistic and aesthetic experience. Naturalism so far takes us but a little way toward explaining these in terms of neurons and ganglia, physiological drives and appetites, satisfactions and frustrations. Supernaturalists, believing in the independence and priority of the psychic, have done more observing and describing of subjective phenomena than their opponents have. In many areas their point of view has led to deeper insights than those of naturalism, especially within the inner world of artistic creation and contemplation. Naturalism, on the other hand, has been more observant toward overt behavior in art and toward the relations between aesthetics, physiology, and sociology. Dualism and idealism have been, ever since Plato, more active in describing the complex conceptual, intellectual life of man as well as the mystical, intuitive, ecstatic modes of experience. Naturalism has been, since Epicurus, more active in describing the sensuous, hedonistic phases of experience and the dependence of mind on its physical basis.

Metaphysical materialism does not imply a materialistic attitude toward values: i.e., that material possessions and bodily pleasures (as of eating and drinking) are the highest values of life. It does not deny the influence of psychic, spiritual factors. It does not, necessarily, hold that economic factors are the chief determinants of art. It denies only that mind or spirit is a separate substance or the activity of one—e.g., a soul. It explains "spiritual" phenomena, including philosophy, art, and science, as the actions of organic matter. The aesthetic, moral, intellectual, and other psychic factors in cultural history are not excluded as causal agencies. On the contrary, their power and value are explicitly affirmed. Their causal efficacy is regarded as ultimately material, operating through the movements of matter and energy in the brain and elsewhere. Thus the important distinction between material and spiritual ends and causes is preserved but stated in terms of a naturalistic psychology.

Conditions change in the realm of theory as well as in that of action. A theory which worked well or ill in the mid-nineteenth century may work very differently now. Hegel's philosophy of history, while of little value in explaining physical, biological, or prehistoric evolution, is *becoming* truer as civilization progresses. It is truer in that human events are more and more dominated by psychic, intellectual factors; by a process of collective thinking which tends toward greater mental differentiation and self-awareness. Following this line of thought, it may be true that art will become in future more independent of the accidents of any one physical or socio-economic environment. The artist and his public, knowing all the possibilities and values concerned, may in a free society choose more freely from the great variety of available types and styles of art. A knowledge of specific, socio-economic conditions will be of less and less value in explaining or predicting the specific styles of art produced. A causal theory can be temporarily, provisionally superior and in a pragmatic sense truer, without being permanently so.

It is also wise to proceed today in the historical and cultural sciences *as if* pluralism were true. No one monistic theory of metaphysics—materialistic, spiritualistic, or other—suffices to explain all the diverse phenomena with which we have to deal. Neither does any one of the nineteenth-century

concepts, such as parallelism and diffusionism, orthogenesis and natural selection. Each seems to help us understand some types of phenomena but not others. Hence we must proceed as if there were many causal factors, any one of which, or any accidental combination of which, might provide the best explanation in a particular case. Pluralism in itself is not an adequate explanation of phenomena. It is a disposition to be open-minded while testing out many proposed explanations, and not to be in a hurry to reduce them all to one. Philosophers will continue to look for more underlying connections and for hitherto unknown factors.

4. DETERMINISM AND INDETERMINISM IN THE EXPLANATION OF HISTORY. EXTREME AND MODERATE VARIETIES OF EACH

Determinism in philosophy is defined as "the doctrine that all the facts in the physical universe, and hence also in human history, are absolutely dependent upon and conditioned by their causes. In psychology, the doctrine that the will is not free but determined by psychical or physical conditions." (*Dictionary of Philosophy*). It is sometimes understood as affirming the universality of causal relations: that every event is caused; that there is no event without a cause; *ex nihilo nihil fit.* The nature of every event, it is said, follows inevitably from the sum total of previous events and conditions; hence there is no real spontaneity, chance, or plurality of alternatives. If we knew all the previous events and conditions, the determinist argues, we could predict all later events exactly. He does not imply that there would be no variation in cosmic laws and processes, but that the possibility of such later variation must be somehow implicit in their original nature. Indeterminism is the denial of such universal causation and necessary sequence.

There has been comparatively little recent opposition to determinism in the physical sciences, with the exception of some aspects of the quantum theory. But in theories of human history, psychology, and art there has been a great deal of opposition, not only to determinism in general but to some of its special forms.

Determinism can be interpreted in terms of divine predestination, as in Mohammedanism and Calvinism. It can be dualistic or idealistic; the latter being a kind of metaphysical monism. However, most varieties of Christian doctrine have insisted on the freedom of the will, partly as a way of explaining the existence of evil and suffering in the world. If Adam's sin had been divinely predestined, it would seem unjust to punish him for it; but since he had received the divine gift of free choice, his sin was voluntary and his punishment deserved. This theory left some critics asking whether God, as omniscient and omnipotent, must not have foreseen that sin and knowingly created Adam with a predisposition to it; also why the Devil was allowed to exist as an active, evil influence. Modern theorists of civil law and punishment have found it hard to fix responsibility and blame if a criminal's acts are due to his heredity and environment. Assigning credit for a good deed or creative achievement becomes likewise problematic if all the individual does has been predetermined by factors beyond his control.

In times past the artist has thought it not unworthy to be the mouthpiece of a Muse or other deity, but the situation is different if his creative work is attributed to prosaic material and social factors. In our day many artists and their admirers resent the idea that art (their own, at least) is influenced by previous art or trends in style. They like to feel that their work is purely original; not uncaused, but determined by their own individual personality and genius. This attitude, though encouraged by the modern ideals of originality and progress, tends to make the artist hostile toward evolutionary determinism. He resents its effort to explain art and personality in terms of huge, impersonal forces. To explain art by a series

of miraculous messages from heaven is more flattering to the ego. Even more so is the self-image of the romantic artist as acting on the outside world but not acted on by it; as studying nature, then improving on it; as creating *de novo*, like the heavenly Creator, from the depths of his own spirit.

On the whole, a general, modified determinism appears to naturalists to have a stronger case than complete indeterminism in explaining artistic and other cultural phenomena. This does not necessarily lead to a fatalistic attitude in conduct, individual or social. A modified determinism does not deny that the human will and psyche, whether spiritual or material in substance, is a determining factor as well as a determined one. The thinking brain helps to direct the course of events. As man undertakes to control his affairs more actively and purposefully, the psychic, teleological factors in human behavior become more influential; psychic determinism becomes more true in human history even though the power of man is slight in the universe. (This does not make teleology true of the universe as a whole.) The possibly depressing effect of physical determinism is partly relieved for the naturalist by realizing, first, that the "laws" of nature seem so flexible as to allow us considerable range of variation. The most important question in practice is the extent to which our main, characteristic, deeply ingrained desires can be achieved; not thwarted by external conditions or forced by fear and coercion into paths otherwise unacceptable.

In everyday conduct it is possible, and for the artist often imperative, to act *as if* one's choices were completely free. We never know exactly what our determinants are; they reveal themselves in our action or inaction. They may include potentialities not apparent in our ancestors or early life. By acting as if we were destined to overcome great obstacles, we may show that we were so destined. A society can achieve freedom by asuming that it has the power to do so and acting accordingly. A general determinism does not, in logic or practice, lead necessarily to any particular form of government, free or tyrannical, open or closed. On the other hand, it is often wise and realistic to recognize the influence of conditions on ourselves and others. One living in a slum environment, or one whose family history contains a hereditary weakness, will do well to guard against it in himself and his children. In trying to avoid bad effects and achieve the good by education or other social means, it is well to believe in the potential efficacy of these means. To say in advance that genius in art is born and not made, that nothing we can do will help or hinder it, is premature defeatism. We can never be sure until we try many possible ways of making and fostering it.

We have already noticed the difference between an idealistic determinism, in which the cosmic spirit determines everything, and a materialistic or mechanistic determinism, in which the original nature of matter does so. Both of these are basically monistic, in that only one basic, determining agency is involved. By adopting a dualism of mind and matter instead of idealism, we do not necessarily abandon monistic determinism. Mind can still be taken as the only creative, directive agency. The case is different in extreme dualisms of good and evil, as in Zorastrianism, where both opposing agencies are personal and willful.

In a dualistic ontology, the determinism is in one way external rather than immanent: matter is acted on from outside as when the potter moulds his clay. But it is easily construed in a more immanent way. The soul inhabits the body; the life force inhabits plants and animals. Thus spirit acts from within the total form and process.

Immanent determinism in theories of history can be naturalistic and mechanistic. It becomes less immanent and more external when environmental factors are assigned a more powerful role in the development of art and culture. It can still be monistic in a metaphysical sense, regarding all the factors as material, but pluralistic in recognizing many kinds of material cause, acting somewhat independently and diversely. Environmental determinism tends to be more loose and flexible than immanent determinism, because the environments of life contain so many different, changing factors.

Pluralistic determinism, through admitting so many kinds of unknown and largely unpredictable variables, amounts in practice to a moderate indeterminism. It is flexible and multilinear. It is ready to grant that any one type of influence may be subordinate, weak, short-lived, easily overcome by different ones. Each event or trend is explained in principle as a joint result of many factors; but no claim is made to explain any event completely or predict the future accurately. Most of the factors involved in a given case cannot be observed or their relative influence accurately compared. So modified, a general determinism is not a dogmatic or restrictive attitude in science, but a fruitful hypothesis. As Ernest Nagel points out (1960, p. 317), scientific determinism opens the door to a progressive liberation from illusion, by furthering objective inquiry into the conditions upon which the occurrence of events is contingent.

Even a theory which stresses some one law or causal agency as basic can be flexibly construed. As we have seen, even the nineteenth-century evolutionists did not conceive of evolution quite as rigidly and simply as their modern critics charge; the difference is one of degree. The metaphysician can, in a sense, "reduce" all phenomena to the single agency of matter or mind, yet recognize the infinite diversity of its effects and manifestations. Evolutionism today can move several steps toward pluralism by recognizing that evolution is not the only widespread cosmic tendency, and that it proceeds along many different lines. It is not "reductionism" in a harmful sense to try to classify phenomena under as few headings as possible, if one does not ignore or falsify their variety at the same time. There is no false reduction or oversimplicity in classing all animals as vertebrates and invertebrates. The three concepts of evolution, devolution, and arrested development or equilibrium are inclusive enough to cover practically all historical phenomena, but they are not oversimplified if we recognize that each allows for infinite variety in detail.

What pluralists object to most in theories of history is a different kind of monism, which we may call cultural rather than metaphysical monism. It picks out some one type of causal factor and treats it as the only one, or the only one important enough to deserve attention.

Are pluralists also determinists? Some accept the label while others do not. They are moderate determinists in holding that everything in art and culture is somehow caused. Some insist on a real element of chance and freedom in events, but they do not explain it very clearly. A more consistent determinism would imply that everything follows necessarily from the sum total of its causes and conditions. The course of history thus follows inevitably from its preconditions, but not from any single law or specific factor. It does not, necessarily, pursue any one consistent direction, since its causal factors keep on recombining in divergent ways according to no regular pattern now discernable by man.

A flexible, pluralistic determinism can be applied in the attempt to explain the genesis of styles, creative epochs, and individual talents. Naturalistic analysis, following the initiatives of Marx, Taine, Freud, and others, has marked off a few broad, overlapping types of factor such as that of biological inheritance, early family and local environment, socio-economic conditioning, general culture-pattern, education, and special training. Each includes an enormous range of variables whose specific character and relative strength in a particular case is almost undiscoverable with our present resources. Some one or two sets of factors may stand out conspicuously in a given case, perhaps because of sensational publicity or the concealment of other factors. Then we tend to explain, as in the Bach family, in terms of heredity and family influence. Elsewhere, as in Byron's case, we may tend to emphasize social class and physical defects. But at most, in such cases, we have the right to say that this is an unusually influential factor; never that it is the sole or sufficient one. There is usually evidence enough to show that a similar cause in another man has produced a very different result, or that different causes have led to a similar result.

Many of the constituent processes and sequences of cultural evolution are almost inevitable under the circumstances. Their necessity is contingent, however, not absolute. It does not follow from any universal law of evolution or of nature. It depends on the nature of man and his environment on this planet, and these might conceivably have been otherwise.

As to stages in art, it was inevitable that, if complex types and styles appeared at all, they would come after and not before the simpler ones. The simpler and less evolved are prerequisite for the complex, highly developed ones. As a child cannot go directly from infancy to logarithms, man could not go directly from total savagery to novels, cathedrals, and symphonies. Such inevitability is contingent in the sense that no development at all might have occurred. But development along every line *must* follow certain general sequences or none at all. Some of these are more exclusive and rigidly determined than others. The embryo of a man cannot become an ape; it cannot skip or reverse its fixed order of stages, although each individual develops a little differently. In the development of art or of a single style there is much more room for variation and more divergence actually occurs. But the variability is not infinite. Culture, like nature, does nothing by leaps, although it often seems so. The range of possibilities at each stage is broadly determined by the configuration of causal factors at that particular moment of history.

In a complex, diversified civilization such as ours, one is under many different pressures: e.g., from different styles and fashions in art, different religious and political tendencies. Furthermore, in spite of tendencies to conformity, our culture encourages certain types of non-conformity; also the general right to decide for oneself which alternatives to follow. It is harder to predict how a given artist will respond to a given set of pressures. There are more different pressures today, and more variable factors within the individual in an urban civilization.

There is a middle ground in historical generalization, between a falsely rigid determinism, which regards everything as the necessary working out of a single law, and excessive pluralism or indeterminism, which believes that anything can happen at any moment. The middle course consists in observing the direction, relative force, extent, and duration of the various tendencies in culture history which assume important proportions; in analyzing them and their motives; in relating them to other tendencies as cooperating or conflicting. The result will often be to show, not that the outcome was 100% certain, but that it was likely to happen under the circumstances. With increasing knowledge of the factors involved, we refine our rough predictions in personal life; we say that, "other things being equal," or "barring accidents," this will happen. Experience teaches how to distinguish the stronger motives and pressures from the weaker, the immediate but short-lived from the gentle but persistent. In between such opposites as "necessary" and "unnecessary," "avoidable" and "inevitable," we use such terms as "fairly probable" or "unlikely, but with one chance in a hundred for success."

Scientific progress in culture history will come about through refining and elaborating such estimates of relative causal potency in regard to both past and future trends; not in trying for impossible exactitude or timidly avoiding general explanation.

Evolution, as we have defined it, is not only a process but also a persistent tendency toward complication in matter and its various activities, including man and culture. This tendency is strong enough to bring considerable pressure on individuals and groups to join in it, even if they do not wish to do so. Even by revolting from certain kinds of development and trying to reverse the process, they tend to contribute to it willy-nilly. Many activities, supposedly anti-evolutionary, are really evolutionary in their net effect: especially the breaking down of complex forms in government, art, and other institutions which crystallize and hamper growth. Obedience to the evolutionary tendency, along one of its myriad possible lines, appears more inescapable in the light of these facts. But it is never completely so, for the whole tendency may reverse itself at any time and is not now universal. Some activities which seem anti-evolutionary are really so; that is, permanently destructive and obstructive to further cultural development. The burning of the library at Alexandria was of this type. The indefinite continuance of evolution is neither necessary nor inevitable, but it seems highly probable in view of its long past. Without evidence for a fundamental change of trend, we are justified in projecting it hypothetically into the future.

5. ANALOGIES BETWEEN THE ARTS OF UNCONNECTED PEOPLES

It is a major theoretical problem in art history to explain the occasional, striking resemblances between styles of art in widely distant times and places, where there is no possibility of much direct influence. How, one asks, could environment be the main determining factor when environments are so diverse and changing? What, if not a persistent inner drive, makes so many separate groups develop songs and dances, religions and technologies, statues and temples, without the possibility of learning from each other?

As an example, we have noted the analogy between ancient Egyptian and Mayan culture, with their monumental stone pyramids and temples, frontal sculpture, astronomic and calendar lore, hieroglyphic writing, mural paintings, and stylized but expressive sculptural reliefs. The Mayan jungle environment was considerably different from the valley of the Nile. Some diffusion from Egypt is conceivable, but there is no adequate evidence for supposing enough to cause these similarities.

Another example is the analogy between the ancient Greek and Chinese attitudes toward music. That of Pythagoras and Plato is well known. They interpreted it in terms of number, to which Pythagoras attributed a magical and Plato a transcendental importance. Number magic was also prominent in the classical Chinese writings. The two Greek philosophers, as well as Confucius and his followers, assigned to music an important moral and educational role, especially as inculcating a spirit of harmony and order. Both Plato and Confucius lived in a time of troubles; of civil wars and revolutions. They reacted against it with what seems now a conservative doctrine. They emphasized order rather than freedom. Both advised that the educated sage or philosopher be given a powerful role in government and spend much of this time here. Both advocated respect for old age and the past. Both made music a leading subject in education. Plato coupled it with gymnastic; the Confucians, with ceremonial rites. Both thought that music should be stately, simple, and regulated by the state. Plato believed it should be directed by a committee of elders.

Hsün Tzu, called "the father of Han Confucianism," wrote of music in a way that Plato would have liked on the whole. One difference is that he emphasized the peaceful character of good music, while Plato approved vigorous, martial music in the training of the future guardians. "The music of a well-ruled state, writes Hsün Tzu, "is peaceful and joyous and its government is orderly; that of a country in confusion is full of resentment and anger and its government is disordered; and that of a dying country is mournful and pensive and its people are in distress. The ways of music and of government are thus directly related." (Like Plato, he thus discerns a two-way causal relationship between the art of a people and its "psychological climate"; also between art and individual temperament; each affects the other.) "The former kings," Hsün Tzu continues, "set up rites and music that men might be controlled by them... Great music must be easy, great rites simple. Music induces an end to anger... Music is the harmony of heaven and earth...Through harmony all things are transformed."[4] By "music," both the Greek and Chinese sages meant a fairly diversified art including instrumental music, singing, and sometimes dancing. Under Confucian influence, state and ritual music was regulated for centuries, more or less in accordance with these ideals. Platonic ideals influenced the Western tradition in music through Plotinus, St. Augustine, Gregorian chants, and the medieval modes.

The usual question arises, of whether there was any direct or indirect influence between Greek and Chinese culture in the theory and practice of music. At present, there seems to be no good reason to think so. There was considerable trade between far east and west in Han times, but little during the lives of Pythagoras, Plato, and Confucius. Plato and other Greek philosophers received some influence from near eastern religious mysticism. But such communications are not enough to explain the resemblances.

The analogy is not limited to ancient times, or to a single style. Down through the centuries there has been in China, and to some extent in Japan, a fairly definite neo-Confucian tradition in the visual arts and literature. In landscape painting especially, it has emphasized rational order and balance, the expression of inner peace and harmony. It has symbolized respect for old age and experience, as in the old, gnarled pine tree. The monumental landscapes of the Northern Sung tradition, in which tree-covered mountains tower upward to the sky, sometimes with humans toiling up rugged paths to a mountain temple, express a philosophic breadth and dignity. This is comparable to the main, classic tradition of Euro-

---

[4] Quoted from the *Book of Rites*, §19, in W. T. de Bary, *Sources of Chinese Tradition*, p. 183. *Cf.* Y. L. Fung, *A Short History of Chinese Philosophy*, p. 150.

pean painting, which stressed the Greek ideals of balance, restraint, proportion, calmness, and nobility of character. In contrast, both East and West also developed more agitated, impulsive, unbalanced styles of art, variously described as romantic, Dionysian, mannerist, expressionist, and otherwise. They were more characteristic of Japanese than of Chinese art, but appeared in China in the "flung ink" style of Southern Sung landscape and elsewhere.

As we come down the centuries through the times of Marco Polo, the Portuguese, and the opening of Japan to Western commerce, the probability of direct, mutual influence grows larger. It is possible in the case of the great Chinese novels of the seventeenth and eighteenth centuries, which express a popular, indecorous tradition rather than the staid Confucian one. Aside from possible influence in art, there was much interchange of commerce, religious teaching, and general ideology. From these, artistic parallels might easily arise.

6. IMMANENT DETERMINISM, PARALLELISM, AND DIFFUSIONISM AS PROPOSED EXPLANATIONS OF HISTORICAL ANALOGIES. EXTREME AND MODERATE VIEWS.

The term "immanent" has several senses in philosophy and must be used with caution. We are using it here in a comparatively literal, broad sense, roughly equivalent to "inherent" or "intrinsic." (Webster, definition 1). As applied to the historical or evolutionary process, "immanent determinism" implies that the main factors which direct it along certain lines exist within the nature of human beings, rather than in their physical environments. The word "immanent" is used by idealists to signify "the indwelling presence of God in the world, including man." That indwelling presence is seen as the essential, directive force in evolution and human history, including

cultural history. We have seen that the directive force can also be conceived as inherent in human life and mind but not divine or essentially spiritual. A naturalist can hold that matter, organized into living organisms, has an inherent tendency to change in certain ways whatever the specific environment may be, as long as that environment provides the basic necessities for life and health. This would be one way of trying to explain independent, parallel invention in the arts.

The issues here depend in part on how we distinguish "immanent" from "external" factors. A historian of art such as Focillon tends to think of painting as a somewhat independent, self-enclosed domain, surrounded by all the rest of the world, physical and cultural. He tends to explain its sequences of style as due to factors within the art itself—e.g., the influence of Giotto on Masaccio, of Masaccio on Leonardo, and so on, rather than as due to social environment. Specific parallelisms, such as those between ancient Roman, Chinese, and European baroque landscape painting, are explained as due to the "inherent life and logic" of the forms. But from the standpoint of an individual artist, the traditions of his own art are parts of the social and cultural environment. The painter is surrounded by other painters and their works, old and new; he observes their methods, products, and statements of purpose. To a painter, the art of painting as it exists in his time is largely an external influence. He feels himself, his own personality, as interacting with it. He accepts part of it, rejects other parts, and exerts an influence upon the art as a whole. The issue between "immanent" and "external" determinism is between factors within himself and those outside, the latter including other artists and their works.

The attempt to explain art history in terms of immanent determinism is still more common among idealists and dualists than among naturalists. Those who do so may not acknowledge their debt to Hegel, Bergson, or other precursors, or state their philosophic creed explicitly. As historians of art, their attention is consciously fixed on works of art and related documents. But their philosophic orientation shows itself in the way they explain the sequence of events in art and the genesis of styles. The restriction of history-writing to a sequence of art-works in the same medium often indicates a tacit assumption that events within that art can be explained without going outside its limits. All or most events and conditions external to that art are ignored or minimized: not only the socio-economic and other environmental but the hereditary; not only religion and science but other arts as well.

When such an approach to art history proceeds from Hegelian assumptions, as it often did in pre-war Germany, it implies that the sequence of styles in a given art such as painting is a self-enclosed, inherently propelled stream of history, influenced only superficially by other streams and accidental circumstances. The various concurrent streams, such as those in architecture, music, literature, religion, industry, and science, are not unrelated causally; for all are said to be directed by the same cosmic mind along more or less parallel lines. But their incidental effects on each other, as crosswise interactions, are not their main determinants. Each would proceed in much the same way in a different environment, for each follows its own inherent logic.

The concept of immanent determinism is also used to explain and support the theory of art history as cyclical and organismic, rather than evolutionary. As we have seen, it is based on an assumed analogy between the life of styles and that of individual organisms. It also assumes as a rule that both are directed by a spiritual force. This leads to the literal attribution of a "life" and "death" to each style. We have rejected this theory as without empirical foundation.

The unilinear evolutionism of the nineteenth century is sometimes described as "parallelism." This theory, in its extreme form, is rejected by contemporary evolutionists. In a more moderate form it is still a tenable hypothesis with special relevance to the history of art.

Hoebel (1958, p. 655) offers an extreme definition of parallelism as "the development of similar cultural forms through identical steps without historical interaction or contact." No one today would accept the idea of "identical steps," and no one in the past—even Morgan and Tylor in their most unilinear moments—has gone that far. If "identical" is changed to "somewhat similar", the theory becomes a little more acceptable today. Parallelism then becomes almost equivalent to the concept of "independent invention," which is a name for the unquestioned fact that some analogous cultural developments occur in unconnected social groups. In the theory called "parallelism," such analogies are held to occur on a large scale in very different environments, as a result of immanent determinism. This implies a proportionately smaller role for chance variation and environmental factors.

The existence of diffusion on a large scale is an unquestioned fact. It means "the spread of cultural elements from one area, tribe, or people to others, as by migration, war, and trade." (Webster). Such a spread may go in one or both directions. Extreme diffusionism holds this process to be responsible for most if not all cultural change. Denying immanent determinism, it belittles independent analogies and explains them as due entirely to chance variation and environmental influence, physical and cultural. Some extreme diffusionists have gone on to assert that all civilization came from one central source, perhaps in Egypt or Mesopotamia, and radiated from there throughout the world.[5] No one would deny that *much* civilization came from there; but again it is going too far to reduce the origins to one single source.

Extreme diffusionism is weak in minimizing or failing to explain the analogies among remote cultures. Extreme parallelism is weak in postulating a rigid, inherent determinism for which there is insufficient evidence. However, there is no good reason today for going to either extreme. As

---

[5] See the discussion of Lord Raglan's "culture hero" theory, above; also the works of Elliot Smith and W. J. Perry.

Tylor clearly stated, it is reasonable to suppose that both kinds of causation occur, in varying degrees at different times and places.

Some of the anthropologists who have been most severe in attacking L. H. Morgan's "unilinear evolutionism" have come around to a moderate, partial form of parallelism. Among them is Lowie, who recognizes independent invention and parallel development in such traits as moieties, a dual system of numbers, and messianic cults. He further accepts, says Steward,[6] a kind of necessity in cultural development, to the extent that certain achievements presuppose others. Metallurgy presupposes an advance from savagery to stockbreeding and farming. Kroeber went so far as to say that "culture relations or patterns develop spontaneously or from within probably more frequently than as a result of direct taking-over." Also, the types of culture forms being limited in number, the same type is frequently evolved independently. Monarchical, feudal, caste-divided, and democratic societies "evolve over and over again," he said, as do priest-ridden and relatively irreligious ones. So do expansive, mercantile, and self-sufficient agricultural nations.

Cultural orthogenesis is in some ways more plausible than biological orthogenesis. It deals with only one biological type: *Homo Sapiens*. Since humans as a genus are obviously alike in many psychophysical predispositions, it is easier to believe of this one genus than of life as a whole that it has a characteristic drive along certain lines of development.

On the other hand, *Homo Sapiens* is the most flexible and variable, the least rigidly predetermined of all organic types as to mental and social development. His innate structure and proclivities determine his cultural development only in broad outlines, leaving it possible for different human groups to diverge and take unpredictable turns at any moment.

Many strong points of moderate parallelism and diffusionism can be combined while awaiting further evidence. A moderate form of parallelism,

immanent determinism, and cultural orthogenesis recognizes *some* inherent pressure toward similar lines of evolution in all human groups, however distant in space and time, if only because they are all human and inhabitants of the same terrestrial scene. But it recognizes also that this directive tendency is often weak or non-existent; that it is easily counteracted or diverted. Inherent determinism of this moderate, partial type differs considerably from parallelism in the literal sense of that word. It does not assert that the lines of cultural evolution always run side by side. It recognizes much divergence, many radiating, zigzag, and converging movements.

Naturalists maintain that any immanent drive toward evolution which exists in plants, animals, and man is basically non-psychic and non-purposeful. At the same time they recognize that it gradually becomes more psychic and purposeful in man, especially in civilized man as he begins to plan his own destiny. The increasingly conscious, teleological nature of the drive has nothing to do with independent spiritual forces. It is due primarily to the evolution of the human brain as capable of intelligent planning. Secondly, it is due to the development of culture to the point where people can think and plan collectively in general, long-range terms.

The origins of planful evolution can be seen in primitive man's behavior toward concrete, immediate situations. More than other animals he has shown a persistent (though not universal) tendency to be dissatisfied with whatever he had at the moment. In addition, he has felt impelled to do something about it, and to use his wits as well as his muscles in the attempt. He has wandered and experimented restlessly in search of something better than what he had.

---

[6] "Evolution and Progress," in *Anthropology Today*, p. 319, quoting Lowie, *An Introduction to Cultural Anthropology* (New York, 1940) and Kroeber, *Anthropology* (New York, 1948), p. 241.

7. PERSISTENCE AND CHANGE IN ART; SOME PSYCHOLOGICAL AND SOCIAL ASPECTS

Man's restless drive for more and better possessions and enjoyments leads at times to continued effort along one line; at other times to radical changes in direction. The latter may be largely due to environmental changes. But it is probable that innate human nature is again partly responsible.

Two opposite tendencies appear to be innate in man, and perhaps in many other species. Both appear in the history of art. One is the tendency to continue doing that which one has found to be satisfying; to stop only when fatigue sets in or appetite is satiated, then to resume the same activity after a period of rest. This involves a disposition to seek and keep the same kind of object which has been found satisfying in the past, or to make or alter one to suit if necessary. This predisposition develops into habit in the individual and custom in society. The other is to become bored and restless after much repetition of the same activity toward the same kind of object; to seek for something radically new and to welcome it when it appears, casting aside the old one. Both tendencies show themselves early in human childhood. The second becomes stronger as the individual matures and develops more diversified interests, including a taste for diversity itself. Fickleness, desire for change and novelty, becomes a habit and a custom. It is stronger in man than in any other animal. It is stronger in modern, Western man than in any other civilization. "Faustian" man is reluctant to say to any one moment, any object or type of experience, "Stay, thou art so fair!" The two tendencies are not irreconcilable. We hold to some of the old along with the new. The new toys, tools, and pleasures which we keep adding to our program for living are never completely new; they have qualities in common with the older ones. We apply our previously developed powers in experiencing them; we interrelate them as contrasting elements in a more or less consistent program of life, as in the cycle of work, play, and rest.

That we are so equipped by nature, and still more by modern Western culture, suggests a partial, basic explanation of the two facts, mentioned above, which often puzzle art historians. One is the fact that certain styles and lines of stylistic development—e.g., realistic perspective in painting and polyphony in music—often continue in a certain group for a considerable time. The other is the fact that such styles and progressions are often dropped, discontinued in favor of others. The first fact helps to give some unilinear direction to the history of an art. While it lasts, a certain kind of creative work seems to acquire almost a physical inertia and momentum of its own. It seems to have an immanent determinism, holding and impelling it indefinitely along the same path in spite of all distractions. Artists and craftsmen who have learned a certain technique, accepting certain general goals and value-standards, often want to continue along that line. Patrons, having acquired a taste for such art and endowed it with sentimental values, often want more of it. Each step ahead, each technical, formal, and expressive problem solved, suggests related ones. Even the most creative artists may want to do the same kind of thing a little better with only minor variations.

The problem for historians is to explain why this momentum does not last forever; why the old style comes to seem, slowly or gradually, as tedious and unprofitable, stale and flat, distasteful to the younger generation. Why does the perennial conflict of younger against older generation break out into open rebellion at certain times and not others? If we have personified the old style and its attendant *Zeitgeist*, as some historians do, we are mystified as to why they became "exhausted" and "died"; why and how this particular new, infant style was "born." What has happened to the immanent determinism which so long preserved the old, steady course of art?

There is nothing essentially mysterious about the

double fact of persistence and change in art. They occur in both the organic and the cultural worlds. Is it especially puzzling that artists and their patrons should want to keep on the same track for a while, achieving one set of values more fully and clearly, then shift to a different set? Not if we start with the hypothesis that both are derived from innate human tendencies, basically physiological. Both are always present and contending in unstable equilibrium: each at times is stronger than the other. But the question still remains of why continuity prevails at one time and place, discontinuity at another.

The general answer of pluralistic naturalism is again that no one factor can be always or exclusively responsible. Man's innate predisposition to both permanence and change is one contributing set of factors. Social structure, technological level, physical environment, religion, and intellectual climate are others. No one of these holds universal priority as the basic determinant. Empirical research must seek to discover which are present in each case, and in what relative strength and configuration.

Drastic social change, unrest, or premonitions of drastic change to come, would naturally strengthen the forces making for change and diversity in art.[7] This occurred in the late nineteenth and twentieth centuries. At the same time, they would tend to arouse counter-tendencies in certain areas, seeking to reinforce conservative symbols and patterns. In times of peace and order where the status quo is not seriously threatened, in times without great technological change, there is less pressure toward radical changes in art. Aberrations in art may then be feared and resisted, put down by force if possible and necessary. In modern times we have become more flexible, more secure in some respect though not in all. We have learned that democracy and art both thrive when many different, even hostile, styles and movements are permitted free rein to struggle for survival. In the democracies we encourage and demand constant change and novelty in art instead of trying to repress it.

There seems to be in healthy human nature a basic tendency toward psychic balance; toward maintaining and restoring an approximate equilibrium between the various elements in personality and experience, individual and social. Natural selection operates to preserve it as it does in the case of diet: those individuals and groups which veer too far off balance eventually weaken themselves and are eliminated. Those fanatical cults which preach and practice celibacy, self-mutilation or other types of extreme asceticism eliminate themselves in due time, though others may take their place. Extremist ideologies, moral and religious principles too much at variance with human nature, often eliminate themselves. They give rise to counter-movements, correctives emphasizing opposite goals and values. Strong natural desires and impulses, too long repressed and undernourished, burst forth into opposite excesses. These too are out of balance, as in the crude sensualities of late Roman Epicureanism; but periodic syntheses are achieved, for which Aristotle's "golden mean" remains the perennial, classical statement. Neo-classical overemphasis on a narrow, cold, restrictive type of reasoning gives rise in time to its antithesis, an anti-rational, emotional, Dionysian counter-trend, as in the romantic spirit. This may manifest itself simultaneously in political revolt, social egalitarianism, and many other concurrent trends; but no one of these is necessarily prior and basic. All contribute toward the vast, semi-conscious, collective effort of civilized man to restore his mental and emotional balance; to live more fully and achieve all the different kinds of value of which he is capable.

This trend expresses itself in all the arts in varying degrees of force and clarity. While a cultural phenomenon, it is, like all culture, deeply rooted in human nature, and hence to some extent inherently determined. The appearance in poetry, philosophy, or elsewhere in the cultural fabric of this gyroscope-like pressure to maintain a psychic

---

[7] *Cf.* Kroeber's comment on the relation between unsettled social conditions and rapid change in women's dress design.

equilibrium is not a mere resultant of environmental factors; it can spring up in any cultural component, in any sort of environment. It can spread throughout the culture, and thence transform the environment itself.

8. SOME WEAKNESSES OF IDEALISTIC EXPLANATION

One common error in theories of history comes from believing that universals, abstract qualities and relations, can exist independently and influence the course of events. To speak and think as if they could is a common, convenient device, far older than Platonism. Thus we say, "faith can move mountains" and " 'Tis love that makes the world go round." It is no error of thought to speak so if we realize that these are merely figures of speech to indicate ways in which concrete, individual humans feel and act. It is a pardonable and often beneficial error for a poet to believe that faith and love are real forces, independent of human individuals. This may lead him to worthwhile imaginings in which literal truth is not the main value to be sought. John Donne, whose poetry is full of abstract causes, wrote:

Absence, hear thou my protestation
  Against thy strength,
  Distance and length:
Do what thou canst for alteration,
  For hearts of truest mettle
  Absence doth join and Time doth settle.

When Plato asserted that universals have a real, independent existence apart from particulars, he confused philosophic thinking for many centuries, in the opinion of naturalists and empiricists. He reinforced the naïve realism of ordinary speech and poetry, which projects the results of human thought into the outer world as objective existences. He obstructed the scientific effort to distinguish between thoughts and things, figures of speech and sober accounts of fact. One can see the ramifications of this mistaken line of thought today in the popular tendency to explain things as due to some abstraction. For example, "gravity holds the universe together." Even some physicists, brought up in the philosophy of idealism as many are in Germany, find it easy to slip over from empirical to Platonic ideology in handling such concepts as "energy." They define it as "capacity for performing work" and as a property of material particles; then write as if such energy or power could exist by itself, apart from all concrete things as an abstract conceptual reality.

Naturalism is nominalistic in its theory of universals and of causation. Abstractions as such have no independent existence and no causal efficacy, according to this view. The only things which exist and have power are material, space-occupying objects—whether as particles, waves in some medium, or otherwise. For reasons and in ways we do not understand, particles of matter have power, not only to move themselves, but to make others move and combine into various forms. This is the only basically real causation, according to naturalism. All other kinds of cause and effect, such as that of medicine on health or music on the soul, are complex movements and configurations of matter. They include the ways in which human brains and nervous systems respond to outer physical stimuli, including waves of light or sound from works of art.

Plato himself was cautious about attributing causal efficacy to the ideas. He assigned it rather to the Demiurge of the *Timaeus.* But Christian neo-Platonism attributed both ideas and first cause to the deity. Once we have attributed independent existence to abstract ideas, it is easy to go a step farther and give them power to influence events: first in the realm of thought, then in nature. Cartesian dualism asserted an interaction between the soul and body, between thoughts and material stimuli, each influencing the other in the brain. Thus the chain of causation could be mixed, material and spiritual. Mind could dominate matter. Other dualists preferred to think of two parallel lines of causation, exactly concurrent but not influencing each other. Kant and Schiller emphasized the freedom of the spiritual world, including art, from laws of causal necessity. In this respect they contrasted it with the realm of nature, in which man is subject to physical laws and bodily needs. This led to a further distinction between the useful arts, as somewhat bound by these laws, and the fine arts as more free. Especially in literature and painting, the artist is free to imagine as he wishes, and music is even less bound by natural facts and appearances. Having no solid material embodiment, the romanticists thought, it comes the nearest of all the arts to escaping from the chains of causality and expressing the free life of pure spirit.

While stressing the freedom of spirit from material bonds, especially in the case of art, the supernaturalists had also to maintain some kind of causation in the spiritual world itself. That world had, perhaps, its own divinely established laws. Among these, it was suggested, were the logical laws of implication among ideas. Hegel developed the principle of contradiction into the dialectic of history. In any case, the world of spirit was subject to, or identical with, divine mind, will, and creativity.

Thoughts, ideas, concepts, and other mental forms can thus enter into causal sequences of their own, according to some forms of panpsychism. The world and all its history is but a thought or momentary dream of Brahma, said the Indian mystics. All apparently material phenomena are but ideas in the mind of God, said Bishop Berkeley. Causality is a category of the mind, said Kant. Panpsychism opens the door in philosophies of history to the belief that styles of art and other abstractions can have an active influence, on each other and on the general course of events.

Once more, let us note the difference between saying this in a figurative, and in a literal sense. The naturalist or nominalist can say it figuratively, and often does. "The Greek styles of architecture influenced the Roman," he will say, and "Florentine naturalism conquered Byzantine decoration." He is well aware that this is but a metaphorical, abbreviated way of saying that certain artists and patrons, having seen some works of art in a new style, decided to imitate it. Neither "style" nor "realism," as a pure abstraction, can influence or conquer anything. But the Platonizing habit of thought can lead one on to believe that, in some mysterious way, a style can really give birth to another, that styles descend through the ages in causal sequence; that one style dies as another is born. It can lead one to believe, with Kroeber, that a style dies out because it is "exhausted" or "lacks the vitality" to develop further. It can lead one to think of styles as struggling for existence in a process of natural selection through the ages.

That there is an element of truth in all these statements, if taken in a figurative sense, we have seen in the foregoing chapters. But when we reach a point in theory where cause and explanation must be clearly analyzed, we should be careful not to take the metaphors too seriously. A style in art is a real existence and a causal factor in cultural evolution to precisely the same extent that a genus or species is in organic evolution. Neither exists independently: neither can cause anything; they cannot directly struggle for survival. The actual, effective agencies are concrete, living animals and humans, their material environments and products. What we call their psychological environment or cultural climate, the "spirit of the age," is only a description of certain recurrent configurations in the feelings, thoughts, and actions of individual men and women.

We have noticed the false implications of thinking that "natural selection" causes evolution, or that "the law of gravity" makes apples drop and planets whirl around the sun. Such abstractions are all, strictly speaking, names for certain ways in which things appear to happen; to move and change their shape in relation to each other. As an abstraction, natural selection causes nothing. We have still to explain just what makes it work in some cases, not in others. "Heredity" and "environment," as abstractions, cause nothing; but the things and events they refer to have far-reaching consequences. The acts of scientists in thinking and writing about them have still others. When cultural evolution shifts gradually from "natural" or humanly unplanned selection to "artificial" or planful selection, we do not have to explain it by the introduction of a new, spiritual factor. From the naturalistic point of view, both are still ultimately caused by the purposeless movements of matter; but in a very small, infinitesimal area of that motion on the earth, there has been a slight increase in the relative influence of brain particles organized as cortical mechanisms—those performing the functions called reasoning, planning, and purposeful control.

9. EMPIRICAL EXPLANATIONS, GENERAL AND PARTICULAR

Scientists and historians in the cultural field now spend little time debating metaphysical explanations, even those which are frankly empirical or naturalistic. They mention such concepts as teleology and determinism chiefly to reject or exclude them from scientific discussion as too speculative and unverifiable. Some times they charge their adversaries with making metaphysical assumptions, without realizing that they themselves are making different ones. But there is a conscious effort to restrict discussion to verifiable hypotheses, especially those susceptible to quantitative demonstrations. Scientists try accordingly to avoid all theorizing on first principles, ultimate causes, and general concepts of reality; to deal only with observable recurrences in phenomena and proximate causes (in the sense opposed to "ultimate"). The sequence of events and proximate causes can be traced back indefinitely—perhaps for billions of years, to the formation of the oldest galaxies—without raising metaphysical questions as to how

there came to be any formation at all, or anything to form. Matter, space, and time can be indefinitely described and explained in purely empirical terms without raising epistemological questions about their relation to underlying reality or the *Ding an sich*. Evolution can be described and partially explained in terms of modes and mechanisms, pervasive trends and processes like complication and diffusion, without asking what originated these patterns in phenomena or what propels them along whatever paths they take.

A partial explanation of this sort may take the form of an assertion that events or conditions of type A tend to cause events or conditions of type B. It may be based on empirical observation or made arbitrarily, as a hypothesis to be tested in later observation. It may be comparatively broad in scope, as in the Marxist theory that socio-economic changes tend to produce changes in artistic style, or more specific, as in saying that modern formalistic art "expresses" (i.e., is caused by) the decadence of capitalistic civilization. Such a generalization implies an attempted explanation of historical events of the type specified: e.g., of the formalistic trend in post-impressionist and abstract European paintings in the twentieth century. It also implies a prediction that capitalistic decadence will tend in future to produce such art. It suggests a means of control, through social revolution. Negatively, it implies that decadent capitalism does not usually produce other kinds of art (e.g., realistic) and that formalism does not usually occur in other socio-economic situations (e.g., communistic). Such a generalization, if accepted as true, would be taken as a partial explanation of any particular case of formalism in modern art. It will not, of course, be accepted by science as true or probable without a considerable amount of evidence.

To explain a particular event in art more and more fully, one should in the first place analyze the event or effect objectively and carefully. In what ways and to what extent is this work or style of art "formalistic"? In the second place, one should know as fully as possible the various sequences of related events which preceded and accompanied it. Third, one should link these up with well-supported generalizations as to the usual causal relations between such variables. Something of this sort is done in the medical diagnosis of a disease. To explain and perhaps control it, one tries to fit it into the context of relevant general knowledge about such symptoms or effects. The general knowledge lies at hand in technological manuals, classified so as to offer tentative explanations for various sets of effects under various circumstances. The diagnostician must be on the watch for unexpected variables which may have produced an unusual sequence of events.

Are we asking too much? Is it impossible to explain historical events to this extent? Yes, say the extreme historicists, for there can be no laws or valid generalizations about unique events and no predictions on the basis of past experience. We have rejected this extreme view. Certainly there are no absolute laws, no exact recurrences, and no certain predictions; but there can be rough approximations to these, and they have some theoretical as well as practical validity. All culture, all accumulation of wisdom, is a process of learning by past experience, of oneself and others. We could not learn by experience if life and history did not constantly repeat themselves in some ways. Every event is the joint result of many different factors, some known or discoverable and others not. There are always unpredictable variables, but not always enough to prevent things from taking their usual course. Thus we come to expect certain outcomes with more and more reliability in fields where much analysis of contributing causes has been done, as in medicine and meteorology. We predict with more and more accuracy and plan more successfully as a result. We have learned in democracy that putting great power in the hands of a military leader, not subject to popular election, runs the risk of dictatorship. We have learned that when an artist's livelihood depends on the approval of officials,

he is apt to produce in ways which will please them. We also see occasional exceptions to these rules.

The limitations of historical explanation are shared to some extent by all sciences. Except perhaps for formal logic and pure mathematics, whose grounds of demonstration are still controversial, all the sciences are definitely based on empirical observation. They describe, not ultimate reality, not what must be by the very nature of things, but what has been observed in human experience or directly inferred from it. The "laws" and principles of causation they imply describe certain observed recurrences within a certain realm of phenomena which have apparently persisted for a long time and will probably, but not necessarily, continue to do so. The physical, biological, social, psychological, and cultural sciences offer no fundamental explanations, but only describe how things are happening, have happened, and will probably happen in their respective realms. They explain particular instances in part by showing how these fit into larger processes and recurrent sequences within the phenomenal world, including that of inner experience.

Phenomena in the social, psychological, and cultural sciences (including aesthetics) are much more variable than those in the physical sciences and therefore harder to describe in laws of uniform recurrence. Statistical correlations and estimates of frequency and probability are usually the most they can achieve. Accordingly, they cannot explain a particular event or type of phenomenon —e.g., the occurrence of artistic genius or of Shakespeare in particular—as neatly as astronomy can explain an eclipse. It is not an example of one, great, regular process or the result of similar, interacting forces like the simultaneous movements of several planets. It is the result of many diverse, irregular processes and influences, such as those of biological heredity, physical environment, psychological and cultural environment, all at a certain moment of history. Their multiplicity, diversity, variability, and inaccessibility to observation reduce the explanatory power of science in such a case to a minimum. As the sciences learn more about the various causal factors involved, they increase the possibility of fuller understanding. But this will require cooperation between the sciences, in describing the relative strength and specific interaction of factors.

The difficulty of explaining particular events does not imply that history or cultural evolution in general is completely inexplicable. The behavior of large numbers of cases and long-range trends is often understood and predicted, as in actuarial statistics. One may not be able to tell which individuals will die from a certain cause in a certain year, but one can predict fairly well how many individuals of different types will do so. One can tell whether certain causal factors (e.g., tuberculosis and automobile accidents) are increasing proportionately. Rises and falls in some of the factors affecting artistic ability are fairly obvious, such as the decrease in ecclesiastical influence on education and art, the shift of patronage to secular agencies, the decline in influence of academic rules of art production, the increase in worldwide diffusion of styles. In so large a process as the evolution of art, many minor, local, temporary, individual factors cancel out and leave fewer types of causal factor to be considered as widespread, long-range influences on the total flow of events.

To explain an event in terms of an unbroken "chain of causes" leading up to it is nearer the truth than one which admits of intervening miracles, magic transformations, creations *ex nihilo*, events without causes, or events without effects. But it is still oversimplified in reducing causation to a single line.[8] Every effect has many joint causes, simultaneous and successive, along with factors in its history which have worked in a contrary or neutral way. Every cause contributes to many joint effects, branching out indefinitely and uncertainly into the future. No end can be assigned, except arbitrarily, to the dense fabric of interacting factors which branch out forward,

backward, and sidewise into space-time from any given event.

Some of those leading up to the event are always more powerful than others, more unusual and therefore striking in this context, or suddenly active while the rest remain constant. It is usually easy to list a number of factors which seem to have contributed, to the event in question. The difficulty is to estimate their relative strength or to be sure one has listed all the important ones.

Some of the things to be explained in history are singular events, such as a sudden, violent death. Any such event has innumerable contributing causes: In crime detection the main explanation sought is an account of who or what killed the person, how and for what motive; also, perhaps, whether the killer was psychologically responsible for his act and planned it in advance. A criminologist or sociologist might be interested more in the type or phenomenon of which this was an instance. What causes such homicides? What has caused a recent increase or decrease? One might try to explain this in terms of widespread socioeconomic trends; e.g., by showing a general correlation between crimes of violence and unemployment. Such correlations, if established, would be thought to help explain a particular case: e.g., if the killer had been unemployed, and had been raised in a slum environment. A psychologist might also say that man's innate, universal, aggressive impulses were basically responsible, though aided by the occasional breakdown of moral, socializing institutions.

The detective story and other types of mystery

[8] The article on "Causality," in the *Dictionary of Philosophy* (1942, p. 47), begins by defining it as "a relation between events, processes, or entities in the same time series, such that when one occurs, the other necessarily follows (sufficient conditions)." Other varieties of causal relation listed are necessary, sufficient, and contributory condition. "Multiple causality" is said to involve several causes which are severally contributory and jointly sufficient. Causality, the article continues, has been said to occur between processes, parts of one process, changing parts of a whole, objects, events, ideas, or something of one and something of another of these types. When one is said to follow causally this may mean that it must succeed but can not be contemporaneous with or prior to the other.

story illustrate in literary form some of the chief problems of historical explanation. A's body is found, let us say, with a wound easily explained as the immediate cause of death and as made by a bullet. "Who fired it and from what motive?" are the main problems. Other observable phenomena point to various characters as possible killers, and perhaps confirm that they have contributed somewhat to the death. But the act of X in firing the shot is singled out among all contributing factors as *the* important cause. Its role was most active and decisive, precipitating a sudden, drastic change in the total situation. In this it may be like the straw that breaks the camel's back or the final vote that breaks the tied election, having no more influence (except by temporal order) than many other like events.

For dramatic purposes, it is quite justifiable to emphasize the conspicuous, precipitating causes. Hence they feature largely in the biographies of artists, as well as in plays and novels. But for purposes of deeper understanding and control this may be misleading. However explosive, they are never the whole cause; the situation may have been such that some other spark would have touched it off before long, as when two hostile armies stand glaring at each other.

From a metaphysical standpoint, in relation to the cosmos as a whole, it may be true that every event is the joint result of an infinite number of interacting factors, reaching outward infinitely far in space and backward infinitely in time. At least, one can draw no sharp line in retrospect, as to where the chain of predisposing causes started. But from the practical standpoint of human affairs, one must stop at a reasonable distance from the event to be explained. Granting the broad, enveloping power of cosmic structure over each of its manifestations, one must arbitrarily limit the explanation to those previous events and conditions which seem fairly closely concerned. They will be (a) fairly *near* to the result in space and time (or connected with it by a bridge of events, as in the influence of an ancient manuscript, just

discovered, on a modern writer). (b) There must be some evidence to show them *actually* operative on the antecedents of the event in question. Thus if Beethoven's late style is the problem, one may take account of his age, increasing deafness, illnesses, and emotional disappointments. These are known to have affected his personality, attitude toward life, and musical expression.[9] (c) One must look for *differential* factors as well as those equally affecting many other artists of his time; factors which may throw some light on ways in which he and his works were more or less unique. The opportunity to take lessons from Mozart was more unusual than that of hearing his music.

It is a partial explanation to show that a trait in the artist's work is connected with his personality or mood at a certain time. But one must guard against implying that any one such correlate is the whole cause. One must guard against overstressing any one type of cause, such as the physiological, emotional, or economic. The artistic traditions inherited at successive periods of the artist's life must be, if possible, related to his personal tendencies to react to them in certain ways: rejecting some elements, accepting and altering others.

A partial explanation, based on incomplete knowledge of previous events and causes, may be worse than none at all. It may be so misleading as to give a false interpretation of the whole, with disastrous consequences. As in Othello's misinterpretation of the handkerchief, many clues may point to the wrong person and strengthen false hypotheses until a single fact is known, which makes them fall into place along a different causal pattern.

Analogous problems and partial solutions can be found in relation to any single artistic event. Mention has been made of Picasso's painting, the

---

[9] *Cf.* J. W. N. Sullivan, *Beethoven: His Spiritual Development* (Knopf, New York, 1927), pp. 79, 243. The late quartet in A minor is here explained in part as "connected with a serious illness."

Demoiselles d'Avignon. In explaining it, some historians would stress previous influences in the visual arts, such as the discovery of African Negro sculpture by Paris artists and the general trend away from realistic representation. Some would stress individual, psychological factors such as a "regressive," "primitivistic" impulse in the painter toward symbols of savage aggression.

Where did Mallarmé get the idea for "The Afternoon of a Faun"? Was it from a picture by Boucher of a pair of nymphs like those in the poem? For such questions of past causation, one must analyze evidence internal and external to the work of art. Nuances in a picture can show, by their similarity to known works of the master, whether they are probably by the same hand. If not, could they be due to a change in his style? If so, is there any discrepancy in style, material, or technique which shows he could not have painted it?

Certain types of cause or antecedent may seem especially important in the light of present interests. Thus an heir to property or title traces back his ancestry with special concern on the male side through each generation, sometimes forgetting that those on the maternal side were equally his progenitors. Sometimes a certain type of factor attracts attention once or twice by conspicuous association with some important artistic effect. Genius runs in one family; insanity in another; both in a third. Tradition says that genius is born, not made. Some theorists jump to the conclusion that it is hereditary; others that it is allied with insanity. Still others, more cautious, treat both as mere hypotheses, to be tested out in a wide sampling of biographies of artists. From the days of Galton and Lombroso to the present such research has gone on sporadically, with no very positive conclusion. For every case where genius runs in a family, there are others in isolation, arising from the most undistinguished parentage. Then one turns to environment for an explanation. In the Bach family, was it perhaps the musical atmosphere, the pressure to follow in one's elders' footsteps, that was chiefly responsible? What of the Bruegel, Tiepolo, Scarlatti, Dumas, and other artistic successions? Is there any special type of family environment, of school and neighborhood environment, of class and social structure, persistently favorable to artistic genius? So runs the search for possible lines of explanation; each a hypothesis to be tested empirically. So far no psychological or social type seems to provide a very high correlation with genius in general or with any particular kind of art.[10]

Meanwhile, another approach to the causation of individual and social creativeness in art goes on in the educational process. When conducted experimentally, education becomes the greatest of all possible laboratories for psychosocial technology, in the arts and elsewhere. During the twentieth century the experimental attitude has been especially active in art education on the lower grades of school, with the aid of other institutions such as the art museum. Dedicated to the aim of stimulating and fostering creativeness in children of all racial and socio-economic groups, it assumes as a hypothesis that proper educational methods can achieve this aim. In other words, it assumes that education is or can be one factor in the production of artistic ability. Probable as this seems in general, no one kind of artistic education has yet proved its superiority in that respect. Freedom of expression, ample equipment, every conceivable encouragement, have so far produced many incidental values including widespread competence and cultivated taste, but so far little outstanding genius. In the most baffling way, genius insists on arising in the most unlikely places and often after what seem to be the worst possible methods of education.

[10] On psychological studies of artists' biographies and related subjects, see Munro, "Methods in the Psychology of Art," in *Art Education: its Philosophy and Psychology* (New York, 1956), pp. 179 ff.

10. WHAT CAUSES EVOLUTION IN ART?
A PLURALISTIC HYPOTHESIS

Assuming that evolution has occurred and is still occurring in the arts, in the sense defined above, how can it be explained in causal terms? We have just seen that no complete or theoretically satisfying answer is possible. One may take one's pick of the existing metaphysical theories of the ultimate cause or prime mover of all events, as material or spiritual. Such an answer, if true, explains everything in a general way and nothing in a specific way.

By showing the operation of certain more specific principles or processes, such as natural selection, immanent determinism, socio-economic determinism, cultural diffusion, and independent invention, we begin to give a somewhat clearer conception of "how it happened." But even these are still very general concepts, and do not take us much closer to an understanding of specific styles or style trends. Each is infinitely variable in itself as to specific content and details of operation. Their interrelations and relative influence—e.g., that of diffusion as compared with independent invention—are still in dispute and our present information does not warrant any definite answer.

If we begin at the empirical end, rather than with general hypotheses, we must specialize on the particular data of some one time and place, or else be overwhelmed by the diversity of phenomena. At the present stage of historical theory, there is no continuous bridge between the very particular and the very general. Conflicting philosophies of art history, would-be scientific hypotheses, swim in suspense above the infinite variety of events, waiting for some place to put their feet down.

As to the immanent phase, let us assume that there is some hereditary, endogenous drive in the human species toward development, mental and social growth with complication; but that this drive is often weak and easily deflected or reversed by outer pressures.

As to the environmental phase, let us assume that physical and social environments interact in the process of cultural selection, which is somewhat analogous to natural selection in the organic world. This would imply that cultural products, including works and styles of art, tend to vary in each generation; that environments determine which shall survive and which die out; also how the surviving types shall adapt themselves to different conditions.

The facts show a long-range, over-all tendency of art to complication, and many complex types survive. Not all complex types survive, and some simple ones do. (The facts are similar in regard to organic evolution.) When the more complex types of art survive, it may be because they help the groups which make and use such art to gain security, prosperity, and power. Or it may be because they succeed in winning and holding the favor of influential groups through successive generations for aesthetic or other reasons. This they can do only through satisfying some innate, potential desire in man.

Amplifying this hypothesis a little, we may suppose that man developed as an organic species through natural selection, with an innate physical equipment capable of and inclined toward complex cultural development in general. He was predisposed to experimenting, learning, and transmitting cultural achievements; to producing and enjoying what later evolved into art. He was, on the whole, predisposed to wanting to improve and develop his cultural possessions along more complex lines, though with important exceptions and regressions. This predisposition was perhaps, from the biological viewpoint, a freak or hypertrophy, innately developed far beyond the requirements of physical survival; but, having it, man has felt at times impelled to use it constructively. Hence the term *homo faber*. This was not his only predisposition, obviously; he is also predisposed to fight, seize, and destroy; but on the whole the constructive side has made considerable headway. The impulse to construct and enjoy complex cultural products and activities, including art, did not become fully conscious, rational, and explicit until a fairly advanced stage of civilization. On the earlier stages, it was less conscious and less differentiated from primary needs and satisfactions. Man's ancestors took the road of competing for survival and power through intelligence, practical ingenuity, symbolic learning, and culture. In the long process, man found that many complex activities and products were not only useful but aesthetically satisfying. The arts developed out of primitive culture in more and more specialized ways, as man developed stronger tastes for aesthetic satisfactions, whether combined with utilitarian devices or apart from them.

Thus the complicative, evolutionary tendency of art was an integral part of the complicative tendency of culture in general. It did not need or have a separate motivation or a distinctive set of causes. It was carried along through early cultural stages by the same motives which impelled the evolution of culture as a whole; by the increasing practical value, intellectual interest, and aesthetic satisfaction of growing mentally and building more elaborate cultural forms. Only in urban civilizations such as the Greek was the process of artistic complication explicitly recognized and evaluated. Then it was sometimes denounced, as by Plato; but by that time its momentum had become too strong to be stopped. It appealed to popular taste if not to philosophers, and this helped to accelerate it. However, strong resistances to cultural complication developed in certain branches of ancient civilization, including utilitarian technology and art. Hence the evolution of art remained slow and irregular. Not until the late eighteenth and nineteenth centuries was it recognized as a large-scale process and approved as desirable by leading philosophers and scientists.

II. SUMMARY

To demonstrate the fact of evolution in the arts, it is not strictly necessary to offer any explanation of *why* it happens or what makes it happen. Attempts at fundamental explanation of historical events and cultural phenomena encounter serious difficulties. The theory of evolution can be stated simply as a description of observable types and tendencies in phenomena, without reference to what causes them. However, a thorough discussion should include some attention to both. The foregoing chapter compares the implications and the strong and weak points of several past attempts.

Complete, certain, ultimate explanations of the universe and human history are impossible. Partial, tentative, empirical ones are not. Historical events vary so much that no exact "covering law" has been found. To show the sequence of events leading up to a certain phenomenon, or the larger processes of which it is a part, is not a complete explanation, but it may be useful and enlightening. The theory of evolution, if true, can provide a partial explanation of artistic phenomena to the extent of showing some of their antecedents and causal relations.

Attempts at historical explanation are on various levels of depth. Those of empirical science are more far-reaching and reliable than those of naïve guess-work. Those of metaphysics try to reach the deepest level, but are speculative or fanciful. They apply the main traditional world-views in postulating a natural or supernatural, material or spiritual first cause and present directive force. All such theories leave much unanswered.

Determinism and indeterminism, parallelism and diffusionism, can all be interpreted in extreme or moderate ways. They can lean toward naturalism or supernaturalism. Determinism can stress the role of environment or that of heredity. The position taken here is one of moderate, pluralistic, flexible determinism. It is naturalistic and empirical as opposed to metaphysical idealism.

Analogies among the arts of unconnected peoples seem to point to some amount of inherent determinism, but not of compelling strength. Persistence and change of direction in the processes of art are both causally related to basic human traits as well as to environmental factors. Art and life often veer toward one extreme type or another, then move to correct the balance.

Much empirical study is needed to discover partial correlations, positive or negative, between various types and trends in art and those in other fields of phenomena. A wide range of variables, both hereditary and environmental, must be examined. Observed correlations can be used as partial, tentative explanations of particular events.

CHAPTER XXII

CAUSAL FACTORS
IN THE HISTORY OF ART

I. MAIN TYPES OF CAUSAL FACTOR IN ART. DETERMINANTS OF STYLE

From a naturalistic standpoint, it seems a reasonable hypothesis that all the determinants of artistic change are covered by the following list, explicitly or by implication. (Supposed supernatural factors, such as divine inspiration and immanent spiritual determinism, are omitted.) The list is a step toward pluralistic explanation on the empirical level, but it is too general to explain or predict any specific event, style, or trend. It may be of use in the general orientation of research and theory, a preliminary survey of the range of possible determinants. Here it may serve to caution the reader against too narrowly simplified explanations. Instead of trying to explain an artistic event in terms of any single causal factor, one may tentatively assume that *all* these types of cause contribute somehow, directly or indirectly, to the nature of *every* artistic event. They do so with varying degrees of strength, some cooperating and some counteracting. Different ones at different times will stand out as most immediate, active, and precipitating causes. The influence of others will be lasting, inconspicuous but deeply pervasive. That of still others may be slight or negligible. Each type listed below includes a great variety of specific factors, capable of operating and interacting in countless different ways. They change, overlap, and mix to such an extent that only rough distinctions between them are possible.

These are determinants, not only of art, but to some extent of all cultural change; also of individual personality and social structure. They determine both persistent trends and divergences. The extent to which their influence is channeled into art, and into a certain type and style of art, depends on their specific nature at a given moment of history. It is influenced by the status and functions already attained by each kind of art in its cultural context and by the artistic materials, technics, and stylistic traditions previously developed there.

I. EXTREMELY WIDESPREAD, STABLE, CONSTANT, LONG-ENDURING FACTORS; ubiquitous forms and tendencies in human nature, environment, and culture; those comparatively universal in humans regarded as normal. They can be roughly divided for our purpose into three main subtypes (A, B, C). These interact to determine the main, general, persistent outlines of art and culture in all civilized periods, places, and peoples. They are subject to evolutionary change, mostly slow and gradual.

A. *Hereditary, biological, endogenous factors*; those characterizing *Homo Sapiens* as a distinct type of mammal and as male or female. These include innate psychological structures and functions, basic human drives, reflexes, appetites, instincts. They determine the main potentialities and limitations of all mental life, personality, art, and culture. They include erect posture, muscular agility and opposable thumb, large cranial capacity and cortex, powers of sense perception, imagination, and reasoning; ability to feel pleasure, pain, and many intermediate and mixed hedonic tones in experience; long infancy and slow maturation; the appearance of major physiological and psychological changes at adolescence. Innate tendencies toward certain general conative and emotional attitudes such as desire and aversion, likes and dislikes, become gradually differentiated, systematized, and attached to a wide range of outer and inner objects. Humans learn to respond intelligently and affectively to symbolic forms such as words and visual signs. They develop tendencies to acquisitiveness, aggression, dominance and submission, playfulness, mutual aid, love and hate, gratitude, resentment, desire for affection. They learn by the experience of themselves and others, thus taking part in the cultural process. Physical sex predisposes to a basic psychological differentiation, much influenced by culture. Man's tendency to sexual desire at all periods of the year has helped predispose him to stable family life; thence to social organization and culture. He is equipped with so many innate tendencies to respond in different ways to different stimuli and situations that they frequently conflict with each other, raising difficulties of choice, integrative adjustment, practical expediency, and ethics. His behavior, individually and socially, cannot be as automatically predetermined by instinct as that of many less intelligent species. His systems of habit and evaluation are comparatively flexible and subject to change. Still awaiting definite empirical confirmation are the psychoanalytic hypotheses that a generic or collective unconscious, preserving residues of past human experience, is transmitted innately in the form of archetypal images or predisposition to an Oedipus conflict. In the meantime it must be assumed that no acquired psychological characters or predispositions are transmitted in the genes.

B. *Factors in the physical and biological environment of man.* Those characteristic of the earth as a whole or of its main habitable parts. They are permanent or slowly changing, hard to modify or escape from. They pertain to geography, topography, climate, natural resources of the earth, water, and atmosphere; flora and fauna as parts of the human environment; plants and animals as potential foods or enemies; as providing materials and subjects for art; animals as potential labor-power.

C. *Relatively widespread, persistent factors in the social and cultural environment of civilized man.* Common types of institution, organization, activity, product and process. Kinship, the family, marriage, government and political organization, military organization, property, wealth, capital, finance, economic organization, labor and management, technics and technology, socio-economic classes, levels, subgroups, education, law and law enforcement, religion, ethics, language (spoken and written), the arts, philosophy, science, sports, amusements. Conflicts between all civilization and some basic psychophysical drives, arising from the effort to restrain impulses to violent, aggressive, lustful, and acquisitive behavior. Those arising from taboos on incestuous and other types of erotic relation. From the need for prudent foresight and social adjustment. Widespread repressions and unconscious conflicts leading to symbolic expressions in folklore, dreams, and art. Attempts at conscious, rational adjustment.

II. FACTORS INTERMEDIATE IN SCOPE AND STABILITY; CHARACTERISTIC OF MEDIUM-SIZED GROUPS, REGIONS, CULTURES, AND PERIODS. Main divisions and varieties of the factors listed in Group I. Subject to somewhat wider, faster changes.

A. *Hereditary.* Factors and forms characteristic of main human types and divisions, especially racial and physiological types; also levels of intelligence and other mental ability. Scientists now agree on the whole that there is no significant correlation between racial differences and general mental ability. As to whether such differences are correlated with any special aptitudes such as that for music, or with a predisposition to any particular styles of art (as Taine supposed), there is little evidence. If any exists, it is presumably slight. However, obvious racial differences can have far-reaching cultural and psychological effects by interaction with specific cultural environments; as helping to determine the status of an individual and family in the social context; his religious and other traditions; the attitudes of others toward him; opportunities, occupations, satisfactions and resentments; his identification with certain subgroups and antagonism toward others. Racial types are blurred by mixture and their social consequences vary according to the culture-pattern.

Other physiological types, thought to help determine temperament and character, have been distinguished on the basis of body structure, glandular functioning, etc. These types, like the levels of intelligence and artistic aptitude, cut across racial and national divisions. Another hypothesis (noted above in connection with Focillon) is that certain innate types of personality tend, in artists, to produce certain kinds of art. To what extent, if any, is a predisposition to mysticism, empiricism, or rationalism inherited? The extent to which characteristics determining personality types are genetically transmitted is not known at present. There seem to be, throughout the world, some types of person born with acute auditory systems and hence the possibility of musical aptitudes; others with visual, still other with intellectual aptitudes, etc. Their correlation with specific physiological and cultural factors, if any, is not known.

B. *Distinctive physical and biological environments in medium-large regions and periods.* Topography, climate, flora, fauna, etc., in main geological eras since the beginnings of culture, in various parts of the world. Prehistoric (glacial, interglacial); important changes of terrain as in land bridge from Asia to Alaska; deforestation, erosion, deserts; disappearance of wild animals from many regions. Domesticated animals and plants. Largescale human alterations in the physical and biological scene. (E.g., dams, canals, irrigation).

C. *Cultural components and patterns of medium-large regions and periods.* Artistic and non-artistic influences pervading a major group at a certain time. Traditions inherited, in art and other cultural components. The socio-economic order as a whole: e.g., tribal, agricultural village, feudal, capitalistic; differences from others of the type; class structure; rigidity or mobility; concentration or diffusion of wealth and power. Technological advancement in various fields including the arts. Other components in the culture-pattern of the national, religious, racial, or other large social group at a certain time; whole-culture styles (e.g., European baroque). Roles of kinship, government, religion, philosophy, ethics, science, and other components therein. Styles and trends in various arts as parts of these larger patterns. As symbolizing moral conflicts and repressions. Dialectical struggles and changes in status among groups, subgroups, and their ideological patterns; among contending types, styles, and theories of art in the group as a whole. Morals and manners in the group as a whole and in different classes and subgroups. The status and role of women; their influence in the arts. The prevailing value-system on different social levels; established attitudes toward sexual, intellectual, artistic, and other types, especially the non-conformist. The influence of these conditions on artistic tastes and trends on various social levels. Technics, styles, traditions, trends and countertrends in particular arts at a given place and time. Religious, intellectual, scientific, technological, and other factors influencing the psychological climate of a social group or major subgroup at a certain moment of history. Status of particular arts in the culture at the time; socio-economic position; prestige and respect; type of patronage; pressures on the artist to conform or revolt. Activity and position of each art, as a creative and prerogative focus of cultural energies or as imitative, obsolescent, perfunctory, routine.

III. LOCAL, SHORT-LIVED, TRANSITORY FACTORS AND PATTERNS; RELATIONS BE-

TWEEN AN INDIVIDUAL ARTIST AND HIS SMALL, IMMEDIATE, SOCIAL AND CULTURAL ENVIRONMENT. INFLUENCES ON HIM FROM THE SMALL SUBGROUPS TO WHICH HE BELONGS AT VARIOUS PERIODS OF HIS LIFE

A. Hereditary: factors and patterns characteristic of particular lineages, families, and individuals during a short period of years. Resultant individual predispositions, aptitudes, limitations, levels of general and special ability, strong and weak traits related to the arts. Types considered as normal, abnormal, supernormal, subnormal, neurotic, psychotic. (Social attitudes vary on this; what is "insane" in one group is "normal" in others.) It is not definitely known to what extent a predisposition to types of personality and ability can be inherited. Some psychotic tendencies are definitely heritable; there is reason to think that some individuals are innately endowed with greater ability than others to resist pressures and unfavorable conditions, psychologically as well as physiologically. It is also not definitely known how or to what extent predispositions to specific types of personality, such as those mentioned in *II A* above, are genetically transmitted and run in certain family lineages. To what extent is homosexuality or other sexual deviation predisposed innately? The problem here is to distinguish, in traits which manifest themselves in maturity, what is due to culture and nurture from what is due to biological inheritance. To what extent and how are individual genius, taste, and talent transmitted, in general and along special lines?

B. Physical and biological environments of small, transitory groups and individuals. The immediate context of a certain family or individual life: e.g., arctic, tropical, or temperate climate; rural or urban, isolated or crowded; barren or fertile; with or without varied natural life, plant and animal; agricultural or hunting; city streets, the "asphalt jungle," mountains, deserts, or seashores. Resultant influences on social and psychological development of the small group and individual.

C. Cultural components and patterns as focusing upon the small, transitory group and the individual. Social, psychological, and artistic factors in the immediate environment. Their contribution to important, brief events and attitudes in the individual, his interests, activities, preferences, desires, aversions, aims and moods at any one time and place. The individual artist as related to his family pattern in infancy, childhood, and youth; to parents, siblings, friends, teachers, servants, clergy. Status of the family in the neighborhood and in the larger social context. Religious or secular traditions. Influences from school, church, and other institutions. Traditions imparted; attitudes fostered. Other interpersonal relations; colleagues, rivals, enmities, love affairs, marriage. Successes and failures, enjoyments, misfortunes, sickness and health. His general and artistic education; history, techniques, appreciation, ideals, interests. Small groups of artists, critics, patrons, as influencing each other and general trends in art; guilds, coteries, movements, local schools, ateliers; their current attitudes toward trends in style; their relation to the larger socio-economic and ideological context. Types, styles, technics, and traditions to which an individual artist is exposed at various times in his career. His participation in collective artistic enterprises, as in architecture and cinema; its influence on his work and character.

IV. THE INDIVIDUAL ARTIST AS CAUSED AND CAUSING. As receiving influences and as actively changing, selecting, reorganizing, and transmitting some of them through his personality, life, and art. His influence, immediate and deferred, on larger cultural and stylistic trends. The nature and influence of particular periods in his life and of outstanding particular works.

Selected elements from all the above types and subtypes of factor pour in upon the individual artist as through a funnel; the selection being largely by chance except for some planful fostering and education. Their relative proportion and strength cannot be directly observed or predicted at birth, but can be conjectured from his later life. After conception, congenital and environmental influences begin to play upon him; at first mainly local and transitory, then increasingly from the greater worlds of adult life, culture, and artistic tradition. At first he is largely a receiver of influence; then increasingly a giver, perhaps locally and then to the greater worlds outside.

The socio-economic status of the artist himself at various stages of his career. As similar to or different from that of his family and early associates; higher or lower. His class status as fixed or mobile; as affecting his prestige, opportunities, self-esteem, and attitudes toward the world. His means of support: by inherited wealth, marriage or own earnings (small or large); by work in art or otherwise. Dependence on certain types of patron, individual or institutional; political, ecclesiastical, popular, élite; as making for conformity or non-conformity to the status quo, in and out of art.

The nature of his physique and personality as determined by the combination of influences before birth and during childhood and adolescence. Normal or neurotic, healthy or unhealthy growth in various respects. Development of attitudes and general abilities relevant to his later work. Traumatic, frustrating experiences; ego-enhancing, satisfying, stimulating, encouraging ones. Characteristic attitudes toward other persons; early friendships and love affairs; attitudes toward various groups, classes, institutions, authorities. Religious, philosophic, moral, and other ideological upbringing; conformity or non-conformity with it. Early manifestations of artistic interest and talent. The artist's mature personality and character in general: normal or neurotic, largely integrated and adjusted or showing inner tensions, conscious and unconscious conflicts, ability to deal with human situations and practical realities; extroverted or introverted tendencies; attitudes toward same and opposite sex. Broad and diverse or specialized education and interests. Major changes in personality at different stages of life, as related to outer and inner events; to successes and failures, accidents, illnesses, happy or unhappy personal and professional relationships. Calm and balanced or volatile, mature or immature, rational and self-disciplined or erratic and uncontrolled; given to alternate elation and depression, love and hate. Moods, attitudes, interests, activities, decisions at particular important moments of his career; e.g., quarrels with patrons; mystic, ecstatic moments of inspiration; gradual or sudden changes of taste and purpose.

Causal relations of all the above to specific traits of his art production; to his general stylistic developments and changes; to the nature of specific works. To what extent these seem to express or result from various types of influence listed above: from the general or local psychological climate, the spirit of the time, current events and trends in art and elsewhere; the effect of personal traits and events such as physical abnormality, illness, or sudden success, health, wealth, fame; the influence of particular artists, living or dead, or of current trends.

In asking how the artist fits into the larger patterns of his age, one should compare his work with previous styles and contemporary trends, asking how and to what extent he is conformist and conservative or rebellious and radical; what he is reacting against and trying to avoid in art as well as what new effects he is trying to produce. In these attitudes, how is he influenced by factors in and outside of his own art, in other arts, in science, technology, and general world-view?

2. THE INTERACTION OF THESE FACTORS

The more general, stable, widespread factors, listed in Group I, combine to form and direct the general nature and broad changes of the arts; their main outlines, ranges, limitations, and common traits of form and function throughout history. They tend to maintain an over-all consistency of form and function in cultural evolution and in the arts of all civilized peoples. They tend to reinforce analogies, parallelisms, and recurrences and thus to make for whatever unilinear direction persists. Groups II, III, and IV tend to diversify the arts in various times, places, media, types, and styles; to determine the more unique, distinctive traits and trends of art history, including those peculiar to individual artists. They make for divergence and multilinear movements, large and small. The influence of Group II appears more in the regional and period styles of larger scope and duration; that of Groups III and IV in individual artists, works of art, and small-scale period styles.

In attempting causal explanations of particular, local and individual phenomena in art, one tends to find in Groups III and IV the more immediate, conspicuous, directly precipitating kinds of cause which are featured in artists' biographies: e.g., a commission from the king or pope; a change of residence to Florence or Paris; an unhappy love affair; a trip to Italy and study with a famous master, rejection by patrons of a completed work. These are not necessarily the most important, influential causes, however. Group I (often ignored entirely) and Group II provide the slow, enveloping causes which are taken for granted; which apply to all or many artists in the same place and period, and hence do not account for their peculiarities.

The various groups cannot be sharply distinguished. The same general factors appear throughout, their more constant aspects being noted in I, their more variable ones in II, III, and IV. They interact in countless ways. If a national culture-pattern is characterized by a belief in progress and by laissez-faire, individualistic liberalism, this tends to favor wider swings of ideology and artistic style among the individuals and subgroups in it, without the necessity of violent revolt for the sake of freedom. A highly stable, relatively simple culture-pattern, centrally directed as in ancient Egypt, tends to favor comparative constancy and persistence of styles. In a relatively free society, the distinctive traits of individual artists can have more influence on style and culture.

In trying to explain the evolution of art and culture as a whole, one will tend to emphasize the general, stable factors, trends, and recurrences more than in the case of a particular artist or local style. The local, short-lived factors and conditions, the individual idiosyncrasies, tend to cancel out to some extent in a broader survey. One is justified in ignoring them to bring out the large patterns, usually ignored by specialized art historians and often misrepresented through ideological prejudice. The danger here is to overemphasize the similarities and produce an oversimplified, unilinear pattern. While a study of this sort cannot notice all or most of the minor diversities, it must keep in mind that such diversities exist and bulk large in the aggregate. As evolution proceeds, cultural differentiation multiplies. The Group III and IV factors and their consequences become increasingly important in the scheme of things.

It is also necessary to distinguish between great individuals (in terms of influence; not necessarily of value) and trivial ones. The scope in time and space of an individual like Sophocles, and of a city like Athens, is no measure of their importance as determinants of cultural history. Their influence far overflows the confines of their lives and shapes the form of subsequent history far more than do the centuries of mediocrity in populous but uncreative areas. Especially puzzling, yet important to explain, are the odd, apparently anomalous geniuses who seem inconsistent with their age or far ahead of their time. Yet it is often hard to tell whether they are so or not; we may have a false conception of their time, and fail to see their connection with it. El Greco now seems more a man of his age than he did some half century ago. Socrates must have seemed an odd, obstreperous figure to many of his contemporaries, but to us he seems in many ways the personification of Athenian culture at its best. Roger Bacon exemplifies incipient trends in medieval culture whose importance did not appear until centuries later.

The factors usually called "psychological" are included mostly under Group I, as organic structures, functions, and tendencies common to all normal humans. The psychology of various types of individual (normal, subnormal, supernormal, abnormal, deviate, neurotic, psychotic, etc.), sometimes called "characterology" or "individual psychology," is covered under groups III and IV. These types of personality, variously conceived, occur in many if not all cultures and periods. A particular individual, such as Vincent van Gogh, is not merely a type, although he exemplifies many types. As a changing, unique selection and combination of traits, he is to be considered under Group IV.

Psychology until the twentieth century dealt comparatively little with the effects on human nature of specific cultures, institutions, and social systems; with the different ways in which basic human predispositions are culturally modified. Much that early psychologists considered as universally human has been found symptomatic of the culture in which the psychologists belonged. More objective, comparative studies of such phenomena have developed in recent decades as "social psychology" and "cultural psychology." As "social factors" in art, they are included under Groups II and III. The older social sciences have paid more attention to the larger, more enduring patterns listed under Group II. The smaller, more brief and local ones listed in Group III—not "the family," but specific types of family situation—have been more discussed by psychiatrists and psychoanalysts than by general sociology. The social and cultural sciences tend to pay somewhat more attention to objective artifacts, overt collective behavior, and institutional patterns, than to the inner thoughts, feelings, and motives which accompany them. In psychology the emphasis is often opposite.

The difficulty thus apparent, of distinguishing sharply between the "social" and "psychological" determinants of art, underlines the statement made in previous sections, that the two are almost inextricably interwoven. Almost all psychological phenomena after early infancy are partly social; almost all social phenomena consist of psychically motivated group behavior. The loneliest hermit or recluse, the artist seeking to escape society, is affected in his innermost thoughts by whatever care and teaching he received in childhood. There is no use in trying to separate the social and the psychic definitely, but it is well to be sure we take the individual, subjective, experiential aspects into account in our explanations of art, as well as the patterns and products of collective behavior.

Cultural evolution is psychic in a broad, naturalistic sense. It is a process of change and development in human thoughts, attitudes, actions, and products through learning by experience. All the thoughts and actions of an individual within a culture involve his relations with other individuals, groups, and institutions. But some are more directly and fully social than others. Some emphasize his relation to material objects such as tools, houses, food, money, clothes, weapons, and vehicles. He desires and uses them; they help to shape his thoughts. A "material" or "economic" factor in his life, or a "social, collective" factor, is always psychological also; it is one selected phase of his total conscious functioning. Antitheses between them, or arguments over which is most influential, usually rest on some arbitrary simplification, as in defining "psychological" to include only the more universal traits of thought and behavior. For socio-economic status to influence art or taste, it must affect people's thinking and thus be a psychic as well as a socio-economic one. Even individual heredity is, through mating and marriage customs, partly a social and cultural resultant. The individual's hereditary predisposition realizes itself only through his interaction with other persons and their products. It is misleading, then, to state the issue in historical explanation as a simple dualism between the psychic and the material or socio-economic. It can be stated in psychological terms, as to the relative strength of different kinds of motivations at different times and places: for example, between the desire for luxury, power, prestige in this world and the frugal joys of a simple life, or between both and the hope of heaven or escape from existence. On the other hand, it can be stated entirely in material terms, as in the belief that all thought is ultimately the behavior of energetic atoms. On either basis, the various organic and cultural components must be described as constantly interpenetrating, dividing, and recombining. Each affects all the others, as in the artistic sublimation of sexual and aggressive impulses and in the reciprocal influence of art, society, technology, and religion.

Rather than to keep debating the relative influence on art of these overlapping abstractions, it would be more enlightening to trace the correlations among a great variety of more specific factors. A prerequisite for such study is the clearer definition of many morphological types and styles in all the arts. These should be correlated with equally clear and specific types of individual (artist and appreciator) and of social structure: for example, in the factors with which art interacts: (a) those of biological predisposition such as racial and physiological types; (b) psychological types, normal and neurotic, such as the intellectual, practical, the mystic visionary, the hysterical, the obsessive, the manic, the homosexual, the heterosexual, the classic or Apollonian, the romantic or Dionysian; (c) socio-economic types such as the primitive agricultural village, the feudal, the capitalistic, and the communistic, with reference to varieties of possible status within each.

In such inquiries, we need to know not only the degree of positive or negative correlation between different sets of variables, but also the relative influence of different factors on the styles and trends in art. For this, we need to know not only that a causal relation exists, but which factor tends to be prior chronologically and hence more determining.

To be thorough, causal explanation should take some account of the forces which tend to make all art and artists alike in some respects, and all artists working in the same period style alike in additional respects. Historians and biographers emphasize the diversities. People think of explanation as the problem of explaining differences, and are often satisfied with a few dramatic events and conditions in the life of an artist which seem unusual enough to explain them. Instead, explanation should take account of all three groups of factors, with due emphasis on the ones which seem most important from one's present point of view. This is not necessarily the most influential set of factors on the whole. In relation to a certain research or practical aim, one set may stand out as deserving most attention: e.g., if one is interested in what can be done to stimulate art production by improving the artist's economic status.

When the problem is narrowly specialized, as in explaining van Gogh's change of style on moving to Paris, or the difference between El Greco and Velázquez as seventeenth-century Spaniards, one can reasonably ignore the vast majority of causal factors involved. One can ignore most of those which remained constant, like the air we breathe and the water we drink, seeking instead for some important factor which changed or differed significantly in relation to the differences in artistic style. These may be found in Group II, III, or IV; in heredity, physical and biological environment, or social, cultural, and artistic environment; or in selected factors from all of these.

It is well to remember again at this point that the "types of causal factor," such as heredity, environment, and local culture-patterns, are names for complex ways in which physical energy flows and manifests itself, especially in the activities of human organisms. But it would be clumsy and tedious, as well as impossible in our present state of knowledge, to describe them in such terms. It is more convenient to say that heredity and environment make us what we are: that patterns of culture influence patterns of art and vice versa.

But for deeper understanding, we must analyze these vague abstractions into more specific ones, and link them up with particular cases.

3. HISTORIC TYPES OF SOCIAL ORGANIZATION. RELATED TYPES OF IDEOLOGY, TECHNOLOGY, AND ART

The next few sections will briefly outline some recurrent associations between (a) modes of social, political, and economic life, (b) technology, (c) religious and philosophic beliefs and attitudes toward the world, and (d) general types and trends in art. They are distinguished, not on a purely sociological basis, but as diversified modes of life involving several cultural components.

This is not a unilinear scheme. No exact, rigid, necessary sequence of all-embracing stages is proposed. Some frequent, and apparently necessary, connections between the social and artistic are shown, but it is also emphasized that many different styles may arise within a single type of social structure.

No exact correlation exists between stages in art and those in other cultural components. None exists between stages in the various arts. A major social and political stage such as the despotic military empire, if long-enduring in a certain place, may include a varied sequence of artistic styles, as in Rome between Augustus and Theodoric. A general socio-political type such as the independent, small city-state or the feudal system is not a single stage in a single chronological sequence, but a persistent and recurrent type. It is highly variable in cultural content. It can die out in a certain place, as the city-state is absorbed in a larger kingdom or empire, then revive there when the larger unit is dissolved. Such changes in status happened repeatedly in Italy, to such cities as Ravenna, Florence, Pisa, and Venice.

A socio-political type, considered abstractly, is only part of the skeleton of a total culture-pattern. The military empire type is flexible enough to include artistic styles and total cultures as varied as those of Assyria, China under the Chou and Sung empires, Rome, Byzantium, and the Aztec rule in Mexico. Late examples of a given type tend to inherit and absorb much of the art and other culture of previous examples, of their own and other types. Thus the Roman Empire absorbed elements from a long list of previous empires, city-states, and villages; some with tyrannical, some with oligarchical, some with feudal, and some with democratic governments. A small city such as Venice or Kyoto can inherit vast cultural wealth from larger predecessors such as Rome and T'ang China. In such cases, the types and styles of art produced seem to be due, not so much to the type of social, political, or economic framework as to the other cultural components with which that framework has been filled by the previous efforts of its own and other peoples.

Some arts and types of art are more dependent than others on the socio-economic and political framework. They depend more on the wealth and power of patrons, private or official, ecclesiastical or secular. They exhibit the tastes and desires of those patrons more obviously by their functional adaptations, costly materials and workmanship, and glorification of aristocratic status-symbols. Architecture (as in churches and palaces), city planning (as in Mycenae and Carcassonne), ornate furniture and costume, painting and sculpture depicting the heroes of church and state, the music and ritual of court circles, all belong in this category. Simple songs and peasant dances, fairy tales and legends are less closely bound up with any particular type of social framework. Nomadic exiles with little or no tangible property can carry folk-songs with them wherever they go, preserving memories of the past and adding to them. Revolutions and conquests do not destroy them easily, although the new régime often tries to abolish those offensive to it.

Folk art is not lacking in social significance, however. One can infer a good deal about the history of a group by noting what the songs and stories praise, yearn for, and commemorate: a folk hero with certain kinds of exploit; an image of woman as goddess or demon, mother, wife, or mistress; a homeland for which captives long. ("By the rivers of Babylon, there we sat down, yea, we wept, when we remembered Zion... We hanged our harps upon the willows.") Even pure, instrumental music can reveal its fitness for use in a cathedral, a military parade, a dance hall, or the salon of a wealthy patron.

In almost any art, the social background is usually more obvious in the examples made for élite, upper-class circles; in rich houses, parks, and furnishings; in theaters, carriages, pageants, and costumes. These require much expenditure of wealth and are usually addressed to the tastes of the high and mighty, both human and divine. Early folk-art is more likely to be made by and for the common people, whose lot until recent centuries has been more alike. It is full of references to kings and queens, palaces, gold and jewels, but as things fantastic and remote. Folklore cannot be stolen or confiscated; it is easily transportable. Bards, minstrels, and wandering musicians are welcomed in huts and palaces. Their anonymous works often survive the fall of empires.

Social structure is never the sole determinant of art. It is a strong and far-reaching influence, however, not only on art but on other components and patterns of culture as well. Distinctive, large-scale types of social organization, including its economic basis, are characteristically associated with certain broad, flexible types of art. From a knowledge of the general socio-economic type one can never predict specifically what the styles of art will be, or the religious and other ideological content of the culture. But one can expect with some assurance that these will follow certain general outlines; the more specific details being determined by other factors. It is these general outlines that we shall consider in the present sec-

tion. Some of the associations are fairly obvious and may seem hardly worth stating; but they deserve attention in view of the denial, by some schools of thought, of any association at all except a purely accidental one.

The association is frequent enough to indicate some causal connection, though a loose and variable one. It runs to some extent in both directions; art has an influence on social trends, and vice versa. There is truth in the aphorism of Andrew Fletcher (1703), "Give me the making of the songs of a nation, and I care not who makes its laws." One thinks of *La Marseillaise* and the *Internationale* as revolutionary; of *Rule, Britannia!* and *God Save the King* as nationalistic. Art often reinforces social attitudes and trends, integrative or disintegrative, which are already under way in the social fabric itself, instead of initiating them. But the two run so closely together on the whole that it is hard to suggest a uniform priority of either.

It is hard to find an example of any art which does not have some social implications or effects, directly or indirectly. Even the complete ignoring of social and other realistic themes, as in rococo decorative and erotic art, may be significant; perhaps as an escape from social problems on the part of a long-entrenched, luxurious aristocracy; perhaps as expressing indifference or contempt. On the whole, the socio-economic factors are undoubtedly more basic and far-reaching than the artistic. They reach every corner of the life of a group, including its arts, while many corners of that life may be almost untouched by art beyond the most drab and rudimentary forms. We are justified in assuming that the sociological approach to art will continue to provide a significant, partial explanation of artistic phenomena, both general and particular.

There are many other aspects of social organization which, at times, throw more light on the genesis of styles. Among these are the infinitely varied patterns and dramas of family life, the relations among close relatives living together, and the perennial relations between old and young, older and younger generations in every kind of social order. "Crabbèd age and youth," said Shakespeare, "cannot live together. Youth is full of pleasure, age is full of care." This is a half-truth. It is not so much the difference in capacity for pleasure that counts as the conflict of desires; the wish of age to restrain desires and inculcate prudent self-discipline in the young; the wish of youth to break away and follow present impulse. Each may envy the others at times. This is an eternal theme of art, distinct to some extent, yet related to the general social pattern, since modern democracy tends to grant much freedom to youth.

The types of social life to be described in this chapter are not definite chronological stages. On the whole, they are listed in the approximate order in which they first appeared and flourished, although some peoples have not gone through all of them. Some types have persisted in altered form in later periods, even to the present day. Most of them have partial analogues in the contemporary world; the more primitive types occurring far from centers of advanced civilization. A group or culture which preserves some primitive traits in an urban-industrial, mechanized world, unless completely isolated, absorbs some traits from more advanced neighbors. Thus a modern tribe whose ideology contains vestiges of animism and magic may use electrical machines and motion pictures, automobiles and airplanes. It may be very primitive in some respects, advanced in others, and mixed in still others, as in the combination of witchcraft with Christianity. The same saint or deity may be called by a Christian and a non-Christian name, with very different implications. Such changes influence art; not only what the people buy from outside but what they make and perform. Their traditional arts may be totally lost, or lost and revived for commercial purposes, or mixed with civilized popular arts.

Far-reaching ideological changes can, under certain circumstances, proceed while the social and political structure remains fairly stable, or

vice versa. Preservation of a relatively primitive social structure, or reversion to it after previous advance, does not always prevent the group from important production in the arts. Although a complex social order and scientific technology are required for some kinds of art, they are not required for all. In fact, they tend to obstruct some other kinds. Hence the frequent primitivism of artists in a complex society; their feeling that science and civilization, bureaucracy and government, are hostile to them.

4. MOBILE KINSHIP GROUPS, HUNTING AND PASTORAL.

PREHISTORIC TYPES AND MODERN SURVIVALS

In general, the paleolithic mode of life was less fixed and stable as to locality than the neolithic. Food was secured through hunting, fishing, and gathering wild vegetable products such as nuts and roots. Where there was enough of this wild food supply and no great pressure from enemies, paleolithic man often remained for long periods in the same geographical area. Loose kinship groups, later organized into tribes, built villages on hills and river-banks near plentiful sources of food. In glacial periods and when attacked, they stayed more in caves; but caves were not otherwise preferred as habitations. Dwellings were flimsy and impermanent, but some camp sites and caves were used for hundreds or thousands of years. Many of the latter were used for ritual and magical purposes rather than as dwellings.

On their walls and on outside rocks, drawings were painted and incised. They depict herds of animals and scenes of humans hunting, fighting, and dancing. Styles vary from crude stick figures to skilful, terse realism. Some small figurines, probably magical fetishes, emphasize stylization and design in three dimensions rather than visual realism. We cannot say at present which came first. Paintings on inside walls and clay sculpture on the floors were more or less immovable. In many secluded caves, later abandoned, closed by nature, and forgotten, such works of art have lasted to the present day. They are exceptions to the general rule that paleolithic man had little or no art of a fixed, heavy, or bulky character. Otherwise, his possessions were few and mostly small and light, easily carried or abandoned after use. During long periods, he had to follow moving wild herds and seek new supplies of wild vegetable food as the former sources were exhausted, or as enemy groups forced him along.

Pastoral life with tamed herds, animal breeding, and husbandry was more characteristic of the neolithic stage in technology and in some areas coincided with the growth of agriculture. Sometimes one preceded and predominated; sometimes the other. Pastoral life was essentially more mobile than agriculture, but it varied from the nomadic extreme to the more settled type in which flocks and herds were shuttled back and forth within a limited area for seasonal access to better grazing. Not until later was the pasturage itself secured or supplemented by agriculture, and confined within still narrower limits. Then it could be centered more stably in a village or urban center. Social organization in the pastoral, as in the hunting and early farming stages, developed mainly along kinship lines, patrilineal or matrilineal. Rule was exercised by hereditary or elected chiefs and councils of elders. Power tended gradually, but with many exceptions, to center in hereditary chiefs and kinglets. Priests and shamans were also powerful. Political and magico-religious powers were often combined.

The early stages of mobile tribal life must, from our point of view, have been extremely insecure and precarious as to food supply and safety from enemies. Prehistoric man was, perhaps, often happily unaware of his own insecurity, and we must not attribute to him all the feelings we would have in his place. But modern tribal life under such conditions shows a tendency toward fears of the unknown, with anxious efforts to avoid taboos

and ward off evil spirits, monstrous or ancestral.[1] Images of animals and other natural phenomena are projected as totems and as potentially hostile or protective spirits. The beginnings of simple art inspired by animism and totemism in various media must often have occurred in paleolithic culture. More universal were the portable tools, weapons, and garments of stone, bone, wood, shell, skins, and vegetable fibers. Of these, some indicate an aesthetic interest in form and decoration over and above utilitarian requirements. Recent evidence indicates early commerce over wide areas in such objects as flints, amber, shells, and bits of unsmelted metal.

Permanent property is relatively small in amount and variety in a group with no fixed abode, although pastoral groups can accumulate rich supplies of animals, tents, harness, and utensils. Apparently some of the oldest human and even prehuman groups tried to repel others from their territory, but ownership of specific areas would be hard for a mobile tribe to maintain.

In the tribal type of social order, kinship relations are highly important in determining attitudes and actions within the group and with other groups. These are eventually developed into elaborate rules determining consanguinity, inheritance, endogamy and exogamy. Conceptions of incest and taboos against certain relationships within the family are often severe. Many varieties of family and kinship evolve, with different attitudes toward polygamy, polyandry, monogamy, virginity, chastity, and adultery. Jealousy may be a strong motive or almost non-existent. All these social attitudes and relations are expressed in folk arts of the tribal stage.

The mobile type of life, with no fixed dwelling, has lasted in modified form to the present day. Wandering bands of robbers and pirates have

---

[1] Walter Abell suggests that, in the neolithic and early metal periods, myths portrayed monsters and demons as powerful, heroes and positive beings as weak. The balance shifted until (as in the European Gothic) evil beings were conceived as powerless against an omnipotent savior and saints. *The Collective Dream in Art* (Cambridge, Mass., 1957), pp. 144 ff.

appeared throughout history. Remote from cities, especially in the Near East, Africa, and Asia, kinship groups of herdsmen, shepherds, and desert Bedouins still roam in search of grass, water, salt, and safety from enemies. In great migrations, large peoples like Mongols and Huns have been temporary wanderers in search of permanent lands. Today, Gypsy bands still maintain their semi-nomadic tradition.

When a roving life persists within occasional reach of settled, civilized groups, it tends to incorporate certain purchases and cultural traits from the latter. Others, inconsistent with mobility, are rejected. This allows, for example, the use of modern light fire-arms and utensils powered by electric batteries; even, as among the Gypsies, automobiles and radios. Temporary encampments allow some commerce and handicrafts for money to buy civilized products. A tribe and individual members can own land and houses even though they do not stay in them.

About these very different stages and varieties of mobile life, a few things can be said in general. Such life tends to exclude the production, care, and use of bulky, heavy works of art such as large statues and elaborate, fragile pottery or glass like that of Venice. It excludes or limits the development of architecture, gardening, and town-planning, with all the developed arts requiring these, such as theater arts, easel painting, and usually mural painting on walls of buildings. It excludes large libraries; there is little bookish education or literary writing. It excludes music requiring heavy instruments, diversified orchestras, and concert halls.

What is left? Along what lines can art develop? Certain types have persisted since paleolithic times: in the visual arts, small carved or molded figurines of bone, stone, or clay; incised drawings on bone, shell, rocks, and leather; painting on cave walls and rock surfaces. The modern nomad can use cloth or paper. One can decorate oneself by painting or tattooing the skin, arranging coiffures, etc. One can make and carry light baskets, skin cloth-

ing and containers for liquids (metal and some durable glass and pottery at a later stage). Light tools, utensils, and weapons can be of any material from rough stone to iron and steel, but those of metal must be acquired from groups with settled residence for metalworking. The same is true of jewelry and complex rugs. Simple weaving is possible; also developed leatherwork for saddles, harnesses, and boots. Tents of skin or cloth can become complex and ornate, with light, portable wooden parts and structures. Wheeled vehicles, superseding those dragged along the ground, greatly facilitate mobility. They can be elaborately decorated.

Available also are the simpler types of music: songs and simple instruments, folk dances, stories, and poems. Love, adventure, and heroism are favorite themes. In happy moods, they praise the free, wandering life; in melancholy ones, they long for some happy homeland left behind. At first they are unwritten. Oral folklore, myths and legends, genealogies, religious texts and rituals, can develop considerably in this type of social setting. They provide sources for later urban literature, music, and dance.

The relative simplicity of these arts is not necessarily a bar to high quality or to respect for them by modern city-dwellers. As an immemorial way of life, supposedly free, adventurous, close to nature, and unconventional, the nomadic ideal is a favorite dream of romantic primitivists in the midst of urban civilization. City people try to incorporate some of it, as in vacation travel, but without considerable isolation from urban influence it ceases to be a distinctive mode of life.

5. THE SEDENTARY VILLAGE WITH SIMPLE AGRICULTURE, ANIMAL HUSBANDRY, HANDICRAFTS, AND TRADE

In its early stages, prehistoric and protohistoric, this mode of life was often associated with the neolithic period and with smooth stone tools. It lasted after the introduction of metals, but with gradual incorporation into larger units. Primitive independent villages were often linked in loose federations, primarily on a kinship basis, with organized systems of marriage and descent. Government was mainly by hereditary chiefs, priests, and councils; occasional limited democracies. Other features were domesticated animals, gardening, and settled crafts; specialization of labor; some slavery and growing class distinctions. Weak protection was afforded by natural features (lake, hill, cliff), or fences, palisades, earthworks, and walls. Village life still persists on a fairly primitive level in remote parts of both hemispheres, but with steady encroachment from the urban centers; hence the disappearance of the quasi-independent village as a distinctive setting for social life.

One outstanding innovation of prehistoric village life, as a stimulus to the arts, was the opportunity for somewhat larger, heavier tools and products, including small houses and equipment for pottery, weaving, and simple metalry. Another was the greater opportunity for developing specialized skills through instruction and regular practice. Still another was the mental stimulation of commerce with outsiders, including some diffusion of artistic styles.

Adoption of a fixed abode led to the ownership of land, buildings, and means of production such as plows and mills. This was often vested in the group or its chiefs, but private property increased, with all the changes in ideology which individual and family wealth brings about. Ownership was often largely hereditary, together with inherited class privileges, transmitted along the male or female line. Increase in trade and barter eventually included the sale of land and buildings, but this was long restricted by tribal regulations. Traces of early matrilineal descent and inheritance, with occasional matriarchy, persist in rites and legends up to recent times. Present scientific opinion, as we have seen, denies the universal priority of matrilineal descent and matriarchy.

With the development of private property and settled family life, jealousy and severity toward extra-marital sex relations became increasingly powerful motives, reflected in the arts. Sex mores remain extremely varied in different parts of the world, however.

The rudiments of writing are said to have originated in the neolithic stage of village life, in simple ideographic symbols scratched or drawn on pebbles, shells, pottery, etc. They may have had magical and totemistic meanings, as well as serving to decorate and to identify property. Although magic persisted, there was apparently less sense of need for realism in figures used for such purposes. Pictorial representation is said to have "degenerated" from the best paleolithic types (as at Lascaux) into very simple, schematic stylizations of human and animal figures. Drawing and decoration (e.g., on pottery and textiles) were often geometric and sometimes complex. They also developed into archaic, semi-realistic styles, including incisions on metal—all within the general framework of village life. Totem poles and other carvings contained both stylized and realistic animal and human figures. Skulls of ancestors and enemies were preserved and decorated. Later village life included more development of writing and, in some cases, the transition from stone tools and weapons to bronze and iron. Writing and pictorial representation diverged somewhat as the former developed arbitrary, non-mimetic symbols.

During the early stages of settled village life, magic and religion were developed and systematized from previous beginnings. Magic assumed a belief in comparatively weak, petty spirits and supernatural agencies behind natural phenomena which could sometimes be controlled by individuals possessing the necessary innate gifts and techniques. It was practiced by shamans or sorcerers, who became increasingly specialized as a class. They could secure the help of friendly spirits and ward off unfriendly ones or expel them from the sick. The principal aims were to insure health and success in hunting, farming, and war; the fertility of domestic animals and women. Certain objects, places, acts, words, and persons could possess mana or magical power, temporarily or permanently. Accordingly, certain acts were taboo—to be avoided or performed only ritually, for fear of evil consequences— such as touching certain objects, entering sacred places, eating certain foods, or killing certain animals. The person of the chief was often surrounded with special taboos.

As instruments of magical practice, early forms of what we now call art were sometimes used: visual and auditory representations of animals, humans, and natural phenomena such as rain and lightning, in pictures, fetishes, masks, and mimetic dances. These were used for sympathetic magic, as in causing rain by pouring water; thunder by sounding drums and rattles. Amulets and talismans, often carved and decorated, could bring good luck and repel evil spirits. The magician might have a set of implements, including masks and costumes, wands and charms, magic ointment, rattles and traps to catch spirits. Ritual acts, speeches, songs, and dances had to be performed with scrupulous accuracy to insure success, and in this effort elaborate techniques were sometimes developed. But magic did not always use or stimulate artistic development. Some of the holiest and most powerful objects were natural, such as rough stones, meteorites, sacred trees, bones, skin, hair, and other relics. As an incentive to the arts, it was less consistently strong than religion.

Religion, in Frazer's sense, involves a belief in stronger spirits who cannot be directly controlled by humans. They must be propitiated and induced to grant human desires. Magic is often combined with religion. One can believe in both strong and weak spirits, and in the idea that the strong ones

sometimes allocate a limited magical power to certain humans, acts, and objects: e.g., to an image of the god or to his name. But the characteristic methods of religion are worship, prayer, sacrifice, and obedience to the supposed divine commands. One appeals to the unseen god as to a human ruler or official, trying to please him in ways which would be likely to succeed on the human level.

The growth of such a belief and attitude is associated with the rise of more and more powerful human chiefs, kings, sorcerers, and priests; the gods are, in part, superhuman projections of them as occupational and personal types, and of human fears and hopes directed toward them. They grow in power and majesty, more or less in proportion to the growth of actual kingly power and scope. Primitive ones are often local or tribal deities: later ones rule and protect larger nations; still later ones, empires and the world. On the early village level, they are often comparatively weak and tribal. Some are animal or plant spirits. A certain species such as the bear or hawk is worshipped as a patron of the tribe and never killed or eaten except ritually. Such animals are portrayed in various styles, from partial realism to abstract symbolism. The representations may possess magical power, and may portray myths and legends connected with the totem animal. These are also recounted verbally and perhaps acted out in dance or pantomime. The ritual killing and eating of the totem-animal was paralleled by the ritual killing, and perhaps eating, of the chief or king to insure the vitality of the group. Vestiges of the totemistic, animal deities survive in the theriomorphic and animal-headed deities of Egypt, some of which change later into anthropomorphic ones carrying animal symbols. Anthropomorphism grows with agricultural and urban life and the diminishing importance of wild animals as food, enemies, and constant neighbors.

There is evidence that the concept of a High God or Supreme Being originated in some primitive cultures before Hebrew monotheism. "Tylor's greatest error," says Hoebel,[2] "was to infer that the High God concept could be only the end product of a long intellectual evolution, beginning with the soul concept and leading through ghost and ancestor worship to polytheistic nature worship on to monotheism." Some primitive minds, it is said, were philosophic and idealistic, seeking a unified cause to explain the universe. They conceived a god who is not anthropomorphic or natural, who created the world and man but lives in the sky far from the petty desires and acts of humans; who is on the whole unapproachable and disinterested. Such a god tends to receive less worship and less artistic tribute. He is said to have created lesser deities who actually run the world. This type of religion could hardly have developed far before the rise of moderately powerful kings, ruling over many villages and towns.

Ancient Indian religion conceived of Brahma as creating the world, but as sleeping through long ages while the lesser gods and spirits whom he created, or through whom he manifested himself, were active in this illusory world. Greek philosophers in the city-state era speculated on an abstract, impersonal cosmic mind (*Nous*) which brings order out of chaos. It is not a complete, pure monotheism when the concept of a single deity is coupled with the belief in many lesser gods or spirits. Artists, like most ordinary, unphilosophic persons, tend to be more interested in the personal, human-like deity—and even, at times, in the animal-like deity— because such a being is more concrete and imaginable. His or her acts, words, and motives can be more easily understood and sympathized with, even if disapproved, than can an abstract, impersonal spirit or causal principle. His or her doings make more exciting stories and pictures.

At this late date, there is no way of knowing certainly how far the development of religious ideas had proceeded before the rise of cities. It seems reasonable to suppose that the concept of a great god, too remote and mighty to be seen by men, who tries to order things but is partly thwarted by corrupt and inefficient subordinates, developed somehow in relation to analogous political conditions. Such a religious idea would have been more comprehensible to the masses when its analogue already existed in the person of a great king or emperor. But it is also possible that, on the tribal and village levels, a few primitive philosophers and dreamers looked both forward and backward in time: backward to a world creation and forward to an age when some great chief would unify all warring tribes. Hopeful dreams and achievements can develop together and influence each other. It is not surprising when the dream precedes the fact by centuries or millennia; but as a rule people dream of something not too far off for them to want and imagine. For this, it must be something like what now exists. Primitive man dreamed of flying like a bird, but not of atomic-powered airplanes.

Religion, with all its ramifications, has doubtless been the strongest single, institutionalized motivation of the arts. From primitive to recent stages, it has given a persistent impetus toward producing types of art which seemed likely to please and influence divine Providence, thus securing blessings in this life and the next. The nature of the offering has depended on current conceptions of the gods and their desires: from human sacrifice and self-torture to quiet expressions of love and thanks; from painted and sculptured image of cruelty and destruction to those of paternal and maternal tenderness; from ascetic chastity to robust sexuality; from costly display to simple plainness. All these types of offering, of hope and fear, of moral and religious attitude and wishful fantasy, have been expressed in art through the centuries. The gods of the primitive village were of opposite sorts: some terrible, to be placated; some benign, to be invoked and thanked.

Largely from these motives, cooperating with more purely aesthetic ones, arose such perennial

[2] Pp. 552–4, citing Andrew Lang, Wilhelm Schmidt (*Der Ursprung der Gottesidee*) and P. Radin, *Monotheism in Primitive Religion.*

types of art as temples and churches, paintings and statues of deities, altars, ecclesiastical vestments, ritual hymns, dances, and dramas. As human taste improved, with more appreciation of refinements in artistic form and style, the gods themselves were expected to appreciate the product and the effort. This in turn helped to motivate increasing refinement of form and technique. Ancient taboos and rules for religious art provided both a limiting and a directing factor. Much of this long development occurred in the later, urban stages of civilization, but the beginnings were older.

6. THE CITY-STATE.
MORE OR LESS INDEPENDENT, FORTIFIED TOWNS AS CENTERS OF AGRICULTURAL, PASTORAL, INDUSTRIAL, AND COMMERCIAL REGIONS

The early stage of urban civilization occurred in Mesopotamia, Egypt, the Indus Valley, and corresponding sites in Guatemala and Peru, at various dates. It often but not always involved the use of metal, wheeled vehicles, and boats if near water; also that of human, animal, and wind power. The typical form was an acropolis or strongly fortified town on a hill, with stone or brick walls and internal facilities to withstand a short siege. These included fresh water supply, reservoirs, and storage for food and weapons. The nearby countryside might contain many subject villages and lands for agriculture and grazing under the protection of the ruler and a citizen army or small standing army. In time of heavy attack, peasants and villagers might enter the town, perhaps with some livestock. Commerce by land or water was adapted to the site. Rule was usually by hereditary kinglets or by conquest or usurpation; sometimes by theocracies, oligarchies, or limited democracies. Kinship organization persisted in clans and gentes, with considerable influence

on class status through descent. It remained active in the Greek, Roman, and Chinese empires, but with gradually diminishing power as travel, migration, and trade substituted other bases for power and prestige. Slavery flourished as a substitute for killing captives; it provided a labor supply and encouraged some forms of large-scale economic management. Specialization of function proceeded. Wealth increased and often tended to concentrate in the ruling class, but a middle class also arose in many cities, composed of successful merchants, small land-owners, skilled artisans and craftsmen, scribes, and minor officials. This tended to weaken the influence of hereditary power and wealth. The status of women varied greatly. All these changing relationships are reflected in the literature and visual art of city-states.

A tendency toward larger units appeared in the alliance or loose federation of semi-independent city-states, often under the hegemony of one such as Athens or Venice.

A characteristic of the city-state mode of life under precarious conditions, when subject to sudden attack, was the huddling of fairly large populations on a small hilltop. Buildings were small by comparison with later standards, but stronger and more permanent than in the village, with differentiation of dwellings according to class and wealth, and of rooms within houses. Important public buildings such as temples and palaces were constructed under supervision of specialized architects and were furnished and decorated by skilled craftsmen. City-planning as an art arose, often with two main streets at right angles, intersecting at a public square, palace, or temple. Streets were sometimes curved or angled to obstruct invaders. Buildings often required thick walls, for defense within the city. Wealth concentrated in successful cities by trade, piracy, and conquest. Travel became wider, with more exchange of arts and ideas. More precious materials were used and more foreign products imported; also foreign styles of music, dance, and costume. There was great development of the arts under these circumstances: both religious and secular, fine and useful. They served to delight and glorify priests and rulers and to develop civic pride through magnificent display and celebration in festivals; also to awe the foreigner. Poetry, music, and ritual developed veneration for ancestral heroism and moral ideals for different classes and sexes.

In this social setting arose the Homeric epics and poetic cycles on the exploits of Hercules, Gilgamesh, Sinbad, Samson, and other folk heroes. Opinions differ on the historicity of these legendary heroes and heroines, as well as of the gods and demigods with whom their adventures were linked. Some scholars hold that many are based on actual, living persons, later endowed with superhuman powers; others that most were derived from imaginary cult deities and demons, characters in ritual dramas for magical purposes. Both theories may have some truth. In any case, different gods and goddesses, heroes and heroines, were venerated by particular tribes, nations, and cities. Some became the protectors of occupational guilds, professions, and craft mysteries. This helped to give the artist greater dignity and sanction for his rights and rules.

Varied musical instruments and skilled dancers were found in large palaces; bards traveled from court to court. Plato, in the Republic, describes the growing luxury and specialization of arts in a city-state. Several trends favored increasing differentiation of artistic skills and styles. One was the progressive differentiation of labor in general; another the mixing of cultures, with conflict and syncretism of ideologies and artistic styles, especially in the Mediterranean. A third was increasing individualism and democracy.

Since the city-state as a more or less independent unit endured for millennia, often along with large empires, it included many types and styles of art, from the geometric and archaic through the classic and baroque. Highly developed realism and idealism flourished in the representational arts, together with complex non-representational design. The Parthenon exemplifies their classical synthesis.

It was largely in the city-states and small, early empires that organized polytheism took form: a form which it was to keep, substantially, throughout succeeding centuries. Analogous tribal, village, and other local deities under various names and aspects combined to form the typical pantheon of gods and goddesses, such as that of Olympus. Through trade and conquest, people over larger areas came to adopt the same names for analogous deities, or to recognize that gods with different names and ceremonies, worshipped by different peoples, were really one and the same. Herodotus describes this syncretistic process in the Mediterranean world, with special reference to the Greek acceptance of Egyptian concepts. Similar trends occurred in India as the Vedic deities of the Aryan conquerors, such as Indra and Brahma, absorbed countless local deities and enlarged their circle to include some powerful newcomers, such as Krishna. Brahmanism, Hinduism, and Buddhism employed the useful principle of avatars, by which a certain god can manifest himself in different forms at different times, including human incarnations. Thus Vishnu assumed the form, life, and adventures of Krishna in an earthly incarnation.

Stories of the deeds and characters of the gods and goddesses were gradually refined and expurgated in accordance with changing moral standards. Plato urged this in criticizing the myths of Homer and Hesiod. Vestiges of totemism remained in myths of the gods assuming animal form as Jupiter did in many of his amorous intrigues, or transforming someone else into one. Seasonal myths such as that of Persephone, portrayed in art and acted out in ritual, symbolized the annual death and rebirth of the sun and vegetation, with the magic hope of insuring that resurrection. Systematic cosmogonies and cosmologies explained the creation of the world, the birth of the gods, and the motions of the stars. Laws and mores were sanctified by doctrines of reward and punishment in a future life. The pantheons of great gods were supplemented by hosts of minor spirits, angels and demons, nymphs and satyrs, demigods and monsters. Largely derived from ancient folklore, their stories were gradually collected, expurgated, and retold by literary artists. The cruel, horrible, and bestial in the spirit world was gradually minimized, leaving chiefly the images of beauty and serenity which prevailed in Periclean Athens and the Renaissance.

No more prolific source and stimulus to the artistic imagination has ever been provided than the cosmology and iconology of polytheism. Beside it, both monotheism and the impersonal theories of science and metaphysics tend, in pure form, to seem abstract and difficult to the popular mind. Early religious and philosophical trends along those lines have never satisfied the masses or the artists, who insist on rebuilding a new, colorful pantheon, as in Mahayana Buddhism and Taoism. If not of gods, strictly speaking, it may be of divine or semi-divine personages, such as the Bodhisattvas or the Holy Family and hierarchy of archangels, angels, saints, and martyrs shown by Dante. A humble person could appeal and offer gifts to a saint or minor deity, asking him to intercede with the all-powerful ruler of heaven.

In the pantheon of a small city-state, such as Athens before its great hegemony, we see a projection of the intimate circle of small-city types. They were interrelated by birth as in a human kinship group. Like the petty kings, knights, and their families, the gods and goddesses are not far away or too superhuman to be understood and vividly imagined. Though strong and immortal, they share many human faults and weaknesses; they quarrel and cheat. They have not always ruled; they drove out the Titans long ago. Particular ones can be bribed or flattered into helping a man against other men and gods. They interfere constantly in great and trivial human affairs. Though Zeus is theoretically absolute, he is often henpecked and disobeyed. The gods personify many of the universal human types, occupations, and motives, such as war, agriculture, hunting, fatherhood, motherhood, and mischievous youth. They express class and occupational levels, as in

contempt for the grimy, crippled blacksmith, Vulcan, cuckolded by the handsome god of war.

Religious hopes and fears, centered on conceptions of benevolent and cruel deities, extended from this world to the next. Some cultures, especially in Asia Minor, developed a sense of sin and guilt, with fears of future punishment. Rites of purification, expiation, and salvation arose, such as the Orphic and Eleusinian mysteries. They were expressed in arts of ritual, painting, and otherwise. The priestly class was looked to for guidance in achieving salvation.

Established religion and ethics, later rationalized by conservative philosophers, cooperated to praise traditional ideals of valor and loyalty in the service of the state; of industry and obedience in carrying out the duties of one's station in life; of care in fulfilling ritual sacrifices and ceremonies. Rewards and pleasures were promised in this life and the next. These ideals were expressed in all the arts. But in partial opposition to them, early religious reformers urged renunciation of pleasures and of political and military ambitions, with escape from the world into ascetic seclusion. These ideals were also expressed in the arts: e.g., in the *Mahabharata* and *Ramayana*. Before political union among cities occurred on a large scale, religious and moral ideas and folkways helped to unify people culturally over large areas. Traveling bards and religious teachers contributed to this work. Holy cities such as Benares, Delphi, and Mecca became, with the aid of artists, ornate shrines respected by otherwise hostile factions. Seasonal festivals promoted truces in warfare, political alliances, and the formation of a sympathetic ideology. This provided a basis for larger political integration in later stages.

In Athens and some other city-states, ancestral clan systems developed into a hereditary, conservative aristocracy of citizens, as distinguished from slaves and foreign residents with limited rights. This system was gradually loosened by a rising middle class, some of whose members were disposed to democracy, naturalism, and individualism.

The authority of traditional religion and ethics was weakened among intellectuals, but not before it had contributed some precarious unity among the rival, often warring cities. Delphi became a religious and artistic center for the Hellenic world, and might conceivably have led to political union. But further interurban wars prevented that.

Pericles' appropriation of funds provided a financial basis for the great artistic and intellectual flowering of Athens. Constant strife among social classes and rival cities, aggravated by epidemics and foreign wars, weakened the state. Increasing individualism in art and ethics, while a cultural asset in itself, reinforced the disintegrative trend which led at last to absorption in the empires of Alexander and Rome. The ideal state, said the pessimistic Plato, could exist only in heaven. The only hope on earth was through a tightly but rationally organized collectivism, with little place for popular arts and luxuries. In both Greece and Rome, the bases for effective democracy were lacking; especially an educated public and the administrative machinery for large-scale representative government.

In Plato's moralizing about art we see the rise of different critical attitudes: especially that of the ascetic, aristocratic, conservative philosopher as against the taste of the masses for exciting, complex, naturalistic, highly differentiated arts. This went along with dissension and skepticism toward the traditional religion and morality; from one extreme to the other, with efforts by the philosophers to find a new, rational basis for self-discipline and social harmony.

Although many cities were absorbed into empires, especially between 2,000 B.C. and the height of the Roman Empire, city-state organization persisted until recent times on the margins of empires, and revived in times of imperial weakness. It flourished, in modified form, during the European middle ages and Renaissance. Thousands of people still lead cramped lives in the hilltop towns then built, though with freedom to come and go. Vestiges of the quasi-independent city are found in such localities as San Marino and Monaco, but their cultures are those of surrounding large nations.

7. THE MILITARY EMPIRE; LARGE, POWER-CENTERED MONARCHIES

As villages and farm-lands had coalesced under the rule of fortified towns, the towns coalesced into small and large empires, often under the rule of some one city, governed by a king of kings or mighty emperor. This assembling was largely involuntary and achieved by conquest. Cities were plundered and burned, the capitals moved with the tides of victory, but new cities were built on the ruins of old and on new sites. The size of large units persisted and grew, while boundaries and capitals shifted. Rule was hereditary and supposedly by divine right, often shared with a powerful priesthood and sometimes with powerful nobles, as in a feudal system. It was also shared with provincial viceroys or satraps as the empire grew.

Great concentration of wealth and specialized skill in large cities, with accumulating knowledge in writing, permitted the use of larger equipment for manufacturing, commerce, and war. Some fairly complex machines were invented in the Alexandrian period; some are described in Vitruvius' book on architecture. Under enlightened monarchs, peace and order could endure long enough to permit the rise of an industrious middle class, including skilled artists. A humble social status and coercion from above did not prevent them from producing majestic art. Commerce was spread far and wide, with resultant convergence and cosmopolitanism of styles and ideologies in the metropolis.

One feature of the growth of empires and, to a less extent, of powerful city-states and hegemonies such as Athens, was to let civilization move out of its crowded hilltops and fortifications. Urban dwellers spread into the countryside in suburbs, rural villas, farms, and vineyards. The army guaranteed some security, subject to occasional plundering and exploitation, but enough to allow expansive, profitable living while the royal power endured. Cities tore down their walls or overflowed them; new ones were built in unprotected places, trusting to the *Pax Romana* or its equivalent. This occurred again in Europe with the gradual restoration of order in the late middle ages, the Renaissance, and especially under the grand monarchs of the seventeenth century.

The prolonged assurance of internal security has a radical, explosive effect on architecture and related arts. Roads and buildings multiply, permitting farther travel and settlement. Thick walls give way to thin, fragile ones or none at all; windows and doors enlarge and lose their bars; rooms expand and admit large, ornate furniture and decoration, paintings, statues, ceramics, tapestries in the wealthier houses. There are solid comforts for the middle class and rustic cottages for the peasantry. Parks and gardens extend over wild areas; luxurious private ones for the rich, small ones for the modest. Public squares and highways are beautified, extended outward by demolishing old walls. Larger and more magnificent palaces and temples arise; not only one of each in a town, but more as the metropolis expands. There are summer and winter palaces, local temples and shrines, mansions for the newly rich and noble, aqueducts and fountains, public baths, stadia, and bridges. There are specialized public buildings for the expanding military and administrative machinery: council chambers, arenas, theaters, law-courts, army barracks, financial bureaus; also large, private banks and business enterprises. Rich costumes and jewelry are in demand, along with finer foods, drinks, and perfumes.

All this brings, of course, a vast development of artistic production along many lines, with more money to finance it through public and private patronage, and with increasing public taste for such refinements. Theater, ballet, and orchestral music may flourish, as well as circuses for the masses, with arts of pageantry and military display. Luxurious vehicles are wanted for distant travel: chariots or carriages, ships and river-barges, floats for festivals. Written literature, in manuscript or printed, reaches a wider public. There is a demand for stories, poetry and plays to entertain the gentry and to glorify the régime. Histories and biographies are written under official patronage. Colossal statues and painted portraits idealize the rulers and nobles; smaller ones do the same for wealthy commoners. Artistic and other cultural standards fluctuate from one extreme to the opposite according to the tastes and interests of the ruler.

As the power and domain of the Roman emperors increased, taking in more and more subject peoples, the process of religious syncretism continued. More and more local and national deities were identified with Roman ones. This had a practical function in helping to unite heterogeneous national groups in a common worship, and in making them regard the emperor as their rightful religious leader. The refusal of the Jews to identify Jehovah with Jupiter obstructed Hadrian's dream of imperial unity. Artists were employed to combine the symbols of various gods, such as Zeus, Osiris, Mercury, and the Persian Mithras, in one composite figure. Their merging in one supreme deity symbolized the union of all nations under one supreme ruler. Meanwhile, as the emperor himself became more awesomely powerful and more inaccessible to his subjects, the tendency grew to regard him as divine or semi-divine. This occurred in Egypt. Nero welcomed and confirmed the idea.

In an absolute monarchy, people and rulers alike tend to assume that the universe must be governed by an absolute, omnipotent ruler, analogous to the human monarch who serves as his vicar on earth. As in previous eras, the conception of deity again involves the projection of a political image into the religious realm. The supreme deity is now conceived as lord of heaven and earth, king of kings, mighty in battle. The traditional image of divine shepherd and patriarch recedes, but it can revive again in times of imperial disintegration and cultural regression to ideals based upon the small, pastoral, kinship unit. This occurred in Christian art before Constantine. After Constantine, Christian art and ideology tended to adopt the imperial world-view in accord with the new, imperial status of Christianity. But the ideas of divine shepherd and father remained as traditional elements in Christian iconography and literary imagery.

In a large, heterogeneous empire, subject to attacks from without and subversive pressures from within, a huge military and administrative hierarchy was required. It was usually in alliance with the ecclesiastical hierarchy. The arts were under pressure to serve and enhance the prestige of this combined hierarchy with all the aesthetic and emotive means at their disposal. As against this some artists protested, comparing the present system unfavorably with past and ideal ones. These protests developed periodically into waves of primitivistic and romantic-revolutionary expression, sometimes along with actual revolutionary movements. Moral and religious thinking took part in this conflict and influenced artistic expressions of attitude. The dominant, official value-system of state and established religion continued to glorify active, patriotic support of the civic and imperial hierarchy. *Dulce et decorum est pro patria mori.* Virgil's *Aeneid* exemplifies the type of art which serves to glorify the empire and its ruler, its traditions, moral and aesthetic ideals.

Such conditions tend to favor an art of spacious, monumental city-planning and one of heroic or colossal sculpture. The ruler is portrayed in superhuman form, perhaps with symbols of divine favor such as a protecting Osiris. In reliefs or pictorial compositions dealing with the ruler and his exploits, there is a tendency to hierarchical design. The figure of the ruler, the great god, or both, tends to be placed at the top or center, larger and more resplendent than the others. These are farther away or lower as their rank diminishes,

as in relative positions at the table or around the throne. Symbols of the division of the universe and man into a hierarchy of levels abound in official art, while depictions of humbler subjects may be more naturalistic and relaxed in form. Styles diversify even more than in the city-state.

As against the glorification of empire, ideologies of renunciation and escape, mysticism and asceticism, persisted from an earlier age and sometimes gained new strength in opposing greater empires. As against civic virtue, patriotism, industry, family life, rank, and valor, they preached pacifism, poverty, and celibacy. They preached that earthly ambition is vain, the world an illusion, life disappointing. Even books and knowledge are deceptive and a weariness of the flesh, except for the few words necessary to find the true path to Heaven or Nirvana. This world-view, antithetical to that of civic and imperial building, tended also to discourage those arts which the official state and church had encouraged. On the whole, it was unfavorable to all arts except the most simple and frugal; especially to those of visual, auditory, and other sensuous enjoyment. Suitable religious and moral poetry could flourish in a limited way.

In time, partial reconciliations were made between these two antithetical world-views within the framework of the state and established religion itself. Radical religious founders and reformers, such as Gautama and Jesus, were given divine or semi-divine status, worshipped, and portrayed in the arts. Visual and literary art contributed to the reconciliation by praising both world-views as admirable. An officially approved, and often subsidized, channel for those who preferred renunciation was provided in monasticism. In India, the spiritual mode of life was partly channeled, theoretically, into the Brahmin caste; but never exclusively or consistently so. Another compromise was made there in the mendicant ideal, of wandering with a begging-bowl in old age, after rearing a family and doing one's civic duties. These ideals figured prominently in the iconography of Buddhist and Hindu art.

Another, less extreme type of liberal dissension from the official world-view was expressed in some cultures, especially Greece and Rome. This was the naturalistic humanism of such individualists as Epicurus and Lucretius. Less civic-minded than Aristotle, they preached the peaceful cultivation of the individual mind along intellectual and aesthetic lines, without the need of wealth, rank, or power. They influenced poets such as Horace and favored a bucolic, gently regressive mode of life, away from the metropolis with family and friends.

8. FEUDALISM

This is sometimes a transitional stage toward absolute monarchy, in which subordinate nobles and officials retain some power. More characteristically, it involves a regression from the large-scale kingdom or empire; a weakening of the monarch in favor of the higher nobles and warlords. It involves a tendency to decentralize authority, administration, wealth, and cultural life from the capital city to smaller, outlying towns and villages with their surrounding domains. Such a tendency occurred in Egypt, in Europe after the death of Charlemagne, and in Japan in the Kamakura period. The effect is unlike that of conquest by a rival empire, or destruction by a barbarian horde. It may produce a new and fairly stable social system, with some remaining political and cultural influence from the emperor and court, and with a precarious peace among the nobles through the system of feudal loyalties. Outbreaks among them are likely, however. The system is, in theory, a continuous ladder or hierarchy from serf to emperor; perhaps a double, parallel hierarchy of church and state as in the political theories of St. Thomas and Dante, with either pope or emperor as supreme head. There is less gulf between the emperor and the next highest than in a despotic empire. Those on each step of the ladder have their traditional and perhaps legal rights, including the serf, who may be attached to the land and more secure with his family than the chattel slaves of the Roman Empire.

Obedient loyalty to one's feudal lord is a powerful motive, often celebrated in the arts. Dramatic conflicts, recorded in literature, often arise between it and other loyalties such as those to one's parents, wife, or siblings. The lord may have power of death over his peasants. Trade and travel are apt to be restricted more than in the large empire. Art and thought may become more provincial. Contact with one's immediate superiors and inferiors (if any) is close; that with foreigners infrequent. Life in the manor tends to become self-sufficient and isolated. Agriculture is inefficient and craftwork may decline through lack of an outside market.

If disintegration proceeds, it tends toward reestablishment of small, independent nations or city-states; perhaps of walled hill-top towns, as in medieval Europe. A strong noble may rule several cities and domains within the empire, maintaining his own army, taxes, and laws. The emperor may regain power with the help of a rising bourgeoisie. Feudalism is unstable, and tends to end in the establishment of a new, strong empire or of separate, small states renouncing all allegiance to the emperor. The latter finally happened in Europe with the weakening of the Holy Roman Empire in the sixteenth century. But as the nations separated, some pursued an opposite course internally in strengthening their monarchs (especially England, France, and Spain). The ecclesiastical hierarchy had been, on the whole, a conservative, stabilizing, international influence, peaceful though often severely repressive as in the Inquisition.

In a feudal system a brilliant cultural life, including the arts, may develop in the courts of powerful nobles such as the dukes of Burgundy and prelates of the church. It tends to inherit some of the culture of previous empires, but on a smaller scale.

The arts in a developed, fairly stable feudalism

tend to express a hierarchical world-view and value-system. This is fully elaborated in Dante's *Divine Comedy*, as a conception of the universe and of the levels of sin and virtue. The visual arts also, especially in complex pictures and sculptural reliefs, continue to symbolize hierarchy in their scale and composition: with the highest personages (divine or human) shown as large and at top or center; others descending or radiating from them in order or rank. This is frequently exemplified in the tympanum reliefs and stained glass windows of cathedrals. The hierarchical type may be stronger and more complex in feudalism than in an absolute monarchy because of its many graded ranks. In a grand monarchy the ruler is far above the highest nobles and sometimes allied with the bourgeoisie against them.

In principle, rank and power are hereditary in a feudal system. Hence emphasis is placed on such genealogical arts as heraldry and tables of consanguinity, as guides to marriage and inheritance. (The Tree of Jesse is a related diagram of Christ's descent on earth.) In practice, however, there is much usurpation of titles by intrigue and conquest, as in Italy during the late middle ages and Renaissance. This tends to weaken the hereditary feudal system. It may bring to power patrons of culture like the Medici or rough soldiers of fortune. There is great variety of cultural climate in feudal courts, as in empires, according to the education and personality of the lord.

9. LIBERAL, CAPITALISTIC DEMOCRACIES; URBAN-INDUSTRIAL REPUBLICS AND CONSTITUTIONAL MONARCHIES. LARGE-SCALE PRIVATE ENTERPRISE, REPRESENTATIVE GOVERNMENT, AND PROTECTION OF MINORITIES

Huge political units, comparable in size to the Roman and Chinese Empires, but managed by governments responsible to the people, are a distinctively modern type in social evolution. Genuinely representative governments, as distinct from those only ostensibly so, are characterized by free elections at stated intervals, with universal, adult suffrage and secret ballots. Officials are elected by their constituents or appointed by elected officials; both types being subject to removal for just cause by the people through process of law. Opposition parties are protected in their right to oppose the party in power and to campaign for election. It is not genuine representative government or democracy to have a hierarchy of delegates in which only the lower ranks are elected by the people, in which the top officials form a comparatively independent, self-perpetuating oligarchy, and in which the delegates have no real power to oppose or oust the party in power by majority vote. Both the British parliamentary system and the American congressional system are representative; the former being more quickly responsive to changing alignments in the legislative body. Liberal democracies depend on constitutional safeguards to protect the basic rights of individuals and minorities, such as equality before the law, freedom from arrest and confiscation of property without due legal process, the right to vote and be represented by delegates actively participating in government, equality of educational opportunity, and freedom of expression and assemblage within defined limits.

Their economic systems retain the capitalistic traditions of free enterprise and private profit, though with varying degrees of modification through graduated taxes, government regulation of business and finance, and government ownership and operation in certain fields such as steel, utilities, railroads, banks, postal and telegraph services. They differ in degree of centralization of powers, in reliance on free trade or protective tariffs, in the relative power of organized labor, and in other ways. The American system emphasizes checks and balances between the arms of government, a strong chief executive elected for a term of years, and little interference by the central government in educational and cultural affairs. Some European democracies retain a tradition of stronger centralized government with more control of business and of cultural institutions. Opposition parties in genuine democracies are protected by regular, free elections with secret ballots and by the right of debate in legislative sessions. Accused are guaranteed legal defense and fair trial. Modern capitalistic democracies are variable and flexible as to the extent of governmental or other public and institutional ownership and operation; also as to the relative strength of farm and factory workers, capital, management, and government on the national, state, and local levels.

Large, incorporated, non-profit foundations are increasing in power over cultural life. They can receive and hold through private gift and bequest huge sums of money and administer them with considerable freedom through self-perpetuating boards of trustees, subject to the general supervision of the government. They are granted many tax immunities. Foundations are exerting a more and more powerful influence on the arts (élite and popular) as well as on education, religion, science, technology, philanthropy, and other cultural components.

A capitalistic state can move in some respects, by legal processes without violence, toward more or less of socialization and collectivization. Completely free enterprise, in the old sense of laissez-faire individualism and unrestricted private profits, is a thing of the past. Large fortunes and incomes can be reduced and held to any desired minimum by graduated taxes on personal income and corporate profits. The power of organized labor has risen greatly in recent years. Labor plays an increasing role in business operation; it is protected by safety laws, wage scales, and restrictions on the right to hire and fire. Public insurance against unemployment, old age, sickness, and private insurance against other hazards, moves the democracies at varying speeds in the direction of welfare states.

The operation of all these mechanisms, governmental and otherwise, is dependent on modern technological means of rapid, cheap communication, transportation, and mass production. Technology in turn is fostered by them. Modern democracy is also dependent for success on the wide diffusion of free, public education; not only basic education for all, but general and specialized education for all according to their interests, aptitudes, and abilities. It implies freedom to determine one's career and mode of life within broad limits, as well as to travel and change one's residence and work at will. Special public and private subsidies are available to talented youth in many fields including the arts.

In spite of the trend to collectivization through expanded powers of government and corporate groups, much of the social mechanism is devoted to preserving competition and free variation, in the belief that this is favorable to general welfare, progress, and prosperity. While the need of centralized authority is recognized in certain fields of basic importance, such as police and defense, a strong effort is made to keep them under responsible civilian control and to prevent them from encroaching on individual freedom in personal, religious, and cultural life. Large, organized pressure groups representing different interests in capital, management, labor, commerce, politics, religion, education, race-relations, philanthropy, and other fields contend with each other more or less peacefully, though often bitterly. They do so through the machinery of representative government, propaganda, and discussion in the mass media of communication.

It is recognized that in a competitive society some individuals will lose while others win the highest rewards, but an attempt is made to set a floor beneath all competition, preserving a decent, minimum standard of living for all. An attempt is also made to regulate the methods of competition, restraining unfair practices and protecting the weaker bargainers to some extent. It is recognized that individuals with similar interests will organize themselves into groups for mutual benefit. In some cases they will contend with rival pressure groups: e.g., through trade unions and associations of manufacturers, managers, and technologists. These rivalries can never be permanently settled, but the struggle between them can be restrained in intensity while areas of possible agreement and cooperation are sought. Government operates, not to prevent them, but to provide rules and arenas for peaceful struggle under conditions of fair play as in games and sports. The extent to which fair play and justice are thus achieved is variable and debatable. At best, the competition of individuals and groups within the whole society goes on without excessive violence. It is no longer between two sharply divided classes such as capital and labor, exploiting and exploited, but between many overlapping groups, all of which have some interests in common. An individual may belong to several different ones in respect to different interests.

Many rival interests use some art as a weapon, especially in advertising and propaganda. The arts themselves tend to organize into professional, commercial, and ideological groups promoting this or that kind of art and expenditure for it.

Success in this competitive system is often richly rewarded in material goods, prestige, and the esteem of oneself and one's family. Failure can be a cause for intolerable shame and sometimes for suicide. Success often goes to the conformist or the one who rides on the crest of some wave of fashion. Its standards are controversial, and many critics challenge them as false, empty, materialistic. The charge is exaggerated in many cases, but the tendency to extreme attitudes persists. Competition makes many young people anxious and overworked; many executives break down under the strain. Such anxieties and frustrations, along with intergroup rivalries, are favorite subjects in contemporary art.

A liberal democracy is largely a consumer-directed economy. Sumptuary laws are absent. A large share of the national income is privately spent and freely allocated by individuals and families. Tax money is spent largely on public necessities. Individuals rather than government officials determine the share of national production devoted to things regarded as luxuries, such as cosmetics, tobacco, liquor, chewing-gum, and art. Even the desires of young children are catered to by advertising for breakfast foods, toys, and clothing. Children's tastes in story pictures are appealed to in the picture sequences of newspapers and comic booklets.

Living in a modern, capitalistic democracy tends to give most of its members certain attitudes in common: for example, that of regarding individual wealth and social status as mobile and variable rather than divinely established and hereditary. It tends to emphasize money and success (e.g., in business, politics, athletics, or popular art) as a goal and standard of the good life. It tends to admire those who rise by their own unaided efforts.

Great social mobility in modern civilization tends to weaken loyalty to, and permanent interest in, one's relatives and any particular town, region, institution, or set of friends. It induces a rather superficial ease, breadth, and fickleness of social adjustment. Divorces and brief, casual, extra-marital affairs multiply. Extreme mobility in the environment encourages frequent changes in a student's educational program and in his later employment; also in his cultural interests, including those of art. In prosperous times, young people see some individuals rise to wealth with little work or education, and wonder whether hard work is worth while. Among the upper classes, there is a taste for constant novelty; an eagerness to keep up with the latest fashion in arts and ideas. No institution and no individual authority commands enduring respect. Experts disagree, especially on aims and values in art. Older ones are quickly replaced by younger ones, equally short-lived. The layman is likely to become at times perplexed, repelled, and indifferent toward the whole controversy. A restless, unstable, extreme relativism sets in among the avant-garde; all permanent, general values are denied and a sterile nihilism becomes fashionable. But even this is transitory; no sooner has a certain belief and attitude spread from the élite to the masses than the élite discards it, turning to something quite different.

Since it is characteristic of the democracy to be volatile and variable, no one ideology pervades it completely. Much depends on one's individual and family status therein: whether rich or poor, managerial or managed; whether one is a strong or weak bargainer in the career and marriage markets. Much depends also on the stage and moment in history. A capitalistic democracy can be vigorous and growing at times, as in the Italian Renaissance; subject to internal splits and splintered factions, as in twentieth-century France, or snugly stabilized as in the Scandinavian countries. The most prosperous and strong, like the United States, can experience wide swings between optimism and pessimism, the "American Dream" and black nihilism, especially in the young intelligentsia. Even the emphasis on money and success is capable of drastic reversals. It leads some sensitive persons to reject them both to an unrealistic extent, and others to think that all the world's evils can be corrected by pouring out money to the "underprivileged." (The word "poor" is considered as insulting.) Meanwhile, many individuals and groups lead their lives and do their jobs in a steady, balanced, undramatic way, ignoring the wide swings in psychological temperature around them.

The growth of modern urban-industrial democracies has been accompanied to a large extent by decline in the power of the church as well as that of the old, hereditary, landed aristocracies. Hereditary upper-class status and membership in a long-wealthy, prominent family still convey some prestige. But they are increasingly overshadowed by achieved rank, money, and fame in any recognized field including the popular arts. Church and state are increasingly separated, al-though churches receive many tax benefits. There is no serious defense of the old principles of divine right or divine sanction for class hierarchies. The right of individuals and minorities to try to better themselves and rise in the socio-economic scale is taken for granted in theory though often resisted in practice.

The spread of democracy has been accompanied by spread of the secular, naturalistic world-view. This world-view and its expressions in art involve, as did the older ones, a projection of current social and political images into one's conception of the universe. The image of a deity as absolute, eternal ruler of the universe may tend to recede into the background of social thought and action, while still influential in conservative groups and individuals. It may be partly replaced by the scientific and democratic image of the universe as self-operative, self-regulative and evolving through natural laws and thus requiring no superhuman, personal direction. Education is increasingly secular, non-partisan, and supervised by public authorities. No explicit, conscious rejection of the older beliefs is common or much discussed outside intellectual circles. They tend to survive as venerated traditions while the newer ones increasingly determine action. Some philosophers adopt an explicit naturalism; others continue some variant of the Hegelian, idealistic tradition; some propose new forms of vitalism and dualism; some avoid all metaphysics in order to analyze the forms of thought and verbal expression. Churches preserve a considerable prestige as custodians of spiritual values. These are largely identified with religious and moral ones as contrasted with the supposedly inferior values of science and material goods. The churches remain as active centers for community sociability and for ceremonials on important occasions of life.

In the arts, there are some significantly related trends. First, there is a tendency to further secularization as to patronage and subject-matter; a continuing decrease of churchly themes as compared with man and his natural environment on earth and in outer space. Second, there is a tendency to democratization. This has shown itself as a greater interest in the common man, his appearance, activities, personality, and social problems, as opposed to the glorification of nobility. It has shown itself in the great increase in production of popular arts: cheaply produced and widely sold books, magazines, phonograph records, newspaper cartoons, phonograph records, and television programs. They are suited to the tastes and interests of children, adolescents, and adults on all economic and educational levels. Third, and closely related to democracy, is a certain leveling in art as contrasted with the concentrated expenditure of taste, skill, and materials on products for the élite. Patronage has been partly decentralized and commercialized; partly directed into the hands of corporate institutions.

Elected legislators hesitate to spend large sums on public art projects, especially those of a controversial nature, while poverty remains. This tends to restrict public expenditure on the arts as compared with private, or to keep it on a level of popular taste. Endowed institutions are somewhat freer to experiment; individuals still more so. There is some pressure of public opinion against too lavish displays and expenditures as "conspicuous waste." A large share of democratic expenditure for art goes to relatively cheap, mass-produced popular art and reproductions of the classics. Some partial democracies, republican and capitalistic in form, still have great inequality of wealth and a concentration of luxurious arts in the hands of a few. This situation is precarious under modern conditions, however.

A fourth tendency of art in a modern democracy is the increase in scientific and technological approaches to art, as to its production, education, history, and theory. This has been aided by the development of related sciences and by the accumulation of examples of the art of many cultures and periods. Fifth, this has been accompanied by an accelerated convergence among styles of art as parts of world civilization, including the revival of primitive styles and the importation of exotic ones. Taste has widened and become more cosmopolitan; no one style or tradition is assumed as best, and the artist feels free to experiment with any of them. The general public tends to prefer a pleasant amount of realism and wishfulfilling fantasies in representational art. Intellectual élites call for more incisive realism and also for nonrealistic styles emphasizing design or expression. Sixth, artists have tended to experiment widely on specialized types of form and style in all the arts, often incorporating some of these exotic elements. These have led them into styles which are often incomprehensible to the general public. Consequently, a gulf has opened between avant-garde artists and their public on the other hand, and popular, commercialized art for conservative tastes.

Some of these tendencies are temporary and confined to particular countries. The leveling process may in time create a broader base on which new élites may arise. This is apparent in the wide diffusion of taste for serious classics in music, literature, and visual art, and in the increasing number of persons who follow a career in art. With more surplus wealth in public and corporate hands, there may be more lavish expenditure on art for public use and enjoyment. The existence of much popular art on a naïve level does not necessarily prevent the rise of élite art, and sometimes provides a ladder for ascent. Accordingly the present wide gulfs in taste between different groups in a democracy may diminish. When a difficult new style of art is accepted by the socially and intellectually élite, many others tend to accept it in the hope of learning to appreciate it or of gaining prestige by association with it. This is now happening with post-impressionist and abstract expressionist painting and sculpture. Further diffusion and familiarity may bring a wider understanding and tolerance toward experimental art and also the rise of intermediate styles, somewhat between the extremes of conservatism and radicalism. Signs of this are apparent in the present use of modernistic idioms in semi-popular advertising and magazine illustration. Some kinds of art appeal to both élite and popular taste: e.g., the Disney films and "progressive jazz" music.

The quantity and quality of art production in a liberal democracy depend on many factors besides the social and political system itself. They depend in part on the wealth and prosperity of the country; in part on the cultural traditions and artistic tastes it has inherited. These may be carried over from an earlier epoch with a very different social order. Communist Russia preserves to some extent the music, dance, and architecture of Czarist Russia. Republican France and Italy, the constitutional monarchies of Great Britain, Holland, and the Scandinavian countries, all inherit and build to some extent upon the arts and tastes of earlier, more aristocratic régimes. The United States of America inherits many artistic traditions from Europe and elsewhere and has now the wealth to build upon them. But its early, frontier traditions were not favorable to most of the arts. Its officials and tax-payers have not yet been educated, as much as in France, to see the value of expenditure for art as a national asset from the economic as well as the cultural point of view. But in recent years there has been a tremendous acceleration of the rush to import, collect, perform, teach, emulate, and if possible excel the art of the rest of the world. The national conception of progress and success is expanding to take in the field of art. However, the traits of a capitalistic democracy persist in great emphasis on the market value of works of art and the sums paid to popular artists; also in the amounts paid for advertising and other commercial and industrial art.

A genuine democracy tries to be a free, open society to the extent that it can be so and yet preserve its existence and its basic institutions and moral standards. In extreme crises, dangers from within or without, it restricts individual liberties and the rights of minorities in certain respects, but restores them as soon after as possible. To a less extent such rights (including that of free expression, publication, and performance in the arts) are now limited in normal times in ways considered essential by the public. These include laws against libel, slander, incitement to riot, and advocating violent overthrow of the government. They also include the censorship or prohibition of works of art considered extremely obscene. But standards change in this regard, and have been greatly relaxed in recent years. All kinds of art are made available to mature students for purposes of study and research. Some films are still restricted to adult audiences. Such restrictions are left mostly for state or local authorities to decide. In a social order emphasizing freedom rather than unity and discipline, the main tendency is toward gradual diminution of the areas of coercion and restriction in the cultural field. Public regulation is mainly concerned with protecting life, health, and property and enforcing a minimum of basic education. However, strong pressures toward conformity are exerted by public opinion. Industries concerned with producing and distributing art for the general public, such as films and television, are pressed to develop their own standards and censor themselves. Church groups have considerable influence in upholding the traditional moralities, while advertisers and marketers often find it profitable to conform even when they are not forced to. Conspicuous exceptions occur and arouse heated controversy.

There seems to be no compelling reason why a liberal democracy, if prosperous, secure, and educated in the humanistic values of life, cannot develop superior creative artists as well as appreciation of their work. But art must compete for high status with many other enjoyments and values intellectual and otherwise. Art can be aided in competition by the powerful and wealthy institutions (such as foundations, universities, libraries, art museums, theaters, and orchestras) which are now emerging. In quantity and quality, the democracies can hope to rival and surpass the artistic achievements of absolutism and feudalism. But it is doubtful whether they will achieve equal coherency in national style or equal persistency in developing art along any one continuous line. The spirit of democracy is more favorable to variation and innovation; to free, experimental expression of many different approaches, rather than to the enforced perfection of one approach. This is true even of the more homogeneous, small democracies of northern Europe, and much more so of the large, heterogeneous ones. Differentiation rather than integration will probably be their characteristic emphasis in art, unless and until the democracies tend more strongly toward integration in the social, political, and other cultural fields.

However, cultural differentiation in a democracy often takes the form of rapid, fickle changes of fashion in the nation as a whole, rather than of individual variation in taste and creative expression at any one time. As such, it is consistent with a large amount of uniformity during each successive period. This is especially true among families eager to be up to date in patronizing the latest styles. Even the artists of the democratic avant-garde sometimes display a sheep-like tendency to follow the latest radical style-leaders, under the mistaken impression that they are being individualistic.

Meanwhile the trend toward large-scale financial, commercial, and industrial organization spreads through the arts, requiring and appealing to huge audiences on various economic and educational levels. It spreads from the mass media of radio, television, and film, from public housing and urban planning through concert bureaus, the publication of books and magazines, and the reproduction of paintings. Large-scale organization on the levels of ownership, management, and labor unions often tends to make production and performance more expensive. It may then be harder for the individual artist to create or perform along experimental lines for a small audience. Artists working for large corporations and appealing to the taste of large publics may be

handsomely paid, while the composer of a symphony or the author of a book of poems may have to pay the cost of publication without much hope of return unless and until he becomes famous. Meanwhile, as against the standardizing trend, some foundations and endowed institutions try to subsidize the young unknown and the lonely pioneer in art. Thus the currents of pressure and counterpressure in a democratic order continue to shift and realign themselves.

10. MODERN DICTATORSHIPS; FASCIST AND COMMUNIST

In the past, dictatorships have usually been brief interludes of one-man rule between more stable forms of government. They have occurred after the collapse of monarchies, grown soft and unable to enforce their claims to power, as in the rise of Cromwell and Napoleon. They have also occurred after the collapse of republics paralyzed by dissension, as in Athens before Philip of Macedon and Rome before Julius Caesar. They have often been preceded by oligarchies in which one man soon wrests the power from others. Sometimes they are followed by a return to hereditary monarchy: either that of the dictator as founder of a new dynasty or that in which the former, "legitimate" dynasty is restored. They are often announced, and perhaps intended, as temporary means of restoring order. But it is hard for those who have risen to great power through violence, thus making many enemies, to give it up with safety or contentment. One has a lion by the tail. Also, the exercise of absolute power is habit-forming; one may enjoy it too much to give it up without a struggle.

Twentieth-century dictatorships have much in common with the old ones, including the fact that they are announced as temporary expedients, steps toward a better form of stable government in which the people, or the best elements of the people, will rule peacefully by universal consent. Many of them came to power on the ruins of past monarchies, as in Germany and Russia, or on those of past, weak republics, as in China. Some constitute partial regressions from representative government to the despotic, military empire. They differ from the latter in avoiding or postponing a return to hereditary monarchy, and in maintaining some vestiges of representative government. The rule of the dictator or the dictatorial junta depends precariously on control of a somewhat larger oligarchy of military and party chiefs, often secretly scheming against each other. Fascist control rests, in theory at least, on a property-owning, managerial class opposed to domination of the workers. Communist control is said to rest primarily on the urban workers and farmers. But in practice there is much resemblance; each tends to develop its own bureacracy with elements descended from various former classes. Both have to gain some support from the masses as well as from the intellectuals, managers, and other brain-workers. A communist dictator may replace a fascist one by a violent coup or vice versa; the change is seldom bloodless.

In any case, the modern dictator sees the need to build up as soon as possible a complex machinery of military and bureaucratic administration under his control. A liberal, democratic constitution may be adopted but indefinitely suspended in practice. Meanwhile, both fascist and communist states tend to be "closed," by contrast with the open democracies. They are comparatively closed internally to the expression of views opposed to the régime and its doctrine; externally to the entrance of such influences from without and perhaps to free travel by their own citizens. There is much variation in these respects among particular nations, however, and the régime may stiffen or relax in proportion to the current threats against it from within and without. Like the fascist dictatorship, the communist usually has a totalitarian, monolithic party system: only one permitted party, containing an élite of the total

population. Differences of policy arise, but are usually settled on a high level by vote, intrigue, or violence within the oligarchy. Criticism of minor officials is allowed in regard to their fulfillment of approved goals. Dictatorships often look forward in theory to a future state of peace and prosperity; communism, to a classless utopia without revolutions but with continued growth. Both are sometimes vague on the time and details, being more concerned with the first stages. Communism tends to conceive it in terms of the welfare state with many benefits conferred by the government. It conceives the first stages as a gradual process of increased socialization, including the elimination of vestiges of private enterprise as in farming.

A fascist dictatorship, as in Franco's Spain, is more likely to invoke religious and ecclesiastical sanction than a communist one; the latter being traditionally atheistic. Churches have often been allied with monarchy and capitalism, as in eighteenth-century France and Russia; hence a proletarian revolution tends at first to oppose both together.

Both types of dictatorship, along with monarchies and democracies, have at times accepted evolutionism in general, including social and cultural evolution. But they tend to interpret it in terms of their own assumptions and objectives. Both fascist and communist philosophers have been attracted by the Darwinian concept of the survival of the fittest through ruthless struggle. Each, of course, regards its own group and ideology as the fittest. It looks forward to eliminating or dominating all rivals. As we have noted, evolutionism does not imply, and is not essentially linked with, any of these political types or ideologies; it is quite as adaptable to the liberal social philosophies of Spencer and Dewey.

Modern dictatorships tend to use science as a means to strengthening their régimes: not only the physical sciences and technologies, but those of psychology and social science as techniques of influencing the public mind at home and abroad. Art is systematically used as a psycho-social technic, often for oppressive and aggressive political ends. At the same time and in the same way, religious and philosophical ideologies and institutions are employed as means to practical ends, often with more cynical disbelief than in the ancient empires. The modern dictator makes use for his purposes of whatever ideology is best suited to sway public attitudes and emotions within his own and other peoples. In the communist states, the official ideology is the Marxist tradition; in fascist ones, it may be ostensibly Christian or Moslem. But foreign ideologies also are studied as to their effects in strengthening or weakening a rival régime. By an authoritarian state, the freedom, individualism, stylistic formalism, and easy-going hedonism of art in a liberal democracy are regarded as socially weakening. It prefers that art should be understandable and appealing to the masses, but convey the desired message of obedience and conformity.

Modern dictators tend, like the ancient ones, to use the arts for reinforcing their régimes through indoctrination of the public. When the dust of revolution has settled, art is again patronized and regimented. In the past, some great artists have flourished under somewhat dictatorial conditions, as in Renaissance Italy; but it is hard for the modern artist to do so after he has acquired a taste for freedom. Much depends on the individual. Augustus Caesar, the Medici, Napoleon, and Lenin were men with a taste for art and learning. So were some of Hitler's henchmen, but he and Stalin showed little interest in that side of life.

Both fascism and communism tend to favor somewhat realistic art, easy for the masses to understand and enjoy, but altered in the direction of idealizing the régime and its heroes and caricaturing its enemies. Sometimes, as in Russia, the policy changes as to who the heroes were. Much poster-like painting is produced as a means of indoctrination. This may change if and when the régime as a whole relaxes and decentralizes, allowing a little more freedom of expression to artists and intellectuals. Although communism is in principle international, communist states have often resembled fascist ones in fostering revivals of traditional national and local arts.

These are usually docile on the whole, and tend to strengthen national unity. Before World War II, the Nazi German leaders condemned the flat-roofed modern type of architecture, linking it with nudism and liberalism. They praised instead the German gothic, with its associations of conservative nationalism. Soviet Russia has encouraged ethnic dancing and folk-song along approved lines. Totalitarian régimes, following Plato, do not usually encourage the wistful, yearning romanticism of Gypsy music and other pre-revolutionary folk-art. Brisk, vigorous, positive, constructive music is favored, as conducive to military and industrial zeal. Art considered favorable to the right attitudes, including serious, classical art of the past, is often subsidized on a scale seldom equalled in the liberal democracies. Theaters, concert-halls, opera-houses, art galleries, libraries, and festivals of art are provided lavishly. Older styles and master-works are reinterpreted and sometimes edited from the standpoint of officially approved aesthetic and political principles.

The closed state is not consumer-directed but government-directed in matters of art and other consumer goods. People are given what is thought to be good for them, and art is often allotted a share of the national income in proportion to its value as a means to social goals.

With individual and local differentiation thus restricted in the arts, their tendency is more unilinear than in the democracies. There is also a regressive tendency toward simplification in certain respects, when this is conducive to easier appreciation and enjoyment by the masses. But the bare, simple, functional forms produced by some twentieth-century styles, especially in architecture, are not always pleasing and impressive to the masses or conducive to desired attitudes. Soon after the Russian Revolution, after some experiment with the architectural styles of Frank

Lloyd Wright and other moderns, there was a tendency to revive the elaborate neo-classicism and neo-baroque of Czarist public buildings. Modern functional styles are also used at times. Much post-impressionist, expressionist, and abstract painting and sculpture was condemned by Nazi and Communist leaders alike as "degenerate, decadent formalism," suited only to a declining culture. The same attitude was taken toward bitter, sordid realism and pessimism of the type which had prevailed in pre-revolutionary Russian novels and has spread through the democratic West.

These specific attitudes and policies toward styles in the various arts are not necessarily permanent. While more controlled and rigid under stress than the democracies, dictatorship is capable of rapid, sudden changes in every field to meet a changing situation, internal or external. This may easily indicate the desirability of a shift in art toward "formalism" or some other previously disapproved type, or toward more freedom for the artist in the non-political aspects of his work. If it goes very far toward freedom, a nation will have ceased to be a dictatorship. It will have ceased to be a fascist or communist state of the present type. But all such types are subject to evolutionary change; none can be frozen indefinitely.

II. CULTURAL DISADVANTAGES
OF LARGE POLITICAL UNITS.
FAVORABLE POSITION
OF THE INDEPENDENT, SMALL INHERITOR

Why does artistic development so often fail to keep pace with political and social? Why does it seem so often to reach its peak of originality and quality at a fairly early stage in the history of a people, and in relatively small political units such as Athens and Florence? Why does a people often originate and outline, at an early stage in

its history, all the main paths of its future progress, so that later stages seem only to follow them out in a somewhat imitative, eclectic way? Why is further political enlargement into complex nations often followed by a decrease in creative genius; by colossal, showy, vulgar works like those of the later Roman Empire?

These are puzzling questions, often asked of the cultural historian. They suggest that artistic evolution can not keep pace, in creative ability at least, with social and political evolution; that creative ability, the poetic mind as contrasted with the scientific and administrative, is essentially a phenomenon of early civilization, doomed to die as evolution proceeds. Many pessimistic philosophers of history have argued along these lines.

The assumptions implied in these questions are open to dispute. They spring from the old, familiar doctrine of degeneration from a Golden Age, and from the tendency to idealize antiquity. Neither Athens nor Florence was a paradise for artists or philosophers. Many original, important developments in art have been made in great empires, as in the public and domestic architecture of Rome under Hadrian. Great modern nations have developed orchestral music, the theater, film, and novel. Art can enjoy advantages in a large nation under enlightened government, not only in the shape of economic support and commissions for expensive works, but in the cosmopolitan blending of styles and cultures, the stimulation of contact with different minds. All kinds of art can flourish in a large state, including the delicate and modest kind as well as the strident.

Nevertheless, there is another side of the picture. Certain disadvantages are typical of the large state. In huge, heterogeneous nations like the Roman and British Empires, especially when threatened by rebellion within and attack from without, there is a need to channel much of the best human ability into complex administrative functions: those of public and ecclesiastical administration, war, commerce, and utilitarian technology. There is no way of knowing how many potential geniuses in art are drawn away from artistic careers into others.

Many artists tell us of an early struggle with the parental wish to send them into other fields, such as law and business, and presumably others have yielded. Psychologists today incline to the belief that artistic ability is not purely unique, but a special application of abilities which can be otherwise used. Many great artists have shown ability and interest in other fields as well. When a large proportion of the best brains of a country turns into the arts, as in Athens and Florence, it is partly due to contemporary social pressures and inducements. When art is belittled and poorly rewarded, many undecided youths may turn to something more promising, of their own accord or through family pressure. A native bent toward art may not be strong enough to swing the balance. In centrally directed nations, such as the ancient empires and modern dictatorships, young men and women are sent into lines where they are wanted, with little regard for their personal preference. The arts have usually not been the most effective paths to wealth and social advancement. They were often (though not always) treated with respect and interest in Athens and Florence, by the public and by statesmen such as Pericles and Lorenzo de' Medici. There was a fairly regular demand for art, though its rewards were precarious. In a small, self-sufficient culture, division of labor did not have to be carried far; the arts were not overly specialized. A man could try his hand at different media and technics, as did Leonardo. Those who were not artists could easily have some contact with a number of arts, if only in religious ceremonials. Civic festivals with athletics, dances, songs, plays, and military drills brought in the able-bodied youth of the upper classes. In a small state, there was often less demand for capable youths to spend a lifetime in military or governmental work. All free citizens could take their turns at it and be ready for call in emergencies. As the state grew, the citizen army became inadequate and a standing army of professional soldiers developed along with a civilian bureaucracy.

Much of the creative art production of Greece, Rome, England, France, Holland, Belgium, and Germany was done before they had gone very far along the road of empire-building, with all its drain of able men into military, commercial, and colonial administration. Large-scale empire-building by the modern European nations reached its height in the eighteenth and nineteenth centuries. Kipling describes a late phase of it in his stories of the British in India. Some of North America's outstanding work in literature was done before the complex fabric of industrialized administration spread across the continent. In the large, centralized state, there is a tendency for cultural pursuits to become impersonal and bureaucracy-ridden. People are caught up in vast institutions and collective enterprises like the film or television, with tasks divided and subdivided. They may have little chance to make a whole product or to compose and present a sonata or simple play before a few discriminating patrons. The cost of producing a play or film in America today is so high as to discourage those not fairly sure of a large audience. Urban life is busied with countless distractions and amusements, leaving little time for quiet imagining and careful craftsmanship.

To be sure, the mere fact of living in a small, primitive community is no guarantee of artistic or intellectual opportunity. As compared with the metropolis, one lacks resources and stimuli. One may have no access to the necessary skills and instruments, or to the great, civilized traditions. Shepherds under the stars and small prairie farmers do not necessarily think great thoughts or write great poetry.

There is a third possibility, and it has at times been the scene of great creative flowerings. This is the situation in which a small state, with simple administrative machinery, inherits the accumulated cultural wealth of larger, older nations. Thus early Athens became a cultural receptacle into which poured, as if through a funnel, much of the art, religion, and science of Egypt and the Middle East. The same was true to some extent of Israel, but Israel despised and rejected much of its surrounding culture—especially of Egypt, Babylon, and Rome—as corrupt and idolatrous. Its solemn piety discouraged the lighter, gayer kinds of art. Its taboo on visual representation deflected much artistic imagination into religious literature. At times in its career (e.g., under Solomon) it had complex administrative responsibilities and a complex architecture; at other times not. Florence, Venice, Padua, Siena, and Milan in the Renaissance were sometimes independent city-states. They inherited a growing stream of rediscovered classical civilization in addition to the Hebrew-Christian, along with some infusions from the Near and Far East. Personal relations within them were intimate though often quarrelsome; the artist knew his patron, and the ruler could easily know in person the leading arts and artists in his realm.

China laid the foundations of its literature and originated many lasting designs in bronze and jade during the small Shang empire; those of its philosophic, moral, social, and political ideology in the Chou dynasty. Confucius and Lao-Tzu taught before 500 B.C. In the Han dynasty, Buddhism entered from the south with its wealth of Indian traditions. From the Wei dynasty onward, these merging streams helped to nourish and stimulate Chinese art and culture, especially painting, sculpture, and literature. Respect for scholarship and aesthetic taste was maintained through later centuries along with an expanding administrative mechanism, partly through an examination system which required some knowledge of the classics by future officials. From the T'ang dynasty onward, a stream of Chinese art and Sino-Indian tradition poured into Japan, then a small and somewhat sheltered island empire. A few centuries of prosperity in the hands of a secure, aesthetically refined aristocracy led to the flowering of decorative, ceremonial, and literary arts

in the Fujiwara (late Heian) period. Its literature set the basic ideals of literary excellence and cultivated aristocracy for centuries to come. Aside from a few brief European incursions, Japan remained isolated from European civilization until the middle of the nineteenth century.

The status of a small, independent city-state in Europe was always somewhat precarious. Athens was able to resist for several centuries absorption into an empire, but eventually succumbed. Small states persisted in Italy until the nineteenth century. Elsewhere, many independent cities and small kingdoms of Europe were gradually combined into grand monarchies. To be a small, weak state in perpetual fear of conquest is not conducive to peaceful work; it may impel the state to a heavy military outlay or to constant intrigues and alliances, as in Machiavelli's time. Some security for several generations would seem to be necessary for the best results. This may be provided by geographical isolation, the weakness of neighbors, or the agreement of great powers to respect the small one's independence, as in the case of a buffer state.

It cannot be said that such factors are a necessary or sufficient cause of cultural creativeness. Other factors must be involved, and may be more decisive. Switzerland and the Scandinavian countries are small, secure, independent states which have inherited great civilized traditions, but they have not been among the greatest contributors to world art.

Can a large, complex, democratic nation be a favorable place for artistic creation, over and above the appreciation of art created elsewhere? That remains to be seen. It may depend in part on freedom from the fear of war and poverty. It will be hard to simplify administrative machinery, for each labor-saving device, each increase in power and efficiency, tends to bring still more administrative expansion. A large share of the financial awards and prestige in an industrial democracy goes to those who please a large public. But time and peaceful evolution may bring a

[487]

further rise in the status and support of art, as well as more public leisure and interest in its cultivation. A systematic effort can be made to provide the artist with the necessary seclusion, leisure, and materials for slow creative work. This would be analogous to basic research in science in that it frees the worker from the need to finish something marketable quickly.

The situation has changed somewhat in regard to the inheritance of cultural traditions. The culture of the entire world now pours into each modern nation, large and small, that is willing to accept it. On a larger scale, the situation is analogous to that in which ancient Mediterranean culture poured into Greece, Alexandria, Rome, and Byzantium. We inherit an embarrassment of cultural riches; far more than we can properly digest, interpret, and employ. But we also inherit a more scientific understanding of the nature and evolution of art, including its relation to the social context. Perhaps, with this knowledge, we can deal effectively with the problem of stimulating artistic development in the most desirable ways.

12. DOES ART EXPRESS ITS AGE?
SOCIAL AND PSYCHOLOGICAL ASPECTS

To say that art "expresses its age" implies that the kinds of art then produced are largely caused or influenced by factors and conditions peculiar to that age. It implies that, as a result, there is a basic harmony or consistency between the art and other cultural manifestations of the time and place.

As to which determines which, there is some disagreement. The usual view is that art puts into explicit, objective, communicative form certain distinctive thoughts, feelings, and desires which have been current for a while but not clearly stated. They may have been vaguely hinted or implied by people's actions, or abstractly and partially stated by philosophers and scientists;

but works of art can put them into concrete, personal symbols which make people more vividly aware of their human significance. Through their influence, the group can become more fully aware of what it is trying to achieve and why; of where it has been moving for a long time without realizing the fact. There is much truth in this idea, which Hegel, Comte, Marx, and Taine all helped to formulate. Art does, to some extent, express its "psychological climate," the "spirit of the age."

On the other hand, it has also been truly said that art does not merely give voice to thoughts and feelings which have already developed elsewhere. Art helps to originate and develop them.[3] It is a creative force, not merely a mouthpiece of its age. "Life imitates art," said Oscar Wilde. Where can one find the "spirit of the age," in any empirical, naturalistic sense of the term, if one disregards the art of the time? What an art historian thinks of as the spirit of an age is largely what he finds in its art; then he turns to other factors, such as its philosophy, and looks for analogous expressions, perhaps ignoring the discrepancies between them.

One might say with some truth, then, that each age expresses its art. The influence is mutual, reciprocal. To analyze it empirically, one must avoid the traditional assumption that "ages" are in fact separate epochs or universal stages, clearly marked off from each other, each with its own distinct identity. Such demarcations are always somewhat arbitrary in the history of art and of culture. Skeptics can argue, then, that there is really no such thing as an "age" in the traditional sense. But some real problems do remain.

One, just noted, is that of whether art is determined by other factors of the time or is itself a determining one. Another is that of which outside factors influence art most strongly. As we have seen, there are two main answers to this second question. One, favored by idealists and dualists, is

[3] See George Boas, *Wingless Pegasus* (Baltimore, 1950), pp. 194–210.

that psychic or spiritual factors are the stronger. The other is that material or socio-economic ones dominate. Neither answer is adequate. Both sets of factors must be somehow recognized and their interrelations noted.

However interpreted, the simple statement "art expresses its age" does not convey the whole truth. Art always expresses something of its age, something more than its age, and something less. In any age, it expresses certain broadly human traits, interests, and attitudes, as impelled by the generically human traits of its makers and users. It also expresses certain traits of its local, momentary cultural setting. A late painting by El Greco is in some ways characteristic of seventeenth-century Spain, in some ways characteristic of Byzantine Greece, and in other ways individual. Art is certainly a medium and technic through which individual and collective attitudes can speak, in some respects more clearly and fully than through any others. Also, it is one in which the problems of life and the possible answers to them can be raised to a more conscious level and communicated, not merely felt in a vague and helpless way. Every art, in every stage of history, is also influenced by other cultural factors and by the special configurations they have taken at that moment. This influence is exerted most obviously on the instruments and technics of art, such as writing, oil paints, pipe organs, and motion picture cameras. It is also fairly obvious in the subject-matter of art, the distinctive choice of ideas, images, and attitudes at a particular time, such as idealized portraits of kings, religious dreams of heaven and hell, or realistic scenes of factories and workers.

In recent years, the interest of theoretical historians has shifted somewhat from these manifest relations to others of a less conscious type, often unrealized by artist and public. These are, especially, the ways in which a certain abstract form or pattern in any art can symbolize certain underlying thoughts and attitudes in the group as a whole. They may be repressed by conventional taboos, as in the case of erotic symbols employed unwittingly by Puritanical artists, or they may be vague, incipient desires at an early stage of cultural evolution.

Following the hypotheses of Freud on the Oedipus complex and of Jung on archetypal images, there has been a flood of psychoanalytical interpretations of the arts. These emphasize certain permanent mechanisms, operative in every civilized age, rather than the distinctive traits of a particular age. Modern refinements are shown as not having eliminated the basic, animal impulses of man, but having glossed them over and partially redirected them. Nevertheless, the stark images of physical sex and sadistic violence, expressed in some primitive and ancient art, stand out in contrast with the expurgated refinements of later ages such as the Victorian. Both contrast with the conscious, sophisticated release of formerly repressed attitudes in present literature. The distinctive ways in which each age and culture tries to restrain certain impulses, especially those of sex and aggression, and its distinctive ways of doing so, such as threats of hell-fire or social ostracism, are historically significant as changing culture-traits, expressed in art.

There is less repression or disapproval in some other kinds of artistic symbolism. Certain typical forms recur, we have seen, in the art of certain periods and peoples: the heavy, thick column and slab in Egypt; Hogarth's "line of grace and beauty" in late Greek and Roman art; the pointed arch in gothic; the asymmetrical, heavy swirl in baroque, the light, small, delicate curve in rococo; the stream-lined, pointed shape of modern vehicles. The landscape in three dimensions is an imaginary journey into infinite space, expressing somewhat the same desire as do explorations and moon-rockets. There are analogues in other arts, such as the fugue in baroque music and the heroic couplet in English rococo verse. Faust symbolizes modern Western man.

The question arises, then: how and why does a certain age and group select a certain characteristic symbol? How does the symbol "express" the cultural configuration in ways of which people are only vaguely conscious, if at all, at the time? A multitude of answers is given: utilitarian, psychoanalytic, and otherwise. The steeply pitched roof with pointed arch helps keep the snow off, and also expresses religious aspiration; the spire, the column, and the stream-lined car are phallic and thus ego-strengthening. What seems non-functional in one age, such as the "fussy," dust-catching ornamentation of rococo furniture, is less so when one has many servants to keep busy, and when one's aim is to display wealth and luxury. The different systems of perspective in Roman, Byzantine, Chinese, and Renaissance painting all express, or coincide with, analogous conceptions of physical space held by scientists at the time. All these current ways of explaining artistic phenomena probably indicate real causal relationships within the culture: not so much of direct cause and effect as of simultaneous response to certain pervasive situations.

In retrospect, we tend to ignore the diversity of each age. We conceive it in terms, not only of our favorite works of art, but of those selective summaries which historical textbooks have given us. They tend to perpetuate oversimplified images of each age and culture, such as the serenity of Greece, the cruelty and corruption of Rome, the materialism of the West. As we look more closely with the aid of scientific historiography, we discover more conflicts, dissenting beliefs and attitudes, within each one. Quarrelsome and peaceful, emotional and logical, religious and irreligious, conservative and radical, grave and frivolous, industrious and lazy—every large group has some of all these, but only in the art of advanced civilizations do all find expression in art. In the earliest tribes and villages, no doubt, some women were urging their men to more peaceful industry and care for children; but the woman's point of view, or the child's, has been given little chance to express itself in art until recent times. The same is true of all subordinate groups—the peasant, the slave, the serf, the urban manual worker, the common soldier. These have been mostly inarticulate or represented by outsiders, often with unsympathetic stereotypes based on class condescension.

What we include and emphasize in our histories of art is largely the official, approved art of dominant groups in each periods; of the wealthy and powerful in church and state. It is art expressing the approved moral and religious attitudes of the time, or those which afterward became so. It is further censored by the attitudes of present historians and readers. To what extent a popular, lower-class art may have flourished in past ages, as in the fabliaux and folklore, the tavern songs and rustic dances of the middle ages, we can only guess. Not until modern democracy does a genuinely popular art, an art of and for the humble and uneducated, the man, woman, and child in the street and on the farm, find strong and wide public expression. If we include these types in our concept of an "age," then art has not undertaken to express it fully until now. Still less does the art enshrined in our histories, museums, and libraries express the whole of the past, or of any past age. It does so only in a highly selective, biased way, which may or may not include the best and most typical. So much has been destroyed or suppressed, as in the loss of Greek wall-painting, that what is left cannot be taken as fairly representative.

Within a dynamic civilization at any time, some groups are pressing for change while others are content with the *status quo*. This is true in art as in other fields. In the modern West, the clamor for change and the conflict of many rival pressures is highly conscious and diverse, but on a smaller scale it has long been common. The artists and their works, the styles and attitudes expressed at any one time, may represent a conservative, a forward-looking, or reactionary trend in general cultural attitude. Often those regarded as dangerous radicals at the time, for their ideas as well as for their art, are afterward venerated as classics. This is true of Shelley and Byron, Wagner and Courbet, to name only a few. In what sense, then, shall we say that these artists "expressed their age"? They expressed a discontented, forward-looking or backward-looking part of it, in criticizing and reacting against the contented, conservative parts of it. We may be justified in judging the cultural leaders to be the most important parts of their age, in the light of progress, but they are certainly not all of it. Much moral and religious preachment, together with its expression in art, constitutes a biting attack on the actual customs and attitudes of the day. Shall we say that the denunciations of the Hebrew prophets against idolatry and harlotry or those of Plato against the exciting, sensual arts of the masses, expressed their age? Or were the sins and sensualities themselves, whose expressions in popular art have long since disappeared, more typical of the age? Each age not only expresses itself in a variety of arts, élite and popular, but also censors that expression and those of previous ages, in handing down its contribution to the future. What it eliminates, as well as what it preserves and distributes, expresses its spirit.

In a changing civilization, some art seems to express the previous age rather than the present one. We call it conservative, retarded, or reactionary art. That which does only this, the purely academic, tends to be ignored by art historians. It may, however, evince a cultural regression, as in the return to official style in Egypt after Ikhnaton. In that case it expresses also its present age. Some art is definitely forward-looking in its content of ideas, such as Bacon's travel-tale, *The New Atlantis*. De Saint-Pierre's *Paul and Virginia* and Burns's *A Man's a Man for A' That* were forward-looking in some ways, regressive in others. C.P.E. Bach's experiments with the sonata were pioneer steps in form. J.S. Bach's polyphonic emphasis was, in a way, a step backward to the baroque age, which he thus expressed more fully than the baroque had done for itself. But J.S. Bach also anticipated the future

in some of his works, as in the rococo spirit of some of his chamber music and the strongly romantic spirit of the *Goldberg Variation 25*.

Insofar as such tendencies are incipient elsewhere in the age, vanguard art can be said to express them. It would not be eagerly accepted and attacked if the aesthetic climate were not, to some extent, ready for it. Each type of art expresses certain constituent attitudes of its age, some of which are growing and some declining. With our interest in progress, we tend to pick out the forward-looking ones as typical, even though they represented only a small weak voice at the time.

A great amount of classical style remained in the work of the acknowledged leaders of romanticism: of classic harmony, rhythm, and sonata-structure in Beethoven; of classic drawing and composition in Delacroix; of classic diction and verse-form in Keats, Shelley, Goethe, and Schiller. Byron, though a romanticist *par excellence* in some respects, was also a rococo wit whose couplets often followed the tradition of Pope and Dryden. Such exceptions complicate the picture, but do not invalidate the general interpretation. It is essential to the understanding of both romanticism and neo-classicism to remember that neither movement was carried to the ultimate extreme by its greatest exponents. A literal, dogmatic application of selected neo-classical principles could have led the artist to extremes of lifeless, monotonous geometry; to the dry, mechanical application of ancient rules. But this would have overlooked other, equally important classical maxims: "nothing too much"; "know thyself"; "the aim of art is to instruct and delight." So in fact, the greatest neo-classicists of the baroque and rococo eras—Racine and Poussin, Haydn and Mozart, put into their work a perceptible amount of emotion, freedom, irregularity, and other traits which were still more emphasized by the romanticists. These traits, if the romanticists had carried them to extremes, would have led to confusion and chaos, and the resultant art would have been far from expressing the diversity of its age.

Great artists seldom, except in a whimsical or experimental mood, carry any one stylistic tendency to its ultimate extreme; they feel the need of some balance from the opposite type. But their movement from a little left of center to a little right of center, or *vice versa*, can be highly expressive and significant culturally. And while the leaders of the movement often go cautiously, retaining much from the previous style, their followers tend to go farther. Thus Whitman is more romantic in verse-form than Keats; Wagner and Debussy in orchestration and rhythm than Beethoven; Monet in blurred atmospheric texture than Delacroix. The later men are not usually called romanticists, and in many ways they were not, having already moved toward the next age; but in other respects they carried romanticism farther toward its possible extremes.

13. SUMMARY

This chapter has offered a more specific answer to the question of what determines artistic phenomena, including changes in style. It has analyzed such very broad, ubiquitous factors as heredity and environment into a list of subordinate types. The basis for this division is not the particular kind of heredity or environment. It is the difference between comparatively widespread, lasting factors (both hereditary and environmental) and those characteristic of smaller, more transitory groups, individuals, and moments in their lives. The former tend on the whole to produce uniformities and continuities; the latter, divergent trends and unique configurations.

Pursuing the hypothesis of some correlation between social and artistic types, later sections of the chapter examine several of each. The list is given in roughly chronological order, but is not proposed as an exact or necessary sequence of stages. Certain types of art, technology, and ideology often accompany certain types of social organization, such as the agricultural village and the city-state. But great variation in art occurs within each social type, especially when an ancient type persists with modification into later times and inherits the culture of larger groups. As to cultural creativeness, certain disadvantages were found to be connected with large political units. The independent, small, secure inheritor has had some corresponding advantages in the past, but the situation is rapidly changing.

Art always expresses something characteristic of its age in general. It also expresses certain broadly human traits, characteristic of many ages. In other ways it expresses only part of its age. In the past, only the dominant groups achieved any approach to full artistic expression; in a modern democracy the expression is more widespread. Some art in every age is backward-looking; other art is forward-looking. There is more artistic diversity in each age than is usually realized.

CHAPTER XXIII

THE MULTIPLE DIALECTIC OF
CULTURAL EVOLUTION

I. CONFLICT AND COMPROMISE
IN CIVILIZATION AND ITS ARTS

Julian Huxley says of the cultural process that "Evolutionary change is always a dialectic process, in which stability, even if reached, is reached slowly and gradually."[1] Such stability, one might add, is never complete or permanent. This conception of cultural dialectic, in a broad sense not restricted to Hegelian or Marxist theory, will be applied to the arts in the present chapter.

The idea of a struggle between opposing forces throughout the cosmic process is older than written philosophy. In Zoroastrianism the struggle was conceived as a fairly equal one between two great powers of good and evil, opposing deities who alternately gained the upper hand. Heraclitus viewed the world as a process of unceasing change and conflict of opposites, only temporarily and partially reconciled. For him the conflict was not wholly bad. Aristotle quotes him as disagreeing with the poet who wished "that strife might perish from among gods and men." For, he said, "there would be no harmony without high and low, no animals without the opposition of female and male." (Gilbert and Kuhn, 1953, p. 1). As an aesthetic principle and a recurrent type of composition, Greek art emphasized the integration of opposing forces as contrasting themes. Among the polarities often contrasted were those of chaos and rational order, creation and destruction (personified in Lucretius by Venus and

Mars), poetry and philosophy, divine madness and reason, recalcitrant matter and the eternal forms of perfection, the world of sense and the world of spirit, virtue and vice, ignorance and wisdom, the one and the many, permanence and change.

While Platonism looked askance at change and conflict as evil and illusory, longing for the static perfection of the ideal world, Hegel's nineteenth-century version of idealism accepted them as basic attributes of cosmic evolution. This involved recurrent intellectual conflicts between partial insights: first a thesis, then an antithesis, then a synthesis or partial combination of them. Out of each clash came a step toward higher knowledge and self-awareness. Hegel's term "dialectic" recalled the Socratic method of Plato's dialogues, in which opposing views were argued until a satisfactory conclusion was reached. The idea that right decisions are to be reached by free discussion and orderly adjustment of opposing interests has remained a basic principle of representative government. We have seen how Marx, at first following Hegel, went on to develop the concept of historical dialectic as a persistent struggle for power and wealth, in which different social classes oppose each other and successively gain control until the final victory of the workers. This conception fitted in with the Darwinian concepts of

[1] "Cultural Process and Evolution," in A. Roe and G. G. Simpson, *Behavior and Evolution*, (New Haven, Conn., 1958), p. 442.

[493]

natural selection and the struggle for survival. Through struggle, Nietzsche added, evolution and progress would produce a higher species, the Superman.

Art played an important role in these theories. It was regarded as a weapon in the struggle for power, a means of indoctrinating the masses or fomenting revolt, a medium for expressing the various contending interests and world-views. Nietzsche further added the concept of a polarity between the Apollonian and Dionysian strains in early Greek art and religion, a conflict partly reconciled in classic Greek tragedy but recurrent in later art and culture. Modern art has tried to reconcile them. Goethe synthesized classic and romantic elements in the second part of *Faust*; Hugo did so in his theory of the stages in literary history. These partial syntheses included, not only the recurrent spirit-flesh and classic-romantic dualisms, but also recognition of the creative aspects of the primitive, savage, demonic forces.

In the present century, Freud developed his theory of a perpetual unsolved struggle between man's innately aggressive, destructive impulses and the restraints of civilization, morality, and practical wisdom. This struggle, he showed, is partly reconciled in the ego as a mediator between the psyche and the world, and in art as a symbolic representation and sublimation of the conflict. It operates partly on the unconscious level in both artist and public. Though formed and expressed mainly by the ego, art receives and incorporates, in modified form, influences from the id and super-ego of the artist as well as from the cultural environment. In every generation of art, further attempts at reconciliation are attempted. Much art, from the Freudian point of view, can be interpreted as a means to this end, though only partly realized as such at the time. The public, like the artist, can respond affectively to symbolic forms of whose meaning neither is fully conscious.

The world's art, especially in drama and fiction, helps us to cope with our moral conflicts on a conscious or partly conscious level by dramatizing them in concrete examples of men and women faced by problems somewhat like our own. It illustrates the various extremes of excess and deficiency, of unbridled violence, cruelty, and lust on one hand and of saintliness beyond the reach of ordinary humans on the other. It shows various possible compromises; attempts to combine opposite values. It shows the consequences of all these ways of thinking and acting. It may suggest a moral and a general solution, a policy of action; but this is the task of ethics rather than of art. Whether or not one can accept the moral and metaphysical implications of the story—e.g., the inheritance of guilt and the punishment of unintentional crime in Oedipus—it may at least stimulate one to think out one's own solution, in general and in one's own particular case. Different ages and cultures express themselves in the solutions and types of character they praise or condemn, the traits they regard as flaws or virtues. Much Japanese traditional art glorified feudal loyalty; Christian medieval art, chastity and heroic self-sacrifice. But conflicting feelings often appear beneath the surface as in the portrayal of a guilty person with some sympathy (Lucifer, Macbeth) or in the humorous caricature of an extreme idealist (Quixote) or hypocrite (Tartuffe).

Using and praising one set of stylistic traits and denouncing another, cultural leaders of the new age make them into symbols: one set to be admired and glorified, the other to be detested and ridiculed. For polemic purposes, the champions of each style select symbols which will tend to glorify it, and symbols of the opposite style which will demean it. The long-haired, Wildean artist with a sunflower became a ridiculous symbol of romanticism to its enemies. Concepts such as "sweetness and light" or "the patient Griselda" are idealized in one age and ridiculed in another; sometimes both by different groups at the same time. Deeper changes and conflicts in the psychological climate are expressed in such contrasting attitudes toward the same symbol.

Each great civilization works out its own persistent series of attempts at synthesis and compromise between its inherent, antithetical tendencies, which are mostly variants of the deeper conflict between man's animal nature and the demands of civilization. The descending sequence of such synthetic, compromise art, which acts as a guide to practical compromise in life, forms a tradition of its own within each great tradition. So do the antithetical sequences of art expressing one extreme or the other, less approved in practice by the group as a whole, but useful as opposite poles, between which life can be steered. Though not followed exactly by most humans, both provide emotive images for aesthetic contemplation and moral evaluation.

Political and ecclesiastical officials often try, with varying success, to crush out expressions of disapproved traditions, however old and previously venerated. Both Greek and Hebrew religion went through a process of expurgation and refinement, in which primitive elements of totemism, animism, demon-worship, cruel sacrifice, and orgiastic rites were gradually eliminated. Traces remain to help scholars reconstruct the past, as in references to Hecate and the Witch of Endor.[2] Much of the Dionysian strain in Greek art is lost, because expressed in dithyrambic song and secret ritual. The Apollonian type has exerted more influence in modern centuries. A narrow, stiffened version of it dominated neo-classical art and theory from the late Renaissance onward. Books have been burned and art destroyed in Greece and China to eliminate a hated set of ideas. But elements of these can survive for centuries *sub rosa*, as in modern Haitian Voodoo, perhaps reviving later in some regressive, back-to-the-primitive movement.

Again and again, some leader and his party make a certain strong affirmation, a selective gesture in art, perhaps along with attacks on previous attitudes. On this basis, they build up a selective, dynamic style of art: let us say, the severe neo-classicism of David as opposed to previous rococo frivolities. It is developed and varied by Ingres.

This phase may be called a thesis, even though it is really antithetical to the previous style. Any vigorous movement in a series of such reactions is both thesis and antithesis, according to one's point of view. As against the neo-classical thesis came the romantic antithesis of Delacroix. But it was not an attempted return to the previous rococo; it was, to some extent, antithetical to both. Courbet's naturalism tried to break away from all three; it was another antithesis. After another specialized gesture in impressionism, the post-impressionist styles of Cézanne and Renoir attempted a new synthesis. There are traits of Fragonard's rococo style in Renoir, and of Courbet's naturalism in Cézanne; of Poussin's classicism and Delacroix's romanticism in both. Some artists, styles, and cultures are comparatively synthetic; they try to combine and reconcile many different values. Euripides, Shakespeare, Goethe, Titian, Beethoven, and Hugo are of this type. Others, such as Vivaldi, Dryden, Reynolds, Blake, Rimbaud, Debussy, and Mallarmé are of narrower scope, and can be placed more completely in one camp or another.

Whether called thesis, antithesis, or synthesis, each strong stylistic movement implies a protest against some apparent lack, deficiency, or excess in the previous style, as too much this or too little that. The new style will correct it. But it never does this completely, or only this; it goes on to some new emphasis of its own, and hence to a choice which is sure to seem excessive or deficient to someone later on. The attempted synthesis is never complete, and cannot be; it will give rise to new counter-gestures in its turn, as did the "golden mean" of Aristotle, the Summa of St. Thomas, and the cosmic vision of Dante.

No cultural synthesis can be fixed or final while life remains dynamic; all are unstable and contain the seeds of their own partial disintegration as

---

[2] See, for example, the theoretical and fictional reconstructions by James Frazer (*The Golden Bough*), Robert Graves (*The White Goddess; King Jesus*), and Mary Renault (*The King Must Die*).

life expands and outgrows them. But modern Western civilization understands and accepts this fact, even enjoys it at times, whereas previous civilizations tended more to hope for a final perfection in heaven or on earth, or at least (as in Buddhism) an escape from endless striving. No philosopher today tries to write the complete and final synthesis; he knows that his own is only one way of looking at the universe, the expression of one perennial world-view. No artist aspires to combine in his own style the best features of all previous styles. Contemporary art tries to approach this by combining elements from all past styles; but not into a single style; rather into a profusion of eclectic styles which are all unstable and competing.

2. COMPETING TRADITIONS AND PARTIAL SYNTHESES

One way to analyze the dialectic of cultural history is in terms of traditions. In a previous chapter, we noted their relation to styles in art, as descending farther in time. The larger traditions, like the Greek and Chinese, include many arts, types and styles of art, and stylistic variations through centuries or millennia. World civilization as a whole has been called "the great tradition"; it might also be called the "greatest" or the total, whole-culture tradition; that which descends everywhere, in all peoples and all cultural components. Within it are many major parts. Traditions are distinguished on an ethnic, national, regional, or religious basis, such as the Hellenic, French, European, or Islamic. They are never completely unified. Early, separate cultures merge to form larger and larger ones, as in Mesopotamia and Central America. Past political and ideological disputes, as between rival Greek schools or Jewish sects, gradually melt away and are forgotten except by specialized historians. New schisms, new tensions arise within each, yet some distinctive traits remain. Sub-

traditions are marked off on the same bases (e.g., the Florentine and Sienese within the Italian) and also in terms of cultural components.

Within world civilization as a whole, art is one great, component tradition, rapidly becoming conscious of itself on a world scale. Religion and technology are others. Each particular art has its own tradition on a world scale, as summarized in histories of painting and comparative literature. Also each regional tradition contains its artistic components, such as French literature within the total French tradition. Needless to say, all these traditions overlap and interpenetrate, especially in modern times.

Sometimes tradition is regarded as a burden or a straitjacket, especially by the modern, rebellious artist; sometimes, as in Confucian China, as a firm foundation on which to build. It has been compared to a great river flowing through time, which suggests a gentle merging. When tradition is conceived as static and conservative, revolt becomes antithetical to it, and the history of art is then seen as an endless conflict between tradition and revolt. But revolt itself has its own traditions and its venerated heroes. In storming their particular Bastilles, rebels like to invoke the name of ancient rebels like Spartacus. Marxism is at once a revolutionary tradition and a restrictive force on modern "revisionists."

Tradition can be all of these things, but in the present connection it is well to remember that traditions are also competitors in the struggle for power and survival. Or, to speak more literally, one can say that groups of humans struggle on behalf of one tradition or another. They contend for the right to preach and practice it; to spread it as widely as possible. People fight directly for their beliefs and ideals; not always along economic lines. As civilization diversifies, the alignments grow more confused. In the name of some religion or creative urge in art, men sometimes disregard all other loyalties: those of family, class, nation, and strong personal inclination. Ideologies (or the people holding them) compete in every cultural arena on innumerable issues, general and special, moral and aesthetic, theoretical and practical. Some reinforce each other and form temporary alliances; some clash with physical violence; some compete gently, with emotional and rational appeals.

Through such confused and shifting *mêlées*, styles and trends of art develop. Causes of the latter are to be sought in the temporary configuration of traditional, cultural factors at the time and just before it. All the determinants of art mix into the fray. We have noted them as contributing factors, pouring as through a funnel into the mind and art of the individual artist. True in part; but the process is also dialectical, in that any of these factors may, at a particular time and place, oppose and partly counteract any other. Innate predispositions clash with family and civil authority; rival artistic movements compete for the young artist's favor. Old and new, conservative and radical, foreign and domestic traditions beckon him to follow. Similar conflicts recur throughout the same culture-area in successive generations.

Historians of art, becoming more aware of styles and their social and psychological significance, now tend to interpret each successive style and trend in terms of action and reaction. The Renaissance revolted from the Byzantine and gothic traditions. Contemporary abstract painting is rebelling against classicism, romanticism, and realism. Any cultural movement can be so interpreted: Buddhism as a revolt from Brahmanism, later Hinduism from Buddhism; early Christianity from legalistic Judaism; the Protestant Reformation from Catholicism, but leading to a Catholic Counter-reformation. Evolutionism in culture history rejected the theories of special creation and degeneration, but it led to the Boasian reaction of the 1920's.

The attempt to reduce cultural history to a series of conflicts and revolts can be overdone. It never fully explains why a particular movement arose or to what it led. History is more than a perpetual conflict; more than an endless fluctuation between polar opposites, however these are conceived. It contains these, but also long intervals of peaceful, cooperative work along continuous lines. To differ and diverge is not necessarily to revolt or conflict. It becomes so, however, when those who differ compete for favor and support. Artists themselves often feel more conscious of the difference and rivalry between themselves and their contemporaries than posterity does. This is true of Michelangelo, Tintoretto, and Courbet; of Beethoven, Wagner, and Hugo. Today we see them as closer to their rivals; all as contributing to the larger stylistic developments of their time. Both aspects of history deserve recognition: the antithetic and the synthetic.

The dialectical theory of art history is a useful tool of description and explanation if it is not reduced to a single component in the cultural process, such as the class struggle or the classic-romantic, classic-baroque, or Apollonian-Dionysian polarity. In any issue, more than two alternatives are usually possible. Thus the historical dialectic is not single but *multiple*, a constant interaction of innumerable factors. Some operate in groups, but they do not fall into any single rhythm—at least, not any now perceptible.

At the present stage of theory, the dialectic of culture history seems overwhelmingly, bewilderingly complex and irregular, like the teeming life of a tropical rain forest. Yet biologists have been able to analyze that life into constituent processes, and culturologists may do so for history in the future.

The diversity seems to be increasing as civilization continues to differentiate. In a liberal democracy especially, each individual may select and integrate from the mass of warring ideologies and styles those which suit him most. He plays many roles in life and can identify himself with somewhat different attitudes in each. By contrast, the individual in a rigid, hierarchical culture was under more pressure to conform to his class and occupational norms in every respect. When one class in the hierarchy rebelled, as in the French and Russian Revolutions, the clash was more likely to be total and terrible. Now it usually dissolves into a permanent process of minor disputes, more capable of peaceful, piecemeal settlement.

Here again, however, the trend is not a simple one. We are constantly discovering the complexity of past conflicts which seemed at first very simple, all black on one side, all white on the other, as in the Crusades and Reformation. Meanwhile, the integrating phase of present cultural evolution is also strong. Even between the great, rival political and military blocs, in spite of ideological differences, converging trends persist. Mechanical industrialization and other technological developments are universal. World art is growing more similar in many respects in spite of all attempts to preserve local differences.

Western civilization since the time of Christ has involved several main religious traditions, each the core of a diversified, changing complex of cultural traits extending into every phase of life. These are sometimes reduced to two: the Classical (Greek and Roman) and the Hebrew-Christian. They have been constantly warring and compromising since their encounter in the late Roman Empire, with the tides of battle going this way and that. Each includes at least two major traditions of its own, persistently antithetical to each other. Within the Greek is the struggle, not only of Apollonian and Dionysian strains in art and religion, but of religious faith and mysticism against the rationalism and naturalism of the early philosophers. Platonism was a monumental synthesis of the rational and mystical approaches, which later separated again into Neo-Platonic mysticism and Epicurean naturalism. Within the Hebrew-Christian tradition are the Hebrew and the Christian, reconciled in the Christian mind by its recognition of the Old Testament as prelude and prophecy of the New. Christian-Jewish tensions have remained in the twentieth-century, and so has the struggle between science (based on Greek rationalism) and Christian faith.

Each of these diverse, contending elements has found expression in one or more arts throughout the history of Western civilization. What seems like a radical rejection of the past, and of traditionalism in general, is often a shift in emphasis from one to another of these persistent strains in the Western tradition, as men of genius follow one or the other. In the Italian Renaissance, Fra Angelico and Savonarola stand for the otherworldly emphasis, prolonging in some ways the medieval outlook, while Botticelli (of the "Spring" and "Birth of Venus"), Petrarch, Boccaccio, Giorgione, Veronese, and Monteverdi exemplify the other. In El Greco, the mystic-religious strain again finds powerful expression. Minor shifts from one to the other can be largely an expression of individual temperament. Major shifts, as in the general trend toward naturalistic humanism in the Renaissance, express more profound, collective trends in the whole culture-pattern.

Within the complex, diversified stream of Western civilization, with its Greek-Roman, Hebrew, and other elements, one can discern many sets of polarities, expressed in art as antithetical characteristics and in life as opposite strivings, goals and standards of value, conflicting attitudes toward life, oneself, God, and the world. In Spain they appear in such figures as the calmly satirical, worldly Cervantes on one side, and the mystical John of the Cross on the other. Throughout the Chinese, Indian, Persian, and other traditions, analogous polarities can be found. They are often obscured from the historian by past elimination and suppression on the part of a dominant group—for example, the wholesale destruction of Epicurean writings and pagan art in the early Christian period.

Old, complex civilizations tend to find a place for each of these different attitudes, somewhere in the social fabric where it can find satisfaction without too much disturbance to others. Thus the Hindu and Christian cultures both made room for the warrior and the saint, the nun and the housewife, the recluse and the gregarious worker. Many kinds of art were produced in each, though not with equal favor. Under ascetic Christian control, worldly art (e.g., the theater) often has to live under scorn and persecution. Other Christian rulers and prelates, especially in the Byzantine and baroque periods, developed the arts in a splendid but transitory synthesis of Church and State.

The Renaissance in Italy did not achieve a complete revival of both Greek traditions. Intellectually, what it revived at first was mainly the Platonic and Neo-Platonic strain, whose mystic symbolism had influenced Augustinian Christianity. Revival of the naturalistic strain, of Greek atomism and of Aristotle in full scope, came in later centuries. Artistically, what it revived as neo-classic theory and practice was Apollonian rather than Dionysian, in its emphasis on order, clarity, balance, and restraint. These qualities, in spite of the shock of nudity with which pagan art combined them, were not impossible to synthesize with Catholic ideals of order and restraint. The more violent, disorderly elements in the Greek tradition were to come to the surface later. Dominated by an angry, nude Apollo in the role of Christ, they appear in the damned souls of Michelangelo's mannerist *Last Judgment*. On the Sistine ceiling, his combination of classical sibyls and Hebrew prophets, of Bible stories and Roman sculptural forms, is an uneasy synthesis of diverse traditions in the Renaissance mind. No later Western painter of first rank attempted so gigantic a synthesis.

As the interest in expository symbolism drained away from Western visual art, as it left the expression of abstract ideas more to science and philosophy, religious art in the West fell into a repetitious sequence of conventional scenes, charmingly varied in form but weak in intellectual meaning. Modern Western literature has faced, more frankly and vigorously, the task of analyzing and if possible solving the main issues in our culture, by victory or compromise. Through action, reason, and imagination, some antitheses

are resolved, but others keep reviving in new forms.

To achieve an ampler, more selective synthesis as time goes on, it is necessary for antithetical views to be able to express themselves, each in sharp and vigorous opposition to the other. Hence the value of the dialectical process, in art as elsewhere. It is at its best in a democracy. Only through opposed extremists do we learn what the possibilities are for a synthesis combining some of both sets of values. A persistent golden mean might have left them all in a rudimentary condition. But the most fruitful kind of dialectic is not a mere struggle for power and wealth among persons or groups with similar though conflicting desires. That kind can go on forever without constructive effect. More significant for cultural evolution are the conflicts which involve moral, intellectual, and aesthetic issues. The two kinds are often bound together and lofty ideals are often a mask for crudely selfish interests. Only the naïve are confident today that victory is always on the side of those with the highest ideals or the most refined tastes. But intellectual and artistic efforts have a way of outliving those who made and those who fought for them; hence their defeats are not all final.

Greek philosophy showed the possibility of arguing, in friendly, theoretical dialectic, the issues of abstract truth and value. Such conflicts can be waged without bloodshed, like those of athletics, in the symbolic arenas of philosophy, science, and art. Gradually, man perfects the technic and the mental attitude required for detaching them from personalities and fighting them out in a more disinterested way, or in the interest of all humanity, with a view to partial agreement. That attitude is far from universal yet. Often some personal interest or animosity impels the partisan to cultural achievements which he would not otherwise have performed. Modern philosophy has tried with some success to demolish partisan barriers on a rational level. This it has done through devotion to the Greek ideal of reason as opposed to obedient faith. Its recent skepticism and empiricism have weakened the claim of reason to know absolute truth; pragmatism tolerates different theories as hypotheses. But there are other roads to cultural synthesis. Western civilization has achieved its fair degree of unity, not so much by theoretical agreement among ideological factions, or even by agreement that partisan creed is non-essential, as by finding other things to agree upon; other satisfactions to share. Conservative groups are slow to abandon their traditional beliefs in principle; but all the main rival factions in the West have compromised somewhat in practice. Other-worldliness has yielded substantially to the pursuit of earthly progress, including normal family life, nationalistic and humanitarian efforts. When avoiding acrimonious subjects, art has provided a basis for common enjoyment by persons of all creeds. When frankly realistic or experimental, it has cooperated with science. Becoming broadly eclectic in style, and appealing to different levels of education, Western art has furthered a loose, democratic synthesis of common interests. In America, it tends to diminish sectional and religious antagonisms.

Regardless of motivation, the results of cultural conflict seem to be, like those of biological struggle for survival, favorable to evolution on the whole. These outweigh the cases of wholesale cultural destruction in the name of an opposing world-view, like the destruction of Mayan-Aztec art and literature by sixteenth-century Christians. Ikhnaton's attempted monotheistic reformation was perhaps the first great civilized conflict of world-views. It was expressed by some unknown artists in a peculiarly free, expressionistic, animated style of art. That clash of ideas and artistic forms, like many later ones, was settled on the level of power. The reformation ended, apparently in total defeat and destruction. But its gift to world culture lay dormant for millennia, to resume in modern times its place in the great tradition of world art.

3. STAGES AND SEQUENCES IN THE FORMS AND TECHNICS OF ART

Previous chapters have described various ways of marking off sequences of types and styles in the various arts and of explaining their causation. There is still much disagreement as to whether they fit into a general process of evolutionary development or one of cyclical recurrence. There seems to be some general development and some recurrence, but neither one occurs in a uniform, regular way; both are blurred by much diversity. Some writers think they see enough diversity to refute the whole idea of stages and recurrences.

Much depends on how we define "stages" and describe their various cultural components. One can hardly compare the art of two successive periods, such as Louis XV and Louis XVI furniture without marking off what amount to "stages," broadly speaking, in the history of that art. One enters more dubious ground in trying to make sharp chronological divisions between the stages in a particular art; also in trying to show that the stages in different arts and activities coincide with each other in all parts of the world. No one tries to do so today. But there are many intermediate positions between that and a complete rejection of stages and recurrences. One can describe them more roughly and sketchily, indicating what seem to be partial or occasional correspondences and possible contributing causes.

Stages and sequences in all the arts can be marked off in terms of far-reaching technical innovations. Some coincide approximately with each other and with stages in social evolution. As we have seen, the adoption of sedentary village life made possible the development of architecture and other bulky, heavy types of product, such as wooden totem poles and stone statues. Other technical innovations have been more limited in direct effect to one or a few arts: for example, the development of the musical modes in antiquity. They serve to indicate stages or main periods in the history of one art, but these may not coincide with the main chronological divisions in other arts. Some great cultural break-throughs, such as the use of iron, occurred at very different dates in different parts of the world. The origin of spoken language, perhaps the most far-reaching step in all man's cultural evolution, must have occurred so long ago and so slowly that its dates and causes are conjectural. Others, such as the printing press and the motion picture camera, are recent historical events.

Many past innovations in technology have been described as revolutionary break-throughs. Some, like the domestication of animals and the invention of the steam engine, have led to vast increases in the human control of physical energy. They have led to far-reaching changes in mode of life, social organization, and culture in all fields. Some, such as steam power, have affected the arts only indirectly and generally; some, such as the smelting and casting of metals, have provided specific technics directly usable in one or more arts. Writing and the printing press are not exclusively artistic innovations, but have revolutionized literature and the graphic arts as well as other fields. By affecting many branches of culture at once, far-reaching inventions tend to produce new, contemporaneous stages in all of them. Science and industry entered a new era in many respects when printing was invented; so did fiction, pictorial engraving, and musical notation. All the arts were affected by it directly or indirectly, because of the wider distribution of books and articles on the arts and the consequent expansion of public knowledge.

As some inventions have led to revolutionary increases in the physical energy at man's disposal, others have led to similar ones in mental energy in art and elsewhere. The invention of writing made the recording and deferred communication of ideas possible; hence the cultural transmission of knowledge, skill, and verbal forms in art and science. Marked improvements in its efficiency, as in advancing from pictographic to alphabetic signs, are comparable to physical break-throughs like the control of water-power and electricity. They make possible, not only more communication and recording, but the expression of abstract, subtle, complex ideas, patterns and trains of thought, which could not be clearly expressed in sounds alone or pictorial images alone.

Each great invention or discovery marks the beginning of a new stage in certain respects. The stage may last indefinitely, as the age of writing has done, or come to an end if superseded by a more advanced one. The pictographic stage has ended on the whole, although pictographic symbols are still used for special purposes. Likewise the bronze age and the age of modal music have ended for the most part, although bronze and modes are still used in subordinate roles.

Among the important technical advances in the arts are some pertaining to types of form and developed components in it, rather than to materials and methods. They are culturally transmitted and can be taught to prospective artists, but are more broad and general than styles. Among these are key-relations and counterpoint in music, as well as the use of conventional patterns such as the fugue and sonata. Poetic technics include prosody or versification, comprising the use of meter, rhyme, stanza patterns, and conventional form-types such as the sonnet and rondeau. Painting technics include, not only the use of brushes, paints, and varnishes, but also perspective, color-harmony, etc.

The following are a few major technical and formal developments in various arts and in outside fields related to the arts. They are not listed in exact chronological order. The stages they define overlap greatly.

Literature: Oral: development of spoken languages; vocabulary, foundations of grammar and syntax; verse forms and developed components in form such as meter, quantitative and accentual rhythms, rhyme, alliteration. Preliterate origins of types such as wisdom literature, myths, proverbs, genealogies, odes, ballads, heroic tales.

Written: pictographs and ideographs, rebuses, syllabic and alphabetical characters; hieratic and demotic scripts. Reorganization and further development of all the foregoing types and others with the aid of writing and later of printing.

Music: Development of song and instrumental music into systematic scales, modes, keys, meters and rhythmic phrases; development of melody; homophonic and polyphonic composition; chord structure and chord progressions. Differentiation of conventional patterns such as hymns, dance music, war and work songs, triumphal and funeral marches, fugues and sonatas. Development of notation, including indications of phrasing, expression, nuances.

Architecture: Post and lintel construction; corbelled arch; true arch; the dome, without and with pendentives; barrel vaulting; ogive arches and ribbed vaults; stained glass windows; buttresses; trusses; cantilever construction; use of steel; reinforced concrete; curtain walls.

Sculpture: Clay shaping, cutting, drilling, and polishing wood, stone, and bone into small figures of animals and humans. From stylization and rigid frontality to a variety of active, realistic poses; development of anatomical realism and animated expression, including surface rendering of musculature. Development of technics in stone, bronze and other metals, polychromy on stone, wood and plaster. Sculpture as subordinate to architecture and as free-standing; relief and round.

Pictorial arts: Technical and formal developments in realistic and stylized, decorative drawing and painting. Use of various pigments and vehicles; earth-colors, chemicals; water-colors, tempera, fresco, encaustic, oils. Graphic arts of engraving, etching, lithography, etc., on paper. Painting on stone, wood, plaster, pottery, glass; enameling on metals. Invention of the camera and magic lantern; the motion-picture camera and projector. Development of photographic and cinematographic technics. Animated drawings and paintings in the cinema. Applications of photography in printing and graphic arts.

Specialists in any art tend to mark off historical divisions in it on the basis of the technical advances which interest them most; e.g., to speak of "the age of photography," "the atonal stage in music," etc. Obviously, such conceptions are much narrower in scope than those of general cultural stages such as "neolithic" or "barbarous." As the arts differentiate from each other, more and more such divisions in their history are made. Some of them coincide and others do not.

Rapid technical advances in several or all arts may occur at about the same time, because of some far-reaching discovery or invention in one field which sends them all ahead, suggesting specific applications in every field and giving rise to long trains of specialized invention. The Pythagorean discovery of the mathematical relation between the length of a string and its pitch was of this sort. Technical advance in many arts at once may also be due in part to a general rise in energy, wealth, power, and ambition, perhaps because of commercial, political, or military success. Prosperity may be shared in part with inventors, intellectuals, artists, craftsmen, and their patrons. A desire for change and improvement in every line is in the air. People take a new look at old, clumsy tools and methods and wonder how they could be more efficient. A mixture of peoples, with the attendant breakdown of old customs and beliefs, often helps to produce this state of mind.

On the other hand, one or more arts or types of art may go ahead much faster than others, passing through several stages while the latter remain static. Certain arts, such as small sculpture and wall painting, pottery and textiles, characteristically move ahead before others because they can be managed with simple technical skills and apparatus, as contrasted with symphonic and operatic music. Symbolic string figures on the hands were highly developed in some Pacific islands. A certain art or groups of arts may move ahead rapidly in a certain culture because it is given prerogative status there, as mosaic was in

Byzantine culture and stained glass in gothic.

A far-reaching social or political change usually tends to affect some arts adversely, others favorably. The victory of a new religion, as in its official adoption by a large state, has been a powerful stimulus to artistic imagination along many lines. It provides the material for iconography to the representational arts, visual and literary. It offers deities for worship in music and ritual: it calls for new kinds of temple and ceremonial utensil. This was true of the worship of Ra and of Ammon in Egypt, the short-lived cult of Aten, the introduction of the early Brahman pantheon in Vedic India, the systematization of Mediterranean polytheism in the pantheon of Olympus, and the development of Christian iconography after Constantine. Where the theology is explicitly monotheistic, an iconographic substitute can be provided by such means as the Trinity and hierarchies of angels and demons. Thus new religions, or great upheavals, schisms, and reforms in a single religion, can mark off stages and sequences in the arts through changes in their subject-matter, symbolic meanings, and ritual functioning.

On the other hand, each major social or intellectual change tends to downgrade certain arts and types of art, thus leading to their decline and marking the end of a stage in their career. The decline of hereditary aristocracy tended to demote heraldry and related types of art expressing genealogical relationships, as in tables of consanguinity and the Jesse Tree in medieval glass and painting. From being useful and emotionally important, they sink toward a level of merely casual interest; e.g., for decorative and sentimental values. Prestige and economic support to other arts, and with them go artistic leaders.

In the technical and conventionally formal aspects of art, the evolutionary tendency has been comparatively obvious and persistent. In every art, successive inventions have provided the artist with a more versatile set of tools, materials, and methods; a more varied set of patterns, to deal with the expanding world of human ex-perience, the expanding range of aesthetic tastes. While the order of inventions has differed somewhat in different places, it has normally followed the developmental path of persistent differentiation and integration: more possible effects, and more ways of interrelating them. When the advance has been stopped or radically deflected, this has usually been due to events outside the art itself.

4. STAGES AND SEQUENCES IN STYLE. POLARITIES, PENDULUM-SWINGS, ACCUMULATIONS

Stages and sequences in the arts are also marked off in terms of what we have called "recurrent stylistic types," such as classic and romantic. As we have seen, these concepts refer to analogies (a) among different arts of the same period and culture, as in romantic painting, poetry, and music of the early nineteenth century, and (b) among the arts of different periods and cultures, as in some kinds of ancient Roman, Chinese, and Indian sculpture. Such types are necessarily defined in terms of fewer traits than most period or individual styles, because fewer traits recur together in different periods. They are stylistic in referring primarily to the kind of product as a whole, rather than to materials, technics, or conventional framework-types such as "chair" or "portrait." But all these categories overlap and resist sharp definition.

A succession of stylistic types such as "archaic, classic, baroque," conceived as following one another more or less directly in a single culture, is a *stylistic type-sequence*. Hegel described one in his triad of "symbolic, classic, romantic." According to him, they were not recurrent or cyclical; each stood for one main stage in cultural history. Other theorists, as we have seen, maintain that certain sequences of stylistic types recur and must recur, since the life cycle of a style is analogous to that of a living organism. An archaic style would thus come at an early, childish or youthful period in the history of a style; a classic one in its maturity, and a baroque one in its approaching senescence and decline.

Some ambiguity arises in the fact that the same word, "style," is often used for a single stage (e.g., sixth-century, severe, black-figured style) and also for the history of the whole art or succession of period styles (e.g., of Greek vase-painting as a whole). When the cyclical theorists refer to the "life and death" of a style, they usually refer to the history of a whole art or branch of art in a certain culture, such as that of Greek tragedy. It might be clearer to refer to this as a *stylistic sequence, progression,* or *development*; i.e., a sequence of different but related styles such as those of Aeschylus, Sophocles, and Euripides. Each style in such a sequence, whether of an individual artist or a brief period, comprises a large number of traits. (Aristotle gives only a brief, partial description of them in the *Poetics*, as to the number of actors, chorus, and other technical means involved.) A *recurrent, stylistic type-sequence*, as we have just seen, could comprise only a few traits at each stage, since only a few could recur in many different contexts.

Kroeber[3] describes what he regards as the main sequence of stages in the life of a style; one which, he thinks, recurs in "many unconnected art styles." It begins with "crude stiffness or ineptitude at the emergence"; then follows "an archaic phase with form developing into definiteness but still rigid; then the freeing from archaism..." After full achievement, he says, comes a straining for effect, "flamboyant rococo," overexpressionism, ultrarealism or overornamentation, repetitive atrophy, and death of feeling in the style. After this, "the great arts soon wither away and have to begin all over again." This cycle, from archaic to rococo, he finds recurring in European sculpture and architecture; also in India, China, Egypt, and aboriginal Mexico, with analogies in painting, music, and literature.

Other historians would include a "geometric" type as almost universal in the neolithic stage of pottery and textiles. In the latter art, it is partly due to the ease of making rectilinear designs in weaving, as in American Indian blankets. But rectilinear and simple curves are common in early pottery and pictographs also. The stage after "archaic" is often called "classic" and defined as a balance between free-flowing, biomorphic shapes, expressing dynamic life, and more rigid geometrical frameworks, as in a Greek temple with pediment sculptures. It also strikes a balance between unity and multiplicity; between restrained simplicity and fullness of detail. This aspect of the classic is summarized in the Greek maxim, "Nothing too much."

After "classic," in this sense, some would place "baroque" and then "rococo." "Baroque" as a recurrent type connotes power, heaviness, swirling masses, exuberant ornamentation, irregularity and partial disbalance, a tendency to merge and blur the outlines of things in building up a unified form; a tendency to work up to strong climaxes. "Rococo," as we have seen, connotes an emphasis on lighter, smaller curves, light colors and gilt, fluffy and lacy ornamentation, asymmetrical compositions, suggestions of delicate feminine grace and luxury rather than of heavy power. After the rococo in Europe came the romantic style, which branched out in various ways. It included a regressive trend toward nature and primitive simplicity; an emphasis on impulse, emotion, and imagination instead of reason, freedom instead of unity and order. It often glorified the peasant, child, or noble savage. Another variety emphasized the heroic, exotic, medieval, passionate and grandiose.

After the romantic in European visual art came a rapid succession of overlapping styles such as naturalism, impressionism, fauvism, expressionism, post-impressionism, cubism, futurism, surrealism, and abstractionism. Some of these can be regarded as continuations of certain elements in romanticism; others as reversions to earlier

[3] *Style and Civilizations*, pp. 35 ff.

styles. According to the pessimistic, cyclical view this diversity indicates confusion, dissolution, and decadence. Others look on it as a period of constructive, multilinear experimentation. No one, specific style has taken the place of romanticism in scope and influence. "Eclecticism" and "experimentation" are general traits but not styles.

The history of European visual styles from the neolithic stage to the present can hardly be reduced to repetitions of Kroeber's triad, "archaic-classic-rococo." One would have to include at least three others: geometric, baroque, and romantic; perhaps also mannerist, naturalist, impressionist, expressionist, surrealist, cubist, and abstract or non-objective. Much would depend on how these styles are interrelated; e.g., are "romantic" and "impressionist" continuations of "baroque," as would appear from Wölfflin's definition of baroque, or distinct and independent? What should be done with "Byzantine" in such a sequence? Is it a separate art or style with a "life" of its own and hence an archaic, classic, and rococo stage? Or is it a regression from Roman classicism to oriental archaism, with decorative enrichments?

Greek visual art from the neolithic through the Hellenistic periods displays a fairly definite sequence from geometric and archaic to classic and baroque. There are hints of romanticism in Hellenistic and Roman pastoral poetry and of baroque exuberance in imperial Roman architecture and sculpture.

Geometric and archaic styles abound in all art-producing cultures, but fully developed classic and baroque styles are more limited, as one might expect, to advanced civilizations such as those of Persia, India, China, and Japan. There, one can find occasional recurrences of Kroeber's three-stage sequence, preceded by "geometric" to make a four-stage one. After and along with these, there is much confusion and merging of styles through conquest, the rise and fall of dynasties, migrations of peoples, religious conversions, and other external causes. Peoples and styles like the Scythian flash out into history for a while, then disappear without extended growth.

As to the history of extensive styles, investigation has not confirmed the organismic theory of definite cyclical growth and decline. It is certainly not proven that rococo or romantic style is necessarily followed by decline and death.

An alternative hypothesis is possible. This is, that the recurrent sequence from geometric to rococo is more like the repeated attempt of men in different places to build a house of many floors. They build from the basement up through one, two, or three stories, only to have the building collapse through internal weakness or outside pressure. Sometimes the building stands a while, but the supply of materials is exhausted and nothing very new can be added. In contemporary civilization, the arts have kept on trying to go beyond the rococo and romantic, but with such different materials and forms that no strong construction of higher levels has yet been achieved. The upper floors may crash again, so that art must begin again farther down; or the storms may be weathered and further floors be raised with strong, new methods.

This hypothesis implies that there is something necessary in the sequence of stages. One does not have to accept the organismic theory in full, or any rigid determinism, to grant that some kinds of art must come before others if any growth is to occur. This is true in all the arts as it is in science and social organization. On the whole, though not always, the simple, easy, and undifferentiated must come before the complex, difficult, and specialized. Regressive movements to simplicity are exceptions. They do not affect the general rule that art in its early stages must proceed in evolutionary sequence. The foundations and walls must come before the roof; simple tunes and drum-beats come before symphonies, and folk-tales before novels. The rudiments of a style must come before its complex and varied fulfilments, as the beginnings of a spinal cord preceded the diversity of complex vertebrate types. The rudiments of Bach's polyphony are to be found in the slow separation of voices in late Gregorian music.

It is the earliest sequences of cultural history that seem most necessary and, accordingly, most unilinear. Man must first develop the prerequisites for all advanced art and culture, such as oral and written language, musical instruments with variable pitch, and the ability to draw, carve, or model a definite shape. He can then go on to modern complexities. By the same token, prehistoric sequences appear to be less dissimilar throughout the world than modern civilized ones. The diversities which anthropologists emphasize (such as those in primitive kinship and drawing) seem few and slight by contrast with those in the arts of advanced civilizations. As man accumulates more civilized technics and styles, he has an increasing range of possible choices. The sequence of steps in art becomes less necessary and less uniform; increasingly optional and subject to variation in different environments. Having invented a workable language, one can do any of a great number of things with it. Each technical advance opens up another wide range of alternatives.

The gradual separation of art from religion, politics, and utilitarian technology has freed it in certain respects, and thus further increased the possibility of variation among artists and local styles. Cut off from their former roots in basic need and collective ideology, cultivated more for aesthetic and hedonic values, the arts are let loose to float about more freely in the shifting winds of taste and doctrine. The sequences of styles are no longer held in step with changes in other cultural components. Increasing diversity results.

The early stages of culture and of art were more liable to disastrous breaks. Less of what had been achieved was safely recorded. The loss of a single library, a single manuscript, or even of one man's skill and memory, could destroy the previous work of centuries. Small wonder that early history seems a perpetual round of cultural deaths and new beginnings. Men can kill each other today

on a larger scale, but it is harder than ever to destroy the inanimate products and records of civilization, and thus to drive art back to new beginnings.

The sequence of stages was not rigidly compulsory, even in prehistoric times. No one knows yet what the exact sequence was in paleolithic painting: whether or not the developed archaic style of the Lascaux cave was preceded by a quasi-geometric style, now lost. What necessity there is in the sequence of styles depends on the nature of all mental growth; that in each step ahead we utilize some of what we learned before. Developed archaic drawing of a realistic type does not necessarily presuppose an earlier stage of precise geometric drawing, or vice versa. It seems more likely that a comparatively undifferentiated type, rougher and simpler, preceded both.

There is a real difference between styles which tend toward emotional exuberance, with expressions of dynamic energy, power, and grandeur, and those which do not. On the whole, baroque is of the former type, as in Milton, Rubens, and the church of Sta. Maria della Salute. "Classic" forms tend to be more restrained; archaic and geometric, still more so. Precise geometric design suggests extreme, tight control. On a primitive level, it suggests the delight of early craftsmen in regular patterns. On a modern level, it suggests rational order and scientific measurement. The sequence from primitive geometric to baroque and romantic involved, on the whole, increasing power to express active human life, will, and emotion.

Instead of regarding baroque and rococo as essentially decadent or senile, it would be more accurate to say that *any* style, any stage in a sequence of styles, may become so. It becomes so when it is practiced without imagination and inventive power, becoming a monotonous, mechanical repetition of established formulas. A work in any style can suffer from a deficiency of expected values, or can expand and multiply details beyond control.

Inasmuch as baroque tends to emphasize multiplicity and complexity, exuberance, power, and grandeur, it is subject to the same fate as other stylistic types: namely, that people eventually tire of it and want the opposite. What had seemed majestically grand comes to seem grandiose, bombastic; what had seemed magnificent seems vulgarly ornate, pompous, ostentatious. By the same token, what had seemed bare and empty, tight and cold in the early stage now comes to seem admirably restrained, austere, and economical.

Such fluctuations in taste influence trends in art and are influenced by them. They are related to the alternating movements, the recurrent "pendulum-swings" in art history which various writers have described in such terms as Apollonian-Dionysian, classic-romantic, and ethos-pathos. This alternation is irregular and varied, involving such component polarities as reason-emotion, science-art, unity-multiplicity, order-freedom, and simplicity-complexity. It is related to the sequence of stylistic types in that baroque and romantic types often incline toward the Dionysian through emphasizing emotional expression, while classic, archaic, and geometric types often emphasize (or seem at the time to emphasize) Apollonian order and clarity. The opposition between these various polarities contributes to the multiple dialectic of cultural history. While one type is ascendant or at its crest, the climate of taste is correspondingly unfavorable to the opposite type.

Such trends seldom embrace the whole culture. They do not involve all the arts, or all factions within a given art, to the same extent at the same time. Some arts will be conservative, resistant, as architecture was toward romanticism. Within each art there is an increasing differentiation of factions: conservative and radical, academic and avant-garde; élite or intellectual, "high-brow" or "long-haired" and popular; adult, adolescent, and juvenile.

In summarizing major trends such as romanticism, one is tempted to oversimplify them as involving simultaneous, concurrent trends along many lines. Thus one may oversimplify the "pendulum-swing" of stylistic change, as if the shift in all polarities occurred together. A romantic trend of taste toward freedom, emotion, and irregularity is combined in some artists with a swing toward naïve, simple unity (in the lyrics of Heine, for example); in others such as Wagner and Hugo, with a swing toward complexity and multiplicity. The escape from neo-classical rules can lead some to liberal democracy (Shelley, Whitman) and others to reactionary medievalism (de Bonald, de Maistre). What seems at first view to be a single, whole-culture pendulum-swing discloses many partly independent, uncoordinated swings within it.

The "pendulum" figure is oversimplified in another way. As we have previously noted, art never goes back to exactly its previous condition. Elements accumulate form one swing to the next, and evolutionary changes intervene to make the swing a zigzag progression.

In the visual arts of early civilizations, the sequence from geometric to archaic to classic to baroque is basically evolutionary in that it involves, on the whole, increasing complexity of form and mental content. It tries to integrate an increasing variety of shapes: from straight lines, angles, and simple arcs to more and more irregular, free-flowing curves; from flat areas to modeled masses and deep vistas; from plain colors to richer textures and atmospheric lighting; from abstract patterns to realistic and fantastic representation in great detail. Geometric and archaic styles are, on the whole, simpler than classic and baroque ones, having fewer details and fewer developed components. This is not true in every case. Forms can be complicated indefinitely within the limits of geometric or archaic style, by the multiplication and interweaving of straight lines and simple curves. But the usual tendency, in a dynamic and long-lived culture, is to pass on to different, more flexible types of form after attaining some proficiency in the simpler ones. As mind and culture evolve in other fields, with diversified activities, experiences, and desires, they call for new styles, more capable of expressing and satisfying them. Greek vase-painting did so, instead of staying forever on the geometric or archaic level, trying to complicate its patterns indefinitely. The same thing happened in social organization: tribal complexities eventually gave way to a new, more flexible kind of social life permitting more varied activity and experience. Neither geometric nor archaic drawing, nor rigidly frontal sculpture, is adequate to express the interest of a maturing civilization in the rich variety of natural forms and human feelings. They had to give way to the classic and baroque for a while, but not necessarily forever.

Regressions from the classic and baroque to the geometric and archaic, or revivals of the latter, often occur as we have noted. The regression or revival is never complete and cannot be so when accumulated traditions remain. A geometric or archaic form produced after the classic stage has been reached is very different from a really primitive example. To go from baroque to geometric is not as devolutionary as it may seem. We have noticed in previous chapters how it may be, in part, an attempt to recapture lost values and exploit abandoned resources; to revive the earlier type in addition to the later one. This is, or can be, also evolutionary.

The possibilities of geometric and archaic style had not been exhausted when Greek artists moved on to the classic stage. Much primitive geometric and archaic had been stiff, clumsy, and groping. It was possible, after a few centuries of illusionistic realism, to realize that some interesting things could still be done in the older types of form. One could return to complicate a geometric or archaic style indefinitely. In some cultures a further motive for such regression was supplied by a mystical religious trend or a taboo on realistic representation. Islamic Egyptian surface carving on wooden doors and wall decoration achieved a high degree of complexity along purely geometric lines. Byzantine paintings and mosaics have many archaic

traits of drawing and modeling along with high complexity of decorative design. Both of these were, in part, conscious, voluntary regressions from the realistic, three-dimensional classic and baroque of the early Roman Empire.

In recent times, we have had several examples of a voluntary return to the geometric and archaic. Picasso has done both. After the softness of impressionist painting, Cézanne led a movement back to the solid designs of the neo-classical masters, especially Poussin and Raphael, while retaining impressionist color. Later generations went on to cubist and other geometrical abstractions, including the flat, rectilinear designs of Mondrian. This was a more drastic regression, but it was also inspired by current factors: at times by an admiration for science and machine forms, as in Léger; at times by primitive Negro sculpture with its quasi-geometrical solids. At times it was inspired by a scientific interest in optical analysis (as in Braque) or in solid geometry (as in Naum Gabo and Antoine Pevsner). In all such cases, the regression to an earlier stage is only partial and superficial; the attitude and motive of the artist are different, and so are the meanings of the forms produced. The modern artist, working in a geometrical or archaic idiom, has a sophisticated background of knowledge and comparison with many other, later styles which he is consciously avoiding for the moment. He revives the primitive and at the same time transforms it into something essentially modern, a part of his own civilization. He can also experiment with neo-classic, neo-baroque, and neo-rococo styles. A Picasso or Stravinsky uses any or all of these at will, as optional resources in a cumulative art.

5. DIALECTICAL INTERACTIONS AMONG THE ARTS.
INCREASING MULTILINEAR DIFFERENTIATION AMONG STAGES AND SEQUENCES

Some of these trends and countertrends, progressions and regressions, occur in several arts at the same time; some in one only. Different arts can move in opposite directions in certain respects. This complicates the relations among the arts and increases the diversity of an epoch. It prevents the stages and sequences in various arts from coinciding completely with each other or with those in other cultural components. It thus diversifies and sometimes obscures the main evolutionary trend.

When a certain style such as romanticism extends widely through culture at a certain time, it gives some consistency to the age, though never completely. A similar effect can occur through comparative harmony between church and state, art and science, economic and other cultural components.

Consistency can be further heightened by the influence of one art on another. The interlacing forms characteristic of basketry, cordwork, and weaving are imitated in painted pottery and manuscript illumination. A prerogative art, as style leader, often influences minor ones. Thus Renaissance painting influenced stained glass and tapestry. Poetry has imitated musical forms and vice versa. This is sometimes acknowledged in the titles of the works. (E.g., Chopin's *Ballades*; Conrad Aiken's poems, "Variations" and "Improvisations"; Amy Lowell's "Music").

Such *rapprochements* between the arts in modern times are often partial and short-lived. Each art eventually discovers the disadvantages of trying to follow another art closely. Stained glass and tapestry found that they had sacrificed much of their effectiveness in color-design, while failing to rival painting in realism. In recent years they have moved away from Renaissance pictorial style and back to their own earlier traditions. In the meantime, painting has also moved away from the Renaissance tradition, and in some cases (such as Rouault) has imitated stained glass. Such attractions and repulsions still continue, with occasional syntheses like Matisse's chapel at Vence. It combines distinctive traits of both stained glass and painting in a unifying decorative and symbolic style.

It was mentioned above that stages in the history of styles do not correspond exactly with those in the history of artistic technics. We have just been considering some of their apparently cyclical aspects. Anti-evolutionists exaggerate this difference in denying all cumulative evolution to style and thus to the "essentials" of art. There is some correspondence, and both types of sequence fit into the larger process of artistic and cultural evolution. But there is a real difference which arises from the nature of styles and of creative artistry.

Great technical advances in the arts are not necessarily made by great artists, or by artists at all. They are often by engineers, technologists, or inventors in other fields, such as Gutenberg and Edison, whose inventions incidentally turn out to be useful and perhaps revolutionary in the arts. Sometimes they are made by humble, anonymous craftsmen working along with master artists. Of this type, perhaps, were the unknown inventors of the lyre and flute, attributed by legend to the gods, and those of lost-wax casting, fresco and tempera painting, the arch and dome; the ode and epic—often mistakenly assigned to some great artist who merely utilized them. This is true of the formal components and conventional framework patterns in any art, such as counterpoint and fugue in music. One does not have to be an artist, in the full sense of the word, to invent or improve them. Great artists seldom invent them, although they sometimes receive the credit for doing so. They are often quick to utilize new forms and technics, which they proceed to fill out with images and meanings, endow with unsuspected potentialities, vary with surprising nuances, and enrich with original details. Some artist-inventors, such as Walt Disney, have done both. They have pioneered along technical and formal lines, but filled them out with specific details of form and meaning, not necessarily great. They are often followed by greater artists who work along the lines thus indicated. All belong to one total cultural evolution. Giotto could not have achieved what he did without the invention of fresco painting, or Beethoven without notation and the instruments of the orchestra.

As we have seen, the evolution of the arts has included increasing differentiation in many respects: e.g., as occupations, technics, forms, and details within forms. Nationalism and the use of vernacular languages instead of Latin for scholarly writing tended to differentiate the European literatures, but at the same time to release local resources and stimulate national types of cultural integration. Artistic differentiation along many lines continues at an accelerating rate.

Western culture has given the arts and individual artists increasing freedom to follow their own autonomous impulses; it has freed them from the obligation to follow uncongenial styles. It has not, so far, provided them with any one conscious, explicit, convincing world-view or new set of aims and value-standards. One result has been to increase the dialectical interaction *among the arts*. It was less developed in a comparatively homogeneous, unified age such as that of Pericles' Athens or Hadrian's Rome, although such ages were less unified than is often supposed. The dialectic is not only between styles and aesthetic principles —e.g., classic and romantic or liberal and Marxist—but also between stylistic tendencies in various arts.

The arts have never, in advanced cultures, followed any one stylistic trend in the same way or to an equal extent. This is impossible because of their increasingly different materials, forms, and functions. In the romantic period, garden and landscape design accepted and fulfilled the prevailing trend much more than architecture did, partly because architecture is forced by human

requirements to be largely geometrical. Its floors and ceilings must be mostly flat and horizontal, its walls mostly vertical, or people will be dizzy and uncomfortable within it. (Minor exceptions are in amusement parks where houses are deliberately put askew or upside down for the fun of temporary visitors. Thatched roofs and neogothic details are also minor concessions to romanticism.) Architecture tended in its main concerns to resist and oppose the romantic movement, or at least to lag behind other arts in following it. As Hegel rightly perceived, music and poetry, as arts of time and motion suited to express the evanescent subtleties of will and feeling, are far removed from architecture. In being essentially "frozen," so that men can move about in it securely, architecture cannot follow very far a trend toward instability and evanescence. It must resist such trends as the "stream of thought" technique in Proust and other twentieth-century novelists. Gaudi's strangely melting architecture in the *Sagrada Familia* in Barcelona is an exceptional tour de force.

The perennial gulf between the arts of rest and the arts of movement has, at the same time, been ingeniously bridged over in several ways. Besides the motion picture, which has given life to painting, the twentieth century has given prerogative status to the arts of transportation. Automobiles, trailers, sleeping cars, passenger ships, and airplanes are, to some extent, mobile architecture. The geometrical house and the picturesque garden have been joined in a complementary synthesis. This eighteenth-century combination, like the picturesque garden itself, was heavily indebted to Japanese and Chinese traditions, which were strong in Europe in the eighteenth century. Geometric, "formal" gardens still remain, but the tendency is strong to soften hard building-lines with irregular soft, green foliage. In recent years domestic architecture has made a further effort to integrate house and garden by glass walls, covered patios, and indoor conservatories.

Other examples of this interaction are numerous

but often short-lived. Notwithstanding Pater's dictum that all arts aspire toward the condition of music, it is not always clear what the condition or aspiration of music is. Romantic music tended toward the programmatic and often toward the descriptive or narrative, as in Berlioz and Wagner. Brahms and others, while somewhat romantic, moved back toward non-representational formalism; an emphasis on thematic design in music. But the programmatic type persisted in Debussy and Stravinsky. Avant-garde painting joined "pure music" in the trend away from so-called "literary values"—i.e., from emphasis on representation. But meanwhile, the newer pictorial media such as photography, cinema, and television, remained in general stubbornly realistic, with strong emphasis on subject-matter and action. Avant-garde trends in these arts toward formalism and abstraction have not been as influential as in painting and sculpture. As photography provided an easier, cheaper means of realism in pictures, painting has moved away from realism; for how long, no one can predict. As the film has emphasized action, some types of literature have tried to get along without it, as in certain examples of existentialist drama and fiction. Literature has tried without much success, along the lines of Gertrude Stein, to develop word-patterns apart from definite meanings, thus approximating "pure" music and painting. Painting and music fell into step for a moment in French impressionism; but many composers have tired of suggesting moods and pictures. Instead, Prokofieff and Stravinsky often try to exploit the distinctive qualities of a given musical medium, such as the percussive nature of the piano. This takes them far away from the gentle, rippling arpeggios of musical impressionism. Mary Wigman tried to free the dance from the domination of music.

Thus whole arts as well as styles and particular artists move at times in opposite directions, at times toward partial syntheses. Certain arts feel at times sympathetic, disposed to cooperate toward similar effects or even in a single work, as in opera and sound-film. At other times they, or individual leaders in them, scorn such resemblance and cooperation. Heightened egotism in the artist, or a craving for complete, original uniqueness, can increase the tendency toward separatism among the arts.

One result of this dialectic is to dislocate still further the sequences in style within the various arts. The more they try to fly apart from each other, the more they cease, for a time at least, to follow analogous series of steps or to produce in similar styles at any one time. While a regressive, back-to-the-primitive movement is in vogue in one (e.g., in Gauguin and Modigliani), a new flowering of the neo-classical tradition appears in Renoir and Seurat and a gothic revival in Rouault. The prerogative arts just mentioned—vehicle design and cinema—shoot ahead of the others with rapid technical improvements and experiments in form. Like architecture and city-planning, however, they are restrained by a host of economic and other outside considerations from evolving as fast along artistic lines as they wish to do. Others, such as poetry, remain in placid, rather neglected backwaters; holding some prestige from the past but slower to develop new types and styles.

The many diverse and short-lived movements in the arts today, the frequent, radical changes in trend, the fluttering attractions and repulsions among arts and factions, present an unusual phenomenon in cultural history and one which is difficult to chart. It is, no doubt, related to the pervasive contemporary mood of nervous, anxious uncertainty. It may decrease as political stability is restored. Meanwhile, unifying trends are not lacking. We have noted them in extensive styles, common themes, cooperative projects, and the decrease of petty sectionalism. Educational, historical, and theoretical studies help to interrelate the arts. Similar trends in future, through cultural interchange and cooperation on a larger scale, may tend to bring the arts somewhat more into step with each other and with the rest of cultural evolution.

But the dialectical rhythm of thesis, antithesis, and temporary synthesis is too integral a part of cultural evolution to be entirely eliminated. It is distinctively human and cultural, since it depends on preserving and transmitting selected elements from all previous stages. Only through vigorous opposition and competition, experimenting with extremes along many lines as well as with the golden mean, can art explore the potential values of every kind of art, experience, and style.

6. SUMMARY

Cultural evolution is "dialectical" in a sense broader than that used by Hegel or Marx. In addition to sequences of change in the same direction, it includes many examples of conflict followed by partial synthesis. Some of these are obviously related to socio-economic and ideological alignments; others are not. Many are concerned, at least on the conscious, explicit level, with more purely aesthetic disputes about content, form, and style. Such conflicts are often expressed as issues between rival movements, aims, and value-standards. What seems like a steady progression may involve a series of compromises between opposing pressures. Issues are not always promptly settled by a moderate compromise along the middle of the road. Each extreme course tends to beget its opposite, as Hegel asserted, but this may be long delayed. The opposition is not necessarily a simple antithesis: many rival alternatives may compete.

Art often takes sides in moral and social conflicts. It can also help one to decide them consciously and rationally by dramatizing them in concrete examples. Continued struggle and partial compromise may go on for many centuries in the same civilization without final resolution. One example is the persistent conflict between the mystic-religious and the naturalistic-humanistic traditions in Western civilization.

Fairly well-marked stages may occur in the technical and formal development of a particular art, but those in various arts do not always coincide. The arts often change in different directions and at different speeds. Major events in other cultural realms may have a different effect on different arts, exalting some and depressing others.

Recurrent pendulum-swings in various arts, such as that between the classic and romantic spirit, do not always occur simultaneously. A trend in one art may stimulate an opposite, compensatory trend in other arts. No one universal, necessary sequence of stages in style has yet appeared. The diversity of trends and counter-trends in the arts is at present increasing and accelerating.

CHAPTER XXIV

CAUSATION, SELECTION,
AND CONTROL

1. WHAT CAUSES CREATIVE EPOCHS
IN THE ARTS?

What can cause a nation or other social group to blossom out into a period of brilliant creativity in art and other fields? In addition to its theoretical interest, no question in the philosophy of history is more important from the standpoint of possible control. If we knew what caused creative epochs, we might find out whether anything could be done to stimulate them by providing the necessary preconditions. Could this be done, for example, by changes in social and economic structure, by generous subsidies to artists, by better methods of education, or in some other way? We have too little knowledge to be confident of any specific explanation. But at least we can analyze the problem and consider some possible causes.

That some peoples and some periods in their history have been more creative in the arts than others is not disputed. Egypt, Sumeria, Greece, Rome, India, China, Japan, Persia, the Mayans, modern Europe—these are a few of the names which come at once to mind. Only in certain periods of their history have they produced notable galaxies of great artists and original styles of art. At other times, and in much of the earth at all times, historians of art find little of importance to record. Some peoples, such as the Chinese, have had several periods of artistic flowering; others, like the Dutch, have had one main period which overshadows all the rest.

Various problems of explanation arise in studying them. What can cause one group to have a persistent, over-all superiority in artistic production over many others? What causes some to be relatively unproductive, static, or imitative in art throughout their history? In a previously undistinguished group, what can cause a short, intense burst of artistic creation?

These questions are analogous to others which arise in evolutionary theory. What causes the obvious difference in creative ability among individuals in the same ethnic or political group at the same time? In organic evolution, what causes certain types of life to be intensely active and successful at a certain time, radiating over large parts of the earth and in many varieties? (For example, the reptiles in the Jurassic and mammals in the Cretaceous period?) Why do these types often relapse into a static, subordinate position? Are genetic or environmental factors chiefly responsible?

Much remains to be done in describing the peaks of artistic evolution, the depressions which surround them, and other phenomena correlated with them. It seems obvious that evolution in art has proceeded at very different rates of speed, not only among different peoples, but within the same people at different times. Just how uneven it is has not been definitely ascertained. There have been times when momentous cultural developments occurred in many widely separate parts of the earth at about the same time—notably the moral, religious, and philosophical movements of about 600 B.C. This is used as an argument for immanent determinism; but perhaps there are better explanations, or at least other, contributing causes. In any case, we need to chart more accurately the geographical and chronological distribution of such spurts in cultural advance, before we can hope to explain them specifically.

The fact of difference in creativity among peoples and periods has long been recognized. The ancient theory of man's degeneration from a Golden Age included an extreme veneration for Homer and for even more legendary founders of the arts. Hebrew culture looked back to the glories of Solomon's temple and the Psalms of David. In the Renaissance, the classical Greeks and Romans were themselves put on a pedestal as unsurpassable. They are still respected highly, though perhaps a little less than in the fifteenth century; as great artists, but not the only ones or in all respects the greatest. Today, we tend to one extreme or the other. Some critics and historians praise the recent art of their own localities in rhapsodic terms; others despise it. Modern taste, including that of experts, is fickle and divided. It inclines to frequent changes in judging artists, styles, and periods. Since the question is largely one of value, as to which ones were really great or creative in a eulogistic sense, it can hardly be answered quite objectively. There is a fair amount of agreement among experts at any one time and place, but the consensus differs considerably from one country and generation to another. However objective they try to be, critics in each nation tend to magnify the role of that country, its artists and creative epochs, in the history of world art.

On the whole, the list of epochs and individuals recognized as great in art has grown steadily during the past few centuries. The late nineteenth-century tendency to admire the arts of primitive cultures has extended ever more widely. Instead of limiting the list to the familiar Mediterranean and European sequences, historians now include such peoples as the African Bushmen, the Negroes of West Central Africa, the Melanesians and Australian Aborigines; also the early urban cultures of the Indus and Tigris-Euphrates valleys, the Mayan, Inca, and pre-Inca cultures of the Western Hemisphere. Even in regard to Egypt, Greece, India, and China, long known for the works of their late and "classical" periods, more respect has been paid to their archaic styles, as in Shang Dynasty China, Minoan Crete, and the Mycenean mainland. The result, while not detracting from the merit of the well-known classical epochs, has been to show that these were not as rare or as completely original as had been supposed. They were often the culmination of long, gradual developments. As in the case of individual genius, the mystic-romantic theory of creative ability as a sudden flash from heaven has lost ground in explaining social genius. Such ability now seems more widespread, less limited to any short list of "superior races." As we rediscover and learn to appreciate the arts of primitive peoples and distant cultures, we find more kinds of creativity, more outlets and expressions of it, than we had known before.

In praising the art of primitives and children, some enthusiasts have used the terms "creative" and "genius" much too loosely. Genius in art is not the same as high I.Q., as measured by our present intelligence tests. Not all spontaneous expressions in an art medium, all childish tunes or scribbles, deserve to be called "creative" in the strict sense. We shall limit the term in this discussion to persons and products which are thought to be important as well as original; to contribute something of potentially enduring value to the world's artistic heritage. The lists made up by contemporary Western historians and critics naturally reflect their own personal and cultural standards. Many nations and individuals, proud and famous for their art at the time, are not so rated now. In order to be ranked today as great, an age must have produced a large amount of art which can hold the high esteem of connoisseurs in later times and other places.

The changing value-standards used by historians, often more or less unconsciously, lead to different judgments as to which periods, cultures, styles, and individuals are outstanding in each art; also as to where the peaks and depressions lie chronologically. Even when the writer makes considerable use of statistical and other scientific methods, personal opinions enter. A. L. Kroeber makes the very debatable assertion that "Modern philosophy reached its zenith with Kant." If one writer sees only a decline in philosophy and art where others see the rise of new, important patterns, their description of "florescent periods," growths and dissolutions, will differ widely. "All European fine arts since about 1880," Kroeber continues, "and more strongly since 1900, have displayed increasing symptoms of what may be called pattern dissolution: jagged rhythms and dissonance in music, free verse in poetry, plotless novels, cubism, abstractionism, and surrealism in sculpture and painting." "Modern painting," he says, culminates with men born about 1790 to 1830."[1] Obviously, any generalization on this basis about the "configurations of culture growth" in modern Europe is debatable.

Kroeber exhibits here the common difficulty of laymen, and of some professionals, in perceiving the new patterns which develop at the expense of older ones. Having formed a narrow taste for certain ones, they notice only the loss of these, the negative aspects of art history; not the unfamiliar forms toward which art is groping. Even the artists who are developing these are sometimes more conscious of what they are rejecting as obsolete than of what they are putting in its place.

The positive side of early twentieth-century painting should now be obvious, including the new patterns in the abstractions of Kandinsky, the cubism of Picasso and Braque. The use of jagged visual forms, jagged rhythms and dissonances, free verse and plotless fiction is not necessarily a mere dissolution. It may be so at times, but it is not so in recent art as a whole. Out of these ingredients, new styles are being made. In philosophy, some

very important developments occurred after Kant. These were not all, like the philosophy of Hegel, along the idealistic lines to which Kant pointed. Some belonged to the traditions of empiricism, naturalism, and pragmatism from Comte to Dewey, Santayana, and Russell.

One's definitions of the fields, activities, or cultural components also affect one's description of the facts. Here, too, Kroeber's ideas were in some respects narrow and restrictive. "Sculpture," he said, "represents objects in nature simply and directly" (p. 781). This excludes or misinterprets all abstract or highly stylized sculpture, including the primitive and archaic. Philosophy, he added, deals primarily with "problems of human existence and the psyche, science with the world outside man" (p. 782). This ignores the whole line of philosophers since Thales who have dealt with problems of the outside world, and of scientists who have dealt with man. Philosophy, said Kroeber, aims "to build up a system of related ideas as such, with only secondary reference to factual observation" (p. 98). "Excluded from consideration" as sciences, in Kroeber's view, are history and "the so-called social sciences" (p. 100). These narrow, inadequate conceptions of the major cultural fields led Kroeber to correspondingly inadequate lists of great individuals and productions in every field.

Notwithstanding these weaknesses, however, Kroeber succeeds in establishing some interesting theses. These are: that cultural growth usually comes in concentrated bursts or constellations, with many geniuses at about the same place and time; that some isolated cases occur, but as rare exceptions; that such florescences may or may not occur in many different activities at about the same time; that no one activity is a necessary, universal part of the florescence; that there is no genuine law or regular order in the growth of various activities, although some, such as sculpture, tend to come early in a culture while others, such as

[1] *Configurations of Culture Growth* (Berkeley, Calif., 1944), pp. 764, 780.

science and the novel, tend to come fairly late. The former deal with simpler materials and ideas; the latter presuppose more previous intellectual and social development.

Kroeber adds that cultural flowering proceeds as a gradual realization of certain patterns, peculiar to each culture. (In this he follows Spengler.) The development of a set of patterns may come in several steps, with less active intervals between them. A small civilization, population, or territory may have a brief growth and decline in which it works out a set of culture patterns in conformity with the culture content (p. 798). A larger one, as in China, may bring one set of patterns to high pitch, then disrupt it and begin a new one after receiving a mass of new material. China did so after the introduction of Buddhism, and achieved anew culmination during the first two T'ang centuries. Something similar happened in India (p. 798). After organizing all its material into patterns, says Kroeber, the culture may become exhausted and die.

He carefully disclaims any effort at ultimate or general causal explanation; especially in terms of any one factor. But some of his statements have significant causal implications. Geniuses, he says (p. 839), are not only persons with eminently superior mental endowment; they are also the "indicators of the realization of coherent pattern growths of cultural value." "Most of the potential geniuses born are never realized," he says, "so far as history or human values are concerned." (Taine had advanced a similar idea.) "The supply of genius," Kroeber continues, "physiologically or psychologically speaking, ought to remain essentially constant in any one race within any period which is not unduly long." This hypothesis, that each race produces a constant supply of potential geniuses, is highly speculative. It could hardly be otherwise considering the evaluative conception of genius and the fact that we have no way of recognizing or counting potential geniuses. It is reasonable, but does not exclude the possibility of differences in the birth rate of potential geniuses

as between various places, peoples, and periods.

In any case, to assume a constant supply of potentially great artists throws no light on why a certain group of them are able to realize their innate capacities at a certain time and place. To approach an explanation, we need some differential factor which may, conceivably, operate or become effective only before and during a particular creative wave. Neither Spencer nor Taine, nor any of the unilinear evolutionists, offers much help in this connection. The organismic theory, toward which Kroeber inclines, claims to do so by analogy with cyclical growth, maturity, and decline in a single plant or animal. The rise and fall of each civilization as a whole is so explained; also the sequence of particular styles and stages in each; some as belonging to the springtime, others to the fall or winter of the civilization. This theory is not convincing to philosophic naturalists because of its tendency to mystical vitalism. It does not fully demonstrate the cyclical character of cultural growths or explain in naturalistic terms how they can really have any such life of their own. It does not explain the pre-eminence of certain groups within the civilization.

Marxism offers its dialectical theory of successive revolutions, with power and wealth passing in each from a small class of exploiters to a larger, previously exploited class. Each revolution would release hitherto inhibited energies and inventive powers as well as providing the material means for increased art production. This does suggest a naturalistic, differential factor and a partial explanation; but not one which Western scholars regard as adequate. Social revolutions can be a contributing cause though not the main one. Many revolutions have not been followed by creative waves, and many creative waves have not followed revolutions.

Kroeber's theory owes much to both Taine and Spengler. He points to the cultural situation (the milieu and moment, as Taine would say) as the active agency in selecting which potential geniuses shall come to fruition. More potential geniuses must have been "inhibited by the cultural situations into which they were born than have been developed by other cultural situations" (p. 840). Within these situations, the important factors are certain "high-value culture patterns" in various activities including art. Within a given group, a certain pattern gradually develops, being indicated and developed by early geniuses. It tends to eliminate some later, potential geniuses, presumably because they would not or could not fit into it, while favoring others more adaptable to that particular pattern.

How this selective process operates is an important question which Kroeber does not pursue. To say that some individuals are innately adapted to a certain culture-pattern and others not would imply a rather specific, rigid predisposition on the part of each individual, so that he could not be conditioned by the culture along any other line. This would be denied by psychologists who stress the power of conditioning. But broader kinds of environmental selection certainly occur: first, when opportunities for development in art are restricted by a rigid, hierarchical system to a very few; second, when the culture is unfavorable to certain kinds of art in general—e.g., to painting, so that a child with pictorial aptitude has no outlet for it.

How and why the group gets started on a particular line of pattern-formation, Kroeber does not say. But his way of describing the process brings him close to Spengler, for whom he has both good and bad to say. He often speaks as if the pattern had a life and power of its own, and fails to indicate how literally he means it. Patterns, he says, "begin to select, early in their formation"; they "commit themselves to certain specializations and exclude others" (p. 763). The selected pattern "tends to develop cumulatively, in the direction in which it first differentiated, by a sort of momentum." It may explore new opportunities lying in its path, but has fulfilled itself when these have been exhausted (p. 763).

Kroeber does not try to prove this explanation, but takes it for granted in case after case. For

instance, "the pattern possibilities of the Goethe and Beethoven configurations are obviously exhausted" (p. 765). This sounds plausible at first, since obviously no later, first-class genius has actually created in exactly the same patterns. Twentieth-century ones are very different. But in terms of stylistic morphology, the patterns of Goethe and Beethoven are still theoretically capable of endless variation and development. Brahms continued some pattern-traits of Beethoven, together with some from later romanticists and others of his own. At the time of Giotto, and still more at the fall of Constantinople, one might have thought the Byzantine style of painting exhausted. El Greco showed that it was not, and it went on to new developments in Russia, Jugoslavia, and Greece well into the twentieth century.

In this sense, no major, complex style ever becomes exhausted. Gothic architecture, impressionist painting, polyphonic music—all contain infinite possibilities of further development. But it is also true that, after varying and developing one style for a time, people eventually tire of it and want to try a different one. To that extent no further development is possible there and then. Artists may turn to the new one with undiminished vitality, as Bach's successors turned to the homophonic style. The important question to ask, then, is why people tire of the old one at a certain time and place, or abandon it for other reasons.

There may be, of course, real exhaustion in the people concerned: in a nation, class, or group of artists and patrons. This can be a physical debility, as in illness or malnutrition. It may be due to political defeat and discouragement, to economic impoverishment, to disintegration of traditional religious and educational institutions, or other causes. Whatever the cause, improved conditions may in time revive the energies of the group. Such genuine exhaustion, temporary or permanent, may come at any stage in a sequence of styles. No one can tell, from the nature of the style itself, exactly what the next will be or how much longer the creative period will last. Symptoms of decline may appear in connection with any style, such as diminishing quantity of production, unvaried repetition, unintended crudities, failures to achieve a desired end such as realism or precision of detail, inability to integrate parts, or reliance on mere size, number, duration, intensity, or costliness instead of organized form. All these are often hard to distinguish from intentional traits, justifiable as means to some positive effect.

The persistence of a distinctive, growing culture-pattern in a social group does not fully explain the rise of creativity there at a certain time. It is not a differential cause as between one period and another. The growth of the general culture-pattern and the rise of creativity within it are both phenomena to be explained. The nature of the culture-pattern at any one time does not help us much in understanding or predicting what is going to happen next in any art. Culture-patterns are always changing, and as civilization evolves they combine more and more different, often conflicting elements, including antithetical traditions in the arts. If one can accurately speak of any single pattern in a modern civilized culture such as that of Italy, it must be recognized as highly flexible and change-able, irregular, diversified, and full of inconsistencies. It is constantly receiving elements from other cultures. Through the multiple dialectic of cultural history, it is constantly developing antithetical movements and partially reconciling them. It is easy to look back on the cultural history of a nation and to say of each event that it was a consistent step in the growth of one unified, distinctive, national pattern. But one must also recognize the flexibility and diversity of a pattern which includes Dante, Savonarola, Aretino, Lorenzo de' Medici, Cesare Borgia, St. Francis, Machiavelli, Fra Angelico, Cellini, Paolo Veronese, Mazzini, and Mussolini.

There is truth in Kroeber's theory that culture-patterns, formed early in the history of a group, act thereafter as selective, directive agencies. Such patterns, including styles and principles of art, do tend to develop cumulatively, along the line first chosen, by "a sort of momentum." But this tendency is not unopposed or all-powerful. It is much less powerful than the innate determinism of a seed or egg. It is one of many determinants in the subsequent history of art and culture in the group, and may be overcome by stronger forces along the way so that the course of events takes a very different direction from that on which it had seemed to be starting. Familiar examples are the influx of Buddhism into Chinese culture and that of Christian Hebraism into Roman culture. It oversimplifies the process to ignore such radical changes in the culture-pattern, or to say that the old culture is dead and a new one born. This ignores the fact of continuity and cumulative tradition throughout the changes. Much pre-Buddhist culture remained active throughout Chinese history, and so did much pre-Christian Roman culture after Constantine. These continuities are evident in the arts.

As to the relative influence of the early, incipient culture-pattern, much will depend on what strong factors enter the situation later on, either from outside or from hitherto latent forces within the group itself. Much will depend on the ethnic and cultural elements which entered at an early stage, such as the fusion of Minoan, Ionian, Mycenean, and Dorian elements in Greece. An isolated, homogeneous group may retain its early patterns for millennia without radical change. The Byzantine empire is commonly used as an example of rigid, hierarchical conservatism. Attempts in such a culture to break away from it in art or any other field are likely to fail as iconoclasm did in Byzantium. But Byzantine culture itself was a fusion of many diverse and discordant elements at the meeting-place of East and West. Its history was not entirely devoid of cultural change, and its conservatism was in part a protective reaction against the disruptive forces that constantly threatened it until the final Moslem conquest. Its art was in many ways a fusion of Persian, Near Eastern, and Hellenistic traditions.

Early culture-patterns exert a much less permanent, restrictive influence in the modern, liberal democracies of Europe and North America. Puritan culture in seventeenth-century New England is not a dominant force in the United States today. It still retains prestige as an object of patriotic sentiment, but in art and other fields it is often rejected in favor of later importations. In Western culture as a whole the ideals of unceasing change and progress, variety of experience, worldwide cosmopolitanism, originality and multiformity, have been explicitly included in the pattern since the seventeenth century. Western culture has become more flexible and tough, more capable of resisting disruption, through long experience in recovering from wars and revolutions, religious and artistic dissensions. It is used to dealing patiently with violence and working out compromises. In a culture of this modern, Western type, inner conflicts and radical changes of direction are often less dangerous than in rigid, simple cultures. Even a phase of total nihilism and blackest pessimism like that of some present avant-garde literature, with reverberations in other arts, is not as foreign to the traditional pattern as it seems. Though felt by some of its leaders and sympathizers as a total rejection of previous styles (classic and romantic alike) and of the concept of art itself, it is still at home in a culture which has praised the free expression of all points of view, all attitudes and ideologies. In attacking what it feels to be false and hypocritical in the old ideals of beauty, harmony, and serenity, in calling attention to the ugliness, viciousness, and sordid misery of much human life beneath the surface, it is following out another element in the Western tradition since Greek philosophy—that of scientific truth and honest realism.

There is a danger, of course, that the confusing flood of rival styles and ideologies, domestic and exotic, will produce no more than sterile eclecticism and eventual cultural death. Many historians believe that a considerable slump in artistic creativeness is now occurring, by contrast with the first third of the century. Events appear at times to verify the dire predictions of Spengler. But it is far too soon to be sure that revival will not follow as it has before. The great task of the next century, once international political stability is reached, will be to work out a new, flexible synthesis from the flood of different cultural elements now pouring together. Besides the danger of too much diversity, there is an opposite danger in trying to perpetuate narrow, restrictive ancestral patterns; of assuming that our culture must grow within these only or be broken apart and die. This can lead to fear and hatred toward foreign kinds of art and ideology.

Kroeber's theory of cultural configurations tends to imply that, once started on a certain line of artistic development, a culture is committed to that line throughout its career. Potential geniuses who cannot or will not fit into it are apparently doomed to be frustrated. Any attempt to broaden and diversify it by experimenting too far afield, or by introducing traits from other cultures and periods, is, according to the theory, sure to weaken and dilute it. At best, new "material" can be added, to be organized into the same basic patterns. "A sophisticated and mature style of sculpture is already too nearly exhausted to be developed profitably by newcomers" (p. 782). Having adopted this fatalistic belief, Kroeber protects it by ignoring negative instances, such as the reinvigoration of twentieth-century sculpture by traits from primitive African and other styles. Kroeber and Spengler ignore the vast amount of selective, cumulative development in styles and traditions which carries over from each period and culture to the next. Kroeber himself was too liberal and optimistic, too empirical and cautious, to fall completely into extreme determinism, either of the cyclical or the evolutionary type. He often flirted with Hegelian and Spenglerian ideas, then drew back before endorsing them completely. But his theory of cultural configurations remains somewhat slanted toward them because of his vagueness on the subject of causes, together with his emphasis on the determining power of early patterns and the cyclical character of styles. The elements of truth in his theory can be combined with a broader pluralism; also with more recognition of the fact and potential value of dialectical change and cumulative evolution in the arts.

Such a pluralistic approach would assume that major cultural events are always due to a variety of factors. As to creative periods in art, environmental factors seem to be the most likely causes, but hereditary ones are not necessarily ruled out in advance.

Let us glance again at some of the latter. The theory of racial inequality—of innate racial differences in potential genius—is not only discredited at present; even if true it would not explain why the same race could be creative at certain times and at others not. But hereditary factors are not necessarily racial. We appeal to them constantly in explaining individual differences in mental ability. "Genius is born, not made," and "genius can not be taught." Why, then, should we rule them out entirely in explaining collective, social differences? We are concerned here, not so much with racial as with political and social differences: with the pre-eminence, for example, of Athens and Florence; not of the larger racial strains in and around them. A certain region, town, or country may certainly attract superior individuals and their families (for a while) by social and economic inducements. Venice and Spain in their heyday attracted many of the world's best artists and craftsmen. Their descendants, perhaps, helped to raise the genetic level for a while. After a few generations, some of these lineages were attracted elsewhere. When a city lost its political and economic ascendancy, many of its artists and intellectuals left for more promising places. They went from Athens to Alexandria and Rome; from Rome to Byzantium; from Byzantium to Venice and Spain; from there to Paris, England, and the Netherlands. All through the middle ages and the Renaissance, architects and craftsmen journeyed internationally to work on churches and other costly projects. In Germany before Hitler, the Bauhaus attracted a notable group of foreign artists. Kandinsky went from Russia to Germany and then on to Paris. Such movements are temporary and primarily socio-economic; but they also lead to genetic shifts insofar as the migrating artists and scholars bring or establish families whose members mix with the local populations.

Nazi German theories of history exalted racial "purity" as an ideal. Ignoring the well-known racial mixtures in Germany, they denounced their enemies as "mongrel." The racist theory has been used to explain, not only differences in ability, but those in style as well, as in contrasting Nordic and Mediterranean art. In this connection it is interesting that another German philosopher of history, Hermann Schneider of the University of Leipzig,[2] advanced in the early twentieth century a racial theory of creative epochs which is directly opposite to the Nazi one. Instead of racial purity, he considered racial and national mixture as the basic cause of cultural flowerings. He maintained that, about five hundred years after each great mixture of peoples, a creative period often occurs. It is followed in a long-lived civilization, he said, by a romantic-revolutionary phase and a second flowering. New racial mixtures, such as occurred repeatedly in Egypt, India, and China, can produce repeated bursts of creativity. Schneider documented his theory with elaborate references to the dates of creative epochs in all major civilizations, including the oriental. His theory was naturalistic, involving no vitalistic or teleological principle, and no immanent determinism along specific, stylistic lines. Thus in some respects it is more plausible from a scientific standpoint than the theories of Spengler and Bergson. Some of the historic intervals seem to corroborate it, as for example that from the Norman Conquest to the birth of Shakespeare. But, as usual in such systems, negative instances are ignored and the facts are forced into an artificial framework of uniform

[2] *Philosophie der Geschichte* (Breslau, 1923); *Die Kulturleistungen der Menschheit* (Leipzig, 1932); *The History of World Civilization* (2 vols.; New York, 1931).

stages and intervals. Like Spengler's, it is full of suggestive analogies, and deserves more attention than it has received.

Certainly, the mixture of races and nations is not always followed by cultural creativeness. The differential factor would have to lie, as in the case of individuals, in a peculiar selection and combination of genes rather than in mixture *per se*. It remains to be discovered how any combination of factors can produce a period of creativeness in the history of a certain people, whether of comparatively pure or mixed descent, and how its descendants can relapse (as some of the Arabs and Mayans have done) into a long period of cultural decline. Are environmental factors, such as conquest by outsiders, sufficient to explain the ups and downs, or must we postulate some temporary alterations in the genetic structure of the group?

We have become so accustomed to surprising, long-range influences in recent science that even the most fanciful may deserve some consideration. It has been suggested, for example, that sunspots and other physical phenomena may exert a temporary influence on human energy, perhaps through changes in radioactivity; but this is not confirmed. Such influences would have to affect some parts of the earth and not others at a particular time, and be especially stimulative along cultural lines. It is less fanciful to suggest that non-hereditary, physiological factors such as diet may affect the creative energies of a group or of a class within that group. A disease, such as malaria, may be endemic for centuries in a certain region, thus lowering the energy potential, and then be overcome. Major plagues like the Black Death, destructive migrations and invasions like the Mongol, and extended wars like the Hundred Years War, can lower physical energy and destroy cultural institutions on a large scale. What seems like the "exhaustion of a style" or the "death of a culture" may be chiefly due to such events.

Physical environment—climate, topography, natural resources, and the like—has a limited explanatory power. Innumerable social groups inhabit similar climates in the temperate and subtropical zones, yet evolve very different cultures and produce creative bursts, if at all, at different times. Similar cultural phenomena occur in different climates. However, so tremendous a physical change as the coming and going of the glaciers, affecting all plant, animal, and human life within the regions concerned, certainly affected culture also. Hence types and stages of prehistoric cultural evolution are marked off in terms of these intervals. The limited physical accessibility of Australia and America (over temporary land bridges) had much to do with the cultural development of migrant groups in those places.

Rises and falls in the wealth and political power of a social group seem to have some positive correlation with artistic production and decline. In themselves, they are no guarantee of high quality in art; for example, in the Roman Empire and so far in the modern communist states. But it is hard to find a great artistic period which is not based in part on accumulated wealth and power. In Athens, Florence, Venice, Spain, and Holland, art came on the heels of national wealth and influence; it declined when they declined. Obviously, such factors provide the economic means for art-production and importation; they attract foreign artists and they allow the development of an élite of cultivated patrons, official or private. They provide a motivation for art in the form of religious and secular themes to be glorified with a view to divine blessing, prestige, indoctrination of the public, and other typical ends. But their beneficial effects on culture often seem to be transitory. The thrill of sudden wealth and power can evaporate while corruption and dissension spread. Military and political problems multiply. The inclination to spend much money and energy on art may weaken.

A similar sequence often occurs after a social revolution. The histories of France, Mexico, and Russia after their revolutions all show a great release of mental energies and abilities. In the first flush of victory, perhaps after some destruction of art which glorified the old régime, the new leaders stress liberal ideals and encourage their expression in new forms of art. A considerable portion of the liberated energy may find its way into the arts, producing a small or large wave of original production. But the recurrent, post-revolutionary phase soon follows.[3] The liberal idealists who overthrew the old régime are themselves overthrown by equally ruthless but more practical, hard-headed men. Freedom may give way to oligarchy, dictatorship, the call for solidarity and discipline. Completely free art is then seen as dangerous; instead, art is used more and more as a means to strengthen the new régime and is accordingly regimented. Funds and capable men are diverted from art to administration, heavy industry, and military build-up. This not only weakens art production, but also reverses the main evolutionary trend from emphasis on basic utilitarian ends to emphasis on artistic and intellectual luxuries.

A series of revolutions in France was necessary to pass from monarchy to some degree of democracy, and the latter is not yet secure; but each victory over foreign or counter-revolutionary forces was followed by a brief new wave of artistic invention. Even the defeat by Prussia in 1871, which might have been disastrous culturally, was followed by another liberating change of government, then another surge of prosperity and artistic brilliance. The years immediately after the Russian Revolution of 1917 and after the overthrow of the German monarchy produced active avant-garde movements in the arts of those countries.

An artistic florescence can occur in any of the major types or stages of political evolution. Transition to a more advanced one, by revolution or otherwise, is no guarantee of increased creativity. Such an increase can appear in a military despotism, a feudal hierarchy, a theocracy, an aristocratic republic, a feudal hierarchy, or a constitutional democracy. The history of Egypt, Persia, Athens, Venice, Rome, and France discloses all these and other social frameworks for artistic flowering.

It does not appear that great individual freedom of thought and expression, or social justice, democracy, and fair distribution of wealth have been necessary for artistic florescence in general, however desirable they are on other grounds. A certain minimum of these conditions does seem necessary, to permit the development of a strong, active professional class of artists and intellectuals not entirely devoted to war and political power. Until modern times they have usually come from an upper or middle class. Most artists need at least the basic means of healthy individual and family life, some self-respect and appreciation, and adequate tools, materials, time, and assistance for their work. They must not have outsiders dictating the form and technique of their work too strictly, if innovation is to develop. But in the past, outsiders have often told them whom and what to glorify and in what accepted symbolism. Many great periods in art have been absolute monarchies in which individual freedom was at a minimum, and in which any deviation from the established religion was punishable by death. The artist may be content if he can accept these dictates willingly and devotedly; if he believes whole-heartedly in the religious, moral, and social systems they imply. But many great artists have had conflicting feelings about them, and the expression of their non-conformity in art has helped to give them lasting fame. Euripides, Dante, Michelangelo, Cervantes, Rousseau, Burns, Keats, Shelley, and Tolstoy are examples. Virgil, Titian, Velasquez, Rubens, and Bach seem to have fitted fairly smoothly into their social and religious contexts, at least during important periods of their lives.

Great inequality of wealth, power, and privilege may tend to favor a concentration of effort and ability in certain kinds of art, especially when the ruler has developed artistic tastes. Such tastes may coexist with cruelty, moral depravity, and bad

---

[3] For more details on events in art after the Mexican revolution, see T. Munro, "Modern Art and Social Problems," in *Art Education: its Philosophy and Psychology* (1956), pp. 274 ff.

government in other respects, as in the case of Nero. The kinds of art most likely to develop under such conditions are those of sensuous luxury and magnificence, with glorification of the ruler and his patron deities. They include certain types of architecture, furniture and decoration, costume and jewelry, painting and sculpture, music, dance, poetic odes and epics, ballet, and pageantry.

Such a régime is not likely to encourage artistic expressions of humanitarian, egalitarian ideals, wealth-sharing, voluntary poverty, or asceticism. These are dangerous, potentially revolutionary ideas, as in early Buddhism and the Christian Gospels. Astute rulers and priests of the old régimes often took steps to deflect their revolutionary force into artistic and religious bypaths, including worship of the person of the reformer after his death.[4] As means of worship and ritual, the arts can be inspired and stimulated by the new ferment of ideas and the new symbols for iconographic treatment. Meanwhile the political and ecclesiastical hierarchy, allying itself with the new art, can be strengthened by the new synthesis. Occasionally, the ruler himself may (like Asoka in India) adopt the new humanitarian ideals and try to put them into practice; but this is sure to be temporary at first. Occasionally, too, the old régime is overthrown by revolution, but twenty-five centuries have not sufficed to put humanitarian ethics on a firm social and political basis.

Each of the main types of socio-political organization can be flexible enough to admit a considerable variety of cultural developments. There is no exact correlation between such political types and styles of art or degrees of creative ability. Much depends, as we have seen, on the cultural traditions which the nation inherits and maintains within its political framework. In the more autocratic forms, more depends on the personal character of the ruler and his chief supporters than in a limited monarchy or a democratic republic. An autocratic régime, small or large, can be cruel and oppressive at one time, devoted mainly to aggression abroad and exploitation of the masses at home; at another benevolent, enlightened, humanitarian, encouraging to new forms of thought. The lives of the Roman emperors cover the whole range from infamy to excellence in human nature; from Caligula and Elagabalus to Hadrian and Marcus Aurelius. A philosopher-king is often followed by a fool or sadist. If liberal ideals gain a strong following, a social revolution may ensue and change the whole structure of the state for better or worse, with a flood of new problems.

While it lasts, enlightened monarchy or feudalism can favor, not only continued support of the luxurious arts which flourish also under tyranny, but also the rise of artistic naturalism and humanism. This can include a broad, sympathetic interest in all life and nature and in the lives and humans of every kind and class. "I count nothing human indifferent to me," said Terence. Apuleius, Montaigne, Boccaccio, Shakespeare, Cervantes, and Molière all lived in somewhat autocratic régimes. The prospect of a humanistic approach to art, escaping from old restraints of ideology and style, can be as exhilarating as the first view of a rich, inviting, unexplored land. Once started, it is hard to suppress. The arts and types most able to profit from a liberation of humanistic thought are, as a rule, the drama and theater, the novel, lyric, essay, painting, and sculpture.

Favorable conditions for a creative period are, besides wealth, power, and some economic support for the arts, a local tradition of previous achievement in them. A high creative peak does not suddenly emerge from a soil completely devoid of art. There must be a developed interest in them, respect for their values, and some foundation of techniques and local styles. This was present in sixteenth-century Venice, as for example in the Basilica of St. Mark. It was present in Athens as a sculptural, architectural, poetic, and dramatic center long before Pericles. With such a preliminary tradition less wealth and power are necessary; without it those resources may be used for other

---

[4] Cf. "The Grand Inquisitor" in Dostoyevsky's *Brothers Karamazov*.

things. Art was no novelty in Spain and the Netherlands before the seventeenth century, in Rome before Augustus, or China before the T'ang emperors.

Lady Murasaki's *Tale of Genji* is an example of refined, humanistic interest in character analysis, especially as to subtle, emotional relations between the sexes. It seems surprising and precocious for its time. It clearly portrays the aristocratic social context and expresses an appropriate ideology. But it profits also from a previous tradition of inferior fictional romance and decorative art, most of which has disappeared. It profits also from the contemporary importation of Chinese art and culture, including Buddhist and Confucian ideas. Women writers were spared, at the same time, the need of having to write in the stilted, formal Chinese literary style. All these external factors fail, as usual, to explain the tremendous difference between previous mediocrity and outstanding genius. For that, we must still fall back on the vague hypothesis of innate ability. Not all in Murasaki's milieu was favorable. She herself was ridiculed as "Lady Annals" for her interest in books and writing. What gave her the strength and ability to be different?

Neither wealth nor power nor social structure, nor all three together, can determine the quality or the specific styles and patterns which a culture or a genius will develop. For these we must look to a combination of innate ability with specific determinants in the cultural heritage of the group along artistic, religious, intellectual, technological, and other related lines. These externals can provide the materials and instruments of art, both physical and mental, together with suggestions as to style.

A general survey of especially creative periods in cultural growth, such as that of Kroeber, does well to include a wide range of types and styles of art, as well as of philosophic and scientific theories. In asking what causes such periods we have been, for the most part, thinking of art in general, rather than of any particular kind of art.

But the more deeply we look into the problem, the more we see that different kinds arise under different conditions and are due to somewhat different causes. They express different motivations, fulfill different psychological and social functions, aim at different ends and values. As we have just observed, the arts of aristocratic luxury, of elegant display and entertainment, can flourish under socio-economic conditions of great inequality and injustice, with arduous labor and a low standard of living for the humbler craftsmen. On the other hand, the rise of a more humanitarian, humanistic type of art, expressing a respect for human dignity, a broad sympathy for the poor, and praise for ascetic sacrifice on the part of the rich and powerful, presupposes a tradition of moral reform such as those of the early Taoists, Buddhists, Essenes, and primitive Christians. It can start to grow in an autocratic state, but if it does so long the total culture-pattern must change considerably. Each influences the other.

One might go on to contrast the arts and styles concerned with primitive magic and developed polytheism, with civic festivals and solitary, inward meditation, with patriotism and revolution, with religious, commercial, and military propaganda, and with wishful, exciting fantasies for sedentary, modern city-dwellers. All these and other types, expressing different needs and motivations both social and individual, spring from somewhat different sets of causes. A creative surge in one type does not necessarily coincide with one in another type. In fact, the various types often conflict and attack one another, as when the preachers of poverty denounce the extravagance and formalism of the rich, or when governments try to suppress a revolutionary song. Thus conditions favorable to creativeness in one kind of art may be unfavorable to that in others. A choice must be made between rival sets of values such as magnificent display and simple piety, or between great enjoyment for one class and a moderate amount for all. These choices are made, usually somewhat unconsciously. For a time, while the issue is heated, no compromise or synthesis may be possible.

Some kinds of art, as in the Christian middle ages, express wishful fantasies of a future life; they spring in part from a sense of frustration and deep dissatisfaction with the here and now. Such dissatisfaction can be diminished by social reforms and technological progress. Some psychoanalysts have argued that all art springs from some kind of frustration and dissatisfaction on the part of the artist, impelling him to fantasy fulfillments. This is no doubt exaggerated, but certainly occurs in some cases. It is never the only cause. But insofar as it is an actual motive, removing the causes of dissatisfaction with the here and now may weaken the impulse toward certain kinds of art.

Some kinds of physical and mental disease can help to direct an unusual share of one's mental and emotional energies into an artistic channel, there to be intensely and rapidly consumed. Frustrations and shocks in some normal type of human experience may help redirect an artist's energies into an artistic substitute. In all such cases, correcting the cause may also prevent or weaken artistic creation, at least along certain lines. This is not to say that all kinds of art are pathologically caused or would be injured by making the world a better, healthier place. Other kinds may flourish instead. Even if they did not, the sacrifice might be, from some points of view, well worth while.

The scientific, naturalistic world-view, by branding as false many of the religious beliefs on which artistic fantasies of the past have been based, tends to render such art unconvincing and weakens its motivation. Other grounds remain for admiring past religious art, but these are not enough to foster its creative development as much as before. Critics have lamented the decline of the age of myth as a necessary stimulus to great art. Can the scientific outlook produce its own myths? Is it in fact now producing some? Can art flourish without them? If not all art, what kinds can do so? Can realistic art satisfy the demand for artistic fantasy? Can artistic fantasy thrive in its own right without the need of believing in the truth of its dreams?

These are difficult questions, and can be definitely answered only by events themselves. They concern us here only indirectly: as emphasizing the complexity of historical causation in the arts and the difficulty of learning what causes creative epochs. Events and conditions which produce one at a certain stage of history, or in a certain cultural context, may not do so in others. Even if we knew what caused one in fifteenth-century Florence, we could not be sure that similar conditions would have the same effect today. The total cultural situation of that time could not be reproduced, of course, and each is to some extent unique. But it is never wholly so; some factors and configurations recur, and therein lies the hope of some increase in understanding and control. Even if complete understanding and control are impossible, there can be some partial approaches to them.

Assuming that a general increase in the quantity and quality of all kinds of art production is desirable (an assumption which not all would accept), the next step would be an extensive study of the possible causes and means to that end. Some are relatively inaccessible to experimental study, at least for the present. These include the hereditary factors of genius, as an individual and a social phenomenon. They also include the formation, differentiation, and integration of major culture-patterns, ideologies, or world-views, whose power to select and direct in art we have been discussing. This is too vast and powerful a current for any individual or group of scholars to influence much. We cannot predict its future course with assurance, or what kinds of art and genius it will raise to eminence in future.

On the other hand, some possible factors do seem relatively understandable and controllable, if a social will to do so develops. They may not, in themselves, be adequate means to social creativity. They may be unfavorable to some kinds of art while favoring others. But they are potentially beneficial on many grounds. One is a general increase in physical health and energy throughout the population. Another is increased distribution of the financial, institutional, and technical means to artistic production. A third is increased respect and prestige for the arts and those who participate in them, with opportunities for greater influence in social policy and management. A fourth is increased opportunity for education in the arts, as to production, performance, understanding, and appreciation in the arts, both in school and out.

No one specific method of education, in general or in particular arts, has yet proved itself as a means to important creative achievement.[5] All that we can say at present is that certain ones seem promising; but they have not yet produced the hoped-for geniuses. By investigating further the psychological and social factors which make for genius, we may be able to devise better ways of fostering it. Little is being done at present along this line, or in scientifically controlled experiment with different educational methods. On the other hand, genius has often arisen in the past and is still arising occasionally, under what seem to be the most adverse family, social, and educational conditions.

It does seem evident that freedom to express oneself, as a student or adult practitioner of art, is not enough. The reservoir and the motivation may too soon be exhausted. For the same reason, mere play with art materials is not enough for an older child. Wealth, power, and talent are probably not enough to turn a potential genius into an actual genius in art. There must also be something in the external situation, capable of arousing and holding interest and a will to achieve along a certain line in a certain artistic medium. One must feel that to create a particular kind of art is somehow important in the scheme of things, worthy of respect in the eyes of God or man, of rulers, officials, patrons, experts, critics, family, friends, colleagues, or the general public. Only in that way can the artist, like any other workman, achieve the self-respect and faith in the value of what he is trying to do which he needs to motivate

persistent effort. But once again, self-esteem and public respect are not enough. Too often they coexist with mediocrity.

We are left once more with the general hypothesis that no one type of cause is adequate; that many must combine to produce a creative epoch. There must be (a) innately potential geniuses; (b) materials and conditions adequate to implement and channel their voluntary energies into some artistic medium; (c) institutions capable of giving them technical training and some knowledge of their own artistic heritage; and (d) other persons with the taste, power, and will to appreciate artistic merit and help to give it wider recognition.

2. NATURAL AND ARTIFICIAL SELECTION IN THE EVOLUTION OF ART

In contrasting organic with cultural evolution, we noted that the latter includes more purposeful action. It is increasingly artificial, in a sense opposed to "natural." Adaptive change in the cultural realm is also said to be increasingly "active," in that man tends to change his environment instead of undergoing involuntary changes in his own structure. The present section will summarize what has been said on these points in previous chapters, and show in more detail how these types of evolution occur in the arts.

We have seen that the genetic, hereditary factors in organic evolution include the tendency of like to reproduce like, and also the tendency to produce a certain range of variations, usually within the parental type. They are called "chance variations" insofar as the mixture of genes takes place without planned control. Darwin conceived them as slight and gradual; De Vries showed that large, sudden mutations also occur. In either case, the struggle for existence within each environment tends to

[5] Cf. T. Munro, "Creative Ability in Art and its Educational Fostering," in *Art Education: its Philosophy and Psychology* (1956), pp. 77-112.

select the fittest in each generation for survival and to eliminate the less fit. In the next generation again, the survivors often produce offspring somewhat like themselves, so that the group as a whole tends to perpetuate the type which is proving fittest under the conditions. This is still called "natural" selection, since it is conceived as operating automatically through the forces of nature, rather than through direct, divine intervention; also in the sense opposed to "artificial" or purposeful selection and breeding by humans, as in eugenics and other applications of genetic science.

Nineteenth-century theists who accepted evolutionism in general argued that what appeared to be "natural" in organic change was divinely directed through the laws of nature. In that sense it was artificial: the work of a "divine Artificer." On the other hand, philosophic naturalists argued that man and all his works were parts of nature, in a broad sense of that term. The human mind with its powers of purposeful control had developed through natural selection and was an integral part of the present order of nature. Cultural evolution, they said, was a part of natural evolution; an outgrowth of organic evolution. The products and processes of art and science, they insisted, are all natural in this sense.

Both schools of thought agreed on the importance of the distinction between evolutionary change which operates without direct, purposeful intervention by man and that which is to some extent so directed. In this narrower sense, "natural" selection and adaptation become less natural and more artificial as man learns to manage his own affairs more purposefully, rather than by animal impulse.

To some extent, man has undertaken the selective breeding of animals and plants. Artificial insemination is increasingly used by humans. Man may in future control human breeding through eugenics. Thus he may, in some degree, direct his own organic as well as cultural evolution. Many types of plant and animal have already been greatly changed in this way, and new ones origi-nated. Since prehistoric times, human breeding has been somewhat affected by culture and purpose, through marriage customs and laws, including the religious, moral, ethnic, and aesthetic standards which influence choice in mating. In this way, human reproduction ceased long ago to be purely "natural" and became partly artificial. Cultural change in general becomes more "artificial" as social behavior becomes more planful.

Lamarck's conception of the evolutionary process, which turned out to be false as applied to organic evolution, becomes more and more true of cultural evolution as the latter proceeds. Culture, including art, evolves through the transmission of acquired characteristics. The mode of transmission has been cultural rather than organic, but becomes organic also insofar as genes are planfully combined according to cultural aims and methods. (This does not imply that traits acquired in an individual's life are passed on through his genes.) Cultural evolution shows increasingly another tendency which Lamarck mistakenly attributed to all evolution: namely, that a species can aspire toward some future condition, and through effort move toward it.

As conscious planning comes to play a greater role in art, the idealistic theory of a psychic "will" to certain kinds of form becomes increasingly true; not of all art or all history, but of modern art and civilization. This will is a purely natural phenomenon of social thinking and desiring. It is becoming more conscious and purposeful, though it still has far to go in that direction. Such collective desiring, as interpreted by naturalism, does not pursue any definitely predetermined course. Like art itself, it is the joint product of many interacting factors, and is still subject to natural selection.

The change from automatic instinct to conscious purpose is no guarantee of greater success in surviving. In gaining more power, not only over nature but also over his own future actions, man runs increasing risk of making disastrous, far-reaching mistakes. Fear of this, and distrust of those officials and supposedly wise men who would make decisions on a world scale, have led many evolutionists from Spencer on to urge that man let nature take its course, and not be too quick to seize the helm. In this they resemble the Chinese Taoists. Others point out that beneficial plans have also been made; that all civilization is the result of intelligent effort. Intelligent planning is the distinctively human method of competing. It has worked fairly well so far, say the optimists, and deserves to be tried on a larger scale with more aid from the social and psychological sciences.

The arts have played many different roles in cultural evolution. At first, and still to some extent, they can be regarded as having some survival value, and hence as factors in natural selection. Even when not intended as means of survival, they often contribute to it, as do the nest-building instincts of birds. Religious and civic arts are known to have this naturalistic function through strengthening group solidarity, encouraging confidence and martial enthusiasm, and other effects. They help some groups and types of human to prevail while others are eliminated. Art has often been regarded as having a supernatural power or mana, as in amulets, statues of gods, and ritual dances. When used to add glamor and prestige to the person of the chief or shaman, or to established codes of laws such as that of Moses or Hammurabi, they can strengthen social organization at crucial points.

However, it is not to be assumed that art originated and evolved entirely because of its survival value. Some anthropologists doubt whether art, especially the aesthetic, non-utilitarian aspects of art, had that much value to primitive man. It may be only in part a product of natural selection. To explain the rest of its huge development, one hypothesis contends that man acquired, perhaps through one or more sudden mutations, a physiological equipment capable of much more artistic and intellectual growth than he needed for survival. Having the mechanism, he has gone on to use it for creating things not strictly needed, but valued for other reasons.[6] From this hypothesis arose

Spencer's theory of art as play involving energies and simulated actions, not required in the struggle for existence.

By the same token, it is not to be assumed that art is always valuable today as a means to physical survival or political power. As Plato rightly saw, some kinds of art can weaken morale, soften physique and military ardor, dull clear thinking, instil a spirit of defeatism, or otherwise handicap an individual or group in the struggle for survival. The destruction of Sybaris is a classical example. Such weakening may not be noticed, or make much difference in actual survival, if the individual or group is securely sheltered from attack or serious competition. Then he or it can afford, at least for a while, to spend much energy in luxurious living, enjoying the Petronian arts of pleasure. Not only the more obvious kinds of luxury and dissipation, but even serious, great art with high aesthetic merit and profound intellectual and moral content, may be pursued to excess, as judged from the biological standpoint, if it distracts from necessary practical efforts. When the struggle for existence is keen and people live at or near the level of bare subsistence, the kinds of art they prefer and practice may have a considerable effect on their power to survive. War-dances and stirring drum or bagpipe music may stimulate one group to decisive martial efforts, while another is lulled to costly inaction by "soft, Lydian airs" or the equivalent. As in Athens, when faced by Sparta and then by Rome, art and intellectual culture are no substitute for political unity or for industrial and military efficiency. However fine in themselves they can, under certain conditions, weaken the same basic virtues which, at an earlier age, they helped to strengthen. Philosophical disputation and individualism, however valuable on the whole, can at times promote dissension and weaken collective resistance. At other times, as in modern liberal states, they contribute to more flexible unities, capable of resisting internal and external pressures.

[6] Cf. L. Eiseley, The Immense Journey (New York 1957), p. 84.

In applying the principle of natural selection to art history, Taine pointed out that works and styles of art are themselves subject to natural selection; that they struggle for survival within their physical, social, and psychological environments. Many kinds are produced like seeds in a given environment, but some fall on soil unfavorable to that kind of plant. We have seen the danger of taking too literally this idea of struggle between styles. Like religions and scientific theories, they are abstractions, without causal power of their own. Concrete human beings do the struggling, alone or in social groups or classes. They struggle for and against abstract ideas, including styles and principles of art, as well as for more concrete goods. Within this qualification it is not too far-fetched to speak of styles "struggling" with each other in a process of natural selection. "Survival" means here persistent public favor. It was mentioned above that there are many degrees of cultural survival, as opposed to obsolescence or oblivion. The most complete survival for a style consists in its being practiced by artists as a dynamic mode of creation, capable of further variation and growth. Short of being totally forgotten or destroyed, there are many less active levels of survival. On all, there is some amount of competition: e.g., for a place on concert programs, in art museums or libraries, and in histories of the art concerned.

In using the term "struggle," we should not exaggerate the violence of the process. Sometimes it is bloody, as when styles of art follow conquest and colonization. Thus Roman architecture and sculpture spread throughout Europe and North Africa, displacing indigenous styles. Sometimes art conquers the conqueror, as when the Mongol emperors adopted Sung culture for the sake of enjoyment and to show themselves cultivated in the finer things of life. Social revolutions often destroy the hated, artistic symbols of the old régime, as in France and Russia; at least until their own leaders call a halt for reasons of public interest. At other times the issue between styles is peaceful though sharp and vehement, as in the controversy over Brahms vs. Wagner, in which Hanslick took the part of the formalists. Riots have broken out in Paris over aesthetic issues, as in the stormy reception of Hugo's *Hernani* and Stravinsky's *Sacre*; chairs have been broken over heads and duels fought. But for the most part the selection goes on more quietly.[7] In a free, consumer-directed society, it is simply a question of whose works of art are sold or otherwise supported; of what artists and what styles continue to be published, performed, exhibited, patronized, and discussed. Many sink gently into oblivion each year; a few manage somehow to keep their heads above water.

Even in the organic world, natural selection was not entirely ruthless, red in tooth and claw. That conception was promptly criticized in the nineteenth century, with the assertion that man's survival had been partly due to his impulses of mutual aid and tenderness, at least toward his immediate kin and comrades. Small fish and birds survive by being useful to, or at least tolerated by, ferocious sharks and rhinoceros. Horses, dogs, and cats were able to survive, partly through pleasing and serving man, who now breeds them artificially. They have become, to some extent, works of human art, produced for aesthetic as well as other values. Ferocious warlords and tyrants have kept gentle artists close around them as long as the latter proved useful or amusing. Homer and his *Odyssey* survive, along with the classical orders of architecture, by continuing to attract the admiration of influential persons in successive generations. Styles may not compete directly except when critics and patrons debate their respective merits.

The active survival of styles involves, necessarily, continued adaptation to new and changing cultural conditions. The classical orders are adapted to new materials and functions in modern cities. Lengthy plays and music are cut down for brief perform-

7 "Cultural selection," says Clyde Kluckhohn, "centers increasingly around struggles over competing sets of values." *Mirror for Man* (New York, 1949), p. 75.

ance on radio and television. Chinese decorative styles are transformed in French rococo; Hindu and African dances are adapted to a New York theater stage. Armor decreases in size and heaviness as social and military conditions change, as knightly tournaments lose their importance, and as gunpowder and bullets penetrate thin steel. Swords change in size and shape from the hacking broadsword to the piercing rapier, and then to the small, ornamental sword of the courtier. The heavy walls of cities, houses and churches melt away in a climate of social order and security.

Individual purposes do not, necessarily, make a social process artificial or planful as a whole. Primitive man could direct his daily actions with some foresight and intelligence. But neither primitive man nor his ancestors could conceive of culture or of evolution on a large scale, or plan for it. Hence the process as a whole could not be planful. Only slowly did man learn to plan any large-scale, long-range policies, as Augustus and Diocletian planned their empires. An enormous multiplicity of small, individual or local schemes and wishes, mostly in conflict with each other over short-range, tangible goods, does not make social conduct planful.

Art itself, although traditionally contrasted with nature, is not necessarily planful or "unnatural." On the contrary, it often tries to follow nature, not in merely representing it, but in avoiding all purposeful direction. We have seen how this was true of Zen Buddhism and European romanticism; how they favored the production of art by sudden impulse, intuition, or free fantasy. The spread of such ideas about art and its methods tends to favor a laissez-faire attitude toward art in education and social policy. It encourages free expressionism in the schools instead of systematic training in a particular style. It encourages a hands-off policy by governments and institutions toward artistic production and consumption. It tends to let the artist express himself as he wishes and the public have whatever art it wants, within broad limits.

All these tendencies increase the element of chance variation in the productive phase of art. They increase the element of free competition among works and styles of art in the struggle for public favor. They tend to make the whole artistic process less artificial and more natural, thus reversing the main trend of cultural evolution.

Even when an individual artist creates in a highly purposeful way, many forces outside of his control help determine what his purposes shall be. Others operate to make his work survive or disappear. Many of the cultural factors which go to make up demand and taste are non-rational. The maelstrom of desires and purposes which struggle in a competitive society, including those of rival artists, critics, and patrons, is not as a whole consistently planful. Artists are induced by the success of a style to produce more in that style, even though the "success" is limited to critical approval by a few critics. Even when the artist thinks he is following his own spontaneous impulses, he is influenced by current tastes, conservative or radical, and by current theories of what is good in art.

Under early, "natural" conditions, art adapts itself more or less to its local environment, physical and social. In an island, maritime people, it may focus on the ornamentation of boats and paddles. Among a forest people, wood and vegetable fibers are much used and woodland spirits are propitiated. The use of stone or clay is largely determined by local resources. Taine's emphasis on the role of physical environment in determining style is more true of primitive than of modern civilized art, and the same can be said of Semper's emphasis on the influence of utilitarian functions and technics. International commerce now brings any desired material to the artist's door. In addition, desired materials are increasingly made to order, as in plastics, synthetics, alloys, and enameled metals. The physical environments of art and of all human activity are fast becoming artificial. Heating, lighting, air-conditioning, rapid transportation and communication, all have a part in this. In varying degrees, art transforms the physical environment for aesthetic ends through city and regional planning, architecture, highways, and landscape design.

Art is still much influenced by its particular social environment. Increasingly in this century, totalitarian states have regimented it with some success. Under any social system, however liberal, each art has to adapt itself to a changing environment of other arts and technics. As in primitive times, certain artistic types and styles tend to flourish and decline together, as in biological symbiosis and the diversified colonies which ecology describes. Thus a given style of architecture fosters certain styles of art, and is itself fostered by the geographical and social environment. Broad, unbroken interior walls make a favorable environment for mosaic, mural painting, and tapestry. Large windows and thin walls, as in a gothic church, favor the development of stained glass. Police protection and cheap, rapid transportation stimulate highway construction with new types of architecture such as motels, restaurants, and inexpensive housing through the countryside. Enormous heavy skirts, as in the baroque Spanish court and the later hoop-skirt, require much space and hamper active movement. They cannot survive for daily use where people have to crowd into small spaces, as in modern transportation, or when a democratic, naturalistic ideology encourages free physical activity on women's part.

Art is gradually freeing itself from extreme subservience to specific social environments. The patronage and financial support of art are more diversified; not limited to any one group such as church, state, nobility, or a few rich families. Under normal conditions of free travel, the artist who does not like Boston or Paris can move to Walden Pond or Tahiti. In spite of dictatorial efforts, it is hard to keep out of one's country all art of foreign countries. Worldwide interchange of art and ideas about art tends to create a cosmopolitan intellectual milieu in which very different kinds of art can thrive.

In ancient and primitive cultures, art was in many ways less free than in modern liberal countries. The processes of art were in some respects more artificially controlled than at present. Artists were less free to depart from traditional models and thus to produce a wide range of variants for the environment to select from. The public as a whole had less power to choose and get what it liked individually. Yet such control was hardly rational in a full sense of the word, since it was largely based on unanalyzed custom and on slight knowledge of the nature and possible values of the arts. In tribal cultures custom and taboo, sanctified by religious and magical beliefs, largely directed the production and the use of art. In the early, military empires, such rules were rationalized more explicitly, but did not often lead to much freedom for the artist or the masses. There was more in Athens, as indicated by Plato's denunciation of it and his call for a return to conservative regulations.

The evolution of art resembles organic natural selection more when artists are comparatively free to produce any kind of art they wish to produce at any moment; free economically and psychologically as well as legally. Such freedom is encouraged by the existence of a large, diversified, liberal public in which almost any kind of art will be patronized by some subgroup with purchasing power. It is favored by the availability for choice of many different types and styles of art, old and recent, native and exotic. Thus the artist's imagination is not channeled along a few established lines, but free to wander. Public taste is comparatively free to choose what it will. Under such conditions, a great variety of styles is produced continuously. This corresponds to chance variation and mutation in the organic realm. A comparatively high degree of such freedom to vary exists in the great, complex, modern democracies such as France and the United States. Each year, accordingly, there is a tremendous variety of art products, some for the élite and some for the masses. Much of it is widely accepted but ephemeral, as in radio- television entertainment and illustrated magazine stories.

In a large, heterogeneous population such as that of modern Europe or America, many different subgroups, based on age, sex, wealth, socio-economic class and the like are able to support the varied forms of art which they prefer. In a free society, artists and intellectuals of many types and tastes form their own subgroups. When an artist consciously reacts against society, denouncing its prevailing styles and principles, he is seldom alone in his revolt. Similar rebels will soon flock to his side, perhaps because they share his views and like his art, perhaps because they favor rebellion in general. Whatever he does, he has some part of society on his side. Thus the fact that artists often react against their cultural milieu, or some aspects of it, does not disprove the theory of environmental selection in art. It only shows that a modern democratic environment is highly varied. If a seed falls on unfriendly soil at first, it may soon be carried to a friendly one which fosters it for a while at least.

A modern totalitarian state, fascist or communist, tends to regulate the production and consumption of art from above; thus to make selection again more artificial than natural. Modern democracies vary considerably as to the extent to which they influence the production and consumption of art through governmental regulation, support, and censorship, as well as through endowed institutions and pressure groups. America is a consumer-directed economy in that the tastes and desires of the public have great power in determining production. In a dictatorship, the government tends to select and adapt its art production in a more planful way. If such a centralized government is motivated by political, economic, and military aims rather than the immediate satisfaction of consumers, its choice of art will be influenced by considerations of utility along these lines. Art tends again to become an instrument of political survival and conquest, as in primitive times, but with more scientific understanding of the technological principles determining its efficacy.

In an enlightened, peaceful autocracy or centralized collectivism, the choice may be made on more humanistic, aesthetic, and hedonistic lines, to encourage what officials believe will be for the best interest and enjoyment of the public. In that case, the taste of these officials will be an actively determining factor in the environment, for better or worse.

3. THE EXTENSION OF PURPOSEFUL CONTROL IN THE ARTS. SOCIAL POLICY TOWARD ART IN LIBERAL SOCIETIES

The tendency to more and more social planning and control in modern civilization gives rise to many questions about the future. To what extent does such control already exist in the arts? To what extent is it likely to increase? To what extent is such increase desirable? If at all, of what kinds? Toward what goals should future evolution be directed?

As to the present policies toward art, it is obvious that more planning and control exist in the totalitarian states than elsewhere. It is an avowed and systematic policy there, whereas the liberal states tend to avoid it as harmful regimentation. In the former it is often a recognized activity of the central government, whether done directly by government agencies or by artists' congresses and the like, which have to follow government policy on the whole. Some communist and some fascist régimes are more strict than others in this respect. All of them change their policies a little from time to time.

On the other hand, it would be a mistake to suppose that, even in the most liberal states, the arts are completely individualistic, subject to no social planning whatever. The difference is one of degree. The choice is not between all or none; it is between more or less and between different kinds of social planning. More is done at present in the liberal states than is commonly realized. If not by government agencies, much is done by large corporate institutions, their officials and advisers. These are often in close touch with public officials. They occupy an intermediate position between the central government at one extreme and the individual artist or patron at the other, Their power is limited; their influence is exerted, not so much by laws, police, or soldiers as by economic and psychological pressures. In cultural as in economic and political affairs, the democracies show many signs of moving toward collectivism and away from the laissez-faire tradition. It would be unrealistic to ignore the non-governmental aspects of social planning and control, which are often more influential than governments in helping to determine the arts of liberal peoples.

In a previous chapter we examined some early theories (Indian and European) of how to control an observer's emotional attitudes by means of art. This is not quite the same as controlling art itself by social agencies for social ends; but the two are related as applications of the technical approach to art, in which art is treated as a psychosocial means to desired ends. All such attempts up to date have been hampered by inadequate psychological knowledge. In the West, at times, they have been further obstructed by the romantic reaction against all science and rational planning in art. We have seen also how that hostility was aggravated, first by the series of wars and calamities in the twentieth century, mistakenly blamed upon science; second by the pessimistic rejection of belief in progress, and third, by the association of control in art with totalitarian oppression. "Control" has been widely associated with "thought control" by dictators for their own selfish, oppressive ends.

According to the romantic liberal tradition, still highly influential in the West, it would be harmful to art and culture for anyone or any group of artists or experts, however learned in the arts, to try to direct them along specific lines. They dis-

agree too much to allow any consistent, widely approved social policy, but even if they agreed they should not be allowed to manage art. The result (according to this view) would be the death of creative originality and the reduction of art to a sterile, mechanical process. Even if one could be sure such control would be purely non-political and sincerely for the good of art, still it is felt that no one can know the best ways for art to develop in future. Let it alone and it will find its own best course intuitively, by trial and error. This is obviously a modern survival of the laissez-faire philosophy of Adam Smith and other eighteenth-century liberal economists. Let the free enterpriser alone and he will be led "as by a hidden hand" to serve society best. Those who do not will be eliminated by free competition—in other words, by natural selection, as the evolutionists called it a half century later. This attitude is pessimistic about the power of science to benefit art and about the power of man to guide his own destiny wisely. Some of its exponents are rather too optimistic, on the other hand, about the power of natural selection or blind, automatic evolution to do a better job. Others are none too hopeful about either alternative.

Those who count on the automatic working of cultural change to benefit the arts can draw little assurance from recent scientific thinking in the field. The critical attacks on nineteenth-century evolutionism, which we have reviewed in some detail, have insisted mainly on the diversity of cultural change and on its lack of any one definite, inevitable line of progress. Past cultural change has produced great differentiation; present change, in spite of the antagonism between two large political and ideological blocs, appears to be increasing cultural similarity throughout the earth in many respects. One of these is art, in which the rapid convergence of many local and national traditions into one great stream, plus the ease of world-wide communication, threatens to produce more uniformity of taste and style than most liberals would like. This suggests that if we want to insure enough variety and personal touch in the art of the future, we must plan and work for it.

Some social control in art is consistent with liberalism if it is aimed primarily at preserving and increasing the freedom of the individual in cultural affairs. This refers both to the artist (the designer, producer, or performer of art) and to the consumer. One can be free to create art as he wishes; the other to have the kind of art he wants, within broad limits defined by society for its basic safety and welfare. The way to insure this freedom in the present age is not, as extreme liberals suppose, to keep hands off the whole affair. Innumerable forces, some domineering, some rapacious, some well-meaning but misguided, are constantly at work to nibble it away. Moreover, art needs active financial and other support far beyond that which it now gets in the open market or from private philanthropy. This applies especially to the more experimental and difficult kinds, often costly in labor, materials, and instruments.

Intelligent liberalism can approve some planning and control in the arts provided it is carefully and explicitly self-limiting. Control can be largely self-control, with most decisions left to artists themselves and to others professionally active in the field. The cooperation of other kinds of expert will certainly be needed, since artists often have little interest or skill in social planning and management. Extreme individualists among them will oppose it actively. But the artist is not the only person concerned with the nature and quality of art. In a free society, art is not made entirely for the artists, or for any one group or class. The artist can and should take the lead, but he is not all-powerful in deciding what shall be made, published, and performed. The consumer also has a right to make his wants known, and so have teachers and parents, tax-payers and cultural institutions. The democratic determination of social policy in so important a realm is necessarily a cooperative task, involving some compromise among different points of view. This does not mean that the general public shall decide on technical questions, about which it lacks the necessary knowledge. Ways are easily found in every technical field to give recognized experts the temporary power to make such decisions, while keeping ultimate control in the hands of the public.

The current association of control in art with dictatorial regimentation is natural enough in the light of recent history. Certainly the dictators and the totalitarian states have shown most disposition to practice it. Certainly the liberals are justified in denouncing this kind of control. But to assume that all social control in the arts must be of this kind is quite unwarranted. The arts are and always have been capable of use for good or bad ends. That depends on what kind of person uses them, what kind of art is produced, and how it is used. The arts are basically neutral in the same way that nuclear energy and weapons of war are neutral. Every kind of power, every major break-through in technology, has been used by malevolent people for aggressive and destructive ends—for example, the use of sails and firearms by pirates. The response of intelligent, peaceful people is not to denounce and avoid these means but to see that their use is limited, so far as possible, to the right sort of person and purpose. For liberals to reject all social controls in art is like rejecting atomic weapons; it merely leaves the advantage to others who are all too eager to use them.

Social control in art is not necessarily conducted for political or economic ends. It is not necessarily coercive or imposed from above. It is not necessarily puritanical, reactionary, or censorious. It can be conducted by democratic processes of discussion and collective decision. It can be slow, cautious, experimental, and tentative, restricted to areas on which there is basic agreement and little possibility of harm. To be sure, there is always danger of its getting out of hand, of becoming dictatorial in the wrong hands. But this danger exists throughout liberal society. One must be ever watchful to preserve essential individual freedoms and the rights of minorities, while also achieving the benefits of moderate social control.

What is "control?" In a broad sense it means "having power over something"; being able to direct or influence it. As such it is exerted by all living things. They automatically control some part of nature in eating and breathing. But only humans, and few of them, understand how and why these processes operate and try to direct them purposefully on a basis of that knowledge. To control a certain type of phenomenon, one does not need to understand it or aim at any conscious goal. A young child or a lunatic can press an electric button, give poison, or cause an explosion without intending it. Art can be made, performed, and used by persons who do not understand its possible effects, with beneficial or disastrous consequences. The control of art, and of human thought, feeling, and action by means of art, has been practiced to some extent for thousands of years with very little understanding or deliberate purpose as to the psychological causes and effects involved. Even with erroneous, mythical theories about the origin and operation of the arts, man did a good deal of efficient controlling of sculptures, pigments, musical sounds, words, tastes, and odors.

Even in scientific technology, control often comes before thorough understanding. Methods are tried, such as tranquilizing drugs and shock treatments in psychiatry, with very little understanding of how they work. This is partly trial and error, with many methods tried and rejected; but it is not entirely in the dark since based on a general understanding of the situation. We are constantly trying new methods in the arts, and especially in art education, whose effects we cannot be sure of in advance or understand fully afterwards. If we like the effects, we keep on using the method, and meanwhile try to understand the phenomena better so as to achieve still more desirable results. Science helps in the understanding and helps the technician to be more sure of getting the results intended. By explaining the various possible results and means to them, science also helps us to decide which ones we want and which are consistent with our ultimate moral, aesthetic, social, and individual aims. It does not prove or try to prove that any one set of aims is universally right or desirable.

From prehistoric times, art has been partly a matter of impulse, custom, and habit; partly a matter of rational control. Its activities, plans, and decisions have been partly individual and partly social, managed by such groups as the family, tribe, village, city, church, empire, and medieval guild. In modern times, man has been gradually increasing his knowledge and control of the materials and processes of art, and using its product for consciously desired social ends. He could not stop doing so if he tried. Partial social control in art is not a radical innovation which can be avoided entirely, or postponed until all can agree on its methods, aims, and scope.

Much social planning and control in and for the arts is willingly accepted by liberals and conservatives alike. Its loss would be regretted by artists as well as the public. Copyright laws to protect the author and composer are of this type. Like traffic laws, these do not try to tell art where to go, but try to make it easier to go wherever one wishes and to carry on any kind of worth-while activity. They ask one to sacrifice small liberties in exchange for larger ones. They limit the right of publication and sale in order to stimulate creative art, which is considered as a greater value to both artist and society. Protecting some rights always involves taking others away: e.g., the right of selfish interests to exploit the artist and lower his standard of living.

Society asks the artist to surrender some rights also: to refrain from libel and slander, from inciting to riot, from aiding an enemy in time of war or public danger, and from distributing publicly works which offend strong moral attitudes on the part of influential groups. How far a free society should go in this is always debatable, and some extreme liberals would abolish all censorship. Liberal law and tradition take a middle course in providing that freedom of speech and related freedoms shall not be arbitrarily curtailed, but only by legally appointed officials, responsive to public opinion. On the whole, the moral censorship of art has been decreasing steadily in recent years. There is practically none where works restricted to adult scholarship are concerned.

Censorship laws are negative and preventative. There is little or no attempt at positive coercion of artists in a free society; i.e., to make them create or perform the kind of art which officials or parties in power would like to have them produce. On the positive side, liberal social policy is designed primarily to establish social conditions favorable to education and cultural production in general, leaving it to individual taste to select what it wants in the open market.

Art education, too, has tried increasingly in recent years to be very broad and neutral in what it asks the prospective artist to do. It encourages all sorts of free, personal expression, especially in painting and sculpture, letting the student decide what specific line he will follow. The net result is a kind of planful planlessness; a careful development of educational technics to avoid and prevent the "imposition" of teachers' tastes or adult standards upon the student, especially the young child. But completely free expression and spontaneous creation have proven impossible. How could one prevent children in a modern city from seeing and hearing adult art? If kept away from art museums and symphony halls, they still see and hear popular—and perhaps inferior—art on all hands, in shop windows, newspapers and magazines, films, radio and television. By withholding serious adult art, old and new, one merely leaves the field entirely to popular art as a formative influence. To urge a student of art to do whatever he wants to is, in effect, to press him toward a certain kind of art production: that of direct, impulsive, individual self-expression. It is to guide him away from the study and practice of any previous style or technique. When he or his classmates are praised for doing a certain kind of work, such as abstract expressionism, and when their works are exhibited with admiration, this encourages them

to continue along the same line. This is not necessarily bad, but it is a step toward purposeful direction, whether so intended or not.

To refrain entirely from selective support of what we consider best in art would be, in effect, to leave the whole process of selection and survival to the public taste of the moment. It would be, again, a return from artificial to natural selection and unregulated competition. By doing nothing to encourage any particular kind of art and artist, we would encourage those kinds which can most easily win the favor of the general public or of wealthy patrons.

Cultural institutions in a liberal society do not refrain from active selection and support of what they regard as best. No one seriously argues that they should. Granted that it is impossible to prove which artists and works are best, the public still relies largely on the consensus of experts in each field and on the judgment of posterity. Differences and changes in taste are taken for granted. Competition is not entirely eliminated, especially among contemporary works. But it is limited in practice. The judgment of experts and institutional officials is followed to a large extent in deciding who are the great artists of past generations, and which of their works are most important. These are included for study in the curricula of schools and universities, in the collections of art museums, in concert programs and phonograph records, in libraries, bibliographies, and historical accounts. Society thus creates an artificially restricted, sheltered environment in which selected types and examples are preserved and recommended. Many of them could not win public favor in completely open competition. Students are under some compulsion to study them in working for diplomas, degrees, and positions. The opinion of experts is followed also in judging contemporary, experimental works. They do not agree completely, but a rough consensus of avant-garde critics and another of conservative ones forms quickly in each main center of the arts. Their opinion weighs heavily in deciding what pictures shall be bought for museums,

[536]

what music played, and what books published. Old masters and contemporary artists must still compete for their approval, and some artists are constantly being eliminated in favor of others. But once given a place among the great, an artistic reputation is raised above the battle for a while at least. Thus to keep selecting and honoring certain works and artists is to increase their influence, and to encourage younger artists to emulate them. Even when the latter try to refuse and avoid all tradition, they are often influenced by some newly introduced, unfamiliar style of art, old or new.

Professional experts on various arts, including prominent artists, critics, scholars, teachers, educational administrators, museum directors, officials and advisers of foundations, constitute a loosely interrelated subgroup within a modern, liberal culture. Though under no direct, systematic coercion and more or less free to act independently, they tend to develop an *esprit de corps* through interlocking organizations, prestige, and personal acquaintance in large cities. Many of them are in touch with governmental bureaus related to education and culture, as well as with commerical and industrial corporations which are donors or potential donors to the arts and to art education. In spite of some competition and dissension, leaders in all areas tend to develop considerable agreement on policy and to act along similar lines.

In some liberal countries such as France, government funds are much used to subsidize cultural institutions: universities, orchestras, museums, and theaters. Efforts are made to protect them from political influence, with varying success. Even where there is comparatively little government activity in the arts, as in the United States, there is often more than is commonly realized. National, state, and local officials award commissions for public works involving art, such as monuments, buildings, and entertainments for the army and navy. They grant tax immunity to educational and cultural institutions and operate some of them under direct governmental control. In the United States, tax deductions are granted to individuals

for gifts and bequests to such institutions. We have already noted the growing influence of foundations, tax exempt and heavily endowed with funds available for grants to individual artists and to art education. Scholarships and travel grants are awarded; subsidies are given for the publication of scholarly books and magazines on art and for serious literature not likely to succeed otherwise. Original symphonies are printed and performed at foundation expense.

All these and other activities, governmental and private, individual and institutional, combine to form an increasingly active social program in support of the arts in liberal countries. Whether so intended or not, such a program inevitably tends to direct the course of the arts to some extent. In practice, there is no such thing as art in general or artists in general. In trying to support and encourage them, one necessarily favors certain kinds which seem most worthy of support. Funds must be distributed to particular institutions and individuals. The combined weight of institutionalized preference, taste, and desire operates as a directive force in the art of liberal democracies, comparable to that of governments and governmentally controlled organizations in the totalitarian states.

To be sure, art does not always go where it is officially steered. Financial subsidies are never enough to direct the best artists in a generation along some particular line. They must want to go there for other reasons. What makes them want to go in a certain direction is still far from being understood, and far from being easy to control. The mere hint of political, commercial, or institutional pressure in a liberal society is often enough to set off a revolt among rebellious artists, thus adding one more flutter to the multiple dialectic of art history. However, the social forces at work are too strong for any but the strongest individuals to oppose with much success. The anxiety of artists in liberal cultures to resist outside influence helps to restrain both centralized control and large-scale public subsidy.

The control of art, and of people by means of art, is not only far greater in totalitarian states, but on the whole more dogmatic and arbitrary. It is usually based upon and guided by some accepted doctrine such as that of Marx. Room is left for debate on specific applications and interpretations of it, as in the Soviet policy of "socialist realism," but basic principles are seldom frankly and freely debated once the party line is authoritatively announced.

In the liberal states, along with greater freedom of choice, another kind of direction is prevalent. This is the arbitrary decision of supposedly expert officials, judges, juries of award, and the like, who have power to allocate vast funds and opportunities in the arts without defending or justifying them in terms of explicit standards. Seldom indeed is the jury of award in an art exhibition or the purchasing official in an art museum required to defend or even explain his judgment to the public. The same can be said of awards for musical composition, for motion picture directing and acting, for literary excellence and so on. In most cases the judges are responsible only to other officials and trustees. Understandably, they do not wish to provoke public argument. Sometimes they hide behind the questionable excuse that "these things can't be put into words." At other times, they appeal to vague, high-sounding terms of praise which have no clear connection with the examples being judged or with reasoned theories of value.

Any thorough attempt to think out, explain, and defend one's preferences in art leads to the subject of aesthetics. In aesthetics, it leads especially to axiology or value-theory, which deals with general principles of criticism. Discussions of the future of art in human society require some understanding of its place in cultural evolution, past and present—the subject of this book.

More active attention has been given in recent years to these problems by Marxists than by scholars and officials in the liberal democracies. For those who can or must accept it, the Marxist doctrine provides a clear and workable philosophy to guide the social planning and control of art. In the liberal states, on the whole, aesthetics has been taken much less seriously. It is usually taught as a highly abstract, specialized subject, remote from the arts and from practical management. To many liberals, the Marxist theory of art history and aesthetic value seems largely erroneous and worse than none at all. But why should Western liberalism not develop its own philosophy of art into something constructive and workable in the practical guidance of artistic progress? Instead of the ends and means to which it objects, it could substitute others more acceptable.

4. QUESTIONS OF VALUE

As indicated at the beginning of this book, evaluative questions have been largely excluded from its scope. The main reason is that the factual problems raised in the long argument over cultural evolutionism are intricate enough to require extended study. The evaluative ones are important enough, and difficult enough, to need equally careful consideration. In the past, much confusion has arisen from trying to handle both at once; to decide at the same time not only what has happened, is happening, and may happen, but also what ought to happen. In this book we have not been able to separate the two entirely, but have touched on questions of value only incidentally. Sooner or later, they must be carefully considered in any comprehensive theory of art history. It may be useful, therefore, to close with a brief note on some of those which remain.

The chief attacks on nineteenth-century evolutionism, which we have analyzed in previous chapters, were mainly concerned with the facts of the case: with demolishing the belief that cultural evolution went on everywhere along the same line and must do so in future. Many hostile critics also attacked the related belief that evolution coincides with progress; that it will inevitably move toward better things in art and otherwise. With this criticism we have agreed, adding that if evolution is to be progressive, that result will not be automatic. It must be insured by social thought and effort. As to the meaning of progress in art and culture—what constitutes improvement and by what standards it can be judged—there was also disagreement with the Spencerian doctrine. Supernaturalists attacked it as too hedonistic and materialistic, in that it often emphasized increasing pleasure and happiness as the goal of evolution and the principal aim of art. Scientific writings on evolution in biology, anthropology, and culture history have usually avoided such issues as too subjective and speculative. Only a few have ventured to express their conceptions of progress, as well as of evolution, in both the organic and cultural fields.

On the whole, the evaluative issues have played a much smaller part in recent evolutionary discussion than the purely factual ones. They have added little to the perennial conflict of a few traditional world-views, philosophic theories of value in ethics and aesthetics. Whatever value-system one accepts, one applies it to the question of what change in art is good and what is bad; what would or would not be a change for the better. Thus the supernaturalists tend to disparage, not only sensuous pleasure as a goal and standard, but also the recent tendency of art to neglect religious subjects and religious service; they condemn it for emphasizing immoral aspects of life. The more extreme supernaturalists regard most art since the Renaissance as a decline in value, an aesthetic and spiritual retrogression. They see little hope of good to come from any social planning or control by leaders of contemporary, materialistic culture. On the other hand, naturalistic humanists restate the traditional value-system of that philosophy, stemming from Aristotle and Lucretius, in relation to the new discoveries of evolutionary science. They reaffirm in modern terms the classical conception of art as a means to the good life on earth, or on whatever planets man and his descendants may inhabit. How to define the good life on earth is, of course, a perennial problem in itself. Here the humanists, while following Epicurus in stressing the quality of experience, differ from him in refusing to accept the concept of pleasure, in a narrow sense, as an adequate summum bonum or criterion of value. They insist, with Aristotle, on a more diversified conception in which the exercise and development of the whole personality in a social environment is sought, together with the use of intelligence and active effort in solving human problems.

Many humanists emphasize the potentially great and growing role of art in future evolution. Thus Sir Julian Huxley, whom we have quoted as one of the most philosophical of present evolutionists, links art with science and religion as one of the three main fields of man's creative activity. "All," he says, "are indispensable for his fulfilment and the greater realization of his possibilities."[8] The practice of the arts, he continues, can play an important part in the development of personality. Art is and should be, not mere self-expression for the artist, or on the other hand a mere tool of the state as in the U.S.S.R. "Both science and art are instruments for comprehending the world, and for communicating that comprehension." (It is significant, as implying a technical conception of art, that Huxley thus refers to art as an *instrument*.) "The essential function of the arts," he says in other words, "is one of bearing witness to the wonder and variety of the world and of human experience... it is to create vehicles for the effective expression and communication of complex emotionally charged experiences, which are of value in the process of human fulfilment." Other humanists would emphasize somewhat different functions of art, both actual and possible.

Such general appraisals offer starting-points for further theories of value in the arts in relation to cultural evolution. Being brief and abstract, they take us only a little way into the subject. In regard

---

[8] Huxley, J., "Evolutionary Humanism," in *New Bottles for New Wine* (London, 1957), p. 306.

to social planning and control, many other questions arise. For a developed value-theory, it is not enough to say that art as a whole is valuable for the good life and human fulfilment. One must try to be more selective in deciding what kinds of art are better than others, for whom and under what conditions. What kinds deserve to be encouraged most? What constitutes improvement in art, and by what standards can it be judged? In what specific ways can art become better or worse? What is, or would be, real progress in the arts?

Such philosophic problems are, of course, not to be answered in a day, and no final solutions of them are to be expected. Each age must work out partly new ones in the light of its own experience and culture-pattern. Science can throw some light on them, especially as to relevant information and techniques of decision; but it cannot be expected to make the ultimate decisions or establish definite, universal standards of value in art.

Important as it is to try to answer these questions in aesthetics and criticism, it is fortunately unnecessary to delay social action until they are solved. A liberal, affluent society runs no great risk in adopting at any time a moderately active program of increased support for the whole field of art. Even if it were possible, it would be unwise at the present time to decide in advance exactly what kinds of art and artist most deserve encouragement in future. We know too little about the facts and values involved. It would be unwise, at the present stage of thinking in ethics and aesthetics, to commit oneself too completely to any theoretical hierarchy of values, any fixed program of steps, or any rigid formula for progress in the arts. Any such formulations should be extremely tentative and subject to revision in the light of experience.

Between the extremes of neglect and regimentation, liberal social policy toward art can seek a middle road of flexible planning, as in modern liberal education, which will give ample scope for individual choice. It can move persistently but cautiously and slowly from blind natural selection to intelligent self-control in art as in other fields.

Progress, as well as evolution, requires both differentiation and reintegration, proceeding together and balancing each other. Society can outline and support certain broad paths of organized study and experiment which promise obvious, important values to all concerned, while leaving to the workers in those fields the main initiative in deciding specific directions, ends, and means.

No generation has the right or power to commit succeeding ones to any controversial, narrowly predetermined policy. But each can try to provide its successors with a firm inheritance of knowledge, skills, products, and ideals to build upon. While pointing out what it regards as the line of greatest progress, it can and must leave all subsequent decisions to the wisdom and creative vision of those who will, in their own time, assume the control of human destiny.

In the growing heritage of democratic peoples, one invaluable treasure is the record of their experiments in collective self-direction. These involve the making of innumerable errors, some of them costly. Increasing power has multiplied the danger of catastrophic mistakes. It is alarming indeed to think of what could happen if the control of human physical inheritance or of art and science as a whole fell into the wrong hands—into the hands of criminals or of well-meaning fanatics like some who have held despotic power in the past.

These are real dangers, and they justify great caution. But caution is not the only virtue, and as Aristotle showed, it can be carried to excess. The decision of many nations to embark on democratic self-government was itself a daring venture. As in representative government, so in art and all other areas of culture, it is only by making collective decisions, running risks, and learning from experience that we can hope to develop wisdom in the conduct of human affairs.

5. SUMMARY

High creative ability in the arts and other cultural fields has been found to occur in irregular bursts, in certain social groups at certain times. Geniuses in many fields often appear in about the same place and period. This raises another problem of causation: what makes these creative bursts occur when and where they do?

Creativeness is not as exceptional as once supposed, but it is certainly uneven in historical distribution. To explain its appearance, one should be able to find causal factors or combinations of them which operate with unusual strength in certain times and places. Neither the evolutionary, the cyclical, the Marxist, nor any other current theory of history is adequate to explain the facts. A pluralistic approach with emphasis on environmental factors seems most reasonable at present.

Empirical research may reveal types of event and condition significantly correlated with high creativity. Both environmental and hereditary factors deserve consideration. Theories emphasizing heredity do not necessarily imply innate racial inequality; some credit racial mixture with favoring creativeness. Diet and health, economic prosperity and political power, are also to be considered. No one kind of social order is necessary. Certain social and cultural conditions may favor creativity in one type of art and discourage it in others. It seems worth while to experiment with some of the most promising methods of encouraging it.

The history of human and prehuman evolution shows a gradual substitution of cultural change for organic, and of "artificial" or purposeful selection for "natural" selection. This tendency is continuing in art and other cultural fields. Art is still subject to partly natural selection through open competition for public favor, but the growth of social planning in general tends to include the arts. This is often associated with regimentation and is resisted by liberals.

However, social planning in, for, and with the arts is not necessarily devoted to political ends or dictatorial methods. It is growing spontaneously in liberal countries through democratic, institutional management as well as governmental subsidy and censorship. Growing knowledge of the psychological and social effects of art makes it likely that a further extension of social planning in this field will occur.

Some amount of this is consistent with liberal ideals and is not necessarily harmful to art and culture. It can be carefully self-limiting and devoted largely to encouraging free, multiform creation and enjoyment in the arts. Instead of trying to resist the powerful trend to purposeful social control in art and culture, democratic societies might consider more carefully how it could be devoted to the best possible ends, while avoiding the harm which often attends its misuse. This raises questions of aesthetic and moral value which lie beyond the scope of the present book.

BIBLIOGRAPHY

NOTE: *JAAC = Journal of Aesthetics and Art Criticism.*

Adams, Robert M. "The Evolutionary Process in Early Civilizations," *The Evolution of Man*, Vol. II of *Evolution After Darwin*, ed. Sol Tax.

Adler, Guido. *Handbuch der Musikgeschichte*. Frankfort, 1924.

Allen, Grant. "The Aesthetic Evolution of Man," *Mind*, V (1880).

—. *The Colour-Sense: its Origin and Development*. London, 1879.

—. *Physiological Aesthetics*. New York, 1877.

Allen, Warren D. *Philosophies of Music History*. New York, American Book Co., 1939.

Antal, Frederick. *Florentine Painting and its Social Background*. London, Kegan, Paul, 1948.

—. "Remarks on the Method of Art History," *The Burlington Magazine*, XCI, 550–561 (February–March 1949).

Appleman, Philip. "Evolution and Two Critics of Art and Literature," *Proceedings of the Third International Congress on Aesthetics, Venice, 1956*. Torino, 1957.

Aristotle. *Poetics*. (Butcher tr.).

—. *Rhetoric*.

Aristoxenus. *Harmonics*.

Augustine, St. *Confessions*.

—. *The City of God*.

Bacon, Francis. *The New Atlantis*.

—. *Novum Organum*.

Baer, Karl Ernst von. *Über Entwicklungsgeschichte der Thiere*. Königsberg, 1827–37.

Baird, James. *Ishmael*. Baltimore, Johns Hopkins Press, 1956.

Bairstow, Edward C. *The Evolution of Musical Form*. London, Oxford U. P., 1943.

Baldwin, James M. *Dictionary of Philosophy and Psychology*. New York, 1901; Gloucester, Mass., Peter Smith, 1957.

Balfour, Henry. *The Evolution of Decorative Art*. London, 1893.

Barnes, Harry E. *Historical Sociology: its Origins and Development*. New York, Philos. Libr., 1948.

—, and Howard Becker. *Social Thought from Lore to Science*. New York, D. C. Heath, 1938.

Barth, Karl. *Die Philosophie der Geschichte als Soziologie*. 1897–1922.

Bayet, Charles. *Précis d'histoire de l'art*. Paris, 1905.

Benedict, Ruth F. "The Science of Custom," *Century Magazine* (April 1929). Reprinted in V. F. Calverton, ed., *The Making of Man*.

—, and Margaret Mead. "The Growth of Culture," *Man, Culture, and Society*, ed. H. L. Shapiro. New York, Oxford U. P., 1956.

Benfey, Theodor. *Geschichte der Sprachwissenschaft*. Munich, 1869.

Bergson, Henri. *L'évolution créatrice*. Paris, 1912.

Berlin, Isaiah. *Historical Inevitability*. Oxford, 1954.

Bharata. *Natya Sastra*.

Bidney, David. *Theoretical Anthropology*. New York, Columbia U. P., 1953.

Blake, William. *On Reynolds' Discourses*, in *Poetry and Prose of William Blake*, ed. Geoffrey Keynes. London, Nonesuch Press, 1939.

Blau, Joseph L. "John Dewey's Theory of History," *Journal of Philosophy*, LVII, 3 (February 4, 1960).

Boas, Franz. *Primitive Art*. Oslo, Aschehoug, 1927.

—. "Anthropology," *Encyclopedia of the Social Sciences*.

Boas, George. *The Happy Beast in French Thought of the Seventeenth Century*. Baltimore, Johns Hopkins Press, 1933.

Boisdeffre, Pierre de. *Une histoire vivante de la littérature d'aujourdhui*. Paris, Le Livre Contemporain, 1958.

Bosanquet, Bernard. *History of Aesthetic*. London, 1892.

Bossuet, Jacques B. *Discourse on Universal History*. 1681.

Boyd, William C. "The Contributions of Genetics to Anthropology," *Anthropology Today*, ed. A. L. Kroeber.

Brunetière, Ferdinand. *Études critiques sur l'histoire de la littérature française*, 3rd series, 2nd ed.

—. *L'évolution des genres dans l'histoire de la littérature*. Paris, 1890.

Buckle, Henry T. *History of Civilization in England*. London, 1857-62

Bukofzer, Manfred F. *Music in the Baroque Era*. New York, W. W. Norton, 1947.

Burckhardt, Jacob C. *Civilization of the Renaissance in Italy*. London, Harrap, 1929.

Bury, John B. *The Idea of Progress*, introd. Charles A. Beard. London & New York, Macmillan, 1920, 1932.

Caird, John. "The Progressiveness of Art," 1887.

Calverton, Victor F., ed. *The Making of Man*. New York, Modern Library, 1931.

—. *The Making of Society*. New York, Modern Library, 1937.

Caramaschi, E. "Brunetière critique," *Revue d'Esthétique*, XI, 3-4 (July–December 1958).

Casella, Alfredo. *The Evolution of Music*. London, J. & W. Chester, 1924.

Cassirer, Ernst. *Language and Myth*, tr. Susanne K. Langer. New York, Harper, 1946.

Chadwick, Hector M. *The Heroic Age*. Cambridge, 1912.

—, and N. Kershaw. *The Growth of Literature*. Cambridge, 1932-40.

Chandler, Albert R. *Beauty and Human Nature*. New York, D. Appleton-Century, 1934.

Childe, V. Gordon. *Social Evolution*. New York, H. Schuman, 1951.

Chuang-Tzu. *Musings of a Chinese Mystic*, ed. Lionel Giles. London, 1911.

Coerne, L. A. *The Evolution of Modern Orchestration*. New York, 1908.

Cohen, Morris. *The Meaning of Human History*. La Salle, Ill., Open Court Publishing Co., 1947.

Cohn, William. *Indische Plastik*. Berlin, B. Cassirer, 1923.

Coleman, Satis N. *Creative Music for Children: a Plan of Training Based on the Natural Evolution of Music, Including the Making and Playing of Instruments*. New York, G. P. Putnam's, 1922.

Collingwood, R. G. *The Idea of History*. Oxford, Clarendon Press, 1946.

—. *The Principles of Art*. Oxford, Clarendon Press, 1938.

Colvin, Sydney. "Fine Arts," *Encyclopedia Britannica* (11th ed., 1910).

Combarieu. *La musique, ses lois, son évolution*, Paris, 1907.

Comte, Auguste. *Cours de philosophie positive*. 1830–1842.

—. *A General View of Positivism*, tr. J. H. Bridges. New York, 1957.

Condillac, E. B. *Essay on the Origin of Human Knowledge*. Paris, 1716.

Condorcet. *Esquisse d'un tableau historique des progrès de l'esprit humain*. Paris, 1795. Tr. June Barraclough as *Sketch for a Historical Picture of the Progress of the Human Mind*. London, Weidenfeld & Nicolson, 1955.

Cooley, C. H. "Art, Science, and Sociology," *The Making of Society*, ed. V. F. Calverton. New York, Modern Library, 1937.

Coomaraswamy, Ananda. *The Dance of Siva*. New York, Sunwise Turn, 1924.

—. "The Theory of Art in Asia," Ch. I of *The Transformation of Nature in Art*. Cambridge, Harvard U. P. 1934.

Croce, Benedetto. *Aesthetic*, tr. Douglas Ainslie. London, Macmillan, 1922.

—. *History: its Theory and Practice*, tr. Douglas Ainslie. New York, Harcourt, Brace, 1921.

Dante. *Divine Comedy*.

Darwin, Charles R. *The Descent of Man and Selection in Relation to Sex*. New York, 1871.

Dean, Bashford. *Catalogue of European Court Swords and Hunting Swords*. New York, Metropolitan Museum of Art, 1929.

—. *Catalogue of European Daggers*. New York, Metropolitan Museum of Art, 1929.

Delacroix, Eugène. *Journal*, February 19, 1850.

Déonna, Waldemar. *L'archéologie, sa valeur, ses méthodes*. 3 vols. Paris, 1912.

Dewey, John. *The Influence of Darwin on Philosophy and Other Essays*. New York, Henry Holt, 1910.

—. *Logic: the Theory of Inquiry*. New York, Henry Holt, 1938.

Diderot. D. *Œuvres Complètes*.

—. *Penseés sur l'interprétation de la nature*. 1754.

Dorner, Alexander. *The Way Beyond Art*. New York U. P., 1958.

Droysen, J. G. *Grundriss der Historik*. 1858–62. Tr. E. B. Andrews as *Outlines of the Principles of History*. Boston, 1893.

Durkheim, Émile. *The Rules of Sociological Method*. 8th ed., tr. Sarah A. Salovay and John H. Mueller, ed. E. G. Catlin, U. Chicago P., 1938.

Dussieux, L. *L'art considéré comme le symbole de l'état social, ou Tableau historique et synoptic du développement des beaux arts en France*. 1838.

Dvořák, Max. *Das Rätsel der Brüder van Eyck*. 1904.

—. *Kunstgeschichte als Geistesgeschichte*. Munich, Piper, 1928.

Eastman, Max. "The Marxian Philosophy," in V. F. Calverton, ed., *The Making of Society*.

Eimer, Theodor. *Die Entstehung der Arten*. 1888.

—. *Orthogenesis der Schmetterlinge*. 1897.

Eliot, T. S. *The Sacred Wood*. London, Methuen, 1920.

Elliot, Hugh. *Herbert Spencer*. New York, Henry Holt, 1917.

Eng, Helga K. *The Psychology of Children's Drawings*. New York, Harcourt, Brace, 1931.

Fairchild, Henry P., ed. *Dictionary of Sociology*. New York, Philos. Libr., 1944.

Fechner, Gustav T. *Vorschule der Ästhetik*, Vol. I. Leipzig, 1876.

Felibien, André. *Entretiens*. 1685.

Feuer, Lewis S., ed. *Marx and Engels, Basic Writings on Politics and Philosophy*. New York, Doubleday Anchor Books, 1959.

Fiedler, Konrad. *Schriften über Kunst*. 1913–14.

Fingesten, Peter. "The Theory of Evolution in the History of Art," *College Art Journal*, XII (Summer 1954).

Fischer, J. M. *Die Grundbegriffe der Tonkunst in ihren Zusammenhange nebst einer geschichtlichen Entwickelung derselben*. Leipzig, 1836.

Fleck, A. "Technology and the Arts," Charles Singer, and others, eds., *History of Technology*. 5 vols. New York, Oxford U. P., 1954–58.

Fleming, W. "The Element of Motion in Baroque Art and Music," *JAAC*, V (December 1946).

Fletcher, Banister. *History of Architecture*. London, 1896.

—. *History of Architecture on the Comparative Method*. 9th ed., rev. & enl., New York, C. Scribner's, 1931.

Flint, Robert. *History of the Philosophy of History in France*. New York, 1894.

Florus. *Epitome Rerum Romanorum*, in Sallust, Florus, and Velleius Paterculus, *Historical Works*, tr. J. S. Watson. London, 1872.

Focillon, Henri. *La vie des formes*. Paris, 1934. Tr. Charles B. Hogan and George Kubler, as *The Life of Forms in Art*. New York, Wittenborn, Schultz, 1948.

Frazer, Sir James G. *The Golden Bough*. London, 1900.

—. *Totemism*. 1898.

Freedman, L. Z., and A. Roe. "Evolution and Human Behavior," *Behavior and Evolution*, ed. A. Roe and G. G. Simpson. New Haven, Yale U. P., 1958.

Freud, Sigmund. *Civilization and its Discontents*, tr. Joan Riviere. New York, J. Cape & H. Smith, 1930.

—. *Totem and Taboo*. 1912–13.

Friedrich, Carl J. *The Age of the Baroque*. New York, Harper, 1952.

—. "Style and Historical Interpretation," *JAAC*, XIV (December 1955).

Frobenius, Leo. *Das Unbekannte Afrika*. Munich, 1923.

Fyfe, William H. *Aristotle's Art of Poetry*. Oxford, Clarendon Press, 1940.

Galton, Francis. *Hereditary Genius—an Inquiry into its Laws and Consequences*. 1869.

Gardiner, Patrick. *The Nature of Historical Explanation*. Oxford U.P., 1952.

—, ed. *Theories of History*. Glencoe, Ill., Free Press, 1959.

Gautier, Théophile. "Du beau dans l'art," *Revue des Deux Mondes*, XIX (1847).

Gayley, Charles M., and Benjamin P. Kurtz. *Methods and Materials of Literary Criticism.* Boston, Ginn & Co., 1920.

Gide, André. *The Counterfeiters,* tr. Dorothy Bussy. New York, A. A. Knopf, 1947.

Gilbert, Katherine, and Helmut Kuhn. *A History of Esthetic.* Rev. & enl. ed., Bloomington, Indiana U. P., 1953.

Giles, Lionel, tr. *The Sayings of Lao Tzu.* London, 1904.

Ginsberg, M. *Evolution and Progress.* New York, Macmillan, 1961.

Glyn, Margaret H. *Analysis of the Evolution of Musical Form.* London, 1909.

Gnoli, R. *The Aesthetic Experience According to Abhinavagupta.* Rome, Istituto Italiano per il Medio ed Extremo Oriente, 1956.

Goldenweiser, Alexander. "Evolution, Social," *Encyclopedia of the Social Sciences.*

—. *History, Psychology, and Culture.* New York, A. A. Knopf, 1933.

Golding, William G. *Lord of the Flies.* New York, Capricorn Books, 1955.

Goldschmidt, W., ed. *The Anthropology of Franz Boas.* Memoir 89 of the American Anthropological Association, Vol. 61, No. 5, Part 2 (October 1959).

Goldwater, Robert J. *Primitivism in Modern Painting.* New York, Harper, 1938.

Gombrich, Ernst H. *Art and Illusion.* New York, Pantheon Books, 1960.

—. "Psychoanalysis and Art," in Benjamin N. Nelson, ed., *Freud and the Twentieth Century.* New York, Meridian Books, 1957.

—. Review of Arnold Hauser's *Social History of Art, Art Bulletin,* XXV (March 1953).

Goodrich, E. S. "Evolution," *Encyclopedia Britannica* (14th ed.).

Grene, Marjorie. "The Faith of Darwinism," *Encounter,* XIII, 5 (November, 1959).

Grinten, E. van der. *Enquiries into the History of Art-Historical Writing.* Amsterdam, Municipal University, 1952.

Grosse, Ernst. *Die Anfänge der Kunst.* Freiburg, 1893. Tr. *The Beginnings of Art.* New York, 1897, 1900.

Grousset, René. *Civilizations of the East,* tr. Catherine A. Phillips. New York, A. A. Knopf, 1931, 1934.

Guérard, Albert L. *Literature and Society.* Boston, Lothrop, Lee, & Shepard, 1935.

Guyau, Jean-Marie. *L'art au point de vue sociologique.* Paris, 1887.

—. *Les problèmes de l'esthétique contemporaine.* Paris, 1884.

Haddon, Alfred C. *Evolution in Art.* London, 1895.

Hanslick, Eduard. *Vom musikalisch Schönen.* 1854.

Harap, L. *Social Roots of the Arts.* New York, International Publishers, 1946.

Hauser, Arnold. *The Philosophy of Art History.* London, Routledge & Kegan Paul, 1958.

—. *Social History of Art,* tr. Stanley Godman. 2 vols., New York, A. A. Knopf, 1951.

Haweis, H. R. *Music and Morals.* London, Harper, 1871.

Hegel, G. W. F. *Aesthetik* (1835). Tr. F. P. B. Osmaston as *Philosophy of Fine Art.* London, G. Bell, 1920.

—. *The Philosophy of History,* tr. J. Sibree. London, 1900.

Hempel, C. G., "The Function of General Laws in History." *Journal of Philosophy,* Vol. 39 (1942), pp. 40 ff.

Hennequin, Émile. *La critique scientifique.* Paris, 1888.

Hesiod. *The Shield of Herakles.*

—. *Theogony.*

—. *Works and Days.*

Hirn, Yrjö. *The Origins of Art—a Psychological and Sociological Inquiry.* London, 1900.

Hobhouse, Leonard T. *Morals in Evolution.* New York, Henry Holt, 1915.

—. "Evolution, Social," *Encyclopedia of the Social Sciences.*

Hoebel, E. A., *Man in the Primitive World.* New York, McGraw-Hill, 1958.

Hoijer, Harry. "Language and Writing," in H. L. Shapiro, ed., *Man, Culture and Society.* New York, Oxford U. P., 1956.

Holmes, William H. *Ancient Art of the Province of Chirique* (Bureau of American Ethnology, Annual Report 6, 1888).

Holt, Elizabeth G., ed. *Literary Sources of Art History.* Princeton U. P., 1947, 1958.

Horace. *Art of Poetry.*

Hugo, Victor. "Preface" to *Cromwell.* 1827.

Huxley, Aldous *Brave New World.* Garden City, N. Y., Doubleday, Doran, 1932.

—. "A Night at Pietramala," *Along the Road.* New York, George H. Doran, 1925.

Huxley, Julian. *Evolution in Action*. London, Harper, 1952.

—. "Evolution, Cultural and Biological," reprinted in *New Bottles for New Wine*. London, Chatto & Windus, 1957.

—. *Evolution: the Modern Synthesis*. New York, Harper, 1942.

—. "The Evolutionary Vision," *Issues in Evolution*, Vol. III of *Evolution After Darwin*, ed. Sol Tax. U. Chicago P., 1960.

Huxley, Thomas H. Address to the Geological Society (1862), *Collected Essays*, Vol. VIII.

—. Article on Evolution, *Encyclopedia Britannica* (9th ed.).

Janson, H. W. Review of Curt Sachs, *The Commonwealth of Art: Style in the Fine Arts, Music, and the Dance* (New York, W. W. Norton, 1946), *Magazine of Art* (April 1947).

Jastrow, Morris. *The Study of Religion*. London, W. Scott, 1902.

Jolles, André. *Einfache Formen*. Halle, 1930.

Jouveau-Dubreuil, G. *Archéologie du sud de l'Inde*. Paris, 1914.

Kahn, Sholom J. *Science and Aesthetic Judgment: a Study in Taine's Critical Method*. London, Routledge & Kegan Paul, 1953.

Kant, Immanuel, *Critique of Judgment*. (Meredith tr.).

Kardiner, Abram, and Ralph Linton. *The Psychological Frontiers of Society*. New York, Columbia U. P., 1945.

Keller, A. G. *Societal Evolution*. 1915.

Kepes, Gyorgy. "Art and Science," *Art and Architecture* (October 1956).

Ker, William P. *Collected Essays*, Vol. I. London, Macmillan, 1922.

Kerschensteiner, Georg. *Die Entwickelung der zeichnerischen Begabung*. Munich, 1905.

Kiesewetter, Georg. *History of the Modern Music of Western Europe*. Leipzig, 1834.

Kluckhohn, Clyde. "The Place of Theory in Anthropological Science," *The Philosophy of Science*, Vol. 6 (1939).

Koestler, Arthur. *The Lotus and the Robot*. New York, Macmillan, 1961.

Kramrisch, Stella. *The Art of India Through the Ages*. London, Phaidon, 1955.

Krappe, Alexander H. *The Science of Folk-lore*. London, Methuen, 1930.

Kroeber, Alfred L. *Anthropology*. New York, Harcourt, Brace, 1923, 1948.

—, ed. *Anthropology Today*. U. Chicago P., 1953.

—. *Configurations of Culture Growth*. Berkeley & Los Angeles, U. California P., 1944.

—. "History and Science in Anthropology," *American Anthropologist*, XXXVII (1935).

—. *The Nature of Culture*. U. Chicago P., 1952.

—. "The Novel in Asia and Europe," *The Nature of Culture*.

—. *Style and Civilizations*. Ithaca, Cornell U. P., 1957.

—, and Clyde Kluckhohn. *Culture: a Critical Review of Concepts and Definitions*. Cambridge, Mass., The Museum, 1952.

Kühn, Herbert. *Die Kunst der Primitiven*. Munich, Delphin-Verlag, 1923.

Lalande, André. *Vocabulaire technique et philosophique*. Paris, Presses Universitaires, 1947.

Lalo, Charles. *Éléments d'une esthétique musicale scientifique*. 2nd ed., Paris, J. Vrin, 1939.

Lamarck. *Zoological Philosophy*. 1809.

Laufer, Berthold. Review of R. H. Lowie's *Culture and Ethnology*, in *American Anthropologist*, Vol. 20 (1918).

Leacock, E. "Social Stratification and Evolutionary Theory," *Ethnohistory*, Vol. V.

Le Bossu, René. *Traité du poème épique*. Paris, 1708.

Lee, Sherman E. "The Two Styles of Chu Ta," *Bulletin of the Cleveland Museum of Art* (November 1958).

—. *Japanese Decorative Style*. Cleveland Museum of Art, 1961.

—, and Wen Fong. *Streams and Mountains Without End*. Ascona, Artibus Asiae, 1955.

Levinstein, S. *Kinderzeichnungen bis zum 14ten Lebensjahr*. Leipzig, 1905.

Leyen, Friedrich von der. *Das Märchen*. Leipzig, Quelle & Meyer, 1925.

Lévy-Bruhl, Lucien. *The Philosophy of Auguste Comte*. New York & London, 1903.

Liepmann, Klaus. *The Language of Music*. New York, Ronald Press, 1953.

Lifshitz, Mikhail. "Leninist Criticism," *Literature and Marxism: a Controversy by Soviet Critics*, ed. Angel Flores. (Critics Group Series, No. 9, New York).

Ligeti, Paul. *Der Weg aus dem Chaos*. 1931.

Linton, Ralph. "Primitive Art," *American Magazine of Art* (January 1933).

—. *The Tree of Culture*. New York, A. A. Knopf, 1955.

Lippert, Julius. *The Evolution of Culture*, tr. & ed. George P. Murdock. New York, Macmillan, 1931.

—. *Kulturgeschichte der Menschheit in ihrem organischen Aufbau.*. 2 vols. Stuttgart, 1886-7.

Listowel, William F. H. *A Critical History of Modern Aesthetics*. London, G. Allen & Unwin, 1933.

Lorenz, Alfred. *Abendländische Musikgeschichte im Rhythmus der Generationen*. Berlin, M. Hesse, 1928.

Lovejoy, Arthur O., and George Boas. *Primitivism and Related Ideas in Antiquity*. Baltimore, Johns Hopkins Press, 1935.

Lowie, Robert H. "Evolution in Cultural Anthropology: a Reply to Leslie White," *American Anthropologist*, XLVIII (1946).

—. *An Introduction to Cultural Anthropology*. New York, Farrar & Rinehart, 1940.

—. *Primitive Society*. New York, Boni & Liveright, 1920.

Lucretius. *On the Nature of Things*, BkV. (Tr. W. E. Leonard, Everyman Ed.).

Lundin, Robert W. *An Objective Psychology of Music*. New York, Ronald Press, 1953.

Luquet, G. H. *Le dessin enfantin*. Paris, 1927.

—. *Les dessins d'un enfant*. Paris, 1913.

Lyell, C. *Principles of Geology*. London, 1830.

MacIver, Robert M. *Society: its Structure and Change*. New York, R. Long & R. R. Smith, 1931.

Mackenzie, Alastair S. *The Evolution of Literature*. New York, T. Y. Crowell, 1911.

MacLeod, William C. *The Origin and History of Politics*. New York, J. Wiley, 1931.

Maistre, J. M. C. de. *Les Soirées de Saint-Pétersbourg*, Vol. II. Paris, 1821.

Maitland, Frederic W. *The Life and Letters of Leslie Stephen*. London, 1906.

Malinowski, Bronislaw. "Culture," *Encyclopedia of the Social Sciences*, Vol. IV (1931).

Malraux, André. *Voices of Silence*, tr. Stuart Gilbert. Garden City, N. Y., Doubleday, 1953.

Malthus. *Essay on Population*. 1798.

Mannhardt, Wilhelm. *Die lettischen Sonnenmythen*. Berlin, 1875.

—. *Mythologische Forschungen*. Strassburg & London, 1884.

—. *Wald- und Feldkulte*. Berlin, 1875-77.

March, Colley. "Evolution and Psychology in Art," *Mind*, V (1896).

Martineau, Harriet, tr. *The Positive Philosophy of Auguste Comte*. New York, 1858.

Marx, Karl. *A Contribution to the Critique of Political Economy*, tr. N. J. Stone. Chicago, 1904.

—. Preface to the second edition of *Das Kapital*.

—. Letter to Margaret Harkness, April 1888. Reprinted in Karl Marx and Frederick Engels, *Literature and Art*.

—, and Friedrich Engels. *Communist Manifesto*. 1847.

—. *Literature and Art: Selections from their Writings*. New York, International Publishers, 1947.

Mason, Daniel G. *From Song to Symphony*. Boston, Oliver Ditson, 1924.

Mead, Margaret. "Cultural Determinants of Behavior," in A. Roe and G. G. Simpson, *Behavior and Evolution*. New Haven, Yale U. P., 1958.

Meinecke, Friedrich. "Causalities and Values in History," *Staat und Persönlichkeit*. Berlin, 1933.

Merz, John T. *A History of European Thought in the Nineteenth Century*. Edinburgh & London, 1903.

Meyerhoff, Hans. *The Philosophy of History in Our Time, an Anthology*. Garden City, N. Y., Doubleday Anchor Books, 1959.

Morgan, C. L. "Evolution and Mind," *Encyclopedia Britannica* (14th ed.).

Morgan, Lewis H. *Systems of Consanguinity and Affinity of the Human Family*. 1869.

—. *Ancient Society: Researches in the Lines of Human Progress through Barbarism in Civilization*. 1877.

Moulton, Richard G. *The Modern Study of Literature*. U. Chicago P., 1915.

—. *World Literature and its Place in General Culture*. New York, Macmillan, 1911, 1930.

Müller, Max. Preface to *Contribution to the Science of Mythology*. 2 vols. London, 1897.

—. "The Philosophy of Mythology," *The Science of Religion*. London, 1873.

Munro, Thomas. *Art Education: its Philosophy and Psychology*. New York, Liberal Arts Press, 1956.

—. *The Arts and Their Interrelations*. New York, Liberal Arts Press, 1949.

—. "Do the Arts Progress?", *JAAC*, XIV (December 1955).

—. "The Failure Story: a Study of Contemporary Pessimism," *JAAC*, XVII (December 1958 & March 1959).

—. "The Psychology of Art: Past, Present, Future," *JAAC*, XXI (Spring 1963).

—. *Toward Science in Aesthetics*. New York, Liberal Arts Press, 1956.

—, and Paul Guillaume. *Primitive Negro Sculpture*. New York, Harcourt, Brace, 1926.

Murdock, George P. *Social Structure*. New York, Macmillan, 1949.

Murphy, Gardner. *Historical Introduction to Modern Psychology*. New York, Harcourt, Brace, 1932.

Murphy, John. *The Origins and History of Religions*. Manchester, 1949.

Nagel, Ernest. "Determinism in History," *Philosophy and Phenomenological Research*, XX (March 1960).

Nägeli, Carl Wilhelm. *Mechanisch-physiologische Theorie der Abstammungslehre*. 1884.

Naumburg, Margaret. *Psychoneurotic Art*. New York, Grune & Stratton, 1953.

Needham, H. A. *Le développement de l'esthétique sociologique*. Paris, Librairie Ancienne Honoré Champion, 1926.

—. "Evolution," *Encyclopedia of the Social Sciences*. New York, 1931.

Nelson, Benjamin N., ed. *Freud and the Twentieth Century*. New York, Meridian Books, 1957.

Nicholls, F. *The Language of Music or Musical Expression and Characterization*. London, P., 1924.

Nilsson, Sven. *Primitive Inhabitants of Scandinavia*, ed. John Lubbock. London, 1868.

Nietzsche, F. *The Birth of Tragedy*.

Nordenskiöld, Erik. *The History of Biology*. New York, 1928.

Ogier, François. Preface to *Tyre and Sidon*. 1628.

Osgood, Cornelius. "Culture: its Empirical and Non-empirical Character," *Southwestern Journal of Anthropology*, VII (1951).

Ovid. *Metamorphoses*, Bk I, Fable III.

Pandey, K. C. *Comparative Aesthetics*. Vol. I, *Indian Aesthetics*. Varanasi, India, Chowkhambra Sanskrit Series Office, P., 1959.

Panofsky, Erwin. "The First Page of Giorgio Vasari's 'Libro,'" *Meaning in the Visual Arts*. New York, Doubleday, 1955.

Parry, Charles H. *The Art of Music*. London, 1893. Later republished as *The Evolution of the Art of Music*, ed. H. C. Colles. New York, D. Appleton, 1930.

Payne-Gaposchkin, C. H. "Why Do Galaxies have a Spiral Form?," *Scientific American* (September 1953).

Perry, Ralph B. *Realms of Value*. Cambridge, Harvard U. P., 1954.

Persons, Stow, ed. *Evolutionary Thought in America*. New York, George Braziller, 1956.

Pizer, Donald. "Evolutionary Ideas in Late Nineteenth-Century English and American Literary Criticism," *JAAC*, XIX (Spring 1961).

Plato. *Laws*.

—. *Philebus*.

—. *Republic*, Bk. VIII.

Plekhanov, G. V. *Art and Social Life*. London, 1953.

—. *Essays in the History of Materialism*. London, 1934.

Pliny. *Natural History*, Bk. XXXV.

Popper, Karl R. *The Open Society and its Enemies*. London, G. Routledge, 1945; rev. ed., Princeton U. P., 1950.

—. *The Poverty of Historicism*. London, Routledge & Kegan Paul, 1957.

Praetorius, Michael. *Syntagma musicum*. Leipzig, 1615.

Praz, Mario. *The Romantic Agony*, tr. Angus Davidson. London, Oxford U. P., H. Milford, 1933.

Quantz, J., and P. E. Bach. *Affektenlehre* in Willi Apel, ed., *Harvard Dictionary of Music*. Cambridge, Harvard U. P., 1950.

Radcliffe-Brown, Alfred R. *Method in Social Anthropology*, U. Chicago, P., 1958.

Raglan, Lord. *The Hero*. London, 1936; New York, 1956.

Randall, John H., Jr. *Nature and Historical Experience*. New York, Columbia U. P., 1958.

Ranke, Leopold von. *The Varieties of History from Voltaire to the Present*, ed. Fritz Stern. New York, 1960.

Read, Herbert. "Art and the Evolution of Consciousness," *JAAC*, XIII (December 1954).

Reinach, Salomon. *Cultes, mythes, et religions*. 5 vols. 1904–23.

—. *Orpheus: a History of Religions*, tr. Florence Simmonds from the 38th French ed. New York, H. Liveright, 1930.

Ribot, T. *L'hérédité—Étude psychologique sur ses phénomènes, ses causes, ses conséquences*. 1873.

Ricci, C. *L'arte dei bambini*. Bologna, 1887; Leipzig, 1906.

Richards, I. A. *Principles of Literary Criticism*. London, K. Paul, Trench, Trubner, 1926.

Riegl, Alois. *Kunstgeschichte als Universalgeschichte.* 1898.

—. *Die spätrömische Kunstindustrie nach den Funden in Österreich-Ungarn.* 1901.

—. *Stilfragen.* 1893.

Rieser, Max. "The Aesthetic Theory of Social Realism," *JAAC,* XVI (December 1957).

—. "The Language of Shapes and Sizes in Architecture or Morphic Semantics," *Philosophical Review* (March 1946).

Robertson, J. D. *The Evolution of Clockwork.* London, 1931.

Roe, Anne, and George G. Simpson, eds. *Behavior and Evolution.* New Haven, Yale U. P., 1958.

Romanes, G. J. *Darwin and After Darwin.* Chicago, 1892–7.

Røstvig, M.-S. *The Happy Man.* 2 vols. Oslo, Akademisk Forlag, 1954–1958.

Rousseau, J. J. "A Discourse on the Moral Effects of the Arts and Sciences" (1750), *The Social Contract and Discourses,* ed. Ernest Rhys. Everyman ed., New York, E. P. Dutton, 1932.

—. *Émile.*

Rowbotham, John F. *A History of Music to the Time of the Troubadours.* London, 1885–87.

Rowley, George. *Principles of Chinese Painting.* Princeton U. P., 1947.

Runes, Dagobert D., ed. *Dictionary of Philosophy.* New York, Philos. Libr., 1942.

Sachs, Curt. *The Commonwealth of Art: Style in the Fine Arts, Music, and the Dance.* New York, W. W. Norton, 1946.

Sahlins, Marshall D. Review of Carl Resek, *Lewis Henry Morgan, American Scholar.* (U. Chicago P., 1960), *Science,* Vol. 131 (May 13, 1960).

—, and E. R. Service. *Evolution and Culture.* Ann Arbor, U. of Michigan, 1960.

St. Exupéry, Antoine de. *Wind, Sand, and Stars,* tr. Lewis Galantière. New York, Reynal & Hitchcock, 1939.

Santayana, George. "The Progress of Philosophy," *Soliloquies in England and Later Soliloquies.* New York, C. Scribner's, 1922.

—. *Realms of Being.* New York, 1937.

Sapir, Edward. *Language.* New York, Harcourt, Brace, 1921.

Sarton, George. *The Life of Science.* New York, H. Schuman, 1941, 1948.

—. *History of Science.* 2 Vols. Cambridge, Harvard U. P., 1959.

Schaefer-Simmern, Henry. *The Unfolding of Artistic Acitivity.* Berkeley, U. California P., 1948.

Schapiro, Meyer. "Style," *Anthropology Today,* ed. A. L. Kroeber. U. Chicago P., 1953.

Scheltema, F. A. van. *Die altnordische Kunst.* Berlin, 1923.

Schilpp, Paul A., ed. *The Philosophy of Ernst Cassirer.* Evanston, Ill., Library of Living Philosophers, 1949.

Schmidt, Wilhelm. Foreword of *The Culture Historical Method of Ethnology* (Vienna, 1937). Tr. S. A. Sieber. New York, Fortuny's, 1939, with Preface by Clyde Kluckhohn.

—. *Handbuch der Methode der Kulturhistorischen Ethnologie.* Münster, P., 1937.

Schneider, Hermann. *Philosophie der Geschichte.* Breslau, 1923. *History of World Civilization* (2 vols.). New York, 1931.

Schoen, Max, ed. *The Effects of Music.* New York, Harcourt, Brace, 1927.

—. *The Psychology of Music.* New York, Ronald Press, 1940.

Scholes, Percy A. "The History of Forms," *Oxford Companion to Music.* London, Oxford U. P., 1938.

Schücking, Levin L. *The Sociology of Literary Taste.* London, K. Paul, Trench, Trubner, 1944.

Scoon, Robert. "The Rise and Impact of Evolutionary Ideas," *Evolutionary Thought in America,* ed. Stow Persons. New York, George Braziller, 1956.

Semper, Gottfried. *Kleine Schriften.* 1884.

—. *Der Stil in den technischen und tektonischen Künsten oder praktische Aesthetik.* Munich, 1861–63.

Seznec, Jean. *The Survival of the Pagan Gods,* tr. Barbara F. Sessions. New York, Pantheon Books, 1953.

Shapiro, Harry L., ed. *Man, Culture, and Society.* New York, Oxford U. P., 1956.

Shipley, Joseph T., ed. *Dictionary of World Literature.* New York, Philos. Libr., 1943.

Sinclair, Upton. *Mammonart, an Essay in Economic Interpretation.* Pasadena, Calif., 1925.

Singer, Charles, and others, eds. *History of Technology.* 5 vols. New York, Oxford U. P., 1954–58.

—. *Short History of Science.* London & Oxford, Clarendon Press, 1941.

Sloane, Joseph. "Baudelaire, Chenevard, and Philosophic Art," *JAAC,* XIII (March 1955).

Smith, Marian W. "Boas' 'Natural History' Approach to Field Method," *The Anthropology of Franz Boas*, ed. W. Goldschmidt (Memoir 89 of the American Anthropological Association, Vol. 61, No. 5, Part 2, October 1959).

Smith, William Robertson. *The Religion of the Semites.* 1889, new ed. 1906.

Somerville, John. *Soviet Philosophy.* New York, Philos. Libr., 1946.

Sorokin, Pitirim A. *Social and Cultural Dynamics: Fluctuation of Forms of Art.* New York, American Book Co., 1937.

Spearing, Herbert G. *The Childhood of Art.* London, 1912.

Spencer, Herbert. "Barbaric Art," *Facts and Comments.* New York, 1902.

—. "Developed Music," *Facts and Comments.*

—. "The Development Hypothesis." 1852.

—. *First Principles.* New York, 1895.

—. *Illustrations of Universal Progress.* 1854.

—. "The Origin and Function of Music." 1857.

—. "The Origin of Music," *Facts and Comments.*

—. *Principles of Sociology.* New York, 1897.

—. "Progress: its Law and Cause. First published in *The Westminster Review* for April 1857. Reprinted in *Essays Scientific, Political, and Speculative.* New York, 1892.

—. *Study of Sociology,* Vol. 98. 1873.

—. "What Knowledge Is of Most Worth?," *Education: Intellectual, Moral, and Physical.* New York, 1896.

Spengler, Oswald. *The Decline of the West.* New York, A. A. Knopf, 1929. Tr. Charles F. Atkinson from *Der Untergang des Abendlandes.* Munich, 1917, 1921.

Stechow, Wolfgang. "Definitions of the Baroque in the Visual Arts," *JAAC,* V (December 1946).

Stephen, Leslie. *History of English Thought in the Eighteenth Century.* London, 1876.

—. *English Literature and Society in the Eighteenth Century.* London, 1904.

Stern, W. "Die zeichnerische Entwicklung eines Knaben vom 4. bis zum 7. Jahre," *Zeitschrift für angewandte Psychologie.* 1909.

Steward, Julian H. "Evolution and Progress," *Anthropology Today,* ed. A. L. Kroeber.

—. *Theory of Culture Change: the Methodology of Multilinear Evolution.* Urbana, U. Illinois P., 1955.

Stoddard, Richard H. Preface to the English translation of Taine's *History of English Literature,* tr. H. Van Laun. New York, 1891.

Strong, Herbert A., W. S. Logeman, and B. I. Wheeler. *Principles of the History of Language.* London, 1891.

Strong, W. D. "Historical Approach in Anthropology." *Anthropology Today,* ed. A. L. Kroeber. U. Chicago, P., 1953.

Strzygowski, J. "The Afghan Stuccos of the N. R. F. Collection." New York, Stora Gallery, n. d.

Stumpf, Carl. *Die Anfänge der Musik.* Leipzig, 1911.

Sturtevant, Edgar H. *An Introduction to Linguistic Science.* New Haven, Yale U. P., 1947.

Sully, James. "L'art et la psychologie," *Revue Philosophique,* Vol. II (1876).

—. Review in *Mind,* II (1876).

—. *Sensation and Intuition: Studies in Psychology and Aesthetics.* London, 1880.

Symonds, John A. *Essays Speculative and Suggestive.* London, 1893.

—. "On the Application of Evolutionary Principles to Art and Literature," *Essays Speculative and Suggestive.* London, 1893.

Sypher, Wylie. *Four Stages of Renaissance Style.* Garden City, N. Y., Doubleday, 1955.

Taine, H. *History of English Literature,* tr. H. Van Laun. New York, 1891.

—. "The Ideal in Art," *Lectures on Art,* Vol. I.

—. *Lectures on Art,* tr. John Durand. New York, 1875. Contains *The Philosophy of Art* and other series in two volumes.

—. *Voyage in Italy,* Vol. II, Book III. Paris, 1866.

Tax, Sol, and others. *An Appraisal of Anthropology Today.* U. Chicago P., 1953.

—, ed. *Evolution After Darwin.* 3 vols. U. Chicago P., 1960.

—. "The Celebration: a Personal View," *Issues in Evolution,* Vol. III of *Evolution After Darwin.* U. Chicago P., 1960.

Teggart, Frederick J., and George H. Hildebrand. *The Idea of Progress.* Berkeley, U. California P., 1949.

Torrend, J. *Specimens of Bantu Folk-lore from Northern Rhodesia.* London, K. Paul, Trench, Trubner, 1921.

Toynbee, Arnold J. *A Study of History.* London, Oxford U. P., 1939; 1-vol. ed., New York, 1947.

Tsui Chi. *A Short History of Chinese Civilization*. New York, G. P. Putnam's, 1943.

Turgot, R. *Tableau philosophique des progrès successifs de l'esprit humain*. 1750.

Tylor, Edward B. *Anthropology*, New York, 1891.

—. "On a Method of Investigating the Development of Institutions: Applied to Laws of Marriage and Descent," *Journal of the Royal Anthropological Institute of Great Britain and Ireland*, Vol. 18 (1888).

—. *Primitive Culture: Research into the Development of Mythology, Philosophy, Religion, Language, Art, and Custom*. 1st ed., London, 1871, 1913.

—. *Researches into the Early History of Mankind*. 1865.

Vasari, Giorgio. *Lives of Seventy of the Most Eminent Painters, Sculptors, and Architects*, ed. & annotated by E. H. & E. W. Blashfield & A. A. Hopkins. 4 vols. New York, C. Scribner's, 1927.

Venturi, Lionello. *History of Art Criticism*, tr. Charles Marriott. New York, E. P. Dutton, 1936.

Véron, Eugène. *L'esthétique*. Paris, 1878.

Vico, Giambattista. *Principles of a New Science*. 1725.

Villani, Filippo. *De Origine Civitatis Florentiae*. c. 1400.

Von Conze. *Beiträge zur Geschichte der griechischen Plastik*. Halle, 1869.

Waley, Arthur. *The Way and its Power: a Study of the Tao Tê Ching*. London, G. Allen & Unwin, 1956.

Wallach, Michael A. "Art, Science, and Representation: Toward an Experimental Psychology of Aesthetics," *JAAC*, XVIII (December 1960).

Wallaschek, Richard. *Primitive Music*. London, 1893.

Washburn, S. L. "The Strategy of Physical Anthropology," *Anthropology Today* ed. A. L. Kroeber.

Watkins, J. W. N. "Philosophy of History," *Philosophy in the Mid-century*, ed. R. Klibansky, Vol. III. Florence, 1958.

Watts, Alan. *The Spirit of Zen*. London, 1946.

Wellek, René. "The Concept of Baroque in Literary Scholarship," *JAAC*, V (December 1946).

—. "Hippolyte Taine's Literary Theory and Criticism," *Criticism* (Winter 1959).

—. "Development," *Dictionary of World Literature*. New York, 1943.

—, and Austin Warren. *Theory of Literature*. New York, Harcourt, Brace, 1949.

Wendt, H. *In Search of Adam*, tr. James Cleugh. Cambridge, Harvard U. P., 1955.

Werner, H. *Die Ursprünge der Lyrik*. Munich, 1924.

Westermarck, Edvard A. *History of Human Marriage*. London, 1891.

—. *Origin and Development of the Moral Ideas*. 1906–8.

White, Leslie A. *The Science of Culture*. New York, Farrar, Straus, 1949.

Whitney, W. D. *History of Language*. New York, 1899.

Wilde, Oscar. *The Soul of Man Under Socialism*, in *Works*, Vol. 13. New York & London, n. d.

Willey, Gordon R. "Archeological Theories and Interpretation: New World," *Anthropology Today*, ed. A. L. Kroeber.

—. "Patterns in New World Culture," *Mind, Evolution, and Culture* (Vol. II of *The Evolution of Man*, ed. Sol Tax).

—, and Philip Phillips. *Method and Theory in American Archaeology*. U. Chicago P., 1958.

Winckelmann, J. J. *Gedanken über die Nachahmung der griechischen Werke in der Malerei u. Bildhauerkunst*. Dresden & Leipzig, 1755.

Wölfflin, Heinrich. *Kunstgeschichtliche Grundbegriffe*. Munich, 1915. Tr. M. D. Hottinger as *Principles of Art History: the Problem of the Development of Style in Later Art*. New York, Henry Holt, 1932.

Wollheim, Richard. "Sociological Explanation of the Arts: Some Distinctions," *Proceedings of the Third International Congress on Aesthetics*. Torino, 1957.

Wundt, Wilhelm. Elements of Folk-Psychology. New York, Macmillan, 1916.

—. *Völkerpsychologie*, Vol. III. 1900–1920.

INDEX

OF CONCEPTS AND WRITERS
CONCERNED WITH THEORIES OF ART AND CULTURE HISTORY

This book was composed in Monotype Bembo 270 and printed on Woodfree Antique by N. V. Drukkerij G. J. Thieme, Nijmegen, the Netherlands. Bound in mat cloth binding by C. H. F. Wöhrmann & zonen, Zutphen, the Netherlands. Design and typography by Merald E. Wrolstad.